Shih-Yao Lin
Tsung-Yi Lin
Weiyao Lin
Yen-Yu Lin
Haibin Ling
Or Litany
Roee Litman
Anan Liu
Changsong Liu
Chen Liu
Ding Liu
Dong Liu
Feng Liu
Guangcan Liu
Luoqi Liu
Miaomiao Liu
Nian Liu
Risheng Liu
Shu Liu
Shuaicheng Liu
Sifei Liu
Tyng-Luh Liu
Wanquan Liu
Weiwei Liu
Xialei Liu
Xiaoming Liu
Yebin Liu
Yiming Liu
Ziwei Liu
Zongyi Liu
Liliana Lo Presti
Edgar Lobaton
Chengjiang Long
Mingsheng Long
Roberto Lopez-Sastre
Amy Loufti
Brian Lovell
Canyi Lu
Cewu Lu
Feng Lu
Huchuan Lu
Jiajun Lu
Jiasen Lu
Jiwen Lu
Yang Lu
Yujuan Lu

Simon Lucey
Jian-Hao Luo
Jiebo Luo
Pablo Márquez-Neila
Matthias Müller
Chao Ma
Chih-Yao Ma
Lin Ma
Shugao Ma
Wei-Chiu Ma
Zhanyu Ma
Oisin Mac Aodha
Will Maddern
Ludovic Magerand
Marcus Magnor
Vijay Mahadevan
Mohammad Mahoor
Michael Maire
Subhransu Maji
Ameesh Makadia
Atsuto Maki
Yasushi Makihara
Mateusz Malinowski
Tomasz Malisiewicz
Arun Mallya
Roberto Manduchi
Junhua Mao
Dmitrii Marin
Joe Marino
Kenneth Marino
Elisabeta Marinoiu
Ricardo Martin
Aleix Martinez
Julieta Martinez
Aaron Maschinot
Jonathan Masci
Bogdan Matei
Diana Mateus
Stefan Mathe
Kevin Matzen
Bruce Maxwell
Steve Maybank
Walterio Mayol-Cuevas
Mason McGill
Stephen Mckenna
Roey Mechrez

Christopher Mei
Heydi Mendez-Vazquez
Deyu Meng
Thomas Mensink
Bjoern Menze
Domingo Mery
Qiguang Miao
Tomer Michaeli
Antoine Miech
Ondrej Miksik
Anton Milan
Gregor Miller
Cai Minjie
Majid Mirmehdi
Ishan Misra
Niloy Mitra
Anurag Mittal
Nirbhay Modhe
Davide Modolo
Pritish Mohapatra
Pascal Monasse
Mathew Monfort
Taesup Moon
Sandino Morales
Vlad Morariu
Philippos Mordohai
Francesc Moreno
Henrique Morimitsu
Yael Moses
Ben-Ezra Moshe
Roozbeh Mottaghi
Yadong Mu
Lopamudra Mukherjee
Mario Munich
Ana Murillo
Damien Muselet
Armin Mustafa
Siva Karthik Mustikovela
Moin Nabi
Sobhan Naderi
Hajime Nagahara
Varun Nagaraja
Tushar Nagarajan
Arsha Nagrani
Nikhil Naik
Atsushi Nakazawa

Martin Kampel
Kenichi Kanatani
Angjoo Kanazawa
Melih Kandemir
Sing Bing Kang
Zhuoliang Kang
Mohan Kankanhalli
Juho Kannala
Abhishek Kar
Amlan Kar
Svebor Karaman
Leonid Karlinsky
Zoltan Kato
Parneet Kaur
Hiroshi Kawasaki
Misha Kazhdan
Margret Keuper
Sameh Khamis
Naeemullah Khan
Salman Khan
Hadi Kiapour
Joe Kileel
Chanho Kim
Gunhee Kim
Hansung Kim
Junmo Kim
Junsik Kim
Kihwan Kim
Minyoung Kim
Tae Hyun Kim
Tae-Kyun Kim
Akisato Kimura
Zsolt Kira
Alexander Kirillov
Kris Kitani
Maria Klodt
Patrick Knöbelreiter
Jan Knopp
Reinhard Koch
Alexander Kolesnikov
Chen Kong
Naejin Kong
Shu Kong
Piotr Koniusz
Simon Korman
Andreas Koschan

Dimitrios Kosmopoulos
Satwik Kottur
Balazs Kovacs
Adarsh Kowdle
Mike Krainin
Gregory Kramida
Ranjay Krishna
Ravi Krishnan
Matej Kristan
Pavel Krsek
Volker Krueger
Alexander Krull
Hilde Kuehne
Andreas Kuhn
Arjan Kuijper
Zuzana Kukelova
Kuldeep Kulkarni
Shiro Kumano
Avinash Kumar
Vijay Kumar
Abhijit Kundu
Sebastian Kurtek
Junseok Kwon
Jan Kybic
Alexander Ladikos
Shang-Hong Lai
Wei-Sheng Lai
Jean-Francois Lalonde
John Lambert
Zhenzhong Lan
Charis Lanaras
Oswald Lanz
Dong Lao
Longin Jan Latecki
Justin Lazarow
Huu Le
Chen-Yu Lee
Gim Hee Lee
Honglak Lee
Hsin-Ying Lee
Joon-Young Lee
Seungyong Lee
Stefan Lee
Yong Jae Lee
Zhen Lei
Ido Leichter

Victor Lempitsky
Spyridon Leonardos
Marius Leordeanu
Matt Leotta
Thomas Leung
Stefan Leutenegger
Gil Levi
Aviad Levis
Jose Lezama
Ang Li
Dingzeyu Li
Dong Li
Haoxiang Li
Hongdong Li
Hongsheng Li
Hongyang Li
Jianguo Li
Kai Li
Ruiyu Li
Wei Li
Wen Li
Xi Li
Xiaoxiao Li
Xin Li
Xirong Li
Xuelong Li
Xueting Li
Yeqing Li
Yijun Li
Yin Li
Yingwei Li
Yining Li
Yongjie Li
Yu-Feng Li
Zechao Li
Zhengqi Li
Zhenyang Li
Zhizhong Li
Xiaodan Liang
Renjie Liao
Zicheng Liao
Bee Lim
Jongwoo Lim
Joseph Lim
Ser-Nam Lim
Chen-Hsuan Lin

Venu Govindu
Helmut Grabner
Petr Gronat
Steve Gu
Josechu Guerrero
Anupam Guha
Jean-Yves Guillemaut
Alp Güler
Erhan Gündoğdu
Guodong Guo
Xinqing Guo
Ankush Gupta
Mohit Gupta
Saurabh Gupta
Tanmay Gupta
Abner Guzman Rivera
Timo Hackel
Sunil Hadap
Christian Haene
Ralf Haeusler
Levente Hajder
David Hall
Peter Hall
Stefan Haller
Ghassan Hamarneh
Fred Hamprecht
Onur Hamsici
Bohyung Han
Junwei Han
Xufeng Han
Yahong Han
Ankur Handa
Albert Haque
Tatsuya Harada
Mehrtash Harandi
Bharath Hariharan
Mahmudul Hasan
Tal Hassner
Kenji Hata
Soren Hauberg
Michal Havlena
Zeeshan Hayder
Junfeng He
Lei He
Varsha Hedau
Felix Heide

Wolfgang Heidrich
Janne Heikkila
Jared Heinly
Mattias Heinrich
Lisa Anne Hendricks
Dan Hendrycks
Stephane Herbin
Alexander Hermans
Luis Herranz
Aaron Hertzmann
Adrian Hilton
Michael Hirsch
Steven Hoi
Seunghoon Hong
Wei Hong
Anthony Hoogs
Radu Horaud
Yedid Hoshen
Omid Hosseini Jafari
Kuang-Jui Hsu
Winston Hsu
Yinlin Hu
Zhe Hu
Gang Hua
Chen Huang
De-An Huang
Dong Huang
Gary Huang
Heng Huang
Jia-Bin Huang
Qixing Huang
Rui Huang
Sheng Huang
Weilin Huang
Xiaolei Huang
Xinyu Huang
Zhiwu Huang
Tak-Wai Hui
Wei-Chih Hung
Junhwa Hur
Mohamed Hussein
Wonjun Hwang
Anders Hyden
Satoshi Ikehata
Nazlı Ikizler-Cinbis
Viorela Ila

Evren Imre
Eldar Insafutdinov
Go Irie
Hossam Isack
Ahmet Işcen
Daisuke Iwai
Hamid Izadinia
Nathan Jacobs
Suyog Jain
Varun Jampani
C. V. Jawahar
Dinesh Jayaraman
Sadeep Jayasumana
Laszlo Jeni
Hueihan Jhuang
Dinghuang Ji
Hui Ji
Qiang Ji
Fan Jia
Kui Jia
Xu Jia
Huaizu Jiang
Jiayan Jiang
Nianjuan Jiang
Tingting Jiang
Xiaoyi Jiang
Yu-Gang Jiang
Long Jin
Suo Jinli
Justin Johnson
Nebojsa Jojic
Michael Jones
Hanbyul Joo
Jungseock Joo
Ajjen Joshi
Amin Jourabloo
Frederic Jurie
Achuta Kadambi
Samuel Kadoury
Ioannis Kakadiaris
Zdenek Kalal
Yannis Kalantidis
Sinan Kalkan
Vicky Kalogeiton
Sunkavalli Kalyan
J.-K. Kamarainen

Achal Dave
Shalini De Mello
Teofilo deCampos
Joseph DeGol
Koichiro Deguchi
Alessio Del Bue
Stefanie Demirci
Jia Deng
Zhiwei Deng
Joachim Denzler
Konstantinos Derpanis
Aditya Deshpande
Alban Desmaison
Frédéric Devernay
Abhinav Dhall
Michel Dhome
Hamdi Dibeklioğlu
Mert Dikmen
Cosimo Distante
Ajay Divakaran
Mandar Dixit
Carl Doersch
Piotr Dollar
Bo Dong
Chao Dong
Huang Dong
Jian Dong
Jiangxin Dong
Weisheng Dong
Simon Donné
Gianfranco Doretto
Alexey Dosovitskiy
Matthijs Douze
Bruce Draper
Bertram Drost
Liang Du
Shichuan Du
Gregory Dudek
Zoran Duric
Pınar Duygulu
Hazım Ekenel
Tarek El-Gaaly
Ehsan Elhamifar
Mohamed Elhoseiny
Sabu Emmanuel
Ian Endres

Aykut Erdem
Erkut Erdem
Hugo Jair Escalante
Sergio Escalera
Victor Escorcia
Francisco Estrada
Davide Eynard
Bin Fan
Jialue Fan
Quanfu Fan
Chen Fang
Tian Fang
Yi Fang
Hany Farid
Giovanni Farinella
Ryan Farrell
Alireza Fathi
Christoph Feichtenhofer
Wenxin Feng
Martin Fergie
Cornelia Fermuller
Basura Fernando
Michael Firman
Bob Fisher
John Fisher
Mathew Fisher
Boris Flach
Matt Flagg
Francois Fleuret
David Fofi
Ruth Fong
Gian Luca Foresti
Per-Erik Forssén
David Fouhey
Katerina Fragkiadaki
Victor Fragoso
Jan-Michael Frahm
Jean-Sebastien Franco
Ohad Fried
Simone Frintrop
Huazhu Fu
Yun Fu
Olac Fuentes
Christopher Funk
Thomas Funkhouser
Brian Funt

Ryo Furukawa
Yasutaka Furukawa
Andrea Fusiello
Fatma Güney
Raghudeep Gadde
Silvano Galliani
Orazio Gallo
Chuang Gan
Bin-Bin Gao
Jin Gao
Junbin Gao
Ruohan Gao
Shenghua Gao
Animesh Garg
Ravi Garg
Erik Gartner
Simone Gasparin
Jochen Gast
Leon A. Gatys
Stratis Gavves
Liuhao Ge
Timnit Gebru
James Gee
Peter Gehler
Xin Geng
Guido Gerig
David Geronimo
Bernard Ghanem
Michael Gharbi
Golnaz Ghiasi
Spyros Gidaris
Andrew Gilbert
Rohit Girdhar
Ioannis Gkioulekas
Georgia Gkioxari
Guy Godin
Roland Goecke
Michael Goesele
Nuno Goncalves
Boqing Gong
Minglun Gong
Yunchao Gong
Abel Gonzalez-Garcia
Daniel Gordon
Paulo Gotardo
Stephen Gould

Jesus Bermudez-Cameo
Leonard Berrada
Gedas Bertasius
Ross Beveridge
Lucas Beyer
Bir Bhanu
S. Bhattacharya
Binod Bhattarai
Arnav Bhavsar
Simone Bianco
Adel Bibi
Pia Bideau
Josef Bigun
Arijit Biswas
Soma Biswas
Marten Bjoerkman
Volker Blanz
Vishnu Boddeti
Piotr Bojanowski
Terrance Boult
Yuri Boykov
Hakan Boyraz
Eric Brachmann
Samarth Brahmbhatt
Mathieu Bredif
Francois Bremond
Michael Brown
Luc Brun
Shyamal Buch
Pradeep Buddharaju
Aurelie Bugeau
Rudy Bunel
Xavier Burgos Artizzu
Darius Burschka
Andrei Bursuc
Zoya Bylinskii
Fabian Caba
Daniel Cabrini Hauagge
Cesar Cadena Lerma
Holger Caesar
Jianfei Cai
Junjie Cai
Zhaowei Cai
Simone Calderara
Neill Campbell
Octavia Camps

Xun Cao
Yanshuai Cao
Joao Carreira
Dan Casas
Daniel Castro
Jan Cech
M. Emre Celebi
Duygu Ceylan
Menglei Chai
Ayan Chakrabarti
Rudrasis Chakraborty
Shayok Chakraborty
Tat-Jen Cham
Antonin Chambolle
Antoni Chan
Sharat Chandran
Hyun Sung Chang
Ju Yong Chang
Xiaojun Chang
Soravit Changpinyo
Wei-Lun Chao
Yu-Wei Chao
Visesh Chari
Rizwan Chaudhry
Siddhartha Chaudhuri
Rama Chellappa
Chao Chen
Chen Chen
Cheng Chen
Chu-Song Chen
Guang Chen
Hsin-I Chen
Hwann-Tzong Chen
Kai Chen
Kan Chen
Kevin Chen
Liang-Chieh Chen
Lin Chen
Qifeng Chen
Ting Chen
Wei Chen
Xi Chen
Xilin Chen
Xinlei Chen
Yingcong Chen
Yixin Chen

Erkang Cheng
Jingchun Cheng
Ming-Ming Cheng
Wen-Huang Cheng
Yuan Cheng
Anoop Cherian
Liang-Tien Chia
Naoki Chiba
Shao-Yi Chien
Han-Pang Chiu
Wei-Chen Chiu
Nam Ik Cho
Sunghyun Cho
TaeEun Choe
Jongmoo Choi
Christopher Choy
Wen-Sheng Chu
Yung-Yu Chuang
Ondrej Chum
Joon Son Chung
Gökberk Cinbis
James Clark
Andrea Cohen
Forrester Cole
Toby Collins
John Collomosse
Camille Couprie
David Crandall
Marco Cristani
Canton Cristian
James Crowley
Yin Cui
Zhaopeng Cui
Bo Dai
Jifeng Dai
Qieyun Dai
Shengyang Dai
Yuchao Dai
Carlo Dal Mutto
Dima Damen
Zachary Daniels
Kostas Daniilidis
Donald Dansereau
Mohamed Daoudi
Abhishek Das
Samyak Datta

Tinne Tuytelaars	KU Leuven, Belgium
Jasper Uijlings	Google, Switzerland
Joost van de Weijer	Computer Vision Center, Spain
Nuno Vasconcelos	University of California, San Diego, USA
Andrea Vedaldi	University of Oxford, UK
Olga Veksler	University of Western Ontario, Canada
Jakob Verbeek	Inria, France
Rene Vidal	Johns Hopkins University, USA
Daphna Weinshall	Hebrew University, Israel
Chris Williams	University of Edinburgh, UK
Lior Wolf	Tel Aviv University, Israel
Ming-Hsuan Yang	University of California at Merced, USA
Todd Zickler	Harvard University, USA
Andrew Zisserman	University of Oxford, UK

Technical Program Committee

Hassan Abu Alhaija	Peter Anderson	Arunava Banerjee
Radhakrishna Achanta	Juan Andrade-Cetto	Atsuhiko Banno
Hanno Ackermann	Mykhaylo Andriluka	Aayush Bansal
Ehsan Adeli	Anelia Angelova	Yingze Bao
Lourdes Agapito	Michel Antunes	Md Jawadul Bappy
Aishwarya Agrawal	Pablo Arbelaez	Pierre Baqué
Antonio Agudo	Vasileios Argyriou	Dániel Baráth
Eirikur Agustsson	Chetan Arora	Adrian Barbu
Karim Ahmed	Federica Arrigoni	Kobus Barnard
Byeongjoo Ahn	Vassilis Athitsos	Nick Barnes
Unaiza Ahsan	Mathieu Aubry	Francisco Barranco
Emre Akbaş	Shai Avidan	Adrien Bartoli
Eren Aksoy	Yannis Avrithis	E. Bayro-Corrochano
Yağız Aksoy	Samaneh Azadi	Paul Beardlsey
Alexandre Alahi	Hossein Azizpour	Vasileios Belagiannis
Jean-Baptiste Alayrac	Artem Babenko	Sean Bell
Samuel Albanie	Timur Bagautdinov	Ismail Ben
Cenek Albl	Andrew Bagdanov	Boulbaba Ben Amor
Saad Ali	Hessam Bagherinezhad	Gil Ben-Artzi
Rahaf Aljundi	Yuval Bahat	Ohad Ben-Shahar
Jose M. Alvarez	Min Bai	Abhijit Bendale
Humam Alwassel	Qinxun Bai	Rodrigo Benenson
Toshiyuki Amano	Song Bai	Fabian Benitez-Quiroz
Mitsuru Ambai	Xiang Bai	Fethallah Benmansour
Mohamed Amer	Peter Bajcsy	Ryad Benosman
Senjian An	Amr Bakry	Filippo Bergamasco
Cosmin Ancuti	Kavita Bala	David Bermudez

Yasuyuki Matsushita	Osaka University, Japan
Dimitris Metaxas	Rutgers University, USA
Greg Mori	Simon Fraser University, Canada
Vittorio Murino	Istituto Italiano di Tecnologia, Italy
Richard Newcombe	Oculus Research, USA
Minh Hoai Nguyen	Stony Brook University, USA
Sebastian Nowozin	Microsoft Research Cambridge, UK
Aude Oliva	MIT, USA
Bjorn Ommer	Heidelberg University, Germany
Tomas Pajdla	Czech Technical University in Prague, Czechia
Maja Pantic	Imperial College London and Samsung AI Research Centre Cambridge, UK
Caroline Pantofaru	Google, USA
Devi Parikh	Georgia Tech and Facebook AI Research, USA
Sylvain Paris	Adobe Research, USA
Vladimir Pavlovic	Rutgers University, USA
Marcello Pelillo	University of Venice, Italy
Patrick Pérez	Valeo, France
Robert Pless	George Washington University, USA
Thomas Pock	Graz University of Technology, Austria
Jean Ponce	Inria, France
Gerard Pons-Moll	MPII, Saarland Informatics Campus, Germany
Long Quan	Hong Kong University of Science and Technology, SAR China
Stefan Roth	TU Darmstadt, Germany
Carsten Rother	University of Heidelberg, Germany
Bryan Russell	Adobe Research, USA
Kate Saenko	Boston University, USA
Mathieu Salzmann	EPFL, Switzerland
Dimitris Samaras	Stony Brook University, USA
Yoichi Sato	University of Tokyo, Japan
Silvio Savarese	Stanford University, USA
Konrad Schindler	ETH Zurich, Switzerland
Cordelia Schmid	Inria, France and Google, France
Nicu Sebe	University of Trento, Italy
Fei Sha	University of Southern California, USA
Greg Shakhnarovich	TTI Chicago, USA
Jianbo Shi	University of Pennsylvania, USA
Abhinav Shrivastava	UMD and Google, USA
Yan Shuicheng	National University of Singapore, Singapore
Leonid Sigal	University of British Columbia, Canada
Josef Sivic	Czech Technical University in Prague, Czechia
Arnold Smeulders	University of Amsterdam, The Netherlands
Deqing Sun	NVIDIA, USA
Antonio Torralba	MIT, USA
Zhuowen Tu	University of California, San Diego, USA

Sanja Fidler	University of Toronto, Canada
Andrew Fitzgibbon	Microsoft, Cambridge, UK
David Forsyth	University of Illinois at Urbana-Champaign, USA
Charless Fowlkes	University of California, Irvine, USA
Bill Freeman	MIT, USA
Mario Fritz	MPII, Germany
Jürgen Gall	University of Bonn, Germany
Dariu Gavrila	TU Delft, The Netherlands
Andreas Geiger	MPI-IS and University of Tübingen, Germany
Theo Gevers	University of Amsterdam, The Netherlands
Ross Girshick	Facebook AI Research, USA
Kristen Grauman	Facebook AI Research and UT Austin, USA
Abhinav Gupta	Carnegie Mellon University, USA
Kaiming He	Facebook AI Research, USA
Martial Hebert	Carnegie Mellon University, USA
Anders Heyden	Lund University, Sweden
Timothy Hospedales	University of Edinburgh, UK
Michal Irani	Weizmann Institute of Science, Israel
Phillip Isola	University of California, Berkeley, USA
Hervé Jégou	Facebook AI Research, France
David Jacobs	University of Maryland, College Park, USA
Allan Jepson	University of Toronto, Canada
Jiaya Jia	Chinese University of Hong Kong, SAR China
Fredrik Kahl	Chalmers University, USA
Hedvig Kjellström	KTH Royal Institute of Technology, Sweden
Iasonas Kokkinos	University College London and Facebook, UK
Vladlen Koltun	Intel Labs, USA
Philipp Krähenbühl	UT Austin, USA
M. Pawan Kumar	University of Oxford, UK
Kyros Kutulakos	University of Toronto, Canada
In Kweon	KAIST, South Korea
Ivan Laptev	Inria, France
Svetlana Lazebnik	University of Illinois at Urbana-Champaign, USA
Laura Leal-Taixé	Technical University of Munich, Germany
Erik Learned-Miller	University of Massachusetts, Amherst, USA
Kyoung Mu Lee	Seoul National University, South Korea
Bastian Leibe	RWTH Aachen University, Germany
Aleš Leonardis	University of Birmingham, UK
Vincent Lepetit	University of Bordeaux, France and Graz University of Technology, Austria
Fuxin Li	Oregon State University, USA
Dahua Lin	Chinese University of Hong Kong, SAR China
Jim Little	University of British Columbia, Canada
Ce Liu	Google, USA
Chen Change Loy	Nanyang Technological University, Singapore
Jiri Matas	Czech Technical University in Prague, Czechia

Publicity Chair

Giovanni Maria   University of Catania, Italy
  Farinella

Industrial Liaison Chairs

Florent Perronnin   Naver Labs, France
Yunchao Gong   Snap, USA
Helmut Grabner   Logitech, Switzerland

Finance Chair

Gerard Medioni   Amazon, University of Southern California, USA

Publication Chairs

Albert Ali Salah   Boğaziçi University, Turkey
Hamdi Dibeklioğlu   Bilkent University, Turkey

Area Chairs

Kalle Åström   Lund University, Sweden
Zeynep Akata   University of Amsterdam, The Netherlands
Joao Barreto   University of Coimbra, Portugal
Ronen Basri   Weizmann Institute of Science, Israel
Dhruv Batra   Georgia Tech and Facebook AI Research, USA
Serge Belongie   Cornell University, USA
Rodrigo Benenson   Google, Switzerland
Hakan Bilen   University of Edinburgh, UK
Matthew Blaschko   KU Leuven, Belgium
Edmond Boyer   Inria, France
Gabriel Brostow   University College London, UK
Thomas Brox   University of Freiburg, Germany
Marcus Brubaker   York University, Canada
Barbara Caputo   Politecnico di Torino and the Italian Institute
                          of Technology, Italy
Tim Cootes   University of Manchester, UK
Trevor Darrell   University of California, Berkeley, USA
Larry Davis   University of Maryland at College Park, USA
Andrew Davison   Imperial College London, UK
Fernando de la Torre   Carnegie Mellon University, USA
Irfan Essa   GeorgiaTech, USA
Ali Farhadi   University of Washington, USA
Paolo Favaro   University of Bern, Switzerland
Michael Felsberg   Linköping University, Sweden

Organization

General Chairs

Horst Bischof	Graz University of Technology, Austria
Daniel Cremers	Technical University of Munich, Germany
Bernt Schiele	Saarland University, Max Planck Institute for Informatics, Germany
Ramin Zabih	CornellNYCTech, USA

Program Committee Co-chairs

Vittorio Ferrari	University of Edinburgh, UK
Martial Hebert	Carnegie Mellon University, USA
Cristian Sminchisescu	Lund University, Sweden
Yair Weiss	Hebrew University, Israel

Local Arrangements Chairs

Björn Menze	Technical University of Munich, Germany
Matthias Niessner	Technical University of Munich, Germany

Workshop Chairs

Stefan Roth	TU Darmstadt, Germany
Laura Leal-Taixé	Technical University of Munich, Germany

Tutorial Chairs

Michael Bronstein	Università della Svizzera Italiana, Switzerland
Laura Leal-Taixé	Technical University of Munich, Germany

Website Chair

Friedrich Fraundorfer	Graz University of Technology, Austria

Demo Chairs

Federico Tombari	Technical University of Munich, Germany
Joerg Stueckler	Technical University of Munich, Germany

existing AC assignment, as well as minimizing the fragmentation across ACs, so that each AC had on average only 5.5 buddy ACs to communicate with. The largest number was 11. Given the complexity of the conflicts, this was a very efficient set of assignments from OpenReview. Each paper was then evaluated by its assigned pair of ACs. For each paper, we required each of the two ACs assigned to certify both the final recommendation and the metareview (aka consolidation report). In all cases, after extensive discussions, the two ACs arrived at a common acceptance decision. We maintained these decisions, with the caveat that we did evaluate, sometimes going back to the ACs, a few papers for which the final acceptance decision substantially deviated from the consensus from the reviewers, amending three decisions in the process.

We want to thank everyone involved in making ECCV 2018 possible. The success of ECCV 2018 depended on the quality of papers submitted by the authors, and on the very hard work of the ACs and the Program Committee members. We are particularly grateful to the OpenReview team (Melisa Bok, Ari Kobren, Andrew McCallum, Michael Spector) for their support, in particular their willingness to implement new features, often on a tight schedule, to Laurent Charlin for the use of the Toronto Paper Matching System, to the CMT3 team, in particular in dealing with all the issues that arise when using a new system, to Friedrich Fraundorfer and Quirin Lohr for maintaining the online version of the program, and to the CMU staff (Keyla Cook, Lynnetta Miller, Ashley Song, Nora Kazour) for assisting with data entry/editing in CMT3. Finally, the preparation of these proceedings would not have been possible without the diligent effort of the publication chairs, Albert Ali Salah and Hamdi Dibeklioğlu, and of Anna Kramer and Alfred Hofmann from Springer.

September 2018

Vittorio Ferrari
Martial Hebert
Cristian Sminchisescu
Yair Weiss

refining conflict definitions and in generating quality matches. The only glitch is that, once the matches were generated, a small percentage of papers were unassigned because of discrepancies between the OpenReview conflicts and the conflicts entered in CMT3. We manually assigned these papers. This glitch is revealing of the challenge of using multiple systems at once (CMT3 and OpenReview in this case), which needs to be addressed in future.

After assignment of papers to ACs, the ACs suggested seven reviewers per paper from the Program Committee pool. The selection and rank ordering were facilitated by the TPMS affinity scores visible to the ACs for each paper/reviewer pair. The final assignment of papers to reviewers was generated again through OpenReview in order to account for refined conflict definitions. This required new features in the OpenReview matching system to accommodate the ECCV workflow, in particular to incorporate selection ranking, and maximum reviewer load. Very few papers received fewer than three reviewers after matching and were handled through manual assignment. Reviewers were then asked to comment on the merit of each paper and to make an initial recommendation ranging from definitely reject to definitely accept, including a borderline rating. The reviewers were also asked to suggest explicit questions they wanted to see answered in the authors' rebuttal. The initial review period was five weeks. Because of the delay in getting all the reviews in, we had to delay the final release of the reviews by four days. However, because of the slack included at the tail end of the schedule, we were able to maintain the decision target date with sufficient time for all the phases. We reassigned over 100 reviews from 40 reviewers during the review period. Unfortunately, the main reason for these reassignments was reviewers declining to review, after having accepted to do so. Other reasons included technical relevance and occasional unidentified conflicts. We express our thanks to the emergency reviewers who generously accepted to perform these reviews under short notice. In addition, a substantial number of manual corrections had to do with reviewers using a different email address than the one that was used at the time of the reviewer invitation. This is revealing of a broader issue with identifying users by email addresses that change frequently enough to cause significant problems during the timespan of the conference process.

The authors were then given the opportunity to rebut the reviews, to identify factual errors, and to address the specific questions raised by the reviewers over a seven-day rebuttal period. The exact format of the rebuttal was the object of considerable debate among the organizers, as well as with prior organizers. At issue is to balance giving the author the opportunity to respond completely and precisely to the reviewers, e.g., by including graphs of experiments, while avoiding requests for completely new material or experimental results not included in the original paper. In the end, we decided on the two-page PDF document in conference format. Following this rebuttal period, reviewers and ACs discussed papers at length, after which reviewers finalized their evaluation and gave a final recommendation to the ACs. A significant percentage of the reviewers did enter their final recommendation if it did not differ from their initial recommendation. Given the tight schedule, we did not wait until all were entered.

After this discussion period, each paper was assigned to a second AC. The AC/paper matching was again run through OpenReview. Again, the OpenReview team worked quickly to implement the features specific to this process, in this case accounting for the

Preface

Welcome to the proceedings of the 2018 European Conference on Computer Vision (ECCV 2018) held in Munich, Germany. We are delighted to present this volume reflecting a strong and exciting program, the result of an extensive review process. In total, we received 2,439 valid paper submissions. Of these, 776 were accepted (31.8%): 717 as posters (29.4%) and 59 as oral presentations (2.4%). All oral presentations were presented as posters as well. The program selection process was complicated this year by the large increase in the number of submitted papers, +65% over ECCV 2016, and the use of CMT3 for the first time for a computer vision conference. The program selection process was supported by four program co-chairs (PCs), 126 area chairs (ACs), and 1,199 reviewers with reviews assigned.

We were primarily responsible for the design and execution of the review process. Beyond administrative rejections, we were involved in acceptance decisions only in the very few cases where the ACs were not able to agree on a decision. As PCs, and as is customary in the field, we were not allowed to co-author a submission. General co-chairs and other co-organizers who played no role in the review process were permitted to submit papers, and were treated as any other author is.

Acceptance decisions were made by two independent ACs. The ACs also made a joint recommendation for promoting papers to oral status. We decided on the final selection of oral presentations based on the ACs' recommendations. There were 126 ACs, selected according to their technical expertise, experience, and geographical diversity (63 from European, nine from Asian/Australian, and 54 from North American institutions). Indeed, 126 ACs is a substantial increase in the number of ACs due to the natural increase in the number of papers and to our desire to maintain the number of papers assigned to each AC to a manageable number so as to ensure quality. The ACs were aided by the 1,199 reviewers to whom papers were assigned for reviewing. The Program Committee was selected from committees of previous ECCV, ICCV, and CVPR conferences and was extended on the basis of suggestions from the ACs. Having a large pool of Program Committee members for reviewing allowed us to match expertise while reducing reviewer loads. No more than eight papers were assigned to a reviewer, maintaining the reviewers' load at the same level as ECCV 2016 despite the increase in the number of submitted papers.

Conflicts of interest between ACs, Program Committee members, and papers were identified based on the home institutions, and on previous collaborations of all researchers involved. To find institutional conflicts, all authors, Program Committee members, and ACs were asked to list the Internet domains of their current institutions. We assigned on average approximately 18 papers to each AC. The papers were assigned using the affinity scores from the Toronto Paper Matching System (TPMS) and additional data from the OpenReview system, managed by a UMass group. OpenReview used additional information from ACs' and authors' records to identify collaborations and to generate matches. OpenReview was invaluable in

Foreword

It was our great pleasure to host the European Conference on Computer Vision 2018 in Munich, Germany. This constituted by far the largest ECCV event ever. With close to 2,900 registered participants and another 600 on the waiting list one month before the conference, participation more than doubled since the last ECCV in Amsterdam. We believe that this is due to a dramatic growth of the computer vision community combined with the popularity of Munich as a major European hub of culture, science, and industry. The conference took place in the heart of Munich in the concert hall Gasteig with workshops and tutorials held at the downtown campus of the Technical University of Munich.

One of the major innovations for ECCV 2018 was the free perpetual availability of all conference and workshop papers, which is often referred to as open access. We note that this is not precisely the same use of the term as in the Budapest declaration. Since 2013, CVPR and ICCV have had their papers hosted by the Computer Vision Foundation (CVF), in parallel with the IEEE Xplore version. This has proved highly beneficial to the computer vision community.

We are delighted to announce that for ECCV 2018 a very similar arrangement was put in place with the cooperation of Springer. In particular, the author's final version will be freely available in perpetuity on a CVF page, while SpringerLink will continue to host a version with further improvements, such as activating reference links and including video. We believe that this will give readers the best of both worlds; researchers who are focused on the technical content will have a freely available version in an easily accessible place, while subscribers to SpringerLink will continue to have the additional benefits that this provides. We thank Alfred Hofmann from Springer for helping to negotiate this agreement, which we expect will continue for future versions of ECCV.

September 2018

Horst Bischof
Daniel Cremers
Bernt Schiele
Ramin Zabih

Editors
Vittorio Ferrari
Google Research
Zurich
Switzerland

Martial Hebert
Carnegie Mellon University
Pittsburgh, PA
USA

Cristian Sminchisescu
Google Research
Zurich
Switzerland

Yair Weiss
Hebrew University of Jerusalem
Jerusalem
Israel

ISSN 0302-9743 ISSN 1611-3349 (electronic)
Lecture Notes in Computer Science
ISBN 978-3-030-01257-1 ISBN 978-3-030-01258-8 (eBook)
https://doi.org/10.1007/978-3-030-01258-8

Library of Congress Control Number: 2018955489

LNCS Sublibrary: SL6 – Image Processing, Computer Vision, Pattern Recognition, and Graphics

This Springer imprint is published by the registered company Springer Nature Switzerland AG
The registered company address is: Gewerbestrasse 11, 6330 Cham, Switzerland

Vittorio Ferrari · Martial Hebert
Cristian Sminchisescu · Yair Weiss (Eds.)

Computer Vision – ECCV 2018

15th European Conference
Munich, Germany, September 8–14, 2018
Proceedings, Part XII

 Springer

More information about this series at http://www.springer.com/series/7412

Lecture Notes in Computer Science 11216

Commenced Publication in 1973
Founding and Former Series Editors:
Gerhard Goos, Juris Hartmanis, and Jan van Leeuwen

P. J. Narayanan
Charlie Nash
Lakshmanan Nataraj
Fabian Nater
Lukáš Neumann
Natalia Neverova
Alejandro Newell
Phuc Nguyen
Xiaohan Nie
David Nilsson
Ko Nishino
Zhenxing Niu
Shohei Nobuhara
Klas Nordberg
Mohammed Norouzi
David Novotny
Ifeoma Nwogu
Matthew O'Toole
Guillaume Obozinski
Jean-Marc Odobez
Eyal Ofek
Ferda Ofli
Tae-Hyun Oh
Iason Oikonomidis
Takeshi Oishi
Takahiro Okabe
Takayuki Okatani
Vlad Olaru
Michael Opitz
Jose Oramas
Vicente Ordonez
Ivan Oseledets
Aljosa Osep
Magnus Oskarsson
Martin R. Oswald
Wanli Ouyang
Andrew Owens
Mustafa Özuysal
Jinshan Pan
Xingang Pan
Rameswar Panda
Sharath Pankanti
Julien Pansiot
Nicolas Papadakis
George Papandreou
N. Papanikolopoulos

Hyun Soo Park
In Kyu Park
Jaesik Park
Omkar Parkhi
Alvaro Parra Bustos
C. Alejandro Parraga
Vishal Patel
Deepak Pathak
Ioannis Patras
Viorica Patraucean
Genevieve Patterson
Kim Pedersen
Robert Peharz
Selen Pehlivan
Xi Peng
Bojan Pepik
Talita Perciano
Federico Pernici
Adrian Peter
Stavros Petridis
Vladimir Petrovic
Henning Petzka
Tomas Pfister
Trung Pham
Justus Piater
Massimo Piccardi
Sudeep Pillai
Pedro Pinheiro
Lerrel Pinto
Bernardo Pires
Aleksis Pirinen
Fiora Pirri
Leonid Pischulin
Tobias Ploetz
Bryan Plummer
Yair Poleg
Jean Ponce
Gerard Pons-Moll
Jordi Pont-Tuset
Alin Popa
Fatih Porikli
Horst Possegger
Viraj Prabhu
Andrea Prati
Maria Priisalu
Véronique Prinet

Victor Prisacariu
Jan Prokaj
Nicolas Pugeault
Luis Puig
Ali Punjani
Senthil Purushwalkam
Guido Pusiol
Guo-Jun Qi
Xiaojuan Qi
Hongwei Qin
Shi Qiu
Faisal Qureshi
Matthias Rüther
Petia Radeva
Umer Rafi
Rahul Raguram
Swaminathan Rahul
Varun Ramakrishna
Kandan Ramakrishnan
Ravi Ramamoorthi
Vignesh Ramanathan
Vasili Ramanishka
R. Ramasamy Selvaraju
Rene Ranftl
Carolina Raposo
Nikhil Rasiwasia
Nalini Ratha
Sai Ravela
Avinash Ravichandran
Ramin Raziperchikolaei
Sylvestre-Alvise Rebuffi
Adria Recasens
Joe Redmon
Timo Rehfeld
Michal Reinstein
Konstantinos Rematas
Haibing Ren
Shaoqing Ren
Wenqi Ren
Zhile Ren
Hamid Rezatofighi
Nicholas Rhinehart
Helge Rhodin
Elisa Ricci
Eitan Richardson
Stephan Richter

Gernot Riegler
Hayko Riemenschneider
Tammy Riklin Raviv
Ergys Ristani
Tobias Ritschel
Mariano Rivera
Samuel Rivera
Antonio Robles-Kelly
Ignacio Rocco
Jason Rock
Emanuele Rodola
Mikel Rodriguez
Gregory Rogez
Marcus Rohrbach
Gemma Roig
Javier Romero
Olaf Ronneberger
Amir Rosenfeld
Bodo Rosenhahn
Guy Rosman
Arun Ross
Samuel Rota Bulò
Peter Roth
Constantin Rothkopf
Sebastien Roy
Amit Roy-Chowdhury
Ognjen Rudovic
Adria Ruiz
Javier Ruiz-del-Solar
Christian Rupprecht
Olga Russakovsky
Chris Russell
Alexandre Sablayrolles
Fereshteh Sadeghi
Ryusuke Sagawa
Hideo Saito
Elham Sakhaee
Albert Ali Salah
Conrad Sanderson
Koppal Sanjeev
Aswin Sankaranarayanan
Elham Saraee
Jason Saragih
Sudeep Sarkar
Imari Sato
Shin'ichi Satoh

Torsten Sattler
Bogdan Savchynskyy
Johannes Schönberger
Hanno Scharr
Walter Scheirer
Bernt Schiele
Frank Schmidt
Tanner Schmidt
Dirk Schnieders
Samuel Schulter
William Schwartz
Alexander Schwing
Ozan Sener
Soumyadip Sengupta
Laura Sevilla-Lara
Mubarak Shah
Shishir Shah
Fahad Shahbaz Khan
Amir Shahroudy
Jing Shao
Xiaowei Shao
Roman Shapovalov
Nataliya Shapovalova
Ali Sharif Razavian
Gaurav Sharma
Mohit Sharma
Pramod Sharma
Viktoriia Sharmanska
Eli Shechtman
Mark Sheinin
Evan Shelhamer
Chunhua Shen
Li Shen
Wei Shen
Xiaohui Shen
Xiaoyong Shen
Ziyi Shen
Lu Sheng
Baoguang Shi
Boxin Shi
Kevin Shih
Hyunjung Shim
Ilan Shimshoni
Young Min Shin
Koichi Shinoda
Matthew Shreve

Tianmin Shu
Zhixin Shu
Kaleem Siddiqi
Gunnar Sigurdsson
Nathan Silberman
Tomas Simon
Abhishek Singh
Gautam Singh
Maneesh Singh
Praveer Singh
Richa Singh
Saurabh Singh
Sudipta Sinha
Vladimir Smutny
Noah Snavely
Cees Snoek
Kihyuk Sohn
Eric Sommerlade
Sanghyun Son
Bi Song
Shiyu Song
Shuran Song
Xuan Song
Yale Song
Yang Song
Yibing Song
Lorenzo Sorgi
Humberto Sossa
Pratul Srinivasan
Michael Stark
Bjorn Stenger
Rainer Stiefelhagen
Joerg Stueckler
Jan Stuehmer
Hang Su
Hao Su
Shuochen Su
R. Subramanian
Yusuke Sugano
Akihiro Sugimoto
Baochen Sun
Chen Sun
Jian Sun
Jin Sun
Lin Sun
Min Sun

Qing Sun
Zhaohui Sun
David Suter
Eran Swears
Raza Syed Hussain
T. Syeda-Mahmood
Christian Szegedy
Duy-Nguyen Ta
Tolga Taşdizen
Hemant Tagare
Yuichi Taguchi
Ying Tai
Yu-Wing Tai
Jun Takamatsu
Hugues Talbot
Toru Tamak
Robert Tamburo
Chaowei Tan
Meng Tang
Peng Tang
Siyu Tang
Wei Tang
Junli Tao
Ran Tao
Xin Tao
Makarand Tapaswi
Jean-Philippe Tarel
Maxim Tatarchenko
Bugra Tekin
Demetri Terzopoulos
Christian Theobalt
Diego Thomas
Rajat Thomas
Qi Tian
Xinmei Tian
YingLi Tian
Yonghong Tian
Yonglong Tian
Joseph Tighe
Radu Timofte
Massimo Tistarelli
Sinisa Todorovic
Pavel Tokmakov
Giorgos Tolias
Federico Tombari
Tatiana Tommasi

Chetan Tonde
Xin Tong
Akihiko Torii
Andrea Torsello
Florian Trammer
Du Tran
Quoc-Huy Tran
Rudolph Triebel
Alejandro Troccoli
Leonardo Trujillo
Tomasz Trzcinski
Sam Tsai
Yi-Hsuan Tsai
Hung-Yu Tseng
Vagia Tsiminaki
Aggeliki Tsoli
Wei-Chih Tu
Shubham Tulsiani
Fred Tung
Tony Tung
Matt Turek
Oncel Tuzel
Georgios Tzimiropoulos
Ilkay Ulusoy
Osman Ulusoy
Dmitry Ulyanov
Paul Upchurch
Ben Usman
Evgeniya Ustinova
Himanshu Vajaria
Alexander Vakhitov
Jack Valmadre
Ernest Valveny
Jan van Gemert
Grant Van Horn
Jagannadan Varadarajan
Gul Varol
Sebastiano Vascon
Francisco Vasconcelos
Mayank Vatsa
Javier Vázquez-Corral
Ramakrishna Vedantam
Ashok Veeraraghavan
Andreas Veit
Raviteja Vemulapalli
Jonathan Ventura

Matthias Vestner
Minh Vo
Christoph Vogel
Michele Volpi
Carl Vondrick
Sven Wachsmuth
Toshikazu Wada
Michael Waechter
Catherine Wah
Jacob Walker
Jun Wan
Boyu Wang
Chen Wang
Chunyu Wang
De Wang
Fang Wang
Hongxing Wang
Hua Wang
Jiang Wang
Jingdong Wang
Jinglu Wang
Jue Wang
Le Wang
Lei Wang
Lezi Wang
Liang Wang
Lichao Wang
Lijun Wang
Limin Wang
Liwei Wang
Naiyan Wang
Oliver Wang
Qi Wang
Ruiping Wang
Shenlong Wang
Shu Wang
Song Wang
Tao Wang
Xiaofang Wang
Xiaolong Wang
Xinchao Wang
Xinggang Wang
Xintao Wang
Yang Wang
Yu-Chiang Frank Wang
Yu-Xiong Wang

Zhaowen Wang
Zhe Wang
Anne Wannenwetsch
Simon Warfield
Scott Wehrwein
Donglai Wei
Ping Wei
Shih-En Wei
Xiu-Shen Wei
Yichen Wei
Xie Weidi
Philippe Weinzaepfel
Longyin Wen
Eric Wengrowski
Tomas Werner
Michael Wilber
Rick Wildes
Olivia Wiles
Kyle Wilson
David Wipf
Kwan-Yee Wong
Daniel Worrall
John Wright
Baoyuan Wu
Chao-Yuan Wu
Jiajun Wu
Jianxin Wu
Tianfu Wu
Xiaodong Wu
Xiaohe Wu
Xinxiao Wu
Yang Wu
Yi Wu
Ying Wu
Yuxin Wu
Zheng Wu
Stefanie Wuhrer
Yin Xia
Tao Xiang
Yu Xiang
Lei Xiao
Tong Xiao
Yang Xiao
Cihang Xie
Dan Xie
Jianwen Xie

Jin Xie
Lingxi Xie
Pengtao Xie
Saining Xie
Wenxuan Xie
Yuchen Xie
Bo Xin
Junliang Xing
Peng Xingchao
Bo Xiong
Fei Xiong
Xuehan Xiong
Yuanjun Xiong
Chenliang Xu
Danfei Xu
Huijuan Xu
Jia Xu
Weipeng Xu
Xiangyu Xu
Yan Xu
Yuanlu Xu
Jia Xue
Tianfan Xue
Erdem Yörük
Abhay Yadav
Deshraj Yadav
Payman Yadollahpour
Yasushi Yagi
Toshihiko Yamasaki
Fei Yan
Hang Yan
Junchi Yan
Junjie Yan
Sijie Yan
Keiji Yanai
Bin Yang
Chih-Yuan Yang
Dong Yang
Herb Yang
Jianchao Yang
Jianwei Yang
Jiaolong Yang
Jie Yang
Jimei Yang
Jufeng Yang
Linjie Yang

Michael Ying Yang
Ming Yang
Ruiduo Yang
Ruigang Yang
Shuo Yang
Wei Yang
Xiaodong Yang
Yanchao Yang
Yi Yang
Angela Yao
Bangpeng Yao
Cong Yao
Jian Yao
Ting Yao
Julian Yarkony
Mark Yatskar
Jinwei Ye
Mao Ye
Mei-Chen Yeh
Raymond Yeh
Serena Yeung
Kwang Moo Yi
Shuai Yi
Alper Yılmaz
Lijun Yin
Xi Yin
Zhaozheng Yin
Xianghua Ying
Ryo Yonetani
Donghyun Yoo
Ju Hong Yoon
Kuk-Jin Yoon
Chong You
Shaodi You
Aron Yu
Fisher Yu
Gang Yu
Jingyi Yu
Ke Yu
Licheng Yu
Pei Yu
Qian Yu
Rong Yu
Shoou-I Yu
Stella Yu
Xiang Yu

Yang Yu
Zhiding Yu
Ganzhao Yuan
Jing Yuan
Junsong Yuan
Lu Yuan
Stefanos Zafeiriou
Sergey Zagoruyko
Amir Zamir
K. Zampogiannis
Andrei Zanfir
Mihai Zanfir
Pablo Zegers
Eyasu Zemene
Andy Zeng
Xingyu Zeng
Yun Zeng
De-Chuan Zhan
Cheng Zhang
Dong Zhang
Guofeng Zhang
Han Zhang
Hang Zhang
Hanwang Zhang
Jian Zhang
Jianguo Zhang
Jianming Zhang
Jiawei Zhang
Junping Zhang
Lei Zhang
Linguang Zhang
Ning Zhang
Qing Zhang

Quanshi Zhang
Richard Zhang
Runze Zhang
Shanshan Zhang
Shiliang Zhang
Shu Zhang
Ting Zhang
Xiangyu Zhang
Xiaofan Zhang
Xu Zhang
Yimin Zhang
Yinda Zhang
Yongqiang Zhang
Yuting Zhang
Zhanpeng Zhang
Ziyu Zhang
Bin Zhao
Chen Zhao
Hang Zhao
Hengshuang Zhao
Qijun Zhao
Rui Zhao
Yue Zhao
Enliang Zheng
Liang Zheng
Stephan Zheng
Wei-Shi Zheng
Wenming Zheng
Yin Zheng
Yinqiang Zheng
Yuanjie Zheng
Guangyu Zhong
Bolei Zhou

Guang-Tong Zhou
Huiyu Zhou
Jiahuan Zhou
S. Kevin Zhou
Tinghui Zhou
Wengang Zhou
Xiaowei Zhou
Xingyi Zhou
Yin Zhou
Zihan Zhou
Fan Zhu
Guangming Zhu
Ji Zhu
Jiejie Zhu
Jun-Yan Zhu
Shizhan Zhu
Siyu Zhu
Xiangxin Zhu
Xiatian Zhu
Yan Zhu
Yingying Zhu
Yixin Zhu
Yuke Zhu
Zhenyao Zhu
Liansheng Zhuang
Zeeshan Zia
Karel Zimmermann
Daniel Zoran
Danping Zou
Qi Zou
Silvia Zuffi
Wangmeng Zuo
Xinxin Zuo

Contents – Part XII

Poster Session

Physical Primitive Decomposition 3
    Zhijian Liu, William T. Freeman, Joshua B. Tenenbaum, and Jiajun Wu

Deep Attention Neural Tensor Network for Visual Question Answering. 21
    Yalong Bai, Jianlong Fu, Tiejun Zhao, and Tao Mei

Shuffle-Then-Assemble: Learning Object-Agnostic Visual
Relationship Features. 38
    Xu Yang, Hanwang Zhang, and Jianfei Cai

Combining 3D Model Contour Energy and Keypoints for Object Tracking. . . 55
    Bogdan Bugaev, Anton Kryshchenko, and Roman Belov

Pairwise Confusion for Fine-Grained Visual Classification 71
    Abhimanyu Dubey, Otkrist Gupta, Pei Guo, Ramesh Raskar,
    Ryan Farrell, and Nikhil Naik

Interpretable Intuitive Physics Model 89
    Tian Ye, Xiaolong Wang, James Davidson, and Abhinav Gupta

Deep Multi-task Learning to Recognise Subtle Facial Expressions
of Mental States 106
    Guosheng Hu, Li Liu, Yang Yuan, Zehao Yu, Yang Hua, Zhihong Zhang,
    Fumin Shen, Ling Shao, Timothy Hospedales, Neil Robertson,
    and Yongxin Yang

SRDA: Generating Instance Segmentation Annotation via Scanning,
Reasoning and Domain Adaptation 124
    Wenqiang Xu, Yonglu Li, and Cewu Lu

Unsupervised Domain Adaptation for 3D Keypoint Estimation
via View Consistency 141
    Xingyi Zhou, Arjun Karpur, Chuang Gan, Linjie Luo, and Qixing Huang

Practical Black-Box Attacks on Deep Neural Networks Using Efficient
Query Mechanisms 158
    Arjun Nitin Bhagoji, Warren He, Bo Li, and Dawn Song

DYAN: A Dynamical Atoms-Based Network for Video Prediction 175
    Wenqian Liu, Abhishek Sharma, Octavia Camps, and Mario Sznaier

Sparsely Aggregated Convolutional Networks.   192
  Ligeng Zhu, Ruizhi Deng, Michael Maire, Zhiwei Deng, Greg Mori,
  and Ping Tan

Revisiting the Inverted Indices for Billion-Scale Approximate
Nearest Neighbors.   209
  Dmitry Baranchuk, Artem Babenko, and Yury Malkov

Diverse Feature Visualizations Reveal Invariances in Early Layers
of Deep Neural Networks.   225
  Santiago A. Cadena, Marissa A. Weis, Leon A. Gatys, Matthias Bethge,
  and Alexander S. Ecker

End-to-End Incremental Learning   241
  Francisco M. Castro, Manuel J. Marín-Jiménez, Nicolás Guil,
  Cordelia Schmid, and Karteek Alahari

Conditional Image-Text Embedding Networks   258
  Bryan A. Plummer, Paige Kordas, M. Hadi Kiapour, Shuai Zheng,
  Robinson Piramuthu, and Svetlana Lazebnik

Sampling Algebraic Varieties for Robust Camera Autocalibration   275
  Danda Pani Paudel and Luc Van Gool

Attribute-Guided Face Generation Using Conditional CycleGAN   293
  Yongyi Lu, Yu-Wing Tai, and Chi-Keung Tang

Deep Structure Inference Network for Facial Action Unit Recognition.   309
  Ciprian Corneanu, Meysam Madadi, and Sergio Escalera

Learning Priors for Semantic 3D Reconstruction.   325
  Ian Cherabier, Johannes L. Schönberger, Martin R. Oswald,
  Marc Pollefeys, and Andreas Geiger

Object Detection in Video with Spatiotemporal Sampling Networks   342
  Gedas Bertasius, Lorenzo Torresani, and Jianbo Shi

Video Summarization Using Fully Convolutional Sequence Networks   358
  Mrigank Rochan, Linwei Ye, and Yang Wang

Modeling Visual Context Is Key to Augmenting Object
Detection Datasets.   375
  Nikita Dvornik, Julien Mairal, and Cordelia Schmid

Learning Region Features for Object Detection.   392
  Jiayuan Gu, Han Hu, Liwei Wang, Yichen Wei, and Jifeng Dai

End-to-End Deep Structured Models for Drawing Crosswalks.   407
  Justin Liang and Raquel Urtasun

Sidekick Policy Learning for Active Visual Exploration.   424
  Santhosh K. Ramakrishnan and Kristen Grauman

Coloring with Words: Guiding Image Colorization Through Text-Based
Palette Generation.   443
  Hyojin Bahng, Seungjoo Yoo, Wonwoong Cho, David Keetae Park,
  Ziming Wu, Xiaojuan Ma, and Jaegul Choo

Efficient Global Point Cloud Registration by Matching Rotation Invariant
Features Through Translation Search.   460
  Yinlong Liu, Chen Wang, Zhijian Song, and Manning Wang

Facial Dynamics Interpreter Network: What Are the Important Relations
Between Local Dynamics for Facial Trait Estimation?.   475
  Seong Tae Kim and Yong Man Ro

Visual Question Generation for Class Acquisition of Unknown Objects.   492
  Kohei Uehara, Antonio Tejero-De-Pablos, Yoshitaka Ushiku,
  and Tatsuya Harada

Efficient Dense Point Cloud Object Reconstruction Using Deformation
Vector Fields   508
  Kejie Li, Trung Pham, Huangying Zhan, and Ian Reid

Improving DNN Robustness to Adversarial Attacks Using
Jacobian Regularization.   525
  Daniel Jakubovitz and Raja Giryes

Concept Mask: Large-Scale Segmentation from Semantic Concepts.   542
  Yufei Wang, Zhe Lin, Xiaohui Shen, Jianming Zhang, and Scott Cohen

Descending, Lifting or Smoothing: Secrets of Robust Cost Optimization   558
  Christopher Zach and Guillaume Bourmaud

Geolocation Estimation of Photos Using a Hierarchical Model
and Scene Classification.   575
  Eric Müller-Budack, Kader Pustu-Iren, and Ralph Ewerth

License Plate Detection and Recognition in Unconstrained Scenarios.   593
  Sérgio Montazzolli Silva and Cláudio Rosito Jung

Self-produced Guidance for Weakly-Supervised Object Localization   610
  Xiaolin Zhang, Yunchao Wei, Guoliang Kang, Yi Yang,
  and Thomas Huang

Occlusions, Motion and Depth Boundaries with a Generic Network
for Disparity, Optical Flow or Scene Flow Estimation   626
   Eddy Ilg, Tonmoy Saikia, Margret Keuper, and Thomas Brox

Is Robustness the Cost of Accuracy? – A Comprehensive Study
on the Robustness of 18 Deep Image Classification Models   644
   Dong Su, Huan Zhang, Hongge Chen, Jinfeng Yi, Pin-Yu Chen,
   and Yupeng Gao

Improving Shape Deformation in Unsupervised
Image-to-Image Translation   662
   Aaron Gokaslan, Vivek Ramanujan, Daniel Ritchie, Kwang In Kim,
   and James Tompkin

SwapNet: Image Based Garment Transfer   679
   Amit Raj, Patsorn Sangkloy, Huiwen Chang, James Hays,
   Duygu Ceylan, and Jingwan Lu

Optimization

Deterministic Consensus Maximization with Biconvex Programming   699
   Zhipeng Cai, Tat-Jun Chin, Huu Le, and David Suter

Robust Fitting in Computer Vision: Easy or Hard?   715
   Tat-Jun Chin, Zhipeng Cai, and Frank Neumann

Highly-Economized Multi-view Binary Compression for Scalable
Image Clustering   731
   Zheng Zhang, Li Liu, Jie Qin, Fan Zhu, Fumin Shen, Yong Xu,
   Ling Shao, and Heng Tao Shen

Efficient Semantic Scene Completion Network with Spatial
Group Convolution   749
   Jiahui Zhang, Hao Zhao, Anbang Yao, Yurong Chen, Li Zhang,
   and Hongen Liao

Asynchronous, Photometric Feature Tracking Using Events and Frames   766
   Daniel Gehrig, Henri Rebecq, Guillermo Gallego,
   and Davide Scaramuzza

Author Index   783

Poster Session

Physical Primitive Decomposition

Zhijian Liu[1], William T. Freeman[1,2], Joshua B. Tenenbaum[1],
and Jiajun Wu[1(✉)]

[1] Massachusetts Institute of Technology, Cambridge, USA
jiajunwu@mit.edu
[2] Google Research, Cambridge, USA

Abstract. Objects are made of parts, each with distinct geometry, physics, functionality, and affordances. Developing such a distributed, physical, interpretable representation of objects will facilitate intelligent agents to better explore and interact with the world. In this paper, we study *physical primitive decomposition*—understanding an object through its components, each with physical and geometric attributes. As annotated data for object parts and physics are rare, we propose a novel formulation that learns physical primitives by explaining both an object's appearance and its behaviors in physical events. Our model performs well on block towers and tools in both synthetic and real scenarios; we also demonstrate that visual and physical observations often provide complementary signals. We further present ablation and behavioral studies to better understand our model and contrast it with human performance.

1 Introduction

Humans use a hammer by holding its handle and striking its head, not vice versa. In this simple action, people demonstrate their understanding of *functional parts* [33,39]: a tool, or any object, can be decomposed into primitive-based components, each with distinct physics, functionality, and affordances [17].

How to build a machine of such competency? In this paper, we tackle the problem of *physical primitive decomposition (PPD)*—explaining the shape and the physics of an object with a few shape primitives with physical parameters. Given the hammer in Fig. 1, our goal is to build a model that recovers its two major components: a tall, wooden cylinder for its handle, and a smaller, metal cylinder for its head.

For this task, we need a physical, part-based object shape representation that models both object geometry and physics. Ground-truth annotations for such representations are however challenging to obtain: large-scale shape repositories like ShapeNet [8] often have limited annotations on object parts, let alone physics. This is mostly due to two reasons. First, annotating object parts and

Electronic supplementary material The online version of this chapter (https://doi.org/10.1007/978-3-030-01258-8_1) contains supplementary material, which is available to authorized users.

© Springer Nature Switzerland AG 2018
V. Ferrari et al. (Eds.): ECCV 2018, LNCS 11216, pp. 3–20, 2018.
https://doi.org/10.1007/978-3-030-01258-8_1

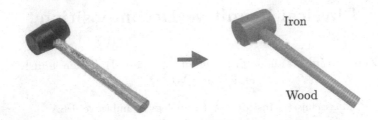

Fig. 1. A hammer (left) and its physical primitive decomposition (right).

physics is labor-intensive and requires strong domain expertise, neither of which can be offered by current crowdsourcing platforms. Second, there exist intrinsic ambiguity in the ground truth: it is impossible to precisely label underlying physical object properties like densities from only images or videos.

Let's think more about what these representations are *for*. We want our object representation to faithfully encode its geometry; therefore, it should be able to explain our visual observation of the object's appearance. Further, as the representation models object physics, it should be effective in explaining the object's behaviors in various physical events.

Inspired by this, we propose a novel formulation that learns a part-based object representation from both visual observations and physical interactions. Starting with a single image and a voxelized shape, the model recovers the geometric primitives and infers their physical properties from texture. The physical representation inferred this way is of course rather uncertain; it therefore only serves as the model's prior of this physical shape. Observing object behaviors in physical events offers crucial additional information, as objects with different physical properties behave differently in physical events. This is used by the model in conjunction with the prior to produce its final prediction.

We evaluate our system for physical primitive decomposition in three scenarios. First, we generate a dataset of synthetic block towers, where each block has distinct geometry and physics. Our model is able to successfully reconstruct the physical primitives by making use of both appearance and motion cues. Second, we evaluate the system on a set of synthetic tools, demonstrating its applicability to daily-life shapes. Third, we build a new dataset of real block towers in dynamic scenes, and evaluate the model's generalization power to real videos.

We further present ablation studies to understand how each source of information contributes to the final performance. We also conduct human behavioral experiments to contrast the performance of the model with humans. In a 'which block is heavier' experiment, our model performs comparably to humans.

Our contributions in this paper are three-fold. First, we propose the problem of physical primitive decomposition—learning a compact, disentangled object representation in terms of physical primitives. Second, we present a novel learning paradigm that learns to characterize shapes in physical primitives to explain both their geometry and physics. Third, we demonstrate that our system can achieve good performance on both synthetic and real data.

2 Related Work

Primitive-Based 3D Representations. Early attempts on modeling 3D shapes with primitives include decomposing them into blocks [34], generalized cylinders [6], and geons [5]. This idea has been constantly revisited throughout the development of computer vision [2,11,13]. To name a few, Gupta *et al.* [11] modeled scenes as qualitative blocks, and van den Hengel *et al.* [13] as Lego blocks. More recently, Tulsaini *et al.* [40] combined the new and the old—using deep convolutional network to generate primitives of a given 3D shape; later, Zou *et al.* proposed 3D-PRNN [53], enhancing the flexibility of the system by leveraging modern advancement in recurrent generative models [41].

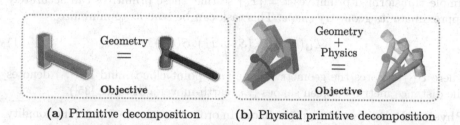

(a) Primitive decomposition   (b) Physical primitive decomposition

Fig. 2. Primitive decomposition (a) and physical primitive decomposition (b). Both tasks attempt to convert an object into a set of primitives yet with different purposes: the former problem targets at shape reconstruction, while the latter one aims to recover both geometric and physical properties.

Primitive-based representations have profound impact that goes far beyond the field of computer vision. Scientists have employed this representation for user-interactive design [16] and for teaching robots to grasp objects [29]. In the field of computer graphics, the idea of modeling shapes as primitives or parts has also been extensively explored [2,19,21,27,47,50]. Researchers have used the part-based representation for single-image shape reconstruction [15], shape completion [37], and probabilistic shape synthesis [14,25].

Physical Shape and Scene Modeling. Beyond object geometry, there have been growing interests in modeling physical object properties and scene dynamics. The computer vision community has put major efforts in building rich and sizable databases. ShapeNet-Sem [36] is a collection of object shapes with material and physics annotations within the web-scale shape repository ShapeNet [8]. Material in Context Database (MINC) [4] is a gigantic dataset of materials in the wild, associating patches in real-world images with 23 materials.

Research on physical object modeling dates back to the study of "functional parts" [17,33,39]. The field of learning object physics and scene dynamics has prospered in the past few years [1,3,7,18,20,23,26,30,32,38,48]. Among them, there are a few papers that explicitly build physical object representations [30, 43–45,49]. Though they also focus on understanding object physics [43,45], functionality [46,51], and affordances [10,22,52], these approaches usually assume a homogeneous object with simple geometry. In our paper, we model an object using physical primitives for richer expressiveness and higher precision.

3   Physical Primitive Decomposition

3.1   Problem Statement

Both primitive decomposition and physical primitive decomposition attempt to approximate an object with primitives. We highlight their difference in Fig. 2.

Primitive Decomposition. As formulated in Tulsaini *et al.* [40] and Zou *et al.* [53], primitive decomposition aims to decompose an object O into a set of simple transformed primitives $x = \{x_k\}$ so that these primitives can accurately approximate its geometry shape. This task can be seen as to minimize

$$\mathcal{L}_{\mathrm{G}}(x) = \mathcal{D}_{\mathrm{S}}\big(\mathcal{S}(\underset{k}{\cup}\, x_k), \mathcal{S}(O)\big), \tag{1}$$

where $\mathcal{S}(\cdot)$ denotes the geometry shape (*i.e.* point cloud), and $\mathcal{D}_{\mathrm{S}}(\cdot, \cdot)$ denotes the distance metric between shapes (*i.e.* earth-mover's distance [35]).

Physical Primitive Decomposition. In order to understand the functionality of object parts, we require the decomposed primitives $x = \{x_k\}$ to also approximate the physical behavior of object O. To this end, we extend the previous objective function with an additional physics term:

$$\mathcal{L}_{\mathrm{P}}(x) = \sum_{p\in\mathcal{P}} \mathcal{D}_{\mathrm{T}}\big(\mathcal{T}_p(\underset{k}{\cup}\, x_k), \mathcal{T}_p(O)\big), \tag{2}$$

where $\mathcal{T}_p(\cdot)$ denotes the trajectory after physics interaction p, $\mathcal{D}_{\mathrm{T}}(\cdot, \cdot)$ denotes the distance metric between trajectories (*i.e.* mean squared error), and $\mathcal{P}$ denotes a predefined set of physics interactions. Therefore, the task of physical primitive decomposition is to minimize an overall objective function constraining both geometry and physics: $\mathcal{L}(x) = \mathcal{L}_{\mathrm{G}}(x) + w \cdot \mathcal{L}_{\mathrm{P}}(x)$, where w is a weighting factor.

(a) **Above**: Aluminum and Wood;   (b) **Above**: Wood and Iron;
      Below: Iron and Wood.   **Below**: Two Coppers.

Fig. 3. Challenges of inferring physical parameters from visual and physical observations: objects with different physical parameters might have (a) similar visual appearance or (b) similar physics trajectory.

3.2 Primitive-Based Representation

We design a structured primitive-based object representation, which describes an object by listing all of its primitives with different attributes. For each primitive x_k, we record its size $x_k^S = (s_x, s_y, s_z)$, position in 3D space $x_k^T = (p_x, p_y, p_z)$, rotation in quaternion form $x_k^R = (q_w, q_x, q_y, q_z)$. Apart from these geometry information, we also track its physical properties: density x_k^D.

In our object representation, the shape parameters, x_k^S, x_k^T and x_k^R, are vectors of continuous real values, whereas the density parameter x_k^D is a discrete value. We discretize the density values into $N_D = 100$ slots, so that estimating density becomes a N_D-way classification. Discretization helps to deal with multi-modal density values. Figure 3a shows that two parts with similar visual appearance may have very different physical parameters. In such cases, regression with an $\mathcal{L}_2$ loss will encourage the model to predict the *mean* value of possible densities; in contrast, discretization allows it to give high probabilities to every possible density. We then figure out which candidate value is optimal from the trajectories.

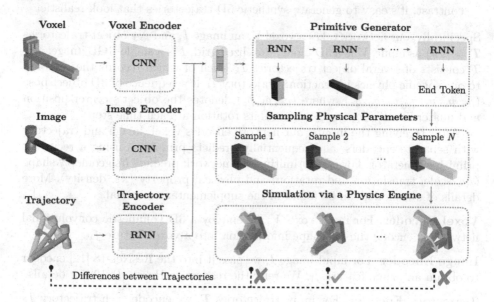

Fig. 4. Overview of our PPD model.

4 Approach

In this section, we discuss our approach to the problem of physical primitive decomposition (PPD). We present an overview of our framework in Fig. 4.

4.1   Overview

Inferring physical parameters from solely visual or physical observation is highly challenging. This is because two objects with different physical parameters might have similar visual appearance (Fig. 3a) or have similar physics trajectories (Fig. 3b). Therefore, our model takes both types of observations as input:

1. **Visual Observation.** We take a voxelized shape and an image as our input because they can provide us with valuable visual information. Voxels help us recover object geometry, and images contain texture information of object materials. Note that, even with voxels as input, it is still highly nontrivial to infer geometric parameters: the model needs to learn to segment 3D parts within the object—an unsolved problem by itself [40].
2. **Physics Observation.** In order to explain the physical behavior of an object, we also need to observe its response after some physics interactions. In this work, we choose to use 3D object trajectories rather than RGB (or RGB-D) videos. Its abstractness enables the model to transfer better from synthetic to real data, because synthetic and real videos can be starkly different; in contrast, it's easy to generate synthetic 3D trajectories that look realistic.

Specifically, our network takes a voxel V, an image I, and N_{T} object trajectories $T = \{T_k\}$ as input. V is a 3D binary voxelized grid, I is a single RGB image, and T consists of several object trajectories T_k, each of which records the response to one specific physics interaction. Trajectory T_k is a sequence of 3D object pose $(p_x, p_y, p_z, q_w, q_x, q_y, q_z)$, where (p_x, p_y, p_z) denotes the object's center position and quaternion (q_w, q_x, q_y, q_z) denotes its rotation at each time step.

After receiving the inputs, our network encodes voxel, image and trajectory with separate encoders, and sequentially predicts primitives using a recurrent primitive generator. For each primitive, the network predicts its geometry shape (*i.e.* scale, translation and rotation) and physical property (*i.e.* density). More details of our model can be found in the supplementary material.

Voxel Encoder. For input voxel V, we employ a 3D volumetric convolutional network to encode the 3D shape information into a voxel feature f_V.

Image Encoder. For input image I, we pass it into the ResNet-18 [12] encoder to obtain an image feature f_I. We refer the readers to He *et al.* [12] for details.

Trajectory Encoder. For input trajectories T, we encode each trajectory T_k into a low-dimensional feature vector h_k with a separate bi-directional recurrent neural network. Specifically, we feed the trajectory sequence, T_k, and also the same trajectory sequence in reverse order, T_k^{reverse}, into two encoding RNNs, to obtain two final hidden states: $\overrightarrow{h_k} = \overrightarrow{\mathrm{encode}}_k(T_k)$ and $\overleftarrow{h_k} = \overleftarrow{\mathrm{encode}}_k(T_k^{\mathrm{reverse}})$. We take $[\overrightarrow{h_k}; \overleftarrow{h_k}]$ as the feature vector h_k. Finally, we concatenate the features of each trajectory, $\{h_k \mid k = 1, 2, \ldots, N_{\mathrm{T}}\}$, and project it into a low-dimensional trajectory feature f_{T} with a fully-connected layer.

Primitive Generator. We concatenate the voxel feature f_V, image feature f_I and trajectory feature f_{T} together as $\hat{f} = [f_V; f_I; f_{\mathrm{T}}]$, and map it to a low-dimensional feature f using a fully-connected layer. We predict the set of physical primitives $\{x_k\}$ sequentially by a recurrent generator.

At each time step k, we feed the previous generated primitive x_{k-1} and the feature vector f in as input, and we receive one hidden vector h_k as output. Then, we compute the new primitive $x_k = (x_k^D, x_k^S, x_k^T, x_k^R)$ as

$$x_k^D = \text{softmax}(W_D \times h_k + b_D), \quad x_k^S = \text{sigmoid}(W_S \times h_k + b_S) \times C_S,$$

$$x_k^T = \tanh(W_T \times h_k + b_T) \times C_T, \quad x_k^R = \frac{W_R \times h_k + b_R}{\max(\|W_R \times h_k + b_R\|_2, \epsilon)}, \quad (3)$$

where C_S and C_T are scaling factors, and $\epsilon = 10^{-12}$ is a small constant for numerical stability. Equation eqn:primitive guarantees that x_k^S is in the range of $[0, C_S]$, x_k^T is in the range of $[-C_T, C_T]$, and $\|x_k^R\|_2$ is 1 (if ignoring ϵ), which ensures that x_k will always be a valid primitive. In our experiments, we set $C_S = C_T = 0.5$, since we normalize all objects so that they can fit in unit cubes. Also note that, x_k^D is an $(N_D + 2)$-dimensional vector, where the first N_D dimensions indicate different density values and the last two indicate the "start token" and "end token".

Sampling and Simulating with the Physics Engine. During testing time, we treat the predicted x_k^D as a multinomial distribution, and we sample multiple possible predictions from it. For each sample, we use its physical parameters to simulate the trajectory with a physics engine. Finally, we select the one whose simulated trajectory is closest to the observed trajectory.

An alternative way to incorporate physics engine is to directly optimize our model over it. As most physics engines are not differentiable, we employ REIN-FORCE [42] for optimization. Empirically, we observe that this reinforcement learning based method performs worse than sampling-based methods, possible due to the large variance of the approximate gradient signals.

Simulating with a physics engine requires we know the force during testing. Such an assumption is essential to ensure the problem is well-posed: without knowing the force, we can only infer the relative part density, but not the actual values. Note that in many real-world applications such as robot manipulation, the external force is indeed available.

4.2   Loss Functions

Let $x = (x_1, x_2, \ldots, x_n)$ and $\hat{x} = (\hat{x}_1, \hat{x}_2, \ldots, \hat{x}_m)$ be the predicted and ground-truth physical primitives, respectively. Our loss function consists of two terms, geometry loss $\mathcal{L}_G$ and physics loss $\mathcal{L}_D$:

$$\mathcal{L}_G(x, \hat{x}) = \sum_k \left(\omega_S \cdot \|x_k^S - \hat{x}_k^S\|_1 + \omega_T \cdot \|x_k^T - \hat{x}_k^T\|_1 + \omega_R \cdot \|x_k^R - \hat{x}_k^R\|_1 \right), \quad (4)$$

$$\mathcal{L}_P(x, \hat{x}) = -\sum_k \sum_i \hat{x}_k^D(i) \cdot \log x_k^D(i), \quad (5)$$

where ω_S, ω_T and ω_R are weighting factors, which are set to 1's because x^S, x^T and x^R are of the same magnitude (10^{-1}) in our datasets. Integrating Equation eqn:loss:g and Equation eqn:loss:p, we define the overall loss function as $\mathcal{L}(x, \hat{x}) = \mathcal{L}_G(x, \hat{x}) + w \cdot \mathcal{L}_P(x, \hat{x})$, where w is set to ensure that $\mathcal{L}_G$ and $\mathcal{L}_P$ are of the same magnitude.

Part Associations. In our formulation, object parts (physical primitives) follow a pre-defined order (*e.g.*, from bottom to top), and our model is encouraged to learn to predict the primitives in the same order.

5   Experiments

We evaluate our PPD model on three diverse settings: synthetic block towers where blocks are of various materials and shapes; synthetic tools with more complex geometry shapes; and real videos of block towers to demonstrate our transferability to real-world scenario.

5.1   Decomposing Block Towers

We start with decomposing block towers (stacks of blocks).

Block Towers. We build the block towers by stacking variable number of blocks (2–5 in our experiments) together. We first sample the size of each block and then compute the center position of blocks from bottom to top. For the kth block, we denote the size as (w_k, h_k, d_k), and its center (x_k, y_k, z_k) is sampled and computed by $x_k \sim \mathcal{N}(x_{k-1}, w_{k-1}/4)$, $y_k \sim \mathcal{N}(y_{k-1}, h_{k-1}/4)$, and $z_k = z_{k-1} + (d_{k-1} + d_k)/2$, where $\mathcal{N}(\mu, \sigma)$ is a normal distribution with mean μ and standard deviation σ. We illustrate some constructed block towers in Fig. 5. We perform the exact voxelization with grid size of $32 \times 32 \times 32$ by binvox, a 3D mesh voxelizer [31].

Materials. In our experiments, we use five different materials, and follow their real-world densities with minor modifications. The materials and the ranges of their densities are listed in Table 1. For each block in the block towers, we first assign it to one of the five materials, and then uniformly sample its density from possible values of its material. We generate 8 configurations for each block tower.

Textures. We obtain the textures for materials by cropping the center portion of images from the MINC dataset [4]. We show sample images rendered with material textures in Fig. 5. Since we render the textures only with respect to the material, the images rendered do not provide any information about density.

Physics Interactions. We place the block towers at the origin and perform four physics interactions to obtain the object trajectories ($N_T = 4$). In detail, we exert a force with the magnitude of 10^5 on the block tower from four pre-defined positions $\{(\pm 1, -1, \pm 1)\}$. We simulate each physics interaction for 256 time steps using the Bullet Physics Engine [9]. To ensure simulation accuracy, we set the time step for simulation to $1/300$s.

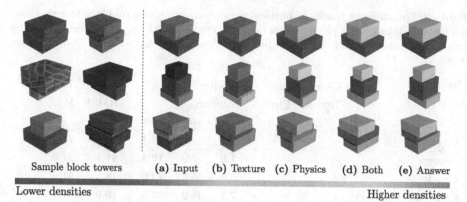

Sample block towers   **(a)** Input   **(b)** Texture   **(c)** Physics   **(d)** Both   **(e)** Answer

Lower densities   Higher densities

Fig. 5. Sample objects in our block towers dataset (left) and qualitative results of our model with different combinations of observations as input (right).

Table 1. Materials and their real-world density values (unit: $\times 10^2 \cdot$ kg/m^3). Objects made of similar materials (different types of metals) may have different physical properties, while different materials (*i.e.*, stone and metal) may have same physical properties.

Material	Wood	Brick	Stone	Ceramic	Metal
Density	$[1, 10]$	$[11, 20]$	$[21, 30]$	$[31, 60]$	$[21, 35] \cup [71, 100]$

Metrics. We evaluate the performance of shape reconstruction by the F_1 score between the prediction and ground truth: each primitive in prediction is labeled as a true positive if its intersection over union (IoU) with a ground-truth primitive is greater than 0.5. For physics estimation, we employ two types of metrics, (i) density measures: top-k accuracy ($k \in \{1, 5, 10\}$) and root-mean-square error (RMSE) and (ii) trajectory measure: mean-absolute error (MAE) between simulated trajectory (using predicted the physical parameters) and ground-truth trajectory.

Methods. We evaluate our model with different combinations of observations as input: (i) texture only (*i.e.*, no trajectory, by setting $f_T = 0$), (ii) physics only (*i.e.*, no image, by setting $f_I = 0$), (iii) both texture and physics but without the voxelized shape, (iv) both texture and physics but with replacing the 3D trajectory with a raw depth video, (v) full data in our original setup (image, voxels, and trajectory). We also compare our model with several baselines: (i) predicting the most frequent density in the training set (*Frequent*), (ii) nearest neighbor retrieval from the training set (*Nearest*), and (iii) knowing the ground-truth material and guessing within its density value range (*Oracle*). While all these baselines assume perfect shape reconstruction, our model learns to decompose the shape.

Results. For the shape reconstruction, our model achieves 97.5 in terms of F1 score. For the physics estimation, we present quantitative results of our model

Table 2. Quantitative results of physical parameter estimation on block towers. Combining appearance with physics does help our model to achieve better estimation on physical parameters, and our model performs significantly better than all other baselines.

Methods	Observations		Density			Trajectory	
	Texture	Physics	Accuracy			RMSE	MAE
			Top 1	Top 5	Top 10		
Frequent	−	−	2.0	9.7	13.4	25.4	74.4
Nearest	−	+	1.9	7.9	12.4	41.1	91.0
Oracle	+	−	6.9	35.7	72.0	18.5	51.3
PPD (no trajectory)	+	−	7.2	35.2	69.5	19.0	51.7
PPD (no image)	−	+	7.1	31.0	50.8	16.7	36.4
PPD (no voxels)	+	+	15.9	56.3	82.4	10.3	29.9
PPD (RGB-D)	+	+	11.6	50.5	79.5	12.8	30.2
PPD (full)	+	+	16.1	56.4	82.5	9.9	21.0
PPD (full) + Sample	+	+	**18.2**	**59.7**	**84.0**	**8.8**	**13.9**

with different observations as input in Table 2. We compare our model with an oracle that infers material properties from appearance while assuming ground-truth reconstruction. It gives *upper-bound* performance of methods that rely on only appearance cues. Experiments suggest that appearance alone is not sufficient for density estimation. From Table 2, we observe that combining appearance with physics performs well on physical parameter estimation, which is because the object trajectories can provide crucial additional information about the density distribution (*i.e.* moment of inertia). Also, all input modalities and sampling contribute to the model's final performance.

We have also implemented a physics engine–based sampling baseline: sampling the shape and physical parameters for each primitive, using a physics engine for simulation, and selecting the one whose

Table 3. Comparison between our model and a physics engine based sampling baseline

	1×	8×	64×	512×
Sample Phys. + Shape	142.2	87.1	70.8	58.7
Sample Phys.	89.7	60.1	38.7	22.7
PPD (ours)	**21.0**	**15.1**	**13.9**	**13.2**

trajectory is closest to the observation. We also compare with a stronger baseline where we only sample physics, assuming ground-truth shape is known. Table 3 shows our model works better and is more efficient: the neural nets have learned an informative prior that greatly reduces the need of sampling at test time.

5.2 Decomposing Tools

We then demonstrate the practical applicability of our model by decomposing synthetic real-world tools.

Table 4. Quantitative results of physical parameter estimation on tools. Combining visual appearance with physics observations helps our model to perform much better on physical parameter estimation, and compared to all other baselines, our model performs significantly better on this dataset.

Methods	Observations		Density				Trajectory
	Texture	Physics	Accuracy			RMSE	MAE
			Top 1	Top 5	Top 10		
Frequent	−	−	2.5	10.2	13.6	25.9	348.2
Nearest	−	+	2.9	8.3	12.4	25.8	329.7
Oracle	+	−	7.4	35.2	72.0	19.1	185.8
PPD (no trajectory)	+	−	7.7	36.4	71.1	16.8	206.8
PPD (no image)	−	+	15.0	56.3	80.2	5.9	143.6
PPD (full)	+	+	35.7	**85.2**	95.8	2.6	103.6
PPD (full) + Sample	+	+	**38.3**	85.0	**96.1**	**2.5**	**74.4**

Tools. Because of the absence of tool data in the ShapeNet Core [8] dataset, we download the tools from 3D Warehouse[1] and manually remove all unrelated models. In total, there are 204 valid tools, and we use Blender to remesh and clean up these tools to fix the issues with missing faces and normals. Following Chang et al. [8], we perform PCA on the point clouds and align models by their PCA axes. Sample tools in our dataset are shown in Fig. 6.

Primitives. Similar to Zou et al. [53], we first use the energy-based optimization to fit the primitives from the point clouds, and then, we assign each vertex to its nearest primitive and refine each primitive with the minimum oriented bounding box of vertices assigned to it.

Other Setups. We make use of the same set of materials and densities as in Table 1 and the same textures for materials as described in Sect. 5.1. Sample images rendered with textures are shown in Fig. 6. As for physics interactions, we follow the same scenario configurations as in Sect. 5.1.

Training Details. Because the size of synthetic tools dataset is rather limited, we first pre-train our PPD model on the block towers and then finetune it on the synthetic tools. For the block towers used for pre-training, we fix the number of blocks to 2 and introduce small random noises and rotations to each block to fill the gap between block towers and synthetic tools.

Results. For the shape reconstruction, our model achieves 85.9 in terms of F1 score. For the physics estimation, we present quantitative results in Table 4. The shape reconstruction is not as good as that of the block towers dataset because the synthetic tools are more complicated, and the orientations might introduce

---

[1] https://3dwarehouse.sketchup.com.

14   Z. Liu et al.

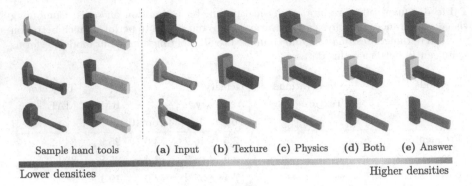

Sample hand tools   (a) Input   (b) Texture   (c) Physics   (d) Both   (e) Answer

Lower densities   Higher densities

Fig. 6. Sample objects in synthetic tools dataset (left) and qualitative results of our model with different combinations of observations as input (right).

some ambiguity (there might exist multiple bounding boxes with different rotations for the same part of object). The physics estimation performance is better since the number of primitives in our synthetic tools dataset is very small (≤ 2 in general). We also show some qualitative results in Fig. 6.

5.3   Decomposing Real Objects

We look into real objects to evaluate the generalization ability of our model.

Real-World Block Towers. We purchase totally ten sets of blocks with different materials (*i.e.* pine, steel, aluminum and copper) from Amazon, and construct a dataset of real-world block towers. Our dataset contains 16 block towers with different configurations: 8 with two blocks, 4 with three blocks, and another 4 with four blocks.

Physics Interaction. The scenario is set up as follows: the block tower is placed at a specific position on the desk, and we use a copper ball (hang by a pendulum) to hit it. In Fig. 7, we show some objects and their trajectories in our dataset.

Video to 3D Trajectory. On real-world data, the appearance of every frame in RGB video is used to extract a 3D trajectory. A major challenge is how to convert RGB videos into 3D trajectories. We employ the following approach:

1. **Tracking 2D Keypoints.** For each frame, we first detect the 2D positions of object corners. For simplicity, we mark the object corners using red stickers and use a simple color filter to determine the corner positions. Then, we find the correspondence between the corner points from consecutive frames by solving the minimum-distance matching between two sets of points. After aligning the corner points in different frames, we obtain the 2D trajectories of these keypoints.
2. **Reconstructing 3D Poses.** We annotate the 3D position for each corner point. Then, for each frame, we have 2D locations of keypoints and their

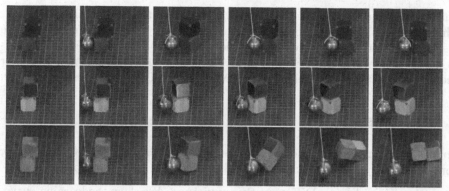

(a) Frame i_1 (b) Frame i_2 (c) Frame i_3 (d) Frame i_4 (e) Frame i_5 (f) Frame i_6

Fig. 7. Objects and their physics trajectories in six sampled frames from our real-world block towers dataset. As in the last two rows, objects with similar visual appearances may have distinct physical properties that we can only distinguish from their behaviors in physical events.

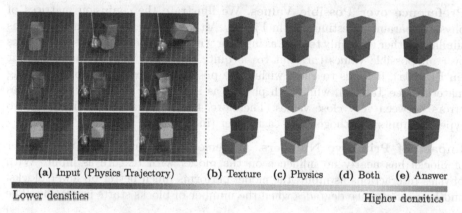

(a) Input (Physics Trajectory)   (b) Texture   (c) Physics   (d) Both   (e) Answer

Lower densities   Higher densities

Fig. 8. Qualitative results (on real-world block towers) of our model with different combinations of observations as input.

corresponding 3D locations. Finally, we reconstruct the 3D object pose in each frame by solving the Perspective-n-Point between 2D and 3D locations using Levenberg-Marquardt algorithm [24,28].

Training Details. We build a virtual physics environment, similar to our real-world setup, in the Bullet Physics Engine [9]. We employ it to simulate physics interactions and generate a dataset of synthetic block towers to train our model.

Results. We show some qualitative results of our model with different observations as input in Fig. 8. In the real-world setup, with only texture or physics information, our model cannot effectively predict the physical parameters because images and object trajectories are much noisier than those in synthetic dataset, while combining them together indeed helps it to predict much more accurate results. In terms of quantitative evaluation, our model (with both observations as input) achieves an RMSE value of 18.7 over the whole dataset and 10.1 over the block towers with two blocks (the RMSE value of random guessing is 40.8).

6   Analysis

To better understand our model, we present several analysis. The first three are conducted on synthetic block towers and the last one is on our real dataset.

Learning Speed with Different Supervisions. We show the learning curves of our PPD model with different supervision in Fig. 9. Model supervised by physics observation reaches the same level of performance of model with texture supervision using much fewer training steps (500K *vs.* 2M). Supervised by both observations, our PPD model preserves the learning speed of the model with only physics supervision, and further improves its performance.

Preference over Possible Values. We illustrate the confusion matrices of physical parameter estimation in Fig. 10. Although our PPD model performs similarly either with only texture as input or with physics as input, its preferences over all possible values turn out to be quite different. With texture as input (in Fig. 10a), it tends to guess within the possible values of the corresponding material (see Table 1), while with physics as input (in Fig. 10b), it only makes errors between very close values. Therefore, the information provided by two types of inputs is orthogonal to each other (in Fig. 10c).

Impact of Primitive Numbers. As demonstrated in Table 5, the number of blocks has nearly no influence on the model with texture as input. With physics interactions as input, the model performs much better on fewer blocks, and its performance degrades when the number of blocks starts increasing. The

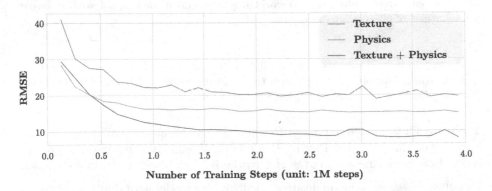

Fig. 9. Learning curves with different observations as input. Our model learns much better and faster when both texture and physics supervisions are available.

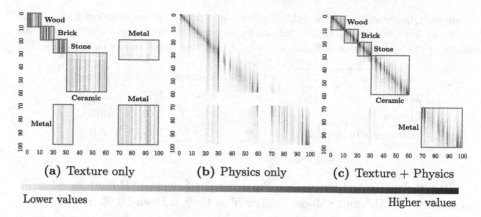

(a) Texture only   (b) Physics only   (c) Texture + Physics

Lower values   Higher values

Fig. 10. Confusion matrices of physical parameter estimation. The information provided by two types of observations are different: (a) with texture as input, our model tends to guess within the material's possible density values (see Table 1); (b) with physics as input, our model only makes errors between close values.

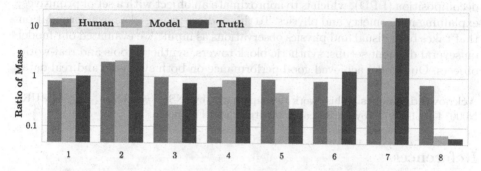

Fig. 11. Human's, model's and ground-truth predictions on "which block is heavier". Our model performs comparable to humans, and its response is correlated with humans

degradation is probably because the physical response of any rigid body is fully characterized by a few object properties (*i.e.*, total mass, center of mass, and moment of inertia), which provides us with limited constraints on the density distribution of an object when the number of primitives is relatively large.

Human Studies. We select the block towers with two blocks from our real dataset, and study the problem of "which block is heavier" upon them. The human studies are conducted on the Amazon Mechanical Turk. For each block tower, we provide 25 annotators with an image and a video of physics interaction, and ask them to estimate the ratio of mass between the upper and the lower block. Instead of directly predicting a real value, we require the annotators to make a choice on a log scale, *i.e.*, from $\{2^k \mid k = 0, \pm 1, \ldots, \pm 4\}$. Results of average human's predictions, model's predictions and the truths are shown in Fig. 11. Our model performs comparably to humans, and its response is also

Table 5. Quantitative results (RMSE's) on block towers (with different block numbers): (a) with texture as input, our model performs comparably on different block numbers; (b) with physics as input, our model performs much better on fewer blocks.

Observation	2 blocks	3 blocks	4 blocks	5 blocks	Overall
Texture	18.2	18.5	18.8	19.7	19.1
Physics	3.6	7.9	15.8	20.0	14.7
Texture + Physics	2.3	4.9	7.8	10.9	8.0

highly correlated with humans: the Pearson's coefficient of "Human *vs.* Model", "Human *vs.* Truth" and "Model *vs.* Truth" is 0.69, 0.71 and 0.90, respectively.

7   Conclusion

In this paper, we have formulated and studied the problem of physical primitive decomposition (PPD), which is to approximate an object with a set of primitives, explaining its geometry and physics. To this end, we proposed a novel formulation that takes both visual and physics observations as input. We evaluated our model on several different setups: synthetic block towers, synthetic tools and real-world objects. Our model achieved good performance on both synthetic and real data.

Acknowledgements. This work is supported by NSF #1231216, ONR MURI N00014-16-1-2007, Toyota Research Institute, and Facebook.

References

1. Agrawal, P., Nair, A., Abbeel, P., Malik, J., Levine, S.: Learning to poke by poking: experiential learning of intuitive physics. In: NIPS (2016)
2. Attene, M., Falcidieno, B., Spagnuolo, M.: Hierarchical mesh segmentation based on fitting primitives. Vis. Comput. **22**(3), 181–193 (2006)
3. Battaglia, P.W., Hamrick, J.B., Tenenbaum, J.B.: Simulation as an engine of physical scene understanding. PNAS **110**(45), 18327–18332 (2013)
4. Bell, S., Upchurch, P., Snavely, N., Bala, K.: Material recognition in the wild with the materials in context database. In: CVPR (2015)
5. Biederman, I.: Recognition-by-components: a theory of human image understanding. Psychol. Rev. **94**(2), 115 (1987)
6. Binford, T.O.: Visual perception by computer. In: IEEE Conference on Systems and Control (1971)
7. Brubaker, M.A., Fleet, D.J., Hertzmann, A.: Physics-based person tracking using the anthropomorphic walker. IJCV **87**(1–2), 140 (2010)
8. Chang, A.X., et al.: ShapeNet: an information-rich 3D model repository. arXiv:1512.03012 (2015)
9. Coumans, E.: Bullet physics engine. Open Source Software (2010). http://bulletphysics.org
10. Grabner, H., Gall, J., Van Gool, L.: What makes a chair a chair? In: CVPR (2011)

11. Gupta, A., Efros, A.A., Hebert, M.: Blocks world revisited: image understanding using qualitative geometry and mechanics. In: Daniilidis, K., Maragos, P., Paragios, N. (eds.) ECCV 2010. LNCS, vol. 6314, pp. 482–496. Springer, Heidelberg (2010). https://doi.org/10.1007/978-3-642-15561-1_35

12. He, K., Zhang, X., Ren, S., Sun, J.: Deep residual learning for image recognition. In: CVPR (2015)

13. van den Hengel, A., et al.: Part-based modelling of compound scenes from images. In: CVPR (2015)

14. Huang, H., Kalogerakis, E., Marlin, B.: Analysis and synthesis of 3D shape families via deep-learned generative models of surfaces. CGF **34**(5), 25–38 (2015)

15. Huang, Q., Wang, H., Koltun, V.: Single-view reconstruction via joint analysis of image and shape collections. ACM TOG **34**(4), 87 (2015)

16. Igarashi, T., Matsuoka, S., Tanaka, H.: Teddy: a sketching interface for 3D freeform design. In: SIGGRAPH (1999)

17. Gibson, J.J.: The theory of affordances. In: The Ecological Approach to Visual Perception, chap. 8 (1977)

18. Jia, Z., Gallagher, A., Saxena, A., Chen, T.: 3D reasoning from blocks to stability. IEEE TPAMI **37**(5), 905–918 (2015)

19. Kalogerakis, E., Chaudhuri, S., Koller, D., Koltun, V.: A probabilistic model for component-based shape synthesis. ACM TOG **31**(4), 55 (2012)

20. Kim, M., et al.: Data-driven physics for human soft tissue animation. In: SIG-GRAPH (2017)

21. Kim, V.G., Li, W., Mitra, N.J., Chaudhuri, S., DiVerdi, S., Funkhouser, T.: Learning part-based templates from large collections of 3D shapes. ACM TOG **32**(4), 70 (2013)

22. Koppula, H.S., Saxena, A.: Physically grounded spatio-temporal object affordances. In: Fleet, D., Pajdla, T., Schiele, B., Tuytelaars, T. (eds.) ECCV 2014. LNCS, vol. 8691, pp. 831–847. Springer, Cham (2014). https://doi.org/10.1007/978-3-319-10578-9_54

23. Lerer, A., Gross, S., Fergus, R.: Learning physical intuition of block towers by example. In: ICML (2016)

24. Levenberg, K.: A method for the solution of certain non-linear problems in least squares. Q. Appl. Math. **2**(2), 164–168 (1944)

25. Li, J., Xu, K., Chaudhuri, S., Yumer, E., Zhang, H., Guibas, L.: GRASS: generative recursive autoencoders for shape structures. In: SIGGRAPH (2017)

26. Li, W., Leonardis, A., Fritz, M.: Visual stability prediction for robotic manipulation. In: ICRA (2017)

27. Li, Y., Wu, X., Chrysathou, Y., Sharf, A., Cohen-Or, D., Mitra, N.J.: GlobFit: consistently fitting primitives by discovering global relations. ACM TOG **30**(4), 52 (2011)

28. Marquardt, D.W.: An algorithm for least-squares estimation of nonlinear parameters. J. Soc. Ind. Appl. Math. **11**(2), 431–441 (1963)

29. Miller, A.T., Knoop, S., Christensen, H.I., Allen, P.K.: Automatic grasp planning using shape primitives. In: ICRA (2003)

30. Mottaghi, R., Rastegari, M., Gupta, A., Farhadi, A.: "What happens if..." learning to predict the effect of forces in images. In: Leibe, B., Matas, J., Sebe, N., Welling, M. (eds.) ECCV 2016. LNCS, vol. 9908, pp. 269–285. Springer, Cham (2016). https://doi.org/10.1007/978-3-319-46493-0_17

31. Nooruddin, F.S., Turk, G.: Simplification and repair of polygonal models using volumetric techniques. IEEE TVCG **9**(2), 191–205 (2003)

32. Pham, T.H., Kheddar, A., Qammaz, A., Argyros, A.A.: Towards force sensing from vision: observing hand-object interactions to infer manipulation forces. In: CVPR (2015)
33. Rivlin, E., Dickinson, S.J., Rosenfeld, A.: Recognition by functional parts. CVIU **62**(2), 164–176 (1995)
34. Roberts, L.G.: Machine perception of three-dimensional solids. Ph.D. thesis, Massachusetts Institute of Technology (1963)
35. Rubner, Y., Tomasi, C., Guibas, L.J.: The earth mover's distance as a metric for image retrieval. IJCV **40**(2), 99–121 (2000)
36. Savva, M., Chang, A.X., Hanrahan, P.: Semantically-enriched 3D models for common-sense knowledge. In: CVPR Workshop (2015)
37. Schnabel, R., Degener, P., Klein, R.: Completion and reconstruction with primitive shapes. CGF **28**(2), 503–512 (2009)
38. Soo Park, H., Shi, J., et al.: Force from motion: decoding physical sensation in a first person video. In: CVPR (2016)
39. Tenenbaum, J.B.: Functional parts. In: CogSci (1994)
40. Tulsiani, S., Su, H., Guibas, L.J., Efros, A.A., Malik, J.: Learning shape abstractions by assembling volumetric primitives. In: CVPR (2017)
41. Van Oord, A., Kalchbrenner, N., Kavukcuoglu, K.: Pixel recurrent neural networks. In: ICML (2016)
42. Williams, R.J.: Simple statistical gradient-following algorithms for connectionist reinforcement learning. MLJ **8**(3–4), 229–256 (1992)
43. Wu, J., Lim, J.J., Zhang, H., Tenenbaum, J.B., Freeman, W.T.: Physics 101: Learning physical object properties from unlabeled videos. In: BMVC (2016)
44. Wu, J., Lu, E., Kohli, P., Freeman, W.T., Tenenbaum, J.B.: Learning to see physics via visual de-animation. In: NIPS (2017)
45. Wu, J., Yildirim, I., Lim, J.J., Freeman, W.T., Tenenbaum, J.B.: Galileo: perceiving physical object properties by integrating a physics engine with deep learning. In: NIPS (2015)
46. Yao, B., Ma, J., Fei-Fei, L.: Discovering object functionality. In: ICCV (2013)
47. Yumer, M.E., Kara, L.B.: Co-abstraction of shape collections. ACM TOG **31**(6), 166 (2012)
48. Zhao, Y., Zhu, S.C.: Scene parsing by integrating function, geometry and appearance models. In: CVPR (2013)
49. Zheng, D., Luo, V., Wu, J., Tenenbaum, J.B.: Unsupervised learning of latent physical properties using perception-prediction networks. In: UAI (2018)
50. Zheng, Y., Cohen-Or, D., Averkiou, M., Mitra, N.J.: Recurring part arrangements in shape collections. CGF **33**(2), 115–124 (2014)
51. Zhu, Y., Zhao, Y., Zhu, S.C.: Understanding tools: Task-oriented object modeling, learning and recognition. In: CVPR (2015)
52. Zhu, Y., Fathi, A., Fei-Fei, L.: Reasoning about object affordances in a knowledge base representation. In: Fleet, D., Pajdla, T., Schiele, B., Tuytelaars, T. (eds.) ECCV 2014. LNCS, vol. 8690, pp. 408–424. Springer, Cham (2014). https://doi.org/10.1007/978-3-319-10605-2_27
53. Zou, C., Yumer, E., Yang, J., Ceylan, D., Hoiem, D.: 3D-PRNN: generating shape primitives with recurrent neural networks. In: ICCV (2017)

Deep Attention Neural Tensor Network
for Visual Question Answering

Yalong Bai[1,2]([✉]), Jianlong Fu[3], Tiejun Zhao[1], and Tao Mei[2]

[1] Harbin Institute of Technology, Harbin, China
tjzhao@hit.edu.cn
[2] JD AI Research, Beijing, China
{baiyalong,tmei}@jd.com
[3] Microsoft Research Asia, Beijing, China
jianf@microsoft.com

Abstract. Visual question answering (VQA) has drawn great attention in cross-modal learning problems, which enables a machine to answer a natural language question given a reference image. Significant progress has been made by learning rich embedding features from images and questions by bilinear models, while neglects the key role from answers. In this paper, we propose a novel deep attention neural tensor network (DA-NTN) for visual question answering, which can discover the joint correlations over images, questions and answers with tensor-based representations. First, we model one of the pairwise interaction (e.g., image and question) by bilinear features, which is further encoded with the third dimension (e.g., answer) to be a triplet by bilinear tensor product. Second, we decompose the correlation of different triplets by different answer and question types, and further propose a slice-wise attention module on tensor to select the most discriminative reasoning process for inference. Third, we optimize the proposed DA-NTN by learning a label regression with KL-divergence losses. Such a design enables scalable training and fast convergence over a large number of answer set. We integrate the proposed DA-NTN structure into the state-of-the-art VQA models (e.g., MLB and MUTAN). Extensive experiments demonstrate the superior accuracy than the original MLB and MUTAN models, with 1.98%, 1.70% relative increases on VQA-2.0 dataset, respectively.

Keywords: Visual question answering · Neural tensor network
Open-ended VQA

1 Introduction

After deep learning techniques have achieved great success in solving natural language processing and computer vision tasks, automatically understanding the semantics of images and text and eliminating the gap between their representations has received intensive research attention. It has stimulated many new

© Springer Nature Switzerland AG 2018
V. Ferrari et al. (Eds.): ECCV 2018, LNCS 11216, pp. 21–37, 2018.
https://doi.org/10.1007/978-3-030-01258-8_2

research topic like image captioning [8], text to image synthesis [23] and visual question answering [4, 10].

The Visual Question Answering (VQA) is a task about answering questions which posed in natural language about images. The answers can either be selected from multiple pre-specified choices or generated by a model. A natural solution for VQA is to combine the visual based image understanding with the question based on natural language understanding and reasoning. Recently, many studies have explored the multi-modal feature fusion of image representation learned from deep convolutional neural network and question representation learned from time sequential model. Nearly all of these previous works train a classifier based on the fusion of image and question feature to predict an answer, and the relationship of image-question-answer triplets is ignored. While in theory, "these approaches have the potential simple reasoning, it is still not clear whether they do actually reason, or they do so in a human-comprehensible way" as Allan *et al.* [12] mentioned. To model the relational information in triplet, there are some other related works try to use pretrained answer representations to help reasoning, by simply concatenating the features of image, question and answer [12], or projecting the image-question feature into answer feature space [27], but the relational information of image-question-answer triplet is too complex to be modeled by using simply concatenating feature vectors or applying element-wise sum or product. Moreover, the answer representations learned from natural language corpus, which is supervised by the syntactic and semantic information in the corpus, still has a certain gap to describe visual information.

Inspired by the success of neural tensor network for explicitly modeling multiple interactions of relational data [22, 26], we proposed a neural tensor network based framework to model the relational information of image-question-answer triplets and learn the VQA task-specific answer representations from scratch. As we know, typically different triplets in VQA correspond to different kinds of relationship and different reasoning process. In most cases, these relationship is associated with the type of question well. Moreover, the responses of candidate answers are also helpful to predict the question's type. Thus we introduce a novel question and answers' responses guided attention mechanism into our proposed deep neural tensor VQA framework by adaptively reasoning for different triplets according to their implicit relation types. After that, we use a regression-based method to approximate the distributions of image-question-candidate answers instead of the traditional classification-based method. We optimize our proposed model by learning a label regression with KL-divergence losses. Such a design enables scalable training and fast convergence over a large number of answer set.

Different from the previous works, we introduce the answer embedding learning in our method for three purposes. First, we want to model the relationship among image-question-answer triplet to help to reason. Second, the answer embedding may correct the question misunderstanding especially for questions with complex syntactic structures. Third, the answer embedding can help to determinate the type of question and to decide using which kind of reasoning process.

We evaluate the impact of our proposed framework on VQA-1.0 and VQA-2.0 datasets. Since our proposed framework is designed to be applicable to most of the previous image-question multimodal feature learning based models, we selected two of the most powerful bilinear pooling based VQA models to equip our proposed framework, and prove that our proposed method can achieve more reasonable answer representations and further result in significant improvement on the VQA performance.

In the next section, we provide more details on related works and highlight our contributions. Our proposed method is presented in Sect. 3, and the successful experiments are reported in Sect. 4. We analyzed the result of experiments in Sect. 5, and conclude with a discussion in Sect. 6.

2 Related Works

The task of VQA has gathered increasing interest in the past few years. Most of the previous works pose the visual question answering as a classification problem and solved with a deep neural network that implements the joint representation of the image and question. Only a few related works introduce answer representation for reasoning. Meanwhile, the question-guided visual regions attention is also very important for VQA. In this section, we briefly review these related works.

Attention mechanisms have been a real breakthrough in VQA task. Chen et al. [7] proposed a question-guided attention mechanism to adaptively learn the most relevant image regions for a given question. Zichao et al. [31] proposed to stack multiple question-guided attention mechanisms to learn the attention in an iterative way. Fukui et al. [9] and Hedi et al. [6] used bilinear pooling to integrate the visual features from the image spatial grids with question features to predict attention. Considering the questions in natural languages may also contain some noise or useless information or words, some co-attention based frameworks designed for jointly learn the attention for both the image and question are also proposed [17,32]. In this paper, we apply the attention mechanisms used in [6,9] to learn the attention on the relevant visual regions and discard the useless information regarding the question.

Classification Based Methods. The answers in the current VQA datasets only span a small set of words and phrases. Thus most of the related works posed the VQA task as a classification over a set of candidate answers. As a result, the image and question feature fusion strategies become the key factor for improving the performance of VQA. Early works modeled interactions between image and question with first order interactions like concatenation [24] or element-wise product [13,16,32]. Second order pooling is a more powerful way to model interactions between two feature spaces. It has shown great success in the fine-grained visual recognition task. Fukui et al. [9] first introduced the bilinear pooling on VQA task. They proposed the Multimodal Compact Bilinear pooling (MCB), which use the outer product of image and question feature vectors in different modalities to produce a very high-dimensional feature for quadratic expansion. However, MCB usually needs high-dimensional features to guarantee robust performance, which may seriously limit its applicability for VQA due to the limitations in GPU memory. To overcome this problem, Multi-modal Low-rank Bilinear pooling (MLB) [14] are proposed, in which the bilinear interactions between image and question feature spaces are parametrized by a tensor and the tensor is constrained to be a low rank. After that, Hedi *et al.* proposed Multimodal Tucker Fusion (MUTAN) [6] which is also a multimodal fusion scheme based on bilinear interactions between modalities but relying on a low-rank Tucker tensor-based decomposition to explicitly constrain the interaction rank.

Image-Question-Answer Triplet Based Reasoning. Different from the classification based methods, there are some other related works try to introduce the answer representations into the reasoning for visual question answers. Shih *et al.* [25] combined the question and answer as input for the model to determine whether a question-answer pair is a good match given evidence from the image. Allan *et al.* [12] concatenate image feature vector, question feature vector and answer embedding as input variables and predict whether or not an image-question-answer triplet is correct. The work in [27] try to project the image-question jointly representation into the answer embedding space learned from a text corpus. Both the work of Allan *et al.* [12] and Teney *et al.* [27] used the answer embedding learned from text corpus which has been proved as having limited ability to represent visual information [5]. Moreover, reasoning about the relations among image-question-answer triplets should be very complex, it should be hard to be model by using simple concatenating feature vectors or element-wise product.

In this work, we introduce DA-NTN, a deep attention based neural tensor network for reasoning the complex relations between image-question-answer triplet. The answer embedding used in this work is learned from scratch by supervision of VQA task. DA-NTN can be applied to traditional classification based VQA models easily and significantly boost the performance of these methods.

3   Approach

Figure 1 provides an overview of the architecture of our open-ended visual question answering framework. The goal of the VQA task is to provide an answer given an image $I \in \mathcal{I}$ and a corresponding question $q \in \mathcal{Q}$. Most of the previous works regard the open-ended VQA as a classification task:

$$\arg \max_{a_i \in \mathcal{A}} p_\theta(a_i | q, I) \tag{1}$$

where θ means the whole set of parameters of the model, and $\mathcal{A}$ is the set of candidate answers. However, in our proposed model, we treat the open-ended VQA as a regression task, that our proposed method target at measure the relevance score $s_\theta(q, I, a_i)$ among image I, question a, and answer a_i, and then predicts whether or not an image-question-answer triplet is correct.

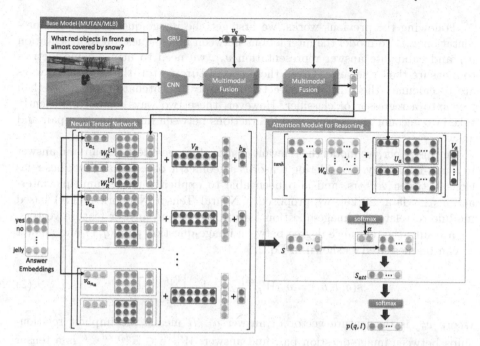

Fig. 1. Overview of our proposed framework for visual question answering. Image, question and all candidate answers are jointly fed into this framework. The structure in the red box is the base model used to generate question representation v_q and the fusion of image and question feature vector v_{qI}. The structure in two blue boxes is our proposed Deep Attention Neural Tensor Network. The blue box named neural tensor network is applied to measure the relevance among image-question-answer triplet, the tensor can represent the implicit relations among triplets. The blue box named attention module for reasoning is designed to adaptively reason for different triplets according to their implicit relation types. (Best viewed in color)

The inputs to our model contain a question and a corresponding image and candidate answers. A convolutional neural network and a GRU recurrent network are used for extracting feature vectors for image and question respectively. Then the representations of image and question are integrated as multi-modal features by using bilinear pooling module such as MLB [14], MUTAN [6]. At last, a DA-NTN module is applied to measure the correlation degree between the integrated feature vector v_{qI} of question-image pair and representation of input answer.

3.1 Neural Tensor Networks for VQA

As we show in Fig. 1, DA-NTN module target to measure the relevance score of the image-question-answer triplet. For the VQA task, the image-question pairs are predefined. Thus the relevance of image-question-answer triplet can be rewritten as the relevance between image-question pair and answer.

Following the previous works, we first get the image-question pair's representation v_{qI}. To model the interactions between image-question representation v_{qI} and candidate answer representation v_{a_i}, we need to utilize some metrics to measure their relevance. Given these two feature vector, the traditional ways are to calculate their distance directly or simply concatenate the vectors then feed into a regressor or classifier. However, these two ways cannot sufficiently take into account the complicated interactions between image-question pair and answer.

In this paper, we model the relevant degree of image-question pair and answer in a non-linear way. Considering tensor is a geometric object that describes relations between vectors, and also been able to explicitly model multiple interactions in data [22,26], we proposed a Neural Tensor Network (NTN) based module to relate the image-question feature vector and answer feature vectors. As a result, the relevance degree between image-question pair $\langle q, I \rangle$ and answer a_i can be measured as shown in Eq. 2.

$$s(q, I, a_i) = v_{qI} W_R^{[1:k]} v_{a_i} + V_R \begin{bmatrix} v_{qI} \\ v_{a_i} \end{bmatrix} + b_R \tag{2}$$

where v_{a_i} is the feature vector of answer a_i. R means the implicit relationships between image-question pair and answer. $W_R^{[1:k]} \in \mathbb{R}^{d_{qI} \times d_a \times k}$ is a tensor and the bilinear tensor product $v_{qI} W_R^{[1:k]} v_{a_i}$ results in a k-d vector $h \in \mathbb{R}^k$, where each $\langle q, I, a_i \rangle$ with a special relationship type $rel_r \in R$ can be computed by a corresponding slice $r = 1, ..., k$ of the tensor: $h_i = v_{qI} W_R^{[i]} v_{a_i}$. The other parameters for implicit relationships R are the standard form of a neural network: $V_R \in \mathbb{R}^{k \times (d_{qI} + d_a)}$ and $b_R \in \mathbb{R}^k$. As a result, we can get a k-d vector $s(q, I, R, a_i)$ to measure the relevance degree between image-question pair and answer, and each element in the vector represent the response of image-question-answer triplet with a specific implicit relationship.

Following the settings of previous works, both of the visual representation v_I and question representation v_q are initialized from a pre-trained model, then fine-tuned during the training procedure of VQA task. But for answer a_i, its representation v_{a_i} should be provided with visual information for reasoning. Traditional word embeddings learned from natural language corpus are not suitable for modeling visual information. For example, the nearest words of "dog" in word representations space learned from the natural language corpus are some other words describing animals like "pet", "cat", etc. The word embeddings learned from natural language corpus can distinguish the semantic and syntax differences between answers but it is hard to be used for visual question answering task which requires the ability to describe visual information [5]. Thus, We try to learn the answer representation v_{a_i} for VQA task from scratch instead of directly using the word representations learned from natural language corpus, which is different with previous related works.

3.2   Attention Module for Reasoning

Since each element in the vector $s(q, I, a_i)$ is designed to correspond to one particular relationship and reasoning process of $\langle q, I, a_i \rangle$, we propose an attention mechanism to combine them by dynamically adjusting the weight of each element in the vector. For VQA task, the relationship of $\langle q, I, a_i \rangle$ triplet usually be decided by the type of question q. For example, the relationships of triplets can be split as object recognition, object location, object counting, object attributes, etc. All of these relationship classes can be recognized according to the meaning of the question. Moreover, the responses of all candidate answers can also provide more detail information about the question type. For example, if one question is answering about colors, the responses of candidate answers about color should have larger responses than other candidate answers.

Specifically, we use the attention mechanism to obtain the weighted average of each element in the relevant vector $s(q, i, a_i)$ as the output of the finally score about whether or not $\langle q, I, a_i \rangle$ is correct, which is denoted as

$$s_{att}(q, I, a_i) = \sum_{j=1}^{k} s_{i,j} \alpha_j \qquad (3)$$

where $s_{i,j}$ is the j-th element in relevance vector $s(q, I, a_i)$, α_j is the attention weight for the j-th element. The attention score α_j is calculated by

$$\alpha_j = \frac{\exp(c_j)}{\sum_{e=1}^{k} \exp(c_e)} \qquad (4)$$

and c_j is defined as

$$c_j = V_a \cdot \tanh(W_a S_j + U_a v_q) \qquad (5)$$

where $S_j = \{s_{1,j}, s_{2,j}, ..., s_{n_a,j}\}$ is a vector to represent the responses of all candidate answers given image I, question q and one special implicit relationship type. $W_a \in \mathbb{R}^{n_a \times n_a}$, $U_a \in \mathbb{R}^{n_a \times |v_q|}$, $V_a \in \mathbb{R}^{n_a \times 1}$ are weight matrices of the attention module. The combination weights are determined by the response of all candidate answers and question representations. In this way, multiply image-question-answer implicit relationships are taken into consideration and different reasoning results are integrated according to the responses of candidate answers and the contextual information in question.

3.3   Label Distribution Learning with Regression

In practice, an image-question pair is associated with one or several similar answers. In dataset like VQA [4] and VQA-2.0 [10], each image-question pair is annotated with multiple answers by different people. The answers for each sample can be represented as a distribution vector of all the possible answers $y \in \mathbb{R}^{n_a}$, where $y_i \in [0, 1]$ indicates the occurrence probability of the i-the answer in $\mathcal{A}$ across human labeled answers for this image-question pair.

Since our proposed model output as regression of answer scores, a typical training strategy is to use margin-based loss function to maximize the distance between correct answers and any incorrect answers. However, for open-ended VQA task, there are lots of candidate answers need to be considered. The increasing of negative samples lead to much more positive-negative pairs to train and more complex training procedure. As a result, it is very complex to model the structure of VQA reasoning space by using margin-based loss function with limited negative samples and may also introduce uncertainty to the learned model and take much more iterations to converge. To overcome this problem, we transform the margin based learning problem with negative sampling to label distribution learning (LDL) problem with all answers distributions y.

For each image-question pair, we compute the regression score $s_{att}(q, I, a_i)$ for each answer a_i in overall answer candidate set $\mathcal{A}$. Then use a softmax regression to approach the answers distributions:

$$p_i(q, I) = \frac{\exp(s_{att}(q, I, a_i))}{\sum_{j=1}^{n_a} \exp(s_{att}(q, I, a_j))} \tag{6}$$

The KL-divergence loss function is applied to penalize the prediction $p_i \in \mathbb{R}^{n_a}$, our model is trained by minimizing

$$l = \frac{1}{N} \sum_{j=1}^{N} \sum_{i=1}^{n_a} y_i \log \frac{y_i}{p_i(q_j, I_j)} \tag{7}$$

where N is the amount of image-question pairs for training.

During inference procedure, we just feed the embeddings of all candidate answers into DA-NTN, and then select the answer a_i with biggest triplet relevance score $s_{att}(q, I, a_i)$ as the final answer.

4 Experiments

In this section, we evaluate the performance of our proposed DA-NTN model on VQA task. We also analyze the implicit relationship used for guiding reasoning and the answer representations learned from VQA task.

Existing VQA approaches usually have three stages: (1) getting the representation vectors of image and question respectively; (2) combining these multimodal features to obtain fused image-question representation; (3) using the integrated image-question features to learn a multi-class classifier and to predict the best-matching answer. Bilinear pooling based methods have been widely used for fusing image-question feature in step 2. We build our model based on below two widely used VQA models by applying the attention-based neural tensor network after step 2 to measure the relevance scores of image-question-answer triplets.

MLB [14]. Using low-rank bilinear pooling in step 2 to approximate full bilinear pooling between image representations and question representations.

MUTAN [6]. A multimodal tensor-based tucker decomposition to efficiently parametrize bilinear interactions between image and question representations.

In order to get convincing comparison between baseline methods and our method, we directly apply the best hyper-parameters on MLB and MUTAN to DA-NTN based MLB and MUTAN respectively. We also reference other previous works for comparison with our DA-NTN based MUTAN and MLB models.

4.1 Dataset

In this paper, we use the VQA-1.0 dataset [4] and VQA-2.0 dataset [10] for evaluating our proposed method.

The VQA-1.0 dataset consists of approximately 200,000 images from MS-COCO dataset with nearly 3 questions per images and each question is answered by 10 annotators. There are 248k question-answer pairs for the training set, 121k pairs for validation and 244k pairs for testing. Additionally, there is a 25% test split subset named *test-dev*.

VQA-2.0 is another dataset for VQA task. Compared to the VQA-v1.0 dataset, it contains more training samples (440k question-answer pairs for training and 214k pairs for validation) and is more balanced to weaken the potential that an overfitted model may achieve good results. Thus we use VQA-2.0 dataset for experimental results analysis.

In this paper, we focus on the open-ended VQA task, where the ground truth answers are given in free natural language phrases. And we evaluate the VQA accuracy by using the tools provided by Antol *et al.* [4], where the accuracy of a predicted answer a_i is given by:

$$\min\left(1, \frac{\# \text{ annotators the provided } a_i}{3}\right) \tag{8}$$

It means that if the predicted answer a_i appears greater than or equal to three times in human labeled answer list, the accuracy is calculated as 1.

4.2 Experimental Settings

To be fair, we use the same image representations and question representations models for all of the experiments in this paper. We used image features with bottom-up attention [1] from Faster R-CNN as the visual features which produce feature maps of size $K \times 2048$, since the features can be interpreted as ResNet features centered on the top-K objects in the image, where $K < 100$. A GRU initialized with the parameters of a pre-trained Skip-thoughts model [15] is used for learning question representations.

We use the Adam solver as the optimizer for training. The hyper-parameters such as initial learning rate, dropout ratio, the dimension of the image-question feature are set as same with the best settings in the original publications about MLB and MUTAN respectively. Both of them are equipped with visual regions attention module.

DA-NTN Setup. For our proposed attention-based neural tensor network module, we set the dimension of answer representation as 360 for all of the experiments in this paper. The candidate answer set $\mathcal{A}$ is fixed to the top-2000 most frequent answers since the answers in VQA-2.0 dataset follow the long-tail distribution. For the inference procedure, only image and question are required as inputs, then embedding of all candidate answers will be fed into the model, and the answer with biggest triplet relevance score s_{att} will be selected as predicted answer of DA-NTN. To avoid over-fitting, we apply L2-regularization for embeddings of all candidate answers. By default, we set $k = 6$ by considering the trade-off between training complex and performance on the validation set.

4.3 Experimental Results

In Table 1, we compare the performance of our proposed method with the base models. The models are trained on the train set and evaluated on the validation set. Furthermore, we explore different hyper-parameters for our proposed attention-based neural tensor network. It worth to note that the average accuracies of our implemented baseline MLB and MUTAN on VQA-2.0 dataset are already 5.7% and 4.9% higher than the performance reported in previous works [6] respectively.

From Table 1, we can find that: (1) MUTAN + NTN gives better results than MUTAN, even with a small number of implicit triplet relationship, like $k = 3$. This shows that the neural tensor network is able to learn powerful

Table 1. Comparison between different models for open-ended VQA on the validation split of VQA-2.0 dataset. The model size indicates the number of all learnable parameters, including the parameters of GRU for question representation learning. NTN means neural tensor network without attention module for reasoning. For NTN we use sum-pooling instead of our proposed attention module for reasoning. All: overall accuracy in percentage, Yes/No: accuracy on yes-no questions, Numb: accuracy on questions that can be answered by numbers or digits, Other: accuracy on other types of questions.

Model	Model size	VQA-2.0 val set			
		Yes/no	Numb.	Other	All
MUTAN	38.0M	81.09	42.25	54.41	62.84
MUTAN + NTN ($k = 3$)	39.3M	81.69	43.88	55.35	63.74
MUTAN + NTN ($k = 6$)	39.9M	81.96	43.63	55.39	63.83
MUTAN + NTN ($k = 10$)	40.6M	82.23	43.34	55.33	63.86
MUTAN + DA-NTN ($k = 3$)	48.1M	81.96	44.59	55.63	64.07
MUTAN + DA-NTN ($k = 6$)	48.7M	81.98	44.85	55.72	64.16
MUTAN + DA-NTN ($k = 10$)	49.4M	82.24	44.55	55.43	64.07
MLB	67.2M	81.89	42.97	53.89	62.98
MLB + DA-NTN ($k = 6$)	87.5M	83.09	44.88	55.71	**64.58**

Table 2. The performance of different single model for open-ended VQA on the test-dev and test-stand set of VQA-2.0 dataset.

Model	VQA-2.0 test-dev set				VQA-2.0 test-standard set			
	Y/N	No.	Other	All	Y/N	No.	Other	All
Prior [10]	-	-	-	-	61.20	0.36	1.17	25.98
LSTM (blind) [10]	-	-	-	-	67.01	31.55	27.37	44.26
MCB [10]	-	-	-	-	78.82	38.28	53.36	62.27
MUTAN	82.88	44.54	56.50	66.01	83.06	44.28	56.91	66.38
MLB	83.58	44.92	56.34	66.27	83.96	44.77	56.52	66.62
MUTAN + DA-NTN	83.58	46.78	57.77	67.15	83.92	46.64	58.0	67.51
MLB + DA-NTN	84.29	47.14	57.92	**67.56**	84.60	47.13	58.20	**67.94**

correlations among image-question-answer triplets. (2) The attention module for reasoning benefit the performance of NTN, we can see that the DA-NTN achieves better performance than NTN. This phenomenon proved, that different types of image-question-answer triplets should correspond to different reasoning process, and the attention module for associating the triplet with its relevant reasoning process is important for VQA. (3) Even using the same DA-NTN hyper-parameter settings of MUTAN ($v_{qI} \in \mathbb{R}^{512}$) for MLB ($v_{qI} \in \mathbb{R}^{4800}$), our proposed DA-NTN still can significantly boost the accuracy of MLB.

Table 2 reports the experimental results on *test-dev* and *test-stand* set of VQA-2.0 dataset. All of the models in Table 2 are trained on the combination of train set and validation set, without any data augmentation. From the results, We can find that the models with DA-NTN have stable improvements than base models, and our DA-NTN based models archived the best accuracy on all of the three different types of questions.

Considering that most of the previous works compare their performance on VQA-1.0 dataset, we also provide the experimental results on the VQA-1.0 dataset in Table 3. Similar with the experimental results on VQA-2.0 dataset, our proposed DA-NTN can provide steady improvement.

5   Analysis

To get the deep insight of our proposed method, in this section, we conduct the studies to investigate how the reasoning attention module helps to improve the performance of the base model, and we also analyze the answer embedding learned from VQA task.

5.1   Attention Module Analysis

As we mentioned in Sect. 3.2, the relationship among image-question-answer triplet and its relevant reasoning process should be decided by the type of question. To further analyze, how the reasoning attention module works, we counted

Table 3. Comparison between different single models for open-ended VQA on the test-dev and test-stand set of VQA-1.0 dataset. [†]: use GloVe [21] as pretrained word embedding model for question representation. [‡]: use Skip-thought [15] as pretrained word embedding model for question representation. [*]: use image features with bottom-up attention [1].

Model	VQA-1.0 test-dev set				VQA-1.0 test-standard set			
	Y/N	No.	Other	All	Y/N	No.	Other	All
iBOWIMG [33]	76.5	35.0	42.6	55.7	76.8	35.0	42.6	55.9
DPPnet [20]	80.7	37.2	41.7	57.2	80.3	36.9	42.2	57.4
VQA team [4]	80.5	36.8	43.1	57.8	80.6	36.5	43.7	58.2
SMem [30]	80.9	37.3	43.1	58.0	80.9	37.5	43.5	58.2
AYN [18]	78.4	36.4	46.3	58.4	78.2	36.3	46.3	58.4
NMN [3]	81.2	38.0	44.0	58.6	81.2	37.7	44.0	58.7
SAN [31]	79.3	36.6	46.1	58.7	-	-	-	58.9
AMA [28]	81.0	38.4	45.2	59.2	81.1	37.1	45.8	59.4
D-NMN [2]	81.1	38.6	45.5	59.4	-	-	-	59.4
FDA [11]	81.1	36.2	45.8	59.2	-	-	-	59.5
DMN+ [29]	80.5	36.8	48.3	60.3	-	-	-	60.4
MRN [13]	82.3	38.9	49.3	61.7	82.4	38.2	49.4	61.8
HieCoAtt [17]	79.7	38.7	51.7	61.8	-	-	-	62.1
RAU [19]	81.9	39.0	53.0	63.3	81.7	38.2	52.8	63.2
MCB[†] [9]	82.5	37.6	55.6	64.7	-	-	-	-
MLB[‡] [14]	84.1	38.2	54.9	65.1	84.0	37.9	54.8	65.1
MFB[†] [32]	84.0	39.8	56.2	65.9	83.8	38.9	56.3	65.8
MUTAN[‡*]	83.3	39.7	56.6	65.7	83.2	40.3	56.4	65.8
MLB[‡*]	85.1	39.9	55.4	65.9	84.7	39.5	55.5	65.9
MUTAN[‡*] + DA-NTN	84.5	41.8	57.8	67.1	84.3	41.9	58.0	67.1
MLB[‡*] + DA-NTN	85.8	41.9	58.6	**67.9**	85.8	42.5	58.5	**68.1**

the average attention scores corresponding to different implicit relationships for each type of question. Figure 2 presents the distributions of attention score computed by MUTAN + DA-NTN on different types of questions in the validation set of VQA-2.0. Since we set $k = 6$ in this experiment, each question type has six attention scores corresponding to six different kinds of implicit relationship and reasoning process.

From Fig. 2, we can observe that each implicit relationship pay attention to at least one specific question type. For example, the attention score α_1 for implicit relationship rel_1 is significantly bigger than others on questions about color. α_2 is bigger than other attention scores on questions about the number of objects. The combination of rel_3 and rel_4 is focussing on questions that have

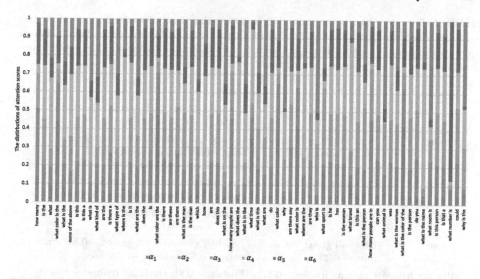

Fig. 2. The distributions of average attention scores across different types of questions. Each attention score α_i is relevant to one specific implicit relationship rel_i. The length of column in different colors indicates the value of attention score of different implicit relationship, higher column means higher attention score. Since we use the softmax function (Eq. 4) normalized the distribution of attention score α_i, the sum of average attention scores for each type of question is 1. (Best viewed in color)

Yes or No answers, meanwhile, the combination of rel_4 and rel_6 usually focus on questions about "what" and "how".

We can also find that some implicit relationships which are hard to distinguish by simple classification based method also can be detected. For example, all questions with answers related to number or digit are treated in the same way by using traditional methods. However, in practice, the questions about "how many objects" should have totally different reasoning process comparing to questions about "what number is", because the former target at counting objects in images, while the latter target at recognizing the digits in images. By using our proposed DA-NTN, these two types of questions can be classified into two different implicit relationships and associated with two different reasoning process. In Fig. 2 we can find that questions asking about "what number is" have biggest attention score on rel_5, while question asking about "how many (people are/people are in/)" have biggest attention score on rel_2.

With these observations, we can conclude that DA-NTN can effectively model diverse relationships among image-question-answer triplets and benefit the reasoning process of visual question answering.

5.2 Answer Representations Analysis

To gain a deeper understanding of how proposed DA-NTN learn answer representations according to the supervision from VQA, we look at nearest neighbors

Table 4. For query words, we show their most similar words based on our method and context based word embedding [21]. We also show the cosine similarity scores between query word and its nearest neighbors, only the words whose cosine similarity scores are smaller than −0.3 are shown in this table.

Answers	DA-NTN	GloVe
0	1: −0.43, 2: −0.32	1: −0.60, 5: −0.53, 9: −0.51, 6: −0.51, 3: −0.50, 4: −0.50, 8: −0.50, etc.
Orange	Red: −0.39, yellow: −0.33, brown: −0.32	Orange and yellow: −0.90, orange and blue: −0.89, orange juice: −0.88, green and orange: −0.87, etc.
Table	On table: −0.35, desk: −0.30	On table: −0.84, picnic table: −0.84, chairs: −0.62, dining room: −0.60, etc.
Rectangle	Square: −0.34	Triangle: −0.64, squares: −0.61, circle: −0.60, oval: −0.59, etc.
Glove	Baseball glove: −0.34, mitt: −0.33	Baseball glove: −0.82, gloves: −0.81, knee pads: −0.57, helmet: −0.56, etc.
Playing frisbee	Catching frisbee: −0.37, throwing frisbee: −0.35	Frisbee: −0.81, throwing frisbee: −0.80, playing tennis: −0.80, playing: −0.80, etc.
River	Lake: −0.32, pond: −0.32	Lake: −0.72, shore: −0.63, railroad crossing: −0.58, bridge: −0.58, water: −0.58, etc.
Middle	Center: −0.30	End: −0.64, in corner: −0.64, right side: −0.63, left one: −0.63, etc.

of several exemplary answers given by word embeddings, where cosine similarity is used as a distance metric. We compare word embeddings learned by DA-NTN with GloVe [21] word embeddings, since GloVe has been used for many previous VQA models [9,27,32]. For GloVe, if the answer is a phrase, we averaged the word embedding of each word in the phrase as phrase representation. The experimental results are shown in Table 4.

Obviously, our word representations reflect more about visually similar. For example, it returns "red", "yellow" and "brown" as the nearest neighbors of word "orange", since these three colors are very close to red in the standard gradual color bar. Due to lack of the supervision from VQA, the words in GloVe embedding space distribute in a mess, we can find that for each answer, there are many nearest neighbors, and all of these nearest neighbors usually have very small cosine distance with the central word. This makes it more difficult to distinguish candidate answers. Moreover, since the GloVe word vectors are learned from natural language corpus without visual supervision, there are many semantic or syntactic similarity but visual irrelevance and noisy words are introduced for nearest neighbors during using GloVe. For example, all of nearest neighbors of "middle" (like "end", "in corner", "right side") in the GloVe space has no visual relevance with "middle". This kind of noisy words can mislead the reasoning process for visual question answering.

6 Conclusion

In this paper, a reasoning attention based neural tensor network is designed for visual question answering. We applied our proposed method to different VQA models and got substantial gains for all types of questions. Our analysis demonstrates that our proposed method can not only model the diverse implicit relationship among image-question-answer triples to benefit the reasoning of visual question answering, but also learn reasonable answer representations.

One direction for future work is to apply our DA-NTN to more VQA models, the other direction is to model the relationships of triplet by measuring the relevance between question-answer pair and image, image-answer pair and question, or some more complex combinations of image, question, and answer. We are also interested in learning better answer representations for some specialized tasks such as reading.

References

1. Anderson, P., et al.: Bottom-up and top-down attention for image captioning and VQA. arXiv preprint arXiv:1707.07998 (2017)
2. Andreas, J., Rohrbach, M., Darrell, T., Klein, D.: Learning to compose neural networks for question answering. arXiv preprint arXiv:1601.01705 (2016)
3. Andreas, J., Rohrbach, M., Darrell, T., Klein, D.: Neural module networks. In: Proceedings of the IEEE Conference on Computer Vision and Pattern Recognition, pp. 39–48 (2016)
4. Antol, S., et al.: VQA: visual question answering. In: Proceedings of the IEEE International Conference on Computer Vision, pp. 2425–2433 (2015)
5. Bai, Y., Yang, K., Yu, W., Xu, C., Ma, W.Y., Zhao, T.: Automatic image dataset construction from click-through logs using deep neural network. In: Proceedings of the 23rd ACM International Conference on Multimedia, pp. 441–450 (2015)
6. Ben-younes, H., Cadene, R., Cord, M., Thome, N.: MUTAN: multimodal tucker fusion for visual question answering. In: The IEEE International Conference on Computer Vision (ICCV), vol. 1, p. 3 (2017)
7. Chen, K., Wang, J., Chen, L.C., Gao, H., Xu, W., Nevatia, R.: ABC-CNN: an attention based convolutional neural network for visual question answering. arXiv preprint arXiv:1511.05960 (2015)
8. Donahue, J., et al.: Long-term recurrent convolutional networks for visual recognition and description. In: Proceedings of the IEEE Conference on Computer Vision and Pattern Recognition, pp. 2625–2634 (2015)
9. Fukui, A., Park, D.H., Yang, D., Rohrbach, A., Darrell, T., Rohrbach, M.: Multimodal compact bilinear pooling for visual question answering and visual grounding. arXiv preprint arXiv:1606.01847 (2016)
10. Goyal, Y., Khot, T., Summers-Stay, D., Batra, D., Parikh, D.: Making the V in VQA matter: elevating the role of image understanding in visual question answering. In: CVPR, vol. 1, p. 9 (2017)
11. Ilievski, I., Yan, S., Feng, J.: A focused dynamic attention model for visual question answering. arXiv preprint arXiv:1604.01485 (2016)

12. Jabri, A., Joulin, A., van der Maaten, L.: Revisiting visual question answering baselines. In: Leibe, B., Matas, J., Sebe, N., Welling, M. (eds.) ECCV 2016. LNCS, vol. 9912, pp. 727–739. Springer, Cham (2016). https://doi.org/10.1007/978-3-319-46484-8_44
13. Kim, J.H., et al.: Multimodal residual learning for visual QA. In: Advances in Neural Information Processing Systems, pp. 361–369 (2016)
14. Kim, J.H., On, K.W., Lim, W., Kim, J., Ha, J.W., Zhang, B.T.: Hadamard product for low-rank bilinear pooling (2017)
15. Kiros, R., Zhu, Y., Salakhutdinov, R.R., Zemel, R., Urtasun, R., Torralba, A., Fidler, S.: Skip-thought vectors. In: Advances in Neural Information Processing Systems, pp. 3294–3302 (2015)
16. Li, R., Jia, J.: Visual question answering with question representation update (QRU). In: Advances in Neural Information Processing Systems, pp. 4655–4663 (2016)
17. Lu, J., Yang, J., Batra, D., Parikh, D.: Hierarchical question-image co-attention for visual question answering. In: Advances in Neural Information Processing Systems, pp. 289–297 (2016)
18. Malinowski, M., Rohrbach, M., Fritz, M.: Ask your neurons: a deep learning approach to visual question answering. Int. J. Comput. Vis. 125(1–3), 110–135 (2017)
19. Noh, H., Han, B.: Training recurrent answering units with joint loss minimization for VQA. arXiv preprint arXiv:1606.03647 (2016)
20. Noh, H., Hongsuck Seo, P., Han, B.: Image question answering using convolutional neural network with dynamic parameter prediction. In: Proceedings of the IEEE Conference on Computer Vision and Pattern Recognition, pp. 30–38 (2016)
21. Pennington, J., Socher, R., Manning, C.D.: Glove: global vectors for word representation. In: Proceedings of the Empiricial Methods in Natural Language Processing (EMNLP 2014), vol. 12 (2014)
22. Qiu, X., Huang, X.: Convolutional neural tensor network architecture for community-based question answering. In: IJCAI, pp. 1305–1311 (2015)
23. Reed, S., Akata, Z., Yan, X., Logeswaran, L., Schiele, B., Lee, H.: Generative adversarial text to image synthesis. arXiv preprint arXiv:1605.05396 (2016)
24. Ren, M., Kiros, R., Zemel, R.: Exploring models and data for image question answering. In: Advances in Neural Information Processing Systems, pp. 2953–2961 (2015)
25. Shih, K.J., Singh, S., Hoiem, D.: Where to look: focus regions for visual question answering. In: Proceedings of the IEEE Conference on Computer Vision and Pattern Recognition, pp. 4613–4621 (2016)
26. Socher, R., Chen, D., Manning, C.D., Ng, A.: Reasoning with neural tensor networks for knowledge base completion. In: Advances in Neural Information Processing Systems, pp. 926–934 (2013)
27. Teney, D., Anderson, P., He, X., Hengel, A.V.D.: Tips and tricks for visual question answering: learnings from the 2017 challenge. arXiv preprint arXiv:1708.02711 (2017)
28. Wu, Q., Wang, P., Shen, C., Dick, A., van den Hengel, A.: Ask me anything: free-form visual question answering based on knowledge from external sources. In: Proceedings of the IEEE Conference on Computer Vision and Pattern Recognition, pp. 4622–4630 (2016)
29. Xiong, C., Merity, S., Socher, R.: Dynamic memory networks for visual and textual question answering. In: International Conference on Machine Learning, pp. 2397–2406 (2016)

30. Xu, H., Saenko, K.: Ask, attend and answer: exploring question-guided spatial attention for visual question answering. In: Leibe, B., Matas, J., Sebe, N., Welling, M. (eds.) ECCV 2016. LNCS, vol. 9911, pp. 451–466. Springer, Cham (2016). https://doi.org/10.1007/978-3-319-46478-7_28
31. Yang, Z., He, X., Gao, J., Deng, L., Smola, A.: Stacked attention networks for image question answering. In: Proceedings of the IEEE Conference on Computer Vision and Pattern Recognition, pp. 21–29 (2016)
32. Yu, Z., Yu, J., Fan, J., Tao, D.: Multi-modal factorized bilinear pooling with co-attention learning for visual question answering. In: Proceedings of IEEE International Conference on Computer Vision, vol. 3 (2017)
33. Zhou, B., Tian, Y., Sukhbaatar, S., Szlam, A., Fergus, R.: Simple baseline for visual question answering. arXiv preprint arXiv:1512.02167 (2015)

Shuffle-Then-Assemble: Learning Object-Agnostic Visual Relationship Features

Xu Yang[✉], Hanwang Zhang, and Jianfei Cai

School of Computer Science and Engineering, Nanyang Technological University,
Singapore, Singapore
s170018@e.ntu.edu.sg, {hanwangzhang,asjfcai}@ntu.edu.sg

Abstract. Due to the fact that it is prohibitively expensive to completely annotate visual relationships, *i.e.*, the (obj1, rel, obj2) triplets, relationship models are inevitably biased to object classes of limited pairwise patterns, leading to poor generalization to rare or unseen object combinations. Therefore, we are interested in learning object-agnostic visual features for more generalizable relationship models. By "agnostic", we mean that the feature is less likely biased to the classes of paired objects. To alleviate the bias, we propose a novel Shuffle-Then-Assemble pre-training strategy. First, we discard all the triplet relationship annotations in an image, leaving two unpaired object domains without obj1-obj2 alignment. Then, our feature learning is to recover possible obj1-obj2 pairs. In particular, we design a cycle of residual transformations between the two domains, to capture shared but not object-specific visual patterns. Extensive experiments on two visual relationship benchmarks show that by using our pre-trained features, naive relationship models can be consistently improved and even outperform other state-of-the-art relationship models. Code has been made available at: https://github.com/yangxuntu/vrd.

1 Introduction

Thanks to the maturity of mid-level vision solutions such as object classification and detection [15,19,41], we are more ambitious to pursue higher-level vision-language tasks such as image captioning [5,13,14,31], visual Q&A [18,22,27], and visual chatbot [7]. Unfortunately, we gradually realize that many of the state-of-the-art systems merely capture training set bias while not the underlying reasoning [22,49,64]. Recently, a promising way is to use visual compositions such as scene graph [23,52] and relationship context [21,61] for explainable visual reasoning. Therefore, visual relationship detection (VRD) [28,56,59,60]—the task of predicting elementary triplets such as "person ride bike" and "car park on road" in an image—is becoming an indispensable building block connecting vision with language.

Despite the relatively preliminary stage of VRD compared to object detection, a major challenge of VRD is the high cost of annotating the (obj1, rel, obj2)

© Springer Nature Switzerland AG 2018
V. Ferrari et al. (Eds.): ECCV 2018, LNCS 11216, pp. 38–54, 2018.
https://doi.org/10.1007/978-3-030-01258-8_3

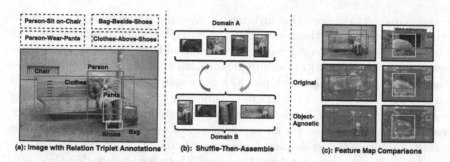

Fig. 1. (a) The triplet annotations of visual relationships in an image. (b) The key idea of the proposed `Shuffle-Then-Assemble` strategy is to discard the paired annotation of any relationship and leave two unpaired object domains. (c) Comparisons between the original feature maps obtained from base CNN (middle) and the object-agnostic ones (bottom) obtained by our pre-training (averaged over all the channels). We can see that our feature maps focus more on the overlapped regions of objects.

triplets as shown in Fig. 1(a). Unlike labeling objects in images, labeling visual relationships is prohibitively expensive as it requires combinatorial checks of the three entries. Therefore, the relationships in existing VRD datasets [26,32] are long-tailed, and the resultant relationship models are inevitably biased to the dominant obj1-obj2 combinations. For example, as reported in pioneering works [32,59], the recognition rate of unseen triplet compositions is significantly lower than the seen ones. This deficiency clearly limits the VRD potential in compositional reasoning. Though it can be alleviated by exploiting external knowledge such as language priors [32] and large-scale weak supervision [60], we still lack a principled solution in the visual modeling perspective.

Unsupervised feature learning (or pre-training) is arguably the most popular remedy for training deep models with small data [10,11,36,39,47,63]. Therefore, we are inspired to learn object-agnostic convolutional feature maps that are less likely biased to certain obj1-obj2 combinations. Such features should be highly responsive to object parts[1] involved in a relationship. A plausible way is to append additional conv-layers to the original base CNN (*e.g.*, VGG16 [44] or ResNet-150 [19]) to remove the object-sensitive responses inherited from image classification pre-training dataset (*e.g.*, ImageNet [8]). For example, as shown in Fig. 1(c), compared with the base CNN's feature map, the object-agnostic one ignores object patterns but focuses on the shared patterns of interacted objects. Therefore, we raise a question: how to learn the object-agnostic feature maps without additional relationship labeling cost?

In this paper, we propose a novel `Shuffle-Then-Assemble` feature learning strategy. As shown in Fig. 1(b), "shuffle" is to discard the original one-to-one paired object alignments, and thus no explicit obj1-obj2 class information is used; "assemble" is to pose the relationship modeling into an unsupervised pair recover problem by transferring Region-of-Interest (ROI) features between

---

[1] The parts can be at the pixel-level as well as the receptive field-level.

the two unpaired domains. Our intuitive motivation is two-fold: (1) if the ROI features extracted from the resultant feature maps still encode object-specific information, features are not likely to be transferred between the two domains of heterogeneous objects; (2) the unsupervised fashion encourages the exploration of many more possible relationships which are usually missing in annotation. As shown in Fig. 1(a), some simple spatial relationships such as "chair beside bag" are missing, and equivalent relationships are usually ignored, *i.e.*, "chair under person" is missing as "person sit on chair" is labeled. Inspired by the recent advances in unsupervised domain transfer methods [20,24,55,65], we design a cycle of transformations to establish the transfer between the two domains: either transfer direction maps an RoI from domain A (or B) to B (or A), and then an adversarial network is used to confuse the mapping with RoIs in B (or A). In particular, we use a residual structure for the transformation network, where the identity mapping encourages the feature map to capture shared but not object-specific visual patterns and the residual allows feature transformation.

We demonstrate the effectiveness of the proposed Shuffle-Then-Assemble strategy on two benchmarks: VRD [32] and VG [26]. We observe consistent improvement of using our pre-trained features against various ablative baselines and other state-of-the-art methods. For example, compared to feature maps without pre-training, we can boost the Recall@100 of supervised, weakly supervised, and zero-shot relationship prediction by absolute 4.74%, 4.42%, 4.04%, respectively on VRD, and 4.41%, 4.2%, 5.81%, respectively on VG.

2   Related Work

Visual Relationships. Modeling the object interactions such as verbs [3,16], actions [17,40,53], and visual phrases [1,9,43,54] has been extensively studied in literature. In particular, our relationship model used in this paper follows the recent progress on modeling generic visual relationships, *i.e.*, the (obj1, rel, obj2) triplets detected in images [32,59]. State-of-the-art relationship models fall into two lines of efforts: (1) message passing between the two object features [28,52,56], and (2) exploitation of subject-object statistics such as language priors [29,32,66] and dataset bias [6,58,62]. However, they are still limited in the inherent issue of insufficient training triplets due to combinatorial annotation complexity, leading the resultant relationship model to be brittle to rare or unseen compositions. Though weakly-supervised methods [38,50,60] can reduce the labeling cost, its performance is still far from practical use compared to supervised models. Unlike previous methods, in this paper, we propose to resolve this challenge in pairwise modeling of relationship, that is, given two regions, we want to improve the predicate classification without additional object information and extra supervision. We believe that the improvement can boost most of the above relationship models by replacing their pairwise modeling counterparts with our method.

Unsupervised Feature Learning. By exploiting large-scale unlabeled data, unsupervised feature learning methods [2] learn more generalizable intermediate

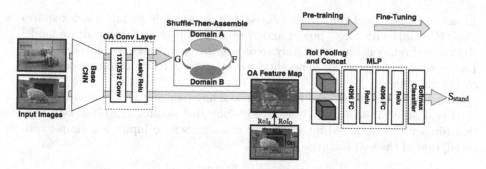

Fig. 2. The overview of the proposed `Shuffle-Then-Assemble` pre-training strategy (red arrow) and relationship detection model (blue arrow). The goal at the pre-training stage is to learn the Object-Agnostic (OA) conv-layers using `Shuffle-Then-Assemble` objective. Then, the traditional supervised training for the relation model can be considered as the fine-tuning stage using the desired OA feature map. (Color figure online)

data representation for solving some other machine learning tasks. Our motivation for visual relationship feature learning follows the common practice: feature transfer in today's computer vision [57], which fine-tunes a base network which has been pre-trained on other datasets and tasks. Different from the popular auto-encoder fashion [11,63], our strategy is more similar to the recent works on self-supervised training, where the learning objective is to discover the inherent data compositions such as predicting the context of image patches [10,33,34,36,37,45]. In particular, we propose to discover the alignment of RoI pairs and pose this discovery into the task of unsupervised domain transfer using adversarial learning [20,24,55,65]. Inspired by them, we use a cycle of transformations to remove the trivial alignment caused by mode collapse and thus build non-trivial connections between the paired RoIs.

3   Method

Figure 2 illustrates the overview of using `Shuffle-Then-Assemble` to enhance the relationship model. The goal of the feature learning process is to pre-train the Object-Agnostic (OA) conv-layers, which result in the desired OA feature map for better relationship modeling. We will first introduce the widely-used relationship modeling framework and its limitations, and then detail how to use the proposed feature learning method to overcome them.

3.1   Visual Relationship Model

The input of the visual relationship model is an image with a pair of object bounding boxes, and the output is an "obj1-rel-obj2" triplet, where "obj1" and "obj2" are the object classes of the two bounding boxes, and "rel" is the relationship class. In this paper, we adopt the common practice as in [32,59] that we do not directly model the triplet composition as a whole [6,43], which requires $\mathcal{O}(C^2 R)$ complexity for C object and R relationship classes; instead, we model objects and relationships separately to reduce the complexity down to $\mathcal{O}(C+R)$. Therefore, without loss of generality, we refer to a relationship model as an R-way classifier.

Suppose $\mathbf{x}_i$ and $\mathbf{x}_j$ are the RoI features of any pair of object bounding boxes (i,j) (e.g., the red and blue cubes in Fig. 2 by RoI pooling [12]), the r-th relationship score is obtained by a softmax classifier whose input is a simple concatenation of the two features:

$$S(i,j,r;\theta) = \frac{\exp\left(\mathbf{w}_r^T \mathrm{MLP}([\mathbf{x}_i, \mathbf{x}_j])\right)}{\sum\limits_{t=1}^{R} \exp\left(\mathbf{w}_t^T \mathrm{MLP}([\mathbf{x}_i, \mathbf{x}_j])\right)}, \tag{1}$$

where $\mathbf{w}_t \in \theta$ is the parameter of the classifier and the configuration of $MLP(\cdot)$ is detailed in Fig. 2. Note that although Eq. (1) is a naive model and there are fruitful ways of combining $\mathbf{x}_i$ and $\mathbf{x}_j$ in the literature, such as appending independent MLPs for each RoI [59], the union RoI [28], and even the fusion with textual features [21], our feature learning can be seamlessly incorporated into any of them. We will leave the evaluations of applying these tweaks for future work.

The relationship model can be trained by minimizing the cross-entropy loss of Eq. (1), summing over all the relationship pairs. However, due to the limited annotation of the relationship triplets, relationship models trained on these extremely long-tailed annotations are inevitably biased to the dominant object classes. One may wonder why it is object-biased as Eq. (1) does not use any object class information at all? The reason resides in the base CNN feature map. Almost all state-of-the-art visual recognition systems deploy the base CNN [19,44,46] pre-trained on ImageNet [8] or ImageNet+MSCOCO [30], where the training task is object recognition. Therefore, the resultant feature map for extracting RoI will naturally favor the sensitivity to object classes—each RoI feature encodes the discriminative information of the object inside the RoI (cf. the original feature map of Fig. 2), and leads the parameters in Eq. (1) over-fitted to specific object patterns. For example, if most of the triplets of "stand on" is "person stand on street", then the "stand on" classifier will mistakenly consider the joint pattern "person" and "street" into "stand on", and fails in cases of "person stand on chair" or "dog stand on street".

3.2   Shuffle-Then-Assemble Feature Learning

To alleviate the bias, we detail our proposed Shuffle-then-Assemble strategy to pre-train the Object-Agnostic (OA) conv-layers for obtaining the OA feature map. As discussed above, the bias is mainly due to the dominant object pairs in training data, therefore, our key idea is to discard the original one-to-one pairwise annotations, i.e., "shuffle", leaving two unaligned domains of RoIs for "obj1" and "obj2", and then we attempt to recover the one-to-one alignment,

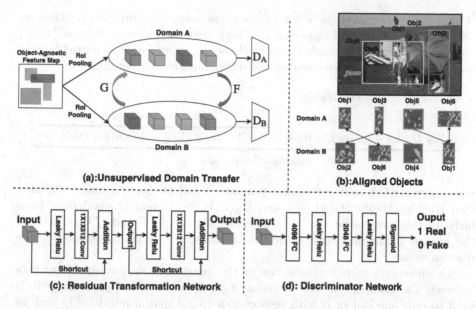

Fig. 3. (a) The overview of unsupervised domain transfer for `Shuffle-Then-Assemble`. It contains a cycle of transformations $F\colon A \mapsto B$ and $G\colon B \mapsto A$, and a pair of discriminators D_A and D_B to measure the quality of the transfer. (b) Qualitative transfer results. The directed arrow indicates the nearest-neighbor RoI in the target domain to the RoI from the source domain. (c) The residual architecture of the transformation network. (d) The architecture of the discriminator.

i.e., "assemble", by unsupervised domain transfer. Note that this pre-training strategy does not require additional cost of supervision. As shown in Fig. 3(b), we manage to align potential relationships without any one-to-one supervision, *e.g.*, obj1 may relate to obj6 with respect to "sit" and obj3 may relate to obj2 with respect to "hold".

The unsupervised domain transfer method used in `Shuffle-Then-Assemble` follows recent progress on adversarial domain transfer [4,20,24,55,65]. Noteworthy, the motivation of using adversarial domain transfer emphasizes more on the unsupervised alignments but NOT the feature transfer as in traditional domain transfer applications such as [48], where the domain transfer is used to close the gap between conveniently available synthetic data and real data. Here, our idea is more similar to [39] which discovers alignments between images that are very visually different such as "spotted bags" and "spotted shoes", or "frontal faces" and "frontal cars".

As illustrated in Fig. 3(a), we want to guide the pre-training of the OA conv-layers by learning mapping functions between domain A and B, where each of them consists of RoI features, $\mathbf{a} \in A$ and $\mathbf{b} \in B$, extracted from the tentative OA feature map. For the purpose of domain transfer, we have a cycle of two mappings: $F\colon A \mapsto B$ and $G\colon B \mapsto A$, to discover the underlying relationship between

A and B. Recall that there is one-to-one supervision between the two domains, we adopt the adversarial objective $\mathcal{L}_{adv}$ such that the mapped features $\{F(\mathbf{a})\}$ and $\{G(\mathbf{b})\}$ are indistinguishable from B and A, respectively; in particular, the indistinguishability is measured by two discriminators D_A and D_B:

$$\mathcal{L}_{adv}(A, B; \phi, F, G, D_A, D_B) =$$

$$\underbrace{\mathbb{E}_\mathbf{a}[\log D_A(\mathbf{a})] + \mathbb{E}_\mathbf{b}[\log D_B(\mathbf{b})] + \overbrace{\mathbb{E}_\mathbf{b}[\log(1 - D_A(G(\mathbf{b})))] + \mathbb{E}_\mathbf{a}[\log(1 - D_B(F(\mathbf{a})))]}^{\text{minimize by } F \text{ and } G}}_{\text{maximize by } D_A \text{ and } D_B},$$

$$(2)$$

where ϕ is the OA conv-layers that generate A and B, D_A is a binary classifier that tries to classify $D_A(\mathbf{a}) \mapsto 1$ and $D_A(F(\mathbf{b})) \mapsto 0$, and D_B is defined similarly. In this adversarial way, we will eventually obtain F and G that discover the hidden alignment between the two domains, *i.e.*, indistinguishable by the discriminators.

To encourage more explorations of the potential relationship alignments between the RoIs in the two domains, *e.g.*, avoid from mapping many RoIs in A to only one RoI in B with respect to a trivial spatial relationship such as "on" and "by", we further impose the "cycle-consistent" loss to be minimized by G and F:

$$\mathcal{L}_{cycle}(A, B; \phi, F, G) = \mathbb{E}_\mathbf{a}[\|\mathbf{a} - G(\mathbf{b})\|_1] + \mathbb{E}_\mathbf{b}[\|\mathbf{b} - F(\mathbf{a})\|_1]. \qquad (3)$$

The loss penalizes two different RoIs, *e.g.*, $\mathbf{a}$ and $\mathbf{a}'$, mapped to the same RoI $\mathbf{b}$ as it is hard to satisfy $\mathbf{a} \approx G(\mathbf{b})$ and $\mathbf{a}' \approx G(\mathbf{b})$ simultaneously.

By putting Eqs. (2) and (3) together, the full objective for pre-training the OA conv-layers is:

$$\phi^* = \arg\min_\phi \min_{F,G} \max_{D_A, D_B} \mathcal{L}_{adv}(A, B; \phi, F, G, D_A, D_B) + \lambda \mathcal{L}_{cycle}(A, B; \phi, F, G),$$

$$(4)$$

where $\lambda > 0$ is a trade-off hyper-parameter. Then, we can use ϕ^* to obtain $\mathbf{x}_i$ and $\mathbf{x}_j$, and fine-tune a better relationship model θ using existing triplet supervision as in Eq. (1). Next, we will introduce the proposed implementation of F and G.

3.3   Implementation Details

Network Architecture. For base CNN, we adopt Faster RCNN (VGG16) [42], which takes short width to be 600 and outputs the original $1/16 \times 1/16 \times 512$ feature map. As shown in Fig. 2, our OA conv-layer has 1 filter of the size 1×1, stride 1, followed by a Leaky Relu [51]. The transformation network is detailed in Fig. 3(c). Each transformation contains two blocks of residual network. The motivation of applying the residual structure is two-fold. (1) The shortcut encourages to find shared regions of two RoIs, since the shared RoI features will pass directly via the shortcut. This makes the optimization not only more light-weighted, but also easier to find the intrinsic inter-related visual patterns as relationships.

(2) If any object-specific information is still encoded in the RoI feature, the shortcut will make it harder to achieve the final domain transfer as domain A and B usually contain diverse objects. The discriminator network is detailed in Fig. 3(d), which is composed by two fully-connected layers followed by Leaky Relu. It takes a 50,176-d (two $7 \times 7 \times 512$ RoI feature) vectorized RoI feature as input and outputs a sigmoidal scalar between 0 and 1.

Training. At the feature pre-training stage, to collect sufficient RoIs in each domain, we augment the number of original bounding boxes by additional ones with IoU larger than 0.7, extracted by using the Region Proposal Network [42]. For each original bounding boxes, 10 RoIs are sampled. To stabilize the adversarial training in Eq. (4), we adopt three practices: (1) We apply least-square GAN [35] to replace the negative log likelihood by a least square loss. (2) The optimizer for training D_A and D_B is set to SGD and the optimizer for G, F and ϕ is set to Adam [25]. The initial learning rate is set to 1e-4 for both optimizers. (2) D_A and D_B are trained three times more compared with G, F and ϕ. The trade-off λ in Eq. (4) is set to 10. Every mini-batch is one image with randomly selected 128 triplets. The epochs for training these networks are set to 20 on VRD dataset and set to 5 on VG dataset.

At the fine-tune stage for training relationship classifier, the short width of image is still set to 600. Every mini-batch is one image with 128 randomly selected triplets. The optimizer is Adam with initial learning rate set to 1e-5 in all the experiments. The epochs are set to 50 and 30 on VRD dataset and VG dataset, respectively.

4   Experiments

We evaluated our `Shuffle-Then-Assemble` method by performing visual relationship prediction on two benchmark datasets. We conducted experiments under extensive settings: supervised, weakly-supervised, and zero-shot, each of which has various ablative baselines and state-of-the-art methods. We also visualized qualitative object-agnostic features maps compared against others.

4.1   Datasets and Metrics

We used two publicly available datasets: VRD (Visual Relationships Dataset [32]) and VG (Visual Genome V1.2 dataset [26]).

VRD Dataset. It contains 5,000 images with 100 object categories and 70 relationships. In total, VRD contains 37,993 relationship triplet annotations with 6,672 unique triplets and 24.25 relationship per object category. We followed the same train/test split as in [32], *i.e.*, 4,000 training images and 1,000 test images, where 1,877 triplets are only in the test set for zero-shot evaluations.

VG Dataset. We used the pruned version provided by Zhang [59] since the original one is very noisy. As a result, VG contains 99,658 images with 200 object categories and 100 predicates, 1,174,692 relation annotations with 19,237 unique relations and 57 predicates per object category. We followed the same 73,801/25,857

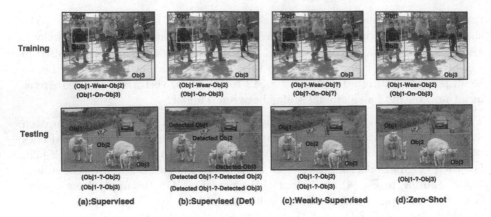

Fig. 4. We evaluate relationship prediction task using four different experiment settings: supervised, supervised (Det), weakly-supervised and zero-shot. "?" denotes the relationship to be predicted. It is noteworthy that the object category is not know under all the experiment settings, and we only use visual features to predict the relationship between object pairs.

train/test split. And this dataset contains 2,098 relationships which never occur in the training set, which can be used for zero-shot evaluations.

Metrics. As conventions [32,59], we used Recall@50 (**R@50**) and Recall@100 (**R@100**) as evaluation metrics. R@K computes the fraction of times a true relationship is predicted in the top K confident relation predictions in an image.

4.2   Settings

In our experiments, we only focused on the relationship prediction task, *i.e.*, classifying any two object regions into relationship classes. The reasons are twofold. First, relationship prediction plays the core role in relationship detection, a more comprehensive task that also needs to detect the two objects. Second, we can exclude the influence of object detection performance, as the improvement of object detection can improve the relationship detection scores [59]. To offer a testbed for application domains of relationship prediction, we designed the following 4 settings according to different pairwise modeling fashions:

Supervised. This setting is the standard supervised relationship prediction. As shown in Fig. 4(a), for training, all the objects are provided with ground truth boxes and the relationship between objects are given; for testing, a pair of objects with bounding boxes are given and their relationship is to be predicted.

Supervised (Det). The above setting assumes a perfect object bounding box detector at testing. However, as shown in Fig. 4(b), a more practical setting is to use detected object bounding boxes using off-the-shelf object detectors. We used Faster RCNN [42] to detect around 100 objects in an image.

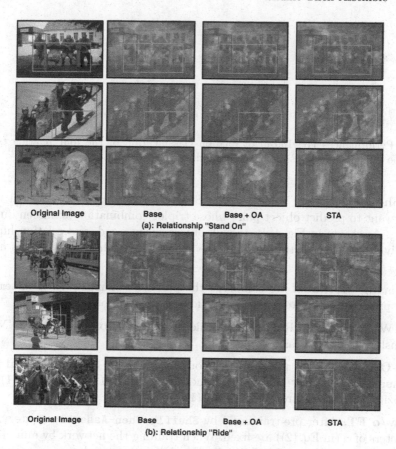

Fig. 5. Qualitative feature maps of two relationships on VRD dataset. For each one, three kinds of feature maps are visualized by averaging over the 512 channels. We can see that by using the proposed `Shuffle-Then-Assemble` (STA), the RoI features are less likely biased to the objects and more focused on the regions of interaction of the two objects. Moreover, the observation is consistent with diverse relationship appearances.

Weakly-Supervised. Compared to Supervised setting, we discard the one-to-one paired object annotation with respect to a relationship. As shown in Fig. 4(c), at training, given objects with boxes, we do not know which object relates to which one. Therefore, we used an average-pooling image-level relationship loss:

$$\mathcal{L}_{weak} = -\sum_{i=1}^{N}\sum_{j=1}^{N}\sum_{r=1}^{R}[y_{ijr}\log S(i,j,r) + (1-y_{ijr})\log(1-S(i,j,r))]; \quad (5)$$

where N is the number of objects, y_{ijr} is 1 if the object pair (i,j) has the r-th relationship, and $S(i,j,r)$ is the relationship score in Eq. (1). Note that the testing stage of this setting is the same as that of Supervised setting.

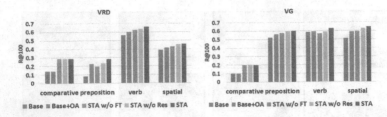

Fig. 6. Performances (R@100%) of relation classification of the four relation types using the different methods in the supervised setting.

Zero-Shot. This setting is the same as Supervised setting except that at testing we want to predict object pairs whose triplet combination is unseen during training. As shown in Fig. 4(d), though object sheep, road, and relationship on are individually seen at training, but the composition "sheep on road" is novel to test.

Comparing Methods. We compared the proposed `Shuffle-Then-Assemble` (**STA**) pre-training strategy with the following ablative baselines:

Base. We directly use RoI features which extracted from the base CNN for relationship prediction task.

Base+OA. We do not pre-train OA conv-layers ϕ (in Eq. (2)) by `Shuffle-Then-Assemble` strategy and directly fine-tune ϕ and $MLP(\cdot)$ (in Eq. (1)) by minimizing the cross-entropy loss of Eq. (1).

STA w/o FT. After pre-training ϕ by `Shuffle-Then-Assemble` strategy, the parameters of ϕ (in Eq. (2)) are fixed. When training the network by minimizing Eq. (1), only parameters of $MLP(\cdot)$ (in Eq. (1)) are updated.

STA w/o Res. The transformation network in Fig. 3 is not a residual network. And the other settings are the same with STA.

We also compared with state-of-the-art visual relationship prediction methods such as **VTransE** [59], **Lu's-V** [32], **Lu's-VLK** [32], and **Peyre's-A** [38]. Note that except for Lu's-VLK which is a multimodal model, all the methods compared here are visual models.

4.3   Results and Analysis

Tables 1 and 2 show the performance of compared methods on two datasets of different experiment settings. As we can see, the proposed STA has the best performances compared with the other baselines and state-of-the-art on both datasets. For example, compared to the Base+OA, the proposed STA can boost the Recall@100 of supervised, weakly supervised, and zero-shot relationship prediction by absolute 4.75%, 4.42%, 4.04%, respectively on VRD, and 4.41%, 4.2%, 5.81%, respectively on VG.

Comparing the results of Base+OA with Base, we can see that by adding OA conv-layers, the performance is improved. This observation is basically as

Table 1. The performances (Recall@K%) of compared methods on two datasets under Supervised setting and Supervised (Det) setting.

Dataset	VRD		VG		VRD(Det)		VG(Det)	
Metric	R@50	R@100	R@50	R@100	R@50	R@100	R@50	R@100
Base	39.25	39.25	52.48	52.61	37.83	37.83	50.12	50.31
Base+OA	43.29	43.29	58.35	58.53	40.78	40.78	57.03	57.31
STA w/o FT	44.30	44.30	58.14	58.32	41.12	41.12	56.88	57.02
STA w/o Res	46.83	46.83	62.08	62.32	44.85	44.85	61.12	61.30
STA	**48.03**	**48.03**	**62.71**	**62.94**	**45.65**	**45.65**	**61.27**	**61.51**
Lu's-V [32]	7.11	7.11	–	–	–	–	–	–
Lu's-VLK [32]	47.87	47.87	–	–	–	–	–	–
VTransE [59]	44.76	44.76	62.63	62.87	–	–	–	–
Peyre's-A [38]	46.30	46.30	–	–	–	–	–	–

Table 2. The performances (Recall@K%) of compared methods on two datasets under Weakly Supervised setting (WS) and Zero-Shot setting (ZS).

Dataset	VRD(WS)		VG(WS)		VRD(ZS)		VG(ZS)	
Metric	R@50	R@100	R@50	R@100	R@50	R@100	R@50	R@100
Base	29.36	29.36	45.78	46.01	14.10	14.10	11.04	11.04
Base+OA	31.47	31.47	47.46	47.72	16.53	16.53	13.09	13.09
STA w/o FT	32.84	32.84	47.23	47.39	18.24	18.24	13.72	13.72
STA w/o Res	35.10	35.10	50.89	51.13	19.01	19.01	18.03	18.03
STA	**35.89**	**35.89**	**51.73**	**51.92**	**20.57**	**20.57**	**18.90**	**18.90**
Peyre's A [38]	34.03	34.03	–	–	16.10	16.10	–	–

expected since the number of parameters have been increased and thus the representation ability of the whole network is improved. By comparing the performance of STA w/o FT with Base+OA, we can find that, even OA conv-layers are not fine-tuned, the features which are pre-trained by Shuffle-Then-Assemble still have comparable performance with the Base+OA. And when the pre-trained OA conv-layers are further fine-tuned (STA w/o Res, STA), the performances will have a considerable boost. Such observations show that the success of the proposed method is not only due to the added small network (OA conv-layers), but also thanks to the proposed Shuffle-Then-Assemble pre-training strategy.

Figure 6 shows the R@100 of relationship prediction of the four relation types which are comparative, preposition, verb and spatial. From this, we can see that the proposed STA has the best performance in each relationship type on both datasets.

Table 3. Computed overlap ratios (%) of two kinds of feature maps

Dataset	OA	Base CNN	Dataset	OA	Base CNN
VRD	**50.27**	42.45	VG	**48.50**	41.32

Analysis of Feature Maps. Figure 5 shows six qualitative examples of feature maps generated by three different strategies. By comparing the STA's feature maps with Base and Base+OA, we can find that STA's feature maps focus more on the overlap regions between subjects and objects. For example, in the second row, STA's feature maps put more attention on people's feet, which would provide cues for predicting the right relationship "stand on".

The ratio: $(\sum_{i \in R_{over}} f(i))/(\sum_{i \in R_{joint}} f(i))$, in Table 3, is used to measure how our model can focus on the overlapped region. In this formula, $f(\cdot)$ is the normalized joint feature map of subject and object region, R_{over} and R_{joint} mean the overlapped region and the joint region of that feature map respectively. We compare the ratios computed by OA feature and Base CNN feature on both VRD and VG datasets. From the results we can see that the proposed `Shuffle-Then-Assemble` pre-training strategy can help the relationship model captures more attention on the shared regions between subject and object.

Analysis of Zero-Shot Setting. From Table 2, we can see that the proposed STA has the best performance on both datasets compared with other baselines and one state-of-the-art. This result can further validate the effectiveness of the proposed `Shuffle-Then-Assemble` pre-training strategy. From the qualitative examples in Fig. 7, we can demonstrate that the reason why STA achieves better performance is due to the learned OA feature maps.

Analysis of Object-Biased Relationships. Figure 8 shows the accuracy of each relationship, listed in an ascending, left-right order according to their biases to specific subject-object configuration by $N_R(r)/N_C(r)$, where $N_C(r)$ is the number of configurations and $N_R(r)$ is the number of training samples of the r-th relationship. Notice that smaller bias indicates more flexible configurations (*e.g.*, "touch") and vice versa (*e.g.*, "wear"). We can find that for relationships which are less biased to specific configurations (left and middle parts), our STA is better as it focuses on object-agnostic features.

Failure Mode. Our model will fail when one relationship depends heavily on specific object combinations. For example, for some relationship listed in the right part of Fig. 8 (like the relationship "read", the subjects and objects are usually "person" and "book"), our model will not defeat the baseline. Under this condition, the object categories will be useful for predicting relationship. Note that such failure can be easily recovered by rules mined from dataset statistics.

Fig. 7. Qualitative feature maps of four zero-shot relationships on VRD dataset. For each one, two feature maps of Base+OA with wrong prediction and STA with correct prediction are visualized by averaging over the 512 channels. We can see that by using the proposed `Shuffle-Then-Assemble` (STA), the RoI features are less likely biased to the objects and more focused on the regions of interaction of the two objects.

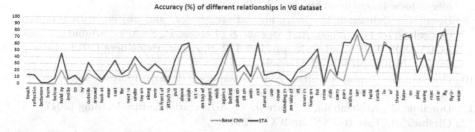

Fig. 8. The accuracy (%) of each relationship in VG dataset. In the horizontal axis, the relationships are listed in an ascending order (from left to right) of their biases to specific object combinations. The vertical axis is the accuracy (%) of each relationship. We can see that for relationships which are less biased to specific combination (left parts), our STA method usually have better performance.

5   Conclusions

We proposed a novel `Shuffle-Then-Assemble` visual relationship feature learning strategy for improving visual relationship models. The key idea is to discard the original one-to-one paired object alignments, and then try to recover them in an unsupervised pair discovery fashion by using a cycle-consistent adversarial domain transfer method. In this way, the object class information in object pairs is excluded and hence the resultant feature map is less likely biased to specific object compositions. On two visual relationship benchmarks, we found a consistent improvement from a naive relationship prediction model using the pre-trained OA feature maps.

Acknowledgments. This research is partially support by NTU-CoE Grant, Alibaba-NTU JRI, and Data Science & Artificial Intelligence Research Centre@NTU (DSAIR).

References

1. Atzmon, Y., Berant, J., Kezami, V., Globerson, A., Chechik, G.: Learning to generalize to new compositions in image understanding. In: EMNLP (2016)
2. Bengio, Y., Courville, A., Vincent, P.: Representation learning: a review and new perspectives. TPAMI **35**(8), 1798–1828 (2013)
3. Chao, Y.W., Wang, Z., He, Y., Wang, J., Deng, J.: HICO: a benchmark for recognizing human-object interactions in images. In: ICCV (2015)
4. Chen, L., Zhang, H., Xiao, J., Liu, W., Chang, S.F.: Zero-shot visual recognition using semantics-preserving adversarial embedding networks. In: CVPR (2018)
5. Chen, L., et al.: SCA-CNN: spatial and channel-wise attention in convolutional networks for image captioning. In: CVPR (2017)
6. Dai, B., Zhang, Y., Lin, D.: Detecting visual relationships with deep relational networks. In: CVPR (2017)
7. Das, A., et al.: Visual dialog. In: CVPR (2017)
8. Deng, J., Dong, W., Socher, R., Li, L.J., Li, K., Fei-Fei, L.: ImageNet: a large-scale hierarchical image database. In: CVPR (2009)
9. Desai, C., Ramanan, D.: Detecting actions, poses, and objects with relational phraselets. In: Fitzgibbon, A., Lazebnik, S., Perona, P., Sato, Y., Schmid, C. (eds.) ECCV 2012. LNCS, vol. 7575, pp. 158–172. Springer, Heidelberg (2012). https://doi.org/10.1007/978-3-642-33765-9_12
10. Doersch, C., Gupta, A., Efros, A.A.: Unsupervised visual representation learning by context prediction. In: ICCV, pp. 1422–1430 (2015)
11. Donahue, J., Krähenbühl, P., Darrell, T.: Adversarial feature learning (2017)
12. Girshick, R.: Fast R-CNN. In: ICCV (2015)
13. Gu, J., Cai, J., Wang, G., Chen, T.: Stack-captioning: coarse-to-fine learning for image captioning. In: AAAI (2018)
14. Gu, J., Wang, G., Cai, J., Chen, T.: An empirical study of language CNN for image captioning. In: ICCV (2017)
15. Gu, J., et al.: Recent advances in convolutional neural networks. Pattern Recognit. **77**, 354–377 (2017)
16. Gupta, A., Davis, L.S.: Beyond nouns: exploiting prepositions and comparative adjectives for learning visual classifiers. In: Forsyth, D., Torr, P., Zisserman, A. (eds.) ECCV 2008. LNCS, vol. 5302, pp. 16–29. Springer, Heidelberg (2008). https://doi.org/10.1007/978-3-540-88682-2_3
17. Gupta, A., Kembhavi, A., Davis, L.S.: Observing human-object interactions: using spatial and functional compatibility for recognition. TPAMI **31**(10), 1775–1789 (2009)
18. Gurari, D., et al.: VizWiz grand challenge: answering visual questions from blind people. In: CVPR (2018)
19. He, K., Zhang, X., Ren, S., Sun, J.: Deep residual learning for image recognition. In: CVPR (2016)

20. Hoffman, J., et al.: CyCADA: cycle-consistent adversarial domain adaptation. arXiv preprint arXiv:1711.03213 (2017)
21. Hu, R., Rohrbach, M., Andreas, J., Darrell, T., Saenko, K.: Modeling relationships in referential expressions with compositional modular networks. In: CVPR (2017)
22. Jabri, A., Joulin, A., van der Maaten, L.: Revisiting visual question answering baselines. In: Leibe, B., Matas, J., Sebe, N., Welling, M. (eds.) ECCV 2016. LNCS, vol. 9912, pp. 727–739. Springer, Cham (2016). https://doi.org/10.1007/978-3-319-46484-8_44
23. Johnson, J., et al.: Image retrieval using scene graphs. In: CVPR (2015)
24. Kim, T., Cha, M., Kim, H., Lee, J., Kim, J.: Learning to discover cross-domain relations with generative adversarial networks. In: ICML (2017)
25. Kingma, D.P., Ba, J.: Adam: a method for stochastic optimization. arXiv preprint arXiv:1412.6980 (2014)
26. Krishna, R.: Visual genome: connecting language and vision using crowdsourced dense image annotations. IJCV **123**(1), 32–73 (2017)
27. Li, Q., Tao, Q., Joty, S., Cai, J., Luo, J.: VQA-E: explaining, elaborating, and enhancing your answers for visual questions. arXiv preprint arXiv:1803.07464 (2018)
28. Li, Y., Ouyang, W., Wang, X., et al.: VIP-CNN: visual phrase guided convolutional neural network. In: CVPR (2017)
29. Li, Y., Ouyang, W., Zhou, B., Wang, K., Wang, X.: Scene graph generation from objects, phrases and region captions. In: ICCV (2017)
30. Lin, T.-Y., et al.: Microsoft COCO: common objects in context. In: Fleet, D., Pajdla, T., Schiele, B., Tuytelaars, T. (eds.) ECCV 2014. LNCS, vol. 8693, pp. 740–755. Springer, Cham (2014). https://doi.org/10.1007/978-3-319-10602-1_48
31. Liu, D., Zha, Z.J., Zhang, H., Zhang, Y., Wu, F.: Context-aware visual policy network for sequence-level image captioning. In: ACMMM (2018)
32. Lu, C., Krishna, R., Bernstein, M., Fei-Fei, L.: Visual relationship detection with language priors. In: Leibe, B., Matas, J., Sebe, N., Welling, M. (eds.) ECCV 2016. LNCS, vol. 9905, pp. 852–869. Springer, Cham (2016). https://doi.org/10.1007/978-3-319-46448-0_51
33. Ma, L., Jia, X., Sun, Q., Schiele, B., Tuytelaars, T., Gool, L.V.: Pose guided person image generation. In: NIPS, pp. 405–415 (2017)
34. Ma, L., Sun, Q., Georgoulis, S., Gool, L.V., Schiele, B., Fritz, M.: Disentangled person image generation. In: CVPR (2018)
35. Mao, X., Li, Q., Xie, H., Lau, R.Y., Wang, Z., Smolley, S.P.: Least squares generative adversarial networks. In: ICCV (2017)
36. Noroozi, M., Favaro, P.: Unsupervised learning of visual representations by solving jigsaw puzzles. In: Leibe, B., Matas, J., Sebe, N., Welling, M. (eds.) ECCV 2016. LNCS, vol. 9910, pp. 69–84. Springer, Cham (2016). https://doi.org/10.1007/978-3-319-46466-4_5
37. Pathak, D., Krahenbuhl, P., Donahue, J., Darrell, T., Efros, A.A.: Context encoders: feature learning by inpainting. In: CVPR (2016)
38. Peyre, J., Laptev, I., Schmid, C., Sivic, J.: Weakly-supervised learning of visual relations. In: ICCV (2017)
39. Radford, A., Metz, L., Chintala, S.: Unsupervised representation learning with deep convolutional generative adversarial networks (2016)
40. Ramanathan, V., et al.: Learning semantic relationships for better action retrieval in images. In: CVPR (2015)
41. Redmon, J., Farhadi, A.: Yolo9000: better, faster, stronger. In: CVPR (2016)

42. Ren, S., He, K., Girshick, R., Sun, J.: Faster R-CNN: towards real-time object detection with region proposal networks. In: NIPS (2015)
43. Sadeghi, M.A., Farhadi, A.: Recognition using visual phrases. In: CVPR (2011)
44. Simonyan, K., Zisserman, A.: Very deep convolutional networks for large-scale image recognition (2015)
45. Sun, Q., Ma, L., Oh, S.J., Gool, L.V., Schiele, B., Fritz, M.: Natural and effective obfuscation by head inpainting. In: CVPR (2018)
46. Szegedy, C., Ioffe, S., Vanhoucke, V., Alemi, A.A.: Inception-v4, inception-resnet and the impact of residual connections on learning. In: AAAI (2017)
47. Tao, Q., Yang, H., Cai, J.: Zero-annotation object detection with web knowledge transfer. arXiv preprint arXiv:1711.05954 (2017)
48. Tsai, Y.H., Hung, W.C., Schulter, S., Sohn, K., Yang, M.H., Chandraker, M.: Learning to adapt structured output space for semantic segmentation. In: CVPR (2018)
49. Vinyals, O., Toshev, A., Bengio, S., Erhan, D.: Show and tell: lessons learned from the 2015 MSCOCO image captioning challenge. TPAMI **39**(4), 652–663 (2017)
50. Wei, Y., Xiao, H., Shi, H., Jie, Z., Feng, J., Huang, T.S.: Revisiting dilated convolution: a simple approach for weakly-and semi-supervised semantic segmentation. In: CVPR (2018)
51. Xu, B., Wang, N., Chen, T., Li, M.: Empirical evaluation of rectified activations in convolutional network. arXiv preprint arXiv:1505.00853 (2015)
52. Xu, D., Zhu, Y., Choy, C.B., Fei-Fei, L.: Scene graph generation by iterative message passing. In: CVPR (2017)
53. Yao, B., Fei-Fei, L.: Modeling mutual context of object and human pose in human-object interaction activities. In: CVPR (2010)
54. Yatskar, M., Zettlemoyer, L., Farhadi, A.: Situation recognition: visual semantic role labeling for image understanding. In: CVPR (2016)
55. Yi, Z., Zhang, H., Tan, P., Gong, M.: DualGAN: unsupervised dual learning for image-to-image translation. In: ICCV (2017)
56. Yin, G., et al.: Zoom-net: mining deep feature interactions for visual relationship recognition (2018)
57. Yosinski, J., Clune, J., Bengio, Y., Lipson, H.: How transferable are features in deep neural networks? In: NIPS (2014)
58. Zellers, R., Yatskar, M., Thomson, S., Choi, Y.: Neural motifs: scene graph parsing with global context. In: CVPR (2018)
59. Zhang, H., Kyaw, Z., Chang, S.F., Chua, T.S.: Visual translation embedding network for visual relation detection. In: CVPR (2017)
60. Zhang, H., Kyaw, Z., Yu, J., Chang, S.F.: PPR-FCN: weakly supervised visual relation detection via parallel pairwise R-FCN. In: ICCV (2017)
61. Zhang, H., Niu, Y., Chang, S.F.: Grounding referring expressions in images by variational context. In: CVPR (2018)
62. Zhang, J., Elhoseiny, M., Cohen, S., Chang, W., Elgammal, A.: Relationship proposal networks. In: CVPR (2017)
63. Zhang, R., Isola, P., Efros, A.A.: Split-brain autoencoders: unsupervised learning by cross-channel prediction. In: CVPR (2017)
64. Zhou, B., Tian, Y., Sukhbaatar, S., Szlam, A., Fergus, R.: Simple baseline for visual question answering. arXiv preprint arXiv:1512.02167 (2015)
65. Zhu, J.Y., Park, T., Isola, P., Efros, A.A.: Unpaired image-to-image translation using cycle-consistent adversarial networks. In: ICCV (2017)
66. Zhuang, B., Liu, L., Shen, C., Reid, I.: Towards context-aware interaction recognition for visual relationship detection. In: ICCV, October 2017

Combining 3D Model Contour Energy and Keypoints for Object Tracking

Bogdan Bugaev[1,2](✉)[iD], Anton Kryshchenko[1,2][iD], and Roman Belov[3][iD]

[1] National Research University Higher School of Economics, St. Petersburg, Russia
bogdan.bugaev@gmail.com, a.s.kryshchenko@gmail.com
[2] Saint Petersburg Academic University, St. Petersburg, Russia
[3] KeenTools, St. Petersburg, Russia
belovrv@gmail.com

Abstract. We present a new combined approach for monocular model-based 3D tracking. A preliminary object pose is estimated by using a keypoint-based technique. The pose is then refined by optimizing the contour energy function. The energy determines the degree of correspondence between the contour of the model projection and the image edges. It is calculated based on both the intensity and orientation of the raw image gradient. For optimization, we propose a technique and search area constraints that allow overcoming the local optima and taking into account information obtained through keypoint-based pose estimation. Owing to its combined nature, our method eliminates numerous issues of keypoint-based and edge-based approaches. We demonstrate the efficiency of our method by comparing it with state-of-the-art methods on a public benchmark dataset that includes videos with various lighting conditions, movement patterns, and speed.

Keywords: 3D tracking · Monocular · Model-based · Pose estimation

1 Introduction

Monocular model-based 3D tracking methods are an essential part of computer vision. They are applied in a wide range of practical areas, from augmented reality to visual effects in cinema. 3D tracking implies iterative, frame-by-frame estimation of an object's position and orientation relative to the camera, with a given initial object pose. Figure 1a shows a scene fragment typical for such a task. A number of characteristics complicate tracking: the object is partially occluded, there are flecks and reflections, and the background is cluttered.

In recent years, a great number of 3D tracking methods have been developed. These can be classified by the image characteristics and 3D model features used

Electronic supplementary material The online version of this chapter (https://doi.org/10.1007/978-3-030-01258-8_4) contains supplementary material, which is available to authorized users.

© Springer Nature Switzerland AG 2018
V. Ferrari et al. (Eds.): ECCV 2018, LNCS 11216, pp. 55–70, 2018.
https://doi.org/10.1007/978-3-030-01258-8_4

(a)   (b)   (c)

Fig. 1. An example of a tracking algorithm applied to a single frame. (a) A fragment of the processed frame. Despite the partial occlusions of the tracked object (*violin*), most of its edges are visible. (b) The result of preliminary pose estimation. The model projection (*white wireframe*) does not coincide with the object image in the frame because the position of the keypoints (*black crosses*) used to determine its position was inaccurately calculated. (c) The object's model with optimized energy 4 of contours (*purple lines*). (Color figure online)

for pose detection. Many approaches [12,18,19,26] are based on calculating keypoints [13,22] on the image and corresponding points on the 3D model. Such methods make it possible to achieve high performance and robustness against partial occlusions and cluttered background and are capable of processing fast object movement. At the same time, their use is limited for poorly textured objects because keypoint calculation requires texture.

Nevertheless, objects tend to have one or other characteristic shape that lends itself to being detected in an image. Therefore, many methods use the information on the edges of the object's 3D model projection—on its *contour* (for illustration, see Fig. 1c). As a rule, the contour of a 3D object corresponds to the areas of an image that are characterized by dramatic and unidirectional change in intensity—its *edges*[1] on an image. Methods [2,4–6,8,9,21,25,29] calculate the object pose from the correspondences between the points on the 3D model contour and points on the image edges. Some approaches are based on optimizing energy functions that determine the degree of correspondence between the object projection in its current position and its silhouette on an image [15,20,23,28]. Authors of [15] propose a tracking method using integral object contour energy optimization; its value is the greater, the more precisely the object contour fits the edges on the image. The energy-based approaches risk detecting local energy function optima that correspond to the wrong object poses. In addition, edge-based methods have a drawback, namely the ambiguity of symmetrical objects, which have identical contours in different positions.

We present an approach that combines a keypoint-based method and integral edge energy optimization. A preliminary object pose is estimated using the Kanade–Lucas–Tomasi (KLT) [14,22,24] tracker. Then, we refine the object pose by optimizing the contour energy. We modify the energy function described in [15] to take into account the image edges' intensity as well as the directions of the model contour and the edges. We limit the search area for the optimal energy function value by using the information obtained from the preliminary object pose estimation. This allows for better convergence and makes it possible to partially overcome the issue of symmetrical objects. For optimization, we use the Basin-Hopping stochastic algorithm [27] to avoid local optima. In particular, we use an efficient Quasi-Newton method [10] considering the search area constraints directly. Contour detection is a time-critical operation that is executed thousands of times during the energy optimization. We propose an algorithm that performs the most time-consuming computations as a preliminary step. This increases tracking performance.

In this paper, we concentrate on frame-to-frame object tracking that relies only on the initial object pose and doesn't require any training using additional data (such as predefined reference frames).

We demonstrate the efficiency of our approach as compared to state-of-the-art 3D tracking methods in a series of experiments conducted on the OPT benchmark dataset [30]. The dataset includes 552 test videos with ground truth object pose annotation. The videos reproduce different lighting conditions and the main movement patterns performed at a various speeds. To compare the tracking efficiency, we use the metric proposed by the authors of the OPT dataset. Our test results demonstrate that, across the whole dataset, our method yielded a value greater by 9.1%–48.9% with respect to the possible maximum than other methods tested. However, it should be noted that our method is not suitable for real-time applications.

Further, we discuss the work related to the topic of this article in Sect. 2. Then, we provide a brief overview of the mathematical notation in Sect. 3. In Sect. 4, we give a detailed description of the proposed tracking method. In Sect. 5, we discuss the experimental results and provide a comparison to other modern tracking methods. And, finally, in Sect. 5.4, we cover the limitations of our method as well as our plans for its further improvement.

2   Related Work

A detailed description of 3D tracking methods can be found in [11,16]. In the present section, we shall discuss solely the approaches based on the information on the contour of 3D objects.

RAPID [8] was one of the first methods where the object pose was estimated based on the correspondences between points on a 3D model contour and points on the edges of the image. To detect correspondences, they use local 1D search of the point with the largest edge intensity along the perpendicular to the contour of the projected 3D model. In subsequent papers [2,4,5,9,21], a number of improvements on the method were proposed; however, they were all based on independent search for correspondences between points on the model contour and points on the edges of the image. The main drawback of this approach lies in the fact that the edge points of different objects can hardly be distinguished from each other. This leads to 3D-2D correspondences containing a great number of outliers, failing to preserve the object's contour, especially in case of cluttered background, occlusions, or fast movement.

Other approaches introduce energy functions, where the value is the greater, the greater the correspondence between the 3D model projection and the image. Therefore, the tracking goal can be achieved through the optimization of such energy. In [15], the authors propose using two variants of integrals along the contour of the 3D model projected onto the image gradient. One variant takes into account only the absolute gradient value, while the other accounts only for the direction of the gradient in points with sufficient absolute gradient value. For energy optimization, the authors propose using coordinate descent. For effective convergence, this method requires a very close approximation to the sought-for optimum, which is calculated with the help of a method similar to RAPID.

The approach described in the present article uses a similar energy function. To improve convergence and overcome the issue of local optima, we use a global optimization technique based on the Basin-Hopping algorithm [27]. Methods in [2,3,9,28] use a particle filter to avoid local optima. In [3], for particle initialization, a keypoint-based approach is used, which leads to a more robust algorithm and less ambiguity during tracking symmetrical objects. For successful convergence in noise conditions and fast object movement, it becomes necessary to use a great number of particles, which has a negative impact on tracking performance. Unlike the particle filter, the Basin-Hopping algorithm takes into account the information on the local optima that have already been identified and makes it possible to use non-trivial termination criteria, thus avoiding excessive calculations.

In addition to the information on the edge on the image, many methods also use the information on color. In [21,29], the color distribution in the object and its background around the edge point is used to eliminate false 3D-2D correspondences. Methods described in [20,23] optimize energy based on the color distribution in the whole object and background. Such approaches are robust against partial occlusions and cluttered scenes; however, they are sensitive to changes in lighting and ambiguities arising from a similar coloring of the object and its background.

3   Input Data and Pose Parametrization

This section provides a brief overview of the mathematical notation used in the present article.

The tracking algorithm accepts input data in the form of sequential grayscale image frames $I_i \colon \Omega \to \mathbb{R}$ (where $\Omega \subset \mathbb{R}^2$ is the image domain). Intensity of point $u \in \Omega$ in the frame i equals $I_i(u)$. In cases where the number of the frame is unimportant, the image is labeled as I.

The intrinsic parameters of the camera used to make the input frames are assumed to be constant. They are given as the matrix

$$K = \begin{bmatrix} f_x & 0 & c_x \\ 0 & f_y & c_y \\ 0 & 0 & 1 \end{bmatrix}. \tag{1}$$

3D model $\mathcal{M}$ describing the tracked object can be defined as $(V_{\mathcal{M}}, F_{\mathcal{M}})$, where $V_{\mathcal{M}} \subset \mathbb{R}^3$ is a finite set of model vertices, while $F_{\mathcal{M}}$ is the set of triplets of vertices defining model faces.

Object pose within frame i has six degrees of freedom and is described as

$$T_i = \left[\begin{array}{c|c} R_i & t_i \\ \hline 0\ 0\ 0 & 1 \end{array} \right] \in SE(3), \tag{2}$$

where $R_i \in SO(3)$ defines the orientation of the model and $t_i \in \mathbb{R}^3$ defines its translation.

The projection $u \in \mathbb{R}^2$ of a point on the model surface $x \in \mathbb{R}^3$ is described by a standard camera model

$$\mathbf{u} = K \cdot [R_i|t_i] \cdot \mathbf{x}, \tag{3}$$

where $\mathbf{u}$ and $\mathbf{x}$ are vectors u and x in homogeneous coordinates. The function performing the projection $x \mapsto u$ in the pose T_i shall be designated as π_{T_i}.

4   3D Tracking by Combining Keypoints and Contour Energy

We solve the tracking task in two steps. During the first step, the Kanade–Lucas–Tomasi (KLT) tracker [14,22,24] is applied to estimate object pose. During the second step, object pose is refined by optimizing the objective function, i.e. the contour energy optimization.

The present section provides a detailed description of the proposed tracking method. First, we give a brief overview of the initial object pose estimation algorithm. Further, we concentrate on the method for pose refinement. First of all, we give a detailed description of the contour energy. Then, we discuss its optimization: we provide an overview of the global optimization method and the local optimization method that it utilizes. Then, we propose a step-by-step procedure to refine the object pose by using the method described. After that, we discuss bound constraints estimation for the energy optimum search area. And, finally, we describe the object contour detection algorithm.

4.1   Initial Object Pose Estimation

We estimate the initial object pose with the help of a wide-known KLT tracker. On the frames where the object pose is known, we identify 2D keypoints and determine corresponding 3D points on the surface of the model. Keypoint movement is tracked with the help of optical flow calculation. On the image, the known 2D-3D correspondences are used to estimate the object pose by solving the PnP problem [11] while using RANSAC [7] to eliminate outliers.

When after a sufficiently great number of iterations RANSAC fails to find a solution with an acceptable percentage of outliers, or when the number of points tracked is very small, we estimate object pose in frame i by extrapolation based on poses in frames $i-1$ and $i-2$.

4.2   Contour Energy

We view pose optimization as the matching of model contour with object edges in the image. Model contours are understood as two types of lines. Firstly, it is the outer contour of the projected model. Secondly, it is the projections of visible sharp model edges. Sharp model edges are the edges where adjacent faces meet at an angle no greater than the pre-selected one φ. Figure 1c provides an example of such matching.

To further ideas described in [15], we suggest the following energy function for a quantitative expression of matching quality:

$$\mathcal{E}(\boldsymbol{T}) = \frac{\displaystyle\int_{C_T} \left| \nabla I(p_T(s)) \cdot n_T(s) \right| \, ds}{\displaystyle\int_{C_T} ds}, \tag{4}$$

where C_T are model contour lines, p_T is the function returning the contour point coordinate in the image, n_T is the function returning the normal unit vector to contour.

The energy is an integral characteristic of the contour (numerator) normalized along the length of the contour (denominator). The division by the length of the contour is done to avoid the case where the long contour is preferred to the shorter one.

Let us consider the numerator expression under integral sign:

$$\left| \nabla I(p_T(s)) \cdot n_T(s) \right|. \tag{5}$$

The image gradient $\nabla I(p_T(s))$ shows the direction and strength of intensity change in a point. If there is an edge, gradient is perpendicular to it. The unit vector $n_T(s)$ is perpendicular to the model contour. The absolute value of their scalar product is the greater, the more visually significant the edge in the image is (i.e. the greater the gradient magnitude) and the higher the correspondence of its direction in the current point and the direction of the model contour.

Therefore, the value $\mathcal{E}(\boldsymbol{T})$ is the greater, the greater the correspondence of the model contour in pose $\boldsymbol{T}$ and the edges in the image and the more visually significant those edges (for example, see Fig. 1c). Given that the object edges are sufficiently visible, the energy, in most cases, will be maximal in the sought-for pose. Therefore, the optimal object pose in frame i can be found as

$$\boldsymbol{T}_i = \arg\max_{\boldsymbol{T}} \mathcal{E}(\boldsymbol{T}). \tag{6}$$

Due to integral nature of the energy function 4, it is sufficiently robust against occlusions. Its disadvantage lies in the fact that, potentially, cases where the wrong object pose will have greater energy than its true pose are possible. However, practical experience shows that such cases are quite rare. In addition, ambiguities in detecting the pose of objects of a symmetrical (e.g., cylindrical) shape may be observed.

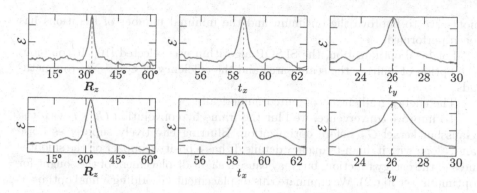

Fig. 2. Examples of contour energy 4 near an optimum. In the top row the energy was calculated from the original image; in the bottom row it was calculated from an image blurred by convolution with a Gaussian kernel. Label R_z denotes the dependence on the rotation around axis z (the other degrees of freedom being fixed), t_x and t_y denote the dependence on translation along axes x and y respectively. The areas demonstrated here correspond 60° for the rotation and approximately 0.2 of object size.

To implement the evaluation of contour energy, it is necessary to perform the discretization of expression 4:

$$\tilde{\mathcal{E}}(T) = \frac{1}{\left|\tilde{C}_T\right|} \sum_{s \in \tilde{C}_T} \left|\nabla I(p_T(s)) \cdot n_T(s)\right|, \tag{7}$$

where $\tilde{C}_T$ is the finite set of points uniformly distributed along the contour lines.

A detailed description of contour line detection is described in Sect. 4.5.

4.3   Energy Optimization Method

In most cases, contour energy 4 has a notable global optimum in the area of the sought-for object pose and, at the same time, shows a plenty of local optima at a certain distance from it (see Fig. 2).

In many cases, the first approximation obtained during object pose estimation is not in the concave region near the sought-for optimum. On the other hand, we may assume that such first approximation will turn out to be good enough; therefore, we propose to limit the search area and then apply an optimization method capable of overcoming the local optima. A detailed description of search area bounds estimation is given in Sect. 4.4.

For optimization, the version of the Basin-Hopping stochastic algorithm described in [27] was selected. Basin-Hopping is an iterative algorithm. At each step, a random hop within the search area is made; after that, local optimization is performed and, then, the obtained local optimum is either accepted or rejected based on the Metropolis criterion [17]. The algorithm stops once the maximum number of iterations has been reached or if several previous steps did not serve to improve the optimum and the minimal number of iterations has been performed.

For local optimization, the SLSQP algorithm was selected [10]. It combines the option of limiting the search area and the efficiency of Quasi-Newton methods.

The energy gradient is computed numerically.

To improve convergence, we blur the frame by convolution $G_\sigma * I$ with the Gaussian kernel G_σ before optimization. Blurring effectively suppresses noise and, along with it, high-frequency details. It has a positive impact on the smoothness of the energy function, but may cause a slight displacement of the sought-for optimum (see Fig. 2). We eliminate this displacement via adding a final optimization step using the original image.

4.4 Search Area Bounds

During initial pose estimation (Sect. 4.1), the object pose can be obtained either with the help of the KLT tracker or through extrapolation based on the previous poses. The former differs from the latter in that there is extra data present; therefore, we shall consider them separately.

In case the object pose could be obtained only through extrapolation, we propose selecting the maximal deviations from the estimated pose based on the assumption on the degree of object movement in consecutive frames. In our experiments, we have limited the rotation around each Euler angle to $\pm 30°$, the translation along the camera axis to ± 0.2 of the object size, and the translation along the other axes to ± 0.1 of the object size.

In case of success, the KLT tracker estimates the object pose by solving the PnP problem on a set of 2D and 3D point correspondences $\{(u_1, x_1), \ldots, (u_m, x_m)\}$ by minimizing the average reprojection error $\widetilde{T} = \arg\min_T e(T)$, where

$$e(T) = \frac{1}{m} \sum_{j=1}^{m} \left\| u_j - \pi_T(x_j) \right\|. \tag{8}$$

The average reprojection error $e(T)$ can be understood as the measure of consistency of object pose T with the position of keypoints used to reach the solution: the smaller the error, the greater the consistency. Due to errors arising during kcypoint tracking, the object pose that is most consistent with them may be different from its true pose, but it will be in its near neighborhood.

We propose selecting search area bounds in such a way that, when approaching them, e does not increase by a value greater than pre-selected one ε, i.e. the consistency with keypoints does not deteriorate below a given threshold:

$$e(T) - e(\widetilde{T}) \leq \varepsilon. \tag{9}$$

The optimization methods proposed in Sect. 4.3 make it possible to set such non-linear constraints on the search area directly.

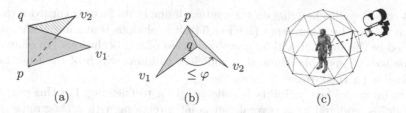

Fig. 3. Edge pq type recognition. (a) Contour edge is formed by front face (v_1, q, p) (marked by *green color*) and back face (v_2, p, q) (marked by *pink hatch*). (b) A sharp edge is formed by two front faces angled at under φ. (c) Our contour detection algorithm rejects the edge if any adjacent front face is invisible from all of three the nearest preprocessed viewpoint directions. (Color figure online)

The size of the search area usually is quite natural in practice. For example, it is often the case that a very noticeable change of object pose in certain directions leads to a relatively small change in average reprojection error. This mostly concerns movement along the camera axes. This can also happen when keypoints are not evenly distributed throughout the object and cover it only partially. Along with errors in keypoint position, this normally results in noticeably inaccurate object pose estimation; for example, see Fig. 1b. Setting the bounds accounting for average reprojection error makes it possible to obtain a broad enough search area and then use energy optimization to find a rather precise pose, as shown in Fig. 1c.

4.5 Model Contour and Sharp Edges Detection

Visible contour and sharp edges detection algorithms can be grouped into two categories. The first type of algorithms is based on model rendering. They are precise and allow for correct processing of self-occlusions. However, rendering requires time-consuming computing. The second type of algorithms is based on the analysis of the model itself: its edges and the spatial relationship between the adjacent faces. They are less complex in terms of computing, but they fail to account for self-occlusion.

We propose a combined approach. Prior to tracking, we perform the most time-consuming calculations and gather data on the visibility of model faces from various points of view. After that, while estimating the contours during tracking, in a single run, we identify sharp and contour edges and process self-occlusion with the help of this data.

When calculating energy 4, the object pose T for which the contours need to be estimated is known. For this purpose, all model $\mathcal{M}$ edges formed by two faces are reviewed. Out of these, the ones lying on the contour or formed by faces meeting at an acute angle are selected.

Let us consider edge pq and its adjacent faces (v_1, q, p) and (v_2, p, q). The edge is considered sharp if both of its faces are turned with their outer surface towards the camera and the angle between them is no greater then φ (see Fig. 3b). The edge is considered to be lying on the contour if one of its faces is turned towards the camera and the other is not (see Fig. 3a). It is obvious that some of the edges identified in this manner will be invisible in case of self-occlusions. To eliminate a major part of invisible edges, it is sufficient to know which of the front faces are invisible for the current point of view.

Data on model face visibility is collected prior to tracking. For this purpose, the model is rendered from several viewpoint directions with orthographic projection camera. To reach uniform distribution of these directions, we use vertices of an icosphere (recursively divided icosahedron) surrounding the model. Given an object pose, we determine three preprocessed viewpoint directions that are close to the current direction and form a face of the icosphere as shown in Fig. 3c. The faces invisible from this three directions will be likely invisible in the current pose. Knowing such faces, we can exclude adjacent contour and sharp edges. More formal description of self-occlusion processing can be found in supplementary material.

Having detected contour and sharp edges and having processed self-occlusion, it is easy to project the edges onto the frame and select points for numerical calculation with the formula 7.

An obvious drawback of the described approach is that it is not perfectly precise in self-occlusion processing, which can lead to a certain percentage of wrongly detected contours. In true model pose, they are unlikely to correspond to the edges on the image, but may potentially occur on some of the edges in the wrong pose. However, in most cases, a small amount of such false contours does not lead to wrong pose estimation.

The advantage of the described algorithm is that the calculations performed during tracking are relatively simple and less computationally complex compared to algorithms that require rendering.

5   Evaluation

To prove the efficiency of the method described in the present article, we have tested it on the OPT dataset [30] and compared our results with those obtained from state-of-the-art tracking approaches. The test dataset includes RGB video recordings of tracked objects, their true pose, and 3D models. The videos are 1920 × 1080 and have been recorded with the help of a programmable robotic arm under various lighting conditions. Object movement patterns are diverse and many in number and the velocity of movement also varies. OPT contains six models of various geometric complexity. For each of these, 92 test videos of varying duration (23–600 frames) have been made, the total number of frames being 79968. The diverse test data covers most of the motion scenarios.

Our method has been implemented in C++ and is part of a software product intended for 3D tracking for film post-production. All experiments were conducted on a computer with an Intel i7-6700 3.4 GHz processor and 32 GB of RAM. Details of our method settings are given in supplementary material.

In the present section, we first describe the approach for results evaluation used to compare our method with other tracking methods. Further, we show the efficiency of object pose optimization based on contour energy. Then, we compare the results from our approach to those obtained by other modern tracking methods. To conclude, we discuss the advantages and drawbacks of our method as well as potential ways for its improvement.

5.1   Evaluation Metric

Given the known true object pose $\hat{T}_i$ in frame i, we calculate the estimated pose T_i error as

$$\delta_i = \operatorname*{avg}_{\mathbf{x} \in V_{\mathcal{M}}} \left\| \hat{T}_i \mathbf{x} - T_i \mathbf{x} \right\|, \tag{10}$$

where $V_{\mathcal{M}}$ is the set of 3D model vertices. We consider the object pose within the frame successfully detected if δ_i is less than kd, where d is the diameter of the 3D model and k is a given error coefficient.

To compare the efficiency of different methods, we create a curve where each point is defined as the percentage of frames where object pose with respect to varying k was successfully determined. The more efficient method of object pose tracking corresponds with the greater value of AUC (area under curve). In our experiments, k varies from 0 to 0.2; therefore AUC varies from 0 to 20.

5.2   Effectiveness of the Contour Energy Optimization

Let us show how the contour energy optimization improves the results of pure Kanade–Lucas–Tomasi tracker using an example; see Fig. 4. When the object poses obtained with the help of KLT tracker are not refined through the contour energy optimization, the object gradually descends onto the background. In the final frames the discrepancy with the actual object pose becomes significant. This behavior is due to frame-by-frame error accumulation. The refinement step using the contour energy optimization eliminates the errors and results in keeping the object close to its actual pose in all frames.

Experiments conducted on the OPT dataset confirm a significant increase in tracking efficiency due to contour energy optimization. Thus, in all tests, the AUC value increased by 18%, while in the group of tests with maximum movement velocity the increase was 27%.

5.3   Comparison with State-of-the-Art Methods

We have compared our approach with the following state-of-the-art methods: GOS [29], PWP3D [20] and ORB-SLAM2 [18]. GOS is an edge-based method improved the approach from [21]. It takes into account color distribution around the edges and contour coherence. PWP3D tracks object by segmenting the frame into object and background and using color distribution statistics. ORB-SLAM2 is state-of-the-art simultaneous localization and mapping approach based on keypoints detection. The authors of [30] proposed modifications that allowed applying this method to 3D model tracking. Tracking results for PWP3D and

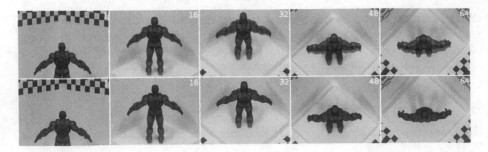

Fig. 4. An example of tracking efficiency increase due to contour energy optimization. Upper and lower rows show video frame fragments (the frame numbers are in the top right corners) with the 3D model (*black wireframe*) projected in the pose estimated with the help of pure KLT tracker and with the help of our method, respectively.

Table 1. Comparison of AUC in tests with different objects

Approach	All tests	Bike	Chest	House	Ironman	Jet	Soda
Our method	**14.79**	**12.55**	14.97	14.48	**14.71**	**17.17**	**14.85**
GOS	7.68	3.38	11.28	8.49	9.91	9.89	3.12
PWP3D	5.01	5.36	5.55	3.58	3.92	5.81	5.87
ORB-SLAM2	12.97	10.41	**15.53**	**17.28**	11.35	9.93	13.44

ORB-SLAM2 applied to the OPT dataset are cited from [30]. Tracking results for GOS were received from testing the open source implementation. During testing, all methods were initialized with the true object pose in the first frame of each video.

Figure 5 demonstrates the results from some of the test groups in OPT. Tables 1 and 2 contain the complete detailed testing results. Overall, all tests show a noticeable disadvantage of other methods as compared to ours: GOS by 35.6%, PWP3D by 48.9%, ORB-SLAM2 by 9.1% (all values have been calculated with respect to the maximum possible value).

Table 3 contains average frame processing times of tested methods. ORB-SLAM2 and PWP3D are positioned as real-time methods and they show the best run time performance. At the same time, our method and GOS are not suitable for real-time applications and our method is in 3.4 times slower than GOS on average. In fact, run time of our method significantly depends on the size of object model as shown in Table 4.

More detailed results of experiments can be found in the supplementary material.

5.4   Discussion and Future Work

Testing results provided in Tables 1, 2 and in Fig. 5 show that our method demonstrated good results under various tracking conditions.

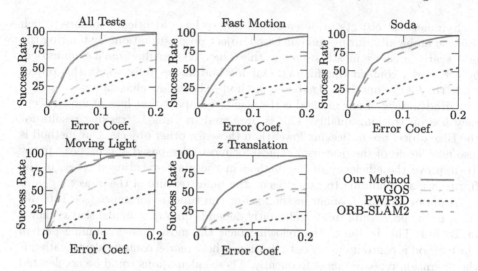

Fig. 5. Comparison of method efficiency on various test groups in OPT

Table 2. Comparison of AUC in tests with different tracking conditions

Approach	Flash light	Free motion	Rotation	Fast motion	Moving light	x-y translation	z translation
Our method	13.96	**13.91**	**15.51**	**14.06**	**16.36**	**14.76**	**13.08**
GOS	10.92	0.95	9.01	2.75	10.51	6.74	6.45
PWP3D	5.08	2.89	5.89	3.76	4.91	8.73	1.83
ORB-SLAM2	**15.91**	9.10	15.24	9.91	15.99	13.30	7.07

Table 3. Comparison of average frame processing time (ms)

Our method	GOS	PWP3D	ORB-SLAM2
683	201	66	67

Table 4. Dependency of our method average frame processing time on object size

Value	Bike	Chest	House	Ironman	Jet	Soda
Time (ms)	1097	358	550	427	1301	364
$|F_{\mathcal{M}}|$	156950	28648	2594	11496	176260	6788

Tests under moving light and flashing light show high performance in spite of the fact that the KLT tracker lacks robustness against dramatic lighting changes. It is also worth noting that our method significantly better processes object movement along the camera axis ('z translation' tests) in comparison with other methods. Edge-based methods are very sensitive to motion blur. Nevertheless, the results of 'Fast Motion' tests demonstrate that our method handles motion blur and fast movement more efficiently than other methods.

Symmetrical objects in different poses may have identical contours, which leads to ambiguity during contour-based object pose estimation. By limiting the pose search area, we mostly overcome this issue. Test results from a symmetrical object, Soda, confirm this finding. Our method successfully tracks this object while the GOS—another edge-based method—shows low efficiency.

Disadvantage of our method is the negative impact that lack of model accuracy has on tracking quality. This is presented in Table 1: tracking results for the Bike object are noticeably lower than those for other objects. Our method is also not devoid of the drawback typical for most edge-based approaches—jitter. To improve the efficiency of the method in the above-mentioned cases, in the future, we are planning to use edges on the inner texture of the object.

A major limitation of our method is low run time performance (see Table 3). Also, frame processing time significantly depends on object model size as shown in Table 4. This is due to the following fact: the most time-consuming part of our method is contour energy optimization, where model contour identification is the operation repeated most frequently. These calculations could be accelerated using GPU.

6   Conclusions

The present article introduced the method for model-based 3D tracking based on combination of model contour energy and keypoints. Kanade–Lucas–Tomasi tracker is used for preliminary pose estimation. Then the pose is refined by the contour energy optimization using the Basin-Hopping stochastic algorithm. To improve optimization, we set search area constraints based on keypoints average reprojection error. Such constraints fix well-tracked parts of the object while allows movement of parts which are failed to be correctly positioned by KLT tracker. The results of experiments on a challenging benchmark dataset show that combining edge-based and keypoint-based approaches can diminish the typical disadvantages of both methods. Contour energy optimization effectively struggle with motion blur and poorly textured surfaces, while keypoints help to correctly process symmetrical objects. We demonstrated the efficiency of our approach by testing it against state-of-the-art methods on a public benchmark dataset.

References

1. Canny, J.: A computational approach to edge detection. IEEE Trans. Pattern Anal. Mach. Intell. PAMI 8(6), 679–698 (1986). https://doi.org/10.1109/TPAMI.1986.4767851
2. Choi, C., Christensen, H.I.: 3D textureless object detection and tracking: an edge-based approach. In: IEEE/RSJ International Conference on Intelligent Robots and Systems, pp. 3877–3884, October 2012. https://doi.org/10.1109/IROS.2012.6386065

3. Choi, C., Christensen, H.I.: Robust 3D visual tracking using particle filtering on the special euclidean group: a combined approach of keypoint and edge features. Int. J. Robot. Res. **31**(4), 498–519 (2012). https://doi.org/10.1177/0278364912437213
4. Comport, A.I., Marchand, E., Chaumette, F.: A real-time tracker for markerless augmented reality. In: The Second IEEE and ACM International Symposium on Mixed and Augmented Reality, pp. 36–45, October 2003. https://doi.org/10.1109/ISMAR.2003.1240686
5. Comport, A.I., Marchand, E., Pressigout, M., Chaumette, F.: Real-time markerless tracking for augmented reality: the virtual visual servoing framework. IEEE Trans. Vis. Comput. Graph. **12**, 615–628 (2006). https://doi.org/10.1109/TVCG.2006.78
6. Damen, D., Bunnun, P., Calway, A., Mayol-cuevas, W.: Real-time learning and detection of 3D texture-less objects: a scalable approach. In: Proceedings of the British Machine Vision Conference, pp. 23.1–23.12. BMVA Press, Guildford (2012). https://doi.org/10.5244/C.26.23
7. Fischler, M.A., Bolles, R.C.: Random sample consensus: a paradigm for model fitting with applications to image analysis and automated cartography. Commun. ACM **24**(6), 381–395 (1981). https://doi.org/10.1145/358669.358692
8. Harris, C., Stennett, C.: RAPID - a video rate object tracker. In: Proceedings of the British Machine Vision Conference, vol. 6, pp. 15.1–15.6. BMVA Press, Guildford, September 1990. https://doi.org/10.5244/C.4.15
9. Klein, G., Murray, D.W.: Full-3D edge tracking with a particle filter. In: Proceedings of the British Machine Vision Conference, pp. 1119–1128. BMVA Press, Guildford, September 2006. https://doi.org/10.5244/C.20.114
10. Kraft, D.: A Software Package for Sequential Quadratic Programming. Forschungsbericht, Wiss. Berichtswesen d. DFVLR, Deutsche Forschungs- und Versuchsanstalt für Luft- und Raumfahrt Köln (1988)
11. Lepetit, V., Fua, P.: Monocular model-based 3D tracking of rigid objects. Found. Trends Comput. Graph. Vis. **1**(1), 1–89 (2005). https://doi.org/10.1561/0600000001
12. Lourakis, M., Zabulis, X.: Model-based pose estimation for rigid objects. In: Chen, M., Leibe, B., Neumann, B. (eds.) ICVS 2013. LNCS, vol. 7963, pp. 83–92. Springer, Heidelberg (2013). https://doi.org/10.1007/978-3-642-39402-7_9
13. Lowe, D.G.: Distinctive image features from scale-invariant keypoints. Int. J. Comput. Vis. **60**(2), 91–110 (2004). https://doi.org/10.1023/B:VISI.0000029664.99615.94
14. Lucas, B.D., Kanade, T.: An iterative image registration technique with an application to stereo vision. In: Proceedings of the 7th International Joint Conference on Artificial Intelligence. IJCAI, vol. 2, pp. 674–679. Morgan Kaufmann, San Francisco, CA, USA (1981)
15. Marchand, E., Bouthemy, P., Chaumette, F.: A 2D–3D model-based approach to real-time visual tracking. Image Vis. Comput. **19**(13), 941–955 (2001). https://doi.org/10.1016/S0262-8856(01)00054-3
16. Marchand, E., Uchiyama, H., Spindler, F.: Pose estimation for augmented reality: a hands-on survey. IEEE Trans. Vis. Comput. Graph. **22**(12), 2633–2651 (2016). https://doi.org/10.1109/TVCG.2015.2513408
17. Metropolis, N., Rosenbluth, A.W., Rosenbluth, M.N., Teller, A.H., Teller, E.: Equation of state calculations by fast computing machines. J. Chem. Phys. **21**(6), 1087–1092 (1953). https://doi.org/10.1063/1.1699114
18. Mur-Artal, R., Tardós, J.D.: ORB-SLAM2: an open-source SLAM system for monocular, stereo and RGB-D cameras. IEEE Trans. Robot. **33**, 1255–1262 (2017). https://doi.org/10.1109/TRO.2017.2705103

19. Pauwels, K., Rubio, L., Díaz, J., Vidal, E.R.: Real-time model-based rigid object pose estimation and tracking combining dense and sparse visual cues. In: IEEE Conference on Computer Vision and Pattern Recognition, pp. 2347–2354. IEEE, Portland, Oregon, USA (Jun 2013). https://doi.org/10.1109/CVPR.2013.304
20. Prisacariu, V.A., Reid, I.D.: PWP3D: real-time segmentation and tracking of 3D objects. Int. J. Comput. Vis. **98**, 335–354 (2012). https://doi.org/10.1007/s11263-011-0514-3
21. Seo, B.K., Park, H., Park, J.I., Hinterstoisser, S., Ilic, S.: Optimal local searching for fast and robust textureless 3D object tracking in highly cluttered backgrounds. IEEE Trans. Vis. Comput. Graph. **20**, 99–110 (2014). https://doi.org/10.1109/TVCG.2013.94
22. Shi, J., Tomasi, C.: Good features to track. Technical report, Ithaca, NY, USA (1993)
23. Tjaden, H., Schwanecke, U., Schömer, E.: Real-time monocular pose estimation of 3D objects using temporally consistent local color histograms. In: IEEE International Conference on Computer Vision, pp. 124–132 (2017). https://doi.org/10.1109/ICCV.2017.23
24. Tomasi, C., Kanade, T.: Detection and tracking of point features. Int. J. Comput. Vis. **9**, 137–154 (1991)
25. Vacchetti, L., Lepetit, V., Fua, P.: Combining edge and texture information for real-time accurate 3D camera tracking. In: Proceedings of the 3rd IEEE/ACM International Symposium on Mixed and Augmented Reality, ISMAR, pp. 48–57. IEEE Computer Society, Washington, DC, USA (2004). https://doi.org/10.1109/ISMAR.2004.24
26. Vacchetti, L., Lepetit, V., Fua, P.: Stable real-time 3D tracking using online and offline information. IEEE Trans. Pattern Anal. Mach. Intell. **26**, 1385–1391 (2004). https://doi.org/10.1109/TPAMI.2004.92
27. Wales, D.J., Doye, J.P.K.: Global optimization by basin-hopping and the lowest energy structures of lennard-jones clusters containing up to 110 atoms. J. Phys. Chem. **101**(28), 5111–5116 (1997). https://doi.org/10.1021/jp970984n
28. Wang, B., Zhong, F., Qin, X.: Pose optimization in edge distance field for textureless 3D object tracking. In: Proceedings of the Computer Graphics International Conference, CGI, pp. 32:1–32:6. ACM, New York (2017).https://doi.org/10.1145/3095140.3095172
29. Wang, G., Wang, B., Zhong, F., Qin, X., Chen, B.: Global optimal searching for textureless 3D object tracking. Vis. Comput.: Int. J. Comput. Graph. **31**(6–8), 979–988 (2015). https://doi.org/10.1007/s00371-015-1098-7
30. Wu, P.C., Lee, Y.Y., Tseng, H.Y., Ho, H.I., Yang, M.H., Chien, S.Y.: A benchmark dataset for 6DoF object pose tracking. In: IEEE International Symposium on Mixed and Augmented Reality, ISMAR-Adjunct, pp. 186–191. IEEE Computer Society, Washington, DC, USA, October 2017. https://doi.org/10.1109/ISMARAdjunct.2017.62

Pairwise Confusion for Fine-Grained Visual Classification

Abhimanyu Dubey[1]([✉]), Otkrist Gupta[1], Pei Guo[2], Ramesh Raskar[1],
Ryan Farrell[2], and Nikhil Naik[1,3]

[1] Massachusetts Institute of Technology, Cambridge, MA 02139, USA
{dubeya,otkrist,raskar,naik}@mit.edu
[2] Brigham Young University, Provo, UT 84602, USA
{peiguo,farrell}@cs.byu.edu
[3] Harvard University, Cambridge, MA 02139, USA
naik@fas.harvard.edu

Abstract. Fine-Grained Visual Classification (FGVC) datasets contain small sample sizes, along with significant intra-class variation and inter-class similarity. While prior work has addressed intra-class variation using localization and segmentation techniques, inter-class similarity may also affect feature learning and reduce classification performance. In this work, we address this problem using a novel optimization procedure for the end-to-end neural network training on FGVC tasks. Our procedure, called Pairwise Confusion (PC) reduces overfitting by intentionally introducing confusion in the activations. With PC regularization, we obtain state-of-the-art performance on six of the most widely-used FGVC datasets and demonstrate improved localization ability. PC is easy to implement, does not need excessive hyperparameter tuning during training, and does not add significant overhead during test time.

1 Introduction

The Fine-Grained Visual Classification (FGVC) task focuses on differentiating between hard-to-distinguish object classes, such as species of birds, flowers, or animals; and identifying the makes or models of vehicles. FGVC datasets depart from conventional image classification in that they typically require expert knowledge, rather than crowdsourcing, for gathering annotations. FGVC datasets contain images with much higher visual similarity than those in large-scale visual classification (LSVC). Moreover, FGVC datasets have minute inter-class visual differences in addition to the variations in pose, lighting and viewpoint found in LSVC [1]. Additionally, FGVC datasets often exhibit long tails in the data distribution, since the difficulty of obtaining examples of different classes may vary. This combination of small, non-uniform datasets and subtle

Electronic supplementary material The online version of this chapter (https://doi.org/10.1007/978-3-030-01258-8_5) contains supplementary material, which is available to authorized users.

V. Ferrari et al. (Eds.): ECCV 2018, LNCS 11216, pp. 71–88, 2018.
https://doi.org/10.1007/978-3-030-01258-8_5

inter-class differences makes FGVC challenging even for powerful deep learning algorithms.

Most of the prior work in FGVC has focused on tackling the *intra-class* variation in pose, lighting, and viewpoint using localization techniques [1–5], and by augmenting training datasets with additional data from the Web [6,7]. However, we observe that prior work in FGVC does not pay much attention to the problems that may arise due to the *inter-class* visual similarity in the feature extraction pipeline. Similar to LSVC tasks, neural networks for FGVC tasks are typically trained with cross-entropy loss [1,7–9]. In LSVC datasets such as ImageNet [10], strongly discriminative learning using the cross-entropy loss is successful in part due to the significant inter-class variation (compared to intra-class variation), which enables deep networks to learn generalized discriminatory features with large amounts of data.

We posit that this formulation may not be ideal for FGVC, which shows smaller visual differences between classes and larger differences within each class than LSVC. For instance, if two samples in the training set have very similar visual content but different class labels, minimizing the cross-entropy loss will force the neural network to learn features that distinguish these two images with high confidence—potentially forcing the network to learn sample-specific artifacts for visually confusing classes in order to minimize training error. We suspect that this effect would be especially pronounced in FGVC, since there are fewer samples from which the network can learn generalizable class-specific features.

Based on this hypothesis, we propose that introducing *confusion* in output logit activations during training for an FGVC task will force the network to learn slightly less discriminative features, thereby preventing it from overfitting to sample-specific artifacts. Specifically, we aim to *confuse* the network, by minimizing the distance between the predicted probability distributions for random pairs of samples from the training set. To do so, we propose Pairwise Confusion (PC)[1], a pairwise algorithm for training convolutional neural networks (CNNs) end-to-end for fine-grained visual classification.

In Pairwise Confusion, we construct a Siamese neural network trained with a novel loss function that attempts to bring class conditional probability distributions closer to each other. Using Pairwise Confusion with a standard network architecture like DenseNet [11] or ResNet [12] as a base network, we obtain state-of-the-art performance on six of the most widely-used fine-grained recognition datasets, improving over the previous-best published methods by 1.86% on average. In addition, PC-trained networks show better localization performance as compared to standard networks. Pairwise Confusion is simple to implement, has no added overhead in training or prediction time, and provides performance improvements both in FGVC tasks and other tasks that involve transfer learning with small amounts of training data.

---

[1] Implementation available at https://github.com/abhimanyudubey/confusion.

2   Related Work

Fine-Grained Visual Classification: Early FGVC research focused on methods to train with limited labeled data and traditional image features. Yao et al. [13] combined strongly discriminative image patches with randomization techniques to prevent overfitting. Yao et al. [14] subsequently utilized template matching to avoid the need for a large number of annotations.

Recently, improved localization of the target object in training images has been shown to be useful for FGVC [1,15–17]. Zhang et al. [15] utilize part-based Region-CNNs [18] to perform finer localization. Spatial Transformer Networks [2] show that learning a content-based affine transformation layer improves FGVC performance. Pose-normalized CNNs have also been shown to be effective at FGVC [19,20]. Model ensembling and boosting has also improved performance on FGVC [21]. Lin et al. [1] introduced Bilinear Pooling, which combines pairwise local feature sets and improves classification performance. Bilinear Pooling has been extended by Gao et al. [16] using a compact bilinear representation and Cui et al. [9] using a general Kernel-based pooling framework that captures higher-order interactions of features.

Pairwise Learning: Chopra et al. [22] introduced a Siamese neural network for handwriting recognition. Parikh and Grauman [23] developed a pairwise ranking scheme for relative attribute learning. Subsequently, pairwise neural network models have become common for attribute modeling [24–27].

Learning from Label Confusion: Our method aims to improve classification performance by introducing confusion within the output labels. Prior work in this area includes methods that utilize label noise (e.g., [28]) and data noise (e.g., [29]) in training. Krause et al. [6] utilized noisy training data for FGVC.

Table 1. A comparison of fine-grained visual classification (FGVC) datasets with large-scale visual classification (LSVC) datasets. FGVC datasets are significantly smaller and noisier than LSVC datasets.

Dataset	Num.classes	Samples per class
Flowers-102 [32]	102	10
CUB-200-2011 [33]	200	29.97
Cars [34]	196	41.55
NABirds [35]	550	43.5
Aircrafts [36]	100	100
Stanford Dogs [37]	120	100
CIFAR-100 [38]	100	500
ImageNet [10]	1000	1200
CIFAR-10 [38]	10	5000
SVHN [39]	10	7325.7

Neelakantan et al. [30] added noise to the gradient during training to improve generalization performance in very deep networks. Szegedy et al. [31] introduced label-smoothing regularization for training deep Inception models.

In this paper, we bring together concepts from pairwise learning and label confusion and take a step towards solving the problems of overfitting and sample-specific artifacts when training neural networks for FGVC tasks.

3   Method

FGVC datasets in computer vision are orders of magnitude smaller than LSVC datasets and contain greater imbalance across classes (see Table 1). Moreover, the samples of a class are not accurately representative of the complete variation in the visual class itself. The smaller dataset size can result in overfitting when training deep neural architectures with large number of parameters—even with preliminary layers being frozen. In addition, the training data may not be completely representative of the real-world data, with issues such as more abundant sampling for certain classes. For example, in FGVC of birds, certain species from geographically accessible areas may be overrepresented in the training dataset. As a result, the neural network may learn to latch on to sample-specific artifacts in the image, instead of learning a versatile representation for the target object. We aim to solve both of these issues in FGVC (overfitting and sample-specific artifacts) by bringing the different class-conditional probability distributions closer together and *confusing* the deep network, subsequently reducing its prediction over-confidence, thus improving generalization performance.

Let us formalize the idea of "confusing" the conditional probability distributions. Consider the conditional probability distributions for two input images $\mathbf{x}_1$ and $\mathbf{x}_2$, which can be given by $p_\theta(\mathbf{y}|\mathbf{x}_1)$ and $p_\theta(\mathbf{y}|\mathbf{x}_2)$ respectively. For a classification problem with N output classes, each of these distributions is an N-dimensional vector, with each element i denoting the belief of the classifier in class $\mathbf{y}_i$ given input $\mathbf{x}$. If we wish to *confuse* the class outputs of the classifier for the pair $\mathbf{x}_1$ and $\mathbf{x}_2$, we should learn parameters θ that bring these conditional probability distributions "closer" under some distance metric, that is, make the predictions for $\mathbf{x}_1$ and $\mathbf{x}_2$ similar.

While KL-divergence might seem to be a reasonable choice to design a loss function for optimizing the distance between conditional probability distributions, in Sect. 3.1, we show that it is infeasible to train a neural network when using KL-divergence as a regularizer. Therefore, we introduce the Euclidean Distance between distributions as a metric for confusion in Sects. 3.2 and 3.3 and describe neural network training with this metric in Sect. 3.4.

3.1   Symmetric KL-Divergence or Jeffrey's Divergence

The most prevalent method to measure dissimilarity of one probability distribution from another is to use the Kullback-Liebler (KL) divergence. However, the standard KL-divergence cannot serve our purpose owing to its asymmetric nature. This could be remedied by using the *symmetric* KL-divergence, defined for two probability distributions P, Q with mass functions $p(\cdot), q(\cdot)$ (for events $u \in \mathcal{U}$):

$$\mathbb{D}_J(P, Q) \triangleq \sum_{u \in \mathcal{U}} \left[p(u) \cdot \log \frac{p(u)}{q(u)} + q(u) \cdot \log \frac{q(u)}{p(u)} \right] = \mathbb{D}_{\mathsf{KL}}(P||Q) + \mathbb{D}_{\mathsf{KL}}(Q||P) \quad (1)$$

This symmetrized version of KL-divergence, known as Jeffrey's divergence [40], is a measure of the average relative entropy between two probability distributions [41]. For our model parameterized by θ, for samples $\mathbf{x}_1$ and $\mathbf{x}_2$, the Jeffrey's divergence can be written as:

$$\mathbb{D}_J(p_\theta(\mathbf{y}|\mathbf{x}_1), p_\theta(\mathbf{y}|\mathbf{x}_2)) = \sum_{i=1}^{N} \left[(p_\theta(\mathbf{y}_i|\mathbf{x}_1) - p_\theta(\mathbf{y}_i|\mathbf{x}_2)) \cdot \log \frac{p_\theta(\mathbf{y}_i|\mathbf{x}_1)}{p_\theta(\mathbf{y}_i|\mathbf{x}_2)} \right] \quad (2)$$

Jeffrey's divergence satisfies all of our basic requirements of a symmetric divergence metric between probability distributions, and therefore could be included as a regularizing term while training with cross-entropy, to achieve our desired confusion. However, when we learn model parameters using stochastic gradient descent (SGD), it can be difficult to train, especially if our distributions P, Q have mass concentrated on different events. This can be seen in Eq. 2. Consider Jeffrey's divergence with $N = 2$ classes, and that $\mathbf{x}_1$ belongs to class 1, and $\mathbf{x}_2$ belongs to class 2. If the model parameters θ are such that it correctly identifies both $\mathbf{x}_1$ and $\mathbf{x}_2$ by training using cross-entropy loss, $p_\theta(\mathbf{y}_1|x_1) = 1 - \delta_1$ and $p_\theta(\mathbf{y}_2|x_2) = 1 - \delta_2$, where $0 < \delta_1, \delta_2 < \frac{1}{2}$ (since the classifier outputs correct predictions for the input images), we can show:

$$\mathbb{D}_J(p_\theta(\mathbf{y}|\mathbf{x}_1), p_\theta(\mathbf{y}|\mathbf{x}_2)) \geq (1 - \delta_1 - \delta_2) \cdot (2 \log(1 - \delta_1 - \delta_2) - \log(\delta_1 \delta_2)) \quad (3)$$

Please see the supplementary material for an expanded proof.

As training progresses with these labels, the cross-entropy loss will motivate the values of δ_1 and δ_2 to become closer to zero (but never equaling zero, since the probability outputs $p_\theta(\mathbf{y}|\mathbf{x}_1), p_\theta(\mathbf{y}|\mathbf{x}_2)$ are the outputs from a softmax). As $(\delta_1, \delta_2) \rightarrow (0^+, 0^+)$, the second term $-\log(\delta_1 \delta_2)$ on the R.H.S. of inequality (3) typically grows whereas $(1 - \delta_1 - \delta_2)$ approaches 1, which makes $\mathbb{D}_J(p_\theta(\mathbf{y}|\mathbf{x}_1), p_\theta(\mathbf{y}|\mathbf{x}_2))$ larger as the predictions get closer to the true labels. In practice, we see that training with $\mathbb{D}_J(p_\theta(\mathbf{y}|\mathbf{x}_1), p_\theta(\mathbf{y}|\mathbf{x}_2))$ as a regularizer term diverges, unless a very small regularizing parameter is chosen, which removes the effect of regularization altogether.

A natural question that can arise from this analysis is that cross-entropy training itself involves optimizing KL-divergence between the target label distribution and the model's predictions, however no such divergence occurs. This is because cross-entropy involves only one direction of the KL-divergence, and the target distribution has all the mass concentrated at one event (the correct label). Since $(x \log x)|_{x=0} = 0$, for predicted label vector $\mathbf{y}'$ with correct label class c, this simplifies the cross-entropy error $\mathcal{L}_{\mathsf{CE}}(p_\theta(\mathbf{y}|\mathbf{x}), \mathbf{y}')$ to be:

$$\mathcal{L}_{\text{CE}}(p_\theta(\mathbf{y}|\mathbf{x}), \mathbf{y}') = -\sum_{i=1}^{N} \mathbf{y}'_i \log(\frac{p_\theta(\mathbf{y}_i|\mathbf{x})}{\mathbf{y}'_i}) = -\log(p_\theta(\mathbf{y}_c|\mathbf{x})) \geq 0 \qquad (4)$$

This formulation does not diverge as the model trains, i.e. $p_\theta(\mathbf{y}_c|\mathbf{x}) \to 1$. In some cases where label noise is added to the label vector (such as label smoothing [28,42]), the label noise is a fixed constant and not approaching zero (as in the case of Jeffery's divergence between model predictions) and is hence feasible to train. Thus, Jeffrey's Divergence or symmetric KL-divergence, while a seemingly natural choice, cannot be used to train a neural network with SGD. This motivates us to look for an alternative metric to measure "confusion" between conditional probability distributions.

3.2 Euclidean Distance as Confusion

Since the conditional probability distribution over N classes is an element within $\mathbb{R}^N$ on the unit simplex, we can consider the Euclidean distance to be a metric of "confusion" between two conditional probability distributions. Analogous to the previous setting, we define the **Euclidean Confusion** $\mathbb{D}_{\text{EC}}(\cdot, \cdot)$ for a pair of inputs $\mathbf{x}_1, \mathbf{x}_2$ with model parameters θ as:

$$\mathbb{D}_{\text{EC}}(p_\theta(\mathbf{y}|\mathbf{x}_1), p_\theta(\mathbf{y}|\mathbf{x}_2)) = \sum_{i=1}^{N}(p_\theta(\mathbf{y}_i|\mathbf{x}_1) - p_\theta(\mathbf{y}_i|\mathbf{x}_2))^2 = \|p_\theta(\mathbf{y}|\mathbf{x}_1) - p_\theta(\mathbf{y}|\mathbf{x}_2)\|_2^2$$

$$(5)$$

Unlike Jeffrey's Divergence, Euclidean Confusion does not diverge when used as a regularization term with cross-entropy. However, to verify this unconventional choice for a distance metric between probability distributions, we prove some properties that relate Euclidean Confusion to existing divergence measures.

Lemma 1. *On a finite probability space, the Euclidean Confusion $\mathbb{D}_{\text{EC}}(P, Q)$ is a lower bound for the Jeffrey's Divergence $\mathbb{D}_J(P, Q)$ for probability measures P, Q.*

Proof. This follows from Pinsker's Inequality and the relationship between ℓ_1 and ℓ_2 norms. Complete proof is provided in the supplementary material.

By Lemma 1, we can see that the Euclidean Confusion is a conservative estimate for Jeffrey's divergence, the earlier proposed divergence measure. For finite probability spaces, the Total Variation Distance $\mathbb{D}_{\text{TV}}(P, Q)^2 = \frac{1}{2}\|P - Q\|_1$ is also a measure of interest. However, due to its non-differentiable nature, it is unsuitable for our case. Nevertheless, we can relate the Euclidean Confusion and Total Variation Distance by the following result.

Lemma 2. *On a finite probability space, the Euclidean Confusion $\mathbb{D}_{\text{EC}}(P, Q)$ is bounded by $4\mathbb{D}_{\text{TV}}(P, Q)^2$ for probability measures P, Q.*

Proof. This follows directly from the relationship between ℓ_1 and ℓ_2 norms. Complete proof is provided in the supplementary material.

3.3   Euclidean Confusion for Point Sets

In a standard classification setting with N classes, we consider a training set with $m = \sum_{i=1}^{N} m_i$ training examples, where m_i denotes the number of training samples for class i. For this setting, we can write the total Euclidean Confusion between points of classes i and j as the average of the Euclidean Confusion between all pairs of points belonging to those two classes. For simplicity of notation, let us denote the set of conditional probability distributions of all training points belonging to class i for a model parameterized by θ as $\mathcal{S}_i = \{p_\theta(\mathbf{y}|\mathbf{x}_1^i), p_\theta(\mathbf{y}|\mathbf{x}_2^i), ..., p_\theta(\mathbf{y}|\mathbf{x}_{m_i}^i)\}$. Then, for a model parameterized by θ, the Euclidean Confusion is given by:

$$\mathbb{D}_{\mathsf{EC}}(\mathcal{S}_i, \mathcal{S}_j; \theta) \triangleq \frac{1}{m_i m_j} \Big(\sum_{u,v}^{m_i, m_j} \mathbb{D}_{\mathsf{EC}}(p_\theta(\mathbf{y}|\mathbf{x}_u^i), p_\theta(\mathbf{y}|\mathbf{x}_v^j)) \Big) \qquad (6)$$

We can simplify this equation by assuming an equal number of points n per class:

$$\mathbb{D}_{\mathsf{EC}}(\mathcal{S}_i, \mathcal{S}_j; \theta) = \frac{1}{n^2} \Big(\sum_{u,v}^{n,n} \|p_\theta(\mathbf{y}|\mathbf{x}_u^i) - p_\theta(\mathbf{y}|\mathbf{x}_v^j)\|_2^2 \Big) \qquad (7)$$

This form of the Euclidean Confusion between the two sets of points gives us an interesting connection with another popular distance metric over probability distributions, known as the **Energy Distance** [43].

Introduced by Gabor Szekely [43], the **Energy Distance** $\mathbb{D}_{\mathsf{EN}}(F, G)$ between two cumulative probability distribution functions F and G with random vectors X and Y in $\mathbb{R}^N$ can be given by

$$\mathbb{D}_{\mathsf{EN}}(F, G)^2 \triangleq 2\mathbb{E}\|X - Y\| - \mathbb{E}\|X - X'\| - \mathbb{E}\|Y - Y'\| \geq 0 \qquad (8)$$

where (X, X', Y, Y') are independent, and $X \sim F, X' \sim F, Y \sim G, Y' \sim G$. If we consider the sets $\mathcal{S}_i$ and $\mathcal{S}_j$, with a uniform probability of selecting any of the n points in each of these sets, then we obtain the following results.

Lemma 3. *For sets $\mathcal{S}_i$, $\mathcal{S}_j$ and $\mathbb{D}_{\mathsf{EC}}(\mathcal{S}_i, \mathcal{S}_j; \theta)$ as defined in Eq. (7):*

$$\tfrac{1}{2}\mathbb{D}_{\mathsf{EN}}(\mathcal{S}_i, \mathcal{S}_j; \theta)^2 \leq \mathbb{D}_{\mathsf{EC}}(\mathcal{S}_i, \mathcal{S}_j; \theta)$$

where $\mathbb{D}_{\mathsf{EN}}(\mathcal{S}_i, \mathcal{S}_j; \theta)$ is the Energy Distance under Euclidean norm between $\mathcal{S}_i$ and $\mathcal{S}_j$ (parameterized by θ), and random vectors are selected with uniform probability in both $\mathcal{S}_i$ and $\mathcal{S}_j$.

Proof. This follows from the definition of Energy Distance with uniform probability of sampling. Complete proof is provided in the supplementary material.

Corollary 1. *For sets $\mathcal{S}_i$, $\mathcal{S}_j$ and $\mathbb{D}_{\mathsf{EC}}(\mathcal{S}_i, \mathcal{S}_j; \theta)$ as defined in Eq. (7), we have:*

$$\mathbb{D}_{\mathsf{EC}}(\mathcal{S}_i, \mathcal{S}_i; \theta) + \mathbb{D}_{\mathsf{EC}}(\mathcal{S}_j, \mathcal{S}_j; \theta) \leq 2\mathbb{D}_{\mathsf{EC}}(\mathcal{S}_i, \mathcal{S}_j; \theta)$$

with equality only when $\mathcal{S}_i = \mathcal{S}_j$.

Proof. This follows from the fact that the Energy Distance $\mathbb{D}_{\mathsf{EN}}(\mathcal{S}_i, \mathcal{S}_j; \theta)$ is 0 only when $\mathcal{S}_i = \mathcal{S}_j$. The complete version of the proof is included in the supplement.

With these results, we restrict the behavior of Euclidean Confusion within two well-defined conventional probability distance measures, the Jeffrey's divergence and Energy Distance. One might consider optimizing the Energy Distance directly, due to its similar formulation and the fact that we uniformly sample points during training with SGD. However, the Energy Distance additionally includes the two terms that account for the negative of the average all-pairs distances between points in $\mathcal{S}_i$ and $\mathcal{S}_j$ respectively, which we do not want to maximize, since we do not wish to push points within the same class further apart. Therefore, we proceed with our measure of Euclidean Confusion.

3.4 Learning with Gradient Descent

We proceed to learn parameters θ^* for a neural network, with the following learning objective function for a pair of input points, motivated by the formulation of Euclidean Confusion:

$$\theta^* = \arg\min_\theta \sum_{\substack{i=1,j \neq i \\ u,v}}^{N,N} \left[\mathcal{L}_{\mathsf{CE}}(p_\theta(\mathbf{y}|\mathbf{x}_u^i), \mathbf{y}_u^i) + \mathcal{L}_{\mathsf{CE}}(p_\theta(\mathbf{y}|\mathbf{x}_v^j), \mathbf{y}_v^j) + \frac{\lambda}{n^2} \mathbb{D}_{\mathsf{EC}}(p_\theta(\mathbf{y}|\mathbf{x}_v^j), p_\theta(\mathbf{y}|\mathbf{x}_u^i)) \right]$$

(9)

This objective function can be explained as: for each point in the training set, we randomly select another point from a different class and calculate the individual cross-entropy losses and Euclidean Confusion until all pairs have been exhausted. For each point in the training dataset, there are $n \cdot (N-1)$ valid choices for the other point, giving us a total of $n^2 \cdot N \cdot (N-1)$ possible pairs. In practice, we find that we do not need to exhaust all combinations for effective learning using gradient descent, and in fact we observe that convergence is achieved far before

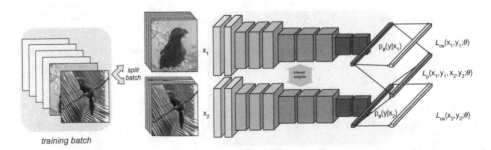

Fig. 1. CNN training pipeline for Pairwise Confusion (**PC**). We employ a Siamese-like architecture, with individual cross entropy calculations for each branch, followed by a joint energy-distance minimization loss. We split each incoming batch of samples into two mini-batches, and feed the network pairwise samples.

all observations are observed. We simplify our formulation instead by using the following procedure described in Algorithm 1.

Training Procedure: As described in Algorithm 1, our learning procedure is a slightly modified version of the standard SGD. We randomly permute the training set twice, and then for each pair of points in the training set, add Euclidean Confusion only if the samples belong to different classes. This form of sampling approximates the exhaustive Euclidean Confusion, with some points with regular gradient descent, which in practice does not alter the performance. Moreover, convergence is achieved after only a fraction of all the possible pairs are observed. Formally, we wish to model the conditional probability distribution $p_\theta(\mathbf{y}|\mathbf{x})$ over the p classes for function $f(\mathbf{x}; \theta) = p_\theta(\mathbf{y}|\mathbf{x})$ parameterized by model parameters θ. Given our optimization procedure, we can rewrite the total loss for a pair of points $\mathbf{x}_1, \mathbf{x}_2$ with model parameters θ as:

$$\mathcal{L}_{\text{pair}}(\mathbf{x}_1, \mathbf{x}_2, \mathbf{y}_1, \mathbf{y}_2; \theta) = \sum_{i=1}^{2}[\mathcal{L}_{\text{CE}}(p_\theta(\mathbf{y}|\mathbf{x}_i), \mathbf{y}_i)] + \lambda\gamma(\mathbf{y}_1, \mathbf{y}_2)\mathbb{D}_{\text{EC}}(p_\theta(\mathbf{y}|\mathbf{x}_1), p_\theta(\mathbf{y}|\mathbf{x}_2))$$

(10)

where, $\gamma(\mathbf{y}_1, \mathbf{y}_2) = 1$ when $\mathbf{y}_i \neq \mathbf{y}_j$, and 0 otherwise. We denote **training** with this general architecture with the term *Pairwise Confusion* or **PC** for short. Specifically, we train a Siamese-like neural network [22] with shared weights, training each network individually using cross-entropy, and add the **Euclidean Confusion** loss between the conditional probability distributions obtained from each network (Fig. 1). During training, we split an incoming batch of training samples into two parts, and evaluating cross-entropy on each sub-batch identically, followed by a pairwise loss term calculated for corresponding pairs of samples across batches. During testing, only one branch of the network is active, and generates output predictions for the input image.

Algorithm 1. Training Using Euclidean Confusion

Training data D, Test data $\hat{D}$, parameters θ, hyperparameters $\hat{\theta}$
for *epoch* $\in$ [0,max_epochs]) **do**
    $D_1 \Leftarrow$ shuffle(D)
    $D_2 \Leftarrow$ shuffle(D)
    for $i \in$ [0,num_batches] **do**
        $\mathcal{L}_{\text{batch}} = 0$
        for $(d_1, d_2) \in$ batch i of (D_1, D_2) **do**
            $\gamma \Leftarrow 1$ if label(d_1) $\neq$ label(d_2), 0 otherwise
            $\mathcal{L}_{\text{pair}} \Leftarrow \mathcal{L}_{\text{CE}}(d_1; \theta) + \mathcal{L}_{\text{CE}}(d_2; \theta) + \lambda \cdot \gamma \cdot \mathbb{D}_{\text{EC}}(d_1, d_2; \theta)$
            $\mathcal{L}_{\text{batch}} \Leftarrow \mathcal{L}_{\text{batch}} + \mathcal{L}_{\text{pair}}$
        end for
        $\theta \Leftarrow$ Backprop($\mathcal{L}_{\text{batch}}, \theta, \hat{\theta}$)
    end for
    $\hat{\theta} \Leftarrow$ ParameterUpdate(epoch, $\hat{\theta}$)
end for

CNN Architectures: We experiment with VGGNet [44], GoogLeNet [42], ResNets [12], and DenseNets [11] as base architectures for the Siamese network trained with **PC** to demonstrate that our method is insensitive to the choice of source architecture.

4 Experimental Details

We perform all experiments using Caffe [45] or PyTorch [46] over a cluster of NVIDIA Titan X, Tesla K40c and GTX 1080 GPUs. Our code and models are available at github.com/abhimanyudubey/confusion. Next, we provide brief descriptions of the various datasets used in our paper.

Table 2. Pairwise Confusion (**PC**) obtains state-of-the-art performance on six widely-used fine-grained visual classification datasets (A-F). Improvement over the baseline model is reported as (Δ). All results averaged over 5 trials.

Method	Top-1	Δ	Method	Top-1	Δ	Method	Top-1	Δ
(A) CUB-200-2011			*(B) Cars*			*(C) Aircrafts*		
Gao *et al.* [16]	84.00	-	Wang *et al.* [17]	85.70	-	Simon *et al.* [49]	85.50	-
STN [2]	84.10	-	Liu *et al.* [48]	86.80	-	Cui *et al.* [9]	86.90	-
Zhang *et al.* [47]	84.50	-	Lin *et al.* [8]	92.00	-	LRBP [50]	87.30	-
Lin *et al.* [8]	85.80	-	Cui *et al.* [9]	92.40	-	Lin *et al.* [8]	88.50	-
Cui *et al.* [9]	86.20	-						
ResNet-50	78.15	(2.06)	ResNet-50	91.71	(1.72)	ResNet-50	81.19	(2.21)
PC-ResNet-50	80.21		**PC**-ResNet-50	**93.43**		**PC**-ResNet-50	83.40	
Bilinear CNN [1]	84.10	(1.48)	Bilinear CNN [1]	91.20	**(1.25)**	BilinearCNN [1]	84.10	(1.68)
PC-BilinearCNN	85.58		**PC**-Bilinear CNN	92.45		**PC**-BilinearCNN	85.78	
DenseNet-161	84.21	**(2.66)**	DenseNet-161	91.83	(1.03)	DenseNet-161	86.30	**(2.94)**
PC-DenseNet-161	**86.87**		**PC**-DenseNet-161	92.86		**PC**-DenseNet-161	**89.24**	
(D) NABirds			*(E) Flowers-102*			*(F) Stanford dogs*		
Branson *et al.* [19]	35.70	-	Det.+Seg. [51]	80.66	-	Zhang *et al.* [3]	80.43	-
Van *et al.* [35]	75.00	-	Overfeat [52]	86.80	-	Krause *et al.* [6]	80.60	-
ResNet-50	63.55	**(4.60)**	ResNet-50	92.46	(1.04)	ResNet-50	69.92	**(3.43)**
PC-ResNet-50	68.15		**PC**-ResNet-50	93.50		**PC**-ResNet-50	73.35	
BilinearCNN [1]	80.90	(1.11)	BilinearCNN [1]	92.52	(1.13)	BilinearCNN [1]	82.13	(0.91)
PC-BilinearCNN	82.01		**PC**-BilinearCNN	**93.65**		**PC**-BilinearCNN	83.04	
DenseNet-161	79.35	(3.44)	DenseNet-161	90.07	**(1.32)**	DenseNet-161	81.18	(2.57)
PC-DenseNet-161	**82.79**		**PC**-DenseNet-161	91.39		**PC**-DenseNet-161	**83.75**	

4.1 Fine-Grained Visual Classification (FGVC) Datasets

1. **Wildlife Species Classification:** We experiment with several widely-used FGVC datasets. The Caltech-UCSD Birds (**CUB-200-2011**) dataset [33] has 5,994 training and 5,794 test images across 200 species of North-American birds. The **NABirds** dataset [35] contains 23,929 training and 24,633 test images across over 550 visual categories, encompassing 400 species of birds, including separate classes for male and female birds in some cases. The **Stanford Dogs** dataset [37] has 20,580 images across 120 breeds of dogs around

the world. Finally, the **Flowers-102** dataset [32] consists of 1,020 training, 1,020 validation and 6,149 test images over 102 flower types.

2. **Vehicle Make/Model Classification**: We experiment with two common vehicle classification datasets. The **Stanford Cars** dataset [34] contains 8,144 training and 8,041 test images across 196 car classes. The classes represent variations in car make, model, and year. The **Aircraft** dataset is a set of 10,000 images across 100 classes denoting a fine-grained set of airplanes of different varieties [36].

These datasets contain (i) large visual diversity in each class [32,33,37], (ii) visually similar, often confusing samples belonging to different classes, and (iii) a large variation in the number of samples present per class, leading to greater class imbalance than LSVC datasets like **ImageNet** [10]. Additionally, some of these datasets have densely annotated part information available, which we do not utilize in our experiments.

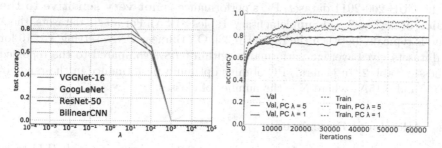

Fig. 2. (left) Variation of test accuracy on CUB-200-2011 with logarithmic variation in hyperparameter λ. (right) Convergence plot of GoogLeNet on CUB-200-2011.

5 Results

5.1 Fine-Grained Visual Classification

We first describe our results on the six FGVC datasets from Table 2. In all experiments, we average results over 5 trials per experiment—after choosing the best value of hyperparameter λ. Please see the supplementary material for mean and standard deviation values for all experiments.

1. **Fine-tuning from Baseline Models**: We fine-tune from three baseline models using the PC optimization procedure: ResNet-50 [12], Bilinear CNN [1], and DenseNet-161 [11]. As Tables 2-(A-F) show, PC obtains substantial improvement across all datasets and models. For instance, a baseline DenseNet-161 architecture obtains an average accuracy of 84.21%, but **PC-DenseNet-161** obtains an accuracy of 86.87%, an improvement of **2.66%**. On NABirds, we obtain improvements of **4.60%** and **3.42%** over baseline ResNet-50 and DenseNet-161 architectures.

2. **Combining PC with Specialized FGVC Models**: Recent work in FGVC has proposed several novel CNN designs that take part-localization into account, such as bilinear pooling techniques [1,9,16] and spatial transformer networks [2]. We train a Bilinear CNN [1] with PC, and obtain an average improvement of 1.7% on the 6 datasets.

We note two important aspects of our analysis: (1) we do not compare with ensembling and data augmentation techniques such as Boosted CNNs [21] and Krause, *et al.* [6] since prior evidence indicates that these techniques invariably improve performance, and (2) we evaluate a single-crop, single-model evaluation without any part- or object-annotations, and perform competitively with methods that use both augmentations.

Choice of Hyperparameter λ: Since our formulation requires the selection of a hyperparameter λ, it is important to study the sensitivity of classification performance to the choice of λ. We conduct this experiment for four different models: GoogLeNet [42], ResNet-50 [12] and VGGNet-16 [44] and Bilinear-CNN [1] on the CUB-200-2011 dataset. PC's performance is **not very sensitive to the choice of** λ (Fig. 2 and Supplementary Tables S1-S5). For all six datasets, the λ value is typically between the range [10,20]. On Bilinear CNN, setting $\lambda = 10$ for all datasets gives average performance within 0.08% compared to the reported values in Table 2. In general, PC obtains optimum performance in the range of $0.05N$ and $0.15N$, where N is the number of classes.

5.2   Additional Experiments

Since our method aims to improve classification performance in FGVC tasks by introducing confusion in output logit activations, we would expect to see a larger improvement in datasets with higher inter-class similarity and intra-class variation. To test this hypothesis, we conduct two additional experiments.

In the first experiment, we construct two subsets of ImageNet-1K [10]. The first dataset, **ImageNet-Dogs** is a subset consisting only of species of dogs (117 classes and 116K images). The second dataset, **ImageNet-Random** contains randomly selected classes from ImageNet-1K. Both datasets contain equal number of classes (117) and images (116K), but ImageNet-Dogs has much higher inter-class similarity and intra-class variation, as compared to ImageNet-Random. To test repeatability, we construct 3 instances of Imagenet-Random, by randomly choosing a different subset of ImageNet with 117 classes each time. For both experiments, we randomly construct a 80–20 train-val split from the training data to find optimal λ by cross-validation, and report the performance on the unseen ImageNet validation set of the subset of chosen classes. In Table 3, we compare the performance of training from scratch with- and without-PC across three models: GoogLeNet, ResNet-50, and DenseNet-161. As expected, PC obtains a larger gain in classification accuracy (1.45%) on ImageNet-Dogs as compared to the ImageNet-Random dataset(0.54% ± 0.28).

In the second experiment, we utilize the CIFAR-10 and CIFAR-100 datasets, which contain the same number of total images. CIFAR-100 has 10× the number of classes and 10% of images per class as CIFAR-10 and contains larger inter-class similarity and intra-class variation. We train networks on both datasets from scratch using default train-test splits (Table 3). As expected, we obtain larger average gains of 1.77% on CIFAR-100, as compared to 0.20% on CIFAR-10. Additionally, when training with $\lambda = 10$ on the entire ImageNet dataset, we obtain a top-1 accuracy of 76.28% (compared to a baseline of 76.15%), which is a smaller improvement, which is in line with what we would expect for a large-scale image classification problem with large inter-class variation.

Moreover, while training with PC, we observe that the rate of convergence is always similar to or faster than training without PC. For example, a GoogLeNet trained on CUB-200-2011 (Fig. 2(right) above) shows that PC converges to higher validation accuracy faster than normal training using identical learning rate schedule and batch size. Note that the training accuracy is reduced when training with PC, due to the regularization effect. In sum, classification problems that have large intra-class variation and high inter-class similarity benefit from optimization with pairwise confusion. The improvement is even more prominent when training data is limited.

Table 3. Experiments with ImageNet and CIFAR show that datasets with large intra-class variation and high inter-class similarity benefit from optimization with Pairwise Confusion. Only the mean accuracy over 3 Imagenet-Random experiments is shown.

Network	ImageNet-Random		ImageNet-Dogs		CIFAR-10		CIFAR-100	
	Baseline	PC	Baseline	PC	Baseline	PC	Baseline	PC
GoogLeNet [42]	71.85	72.09	62.35	64.17	86.63	87.02	73.35	76.02
ResNet-50 [12]	82.01	82.65	73.81	75.92	93.17	93.46	72.16	73.14
DenseNet-161 [11]	78.34	79.10	70.15	71.44	95.15	95.08	78.60	79.56

Table 4. Pairwise Confusion (**PC**) improves localization performance in fine-grained visual classification tasks. On the CUB-200-2011 dataset, PC obtains an average improvement of 3.4% in Mean Intersection-over-Union (IoU) for Grad-CAM bounding boxes for each of the five baseline models.

Method	GoogLeNet	VGG-16	ResNet-50	DenseNet-161	Bilinear-CNN
Mean IoU (Baseline)	0.29	0.31	0.32	0.34	0.37
Mean IoU (PC) - Ours	0.35	0.34	0.35	0.37	0.39

5.3   Improvement in Localization Ability

Recent techniques for improving classification performance in fine-grained recognition are based on summarizing and extracting dense localization information in images [1,2]. Since our technique increases classification accuracy, we wish to understand if the improvement is a result of enhanced CNN localization abilities

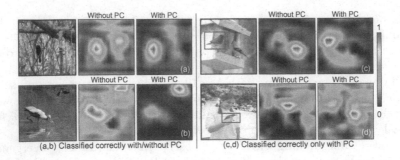

Fig. 3. Pairwise Confusion (**PC**) obtains improved localization performance, as demonstrated here with Grad-CAM heatmaps of the CUB-200-2011 dataset images (left) with a VGGNet-16 model trained without PC (middle) and with PC (right). The objects in (a) and (b) are correctly classified by both networks, and (c) and (d) are correctly classified by PC, but not the baseline network (VGG-16). For all cases, we consistently observe a tighter and more accurate localization with PC, whereas the baseline VGG-16 network often latches on to artifacts, even while making correct predictions.

due to PC. To measure the regions the CNN localizes on, we utilize Gradient-Weighted Class Activation Mapping (Grad-CAM) [53], a method that provides a heatmap of visual saliency as produced by the network. We perform both quantitative and qualitative studies of localization ability of PC-trained models.

Overlap in Localized Regions: To quantify the improvement in localization due to PC, we construct bounding boxes around object regions obtained from Grad-CAM, by thresholding the heatmap values at 0.5, and choosing the largest box returned. We then calculate the mean IoU (intersection-over-union) of the bounding box with the provided object bounding boxes for the CUB-200-2011 dataset. We compare the mean IoU across several models, with and without PC. As summarized in Table 4, we observe an average 3.4% improvement across five different networks, implying better localization accuracy.

Change in Class-Activation Mapping: To qualitatively study the improvement in localization due to PC, we obtain samples from the CUB-200-2011 dataset and visualize the localization regions returned from Grad-CAM for both the baseline and PC-trained VGG-16 model. As shown in Fig. 3, PC models provide tighter, more accurate localization around the target object, whereas sometimes the baseline model has localization driven by image artifacts. Figure 3-(a) has an example of the types of distractions that are often present in FGVC images (the cartoon bird on the right). We see that the baseline VGG-16 network pays significant attention to the distraction, despite making the correct prediction. With PC, we find that the attention is limited almost exclusively to the correct object, as desired. Similarly for Fig. 3-(b), we see that the baseline method latches on to the incorrect bird category, which is corrected by the addition of PC. In Figs. 3-(c-d), we see that the baseline classifier makes incorrect decisions due to poor localization, mistakes that are resolved by PC.

6 Conclusion

In this work, we introduce Pairwise Confusion (PC), an optimization procedure to improve generalizability in fine-grained visual classification (FGVC) tasks by encouraging confusion in output activations. PC improves FGVC performance for a wide class of convolutional architectures while fine-tuning. Our experiments indicate that PC-trained networks show improved localization performance which contributes to the gains in classification accuracy. PC is easy to implement, does not need excessive tuning during training, and does not add significant overhead during test time, in contrast to methods that introduce complex localization-based pooling steps that are often difficult to implement and train. Therefore, our technique should be beneficial to a wide variety of specialized neural network models for applications that demand for fine-grained visual classification or learning from limited labeled data.

Acknowledgements. We would like to thank Dr. Ashok Gupta for his guidance on bird recognition, and Dr. Sumeet Agarwal, Spandan Madan and Ishaan Grover for their feedback at various stages of this work. RF and PG were supported in part by the National Science Foundation under Grant No. IIS1651832, and AD, OG, RR and NN acknowledge the generous support of the MIT Media Lab Consortium.

References

1. Lin, T.Y., RoyChowdhury, A., Maji, S.: Bilinear CNN models for fine-grained visual recognition. In: IEEE International Conference on Computer Vision, pp. 1449–1457 (2015)
2. Jaderberg, M., Simonyan, K., Zisserman, A., Kavukcuoglu, K.: Spatial transformer networks. In: Advances in Neural Information Processing Systems, pp. 2017–2025 (2015)
3. Zhang, Y., et al.: Weakly supervised fine-grained categorization with part-based image representation. IEEE Trans. Image Process. **25**(4), 1713–1725 (2016)
4. Krause, J., Jin, H., Yang, J., Fei-Fei, L.: Fine-grained recognition without part annotations. In: IEEE Conference on Computer Vision and Pattern Recognition, pp. 5546–5555 (2015)
5. Zhang, N., Shelhamer, E., Gao, Y., Darrell, T.: Fine-grained pose prediction, normalization, and recognition. In: International Conference on Learning Representations Workshops (2015)
6. Krause, J., et al.: The unreasonable effectiveness of noisy data for fine-grained recognition. In: Leibe, B., Matas, J., Sebe, N., Welling, M. (eds.) ECCV 2016. LNCS, vol. 9907, pp. 301–320. Springer, Cham (2016). https://doi.org/10.1007/978-3-319-46487-9_19
7. Cui, Y., Zhou, F., Lin, Y., Belongie, S.: Fine-grained categorization and dataset bootstrapping using deep metric learning with humans in the loop. In: IEEE Conference on Computer Vision and Pattern Recognition (2016)
8. Lin, T.Y., Maji, S.: Improved bilinear pooling with CNNs. arXiv preprint arXiv:1707.06772 (2017)
9. Cui, Y., Zhou, F., Wang, J., Liu, X., Lin, Y., Belongie, S.: Kernel pooling for convolutional neural networks. In: IEEE Conference on Computer Vision and Pattern Recognition (2017)

10. Deng, J., Dong, W., Socher, R., Li, L.J., Li, K., Fei-Fei, L.: ImageNet: a large-scale hierarchical image database. In: IEEE Conference on Computer Vision and Pattern Recognition, pp. 248–255 (2009)
11. Huang, G., Liu, Z., van der Maaten, L., Weinberger, K.Q.: Densely connected convolutional networks. In: IEEE Conference on Computer Vision and Pattern Recognition (2017)
12. He, K., Zhang, X., Ren, S., Sun, J.: Deep residual learning for image recognition. In: IEEE Conference on Computer Vision and Pattern Recognition, pp. 770–778 (2016)
13. Yao, B., Khosla, A., Fei-Fei, L.: Combining randomization and discrimination for fine-grained image categorization. In: IEEE Conference on Computer Vision and Pattern Recognition, pp. 1577–1584 (2011)
14. Yao, B., Bradski, G., Fei-Fei, L.: A codebook-free and annotation-free approach for fine-grained image categorization. In: IEEE Conference on Computer Vision and Pattern Recognition, pp. 3466–3473 (2012)
15. Zhang, N., Donahue, J., Girshick, R., Darrell, T.: Part-based R-CNNs for fine-grained category detection. In: Fleet, D., Pajdla, T., Schiele, B., Tuytelaars, T. (eds.) ECCV 2014. LNCS, vol. 8689, pp. 834–849. Springer, Cham (2014). https://doi.org/10.1007/978-3-319-10590-1_54
16. Gao, Y., Beijbom, O., Zhang, N., Darrell, T.: Compact bilinear pooling. In: IEEE Conference on Computer Vision and Pattern Recognition, pp. 317–326 (2016)
17. Wang, Y., Choi, J., Morariu, V., Davis, L.S.: Mining discriminative triplets of patches for fine-grained classification. In: IEEE Conference on Computer Vision and Pattern Recognition, June 2016
18. Ren, S., He, K., Girshick, R., Sun, J.: Faster R-CNN: towards real-time object detection with region proposal networks. In: Advances in Neural Information Processing Systems, pp. 91–99 (2015)
19. Branson, S., Van Horn, G., Belongie, S., Perona, P.: Bird species categorization using pose normalized deep convolutional nets. In: British Machine Vision Conference (2014)
20. Zhang, N., Farrell, R., Darrell, T.: Pose pooling Kernels for sub-category recognition. In: IEEE Computer Vision and Pattern Recognition, pp. 3665–3672 (2012)
21. Moghimi, M., Saberian, M., Yang, J., Li, L.J., Vasconcelos, N., Belongie, S.: Boosted convolutional neural networks (2016)
22. Chopra, S., Hadsell, R., LeCun, Y.: Learning a similarity metric discriminatively, with application to face verification. In: IEEE Conference on Computer Vision and Pattern Recognition, pp. 539–546 (2005)
23. Parikh, D., Grauman, K.: Relative attributes. In: IEEE International Conference on Computer Vision, pp. 503–510 (2011)
24. Dubey, A., Agarwal, S.: Modeling image virality with pairwise spatial transformer networks. arXiv preprint arXiv:1709.07914 (2017)
25. Souri, Y., Noury, E., Adeli, E.: Deep relative attributes. In: Lai, S.-H., Lepetit, V., Nishino, K., Sato, Y. (eds.) ACCV 2016. LNCS, vol. 10115, pp. 118–133. Springer, Cham (2017). https://doi.org/10.1007/978-3-319-54193-8_8
26. Dubey, A., Naik, N., Parikh, D., Raskar, R., Hidalgo, C.A.: Deep learning the city: quantifying urban perception at a global scale. In: Leibe, B., Matas, J., Sebe, N., Welling, M. (eds.) ECCV 2016. LNCS, vol. 9905, pp. 196–212. Springer, Cham (2016). https://doi.org/10.1007/978-3-319-46448-0_12

27. Singh, K.K., Lee, Y.J.: End-to-end localization and ranking for relative attributes. In: Leibe, B., Matas, J., Sebe, N., Welling, M. (eds.) ECCV 2016. LNCS, vol. 9910, pp. 753–769. Springer, Cham (2016). https://doi.org/10.1007/978-3-319-46466-4_45

28. Reed, S., Lee, H., Anguelov, D., Szegedy, C., Erhan, D., Rabinovich, A.: Training deep neural networks on noisy labels with bootstrapping. arXiv preprint arXiv:1412.6596 (2014)

29. Xiao, T., Xia, T., Yang, Y., Huang, C., Wang, X.: Learning from massive noisy labeled data for image classification. In: IEEE Conference on Computer Vision and Pattern Recognition, pp. 2691–2699 (2015)

30. Neelakantan, A., et al.: Adding gradient noise improves learning for very deep networks. arXiv preprint arXiv:1511.06807 (2015)

31. Szegedy, C., Vanhoucke, V., Ioffe, S., Shlens, J., Wojna, Z.: Rethinking the inception architecture for computer vision. In: IEEE Conference on Computer Vision and Pattern Recognition, pp. 2818–2826 (2016)

32. Nilsback, M.E., Zisserman, A.: Automated flower classification over a large number of classes. In: Indian Conference on Computer Vision, Graphics & Image Processing, pp. 722–729 (2008)

33. Wah, C., Branson, S., Welinder, P., Perona, P., Belongie, S.: The caltech-ucsd birds-200-2011 dataset (2011)

34. Krause, J., Stark, M., Deng, J., Fei-Fei, L.: 3D object representations for fine-grained categorization. IEEE International Conference on Computer Vision Workshops, pp. 554–561 (2013)

35. Van Horn, G., et al.: Building a bird recognition app and large scale dataset with citizen scientists: the fine print in fine-grained dataset collection. In: IEEE Conference on Computer Vision and Pattern Recognition, pp. 595–604 (2015)

36. Maji, S., Rahtu, E., Kannala, J., Blaschko, M., Vedaldi, A.: Fine-grained visual classification of aircraft. arXiv preprint arXiv:1306.5151 (2013)

37. Khosla, A., Jayadevaprakash, N., Yao, B., Li, F.F.: Novel dataset for fine-grained image categorization: stanford dogs. In: IEEE International Conference on Computer Vision Workshops on Fine-Grained Visual Categorization, p. 1 (2011)

38. Krizhevsky, A., Nair, V., Hinton, G.: The cifar-10 dataset otkrist (2014)

39. Netzer, Y., Wang, T., Coates, A., Bissacco, A., Wu, B., Ng, A.Y.: Reading digits in natural images with unsupervised feature learning. NIPS Workshop on Deep Learning and Unsupervised Feature Learning, no. 2, p. 5 (2011)

40. Jeffreys, H.: The Theory of Probability. OUP Oxford (1998)

41. Kullback, S., Leibler, R.A.: On information and sufficiency. Ann. Math. Stat. **22**(1), 79–86 (1951)

42. Szegedy, C., et al.: Going deeper with convolutions. In: IEEE Conference on Computer Vision and Pattern Recognition, pp. 1–9 (2015)

43. Székely, G.J., Rizzo, M.L.: Energy statistics: a class of statistics based on distances. J. Stat. Plan. Infer. **143**(8), 1249–1272 (2013)

44. Simonyan, K., Zisserman, A.: Very deep convolutional networks for large-scale image recognition. arXiv preprint arXiv:1409.1556 (2014)

45. Jia, Y., et al.: Caffe: convolutional architecture for fast feature embedding. In: ACM International Conference on Multimedia, pp. 675–678 (2014)

46. Paskze, A., Chintala, S.: Tensors and dynamic neural networks in Python with strong GPU acceleration. https://github.com/pytorch. Accessed 1 Jan 2017

47. Zhang, X., Xiong, H., Zhou, W., Lin, W., Tian, Q.: Picking deep filter responses for fine-grained image recognition. In: IEEE Conference on Computer Vision and Pattern Recognition, pp. 1134–1142 (2016)

48. Liu, M., Yu, C., Ling, H., Lei, J.: Hierarchical joint CNN-based models for fine-grained cars recognition. In: International Conference on Cloud Computing and Security, pp. 337–347 (2016)
49. Simon, M., Gao, Y., Darrell, T., Denzler, J., Rodner, E.: Generalized orderless pooling performs implicit salient matching. In: International Conference on Computer Vision (ICCV) (2017)
50. Kong, S., Fowlkes, C.: Low-rank bilinear pooling for fine-grained classification. In: IEEE Conference on Computer Vision and Pattern Recognition, pp. 7025–7034 (2017)
51. Angelova, A., Zhu, S.: Efficient object detection and segmentation for fine-grained recognition. In: IEEE Conference on Computer Vision and Pattern Recognition, pp. 811–818 (2013)
52. Sharif Razavian, A., Azizpour, H., Sullivan, J., Carlsson, S.: CNN features off-the-shelf: an astounding baseline for recognition. In: IEEE Conference on Computer Vision and Pattern Recognition Workshops, June 2014
53. Selvaraju, R.R., Das, A., Vedantam, R., Cogswell, M., Parikh, D., Batra, D.: Grad-cam: why did you say that? visual explanations from deep networks via gradient-based localization. arXiv preprint arXiv:1610.02391 (2016)

Interpretable Intuitive Physics Model

Tian Ye[1(✉)], Xiaolong Wang[1], James Davidson[2], and Abhinav Gupta[1]

[1] Robotics Institute, Carnegie Mellon University, Pittsburgh, USA
tiany1@andrew.cmu.edu
[2] Third Wave Automation, Pittsburgh, USA

Abstract. Humans have a remarkable ability to use physical common-sense and predict the effect of collisions. But do they understand the underlying factors? Can they predict if the underlying factors have changed? Interestingly, in most cases humans can predict the effects of similar collisions with different conditions such as changes in mass, friction, etc. It is postulated this is primarily because we learn to model physics with meaningful latent variables. This does not imply we can estimate the precise values of these meaningful variables (estimate exact values of mass or friction). Inspired by this observation, we propose an interpretable intuitive physics model where specific dimensions in the bottleneck layers correspond to different physical properties. In order to demonstrate that our system models these underlying physical properties, we train our model on collisions of different shapes (cube, cone, cylinder, spheres etc.) and test on collisions of unseen combinations of shapes. Furthermore, we demonstrate our model generalizes well even when similar scenes are simulated with different underlying properties.

Keywords: Intuitive physics · Interpretable models
Physical properties

1 Introduction

Consider the collision image sequences shown in Fig. 1. When people see these images, they not only recognize the shapes and color of objects but also predict what is going to happen. For example, in the first sequence people can predict that the cylinder is going to rotate while in the second sequence the ball will bounce with no motion on cylinder. But beyond visual prediction, we can even infer the underlying latent factors which can help us explain the difference in visual predictions. For example, a possible explanation of the behavior between the two sequences, if we knew the ball's mass didn't change, is that the first sequence's cylinder was lighter than the ball whereas in the second sequence the cylinder was heavier than the ball. Beyond this we can deduce that the cylinder in the first sequence was much lighter than the one in the second.

Humans demonstrate the profound ability to understand the underlying physics of the world [9,10] and use it to predict the future. We use this physical

V. Ferrari et al. (Eds.): ECCV 2018, LNCS 11216, pp. 89–105, 2018.
https://doi.org/10.1007/978-3-030-01258-8_6

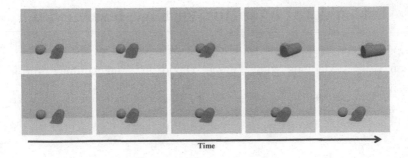

Fig. 1. Interpretable physics models. Consider the sequences shown above. Not only we can predict the future frames of collisions but we can also predict the underlying factors that lead to such an inference. For example, we can infer the mass of cylinder is much higher in second sequence and therefore it hardly moves in the image. Our ability to infer meaningful underlying latent factors inspires us in this paper to learn an interpretable intuitive physics model.

commonsense for not only rich understanding but also for physical interactions. The question arises as to whether this physical commonsense is just an end-to-end model with intermediate representations being a black-box, or explicit and meaningful intermediate representations? For humans, the answer appears to be the latter. We can predict the future if some underlying conditions are changed. For example, we can predict that if we throw the ball in the second sequence with 10x initial speed then the cylinder might rotate.

In this paper, we focus on learning an intuitive model of physics [2,13,17]. Unlike some recent efforts, where the goal is to learn physics in an end-to-end manner with little-to-no constraints on intermediary layers, we focus on learning an **interpretable** model. More specifically, the bottleneck layers in our network model physical properties such as mass, friction, etc.

Learning an interpretable intuitive physics model is, however, quite a challenging task. For example, Wu et al. [25] attempts to build a model but the inverse graphics engine infers physical properties such as mass and friction. These properties are then used with neural physics engine or simulators for prediction. But can we really infer physical properties from the few frames of such collisions? Can we separate friction from mass, restitution by observing the frames? The fact is most of these physical factors are so dependent that it is infeasible to infer the exact values of physical properties. For example we can determine ratios between properties but not the precise values of both (e.g., we can determine the relative mass between two objects but not the exact values for both). This is precisely why in [25] only one factor is inferred from motion and the other factor is directly correlated to the appearance. Furthermore, the learned physics model is domain-specific and will not generalize—even across different shapes.

To tackle these challenges, we propose an interpretable intuitive physics model, where specific dimensions in the bottleneck layers correspond to different physical properties. The bottleneck layer models the distribution rather than infer precise values of mass, speed and friction. In order to demonstrate that our system models these underlying physical properties, we train our model on collision of different shapes (cube, cone, cylinder, spheres etc.) and test on collisions of unseen combinations of shapes altogether. We also demonstrate the richness of our model by predicting the future states under different physical conditions (*e.g.*, how the future frames will look if the friction is doubled).

Our contributions include: (a) an intuitive physics model that disentangles different physical properties in an interpretable way; (b) a staggered training algorithm designed to distinguish the subtleties between different physical quantities; (c) generalization to different shapes and physical quantity combinations; most importantly, (d) the ability to adapt future predictions when physical environments change. Note (d) is different from generalization: the hallucination/prediction is done for a physical scene completely different from the observed first four frames.

2 Related Work

Physical reasoning and learning physical commonsense has raised a lot of interest in recent years [1,5,16–18,28,29,31]. There has been multiple efforts to learn implicit and explicit models of physics commonsense. The underlying goal of most of these systems is to use physics to predict what is going to happen next [6–8,13,14,24,26]. The hope is that if the model can predict what is going to happen next after interacting with objects, it will be forced to understand the physical properties of the objects. For example, [13] tries to learn the physical properties by predicting whether a tower of blocks will fall. [7] proposed to learn a visual predictive model for playing billiards.

However, the first issue is what is the right data to learn this physics model. Researchers have tried a wide spectrum of approaches. For example, many researchers have focused on the task of visual prediction using real-world videos, based on the hypothesis that the predictive model will contain some underlying physical properties [15,21,22]. While videos provide realistic data, there is little to no control on how the data is collected and therefore the implicit models end up learning dynamic models of texture. In order to force physical commonsense learning, people have even tried using videos of physical interactions. For example, Physics101 dataset [24] collects sequences of collisions for this task. But most of the learning still happens passively (random batches). In order to overcome that, recent approaches have tried to learn physics by active interaction using robots [1,6,18]. While there is more control in the process of data collection, there are still issues with lack of diverse data due to most experiments being performed in lab setting with few objects. Finally, one can collect data with full control over several physical parameters using simulation. There has been lot of recent efforts in using simulation to learn physical models [7,13,16,17]. One limitation of these approaches, in terms of data, is the lack of diversity during training, which forces them to learn physics models specific to particular shapes such as blocks, spheres etc. Furthermore, none of these approaches use the full power of simulation to generate a dense set of videos with multiple conditions. Most importantly, none of these approaches learn an interpretable model.

Apart from the question of data, another core issue is how explicit is the representation of physics in these models. To truly understand the object physical properties, it requires our model to be interpretable [3,4,12,23,25]. That is, the model should not only be able to predict the futures, but the latent representations should also indicate the physical properties (e.g., mass, friction and speed) implicitly or explicitly. For example, [3] proposed an Interaction Network which learns to predict the rigid body dynamics of gravitational systems. [25] proposed to explicitly estimate the physical object states and forward this state information to a physics engine for prediction. However, we argue exact values of these physical properties might not be possible due to entanglement of various factors. Instead of estimating the physics states explicitly, our work focuses on separating the dimensions in the bottleneck layer.

Our work is mostly related to the Inverse Graphics Network [12]. It learns a disentangled representation in the graphics code layer where different neurons are encouraged to represent different transformations including pose and light. The system can be trained in an end-to-end manner without providing an explicit state value as supervisions for the graphics code layer. However, unlike the Inverse Graphics Network, where pose and light can be separately inferred from the input images, the dynamics are dependent on the joint set of physical properties in our model (mass, friction and speed), which confound future predictions.

Our model is also related to the visual prediction models [11,15,19,20,22,27,30] in computer vision. For example, [20] proposed to directly predict a sequence of video frames in raw pixels given a sequence of former frames as inputs. Instead of directly predicting the pixels, [22] proposed to predict the optical flows given an input image and then warp the flows on the input images to generate future frames. However, the optical flow estimation is not always correct, introducing errors in the supervisions for training. To tackle this, [30] proposed a bilinear sampling layer which makes the warping process differentiable. This enables them to train their prediction model from pixels to pixels in an end-to-end manner.

3   Dataset

We create a new dataset for our experiments in this paper. The advantage of our proposed dataset is that we have rich combinations of different physical properties as well as different object appearances for different types of collisions (falling over, twisting, bouncing, etc.). Unlike previous datasets, the physical properties in our dataset are independent from the object shapes and appearance. In this way, we can train models which force estimation of physical properties by observing the collisions. More importantly, our testing sets contain novel combinations of object shapes or physical properties that are unseen in the training set. The details of dataset generation is illustrated as following.

We generate our data using the Unreal Engine 4 (UE4) game engine. We use 11 different object combinations with 5 unique basic objects: sphere, cube,

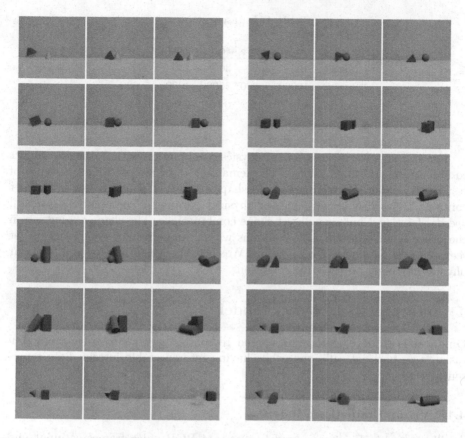

Fig. 2. Our dataset includes 2 object collisions with a variety of shapes. Unlike existing physics datasets which have only one type of shape, our dataset is diverse in terms of different shapes and physical properties of objects.

cylinder, cone, and wedge. We select 3 different physical properties including mass of static object, initial speed of colliding object and friction of floor. For each property, we choose 5 different scales of values as shown in Table 1. For simplicity, we specify a certain scale of parameter by the format {*parameter name*}$_{\{scale\}}$ (e.g., $mass_1$, $friction_4$, $speed_2$). We simulate all the $5 \times 5 \times 5 = 125$ sets of physical combinations. For each set of physical property combination, there are 11 different object combinations and 15 different initial rotation and restitution. Thus in total there are $125 \times 15 \times 11 = 20625$ collisions. Each collision is represented by 5 sample frames with 0.5 s time intervals between them.

The diversity in our dataset is highlighted in Fig. 2. For example, our dataset has cones toppling over; cylinders falling down when hit by a ball and rolling cylinders. We believe this large diversity makes it one of the most challenging datasets to learn and disentangle physical properties.

Table 1. Dataset settings

	$scale_1$	$scale_2$	$scale_3$	$scale_4$	$scale_5$
Mass	100	200	300	400	500
Speed	10000	20000	30000	40000	50000
Friction	0.01	0.02	0.03	0.04	0.05

For training, we use 124 sets of physics combination with 9 different object combinations (16740 collisions). The remaining data are used for two types of testing: (i) parameter testing and (ii) shape testing. The parameter testing set contains 135 collisions with unseen physical parameter combinations ($mass_3$, $speed_3$, $friction_3$) but seen object shape combinations. The shape testing set on the other hand, contains 3750 collisions with 2 unseen shape combinations yet seen physical parameter combinations. We show the generalization ability of our physics model on both testing conditions.

4   Interpretable Physics Model

Our goal is to develop a physics-based reasoning network to solve prediction tasks, *e.g.*, physical collisions, while having interepretable intermediate representations.

4.1   Visual Prediction Model

As illustrated in Fig. 3, our model takes in 4 RGB video frames as input and learns to predict the future 5th RGB frame after the collisions. The model is composed with two parts: an encoder for extracting abstract physical representations and a decoder for future frame prediction.

Encoder for Physics Representations. The encoder is designed to capture the motion of two colliding objects, from which the physical properties can be inferred. Given 4 RGB frames as inputs, they are first forwarded to a ConvNet with AlexNet architecture and ImageNet pre-training. We extract the pool5 feature for each video frame and concatenate the features together as a representation for the input sequence. This feature is then forwarded to two convolutional layers and four fully connected layers to obtain the physics representation.

The physics representation is a 306 dimensional vector, which contains disentangled neurons of mass (dimensions 1 to 25), speed (dimensions 26 to 50), friction (dimensions 51 to 75), and other intrinsic information (dimensions 76 to 306), as shown in Fig. 3. Note that although the vector is disentangled, there is no explicit meanings for each neuron value.

Decoder for Future Prediction. The physics representation is forwarded to a decoder for future frame prediction. Our decoder contains one fully-connected layer followed by six decovolutional layers. Inspired by [22,30], our decoder uses optical flow fields as the output representation instead of directly outputing the RGB raw pixel values. The optical flow is then used to perform warping on the last input frame by a bilinear sampling layer [30] to generate the future frame. Since the bilinear sampling layer is differentiable, the network can be trained in an end-to-end manner with the 5th frame for direct supervision.

There are two major advantages of using optical flow as outputs: (i) it can force the model to learn the factors that cause the changes between two frames; (ii) it allows the model to focus on the changes of the foreground objects.

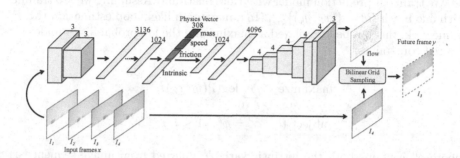

Fig. 3. Model architecture: we follow an encoder-decoder framework. The encoder takes 4 frames of a collision (2 before collision, 1 during collision, and 1 after collision). All inputs are first passed through a pre-trained Alexnet. The Alexnet features are further appended along channels and are sent to two convolution layers and four fully-connected layers. The resulting physics vector is passed through a decoder consisting of one fully-connected layer and six up-sampling convolution layers to produce an optical flow. The number on the convolution layers and transpose convolution layers stands for the kernel size of corresponding layer. The last bilinear grid sampling layer takes the optical flow and the 4th input frame to produce future prediction.

4.2   Learning Objective

Formally, we define the encoder as a function f and the decoder as a function g. Given an image sequence x as inputs (4 frames), our encoder transforms the images into a physically meaningful and disentangled representation $z = f(x)$ and then the decoder transforms this representation into a future frame $y = g(z)$.

The disentangled representation z can be formulated as $z = (\phi^m, \phi^s, \phi^f, \phi^i)$ where $(\cdot, \cdot)$ denotes concatenation. The first part (ϕ^m, ϕ^s, ϕ^f) denotes the combination *physics variable*, which encodes the physical quantities (m, s, f stands for mass, speed, and friction respectively). The second part ϕ^i is the *intrinsic variable*, representing all the other intrinsic properties in the scene (*e.g.*, colors, shapes and initial rotation).

In this paper, we study the effect of varying the values of physical quantities in a two-object collision scenario. Following the strategy in [12], we group our training sequence samples into mini-batches. Inside one mini-batch, only one physical property changes across all the samples and other physical properties remain fixed. We denote $B^p = \{(x_k, y_k)\}_{k=1}^5$ as one mini-batch with 5 sequences, where the only changing property is p (i.e., we use p as a variable to represent either mass, speed or friction).

For each mini-batch B^p during training, we encourage only the dimensions corresponding to the property p to change in z. For example, when training with a mini-batch where only mass is changing, we force the network to have different values in the dimensions for ϕ^m and same values for the rest of the dimensions in z. For simplicity, we further denote the dimensions which relevant to p in z as ϕ_k^p and the rest of the dimensions as $\bar{\phi}_k^p$ for example k.

We train our prediction model with this constraint. Assuming we are training with one batch $B^p = \{(x_k, y_k)\}_{k=1}^5$. In a maximum likelihood estimation (MLE) framework, this can be formulated as maximizing the log-probabilities under the desired constraints:

$$\text{maximize} \quad \sum_{k=1}^5 \log(\mathrm{P}(y_k|x_k)) \tag{1}$$
$$\text{subject to} \quad \bar{\phi}_i^p = \bar{\phi}_j^p, \forall 1 \leq i, j \leq 5$$

where $\bar{\phi}_k^p$ contains both the intrinsic variable inferred from image sequence x_k and inferred physics variables, except for the changing parameter.

In our auto-encoder architecture, the objective function is equivalent to minimizing the l1 distance between the predicted images $\hat{y}_k$ and the ground truth future images y_k:

$$\mathcal{L}_{mle} = \sum_k ||\hat{y}_k - y_k||_1. \tag{2}$$

The constraints in Eq. 1 can be satisfied via minimizing the loss between $\bar{\phi}_k^p$ and the mean of them within the mini-batch $\bar{\phi}^p = \frac{1}{5}\sum_k \bar{\phi}_k^p$ as,

$$\mathcal{L}_{ave} = \sum_k ||\bar{\phi}_k^p - \bar{\phi}^p||_2^2. \tag{3}$$

We apply both losses jointly during training our model with a constant λ balancing between them as,

$$\mathcal{L} = L_{mle} + \lambda L_{ave}. \tag{4}$$

In practice, we set the λ dynamically so that both gradients are maintained in the same magnitude. The value of λ is around $1e-6$.

4.3 Staggered Training

Although we follow the training objective proposed in [12], it is actually non-trivial to directly optimize with this objective. There is a fundamental difference between our problem and the settings in [12]: the physical dynamics are dependent across the set of properties, which confounds training. The same sequence of inputs and output ground-truth might infer different combinations of the physical properties. For example, both large friction and slow speed can lead to small movements of the second object after collision. Thus modifications on training method is required to handle this multi-modality issue.

We propose a staggered training algorithm to alleviate this problem. We first divide the entire training set D into 3 different sets $\{D^p\}$, where p indicates one of the physics properties (mass, speed or friction). Each D^p contains different mini-batches of B^p, inside which the only changing property is indicated by p.

The idea is: instead of training with all the physics properties at the same time in the beginning, we perform curriculum learning. We first train the network with one subset D^p and then progressively add more subsets with different properties into training. In this way, our training set becomes larger and larger through time. By learning the physics properties in this sequential manner, we force the network to recognize new physical properties one by one while keeping the learned properties. In practice, we observe that in the first training session, the network behaves normally. For the following training sessions, the loss will increase in the beginning, and will decrease to roughly the same level as the previous session.

5   Experiments

We now demonstrate the effectiveness and generalization of our model. We will perform two sets of experiments with respect to two different testing sets in our dataset. One tests on unseen physical property combinations but seen shape combinations, and the other tests on unseen shape combinations with seen physical properties. Before going into further analysis, we will first describe the implementation details of our model and the baseline method.

Implementation Details. In total, we trained for 319 epochs. We used ADAM for optimization, with initial learning rate 10^{-6}. During training, each mini-batch mentioned above has 5 sequences. During the training for the first physical quantity, each batch contains 3 mini-batches, which means 15 data in total. For the second round of staggered training, each batch contains 2 mini-batches, one for each physical quantity; similarly, in the third round of training, each batch contains 3 mini-batches, one for each physical quantity.

Baseline Model. Our baseline model learns intuitive physics in an end-to-end manner and post-hoc obtains the dimensions that correspond to different physical properties. We need the disentagled representation because we want to test the generalization when the physical properties are different from input video: *e.g.*, what happens if friction is doubled? What happens if the speed is 1/10th?

For the baseline, we use the same network architecture. Different from our approach, we do not add any constraints on the bottleneck representation layer as in Eq. 1 in the baseline model. However, we still want to obtain the disentangled representation from this baseline for comparison. Recall that we have a subset D^p

for each property p (mass, friction or speed). The examples in each mini-batch inside D^p specify the change of property p. We compute the variances for each neuron in the bottleneck representation for each D^p, and select 25 dimensions with top variances as the vector indicating property p.

5.1   Visual Prediction

Unseen Parameters. First we evaluate if we can predict future pixels when we see a novel combination of physical parameters. Specifically, our model has never seen in training a combination of mass $= 3$, friction $= 3$ and speed $= 3$. Figure 4 shows our interpretable model generalizes well and produces high quality predictions.

Unseen Shape Combinations. Next, we want to explore if our visual prediction model generalizes to different shape combinations using two unseen sets: (a) cone and cuboid; (b) cuboid and sphere. To demonstrate that our model understands each of these physical properties, we show contrasted prediction results for two different values. For example, we will use different friction values $(1, 5)$ but same mass and speed. Comparing these two outputs should highlight how our approach understands the underlying friction values.

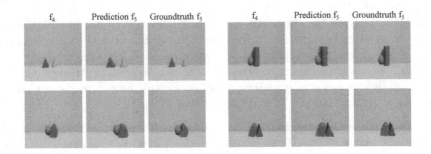

Fig. 4. Prediction results for unseen parameters but seen shapes.

As shown in Fig. 5, our predicted future frame has high quality compared to the ground-truth. We show that our model can generalize the physics reasoning to unseen objects and learn to output different collisions results given different physical environments. For example in the second condition, when the mass of sphere is high (5), our approach can predict it will not move and instead the cube will bounce back. We also compare our approach to baseline quantitatively: our approach has pixel error of 87.3, while baseline has pixel error of 95.6. The results clearly indicate our interpretable model tends to generalize better than an end-to-end model when test conditions are very different.

In addition to the baseline, we also compare our model with two other methods based on optical flow. First, we trained another prediction network using the optical flow computed between the 4th and the 5th frame as direct supervisions,

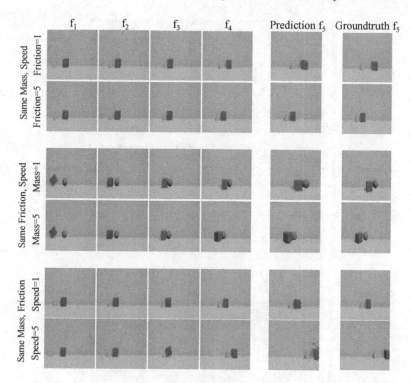

Fig. 5. 4 input frames, the predicted 5th frame and ground-truth for collisions with unseen shape combinations. Contrast the predictions as one of physical property changes. For example, to show our approach understand these shapes, we predict for two different friction values in first case (keeping mass and speed same). The less motion in 2nd case shows that our approach understands the concept of friction.

instead of using the pixels of the 5th frame. For testing, we apply the predicted optical flows on the 4th frame to generate the future frame. The loss between the future frame and the ground-truth 5th frame is 118.8. Second, we computed 3 optical flows of first 4 frames, using which to find a linear model to generate the future optical flow. We apply this optical flow on the 4th frame and compare the result to the ground-truth 5th frame. The error reaches to 292.5. The result shows that our method achieves high precision than using optical flow directly.

5.2   Physical Interpolation

To show our model has actually learnt physics properties, we perform a series of interpolations on the bottleneck representation.

Interpolating Physics Representation Within a Mini-Batch. We first show that the learned bottleneck layer is meaningful and smooth. To demonstrate this, we interpolate between different physical properties and compare our result with the ground-truth. The experiment is conducted in the following way. Let's

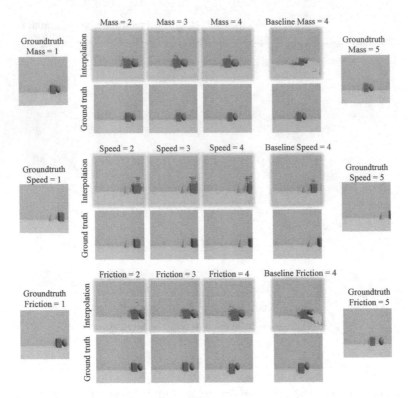

Fig. 6. Interpolation results for physical quantity with different values. Our interpolation results are shown with blue frames. Images with red frame in last column represents the interpolation results for baseline when physical quantities equal to 4. (Color figure online)

take mass as an example: given a mini-batch where only mass changes, we use the encoder to get the physics vector $z_1 = (\phi_1^m, \phi_1^s, \phi_1^f, \phi_1^i)$ from mass$_1$ data and $z_5 = (\phi_5^m, \phi_5^s, \phi_5^f, \phi_5^i)$ from mass$_5$ data. To estimate the physics vector for mass$_i$, we interpolate a new mass variable $\hat{\phi}_i^m = (1 - 0.25i) \cdot \phi_1^m + 0.25i \cdot \phi_5^m$ and use this to create a new physics vector $\hat{z}_i = (\hat{\phi}_i^m, \phi_1^s, \phi_1^f, \phi_1^i)$. We pass the new vector to the decoder to predict the optical flows, which are warped to the 4th image in sequence i via the bilinear sampling layer, and generate the future frame.

We perform the same set of experiments for the baseline model. Quantitatively, we evaluate the prediction using the sum of mean square error for each pixel, as shown in Table 2, which shows that our method is significantly better than the baseline. We also visualized the results in Fig. 6. Interestingly, our interpolation results are also very close to the ground-truth. On the other hand, baseline models failed easily when there is a dramatic change during interpolations.

We also trained another model which takes physics parameters and the optical flows of first 4-frame as inputs, and predicts the future frame. This model performs much worse than our model in the interpolation test as shown in Fig. 6.

Table 2. Interpolation result. The numbers are pixel prediction errors

Method	Shape 2	Shape 3	Shape 4	Shape 5	Parameter 3
Baseline	117.76	130.41	154.78	173.80	299.88
Flow + Physics	272.02	317.79	328.06	336.54	671.51
Ours	**110.93**	**119.73**	**131.70**	**138.04**	**154.09**

We believe a ground-truth physics parameter based approach focuses on classification instead of learning an intuitive physics model. In interpolation experiments, the model cannot separate physics information from the optical flow features.

From these comparison, we can see that only by learning interpretable representations, we can generate reasonable prediction results after interpolations.

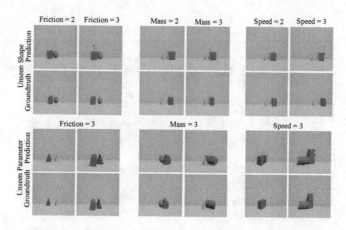

Fig. 7. Prediction by learning double, triple ratio relation for different physical entities. Top: the result with unseen shapes. Bottom: result with unseen parameters.

Changing Physical Properties. In this experiment, we show that physics variables learned by our model are interpretable by finding a mapping between different scale of the same physical property. Specifically, we want to see: can we predict the future if the mass is doubled while all other physics conditions remain the same? For each physical quantity p, we train two networks F_2^p and F_3^p which learns to double or triple the scale of a physical property. For example, we can project the physics representation of $mass_1$ to $mass_3$ by using the network F_3^p. The network architecture for both F_2^p and F_3^p is a simple 2-layer fully connected network with 256 hidden neurons per layer. These two networks can be trained using the physical representations inferred by our encoder with the training data.

In testing time, we apply the similar interpolation as the last experiment. The only difference is that instead of using an interpolation between two relevant representations, we use the fully connected network to generate the new representations. We again evaluate the quantitative results by computing the mean square error over the pixels. As shown in Table 3, we have a larger performance gain in this setting compared to the baseline. Figure 7 shows the prediction results of our model when the physics property is enlarged from scale 1 to 2 and 3, which are all very close to the ground-truth. This is another evidence showing our physics representation is interpretable and generalizes significantly better.

Table 3. Ratio result. Comparing visual prediction when underlying physical parameters are changed by a factor

Method	Shape ratio 2 ($\downarrow$)	Shape ratio 3 ($\downarrow$)	Parameter ratio 3 ($\downarrow$)
Baseline	345.60	310.37	490.92
Ours	**110.79**	**124.00**	**157.10**

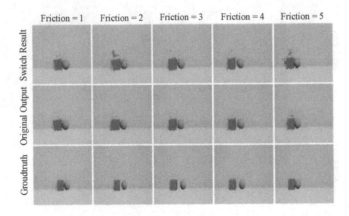

Fig. 8. Prediction when physical property vector from one shape combination is applied to a different shape combinations. The first row shows switched result; the second row shows the prediction without switching; the third row shows ground-truth.

Switching Between the Object Shapes. In experiments above, we interpolate the physics representation and apply them to the same object shape combinations. In this experiment, for a physical property p, we replace the corresponding variable ϕ^p of one collision with the variable from another collision with different objects but the same p value. We visualize the results in Fig. 8, where the first line shows the predictions when we replace current ϕ^p with one from another shape combination. The results are almost same as the original prediction and the ground-truth, which means that the physical variable of same value can be transferred among different shape combinations. It also shows that the dimensions of physics and other dimensions are independent and can be appended easily.

6 Conclusions

We demonstrated an interpretable intuitive physics model that generalizes across scenes with different underlying properties and object shapes. Most importantly, our model is able to predict the future when physical environment changes. To achieve this we proposed a model where specific dimensions in the bottleneck layers correspond to different physical properties. However, often physical properties are dependent and intertangled, so we introduced a training curriculum and generalized loss function that was shown to outperform the baseline approaches.

Acknowledgement. Research was sponsored by the Army Research Office and was accomplished under Grant Number W911NF-18-1-0019. The views and conclusions contained in this document are those of the authors and should not be interpreted as representing the official policies, either expressed or implied, of the Army Research Office or the U.S. Government. The U.S. Government is authorized to reproduce and distribute reprints for Government purposes notwithstanding any copyright notation herein. We would like to thank Yin Li and Siyuan Qi for helpful discussions.

References

1. Agrawal, P., Nair, A., Abbeel, P., Malik, J., Levine, S.: Learning to poke by poking: experiential learning of intuitive physics. In: Neural Information Processing Systems (NIPS) (2016)
2. Battaglia, P., Pascanu, R., Lai, M., Rezende, D.J., et al.: Interaction networks for learning about objects, relations and physics. In: Neural Information Processing Systems (NIPS) (2016)
3. Battaglia, P., Pascanu, R., Lai, M., Rezende, D.J., et al.: Interaction networks for learning about objects, relations and physics. In: Neural Information Processing Systems (NIPS) (2016)
4. Chang, M.B., Ullman, T., Torralba, A., Tenenbaum, J.B.: A compositional object-based approach to learning physical dynamics. In: International Conference on Learning Representations (ICLR) (2017)
5. Edmonds, M., et al.: Feeling the force: integrating force and pose for fluent discovery through imitation learning to open medicine bottles. In: Intelligent Robots and Systems (IROS) (2017)
6. Finn, C., Goodfellow, I., Levine, S.: Unsupervised learning for physical interaction through video prediction. In: Neural Information Processing Systems (NIPS) (2016)
7. Fragkiadaki, K., Agrawal, P., Levine, S., Malik, J.: Learning visual predictive models of physics for playing billiards. In: International Conference on Learning Representations (ICLR) (2016)
8. Grzeszczuk, R., Terzopoulos, D., Hinton, G.: Neuroanimator: fast neural network emulation and control of physics-based models. In: Proceedings of the 25th Annual Conference on Computer Graphics and Interactive Techniques, pp. 9–20. ACM (1998)
9. Hamrick, J., Battaglia, P., Tenenbaum, J.B.: Internal physics models guide probabilistic judgments about object dynamics. In: Proceedings of the 33rd Annual Conference of the Cognitive Science Society (2011)

10. Hamrick, J.B., Battaglia, P.W., Griffiths, T.L., Tenenbaum, J.B.: Inferring mass in complex scenes by mental simulation. Cognition (2016)
11. Kitani, K.M., Ziebart, B.D., Bagnell, J.A., Hebert, M.: Activity forecasting. In: Fitzgibbon, A., Lazebnik, S., Perona, P., Sato, Y., Schmid, C. (eds.) ECCV 2012. LNCS, vol. 7575, pp. 201–214. Springer, Heidelberg (2012). https://doi.org/10.1007/978-3-642-33765-9_15
12. Kulkarni, T.D., Whitney, W.F., Kohli, P., Tenenbaum, J.: Deep convolutional inverse graphics network. In: Neural Information Processing Systems (NIPS) (2015)
13. Lerer, A., Gross, S., Fergus, R.: Learning physical intuition of block towers by example. In: International Conference on Machine Learning (ICML) (2016)
14. Li, W., Azimi, S., Leonardis, A., Fritz, M.: To fall or not to fall: a visual approach to physical stability prediction. arXiv:1604.00066 (2016)
15. Mathieu, M., Couprie, C., LeCun, Y.: Deep multi-scale video prediction beyond mean square error. In: International Conference on Learning Representations (ICLR) (2016)
16. Mottaghi, R., Bagherinezhad, H., Rastegari, M., Farhadi, A.: Newtonian scene understanding: unfolding the dynamics of objects in static images. In: Computer Vision and Pattern Recognition (CVPR) (2016)
17. Mottaghi, R., Rastegari, M., Gupta, A., Farhadi, A.: "What happens if..." learning to predict the effect of forces in images. In: Leibe, B., Matas, J., Sebe, N., Welling, M. (eds.) ECCV 2016. LNCS, vol. 9908, pp. 269–285. Springer, Cham (2016). https://doi.org/10.1007/978-3-319-46493-0_17
18. Pinto, L., Gandhi, D., Han, Y., Park, Y.-L., Gupta, A.: The curious robot: learning visual representations via physical interactions. In: Leibe, B., Matas, J., Sebe, N., Welling, M. (eds.) ECCV 2016. LNCS, vol. 9906, pp. 3–18. Springer, Cham (2016). https://doi.org/10.1007/978-3-319-46475-6_1
19. Qi, S., Jia, B., Zhu, S.C.: Generalized earley parser: bridging symbolic grammars and sequence data for future prediction. In: International Conference on Machine Learning (ICML) (2018)
20. Srivastava, N., Mansimov, E., Salakhutdinov, R.: Unsupervised learning of video representations using LSTMs. In: International Conference on Machine Learning (ICML) (2015)
21. Vondrick, C., Pirsiavash, H., Torralba, A.: Generating videos with scene dynamics. In: Neural Information Processing Systems (NIPS) (2016)
22. Walker, J., Doersch, C., Gupta, A., Hebert, M.: An uncertain future: forecasting from static images using variational autoencoders. In: Leibe, B., Matas, J., Sebe, N., Welling, M. (eds.) ECCV 2016. LNCS, vol. 9911, pp. 835–851. Springer, Cham (2016). https://doi.org/10.1007/978-3-319-46478-7_51
23. Watters, N., Tacchetti, A., Weber, T., Pascanu, R., Battaglia, P., Zoran, D.: Visual interaction networks. In: Neural Information Processing Systems (NIPS) (2017)
24. Wu, J., Lim, J.J., Zhang, H., Tenenbaum, J.B., Freeman, W.T.: Physics 101: learning physical object properties from unlabeled videos. In: BMVC (2016)
25. Wu, J., Lu, E., Kohli, P., Freeman, W.T., Tenenbaum, J.B.: Learning to see physics via visual de-animation. In: Neural Information Processing Systems (NIPS) (2017)
26. Wu, J., Yildirim, I., Lim, J.J., Freeman, W.T., Tenenbaum, J.B.: Galileo: perceiving physical object properties by integrating a physics engine with deep learning. In: Neural Information Processing Systems (NIPS) (2015)
27. Xue, T., Wu, J., Bouman, K.L., Freeman, W.T.: Visual dynamics: probabilistic future frame synthesis via cross convolutional networks. In: Neural Information Processing Systems (NIPS) (2016)

28. Zhang, R., Wu, J., Zhang, C., Freeman, W.T., Tenenbaum, J.B.: A comparative evaluation of approximate probabilistic simulation and deep neural networks as accounts of human physical scene understanding. In: Proceedings of the 38th Annual Conference of the Cognitive Science Society (2016)
29. Zheng, B., Zhao, Y., Yu, J., Ikeuchi, K., Zhu, S.C.: Scene understanding by reasoning stability and safety. Int. J. Comput. Vis. (IJCV) **112**, 221–238 (2015)
30. Zhou, T., Tulsiani, S., Sun, W., Malik, J., Efros, A.A.: View synthesis by appearance flow. In: Leibe, B., Matas, J., Sebe, N., Welling, M. (eds.) ECCV 2016. LNCS, vol. 9908, pp. 286–301. Springer, Cham (2016). https://doi.org/10.1007/978-3-319-46493-0_18
31. Zhu, Y., Jiang, C., Zhao, Y., Terzopoulos, D., Zhu, S.C.: Inferring forces and learning human utilities from videos. In: Computer Vision and Pattern Recognition (CVPR) (2016)

Deep Multi-task Learning to Recognise Subtle Facial Expressions of Mental States

Guosheng Hu[1,2(✉)], Li Liu[3], Yang Yuan[1], Zehao Yu[4], Yang Hua[2],
Zhihong Zhang[4], Fumin Shen[5], Ling Shao[3], Timothy Hospedales[6],
Neil Robertson[1,2], and Yongxin Yang[6,7]

[1] Anyvision, Queens Road, Belfast, UK
huguosheng100@gmail.com
[2] ECIT, Queens University of Belfast, Belfast, UK
[3] Inception Institute of Artificial Intelligence, Abu Dhabi, UAE
[4] Software Department, Xiamen University, Xiamen, China
[5] University of Electronic Science and Technology of China, Chengdu, China
[6] School of Informatics, University of Edinburgh, Edinburgh, UK
[7] Yang's Accounting Consultancy Ltd., London, UK

Abstract. Facial expression recognition is a topical task. However, very
little research investigates subtle expression recognition, which is important for mental activity analysis, deception detection, etc. We address
subtle expression recognition through convolutional neural networks
(CNNs) by developing multi-task learning (MTL) methods to effectively
leverage a side task: facial landmark detection. Existing MTL methods
follow a design pattern of shared bottom CNN layers and task-specific top
layers. However, the sharing architecture is usually heuristically chosen,
as it is difficult to decide which layers should be shared. Our approach
is composed of (1) a novel MTL framework that automatically learns
which layers to share through optimisation under tensor trace norm regularisation and (2) an invariant representation learning approach that
allows the CNN to leverage tasks defined on disjoint datasets without
suffering from dataset distribution shift. To advance subtle expression
recognition, we contribute a Large-scale Subtle Emotions and Mental
States in the Wild database (LSEMSW). LSEMSW includes a variety
of cognitive states as well as basic emotions. It contains 176K images,
manually annotated with 13 emotions, and thus provides the first *subtle*
expression dataset large enough for training deep CNNs. Evaluations on
LSEMSW and 300-W (landmark) databases show the effectiveness of
the proposed methods. In addition, we investigate transferring knowledge
learned from LSEMSW database to traditional (non-subtle) expression
recognition. We achieve very competitive performance on Oulu-Casia
NIR&Vis and CK+ databases via transfer learning.

Electronic supplementary material The online version of this chapter (https://
doi.org/10.1007/978-3-030-01258-8_7) contains supplementary material, which is
available to authorized users.

1   Introduction

Facial expressions convey important information about the emotional and mental states of a person. Facial expression understanding has wide applications and has been most widely studied in the form of emotion recognition. The classic problem is to recognise six basic emotions [39] (Fig. 1, top) based on facial expressions [21]. This problem is now considered solved for posed, exaggerated expressions in lab conditions (Fig. 1, top); but is still an open question for realistic subtly exhibited expressions where, for example, even a slight tightening of the lips can be a sign that someone is angry. Subtle expressions (Fig. 1, Row 2&3) are important for mental activity analysis and deception detection [55].

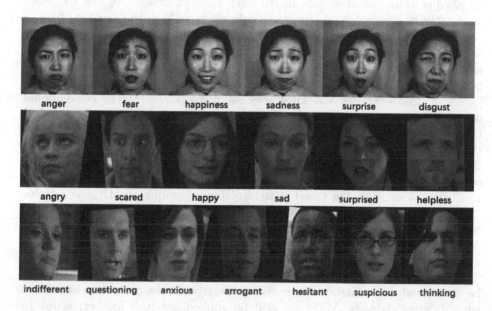

Fig. 1. Conventional emotion recognition (Row 1) vs our LSEMSW (Row 2 and 3). Our dataset contains mental states that are richer – including a variety of cognitive states, conveyed by *subtle* expressions, and exhibited in the wild.

In this paper we go significantly beyond existing work on emotion recognition in two ways, to address: Recognition of *subtly* expressed rather than exaggerated emotions; and recognition of a wider range of mental states beyond the basic six emotions, including for the first time cognitive states. To address these goals we work from two directions: providing (1) improved deep learning algorithms, and (2) a big dataset covering subtle emotions and cognitive states. Specifically, *first*, we introduce a new deep learning approach to subtle expression recognition, based on a novel multi-task learning architecture to exploit a side task: landmark detection. *Second*, in order to benchmark the new proposed task, and to train our deep learning model, we also contribute a new large scale dataset: Large-scale

Subtle Emotions and Mental States in the Wild (LSEMSW). The expressions of this database are much more realistically subtle compared to existing posed and exaggerated benchmarks (Fig. 1). The dataset is also much richer than most existing benchmarks – containing 13 emotions and cognitive states (Fig. 1 Row 2 & 3) defined by 2 psychologists.

Deep MTL Algorithms. We build on deep CNNs, which have achieved great success in many vision tasks. As per classic studies that use landmark locations [54] and distances [50] for basic emotion recognition; we observe that when emotional/mental state is conveyed by subtle expressions, a salient cue is often slight movements of facial landmarks (e.g., eye widening). To provide this prior knowledge as an inductive bias in our deep network design, we aim to detect landmarks and mental state simultaneously via multi-task learning (MTL).

Classic MTL methods focused on improving performance by cross-task knowledge transfer through shared task representations in linear models [2] or kernel-based nonlinear models [10]. More recently, interest in MTL for neural networks has been grown in popularity (again [5]), in order to combine the power of deep networks and knowledge sharing [24,27,61]. The conventional deep MTL pre-defines the first few CNN layers as shared by multiple tasks, and then forks into different layers for different tasks with different losses. However, this approach is heuristic and, without theoretical guidance about how to choose sharing structure, it is often left to 'grad student descent'. This is particularly tricky with increasingly deep CNN architectures. For example ResNet [17] has 156 layers, leading to 156 possible architectures assuming exactly one fork, or $(B_T)^{156}$ architectures (where T is the number of tasks and $B.$ is the Bell number, i.e., the number of partitions of a set) more generally. To address this, we develop a new tensor trace norm approach that automatically determines how much every layer should be shared, and without assuming a single fork point.

Furthermore we address the issue that MTL typically requires all tasks to be annotated on a single dataset to be effective. If the tasks are associated with different datasets, MTL can still be applied but it is ineffective due to the negative effect of cross-dataset distribution shift outweighing the benefit of MTL-based knowledge sharing. By integrating a distribution alignment strategy [13], we can use disjoint training sets (tasks defined on different datasets), thus making MTL much more flexible and widely applicable. In the context of emotion recognition, this allows us to leverage existing datasets to provide auxiliary tasks such as facial landmark localisation in 300-W dataset [45].

Subtle **Expression Database.** Most existing expression databases [8,11,20,37] only contain images with strong expression of exaggerated emotions, and *subtle* expression analysis is rarely investigated. To address this gap, we contribute LSEMSW, the first big database for *subtle* expression analysis. LSEMSW only contains images with realistically subtle expressions. In addition, the existing databases have some limitations: they either contain only emotions without other mental states [8,11], are noisy due to automated annotation [11], or are too small for deep learning [8]. Our LSEMSW contains other (non-emotional) cognitive mental states, compared to existing datasets focusing on six basic emotions [8]. LSEMSW contains 176K images, making it multiple orders of magnitude larger than some alternatives (E.g., 1500 images in AFEW [8]), and all images are manually labelled rather than automatically annotated by algorithms [11]. Finally, we contrast *micro-expression* recognition, which is to recognise an emotion that a person is trying to conceal [25]. This is related in addressing subtle cues, but different in that it is typically performed on video rather than images.

Contributions. In summary, our contributions are: (i) Unlike standard heuristically designed deep MTL, we propose an end-to-end soft sharing strategy that flexibly learns where, what and how much to share by optimising the trace norm regularised parameters. We further embed a distribution alignment method in order to maintain good performance when the per-task training sets are disjoint. (ii) We contribute our LSEMSW dataset consisting of 176K images manually annotated with 13 emotions and cognitive states. This is the first database for *subtle* expression analysis, the first database for recognising *cognitive* states from facial expressions, and it is big enough for deep CNN training. We will release this database to advance mental state recognition in the deep learning era. In addition, the source code and trained models will be made publicly available. (iii) We show that LSEMSW can benefit Traditional (non-subtle) expression recognition (TNER), by using transfer learning to achieve very competitive TNER performance on Oulu-Casia NIR&Vis [62] and CK+ [29] databases.

2   Methodology

2.1   Preliminaries

Matrix-Based Multi-task Learning. Matrix-based MTL is usually built on linear models, i.e., each task is parameterised by a D-dimensional weight vector $\mathbf{w}$, and the model prediction is $\hat{y} = \mathbf{x}^T \mathbf{w}$, where $\mathbf{x}$ is a D-dimensional feature vector representing an instance. The objective function for matrix-based MTL can be written as $\sum_{i=1}^{T} \sum_{j=1}^{N^{(i)}} \ell(y_j^{(i)}, \mathbf{x}_j^{(i)} \cdot \mathbf{w}^{(i)}) + \lambda \Omega(W)$. Here $\ell(y, \hat{y})$ is a loss function of the true label $\mathbf{y}$ and predicted label $\hat{\mathbf{y}}$. T is the number of tasks, and for the i-th task there are $N^{(i)}$ training instances. Assuming the dimensionality of every task's feature is the same, the models $\mathbf{w}^{(i)}$ are of the same size. Then the collection of $\mathbf{w}^{(i)}$s forms a $D \times T$ matrix W where the i-th column is a linear model for the i-th task. A regulariser $\Omega(W)$ is exploited to encourage W to be a low-rank matrix. Some choices include the $\ell_{2,1}$ norm [2], and trace norm [19].

Tensor-Based Multi-task Learning. In standard MTL, each task is indexed by a single factor. But in some real-world problems, tasks are indexed by multiple factors. The collection of linear models for all tasks is then a 3-way tensor $\mathcal{W}$ of size $D \times T_1 \times T_2$, where T_1 and T_2 are two task indices. In this case, tensor norm regularisers $\Omega(\mathcal{W})$ have been used [51]. For example, sum of the trace norms on all matriciations [44] and scaled latent trace norm [56]. However, such prior tensor norm-based regularisers have been limited to shallow models. We develop methods to allow application of tensor norms end-to-end in deep networks.

Deep Multi-task Learning. With the success of deep learning, many studies have investigated deep MTL [28,36,41,58,61]. E.g., using a CNN to find facial landmarks as well as recognise facial attributes [41,61]. The standard approach [28,41,61] is to share the bottom layers of a deep network and use ask-specific parameters for the top layers. We call this type of 'predefined' sharing strategy 'hard' sharing. This 'hard' sharing based architecture can be traced back to 2000s [3]. However, it is impossible to try every hard sharing possibility in modern CNN architectures with many layers. Limited very recent work on automating deep MTL [36,58] suffers from the need to specify discrete ranks at every layer. This introduces an additional sharing-strength hyper-parameter per-layer, and crucially prevents knowledge sharing when working with only two tasks, as it increases rather than decreases the number of parameters. Our approach learns soft sharing at all layers controlled by a single sharing strength hyper-parameter.

2.2   Trace Norm-Based Knowledge Sharing for Deep MTL

In this work, we focus on deep MTL, in particular, CNN-based MTL. One CNN contains multiple convolution layers, each consisting of a number of convolutional kernels. A convolutional layer is parameterised by a 4-way tensor of size $H \times W \times C \times M$ where H, W, C, M are the height, width, number of channels, number of filters respectively. Since convolutional layers are structured as tensors, we use tensor-based theory, in particular, tensor trace norm, to achieve knowledge sharing. Unlike 'hard sharing' strategy, we propose a flexible 'soft' parameter sharing strategy that automatically learns where, what and how much to share by optimising the tensor trace norm regularised parameters.

Knowledge Sharing. To *learn* a parameter sharing strategy, we propose the following framework: For T tasks, each is modelled by a neural network of the same architecture. The T networks are stacked horizontally in a layer-wise fashion, i.e. we assume the architectures of different tasks' networks are the same, so that we can collect the parameters in the same level (layer) then stack them to form a one-order higher tensor, e.g., for convolution layer, $4D \rightarrow 5D$. This process is repeated for every layer. With this stacking of parameters into higher order tensors, we can apply a tensor trace norm regulariser to each in order to achieve knowledge sharing. A schematic example with 2-task learning is illustrated in Fig. 2. Learning the CNN with tensor trace norm regularisation means that the ranks of these tensors are minimised where possible, and thus knowledge is shared where possible. Since trace norm is performed on the stacked parameters of all the layers, we can control the parameter sharing for all layers with a single hyperparameter of regularisation strength.

Tensor Norms. Since tensor trace norm is the core of our approach, we review this topic. Matrix trace norm is the sum of a matrix's singular values $||X||_* = \sum_{i=1} \sigma_i$. It is the tightest convex relation of matrix rank [42]. Thus when directly restricting the rank of a matrix is challenging, trace norm serves as a good proxy. The trace norm of a tensor can be formulated as the sum of trace norms of matrices. However unlike for matrices, the trace norm of a tensor is not unique because tensors can be factored in many ways e.g., Tucker [53] and Tensor-Train [38] decompositions. We propose three tensor trace norms here, corresponding to three variants of the proposed method.

For an N-way tensor $\mathcal{W}$ of size $D_1 \times D_2 \times \cdots \times D_N$. We define

$$\textbf{Last Axis Flattening (LAF)} \quad ||\mathcal{W}||_* = \gamma||\mathcal{W}_{(N)}||_* \tag{1}$$

where $\mathcal{W}_{(i)} := \text{reshape}(\text{permute}(\mathcal{W}, [i, 1, \ldots, i-1, i+1 \ldots, N]), [D_i, \prod_{j \neq i} D_j])$ is the mode-i tensor flattening. This is the simplest definition. Given that in our framework, the last axis of tensor indexes the tasks, i.e., $D_N = T$, it is the most straightforward way to adapt matrix-based MTL – i.e. by reshaping the $D_1 \times D_2 \times \cdots \times T$ tensor to $D_1 D_2 \cdots \times T$ matrix.

To advance, we define two kinds of tensor trace norm that are closely connected with Tucker-rank (obtained by Tucker decomposition) and TT-rank (obtained by Tensor Train decomposition).

$$\textbf{Tucker} \quad ||\mathcal{W}||_* = \sum_{i=1}^{N} \gamma_i ||\mathcal{W}_{(i)}||_* \tag{2}$$

$$\textbf{TT} \quad ||\mathcal{W}||_* = \sum_{i=1}^{N-1} \gamma_i ||\mathcal{W}_{[i]}||_* \tag{3}$$

Here $\mathcal{W}_{[i]}$ is yet another way to unfold the tensor, which is obtained by $\mathcal{W}_{[i]} = \text{reshape}(\mathcal{W}, [D_1 D_2 \ldots D_i, D_{i+1} D_{i+2} \ldots D_N])$. Note that unlike LAF, Tucker and TT also encourage within-task parameter sharing, e.g., sharing across filters in a neural network context.

Optimisation. For the regularisers defined in Eqs. (1)–(3), we see that tensor trace norm is formulated as the sum of matrix trace norms. Gradient-based methods are not commonly used to optimise matrix trace norm. However in order to apply trace norm-based regularisation end-to-end in CNNs, we wish to optimise trace norm and standard CNN losses using a single gradient-based optimiser such as Tensorflow [1]. Thus we derive a (sub-)gradient descent method for trace norm minimisation.

We start from an equivalent definition of trace norm instead of the sum of singular values, $||W||_* = \text{Trace}((W^T W)^{\frac{1}{2}}) = \text{Trace}((WW^T)^{\frac{1}{2}})$ where $(\cdot)^{\frac{1}{2}}$ is the matrix square root. Given the property of the differential of the trace function, $\partial \text{Trace}(f(A)) = f'(A^T) : \partial A$, where the colon : denotes the double-dot (a.k.a. Frobenius) product, i.e., $A : B = \text{Trace}(AB^T)$. In this case, $A = W^T W$, $f(\cdot) = (\cdot)^{\frac{1}{2}}$ thus $f'(\cdot) = \frac{1}{2}(\cdot)^{-\frac{1}{2}}$, so we have,

$$\partial \operatorname{Trace}((W^TW)^{\frac{1}{2}}) = \frac{1}{2}(W^TW)^{-\frac{1}{2}} : \partial(W^TW) = W(W^TW)^{-\frac{1}{2}} : \partial W$$

Therefore we have $\frac{\partial \|W\|_*}{\partial W} = W(W^TW)^{-\frac{1}{2}}$. In the case that W^TW is not invertible, we can derive that $\frac{\partial \|W\|_*}{\partial W} = (WW^T)^{-\frac{1}{2}}W$ similarly. To avoid the check on whether W^TW is invertible, and more importantly, to avoid the explicit computation of the matrix square root, which is usually not numerically safe, we use the following procedure.

First, we assume W is an $N \times P$ matrix $(N > P)$ and let the (full) SVD of W be $W = U\Sigma V^T$. Σ is an $N \times P$ matrix in the form of $\Sigma = [\Sigma_*; \mathbf{0}_{(N-P) \times P}]$. Then we have

$$W(W^TW)^{-\frac{1}{2}} = U\Sigma V^T(V\Sigma_*^2 V^T)^{-\frac{1}{2}} = U\Sigma V^T V\Sigma_*^{-1}V^T$$
$$= U\Sigma\Sigma_*^{-1}V^T = U[I_P; \mathbf{0}_{(N-P) \times P}]V^T$$

This indicates that we only need to compute the truncated SVD, i.e., $W = U_*\Sigma_*V_*^T$, and $W(W^TW)^{-\frac{1}{2}} = U_*V_*^T$. For the case when $N < P$, we have the same result as,

$$(WW^T)^{-\frac{1}{2}}W = (U\Sigma_*^2 U^T)^{-\frac{1}{2}}U\Sigma V^T = U\Sigma_*^{-1}U^T U\Sigma V^T$$
$$= U\Sigma_*^{-1}\Sigma V^T = U[I_N, \mathbf{0}_{(P-N) \times N}]V^T$$

Now we have an agreed formulation: $\frac{\partial \|W\|_*}{\partial W} = U_*V_*^T$ that we can use for gradient descent. Though exact SVD is expensive, we find that a fast randomized SVD [16] works well in practice.

2.3 Adversarial Domain Alignment (ADA)

In our application, the main task's dataset (LSEMSW) is disjoint to the auxiliary task's (300-W) [45]. This leads to the distribution shift problem across the two tasks, reducing the performance of MTL. Inspired by [14] and [13], we propose to confuse the dataset identity for dealing with this problem.

We use ADA to solve this problem: One classifier aims to distinguish which distribution (dataset) the features of each task are from. If features are distinguishable the domain shift is clearly greater than if they are indistinguishable. ADA trains them to be indistinguishable. We assume $T \geq 2$ tasks (indexed by t), each with its own dataset $\{X_t, y_t\}$. Task t is modelled by a CNN parametrised by $\Theta_t = \{\theta_t^{(1)}, \theta_t^{(2)}, \ldots, \theta_t^{(L)}\}$ where L is the number of layers, and we split Θ_t into two sets at the l-th layer. Conventionally we choose $l = L-1$, i.e., the penultimate layer, so we have $\Theta_t = \Theta_t^* \cup \{\theta_t^{(L)}\}$ where $\Theta_t^* = \{\theta_t^{(1)}, \theta_t^{(2)}, \ldots, \theta_t^{(L-1)}\}$. We then build a multi-class classification problem that uses a neural network parametrised by Φ to predict the database identity from $f_{\Theta_t}(X_t)$, the penultimate layer representation. Letting Z be the stacked features for all tasks i.e., $Z = [f_{\Theta_t^*}(X_1) \ldots f_{\Theta_t^*}(X_T)]$, we optimise

$$\max_{\Theta_1^* \ldots \Theta_T^*} \min_{\Phi} \ell(g_\Phi([f_{\Theta_1^*}(X_1) \ldots f_{\Theta_T^*}(X_T)]), y) \tag{4}$$

where y is one-hot label to indicate which distribution the feature is from; g_Φ is a classifier, e.g. softmax; ℓ is a cross entropy loss.

For our application, we have 2 tasks in total, so it is reduced to a binary classification problem. For the task identity prediction neural network, we use a 2-hidden-layer MLP (multilayer perceptron) with 512 (input feature) -128 (hidden layer)-64 (hidden layer) -2 (classifier) architecture.

2.4   CNN Architecture for Deep MTL

In this study, we implement our deep MTL based on the well known Residual Network (ResNet) architecture [17]. We use the compact 34-layer ResNet with 33 convolutional layers and 1 fully connected layer detailed in [17]. We perform trace norm on the weights of all the 33 shareable convolutional layers of the stacked networks. In addition, the original 34-layer ResNet has a 7×7 global average pooling before loss layer, adapting to the 224×224 input. To adapt to our 96×96 input, we use 3×3 average pooling instead. The Adversarial Domain Alignment is performed on the activations (feature map) of this average pooling. The classification loss for mental state recognition is softmax cross-entropy loss, while the loss for landmark detection is l_1 regression loss. The architecture is shown in Fig. 2.

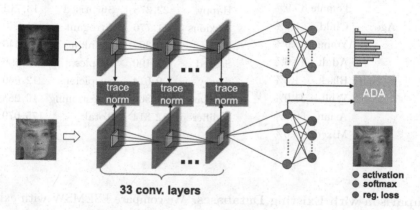

Fig. 2. Our deep MTL framework. For simplicity, layers such as pooling, relu, etc. are not visualised. 'activation'$\in R^{512}$ denotes the feature map after global average pooling.

3   Large-Scale Subtle Emotions and Mental States in the Wild (LSEMSW) Database

Motivation. Subtle expressions occur when a person's emotional response to surroundings is of low intensity. People usually exhibit subtle expressions when they start to feel an emotion. Subtle expression recognition has many applications such as mental activity analysis and deception detection [55]. However, subtle expressions are rarely investigated and the existing facial expression analysis techniques mainly focus on strong or exaggerated expressions. To advance research on subtle expression analysis, we collect the new LSEMSW database.

Collection and Annotation. LSEMSW was collected from more than 200 movies and TV serials such as Big Bang Theory, Harry Potter, Game of Thrones, etc. For each video/clip, we selected the first frame of every 5 ones. Then face detection was performed on the selected frames using MTCNN [60]. The images that contain faces were manually annotated via Amazon Mechanical Turk over nine months. To achieve accurate annotation, we provided detailed instructions to annotators and used Amazon MT Master service to select well-performing reliable annotators based on their historical performance. Each image is assigned to 3 workers for annotation. During the annotation, the subtitle (if available) on the frame is shown to help the workers make their decision. An annotation is accepted only if more than two workers agree on the annotation. The images with strong expressions were manually filtered. More details of our database are shown in Tables 1 and 2 and in the supplementary material.

Table 1. Attribute distribution.

Gender	Male	64.1%
	Female	35.9%
Age	Child	1.5%
	Young	55.9%
	Adult	42.6%
Ethinity	Black	1.3%
	White	31.9%
	Asian	66.2%
	Mixed	0.6%

Table 2. Expression distribution.

Expression	# Images	Expression	# Images
Happy	22,378	Surprised	13,712
Anxious	11,776	Arrogant	11,240
Sad	10,392	Thinking	31,645
Scared	12,190	Helpless	10,699
Angry	9,014	Suspicious	12,666
Hesitant	7,365	Questioning	10,288
Indifferent	12,314	Total	175,679

Comparison with Existing Databases. We compare LSEMSW with existing well known expression/emotion databases in Table 3. We can see that our LSEMSW is the only one with *subtle* expressions rather than strong expressions. Although this research focuses on *subtle* expression recognition, the knowledge learned from LSEMSW can be transferred to standard strong expression recognition, as verified in Sect. 4.2. In terms of size, LSEMSW is smaller than EmotioNet [11] and AffectNet [37]. However while EmotioNet [11] contains 1 million images, only 50K are manually annotated and the labels of the remaining images are noisily predicted by algorithm [4]. Therefore, our database is the second largest with manual expression annotations. It is the only database with cognitive state annotations.

4   Experiments

4.1   Databases and Settings

Expressions. We explore two types of expression recognition: (1) subtle expression recognition and (2) traditional (non-subtle) expression recognition (TNER). For (1), our LSEMSW database is used for evaluation. Specifically, the database is divided to training, validation and test sets according to the ratio: 80%, 10% and 10%. The rank 1 recognition rate on test set is reported. For (2), we explore transferring representation learned from LSEMSW to TNER. Specifically, we train TNER networks by finetuning from the *subtle* expression network trained with LSEMSW. We use two well known TNER databases, Oulu-Casia NIR&Vis (OCNV) facial expression database [62] and Extended Cohn-Kanade database (CK+) [29], for this evaluation. OCNV contains 480 sequences taken under 3 lightings: dark, strong and weak. Following [9], we use VIS videos with strong lighting (80 identities and 6 expressions). Each image sequence varies from neutral to peak formation of one particular expression. The last three frames (strongest expression) are used. 10-fold cross validation is conducted as [9]. On the other hand, CK+ includes 593 video sequences of 123 subjects. Subjects displayed 7 basic (non subtle) expressions in different sequences. We use only the last (strongest) frame of the sequence. Following [23], 5-fold cross validation is conducted. During training, data augmentation (flip, crop, rotation), which we find is very important, is performed. We finetune the LSEMSW-pretrained network using the augmented training images of OCNV and CK+ and evaluate the performance on the testing images of these 2 databases. Evaluations are reported on task (1) except where explicitly specified.

Table 3. Comparison of manually annotated facial expression databases.

Database	Expr. Intensity	Expr. Type	# Expr.	# Images	Environment
JAFFE [32]	strong	emotions	7	213	controlled
SFEW [7]	strong	emotions	7	663	uncontrolled
DISFA [34]	strong	emotions	7	4,845	controlled
FER2013 [15]	strong	emotions	7	36K	uncontrolled
RAF-DB [23]	strong	emotions	18	30K	uncontrolled
EmotioNet [11]	strong	emotions	16	50K (950K)^a	uncontrolled
AffectNet [37]	strong	emotions	7	450K (1M)^b	uncontrolled
LSEMSW	subtle	emotions & cognitive states	13	176K	uncontrolled

^{a} 50K images are manually annotated, and the labels of 950K images are predicted by algorithm [4].

^{b} 450K of 1M images are manually annotated with emotions, valence and arousal.

Facial Landmarks. We use 68-point annotations [46] for landmark detection. Our training set consists of the training images of 300 Faces In-the-Wild Challenge (300-W) [46] and Menpo benchmark [59]. Face detection using MTCNN [60] is performed on original training images. The detected bounding boxes are extended with a scale ratio of 0.2, aiming to cover the whole face area. Due to the limited training images, data argumentation is important. The detected faces are flipped, rotated $(-30°, 30°)$, and disturbed via translation and scaling (0.8, 1.2). During training, the landmark coordinates are normalised to (0, 1). Following [18,52], the test set contains 3 parts: common subset (554 images), challenging subset (135 images) and full set (689 images). Where not explicitly specified, we reports the results on the full set. Following [18,52], we use the normalised mean error (the distance between estimated landmarks and the ground truths, normalised by the inter-pupil distance) to evaluate the result.

Implementation Details. Our end-to-end deep MTL framework is implemented in TensorFlow [1]. The training images for mental state recognition are aligned and cropped to 96×96. Similarly, the images for landmark detection are resized to 96×96 and landmark coordinates are whitened following [43]. The landmark detection data is augmented by horizontal flip, rotation, scale, shift, and adding Gaussian noise following [12]. Only horizontal flip is used for emotion recognition. The learning rates for both networks are set 0.01, and batch sizes are both 256.

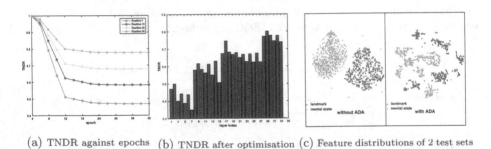

(a) TNDR against epochs (b) TNDR after optimisation (c) Feature distributions of 2 test sets

Fig. 3. Trace Norm and ADA Analysis: Trace Norm changes during (a) and after (b) network optimisation. The feature distributions with and without ADA (c).

4.2 Results

Analysis of Discovered Sharing. To analyse the learned sharing strategy, we define the trace norm decrease rate (TNDR) as $\frac{\text{Norm of Optimised Para}}{\text{Norm of Initialised Para}}$. The smaller TNDR is, the more knowledge one convolutional layer shares. We take ResNet+LAF as an example to investigate the properties of trace norm optimisation. Figure 3a shows the TNDR decreases against network optimisation epochs. We choose the 1st, 10th, 20th, 30th layers LAF trace norms for analysis.

Clearly, the 1st layer LAF decreases more dramatically than others, implying more knowledge is shared in the 1st layer. This is consistent with the common intuition that the lower layers capture more broadly useful low-level features. Figure 3b shows the TNDR of all layers after learning. We observe that: (i) Overall TNDR is smaller (information sharing is greater) at earlier layers as expected. However this trend is continuous rather than discontinuous, supporting the value of continuously varying soft sharing rather than a discrete all-or-nothing fork. Surprisingly (ii) within each residual block TNDR decreases (sharing is less) at higher layers. By *learning* the parameter sharing, our method has discovered a surprising strategy – related to the ResNet block architecture – that a human engineer is unlikely to have tried.

Comparison with Other Deep MTL Methods. Traditional Deep MTL methods use hand designed 'hard' parameter sharing which manually defines which layers are shared and which not. To contrast the manual approach, we compare 4 predefined architectures: 34-layer ResNets with the first {6, 14, 26, 32} convolutional layers shared and the rest task-specific. These increments are chosen to correspond to 4 residual units/blocks in [17]. From Table 4, we see that our automatic soft sharing (without ADA) works much better than 'hard' sharing in both tasks. Among 'hard' methods, ResNet (6) with the first 6 layers shared is best. The fact that such fairly limited sharing works best implies the cross-dataset domain-shift between the two tasks is strong, further motivating our solution for domain invariant feature learning. We also implement the recent deep MTL method 'cross stitch MTL' [36] using the same ResNet. From Table 4, we can see that our MTL strategy outperforms 'cross stitch MTL'. This is because our trace-norm based strategy provides more fine-grained control of information sharing compared to discrete rank setting.

Table 4. Accuracy (%) of Mental State Recognition on LSEMSW using 34-layer ResNet. RN(#) indicates the number of shared layers in standard MTL baseline.

	Single task	Our soft sharing			Hard sharing				Cross stitch [36]
	RN	LAF	Tucker	TT	RN(6)	RN(14)	RN(26)	RN(32)	RN
No ADA	28.39	33.43	33.39	33.41	30.07	28.11	26.90	24.69	30.96
ADA	-	**36.72**	36.51	36.64	33.97	31.95	30.58	28.18	-

Trace Norm Comparison. A key contribution of this work is multi-task parameter sharing through trace norm. Here we compare the three trace norms (LAF, Tucker, TT) introduced in Sect. 2.2 without ADA. The baseline single task method is 34-layer ResNet without any parameter sharing. From the results in Table 4, we can see our MTL methods (LAF, Tucker, TT) perform significantly better than single-task learning. Specifically, for mental state recognition,

LAF, Tucker and TT achieve recognition accuracy around 33.4%, compared with 28.39% of single task learning. For landmark detection, LAF, Tucker and TT reduce the mean error rates vs single task by around 7%. The three trace norms achieve very similar performance. This means that our strategy is not very sensitive to the type of norm/factorisation. The similar performance of TT and Tucker to LAF also mean that there is not much gain from compressing across filters rather than tasks – suggesting that ResNet is not overly 'wide' for mental state recognition. Thus we choose the simplest LAF for subsequent comparisons.

Adversarial Domain Alignment. We proposed ADA to reduce the domain shift across training sets from the tasks. As shown in Table 4, our method ResNet+LAF+ADA achieved 36.72% mental state recognition accuracy and 4.64% mean error rate of landmark detection, compared with ResNet+LAF (33.43%, 4.67%), showing the effectiveness of ADA. To further investigate the effect of ADA, we visualise the data distributions using t-SNE [33] technique. From Fig. 3c, we compare the feature distributions of two test sets (mental state and landmark) with (ResNet+LAF+ADA) and without (ResNet+LAF) using ADA. Clearly, ADA can effectively solve the domain shift problem.

Subtle Expression Recognition (SoA). Finally, we compare to prior state-of-the-art (SoA) methods. The historical lack of big training data, means that most prior approaches to expression/emotion recognition use handcrafted features such as LPQ [6], LBP [47], EOH [35]. A very recent study [40] empirically showed deep learning methods (AlexNet, VGGNet, ResNet) to be effective. Therefore, we compare the proposed method with all these networks. As subtle expression recognition is very challenging, handcrafted features (LPQ, LBP and EOH) do not achieve promising performance. From Table 5, we see that EOH [35] is the best handcrafted feature because EOH captures both spatial and texture information while LBP and LPQ only capture texture information. Nevertheless deep learning methods work better than handcrafted features because the deep features are trained end-to-end to capture subtle facial variations. Our proposed ResNet+LAF+ADA approach performs best overall. The superiority of ResNet+LAF+ADA against ResNet shows the effectiveness of our MTL strategy (LAF) and domain alignment strategy (ADA).

Landmark Detection (SoA). Facial landmark detection is primarily performed to provide an auxiliary task for our main subtle expression recognition task. We nevertheless also evaluate landmark detection here. Some qualitative results are shown in Fig. 4. The images illustrate strong variation of expression, illumination, occlusion, and poses. We can see that our method (ResNet+LAF+ADA) is very robust to these variations. Some failure cases are also shown in Fig. 4. These are mainly caused by the combination of different strong variations, e.g. expression+pose (row 2, col 5 & 6) and expression+pose+illumination (row 2, col 7). We also perform quantitative comparison to SoA methods in Table 6. From the results we can see that our method

Table 5. Comparison of SoA methods on LSEMSW

Method		Acc (%)
Hand-crafted Features	LPQ [6]	10.86
	LBP [47]	10.53
	EOH [35]	13.47
Deep learning	AlexNet [22,40]	26.77
	VGGNet [40,49]	28.07
	RN	28.39
	RN+LAF+ADA	**36.72**

Table 6. Error Rate (%) of Landmark detection on 300-W database.

Method	Common subset	Challenging subset	Full set
TCDCN [61]	4.80	8.60	5.54
TSR [30]	4.36	7.56	4.99
RAR [57]	4.12	8.35	4.94
MSLPR [18]	**3.83**	**7.46**	**4.54**
Ours(l_2 loss)	4.09	7.51	4.76
Ours(l_1 loss)	3.99	7.28	4.64

(RN+LAF+ADA) achieves very promising landmark detection performance. Specifically, we achieve the 2nd best performance on common subset and full set, and best on challenging subset, showing the robustness of our method on various challenging scenarios such as strong pose, illumination and expression variations – as illustrated in Fig. 4. The promising performance results from (1) the strong nonlinear modelling (regression) capacity of ResNet and (2) the effectiveness of LAF and ADA. Both (1) and (2) are also supported by Table 4. We also compare the different loss functions used by landmark detection. From Table 6, we can see that l_1 loss achieves better performance than l_2 loss.

Fig. 4. Samples of Landmark Detection: Faces with expressions (row 1, col 1–2), illuminations (row 1, col 3–4), occlusions (row 1, col 5–6), poses (row 2, col 1–3) and failed cases (row 2, col 4–6)

Traditional (non-subtle) Expression Recognition (TNER). It is interesting to investigate transferring knowledge learned from LSEMSW to TNER. We finetune the LSEMSW-pretrained network using the augmented training images of Oulu-Casia NIR&Vis (OCNV) [62] and CK+ [29] facial expression databases and also 300-W for multi-task learning. From the results in Table 7, we can draw the following conclusions: (i) Finetuning from LSEMSW works significantly better than training from scratch: 87.1% vs 76.0% on OCNV and 96.4% vs 86.3%, thus confirming its benefit as a source of data for representation learning, even if the final goal is TNER. (ii) Our MTL based on LAF and ADA is also beneficial for this TNER task (RN+LAF+ADA (FT) vs RN (FT) scores 87.1% vs 82.9% on OCNV and 96.4% vs 93.2% on CK+), as well as subtle expression recognition. (iii) In terms of comparison to prior state of the art, we achieve very competitive TNER performance via our soft MTL method and fine-tuning from LSEMSW (although it exclusively contains subtle expressions). Our RN+LAF+ADA (FT) achieves state of the art performance on CK+ and second best on OCNV.

Table 7. Comparison against state of the art on traditional non-subtle expression recognition. (FT) indicates fine-tuning from LSEMSW. (S) means training from scratch.

OCNV database		CK+ database	
Method	Acc. (%)	Method	Acc. (%)
LOMO [48]	82.1	FP+SAE [31]	91.1
PPDN [63]	84.6	AUDN [26]	93.7
FN2EN [9]	**87.7**	RAF [23]	**95.8**
RN (FT)	82.9	RN (FT)	93.2
RN+LAF (FT)	85.8	RN+LAF (FT)	95.3
RN+LAF+ADA (FT)	**87.1**	RN+LAF+ADA (FT)	**96.4**
RN+LAF+ADA (S)	76.0	RN+LAF+ADA (S)	86.3

5   Conclusion

In summary we have contributed a large new database to advance subtle expression recognition in the deep learning era. A trace norm based MTL learning method is proposed and ADA is used for domain alignment. Extensive experiments have verified the effectiveness of the propose methods.

References

1. Abadi, M., Agarwal, A., Barham, et al.: TensorFlow: large-scale machine learning on heterogeneous systems (2015). Software available from tensorflow.org
2. Argyriou, A., Evgeniou, T., Pontil, M.: Convex multi-task feature learning. Mach. Learn. **73**, 243–272 (2008)
3. Bakker, B., Heskes, T.: Task clustering and gating for Bayesian multitask learning. J. Mach. Learn. Res. **4**, 83–99 (2003)
4. Benitez-Quiroz, C.F., Srinivasan, R., Feng, Q., Wang, Y., Martinez, A.M.: Emotionet challenge: recognition of facial expressions of emotion in the wild. arXiv preprint arXiv:1703.01210 (2017)

5. Caruana, R.: Multitask learning. In: Thrun, S., Pratt, L. (eds.) Learning to Learn. Springer, Boston (1998). https://doi.org/10.1007/978-1-4615-5529-2_5

6. Dhall, A., Asthana, A., Goecke, R., Gedeon, T.: Emotion recognition using PHOG and LPQ features. In: Automatic Face and Gesture Recognition and Workshops (FG) (2011)

7. Dhall, A., Goecke, R., Lucey, S., Gedeon, T.: Static facial expression analysis in tough conditions: data, evaluation protocol and benchmark. In: ICCV Workshops (2011)

8. Dhall, A., Goecke, R., Lucey, S., Gedeon, T.: Collecting large, richly annotated facial-expression databases from movies. IEEE MultiMed. **19**(3), 0034 (2012)

9. Ding, H., Zhou, S.K., Chellappa, R.: FaceNet2ExpNet: regularizing a deep face recognition net for expression recognition. In: FG (2017)

10. Evgeniou, T., Pontil, M.: Regularized multi-task learning. In: KDD (2004)

11. Fabian Benitez-Quiroz, C., Srinivasan, R., Martinez, A.M.: Emotionet: an accurate, real-time algorithm for the automatic annotation of a million facial expressions in the wild. In: CVPR, pp. 5562–5570 (2016)

12. Feng, Z.H., Kittler, J., Christmas, W., Huber, P., Wu, X.J.: Dynamic attention-controlled cascaded shape regression exploiting training data augmentation and fuzzy-set sample weighting. arXiv preprint arXiv:1611.05396 (2016)

13. Ganin, Y., Lempitsky, V.S.: Unsupervised domain adaptation by backpropagation. In: ICML (2015)

14. Goodfellow, I., et al.: Generative adversarial nets. In: NIPS (2014)

15. Goodfellow, I.J., et al.: Challenges in representation learning: a report on three machine learning contests. In: Lee, M., Hirose, A., Hou, Z.-G., Kil, R.M. (eds.) ICONIP 2013. LNCS, vol. 8228, pp. 117–124. Springer, Heidelberg (2013). https://doi.org/10.1007/978-3-642-42051-1_16

16. Halko, N., Martinsson, P., Tropp, J.: Finding structure with randomness: probabilistic algorithms for constructing approximate matrix decompositions. SIAM Rev. **53**(2), 217–288 (2011)

17. He, K., Zhang, X., Ren, S., Sun, J.: Deep residual learning for image recognition. In: CVPR (2016)

18. Huang, Z., Zhou, E., Cao, Z.: Coarse-to-fine face alignment with multi-scale local patch regression. arXiv preprint arXiv:1511.04901 (2015)

19. Ji, S., Ye, J.: An accelerated gradient method for trace norm minimization. In: ICML, pp. 457–464 (2009)

20. Kossaifi, J., Tzimiropoulos, G., Todorovic, S., Pantic, M.: AFEW-VA database for valence and arousal estimation in-the-wild. Image Vis. Comput. **65**, 23–36 (2017)

21. Krause, R.: Universals and cultural differences in the judgments of facial expressions of emotion. J. Pers. Soc. Psychol. **5**(3), 4–712 (1987)

22. Krizhevsky, A., Sutskever, I., Hinton, G.E.: Imagenet classification with deep convolutional neural networks. In: NIPS, pp. 1097–1105 (2012)

23. Li, S., Deng, W., Du, J.: Reliable crowdsourcing and deep locality-preserving learning for expression recognition in the wild. In: CVPR, July 2017

24. Li, S., Liu, Z.Q., Chan, A.B.: Heterogeneous multi-task learning for human pose estimation with deep convolutional neural network. In: CVPR Workshops (2014)

25. Li, X., et al.: Towards reading hidden emotions: a comparative study of spontaneous micro-expression spotting and recognition methods. IEEE Trans. Affect. Comput. (2017)

26. Liu, M., Li, S., Shan, S., Chen, X.: Au-inspired deep networks for facial expression feature learning. Neurocomputing **159**, 126–136 (2015)

27. Liu, W., Mei, T., Zhang, Y., Che, C., Luo, J.: Multi-task deep visual-semantic embedding for video thumbnail selection. In: CVPR (2015)
28. Liu, X., Gao, J., He, X., Deng, L., Duh, K., Wang, Y.Y.: Representation learning using multi-task deep neural networks for semantic classification and information retrieval. In: HLT-NAACL, pp. 912–921 (2015)
29. Lucey, P., Cohn, J.F., Kanade, T., Saragih, J., Ambadar, Z., Matthews, I.: The extended cohn-kanade dataset (CK+): a complete dataset for action unit and emotion-specified expression. In: CVPR Workshops (CVPRW) (2010)
30. Lv, J., Shao, X., Xing, J., Cheng, C., Zhou, X.: A deep regression architecture with two-stage re-initialization for high performance facial landmark detection. In: CVPR (2017)
31. Lv, Y., Feng, Z., Xu, C.: Facial expression recognition via deep learning. In: International Conference on Smart Computing (SMARTCOMP) (2014)
32. Lyons, M.J., Akamatsu, S., Kamachi, M., Gyoba, J., Budynek, J.: The Japanese female facial expression (JAFFE) database
33. van der Maaten, L., Hinton, G.: Visualizing data using t-SNE. J. Mach. Learn. Res. 9(Nov), 2579–2605 (2008)
34. Mavadati, S.M., Mahoor, M.H., Bartlett, K., Trinh, P., Cohn, J.F.: DISFA: a spontaneous facial action intensity database. IEEE Trans. Affect. Comput. 4(2), 151–160 (2013)
35. Meng, H., Romera-Paredes, B., Bianchi-Berthouze, N.: Emotion recognition by two view SVM_2K classifier on dynamic facial expression features. In: Automatic Face and Gesture Recognition and Workshops (FG) (2011)
36. Misra, I., Shrivastava, A., Gupta, A., Hebert, M.: Cross-stitch networks for multi-task learning. In: CVPR (2016)
37. Mollahosseini, A., Hasani, B., Mahoor, M.H.: AffectNet: a database for facial expression, valence, and arousal computing in the wild. arXiv preprint arXiv:1708.03985 (2017)
38. Oseledets, I.V.: Tensor-train decomposition. SIAM J. Sci. Comput. 33(5), 2295–2317 (2011)
39. Pantic, M., Rothkrantz, L.J.M.: Automatic analysis of facial expressions: the state of the art. TPAMI 22, 1424–1445 (2000)
40. Pramerdorfer, C., Kampel, M.: Facial expression recognition using convolutional neural networks: state of the art. arXiv preprint arXiv:1612.02903 (2016)
41. Ranjan, R., Patel, V.M., Chellappa, R.: HyperFace: a deep multi-task learning framework for face detection, landmark localization, pose estimation, and gender recognition. arXiv (2016)
42. Recht, B., Fazel, M., Parrilo, P.A.: Guaranteed minimum-rank solutions of linear matrix equations via nuclear norm minimization. SIAM Rev. 52(3), 471–501 (2010)
43. Ren, S., He, K., Girshick, R., Sun, J.: Faster R-CNN: towards real-time object detection with region proposal networks. In: NIPS, pp. 91–99 (2015)
44. Romera-Paredes, B., Aung, H., Bianchi-Berthouze, N., Pontil, M.: Multilinear multitask learning. In: ICML (2013)
45. Sagonas, C., Antonakos, E., Tzimiropoulos, G., Zafeiriou, S., Pantic, M.: 300 faces in-the-wild challenge: database and results. Image Vis. Comput. 47, 3–18 (2016)
46. Sagonas, C., Tzimiropoulos, G., Zafeiriou, S., Pantic, M.: 300 faces in-the-wild challenge: the first facial landmark localization challenge. In: ICCV Workshops (2013)
47. Shan, C., Gong, S., McOwan, P.W.: Facial expression recognition based on local binary patterns: a comprehensive study. Image Vis. Comput. 27(6), 803–816 (2009)

48. Sikka, K., Sharma, G., Bartlett, M.: LOMo: latent ordinal model for facial analysis in videos. In: CVPR (2016)
49. Simonyan, K., Zisserman, A.: Very deep convolutional networks for large-scale image recognition. arXiv preprint arXiv:1409.1556 (2014)
50. Tang, H., Huang, T.S.: 3D facial expression recognition based on automatically selected features. In: CVPR Workshops, pp. 1–8 (2008)
51. Tomioka, R., Hayashi, K., Kashima, H.: On the extension of trace norm to tensors. In: NIPS Workshop on Tensors, Kernels, and Machine Learning (2010)
52. Trigeorgis, G., Snape, P., Nicolaou, M.A., Antonakos, E., Zafeiriou, S.: Mnemonic descent method: a recurrent process applied for end-to-end face alignment. In: CVPR (2016)
53. Tucker, L.R.: Some mathematical notes on three-mode factor analysis. Psychometrika **31**(3), 279–311 (1966)
54. Walecki, R., Rudovic, O., Pavlovic, V., Pantic, M.: Variable-state latent conditional random fields for facial expression recognition and action unit detection. In: Automatic Face and Gesture Recognition (FG) (2015)
55. Warren, G., Schertler, E., Bull, P.: Detecting deception from emotional and unemotional cues. J. Nonverbal Behav. **33**(1), 59–69 (2009)
56. Wimalawarne, K., Sugiyama, M., Tomioka, R.: Multitask learning meets tensor factorization: task imputation via convex optimization. In: NIPS, pp. 2825–2833 (2014)
57. Xiao, S., Feng, J., Xing, J., Lai, H., Yan, S., Kassim, A.: Robust facial landmark detection via recurrent attentive-refinement networks. In: Leibe, B., Matas, J., Sebe, N., Welling, M. (eds.) ECCV 2016. LNCS, vol. 9905, pp. 57–72. Springer, Cham (2016). https://doi.org/10.1007/978-3-319-46448-0_4
58. Yang, Y., Hospedales, T.: Deep multi-task representation learning: a tensor factorisation approach. In: ICLR (2017)
59. Zafeiriou, S., Trigeorgis, G., Chrysos, G., Deng, J., Shen, J.: The menpo facial landmark localisation challenge: a step towards the solution. In: Computer Vision and Pattern Recognition Workshop (2017)
60. Zhang, K., Zhang, Z., Li, Z., Qiao, Y.: Joint face detection and alignment using multitask cascaded convolutional networks. IEEE Signal Process. Lett. **23**(10), 1499–1503 (2016)
61. Zhang, Z., Luo, P., Loy, C.C., Tang, X.: Facial landmark detection by deep multi-task learning. In: Fleet, D., Pajdla, T., Schiele, B., Tuytelaars, T. (eds.) ECCV 2014. LNCS, vol. 8694, pp. 94–108. Springer, Cham (2014). https://doi.org/10.1007/978-3-319-10599-4_7
62. Zhao, G., Huang, X., Taini, M., Li, S.Z., Pietikäinen, M.: Facial expression recognition from near-infrared videos. Image Vis. Comput. **29**(9), 607–619 (2011)
63. Zhao, X., et al.: Peak-piloted deep network for facial expression recognition. In: Leibe, B., Matas, J., Sebe, N., Welling, M. (eds.) ECCV 2016. LNCS, vol. 9906, pp. 425–442. Springer, Cham (2016). https://doi.org/10.1007/978-3-319-46475-6_27

SRDA: Generating Instance Segmentation Annotation via Scanning, Reasoning and Domain Adaptation

Wenqiang Xu [id], Yonglu Li [id], and Cewu Lu[(✉)] [id]

Department of Computer Science and Engineering, Shanghai Jiao Tong University,
Shanghai, China
{vinjohn,yonglu_li,lucewu}@sjtu.edu.cn

Abstract. Instance segmentation is a problem of significance in computer vision. However, preparing annotated data for this task is extremely time-consuming and costly. By combining the advantages of 3D scanning, reasoning, and GAN-based domain adaptation techniques, we introduce a novel pipeline named SRDA to obtain large quantities of training samples with very minor effort. Our pipeline is well-suited to scenes that can be scanned, i.e. most indoor and some outdoor scenarios. To evaluate our performance, we build three representative scenes and a new dataset, with 3D models of various common objects categories and annotated real-world scene images. Extensive experiments show that our pipeline can achieve decent instance segmentation performance given very low human labor cost.

Keywords: 3D scanning · Physical reasoning · Domain adaptation

1 Introduction

Instance segmentation [6,21] is one of the fundamental problems in computer vision, which provides many more details in comparison to object detection [28], or semantic segmentation [23]. With the development of deep learning, significant progress has been made in instance segmentation. Many annotated datasets of large quantity were proposed [5,22]. However, in practice, when meeting a new environment with many new objects, large-scale training data collection and annotation is inevitable, which is cost-prohibitive and time-consuming.

Researchers have longed for a means of generating numerous training samples with minor effort. Computer graphics simulation is a promising way, since a 3D

W. Xu and Y. Li—Equal contributions.

C. Lu—Member of MoE Key Lab of Artificial Intelligence, AI Institute, Shanghai Jiao Tong University, and SJTU-SenseTime AI lab.

Electronic supplementary material The online version of this chapter (https://doi.org/10.1007/978-3-030-01258-8_8) contains supplementary material, which is available to authorized users.

V. Ferrari et al. (Eds.): ECCV 2018, LNCS 11216, pp. 124–140, 2018.
https://doi.org/10.1007/978-3-030-01258-8_8

scene can be a source of unlimited photorealistic images paired with ground truths. Besides, modern simulation techniques are capable of synthesizing most indoor and outdoor scenes with perceptual plausibility. Nevertheless, these two advantages are double-edged, rendered images would be painstaking to make the simulated scene visually realistic [31,38,43]. Moreover, for new environment, it is very likely some of the objects in reality are not in the 3D model database.

Fig. 1. Compared with human labeling (red), our pipeline (blue) can significantly reduce human labor cost by nearly 2000 folds and achieve reasonable accuracy in instance segmentation. 77.02 and 86.02 are average mAP@0.5 of 3 scenes. (Color figure online)

We present a new pipeline that attempts to address these challenges. Our pipeline comprises three stages: *scanning, physics reasoning, domain adaptation* (**SRDA**) as shown in Fig. 1. At the first stage, new objects and environmental background from a certain scene are scanned into 3D models. Unlike other CG based methods that do simulation with existing model datasets, images synthesized by our pipeline can ensure realistic effect and well describe the targeting environment, since we use real-world scanned data. At the reasoning stage, we proposed a reasoning system to generate proper layout for each scene by fully considering physically and commonsense plausible. Physics engine is used to ensure physics plausible and commonsense plausible is checked by commonsense likelihood (CL) function. For example, "a mouse on the mouse pad and they on the table" would have a large output in CL function. In the last stage, we proposed a novel *Geometry-guided GAN* (GeoGAN) framework. It integrates geometry information (segmentation as edge cue, surface normal, depth) which helps to generate more plausible images. In addition, it includes a new component *Predictor* which can serve as a useful auxiliary supervision, and also a criterion to score the visual quality of images.

The major advantage of our pipeline is time-saving. Compared with conventional exhausting annotation, we can reduce labor cost by nearly 2000 folds, in the meantime, achieve decent accuracy, preserving 90% performance. (See Fig. 1). The most time-consuming stage is scanning, which is easy to accomplish in most of indoor and some of outdoor scenarios.

Our pipeline can be widely adaptive to many scenarios. We choose three representative scenes, namely a shelf from a supermarket (for a self-service supermarket), a desk from an office (for home robot), a tote similar in Amazon Robotic Challenge[1].

To the best of our knowledge, no current datasets consist of compact 3D object/scene models and real scene images with instance segmentation annotations. Hence, we build a dataset to prove the efficacy of our pipeline. This dataset have two parts, one for scanned object models (SOM dataset) and one for real scene images with instance level annotations (Instance-60K).

Our contributions have two folds:

- The main contribution is the novel three-stage SRDA pipeline. We added a reasoning system to the feasible layout building and proposed a new domain adaptation framework named GeoGAN. It is time-saving and the output images are close to real ones according to the evaluation experiment.
- To demonstrate the effectiveness, we build up a database which contains 3D models of common objects and corresponding scenes (SOM dataset) and scene images with instance level annotations (instance-60K).

We will first review some of the related concepts and works in Sect. 2 and depict the whole pipeline from Sect. 3 on. We describe the scanning process in Sect. 3, reasoning system in Sect. 4, and GAN-based domain adaptation in Sect. 5. In Sect. 6, we illustrate how Instance-60K dataset is built. Extensive evaluation experiments are carried out in Sect. 7. And finally, we discuss the limitation of our pipeline in Sect. 8.

2   Related Works

Instance Segmentation. Instance segmentation has become a hot topic in recent years. Dai et al. [6] proposed a complex multiple-stage cascaded network that does detection, segmentation, and classification in sequence. Li et al. [21] combined a segment proposal system and object detection system, simultaneously producing object classes, bounding boxes, and masks. Mask R-CNN [14] supports multiple tasks including instance segmentation, object detection, human pose estimation. Whereas exhausting labeling is required to guarantee a satisfactory performance, if we apply these methods to a new environment.

Generative Adversarial Networks. Since introduced by Goodfellow [12], GAN-based methods have fruitful results in various fields, such as image generation [27], image-to-image translation [42], 3D model generation [40], etc. The former paper on image-to-image translation inspired our work, it indicates GAN has the potential to bridge the gap between simulation domain and real domain.

---

[1] https://www.amazonrobotics.com/#/roboticschallenge.

Image-to-Image Translation. A general image-to-image translation framework was first introduced by Pix2Pix [16], but it required a great amount of paired data. Chen [4] proposed a cascaded refinement network free of adversarial training, which gets high-resolution results, but still demands paired data. Taigman et al. [36] proposed an unsupervised approach to learn cross-domain conversion, however it needs a pre-trained function to map samples from two domains into an intermediate representation. Dual learning [17,41,42] is soon imported for unpaired image translation, but currently, dual learning methods encounter setbacks when camera viewpoint or object position varies. On the contrary to CycleGAN, Benaim et al. [2] learned one-side mapping. Refining rendered image using GAN is also not unknown [3,32,33]. Our work is a complementary to these approaches, where we deal with more complex data and tasks. We will compare [3,32] with our GeoGAN in Sect. 7.

Synthetic Data for Training. Some researchers attempt to generate synthetic data for vision tasks such as viewpoint estimation [35], object detection [11], semantic segmentation [30]. In [1], Alhaija et al. addressed generation of instance segmentation training data for street scenes with technical effort in producing realistically rendered and positioned cars. However, they focus on street scenes and do not use an adversarial formulation.

Scene Generation by Computer Graphics. Scene generation by CG techniques is a well-studied area in the computer graphics community [9,13,25,26,34]. These methods are capable of generating plausible layout of indoor or outdoor scene, but they have no intention to transfer the rendered images to real domain.

3   Scanning Process

In this section, we describe the scanning process. Objects and scene backgrounds are scanned in two ways due to the scale issue.

We choose the multi-view environment (MVE) [10] to perform dense reconstruction for objects, since it is image-based and thus requires only a RGB sensor. Objects are first videotaped, which can be easily done by most RGB sensors. In the experiment, we use an iPhone5s. The videos are sliced into images with multiple viewpoints, and fed into MVE to generate 3D models. We can videotape multiple objects (at least 4) and generate corresponding models per time, which can alleviate the scalability issue when new objects are too many to scan one by one. MVE is capable of generating dense meshes with a fine texture. As for the texture-less objects, we scan the object with hand holding, and the hand-object interaction can be a useful cue for reconstruction, as indicated in [39].

For the environmental background, scenes without targeting objects were scanned by Intel RealSense R200 and reconstructed by ReconstructMe[2]. We follow the official instruction to operate reconstruction.

---

[2] http://reconstructme.net/.

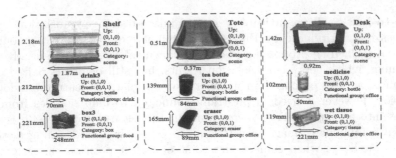

Fig. 2. Representative environmental backgrounds, object models, and corresponding label information.

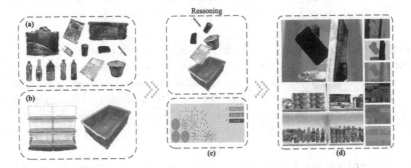

Fig. 3. The scanned objects (a) and background (b) are put into a rule-based reasoning system (c) to generate physics plausible layouts. The upper of (c) is the random scheme, while the bottom is the rule-based scheme. In the end, system output rough RGB images and corresponding annotations (d).

Resolution for iPhone5s is 1920 × 1080 and for R200 is 640 × 480 at 60 FPS. Remaining settings are by default.

4 Layout Building with Reasoning

4.1 Scene Layout Building with Knowledge

With 3D models of objects and environmental background at hand, we are ready to generate scenes by our reasoning system. A proper scene layout must obey physics laws and human conventions. To make scene physics plausible, we select an off-the-shelf physics engine, Project Chrono [37]. However, it is not as direct to make object layout convincing, some commonsense knowledge should be incorporated. To produce a feasible layout, we need to make object pose and location reasonable. For example, a cup has the pose of "standing up", but not "lying down", meanwhile, it is always on the table not the ground. This prior falls in daily knowledge that cannot be achieved by physics reasoning. Therefore, we present how to annotate the pose and location prior in what follows (Figs. 2 and 3).

Pose Prior: For each object, we show annotators its 3D model in 3D graphics environment, and ask annotators to draw all its possible poses that she/he can imagine. For each possible pose, the annotator should suggest a probability that this pose would happen. We record the probability of ith object in pose k as $D_p[k|i]$. We use interpolation to ensure most poses has a probability value.

Location Prior: The same as pose prior, we show annotators the environmental background in 3D graphics environment, thus annotators label all its possible locations that an object may be placed. For each possible location, the annotator should suggest a probability that this object would be placed. We denoted the probability of ith object in location k as $D_l[k|i]$. We use interpolation to make most of location has correponding probability value.

Relationship Prior: Some objects have strong co-occurrence prior. For example, mouse is always close to laptop. Given an object name list, we use language prior to select a set of object pair that have high co-occurrence probability, we call them as occurrence object pair (OOP). For each OOP, annotator suggests a probability of occurrence of corresponding object pairs. For object i^{th} and j^{th}, their probability of occurrence is denoted as $D_r[i,j]$ and a suggested distance (by annotators) is $H_r[i,j]$.

Note that the annotation maybe subjective, but we found that we only need a prior for layout generation guidance. Extensive experiments show that roughly subjective labeling is sufficient for producing satisfactory results. We will report the experiment details in supplementary file.

4.2 Layout Generation by Knowledge

We generate layout by considering both physics laws and human conventions. First, we randomly generate a layout and check its physics plausible by Chrono. If it is not physically reasonable, we reject this layout. Second, we check its commonsense plausible by three priors above. In detail, all object pairs are extracted in layout scene. We denote $(\{c_1(i), c_2(i)\}, (\{p_1(i), p_2(i)\}$ and $(\{l_1(i), l_2(i)\}$ as category, pose and 3D location of ith extracted object pair in scene layout. The likelihood of pose is expressed as

$$K_p[i] = D_p[p_1(i)|c_1(i)]D_p[p_2(i)|c_2(i)]. \tag{1}$$

The likelihood of location for i^{th} object pair is written as,

$$K_l[i] = D_l[l_1(i)|c_1(i)]D_l[l_2(i)|c_2(i)]. \tag{2}$$

The likelihood of occurrence for i^{th} object pair is presented as

$$K_r[i] = \begin{cases} G_\sigma(|l_1(i) - l_2(i)| - D_r[c_1(i), c_2(j)]) & \text{if } H_r[i,j] > \gamma \\ 1, & \text{otherwise.} \end{cases} \tag{3}$$

where G_σ is a Gaussian function with parameter σ ($\sigma = 0.1$ in our paper). We compute occurrence prior in the case where the probability $H_r[i, j]$ is larger than a threshold γ ($\gamma = 0.5$ in our paper).

We denote commonsense likelihood function of a scene layout as

$$K = \prod_i K_l[i]K_l[i]K_r[i] \propto \sum_i \log(K_l[i]) + \log(K_p[i]) + \log(K_r[i]) \qquad (4)$$

Thus, we can judge commonsense plausible by K. If K is smaller than a threshold ($K \leq 0.6$ in our experiments), we reject its corresponding layout. In this way, we can generate large quantities of layouts that is both physics and commonsense plausible.

4.3   Annotation Cost

We annotate scanned model one by one. So, the annotation cost is linear scale with respect to scanned object model number M. Note that only a small set of object have strong object occurrence assumption (e.g. laptop and mouse). So, the complexity of object occurrence annotation is close to $O(M)$. We carry out experiment to find that $10\,\mathrm{s}$ is taken to label knowledge for a scanned object model in average, which is minor (one hour for hundreds of objects).

5   Domain Adaptation with Geometry-Guided GAN

Now, we have collection of the rough (RGB) image $\{I_i^r\}_{i=1}^M \in \mathcal{I}^r$ and its corresponding ground truths, instance segmentation $\{I_i^{s\text{-}gt}\}_{i=1}^M \in \mathcal{I}^{s\text{-}gt}$, surface normal $\{I_i^{n\text{-}gt}\}_{i=1}^M \in \mathcal{I}^{n\text{-}gt}$, depth image $\{I_i^{d\text{-}gt}\}_{i=1}^M \in \mathcal{I}^{d\text{-}gt}$. Besides, the real image captured from targeting environment is denoted as $\{I_j\}_{j=1}^N$. M, N are the sample sizes for rendered samples and real samples. With these data, we can embark on training GeoGAN.

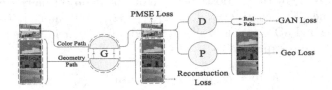

Fig. 4. The GDP structure consists of three components: a generator (G), a discriminator (D), and a predictor (P), along with four loss: LSGAN loss (GAN loss), Structure loss, Reconstruction loss (L1 loss), Geometry-guided loss (Geo loss).

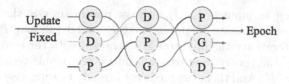

Fig. 5. Iterative optimization framework. As the epoch goes, G, D and P are updated as presented. While one component is updating, the other two are fixed.

5.1 Objective Function

GeoGAN has a "GDP" structure, as sketched in Fig. 4, which comprises a generator (G), a discriminator (D) and a predictor (P) which serves as a geometry prior guidance. Such structure leads to the design of the objective function, which consists of four loss functions that will be presented in what follows.

LSGAN Loss. We adopt a least-square generative adversarial objective (LSGAN) [24] to help G and D training stable. The LSGAN adversarial loss can be written as

$$\mathcal{L}_{GAN}(G, D) = \mathbb{E}_{y \sim p_{data}(y)}[(D(y) - 1)^2] + \mathbb{E}_{x \sim p_{data}(x)}[(D(G(x)))^2], \quad (5)$$

x and y stand for a sample from the rough image and the real image domain respectively.

We denote the output of the generator with parameter Φ_G for i^{th} rough image as I_i^*, i.e. $I_i^* \triangleq G(I_i^r | \Phi_G)$.

Structure Loss. A structure loss is introduced to ensure I_i^* maintains the original structure of I_i^r. A Pairwise Mean Square Error (PMSE) loss is imported from [7], expressed as:

$$\mathcal{L}_{PMSE}(G) = \frac{1}{N} \sum_i (I_i^r - I_i^*)^2 - \frac{1}{N^2} (\sum_{i,j} (I_i^r - I_i^*))^2. \quad (6)$$

Reconstruction Loss. To ensure the geometry information successfully encoded in the network. We also use ℓ^1 as a reconstruction loss for the geometric images.

$$\mathcal{L}_{rec}(G) = ||[I^r, I^s, I^n, I^d | \Phi_G]_{rec}, [I^r, I^s, I^n, I^d]||_1 \quad (7)$$

Geometry-Guided Loss. Given an excellent geometry predictor, a high-quality image should be able to produce desirable instance segmentation, depth map and normal map. It is a useful criterion that judges whether I_i^* is qualified or not. An unqualified image (with artifacts, distorted structure) will induce large geometry-guided loss (Geo Loss).

To achieve this goal, we pretrained the predictor with following formula:

$$[I^s, I^n, I^d] = P(I | \Phi_P), \quad (8)$$

It means given an input image I, with the parameter Φ_P, the predictor can output instance segmentation I^s, normal map I^n and depth map I^d respectively. In the first few iterations, the predictor is pretrained with the rough image, that is, $I = I^r$. When the generator starts to produce reasonable results, Φ_P can be updated with $I = I^*$. And then, the predictor is ready to supervise the generator, and Φ_G will be updated as follow:

$$\mathcal{L}_{Geo}(G, P) = ||P(I_i^*|\Phi_P), [I_i^{s\text{-}gt}, I_i^{n\text{-}gt}, I_i^{d\text{-}gt}]||_2^2. \tag{9}$$

In this equation, Φ_P is not updated, and it is a ℓ^2 loss.

Overall Objective Function. In sum, our objective function can be expressed as:

$$\min_{\Phi_G} \max_{\Phi_D} \lambda_1 \mathcal{L}_{GAN}(G, D) + \lambda_2 \mathcal{L}_{PMSE}(G) + \lambda_3 \mathcal{L}_{rec}(G) + \lambda_4 \mathcal{L}_{Geo}(G, P),$$
$$\min_{\Phi_P} \mathcal{L}_{Geo}(G, P). \tag{10}$$

It reveals the iterative optimization, as shown in Fig. 5.

5.2   Implementation

Dual Path Generator (G). Our generator has dual forward data paths (color path and geometry path), which help to integrate the color and geometry information. For color path, input rough image will firstly pass three convolutional layers, and then downsample to 64×64 and pass 6 resnet blocks [15]. After that, output feature maps are upsampled to 256×256 with bilinear upsampling. During upsampling, color information path will concatenate feature maps from geometry information path.

Geometry information are firstly convolutioned to feature maps and concatenated together, resulting in a 3-dimensional 256×256 feature map before passing to geometry path described below. After the last layer, we split the output of the last layer into three parts, and produce three reconstruction images for three kinds of geometric images.

Let $3n64s1$ denote 3×3-Convolution-InstanceNorm-ReLU layer with 64 filters and stride 1. Rk denotes a residual block that contains two 3×3 convolutional layers with the same number of filters on both. upk denotes a bilinear upsampling layer followed with a 3×3 Convolution-InstanceNorm-ReLU layer with k filters and stride 1.

The generator architecture is:

color path: 7n3s1-3n64s2-3n128s2-R256-R256-R256-R256-R256-R256-up512-up256
geometry path: 7n3s1-3n64s2-3n128s2-R256-R256-R256-R256-R256-R256-up256-up128.

Markovian Discriminator (D). The discriminator is a typical PatchGAN or Markovian discriminator described in [16,19,20]. We also found 70×70 is a proper receptive field size, hence the architecture is exactly like [16].

Geometry Predictor (P). FCN-like networks [23] or UNet [29] are good candidates for the geometry predictor. In implementation, we choose a UNet architecture. *downk* denotes a 3×3 Convolution-InstanceNorm-LeakyReLU layer with k filters and stride 2, the slope of leaky ReLU is 0.2. *upk* denotes a bilinear upsampling layer followed with a 3×3 Convolution-InstanceNorm-ReLU layer with k filters and stride 1. k in *upk* is 2 times larger than that in *downk*, since a skip connection between corresponding layers. After the last layer, feature maps are split into three parts and convolution to a three dimension layer separately, activated by tanh function.

The predictor architecture is: down64-down128-down256-down512-down512-down512-up1024-up1024-up1024-up512-up256-up128.

Training Details. Adam optimizer [18] is used for all three "GDP" components, with batch size of 1. G, D and P are trained from scratch. We firstly trained geometry predictor with 5 epochs to get a good initialization, then began the iterative procedures. In the iterative procedures, learning rate for the first 100 epochs are 0.0002 and linearly decay to zero in the next 100 epochs. All training images are of size 256×256.

All models are trained with $\lambda_1 = 2$, $\lambda_2 = 5$, $\lambda_3 = 10$, $\lambda_4 = 3$ in Eq. 10. The generator is trained twice before the discriminator updates once.

6   Instance-60K Building Process

As we found no existing Instance segmentation datasets [5, 8, 22] can benchmark our task, we have to build a new dataset to benchmark our method.

Instance-60K is an ongoing effort to annotate instance segmentation for scenes can be scanned. Currently it contains three representative scenes, namely supermarket shelf, office desk and tote. These three scenes are chosen since they potentially benefit real-world applications in the future. Supermarket cases are well-suited to self-service supermarkets like Amazon Go[3]. Home robots will always meet the scene of an office desk. The tote is in the same setting as Amazon Robotic Challenge.

To note that our pipeline does not restrict to these three scenes, technically any scenes can be simulated are suitable to our pipeline.

Shelf scene has objects of 30 categories, which items such as soft drinks, biscuits, and tissues. 15 categories for desk scene and tote scene. All are common objects in the corresponding scenes. Objects and scenes are scanned for building SOM dataset as described in Sect. 3.

For instance-60K dataset, these objects are placed in corresponding scenes and then videotaped by iPhone5s under various viewpoints. We arranged 10 layouts for the shelf, and over 100 layouts for desk and tote. Videos are then sliced into 6000 images in total, 2000 for each scene. The number of labeled instance is 60894, that is the reason why we call it instance-60K. We have average

---

[3] https://www.amazon.com/b?node=16008589011.

Fig. 6. Representative images and manual annotations in the Instance-60K dataset.

966 instances per category. This scale is about three times larger than PASCAL VOC [8] level (346 instances per category), so it is qualified to benchmark this problem. Again, we found instance segmentation annotation is laborious, it took more than 4000 man-hours on building this dataset. Some representative real images and annotation are shown in Fig. 6. As we can see, annotating them is time-consuming.

7   Evaluation

In this section, we evaluate our generated instance segmentation samples quantitatively and qualitatively (Fig. 7).

Table 1. mAP results on real, rough, fake, fake$_{plus}$ models of different scenes with Mask R-CNN.

	Shelf				Desk				Tote			
	real	rough	fake	fake$_{plus}$	real	rough	fake	fake$_{plus}$	real	rough	fake	fake$_{plus}$
mAP@0.5	79.75	18.10	49.11	**66.31**	88.24	43.81	57.07	**82.07**	90.06	28.67	61.40	**82.69**
mAP@0.7	67.02	10.53	37.56	**47.25**	73.75	35.14	45.44	**71.82**	85.10	16.87	50.13	**76.84**

7.1   Evaluation on Instance-60K

We employed instance segmentation tasks to evaluate on generated samples. To prove that the proposed pipeline generally works, we will report results using Mask R-CNN [14]. We train segmentation model on resulting images produced by our GeoGAN. The trained model is denoted as "fake-model". Likewise, model trained on rough images is denoted as "rough-model". One question we should ask is that how "fake-model" compare to models train on real images. To answer this question, we train models on training set of instance-60K dataset, which is denoted as "real-model". It is pre-trained on COCO dataset [22].

Training procedures on real images strictly follow the procedures mentioned in [14]. We find the learning rate for real images is not workable to rough and

Rough   Refined   Rough   Refined

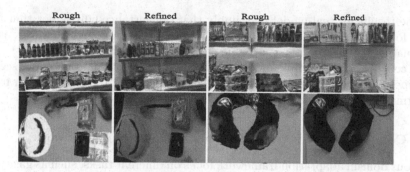

Fig. 7. Refinement of GAN. Refined column is the result of GeoGAN and rough column is the rendered image. Apparent improvement on lighting conditions and texture can be observed.

GAN generated images, so we lower the learning rate and make it decay earlier. All models are trained with 4500 images, though we can generate endless training sample for "rough-model" and "fake-model", since "real-model" only can train on 4500 images in the training set of instance-60K dataset. Finally, all models are evaluated on testing set of instance-60K dataset.

Experiment results shown in Table 1. Overall mAP of the rough image is generally low, while "fake-model" significantly outperformed it. Noticeably, it still has a clear gap between "fake-model" results and real one, though the gap has been bridged a lot. Naturally, we would like to know how many refined training images is sufficient to achieve comparable results with "real-model". Hence, we conducted experiments on 15000 GAN generated images, and named model as "fake$_{plus}$-model". As we can see from Table 1, "fake$_{plus}$" and "real" is really close. We try to augment more training samples to "fake$_{plus}$-model", but, the improvement is marginal. In this way, our synthetic "images + annotation" is comparable with "real image + human annotation" for instance segmentation (Fig. 8).

Rough   Fake   Fake$_{plus}$ Real

Fig. 8. Qualitative results visualization of rough, fake, fake$_{plus}$ and real model respectively.

The results for real-model may imply that our instance-60K is not that difficult for Mask R-CNN. Extension of the dataset is on-going. However, it is undeniable that the dataset is capable of proving the ability of GeoGAN.

In contrast to exhausting annotation using over 1000 human-hours per scene, our pipeline takes 0.7 human-hours per scene. Admittedly, the results suffer from performance loss, but save the whole task 3-order of human-hours.

7.2   Comparison with Other Domain Adaptation Framework

Previous domain adaptation framework focus on different tasks, such as gaze and hand pose estimation [32], object classification and 6D pose estimation [3]. To the best of our knowledge, we are the first to propose a GAN-based framework to do instance segmentation. Comparison with each other is indirect. We reproduced the work of [32] and [3]. For [3], we substituted the task component with our P. The experiments are conducted on the scenes same in the paper. Results are shown in Fig. 9 and Table 2.

Fig. 9. Qualitative comparison of our pipeline and [3], [32]. The background of generated images from [3] are damaged since they use a masked-PMSE loss.

7.3   Ablation Study

Ablation study is carried out by removing geometry-guided loss and structure loss separately. Extended ablation study on the specific geometric information in the geometry path is reported in the supplementary file. We applied Mask R-CNN to train the segmentation models on resulting images from GeoGAN without geometry-guided loss (denoted as "fake$_{plus,w/o\text{-}geo}$-model") or structure loss (denoted as "fake$_{plus,w/o\text{-}pmse}$-model"). As we can see, it suffers a significant performance loss when removing geometry-guided loss or structure loss. Besides, we also need to prove the necessity of reasoning system. After removing reasoning system, resulting in unrealistic images and performance loss. Results are shown in Table 3 (Fig. 10).

Table 2. Quantitative comparison of our pipeline and [3], [32].

mAP			0.5	0.7
Mask R-CNN	Shelf	$fake_{plus,ours}$	66.31	47.25
		$fake_{plus,[25]}$	31.46	20.88
		$fake_{plus,[13]}$	56.16	36.04
	Desk	$fake_{plus,ours}$	82.07	71.82
		$fake_{plus,[25]}$	44.33	29.93
		$fake_{plus,[13]}$	69.54	57.27
	Tote	$fake_{plus,ours}$	82.69	76.84
		$fake_{plus,[25]}$	42.50	33.61
		$fake_{plus,[13]}$	70.73	62.68

Table 3. mAP results of ablation study on Mask R-CNN.

mAP			0.5	0.7
Mask R-CNN	Shelf	$fake_{plus}$	66.31	47.25
		$fake_{plus,w/o\text{-}geo}$	48.52	31.17
		$fake_{plus,w/o\text{-}pmse}$	27.33	19.24
		$fake_{plus,w/o\text{-}reason}$	15.21	8.44
	Desk	$fake_{plus}$	82.07	71.82
		$fake_{plus,w/o\text{-}geo}$	63.99	55.23
		$fake_{plus,w/o\text{-}pmse}$	45.05	34.51
		$fake_{plus,w/o\text{-}reason}$	18.36	9.71
	Tote	$fake_{plus}$	82.69	76.84
		$fake_{plus,w/o\text{-}geo}$	64.22	53.31
		$fake_{plus,w/o\text{-}pmse}$	46.44	35.62
		$fake_{plus,w/o\text{-}reason}$	20.05	12.43

Fig. 10. Samples to illustrate the efficacy of structure loss, geometry-guided loss in GeoGAN and reasoning system in our pipeline.

8 Limitations and Future Work

If the environmental background changes dynamically, we should scan a large number of environmental backgrounds to cover this variance and take much effort. Due to the limitations of the physics engine, it is hard to handle highly non-rigid objects such as a towel. For another limitation, our method does not consider illumination effects in rendering, since it is much more complicated. GeoGAN that transfers illumination conditions of the real image may partially address this problem, but it is still imperfect. In addition, the size of our benchmark dataset is relatively small in comparison with COCO. Future work is necessary to address these limitations.

Acknowledgement. This work is supported in part by the National Key R&D Program of China, No. 2017YFA0700800, National Natural Science Foundation of China under Grants 61772332 and SenseTime Ltd.

References

1. Alhaija, H.A., Mustikovela, S.K., Mescheder, L., Geiger, A., Rother, C.: Augmented reality meets deep learning for car instance segmentation in urban scenes. In: Proceedings of the British Machine Vision Conference, vol. 3 (2017)
2. Benaim, S., Wolf, L.: One-sided unsupervised domain mapping. In: Advances in Neural Information Processing Systems (2017)
3. Bousmalis, K., Silberman, N., Dohan, D., Erhan, D., Krishnan, D.: Unsupervised pixel-level domain adaptation with generative adversarial networks. In: The IEEE Conference on Computer Vision and Pattern Recognition (CVPR), July 2017
4. Chen, Q., Koltun, V.: Photographic image synthesis with cascaded refinement networks. In: IEEE International Conference on Computer Vision (ICCV) (2017)
5. Cordts, M., et al.: The cityscapes dataset for semantic urban scene understanding. In: Proceedings of the IEEE Conference on Computer Vision and Pattern Recognition (CVPR) (2016)
6. Dai, J., He, K., Sun, J.: Instance-aware semantic segmentation via multi-task network cascades. In: 2016 IEEE Conference on Computer Vision and Pattern Recognition (CVPR), pp. 3150–3158, June 2016. DOI: https://doi.org/10.1109/CVPR.2016.343
7. Eigen, D., Puhrsch, C., Fergus, R.: Depth map prediction from a single image using a multi-scale deep network. In: International Conference on Neural Information Processing Systems, pp. 2366–2374 (2014)
8. Everingham, M., Van Gool, L., Williams, C.K.I., Winn, J., Zisserman, A.: The PASCAL Visual Object Classes Challenge 2012 (VOC2012) Results. http://www.pascal-network.org/challenges/VOC/voc2012/workshop/index.html
9. Fisher, M., Ritchie, D., Savva, M., Funkhouser, T., Hanrahan, P.: Example-based synthesis of 3D object arrangements. ACM Trans. Graph. **31**(6), 135 (2012)
10. Fuhrmann, S., Langguth, F., Goesele, M.: MVE-A multi-view reconstruction environment. In: GCH, pp. 11–18 (2014)
11. Georgakis, G., Mousavian, A., Berg, A.C., Kosecka, J.: Synthesizing training data for object detection in indoor scenes. arXiv preprint arXiv:1702.07836 (2017)

12. Goodfellow, I., et al.: Generative adversarial nets. In: Advances in Neural Information Processing Systems, pp. 2672–2680 (2014)
13. Handa, A., Ptucean, V., Stent, S., Cipolla, R.: SceneNet: an annotated model generator for indoor scene understanding. In: IEEE International Conference on Robotics and Automation, pp. 5737–5743 (2016)
14. He, K., Gkioxari, G., Dollár, P., Girshick, R.: Mask R-CNN. arXiv preprint arXiv:1703.06870 (2017)
15. He, K., Zhang, X., Ren, S., Sun, J.: Deep residual learning for image recognition. In: Computer Vision and Pattern Recognition, pp. 770–778 (2016)
16. Isola, P., Zhu, J.Y., Zhou, T., Efros, A.A.: Image-to-image translation with conditional adversarial networks. In: The IEEE Conference on Computer Vision and Pattern Recognition (CVPR), July 2017
17. Kim, T., Cha, M., Kim, H., Lee, J., Kim, J.: Learning to discover cross-domain relations with generative adversarial networks. In: IEEE International Conference on Computer Vision (ICCV) (2017)
18. Kingma, D.P., Ba, J.: Adam: a method for stochastic optimization. In: Computer Science (2014)
19. Ledig, C., et al.: Photo-realistic single image super-resolution using a generative adversarial network (2016)
20. Li, C., Wand, M.: Precomputed real-time texture synthesis with Markovian generative adversarial networks. In: Leibe, B., Matas, J., Sebe, N., Welling, M. (eds.) ECCV 2016. LNCS, vol. 9907, pp. 702–716. Springer, Cham (2016). https://doi.org/10.1007/978-3-319-46487-9_43
21. Li, Y., Qi, H., Dai, J., Ji, X., Wei, Y.: Fully convolutional instance-aware semantic segmentation. In: 2017 IEEE Conference on Computer Vision and Pattern Recognition (CVPR) (2017)
22. Lin, T.Y., et al.: Microsoft COCO: common objects in context. In: Fleet, D., Pajdla, T., Schiele, B., Tuytelaars, T. (eds.) ECCV 2014. LNCS, vol. 8693, pp. 740–755. Springer, Cham (2014). https://doi.org/10.1007/978-3-319-10602-1_48
23. Long, J., Shelhamer, E., Darrell, T.: Fully convolutional networks for semantic segmentation. In: Computer Vision and Pattern Recognition, pp. 3431–3440 (2015)
24. Mao, X., Li, Q., Xie, H., Lau, R.Y.K., Wang, Z., Smolley, S.P.: Least squares generative adversarial networks (2016)
25. Mccormac, J., Handa, A., Leutenegger, S., Davison, A.J.: SceneNet RGB-D: 5M photorealistic images of synthetic indoor trajectories with ground truth (2017)
26. Merrell, P., Schkufza, E., Li, Z., Agrawala, M., Koltun, V.: Interactive furniture layout using interior design guidelines. In: ACM SIGGRAPH, p. 87 (2011)
27. Radford, A., Metz, L., Chintala, S.: Unsupervised representation learning with deep convolutional generative adversarial networks
28. Ren, S., He, K., Girshick, R., Sun, J.: Faster R-CNN: towards real-time object detection with region proposal networks. In: Advances in Neural Information Processing Systems (NIPS) (2015)
29. Ronneberger, O., Fischer, P., Brox, T.: U-Net: convolutional networks for biomedical image segmentation. In: Navab, N., Hornegger, J., Wells, W.M., Frangi, A.F. (eds.) MICCAI 2015. LNCS, vol. 9351, pp. 234–241. Springer, Cham (2015). https://doi.org/10.1007/978-3-319-24574-4_28
30. Ros, G., Sellart, L., Materzynska, J., Vazquez, D., Lopez, A.: The SYNTHIA dataset: a large collection of synthetic images for semantic segmentation of urban scenes. In: 2017 IEEE Conference on Computer Vision and Pattern Recognition (CVPR) (2016)

31. Rusu, A.A., Vecerik, M., Rothrl, T., Heess, N., Pascanu, R., Hadsell, R.: Sim-to-real robot learning from pixels with progressive nets (2016)
32. Shrivastava, A., Pfister, T., Tuzel, O., Susskind, J., Wang, W., Webb, R.: Learning from simulated and unsupervised images through adversarial training. In: The IEEE Conference on Computer Vision and Pattern Recognition (CVPR) (2017)
33. Sixt, L., Wild, B., Landgraf, T.: RenderGAN: generating realistic labeled data. arXiv preprint arXiv:1611.01331 (2016)
34. Song, S., Yu, F., Zeng, A., Chang, A.X., Savva, M., Funkhouser, T.: Semantic scene completion from a single depth image (2016)
35. Su, H., Qi, C.R., Li, Y., Guibas, L.J.: Render for CNN: viewpoint estimation in images using CNNs trained with rendered 3D model views. In: The IEEE International Conference on Computer Vision (ICCV), December 2015
36. Taigman, Y., Polyak, A., Wolf, L.: Unsupervised cross-domain image generation (2016)
37. Tasora, A., et al.: Chrono: an open source multi-physics dynamics engine. In: Kozubek, T., Blaheta, R., Šístek, J., Rozložník, M., Čermák, M. (eds.) HPCSE 2015. LNCS, vol. 9611, pp. 19–49. Springer, Cham (2016). https://doi.org/10.1007/978-3-319-40361-8_2
38. Tzeng, E., et al.: Towards adapting deep visuomotor representations from simulated to real environments. In: Computer Science (2015)
39. Tzionas, D., Gall, J.: 3D object reconstruction from hand-object interactions. In: Proceedings of the IEEE International Conference on Computer Vision, pp. 729–737 (2015)
40. Wu, J., Zhang, C., Xue, T., Freeman, B., Tenenbaum, J.: Learning a probabilistic latent space of object shapes via 3D generative-adversarial modeling. In: Advances in Neural Information Processing Systems, pp. 82–90 (2016)
41. Yi, Z., Zhang, H., Gong, P.T., et al.: DualGAN: unsupervised dual learning for image-to-image translation. In: IEEE International Conference on Computer Vision (ICCV) (2017)
42. Zhu, J.Y., Park, T., Isola, P., Efros, A.A.: Unpaired image-to-image translation using cycle-consistent adversarial networks. In: IEEE International Conference on Computer Vision (ICCV) (2017)
43. Zhu, Y., et al.: Target-driven visual navigation in indoor scenes using deep reinforcement learning (2016)

Unsupervised Domain Adaptation for 3D Keypoint Estimation via View Consistency

Xingyi Zhou[1], Arjun Karpur[1], Chuang Gan[2], Linjie Luo[3], and Qixing Huang[1(✉)]

[1] The University of Texas at Austin, Austin, USA
{zhouxy,akarpur,huangqx}@cs.utexas.edu
[2] MIT-IBM Watson AI Lab, Cambridge, USA
ganchuang1990@gmail.com
[3] Snap Inc., Los Angeles, USA
linjie.luo@snap.com

Abstract. In this paper, we introduce a novel unsupervised domain adaptation technique for the task of 3D keypoint prediction from a single depth scan or image. Our key idea is to utilize the fact that predictions from different views of the same or similar objects should be consistent with each other. Such view consistency can provide effective regularization for keypoint prediction on unlabeled instances. In addition, we introduce a geometric alignment term to regularize predictions in the target domain. The resulting loss function can be effectively optimized via alternating minimization. We demonstrate the effectiveness of our approach on real datasets and present experimental results showing that our approach is superior to state-of-the-art general-purpose domain adaptation techniques.

Keywords: 3D keypoint estimation · Multi-view consistency
Domain adaptation · Unsupervised learning

1 Introduction

A new era has arrived with the proliferation of depth-equipped sensors in all kinds of form factors, ranging from wearables and mobile phones to on-vehicle scanners. This ever-increasing amount of depth scans is a valuable resource that remains largely untapped, however, due to a lack of techniques capable of efficiently processing, representing, and understanding them.

3D keypoints, which can be inferred from depth scans, are a compact yet semantically rich representation of 3D objects that have proven effective for many

Electronic supplementary material The online version of this chapter (https://doi.org/10.1007/978-3-030-01258-8_9) contains supplementary material, which is available to authorized users.

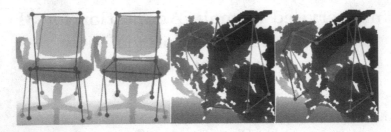

Fig. 1. Our approach improves 3D keypoint prediction results from single depth scans of the Redwood dataset [3]. For each pair: **(Left)** without domain adaptation, the pre-trained keypoint predictor from simulated examples failed to predict accurate 3D keypoints (blue). **(Right)** 3D keypoint predictions (blue) after domain adaptation are significantly improved. Note that the ground-truth keypoints are shown in red for comparison. (Color figure online)

tasks, including reconstruction [10], object segmentation and recognition [17], as well as pose estimation [33]. Despite the wide availability of depth scans of various object categories [3], there is a lack of corresponding 3D keypoint annotations, which are necessary to train reliable keypoint predictors in a supervised approach. This is partially due to the fact that depth scans are inherently partial views of the underlying objects, making it difficult to annotate the object parts occluded from view. One could automate the annotation process by leveraging the "fused" models created using the depth scans, but most depth-fusion methods are susceptible to scanning noise and cascading errors when depth scans are captured at scale [3] (Fig. 1).

In this paper, our goal is to predict 3D keypoints of an underlying object from a single raw depth scan. To train a reliable 3D keypoint predictor, we generate a large dataset of simulated depth scans using large-scale 3D model repositories such as ShapeNet [2] and ModelNet [38]. The 3D keypoint annotations on the 3D models from these repositories can naturally carry over to the simulated depth scans for effective supervised training. A large gap exists, however, between the simulated and real depth scan domains. Particularly, 3D models from repositories are generally designed with interactive tools, inevitably resulting in inaccurate geometries with varying scales. Furthermore, the real depth scans contain noticeable measurement noise and background objects, and the class distributions of 3D models from the repositories and those from real depth scans may be quite different.

To close the gap between the source domain of simulated depth scans and the target domain of real depth scans, we introduce a novel approach for unsupervised domain adaptation of 3D keypoint prediction. Our approach is motivated by the special spatial properties of the 3D keypoints and the relationship between the keypoint distributions of the source and target domains.

First, keypoint predictions from different views of the same 3D model should be consistent with each other up to a pose transformation. This allows us to formulate a *view-consistency* regularization to propagate a good prediction, e.g.

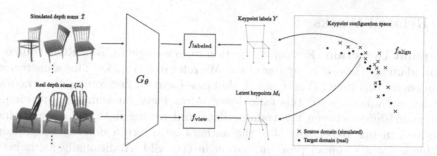

Fig. 2. Approach overview. We train an end-to-end 3D keypoint prediction network G_θ from labeled simulated depth scans $\bar{\mathcal{I}}$ of 3D models and unlabeled and unaligned real depth scans $\{\mathcal{I}_i\}$ of real world objects.

from a well-posed view where the prediction is more accurately adapted, to a challenging view with less accurate adaptation. To this end, we introduce a latent keypoint configuration to fuse the keypoint predictions from different views of the same object. Additionally, we introduce a pose-invariant metric to compare the keypoint predictions, which allows us to leverage depth scans without camera pose calibration for training (Fig. 2).

Second, despite the distinctive differences between the source and target domains, their 3D keypoint distributions are highly correlated. However, naively aligning the 3D keypoint distributions between the two domains is sub-optimal since the occurrences of the same type of objects differ. To address this challenge, we propose a *geometric alignment* regularization that is insensitive to varying densities of the objects in order to align the keypoint distributions of the two domains. We make use of the target domain's latent keypoint configurations from view consistency regularization to compute the geometric alignment with the source domain. Note that since possible keypoint configurations lie on a manifold with much lower dimension over the ambient space, the geometric alignment can provide effective regularization.

Our final formulation combines a standard supervised loss on the source domain with the two unsupervised regularization losses on view-consistency and geometric alignment. Our formulation can be easily optimized via alternating minimization and admits a simple strategy for variable initialization.

We evaluate the proposed approach on unsupervised domain adaptation from ModelNet [38] to rendered depth scans from the synthesized ShapeNet [2] 3D model dataset, and to real depth scans from the Redwood Object Scans [3] and 3DCNN Depth Scans [22] datasets. Experimental results demonstrate that our approach can effectively reduce the domain gap between the online 3D model repositories and the real depth scans with background noise. Our approach is significantly better than without domain adaptation and is superior to general-purpose domain adaptation techniques such as ADDA [35]. We also provide ablation studies to justify the design choice of each component of our approach. Code is available at https://github.com/xingyizhou/3DKeypoints-DA.

2   Related Works

Keypoint Detection. Keypoint detection from a single RGB or RGB-D image is a fundamental task in computer vision. We refer to [7,19,25,45] for some recent advances on this topic. While most techniques focus on developing novel neural network architectures for this task, fewer works focus on addressing the issue of domain shifts between the training data and testing data, e.g., the setting described in this paper. In [45], the authors introduce a domain adaptation technique for 3D human pose estimation in the wild. Additionally for human pose estimation, [7] proposes to align the source and target label distributions using a GAN loss. We opt to use an alternate metric that offers more flexibility in addressing domain shifts. Similarly to our method, [25] also leverages the consistency across multiple views to boost the supervision on the target domain. However, the output of this approach is computed directly from the initial predictions from the source domain. In contrast, our approach only uses the initial predictions to initialize final predictions. Moreover, we utilize a latent configuration for synchronizing the predictions from multiple views, which avoids performing pair-wise analysis.

Multi-view Supervision. RGB and RGB-D video sequences essentially consist of different views of the same underlying 3D environment. In the literature, people have utilized such weak supervision for various tasks such as 3D reconstruction, novel view synthesis and 2D keypoint prediction, e.g.,[15,25,34,40,43]. Our work differs from most works in the sense that we do not assume that relative poses between cameras are known. Instead, we introduce a pose invariant metric to compare keypoint configurations. Concurrent to our work, Helge et al. [23] also introduced a similar viewpoint consistency term for un-supervised 3D human pose estimation. However, the multi-view data for articulated object is still hard to obtain. On the contrary, we use viewpoint consistency for rigid objects, where the views are free from videos.

Supervision from Big 3D Data. Thanks the availability of annotated big 3D data such as ModelNet [38] and ShapeNet [2], people have leveraged synthetic data generated from 3D models for various tasks, including image classification [38], object recognition [21,26,27], semantic segmentation [42], object reconstruction [4,28,32], pose estimation [29] and novel-view synthesis [30,44]. The fundamental challenge of these approaches is that there are domain shifts between synthetic data and real RGB or RGB-D images. Most existing works focus on improving the simulation process to close this gap. In contrast, we focus on developing an unsupervised loss for domain adaptation.

Domain Adaptation. Domain adaptation [1,8,9,12,16,18,20,24,36,39,41] for various visual recognition tasks is an active research area in computer vision, and our problem falls into the general category of domain adaptation. It is beyond the scope of this paper to provide a comprehensive review of the literature, however we refer to a recent survey [6] on this topic. A common strategy for unsupervised domain adaptation is to align the output distributions between source and target domains, e.g., either through explicit domain-wise maps or through use of a GAN. In contrast, our regularizations are tailored for the particular problem we consider, i.e., view-consistency and domain shifts caused by varying densities.

3   Problem Statement

We study the problem of predicting complete 3D keypoints of an underlying object from a single image or depth scan. We assume the input consists of a labeled dataset $\overline{\mathcal{I}}$ and an unlabeled dataset $\mathcal{I}$. Moreover, the unlabeled dataset is comprised of N subsets $\mathcal{I}_i, 1 \leq i \leq N$, where each subset collects depth scans/images of the same object from different views. Such data naturally arises from RGB-D or RGB video sequences.

Each instance $I \in \overline{\mathcal{I}}$ in the labeled dataset possesses a ground-truth label $Y(I) \in \mathbb{R}^{3 \times d}$, which is a matrix that collects the coordinates of the ordered keypoints in its columns. Without losing generality, we assume that the 3D local coordinate system of I is chosen so that the centroid of $Y(I)$ is at the origin:

$$Y(I)\mathbf{1} = 0. \tag{1}$$

It is expected that the source domain of the labeled dataset and the target domain of the unlabeled dataset are different (e.g., the source domain consists of synthetic images/scans but the target domain consists of real images/scans). Our goal is to train a neural network $G_\theta : \mathbb{R}^{m \times n} \to \mathbb{R}^{3 \times d}$ that takes an image from the target domain as input and outputs the predicted keypoints by leveraging both the labeled dataset $\overline{\mathcal{I}}$ and unlabeled subsets $\mathcal{I}_i, 1 \leq i \leq N$. We define this problem as unsupervised domain adaptation for 3D keypoint prediction.

Note that we do not assume the underlying cameras of each unlabeled subset are calibrated, or in other words, the relative transformations between different views of the same object are not required. Although it is possible to align the depth scans to obtain relative transformations, we found that such alignments are not always reliable in the presence of scanning discontinuities where little overlaps between consecutive scans are available. In contrast, our formulation treats relative camera poses as latent variables, which are optimized together with the network parameters.

4   Approach

In this section, we describe our detailed approach to unsupervised domain adaptation for 3D keypoint prediction. We first introduce a pose-invariant distance metric to compare keypoint configurations in Sect. 4.1. This allows us to compare the predictions in different views without knowing the relative transformations for uncalibrated datasets. We then present the formulation of our approach in Sect. 4.2. Finally, we discuss our optimization strategy in Sect. 4.3.

4.1 Pose-Invariant Distance Metric

The pose-invariant distance metric compares two keypoint configurations $X, Y \in \mathbb{R}^{3 \times d}$ described in different coordinate systems. Since the mean of each keypoint configuration is zero, we introduce a latent rotation R to account for the underlying relative transformation:

$$r(X,Y) = \min_{R \in SO(3)} \|RX - Y\|_{\mathcal{F}}^2, \tag{2}$$

where $\| \cdot \|_{\mathcal{F}}$ denotes the matrix Frobenius Norm. It is clear that $r(X,Y)$ is independent of the coordinate systems associated with X and Y, making it particularly suitable for comparing predictions from uncalibrated views and aligning the source domain and the target domain.

In the following, we discuss a few key properties of $r(X,Y)$ that will be used extensively in our approach. First of all, both $r(X,Y)$ and the gradient of $r(X,Y)$ with respect to each of its argument admit closed-form expressions. These are summarized in the following two propositions.

Proposition 1. $r(X,Y)$ admits the following analytic expression:

$$r(X,Y) = \|X\|_{\mathcal{F}}^2 + \|Y\|_{\mathcal{F}}^2 - 2 \cdot trace\big(R \cdot (XY^T)\big)$$

where R is derived from the singular value decomposition (or SVD) of $YX^T = U\Sigma V^T$:

$$R = U \mathrm{diag}(1,1,s)V^T, \quad s = sign(\det(XY^T)). \tag{3}$$

Proof: See [13]. □

Proposition 2. The gradient of $r(X,Y)$ with respect to X is given by

$$\frac{\partial r}{\partial X}(X,Y) = 2(X - R^T Y),$$

where R is given by Eq. (3).

Proof: Please refer to the supplemental material. □

Our optimization procedure also frequently involves the following optimization problem that computes the weighted average $X^\star$ of a set of keypoint configurations $Y_i, 1 \leq i \leq n$ in the quotient space $\mathbb{R}^{3 \times d}/SO(3)$:

$$X^\star = \underset{X \in \mathbb{R}^{3 \times d}}{\mathrm{argmin}} \sum_{i=1}^{n} c_i r(X, Y_i) = \underset{X \in \mathbb{R}^{3 \times d}}{\mathrm{argmin}} \sum_{i=1}^{n} c_i \min_{R_i \in SO(3)} \|X - R_i^T Y_i\|_{\mathcal{F}}^2, \tag{4}$$

where $c_i, 1 \leq i \leq n$ are constants. Although Eq. (4) does not admit a closed-form solution, it can be easily optimized via alternating minimization. Specifically, when X is fixed, each R_i can be computed independently using Proposition 1. When the R_i latent variables are fixed, X is simply given by the mean of $R_i^T Y_i$, i.e., $X = \frac{1}{\sum c_i} \sum_{i=1}^{n} c_i R_i^T Y_i$. To make the solution unique, we always set $R_1 = I_3$.

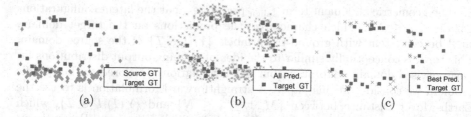

Fig. 3. Latent Distribution and View Selection. This figure provides visualizations of label distributions and view selection for initializing the latent configurations from ModelNet (source domain) to Redwood (target domain) on the Chair category. All visualizations are done by 2D projections using the first two principal components. (a) Label distributions of the source and target domains. (b) Visualizations of all predictions from different views. (c) Visualizations of the best prediction from each object.

4.2   Formulation

To train the keypoint prediction network $G_\theta(\cdot)$, we introduce three loss terms, namely, a labeled term f_{labeled}, a view-consistency term f_{view} and a geometric alignment term f_{align}.

The labeled term f_{labeled} fits predictions on the source domain labeled dataset $\overline{\mathcal{I}}$ to the prescribed ground-truth labels. We use the regression loss under the L2-norm, which works well for 3D keypoint prediction tasks (c.f. [31,45]):

$$f_{\text{labeled}} = \frac{1}{|\overline{\mathcal{I}}|} \sum_{I \in \overline{\mathcal{I}}} \|G_\theta(I) - Y(I)\|_{\mathcal{F}}^2. \tag{5}$$

The view-consistency term f_{view} is defined on the target domain to enforce consistency between the predictions from different views of the same object. In other words, there exist pairwise rotations that transform the predictions from one view to another. A straightforward approach is to minimize $r(G_\theta(I_{ij}), G_\theta(I_{ij'}))$, where I_{ij} and $I_{ij'}$ are different views of the same object. However, we found that such approach introduces a quadratic number of terms as the number of views increases and quickly becomes intractable. Therefore, we introduce a latent configuration $M_i \in \mathbb{R}^{3 \times d}$ for each unlabeled subset $\mathcal{I}_i$ that characterizes the underlying ground-truth in the canonical frame. We then define the view consistency term as:

$$f_{\text{view}} = \frac{1}{N} \sum_{i=1}^{N} \frac{1}{|\mathcal{I}_i|} \sum_{I_{ij} \in \mathcal{I}_i} r(G_\theta(I_{ij}), M_i). \tag{6}$$

It is clear that minimizing f_{view} automatically aligns the predictions across different views. The key advantages of Eq. (6) over enforcing pairwise view-consistency are (i) the number of items is linear to the number of views, and (ii) as we will see immediately, the latent configurations $\{M_i\}$ allow us to easily formulate the geometric alignment term f_{align}.

The geometric alignment term f_{align} prioritizes that the latent configurations $\{M_i, 1 \le i \le N\}$, which characterize the predictions on the target domain, shall be consistent with ground-truth labels $\{Y_I | I \in \bar{\mathcal{I}}\}$ of the source domain. This term is conceptually similar to the idea of aligning output distributions for unsupervised domain adaptation, but our formulation is tailored to the specific problem we consider in this paper. A straightforward formulation is to use the Earth-Mover Distance between $\{M_i, 1 \le i \le N\}$ and $\{Y(I) | I \in \bar{\mathcal{I}}\}$, which essentially aligns the two corresponding empirical distributions. However, we found that this strategy would force the alignment of keypoint configurations that are far apart, since the repetition counts of the same sub-types of an object may be different between the source and target domains (See Fig. 3(a)). To address this issue, we propose to use the Chamfer distance for alignment:

$$f_{\text{align}} = \frac{1}{N} \sum_{i=1}^{N} \min_{I \in \bar{\mathcal{I}}} r(M_i, Y_I) + \frac{1}{|\bar{\mathcal{I}}|} \sum_{I \in \bar{\mathcal{I}}} \min_{1 \le i \le N} r(M_i, Y_I). \tag{7}$$

Intuitively, Eq. (7) still aligns the source and target domains, but it is insensitive to local density variations, and provides an effective way to address domain shifts.

We combine the labeled term f_{labeled}, the view-consistency term f_{view} and the geometric alignment term f_{align} into the final loss function:

$$\underset{\theta, \{M_i\}}{\text{minimize}} f_{\text{labeled}} + \lambda f_{\text{view}} + \mu f_{\text{align}}. \tag{8}$$

In our implementation, we set $\lambda = 1$ and $\mu = 0.1$.

4.3   Optimization

The major difficulty for optimizing Eq. (8) lies in the fact that the alignment term f_{align} is highly non-convex. In our experiments, we found that obtaining good initial values of the network parameters and latent variables is critical to achieving high-quality keypoint prediction network. In the following, we first introduce effective strategies to initialize the variables. We then show how to refine the variables using alternating minimization.

Network Parameter Initialization. The network parameters are initialized by pre-training on the the source domain labeled dataset, i.e.,

$$\theta^{(0)} = \min_{\theta} \sum_{I \in \bar{\mathcal{I}}} \|G_\theta(I) - Y_I\|_{\mathcal{F}}^2. \tag{9}$$

It is then optimized via standard back-propagation.

Latent Configuration Initialization. We use the predictions obtained from the initial network $G_{\theta^{(0)}}(I_{ij}), I_{ij} \in \mathcal{I}_i$ to initialize each latent variable M_i. To this end, we define a score for each prediction and set M_i as the one with the highest score. The scoring function is motivated by the fact that the latent variables are expected to align with the source domain, we thus define an un-normalized density function:

$$p(M) = \sum_{I \in \overline{\mathcal{I}}} \exp(-\frac{r(M, Y(I))}{2\sigma^2}), \tag{10}$$

where σ is chosen as mean of $r(G_{\theta^{(0)}}(I_{ij}), Y(I))$ between the predicted configurations and their closest labeled instances. Given Eq. (10), we set

$$M_i^{(0)} = \underset{M \in \{G_{\theta^{(0)}}(I)|I \in \mathcal{I}_i\}}{\mathrm{argmax}} \; p(M). \tag{11}$$

As illustrated in Fig. 3(b–c), this strategy leads to initial configurations that are close to the underlying ground-truth.

Alternating Minimization. Given the initial network parameter $\theta^{(0)}$ and the initial latent configurations $M_i^{(0)}, 1 \leq i \leq N$, we then refine them by solving Eq. (8) via alternating minimization. With $M_i^{(k)}$ and $\theta^{(k)}$ we denote their values at iteration k. At each alternating minimization step, we first fix the latent variables to optimize the network parameters. This leads to computing

$$\theta^{(k+1)} = \underset{\theta}{\mathrm{argmin}} \; \frac{1}{|\overline{\mathcal{I}}|} \sum_{I \in \overline{\mathcal{I}}} \|G_\theta(I) - Y_I\|_{\mathcal{F}}^2 + \frac{\lambda}{N} \sum_{i=1}^{N} \frac{1}{|\mathcal{I}_i|} \sum_{I \in \mathcal{I}_i} r(G_\theta(I), M_i^{(k)}). \tag{12}$$

Utilizing Proposition 2, we apply stochastic gradient descent via back-propagation for solving Eq. (12).

We then fix the network parameters θ and optimize the latent variables $\{M_i^{(k+1)}\}$. In this case, Eq. (8) reduces to

$$\{M_i^{(k+1)}\} = \underset{\{M_i\}}{\mathrm{argmin}} \; \frac{\mu}{|\overline{\mathcal{I}}|} \sum_{I \in \overline{\mathcal{I}}} \min_{1 \leq i \leq N} r(M_i, Y_I)$$

$$+ \frac{1}{N} \sum_{i=1}^{N} \Big(\frac{\lambda}{|\mathcal{I}_i|} \sum_{I \in \mathcal{I}_i} r(G_{\theta^{(k)}}(I), M_i) + \mu \min_{I \in \overline{\mathcal{I}}} r(M_i, Y_I) \Big). \tag{13}$$

We again apply alternating minimization to solve Eq. (13). In particular, we fix the closest point pairs given $\{M_i^{(k)}\}$:

$$\hat{I}(i) = \underset{I \in \overline{\mathcal{I}}}{\mathrm{argmin}} \; r(M_i^{(k)}, Y_I), \quad \hat{i}(I) = \underset{1 \leq i \leq N}{\mathrm{argmin}} \; r(M_i^{(k)}, Y_I). \tag{14}$$

Given these closest pairs, we can optimize each latent configuration as

$$\underset{M_i}{\mathrm{argmin}} \frac{\mu}{|\overline{\mathcal{I}}|} \sum_{I|\hat{i}(I)=i} r(M_i, Y_I) + \frac{1}{N} \Big(\frac{\lambda}{|\mathcal{I}_i|} \sum_{I \in \mathcal{I}_i} r(G_{\theta^{(k)}}(I), M_i) + \mu r(M_i, Y_{\hat{I}(i)}) \Big).$$

$$\tag{15}$$

Equation (15) admits a form of Eq. (4), and we apply the procedure described above to solve Eq. (15). In our experiments, we typically apply the inner alternating minimizations each 5 epochs for training the network parameters θ.

5   Evaluation

For experimental evaluation, we first describe the experimental setup in Sect. 5.1. We then present qualitative and quantitative results and compare our technique against baseline approaches in Sect. 5.2. We also present an ablation study to evaluate each component of our approach in Sect. 5.3. Finally, we further extend our method to 3D human pose estimation and RGB images in Sects. 5.4 and 5.5, respectively.

5.1   Experimental Setup

Dataset. Rendered depth scans of synthesized object models from the Model-Net [38] dataset serve as our source domain, and we test our domain adaptation method on three different target domains, namely: ShapeNet [2] (another synthesized 3D model dataset), the Redwood Object Scans real depth scan dataset [3], and the 3DCNN real depth scan dataset [22]. We focus our experiments on the chair, motorbike, and human classes, however we provide the most-detailed results on chairs because of their ubiquitousness across many popular 3D model and depth scan datasets. To provide keypoint labels for our source domain, we manually annotate the training samples in ModelNet with Meshlab [5]. To evaluate the accuracy of our system, we also annotate keypoints on our target domain datasets. This annotation is done by recovering each object's 3D mesh and each frame's camera pose from a depth video sequence. We only maintain frames in which all 2D projections of keypoints are within the image and keep the models with at least 20 valid frames. A summary of the four datasets used in our experiments is presented in Table 3. As a natural extension, we also test our method on the RGB images from the same Redwood dataset [3].

Data Pre-processing. We assume the camera intrinsic and object's 3D bounding box are known both in training and testing depth images solely for data pre-processing. We use the 2D projection of the 3D bounding box to crop each depth image. Additionally, the input depth images are centered by the mean depth and the depth values are normalized by the diagonal length of the 3D bounding box. Aside from the images, all keypoints are converted and evaluated in a unified coordinate system. Given a configuration, we subtract their mean and normalize by the diagonal length of the 3D bounding box.

Evaluation Protocol. Similar to [37], we measure the Average distance Error (AE) between each predicted keypoint configuration and the corresponding annotation and plot the Percentage of Correct Keypoint (PCK) with respect to a threshold for each method for detailed comparison. We also introduce a new metric, Pose-invariant Average distance Error (PAE) based on (2), for a better illustration of how our proposed method works. The AE and PAE are shown in percentage and represent the relative ratio to the diagonal length of the 3D bounding box.

Baseline Methods. We consider three baseline methods for experimental evaluation.

- **Baseline I.** We first test performance without any domain adaptation techniques, namely we directly apply the keypoint predictor trained on the source domain to the target domain. This baseline serves as a performance lower bound for accessing domain adaptation techniques.
- **Baseline II.** We implement a state-of-the-art deep unsupervised general domain adaptation technique described in [35], which encourages domain confusion by fine-tuning the feature extractor on the target domain.
- **Baseline III.** We apply supervised keypoint prediction on the target domain. To this end, we annotate 50 additional models from each domain and fine-tune Baseline I on these labeled instances. This baseline serves as a performance upper bound for accessing domain adaptation techniques.

In Table 1 we compare these baselines to our approach on the Chair dataset. In addition, we provide before/after adaptation results for motorbike and human in Table 2. We also conduct an ablation study on the Chair dataset to evaluate each component of our approach (Table 4 and Fig. 4).

Implementation Details. We use ResNet50 [11] pre-trained on ImageNet as our keypoint prediction network G_θ. In order to fit our depth scans to the ResNet50 input (and additionally, to allow for natural extension to the RGB image domain), we duplicate the depth channel three times. The network is first trained on source domain $\overline{\mathcal{I}}$ for 120 epochs, and then fine-tuned on a specific target domain $\mathcal{I}$ for 30 epochs. The network is trained using a SGD optimizer via back-propagation, with learning rate 0.01 (dropped to 0.001 after 20 epochs), batch size 64, momentum 0.9 and weight decay 1e-4, which are all the default parameters in Resnet50 [11]. Our implementation is done in PyTorch.

5.2 Analysis of Results

Tables 1, 2 and 4, Figs. 4, and 5 present the quantitative and qualitative results of our approach.

Table 1. Results of our proposed methods tested on chairs after domain adaptation on different target domains. We show Average distance Error (AE) and Pose-Invariant Average distance Error (PAE) in percentage. For both metrics, the lower the better.

Target-Metric	Default-AE	ADDA-AE	Ours-AE	Supervised-AE	Default-PAE	ADDA-PAE	Ours-PAE	Supervised-PAE
ModelNet [38]	-	-	-	5.56	-	-	-	4.76
ShapeNet [2]	6.97	6.98	**6.60**	5.82	5.77	5.89	**5.32**	4.77
RedwoodDepth [3]	16.01	15.44	**12.76**	8.67	10.73	10.13	**8.27**	5.68
3DCNN [22]	11.61	11.81	**10.60**	6.73	8.15	8.19	**7.25**	4.98
RedwoodRGB [3]	27.59	26.16	**25.24**	11.90	13.44	12.31	**11.38**	7.67

Table 2. Quantitative results - AE

Category	Motorcycle	Human
Before adaptation	21.55%	153.39 mm
After adaptation	18.92%	135.56 mm
Supervised	16.17%	113.44 mm

Table 3. Statistics of the datasets.

Target	#Train models	#Test models	Avg #frames
ModelNet [38]	899	100	Inf
ShapeNet [2]	2500	100	Inf
Redwood [3]	200	35	150
3DCNN [22]	9	3	80

Qualitative Results. As illustrated in Fig. 5, our approach yields keypoint structures that are consistent with the underlying ground-truths. Even under significant background noise and incomplete observations, our approach leads to faithful structures. Exceptions include the case for chair types that involve swivel bases. In this case, the predicted legs may be tilted. This is expected since the annotations may become unreliable in cases when the legs do not fall directly below the seat corners.

Quantitative Assessment. As shown in Table 1, the mean deviations of our approach in the two real depth scan datasets Redwood [3] and 3DCNN [22] for the chair object class are 12.76% and 10.60% of the diagonal length of object bounding box, respectively. This translates to approximately 7–10 cm, which is fairly accurate when compared to the radius of a chair's base. Additional experiments done on the motorbike class yield similar improvements, as indicated by Table 2. For the motorbike training process, we utilize the ShapeNet dataset as our source domain and the Redwood dataset as our target domain.

Analyses of Performance Across Different Datasets. Table 1 shows that our method gives consistent performance improvements on all three target depth domains. For the synthesized dataset ShapeNet [2], which has a relatively small domain shift from the supervised training set, our unsupervised terms are still able to push error rates close to the supervised upper bound. The advantages of our proposed method can be best observed in the Redwood dataset [3], where using our full error terms leads to a 44% step towards the supervised performance upper-bound. Additionally, the improvement in 3DCNN Dataset [22] is still decent despite the very limited available models and poor depth image quality.

Analysis of Performance Gain. Our performance gains can be attributed to our network learning more plausible keypoint configuration shapes, which is supported by the fact that the improvement of AE is always close to that of PAE. This is expected because our unsupervised terms are viewpoint-invariant and focus on improving the keypoint configuration shape.

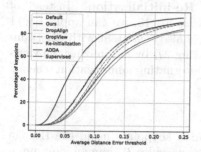

Fig. 4. Baseline & Ablation Study. Comparisons between our approach with alternative approaches on Redwood depth Dataset [3]. The Figure shows Percentage of Correct Keypoints (PCK) under a threshold.

Table 4. Chair ablation study on ShapeNet and Redwood Object Scans dataset. We show the Average distance Error (AE) in percentage for each approach, including the three baselines.

Target domain	ShapeNet(%)	Redwood depth(%)
Ours	**6.60**	**12.76**
Drop view	6.70	13.95
Drop align	6.67	12.97
Re-initialize	6.66	13.43
Default	6.97	16.01
ADDA [35]	6.98	15.44
Supervised lower bound	5.82	8.67

Comparison to ADDA [35]. Our approach is superior to the state-of-the-art unsupervised domain adaptation technique [35] in the keypoint estimation task. ADDA aims to cross the domain gap by aligning the feature distributions of the source and target domains, which is complementary to our approach's constraints on the label space. We argue that there is more structure to rely on in label space than feature space for rigid objects. Another important factor is that view consistency is not incorporated in ADDA [35].

5.3 Ablation Study

We present ablation studies to justify each component of our approach. We restrict our study to a sole object class, chair, and to the representative target domains, ShapeNet and Redwood Object Scans.

Dropping the View-Consistency Term. We test the effects of dropping the view-consistency term. In this case, we simply align the output from all the depth scans with annotations of the source domain. As shown in Table 4 and Fig. 4, the performance drops considerably compared to our full term, while still maintaining better performance than without adaptation. Thus, if the predictions on the majority of views are consistent with one another, the keypoint configuration obtained by averaging all the predictions can serve as a reliable guidance to correct the bad outliers.

Dropping the Alignment Term. Without output alignment, merely utilizing the view consistency term can also significantly reduce the testing error. This can be interpreted as the network updating the latent variables in a self-guided manner, based solely on the consistency between different views.

Latent Configuration Updates Versus Re-initialization. Instead of updating the latent configurations M_i by solving Eq. 15, we can apply Eq. 11 to re-initialize the latent configurations, which is also consistent with our training framework. The results is worse than updating M_i by minimizing the view-consistency term, showing an advantage of our alternating minimization schema.

5.4   Extension to Human Pose

Additionally, we perform experiments for human keypoints using the Human 3.6M dataset [14]. The Human 3.6M dataset [14] provides 3D human joint annotations for 7 subjects (5 for training and 2 for testing) from 4 different camera views. We use 3 of the 5 training subjects as supervised (source) samples and the remaining 2 training subjects as unsupervised (target) samples, trained with the proposed multi-view consistency and output alignment constraints. The result is shown in Table 2 and Fig. 5. The supervised performance upper-bound of our implementation is 113.44 mm, which approximately matches the *3D data-only* state-of-the-art [31].

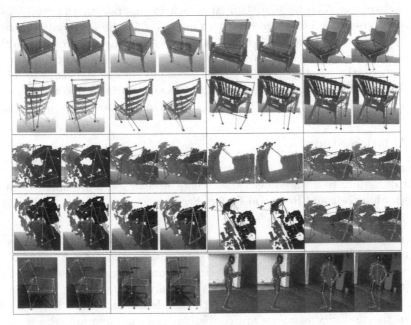

Fig. 5. Qualitative results. We compare 3D keypoint predictions (blue) before (left) and after (right) using our approach on different datasets. For each model we show 2 views. Reference ground-truth are in red (Color figure online).

5.5   Extension to RGB Images

Our approach can seamlessly be applied to keypoint estimation from RGB images. We show our preliminary results on Table 1, which indicate that our proposed method is able to reduce the AE from the baseline without domain adaptation. As shown in Fig. 5, our method helps regularize the output when the before-adaptation baseline predicts a seemingly random point set.

6   Conclusions

In this paper, we introduced an unsupervised domain adaptation approach for keypoint prediction from a single depth image. Our approach combines two task-specific regularizations, i.e., view-consistency and label distributions alignment of the source and target domains. Experimental results show that our approach is significantly better than without domain adaptation and is superior to state-of-the-art generic domain adaptation methods. Additionally, our multi-view consistency and output alignment terms makes it easier to leverage mass amounts of unlabeled 3D data for 3D tasks such as viewpoint estimation and object reconstruction.

Acknowledgement. Qixing Huang would like to acknowledge support of this research from NSF DMS-1700234, a Gift from Snap Research, and a hardware Donation from NVIDIA.

References

1. Bousmalis, K., Silberman, N., Dohan, D., Erhan, D., Krishnan, D.: Unsupervised pixel-level domain adaptation with generative adversarial networks. In: The IEEE Conference on Computer Vision and Pattern Recognition (CVPR), July 2017
2. Chang, A.X., et al.: ShapeNet: an information-rich 3D model repository. CoRR abs/1512.03012 (2015)
3. Choi, S., Zhou, Q.Y., Miller, S., Koltun, V.: A large dataset of object scans (2016). arXiv:1602.02481
4. Choy, C.B., Xu, D., Gwak, J.Y., Chen, K., Savarese, S.: 3D-R2N2: a unified approach for single and multi-view 3D object reconstruction. In: Leibe, B., Matas, J., Sebe, N., Welling, M. (eds.) ECCV 2016. LNCS, vol. 9912, pp. 628–644. Springer, Cham (2016). https://doi.org/10.1007/978-3-319-46484-8_38
5. Cignoni, P., Callieri, M., Corsini, M., Dellepiane, M., Ganovelli, F., Ranzuglia, G.: MeshLab: an open-source mesh processing tool. In: Eurographics Italian Chapter Conference, vol. 2008, pp. 129–136 (2008)
6. Csurka, G.: Domain adaptation for visual applications: a comprehensive survey. CoRR abs/1702.05374 (2017)
7. Fish Tung, H.Y., Harley, A.W., Seto, W., Fragkiadaki, K.: Adversarial inverse graphics networks: learning 2D-to-3D lifting and image-to-image translation from unpaired supervision. In: The IEEE International Conference on Computer Vision (ICCV), October 2017
8. Gebru, T., Hoffman, J., Fei-Fei, L.: Fine-grained recognition in the wild: a multi-task domain adaptation approach. In: The IEEE International Conference on Computer Vision (ICCV), October 2017

9. Gholami, B., (Oggi) Rudovic, O., Pavlovic, V.: PUnDA: probabilistic unsupervised domain adaptation for knowledge transfer across visual categories. In: The IEEE International Conference on computer Vision (ICCV), October 2017
10. Gupta, S., Arbeláez, P.A., Girshick, R.B., Malik, J.: Aligning 3D models to RGB-D images of cluttered scenes. In: Computer Vision and Pattern Recognition (CVPR) (2015)
11. He, K., Zhang, X., Ren, S., Sun, J.: Deep residual learning for image recognition. In: Proceedings of the IEEE conference on computer vision and pattern recognition, pp. 770–778 (2016)
12. Herath, S., Harandi, M., Porikli, F.: Learning an invariant hilbert space for domain adaptation. In: The IEEE Conference on Computer Vision and Pattern Recognition (CVPR), July 2017
13. Horn, B.K.P.: Closed-form solution of absolute orientation using unit quaternions. J. Opt. Soc. Am. A **4**(4), 629–642 (1987)
14. Ionescu, C., Papava, D., Olaru, V., Sminchisescu, C.: Human3.6M: large scale datasets and predictive methods for 3D human sensing in natural environments. IEEE Trans. Pattern Anal. Mach. Intell. **36**(7), 1325–1339 (2014)
15. Kalogerakis, E., Averkiou, M., Maji, S., Chaudhuri, S.: 3D shape segmentation with projective convolutional networks. CoRR abs/1612.02808 (2016)
16. Koniusz, P., Tas, Y., Porikli, F.: Domain adaptation by mixture of alignments of second- or higher-order scatter tensors. In: The IEEE Conference on Computer Vision and Pattern Recognition (CVPR), July 2017
17. Li, Y., Dai, A., Guibas, L., Nießner, M.: Database-assisted object retrieval for real-time 3D reconstruction. In: Computer Graphics Forum, vol. 34. Wiley Online Library (2015)
18. Maria Carlucci, F., Porzi, L., Caputo, B., Ricci, E., Rota Bulo, S.: AutoDIAL: automatic domain alignment layers. In: The IEEE International Conference on Computer Vision (ICCV), October 2017
19. Newell, A., Yang, K., Deng, J.: Stacked hourglass networks for human pose estimation. In: Leibe, B., Matas, J., Sebe, N., Welling, M. (eds.) ECCV 2016. LNCS, vol. 9912, pp. 483–499. Springer, Cham (2016). https://doi.org/10.1007/978-3-319-46484-8_29
20. Panareda Busto, P., Gall, J.: Open set domain adaptation. In: The IEEE International Conference on Computer Vision (ICCV), October 2017
21. Peng, X., Sun, B., Ali, K., Saenko, K.: Learning deep object detectors from 3D models. In: ICCV, pp. 1278–1286. IEEE Computer Society (2015)
22. Qi, C.R., Su, H., Nießner, M., Dai, A., Yan, M., Guibas, L.J.: Volumetric and multi-view CNNs for object classification on 3D data. In: Proceedings of the IEEE Conference on Computer Vision and Pattern Recognition, pp. 5648–5656 (2016)
23. Rhodin, H., et al.: Learning monocular 3D human pose estimation from multi-view images. In: The IEEE Conference on Computer Vision and Pattern Recognition (CVPR), June 2018
24. Sankaranarayanan, S., Balaji, Y., Castillo, C.D., Chellappa, R.: Generate to adapt: aligning domains using generative adversarial networks. CoRR abs/1704.01705 (2017)
25. Simon, T., Joo, H., Matthews, I., Sheikh, Y.: Hand keypoint detection in single images using multiview bootstrapping. In: The IEEE Conference on Computer Vision and Pattern Recognition (CVPR), July 2017
26. Song, S., Xiao, J.: Sliding shapes for 3D object detection in depth images. In: Fleet, D., Pajdla, T., Schiele, B., Tuytelaars, T. (eds.) ECCV 2014. LNCS, vol. 8694, pp. 634–651. Springer, Cham (2014). https://doi.org/10.1007/978-3-319-10599-4_41

27. Song, S., Xiao, J.: Deep sliding shapes for amodal 3D object detection in RGB-D images (2016)
28. Song, S., Yu, F., Zeng, A., Chang, A.X., Savva, M., Funkhouser, T.: Semantic scene completion from a single depth image. In: Proceedings of 30th IEEE Conference on Computer Vision and Pattern Recognition (2017)
29. Su, H., Qi, C.R., Li, Y., Guibas, L.J.: Render for CNN: viewpoint estimation in images using CNNs trained with rendered 3D model views. In: The IEEE International Conference on Computer Vision (ICCV), December 2015
30. Su, H., Wang, F., Yi, E., Guibas, L.J.: 3D-assisted feature synthesis for novel views of an object. In: ICCV, pp. 2677–2685. IEEE Computer Society (2015)
31. Sun, X., Shang, J., Liang, S., Wei, Y.: Compositional human pose regression. In: The IEEE International Conference on Computer Vision (ICCV), October 2017
32. Tatarchenko, M., Dosovitskiy, A., Brox, T.: Multi-view 3D models from single images with a convolutional network. In: Leibe, B., Matas, J., Sebe, N., Welling, M. (eds.) ECCV 2016. LNCS, vol. 9911, pp. 322–337. Springer, Cham (2016). https://doi.org/10.1007/978-3-319-46478-7_20
33. Tulsiani, S., Malik, J.: Viewpoints and keypoints. CoRR abs/1411.6067 (2014)
34. Tulsiani, S., Zhou, T., Efros, A.A., Malik, J.: Multi-view supervision for single-view reconstruction via differentiable ray consistency. CoRR abs/1704.06254 (2017)
35. Tzeng, E., Hoffman, J., Saenko, K., Darrell, T.: Adversarial discriminative domain adaptation. arXiv preprint arXiv:1702.05464 (2017)
36. Tzeng, E., Hoffman, J., Saenko, K., Darrell, T.: Adversarial discriminative domain adaptation. In: The IEEE Conference on Computer Vision and Pattern Recognition (CVPR), July 2017
37. Wu, J., et al.: Single image 3D interpreter network. CoRR abs/1604.08685 (2016)
38. Wu, Z., et al.: 3D ShapeNets: a deep representation for volumetric shapes. In: CVPR, pp. 1912–1920 (2015)
39. Yan, H., Ding, Y., Li, P., Wang, Q., Xu, Y., Zuo, W.: Mind the class weight bias: weighted maximum mean discrepancy for unsupervised domain adaptation. In: The IEEE Conference on Computer Vision and Pattern Recognition (CVPR), July 2017
40. Yan, X., Yang, J., Yumer, E., Guo, Y., Lee, H.: Perspective transformer nets: learning single-view 3D object reconstruction without 3D supervision. CoRR abs/1612.00814 (2016)
41. Zhang, Y., David, P., Gong, B.: Curriculum domain adaptation for semantic segmentation of urban scenes. In: The IEEE International Conference on Computer Vision (ICCV), October 2017
42. Zhang, Y., et al.: Physically-based rendering for indoor scene understanding using convolutional neural networks. In: The IEEE Conference on Computer Vision and Pattern Recognition (CVPR) (2017)
43. Zhao, B., Wu, X., Cheng, Z., Liu, H., Feng, J.: Multi-view image generation from a single-view. CoRR abs/1704.04886 (2017)
44. Zhou, T., Tulsiani, S., Sun, W., Malik, J., Efros, A.A.: View synthesis by appearance flow. In: Leibe, B., Matas, J., Sebe, N., Welling, M. (eds.) ECCV 2016. LNCS, vol. 9908, pp. 286–301. Springer, Cham (2016). https://doi.org/10.1007/978-3-319-46493-0_18
45. Zhou, X., Huang, Q., Sun, X., Xue, X., Wei, Y.: Towards 3D human pose estimation in the wild: a weakly-supervised approach. In: The IEEE International Conference on Computer Vision (ICCV), October 2017

Practical Black-Box Attacks on Deep Neural Networks Using Efficient Query Mechanisms

Arjun Nitin Bhagoji[1]([✉]), Warren He[2], Bo Li[3], and Dawn Song[2]

[1] Princeton University, Princeton, USA
abhagoji@princeton.edu
[2] University of California, Berkeley, Berkeley, USA
[3] University of Illinois at Urbana-Champaign, Champaign, USA

Abstract. Existing black-box attacks on deep neural networks (DNNs) have largely focused on transferability, where an adversarial instance generated for a locally trained model can "transfer" to attack other learning models. In this paper, we propose novel Gradient Estimation black-box attacks for adversaries with query access to the target model's class probabilities, which do not rely on transferability. We also propose strategies to decouple the number of queries required to generate each adversarial sample from the dimensionality of the input. An iterative variant of our attack achieves close to 100% attack success rates for both targeted and untargeted attacks on DNNs. We carry out a thorough comparative evaluation of black-box attacks and show that Gradient Estimation attacks achieve attack success rates similar to state-of-the-art white-box attacks on the MNIST and CIFAR-10 datasets. We also apply the Gradient Estimation attacks successfully against real-world classifiers hosted by Clarifai. Further, we evaluate black-box attacks against state-of-the-art defenses based on adversarial training and show that the Gradient Estimation attacks are very effective even against these defenses.

Keywords: Deep neural networks · Image classification
Adversarial examples · Black-box attacks

1 Introduction

The ubiquity of machine learning provides adversaries with both opportunities and incentives to develop strategic approaches to fool learning systems and achieve their malicious goals. Many attack strategies devised so far to generate adversarial examples that cause learning systems to drastically change their

---

A. N. Bhagoji—Work done while at University of California, Berkeley.

Electronic supplementary material The online version of this chapter (https://doi.org/10.1007/978-3-030-01258-8_10) contains supplementary material, which is available to authorized users.

Single-step   Iterative

White-box Finite Diff. Query-reduced   White-box Finite Diff. Query-reduced

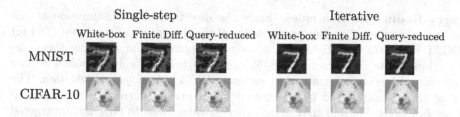

Fig. 1. Targeted adversarial examples for MNIST and CIFAR-10. The '7' from MNIST is classified as a '3' while the *dog* from CIFAR-10 is classified as a *bird* by all attacks. 'Finite Diff.' and 'Query-reduced' refer to Gradient Estimation attacks with and without query reduction respectively. Perturbations generated using Single-step attacks are far smaller than those for Iterative attacks.

predictions with perturbations imperceptible to humans have been in the white-box setting, where adversaries are assumed to have access to the target model [3,8,20,31]. However, in many realistic settings, adversaries may only have black-box access to the model; i.e., they have no knowledge of the details of the learning system, such as its parameters, but may have query access to the model's predictions on input samples, including class probabilities. This is the case in a number of popular commercial AI offerings from IBM [33], Google [9] and Clarifai [5]. With access to model predictions, the loss of the target model for a given input can be found, but without access to the entire model, the gradients required to carry out white-box attacks cannot be accessed.

Most existing black-box attacks on Deep Neural Networks (DNNs) have focused on *transferability* based attacks [19,24,25], where adversarial examples crafted for a local surrogate model (trained on a representative dataset) can be used to attack the target model to which the adversary has no direct access. In this paper, we design powerful new black-box attacks using *limited query access to target models* which achieve attack success rates and distortion levels close to that of white-box attacks[1]. These attacks do not need access to a representative dataset or the training of a local model. Our contributions are as follows:

New Black-Box Attacks. We propose novel *Gradient Estimation* attacks on DNNs, where the adversary is only assumed to have query access to the target model. In these attacks, the adversary adds perturbations proportional to the *estimated gradient*, instead of the true gradient as in white-box attacks [8,16]. Our attacks achieve close to 100% attack success in both the targeted and untargeted attack settings, matching white-box success on state-of-the-art models on the MNIST [17] and CIFAR-10 [15] datasets. We also experimented with Simultaneous Perturbation Stochastic Approximation (SPSA) [29] and Particle Swarm Optimization (PSO) [14] as alternative methods to carry out query-based black-box attacks but found Gradient Estimation to work the best.

---

[1] The code to reproduce our results is at https://github.com/sunblaze-ucb/blackbox-attacks.

Query-Reduction Strategies. Since the direct Gradient Estimation attack requires a number of queries on the order of the dimension of the input (784 for MNIST and 3072 for CIFAR-10), we explore strategies for reducing the number of queries to the target model. We propose two strategies: *random feature grouping* and *principal component analysis (PCA) based query reduction*. The use of these is supported by the notion of directional derivatives for differentiable functions. We find that attack success rates close to 90% for untargeted Single-step attacks and 100% for Iterative attacks in both targeted and untargeted cases are achievable with drastic query reduction to just 200 to 800 queries per sample for Single-step attacks and around 8,000 queries for Iterative attacks. Figure 1 displays some successful targeted adversarial examples generated using our attacks.

Attacking Real-World Systems and State-of-the-Art Defenses. To demonstrate the effectiveness of our Gradient Estimation attacks in the real world, we also carry out a *practical black-box attack* (Fig. 3) using these methods against the Not Safe For Work (NSFW) classification and Content Moderation models developed by Clarifai [5], which we choose due to their socially relevant application. These models have begun to be deployed for real-world moderation [18], which makes such black-box attacks especially pernicious. The Gradient Estimation attack achieves a 95.2% attack success rate on the set of images we chose with around 200 queries per image, taking roughly a minute per image. These black-box attacks help us understand the extent of the threat posed to deployed systems by query-based attacks as the attack was carried out with *no knowledge of the training set*.

In addition, we also evaluate the effectiveness of these attacks on *DNNs made more robust using adversarial training* [8,31] and its variants ensemble [32] and iterative adversarial training [21]. We find that although standard and ensemble adversarial training confer some robustness against Single-step attacks, they are vulnerable to Iterative Gradient Estimation attacks, with attack success rates in excess of 70%.

Comparative Evaluation of Black-Box Attacks. We carry out a thorough empirical comparison of black-box attacks on both the MNIST and CIFAR-10 datasets. We show that our Gradient Estimation attacks outperform the other query-based black-box attacks we tested in terms of attack success rate. In the supplementary material, we also show that black-box attacks requiring zero queries to the learning model, including the addition of perturbations that are either random or proportional to the difference of means of the original and targeted classes, as well as transferability based attacks do not perform as well as query-based attacks.

1.1 Related Work

Existing black-box attacks are mostly based on transferability [24,25,31], where an adversarial example generated for a local model is used to attack a target model. Query-based attacks were first proposed for convex-inducing two-class classifiers by Nelson et al. [23]. Xu et al. [35] use genetic algorithms to craft adversarial examples for malware data, while Dang et al. [6] apply hill climbing algorithms. These methods are prohibitively expensive for non-categorical and high-dimensional data such as images. We now discuss attacks that carry out direct query-based black-box attacks on DNNs. Narodytska & Kasiviswanathan [22] propose a greedy local search for high-impact pixels in input saliency maps to generate adversarial examples. Their method uses 500 queries per iteration and runs the greedy local search for around 150 iterations for each image, resulting in a total of 75,000 queries per image, which is much higher than any of our attacks. Our methods achieve higher targeted and untargeted attack success rates on both MNIST and CIFAR-10 compared to their method. In independent work, Chen et al. [4] propose a black-box attack method named ZOO, which also uses the method of finite differences to estimate the derivative of a function. However, while we propose attacks that compute an adversarial perturbation, approximating FGSM and iterative FGS; ZOO approximates the Adam optimizer, while performing coordinate descent on a logit based loss [3]. While they achieve similar attack success rates and distortion levels, they use around 1.5×10^6 and 5.1×10^5 queries per image for MNIST and CIFAR-10 respectively, which is 192× and 67× greater than our Gradient Estimation attacks with query reduction. This leads to the runtime of their attack being up to 160× as long as ours. Neither of these works demonstrates the effectiveness of their attacks on real-world systems or on state-of-the-art defenses. In concurrent work, Ilyas et al. [13] study the use of natural evolution strategies with Gaussian noise to obtain gradient estimates, which is equivalent to the SPSA method. We find that the Gradient Estimation method achieves higher attack success rates at lower distortion levels compared to SPSA. Further, Ilyas et al. do not analyze the effectiveness of their attack on state-of-the-art defenses. Brendel et al. [2] use the target model's output class to modify a starting image which is misclassified, by following the decision boundaries to gradually make it closer to a benign image. Since their attacks use only the output class, they take up to 1.2×10^6 queries to converge to an adversarial example. For similarly sized images, they use 10× more queries for misclassification at the same distortion rate. More detailed comparisons are given in the supplementary material.

2 Query Based Black-Box Attacks: Gradient Estimation

Deployed learning systems often provide feedback for input samples provided by the user. Given query feedback, different adaptive, query-based algorithms can be applied by adversaries to understand the system and iteratively generate effective adversarial examples to attack it. We explored a number of methods using query feedback to carry out black-box attacks including Particle Swarm Optimization [14] and Simultaneous Perturbation Stochastic Approximation [29] (Sect. 2.4) but found these were not as effective as white-box attacks at finding adversarial examples. Given the fact that many white-box attacks for generating adversarial examples are based on gradient information, we tried *directly estimating the gradient to carry out black-box attacks*, and found it to be very effective in a range of conditions. In other words, the adversary can approximate white-box Single-step and Iterative Fast Gradient Sign (FGS) attacks [8,16] using estimates of the losses that are needed to carry out those attacks. We first propose a Gradient Estimation black-box attack based on the method of finite differences [30]. The drawback of a naive implementation of the finite difference method, however, is that it requires $O(d)$ queries per input, where d is the dimension of the input. This leads us to explore methods such as random grouping of features and feature combination using components obtained from Principal Component Analysis (PCA) to reduce the number of queries.

2.1   Notation and Threat Model

A classifier $f(\cdot; \theta) : \mathcal{X} \rightarrow \mathcal{Y}$ is a function mapping from the domain $\mathcal{X}$ to the set of classification outputs $\mathcal{Y}$ (e.g. $\mathcal{Y} = \{0, 1\}$ in the case of binary classification). The number of possible classification outputs is then $|\mathcal{Y}|$. θ is the set of parameters associated with a classifier. $\mathcal{H}$ denotes the constraint set which an adversarial example must lie in. $\ell_f(\mathbf{x}, y)$ is used to represent the loss function for the classifier f with respect to inputs $\mathbf{x} \in \mathcal{X}$ and their true labels $y \in \mathcal{Y}$. The outputs of the penultimate layer of a neural network f, representing the output of the network computed over all preceding layers, are known as the logits. We represent the logits as a vector $\phi^f(\mathbf{x}) \in \mathbb{R}^{|\mathcal{Y}|}$. The final layer of a neural network f used for classification is usually a softmax layer represented as a vector of probabilities $\mathbf{p}^f(\mathbf{x}) = [p_1^f(\mathbf{x}), \ldots, p_{|\mathcal{Y}|}^f(\mathbf{x})]$, with $\sum_{i=1}^{|\mathcal{Y}|} p_i^f(\mathbf{x}) = 1$ and $p_i^f(\mathbf{x}) = \frac{e^{\phi_i^f(\mathbf{x})}}{\sum_{j=1}^{|\mathcal{Y}|} e^{\phi_j^f(\mathbf{x})}}$.

Threat Model and Justification. We assume that the adversary can obtain the vector of output probabilities for any input $\mathbf{x}$. The set of queries the adversary can make is then $\mathcal{Q}_f = \{\mathbf{p}^f(\mathbf{x}), \forall \mathbf{x}\}$. For untargeted attacks, the adversary only needs access to the output probabilities for the two most likely classes. A compelling reason for assuming this threat model for the adversary is that many existing cloud-based ML services allow users to query trained models [5,9,33]. The results of these queries are confidence scores which can be used to carry out Gradient Estimation attacks. These trained models are often deployed by the clients of these ML as a service (MLaaS) providers [18]. Thus, an adversary can pose as a user for a MLaaS provider and create adversarial examples using our attack, which can then be used against any client of that provider.

2.2   Gradient Estimation Attacks Using Finite Differences

In this section, we focus on the method of finite differences to carry out Gradient Estimation based attacks. All the analysis is presented for untargeted attacks, but can be easily extended to targeted attacks (see supplementary material). White-box attacks such as the FGS attack use the gradient of an appropriately defined loss to create adversarial examples. If the loss function is $\ell_f(\mathbf{x}, y)$, then a white-box FGS adversarial example will be $\mathbf{x}_{\text{adv}}^{\text{FGS}} = \mathbf{x} + \epsilon \cdot \text{sign}(\nabla_{\mathbf{x}}\ell_f(\mathbf{x}, y))$.

In a black-box setting, however, the adversary does not have access to the gradient of the loss and needs to *estimate* it. One way to do this is the method of Finite Differences [30]. Let the function whose gradient is being estimated using be $g(\mathbf{x})$ where $\mathbf{x} \in \mathbb{R}^d$. The elements of $\mathbf{x}$ are represented as $\mathbf{x}_i$, where $i \in [1, \ldots, d]$. The canonical basis vectors are represented as $\mathbf{e}_i$, where $\mathbf{e}_i$ is 1 only in the ith coordinate and 0 everywhere else. Then, a two-sided estimation of the gradient of g with respect to $\mathbf{x}$ is

$$\text{FD}_{\mathbf{x}}(g(\mathbf{x}), \delta) = \left[\frac{g(\mathbf{x} + \delta \mathbf{e}_1) - g(\mathbf{x} - \delta \mathbf{e}_1)}{2\delta}, \ldots \frac{g(\mathbf{x} + \delta \mathbf{e}_d) - g(\mathbf{x} - \delta \mathbf{e}_d)}{2\delta} \right], \quad (1)$$

where δ is a free parameter that controls the accuracy of the estimation. A one-sided approximation can also be used, but will be less accurate [34]. If the gradient of the function g exists, then $\lim_{\delta \to 0} \text{FD}_{\mathbf{x}}(g(\mathbf{x}), \delta) = \nabla_{\mathbf{x}} g(\mathbf{x})$. The Finite Differences method is useful for a black-box adversary aiming to approximate a gradient based attack, since the gradient can be directly estimated with access to only the function values.

Estimating the Logit Loss. To illustrate how the method of Finite Differences can be used to construct adversarial examples, we focus on a loss function based on logits which was found to work well for white-box attacks by [3]. Attacks using the cross-entropy loss [7] are described in the supplementary material. The logit loss is given by $\ell(\mathbf{x}, y) = \phi(\mathbf{x} + \delta)_y - \max\{\phi(\mathbf{x} + \delta)_i : i \neq y\}$, where y represents the ground truth label for the benign sample $\mathbf{x}$ and $\phi(\cdot)$ are the logits.

An adversary can compute the logit values up to an additive constant by taking the logarithm of the softmax probabilities, which are assumed to be available in this threat model. Since the loss function is equal to the difference of logits, the additive constant is canceled out. Then, the finite differences method can be used to estimate the difference between the logit values for the original class y, and the second most likely class y', i.e., the one given by $y' = \text{argmax}_{i \neq y} \phi(\mathbf{x})_i$. The untargeted adversarial sample generated for this loss in the white-box case is $\mathbf{x}_{\text{adv}} = \mathbf{x} + \epsilon \cdot \text{sign}(\nabla_{\mathbf{x}}(\phi(\mathbf{x})_{y'} - \phi(\mathbf{x})_y))$. In the case of a black-box adversary with query access to the softmax probabilities, the adversarial example is

$$\mathbf{x}_{\text{adv}} = \mathbf{x} + \epsilon \cdot \text{sign}(\text{FD}_{\mathbf{x}}(\phi(\mathbf{x})_{y'} - \phi(\mathbf{x})_y, \delta)). \quad (2)$$

This attack is denoted as **FD-logit** and the corresponding one based on the cross-entropy loss is denoted **FD-xent**.

Iterative Attacks with Estimated Gradients. The iterative variant of the FGS attack [16] is a powerful attack that often achieves much higher attack success rates in the white-box setting than the simple single-step gradient based attacks. Thus, it stands to reason that a version of the iterative attack with estimated gradients will also perform better than the single-step attacks described until now. An iterative attack with $t + 1$ iterations using the logit loss is:

Algorithm 1. Gradient estimation with query reduction using random features

---

Input: $\mathbf{x}$, k, δ, $g(\cdot)$
Output: Estimated gradient $\hat{\nabla}_{\mathbf{x}}g(\mathbf{x})$ of $g(\cdot)$ at $\mathbf{x}$
1: Initialize empty vector $\hat{\nabla}_{\mathbf{x}}g(\mathbf{x})$ of dimension d
2: **for** $i \leftarrow 1$ to $\lceil \frac{d}{k} \rceil - 1$ **do**
3:     Choose a set of random k indices S_i out of $[1, \ldots, d]/\{\cup_{j=1}^{i-1} S_j\}$
4:     Initialize $\mathbf{v}$ such that $\mathbf{v}_j = 1$ iff $j \in S_i$
5:     For all $j \in S_i$, set $\hat{\nabla}_{\mathbf{x}}g(\mathbf{x})_j = \frac{g(\mathbf{x}+\delta\mathbf{v})-g(\mathbf{x}-\delta\mathbf{v})}{2\delta k}$, which is the two-sided approximation of the directional derivative along $\mathbf{v}$
6: **end for**
7: Initialize $\mathbf{v}$ such that $\mathbf{v}_j = 1$ iff $j \in [1, \ldots, d]/\{\cup_{j=1}^{\lceil \frac{d}{k} \rceil - 1} S_j\}$
8: For all $j \in [1, \ldots, d]/\{\cup_{j=1}^{\lceil \frac{d}{k} \rceil - 1} S_j\}$, set $\hat{\nabla}_{\mathbf{x}}g(\mathbf{x})_j = \frac{g(\mathbf{x}+\delta\mathbf{v})-g(\mathbf{x}-\delta\mathbf{v})}{2\delta k}$

$$\mathbf{x}_{\text{adv}}^{t+1} = \mathbf{x}_{\text{adv}}^t + \alpha \cdot \text{sign}\left(\text{FD}_{\mathbf{x}_{\text{adv}}^t}\left(\phi(\mathbf{x}_{\text{adv}}^t)_{y'} - \phi(\mathbf{x}_{\text{adv}}^t)_y, \delta\right)\right), \tag{3}$$

where α is the step size and $\mathcal{H}$ the constraint set for the adversarial example. This attack is denoted as **IFD-logit** (**IFD-xent** with the cross-entropy loss).

2.3   Query Reduction Techniques

A drawback of the Finite Differences technique is that the number of queries needed per adversarial sample is exactly $2d$ for a two-sided approximation which could be too large for high-dimensional inputs. So, we examine two techniques to reduce the number of queries the adversary has to make. Both techniques involve estimating the gradient for groups of features, instead of estimating it using a single feature at a time. The justification for the use of feature grouping comes from the relation between gradients and directional derivatives [12] for differentiable functions. The directional derivative of a function g is defined as $\nabla_{\mathbf{v}}g(\mathbf{x}) = \lim_{h \to 0} \frac{g(\mathbf{x}+h\mathbf{v})-g(\mathbf{x})}{h}$. It is a generalization of a partial derivative. For differentiable functions, $\nabla_{\mathbf{v}}g(\mathbf{x}) = \nabla_{\mathbf{x}}g(\mathbf{x}) \cdot \mathbf{v}$, which implies that the directional derivative is just the projection of the gradient along the direction $\mathbf{v}$. Thus, estimating the gradient by grouping features is equivalent to estimating an approximation of the gradient constructed by projecting it along appropriately chosen directions. The estimated gradient $\hat{\nabla}_{\mathbf{x}}g(\mathbf{x})$ of any function g can be computed using the techniques below, and then plugged in to Eqs. 2 and 3 instead of the Finite Differences term to generate an adversarial example. Next, we introduce the techniques applied to group the features for estimation.

Query Reduction Based on Random Grouping. The simplest way to group features is to choose, without replacement, a random set of features. The gradient can then be simultaneously estimated for all these features. If the size of the set chosen is k, then the number of queries the adversary has to make is $\lceil \frac{d}{k} \rceil$. When $k = 1$, this reduces to the Finite Differences method from Sect. 2.2. In each iteration of Algorithm 1, there is a set of indices S according to which $\mathbf{v}$

is determined, with $\mathbf{v}_i = 1$ if and only if $i \in S$. Thus, the directional derivative being estimated is $\sum_{i \in S} \frac{\partial g(\mathbf{x})}{\partial \mathbf{x}_i}$, which is an average of partial derivatives.

Query Reduction Using PCA Components. A more principled way to reduce the number of queries the adversary has to make to estimate the gradient is to compute directional derivatives along the principal components as determined by principal component analysis (PCA) [28], which requires the adversary to have access to a set of data which is representative of the training data. If $\mathbf{U}$ is the $d \times d$ matrix whose columns are the principal components $\mathbf{u}_i$, where $i \in [d]$, then the approximation of the gradient in the PCA basis is $(\nabla_{\mathbf{x}} g(\mathbf{x}))^k = \sum_{i=1}^{k} \left(\nabla_{\mathbf{x}} g(\mathbf{x})^{\mathsf{T}} \frac{\mathbf{u}_i}{\|\mathbf{u}_i\|} \right) \frac{\mathbf{u}_i}{\|\mathbf{u}_i\|}$, where the term on the left represents an approximation of the true gradient by the sum of its projection along the top k principal components. Since in the black-box setting the true gradient is inaccessible, the weights of the representation in the PCA basis are estimated using directional derivatives along the principal components. The supplementary material contains a detailed description of this method.

Iterative Attacks with Query Reduction. Performing an iterative attack with the gradient estimated using Finite Differences could be expensive for an adversary, needing $2td$ queries to the target model, for t iterations with the two-sided Finite Differences estimation of the gradient. To lower the number of queries needed, the adversary can use either of the query reduction techniques described above to reduce the number of queries to $2tk$ ($k < d$). These attacks using the cross-entropy loss are denoted as IGE-QR (RG-k, logit) for the random grouping technique and IGE-QR (PCA-k, logit) for the PCA-based technique.

2.4   Other Query-Based Black-Box Attacks

Other black-box optimization techniques we considered for generating adversarial examples were Particle Swarm Optimization (PSO) [14],[2] a commonly used evolutionary optimization strategy and SPSA method [29]. PSO is a heuristic gradient-free optimization technique which initiates a number of candidate solutions called 'particles' which then move around the search space to find better solutions, previously used to find adversarial examples to fool face recognition systems [27]. SPSA is a special case of natural evolution strategies (NES) [26], where the distribution over the parameters is assumed to be a factored Gaussian. It is similar to the method of Finite Differences, but it estimates the gradient of the loss along a *random direction* $\mathbf{r}$ at each step, instead of along the canonical basis vectors. While each step of SPSA only requires 2 queries to the target model, a large number of steps are nevertheless required to generate adversarial examples. A single step of SPSA does not reliably produce adversarial examples.

---

[2] Using freely available code from http://pythonhosted.org/pyswarm/.

3   Experimental Results

In this section, we compare various black-box attacks in both targeted and untargeted settings to Gradient Estimation attacks as well as comparing them to white-box attacks. We also describe how we carried out a successful targeted attack on a real-world system, Clarifai, in Sect. 3.5.

3.1   Evaluation Setup

We evaluate our attacks on state-of-the-art neural networks on the MNIST [17] and CIFAR-10 [15] datasets. All models were run on a GPU with a batch size of 100. The details are as follows: (i) *MNIST*. Each pixel of the MNIST image data is scaled to $[0, 1]$. We trained two different CNNs on the MNIST dataset, denoted **Model A** and **Model B** [32]. **Model A** has 2 convolutional layers followed by a fully connected layer while **Model B** has only 3 convolutional layers. Both models have a test accuracy of 99.2%; (ii) *CIFAR-10*. Each pixel of the CIFAR-10 image data is in $[0, 255]$. We choose two model architectures for this dataset, which are both ResNet variants. **Resnet-32** [11] is a 32-layer ResNet achieving 92.4% test accuracy while **Resnet-28-10** [36] is a 28-layer ResNet with 10 times width expansion with 94.4% test accuracy. Further architecture details are in the supplementary material.

Attack Parameters. We focus on attacks that use the logit-based loss (**logit**) as it has better performance but also use the cross-entropy loss (**xent**) for comparison. In all attacks, the adversary's perturbation is constrained using the L_∞ distance. For the MNIST dataset, we vary the adversary's perturbation budget ϵ from 0 to 0.4, since at a perturbation budget of 0.5, any image can be made solid gray while for the CIFAR-10 dataset, we vary it from 0 to 28. We use the Finite Difference parameter $\delta = 1.0$ for **FD-xent** and **IFD-xent** for both datasets, while using $\delta = 0.01$ for **FD-logit** and **IFD-logit**. A larger value of δ is needed for **xent** loss based attacks to work well since the probability values used in the **xent** loss are not as sensitive to changes as the **logit** loss. For all Iterative attacks, including white-box attacks, we use $\alpha = 0.01$ and $t = 40$ for MNIST and $\alpha = 1.0$ and $t = 10$ for CIFAR-10. We find these choices work well while maintaining low runtimes for the Gradient Estimation attacks. For the query reduction methods, we use a random group size of 8 for both datasets and the number of principal components to be 100 for MNIST and CIFAR-10. For SPSA, we use around 4000 iterations for both datasets with a step size of 10^{-3} for MNIST and 2×10^{-2} for CIFAR-10. The effect of various hyperparameters on attack success is examined in the supplementary material.

3.2   Metrics

We now define the standard metrics we use to determine attack performance.

Attack Success Rate. The main metric, the attack success rate, is the fraction of samples that meets the adversary's goal: $f(\mathbf{x}_{adv}) \neq y$ for untargeted attacks and $f(\mathbf{x}_{adv}) = T$ for targeted attacks with target T [31,32].

Average Distortion. We also evaluate the average distortion for adversarial examples using average L_2 distance between the benign and adversarial ones as in [10]: $\Delta(\mathbf{X}_{adv}, \mathbf{X}) = \frac{1}{N} \sum_{i=1}^{N} \|(\mathbf{X}_{adv})_i - (\mathbf{X})_i\|_2$ where N is the number of samples. This metric allows us to compare the average distortion for attacks which achieve similar attack success rates, and therefore infer which one is stealthier.

Number of Queries. Query based black-box attacks make queries to the target model, and this metric may affect the cost of mounting the attack. This is an important consideration when attacking real-world systems which have costs associated with the number of queries made.

For *MNIST*, Single-step attacks are carried out on the *test set* of 10,000 samples, while Iterative attacks are carried out on 1,000 randomly chosen samples from the test set. For *CIFAR-10*, we choose 1,000 random samples from the test set for both Single-step and Iterative attacks. In our evaluation of targeted attacks, we choose target T for each sample uniformly at random from the set of classification outputs, except the true class y of that sample.

Table 1. Targeted black-box attacks: attack success rates. The number in parentheses () for each entry is $\Delta(\mathbf{X}, \mathbf{X}_{adv})$, the average L_2 distortion over all examples used in the attack. The number in brackets [] beside the Single-step and Iterative descriptors gives the number of queries needed for each type of attack. The per-pixel perturbation limits are $\epsilon = 0.3$ for MNIST (Top) and $\epsilon = 8$ for CIFAR-10 (Bottom).

Dataset	White-box		Gradient Estimation, FD (ours)		Gradient Estimation, Query Reduction (ours)			
MNIST **Models**	Single-step FGS (logit)	Iterative IFGS (logit)	Single-step [1568] FD logit	Iterative [62720] IFD logit	Single-step [~200] PCA-100	RG-8	Iterative [8000] PCA-100	RG-8
A	30.1 (6.1)	99.6 (2.7)	29.9 (6.1)	**99.7 (2.7)**	23.2 (5.9)	15.9 (5.9)	96.2 (3.3)	73.8 (2.5)
B	29.6 (6.2)	**98.7 (2.4)**	29.3 (6.3)	**98.7 (2.4)**	29.0 (6.3)	17.8 (6.3)	93.9 (2.9)	73.7 (2.6)
CIFAR-10 **Models**	Single-step FGS (logit)	Iterative IFGS (logit)	Single-step [6144] FD-logit	Iterative [61440] IFD-logit	Single-step [~800] PCA-400	RG-8	Iterative [~8000] PCA-400	RG-8
Resnet-32	23.5 (436.0)	**100.0 (89.5)**	23.0 (437.0)	**100.0 (89.5)**	21.0 (438.2)	19.0 (438.1)	81.0 (222.8)	97.0 (126.1)
Resnet-28-10	27.6 (436.5)	**100.0 (99.0)**	28.0 (436.1)	**100.0 (98.3)**	23.0 (433.7)	20.0 (433.7)	72.0 (253.1)	94.0 (132.4)

3.3 Effectiveness of Targeted Gradient Estimation Attacks

We find that Targeted Gradient Estimation attacks match white-box attack success, even with query reduction. The Iterative Gradient Estimation attack using Finite Differences and the logit loss (**IFD-logit**) achieves close to 100% targeted attack success rates on both MNIST and CIFAR-10 models (Table 1). The Single-step attack **FD-logit** achieves about 20 to 30% attack success rates, matching the performance of Single-step white-box attacks such as **FGS-logit**. The average distortion for samples generated using gradient estimation methods is similar to that of white-box attacks. Further, the Iterative Gradient Estimation attacks with query reduction achieve high targeted attack success rates as well. For example, using the random grouping method with a group size of 8 (RG-8) for query reduction and using just around 8000 queries per sample, attack success rates of 97% and 94% are achieved for Resnet-32 and Resnet-28-10 respectively.

3.4 Comparing Untargeted Black-Box Attacks

Single-step Gradient Estimation Attacks Match White-Box Attack Success. The Gradient Estimation attack with Finite Differences (FD-logit) is the most successful *untargeted* Single-step black-box attack for MNIST and CIFAR-10 models as can be seen in Fig. 2. We also compare against black-box attacks that make zero queries to the target model; these are the Difference-of-Means, Random Perturbation and Transfer attacks. The Transfer attack is based on the well-known phenomenon of transferability [24,31]. Further details and experimental results for these attacks are in the supplementary material.

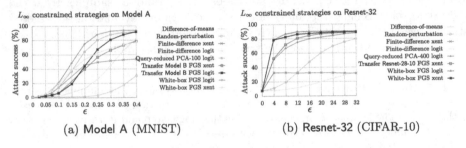

(a) Model A (MNIST)   (b) Resnet-32 (CIFAR-10)

Fig. 2. Effectiveness of untargeted Single-step black-box attacks on Model A (MNIST) and Resnet-32 (CIFAR-10). The y-axis for both figures plots the attack success as the perturbation magnitude ϵ is increased. The most successful black-box attack in both cases is the Gradient Estimation attack using Finite Differences with the logit loss (FD-logit), which matches white-box FGS logit-based attack success (WB FGS-logit). The Gradient Estimation attack with query reduction using PCA (GE-QR (PCA-k, logit)) performs well for both datasets.

The FD-logit attack significantly outperforms transferability-based attacks and closely tracks white-box FGS with a logit loss (WB FGS-logit) on MNIST and CIFAR-10. The Gradient Estimation attack with PCA based query reduction (GE-QR (PCA-k, logit)) is also effective, with performance close to that of FD-logit with $k = 100$ for MNIST (Fig. 2a) and $k = 400$ for CIFAR-10 (Fig. 2b). While random grouping is not as effective as the PCA based method for Single-step attacks, we find it is as effective for Iterative attacks.

Iterative Gradient Estimation Attacks Outperform other Query-Based Black-Box Attacks. A comparative evaluation of all the query-based black-box attacks we experimented with for both MNIST and CIFAR-10 datasets is given in Table 2. For adversarial examples generated iteratively, the Iterative Gradient Estimation attack with Finite Differences (IFD-logit) achieves 100% attack success rate on both datasets. White-box Iterative FGS also achieves 100% attack success rates with distortions of 2.1 for MNIST and 66.1 for CIFAR-10. The attack that achieves the best trade-off between speed and attack success is IGE-QR (RG-k, logit), achieving close to 100% success rates on both datasets with just around 8000 queries. We found PSO to be prohibitively slow (with a swarm size of 100) for a large dataset and outperformed even by the Single-step FD-logit attack, in spite of trying a large range of parameters. While the SPSA method is quite effective, it is outperformed by Iterative Gradient Estimation, with and without query reduction in terms of attack success rate for both MNIST and CIFAR-10. Also, IGE-QR (RG-k, logit) achieves a higher attack success rate with lower distortion for MNIST. In practice, we found the convergence of SPSA to be much more sensitive to the choice of both δ (gradient estimation step size) and α (loss minimization step size).

Table 2. Comparison of attack success (AS) and distortion (dist.) for **untargeted query-based black-box attack** methods. All attacks for MNIST use an L_∞ constraint of $\epsilon = 0.3$ while those for CIFAR-10 use $\epsilon = 8$. The logit loss is used for all methods expect PSO, which uses the class probabilities

Attack Type	MNIST (Model A)			CIFAR-10 (Resnet-32)		
Query-based attack	AS (Dist.)	Queries	Avg. Time (s)	AS (Dist.)	Queries	Avg. Time (s)
Finite Di .	92.9 (6.1)	1568	8.8×10^{-2}	86.0 (410.3)	6144	3.3
Gradient Estimation (RG-8)	61.5 (6.0)	196	1.1×10^{-2}	66.8 (402.7)	768	0.43
Iter. Finite Di .	100.0 (2.1)	62720	3.5	100.0 (65.7)	61440	32.1
Iter. Gradient Estimation (RG-8)	98.4 (1.9)	8000	0.43	99.0 (80.5)	7680	4.2
Particle Swarm Optimization	84.1 (5.3)	10000	21.2	89.2 (262.3)	7700	67.3
SPSA	96.7 (3.9)	8000	1.25	88.0 (44.4)	7680	8.7

3.5   Attacks on Clarifai, a Real-World System

Since the only requirement for carrying out the Gradient Estimation based attacks is query-based access to the target model, a number of deployed public systems that provide classification as a service can be used to evaluate our methods. We choose *Clarifai* [5], as it has models trained to classify image datasets for a variety of practical applications, and it provides black-box access to its models and returns confidence scores upon querying. In particular, Clarifai has models used for the detection of Not Safe For Work (NSFW) content, as well as for Content Moderation. These are important applications where the presence of adversarial examples presents a real danger: an attacker, using query access to the model, could generate an adversarial examples which will no longer be classified as inappropriate. For example, an adversary could upload violent images, adversarially modified, such that they are marked incorrectly as 'safe' by the Content Moderation model.

We evaluate our attack using the Gradient Estimation method on Clarifai's NSFW and Content Moderation models. When we query the API with an image, it returns the confidence scores associated with each category (summing to 1). We use the *random grouping* query reduction technique and take the logarithm of the confidence scores in order to use the *logit loss*. This method achieves 95.2% attack success rate against the NSFW model on our sample set of 21 images. An example of an attack against the Content Moderation model is given in Fig. 3 where the original image (left) depicts a white drug and a syringe. The Content Moderation model classifies it as 'drug' with confidence 1.0. The adversarial image (right) was generated with 197 queries, with an L_∞ constraint of $\epsilon = 16$. While this image can clearly be classified by a human as containing drugs, the target model classifies it as 'safe' with confidence 0.67. More successful attack images and the methodology followed to choose them are included in the supplementary material and at https://sunblaze-ucb.github.io/blackbox-attacks/.

4   Attacking State-of-the-art Defenses

In this section, we evaluate black-box attacks on defenses based on adversarial training and its variants. We focus on adversarial training based defenses as they aim to directly improve the robustness of DNNs, and are among the most effective defenses demonstrated so far in the literature [1]. These defenses make DNNs more robust by adding a loss term dependent on adversarial examples during training to count for adversarial examples. During training, the adversarial examples are computed with respect to the current state of the network using an appropriate method such as FGSM (standard) [8] and Iterative FGSM (iterative) [21]. Adversarial examples from other DNNs may also be included in the training set, leading to ensemble adversarial training [32].

Fig. 3. Sample adversarial images of Gradient Estimation attacks on Clarifai's Content Moderation model. Left: original image, classified as 'drug' with a confidence of 1.0. Right: adversarial example with $\epsilon = 16$, classified as 'safe' with a confidence of 0.67.

Adversarially Trained Model Setup. We train variants of Model A with the 3 adversarial training strategies described above using adversarial samples based on an L_∞ constraint of 0.3. Model A$_{adv-0.3}$ is trained with FGS samples, while Model A$_{adv-iter-0.3}$ is trained with Iterative FGS samples using $t = 40$ and $\alpha = 0.01$. For the model with ensemble training, Model A$_{adv-ens-0.3}$ is trained with pre-generated FGS samples for Models A and two other DNN models as well as FGS samples. The source of the samples is chosen randomly for each minibatch during training. These models all achieve test accuracies of greater than 99%. For CIFAR-10, we train variants of Resnet-32 using adversarial samples with an L_∞ constraint of 8. Resnet-32 $_{adv-8}$ is trained with FGS samples with the same constraint, and Resnet-32 $_{ens-adv-8}$ is trained with pre-generated FGS samples from Resnet-32 and Std.-CNN as well as FGS samples. These have test accuracies of around 92%. Resnet-32 $_{adv-iter-8}$ is trained with iterative FGS samples using $t = 10$ and $\alpha = 1.0$ and has only 79.1% test accuracy.

4.1   Experimental Results

In this section, we focus on *untargeted* attacks on adversarially trained models, so the results in this section can be compared to those for undefended models in Table 2. Results for targeted attacks can be found in the supplementary material. In all cases, we find that Single-step Gradient Estimation attacks match the success rate of their white-box counterparts even with query reduction. Further discussion of these is contained in the supplementary material.

Adversarially Trained Models are not Robust to Gradient Estimation Attacks. Our experiments show that Iterative black-box attacks continue to work well even against adversarially trained networks (Table 3). For example, the Iterative Gradient Estimation attack using Finite Differences with a logit loss (IFD-logit) achieves attack success rates of 76.5% and 96.4% against Models A$_{adv-0.3}$ and A$_{adv-ens-0.3}$ respectively. This attack works well for CIFAR-10 models as well, achieving attack success rates of 100% against both Resnet-32 $_{adv-8}$ and Resnet-32 $_{adv-ens-8}$. This reduces slightly to 98% and 91% respectively when query reduction using random grouping is used. For both datasets, IFD-logit matches white-box attack performance. For MNIST, using PCA for query reduction, a 51% attack success rate is achieved for both Models A$_{adv-0.3}$ and A$_{adv-ens-0.3}$.

Model A$_{adv-iter-0.3}$ is robust even against iterative attacks, with the highest black-box attack success rate achieved being 11.6%—marginally higher than the white-box attack success rate. On CIFAR-10, the iteratively trained model has poor performance on both benign and adversarial examples. The IFD-logit attack achieves an untargeted attack success rate of 55% on this model, which is lower than on the other adversarially trained models, but still significant. This is in line with Madry et al.'s observation [21] that iterative adversarial training needs models with large capacity for it to be effective. This highlights a limitation of this defense, since it is not clear what model capacity is needed, and the models we use already have a large number of parameters.

Table 3. Untargeted black-box attacks for models with adversarial training: attack success rates and average distortion $\Delta(\mathbf{X}, \mathbf{X}_{adv})$. Top: MNIST, $\epsilon = 0.3$. Bottom: CIFAR-10, $\epsilon = 8$.

Dataset	White-box		Gradient Estimation (FD)		Gradient Estimation (Query Reduction)			
MNIST Models	Single-step FGS (logit)	Iterative IFGS (logit)	Single-step [1568] FD-logit	Iterative [62720] IFD-logit	Single-step [∼ 200] PCA-100	RG-8	Iterative [8000] PCA-100	RG-8
A_adv-0.3	2.9 (6.0)	78.5 (3.1)	2.8 (5.9)	76.5 (3.1)	4.1 (5.8)	2.0 (5.3)	50.7 (4.2)	27.5 (2.4)
A_adv-ens-0.3	6.2 (6.2)	96.2 (2.7)	6.2 (6.3)	**96.4 (2.7)**	5.4 (6.2)	3.7 (6.4)	51.0 (3.9)	32.0 (2.1)
A_adv-iter-0.3	7.3 (7.5)	11.0 (3.6)	7.5 (7.2)	11.6 (3.5)	3.5 (4.0)	1.6 (4.2)	9.0 (2.8)	3.0 (1.4)
CIFAR-10 Models	Single-step FGS (logit)	Iterative IFGS (logit)	Single-step [6144] FD-logit	Iterative [61440] IFD-logit	Single-step [∼ 800] PCA-400	RG-8	Iterative [∼ 8000] PCA-400	RG-8
Resnet-32 adv-8	8.9 (438.8)	100.0 (73.7)	8.5 (401.9)	**100.0 (73.8)**	8.0 (402.1)	7.7 (401.8)	97.0 (151.3)	98.0 (92.9)
Resnet-32 adv-ens-8	13.3 (437.9)	100.0 (85.3)	12.2 (399.8)	**100.0 (85.2)**	15.4 (396.1)	13.8 (395.9)	82.7 (178.7)	90.8 (106.6)
Resnet-32 adv-iter-8	50.4 (346.6)	57.3 (252.4)	47.5 (331.1)	54.6 (196.3)	47.5 (344.1)	38.4 (341.4)	51.3 (256.6)	42.4 (153.3)

5 Possible Countermeasures and Conclusion

The Gradient Estimation attacks depend on model output probabilities to generate adversarial examples, so possible countermeasures can modify these to reduce their effectiveness. These modifications would, however, impact legitimate users as well. To validate this idea, we experimented with undefended models and *rounded off the output probabilities to two decimal places*. This successfully reduced the effectiveness of all Gradient Estimation attacks using the same parameters, with even the iterative variants achieving only as high as 28.0% attack success rates. We plan to explore query-efficient attacks that work in spite of these countermeasures in future work.

Overall, in this paper, we conduct a systematic analysis of black-box attacks on state-of-the-art classifiers and defenses. We propose Gradient Estimation attacks which achieve high attack success rates comparable with even white-box attacks. We apply random grouping and PCA-based methods to reduce the number of queries required while maintaining the effectiveness of the Gradient Estimation attack. We also apply our attacks against a real-world classifier and state-of-the-art defenses. All of our results show that Gradient Estimation attacks are very effective in a variety of settings, making the development of better defenses against black-box attacks an urgent task.

References

1. Athalye, A., Carlini, N., Wagner, D.: Obfuscated gradients give a false sense of security: circumventing defenses to adversarial examples. In: Proceedings of the 35th International Conference on Machine Learning (2018)
2. Brendel, W., Rauber, J., Bethge, M.: Decision-based adversarial attacks: reliable attacks against black-box machine learning models. In: International Conference on Learning Representations (2018)
3. Carlini, N., Wagner, D.: Towards evaluating the robustness of neural networks. In: IEEE Symposium on Security and Privacy (2017)

4. Chen, P.Y., Zhang, H., Sharma, Y., Yi, J., Hsieh, C.J.: Zoo: zeroth order optimization based black-box attacks to deep neural networks without training substitute models. In: 11th ACM Workshop on Artificial Intelligence and Security (2017)
5. Clarifai — image & video recognition API. https://clarifai.com. Accessed 22 Aug 2017
6. Dang, H., Yue, H., Chang, E.C.: Evading classifiers by morphing in the dark. In: 24th ACM Conference on Computer and Communications Security (2017)
7. Goodfellow, I., Bengio, Y., Courville, A.: Deep Learning. MIT Press, Cambridge (2016)
8. Goodfellow, I.J., Shlens, J., Szegedy, C.: Explaining and harnessing adversarial examples. In: International Conference on Learning Representations (2015)
9. Vision API - image content analysis—Google cloud platform. https://cloud.google.com/vision/. Accessed 22 Aug 2017
10. Gu, S., Rigazio, L.: Towards deep neural network architectures robust to adversarial examples. arXiv preprint arXiv:1412.5068 (2014)
11. He, K., Zhang, X., Ren, S., Sun, J.: Deep residual learning for image recognition. In: Proceedings of the IEEE Conference on Computer Vision and Pattern Recognition, pp. 770–778 (2016)
12. Hildebrand, F.B.: Advanced Calculus for Applications, vol. 63. Prentice-Hall Englewood Cliffs, NJ (1962)
13. Ilyas, A., Engstrom, L., Athalye, A., Lin, J.: Black-box adversarial attacks with limited queries and information. In: Proceedings of the 35th International Conference on Machine Learning (2018)
14. Kennedy, J.: Particle swarm optimization. In: Sammut, C., Webb, G.I. (eds.) Encyclopedia of Machine Learning, pp. 760–766. Springer, Heidelberg (2011). https://doi.org/10.1007/978-0-387-30164-8
15. Krizhevsky, A., Hinton, G.: Learning multiple layers of features from tiny images (2009)
16. Kurakin, A., Goodfellow, I., Bengio, S.: Adversarial examples in the physical world. arXiv preprint arXiv:1607.02533 (2016)
17. LeCun, Y., Cortes, C.: The MNIST database of handwritten digits (1998)
18. Liu, A.: Clarifai featured hack: block unwanted nudity in blog comments with disqus (2016). https://goo.gl/TCCVrR. Accessed 22 Aug 2017
19. Moosavi-Dezfooli, S.M., Fawzi, A., Fawzi, O., Frossard, P.: Universal adversarial perturbations. In: IEEE Conference on Computer Vision and Pattern Recognition (2016)
20. Moosavi-Dezfooli, S.M., Fawzi, A., Frossard, P.: Deepfool: a simple and accurate method to fool deep neural networks. In: IEEE Conference on Computer Vision and Pattern Recognition (2016)
21. Mądry, A., Makelov, A., Schmidt, L., Tsipras, D., Vladu, A.: Towards deep learning models resistant to adversarial attacks. In: International Conference on Learning Representations (2018)
22. Narodytska, N., Kasiviswanathan, S.P.: Simple black-box adversarial perturbations for deep networks. arXiv preprint arXiv:1612.06299 (2016)
23. Nelson, B., et al.: Query strategies for evading convex-inducing classifiers. J. Mach. Learn. Res. 13(1), 1293–1332 (2012)
24. Papernot, N., McDaniel, P., Goodfellow, I.: Transferability in machine learning: from phenomena to black-box attacks using adversarial samples. arXiv preprint arXiv:1605.07277 (2016)

25. Papernot, N., McDaniel, P., Goodfellow, I., Jha, S., Berkay Celik, Z., Swami, A.: Practical black-box attacks against deep learning systems using adversarial examples. In: ACM Asia Conference on Computer and Communications Security (2017)
26. Salimans, T., Ho, J., Chen, X., Sutskever, I.: Evolution strategies as a scalable alternative to reinforcement learning. arXiv preprint arXiv:1703.03864 (2017)
27. Sharif, M., Bhagavatula, S., Bauer, L., Reiter, M.K.: Accessorize to a crime: real and stealthy attacks on state-of-the-art face recognition. In: ACM Conference on Computer and Communications Security (2016)
28. Shlens, J.: A tutorial on principal component analysis. arXiv preprint arXiv:1404.1100 (2014)
29. Spall, J.C.: Multivariate stochastic approximation using a simultaneous perturbation gradient approximation. IEEE Trans. Autom. Control **37**(3), 332–341 (1992)
30. Spall, J.C.: Introduction to Stochastic Search and Optimization: Estimation, Simulation, and Control, vol. 65. Wiley, Hoboken (2005)
31. Szegedy, C., et al.: Intriguing properties of neural networks. In: International Conference on Learning Representations (2014)
32. Tramèr, F., Kurakin, A., Papernot, N., Boneh, D., McDaniel, P.: Ensemble adversarial training: attacks and defenses. In: International Conference on Learning Representations (2018)
33. Watson visual recognition. https://www.ibm.com/watson/services/visual-recognition/. Accessed 27 Aug 2017
34. Wright, S.J., Nocedal, J.: Numerical optimization. Springer Sci. **35**(67–68), 7 (1999)
35. Xu, W., Qi, Y., Evans, D.: Automatically evading classifiers. In: Proceedings of the 2016 Network and Distributed Systems Symposium (2016)
36. Zagoruyko, S., Komodakis, N.: Wide residual networks. arXiv preprint arXiv:1605.07146 (2016)

DYAN: A Dynamical Atoms-Based Network for Video Prediction

Wenqian Liu, Abhishek Sharma, Octavia Camps$^{(\boxtimes)}$, and Mario Sznaier

Electrical and Computer Engineering, Northeastern University,
Boston, MA 02115, USA
{liu.wenqi,sharma.abhis}@husky.neu.edu,
{camps,msznaier}@northeastern.edu
http://robustsystems.coe.neu.edu

Abstract. The ability to anticipate the future is essential when making real time critical decisions, provides valuable information to understand dynamic natural scenes, and can help unsupervised video representation learning. State-of-art video prediction is based on complex architectures that need to learn large numbers of parameters, are potentially hard to train, slow to run, and may produce blurry predictions. In this paper, we introduce DYAN, a novel network with very few parameters and easy to train, which produces accurate, high quality frame predictions, faster than previous approaches. DYAN owes its good qualities to its encoder and decoder, which are designed following concepts from systems identification theory and exploit the dynamics-based invariants of the data. Extensive experiments using several standard video datasets show that DYAN is superior generating frames and that it generalizes well across domains.

Keywords: Video autoencoder · Sparse coding · Video prediction

1 Introduction

The recent exponential growth in data collection capabilities and the use of supervised deep learning approaches have helped to make tremendous progress in computer vision. However, learning good representations for the analysis and understanding of dynamic scenes, with limited or no supervision, remains a challenging task. This is in no small part due to the complexity of the changes in appearance and of the motions that are observed in video sequences of natural scenes. Yet, these changes and motions provide powerful cues to understand dynamic scenes such as the one shown in Fig. 1(a), and they can be used to predict what is going to happen next. Furthermore, the ability of anticipating

This work was supported in part by NSF grants IIS–1318145, ECCS–1404163, and CMMI–1638234; AFOSR grant FA9550-15-1-0392; and the Alert DHS Center of Excellence under Award Number 2013-ST-061-ED0001.

V. Ferrari et al. (Eds.): ECCV 2018, LNCS 11216, pp. 175–191, 2018.
https://doi.org/10.1007/978-3-030-01258-8_11

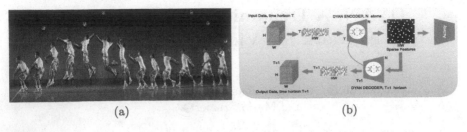

Fig. 1. (a) Dynamics and motion provide powerful cues to understand scenes and predict the future. (b) DYAN's architecture: Given T consecutive $H \times W$ frames, the network uses a dynamical atoms-based encoder to generate a set of sparse $N \times HW$ features that capture the dynamics of each pixel, with $N \gg T$. These features can be passed to its dynamical atoms-based decoder to reconstruct the given frames and predict the next one, or they can be used for other tasks such as action classification.

the future is essential to make decisions and take action in critical real time systems such as autonomous driving. Indeed, recent approaches to video understanding [17, 22, 31] suggest that being capable to accurately generate/predict future frames in video sequences can help to learn useful features with limited or no supervision.

Predicting future frames to anticipate what is going to happen next requires good generative models that can make forecasts based on the available past data. Recurrent Neural Networks (RNN) and in particular Long Short-Term Memory (LSTM) have been widely used to process sequential data and make such predictions. Unfortunately, RNNs are hard to train due to the exploding and vanishing gradient problems. As a result, they can easily learn short term but not long-term dependencies. On the other hand, LSTMs and the related Gated Recurrent Units (GRU), addressed the vanishing gradient problem and are easier to use. However, their design is ad-hoc, with many components whose purpose is not easy to interpret [13].

More recent approaches [20, 22, 35, 37] advocate using generative adversarial network (GAN) learning [7]. Intuitively, this is motivated by reasoning that the better the generative models, the better the prediction will be, and vice-versa: by learning how to distinguish predictions from real data, the network will learn better models. However, GANs are also reportedly hard to train, since training requires finding a Nash equilibrium of a game, which might be hard to get using gradient descent techniques.

In this paper, we present a novel DYnamical Atoms-based Network, DYAN, shown in Fig. 1(b). DYAN is similar in spirit to LSTMs, in the sense that it also captures short and long term dependencies. However, DYAN is designed using concepts from dynamic systems identification theory, which help to drastically reduce its size and provide easy interpretation of its parameters. By adopting ideas from atom-based system identification, DYAN learns a structured dictionary of atoms to exploit dynamics-based affine invariants in video data sequences. Using this dictionary, the network is able to capture actionable information from the dynamics of the data and map it into a set of very sparse features, which can then be used in video processing tasks, such as frame prediction, activity recognition, semantic segmentation, etc. We demonstrate the power of DYAN's autoencoding by using it to generate future frames in video sequences. Our extensive experiments using several standard video datasets show that DYAN can predict future frames more accurately and efficiently than current state-of-art approaches.

In summary, the main contributions of this paper are:

- A novel auto-encoder network that captures long and short term temporal information and explicitly incorporates dynamics-based affine invariants;
- The proposed network is shallow, with very few parameters. It is easy to train and it does not take large disk space to save the learned model.
- The proposed network is easy to interpret and it is easy to visualize what it learns, since the parameters of the network have a clear physical meaning.
- The proposed network can predict future frames accurately and efficiently without introducing blurriness.
- The model is differentiable, so it can be fine-tuned for another task if necessary. For example, the front end (encoder) of the proposed network can be easily incorporated at the front of other networks designed for video tasks such as activity recognition, semantic video segmentation, etc.

The rest of the paper is organized as follows. Section 2 discusses related previous work. Section 3 gives a brief summary of the concepts and procedures from dynamic systems theory, which are used in the design of DYAN. Section 4 describes the design of DYAN, its components and how it is trained. Section 5 gives more details of the actual implementation of DYAN, followed by Sect. 6 where we report experiments comparing its performance in frame prediction against the state-of-art approaches. Finally, Sect. 7 provides concluding remarks and directions for future applications of DYAN.

2   Related Work

There exist an extensive literature devoted to the problem of extracting optical flow from images [10], including recent deep learning approaches [5,12]. Most of these methods focus on *Lagrangian* optical flow, where the flow field represents the displacement between corresponding pixels or features across frames. In contrast, DYAN can also work with *Eulerian* optical flow, where the motion is captured by the changes at individual pixels, without requiring finding correspondences or tracking features. Eulerian flow has been shown to be useful for tasks such as motion enhancement [33] and video frame interpolation [23].

State-of-art algorithms for action detection and recognition also exploit temporal information. Most deep learning approaches to action recognition use spatio-temporal data, starting with detections at the frame level [27,29] and linking them across time by using very short-term temporal features such as optical flow. However, using such a short horizon misses the longer term dynamics of the action and can negatively impact performance. This issue is often addressed by following up with some costly hierarchical aggregation over time. More recently, some approaches detect tubelets [11,15] starting with a longer temporal support than optical flow. However, they still rely on a relatively small number of frames, which is fixed a priori, regardless of the complexity of the action. Finally, most of these approaches do not provide explicit encoding and decoding of the involved dynamics, which if available could be useful for inference and generative problems.

In contrast to the large volume of literature on action recognition and motion detection, there are relatively few approaches to frame prediction. Recurrent Neural Networks (RNN) and in particular Long Short-Term Memory (LSTM) have been used to predict frames. Ranzato et al. [28] proposed a RNN to predict frames based on a discrete set of patch clusters, where an average of 64 overlapping tile predictions were used to avoid blockiness effects. In [31] Srivastava et al. used instead an LSTM architecture with an ℓ_2 loss function. Both of these approaches produce blurry predictions due to using averaging. Other LSTM-based approaches include the work of Luo et al. [21] using an encoding/decoding architecture with optical flow and the work of Kalchbrenner et al. [14] that estimates the probability distribution of the pixels.

In [22], Mathieu et al. used generative adversarial network (GAN) [7] learning together with a multi-scale approach and a new loss based on image gradients to improve image sharpness in the predictions. Zhou and Berg [37] used a similar approach to predict future state of objects and Xue et al. [35] used a variational autoencoder to predict future frames from a single frame. More recently, Luc et al. [20] proposed an autoregressive convolutional network to predict semantic segmentations in future frames bypassing pixel prediction. Liu et al. [18] introduced a network that synthesizes frames by estimating voxel flow. However, it assumes that the optical flow is constant across multiple frames. Finally, Liang et al. [17] proposed a dual motion GAN architecture that combines frame and flow predictions to generate future frames. All of these approaches involve large networks, potentially hard to train.

Lastly, DYAN's encoder was inspired by the sparsification layers introduced by Sun et al. in [32] to perform image classification. However, DYAN's encoder is fundamentally different since it must use a *structured* dictionary (see (6)) in order to model dynamic data, while the sparsification layers in [32] do not.

3   Background

3.1   Dynamics-Based Invariants

The power of *geometric* invariants in computer vision has been recognized for a long time [25]. On the other hand, *dynamics*-based affine invariants have been used far less. These dynamics-based invariants, which were originally proposed for tracking [1], activity recognition [16], and chronological sorting of images [3], tap on the properties of linear time invariant (LTI) dynamical systems. As briefly summarized below, the main idea behind these invariants, is that if the available sequential data (i.e. the trajectory of a target being tracked or the values of a pixel as a function of time) can be modeled as the output of some unknown LTI system, then, this underlying system has several attributes/properties that are invariant to affine transformations (i.e. viewpoint or illumination changes). In this paper, as described in detail in Sect. 4, we propose to use this affine invariance property to reduce the number of parameters in the proposed network, by leveraging the fact that multiple observations of one motion, captured in different conditions, can be described using one single set of these invariants.

Let S be a LTI system, described either by an autoregressive model or a state space model:

$$y_k = \sum_{i=1}^{n} a_i y_{k-i} \qquad \% \text{ Autoregressive Representation} \qquad (1)$$

$$\mathbf{x}_{k+1} = \mathbf{A}\mathbf{x}_k; \; y_k = \mathbf{C}\mathbf{x}_k \qquad \% \text{ State Space Representation} \qquad (2)$$

$$\text{with } \mathbf{x}_k = \begin{bmatrix} y_{k-n} \\ \vdots \\ y_k \end{bmatrix}, \; \mathbf{A} = \begin{bmatrix} 0 & 1 & \dots & 0 \\ \vdots & \ddots & \ddots & 0 \\ 0 & 0 & \dots & 1 \\ a_n & a_{n-1} & \dots & a_1 \end{bmatrix} ; \; \mathbf{C} = [0 \dots 0\, 1]$$

where $y_k{}^1$ is the observation at time k, and n is the (unknown a priori) order of the model (memory of the system). Consider now a given initial condition $\mathbf{x}_o$ and its corresponding sequence $\mathbf{x}$. The Z-transform of a sequence $\mathbf{x}$ is defined as $X(z) = \sum_{k=0}^{\infty} x_k z^{-k}$, where z is a complex variable $z = re^{j\phi}$. Taking Z transforms on both sides of (2) yields:

$$z(\mathbf{X}(z) - \mathbf{x}_o) = \mathbf{A}\mathbf{X}(z) \;\Rightarrow\; \mathbf{X}(z) = z(z\mathbf{I} - \mathbf{A})^{-1}\mathbf{x}_o, \; Y(z) = z\mathbf{C}(z\mathbf{I} - \mathbf{A})^{-1}\mathbf{x}_o \quad (3)$$

where $\mathcal{G}(z) \doteq z\mathbf{C}(z\mathbf{I} - \mathbf{A})^{-1}$ is the transfer function from initial conditions to outputs. Using the explicit expression for the matrix inversion and assuming non-repeated poles, leads to

$$Y(z) = \frac{z\mathbf{C}_{\text{adj}}(z\mathbf{I} - \mathbf{A})\mathbf{x}_o}{\det(z\mathbf{I} - \mathbf{A})} \doteq \sum_{i=1}^{n} \frac{zc_i}{z - p_i} \;\Longleftrightarrow\; y_k = \sum_{i=1}^{n} c_i p_i^k, \; k = 0, 1, \dots \quad (4)$$

where the roots of the denominator, p_i, are the eigenvalues of $\mathbf{A}$ (e.g. poles of the system) and the coefficients c_i depend on the initial conditions. Consider now an affine transformation Π. Then, substituting[2] in (1) we have, $y_k' \doteq \Pi(y_k) = \Pi(\sum_{i=1}^{n} a_i y_{k-i}) = \sum_{i=1}^{n} a_i \Pi(y_{k-i})$. Hence, the order n, the model coefficients a_i (and hence the poles p_i) are affine invariant since the sequence y_k' is explained by the same autoregressive model as the sequence y_k.

---

[1] For simplicity of notation, we consider here y_k scalar, but the invariants also hold for $\mathbf{y}_k \in \mathbb{R}^d$.
[2] (using homogeneous coordinates).

3.2   LTI System Identification Using Atoms

Next, we briefly summarize an atoms-based algorithm [36] to identify an LTI system from a given output sequence.

First, consider a set with an infinite number of atoms, where each atom is the impulse response of a LTI first order (or second order) system with a single real pole p (or two conjugate complex poles, p and p^*). Their transfer functions can be written as:

$$\mathcal{G}_p(z) = \frac{wz}{z-p} \quad \text{and} \quad \mathcal{G}_p(z) = \frac{wz}{z-p} + \frac{w^*z}{z-p^*}$$

where $w \in \mathbb{C}$, and their impulse responses are given by $\mathbf{g}_p = w[1, p, p^2, p^3, \dots]'$ and $\mathbf{g}_p = w[1, p, p^2, p^3, \dots]' + w^*[1, p^*, p^{*2}, p^{*3}, \dots]'$, for first and second order systems, respectively.

Next, from (3), every proper transfer function can be approximated to arbitrary precision as a linear combination of the above transfer functions[3]:

$$G(z) = \sum_i c_i \mathcal{G}_{p_i}(z)$$

Hence, low order dynamical models can be estimated from output data $\mathbf{y} = [y_1, y_2, y_3, y_4, \dots]'$ by solving the following sparsification problem:

$$\min_{\mathbf{c}=\{c_i\}} \|\mathbf{c}\|_o \quad \text{subject to: } \|\mathbf{y} - \sum c_i \mathbf{g}_p\|_2^2 \le \eta^2$$

where $\|.\|_o$ denotes cardinality and the constraint imposes fidelity to the data. Finally, note that solving the above optimization is not trivial since minimizing cardinality is an NP-hard problem and the number of poles to consider is infinite. The authors in [36] proposed to address these issues by (1) using the ℓ_1 norm relaxation for cardinality, (2) using impulse responses of the atoms truncated to the length of the available data, and (3) using a finite set of atoms with uniformly sampled poles in the unit disk. Then, using these ideas one could solve instead:

$$\min_{\mathbf{c}} \frac{1}{2}\|\mathbf{y}_{1:T} - D^{(T)}\mathbf{c}\|_2^2 + \lambda\|\mathbf{c}\|_1 \tag{5}$$

where $\mathbf{y}_{1:T} = [y_1, y_2, \dots, y_T]'$, $D^{(T)}$ is a *structured* dictionary matrix with T rows and N columns:

$$D^{(T)} = \begin{bmatrix} p_1^0 & p_2^0 & \cdots & p_N^0 \\ p_1 & p_2 & \cdots & p_N \\ p_1^2 & p_2^2 & \cdots & p_N^2 \\ \vdots & \vdots & \vdots & \vdots \\ p_1^{T-1} & p_2^{T-1} & \cdots & p_N^{T-1} \end{bmatrix} \tag{6}$$

where each column corresponds to the impulse response of a pole p_i, $i = 1, \dots, N$ inside or near the unit disk in $\mathbb{C}$. Note that the dictionary is completely parameterized by the magnitude and phase of its poles.

---

[3] Provided that if a complex pole p_i is used, then its conjugate p_i^* is also used.

4 DYAN: A Dynamical Atoms-Based Network

In this section we describe in detail the architecture of **DYAN**, a dynamical atoms-based network. Figure 1(b) shows its block diagram, depicting its two main components: a dynamics-based encoder and dynamics-based decoder. Figure 2 illustrates how these two modules work together to capture the dynamics at each pixel, reconstruct the input data and predict future frames.

The goal of DYAN is to capture the dynamics of the input by mapping them to a latent space, which is learned during training, and to provide the inverse mapping from this feature space back to the input domain. The implicit assumption is that the dynamics of the input data should have a sparse representation in this latent space, and that this representation should be enough to reconstruct the input and to predict future frames.

Following the ideas from dynamic system identification presented in Sect. 3, we propose to use as latent space, the space spanned by a set of atoms that are the impulse responses of a set of first (single real pole) and second order (pair of complex conjugate poles) LTI systems, as illustrated in Fig. 2. However, instead of using a set of random poles in the unit disk as proposed in [36], the proposed network learns a set of "good" poles by minimizing a loss function that penalizes reconstruction and predictive poor quality.

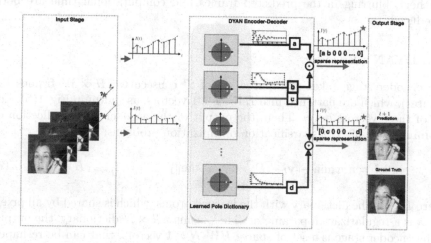

Fig. 2. DYAN identifies the dynamics for each pixel, expressing them as a linear combination of a small subset of dynamics-based atoms from a dictionary (learned during training). The selected atoms and the corresponding coefficients are represented using sparse feature vectors, found by a sparsification step. These features are used by the decoder to reconstruct the input data and predict the next frame by using the same dictionary, but with an extended temporal horizon. See text for more details.

The main advantages of the DYAN architecture are:

- **Compactness:** Each pole in the dictionary can be used by more than one pixel, and affine invariance allows to re-use the same poles, even if the data was captured under different conditions from the ones used in training. Thus, the total number of poles needed to have a rich dictionary, capable of modeling the dynamics of a wide range of inputs, is relatively small. Our experiments show that the total number of parameters of the dictionary, which are the magnitude and phase of its poles, can be below two hundred and the network still produces high quality frame predictions.
- **Adaptiveness to the dynamics complexity:** The network adapts to the complexity of the dynamics of the input by automatically deciding how many atoms it needs to use to explain them. The more complex the dynamics, the higher the order of the model is needed, i.e. the higher the number of atoms will be selected, and the longer term memory of the data will be used by the decoder to reconstruct and predict frames.
- **Interpretable:** Similarly to CNNs that learn sets of convolutional filters, which can be easily visualized, DYAN learns a basis of very simple dynamic systems, which are also easy to visualize by looking at their poles and impulse responses.
- **Performance:** Since pixels are processed in parallel, independently of each other[4], blurring in the predicted frames and computational time are both reduced.

4.1 DYAN's Encoder

The encoder stage takes as input a set of T consecutive $H \times W$ frames (or features), which are flattened into HW, $T \times 1$ vectors, as shown in Fig. 1(b). Let one of these vectors be $\mathbf{y}_l$. Then, the output of the encoder is the collection of the minimizers of HM sparsification optimization problems:

$$\mathbf{c}_l^* = \arg\min_{\mathbf{c}} \frac{1}{2}\|\mathbf{y}_l - D^{(T)}\mathbf{c}\|_2^2 + \lambda\|\mathbf{c}\|_1 \qquad l = 1, \ldots, HW \qquad (7)$$

where $D^{(T)}$ is the dictionary with the learned atoms, which is shared by all pixels and λ is a regularization parameter. Thus, using a $T \times N$ dictionary, the output of the encoder stage is a set of sparse HW $N \times 1$ vectors, that can be reshaped into $H \times W \times N$ features.

In order to avoid working with complex poles p_i, we use instead a dictionary $D^{(T)}_{\rho,\psi}$ with columns corresponding to the real and imaginary parts of increasing powers of the poles $p_i = \rho_i e^{j\psi_i}$ in the first quadrant ($0 \leq \psi_i \leq \pi/2$), of their conjugates and of their mirror images in the third and fourth quadrant[5]: $\rho_i^k \cos(k\psi_i)$,

---

[4] On the other hand, if modeling cross-pixel correlations is desired, it is easy to modify the network to process jointly local neighborhoods using a group Lasso optimization in the encoder.

[5] But eliminating duplicate columns.

$\rho_i^k \sin(k\psi_i)$, $(-\rho_i)^k \cos(k\psi_i)$, and $(-\rho_i)^k \sin(k\psi_i)$ with $k = 0, \ldots, T-1$. In addition, we include a fixed atom at $p_i = 1$ to model constant inputs.

$$D_{\rho,\psi}^{(T)} = \begin{bmatrix} 1 & 1 & 0 & \cdots & 0 \\ 1 & \rho_1 \cos\psi_1 & \rho_1 \sin\psi_1 & \cdots & -\rho_N \sin\psi_N \\ 1 & \rho_1^2 \cos 2\psi_1 & \rho_1^2 \sin 2\psi_1 & \cdots & (-\rho_N)^2 \sin 2\psi_N \\ \vdots & \vdots & \vdots & \vdots & \vdots \\ 1 & \rho_1^{T-1} \cos(T-1)\psi_1 & \rho_1^{T-1} \sin(T-1)\psi_1 & \cdots & (-\rho_N)^{T-1} \sin(T-1)\psi_N \end{bmatrix} \tag{8}$$

Note that while Eq. (5) finds one $\mathbf{c}^*$ (and a set of poles) for each feature $\mathbf{y}$, it is trivial to process all the features in parallel with significant computational time savings. Furthermore, (5) can be easily modified to force neighboring features, or features at the same location but from different channels, to select the same poles by using a group Lasso formulation.

Algorithm 1. FISTA

Require: Dictionary $D \in \mathbb{R}^{n \times m}$, input signal $y \in \mathbb{R}^n$, λ, L the largest eigenvalue of $D^T D$, $A = I - \frac{1}{L}(D^T D)$, $b = \frac{1}{L} D^T y$, $g = \frac{1}{L}$. Initialize iterator $t = 0$, $c_t = 0 \in \mathbb{R}^m$, $\gamma_t = 0 \in \mathbb{R}^m$, $s_0 = 1$.
1: **while** stopping criterion not satisfied **do**
2:     $\gamma = A c_t + b$
3:     if $\gamma > g : c_{t+1} \leftarrow \gamma - g$
4:     else $\gamma < -g : c_{t+1} \leftarrow \gamma + g$
5:     $s_{t+1} \leftarrow (1 + \sqrt{(1 + 4s_t^2)})/2$
6:     $c_t \leftarrow c_{t+1}((s_t - 1)/s_{t+1} + 1)) - c_t((s_t - 1)/s_{t+1})$
7:     $t \leftarrow t + 1$
8: **end while**
9: **return** sparse code c_t

In principle, there are available several sparse recovery algorithms that could be used to solve Problem (7), including LARS [9], ISTA and FISTA [2], and LISTA [8]. Unfortunately, the structure of the dictionary needed here does not admit a matrix factorization of its Gram kernel, making the LISTA algorithm a poor choice in this case [24]. Thus, we chose to use FISTA, shown in Algorithm 1, since very efficient GPU implementations of this algorithm are available.

4.2   DYAN's Decoder

The decoder stage takes as input the output of the encoder, i.e. a set of sparse HW $N \times 1$ vectors and multiplies them with the encoder dictionary, extended with one more row:

$$\begin{bmatrix} 1 & \rho_1^T \cos(T\psi_1) & \rho_1^T \sin(T\psi_1) & \ldots & (-\rho_N)^T \sin(T\psi_N) \end{bmatrix} \tag{9}$$

to reconstruct the T input frames and to predict the $T + 1$ frame. Thus, the output of the decoder is a set of $HW\ (T+1) \times 1$ vectors that can be reshaped into $(T + 1)$, $H \times W$ frames.

4.3 DYAN's Training

The parameters of the dictionary are learned using Steepest Gradient Descent (SGD) and the ℓ_2 loss function. The back propagation rules for the *encoder, decoder* layers can be derived by taking the subgradient of the empirical loss function with respect to the magnitudes and phases of the first quadrant poles and the regularizing parameters. Here, for simplicity, we give the derivation for $D_p^{(T)}$, but the one for $D_{\rho,\psi}^{(T)}$ can be derived in a similar manner.

Let $\mathbf{c}^*$ be the solution of one of the minimization problems in (5), where we dropped the subscript l and the superscript (T) to simplify notation, and define

$$\mathcal{F} = \frac{1}{2}\|\mathbf{y} - D\mathbf{c}^*\|_2^2 + \lambda \sum_{i=1}^{N} c_i^* \text{sign}(c_i^*)$$

Taking subgradients with respect to $\mathbf{c}^*$:

$$\frac{\partial \mathcal{F}}{\partial \mathbf{c}^*} = 0 = -D^T(\mathbf{y} - D\mathbf{c}^*) + \lambda \mathbf{v} = 0$$

where $\mathbf{v} = \begin{bmatrix} v_1 \dots v_N \end{bmatrix}^T$, $v_i = \text{sign}(c_i^*)$ if $c_i^* \neq 0$, and $v_i = g$, where $-1 \leq g \leq 1$, otherwise. Then,

$$\mathbf{c}^* = (D_\Lambda^T D_\Lambda)^{-1} \begin{bmatrix} D_\Lambda^T \mathbf{y} - \lambda \mathbf{v} \end{bmatrix}$$

and

$$\frac{\partial \mathbf{c}^*}{\partial D_{ij}}\bigg|_\Lambda = (D_\Lambda^T D_\Lambda)^{-1} \begin{bmatrix} \frac{\partial D_\Lambda^T \mathbf{y}}{\partial D_{ij}} - \frac{\partial D_\Lambda^T D_\Lambda}{\partial D_{ij}} \mathbf{c}^* \end{bmatrix}$$

where the subscript $.|_\Lambda$ denotes the active set of the sparse code $\mathbf{c}$, D_Λ is composed of the active columns of D, and $\mathbf{c}_\Lambda$ is the vector with the active elements of the sparse code. Using the structure of the dictionary, we have

$$\frac{\partial \mathbf{c}_\Lambda^*}{\partial p_k} = \sum_{i=1}^{M}(i-1)p_k^{i-2}\frac{\partial \mathbf{c}_\Lambda^*}{\partial D_{ik}}; \quad \frac{\partial \mathbf{c}_\Lambda^*}{\partial y_j} = (D_\Lambda^T D_\Lambda)^{-1}\frac{\partial D_\Lambda^T \mathbf{y}}{\partial y_j}; \quad \frac{\partial \mathbf{c}_\Lambda^*}{\partial \lambda} = -(D_\Lambda^T D_\Lambda)^{-1}\text{sign}(\mathbf{c}_\Lambda^*)$$

Figure 3 shows how a set of 160 uniformly distributed poles within a ring around the unit circle move while training DYAN with videos from the KITTI video dataset [6], using the above back propagation and a ℓ_2 loss function. As shown in the figure, after only 1 epoch, the poles have already moved significantly and after 30 epochs the poles move slower and slower.

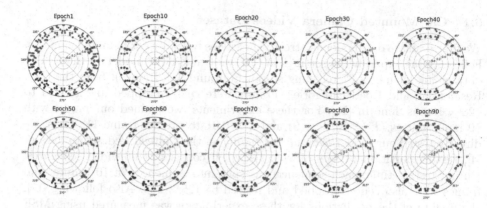

Fig. 3. Temporal evolution of a dictionary trained with the KITTI dataset.

5   Implementation Details

We implemented[6] DYAN using Pytorch version-0.3. A DYAN trained using raw pixels as input produces nearly perfect reconstruction of the input frames. However, predicted frames may exhibit small lags at edges due to changes in pixel visibility. This problem can be easily addressed by training DYAN using optical flow as input. Therefore, given a video with F input frames, we use coarse to fine optical flow [26] to obtain $T = F - 1$ optical flow frames. Then, we use these optical flow frames to predict with DYAN the next optical flow frame to warp frame F into the predicted frame $F + 1$. The dictionary is initialized with 40 poles, uniformly distributed on a grid of 0.05×0.05 in the first quadrant within a ring around the unit circle defined by $0.85 \leq \rho \leq 1.15$, their 3 mirror images in the other quadrants, and a fixed pole at $p = 1$. Hence, the resulting encoder and decoder dictionaries have $N = 161$ columns[7] and T and $T + 1$ rows, respectively. Each of the columns in the encoding dictionary was normalized to have norm 1. The maximum number of iterations for the FISTA step was set to 100.

6   Experiments

In this section, we describe a set of experiments using DYAN to predict the next frame and compare its performance against the state-of-art video prediction algorithms. The experiments were run on widely used public datasets, and illustrate the generative and generalization capabilities of our network.

---

[6] Code will be made available in Github.

[7] Note that the dictionaries do not have repeated columns, for example conjugate poles share the column corresponding to their real parts, so the number of columns is equal to the number of poles.

6.1 Car Mounted Camera Videos Dataset

We first evaluate our model on street view videos taken by car mounted cameras. Following the experiments settings in [17], we trained our model on the KITTI dataset [6], including 57 recoding sessions (around 41k frames), from the City, Residential, and Road categories. Frames were center-cropped and resized to 128×160 as done in [19]. For these experiments, we trained our model with 10 input frames ($F = 10, T = 9$) and $\lambda = 0.01$ to predict frame 11. Then, we directly tested our model *without fine tuning* on the Caltech Pedestrian dataset [4], testing partition (4 sets of videos), which consists of 66 video sequences. During testing time, each sequence was split into sequences of 10 frames, and frames were also center-cropped and resized to 128×160. Also following [17], the quality of the predictions for these experiments was measured using MSE [19] and SSIM [34] scores, where lower MSE and higher SSIM indicate better prediction results.

Qualitative results on the Caltech dataset are shown in Fig. 4, where it can be seen that our model accurately predicts sharp, future frames. Also note that even though in this sequence there are cars moving towards opposite directions or occluding each other, our model can predict all motions well. We compared DYAN's performance against three state-of-the-art approaches: DualMoGAN [17], BeyondMSE [22] and Prednet [19]. For a fair comparison, we normalized our image values between 0 and 1 before computing the MSE score. As shown in Table 1, our model outperforms all other algorithms, even without fine tuning on the new dataset. This result shows the superior predictive ability of DYAN, as well as its transferability.

For these experiments, the network was trained on 2 NVIDIA TITAN XP GPUs, using one GPU for each of the optical flow channels. The model was trained for 200 epochs and it only takes 3 KB to store it on disk. Training only

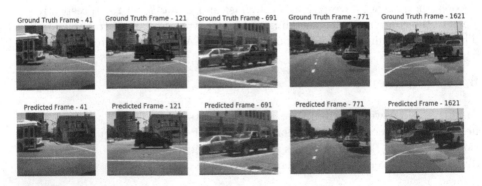

Fig. 4. Qualitative results for our model trained on the KITTI dataset and tested on the Caltech dataset, without fine tuning. The figure shows examples from Caltech test set S10, sequence V010, with ground truth on the top row and predicted frames below. As shown in the figure, our model produces sharp images and fully captures the motion of the vehicles and the camera.

takes 10 s/epoch, and it takes an average of 230 ms (including warping) to predict the next frame, given a sequence of 10 input frames. In comparison, [17] takes 300 ms to predict a frame.

Table 1. MSE and SSIM scores of next frame prediction test on Caltech dataset after training on KITTI datset.

Caltech	CopyLast (F = 10)	BeyondMSE [22] (F = 10)	PredNet [19] (F = 10)	DualMoGan [17] (F = 10)	Ours (F = 10)
MSE	0.00795	0.00326	0.00313	0.00241	0.00087
SSIM	0.762	0.881	0.884	0.899	0.952

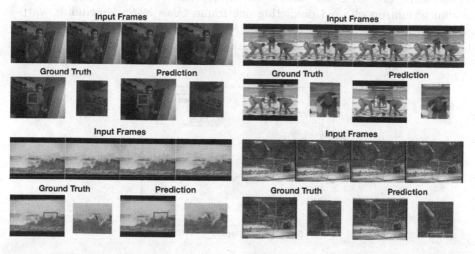

Fig. 5. Qualitative results for next frame prediction test on UCF-101. For each sequence, the first row shows the 4 input frames, while the ground truth and our prediction are shown on the second row. We also enlarge the main moving portion inside each frame to show how similar our predictions are compared to the ground truth.

6.2 Human Action Videos Dataset

We also tested DYAN on generic videos from the UCF-101 dataset [30]. This dataset contains 13,320 videos under 101 different action categories with an average length of 6.2 s. Input frames are 240 × 320. Following state-of-art algorithms [18] and [22], we trained using the first split and using $F = 4$ frames as input to predict the 5th frame. While testing, we adopted the test set provided by [22] and the evaluation script and optical masks provided by [18] to mask in only the moving object(s) within each frame, resized to 256 × 256. There are in total

378 video sequences in the test set: every 10th video sequence was extracted from UCF-101 test list and then 5 consecutive frames are used, 4 for input and 1 for ground truth. Quantitative results with PSNR [22] and SSIM [34] scores, where the higher the score the better the prediction, are given in Table 2 and qualitative results are shown in Fig. 5. These experiments show that DYAN predictions achieve superior PSNR and SSIM scores by identifying the dynamics of the optical flow instead of assuming it is constant as DVF does.

Finally, we also conducted a multi-step prediction experiment in which we applied our $F = 4$ model to predict the next three future frames, where each prediction was used as a new available input frame. Figure 6 shows the results of this experiment, compared against the scores for BeyondMSE [22] and DVF [18], where it can be seen that the PSNR scores of DYAN's predictions are consistently higher than the ones obtained using previous approaches.

For these experiments, DYAN was trained on 2 NVIDIA GeForce GTX GPUs, using one GPU for each of the optical flow channels. Training takes around 65 min/epoch, and predicting one frame takes 390ms (including warping). Training converged at 7 epochs for $F = 4$. In contrast, DVF takes severals day to train. DYAN's saved model only takes 3KB on hard disk.

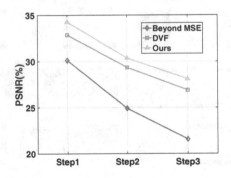

Fig. 6. Qualitative result for our model trained on UCF-101 dataset with $F = 4$. Other scores were obtained by running the code provided by the respective authors. All scores were computed using masks from [18].

Table 2. PSNR and SSIM scores of next frame prediction on UCF-101 dataset. Results for [18,22] were obtained by running the code provided by the respective authors.

UCF-101	CopyLast (F = 4)	BeyondMSE [22] (F = 4)	OpticalFlow [22] (F = 4)	DVF [18] (F = 4)	Ours (F = 4)
PSNR	28.6	30.11	31.6	32.86	34.26
SSIM	0.89	0.88	0.93	0.93	0.96

7 Conclusion

We introduced a novel DYnamical Atoms-based Network, DYAN, designed using concepts from dynamic systems identification theory, to capture dynamics-based invariants in video sequences, and to predict future frames. DYAN has several advantages compared to architectures previously used for similar tasks: it is compact, easy to train, visualize and interpret, it is fast to train, it produces high quality predictions fast, and generalizes well across domains. Finally, the high quality of DYAN's predictions show that the sparse features learned by its encoder do capture the underlying dynamics of the input, suggesting that they will be useful for other unsupervised learning and video processing tasks such as activity recognition and video semantic segmentation.

References

1. Ayazoglu, M., Li, B., Dicle, C., Sznaier, M., Camps, O.I.: Dynamic subspace-based coordinated multicamera tracking. In: 2011 IEEE International Conference on Computer Vision (ICCV), pp. 2462–2469. IEEE (2011)
2. Beck, A., Teboulle, M.: A fast iterative shrinkage-thresholding algorithm for linear inverse problems. SIAM J. Imaging Sci. $2(1)$, 183–202 (2009)
3. Dicle, C., Yilmaz, B., Camps, O., Sznaier, M.: Solving temporal puzzles. In: CVPR, pp. 5896–5905 (2016)
4. Dollár, P., Wojek, C., Schiele, B., Perona, P.: Pedestrian detection: a benchmark. In: IEEE Conference on Computer Vision and Pattern Recognition, CVPR 2009, pp. 304–311. IEEE (2009)
5. Dosovitskiy, A., et al.: Flownet: learning optical flow with convolutional networks. In: Proceedings of the IEEE International Conference on Computer Vision, pp. 2758–2766 (2015)
6. Geiger, A., Lenz, P., Stiller, C., Urtasun, R.: Vision meets robotics: the kitti dataset. Int. J. Robot. Res. $32(11)$, 1231–1237 (2013)
7. Goodfellow, I., et al.: Generative adversarial nets. In: Advances in Neural Information Processing Systems, pp. 2672–2680 (2014)
8. Gregor, K., LeCun, Y.: Learning fast approximations of sparse coding. In: Proceedings of the 27th International Conference on Machine Learning (ICML 2010), pp. 399–406 (2010)
9. Hesterberg, T., Choi, N.H., Meier, L., Fraley, C.: Least angle and l1 penalized regression: a review. Stat. Surv. 2, 61–93 (2008)
10. Horn, B.K., Schunck, B.G.: Determining optical flow. Artif. Intell. $17(1$–$3)$, 185–203 (1981)
11. Hou, R., Chen, C., Shah, M.: Tube convolutional neural network (T-CNN) for action detection in videos. arXiv preprint arXiv:1703.10664 (2017)
12. Ilg, E., Mayer, N., Saikia, T., Keuper, M., Dosovitskiy, A., Brox, T.: Flownet 2.0: evolution of optical flow estimation with deep networks. In: IEEE Conference on Computer Vision and Pattern Recognition (CVPR), vol. 2 (2017)
13. Jozefowicz, R., Zaremba, W., Sutskever, I.: An empirical exploration of recurrent network architectures. In: ICML, pp. 2342–2350 (2015)
14. Kalchbrenner, N., et al.: Video pixel networks. arXiv preprint arXiv:1610.00527 (2016)

15. Kalogeiton, V., Weinzaepfel, P., Ferrari, V., Schmid, C.: Action tubelet detector for spatio-temporal action localization. arXiv preprint arXiv:1705.01861 (2017)
16. Li, B., Camps, O.I., Sznaier, M.: Cross-view activity recognition using hankelets. In: 2012 IEEE Conference on Computer Vision and Pattern Recognition (CVPR), pp. 1362–1369. IEEE (2012)
17. Liang, X., Lee, L., Dai, W., Xing, E.P.: Dual motion GAN for future-flow embedded video prediction. arXiv preprint arXiv:1708.00284 (2017)
18. Liu, Z., Yeh, R., Tang, X., Liu, Y., Agarwala, A.: Video frame synthesis using deep voxel flow. In: International Conference on Computer Vision (ICCV), vol. 2 (2017)
19. Lotter, W., Kreiman, G., Cox, D.: Deep predictive coding networks for video prediction and unsupervised learning. arXiv preprint arXiv:1605.08104 (2016)
20. Luc, P., Neverova, N., Couprie, C., Verbeek, J., LeCun, Y.: Predicting deeper into the future of semantic segmentation. In: ICCV 2017-International Conference on Computer Vision, p. 10 (2017)
21. Luo, Z., Peng, B., Huang, D.A., Alahi, A., Fei-Fei, L.: Unsupervised learning of long-term motion dynamics for videos. arXiv preprint arXiv:1701.01821 vol. 2 (2017)
22. Mathieu, M., Couprie, C., LeCun, Y.: Deep multi-scale video prediction beyond mean square error. arXiv preprint arXiv:1511.05440 (2015)
23. Meyer, S., Wang, O., Zimmer, H., Grosse, M., Sorkine-Hornung, A.: Phase-based frame interpolation for video. In: Proceedings of the IEEE Conference on Computer Vision and Pattern Recognition, pp. 1410–1418 (2015)
24. Moreau, T., Bruna, J.: Understanding the learned iterative soft thresholding algorithm with matrix factorization. arXiv preprint arXiv:1706.01338 (2017)
25. Mundy, J.L., Zisserman, A.: Geometric invariance in computer vision, vol. 92. MIT press Cambridge, MA (1992)
26. Pathak, D., Girshick, R., Dollár, P., Darrell, T., Hariharan, B.: Learning features by watching objects move. In: Computer Vision and Pattern Recognition (CVPR) (2017)
27. Peng, X., Schmid, C.: Multi-region two-stream R-CNN for action detection. In: Leibe, B., Matas, J., Sebe, N., Welling, M. (eds.) ECCV 2016. LNCS, vol. 9908, pp. 744–759. Springer, Cham (2016). https://doi.org/10.1007/978-3-319-46493-0_45
28. Ranzato, M., Szlam, A., Bruna, J., Mathieu, M., Collobert, R., Chopra, S.: Video (language) modeling: a baseline for generative models of natural videos. arXiv preprint arXiv:1412.6604 (2014)
29. Saha, S., Singh, G., Sapienza, M., Torr, P.H., Cuzzolin, F.: Deep learning for detecting multiple space-time action tubes in videos. arXiv preprint arXiv:1608.01529 (2016)
30. Soomro, K., Zamir, A.R., Shah, M.: Ucf101: A dataset of 101 human actions classes from videos in the wild. arXiv preprint arXiv:1212.0402 (2012)
31. Srivastava, N., Mansimov, E., Salakhudinov, R.: Unsupervised learning of video representations using LSTMs. In: International Conference on Machine Learning, pp. 843–852 (2015)
32. Sun, X., Nasrabadi, N.M., Tran, T.D.: Supervised multilayer sparse coding networks for image classification. arXiv preprint arXiv:1701.08349 (2017)
33. Wadhwa, N., Rubinstein, M., Durand, F., Freeman, W.T.: Phase-based video motion processing. ACM Trans. Graph. (TOG) 32(4), 80 (2013)
34. Wang, Z., Bovik, A.C., Sheikh, H.R., Simoncelli, E.P.: Image quality assessment: from error visibility to structural similarity. IEEE Trans. Image Process. 13(4), 600–612 (2004)

35. Xue, T., Wu, J., Bouman, K., Freeman, B.: Visual dynamics: probabilistic future frame synthesis via cross convolutional networks. In: Advances in Neural Information Processing Systems, pp. 91–99 (2016)

36. Yilmaz, B., Bekiroglu, K., Lagoa, C., Sznaier, M.: A randomized algorithm for parsimonious model identification. IEEE Trans. Autom. Control. **63**(2), 532–539 (2018)

37. Zhou, Y., Berg, T.L.: Learning temporal transformations from time-lapse videos. In: Leibe, B., Matas, J., Sebe, N., Welling, M. (eds.) ECCV 2016. LNCS, vol. 9912, pp. 262–277. Springer, Cham (2016). https://doi.org/10.1007/978-3-319-46484-8_16

Sparsely Aggregated Convolutional Networks

Ligeng Zhu[1]([⊠]), Ruizhi Deng[1], Michael Maire[2], Zhiwei Deng[1],
Greg Mori[1], and Ping Tan[1]

[1] Simon Fraser University, Burnaby, Canada
{lykenz,ruizhid,zhiweid,mori,pingtan}@sfu.edu
[2] University of Chicago, Chicago, USA
mmaire@uchicago.edu

Abstract. We explore a key architectural aspect of deep convolutional neural networks: the pattern of internal skip connections used to aggregate outputs of earlier layers for consumption by deeper layers. Such aggregation is critical to facilitate training of very deep networks in an end-to-end manner. This is a primary reason for the widespread adoption of residual networks, which aggregate outputs via cumulative summation. While subsequent works investigate alternative aggregation operations (*e.g.* concatenation), we focus on an orthogonal question: which outputs to aggregate at a particular point in the network. We propose a new internal connection structure which aggregates only a sparse set of previous outputs at any given depth. Our experiments demonstrate this simple design change offers superior performance with fewer parameters and lower computational requirements. Moreover, we show that sparse aggregation allows networks to scale more robustly to 1000+ layers, thereby opening future avenues for training long-running visual processes.

1 Introduction

As convolutional neural networks have become a central component of many vision systems, the field has quickly adopted successive improvements in their basic design. This is exemplified by a series of popular CNN architectures, most notably: AlexNet [25], VGG [32], Inception [34,35], ResNet [16,17], and DenseNet [20]. Though initially targeted to image classification, each of these designs also serves the role of a backbone across a broader range of vision tasks, including object detection [7,14] and semantic segmentation [3,28,41]. Advances in backbone network architecture consistently translate into corresponding performance boosts to these downstream tasks.

We examine a core design element, internal aggregation links, of the recent residual (ResNet [16]) and dense (DenseNet [20]) network architectures. Though vital to the success of these architectures, we demonstrate that the specific

Electronic supplementary material The online version of this chapter (https://doi.org/10.1007/978-3-030-01258-8_12) contains supplementary material, which is available to authorized users.

V. Ferrari et al. (Eds.): ECCV 2018, LNCS 11216, pp. 192–208, 2018.
https://doi.org/10.1007/978-3-030-01258-8_12

structure of aggregation in current networks is at a suboptimal design point. DenseNet, considered state-of-the-art, actually wastes capacity by allocating too many parameters and too much computation along internal aggregation links.

We suggest a principled alternative design for internal aggregation structure, applicable to both ResNets and DenseNets. Our design is a sparsification of the default aggregation structure. In both ResNet and DenseNet, the input to a particular layer is formed by aggregating the output of all previous layers. We switch from this full aggregation topology to one in which only a subset of previous outputs are linked into a subsequent layer. By changing the number of incoming links to be logarithmic, rather than linear, in the overall depth of the network, we fundamentally reduce the growth of parameters in our resulting analogue of DenseNet. Experiments reveal our design to be uniformly advantageous:

- On standard tasks, such as image classification, SparseNet, our sparsified DenseNet variant, is more efficient than both ResNet and DenseNet. This holds for measuring efficiency in terms of both parameters and operations (FLOPs) required for a given level of accuracy. A much smaller SparseNet model matches the performance of the highest accuracy DenseNet.
- In comparison to DenseNet, the SparseNet design scales in a robust manner to instantiation of extremely deep networks of 1000 layers and beyond. Such configurations magnify the efficiency gap between DenseNet and SparseNet.
- Our aggregation pattern is equally applicable to ResNet. Switching ResNet to our design preserves or improves ResNet's performance properties. This suggests that aggregation topology is a fundamental consideration of its own, decoupled from other design differences between ResNet and DenseNet.

Section 4 provides full details on these experimental results. Prior to that, Sect. 2 relates background on the history and role of skip or aggregation links in convolutional neural networks. It places our contribution in the context of much of the recent research focus on CNN architecture.

Section 3 presents the details of our sparse aggregation strategy. Our approach occupies a previously unexplored position in aggregation complexity between that of standard CNNs and FractalNet [26] on one side, and ResNet and DenseNet on the other. Taken together with our experimental results, sparse aggregation appears to be a simple, general improvement that is likely to filter into the standard CNN backbone design. Section 5 concludes with a synthesis of these observations, and discussion of potential future research paths.

2   Related Work

Modern CNN architectures usually consist of a series of convolutional, ReLU, and batch normalization [23] operations, mixed with occasional max-pooling and subsampling stages. Much prior research focuses on optimizing for parameter efficiency within convolution, for example, via dimensionality reduction bottlenecks [16,17,22], grouped convolution [19,39], or weight compression [4]. These efforts all concern design at a micro-architectural level, optimizing structure that fits inside a single functional unit containing at most a few operations.

At a macro-architectural level, skip connections have emerged as a common and useful design motif. Such connections route outputs of earlier CNN layers directly to the input of far deeper layers, skipping over the sequence of intermediate layers. Some deeper layers thus take input from multiple paths: the usual sequential path as well as these shortcut paths. Multiple intuitions motivate inclusion of skip connections, and may share in explaining their effectiveness.

2.1   Skip Connections for Features

Predicting a detailed labeling of a visual scene may require understanding it at multiple levels of abstraction, from edges and textures to object categories. Taking the plausible view that a CNN learns to compute increasingly abstract visual representations when going from shallower to deeper layers, skip connections can provide a pathway for assembling features that combine many levels of abstraction. Building in such connections alleviates the burden of learning to store and maintain features computed early that the network needs again later.

This intuition motivates the skip connection structures found in many semantic segmentation CNNs. Fully convolutional networks [28] upsample and combine several layers of a standard CNN, to act as input to a final prediction layer. Hypercolumn networks [13] similarly wire intermediate representations into a concatenated feature descriptor. Rather than use the end layer as the sole destination for skip links, encoder-decoder architectures, such as SegNet [1] and U-Net [31], introduce internal skip links between encoder and decoder layers of corresponding spatial resolutions. Such internal feature aggregation, though with different connectivity, may also serve to make very deep networks trainable.

2.2   Training Very Deep Networks

Training deep networks end-to-end via stochastic gradient descent requires back-propagating a signal through the entire network. Starting from random initialization, the gradient received by earlier layers from a loss at the end of the network will be noisier than that received by deeper layers. This issue worsens with deeper networks, making them harder to train. Attaching additional losses to intermediate layers [27,35] is one strategy for ameliorating this problem.

Highway networks [33] and residual networks [16] (ResNets) offer a more elegant solution, preserving the ability to train from a single loss by adding skip connections to the network architecture. The addition of skip connections shortens the effective path length between early network layers and an informative loss. Highway networks add a gating mechanism, while residual networks implement skip connections by summing outputs of all previous layers. The effectiveness of the later strategy is cause for its current widespread adoption.

Fractal networks [26] demonstrate an alternative skip connection structure for training very deep networks. The accompanying analysis reveals skip connections function as a kind of scaffold that supports the training processes. Under special conditions, the FractalNet skip connections can be discarded after training.

DenseNets [20] build directly on ResNets, by switching the operational form of skip connections from summation to concatenation. They maintain the same aggregation topology as ResNets, as all previous layer outputs are concatenated.

2.3 Architecture Search

The dual motivations of building robust representations and enabling end-to-end training drive inclusion of internal aggregation links, but do not dictate an optimal procedure for doing so. Absent insight into optimal design methods, one can treat architectural details as hyperparameters over which to optimize [42]. Training of a single network can then be wrapped as a step in larger search procedure that varies network design.

However, it is unclear whether skip link topology is an important hyperparameter over which to search. Our proposed aggregation topology is motivated by a simple construction and, as shown in Sect. 4, significantly outperforms prior hand-designed structures. Perhaps our topology is near optimal and will free architecture search to focus on more consequential hyperparameters.

2.4 Concurrent Work

Concurrent work [18], independent of our own, proposes a modification of DenseNet similar to our SparseNet design. We make distinct contributions in comparison:

- Our SparseNet image classification results are substantially better than those reported in Hu *et al.* [18]. Our results represent an actual and significant improvement over the DenseNet baseline.
- We explore sparse aggregation topologies more generally, showing application to ResNet and DenseNet, whereas [18] proposes specific changes to DenseNet.
- We experiment with networks in extreme configurations (*e.g.* 1000 layers) in order to highlight the robustness of our design principles in regimes where current baselines begin to break down.

While we focus on skip connections in the context of both parameter efficiency and network trainability, other concurrent work examines alternative mechanisms to ensure trainability. Xiao *et al.* [38] develop a novel initialization scheme that allows training very deep vanilla CNNs. Chang *et al.* [2], taking inspiration from ordinary differential equations, develop a framework for analyzing stability of reversible networks [8] and demonstrate very deep reversible architectures.

3 Aggregation Architectures

Figure 1 sketches our proposed sparse aggregation architecture alongside the dominant ResNet [16] and DenseNet [20] designs, as well as the previously

(a) Dense Aggregation (ResNet / DenseNet Topology)

(b) Dense Aggregation: Equivalent Exploded View of **(a)**

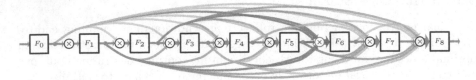

(c) Sparse Aggregation (Our Proposed Topology)

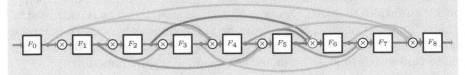

(d) Fractal Aggregation (FractalNet)

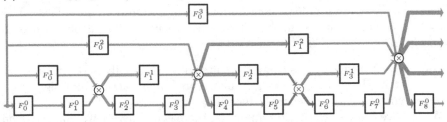

Fig. 1. Aggregation topologies. Our proposed sparse aggregation topology devotes less machinery to skip connections than DenseNet [20], but more than FractalNet [26]. This is apparent by comparing the exploded view (b) of the ResNet [16] or DenseNet topology (a), as well as the fractal topology (d), with our proposal (c). All of these architectures are describable in terms of a basic parameterized functional unit $F(\cdot)$ (*e.g.* convolution-ReLU-batchnorm), an aggregation operator $\otimes$, and a connection pattern. For ResNet, $\otimes$ is addition [+]; for DenseNet, $\otimes$ is concatenation [$\oplus$]; for FractalNet $\otimes$ is averaging [$\mp$]. Note how the compact view (a) feeds the result of one aggregation into the next; the exploded view (b) of DenseNet is the correct visualization for comparison to (c) and (d). For a network of depth N, dense aggregation requires $O(N^2)$ connections, sparse aggregation $O(N\log(N))$, and fractal aggregation $O(2N)$. These differences are visually apparent by comparing incoming links at a common depth. For example, compare the density of the (highlighted red) links into layer $F_6(\cdot)$.(Color figure online)

proposed FractalNet [26] alternative to ResNet. This macro-architectural view abstracts away details such as the specific functional unit $F(\cdot)$, parameter counts and feature dimensionality, and the aggregation operator $\otimes$. As our focus is on a novel aggregation topology, experiments in Sect. 4 match these other details to those of ResNet and DenseNet baselines.

We define a network with a sparse aggregation structure to be a sequence of nonlinear functional units (layers) $F_\ell(\cdot)$ operating on input x, with the output y_ℓ of layer ℓ computed as:

$$y_0 = F_0(x) \tag{1}$$

$$y_\ell = F_\ell(\otimes(y_{\ell-c^0}, y_{\ell-c^1}, y_{\ell-c^2}, y_{\ell-c^3}, \ldots, y_{\ell-c^k})) \tag{2}$$

where c is a positive integer and k is the largest non-negative integer such that $c^k \leq \ell$. $\otimes$ is the aggregation function. This amounts to connecting each layer to previous layers at exponentially increasing offsets. Contrast with ResNet and DenseNet, which connect each layer to all previous layers according to:

$$y_\ell = F_\ell(\otimes(y_{\ell-1}, y_{\ell-2}, y_{\ell-3}, y_{\ell-4}, \ldots, y_0)) \tag{3}$$

For a network of total depth N, the full aggregation strategy of ResNet and DenseNet introduces N incoming links per layer, for a total of $O(N^2)$ connections. In contrast, sparse aggregation introduces no more than $\log_c(N)$ incoming links per layer, for a total of $O(N \log(N))$ connections.

Our sparse aggregation strategy also differs from FractalNet's aggregation pattern. The FractalNet [26] design places a network of depth N in parallel with networks of depth $\frac{N}{2}, \frac{N}{4}, \ldots, 1$, making the total network consist of $2N - 1$ layers. It inserts occasional join (aggregation) operations between these parallel networks, but does so with such extreme sparsity that the total connection count is still dominated by the $O(2N)$ connections in parallel layers.

Our sparse connection pattern is sparser than ResNet or DenseNet, yet denser than FractalNet. It occupies a previously unexplored point, with a fundamentally different scaling rate of skip connection density with network depth.

3.1 Potential Drawbacks of Dense Aggregation

The ability to train networks with depth greater than 100 layers using DenseNet and ResNet architectures can be partially attributed to to their feature aggregation strategies. As discussed in Sect. 2, skip links serve as a training scaffold, allowing each layer to be directly supervised by the final output layer, and aggregation may help transfer useful features from shallower to deeper layers.

However, dense feature aggregation comes with several potential drawbacks. These drawbacks appear in different forms in the ResNet-styled aggregation by summation and the DenseNet-styled aggregation by concatenation, but share a common theme of over-constraining or over-burdening the system.

In general, it is impossible to disentangle the original components of a set of features after taking their sum. As the depth of a residual network grows, the number of features maps aggregated grows linearly. Later features may corrupt or wash-out the information carried by earlier feature maps. This information loss caused by summation could partially explain the saturation of ResNet performance when the depth exceeds 1000 layers [16]. This way of combining features is also hard-coded in the design of ResNets, giving the model little flexibility to learn more expressive combination strategies. This constraint may be the reason that ResNet layers tend to learn to perform incremental feature updates [10].

In contrast, the aggregation style of DenseNets combines features through direct concatenation, which preserves the original form of the previous features. Concatenation allows each subsequent layer a clean view of all previously computed features, making feature reuse trivial. This factor may contribute to the better parameter-performance efficiency of DenseNet over ResNet.

But DenseNet's aggregation by concatenation has its own problems: the number of skip connections and required parameters grows at a rate of $O(N^2)$, where N is the network depth. This asymptotically quadratic growth means that a significant portion of the network is devoted to processing previously seen feature representations. Each layer contributes only a few new outputs to an ever-widening concatenation of stored state. Experiments show that it is hard for the model to make full use of all the parameters and dense skip connections. In the original DenseNet work [20], a large fraction of the skip connections have average absolute weights of convolution filters close to zero. This implies that dense aggregation of feature maps maintains some extraneous state.

The pitfalls of dense feature aggregation in both DenseNet and ResNet are caused by the linear growth in the number of features aggregated with respect to the depth. Variants of ResNet and DenseNet, including the post-activation ResNets [17], mixed-link networks [36], and dual-path networks [5] all use the same dense aggregation pattern, differing only by aggregation operator. They thus inherit potential limitations of this dense aggregation topology.

3.2 Properties of Sparse Aggregation

We would like to maintain the power of short gradient paths for training, while avoiding the potential drawbacks of dense feature aggregation. SparseNets do, in fact, have shorter gradient paths than architectures without aggregation.

Table 1. SparseNet properties. We compare architecture-induced scaling properties for networks of depth N and for individual layers located at depth ℓ.

	Parameters	Shortest gradient path	Aggregated features
Plain	$O(N)$	$O(N)$	$O(1)$
ResNets	$O(N)$	$O(1)$	$O(\ell)$
DenseNets	$O(N^2)$	$O(1)$	$O(\ell)$
SparseNets (sum)	$O(N)$	$O(\log(N))$	$O(\log \ell)$
SparseNets (concat)	$O(N \log N)$	$O(\log(N))$	$O(\log \ell)$

In plain feed-forward networks, there is only one path from a layer to a previous layer with offset S; the length of the path is $O(S)$. The length of the shortest gradient path is constant in dense aggregation networks like ResNet and DenseNet. However, the cost of maintaining a gradient path with $O(1)$ length between any two layers is the linear growth of the count of aggregated features. By aggregating features only from layers with exponential offset, the length of the shortest gradient path between two layers with offset S is bounded by $O((c-1)\log(S))$. Here, c is again the base of the exponent governing the sparse connection pattern.

It is also worth noting that the number of predecessor outputs gathered by the ℓth layer is $O(\log(\ell))$, as it only reaches predecessors with exponential offsets. Therefore, the total number of skip connections is

$$\sum_{\ell=1}^{N} \lfloor \log_c \ell \rfloor = O(N \log N) \tag{4}$$

where N is the number of layers (depth) of the network. The number of parameters are $O(N \log N)$ and $O(N)$, respectively, for aggregation by concatenation and aggregation by summation. Table 1 summarizes these properties.

4   Experiments

We demonstrate the effectiveness SparseNets as a drop-in replacement (and upgrade) for state-of-the-art networks with dense feature aggregation, namely ResNets [16,17] and DenseNets [20], through image classification tasks on the CIFAR [24] and ImageNet datasets [6]. Except for the difference between the dense and sparse aggregation topologies, we set all other SparseNet hyperparameters to be the same as the corresponding ResNet or DenseNet baseline.

For some large models, image classification accuracy appears to saturate when we continue increasing model depth or internal channel counts. It is likely such saturation is not due to model capacity limits, but rather both our model and baselines reach diminishing returns given the dataset size and task complexity. We are interested not only in absolute accuracy, but also parameter-accuracy and FLOP-accuracy efficiency.

We implement our models in the PyTorch framework [29]. For optimization, we use SGD with Nesterov momentum 0.9 and weight decay 0.0001. We train all models from scratch using He et al.'s initialization scheme [15]. All networks were trained using NVIDIA GTX 1080 Ti GPUs. We release our implementation[1] of SparseNets, with full details of model architecture and parameter settings, for the purpose of reproducible experimental results.

---

[1] https://github.com/Lyken17/SparseNet.

4.1 Datasets

CIFAR. Both the CIFAR-10 and CIFAR-100 datasets [24] have 50,000 training images and 10,000 testing images with size of 32×32 pixels. CIFAR-10 (C10) and CIFAR-100 (C100) have 10 and 100 classes respectively. Our experiments use standard data augmentation, including mirroring and shifting, as done in [20]. The mark + beside C10 or C100 in results tables indicates this data augmentation scheme. As preprocessing, we normalize the data by the channel mean and standard deviation. Following the schedule from the Torch implementation of ResNet [11], our learning rate starts from 0.1 and is divided by 10 at epoch 150 and 225.

ImageNet. The ILSVRC 2012 classification dataset [6] contains 1.2 million images for training, and 50K for validation, from 1000 classes. For a fair comparison, we adopt the standard augmentation scheme for training images as in [11,16,20]. Following [16,20], we report classification errors on the validation set with single crop of size 224×224.

4.2 Results on CIFAR

Table 2 reports experimental results on CIFAR [24]. The best SparseNet closely matches the performance of the state-of-the DenseNet. We also show the results for a selection of DenseNet and SparseNet models over multiple runs on the CIFAR-100 dataset in the supplementary material. Multiple runs exhibit similar accuracies with low variance. In all of these experiments, we instantiate each SparseNet to be exactly the same as the correspondingly named DenseNet, but with sparser aggregation structure (some connections removed). The parameter k indicates feature growth rates (how many new feature channels each layer produces), which we match to the DenseNet baseline. Models whose names end with BC use the bottleneck compression structure, as in the original DenseNet paper. As SparseNet does fewer concatenations than DenseNet, the same feature growth rate produces models with fewer overall parameters. Remarkably, for many of the corresponding 100 layer models, SparseNet performs as well or better than DenseNet, while having substantially fewer parameters.

4.3 Going Deeper with Sparse Connections

Table 3 shows results of pushing architectures to extreme depth. While Table 2 explored only the SparseNet analogue of DenseNet, we now explore switching both ResNet and DenseNet to sparse aggregation structures, and denote their corresponding SparseNets by SparseNet[+] and SparseNet[⊕], respectively.

Both ResNet and SparseNet[+] demonstrate better performance on CIFAR100 as their depth increases from 56 to 200 layers. The gap between the performance of ResNet and SparseNet[+] initially enlarges as depth increases. However, it narrows as network depth reaches 1001 layers, and the performance of SparseNet[+]-2000 surpasses ResNet-2000. Compared to ResNet, SparseNet[+] appears better able to scale to depths of over 1000 layers.

Similar to both ResNet and SparseNet[+], the performance of DenseNet and SparseNet[⊕] also improves as their depth increases. The performance of DenseNet is also affected by the feature growth rate. However, the parameter count of DenseNet explodes as we increase its depth to 400, even with a growth rate of 12. Bottleneck compression layers have to be adopted and the number of filters in each layer has to be significantly reduced if we want to go deeper. We experiment with DenseNets of depth greater than 1000 by adopting bottleneck compression (BC) structure and using a growth rate of 4. But, as Table 3 shows, their performance is far from satisfying. In contrast, building SparseNet[⊕] with more than 1000 layers is practical and memory-efficient. We can easily build SparseNet[⊕] with depth greater than 400 using BC structure and a growth rate of 12. At 1001 layers, it achieves far better performance than DenseNet-1001.

Table 2. CIFAR classification performance. We show classification error rate for SparseNets compared to DenseNets, ResNets, and their variants. Results marked with a * are from our implementation. Datasets marked with + indicates use of standard data augmentation (translation and mirroring).

Architecture	Depth	Params	C10+	C100+
ResNet [16]	110	1.7M	6.61	-
ResNet(pre-activation) [16]	164	1.7M	5.46	24.33
ResNet(pre-activation) [16]	1001	10.2M	4.62	21.42*
Wide ResNet [40]	16	11.0M	4.81	22.07
FractalNet [26]	21	38.6M	5.52	23.30
DenseNet (k = 12) [20]	40	1.1M	5.39*	24.79*
DenseNet (k = 12) [20]	100	7.2M	4.28*	20.97*
DenseNet (k = 24) [20]	100	28.3M	4.04*	19.61*
DenseNet (k = 16, 32, 64) [20]	100	61.1M	4.31*	20.6*
DenseNet (k = 32, 64, 128) [20]	100	241.6M	N/A	N/A
DenseNet-BC (k = 24) [20]	250	15.3M	**3.65**	17.6
DenseNet-BC (k = 40) [20]	190	25.6M	3.75*	**17.53***
DenseNet-BC (k = 16, 32, 64) [20]	100	7.9M	4.02*	19.55*
DenseNet-BC (k = 32, 64,128) [20]	100	30.5M	3.92*	18.71*
SparseNet (k = 12)	40	0.8M	5.13	24.65
SparseNet (k = 24)	100	2.5M	4.64	22.41
SparseNet (k = 36)	100	5.7M	4.34	20.50
SparseNet (k = 16, 32, 64)	100	7.2M	4.11	19.49
SparseNet (k = 32, 64, 128)	100	27.7M	3.88	18.80
SparseNet-BC (k = 24)	100	1.5M	4.03	22.12
SparseNet-BC (k = 36)	100	3.3M	3.91	20.31
SparseNet-BC (k = 16, 32, 64)	100	4.4M	3.43	19.71
SparseNet-BC (k = 32, 64, 128)	100	16.7M	**3.22**	**17.71**

Table 3. Depth scalability on CIFAR. *Left:* ResNets and their sparsely aggregated analogue SparseNets[+]. *Right:* DenseNets and their corresponding sparse analogues SparseNets[⊕]. Observe that ResNet and all SparseNet variants of any depth exhibit robust performance. DenseNets suffer an efficiency drop when stretched too deep.

Model	Depth	Params	CIFAR 100+	Model	Depth	Params	CIFAR 100+
	56	0.59M	27.00		40	1.10M	24.79
	110	1.15M	24.70	DenseNet(k=12)	100	7.20M	20.97
ResNet	200	2.07M	23.10		400	117M	N/A
	1001	10.33M	**21.42**	DenseNet-BC(k=24)	250	25.6M	17.6
	2000	20.62M	22.76		400	216.3M	N/A
	56	0.59M	27.70	DenseNet-BC(k=4)	400	1.10M	32.94
	110	1.15M	26.10		1001	6.63M	28.50
SparseNet[+]	200	2.07M	25.77		100	0.40M	27.99
	1001	10.33M	22.10	SparseNet[⊕]-BC (k=12)	400	1.70M	24.41
	2000	20.62M	**21.01**		1001	4.62M	22.10

An important advantage of SparseNet[⊕] over DenseNet is that the number of previous layers aggregated can be bounded by a small integer even when the depth of the network is over 1000 layers. This is a consequence of the slow growth rate of the logarithm function. This feature not only permits building deeper SparseNet[⊕] variants, but allows us to explore hyperparameters of SparseNet[⊕] with more flexibility on both depth and filter count.

We also observe that SparseNet[⊕] generally has better parameter efficiency than SparseNet[+]. For example, on CIFAR-100, the error rate of SparseNet[+]-1001 and SparseNet[⊕]-1001 are (coincidently) both 22.10. However, notice that SparseNet[⊕]-1001 requires less than half the parameters of SparseNet[+]-1001. Similar trends are also seen in the comparison between SparseNet[+]-200 and SparseNet[⊕]-400. The DenseNet *vs.* ResNet advantage of preserving features via concatenation (over summation) also holds for the sparse aggregation pattern.

4.4 Efficiency of SparseNet[⊕]

Returning to Table 2, we can further comment on the efficiency of SparseNet[⊕] (denoted in Table 2 as SparseNet) in comparison to DenseNet. These results include our exploration of parameter efficiency by varying the depth and number of filters of SparseNet[⊕]. As the number of features each layer aggregates grows slowly, and is nearly a constant within a block, we also double the number of filters across blocks, following the approach of ResNets. Here, a block refers to a sequence of layers running at the same spatial resolution, between pooling and subsampling stages of the CNN pipeline.

There are two general trends in the results. First, SparseNet usually requires fewer parameters than DenseNet when they have close performance. Most notably, DenseNet-BC ($N = 190$, $k = 40$) requires 25.6 million parameters to achieve error rate 17.53% on CIFAR100+, while SparseNet-BC can achieve a similar error of 17.71% under setting ($N = 100$, $k = \{32, 64, 128\}$) with only 16.7 million parameters. The 19.71% error rate of SparseNet-BC ($N = 100$,

$k = \{16, 32, 64\}$) is close to the performance of the corresponding DenseNet-BC ($N = 100$, $k = \{16, 32, 64\}$) but requires 4.4 rather than 7.9 million parameters.

Second, when both networks have less than 15 million parameters, SparseNet always outperforms the DenseNet with similar parameter count. For example, DenseNet ($N = 100, k = 12$) and SparseNet ($N = 100, k = \{16, 32, 64\}$) both have around 7.2 million parameters, but the latter shows better performance. DenseNet ($N = 40, k = 12$) consumes around 1.1 million parameters but still has worse performance than the 0.8 million param SparseNet ($N = 40, k = 12$).

Counterexamples do exist, such as the comparison between SparseNet-BC-100-$\{32, 64, 128\}$ and DenseNet-BC-250-24. The latter model, with fewer parameters, performs slightly better (17.6% vs 17.71% error) than the previous one. We argue this is an example of performance saturation considering DenseNet-BC-190-40 only has slightly higher accuracy than DenseNet-BC-250-24, with many more parameters (25.6 million $vs.$ 15.3 million). These large networks may be close to saturating performance on the CIFAR-100 image classification task.

Table 4. ImageNet results. The top-1 single-crop validation error, parameters, FLOPs, and time of each model on ImageNet.

Model	Error	Params	FLOPs	Time
DenseNet-121-32 [20]	25.0*	7.98M	5.7G	19.5ms
DenseNet-169-32 [20]	23.6*	14.15M	6.76G	32.0ms
DenseNet-201-32 [20]	22.6*	20.01M	8.63G	42.6ms
DenseNet-264-32 [20]	**22.2***	27.21M	11.03G	50.4ms
SparseNet[⊕]-121-32	25.6	4.51M	3.46G	13.5ms
SparseNet[⊕]-169-32	24.2	6.23M	3.74G	18.8ms
SparseNet[⊕]-201-32	23.1	7.22M	4.13G	22.0ms
SparseNet[⊕]-201-48	**22.1**	14.91M	9.19G	43.1ms
ResNet-50	23.9	25.5M	8.20G	42.2ms
ResNet-50 Pruned [12]	**23.7**	7.47M	-	-

Note that when we double the number of filters across different blocks, the performance of SparseNets is boosted and their better parameter efficiency over DenseNets becomes more obvious. SparseNets achieve similar or better performance than DenseNets, while requiring at most half the number of parameters uniformly across all settings. These general trends are summarized in the parameter-performance plots in Fig. 2 (left).

4.5   Results on ImageNet

To demonstrate efficiency on a larger-scale dataset, we further test different configurations of SparseNet[⊕] and compare them with state-of-the-art networks on ImageNet. All models are trained with the same preprocessing methods and hyperparameters. Table 4 reports ImageNet validation error.

These results reveal that the better parameter-performance efficiency exhibited by SparseNet[⊕] over DenseNet extends to ImageNet [6]: SparseNet[⊕] performs similarly to state-of-the-art DenseNets, while requiring significantly fewer parameters. For example, SparseNet-201-48 (14.91M params) yields better validation error than DenseNet-201-32 (20.01M params). SparseNet-201-32 (7.22M params) outperforms DenseNet-169-32 with just half the parameter count.

Even compared to pruned networks, SparseNets show competitive parameter efficiency. In the last row of the Table 4, we show the result of pruning ResNet-50 using deep compression [12], whose parameter-performance efficiency significantly outpaces the unpruned ResNet-50. However, our SparseNet[⊕]-201-32, trained from scratch, has even better error rate than pruned ResNet-50, with fewer parameters. See Fig. 2 (right) for a complete efficiency plot.

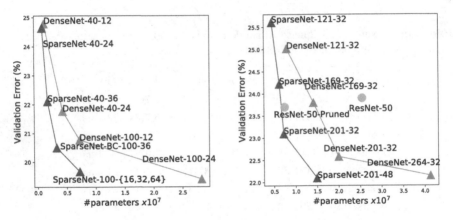

Fig. 2. Parameter efficiency. Comparison between DenseNets and SparseNets[⊕] on top-1% error and number of parameters with different configurations. *Left:* CIFAR. *Right:* ImageNet. SparseNets achieve lower error with fewer parameters.

4.6 Feature Reuse and Parameter Redundancy

The original DenseNets work [20] conducts a simple experiment to investigate how well a trained network reuses features across layers. In short, for each layer in each densely connected block, they compute the average absolute weights of the part of that layer's filters that convolves with each previous layer's feature map. The averaged absolute weights are rescaled between 0 and 1 for each layer i. The jth normalized value implies the relative dependency of the features of layer i on the features of layer j, compared to other layers. These experiments are performed on a DenseNet consisting of 3 blocks with $N = 40$ and $k = 12$.

We perform a similar experiment on a SparseNet model with the same configuration. We plot results as heat maps in Fig. 3. For comparison, we also include

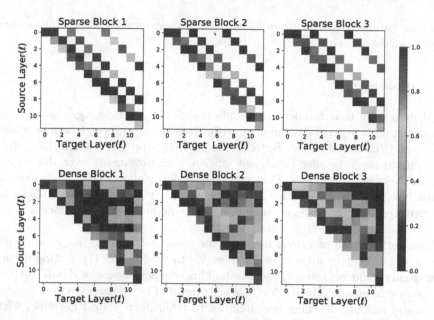

Fig. 3. The average absolute filter weights of convolutional layers in trained DenseNet and SparseNet. The color of pixel (i, j) indicates the average weights of connections from layer i to j within a block. The first row encodes the weights attached to the first input layer of a DenseNet/SparseNet block. (Color figure online)

the heat maps of the corresponding experiment on DenseNets [20]. In these heap maps, a red pixel at location (i, j) indicates layer i makes heavy use of the features of layer j; a blue pixel indicates relatively little usage. A white pixel indicates there is no direct connection between layer i and layer j. From the heat maps, we observe the following:

- Most of the non-white elements in the heat map of SparseNet are close to red, indicating that each layer takes full advantage of all the features it directly aggregates. It also indicates almost all the parameters are fully exploited, leaving little parameter redundancy. This result is not surprising considering the high observed parameter-performance efficiency of our model.
- In general, the layer coupling value at position (i, j) in DenseNet decreases as the offset between i and j gets larger. However, such a decaying trend does not appear in the heat map of SparseNet, implying that layers in SparseNets have better ability to extract useful features from long-distance connections to preceding layers.

The distribution of learned weights in Fig. 3, together with the efficiency curves in Fig. 2, serves to highlight the importance of optimizing macro-architectural design. Others have demonstrated the benefits of a range of schemes [9,19,22,30,37] for sparsifying micro-architectural network structure (parameter structure within layers or filters). Our results show similar considerations are relevant at the scale of the entire network.

5 Conclusion

We demonstrate that following a simple design rule, scaling aggregation link complexity in a logarithmic manner with network depth, yields a new state-of-the-art CNN architecture. Extensive experiments on CIFAR and ImageNet show our SparseNets offer significant efficiency improvements over the widely used ResNets and DenseNets. This increased efficiency allows SparseNets to scale robustly to great depth. While CNNs have recently moved from the 10-layer to 100-layer regime, perhaps new possibilities will emerge with straightforward and robust training of 1000-layer networks.

The performance of neural networks for visual recognition has grown with their depth as they evolved from AlexNet [25] to ResNet [16,17]. Extrapolating such trends could be cause to believe building deeper networks should further improve performance. Much effort has been devoted by researchers in computer vision and machine learning communities to train deep neural networks with more than 1000 layers, with such hope [17,21].

Though previous works and our experiments show we can train very deep neural networks with stochastic gradient descent, their test performance still usually plateaus. Even so, very deep neural networks might be suitable for other interesting tasks. One possible future direction could be solving sequential search or reasoning tasks relying on long-term dependencies. Skip connections might empower the network with backtracking ability. Sparse feature aggregation might permit building extremely deep neural networks for such tasks.

References

1. Badrinarayanan, V., Kendall, A., Cipolla, R.: SegNet: a deep convolutional encoder-decoder architecture for image segmentation. PAMI **39**, 2481–2495 (2017)
2. Chang, B., Meng, L., Haber, E., Ruthotto, L., Begert, D., Holtham, E.: Reversible architectures for arbitrarily deep residual neural networks. In: AAAI (2018)
3. Chen, L.C., Papandreou, G., Kokkinos, I., Murphy, K., Yuille, A.L.: DeepLab: semantic image segmentation with deep convolutional nets, atrous convolution, and fully connected CRFs. arXiv:1606.00915 (2016)
4. Chen, W., Wilson, J.T., Tyree, S., Weinberger, K.Q., Chen, Y.: Compressing neural networks with the hashing trick. In: ICML (2015)
5. Chen, Y., Li, J., Xiao, H., Jin, X., Yan, S., Feng, J.: Dual path networks. In: NIPS (2017)
6. Deng, J., Dong, W., Socher, R., Li, L.J., Li, K., Fei-Fei, L.: ImageNet: a large-scale hierarchical image database. In: CVPR (2009)
7. Girshick, R., Donahue, J., Darrell, T., Malik, J.: Rich feature hierarchies for accurate object detection and semantic segmentation. In: CVPR (2014)
8. Gomez, A.N., Ren, M., Urtasun, R., Grosse, R.B.: The reversible residual network: backpropagation without storing activations. In: NIPS (2017)

9. Gray, S., Radford, A., Kingma, D.P.: GPU kernels for block-sparse weights. Technical report, OpenAI (2017)
10. Greff, K., Srivastava, R.K., Schmidhuber, J.: Highway and residual networks learn unrolled iterative estimation. In: ICLR (2017)
11. Gross, S., Wilber, M.: Training and investigating residual nets (2016). https://github.com/facebook/fb.resnet.torch
12. Han, S., Mao, H., Dally, W.J.: Deep compression: compressing deep neural networks with pruning, trained quantization and huffman coding. In: ICLR (2016)
13. Hariharan, B., Arbelaez, P., Girshick, R., Malik, J.: Hypercolumns for object segmentation and fine-grained localization. In: CVPR (2015)
14. He, K., Gkioxari, G., Dollar, P., Girshick, R.: Mask R-CNN. In: ICCV (2017)
15. He, K., Zhang, X., Ren, S., Sun, J.: Delving deep into rectifiers: surpassing human-level performance on imagenet classification. In: ICCV (2015)
16. He, K., Zhang, X., Ren, S., Sun, J.: Deep residual learning for image recognition. In: CVPR (2016)
17. He, K., Zhang, X., Ren, S., Sun, J.: Identity mappings in deep residual networks. In: Leibe, B., Matas, J., Sebe, N., Welling, M. (eds.) ECCV 2016. LNCS, vol. 9908, pp. 630–645. Springer, Cham (2016). https://doi.org/10.1007/978-3-319-46493-0_38
18. Hu, H., Dey, D., Giorno, A.D., Hebert, M., Bagnell, J.A.: Log-DenseNet: How to sparsify a DenseNet. arXiv:1711.00002 (2017)
19. Huang, G., Liu, S., van der Maaten, L., Weinberger, K.Q.: CondenseNet: an efficient densenet using learned group convolutions. In: CVPR (2018)
20. Huang, G., Liu, Z., van der Maaten, L., Weinberger, K.Q.: Densely connected convolutional networks. In: CVPR (2017)
21. Huang, G., Sun, Y., Liu, Z., Sedra, D., Weinberger, K.Q.: Deep networks with stochastic depth. In: Leibe, B., Matas, J., Sebe, N., Welling, M. (eds.) ECCV 2016. LNCS, vol. 9908, pp. 646–661. Springer, Cham (2016). https://doi.org/10.1007/978-3-319-46493-0_39
22. Iandola, F.N., Moskewicz, M.W., Ashraf, K., Han, S., Dally, W.J., Keutzer, K.: SqueezeNet: AlexNet-level accuracy with 50x fewer parameters and <1MB model size. arXiv:1602.07360 (2016)
23. Ioffe, S., Szegedy, C.: Batch normalization: accelerating deep network training by reducing internal covariate shift. In: ICML (2015)
24. Krizhevsky, A., Hinton, G.: Learning multiple layers of features from tiny images. Technical report, University of Toronto (2009)
25. Krizhevsky, A., Sutskever, I., Hinton, G.E.: ImageNet classification with deep convolutional neural networks. In: NIPS (2012)
26. Larsson, G., Maire, M., Shakhnarovich, G.: FractalNet: Ultra-deep neural networks without residuals. In: ICLR (2017)
27. Lee, C.Y., Xie, S., Gallagher, P., Zhang, Z., Tu, Z.: Deeply-supervised nets. In: AISTATS (2015)
28. Long, J., Shelhamer, E., Darrell, T.: Fully convolutional networks for semantic segmentation. In: CVPR (2015)
29. Paszke, A., et al.: PyTorch: tensors and dynamic neural networks in python with strong GPU acceleration, May 2017
30. Prabhu, A., Varma, G., Namboodiri, A.M.: Deep expander networks: efficient deep networks from graph theory. arXiv:1711.08757 (2017)
31. Ronneberger, O., Fischer, P., Brox, T.: U-Net: convolutional networks for biomedical image segmentation. In: Navab, N., Hornegger, J., Wells, W.M., Frangi, A.F. (eds.) MICCAI 2015. LNCS, vol. 9351, pp. 234–241. Springer, Cham (2015). https://doi.org/10.1007/978-3-319-24574-4_28

32. Simonyan, K., Zisserman, A.: Very deep convolutional networks for large-scale image recognition. In: ICLR (2015)
33. Srivastava, R.K., Greff, K., Schmidhuber, J.: Highway networks. arXiv:1505.00387 (2015)
34. Szegedy, C., Ioffe, S., Vanhoucke, V., Alemi, A.A.: Inception-v4, Inception-ResNet and the impact of residual connections on learning. In: AAAI (2017)
35. Szegedy, C., et al.: Going deeper with convolutions. In: CVPR (2015)
36. Wang, W., Li, X., Yang, J., Lu, T.: Mixed link networks. arXiv:1802.01808 (2018)
37. Wen, W., Wu, C., Wang, Y., Chen, Y., Li, H.: Learning structured sparsity in deep neural networks. In: NIPS (2016)
38. Xiao, L., Bahri, Y., Sohl-Dickstein, J., Schoenholz, S.S., Pennington, J.: Dynamical isometry and a mean field theory of CNNs: how to train 10,000-layer vanilla convolutional neural networks. In: ICML (2018)
39. Xie, S., Girshick, R., Dollár, P., Tu, Z., He, K.: Aggregated residual transformations for deep neural networks. In: CVPR (2017)
40. Zagoruyko, S., Komodakis, N.: Wide residual networks. In: BMVC (2016)
41. Zhao, H., Shi, J., Qi, X., Wang, X., Jia, J.: Pyramid scene parsing network. In: CVPR (2017)
42. Zoph, B., Le, Q.V.: Neural architecture search with reinforcement learning. arXiv:1611.01578 (2016)

Revisiting the Inverted Indices for Billion-Scale Approximate Nearest Neighbors

Dmitry Baranchuk[1,2], Artem Babenko[1,3(✉)], and Yury Malkov[4]

[1] Yandex, Moscow, Russia
artem.babenko@phystech.edu
[2] Lomonosov Moscow State University, Moscow, Russia
[3] National Research University Higher School of Economics, Moscow, Russia
[4] The Institute of Applied Physics of the Russian Academy of Sciences,
Nizhny Novgorod, Russia

Abstract. This work addresses the problem of billion-scale nearest neighbor search. The state-of-the-art retrieval systems for billion-scale databases are currently based on the inverted multi-index, the recently proposed generalization of the inverted index structure. The multi-index provides a very fine-grained partition of the feature space that allows extracting concise and accurate short-lists of candidates for the search queries.

In this paper, we argue that the potential of the simple inverted index was not fully exploited in previous works and advocate its usage both for the highly-entangled deep descriptors and relatively disentangled SIFT descriptors. We introduce a new retrieval system that is based on the inverted index and outperforms the multi-index by a large margin for the same memory consumption and construction complexity. For example, our system achieves the state-of-the-art recall rates several times faster on the dataset of one billion deep descriptors compared to the efficient implementation of the inverted multi-index from the FAISS library.

1 Introduction

The last decade efficient billion-scale nearest neighbor search has become a significant research problem [1–6], inspired by the needs of modern computer vision applications, e.g. large-scale visual search [7], low-shot classification [8] and face recognition [9]. In particular, since the number of images on the Internet grows enormously fast, the multimedia retrieval systems need scalable and efficient search algorithms to respond queries to the databases of billions of items in several milliseconds.

All the existing billion-scale systems avoid the infeasible exhaustive search via restricting the part of the database that is considered for a query. This restriction is performed with the help of an *indexing structure*. The indexing structures partition the feature space into a large number of disjoint regions,

© Springer Nature Switzerland AG 2018
V. Ferrari et al. (Eds.): ECCV 2018, LNCS 11216, pp. 209–224, 2018.
https://doi.org/10.1007/978-3-030-01258-8_13

and the search process inspects only the points from the regions that are the closest to the particular query. The inspected points are organized in *short-lists* of candidates and the search systems calculate the distances between the query and all the candidates exhaustively. In scenarios, when the database does not fit in RAM, the compressed representations of the database points are used. The compressed representations are typically obtained with product quantization [10] that allows to compute the distances between the query and compressed points efficiently. The step of the distances calculation has a complexity that is linear in the number of candidates hence the short-lists provided by indexing structures should be concise.

The first indexing structure that was able to operate on the billion-scale datasets was introduced in [1]. It was based on the inverted index structure that splits the feature space into Voronoi regions for a set of K-Means centroids, learned on the dataset. This system was shown to achieve reasonable recall rates in several tens of milliseconds.

Later a generalization of the inverted index structure was proposed in [2]. This work introduced the inverted multi-index (IMI) that decomposes the feature space into several orthogonal subspaces and partitions each subspace into Voronoi regions independently. Then the Cartesian product of regions in each subspace formes the implicit partition of the whole feature space. Due to a huge number of regions, the IMI space partition is very fine-grained, and each region contains only a few data points. Therefore, IMI forms accurate and concise candidate lists while being memory and runtime efficient.

However, the structured nature of the regions in the IMI partition also has a negative impact on the final retrieval performance. In particular, it was shown in [5] that the majority of IMI regions contain no points and the effective number of regions is much smaller than the theoretical one. For certain data distributions, this results in the fact that the search process spends much time visiting empty regions that produce no candidates. In fact, the reason for this deficiency is that the IMI learns K-Means codebooks independently for different subspaces while the distributions of the corresponding data subvectors are not statistically independent in practice. In particular, there are significant correlations between different subspaces of CNN-produced descriptors that are most relevant these days. In this paper, we argue that the previous works underestimate the simple inverted index structure and advocate its use for all data types. The contributions of our paper include:

1. We demonstrate that the performance of the inverted index could be substantially boosted via using larger codebooks, while the multi-index design does not allow such a boost.
2. We introduce a memory-efficient *grouping* procedure for database points that boosts retrieval performance even further.
3. We provide an optimized implementation of our system for billion-scale search in the compressed domain to support the following research on this problem. As we show, the proposed system achieves the state-of-the-art recall rates up to several times faster, compared to the advanced IMI implementation

from the FAISS library [6] for the same memory consumption. The C++ implementation of our system is publicly available online[1].

The paper is structured as follows. We review related works on billion-scale indexing in Sect. 2. Section 3 describes a new system based on the inverted index. The experiments demonstrating the advantage of our system are detailed in Sect. 4. Finally, Sect. 5 concludes the paper.

2   Related Work

In this section we briefly review the previous methods that are related to our approach. Also here we introduce notation for the following sections.

Product Quantization (PQ) is a lossy compression method for high-dimensional vectors [10]. Typically, PQ is used in scenarios when the large-scale datasets do not fit into the main memory. In a nutshell, PQ encodes each vector $x \in \mathbf{R}^D$ by a concatenation of M codewords from M $\frac{D}{M}$-dimensional codebooks $R_1, \ldots, R_M$. Each codebook typically contains 256 codewords $R_m = \{r_1^m, \ldots, r_{256}^m\} \subset \mathbf{R}^D$ so that the codeword id could fit into one byte. In other words, PQ decomposes a vector x into M separate subvectors $[x_1, \ldots, x_M]$ and applies vector quantization (VQ) to each subvector x_m, while using a separate codebook R_m. Then the M-byte code for the vector x is a tuple of codewords indices $[i_1, \ldots, i_M]$ and the effective approximation is $x \approx [r_{i_1}^1, \ldots, r_{i_M}^M]$. As a nice property, PQ allows efficient computation of Euclidean distances between the uncompressed query and the large number of compressed vectors. The computation is performed via the ADC procedure [10] using lookup tables:

$$\|q - x\|^2 \approx \|q - [r_{i_1}^1, \ldots, r_{i_M}^M]\|^2 = \sum_{m=1}^{M} \|q_m - r_{i_m}^m\|^2 \qquad (1)$$

where q_m is the mth subvector of a query q. This sum can be calculated in M additions and lookups given that distances from query subvectors to codewords are precomputed and stored in lookup tables. Thanks to both high compression quality and computational efficiency PQ-based methods are currently the top choice for compact representations of large datasets. PQ gave rise to active research on high-dimensional vectors compression in computer vision and machine learning community [11–19].

IVFADC [1] is one of the first retrieval systems capable of dealing with billion-scale datasets efficiently. IVFADC uses the inverted index [20] to avoid exhaustive search and Product Quantization for database compression. The inverted index splits the feature space into K regions that are the Voronoi cells of the codebook $C = \{c_1, \ldots, c_K\}$. The codebook is typically obtained via standard K-means clustering. Then IVFADC encodes the displacements of each point from the centroid of a region it belongs to. The encoding is performed via Product Quantization with global codebooks shared by all regions.

---

[1] https://github.com/dbaranchuk/ivf-hnsw.

The Inverted Multi-Index and Multi-D-ADC. The inverted multi-index (IMI) [2] generalizes the inverted index and is currently the state-of-the-art indexing approach for high-dimensional spaces and huge datasets. Instead of using the full-dimensional codebook, the IMI splits the feature space into several orthogonal subspaces (usually, two subspaces are considered) and constructs a separate codebook for each subspace. Thus, the inverted multi-index has two $\frac{D}{2}$-dimensional codebooks for different halves of the vector, each with K subspace centroids. The feature space partition then is produced as a Cartesian product of the corresponding subspace partitions. Thus for two subspaces the inverted multi-index effectively produces K^2 regions. Even for moderate values of K that is much bigger than the number of regions within the IVFADC system or other systems using inverted indices. Due to a very large number of regions only a small fraction of the dataset should be visited to reach the correct nearest neighbor. [2] also describes the *multi-sequence* procedure that produces the sequence of regions that are the closest to the particular query. For dataset compression, [2] also uses Product Quantization with codebooks shared across all cells to encode the displacements of the vectors from region centroids. The described retrieval system is referred to as *Multi-D-ADC*.

The performance of indexing in the Multi-D-ADC scheme can be further improved by using the global data rotation that minimizes correlations between subspaces [3]. Another improvement [4] introduces the Multi-LOPQ system that uses local PQ codebooks for displacements compression with the IMI structure.

Several other works consider the problem of the memory-efficient billion-scale search. [5] proposes the modification of the inverted multi-index that uses two non-orthogonal codebooks to produce region centroids. [16] proposes to use Composite Quantization [15] instead of Product Quantization to produce the partition centroids. While these modifications were shown to achieve higher recall rates compared to the original multi-index, their typical runtimes are about ten milliseconds that could be prohibitively slow in practical scenarios. Several works investigate efficient GPU implementations for billion-scale search [6, 21]. In this paper, we focus on the niche of the CPU methods that operate with runtimes about one millisecond.

3   Inverted Index Revisited

In this section we first compare the inverted index to the IMI. In particular, we show that the simple increase of the codebook size could substantially improve the indexing quality for the inverted index while being almost useless for the IMI. Second, we introduce a modification for the inverted index that could be used to boost the indexing performance even further without efficiency drop.

3.1   Index vs Multi-Index

We compare the main properties of the inverted index and the IMI in the Table 1. The top part of the table lists the features that make the IMI the state-of-the-art indexing structure these days: precise candidate lists, fast indexing and query assignment due to small codebook sizes (typically K does not exceed 2^{14} for billion-sized databases).

Table 1. Comparison of the main properties of the inverted index and the IMI. K denotes the codebook sizes in both systems. The IMI provides more precise candidate lists and has low indexing and query assignment costs due to smaller codebook sizes. On the other hand, the inverted index requires a smaller number of expensive random memory accesses when searching, and could benefit from large codebooks, while the IMI performance saturates with K about 2^{14}. Moreover, the increase of K is memory-inefficient in the IMI as its additional memory consumption scales quadratically.

Structure	Inverted index	Inverted multi-index
Candidate lists quality	Medium	**High**
Query assignment & indexing cost	Medium	**Low**
Number of random memory accesses during search	**Small**	Large
Performance increase from large K	**High**	Small
Memory consumption scalability	**O(K)**	$O(K^2)$

Nevertheless, the fine-grained partition in the multi-index imposes several limitations that are summarized in the bottom part of the Table 1. First, the IMI has to visit much more partition regions compared to the inverted index to accumulate the reasonable number of candidates. Skipping to the next region requires a random memory access operation that is more expensive compared to the sequential PQ-distance computation, especially for short code lengths. A large number of random access operations slows down the search, especially when large number of candidates is needed.

Another property that favors the inverted index is the possibility to increase its codebook size K. To the best of our knowledge, the largest codebook sizes used in the index vs multi-index comparison were 2^{17} and 2^{14} respectively [5]. We argue that the multi-index performance is closer to saturation w.r.t K compared to the inverted index, and the usage of $K > 2^{14}$ would not result in substantially better feature space partition. On the other hand, in the inverted index one could use much larger codebooks compared to $K = 2^{17}$ without saturation in the space partition quality. To support this claim, we compare the distances from the datapoints to the closest centroids for the inverted index and the IMI with different K values for the DEEP1B dataset [5] in Table 2. The smaller distances typically indicate that the centroids represent the actual data distribution better. Table 2 demonstrates that the increase of K in the multi-index results in the much smaller decrease of the closest distances compared to the inverted index. E.g. the 16-fold increase of K from 2^{18} to 2^{22} in the inverted index results in 18% drop in the average distance. On the other hand, the 16-fold increase of regions number in the IMI partition (that corresponds to the fourfold increase in K from 2^{13} to 2^{15}) results only in 11% drop. We also compare amounts of additional memory consumption required by both systems with different K values to demonstrate that the IMI is memory-inefficient for large codebooks. E.g. for $K = 2^{15}$ the inverted multi-index requires about four additional bytes per point for one billion database, that is non-negligible, especially for short code lengths. The reason for the quadratic scalability is that the IMI has to maintain K^2 inverted lists to represent the feature space partition.

Table 2. The indexing quality and the amount of additional memory consumption for the inverted index and the IMI with different codebook sizes on the DEEP1B dataset. The indexing quality is evaluated by the average distance from the datapoints to the closest region centroid. The IMI indexing quality does not benefit from $K > 2^{14}$ while the required memory grows quadratically.

Inverted index			Inverted multi-index		
K	Average distance	Memory	K	Average distance	Memory
2^{18}	0.315	97 Mb	2^{13}	0.345	256 Mb
2^{20}	0.282	388 Mb	2^{14}	0.321	1024 Mb
2^{22}	0.259	1552 Mb	2^{15}	0.305	4096 Mb

The numbers from Table 2 encourage to use the inverted index with larger codebook instead of the IMI, despite the smaller number of the partition regions. The only practical reason, preventing their usage, is the expensive procedure of query assignment that takes $O(K)$ operations. But in the experimental section below we demonstrate that due to the recent progress in the million-scale ANN-search one can use the approximate search of high accuracy for query assignment. We show that the usage of the approximate search does not result in the search performance drop and the overall scheme of the inverted index with approximate query assignment outperforms the state-of-the-art IMI implementation.

3.2 Grouping and Pruning

Now we describe a technique that is especially useful for the IVFADC scheme for compressed domain search. In general, we propose a procedure that organizes the points in each region into several groups such that the points in nearby locations belong to the same group. In other words, we want to split each inverted index region into a set of smaller *subregions*, corresponding to Voronoi cells of a set of *subcentroids*. The naive solution of this problem via K-Means clustering in each region would require storing full-dimensional subcentroids codebooks that would require too much memory. Instead, we propose an almost memory-free approach that constructs the subcentroids codebook in each region as a set of convex combinations of the region centroid and its neighboring centroids. We refer to the proposed technique as *grouping* procedure and describe it formally below.

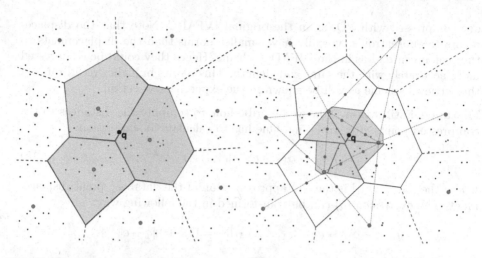

Fig. 1. The indexing and the search process for the dataset of 200 two-dimensional points (small black dots) with the inverted index (left) and the inverted index augmented with grouping and pruning procedures (right). The large green points denote the region centroids, and for each centroid $L = 5$ neighboring centroids are precomputed. For three regions in the center of the right plot, the region subcentroids are denoted by the red points. The fractions of the database traversed by the same query q with and without pruning are highlighted in blue. Here the query is set to visit only $\tau = 40\%$ closest subregions. (Color figure online)

The Model. The grouping procedure is performed independently for all the regions so it is sufficient to describe it for the single region with the centroid c. We assume that the database points $\{x_1, \ldots, x_n\}$ belong to this region. Let us denote by $s_1, \ldots, s_L \in C$ the nearest centroids of the centroid c:

$$\{s_1, \ldots, s_L\} = \mathrm{NN}_L(c) \tag{2}$$

where $NN_L(c)$ denotes the set of L nearest neighbors for c in the set of all centroids. The region subcentroids then taken to be $\{c + \alpha(s_l - c)\}$, $l = 1, \ldots, L$, where α is a scalar parameter that is learnt from data as we describe below. Note that different α values are used in different regions. The points $\{x_1, \ldots, x_n\}$ are distributed over Voronoi subregions produced by this set of subcentroids. For each point x_i we determine the closest subcentroid

$$l_i = \arg\min_l \|x_i - (c + \alpha(s_l - c))\|^2 \tag{3}$$

In the indexing structure the region points are stored in groups, i.e. all points from the same subregion are ordered continuously. In this scheme, we store only the subregion sizes to determine what group the particular point belongs to. After grouping, the displacements from the corresponding subcentroids

$$x_i - (c + \alpha(s_{l_i} - c)) \tag{4}$$

are compressed with PQ, as in the original IVFADC. Note that the displacements to subcentroids typically have smaller norms than the displacements to the region centroid as in the IVFADC scheme. Hence they could be compressed more accurately with the same code length. This results in higher recall rates of the retrieval scheme as will be shown in the experimental section.

Distance Estimation. Now we describe how to compute the distances to the compressed points after grouping. One has to calculate an expression:

$$\|q - c - \alpha(s - c) - [r_1, \ldots, r_M]\|^2 \tag{5}$$

where the $[r_1, \ldots, r_M]$ is the PQ approximation of the database point displacement. The expression (5) can be transformed in the following way:

$$\|q - c - \alpha(s - c) - [r_1, \ldots, r_M]\|^2 = (1 - \alpha)\|q - c\|^2 +$$
$$+ \alpha\|q - s\|^2 - 2 \sum_{m=1}^{M} \langle q_m, r_m \rangle + const(q) \tag{6}$$

The first term in the sum above can be easily computed as the distance $\|q - c\|^2$ is known from the closest centroids search result. The distances $\|q - s\|^2$ are computed online before visiting the region points. Note that the sets of neighboring centroids for the close regions typically have large intersections, and we do not recalculate the distances $\|q - s\|^2$, which were computed earlier for previous regions, for efficiency. The scalar products between the query subvectors and PQ codewords $\langle q_m, r_m \rangle$ are precomputed before regions traversal. The last term is query-independent, and we quantize it into 256 values and explicitly keep its quantized value as an additional byte in the point code. Note that the computation of distances to the neighboring centroids results in additional runtime costs. In the experiments below we show that these costs are completely justified by the improvement in the compression accuracy. The number of subregions L is set in such a way that the additional memory consumption ($K \cdot L \cdot$`sizeof(float)` bytes) is negligible compared to the compressed database size.

Subregions Pruning. The use of the grouping technique described above also allows the search procedure to skip the least promising subregions during region traversal. This provides the total search speedup without loss in search accuracy. Below we refer to such subregions skipping as *pruning*. Let us describe pruning in more details. Consider traversing the particular region with a centroid c, the neighboring centroids $s_1, \ldots, s_L$ and the scaling factor α. The distances to the subcentroids can then be easily precomputed as follows:

$$\|q - c - \alpha(s_l - c)\|^2 = (1 - \alpha)\|q - c\|^2 + \alpha\|q - s_l\|^2 + const(q), \quad l = 1 \ldots L \tag{7}$$

In the sum above the first and the second terms are computed as described in the previous paragraph while the last term is precomputed offline and stored explicitly for each neighboring centroid. If the search process is set to visit k inverted index regions, then kL distances to the subcentroids are calculated, and only a certain fraction τ of the closest subregions is visited. In practice, we observed that the search process could filter out up to half of the subregions without accuracy loss that provides additional search acceleration. Figure 1 schematically demonstrates the retrieval stage with and without pruning for the same query.

Learning the Scaling Factor α. Finally, we describe how to learn the scaling factor α for the particular region with a centroid c and the neighboring centroids $s_1, \ldots, s_L$. α is learnt on the hold-out learning set, and we assume that the region contains the learning points $x_1, \ldots, x_n$. We aim to solve the following minimization problem:

$$\min_{\alpha \in [0;1]} \sum_{i=1}^{n} \min_{l_i} \|x_i - c - \alpha(s_{l_i} - c)\|^2 \tag{8}$$

In other words, we want to minimize the distances between the data points and the scaled subcentroids given that each point is assigned to the closest subcentroid. We also restrict α to belong to the $[0;1]$ segment so that each subcentroid is a convex combination of c and one of the neighboring centroid s.

The exact solution of the problem above requires joint optimization over the continuous variable α and the discrete variables l_i. Instead, we solve (8) approximately in two steps:

1. First, for each training point x_i we determine the optimal s_{l_i} value. This is performed by minimizing the auxiliary function that is the lower bound of the target function in (8):

$$\sum_{i=1}^{n} \min_{l_i, \alpha_i \subset [0;1]} \|x_i - c - \alpha_i(s_{l_i} - c)\|^2 \tag{9}$$

This problem is decomposable into n identical minimization subproblems for each learning point x_i:

$$\min_{\alpha_i \in [0;1], s_{l_i}} \|x_i - c - \alpha_i(s_{l_i} - c)\|^2 \tag{10}$$

This subproblem is solved via exhaustive search over all possible s_{l_i}. For a fixed s_{l_i}, the minimization over α_i has a closed form solution and the corresponding minimum value of the target function (10) can be explicitly computed. Then the solution of the subproblem (10) for the point x_i is:

$$s_{l_i}^* = \arg\min_{s_{l_i}} \left\| x_i - c - \frac{(x_i - c)^T (s_{l_i} - c)}{\|s_{l_i} - c\|^2} (s_{l_i} - c) \right\|^2 \tag{11}$$

2. Second, we minimize (8) over α with the values of $s_{l_i}^*$ obtained from the previous step. In this case the closed-form solution for the optimal value is:

$$\alpha = \frac{\sum_{i=1}^{n} (x_i - c)^T (s_{l_i}^* - c)}{\sum_{i=1}^{n} \|s_{l_i}^* - c\|^2} \tag{12}$$

Discussion. The grouping and pruning procedures described above allow to increase the compression accuracy and the candidate lists quality. This results in a significant enhancement in the final system performance as will be shown in the experimental section. Note that these procedures are more effective for the inverted index, and they cannot be exploited as efficiently in the IMI due to a very large number of regions in its space partition.

4   Experiments

In this section we present the experimental comparison of the proposed indexing structure and the corresponding retrieval system with the current state-of-the-art.

Datasets. We perform all the experiments on the publicly available datasets that are commonly used for billion-scale ANN search evaluation:

1. DEEP1B dataset [5] contains one billion of 96-dimensional CNN-produced feature vectors of the natural images from the Web. The dataset also contains a learning set of 350 million descriptors and 10,000 queries with the groundtruth nearest neighbors for evaluation.
2. SIFT1B dataset [1] contains one billion of 128-dimensional SIFT descriptors as a base set, a hold-out learning set of 100 million vectors, and 10,000 query vectors with the precomputed groundtruth nearest neighbors.

In most of the experiments the search accuracy is evaluated by the $Recall@R$ measure which is calculated as a rate of queries for which the true nearest neighbor is presented in the short-list of length R. All trainable parameters are obtained on the hold-out learning sets. All experiments are performed on the Intel Xeon E5-2650 2.6 GHz CPU in a single thread mode.

Large Codebooks in the Inverted Index. As we show in Sect. 3 the indexing quality of the inverted index does not saturate even with codebooks of several million centroids. As the exhaustive query assignment would be inefficient for large codebooks, we use the approximate nearest centroids search via HNSW algorithm [22]. The algorithm is based on the proximity graph, constructed on the set of centroids. As we observed in our experiments, HNSW allows obtaining a small top of the closest centroids with almost perfect accuracy in a submillisecond time. We also use HNSW on the codebooks learning stage to accelerate the assignment step during K-Means iterations. The only cost of the HNSW search is the additional memory required to maintain the proximity graph. In our experiments each vertex of the proximity graph is connected to 32 other vertices, hence the total memory for all the edge lists equals $32 \cdot K \cdot$`sizeof(int)` bytes, where K denotes the codebook size.

Note that the accuracy and efficiency of the HNSW are crucial for the successful usage of large codebooks with an approximate assignment. The earlier efforts to use larger codebooks were not successful: [2] evaluated the scheme based on the inverted index with a very large codebook where the closest centroids were

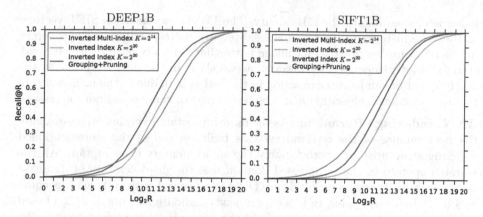

Fig. 2. Recall as a function of the candidate list length for inverted multi-indices with $K = 2^{14}$, inverted index with $K = 2^{20}$ with and without pruning. On DEEP1B the inverted indices outperform the IMI for all reasonable values of R by a large margin. For SIFT1B the candidate lists quality of the inverted index with pruning is comparable to the quality of the IMI for R larger than 2^{13}.

found via kd-tree [23]. It was shown that this scheme was not able to achieve the state-of-the-art recall rates due to inaccuracies of the closest centroids search.

Indexing Quality. In the first experiment we evaluate the ability of different indexing approaches to extract concise and accurate candidate lists. The candidates reranking is not performed here. We compare the following structures:

1. **Inverted Multi-Index (IMI)** [2]. We evaluate the IMI with codebooks of size $K = 2^{14}$ and consider the variant of the IMI with global rotation before dataspace decomposition [3] that boosts the IMI performance on datasets of deep descriptors. In all experiments we used the implementation from the FAISS library [6].
2. **Inverted Index**[20]. We use a large codebook of $K = 2^{20}$ centroids. The query assignment is performed via HNSW.
3. **Inverted Index+Grouping+Pruning.** Here we augment the inverted index setup from above with the grouping and pruning procedures described in Sect. 3.2. The number of subregions is set to $L = 64$, and the pruning ratio is set to $\tau = 50\%$.

The *Recall@R* values for different values of R are demonstrated in Fig. 2. Despite a much smaller number of regions, the inverted index produces more accurate short-lists compared to the IMI for the DEEP1B dataset. Note that the pruning procedure in the inverted index improves short-lists quality even further. The most practically important part of this plot corresponds to $R = 10^4 - 10^5$ and in this range the inverted index outperforms the IMI by up to 10%.

For the SIFT1B dataset, the IMI with $K = 2^{14}$ produces a slightly better candidate lists for small values of R. For $R > 2^{13}$ the quality of the inverted index is comparable to the IMI quality. The IMI is successful on SIFT vectors, as they are histogram-based and the subvectors corresponding to the different halves of them describe disjoint image parts that typically have relatively weak statistical inter-dependency. However, as we show in the next experiment, the runtime cost of candidates extraction in the IMI is high due to the inefficiency of the multi-sequence algorithm and a large number of random memory accesses.

ANN: Indexing+Reranking. As the most important experiment, we evaluate the performance of the retrieval systems built on top of the aforementioned indexing structures for approximately the same memory consumption. All the systems operate in the compressed domain, i.e. the displacements of database points from their region centroids are OPQ-compressed with code lengths equal to 8 or 16 bytes per point. In this experiment candidate lists are reranked based on the distances between the query and the compressed candidate points. The OPQ codebooks are global and shared by all regions. We compare the following systems:

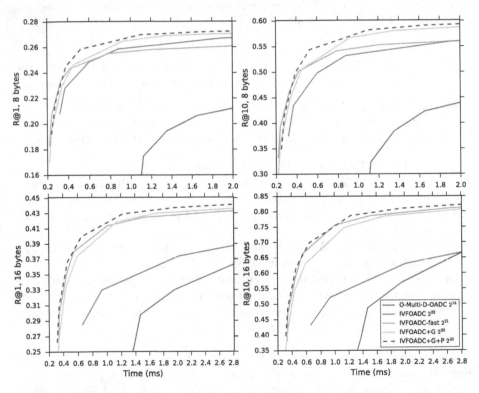

Fig. 3. The $R@1$ and $R@10$ values after reranking as functions of runtime on the DEEP1B. The systems based on the inverted index substantially outperform the IMI-based system. The IVFOADC system with grouping outperforms the IVFOADC systems with larger codebooks for the same memory consumption.

1. **O-Multi-D-OADC** is our main baseline system. It uses the inverted multi-index with global rotation and a codebook of size $K = 2^{14}$. This system requires 1 Gb of additional memory to maintain the IMI structure.
2. **IVFOADC** is based on the inverted index with a codebook of a size $K = 2^{22}$. This system requires 2.5 Gb of additional memory to store the codebook and the HNSW graph.
3. **IVFOADC-fast** is a system that uses the expression (6) for efficient distance estimation with $\alpha = 0$. This system is also based on the inverted index without grouping but requires one additional code byte per point to store the query-independent term from (6). We use $K = 2^{21}$ for this scheme to make the total memory consumption the same as for the previous system. The memory consumption includes 1 Gb for the additional code bytes and 1.25 Gb to store the codebook and the graph that gives 2.25 Gb in total.
4. **IVFOADC+Grouping** additionally employs the grouping procedure with $L = 64$ subcentroids per region. In this system we use a codebook with $K = 2^{20}$ that results in the total memory consumption of 1.87 Gb.
5. **IVFOADC+Grouping+Pruning** employs both grouping and pruning procedures with $L = 64$ subcentroids. The pruning is set to filter out 50% of the subregions. In this system we also use a codebook with $K = 2^{20}$.

We plot *Recall@1* and *Recall@10* on the DEEP1B dataset for different lengths of candidate lists as functions of the corresponding search runtime. The results are summarized in Fig. 3. We highlight several key observations:

1. The systems based on the inverted index outperform the IMI-based system in terms of accuracy and search time. In particular, for a time budget of 1.5 ms, the IVFOADC+G+P system outperforms the O-Multi-D-OADC by 7 and 17% points of $R@1$ and $R@10$ respectively on the DEEP1B dataset and 8-byte codes. As for the runtime, this system reaches the same recall values several times faster compared to O-Multi-D-OADC.
2. The IVFOADC system with grouping and pruning outperforms the IVFOADC systems with larger codebooks without grouping. The advantage is the most noticeable for short 8-byte codes when an additional encoding capacity from grouping is more valuable.

The Inverted Multi-Index Limitations. Here we perform several experiments to demonstrate that both approximate query assignment and grouping are more beneficial for IVFADC than for IMI. In theory, one could also accelerate the IMI-based schemes via using approximate closest subspace centroids search. However, in this case, one would have to find several hundred closest items from a moderate codebook of size $K = 2^{14}$, and we observed that in this setup the approximate search with HNSW takes almost the same time as brute-force. Moreover, such acceleration would not speed up the candidates accumulation that is quite slow in the multi-index due to a large number of empty regions.

Second, the grouping procedure is less effective for the IMI compared to the inverted index. With $K = 2^{14}$ each region in the IMI space partition contains only a few points, hence grouping is useless. To evaluate grouping effectiveness for the IMI with coarser codebooks we perform the following experiment. We compute the relative decrease in the average distance from the datapoints to the closest (sub-)centroid before and after grouping with $L = 64$. Here we compare the inverted index with $K = 2^{20}$ and the IMI with $K = 2^{10}$ that result in the space partitions with the same number of regions. The average distances before and after grouping are presented in Table 3, right. The relative decrease in the average distances is smaller for the IMI that implies that grouping is more effective for the inverted index compared to the IMI. However, we assume that one of the interesting research directions is to investigate if the grouping could be incorporated in the IMI effectively.

Table 3. *Left*: The recall values and the runtimes of the IVFOADC+ Grouping+Pruning system for different numbers of subcentroids per region on the DEEP1B dataset. Here we use the candidate lists of length $30K$ and 16-byte codes. *Right*: The average distances from the datapoints to the closest (sub-)centroids with and without grouping for the inverted index with $K = 2^{20}$ and the IMI with $K = 2^{10}$ on the DEEP1B dataset.

L	R@1	R@10	R@100	$t(ms)$		Inverted Index	Inverted Multi-Index
32	0.417	0.776	0.869	1.22	No grouping	0.282	0.415
64	0.433	0.785	0.878	1.28	With grouping	0.255	0.385
128	0.441	0.791	0.882	1.48	Decrease	**10%**	7%

Table 4. Comparison to the previous works for 16-byte codes. The search runtimes are reported in milliseconds. We also provide the memory per point required by the retrieval systems (the numbers are in bytes and do not include 4 bytes for point ids).

Method	K	DEEP1B					SIFT1B				
		R@1	R@10	R@100	t	Mem	R@1	R@10	R@100	t	Mem
O-Multi-D-OADC [24]	2^{14}	0.397	0.766	0.909	8.5	17.34	0.360	0.792	0.901	5	17.34
Multi-LOPQ [4]	2^{14}	0.41	0.79	-	20	18.68	**0.454**	**0.862**	0.908	19	19.22
GNOIMI [5]	2^{14}	0.45	0.81	-	20	19.75	-	-	-	-	-
IVFOADC+G+P	2^{20}	**0.452**	**0.832**	**0.947**	**3.3**	17.87	0.405	0.851	**0.957**	**3.5**	18

Number of Grouping Subregions. We also demonstrate the performance of the proposed scheme for different numbers of subcentroids per region L. In Table 3, left we provide the evaluation of the IVFOADC+Grouping+Pruning system on DEEP1B for candidate lists of size $30K$ and 16-byte codes. The usage of $L > 64$ is hardly justified due to increase in runtime and memory consumption.

Comparison to the State-of-the-Art. Finally, we compare the proposed IVFADC+G+P with the results reported in the literature on the DEEP1B and SIFT1B, see Table 4. Along with the recall values and timings we also report the amount of additional memory per point, required by each system.

5   Conclusion

In this work, we have proposed and evaluated a new system for billion-scale nearest neighbor search. The system expands the well-known inverted index structure and makes no assumption about database points distribution what makes it a universal tool for datasets with any data statistics. The advantage of the scheme is demonstrated on two billion-scale publicly available datasets.

References

1. Jegou, H., Tavenard, R., Douze, M., Amsaleg, L.: Searching in one billion vectors: re-rank with source coding. In: ICASSP (2011)
2. Babenko, A., Lempitsky, V.S.: The inverted multi-index. In: 2012 IEEE Conference on Computer Vision and Pattern Recognition, Providence, RI, USA, 16–21 June 2012 (2012)
3. Ge, T., He, K., Ke, Q., Sun, J.: Optimized product quantization. Technical report (2013)
4. Kalantidis, Y., Avrithis, Y.: Locally optimized product quantization for approximate nearest neighbor search. In: Proceedings of International Conference on Computer Vision and Pattern Recognition (CVPR 2014). IEEE (2014)
5. Babenko, A., Lempitsky, V.S.: Efficient indexing of billion-scale datasets of deep descriptors. In: CVPR (2016)
6. Johnson, J., Douze, M., Jégou, H.: Billion-scale similarity search with GPUs. arXiv preprint arXiv:1702.08734 (2017)
7. Philbin, J., Chum, O., Isard, M., Sivic, J., Zisserman, A.: Object retrieval with large vocabularies and fast spatial matching. In: CVPR (2007)
8. Douze, M., Szlam, A., Hariharan, B., Jegou, H.: Low-shot learning with large-scale diffusion. In: CVPR (2018)
9. Wang, D., Otto, C., Jain, A.K.: Face search at scale. TPAMI **39**, 1122–1136 (2017)
10. Jégou, H., Douze, M., Schmid, C.: Product quantization for nearest neighbor search. TPAMI **33**(1), 117–128 (2011)
11. Ge, T., He, K., Ke, Q., Sun, J.: Optimized product quantization for approximate nearest neighbor search. In: CVPR (2013)
12. Norouzi, M., Fleet, D.J.: Cartesian k-means. In: CVPR (2013)
13. Babenko, A., Lempitsky, V.: Additive quantization for extreme vector compression. In: CVPR (2014)
14. Babenko, A., Lempitsky, V.S.: Tree quantization for large-scale similarity search and classification. In: CVPR (2015)
15. Zhang, T., Du, C., Wang, J.: Composite quantization for approximate nearest neighbor search. In: ICML (2014)
16. Zhang, T., Qi, G.J., Tang, J., Wang, J.: Sparse composite quantization. In: CVPR (2015)
17. Martinez, J., Clement, J., Hoos, H.H., Little, J.J.: Revisiting additive quantization. In: Leibe, B., Matas, J., Sebe, N., Welling, M. (eds.) ECCV 2016. LNCS, vol. 9906, pp. 137–153. Springer, Cham (2016). https://doi.org/10.1007/978-3-319-46475-6_9
18. Douze, M., Jégou, H., Perronnin, F.: Polysemous codes. In: Leibe, B., Matas, J., Sebe, N., Welling, M. (eds.) ECCV 2016. LNCS, vol. 9906, pp. 785–801. Springer, Cham (2016). https://doi.org/10.1007/978-3-319-46475-6_48

19. Jain, H., Pérez, P., Gribonval, R., Zepeda, J., Jégou, H.: Approximate search with quantized sparse representations. In: Leibe, B., Matas, J., Sebe, N., Welling, M. (eds.) ECCV 2016. LNCS, vol. 9911, pp. 681–696. Springer, Cham (2016). https:// doi.org/10.1007/978-3-319-46478-7_42
20. Sivic, J., Zisserman, A.: Video Google: a text retrieval approach to object matching in videos. In: ICCV (2003)
21. Wieschollek, P., Wang, O., Sorkine-Hornung, A., Lensch, H.P.A.: Efficient large-scale approximate nearest neighbor search on the GPU. In: CVPR (2016)
22. Malkov, Y.A., Yashunin, D.A.: Efficient and robust approximate nearest neighbor search using hierarchical navigable small world graphs. arXiv preprint arXiv:1603.09320 (2016)
23. Bentley, J.L.: Multidimensional binary search trees used for associative searching. Commun. ACM **18**(9), 509–517 (1975)
24. Babenko, A., Lempitsky, V.S.: The inverted multi-index. IEEE Trans. Pattern Anal. Mach. Intell. **37**(6), 1247–1260 (2015)

Diverse Feature Visualizations Reveal Invariances in Early Layers of Deep Neural Networks

Santiago A. Cadena[✉], Marissa A. Weis, Leon A. Gatys, Matthias Bethge, and Alexander S. Ecker

Center for Integrative Neuroscience and Institute for Theoretical Physics, Bernstein Center for Computational Neuroscience, University of Tübingen, Tübingen, Germany
{santiago.cadena,marissa.weis,leon.gatys, matthias.bethge,alexander.ecker}@bethgelab.org

Abstract. Visualizing features in deep neural networks (DNNs) can help understanding their computations. Many previous studies aimed to visualize the selectivity of individual units by finding meaningful images that maximize their activation. However, comparably little attention has been paid to visualizing to what image transformations units in DNNs are invariant. Here we propose a method to discover invariances in the responses of hidden layer units of deep neural networks. Our approach is based on simultaneously searching for a batch of images that strongly activate a unit while at the same time being as distinct from each other as possible. We find that even early convolutional layers in VGG-19 exhibit various forms of response invariance: near-perfect phase invariance in some units and invariance to local diffeomorphic transformations in others. At the same time, we uncover representational differences with ResNet-50 in its corresponding layers. We conclude that invariance transformations are a major computational component learned by DNNs and we provide a systematic method to study them.

Keywords: Feature visualization · Invariance · Phase invariance Deep neural networks · Early visual system

1 Introduction

As deep neural networks have gained popularity in many scientific disciplines and technological applications, there is a growing interest in understanding the representations they learn and the computations they perform. One approach towards achieving such understanding is to visualize the features that activate the neurons in a network. There is a growing body of work that seeks to visualize

Electronic supplementary material The online version of this chapter (https:// doi.org/10.1007/978-3-030-01258-8_14) contains supplementary material, which is available to authorized users.

V. Ferrari et al. (Eds.): ECCV 2018, LNCS 11216, pp. 225–240, 2018.
https://doi.org/10.1007/978-3-030-01258-8_14

features by synthesizing images which maximally drive hidden layer units. While this approach can give us a rough intuition about a unit's selectivity, it provides only a very incomplete picture of its computation. In addition to characterizing feature detectors by the stimulus that elicits the largest response, it is important to identify the nuisance parameters to which the neuron is invariant. As hidden layers build up response invariances gradually with depth, it is not the *image* that most strongly drives a unit that is the most telling about this unit's function, but instead the *set of images* that elicit a strong response. While some previous work has visualized multiple 'facets' of neurons' selectivity, these efforts focused mostly on the highest layers of the network and relied on initialization or random sampling strategies to create multiple images for each unit. However, as we show in the present paper, these approaches underestimate the true diversity of the selectivity of even relatively low-level units. Additionally, these approaches have not offered insights about how the representations of different networks trained on the same task compare. Our contributions are the following:

1. Motivated by the phase invariance of complex cells in the early visual system of the brain, we show why visualizing invariance is as important as visualizing selectivity for understanding the computations of even low-level units.
2. We develop a non-parametric approach to map the manifold of highly-activating inputs as exhaustively as possible.
3. We show that even relatively low-level units exhibit a remarkable degree of invariance in VGG-19 [28], which is not revealed by finding highly activating stimuli from multiple optimization runs with random initializations.
4. We find that in low to intermediate layers of VGG-19, at least two types of invariances emerge: tolerance to local diffeomorphic transformations tuned to specific features, and phase invariance, where units respond well to periodic texture patterns and are insensitive to their phase. We additionally offer a way to quantify these invariances.
5. In contrast, we find that low to intermediate layers of a network with skip connections (ResNet-50 [11]) that was trained on the same task as VGG-19 exhibit far less phase invariance, revealing representational differences between these two networks.
6. We showcase our visualization approach on a CNN trained to predict responses to natural images in primary visual cortex of the primate brain.

We provide the code to replicate our results.[1]

2   Related Work

One way to identify selectivity of hidden units is to look for image patches in the dataset that drive them maximally [6,33]. These image patches can sometimes hint at a unit's selectivity, but it can be difficult to identify their common features. Optimization-based techniques have proven more useful for feature visualization: a common approach is to search for pre-images that drive individual

---

[1] https://github.com/sacadena/diverse_feature_vis.

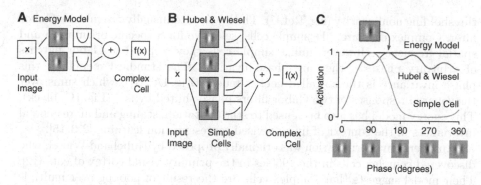

Fig. 1. Simple and complex cells, phase invariance. A. Energy model of complex cell. B. Hubel & Wiesel model of complex cell. C. Neural response as a function of phase of Gabor stimulus with optimal orientation and spatial frequency. (Color figure online)

neurons maximally via gradient ascent [6]. Most previous work focused on deep layers, where finding natural-looking pre-images is challenging. For example, the activation objective leads to adversarial-like patterns [20,29]. As a consequence, much of the follow-up work focused on developing regularization techniques to obtain more natural pre-images, including penalties on high-frequency noise [16,20] or the distance between the generated visualizations and natural images patches [32], or performing gradient descent in the feature space of a deep generator network [19].

Goodfellow et al. [9] were the first (to our knowledge) to study invariances in deep networks. Their approach allows to quantify how invariant a unit is to known transformations such as translation, (3D-) rotation or scaling, but it does not allow to discover these transformations if they are unknown in advance.

Recent work proposes visualizing multiple 'facets' of the neuron's selectivity by obtaining multiple images from different random initializations [17], using a diverse set of highly activating images as initializations [21], or using a generative image model to sample highly-activating images [18].

These methods do not explicitly specify an objective to produce a diverse set of images. In contrast, we optimize a batch of images to drive the neuron of interest strongly while simultaneously being as distinct from each other as possible. Recent concurrent work [22] introduces a similar idea, albeit with a different loss function based on texture representations [7,8].

3 Discovering Invariances

3.1 Motivation: Simple and Complex Cells

We illustrate our point by considering a toy example well known from early vision in the brain (Fig. 1): simple and complex cells [12], which are found in the primary visual cortex, an early stage of visual processing in the mammalian brain. Simple cells can be approximated well by a linear filter followed by a thresholding nonlinearity (e.g. ReLU). The linear filter usually resembles a Gabor filter. Complex cells are, like simple cells, selective for a specific orientation and spatial frequency. However, unlike simple cells they respond to Gabor patches of arbitrary phases – they are phase-invariant. The standard model for this phase invariance is the so-called energy model (Fig. 1A, [1]), which sums over the squared responses of two Gabor filters phase-shifted by 90° (Fig. 1C, black). This energy model has also been used to study rotation, scaling and more general invariances in the context of unsupervised representation learning [2,3,15].

An alternative formulation was originally proposed by Hubel and Wiesel, who discovered complex cells in the 1960ies in the primary visual cortex of cats [12]. Their model suggests that complex cells are the result of pooling over multiple simple cells with a range of phase preferences (Fig. 1B). If the learned weights and phase preferences exhibit some variability, the resulting phase invariance is only approximate (Fig. 1C, blue).

Now, consider what happens when we study simple and complex cells using activity maximization. For a simple cell, we will recover its selectivity. For a complex cell, however, all Gabor patches of optimal orientation and spatial frequency will elicit a high response, irrespective of their phase. In the case of the Energy Model, which is perfectly phase-invariant, we may obtain this set of optimal images by starting with random initializations. However, for an imperfect model more likely to occur in reality (e.g. Hubel & Wiesel model, blue in Fig. 1C), there is a unique maximum, which we will find despite the fact that activations are consistently above 80% of the maximum for all phases. Thus, activity maximization will produce the same result for both simple and complex cells (a single Gabor patch), but this result will miss the key aspect of the complex cell's computation: its phase invariance.

3.2   Mapping Invariances

Objective. The idea behind our approach is to find a batch of images in which each image maximally drives a specific unit while the images are maximally different from one another. Starting with a batch of n images $\{x_1, \cdots, x_n\}$, initialized as white noise, we *maximize* the following objective using gradient ascent:

$$L = \sum_{i=1}^{n} y_{ik}^{(l)} + \alpha \sum_{i=1}^{n} \log P(x_i) + \lambda \min_{i,j} d(x_i, x_j). \tag{1}$$

Here, $y_{ik}^{(l)}$ is the output activation of unit k in layer l for the ith image in the batch, $P(x_i)$ is the likelihood of the image under a generative model of natural images and $d(x_i, x_j)$ is a distance between two images, The likelihood and distance measures are specified below. Note that we set the image size to the receptive field size of units in the layer to be visualized, such that the outputs $y_{ik}^{(l)}$ are 1×1 spatially and we can omit the indices over space. We constrain the norm of the synthesized images to be equal to half the average norm of natural images patches of the same size taken from the ImageNet dataset[2], where we assume that zero in each color channel corresponds to the average value of this channel across the ImageNet training set. For visualization, we add this mean and clip the values between 0 and 255. Very few pixels fall outside this range.

The first and the second term in the objective are similar to previous work, encouraging the optimization to find natural images that strongly activate the unit. The third term forces all images in the batch to be as distinct as possible from all other images, since we penalize the minimum distance between any pair of images. This objective presents a trade-off: we allow for some degree of non-maximal responses if this allows us to increase the set of strongly activating pre-images substantially.

It is important to use the minimum distance in the objective rather than the average. Maximizing the average distance does not necessarily lead to coverage of the invariant subspace. Consider the Energy Model: assuming we generate an even number of n images, the optimal solution maximizing the average L_2 distance is to place all images at either of two distinct phases separated by 180°. Now we fail to generate a diverse set of images but the average distance is high (90°). In contrast, the desired solution of images evenly separated by $360°/n$ will give a smaller average distance for $n > 4$ and can be obtained when maximizing the minimum distance.

It has also some advantages to consider a single unit within a feature map compared to considering the entire feature map. When maximizing the activation of the entire feature map, the resulting image will be shift-invariant by construction and properties such as phase invariance of individual units cannot be detected.

Natural Image Prior. We use PixelCNN++ [27] as a natural image prior, as it allows directly evaluating and optimizing the likelihood of an image patch of arbitrary size. In a nutshell, PixelCNN++ improves upon PixelCNN [23] and earlier autoregressive models [24,30,31] that attempt to capture the distribution of natural images by expressing the joint distribution of all pixels as the product of the distributions of individual pixels conditioned on a causal neighborhood. We use the model pre-trained on Cifar-100 provided by OpenAI[3] which is state-of-the-art in terms of likelihood on natural images.

Distance Metric. To evaluate the distance between two images, we use a feature space given by the neural network to encourage diversity on perceptually interesting image properties. For an output unit y_k in layer l, we compute the Euclidean distance in the feature space of the preceding convolutional layer:

$$d(x_i, x_j) = \|\mathbf{y}_i^{(l-1)} - \mathbf{y}_j^{(l-1)}\|_2; \quad i \neq j \tag{2}$$

where $\mathbf{y}_i^{(l-1)}$ and $\mathbf{y}_j^{(l-1)}$ are vectors of activations in the preceding layer flattened over space and channels.

---

[2] Using half the average norm is a heuristic that we use because the synthesized images tend to be localized to the center of the patch.

[3] https://github.com/openai/pixel-cnn.

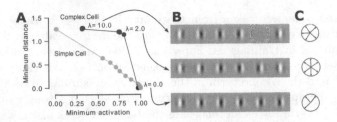

Fig. 2. Mapping invariances as a trade-off between diversity and maximizing activation. A. Trade-off between activation and image diversity. For a complex cell, images can be made quite diverse while keeping the activation level high. When λ gets too large ($\lambda >$ 2), there is a qualitative change. B. Set of images for three different λ. C. Distribution of phases of synthesized Gabor patches, showing that with the optimal $\lambda = 2$ we get equally spaced images, i.e. cover the invariant subspace well. (Color figure online)

Optimization. We optimize the objective defined in Eq. (1) using the Adam optimizer [13] with a learning rate of 0.1 until the objective converges (maximum of 1000 steps). Similar to Olah et al. [22], we precondition the gradient to reduce the effect of high frequencies by dividing each frequency component by $\sqrt{f}$.

We manually set the hyperparameter α, which controls the strength of the natural image prior, based on qualitative inspection of the resulting images in an exploratory experiment. We used $\alpha = 0.0005$ for all experiments.

We sweep a range of values for λ (0.02, 0.04, 0.08, ... 20.48) and for each unit pick the largest such λ that the average activation level remains above a threshold. This threshold is 80% of the maximum for the complex cell model and 90% for VGG-19 and ResNet-50. See Figs. 2A and 4 for a qualitative justification of these thresholds.

3.3   Application to Complex Cell Models

Before applying our approach to a deep neural network, we verify that it works when the units are only approximately invariant to some transformation. To this end, we use the Hubel & Wiesel model of a complex cell outlined above (Fig. 1B), which does not produce perfect phase invariance, but still responds strongly to Gabor patches of all phases.

Indeed, our approach can visualize the entire invariant subspace spanning the full range of phases (Fig. 2). Without the diversity term ($\lambda = 0$), the optimization tends to converge to the same pre-image (Fig. 2B). Four out of six solutions correspond to the globally most strongly driving image (see also Fig. 1C, top). In contrast, with an appropriate choice of λ, the images distribute uniformly (Fig. 2B, C). If we increase λ too much, however, the diversity penalty becomes too large and the optimization will converge to solutions including non-optimal images. Thus, to visualize the invariant subspace, we should pick the largest λ that leads to only a small decrease in activation level. This point depends on how 'clean' the invariance of the cell is. For the Hubel & Wiesel model considered

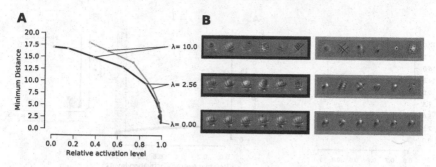

Fig. 3. Invariant subspace of two example units in conv3_2 (feature maps 9 and 26). A. Invariance/activation trade-off. B. Pre-images obtained for different values of λ.

here, this drop in activation occurs when the average activation falls below 80% of the maximum, which corresponds to the response range for images within the approximately invariant subspace (see Fig. 1C, blue line).

Note that for the simple cell, which does not exhibit any such response invariance, the curve looks qualitatively different (Fig. 2A, red line). Thus, we can quantify response invariance of units in a DNN by computing the minimum distance between any two images in the batch at the optimal λ.

4   Invariances in VGG-19

We asked to what extent deep neural networks trained on large-scale object recognition (ImageNet [25]) exhibit response invariances in their convolutional layers. Previous work focused mostly on higher layers and did not find much invariance in low and intermediate layers. However, in neuroscience it is well-known that low- and mid-level neurons in the brain – like complex cells – can exhibit a substantial degree of response invariance. Moreover, there is evidence for a considerable degree of similarity between neural representations in DNNs trained on object recognition and the primate visual system [4,5,10,14]. In particular, we have shown [4] that the convolutional layers of VGG-19 [28] around layer conv3_1 best predict neural activity in primary visual cortex, including that of many complex cells. Therefore we would expect that these layers in the VGG-19 network should also exhibit some degree of invariance to phase and potentially other transformations.

4.1   Convolutional Layers of VGG-19 Exhibit Response Invariances

We start by considering two example units from layer conv3_2 (Fig. 3) of VGG-19. As in the complex cell example, we can increase the diversity of generated images quite substantially while maintaining a high activation level (Fig. 3A). Only when we increase λ too much, the activation level drops substantially and the images start deteriorating (Fig. 3B, top row). Overall, the trade-off between

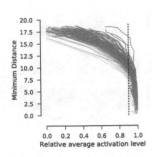

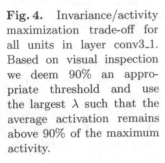

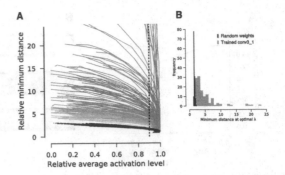

Fig. 4. Invariance/activity maximization trade-off for all units in layer conv3_1. Based on visual inspection we deem 90% an appropriate threshold and use the largest λ such that the average activation remains above 90% of the maximum activity.

Fig. 5. VGG units are more invariant than expected from random weights. A. All 256 units in conv3_1 (colored lines) are more invariant than units in a network with the same architecture but random weights (black lines). B. Histogram of the diversity terms for the optimal λ relative to their value for $\lambda = 0$ (black: random weights; purple: trained conv3_1). This means that for the least invariant units we can increase the diversity of the images two-fold while maintaining the average activation above 90% of the maximum obtained with $\lambda = 0$. (Color figure online)

image diversity and activation level looks qualitatively similar to the complex cell example above.

Moreover, the images generated with the optimal λ look significantly more diverse than those obtained by random initialization at $\lambda = 0$ (Fig. 3B, middle and bottom rows). Indeed, most units showed quite some degree of invariance: we can increase the image diversity considerably while maintaining activation levels above 90% of the maximum (Fig. 4 for conv3_1; see Sect. 1 in the Supp. for additional convolutional layers). Below, we therefore use the largest such λ that maintains the average activation level above 90% of the maximum.

4.2 Response Invariances Are a Learned Property of the Network

Is this invariance a learned property of the network or does it arise trivially from the network architecture? We repeated the analysis on a network with the same architecture as VGG-19 but random weights. To keep the two networks comparable, we normalized both the activations and the distances between images such that they are equal to one for $\lambda = 0$. We found that units in the random network are substantially less invariant than those of VGG-19 (Fig. 5A), suggesting that the neurons' response invariance is indeed a learned property. Remarkably, by introducing the diversity term into the pre-image search, we could increase the minimum distance between any two images in a batch by a factor of at least two and up to 100-fold without 'sacrificing' more than 10% of the unit's activation level (Fig. 5B), a property that the random network does not exhibit.

texture-detector   shape-detector

Fig. 6. Examples of invariant subspaces of texture-like and shape-like detectors of feature maps 13 (left) and 22 (right) in conv3_1. (Color figure online)

4.3 Types of Invariance: Texture Vs. Shape Detectors

We now investigate the types of invariance learned by different units in the network. We start by considering two example units from layer conv3_1 (Fig. 6). The first unit responds to a dark grid on brighter background of arbitrary color. In addition to this selectivity, it appears to be entirely phase- and rotation-invariant: the location of the grid lines and their orientation is irrelevant for the unit's activation, but their general spatial scale and the foreground color are important. We refer to units that exhibit this property as *texture* detectors.

The second unit, in contrast, detects a circular feature in the lower half of its receptive field. While it is sensitive to the location of this pattern within its receptive field, it exhibits a substantial degree of color and scale invariance: the contours have a sinusoidal cross-section whose local phase varies across images, such that by using linear combinations of multiple of these images one can obtain the circular pattern in various different sizes and color combinations. We refer to such units as *shape* detectors: they are sensitive to location but allow for some degree of local diffeomorphic transformation.

The two units shown here are representative of a larger number of units in various layers of VGG-19 (see Fig. 7 and Sect. 2 from Supp. for more examples). As we will quantitatively show below, they lie on two extremes of a spectrum along which we can characterize low- and intermediate-level units.

4.4 Quantification of Phase Invariance (Textures)

So far, we have described texture and shape units only qualitatively. We therefore developed metrics to quantify these properties more systematically. We start by quantifying phase invariance, the property that characterizes texture detectors.

While shift *equivariance* is built into CNNs, phase *invariance* of individual units has to our knowledge not been reported. A perfectly phase-invariant unit would maintain a high activation when presented with shifted versions of its preferred texture. Therefore, to quantify phase invariance, we optimize an image twice as large as the unit's receptive field such that the average activation of all possible windowed crops from this image is maximized (Fig. 8A, 1–4). Indeed, for a decent number of units we had qualitatively labeled as 'texture detectors,' the crops generated in this way (Fig. 8A, 3) resemble the templates we synthesized earlier (Fig. 8A, 4) and elicit similarly high activations (Fig. 8C). On the other hand, 'shape-selective' units expect certain structures in specific locations within their receptive field. Generating a texture where arbitrary crops are highly activating is not possible for these units (Fig. 8B).

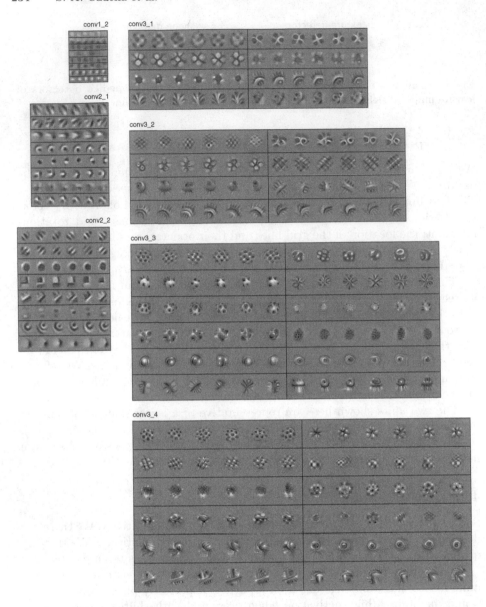

Fig. 7. Invariant subspaces of a selection of units in convolutional layers conv1_2 to conv3_4 of VGG-19. Each horizontal block of six images represents one unit. It contains the six maximally diverse images resulting in an activation of the unit above 90% of its maximum. Images for higher layers are scaled up slightly to improve visibility, but the pixel sizes are not matched across layers (lower layers have comparably larger pixels).

To quantify this intuitive argument, we defined shift invariance as the ratio between the average activation of all crops from the larger texture and the average activation of the diverse templates produced earlier (see example histogram

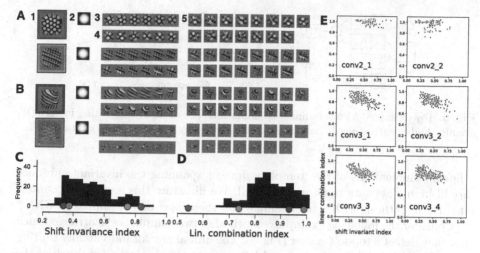

Fig. 8. Quantification of invariances in VGG19. For layer conv3_1, examples of texture (A) and shape (B) units. Left: Phase invariance. We optimize a texture (1) to maximize the average activation of all windowed (2) crops (3). The mask has the form $\exp\left(-(r/\sigma)^4\right)$ where $r = \sqrt{x^2 + y^2}$. We picked σ so that the ratio between the unit's receptive field and σ is ~2.5. (4): individual images maximizing the unit's activation. Right: Invariance to local deformations is supported by features that locally form quadrature pairs. Linear combinations (5) of templates (4) produce images with high activations. C. Histogram of the phase invariance (examples from A + B labeled). D. Histogram of metric measuring invariance to local deformations. E. Scatter plot of the two metrics (shift invariant index and linear combination index) for all units at each convolutional layer of VGG19. (Color figure online)

in Fig. 8C, for conv3_1). Indeed, the units labeled as phase-invariant (Fig. 8A), maintain a high activations despite arbitrary phase shifts, while the activation of the shape-selective units (Fig. 8B) drops substantially (Fig. 8C).

Note that synthesizing a larger image by maximizing all crops is similar to maximizing an entire channel's activity (i.e. feature map) for a sufficiently large input image, an approach other authors have taken for feature visualization [22]. Although insightful in many occasions, the drawback is that this procedure often occludes shape selectivity. For instance, the first unit in Fig. 8B is selective to a circular pattern in the top-right with rays pointing towards the bottom-left when maximized individually. However, the resulting texture looks like a field of oriented edges, thus missing the crucial pattern that drives this unit.

4.5   Tolerance to Local Deformations (Shapes)

The second invariance we identify is tolerance to local deformations. A closer look at some examples (e.g. Fig. 6, right; Fig. 8B, top) reveals that some of the units have local tolerance for phase changes. The patterns these units are tuned for can be locally built by spatially arranging multiple complex-cell-like quadrature pairs. This would suggest, that – although mapped into a nonlinear feature space

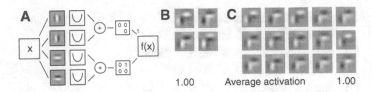

Fig. 9. Toy example (A) where linear combinations (C) of highly activating images (B) are also highly activating. It detects a top-left corner by combining two complex cells.

– linear combinations of the 'template' images spanning the invariant subspace should highly activate these units as well. We illustrate this seemingly counter-intuitive hypothesis with a toy example and then show how it applies to CNNs.

Consider the following example comprised of two complex cells arranged such that they detect a top-left corner (Fig. 9). The unit allows for individually shifting up or down the horizontal edge, and left or right the vertical edge. Each of the two edges is detected by an energy model of a complex cell (Fig. 9A), each at a defined location within the receptive field. Accordingly, the highly activating template images are made up of combinations of odd and even Gabors (Fig. 9B) and any linear combination of them is again a highly activating image (Fig. 9C).

To quantify whether the same property holds for VGG units, we computed the average activation level of linear combinations of the maximally activating images. Specifically, we took the averages (in pixel space) of all 15 pairs of templates (Fig. 8A.5), renormalized them to the same norm as the templates and compared their average activation to that of the templates. For 'texture-selective' units this procedure deteriorates the clear texture patterns revealed by the templates (see for instance Fig. 8A.5). Accordingly, the unit's activation level to these images drops substantially (Fig. 8D, red + orange). We quantify this drop by computing a linear combination index, defined as the ratio between the average activation of average-image pairs and the average activation of the diverse templates. Units tuned to shape patterns that are tolerant to local transformations give average-pairs that are fairly similar to the original templates, producing a high linear combination index.

4.6 Characterization of Invariances Across Layers

We have identified two metrics that quantify two different forms of invariance in VGG units. Our examples from Fig. 8 suggest that these two types of invariance are anticorrelated. As this does not have to be the case a priori – a complex cell would score high on both metrics – we asked whether this was just due to our selection of examples or whether it holds more generally across layers. Indeed, shift invariance and tolerance to local deformations appear to be anticorrelated across a wide range of layers (Fig. 8E; conv3 in particular). We also observe that higher layers tend to be less shift-invariant than lower ones (e.g. compare within conv3 in Fig. 8E).

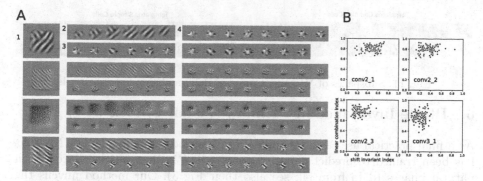

Fig. 10. ResNet-50 results. A, Example units of block conv2_3 (compare to Fig. 8). We noticed that maximizing windowed crops (2) of a big texture (1) are largely different from the maximizing templates (3). 15 template-pair averages (4) are on the other hand highly activating and similar to the templates. B, Scatter plot of the two metrics proposed for said layers of ResNet-50.

5 Diverse Visualizations of Early Layers of ResNet-50

To test whether our results so far are properties of VGG-19 or apply more generally to CNNs trained on ImageNet, we also applied our methods to ResNet-50 [11]. We considered its early layers up to conv3_1 (fourth block), which have receptive field sizes comparable to the layers we studied in VGG-19. We first synthesized diverse image batches with different diversity penalties and found a similar trade-off between activation and diversity as found before (see Sect. 3 in Suppl. Material). However, for the λ that evoked at least 90% of the maximal responses we observed on average a smaller diversity compared to that of VGG-19 units. We then ran our analysis to identify both phase and shape invariance and surprisingly found a much reduced number of phase-invariant units compared to VGG-19 (Fig. 10): there are basically no ResNet-50 units for which the crops from the optimal texture look like the optimized templates (e.g. Fig. 10A, $2 + 3$). On the other hand, template-pair averages do not appear to qualitatively deviate from the synthesized templates (Fig. 10A, 4) indicating a strong presence of tolerance to local changes. The two metrics introduced above confirm this observation quantitatively: the distribution of shift invariance indices is shifted towards zero in ResNet-50 layers (Fig. 10B) with respect to those in VGG-19.

This is a very interesting finding, because it shows that the different architectures learn quite different features in their early layers despite both being trained on ImageNet and achieving comparable classification accuracy. Thus, our novel approach to feature visualization helped us identify strong representational differences in the canonical directions between two architectures that would not have been observed with conventional activity maximization.

Fig. 11. Subspaces of V1 cells. Complex (left) and simple (right) cells

6   Phase Invariance in Primary Visual Cortex (V1)

As a final practical use case, we applied our method to a three-layer CNN that has been trained to predict neural responses in V1 when monkeys are shown natural images (data from [4]; see also their Fig. 3). Our method unveils the known cell types – simple: phase-selective and complex: phase-invariant (Fig. 11). Although complex cells can also be identified using specifically designed stimuli or analysis methods relying on quadratic features (e.g. spike-triggered covariance [26]), our non-parametric approach could in principle also uncover other types of invariance that are not captured by quadratic features. Given that we see no such additional invariances, there are likely no other major features V1 cells are invariant to – a conclusion that could not be drawn using parametric approaches.

7   Conclusion

Motivated by early vision in the brain, we investigated the response invariances in the early to intermediate convolutional layers of DNNs. We found that units in early layers of VGG-19 show invariance to global texture-preserving transformations and invariance to local shape-preserving transformations. In contrast, ResNet-50 does not exhibit the same degree of shift invariance. This difference could explain why practitioners working on texture synthesis and style transfer observe that the features of VGG work substantially better than those of more modern architectures such as residual networks.

We conclude that these methods not only give new insights into the computations performed by DNNs and how they compare with other architectures, but also constitutes an important step towards a unified language for describing neural representations in both biological and computer vision.

Acknowledgements. We thank Jonas Rauber and Andreas Tolias for useful discussions. This work was supported by the German Research Foundation (DFG) grant EC 479/1-1 to A.S.E. The International Max Planck Research School for Intelligent Systems (IMPRS-IS) supported S.A.C. The work was also supported by IARPA via Department of Interior (DoI) contract D16PC00003.

References

1. Adelson, E.H., Bergen, J.R.: Spatiotemporal energy models for the perception of motion. J. Opt. Soc. Am. A **2**(2), 284–299 (1985). https://doi.org/10.1364/JOSAA.2.000284
2. Berkes, P., Wiskott, L.: Slow feature analysis yields a rich repertoire of complex cell properties. J. Vis. **5**(6), 9 (2005)

3. Bethge, M., Gerwinn, S., Macke, J.H.: Unsupervised learning of a steerable basis for invariant image representations. In: Human Vision and Electronic Imaging XII, vol. 6492, p. 64920C. International Society for Optics and Photonics (2007)
4. Cadena, S.A., et al.: Deep convolutional models improve predictions of macaque V1 responses to natural images. bioRxiv (2017). https://doi.org/10.1101/201764
5. Cadieu, C.F., et al.: Deep neural networks rival the representation of primate IT cortex for core visual object recognition. PLoS Comput. Biol. **10**(12), e1003963 (2014). 00152
6. Erhan, D., Bengio, Y., Courville, A., Vincent, P.: Visualizing higher-layer features of a deep network. Technical report 1341, University of Montreal, June 2009. Also Presented at the ICML 2009 Workshop on Learning Feature Hierarchies. Montréal, Canada
7. Gatys, L., Ecker, A.S., Bethge, M.: Texture synthesis using convolutional neural networks. In: Advances in Neural Information Processing Systems, pp. 262–270 (2015)
8. Gatys, L.A., Ecker, A.S., Bethge, M.: Image style transfer using convolutional neural networks. In: Proceedings of the IEEE Conference on Computer Vision and Pattern Recognition, pp. 2414–2423 (2016)
9. Goodfellow, I., Lee, H., Le, Q.V., Saxe, A., Ng, A.Y.: Measuring invariances in deep networks. In: Advances in Neural Information Processing Systems, pp. 646–654 (2009)
10. Güçlü, U., van Gerven, M.A.J.: Deep neural networks reveal a gradient in the complexity of neural representations across the ventral stream. J. Neurosci. **35**(27), 10005–10014 (2015). https://doi.org/10.1523/JNEUROSCI.5023-14.2015
11. He, K., Zhang, X., Ren, S., Sun, J.: Deep residual learning for image recognition. In: Proceedings of the IEEE Conference on Computer Vision and Pattern Recognition, pp. 770–778 (2016)
12. Hubel, D.H., Wiesel, T.N.: Receptive fields, binocular interaction and functional architecture in the cat's visual cortex. J. Physiol. **160**(1), 106 (1962). 09139
13. Kingma, D.P., Ba, J.: Adam: a method for stochastic optimization. arXiv preprint arXiv:1412.6980 (2014)
14. Kriegeskorte, N.: Deep neural networks: a new framework for modeling biological vision and brain information processing. Annu. Rev. Vis. Sci. **1**(1), 417–446 (2015). https://doi.org/10.1146/annurev-vision-082114-035447
15. Lies, J.P., Häfner, R.M., Bethge, M.: Slowness and sparseness have diverging effects on complex cell learning. PLoS Comput. Biol. **10**(3), e1003468 (2014)
16. Mahendran, A., Vedaldi, A.: Understanding deep image representations by inverting them. In: Proceedings of the IEEE Conference on Computer Vision and Pattern Recognition, pp. 5188–5196 (2015)
17. Mahendran, A., Vedaldi, A.: Visualizing deep convolutional neural networks using natural pre-images. Int. J. Comput. Vis. **120**(3), 233–255 (2016)
18. Nguyen, A., Clune, J., Bengio, Y., Dosovitskiy, A., Yosinski, J.: Plug & play generative networks: conditional iterative generation of images in latent space. In: CVPR, vol. 2, p. 7 (2017)
19. Nguyen, A., Dosovitskiy, A., Yosinski, J., Brox, T., Clune, J.: Synthesizing the preferred inputs for neurons in neural networks via deep generator networks. In: Advances in Neural Information Processing Systems, pp. 3387–3395 (2016)
20. Nguyen, A., Yosinski, J., Clune, J.: Deep neural networks are easily fooled: high confidence predictions for unrecognizable images. In: The IEEE Conference on Computer Vision and Pattern Recognition, June 2015

21. Nguyen, A.M., Yosinski, J., Clune, J.: Multifaceted feature visualization: uncovering the different types of features learned by each neuron in deep neural networks. In: Visualization for Deep Learning workshop, ICML (2016)
22. Olah, C., Mordvintsev, A., Schubert, L.: Feature visualization. Distill (2017). https://doi.org/10.23915/distill.00007
23. van den Oord, A., Kalchbrenner, N., Espeholt, L., Vinyals, O., Graves, A., et al.: Conditional image generation with PixelCNN decoders. In: Advances in Neural Information Processing Systems, pp. 4790–4798 (2016)
24. van der Oord, A., Kalchbrenner, N., Kavukcuoglu, K.: Pixel recurrent neural networks. arXiv preprint arXiv:1601.06759 (2016)
25. Russakovsky, O.: ImageNet large scale visual recognition challenge. Int. J. Comput. Vis. (IJCV) **115**(3), 211–252 (2015). https://doi.org/10.1007/s11263-015-0816-y
26. Rust, N.C., Schwartz, O., Movshon, J.A., Simoncelli, E.P.: Spatiotemporal elements of macaque V1 receptive fields. Neuron **46**(6), 945–956 (2005)
27. Salimans, T., Karpathy, A., Chen, X., Kingma, D.P., Bulatov, Y.: Pixelcnn++: a PixelCNN implementation with discretized logistic mixture likelihood and other modifications. In: Submitted to ICLR 2017 (2016)
28. Simonyan, K., Zisserman, A.: Very deep convolutional networks for large-scale image recognition. arXiv preprint arXiv:1409.1556 (2014)
29. Szegedy, C., et al.: Intriguing properties of neural networks. arXiv preprint arXiv:1312.6199 (2013)
30. Theis, L., Bethge, M.: Generative image modeling using spatial LSTMs. In: Advances in Neural Information Processing Systems, pp. 1927–1935 (2015)
31. Theis, L., Hosseini, R., Bethge, M.: Mixtures of conditional Gaussian scale mixtures applied to multiscale image representations. PloS One **7**(7), e39857 (2012)
32. Wei, D., Zhou, B., Torrabla, A., Freeman, W.: Understanding intra-class knowledge inside CNN. arXiv preprint arXiv:1507.02379 (2015)
33. Zeiler, M.D., Fergus, R.: Visualizing and understanding convolutional networks. In: Fleet, D., Pajdla, T., Schiele, B., Tuytelaars, T. (eds.) ECCV 2014. LNCS, vol. 8689, pp. 818–833. Springer, Cham (2014). https://doi.org/10.1007/978-3-319-10590-1_53

End-to-End Incremental Learning

Francisco M. Castro[1]($\boxtimes$), Manuel J. Marín-Jiménez[2], Nicolás Guil[1],
Cordelia Schmid[3], and Karteek Alahari[3]

[1] Department of Computer Architecture, University of Málaga, Málaga, Spain
fcastro@uma.es
[2] Department of Computing and Numerical Analysis, University of Córdoba,
Córdoba, Spain
[3] Univ. Grenoble Alpes, Inria, CNRS, Grenoble INP, LJK, 38000 Grenoble, France

Abstract. Although deep learning approaches have stood out in recent
years due to their state-of-the-art results, they continue to suffer from
catastrophic forgetting, a dramatic decrease in overall performance when
training with new classes added incrementally. This is due to current
neural network architectures requiring the entire dataset, consisting of
all the samples from the old as well as the new classes, to update the
model—a requirement that becomes easily unsustainable as the number
of classes grows. We address this issue with our approach to learn deep
neural networks incrementally, using new data and only a small exemplar set corresponding to samples from the old classes. This is based on a
loss composed of a distillation measure to retain the knowledge acquired
from the old classes, and a cross-entropy loss to learn the new classes.
Our incremental training is achieved while keeping the entire framework
end-to-end, i.e., learning the data representation and the classifier jointly,
unlike recent methods with no such guarantees. We evaluate our method
extensively on the CIFAR-100 and ImageNet (ILSVRC 2012) image classification datasets, and show state-of-the-art performance.

Keywords: Incremental learning · CNN · Distillation loss
Image classification

1 Introduction

One of the main challenges in developing a visual recognition system targeted
at real-world applications is learning classifiers incrementally, where new classes
are learned continually. For example, a face recognition system must handle
new faces to identify new people. This task needs to be accomplished without
having to re-learn faces already learned. While this is trivial to accomplish for
most people (we learn to recognize faces of new people we meet every day), it
is not the case for a machine learning system. Traditional models require all the

Electronic supplementary material The online version of this chapter (https://
doi.org/10.1007/978-3-030-01258-8_15) contains supplementary material, which is
available to authorized users.

© Springer Nature Switzerland AG 2018
V. Ferrari et al. (Eds.): ECCV 2018, LNCS 11216, pp. 241–257, 2018.
https://doi.org/10.1007/978-3-030-01258-8_15

samples (corresponding to the old and the new classes) to be available at training time, and are not equipped to consider only the new data, with a small selection of the old data. In an ideal system, the new classes should be integrated into the existing model, sharing the previously learned parameters. Although some attempts have been made to address this, most of the previous models still suffer from a dramatic decrease in performance on the old classes when new information is added, in particular, in the case of deep learning approaches [2, 8,10,16–18,22,23,30]. We address this challenging task in this paper using the problem of image classification to illustrate our results.

A truly incremental deep learning approach for classification is characterized by its: *(i)* ability to being trained from a flow of data, with classes appearing in any order, and at any time; *(ii)* good performance on classifying old and new classes; *(iii)* reasonable number of parameters and memory requirements for the model; and *(iv)* end-to-end learning mechanism to update the classifier and the feature representation jointly. Therefore, an ideal approach would be able to train on an infinitely-large number of classes in an incremental way, without losing accuracy, and having exactly the same number of parameters, as if it were trained from scratch.

None of the existing approaches for incremental learning [4,9,13,14,16,23,26, 28,30,32,34,37] satisfy all these constraints. They often decouple the classifier and representation learning tasks [23], or are limited to very specific situations, e.g., learning from new datasets but not new classes related to the old ones [9,13, 16,34], or particular problems, e.g., object detection [30]. Some of them [4,26] are tied to traditional classifiers such as SVMs and are unsuitable for deep learning architectures. Others [14,28,32,37] lead to a rapid increase in the number of parameters or layers, resulting in a large memory footprint as the number of classes increases. In summary, there are no state-of-the-art methods that satisfy all the characteristics of a truly incremental learner.

The main contribution of this paper is addressing this challenge with our end-to-end approach designed specifically for incremental learning. The model can be realized with any deep learning architecture, together with our representative memory component, which is akin to an exemplar set for maintaining a small set of samples corresponding to the old classes (see Sect. 3.1). The model is learned by minimizing the cross-distilled loss, a combination of two loss functions: cross-entropy to learn the new classes and distillation to retain the previous knowledge corresponding to the old classes (see Sect. 3.2). As detailed in Sect. 4, any deep learning architecture can be adapted to our incremental learning framework, with the only requirement being the replacement of its original loss function with our new incremental loss. Finally, we illustrate the effectiveness of our image classification approach in obtaining state-of-the-art results for incremental learning on CIFAR-100 [15] and ImageNet [27] (see Sects. 6 and 7).

2   Related Work

We now describe methods relevant to our approach by organizing them into traditional ones using a fixed feature set, and others that learn the features through deep learning frameworks, in addition to training classifiers.

Traditional Approaches. Initial methods for incremental learning targeted the SVM classifier [6], exploiting its core components: support vectors and Karush-Kuhn-Tucker conditions. Some of these [26] retain the support vectors, which encode the classifier learned on old data, to learn the new decision boundary together with new data. Cauwenberghs and Poggio [4] proposed an alternative to this by retaining the Karush-Kuhn-Tucker conditions on all the previously seen data (which corresponds to the old classes), while updating the solution according to the new data. While these early attempts showed some success, they are limited to a specific classifier and also do not extend to the current paradigm of learning representations and classifiers jointly.

Another relevant approach is learning concepts over time, in the form of lifelong [33] or never-ending [5,7,20] learning. Lifelong learning is akin to transferring knowledge acquired on old tasks to the new ones. Never-ending learning, on the other hand, focuses on continuously acquiring data to improve existing classifiers or to learn new ones. Methods in both these paradigms either require the entire training dataset, e.g., [5], or rely on a fixed representation, e.g., [7]. Methods such as [19,25,29] partially address these issues by learning classifiers without the complete training set, but are still limited due to a fixed or engineered data representation. This is achieved by: *(i)* restricting the classifier or regression models, e.g., those that are linearly decomposable [29], or *(ii)* using a nearest mean classifier (NMC) [19], or a random forest variant [25]. Incremental learning is then performed by updating the bases or the per-class prototype, i.e., the average feature vector of the observed data, respectively.

Overall, the main drawback of all these methods is the lack of a task-specific data representation, which results in lower performance. Our proposed method addresses this issue with joint learning of features and classifiers.

Deep Learning Approaches. This class of methods provides a natural way to learn task-specific features and classifiers jointly [3,24,31]. However, learning models incrementally in this paradigm results in *catastrophic forgetting*, a phenomenon where the performance on the original (old) set of classes degrades dramatically [2,8,10,16–18,22,23,30]. Initial attempts to overcome this issue were aimed at connectionist networks [2,8,18], and are thus inapplicable in the context of today's deep architectures for computer vision problems.

A more recent attempt to preserve the performance on the old tasks was presented in [16] using distillation loss in combination with the standard cross-entropy loss. Distillation loss, which was originally proposed to transfer knowledge between different neural networks [12], was adapted to maintain the responses of the network on the old tasks whilst updating it with new training samples [16]. Although this approach reduced forgetting to some extent, in particular, in simplistic scenarios where the old and the new samples come from different datasets with little confusion between them, its performance is far from ideal. This is likely due to a weak knowledge representation of the old classes, and not augmenting it with an exemplar set, as done in our method. Works such as [23,34] demonstrated this weakness of [16] showing significant errors in a sequential learning scenario, where samples from new classes are continuously added, and in particular when the new and the old samples are from related distributions—the challenging problem we consider in this paper.

Other approaches using distillation loss, such as [13], propose to freeze some of the layers corresponding to the original model, thereby limiting its adaptability to new data. Triki *et al.* [34] build on the method in [16] using an autoencoder to retain the knowledge from old tasks, instead of the distillation loss. This method was also evaluated in a restrictive scenario, where the old and the new networks are trained on different datasets, similar to [16]. Distillation loss was also adopted for learning object detectors incrementally [30]. Despite its success for object detection, the utility of this specific architecture for more general incremental learning scenarios we target here is unclear.

Alternative strategies to mitigate catastrophic forgetting include, increasing the number of layers in the network to learn features for the new classes [28,32], or slowing down the learning rate selectively through per-parameter regularization [14]. Xiao *et al.* [37] also follow a related scheme and grow their tree-structured model incrementally as new classes are observed. The main drawback of all these approaches is the rapid increase in the number of parameters, which grows with the total number of weights, tasks, and the new layers. In contrast, our proposed model results in minimal changes to the size of the original network, as explained in Sect. 3.

Rebuffi *et al.* [23] present iCaRL, an incremental learning approach where the tasks of learning the classifier and the data representation are decoupled. iCaRL uses a traditional NMC to classify test samples, i.e., it maintains an auxiliary set containing old and new data samples. The data representation model, which is a standard neural network, is updated as and when new samples are available, using a combination of distillation and classification losses [12,16]. While our approach also uses a few samples from the old classes as exemplars in the representative memory component (cf. Sect. 3.1), it overcomes the limitations of previous work by learning the classifier and the features jointly, in an end-to-end fashion. Furthermore, as shown in Sects. 6 and 7, our new model outperforms [23].

3   Our Model

Our end-to-end approach uses a deep network trained with a cross-distilled loss function, i.e., cross-entropy together with distillation loss. The network can be based on the architecture of most deep models designed for classification, since our approach does not require any specific properties. A typical architecture for classification can be seen in Fig. 1, with one *classification layer* and a classification loss. This *classification layer* uses features from the feature extractor to produce a set of *logits* which are transformed into class scores by a softmax layer (not shown in the figure). The only necessary modification is the loss function, described in Sect. 3.2. To help our model retain the knowledge acquired from the old classes, we use a representative memory (Sect. 3.1) that stores and manages the most representative samples from the old classes. In addition to this

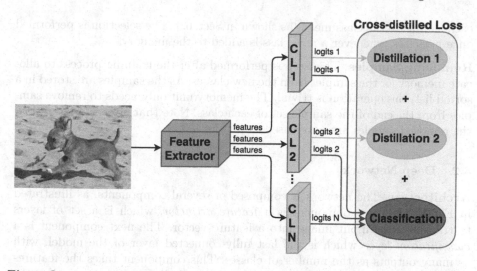

Fig. 1. Our incremental model. Given an input image, the feature extractor produces a set of features which are used by the *classification layers* (CL*i* blocks) to generate a set of *logits*. Grey *classification layers* contain old classes and their *logits* are used for distillation and classification. The green *classification layer* (CL*N* block) contains new classes and its *logits* are involved only in classification. (Best viewed in color.)

we perform data augmentation and a balanced fine-tuning (Sect. 4). All these components put together allow us to get state-of-the-art results.

3.1 Representative Memory

When a new class or set of classes is added to the current model, a subset with the most representative samples from them is selected and stored in the representative memory. We investigate two memory setups in this work. The first setup considers a memory with a limited capacity of K samples. As the capacity of the memory is independent of the number of classes, the more classes stored, the fewer samples retained per class. The number of samples per class, n, is thus given by $n = \lfloor K/c \rfloor$, where c is the number of classes stored in memory, and K is the memory capacity. The second setup stores a constant number of exemplars per class. Thus, the size of the memory grows with the number of classes.

The representative memory unit performs two operations: selection of new samples to store, and removal of leftover samples.

Selection of New Samples. This is based on *herding selection* [36], which produces a sorted list of samples of one class based on the distance to the mean sample of that class. Given the sorted list of samples, the first n samples of the list are selected. These samples are most representative of the class according to the mean. This selection method was chosen based on our experiments testing different approaches, such as random selection, histogram of the distances from each sample to the class mean, as shown in Sect. 6.3. The selection is performed once per class, whenever a new class is added to the memory.

Removing Samples. This step is performed after the training process to allocate memory for the samples from the new classes. As the samples are stored in a sorted list, this operation is trivial. The memory unit only needs to remove samples from the end of the sample set of each class. Note that after this operation, the removed samples are never used again.

3.2 Deep Network

Architecture. The network is composed of several components, as illustrated in Fig. 1. The first component is a *feature extractor*, which is a set of layers to transform the input image into a feature vector. The next component is a *classification layer* which is the last fully-connected layer of the model, with as many outputs as the number of classes. This component takes the features and produces a set of *logits*. During the training phase, gradients to update the weights of the network are computed with these *logits* through our cross-distilled loss function. At test time, the loss function is replaced by a softmax layer (not shown in the figure).

To build our incremental learning framework, we start with a traditional, i.e., non-incremental, deep architecture for classification for the first set of classes. When new classes are trained, we add a new *classification layer* corresponding to these classes, and connect it to the *feature extractor* and the component for computing the cross-distilled loss, as shown in Fig. 1. Note that the architecture of the *feature extractor* does not change during the incremental training process, and only new *classification layers* are connected to it. Therefore, any architecture (or even pre-trained model) can be used with our approach just by adding the incremental classification layers and the cross-distilled loss function when necessary.

Cross-Distilled Loss Function. This combines a distillation loss [12], which retains the knowledge from old classes, with a multi-class cross-entropy loss, which learns to classify the new classes. The distillation loss is applied to the *classification layers* of the old classes while the multi-class cross-entropy is used on all *classification layers*. This allows the model to update the decision boundaries of the classes. The loss computation is illustrated in Fig. 1. The cross-distilled loss function $L(\omega)$ is defined as:

$$L(\omega) = L_C(\omega) + \sum_{f=1}^{F} L_{D_f}(\omega), \qquad (1)$$

where $L_C(\omega)$ is the cross-entropy loss applied to samples from the old and new classes, L_{D_f} is the distillation loss of the *classification layer* f, and F is the total number of *classification layers* for the old classes (shown as grey boxes in Fig. 1).

The cross-entropy loss $L_C(\omega)$ is given by:

$$L_C(\omega) = -\frac{1}{N} \sum_{i=1}^{N} \sum_{j=1}^{C} p_{ij} \log q_{ij},$$ (2)

where q_i is a score obtained by applying a softmax function to the *logits* of a *classification layer* for sample i, p_i is the ground truth for the sample i, and N and C denote the number of samples and classes respectively.

The distillation loss $L_D(\omega)$ is defined as:

$$L_D(\omega) = -\frac{1}{N} \sum_{i=1}^{N} \sum_{j=1}^{C} pdist_{ij} \log qdist_{ij},$$ (3)

where $pdist_i$ and $qdist_i$ are modified versions of p_i and q_i, respectively. They are obtained by raising p_i and q_i to the exponent $1/T$, as described in [12], where T is the distillation parameter. When $T = 1$, the class with the highest score influences the loss significantly, e.g., more than 0.9 from a maximum of 1.0, and the remaining classes with low scores have minimal impact on the loss. However, with $T > 1$, the remaining classes have a greater influence, and their higher loss values must be minimized. This forces the network to learn a more fine grained separation between them. As a result, the network learns a more discriminative representation of the classes. Based on our empirical results, we set T to 2 for all our experiments.

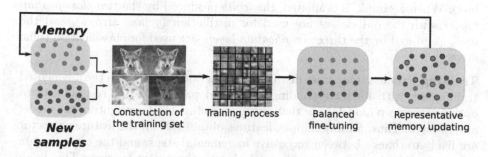

Fig. 2. Incremental training. Grey dots correspond to samples stored in the representative memory. Green dots correspond to samples from the new classes. Dots with red border correspond to the selected samples to be stored in the memory. (Best viewed in color.)

4   Incremental Learning

An incremental learning step in our approach consists of four main stages, as illustrated in Fig. 2. The first stage is the construction of the training set, which prepares the training data to be used in the second stage, the training process, which fits a model given the training data. In the third stage, a fine-tuning with a subset of the training data is performed. This subset contains the same number of samples per class. Finally, in the fourth stage, the representative memory is updated to include samples from the new classes. We now describe these stages in detail.

Construction of the Training Set. Our training set is composed of samples from the new classes and exemplars from the old classes stored in the representative memory. As our approach uses two loss functions, i.e., classification and distillation, we need two labels for each sample, associated with the two losses. For classification, we use the one-hot vector which indicates the class appearing in the image. For distillation, we use as labels the *logits* produced by every *classification layer* with old classes (grey fully-connected layers in Fig. 1). Thus, we have as many distillation labels per sample as *classification layers* with old classes. To reinforce the old knowledge, samples from the new classes are also used for distillation. This way, all images produce gradients for both the losses. Thus, when an image is evaluated by the network, the output encodes the behaviour of the weights that compose every layer of the deep model, independently of its label. Each image of our training set will have a classification label and F distillation labels; cf. Eq. 1. Note that this label extraction is performed in each incremental step.

Consider an example scenario to better understand this step, where we are performing the third incremental step of our model (Fig. 1). At this point the model has three *classification layers* ($N = 3$), two of them will process old classes (grey boxes), i.e., $F = 2$, and one of them operates on the new classes (green box). When a sample is evaluated, the *logits* produced by the two *classification layers* with the old classes are used for distillation (yellow arrows), and the *logits* produced by the three *classification layers* are used for classification (blue arrows).

Training Process. Our cross-distilled loss function (Eq. 1) takes the augmented training set with its corresponding labels and produces a set of gradients to optimise the deep model. Note that, during training, all the weights of the model are updated. Thus, for any sample, features obtained from the feature extractor are likely to change between successive incremental steps, and the *classification layers* should adapt their weights to deal with these new features. This is an important difference with some other incremental approaches like [16], where the *feature extractor* is frozen and only the *classification layers* are trained.

Balanced Fine-Tuning. Since we do not store all the samples from the old classes, samples from these classes available for training can be significantly lower than those from the new classes. To deal with this unbalanced training scenario, we add an additional fine-tuning stage with a small learning rate and a balanced subset of samples. The new training subset contains the same number of samples per class, regardless of whether they belong to new or old classes. This subset is built by reducing the number of samples from the new classes, keeping only the most representative samples from each class, according to the selection algorithm described in Sect. 3.1. With this removal of samples from the new classes, the model can potentially forget knowledge acquired during the previous training step. We avoid this by adding a temporary distillation loss to the *classification layer* of the new classes.

Representative Memory Updating. After the balanced fine-tuning step, the representative memory must be updated to include exemplars from the new classes. This is performed with the selection and removing operations described in Sect. 3.1. First, the memory unit removes samples from the stored classes to allocate space for samples from the new classes. Then, the most representative samples from the new classes are selected, and stored in the memory unit according to the selection algorithm.

5   Implementation Details

Our models are implemented on MatConvNet [35]. For each incremental step, we perform 40 epochs, and an additional 30 epochs for balanced fine-tuning. Our learning rate for the first 40 epochs starts at 0.1, and is divided by 10 every 10 epochs. The same reduction is used in the case of fine-tuning, except that the starting rate is 0.01. We train the networks using standard stochastic gradient descent with mini-batches of 128 samples, weight decay of 0.0001 and momentum of 0.9. We apply L^2-regularization and random noise [21] (with parameters $\eta = 0.3, \gamma = 0.55$) on the gradients to minimize overfitting.

Following the setting suggested by He et al. [11], we use dataset-specific CNN/deep models. This allows the architecture of the network to be adapted to specific characteristics of the dataset. We use a 32-layer ResNet for CIFAR-100, and a 18-layer ResNet for ImageNet as the deep model. We store $K = 2000$ distillation samples in the representative memory for CIFAR-100 and $K = 20000$ for ImageNet. When training the model for CIFAR-100, we normalize the input data by dividing the pixel values by 255, and subtracting the mean image of the training set. In the case of ImageNet, we only perform the subtraction, without the pixel value normalization, following the implementation of [11].

Since there are no readily-available class-incremental learning benchmarks, we follow the standard setup [23,30] of splitting the classes of a traditional multi-class dataset into incremental batches. In all the experiments below, iCaRL refers to the final method in [23], and hybrid1 refers to their variant, which uses a CNN classifier instead of NMC. LwF.MC is the multi-class implementation of LwF [16], as done in [23]. We used the publicly available implementation of iCaRL from GitHub[1]. The results for LwF.MC are also obtained from this code, without the exemplar usage. We report results for each method as the average accuracy over all the incremental batches. Note that we do not consider the accuracy of the first batch in this average, as it does not correspond to incremental learning. This is unlike the evaluation in [23], which is the reason

---

[1] https://github.com/srebuffi/iCaRL.

for difference between the results we report for their method, and the published results.

Data Augmentation. The second and third stages of our approach (cf. Sect. 4) perform data augmentation before the training step. Specifically, the operations performed are:

1. *Brightness*: the intensity of the original image is altered by adding a random intensity value in the range $[-63, 63]$.
2. *Contrast normalization*: the contrast of the original image is altered by a random value in the range $[0.2, 1.8]$. The operation performed is $im_{\text{altered}} = (im - mean) \times contrast + mean$. Where im is the original image, $mean$ is the mean of the pixels per channel, and $contrast$ is the random contrast value.
3. *Random cropping*: all the images (original, brightness and contrast) are randomly cropped.
4. *Mirroring*: a mirror image is computed for all images (original, brightness, contrast and crops).

Other operations applied on each dataset are specified in Sect. 6 for CIFAR-100 and in Sect. 7 for ImageNet.

6 Evaluation on CIFAR-100

We perform three types of experiments on the CIFAR-100 dataset. In the first one (Sect. 6.1), we set the maximum storage capacity of our representative memory unit, following the experimental protocol in [23]. The second experiment (Sect. 6.2) evaluates the methods without a fixed memory size, and uses a constant number samples for each of the old classes instead. Here, the memory size grows with each incremental step, when new classes are stored in the representative memory unit. Finally, in Sect. 6.3, we perform an ablation study to analyze the influence of different components of our approach on the accuracy.

Dataset. CIFAR-100 dataset [15] is composed of 60k 32×32 RGB images of 100 classes, with 600 images per class. Every class has 500 images for training and 100 images for testing. We divide the 100 classes into splits of 2, 5, 10, 20, and 50 classes with a random order. Thus, we will have 50, 20, 10, 5, and 2 incremental training steps respectively. After each incremental step, the resulting model is evaluated on the test data composed of all the trained classes, i.e., old and new ones. Our evaluation metric at each incremental step is the standard multi-class accuracy. We execute the experiments five times with different random class orders, reporting the average accuracy and standard deviation. In addition, we report the average incremental accuracy (mean of the accuracy values at every incremental step). As mentioned earlier, we do not consider the accuracy of the first step for this average as it does not represent incremental learning.

On CIFAR, we follow the data augmentation steps described in Sect. 5 and, for each training sample, generate 11 new samples: one brightness normalization,

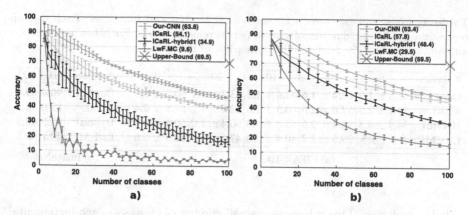

Fig. 3. Accuracy on CIFAR-100. Average and standard deviation of 5 executions with (a) 2 and (b) 5 classes per incremental step. Average of the incremental steps is shown in parentheses for each method. (Best viewed in pdf.)

one contrast normalization, three random crops (applied to the original, brightness and contrast images) and six mirrors (applied to the previously generated images and the original one).

6.1   Fixed Memory Size

We evaluate five different splits with different class order and incremental steps of 2, 5, 10, 20, and 50 classes. The class order is identical for all the evaluated methods, to ensure that the results are comparable. Table 1(a) summarises the results of the experiments and Fig. 3 shows the incremental steps for 2 and 5 classes. The rest of plots are included in the appendix [1]. The 'Upper-Bound' result, shown in Fig. 3 with a large cross (in magenta) in the last step, is obtained by training a non-incremental model using all the classes, and all their training samples.

We observe that our end-to-end approach obtains the best results for 2, 5, 10, and 20 classes. For 50 classes, although we achieve the same score as Hybrid1 (the variant of iCaRL using CNN classifier), we are 1% lower than iCaRL. This behaviour is due to the limited memory size, resulting in a heavily unbalanced training set containing 12.5 times more data from the new samples than from the old classes. To highlight the statistical significance of our method's performance compared to iCaRL, we performed a paired t-test on the results obtained for CIFAR-100. The corresponding p-values are 0.00005, 0.0005, 0.003, 0.0077, 0.9886 for 2, 5, 10, 20, and 50 classes respectively, which shows that the improvement of our method over iCaRL is statistically significant ($p < 0.01$) in all cases, except for 50 classes where both methods show similar performance.

It can be also observed that the performance of our approach remains stable across the incremental step sizes (from 2 to 20 classes per step) in Table 1(a), in contrast to all the other methods, which are dependent on the number of classes

Table 1. Fixed memory size: accuracy on CIFAR-100 and ImageNet. Each column represents a different number of classes per incremental step. Each row represents a different approach. The best results are marked in bold.

# classes	2	5	10	20	50
Our-CNN	**63.8 ± 1.9**	**63.4 ± 1.6**	**63.6 ± 1.3**	**63.7 ± 1.1**	60.8 ± 0.3
iCaRL	54.1 ± 2.5	57.8 ± 2.6	60.5 ± 1.6	62.0 ± 1.2	**61.8 ± 0.4**
Hybrid1	34.9 ± 4.5	48.4 ± 2.6	55.8 ± 1.8	60.4 ± 1.0	60.8 ± 0.7
LwF.MC	9.6 ± 1.5	29.5 ± 2.2	40.4 ± 2.0	47.6 ± 1.5	52.9 ± 0.6

# classes	10	100
Our-CNN	**90.4**	**69.4**
iCaRL	85.0	62.5
Hybrid1	83.5	46.1
LwF.MC	79.1	43.8

(a) CIFAR-100   (b) ImageNet

added in each step. This is because a small number of classes at each incremental step benefits the accuracy in the early stages of the incremental learning process, as only a few classes must be classified. However, as more steps are applied to train all the classes, the accuracy of the final stages decreases.

The behaviour is reversed when larger number of classes are added in each incremental step. Lower accuracy values are seen during the early stages, but this is compensated with better values in the final stages. These effects can be seen in Fig. 3, where two different number of classes per incremental step (2 and 5) are visualized. Figure 3 also shows that our approach is significantly better than iCaRL when a small number of classes per incremental step are employed. With larger number of classes in each step, iCaRL approaches our performance, but still remains lower overall. Our approach clearly outperforms LwF.MC in all the cases, thus highlighting the importance of the representative memory in our model.

6.2 Fixed Number of Samples

In this experiment, we train the models using a constant number of training samples per old class. This limitation is not applied to the samples from the new classes. Thus, we allow the memory to grow in proportion to the number of classes, in contrast to the fixed memory experiment, where the memory size remains constant. Additionally, to measure the impact of the number of samples in the accuracy, we evaluate different number of samples per class: 50, 75 and 100. We focus on experiments with incremental step values of 5, 10 and 20 classes. We consider the same class order for both iCaRL and our approach to ensure that the results are comparable. We focus the comparison on iCaRL and Hybrid1 in this experiment, as LwF.MC shows a lower performance than these two methods; see Sect. 6.1.

Table 2(a) summarizes the results of these experiments. The number of classes per incremental step is indicated in the first row of the table. The second row contains the number of exemplars per old class used during training. The remaining rows show the results of the different approaches evaluated. Comparing the results between Our-CNN and the methods developed in [23], we see that in all scenarios our approach performs better. As in the 'fixed memory size' experiment

Table 2. Accuracy on CIFAR-100. Each row represents a different approach. The best results are marked in bold. See the main text for more details.

# classes	5			10			20		
# img / cls	50	75	100	50	75	100	50	75	100
Our-CNN	**62.4**	**66.9**	**68.6**	**62.7**	**65.7**	**68.5**	**63.3**	**65.4**	**67.3**
iCaRL	56.5	59.9	62.2	60.0	62.3	63.7	61.9	63.0	64.0
Hybrid1	45.7	49.2	50.9	55.3	56.5	57.4	60.4	61.5	62.2

(a) Fixed number of samples

# classes	5	10	20
Our-CNN-Base	57.0	53.7	50.1
Our-CNN-DA	59.2	57.9	57.2
Our-CNN-BF	57.9	58.1	57.1
Our-CNN-Full	**63.8**	**64.0**	**63.2**
iCaRL	58.8	60.9	61.2
Hybrid1	48.7	55.1	59.8

(b) Ablation study

(Sect. 6.1), our approach achieves a similar average accuracy for incremental step sizes ranging from 5 to 20 classes, e.g., 62.4, 62.7, 63.3 with 50 exemplars per class, showing its stability. To measure the impact of the number of exemplars per class on the training, we compare the results in Table 1(a) with those in Table 2(a). In all cases, the more the exemplars used for training, the better the accuracy obtained. For 50 exemplars, the results are worse than those in Table 1 because in the early incremental steps, the number of exemplars available is lower, and these initial models are under trained. This causes a chain effect, and the model obtained in the final stage is worse than expected, even when more exemplars are available.

6.3 Ablation Studies

We now analyze the components of our approach and demonstrate their impact on the final performance. All these ablation studies are performed with the fixed memory setup. We first evaluate the sample selection strategy with an experiment using incremental steps of 10 classes and three methods for selecting samples: herding, random and histogram selection. Herding is our selection method, presented in Sect. 3.1. Random selection refers to choosing samples to be stored in memory randomly. In the histogram selection strategy, samples are chosen according to their distance to the mean of their class. We first compute a histogram of distances, with ten bins, and assign each sample to one of these bins. We then select samples from each bin according to the proportion of samples it contains. From the results (herding: 63.6%, random: 63.1%, and histogram: 59.1%), herding and random selection strategies show the best performance.

In the following ablation study, we analyze the impact of augmentation and fine-tuning. We first train our model with data augmentation, but without balanced fine-tuning ('Our-CNN-DA'). In the second experiment, we train without data augmentation, but with balanced fine-tuning ('Our-CNN-BF'). Finally, we train our model without data augmentation and balanced fine-tuning ('Our-CNN-Base'). Here, we focus on experiments with incremental step values of 5, 10 and 20 classes. As in previous experiments, the first split for iCaRL and our approach is run with the same order of classes, to ensure that the results

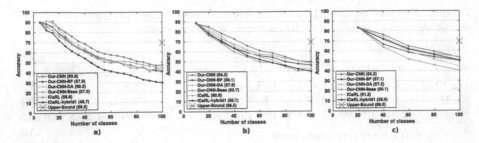

Fig. 4. Ablation study with CIFAR-100. Results for (a) 5, (b) 10, and (c) 20 classes. The average over all the incremental steps is shown in parentheses for each method. (Best viewed in pdf.)

are comparable. Table 2(b) and Fig. 4 summarise the results for this study. The baseline 'Our-CNN-Base' is the worst one for all cases. However, when the data augmentation ('Our-CNN-DA') is added, the results improve in all cases, obtaining the best result for 5 classes (59.2). However, due to the unbalanced number of samples between the old and new classes, with larger incremental steps it is necessary to add our balanced fine-tuning ('Our-CNN-BF'). When balanced fine-tuning ('Our-CNN-BF') is added, it improves the results in all cases, specially with big incremental steps, which highlights the importance of a balanced training set. Finally, when both the components are added to the baseline, obtaining our full model ('Our-CNN-Full'), we observe the best results and a new state-of-the-art is established on this dataset for incremental learning.

7 Evaluation on ImageNet

Dataset. ImageNet Large-Scale Visual Recognition Challenge 2012 (ILSVRC12) [27] is an annual competition which uses a subset of ImageNet. This subset is composed of 1000 classes with more than 1000 images per class. In total, there are roughly 1.2 million training images, 50k validation images, and 150k testing images. We run two experiments with this dataset. In the first one, we randomly select 100 classes, and divide them into splits of 10 classes selected randomly. In the second one, we divide the 1000 classes into splits of 100 classes randomly selected. Note that the same set of classes are considered for all the approaches to ensure that the results are comparable. After every incremental step, the resulting model is evaluated on test data composed of all the trained classes. We execute the experiments once and report the top-5 accuracy for each incremental step. We also report the average incremental accuracy described in Sect. 6.

We use data augmentation described in Sect. 5, and for each training sample, generate its mirror image, and then randomly apply transformations (cf. Sect. 5) for all the images (original and mirror). Thus, with our data augmentation, we double the number of training samples.

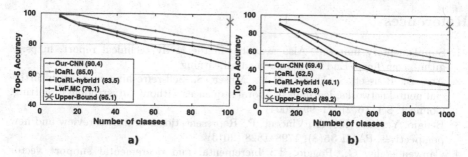

Fig. 5. Accuracy on ImageNet. One execution with (a) 10 and (b) 100 classes per incremental step. Average of the incremental steps is shown in parentheses for each method. (Best viewed in pdf.)

Fixed Memory Size. We maintain identical class order for all the evaluated methods, to ensure that the results are comparable. We also follow the protocol in [23] for a fair comparison with iCaRL and hybrid1. Table 1(b) summarizes the results of this fixed memory size experiment, and Fig. 5 shows the incremental steps with 10 and 100 classes. The 'Upper-Bound' result, shown with a cross in the figure, is obtained by training a non-incremental model using the training samples for all the classes. From the results, we observe that in both cases we establish a new state-of-the-art, improving the previous average results by more than 5%. This suggests that our approach is also suitable for large datasets with many classes. In addition, as the number of samples from new and old classes is more balanced than in CIFAR-100, our approach achieves good accuracy even with large incremental steps of 100 classes.

8 Summary

This paper presents a novel approach for training CNNs in an incremental fashion using a combination of cross-entropy and distillation loss functions. Experimental results on CIFAR-100 and ImageNet presented in the paper lead to the following conclusions. *(i)* Our end-to-end approach is more robust than other recent methods, such as iCaRL, relying on a sub-optimal, independently-learned external classifier. *(ii)* Representative memory, its size, and unbalanced training sets play an important role in the final accuracy. As part of future work we plan to explore new sample selection strategies, using a dynamic number of samples per class.

Acknowledgements. This work was supported in part by the projects TIC-1692 (Junta de Andalucía), TIN2016-80920R (Spanish Ministry of Science and Tech.), ERC advanced grant ALLEGRO, and EVEREST (no. 5302-1) funded by CEFIPRA. We gratefully acknowledge the support of NVIDIA Corporation with the donation of a Titan X Pascal GPU used for this research.

References

1. Supplementary material. Also available in the arXiv technical report. https://github.com/fmcp/EndToEndIncrementalLearning
2. Ans, B., Rousset, S., French, R.M., Musca, S.: Self-refreshing memory in artificial neural networks: learning temporal sequences without catastrophic forgetting. Connect. Sci. **16**(2), 71–99 (2004)
3. Bengio, Y., Courville, A., Vincent, P.: Representation learning: a review and new perspectives. PAMI **35**(8), 1798–1828 (2013)
4. Cauwenberghs, G., Poggio, T.: Incremental and decremental support vector machine learning. In: NIPS (2000)
5. Chen, X., Shrivastava, A., Gupta, A.: NEIL: extracting visual knowledge from web data. In: ICCV (2013)
6. Cortes, C., Vapnik, V.: Support-vector networks. Mach. Learn. **20**(3), 273–297 (1995)
7. Divvala, S., Farhadi, A., Guestrin, C.: Learning everything about anything: webly-supervised visual concept learning. In: CVPR (2014)
8. French, R.M.: Dynamically constraining connectionist networks to produce distributed, orthogonal representations to reduce catastrophic interference. In: Cognitive Science Society Conference (1994)
9. Furlanello, T., Zhao, J., Saxe, A.M., Itti, L., Tjan, B.S.: Active long term memory networks. ArXiv e-prints. arXiv:1606.02355 (2016)
10. Goodfellow, I., Mirza, M., Xiao, D., Courville, A., Bengio, Y.: An empirical investigation of catastrophic forgetting in gradient-based neural networks. ArXiv e-prints. arXiv:1312.6211 (2013)
11. He, K., Zhang, X., Ren, S., Sun, J.: Deep residual learning for image recognition. In: CVPR (2016)
12. Hinton, G., Vinyals, O., Dean, J.: Distilling the knowledge in a neural network. In: NIPS Workshop (2014)
13. Jung, H., Ju, J., Jung, M., Kim, J.: Less-forgetting learning in deep neural networks. ArXiv e-prints. arXiv:1607.00122 (2016)
14. Kirkpatrick, J., et al.: Overcoming catastrophic forgetting in neural networks. Proc. Natl. Acad. Sci. **114**(13), 3521–3526 (2017)
15. Krizhevsky, A.: Learning multiple layers of features from tiny images. Technical report, University of Toronto (2009)
16. Li, Z., Hoiem, D.: Learning without forgetting. PAMI (2018)
17. Lopez-Paz, D., Ranzato, M.A.: Gradient episodic memory for continual learning. In: NIPS (2017)
18. McCloskey, M., Cohen, N.J.: Catastrophic interference in connectionist networks: the sequential learning problem. Psychol. Learn. Motiv. **24**, 109–165 (1989)
19. Mensink, T., Verbeek, J., Perronnin, F., Csurka, G.: Distance-based image classification: generalizing to new classes at near-zero cost. PAMI **35**(11), 2624–2637 (2013)
20. Mitchell, T., et al.: Never-ending learning. In: AAAI (2015)
21. Neelakantan, A., et al.: Adding gradient noise improves learning for very deep networks. ArXiv e-prints. arXiv:1511.06807 (2017)
22. Ratcliff, R.: Connectionist models of recognition memory: constraints imposed by learning and forgetting functions. Psychol. Rev. **97**(2), 285 (1990)
23. Rebuffi, S.A., Kolesnikov, A., Sperl, G., Lampert, C.H.: iCaRL: incremental classifier and representation learning. In: CVPR (2017)

24. Ren, S., He, K., Girshick, R., Sun, J.: Faster R-CNN: towards real-time object detection with region proposal networks. In: NIPS (2015)
25. Ristin, M., Guillaumin, M., Gall, J., Gool, L.V.: Incremental learning of NCM forests for large-scale image classification. In: CVPR (2014)
26. Ruping, S.: Incremental learning with support vector machines. In: ICDM (2001)
27. Russakovsky, O., et al.: ImageNet large scale visual recognition challenge. IJCV 115(3), 211–252 (2015)
28. Rusu, A.A., et al.: Progressive neural networks. ArXiv e-prints. arXiv:1606.04671 (2016)
29. Ruvolo, P., Eaton, E.: ELLA: an efficient lifelong learning algorithm. In: ICML (2013)
30. Shmelkov, K., Schmid, C., Alahari, K.: Incremental learning of object detectors without catastrophic forgetting. In: ICCV (2017)
31. Simonyan, K., Zisserman, A.: Two-stream convolutional networks for action recognition in videos. In: NIPS (2014)
32. Terekhov, A.V., Montone, G., O'Regan, J.K.: Knowledge transfer in deep block-modular neural networks. In: Wilson, S.P., Verschure, P.F.M.J., Mura, A., Prescott, T.J. (eds.) LIVINGMACHINES 2015. LNCS (LNAI), vol. 9222, pp. 268–279. Springer, Cham (2015). https://doi.org/10.1007/978-3-319-22979-9_27
33. Thrun, S.: Lifelong learning algorithms. In: Thrun, S., Pratt, L. (eds.) Learning to Learn, pp. 181–209. Springer, Boston (1998). https://doi.org/10.1007/978-1-4615-5529-2_8
34. Triki, A.R., Aljundi, R., Blaschko, M.B., Tuytelaars, T.: Encoder based lifelong learning. In: ICCV (2017)
35. Vedaldi, A., Lenc, K.: MatConvNet - convolutional neural networks for MATLAB. In: ACM Multimedia (2015)
36. Welling, M.: Herding dynamical weights to learn. In: ICML (2009)
37. Xiao, T., Zhang, J., Yang, K., Peng, Y., Zhang, Z.: Error-driven incremental learning in deep convolutional neural network for large-scale image classification. In: ACM Multimedia (2014)

Conditional Image-Text Embedding Networks

Bryan A. Plummer[1]([✉]), Paige Kordas[1], M. Hadi Kiapour[2], Shuai Zheng[2], Robinson Piramuthu[2], and Svetlana Lazebnik[1]

[1] University of Illinois at Urbana-Champaign, Champaign, USA
{bplumme2,pkordas2,slazebni}@illinois.edu
[2] Ebay Inc., San Jose, USA
{mkiapour,shuzheng,rpiramuthu}@ebay.com

Abstract. This paper presents an approach for grounding phrases in images which jointly learns multiple text-conditioned embeddings in a single end-to-end model. In order to differentiate text phrases into semantically distinct subspaces, we propose a concept weight branch that automatically assigns phrases to embeddings, whereas prior works predefine such assignments. Our proposed solution simplifies the representation requirements for individual embeddings and allows the underrepresented concepts to take advantage of the shared representations before feeding them into concept-specific layers. Comprehensive experiments verify the effectiveness of our approach across three phrase grounding datasets, Flickr30K Entities, ReferIt Game, and Visual Genome, where we obtain a (resp.) 4%, 3%, and 4% improvement in grounding performance over a strong region-phrase embedding baseline (Code: https://github.com/BryanPlummer/cite).

Keywords: Natural language grounding · Phrase localization Embedding methods · Conditional models

1 Introduction

Phrase grounding attempts to localize a given natural language phrase in an image. This constituent task has applications to image captioning [6,12,14,19,34], image retrieval [9,26], and visual question answering [1,7,29]. Research on phrase grounding has been spurred by the release of several datasets, some of which primarily contain relatively short phrases [15,18], while others contain longer queries, including entire sentences that can provide rich context [22,25]. The difference in query length compounds the already challenging problem of generalizing to any (including never before seen) natural language input. Despite this, much of the recent attention has focused on learning a single embedding model between image regions and phrases [7,10,21,22,28,31,32,35].

In this paper, we propose a Conditional Image-Text Embedding (CITE) network that jointly learns different embeddings for subsets of phrases (Fig. 1). This

© Springer Nature Switzerland AG 2018
V. Ferrari et al. (Eds.): ECCV 2018, LNCS 11216, pp. 258–274, 2018.
https://doi.org/10.1007/978-3-030-01258-8_16

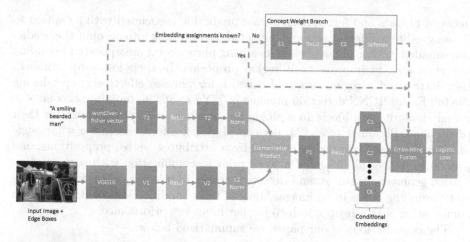

Fig. 1. Our CITE model separates phrases into different groups and learns conditional embeddings for these groups in a single end-to-end model. Assignments of phrases to embeddings can either be pre-defined (*e.g.* by separating phrases into distinct concepts like *people* or *clothing*), or can be jointly learned with the embeddings using the concept weight branch. Similarly colored blocks refer to layers of the same type, with purple blocks representing fully connected layers. Best viewed in color

enables our model to train separate embeddings for phrases that share a concept. Each conditional embedding can learn a representation specific to a subset of phrases while also taking advantage of weights that are shared across phrases. This is especially important for smaller groups of phrases that would be prone to overfitting if we were to train separate embeddings for them. In contrast to similar approaches that manually determine how to group concepts [20,24,30], we use a concept weight branch, trained jointly with the rest of the network, to do a soft assignment of phrases to learned embeddings automatically. The concept weight branch can be thought of producing a unique embedding for each region-phrase pair based on a phrase-specific linear combination of individual conditional embeddings. By training multiple embeddings our model also reduces variance akin to an ensemble of networks, but with far fewer parameters and lower computational cost.

Our idea of conditional embeddings was directly inspired by the conditional similarity networks of Veit et al. [30], although that work does not deal with cross-modal data and does not attempt to automatically assign different input items to different similarity subspaces. An earlier precursor of the idea of conditional similarity metrics can be found in [2]. Our work is also similar in spirit to Zhang *et al.* [37], who produced a linear classifier used to discriminate between image regions based on the textual input.

Our primary focus is on improving methods of associating individual image regions with individual phrases. Orthogonal to this goal, other works have focused on performing global inference for multiple phrases in a sentence and multiple regions in an image. Wang *et al.* [33] modeled the pronoun relationships between phrases and forced each phrase prediction associated with a caption to be assigned to a different region. Chen *et al.* [3] also took into account the predictions made by other phrases when localizing phrases and incorporated bounding box regression to improve their region proposals. In their follow-up work [4], they introduced a region proposal network for phrases effectively reproducing the full Faster RCNN detection pipeline [27]. Yu *et al.* [36] took into account the visual similarity of objects in a single image when providing context for their predictions. Plummer *et al.* [24] performed global inference using a wide range of image-language constraints derived from attributes, verbs, prepositions, and pronouns. Yeh *et al.* [35] used a word prior in combination with segmentation masks, geometric features, and detection scores to select a region from all possible bounding boxes in an image. Many of these modifications could be used in combination with our approach to further improve performance.

The contributions of our paper are summarized below:

- By conditioning the embedding used by our model on the input phrase we simplify the representation requirements for each embedding, leading to a more generalizable model.
- We introduce a concept weight branch which enables our embedding assignments to be learned jointly with the image-text model.
- We introduce several improvements to the Similarity Network of Wang *et al.* [32] boosting the baseline model's localization performance by 3.5% over the original paper.
- We perform extensive experiments over three datasets, Flickr30K Entities [25], ReferIt Game [15], and Visual Genome [18], where we report a (resp.) 4%, 3% and 4% improvement in phrase grounding performance over the baseline.

We begin Sect. 2.1 by describing the image-text Similarity Network [32] that we use as our baseline model. Section 2.2 describes our text-conditioned embedding model. Section 2.3 discusses three methods of assigning phrases to the trained embeddings. Lastly, Sect. 3 contains detailed experimental results and analysis of our proposed approach.

2   Our Approach

2.1   Image-Text Similarity Network

Given an image and a phrase, our goal is to select the most likely location of the phrase from a set of region proposals. To accomplish this, we build upon the image-text similarity network introduced in Wang *et al.* [32]. The image and text branches of this network each have two fully connected layers with batch normalization [11] and ReLUs. The final outputs of these branches are L2 normalized before performing an element-wise product between the image and text representations. This representation is then fed into a triplet of fully connected layers using batch normalization and ReLUs. This is analogous to using the CITE model in Fig. 1 with a single conditional embedding.

The training objective for this network is a logistic regression loss computed over phrases P, the image regions R, and labels Y. The label y_{ij} for the ith input phrase and jth region is $+1$ where they match and -1 otherwise. Since this is a supervised learning approach, matching pairs of phrases and regions need to be provided in the annotations of each dataset. After producing some score x_{ij} measuring the affinity between the image region and text features using our network, the loss is given by

$$L_{sim}(P, R, Y) = \sum_{ij} \log(1 + \exp{(-y_{ij} x_{ij})}). \qquad (1)$$

In this formulation, it is easy to consider multiple regions for a given phrase as positive examples and to use a variable number of region proposals per image. This is in contrast to competing methods which score regions with softmax with a cross entropy loss over a set number of proposals per image (*e.g.* [3, 7, 28]).

Sampling Phrase-Region Training Pairs. Following Wang *et al.* [32], we consider any regions with at least 0.6 intersection over union (IOU) with the ground truth box for a given phrase as a positive example. Negative examples are randomly sampled from regions of the same image with less than 0.3 IOU with the ground truth box. We select twice the number of negative regions as we have positive regions for a phrase. If too few negative regions occur for an image-phrase pair, then the negative example threshold is raised to 0.4 IOU.

Features. We represent phrases using the HGLMM fisher vector encoding [17] of word2vec [23] PCA reduced down to 6,000 dimensions. We generate region proposals using Edge Boxes [38]. Similarly to most state-of-the-art methods on our target datasets, we represent image regions using a Fast RCNN network [8] fine-tuned on the union of PASCAL 2007 and 2012 trainval sets [5]. The only exception is the experiment reported in Table 1(d), where we fine-tune the Fast RCNN parameters (corresponding to the VGG16 box in Fig. 1) on the Flickr30K Entities dataset.

Spatial Location. Following [3, 4, 28, 36], we experiment with concatenating bounding box location features to our region representation. This way our model can learn to bias predictions for phrases based on their location (*e.g.* that *sky* typically occurs in the top part of an image). For Flickr30K Entities we encode this spatial information as defined in [3, 4] for this dataset. For an image of height H and width W and a box with height h and width w is encoded as $[x_{min}/W, y_{min}/H, x_{max}/W, y_{max}/H, wh/WH]$. For a fair comparison to prior work [3, 4, 28], experiments on the ReferIt Game dataset encode the spatial information as an 8-dimensional feature vector $[x_{min}, y_{min}, x_{max}, y_{max}, x_{center}, y_{center}, w, h]$. For Visual Genome we adopt the same method of encoding spatial location as used for the ReferIt Game dataset.

2.2 Conditional Image-Text Network

Inspired by Veit *et al.* [30], we modify the image-text similarity model of the previous section to learn a set of conditional or concept embedding layers denoted $C_1, \ldots C_K$ in Fig. 1. These are K parallel fully connected layers each with output dimensionality M. The outputs of these layers, in the form of a matrix of size $M \times K$, are fed into the embedding fusion layer, together with a K-dimensional concept weight vector U, which can be produced by several methods, as discussed in Sect. 2.3. The fusion layer simply performs a matrix-vector product, *i.e.*, $F = CU$. This is followed by another fully connected layer representing the final classifier (*i.e.*, the layer's output dimension is 1).

2.3 Embedding Assignment

This section describes three possible methods for producing the concept weight vector U for combining the conditional embeddings as introduced in Sect. 2.2.

Coarse Categories. The Flickr30K Entities dataset comes with hand-constructed dictionaries that group phrases into eight coarse categories: *people, clothing, body parts, animals, vehicles, instruments, scene, other*. We use these dictionaries to map phrases to binary concept vectors representing their group membership. This is analogous to the approach of Veit *et al.* [30], which defines the concepts based on meta-data labels. Both the remaining approaches base their assignments on the training data rather than a hand-defined category label.

Nearest Cluster Center. A simple method of creating concept weights is to perform K-means clustering on the text features of the queries in the test set. Each cluster center becomes its own concept to learn. The concept weights U are then encoded as one-hot cluster membership vectors which we found to work better than alternatives such as similarity of a sample to each cluster center.

Concept Weight Branch. Creating a predefined set of concepts to learn, either using dictionaries or K-means clustering, produces concepts that don't necessarily have anything to do with the difficulty or ease in localizing the phrases within them. An alternative is to let the model decide which concepts to learn. With this in mind, we feed the raw text features into a separate branch of the network consisting of two fully connected layers with batch normalization and a ReLU between them, followed by a softmax layer to ensure the output sums to 1 (denoted as the concept weight branch in Fig. 1). The output of the softmax is then used as the concept weights U. This can be seen as analogous to using soft attention [34] on the text features to select concepts for the final representation of a phrase. We use L1 regularization on the output of the last fully connected layer before being fed into the softmax to promote sparsity in our assignments. The training objective for our full CITE model then becomes

$$L_{CITE} = L_{sim}(P, R, Y) + \lambda\|\phi\|_1, \qquad (2)$$

where ϕ are the inputs to the softmax layer and λ is a parameter controlling the importance of the regularization term. Note that we do not enforce diversity of assignments between different phrases, so it is possible that all phrases attend to a single embedding. However, we do not see this actually occur in practice. We also tried to use entropy minimization rather then L1 regularization for our concept weight branch as well as hard attention instead of soft attention, but found all worked similarly in our experiments.

3 Experiments

3.1 Datasets and Protocols

We evaluate the performance of our phrase-region grounding model on three datasets: Flickr30K Entities [25], ReferIt Game [15], and Visual Genome [18]. The metric we report is the proportion of correctly localized phrases in the test set. Consistent with prior work, a 0.5 IOU between the best-predicted box for a phrase and its ground truth is required for a phrase to be considered successfully localized. Similarly to [4,24,32], for phrases associated with multiple bounding boxes, the phrase is represented as the union of its boxes.

Training Procedure. We begin training our models with Adam [16]. After every epoch, we evaluate our model on the validation set. After it hasn't improved performance for 5 epochs, we fine-tune our model with stochastic gradient descent at 1/10th the learning rate and the same stopping criteria. We report test set performance for the model that performed best on the validation set.

Comparative Evaluation. In addition to comparing to previously published numbers of state-of-the-art approaches on each dataset, we systematically evaluate the following baselines and variants of our model:

- **Similarity Network.** Our first baseline is given by our own implementation of the model from Wang et al. [32], trained using the procedure described above. Phrases are pre-processed using stop word removal rather than part-of-speech filtering as done in the original paper. This change, together with a more careful tuning of the training settings, leads to a 2.5% improvement in performance over the reported results in [32]. The model is further enhanced by using the spatial location features (Sect. 2.1), resulting in a total improvement of 3.5%.
- **Individual Coarse Category Similarity Networks.** We train multiple Similarity Networks on different subsets of the data created according to the coarse category assignments as described in Sect. 2.3.

- **Individual K-means Similarity Networks.** We train multiple Similarity Networks on different subsets of the data created according to the nearest cluster center assignments as described in Sect. 2.3.
- **CITE, Coarse Categories.** No concept weight branch. Phrases are assigned according to their coarse category.
- **CITE, Random.** No concept weight branch. Phrases are randomly assigned to an embedding. At test time, phrases seen during training keep their assignments, while new phrases are randomly assigned.
- **CITE, K-means.** No concept weight branch. Phrases are matched to embeddings using nearest cluster center assignments.
- **CITE, Learned.** Our full model with the concept weight branch used to automatically produce concept weights as described in Sect. 2.3.

3.2 Flickr30K Entities

We use the same splits as Plummer *et al.* [25], which separates the images into 29,783 for training, 1,000 for testing, and 1,000 for validation. Models are trained with a batch size of 200 (128 if necessary to fit into GPU memory) and learning rate of 5e-5. We set $\lambda = $ 5e-5 in Eq. (2). We use the top 200 Edge Box proposals per image and embedding dimension $M = 256$ unless stated otherwise.

Grounding Results. Table 1 compares overall localization accuracies for a number of methods. The numbers for our Similarity Network baseline are reported in Table 1(b), and as stated above, they are better than the published numbers from [32]. Table 1(c) reports results for variants of conditional embedding models. From the first two lines, we can see that learning embeddings from subsets of the data without any shared weights leads to only a small improvement ($\leq 1\%$) over the Similarity Network baseline. The third line of Table 1(c) reports that separating phrases by manually defined high-level concepts only leads to a 1% improvement even when weights are shared across embeddings. This is likely due, in part, to the significant imbalance between different coarse categories, as a uniform random assignment shown in the fourth line of Table 1(c) lead to a 3% improvement. The fifth line of Table 1(c) demonstrates that grouping phrases based on their text features better reflects the needs of the data, resulting in just over 3% improvement over the baseline, only slightly better than random assignments. An additional improvement is reported in the eighth line of Table 1(c) by incorporating our concept weight branch, enabling our model to both determine what concepts are important to learn and how to assign phrases to them. We see in the last line of Table 1(c) that going from 200 to 500 bounding box proposals provides a small boost in localization accuracy. This results in our best performance using PASCAL-tuned features which is 3% better than the prior work reported in Table 1(a) and 4.5% better than the Similarity Network. We also note that the time to test an image-phrase pair is almost unaffected using our approach (the CITE, Learned, K = 4 model performs inference on 200

Table 1. Phrase localization performance on the Flickr30k Entities test set. (a) State-of-the-art results when predicting a single phrase at a time taken from published works. (b,c) Our baselines and variants using PASCAL-tuned features. (d) Results using Flickr30k-tuned features

Method	Accuracy
(a) **Single phrase methods (PASCAL-tuned features)**[a]	
NonlinearSP [31]	43.89
GroundeR [28]	47.81
MCB [7]	48.69
RtP [25]	50.89
Similarity Network [32]	51.05
IGOP [35]	53.97
SPC [24]	55.49
MCB + Reg + Spatial [3]	51.01
MNN + Reg + Spatial [3]	55.99
(b) **Our implementation**	
Similarity Network	53.45
Similarity Network + Spatial	54.52
(c) **Conditional models + spatial**	
Individual Coarse Category Similarity Networks, $K = 8$	55.32
Individual K-means Similarity Networks, $K = 8$	54.95
CITE, Coarse Categories, $K = 8$	55.42
CITE, Random, $K = 16$	57.58
CITE, K-means, $K = 16$	57.89
CITE, Learned, $K = 4$	58.69
CITE, Learned, $K = 4$, 500 Edge Boxes	59.27
(d) **Flickr30K-tuned features + spatial**	
PGN + QRN [4]	60.21
CITE, Learned, $K = 4$, 500 Edge Boxes	**61.89**

[a]Performance on this task can be further improved by taking into account the predictions made for other phrases in the same sentence [3,4,24,33], with the best result using Pascal-tuned features of 57.53% achieved by Chen et al. [3] and 65.14% using Flickr30K-tuned features [4].

Edge Boxes at 0.182 s per pair using a NVIDIA Titan X GPU with our implementation) compared with the baseline Similarity Network (0.171 s per pair). Finally, Table 1(d) gives results for models whose visual features were fine-tuned for localization on the Flickr30K Entities dataset. Our model still obtains a 1.5% improvement over the approach of Chen et al. [4], which used bounding box regression as well as a region proposal network. In principle, we could also incorporate these techniques to further improve the model.

Table 2. Comparison of phrase grounding performance over coarse categories on the Flickr30K Entities dataset. Our models were tested with 500 Edge Box proposals

	People	Clothing	Body parts	Animals	Vehicles	Instruments	Scene	Other
PASCAL-tuned Features								
GroundeR [28]	61.00	38.12	10.33	62.55	68.75	36.42	58.18	29.08
RtP [25]	64.73	46.88	17.21	65.83	68.75	37.65	51.39	31.77
IGOP [35]	68.71	**56.83**	19.50	70.07	73.75	39.50	60.38	32.45
MCB + Reg + Spatial [3]	62.75	43.67	14.91	65.44	65.25	24.74	**64.10**	34.62
MNN + Reg + Spatial [3]	67.38	47.57	20.11	73.75	72.44	29.34	63.68	37.88
CITE, Learned, $K = 4$ + Spatial	**73.20**	52.34	**30.59**	**76.25**	**75.75**	**48.15**	55.64	**42.83**
Flickr30K-tuned Features								
PGN + QRN + Spatial [4]	75.05	55.90	20.27	73.36	68.95	45.68	**65.27**	38.80
CITE, Learned, $K = 4$ + Spatial	**75.95**	**58.50**	**30.78**	**77.03**	**79.25**	**48.15**	58.78	**43.24**

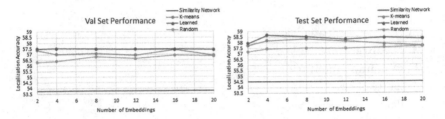

Fig. 2. Effect of the number of learned embeddings (K) on Flickr30K Entities localization accuracy using PASCAL-tuned features

Table 2 breaks down localization accuracy by coarse category. Of particular note are our results on the challenging *body part* category, which are typically small and represent only 3.5% of the phrases in the test set, improving over the next best model as well as the Similarity Network trained on just body part phrases by 10% when using Flickr30K-tuned features. We also see a substantial improvement in the *vehicles* and *other* categories, seeing a 5–9% improvement over the previous state-of-the-art. The only category where we perform worse are phrases referring to scenes, which commonly cover the majority (or entire) image. Here, incorporating a bias towards selecting larger proposals, as in [24,25], can lead to significant improvements.

Parameter Selection. In addition to reporting the localization performance, we also provide some insight into the effect of different parameter choices and what information our model is capturing. In Fig. 2 we show how the number K of learned embeddings affects performance. Using our concept weight branch consistently outperforms K-means cluster assignments. Table 3 shows how the embedding dimensionality M affects performance. Here we see that reducing the output dimension from 256 to 64 (*i.e.*, by 1/4th) leads to a minor (1%) decrease in performance. This result is particularly noteworthy as the CITE network with $K = 4, M = 64$ has 4 million parameters compared the 14 million the baseline Similarity Network has with $M = 256$ while still maintaining a 3% improvement in performance. We also experimented with different ways of altering the Similarity Network to have the same number of parameters to ours at similar points (*e.g.* increasing the last fully connected layer to be K times larger or adding K additional layers), but found they performed comparably to the baseline Similarity Network (*i.e.* their performance was about 4% worse than our approach). In addition to experiments on how many layers to use and the size of each layer, we also explored the effect the number of Edge Boxes has on performance in Table 4. In contrast to some prior work which performed best using 200 candidates (*e.g.* [24,25]), our model's increased discriminate power enables us to still be able to obtain a benefit from using up to 500 proposals.

Concept Weight Branch Examination. To analyze what our model is learning, Fig. 3 shows the means and standard deviations of the weights over the different embeddings broken down by coarse categories. Interestingly, *people* end up being split between two embeddings. We find that people phrases tend to be split by plural vs. singular. Table 5 gives a closer look at the conditional embeddings by listing the ten phrases with the highest weight for each embedding. While most phrases give the first embedding little weight, it appears to provide the most benefit for finding very specific references to people rather than generic terms (*e.g. little curly hair girl* instead of *girl* itself). These patterns generally hold through multiple runs of the model, indicating they are important concepts to learn for the task.

Qualitative Results. Figure 4 gives a look into areas where our model could be improved. Of the phrases that occur at least 100 times in the test set, the lowest performing phrases are *street* and *people* at (resp.) 60% and 64% accuracy. The highest performing of these common phrases is *man* at 81% accuracy, which also happens to be the most common phrase with 1065 instances in the test set. In the top-left example of Fig. 4, the word *people*, which is not correctly localized, refers to partially visible background pedestrians. Analyzing the saliency of a phrase in the context of the whole caption may lead to treating these phrases differently. Global inference constraints, for example, a requirement that predictions for *a man* and *a woman* must be different, would be useful for the top-center example. Performing pronoun resolution, as attempted in [24], would help in the top-right example. In the test set, the pronoun *one* is correctly localized around 36% of the time, whereas *the blond woman* is correctly localized 81% of the time. Having an understanding of relationships between entities may help in cases such as the bottom-left example of Fig. 4, where the extent of the table could be refined by knowing that the groceries are "on" it. Our model also performs relatively poorly on phrases referring to classic "stuff" categories, as shown in the bottom-center and bottom-right examples. The *water* and *street* phrases in these examples are only partly localized. Using pixel-level predictions may help to recover the full extent of these types of phrases since the parts of the images they refer to are relatively homogeneous.

Table 3. Localization accuracy with different embedding sizes using the CITE, Learned, $K = 4$ model on Flickr30K Entities with PASCAL-tuned features. Embedding size refers to M, the output dimensionality of layers P1 and the conditional embeddings in Fig. 1. The remaining fully connected layers' output dimensions (excluding those that are part of the VGG16 network) are four times the embedding size

Embedding size (M)	64	128	256	512
Validation set accuracy	56.32	57.51	**57.53**	57.42
Test set accuracy	57.77	58.48	**58.69**	58.64

Table 4. Localization accuracy with different numbers of proposals using the CITE, Learned, $K = 4$ model on Flickr30K Entities with PASCAL-tuned features

#Edge Box proposals	100	200	500	1000
Validation set accuracy	49.61	57.53	58.48	57.87
Test set accuracy	51.32	58.69	59.27	58.63

3.3 ReferIt Game

We use the same splits as Hu *et al.* [10], which consist of 10,000 images combined for training and validation with the remaining 10,000 images for testing. Models are trained with a batch size of 128, learning rate of 5e-4, and $\lambda = $ 5e-4 in Eq. (2). We generate 500 Edge Box proposals per image.

Results. Table 6 reports the localization accuracy across the ReferIt Game test set. The first line of Table 6(b) shows that our model using the nearest cluster center assignments results in a 2.5% improvement over the baseline Similarity Network. Using our concept weight branch in order to learn assignments yields an additional small improvement.

We note that we do not outperform the approach of Yeh *et al.* [35] on this dataset. This can likely be attributed to the failures of Edge Boxes to produce adequate proposals on the ReferIt Game dataset. Oracle performance using the top 500 proposals is 93% on Flickr30K Entities, while it is only 86% on this dataset. As a result, the specialized bounding box methods used by Yeh *et al.* as well as Chen *et al.* [3] may play a larger role here. Our model would also likely benefit from these improved bounding boxes.

As with the Flickr30K Entities dataset, we show the effect of the number K of embeddings on localization performance in Fig. 5. While the concept weight branch provides a small performance improvement across many different choices of K, when $K = 2$ the clustering assignments actually perform a little better. However, this behavior is atypical in our experiments across all three datasets, and may simply be due to the small size of the ReferIt Game training data, as it has far fewer ground truth phrase-region pairs to train our models with.

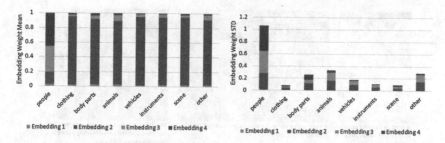

Fig. 3. The mean weight for each embedding (left) along with the standard deviation of those weights (right) broken down by coarse category for the Flickr30K Entities dataset using Flickr30K-tuned features

Table 5. The ten phrases with the highest weight per embedding on the Flickr30K Entities dataset using Flickr30K-tuned features

Embedding 1	Soldiers (0.08), male nun (0.07), rather angry looking woman (0.07), skinny dark complected boy (0.07), little curly hair girl (0.07), middle eastern woman (0.07), first man's leg (0.07), statue athletic man (0.07), referee (0.07), woman drink wine (0.07)
Embedding 2	Red scooter (0.97), blue clothes (0.97), yellow bike (0.97), red bike (0.97), red buckets (0.97), yellow backpack (0.97), street window shops (0.97), red blue buckets (0.97), red backpack (0.97), purple red backpack (0.97)
Embedding 3	Two people (0.94), two men (0.93), two young kids (0.93), two kids (0.93), two white-haired women (0.93), two women (0.93), group three boys (0.93), two young people (0.93), three people (0.92), crowd people (0.92)
Embedding 4	Blond-haired woman (0.91), dark-skinned woman (0.91), gray-haired man (0.91), one-armed man (0.91), dark-haired man (0.91), red-haired man (0.91), boy young man (0.91), man (0.91), well-dressed man (0.91), dark-skinned man (0.91)

3.4 Visual Genome

We use the same splits as Zhang et al. [37], consisting of 77,398 images for training and 5,000 each for testing and validation. Models are trained with a learning rate of 5e−5, and $\lambda = 5e-4$ in Eq. (2). We generate 500 Edge Box proposals per image, and use a batch size of 128.

Results. Table 7 reports the localization accuracy across the Visual Genome dataset. Table 7(a) lists published numbers from several recent methods. The current state of the art performance belongs to Zhang et al. [37], who fine-tuned visual features on this dataset and created a cleaner set during training by pruning ambiguous phrases. We did not perform either fine-tuning or phrase

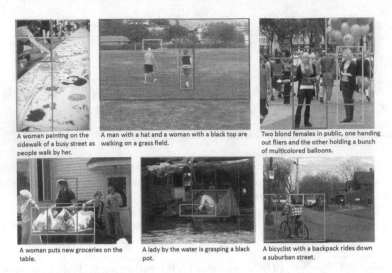

A woman painting on the sidewalk of a busy street as people walk by her.

A man with a hat and a woman with a black top are walking on a grass field.

Two blond females in public, one handing out fliers and the other holding a bunch of multicolored balloons.

A woman puts new groceries on the table.

A lady by the water is grasping a black pot.

A bicyclist with a backpack rides down a suburban street.

Fig. 4. Examples demonstrating some common failure cases on the Flickr30K Entities dataset. See Sect. 3.2 for discussion

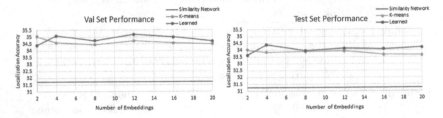

Fig. 5. Effect of the number K of embeddings on localization accuracy on the ReferIt Game dataset

pruning, so the most comparable reference number for our methods is their 17.5% accuracy without these steps.

The baseline accuracies for our Similarity Network with and without spatial features are given in the last two lines of Table 7(a). We can see that including the spatial features gives only a small improvement. This is likely due to the denser annotations in this dataset as compared to Flickr30K Entities. For example, a phrase like *a man* in Flickr30K Entities would typically refer to a relatively large region towards the center since background instances are commonly not mentioned in an image-level caption. However, entities in Visual Genome include both foreground and background instances.

In the first line of Table 7(b), we see our K-means model is 3.5% better than the Similarity Network baseline, and over 6% better than the 17.5% accuracy of [37]. According to the second line of Table 7(b), using the concept weight branch obtains a further improvement. In fact, our full model with pre-trained PASCAL features has better performance than [37] with fine-tuned features.

Table 6. Localization performance on the ReferIt Game test set. (a) Published results and our Similarity Network baseline. (b) Our best-performing conditional models

Method	Accuracy
(a) State-of-the-art	
SCRC [10]	17.93
GroundeR + Spatial [28]	26.93
MCB + Reg + Spatial [3]	26.54
CGRE [21]	31.85
MNN + Reg + Spatial [3]	32.21
IGOP [35]	34.70
Similarity Network + Spatial	31.26
(b) Conditional Models + Spatial	
CITE, K-Means, $K = 2$	34.01
CITE, Learned, $K = 12$	34.13

Table 7. Phrase localization performance on Visual Genome. (a) Published results and our Similarity Network baselines. APP refers to ambiguous phrase pruning (see [37] for details). (b) Our best-performing conditional models

Method	Accuracy
(a) State-of-the-art	
Densecap [13]	10.1
SCRC [10]	11.0
DBNet [37]	17.5
DBNet (with APP) [37]	21.2
DBNet (with APP, V. Genome-tuned Features) [37]	23.7
Similarity Network	19.76
Similarity Network + Spatial	20.08
(b) Conditional Models + Spatial	
CITE, K-Means, $K = 12$	23.67
CITE, Learned, $K = 12$	24.43

As with the other two datasets, Fig. 6 reports performance as a function of the number of learned embeddings. Echoing most of the earlier results, we see a consistent improvement for the learned embeddings over the K-means ones. The large size of this dataset (>250,000 instances in the test set) helps to reinforce the significance of our results.

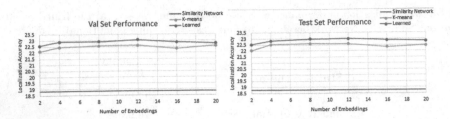

Fig. 6. Effect of the number of learned embeddings on performance on the Visual Genome with models trained on 1/3 of the available training data

4   Conclusion

This paper introduced a method of learning a set of conditional embeddings and phrase-to-embedding assignments in a single end-to-end network. The effectiveness of our approach was demonstrated on three popular and challenging phrase-to-region grounding datasets. In future work, our model could be further improved by including a term to enforce that distinct concepts are being learned by each embedding.

Our experiments focused on localizing individual phrases to a fixed set of category-independent region proposals. As such, our absolute accuracies could be further improved by incorporating a number of orthogonal techniques used in competing work. By jointly predicting multiple phrases in an image our model could take advantage of relationships between multiple entities (*e.g.* [3,4,24,33]). Including bounding box regression and a region proposal network as done in [3,4] would also likely lead to a better model. In fact, tying the regression parameters to a specific concept embedding may further improve performance since it would simplify our prediction task as a result of needing to learn parameters for just the phrases assigned to that embedding.

Acknowledgements. This material is based upon work supported in part by the National Science Foundation under Grants No. 1563727 and 1718221, Amazon Research Award, AWS Machine Learning Research Award, and Google Research Award.

References

1. Antol, S., et al.: VQA: visual question answering. In: ICCV (2015)
2. Babenko, B., Branson, S., Belongie, S.: Similarity metrics for categorization: from monolithic to category specific. In: ICCV (2009)
3. Chen, K., Kovvuri, R., Gao, J., Nevatia, R.: MSRC: multimodal spatial regression with semantic context for phrase grounding. In: ICMR (2017)
4. Chen, K., Kovvuri, R., Nevatia, R.: Query-guided regression network with context policy for phrase grounding. In: ICCV (2017)
5. Everingham, M., Van Gool, L., Williams, C.K.I., Winn, J., Zisserman, A.: The PASCAL visual object classes challenge 2012 (VOC2012) results (2012). http://www.pascal-network.org/challenges/VOC/voc2012/workshop/index.html

6. Fang, H., et al.: From captions to visual concepts and back. In: CVPR (2015)
7. Fukui, A., Park, D.H., Yang, D., Rohrbach, A., Darrell, T., Rohrbach, M.: Multimodal compact bilinear pooling for visual question answering and visual grounding. In: EMNLP (2016)
8. Girshick, R.: Fast R-CNN. In: ICCV (2015)
9. Gordo, A., Almazán, J., Revaud, J., Larlus, D.: Deep image retrieval: learning global representations for image search. In: Leibe, B., Matas, J., Sebe, N., Welling, M. (eds.) ECCV 2016. LNCS, vol. 9910, pp. 241–257. Springer, Cham (2016). https://doi.org/10.1007/978-3-319-46466-4_15
10. Hu, R., Xu, H., Rohrbach, M., Feng, J., Saenko, K., Darrell, T.: Natural language object retrieval. In: CVPR (2016)
11. Ioffe, S., Szegedy, C.: Batch normalization: accelerating deep network training by reducing internal covariate shift. In: ICML (2015)
12. Johnson, J., Karpathy, A., Fei-Fei, L.: DenseCap: fully convolutional localization networks for dense captioning. In: CVPR (2016)
13. Johnson, J., et al.: Image retrieval using scene graphs. In: CVPR (2015)
14. Karpathy, A., Fei-Fei, L.: Deep visual-semantic alignments for generating image descriptions. In: CVPR (2015)
15. Kazemzadeh, S., Ordonez, V., Matten, M., Berg, T.: ReferitGame: referring to objects in photographs of natural scenes. In: EMNLP (2014)
16. Kingma, D.P., Ba, J.: Adam: a method for stochastic optimization. In: International Conference for Learning Representations (2015)
17. Klein, B., Lev, G., Sadeh, G., Wolf, L.: Associating neural word embeddings with deep image representations using fisher vector. In: CVPR (2015)
18. Krishna, R.: Visual genome: connecting language and vision using crowdsourced dense image annotations. IJCV **123**, 32–73 (2017)
19. Liu, C., Mao, J., Sha, F., Yuille, A.: Attention correctness in neural image captioning. In: AAAI (2017)
20. Liu, J., Wang, L., Yang, M.H.: Referring expression generation and comprehension via attributes. In: ICCV (2017)
21. Luo, R., Shakhnarovich, G.: Comprehension-guided referring expressions. In: CVPR (2017)
22. Mao, J., Huang, J., Toshev, A., Camburu, O., Yuille, A., Murphy, K.: Generation and comprehension of unambiguous object descriptions. In: CVPR (2016)
23. Mikolov, T., Chen, K., Corrado, G., Dean, J.: Efficient estimation of word representations in vector space. arXiv:1301.3781 (2013)
24. Plummer, B.A., Mallya, A., Cervantes, C.M., Hockenmaier, J., Lazebnik, S.: Phrase localization and visual relationship detection with comprehensive image-language cues. In: ICCV (2017)
25. Plummer, B.A., Wang, L., Cervantes, C.M., Caicedo, J.C., Hockenmaier, J., Lazebnik, S.: Flickr30k entities: collecting region-to-phrase correspondences for richer image-to-sentence models. IJCV **123**(1), 74–93 (2017)
26. Radenović, F., Tolias, G., Chum, O.: CNN image retrieval learns from BoW: unsupervised fine-tuning with hard examples. In: Leibe, B., Matas, J., Sebe, N., Welling, M. (eds.) ECCV 2016. LNCS, vol. 9905, pp. 3–20. Springer, Cham (2016). https://doi.org/10.1007/978-3-319-46448-0_1
27. Ren, S., He, K., Girshick, R., Sun, J.: Faster R-CNN: towards real-time object detection with region proposal networks. In: NIPS (2015)

28. Rohrbach, A., Rohrbach, M., Hu, R., Darrell, T., Schiele, B.: Grounding of textual phrases in images by reconstruction. In: Leibe, B., Matas, J., Sebe, N., Welling, M. (eds.) ECCV 2016. LNCS, vol. 9905, pp. 817–834. Springer, Cham (2016). https://doi.org/10.1007/978-3-319-46448-0_49

29. Tommasi, T., Mallya, A., Plummer, B.A., Lazebnik, S., Berg, A.C., Berg, T.L.: Solving visual madlibs with multiple cues. In: BMVC (2016)

30. Veit, A., Belongie, S., Karaletsos, T.: Conditional similarity networks. In: CVPR (2017)

31. Wang, L., Li, Y., Lazebnik, S.: Learning deep structure-preserving image-text embeddings. In: CVPR (2016)

32. Wang, L., Li, Y., Lazebnik, S.: Learning two-branch neural networks for image-text matching tasks. arXiv:1704.03470 (2017)

33. Wang, M., Azab, M., Kojima, N., Mihalcea, R., Deng, J.: Structured matching for phrase localization. In: Leibe, B., Matas, J., Sebe, N., Welling, M. (eds.) ECCV 2016. LNCS, vol. 9912, pp. 696–711. Springer, Cham (2016). https://doi.org/10.1007/978-3-319-46484-8_42

34. Xu, K., et al.: Show, attend and tell: neural image caption generation with visual attention. In: ICML (2015)

35. Yeh, R.A., Xiong, J., Hwu, W.M., Do, M.N., Schwing, A.G.: Interpretable and globally optimal prediction for textual grounding using image concepts. In: NIPS (2017)

36. Yu, L., Poirson, P., Yang, S., Berg, A.C., Berg, T.L.: Modeling context in referring expressions. In: Leibe, B., Matas, J., Sebe, N., Welling, M. (eds.) ECCV 2016. LNCS, vol. 9906, pp. 69–85. Springer, Cham (2016). https://doi.org/10.1007/978-3-319-46475-6_5

37. Zhang, Y., Yuan, L., Guo, Y., He, Z., Huang, I.A., Lee, H.: Discriminative bimodal networks for visual localization and detection with natural language queries. In: CVPR (2017)

38. Zitnick, C.L., Dollár, P.: Edge boxes: locating object proposals from edges. In: Fleet, D., Pajdla, T., Schiele, B., Tuytelaars, T. (eds.) ECCV 2014. LNCS, vol. 8693, pp. 391–405. Springer, Cham (2014). https://doi.org/10.1007/978-3-319-10602-1_26

Sampling Algebraic Varieties for Robust Camera Autocalibration

Danda Pani Paudel[1](✉) and Luc Van Gool[1,2]

[1] Computer Vision Lab, ETH Zürich, Zürich, Switzerland
{paudel,vangool}@vision.ee.ethz.ch
[2] VISICS, ESAT/PSI, KU Leuven, Leuven, Belgium

Abstract. This paper addresses the problem of robustly autocalibrating a moving camera with constant intrinsics. The proposed calibration method uses the Branch-and-Bound (BnB) search paradigm to maximize the consensus of the polynomials. These polynomials are parameterized by the entries of, either the Dual Image of Absolute Conic (DIAC) or the Plane-at-Infinity (PaI). During the BnB search, we exploit the theory of sampling algebraic varieties, to test the positivity of any polynomial within a parameter's interval, i.e. outliers with certainty. The search process explores the space of exact parameters (i.e. the entries of DIAC or PaI), benefits from the solution of a local method, and converges to the solution satisfied by the largest number of polynomials. Given many polynomials on the sought parameters (with possibly overwhelmingly many from outlier measurements), their consensus for calibration is searched for two cases: simplified Kruppa's equations and Modulus constraints, expressed in DIAC and PaI, resp. Our approach yields outstanding results in terms of robustness and optimality.

1 Introduction

Estimating the intrinsics of a moving camera is difficult mainly due the nonlinear nature of the problem. Furthermore, it also demands the camera motion to be rich and diverse (with sufficiently large translations and rotations), such that the degenerate motions for autocalibration – so-called Critical Motion Sequences (CMS) – are avoided. Yet, when the camera undergoes a large motion, establishing a good set of correspondences across multiple views becomes very challenging mainly due to the change in viewpoints or occlusions. Failure to establish such correspondences leads to an inaccurate estimation of camera motion, thus demanding a robust method for camera autocalibration. Although the problem of accurate motion estimation may be partially handled by carefully capturing the image sets, such solutions are not always possible especially when the image acquisitions cannot be controlled as desired (e.g. remote cameras, holidays pictures). Furthermore, camera motion estimation is expected to be riddled with inaccuracies and outliers, mainly due to the presence of repetitive patterns, changes in illumination, and partial/no scene overlaps.

© Springer Nature Switzerland AG 2018
V. Ferrari et al. (Eds.): ECCV 2018, LNCS 11216, pp. 275–292, 2018.
https://doi.org/10.1007/978-3-030-01258-8_17

Camera autocalibration has obtained significant attention since the seminal work by *Maybank et Faugeras* [1]. Existing approaches can be broadly divided into three categories: (i) direct estimation of a ubiquitous conic which encodes the camera intrinsics: the so-called Dual Image of the Absolute Conic (DIAC) [2–4], (ii) stratified estimation of the Plane-at-Infinity (PaI) followed by a linear retrieval of the DIAC [5–9], (iii) joint estimation of both PaI and DIAC in the form of the so-called Dual Image of the Absolute Quadric (DIAQ) [10–12]. On the one hand, most of these methods are only locally optimal (requiring a good initialization of the sought intrinsics) and susceptible to even a small number of outliers. On the other hand, globally optimal methods [9,11,12] only focus on the optimality while discarding the criteria for robustness towards outliers.

A relatively robust and globally optimal method [13] performs the interval analysis within the framework of Branch-and-Bound (BnB) to solve the modified robust cost function proposed in [14], which was originally derived in [2]. Unfortunately, due to the inefficiency of the interval analysis technique, the method has proved computationally very expensive and applicable only to rather short image sequences. Furthermore, this method also suffers from the same problem as [14] for high numbers of outliers. To the best of our knowledge, there exist no efficient minimal solver for full camera calibration that offers a practical way of conducting robust estimation within the framework of RANSAC. Furthermore, RANSAC-based methods would still be non-deterministic and fail to provide meaningful solutions in the presence of many outliers. Existing minimal solvers such as [15–17] make strong assumptions on an unknown focal length with known aspect ratio. A detailed study on Minimal Conditions for camera autocalibration is provided in [18]. Note that a variety of methods for solving systems of nonlinear polynomial equations exist. While some are based on Gröbner bases or homotopy continuation [19], others use Sum-of-Squares (SoS) polynomial optimization [20–22]. Yet, such methods are dedicated to solving outlier-free nonlinear systems and dealing with outliers is carried out through RANSAC.

In this work, we address the problem of robustly autocalibrating a moving camera with constant intrinsics. The proposed method uses the BnB search paradigm to solve both direct and stratified calibrations, namely simplified Kruppa's equations [4] and Modulus constraints [7], parameterized by DIAC and PaI, respectively. Although, *Gurdjos et al.* [23] suggest that the solutions to Kruppa's equations or Modulus constraints may suffer from artificial CMS (due to the failure of enforcing the Absolute Conic to lie on the PaI), we argue that the artificial CMS are unlikely to happen for cameras under large motion. In such cases, robustness towards outliers is rather more important to deal with. In fact, the joint estimation of the DIAC and PaI, in the form of rank-3 DAQ, not only makes the problem more challenging but also demands a high quality projective reconstruction, thus making it less suitable for robust camera calibration.

During the BnB search, we explore the DIAC or PaI parameter space. As in [24,25], we rely on establishing optimistic and pessimistic sets of inlier assignments for pruning branches whose most optimistic sets are worse than the best pessimistic one. For any branch, we obtain the pessimistic inlier set using a local refinement method that guarantees the solution to lie within the sought interval. To estimate the optimistic inlier set, we exploit the theory of sampling algebraic varieties for testing the positivity/negativity of polynomials on the given varieties. In this regard, polynomials to be tested, say interval polynomials, are derived from the parameters' current intervals, whereas varieties are represented by the polynomials from either the Kruppa's equations or Modulus constraints. The interval polynomials are quadratic in nature and designed such that they are always negative within the considered interval while being positive elsewhere. If the interval polynomial is positive/negative on any variety, the measurement corresponding to that variety is an outlier, with certainty, for that particular interval. The optimistic inliers are then estimated by discarding such outliers for the total measurements.

The major contributions of this paper can be summarized as: (i) For the first time, we introduce the theory of sampling algebraic varieties to detect the outlier polynomials with certainty, within the considered parameters' intervals. (ii) Based on the rigorous theory of algebraic geometry, we devise an efficient and optimal BnB-based search method to maximize the consensus of the polynomials sharing common real roots. Furthermore, we also provide the common root as the solution to the given polynomial system with many outliers. (iii) The proposed method has been tested on two challenging autocalibration problems, demonstrating outstanding results both in terms of robustness and optimality.

2   Sampling Varieties Theory

Consider the ring $\mathbb{R}[\mathsf{x}] := \mathbb{R}[x_1, ..., x_n]$ of multivariate polynomials and an algebraic variety $\mathcal{V} \subseteq \mathbb{C}^n$ defined such that $\mathcal{V} := \{\mathsf{x} \in \mathbb{C}^n : h_i(\mathsf{x}) = 0, \text{for } i = 1, ..., m\}$. For a given polynomial $p(\mathsf{x}) \in \mathbb{R}[\mathsf{x}]$, we are interested to know whether,

$$p(\mathsf{x}) \geq 0, \text{for all } \mathsf{x} \in \mathcal{V} \cap \mathbb{R}^n. \tag{1}$$

The decision problem in (1) is NP-hard. However, there are some relaxation methods based on sum of squares (SoS) [25,26]. Recall that a polynomial $f(\mathsf{x}) \in \mathbb{R}[\mathsf{x}]$ is SoS, if there exist polynomials $f_i(\mathsf{x}) \in \mathbb{R}[\mathsf{x}]$ such that $f(\mathsf{x}) = \sum_i (f_i(\mathsf{x}))^2$. Given a bound $d \in \mathbb{N}$, it is straightforward to observe that (1) must hold true, if there exists a SoS polynomial $f(\mathsf{x})$ of degree $\leq 2d$ such that,

$$p(\mathsf{z}) = f(\mathsf{z}), \text{for all } \mathsf{z} \in \mathcal{V}. \tag{2}$$

We refer to such $f(\mathsf{x})$ as a d-SoS certificate. Now, we are interested to know the answer to the following problem.

Problem 1. Given a bound $d \in \mathbb{N}$, a polynomial $p(\mathsf{x})$ and a variety $\mathcal{V}$, does there exist a d-SoS certificate?

An affirmative answer to Problem 1 is a sufficient condition for (1) to be true. To answer the Problem 1, we rely on the theory of sampling varieties, originally developed in [27]. This theory uses a generic set of samples $\mathcal{Z} = \{z_1, \ldots, z_S\} \subseteq \mathcal{V}$, while specializing the condition in (2) to $\mathcal{Z}$. Intuitively, if (2) is satisfied for a sufficiently large sample set $\mathcal{Z} \subseteq \mathcal{V}$, it must also be true for all $z \in \mathcal{V}$, as long as both the number of variables and the degree of $p(x)$ are bounded. Then one may be interested to know what is the smallest size of $\mathcal{Z}$ required to conclude that (2) is indeed true.

Unfortunately, there is not an easy way to find the minimal size of $\mathcal{Z}$. But the good news is that, for a given $\mathcal{Z}$, one can test whether it is sufficient to find a d-SoS certificate. Using the method proposed in [27], such certificate can be obtained in two steps; (i) pre-certificate computation, (ii) poisedness test.

Definition 1 (Pre-certificate). *For a variety $\mathcal{V} \subseteq \mathbb{C}^n$, a non negative polynomial $p(x) \in \mathbb{R}[x]$ on $\mathcal{V} \cap \mathbb{R}^n$, and a bound $d \in \mathbb{N}$, a sampling d-SoS pre-certificate is a pair $(f(x), \mathcal{Z})$, where $f(x)$ is a SoS polynomial of degree $\leq 2d$ and $\mathcal{Z} = \{z_1, \ldots, z_S\} \subseteq \mathcal{V}$ a sample set, such that,*

$$p(z_s) = f(z_s), \text{ for } s = 1, \ldots, S. \tag{3}$$

If $f(x)$ is a d-SoS certificate, the pre-certificate is correct.

Finding a pre-certificate with (3), is a Semi-Definite Programming (SDP) problem.

$$\begin{aligned} \text{find} \quad & Q \in \mathcal{S}^N, \quad Q \succeq 0, \\ \text{s.t.} \quad & p(z_s) = u(z_s)^\mathsf{T} Q u(z_s) \qquad \text{for, } s = 1, \ldots S. \end{aligned} \tag{4}$$

Where, $u(x) \in \mathbb{R}[x]^N$ is the vector of all monomials of degree at most d, and $\mathcal{S}^N$ denotes the space of $N \times N$ real symmetric matrices. Recall that, a polynomial $f(x) \in \mathbb{R}[x]$ is d-SoS if and only if, $f(x) = u(x)^\mathsf{T} Q u(x)$ for a positive definite matrix Q (denoted by $Q \succeq 0$). Therefore, if there exists any matrix $Q \succeq 0$ that satisfies (4), the pre-certificate (defined in Definition 1) is correct. Although the per-certificate obtained in this manner does not necessarily guarantee that (2) is satisfied, it can be used for the certainty, if the set $\mathcal{Z}$ is poised.

Definition 2 (Poisedness). *Let $\mathcal{L} \subseteq \mathbb{R}[\mathcal{V}]$ be a linear subspace. For a given set of samples $\mathcal{Z} \subseteq \mathcal{V}$, $(\mathcal{L}, \mathcal{Z})$ is called poised if the only polynomial $p(x) \in \mathcal{L}$ with $p(z) = 0$ for all $z \in \mathcal{Z}$, is the zero polynomial. Furthermore, for any finite dimensional $\mathcal{L}$ there is a finite set $\mathcal{Z}$ such that $(\mathcal{L}, \mathcal{Z})$ is poised [27].*

Let $\mathcal{L}_d \subseteq \mathbb{R}[\mathcal{V}]$ and $\mathcal{L}_{2d} \subseteq \mathbb{R}[\mathcal{V}]$ are the linear spaces spanned by the entries of $u(x)$ and $u(x)u(x)^\mathsf{T}$, respectively. The polynomial $f(x) = u(x)^\mathsf{T} Q u(x) \in \mathcal{L}_{2d}$. There exist a simple strategy to test if the given pair $(\mathcal{L}, \mathcal{Z})$ is poised or not. The test is summarized in Algorithm 1. Please, refer [27] for the details about the poisedness test. Now, the following theorem guarantees the correctness of pre-certificate for a good set of samples, i.e. when $(\mathcal{L}_{2d}, \mathcal{Z})$ is poised.

Algorithm 1. $[testFlag] = \text{poisednessTest}(u(x), \mathcal{Z})$

1. Form vector $u_2(x) = vec(u(x)u(x)^\top)$ spanning $\mathcal{L}_{2d}$.
2. Build a matrix $\hat{U}_2$ with columns $u_2(z)$ for $z \in \mathcal{Z} \cup \overline{\mathcal{Z}}$.
3. If $\hat{U}_2$ has full column rank, return "false". Else, return "true".

Theorem 1 (Poisedness implies correctness [27]). *For any given set of samples $\mathcal{Z}$, its pre-certificate $(f(x), \mathcal{Z})$ is correct, if $(\mathcal{L}_{2d}, \mathcal{Z})$ is poised.*

To summarize, the decision Problem of (1) can be answered with the help of a generic sample set $\mathcal{Z}$. For a general variety $\mathcal{V}$, one can use numerical algebraic geometry tools (such as Bertini [28] and PHCpack [29]) to compute such sample sets. The answer to the Problem (1) is affirmative, if there exists $Q \succeq 0$ satisfying (3) and $\mathcal{Z}$ passes the poisedness test of Algorithm 1. In case of failure, the poisedness test of $\mathcal{Z}$ can be ensured by adding more samples. Recall from Definition 2, for any finite dimensional $\mathcal{L}$ there is a finite set $\mathcal{Z}$ that passes the poisedness test. Needless to say that if $p(z_s)$ is negative for any z_s, the test for Problem of (1) is not really necessary. More importantly, if the pre-certificate cannot be obtained even for the smallest $\mathcal{Z}$ that passes the poisedness test, the answer to the Problem (1) is undetermined.

3 Consensus Within a System of Polynomials

Consider a set of measurements $\{\mathcal{M}_i\}_{i=1}^m$ such that each $\mathcal{M}_i$ can be expressed as a set polynomials $\mathcal{P}_i = \{h_{ij}(x)\}_{j=1}^l$, on the unknown parameter $x \in \mathbb{R}^n$. Let the variety $\mathcal{V}_i := \{x \in \mathbb{R}^n : h_{ij}(x) = 0, \text{for } j = 1, \ldots, l\}$, where $h_{ij}(x) = 0$, for $j = 1, \ldots, l$ are the polynomials obtained from the measurement $\mathcal{M}_i$. Ideally, we are interested to find an $x \in \cap_{i=1}^m \mathcal{V}_i$. However, in the presence of noise and outliers, such x may not even exist. Therefore, we wish to solve the following Problem.

Problem 2. Given a set $\mathcal{S} = \{\mathcal{P}_i\}_{i=1}^m$ and a threshold ϵ,

$$\max_{x, \zeta \subseteq \mathcal{S}} \quad |\zeta|,$$

$$\text{subject to} \quad \mathbf{d}(x, \mathcal{V}_i) \le \epsilon, \quad \forall \mathcal{P}_i \in \zeta, \tag{5}$$

for a sample x to variety $\mathcal{V}$ distance defined by,

$$\mathbf{d}(x, \mathcal{V}) = \min_{y \in \mathcal{V}} \ \|x - y\|. \tag{6}$$

This problem, however, is difficult to solve due to its non-convex and NP-hard combinatorial nature. In this work, we approach this problem using the BnB algorithmic paradigm. Our BnB search is performed by branching on the space of parameters $x \in \mathbb{R}^n$. Every branch is represented by an interval of parameters x in the form of two vectors $[\underline{x}, \overline{x}]$ such that $\underline{x} \le \overline{x}$, for the entry-wise inequality.

3.1 Polynomials Within an Interval

The key idea of this paper is an effective way of estimating the optimistic number of inliers/outliers measurements, represented by a set of polynomials, for each branch by answering the following problem.

Problem 3. For any given measurement $\mathcal{M}_i$ and a parameter's interval $[\underline{x}, \overline{x}]$, does there exist a vector $x \in [\underline{x}, \overline{x}]$ such that $d(x, \mathcal{V}_i) \leq \epsilon$?

In other words, we would like to know whether all the polynomials $h_{ij} \in \mathcal{P}_i$ share at least one common root within the given interval representing a branch, with an ϵ tolerance. If this question is answered affirmatively, then the measurement $\mathcal{M}_i$ is a potential inlier within the considered interval. This problem however, is difficult to answer unless the following proposition is considered.

Proposition 1. *For the given threshold ϵ and parameter's interval $[\underline{x}, \overline{x}]$, let us define a polynomial $p_b(x)$ representing the interval bounds:*

$$p_b(x) = \left\| x - \frac{\underline{x} + \overline{x}}{2} \right\|^2 - \left(\left\| \frac{\overline{x} - \underline{x}}{2} \right\| + \epsilon \right)^2. \tag{7}$$

For any measurement $\mathcal{M}_i$, there exists no $x \in [\underline{x}, \overline{x}]$ such that $d(x, \mathcal{V}_i) \leq \epsilon$, if $p_b(x) \geq 0$ for all $x \in \mathcal{V}_i \cap \mathbb{R}^n$.

Proof. Observe that $p_b(x) \geq 0$ is the interior of a sphere with center $\frac{\underline{x} + \overline{x}}{2}$ and radius $\left\| \frac{\overline{x} - \underline{x}}{2} \right\| + \epsilon$, which includes all $x \in [\underline{x}, \overline{x}]$ with ϵ tolerance. Therefore, if $p_b(x) \geq 0$ for all $x \in \mathcal{V}_i \cap \mathbb{R}^n$, there exists no $x \in [\underline{x}, \overline{x}]$ such that $d(x, \mathcal{V}_i) \leq \epsilon$. $\square$

Proposition 1 allows us to answer the Problem 3 similar to the decision problem of (1). The ability to answer the Problem 3 allows us to reason about whether the measurement $\mathcal{M}_i$ is an inlier or outlier. Recall that a measurement $\mathcal{M}_i$ is an inlier if $d(x, \mathcal{V}_i) \leq \epsilon$. Alternatively, there exists no $x \in [\underline{x}, \overline{x}]$ such that $d(x, \mathcal{V}_i) \leq \epsilon$, then the measurement $\mathcal{M}_i$ is definitely an outlier within the considered bounds. Otherwise, it is a potential inlier. For interval bounds $[\underline{x}, \overline{x}]$ and a threshold ϵ, we summarize the method to test whether the given measurement $\mathcal{M}_i$ is an outlier, in Algorithm 2.

Algorithm 2. $[testFlag]$ = OutlierTest($[\underline{x}, \overline{x}], \mathcal{M}_i, \epsilon$)

  1. Construct $p_b(x)$ using (7), for bounds $[\underline{x}, \overline{x}]$ and threshold ϵ.
  2. For given $\mathcal{M}_i$, construct $\mathcal{P}_i$ to define its variety $\mathcal{V}_i$.
  3. Test if $p_b(x) \geq 0$, for all $x \in \mathcal{V}_i \cap \mathbb{R}^n$, as in (1) in two steps:
  $\rightarrow$ (i) Compute the pre-certificate using (4).
  $\rightarrow$ (ii) Verify the pre-certificate using Algorithm 1.
  4. If the test holds true, return "true". Else, return "false".

Now we are interested to know whether Algorithm 2 often misses the outliers. In other words, even if there exists no $x \in [\underline{x}, \overline{x}]$ with $d(x, \mathcal{V}_i) \leq \epsilon$, could it be possible that Algorithm 2 fails to provide the outlier certificate for the measurement $\mathcal{M}_i$? In fact, this may often happen, especially when the interval gap is large. However, when the gap shrinks towards zero during the BnB search, such occurrences are less and less likely to happen. This can be inferred from the extreme condition of $\epsilon = 0$ and $\hat{x} = \underline{x} = \overline{x}$. In such case, the polynomial $p_b(x)$ becomes an SoS, of the form $p_b(x) = \|x - \hat{x}\|^2$. The d-SoS certificate $f(x)$ of $p_b(x)$, in (2), is $p_b(x)$ itself.

3.2 The BnB Algorithm

The goal of the BnB algorithm is to estimate parameters $x \in \mathbb{R}^n$ that yield the largest number of inlier measurements. We start with a set $\mathcal{S} = \{\mathcal{P}_i\}_{i=1}^m$, where the set of polynomials $\mathcal{P}_i$ defines a variety $\mathcal{V}_i$ for each measurement $\mathcal{M}_i$. During BnB search, a dynamic search tree, whose nodes are parameter intervals, is built to explore the space of parameters. Given measurements and intervals, the BnB algorithm (see Algorithm 3) requires the estimation of both optimistic and pessimistic numbers of inliers.

Optimistic Number of Inliers: We estimate the optimistic number of inliers by exploiting the outlier test method of the Algorithm 2. Since any measurement that passes the test is definitely an outlier for the considered interval, the optimistic inliers are obtained by simply discarding such outliers from the total measurements.

Pessimistic Number of Inliers: A local refinement method is used to obtain a pessimistic number of inliers for each node. The local method iteratively refines x while starting from the mid-values of the parameter intervals. To ensure that the final solution still represents the same node, it searches the optimal solution within the investigated intervals. Given a set of potential inliers $\mathcal{I} \subseteq \mathcal{S}$, the algorithm iteratively updates the parameters to:

$$x^* = \underset{\substack{x \in [\underline{x}, \overline{x}] \\ h_{ij}(x) \in \mathcal{P}_i, \\ \mathcal{P}_i \in \mathcal{I}}}{\operatorname{argmin}} \sum \|h_{ij}(x)\|^2. \tag{8}$$

The pessimistic set of inliers are only those measurements which satisfy the condition $d(x^*, \mathcal{V}) \leq \epsilon$. For the given measurement $\mathcal{M}_i$, following two steps are performed:

(i) If there exists $z \in \mathcal{Z}_i$ (sample set $\mathcal{Z}_i$ of $\mathcal{V}_i$) such that $d(x^*, z) \leq \epsilon$, $\mathcal{M}_i$ is an inlier.
(ii) The entries of x^* are used to solve the polynomial system $\mathcal{P}_i = \{h_{ij}(x)\}_{j=1}^l$ on l variables (by replacing the others). If the solution is ϵ close to x^*, $\mathcal{M}_i$ is an inlier. This step is carried out only if $|h_{ij}(x)| < \eta$ for all $h_{ij}(x) \in \mathcal{P}_i$ and threshold η.

At any instant of the BnB search, we keep track of the biggest set of inliers obtained so far. Let us call $nOpti$ and $nPess$ the number of optimistic and pessimistic inliers, respectively. Similarly, $bPess$ for the maximum of $nPess$ among all nodes. Any node whose $nOpti$ is worse than $bPess$ is rejected. Otherwise, the node is further branched for its parameter with the largest interval, resulting in two new nodes to be processed. The node corresponding to the $bPess$ is processed first. The algorithm terminates when no node has an $nOpti$ that is better than $bPess$.

Algorithm 3. $[flag,bPess]$ = processNode($[\underline{x},\overline{x}],\mathcal{S}$, ϵ, $bPess$)

1. Count $nOpti$ using Algorithm 2 for each $\mathcal{P}_i \in \mathcal{S}$ of $\mathcal{M}_i$.
2. If $nOpti \leq bPess$, set $flag$ = "false" (for pruning), return.
3. Count $nPess$ using local method (8) followed by steps (i) and (ii).
4. If $bPess < nPess$, then $bPess \leftarrow nPess$, $flag$ = "true".

---

4   Polynomials for Camera Autocalibration

We consider that a set of m image pairs $\{\mathcal{I}_i, \mathcal{I}'_i\}_{i=1}^m$ are captured by uncalibrated cameras. For each pair, both 3D scene points and cameras are reconstructed up to a projective ambiguity, from the point correspondences between images [30]. Without loss of generality, we choose the world frame such that it coincides with the camera coordinate frame of the first image. In this case, the projection matrix of the first image becomes $[\mathsf{I}_{3\times3}|0_{3\times1}]$. Let the projection matrix of the second image be $\mathsf{M}_i = [\mathsf{H}_i|\mathsf{e}_i]_{3\times4}$. Given a set of measurements $\mathcal{S} = \{\mathsf{M}_i\}_{i=1}^m$, with possibly many outliers, we wish to calibrate cameras by using the method presented in Sect. 3. To do so, we exploit the formulations of the following two classical camera autocalibration methods.

4.1   Simplified Kruppa's Equations on DIAC

The Kruppa's equations for camera autocalibration rely on an omnipresent line conic lying on the PaI – the so-called the Dual Absolute Conic (DAC). The projection of DAC on the image $\mathcal{I}'_i$, known as Dual Image of Absolute Conic (DIAC), can be expressed in the form of the camera intrinsics K_i of the camera capturing $\mathcal{I}'_i$, as,

$$\omega_i = \mathsf{K}_i\mathsf{K}_i^{\mathsf{T}}. \tag{9}$$

In this work, we assume that the camera intrinsics are constant across all images such that $\mathsf{K} = \mathsf{K}_i$, thus leading to a unique DIAC ω for all image pairs. The simplified Kruppa's equations [4] allow us to express such ω in the form of polynomials, with the help of Fundamental matrices $\mathsf{F}_i = [\mathsf{e}_i]_\times \mathsf{H}_i$.

Let $F_i = U_i D_i V_i$ be the singular value decomposition, with $D = \mathrm{diag}([r_i, s_i, 0])$. For $U_i = [u_{i1}|u_{i2}|u_{i3}]$ and $V_i = [v_{i1}|v_{i2}|v_{i3}]$, two independent polynomials of simplified Kruppa's equations are of the form:

$$h_{i1}(\omega) = (r_i s_i v_{i1}^\mathsf{T} \omega v_{i2})(u_{i2}^\mathsf{T} \omega u_{i2}) + (r_i^2 v_{i1}^\mathsf{T} \omega v_{i1})(u_{i1}^\mathsf{T} \omega u_{i2}),$$
$$h_{i2}(\omega) = (r_i s_i v_{i1}^\mathsf{T} \omega v_{i2})(u_{i1}^\mathsf{T} \omega u_{i1}) + (s_i^2 v_{i2}^\mathsf{T} \omega v_{i2})(u_{i1}^\mathsf{T} \omega u_{i2}). \tag{10}$$

Given a set of projection matrices $\mathcal{S} = \{M_i\}_{i=1}^m$ as measurements, the task of robust camera autocalibration is to estimate ω that maximizes the consensus of these measurements. Note that ω is a 3×3 matrix with $\omega = \omega^\mathsf{T}$ and $\omega_{(3,3)} = 1$. Therefore, one can linearly parameterize ω using only a vector $x \in \mathbb{R}^5$. Let $h_{i1}(x)$ and $h_{i2}(x)$ be the equivalent representations of $h_{i1}(\omega)$ and $h_{i1}(\omega)$ of (10), respectively. For each measurement $M_i \in \mathcal{S}$, we derive two polynomials $\mathcal{P}_i = \{h_{i1}(x), h_{i2}(x)\}$ defining a variety $\mathcal{V}_i := \{x \in \mathbb{R}^5 : h_{i1}(x) = 0, h_{i2}(x) = 0\}$. Now, we cast the task of autocalibration as Problem 2, for a set $\mathcal{S} = \{\mathcal{P}_i\}_{i=1}^m$ and a threshold ϵ, to estimate ω parameterized by $x \in \mathbb{R}^5$. This problem is solved by using our solution proposed in Sect. 3 for both ω and the largest inlier set ζ, simultaneously. The intrinsics K are then recovered by performing the Cholesky decomposition on ω.

4.2   Modulus Constraints on PaI

Modulus constraints [7] allow us to derive polynomials parameterized by the coordinates of the Plane-at-Infinity (PaI) – the plane supporting the Absolute Conic – with the help of the homography between two images induced by any arbitrary plane. The estimation of the PaI is a necessary condition to upgrade projective reconstructions to affine. Once the upgrade is performed, the task of camera calibration boils down to a linear problem [30]. Such methods fall into the category of stratified autocalibration.

In this work, we assume that all the projection matrices M_i are registered to a common coordinate frame. In practice, this can be achieved in several ways: by joint projective factorization [31, 32]; by registering projection matrices using projective homographies [30]; or simply by choosing a fixed image as the reference for all others. Without loss of generality, we assume that M_i are obtained using the latter. Under such circumstances, there exists a unique Plane-at-Infinity, say Π_∞, common to all the views [5]. Let $\Pi_\infty = (\pi_\infty^\mathsf{T}, 1)^\mathsf{T} \in \mathbb{R}^4$ be the coordinate vector of Π_∞. For $M_i = [H_i|e_i]$, the homography between pairs $\mathcal{I}_i$ and $\mathcal{I}'_i$ via Π_∞ can be expressed as,

$$H_{i\infty} = H_i - e_i \pi_\infty^\mathsf{T}. \tag{11}$$

Given M_i, the theory of Modulus constraints relies on the fact that the homography $H_{i\infty}$ must have all three eigenvalues with the same moduli, to recover the unknown π_∞. In [7], *Pollefeys et Van Gool* have shown that the moduli constraint can indeed be expressed as quartic polynomials, parameterize by $\pi_\infty \in \mathbb{R}^3$. At this point, we borrow four linear functions $l_0(\pi_\infty), \ldots, l_3(\pi_\infty)$, from [7] (please, refer [7] for their definitions). Now, the modulus constraints are of the form:

$$h_i(\pi_\infty) = l_{i3}(\pi_\infty)(l_{i1}(\pi_\infty))^3 - l_{i0}(\pi_\infty)(l_{i2}(\pi_\infty))^3. \tag{12}$$

While searching for Π_∞, we make use of projection matrices $\mathcal{S} = \{\mathsf{M}_i\}_{i=1}^m$ as measurements, such that the sought solution maximizes the consensus within $\mathcal{S}$. For each $\mathsf{M}_i \in \mathcal{S}$, we derive a polynomial $\mathcal{P}_i = \{h_i(\pi_\infty)\}$ defining a variety $\mathcal{V}_i := \{\pi_\infty \in \mathbb{R}^3 : h_i(\pi_\infty) = 0\}$. Now, we cast the task of finding Π_∞ as Problem 2, for a set $\mathcal{S} = \{\mathcal{P}_i\}_{i=1}^m$ and a threshold ϵ, to estimate $\pi_\infty \in \mathbb{R}^3$. This problem can be solved by using our solution of Sect. 3 for both π_∞ and the largest inlier set ζ, simultaneously.

5   Discussion

Although we focus on the autocalibration for cameras with constant intrinsics, the solution proposed for estimating PaI does not require this assumption. Note that, a projective reconstruction obtained from cameras with different intrinsics still share a common PaI. Therefore, once the PaI is estimated, one may exploit this information for calibrating cameras with variable focal lengths similar to [33].

The main concern of this paper is finding good initial bounds on the sought parameters (see Algorithm 3). Fortunately, in the context of camera calibration, one can safely assume that a vague guess on camera intrinsics can be known, except for close to affine cameras. For affine (or close to affine) cameras, the task of autocalibration is considered to be rather a simpler problem [34], hence can be attempted accordingly.

In our experiments, we consider that the focal length lies within $[1\ 10]$ interval relative to the image size, aspect ratio lies between 0.7-1.25, principal points lie around image center within a radius of $(\frac{1}{4})^{th}$ of the image size, and the skew is close to zero. With these assumptions, we derive bounds on DAIC using the interval analysis arithmetics [35]. While deriving the bounds on PaI, we assume that the distance of PaI is smaller than 5 units from the reference camera frame, in the normalized projective reconstruction. The projective reconstruction is obtained by normalizing the reference image to 1×1. Note that, the coordinate of PaI, π_∞ is the product of its distance d and the normal $\hat{n}$. Since $\|\hat{n}\| = 1$, the coordinates π_∞ can also be bounded.

6   Experiments

We conducted several experiments with nine different real datasets to test the robustness and optimality of our method. These datasets are, Fountain [36], Herz-Jesu [36], Dino4983 [37], DinoColmap [37], House [37], Courtyard [38], CherubColmap [39], Vercingetorix [32], and Watertower [32]. All reported experiments were conducted on real datasets. The projective reconstruction required for our method was obtained using [40] for Fountain and Herz-Jesu, after piece-wise factorization and registration with projective homography. The projective reconstructions for all other datasets were obtained using [32]. For the experiments with quantitative evaluations, only the outliers were synthetically generated. These synthetic outliers were added either on Fountain or Herz-jesu dataset, by arbitrarily selecting them for any set of experiments, since these two are also the datasets with known ground truth DIAC and PaI. Our algorithm is implemented in MATLAB2015a and all the optimization problems are solved using MOSEK [41]. All experiments were carried out on a 16 GB RAM Pentium i7/3.40 GHz.

To evaluate the calibration quality, five different error measurement metrics were defined: the RMS error on 3D reconstruction, errors in focal length Δf, principal point Δuv, skew Δs and PaI $\Delta \pi_\infty$, similarly as in [12] . The 3D reconstruction error is computed on the normalized pointsets (with mean radius of $\sqrt{3}$), error for camera intrinsics are computed for 1×1 image size, and error for PaI is computed for its normal vector.

6.1 Simplified Kruppa's Equations

To observe the behavior of proposed algorithm with simplified Kruppa's equations, we generated multiple image pairs with dominating number of outliers. Then, we tracked the number of pessimistic and optimistic inliers for increasing BnB iterations, along with the number of nodes remaining to be processed and the volume of the parameter space yet to be explored. For almost all our experiments, it has been observed that the algorithm converges before 1000 iteration, while limiting itself to a reasonable number of nodes across search iterations (showing only a small memory usage). One of these observations is shown in Fig. 1. Note from Fig. 1(left) that our outlier detection method of Algorithm 2 comes into play, to help punning, soon after the algorithm starts. Our algorithm also finds the optimal solution only in a few iterations, while most of the search is performed to obtain the optimality certificate. In Fig. 1(middle), we show the number of nodes and search volume remaining for the same experiment.

We report the computation time of our method in Fig. 1(right), for two different sets of inlier pairs with increasing percentage of outliers. Note that these experiments are conducted with as high as 90% of outliers. Even in such extreme cases, our algorithm successfully results the optimal solution, with optimality

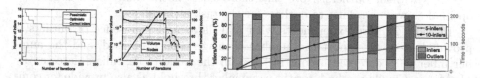

Fig. 1. Convergence graph (left) and remaining nodes/volume during BnB search (middle). Time taken for increasing % outliers with two different cases of fixed inliers (right). Experiments with Kruppa's equations.

certificate, within a reasonable amount of time. Here, 10 inliers with 90% outliers refers to the total of 100 image pairs.

In Fig. 2, we report the results obtained by our method and a randomly started local method for 100 independent experiments. We use the well known Mendonça-Cipolla [14] for local method as it was designed to be robust towards noise. In each experiment, the Mendonça-Cipolla method was started at randomly picked camera intrinsics lying within the initial intervals. The results show that, unlike Mendonça-Cipolla which generates a very low number of inliers and provides very large 3D errors, our method consistently detects the same number of inliers with the same 3D error.

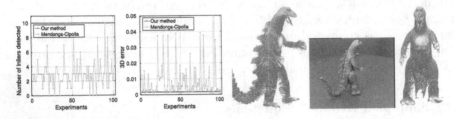

Fig. 2. Left-middle: global vs. local method for 100 experiments with 10 inliers and 20 outliers. Number of detected inliers (left) and 3D reconstruction error (middle). Right: reconstruction of Dino, obtained using our estimated camera intrinsics. One of the input images with two views of the reconstruction. Experiments with Kruppa's equations.

We further compared the results of our method against that of one local and three global methods for autocalibration: a local and practical method from [8], a DAQ rank-3 constrained direct method from [11], a LMI-based direct method from [12] and a stratified method from [9]. All of these methods assume that the input projective reconstruction is free of outliers. Therefore, we conducted experiments with datasets with no outliers. In Table 1, we provide the quantitative results for calibration accuracy, by computing errors in intrinsics and PaI. For the DIAC obtained from Kruppa's equations, we extract camera intrinsics using Cholesky decomposition, whereas the PaI is obtained linearly using the DAQ projection equation. Table 1 shows that our method is very competitive in terms of accuracy and generally faster in terms of speed when compared to global methods without outliers. Note that there exists no method which is globally optimal as well as robust to outliers for the task at hand.

In Table 2, more experiments with real data in the presence of outliers is provided. Here, we report the number of image pairs processed, and the number inlier pairs detected by our method. In the same table, inliers detected by Mendonça-Cipolla method, for the same inlier threshold, is also provide for comparison, along with two other methods discussed later in this paper. For all four methods, their run time is also reported. Although the compared methods of Table 2 are faster, they are only locally optimal and thus do not always provide the globally optimal solutions. As expected, our method consistently detects more (or equal) number of inliers than Mendonça-Cipolla method. To qualitatively evaluate our calibration results, we provided our estimated intrinsics to the calibrated reconstruction framework of [42], whose dense reconstruction is shown in Fig. 2(right). The reconstructions for two more datasets obtained via projective-to-metric upgrade using our method are shown in Fig. 3. Figures 2 and 3 demonstrate that our estimated inlier set provides meaningful metric reconstruction. This also ensures that the obtained inliers are indeed true inliers. Unfortunately, 3D models for all dataset of Table 2 are not available to compute the 3D RMS error.

Table 1. Our method vs. one local [8] and three global [9,11,12] autocalibration methods. Two real datasets without outliers. Outlier-free data is necessary for [8,9,11,12].

Dataset	Method	Δf	Δuv	Δs	$\Delta \pi_\infty$	Time (s)	3D err
Fountain (11-views)	Practical [8]	0.0117	0.0149	0.0037	0.0080	0.36	0.0003
	Stratified [9]	0.0777	0.0969	0.0125	0.0455	388.24	0.0083
	Rank-3 Direct [11]	0.0100	0.0147	0.0044	0.0075	5.75	0.0003
	LMI Direct [12]	0.0506	0.0269	0.0024	0.0199	156.88	0.0018
	Kruppa (ours)	2.93e−05	0.0069	3.23e−05	0.0009	1.88	0.0001
	Modulus (ours)	0.0368	0.0085	0.0033	0.0033	13.71	0.0012
Herz-jesu (8-views)	Practical [8]	0.0017	0.0113	0.0068	0.0006	0.36	0.0004
	Stratified [9]	0.7231	0.4462	0.3232	0.0960	380.72	0.0432
	Rank-3 Direct [11]	0.0026	0.0096	0.0069	0.0008	16.54	0.0003
	LMI Direct [12]	0.0138	0.0086	0.005	0.005	115.61	0.0008
	Kruppa (ours)	4.46e−05	0.0069	3.40e−05	0.0003	0.53	0.0004
	Modulus (ours)	0.0103	0.0070	0.0047	0.0009	52.12	0.0003

Fig. 3. Sample image and two views of 3D reconstruction of Cherubim (left) and Vercingetorix (right) obtained via projective-to-metric upgrade using our method with Kruppa's equations.

6.2 Modulus Constraints

Similar to the case of Kruppa's equations, we also monitored the optimistic/pessimistic inliers as well as the remaining volume/node with the evolution of the BnB search. As expected, we observed that the Algorithm 2 starts rejecting outliers efficiently only after a few iterations of BnB. This is attributed to the weaker initial bounds on PaI, and the higher degree of polynomials of Modulus constraints. For an example experiment, the convergence graph and node/volume information is shown in Fig. 4.

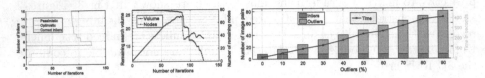

Fig. 4. Convergence graph (left) and remaining nodes/volume during BnB search (middle). Time taken for increasing % of outliers and fixed inliers (right). Our method with Modulus constraints.

In Fig. 4, we also show the time taken for our method for Modulus constraints, for a fixed number of inlier image pairs and increasing number of outliers. To test the robustness, we varied the number of outliers up to 90% and compared the results against an in-house RANSAC method. Every iteration of the RANSAC, (i) randomly generates a PaI hypothesis within the initial interval of consideration; (ii) selects best three modulus constraint polynomials for given hypothesis (based on their residuals) and locally refines the hypothesis similarly for (8); (iii) collects the consensus among all the polynomials using the refined hypothesis. The maximum number of iterations for RANSAC is chosen such that it takes about the same time as our method. Figure 5 (left) shows that our method consistently detects 8 inliers for all the experiments, while RANSAC fails to detect number of correct inliers, starting from 40% of outliers. The numbers of inliers reported are true-positive inliers. Our method does not detect any false positive inlier. In rest of the plots of Fig. 5, we show errors in focal length (second from left), PaI (third from left), and 3D reconstruction (right). Using the estimated PaI, we linearly solve the DAQ projection equation for DIAC, under the assumption of constant intrinsics. If the obtained DIAC is far from being a positive definite matrix, the intrinsics cannot be recovered. We consider such cases as calibration failure. The Missing entries for RANSAC in Fig. 5 refer to such failures.

Our results for Modulus constraints are also compared to a direct method from [12] and a stratified method from [9], in Table 1 alongside with our results for Kruppa's equations. Note that both of our methods perform better than [12] and [9], in terms of time as well as accuracy. In Table 2, time and inliers detected by our method with Modulus constraints are provided. In the same table, inliers detected by RANSAC, for the same inlier threshold, is also provide for comparison.

From our experiments, we observed that the reconstruction obtained form [32] preserves a unique PaI valid for most of the views. However, the projection matrices do not really respect the constraint of constant intrinsics. This

Table 2. Real data with outliers. Total number of image pairs processed (N), number of inliers detected, and time take for our method with Kruppa's equations, Mendonça-Cipolla [14], our method with Modulus constraints, and a in-house RANSAC on Modulus constraints.

Dataset	N	Kruppa (ours)		Mendonça-Cipolla		Modulus (ours)		Modulus-RANSAC	
		Inliers	Time (s)	Inliers	Time (s)	Inliers	Time (s)	Inliers	Time (s)
CherubColmap	20	9	28.76	3	0.49	20	118.51	7	76.92
Courtyard	43	11	81.51	11	0.36	43	29.06	43	0.92
Dino4983	11	8	104.55	6	1.02	11	65.98	11	3.09
DinoColmap	11	8	135.65	4	0.32	11	21.97	11	3.33
House	8	7	22.73	2	0.35	8	387.59	8	7.61
Vercingetorix	22	11	50.02	7	0.79	21	262.43	18	75.34
Watertower	36	22	70.81	22	0.28	36	342.44	36	25.80

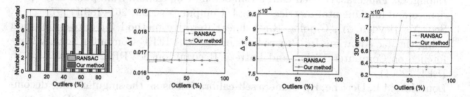

Fig. 5. Global vs. RANSAC with outliers. Left to right: number of detected inliers; focal length error; plane-at-infinity error; 3D reconstruction error. Experiments with Modulus constraints.

is not really surprising since cameras are allowed (or even expected) to have different intrinsics, during reconstruction. This makes the camera calibration with constant intrinsics assumption a difficult problem, since many polynomials derived from Kruppa's equations are not satisfied anymore. This can be observed in Table 2, from the difference between detected inliers for Kruppa and Modulus methods.

Our experiments highlight the robustness of our method, which is also the main focus of this paper. The scaling of our method with image pairs and outliers can be seen in Figs. 1 and 4. Since the algorithm explores the parameters space, the performance depends upon dimensionality of the problem, number of measurements, outlier ratio, and the initial bound gap of the parameters. Therefore, a trade-off between them is necessary for a better scaling.

7   Conclusion

In this paper, we presented a generic framework of consensus maximization for polynomials. The proposed framework was applied to obtain the consensus among polynomials parameterized by DIAC or PaI, which appear during camera autocalibration. We showed with several experiments that our algorithm can calibrate cameras even when an overwhelmingly high number of camera motions are incorrectly estimated. Moreover, the proposed method not only detects the inlier/outlier camera motions correctly, but also results accurate estimation of DIAC and PaI, when searched with the polynomials derived from Kruppa's equations or Modulus constraints. Our framework has potential to be applied in may other Computer Vision problems.

Acknowledgements. This research was supported by the Swiss Commission for Technology and Innovation under the CTI project EXASOLVED, Grant No. 26253.1 PFES-ES.

References

1. Maybank, S.J., Faugeras, O.D.: A theory of self-calibration of a moving camera. Int. J. Comput. Vis. **8**(2), 123–151 (1992)
2. Luong, Q., Faugeras, D.: Self-calibration of a moving camera from point correspondences and fundamental matrices. Int. J. Comput. Vis. **22**, 261–289 (1997)
3. Seo, Y., Heyden, A., Cipolla, R.: A linear iterative method for auto-calibration using the dac equation. In: Proceedings of the 2001 IEEE Computer Society Conference on Computer Vision and Pattern Recognition, CVPR 2001, vol. 1, p. I. IEEE (2001)
4. Lourakis, M.I., Deriche, R.: Camera self-calibration using the singular value decomposition of the fundamental matrix: from point correspondences to 3D measurements. Ph.D. thesis, INRIA (1999)
5. Hartley, R.I., Hayman, E., de Agapito, L., Reid, I.: Camera calibration and the search for infinity. In: 1999 Proceedings of the Seventh IEEE International Conference on Computer Vision, vol. 1, pp. 510–517. IEEE (1999)
6. Nistér, D.: Untwisting a projective reconstruction. Int. J. Comput. Vis. **60**(2), 165–183 (2004)
7. Pollefeys, M., Van Gool, L.: Stratified self-calibration with the modulus constraint. IEEE Trans. Pattern Anal. Mach. Intell. **21**(8), 707–724 (1999)
8. Gherardi, R., Fusiello, A.: Practical autocalibration. In: Daniilidis, K., Maragos, P., Paragios, N. (eds.) ECCV 2010. LNCS, vol. 6311, pp. 790–801. Springer, Heidelberg (2010). https://doi.org/10.1007/978-3-642-15549-9_57
9. Chandraker, M., Agarwal, S., Kriegman, D., Belongie, S.: Globally optimal affine and metric upgrades in stratified autocalibration. In: 2007 IEEE 11th International Conference on Computer Vision, ICCV 2007, pp. 1–8. IEEE (2007)
10. Triggs, B.: Autocalibration and the absolute quadric. In: 1997 Proceedings of IEEE Computer Society Conference on Computer Vision and Pattern Recognition, pp. 609–614. IEEE (1997)
11. Chandraker, M., Agarwal, S., Kahl, F., Nistér, D., Kriegman, D.: Autocalibration via rank-constrained estimation of the absolute quadric. In: 2007 IEEE Conference on Computer Vision and Pattern Recognition, CVPR 2007, pp. 1–8. IEEE (2007)
12. Habed, A., Pani Paudel, D., Demonceaux, C., Fofi, D.: Efficient pruning LMI conditions for branch-and-prune rank and chirality-constrained estimation of the dual absolute quadric. In: Proceedings of the IEEE Conference on Computer Vision and Pattern Recognition, pp. 493–500 (2014)
13. Fusiello, A., Benedetti, A., Farenzena, M., Busti, A.: Globally convergent autocalibration using interval analysis. IEEE Trans. Pattern Anal. Mach. Intell. **26**(12), 1633–1638 (2004)

14. Mendonça, P.R., Cipolla, R.: A simple technique for self-calibration. In: 1999 IEEE Computer Society Conference on Computer Vision and Pattern Recognition, vol. 1, pp. 500–505. IEEE (1999)
15. Heikkila, J.: Using sparse elimination for solving minimal problems in computer vision. In: Proceedings of the IEEE Conference on Computer Vision and Pattern Recognition, pp. 76–84 (2017)
16. Barath, D., Toth, T., Hajder, L.: A minimal solution for two-view focal-length estimation using two affine correspondences (2017)
17. Sturm, P.: On focal length calibration from two views. In: Proceedings of the 2001 IEEE Computer Society Conference on Computer Vision and Pattern Recognition, CVPR 2001, vol. 2, p. II. IEEE (2001)
18. Heyden, A., Åkström, K.: Minimal conditions on intrinsic parameters for Euclidean reconstruction. In: Chin, R., Pong, T.-C. (eds.) ACCV 1998. LNCS, vol. 1352, pp. 169–176. Springer, Heidelberg (1997). https://doi.org/10.1007/3-540-63931-4_212
19. Verschelde, J.: Algorithm 795: PHCpack: a general-purpose solver for polynomial systems by homotopy continuation. ACM Trans. Math. Softw. (TOMS) **25**(2), 251–276 (1999)
20. Lasserre, J.B.: Global optimization with polynomials and the problem of moments. SIAM J. Optim. **11**(3), 796–817 (2001)
21. Parrilo, P.A.: Structured semidefinite programs and semialgebraic geometry methods in robustness and optimization. Ph.D. thesis, California Institute of Technology (2000)
22. Schweighofer, G., Pinz, A.: Globally optimal O(n) solution to the PnP problem for general camera models. In: BMVC, pp. 1–10 (2008)
23. Gurdjos, P., Bartoli, A., Sturm, P.: Is dual linear self-calibration artificially ambiguous? In: 2009 IEEE 12th International Conference on Computer Vision, pp. 88–95. IEEE (2009)
24. Campbell, D., et al.: Globally-optimal inlier set maximisation for simultaneous camera pose and feature correspondence. In: Proceedings of the IEEE International Conference on Computer Vision (2017)
25. Pani Paudel, D., Habed, A., Demonceaux, C., Vasseur, P.: Robust and optimal sum-of-squares-based point-to-plane registration of image sets and structured scenes. In: Proceedings of the IEEE International Conference on Computer Vision, pp. 2048–2056 (2015)
26. Parrilo, P.A.: Semidefinite programming relaxations for semialgebraic problems. Math. Program. **96**(2), 293–320 (2003)
27. Cifuentes, D., Parrilo, P.A.: Sampling algebraic varieties for sum of squares programs. arXiv preprint arXiv:1511.06751 (2015)
28. Bates, D.J., Hauenstein, J.D., Sommese, A.J., Wampler, C.W.: Bertini: software for numerical algebraic geometry. Available at bertini.nd.edu with permanent https://doi.org/10.7274/R0H41PB5
29. Verschelde, J.: PHCpack: a general-purpose solver for polynomial systems by homotopy continuation (1997, preprint)
30. Hartley, R., Zisserman, A.: Multiple View Geometry in Computer Vision. Cambridge University Press, Cambridge (2003)
31. Sturm, P., Triggs, B.: A factorization based algorithm for multi-image projective structure and motion. In: Buxton, B., Cipolla, R. (eds.) ECCV 1996. LNCS, vol. 1065, pp. 709–720. Springer, Heidelberg (1996). https://doi.org/10.1007/3-540-61123-1_183

32. Magerand, L., Del Bue, A.: Practical projective structure from motion (P2SFM). In: 2017 Proceedings of IEEE International Conference on Computer Vision, pp. 39–47 (2017)

33. Pollefeys, M., Van Gool, L., Proesmans, M.: Euclidean 3D reconstruction from image sequences with variable focal lengths. In: Buxton, B., Cipolla, R. (eds.) ECCV 1996. LNCS, vol. 1064, pp. 31–42. Springer, Heidelberg (1996). https://doi.org/10.1007/BFb0015521

34. Quan, L.: Self-calibration of an affine camera from multiple views. Int. J. Comput. Vis. **19**(1), 93–105 (1996)

35. Alefeld, G., Mayer, G.: Interval analysis: theory and applications. J. Comput. Appl. Math. **121**(1), 421–464 (2000)

36. Strecha, C., von Hansen, W., Van Gool, L., Fua, P., Thoennessen, U.: On benchmarking camera calibration and multi-view stereo for high resolution imagery. In: IEEE Conference on Computer Vision and Pattern Recognition (CVPR), pp. 1–8 (2008)

37. Multi-view and oxford colleges building reconstruction (2017). http://www.robots.ox.ac.uk/~vgg/data/data-mview.html

38. Olsson, C., Enqvist, O.: Stable structure from motion for unordered image collections. In: Heyden, A., Kahl, F. (eds.) SCIA 2011. LNCS, vol. 6688, pp. 524–535. Springer, Heidelberg (2011). https://doi.org/10.1007/978-3-642-21227-7_49

39. 3DFLOW SRL: 3DF zephyr reconstruction showcase (2017). http://www.3dflow.net/

40. Oliensis, J., Hartley, R.: Iterative extensions of the sturm/triggs algorithm: convergence and nonconvergence. IEEE Trans. Pattern Anal. Mach. Intell. **29**(12), 2217–2233 (2007)

41. MOSEK ApS: The mosek optimization toolbox for matlab manual, version 8.0. MOSEK ApS, Denmark (2015)

42. Agisoft photoscan (2017). http://www.agisoft.com/

Attribute-Guided Face Generation Using Conditional CycleGAN

Yongyi Lu[1]([✉])[iD], Yu-Wing Tai[2][iD], and Chi-Keung Tang[1][iD]

[1] The Hong Kong University of Science and Technology, Hong Kong, China
{yluaw,cktang}@cse.ust.hk
[2] Tencent Youtu, Shenzhen, China
yuwingtai@tencent.com

Abstract. We are interested in attribute-guided face generation: given a low-res face input image, an attribute vector that can be extracted from a high-res image (attribute image), our new method generates a high-res face image for the low-res input that satisfies the given attributes. To address this problem, we condition the CycleGAN and propose conditional CycleGAN, which is designed to (1) handle unpaired training data because the training low/high-res and high-res attribute images may not necessarily align with each other, and to (2) allow easy control of the appearance of the generated face via the input attributes. We demonstrate high-quality results on the *attribute-guided conditional CycleGAN*, which can synthesize realistic face images with appearance easily controlled by user-supplied attributes (e.g., gender, makeup, hair color, eyeglasses). Using the attribute image as identity to produce the corresponding conditional vector and by incorporating a face verification network, the attribute-guided network becomes the *identity-guided conditional CycleGAN* which produces high-quality and interesting results on identity transfer. We demonstrate three applications on identity-guided conditional CycleGAN: identity-preserving face superresolution, face swapping, and frontal face generation, which consistently show the advantage of our new method.

Keywords: Face generation · Attribute · GAN

1 Introduction

This paper proposes a practical approach, *attribute-guided face generation*, for natural face image generation where facial appearance can be easily controlled by user-supplied attributes. Figure 1 shows that by simply providing a high-res image of Ivanka Trump, our face superresolution result preserves her identity which is not necessarily guaranteed by conventional face superresolution (Fig. 1: top row). When the input attribute/identity image is a different person, our method transfers the man's identity to the high-res result, where the low-res input is originally downsampled from a woman's face (Fig. 1: bottom row).

This work was partially done when Yongyi Lu was an intern at Tencent Youtu.

© Springer Nature Switzerland AG 2018
V. Ferrari et al. (Eds.): ECCV 2018, LNCS 11216, pp. 293–308, 2018.
https://doi.org/10.1007/978-3-030-01258-8_18

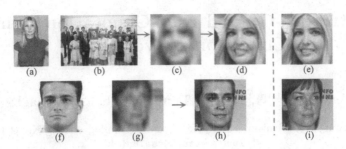

Fig. 1. Identity-guided face generation. Top: identity-preserving face super-resolution where (a) is the identity image; (b) input photo; (c) image crop from (b) in low resolution; (d) our generated high-res result; (e) ground truth image. Bottom: face transfer, where (f) is the identity image; (g) input low-res image of another person provides overall shape constraint; (h) our generated high-res result where the man's identity is transferred. To produce the low-res input (g) we down-sample from (i), which is a woman's face.

We propose to address our face generation problem using conditional Cycle-GAN. The original unconditional CycleGAN [23], where enforcing cycle consistency has demonstrated state-of-the-art results in photographic image synthesis, was designed to handle unpaired training data. Relaxing the requirement of paired training data is particularly suitable in our case because the training low/high-res and high-res attribute images do not need to align with each other. By enforcing cycle consistency, we are able to learn a bijective mapping, or one-to-one correspondence with unpaired data from the same/different domains. By simply altering the attribute condition, our approach can be directly applied to generate high-quality face images that simultaneously preserve the constraints given in the low-res input while transferring facial features (e.g., gender, hair color, emotion, sun-glasses) prescribed by input face attributes.

Founded on CycleGAN, we present significant results on both attribute-guided and identity-guided face generation, which we believe is important and timely. Technically, our contribution consists of the new conditional CycleGAN to guide the single-image super-resolution process via the embedding of complex attributes for generating images with high level of photo-realism:

First, in our *attribute-guided conditional CycleGAN*, the adversarial loss is modified to include a conditional feature vector as part of the input to the generator and intra layer to the discriminator as well. Using the trained network we demonstrate impressive results including gender change, transfer of hair color and facial emotion.

Second, in our *identity-guided conditional CycleGAN*, we incorporate a face verification network to produce the conditional vector, and define the proposed identity loss in an auxiliary discriminator for preserving facial identity. Using the trained network, we demonstrate realistic results on identity transfer which are robust to pose variations and partial occlusion. We demonstrate three applications of identity-guided conditional CycleGAN: identity-preserving face superresolution, face swapping, and frontal face generation.

2   Related Work

Recent state-of-the-art image generation techniques have leveraged the deep convolutional neural networks (CNNs). For example, in single-image superresolution (SISR), a deep recursive CNN for SISR was proposed in [8]. Learning upscaling filters have improved accuracy and speed [3,16,17]. A deep CNN approach was proposed in [2] using bicubic interpolation. The ESPCN [16] performs SR by replacing the deconvolution layer in lieu of upscaling layer. However, many existing CNN-based networks still generate blurry images. The SRGAN [10] uses the Euclidean distance between the feature maps extracted from the VGGNet to replace the MSE loss which cannot preserve texture details. The SRGAN has improved the perceptual quality of generated SR images. A deep residual network (ResNet) was proposed in [10] that produces good results for upscaling factors up to 4. In [7] both the perceptual/feature loss and pixel loss are used in training SISR.

Existing GANs [1,4,21] have generated state-of-the-art results for automatic image generation. The key of their success lies in the adversarial loss which forces the generated images to be indistinguishable from real images. This is achieved by two competing neural networks, the generator and the discriminator. In particular, the DCGAN [14] incorporates deep convolutional neural networks into GANs, and has generated some of the most impressive realistic images to date. GANs are however notoriously difficult to train: GANs are formulated as a minimax "game" between two networks. In practice, it is hard to keep the generator and discriminator in balance, where the optimization can oscillate between solutions which may easily cause the generator to collapse. Among different techniques, the conditional GAN [6] addresses this problem by enforcing forward-backward consistency, which has emerged to be one of the most effective ways to train GAN.

Forward-backward consistency has been enforced in computer vision algorithms such as image registration, shape matching, co-segmentation, to name a few. In the realm of image generation using deep learning, using unpaired training data, the CycleGAN [23] was proposed to learn image-to-image translation from a source domain X to a target domain Y. In addition to the standard GAN loss respectively for X and Y, a pair of cycle consistency losses (forward and backward) was formulated using L1 reconstruction loss. Similar ideas can also be found in [9,20]. For forward cycle consistency, given $x \in X$ the image translation cycle should reproduce x. Backward cycle consistency is similar. In this paper, we propose conditional CycleGAN for face image generation so that the image generation process can preserve (or transfer) facial identity, where the results can be controlled by various input attributes. Preserving facial identity has also been explored in synthesizing the corresponding frontal face image from a single side-view face image [5], where the identity preserving loss was defined based on the activations of the last two layers of the Light CNN [19]. In multi-view image generation from a single view [22], a condition image (e.g. frontal view) was used to constrain the generated multiple views in their coarse-to-fine framework. However, facial identity was not explicitly preserved in their results and thus many of the generated faces look smeared, although as the first generated results of multiple views from single images, the pertinent results already look quite impressive.

While our conditional CycleGAN is an image-to-image translation framework, [13] factorizes an input image into a latent representation z and conditional information y using their respective trained encoders. By changing y into y', the generator network then combines the same z and new y' to generate an image that satisfies the new constraints encoded in y'. We are inspired by their best conditional positioning, that is, where y' should be concatenated among all of the convolutional layers. For SISR, in addition, z should represent the embedding for a (unconstrained) high-res image, where the generator can combine with the identity feature y to generate the super-resolved result. In [11] the authors proposed to learn the dense correspondence between a pair of input source and reference, so that visual attributes can be swapped or transferred between them. In our identity-guided conditional CycleGAN, the input reference is encoded as a conditional identity feature so that the input source can be transformed to target identity even though they do not have perceptually similar structure.

3   Conditional CycleGAN

3.1   CycleGAN

A Generative Adversarial Network [4] (GAN) consists of two neural networks, a generator $G_{X \to Y}$ and a discriminator D_Y, which are iteratively trained in a two-player minimax game manner. The adversarial loss $\mathcal{L}(G_{X \to Y}, D_Y)$ is defined as

$$
\mathcal{L}(G_{X \to Y}, D_Y) = \min_{\Theta_g} \max_{\Theta_d} \big\{ \mathbb{E}_y[\log D_Y(y)] \\
+ \mathbb{E}_x[\log(1 - D_Y(G_{X \to Y}(x)))] \big\}
\tag{1}
$$

where Θ_g and Θ_d are respectively the parameters of the generator $G_{X \to Y}$ and discriminator D_Y, and $x \in X$ and $y \in Y$ denotes the *unpaired* training data in source and target domain respectively. $\mathcal{L}(G_{Y \to X}, D_X)$ is analogously defined.

In CycleGAN, X and Y are two different image representations, and the CycleGAN learns the translation $X \to Y$ and $Y \to X$ simultaneously. Different from "pix2pix" [6], training data in CycleGAN is unpaired. Thus, they introduce Cycle Consistency to enforce forward-backward consistency which can be considered as "pseudo" pairs of training data. With the Cycle Consistency, the loss function of CycleGAN is defined as:

$$
\mathcal{L}(G_{X \to Y}, G_{Y \to X}, D_X, D_Y) = \mathcal{L}(G_{X \to Y}, D_Y) \\
+ \mathcal{L}(G_{Y \to X}, D_X) + \lambda \mathcal{L}_c(G_{X \to Y}, G_{Y \to X})
\tag{2}
$$

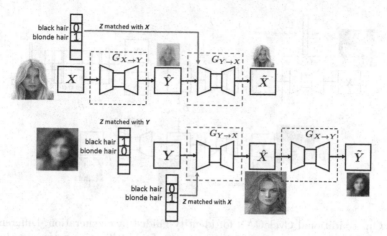

Fig. 2. Our conditional CycleGAN for attribute-guided face generation. In contrast to the original CycleGAN, we embed an additional attribute vector z (e.g., blonde hair) which is associated with the input attribute image X to train a generator $G_{Y \to X}$ as well as the original $G_{X \to Y}$ to generate high-res face image $\hat{X}$ given the low-res input Y and the attribute vector z. Note the discriminators D_X and D_Y are not shown for simplicity.

where

$$
\begin{aligned}
\mathcal{L}_c(G_{X \to Y}, G_{Y \to X}) = &\|G_{Y \to X}(G_{X \to Y}(x)) - x\|_1 \\
+ &\|G_{X \to Y}(G_{Y \to X}(y)) - y\|_1
\end{aligned}
\tag{3}
$$

is the Cycle Consistency Loss. In our implementation, we adopt the network architecture of CycleGAN to train our conditional CycleGAN with the technical contributions described in the next subsections.

3.2 Attribute-Guided Conditional CycleGAN

We are interested in natural face image generation guided by user-supplied facial attributes to control the high-res results. To include conditional constraint into the CycleGAN network, the adversarial loss is modified to include the conditional feature vector z as part of the input of the generator and intra layer to the discriminator as

$$
\begin{aligned}
\mathcal{L}(G_{(X,Z) \to Y}, D_Y) = \min_{\Theta_g} \max_{\Theta_d} \big\{ &\mathbb{E}_{y,z}[\log D_Y(y, z)] \\
+ &\mathbb{E}_{x,z}[\log(1 - D_Y(G_{(X,Z) \to Y}(x, z), z))] \big\}
\end{aligned}
\tag{4}
$$

$\mathcal{L}(G_{(Y,Z) \to X}, D_X)$ is defined analogously.

With the conditional adversarial loss, we modify the CycleGAN network as illustrated in Fig. 2. We follow [13] to pick 18 attributes as our conditional feature vector. Note that in our conditional CycleGAN, the attribute vector is associated with the input high-res face image (i.e., X), instead of the input low-res face image (i.e., Y). In each "pair" of training iteration, the same conditional

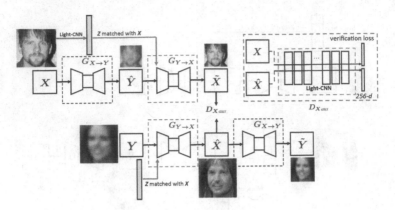

Fig. 3. Our conditional CycleGAN for identity-guided face generation. Different from attribute-guided face generation, we incorporate a face verification network as both the source of conditional vector z and the proposed identity loss in an auxiliary discriminator $D_{X_{aux}}$. The network $D_{X_{aux}}$ is pretrained. Note the discriminators D_X and D_Y are not shown for simplicity.

feature vector is used to generate the high-res face image (i.e., $\hat{X}$). Hence, the generated intermediate high-res face image in the lower branch of Fig. 2 will have different attributes from the corresponding ground truth high-res image. This is on purpose because the conditional discriminator network would enforce the generator network to utilize the information from the conditional feature vector. If the conditional feature vector always receives the correct attributes, the generator network would learn to skip the information in the conditional feature vector, since some of the attributes can be found in the low-res face image.

In our implementation, the conditional feature vector is first replicated to match the size of the input image which is downsampled into a low-res. Hence, for 128×128 low-res input and 18-dimensional feature vector, we have $18 \times 128 \times 128$ homogeneous feature maps after resizing. The resized feature is then concatenated with the *input* layer of the generator network to form a $(18 + 3) \times 128 \times 128$ tensor to propagate the inference of feature vector to the generated images. In the discriminator network, the resized feature (with size $18 \times 64 \times 64$) is concatenated with the *conv1* layer to form a $(18 + 64) \times 64 \times 64$ tensor.

Algorithm 1 describes the the whole training procedure, with the network illustrated in Fig. 2. In order to train the conditional GAN network, only the correct pair of groundtruth high-res face image and the associated attribute feature vector are treated as positive examples. The generated high-res face image with the associated attribute feature vector, and the groundtruth high-res face image with randomly sampled attribute feature vector are both treated as negative examples. In contrast to traditional CycleGAN, we use conditional adversarial loss and conditional cycle consistency loss for updating the networks.

Algorithm 1. Conditional CycleGAN training procedure (using minibatch SGD as illustration)

Input: Minibatch image sets $x \in X$ and $y \in Y$ in target and source domain respectively, attribute vectors z matched with x and mismatching $\hat{z}$, number of training batch iterations S

Output: Update generator and discriminator weights $\theta_{g(X \to Y)}$, $\theta_{g(Y \to X)}$, $\theta_{d(X)}$, $\theta_{d(Y)}$

1: $\theta_{g(X \to Y)}$, $\theta_{g(Y \to X)}$, $\theta_{d(X)}$, $\theta_{d(Y)} \leftarrow$ initialize network parameters
2: **for** $n = 1$ to S **do**
3: $\quad \hat{y} \leftarrow G_{X \to Y}(x)$ {Forward cycle $X \to Y$, fake $\hat{y}$}
4: $\quad \tilde{x} \leftarrow G_{Y \to X}(\hat{y}, z)$ {Forward cycle $Y \to X$, reconstructed $\tilde{x}$}
5: $\quad \hat{x} \leftarrow G_{Y \to X}(y, z)$ {Backward cycle $Y \to X$, fake $\hat{x}$}
6: $\quad \tilde{y} \leftarrow G_{X \to Y}(\hat{x})$ {Backward cycle $X \to Y$, reconstructed $\tilde{y}$}
7: $\quad \rho_r \leftarrow D_Y(y)$ {Compute D_Y, real image}
8: $\quad \rho_f \leftarrow D_Y(\hat{y})$ {Compute D_Y, fake image}
9: $\quad s_r \leftarrow D_X(y, z)$ {Compute D_X, real image, right attribute}
10: $\quad s_f \leftarrow D_X(\hat{y}, z)$ {Compute D_X, fake image, right attribute}
11: $\quad s_w \leftarrow D_X(y, \hat{z})$ {Compute D_X, real image, wrong attribute}
12: $\quad \mathcal{L}_{D_Y} \leftarrow \log(\rho_r) + \log(1 - \rho_f)$ {Compute D_Y loss}
13: $\quad \theta_{d(Y)} \leftarrow \theta_{d(Y)} - \alpha \nabla_{\theta_{d(Y)}} \mathcal{L}_{D_Y}$ {Update on D_Y}
14: $\quad \mathcal{L}_{D_X} \leftarrow \log(s_r) + [\log(1 - s_f) + \log(1 - s_w)]/2$
$\quad$ {Compute D_X loss}
15: $\quad \theta_{d(X)} \leftarrow \theta_{d(X)} - \alpha \nabla_{\theta_{d(X)}} \mathcal{L}_{D_X}$ {Update on D_X}
16: $\quad \mathcal{L}_c = \lambda_1 \|\tilde{x} - x\|_1 + \lambda_2 \|\tilde{y} - y\|_1$ {Cycle consistency loss}
17: $\quad \mathcal{L}_{G_{X \to Y}} \leftarrow \log(\rho_f) + \mathcal{L}_c$ {Compute $G_{X \to Y}$ loss}
18: $\quad \theta_{g(X \to Y)} \leftarrow \theta_{g(X \to Y)} - \alpha \nabla_{\theta_{g(X \to Y)}} \mathcal{L}_{G_{X \to Y}}$
$\quad$ {Update on $G_{X \to Y}$}
19: $\quad \mathcal{L}_{G_{Y \to X}} \leftarrow \log(s_f) + \mathcal{L}_c$ {Compute $G_{Y \to X}$ loss}
20: $\quad \theta_{g(Y \to X)} \leftarrow \theta_{g(Y \to X)} - \alpha \nabla_{\theta_{g(Y \to X)}} \mathcal{L}_{G_{Y \to X}}$
$\quad$ {Update on $G_{Y \to X}$}
21: **end for**

3.3 Identity-Guided Conditional CycleGAN

To demonstrate the efficacy of our conditional CycleGAN guided by control attributes, we specialize it into identity-guided face image generation. We utilize the feature vector from a face verification network, i.e. Light-CNN [19] as the conditional feature vector. The identity feature vector is a 256-D vector from the "Light CNN-9 model". Compared with another state-of-the-art FaceNet [15], which returns a 1792-D face feature vector for each face image, the 256-D representation of light-CNN obtains state-of-the-art results while it has fewer parameters and runs faster. Though among the best single models, the Light-CNN can be easily replaced by other face verification networks like FaceNet or VGG-Face.

Auxiliary Discriminator. In our initial implementation, we follow the same architecture and training strategy to train the conditional CycleGAN for identity-guided face generation. However, we found that the trained network does not generate good results (sample shown in Fig. 12(d)). We believe this is because the discriminator network is trained from scratch, and the trained discriminator network is not as powerful as the light-CNN which was trained from million pairs of face images.

Thus, we add an auxiliary discriminator $D_{X_{aux}}$ on top of the conditional generator $G_{Y \to X}$ in parallel with the discriminator network D_X so there are two discriminators for $G_{Y \to X}$, while the discriminator for $G_{X \to Y}$ remains the same (as illustrated in Fig. 3). Our auxiliary discriminator takes an input of the generated high-res image $\hat{X}$ or the ground truth image X, and outputs a feature embedding. We reuse the pretrained Light-CNN model for our auxiliary discriminator, the activation of the second last layer: the 256-D vector same as our conditional vector Z.

Based on the output of the auxiliary discriminator, we define an identity loss to better guide the learning of the generator. Here we use the L1 loss of the output 256-D vectors as our identity loss. The verification errors from the auxiliary discriminator is back propagated concurrently with the errors from the discriminator network. With the face verification loss, we are able to generate high quality high-res face images matching the identity given by the conditional feature vector. As shown in the running example in Fig. 3, the lady's face is changed to a man's face whose identify is given by the light-CNN feature.

4   Experiments

We use two image datasets, MNIST (for sanity check) and CelebA [12] (for face image generation) to evaluate our method. The MNIST is a digit dataset of 60,000 training and 10,000 testing images. Each image is a 28×28 black and white digit image with the class label from 0 to 9. The CelebA is a face dataset of 202,599 face images, with 40 different attribute labels where each label is a binary value. We use the aligned and cropped version, with $182\,K$ images for training and $20\,K$ for testing. To generate low-res images, we downsampled the images in both datasets by a factor of 8, and we separate the images such that the high-res and low-res training images are non-overlapping.

4.1   MNIST

We first evaluate the performance of our method on MNIST dataset. The conditional feature vector is the class label of digits. As shown in Fig. 4, our method can generate high-res digit images from the low-res inputs. Note that the generated high-res digit follows the given class label when there is conflict between the low-res image and feature vector. This is desirable, since the conditional constraint consumes large weights during the training. This sanity check also verifies that we can impose conditional constraint into the CycleGAN network.

In addition to the label changes based on the high-res identity inputs, we observe that the generated high-res images inherit the appearance in the low-res inputs such as the orientation and thickness. For the '8' example in Fig. 4 the outputs share the same slanting orientation with the low-res '8' which is tilted to

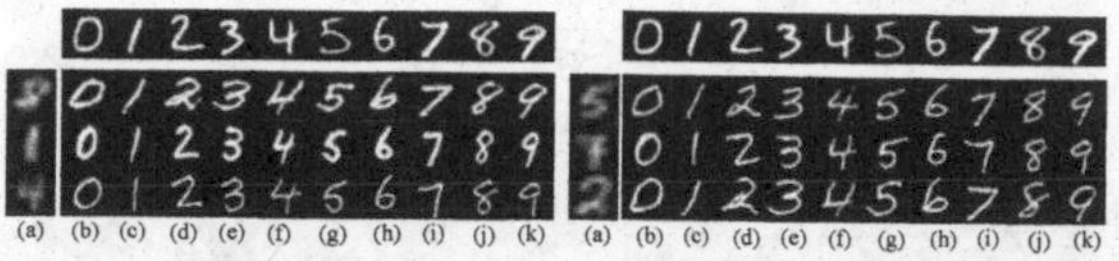

Fig. 4. From the low-res digit images (a), we can generate high-res digit images (b) to (k) subject to the conditional constrain from the digit class label in the first row.

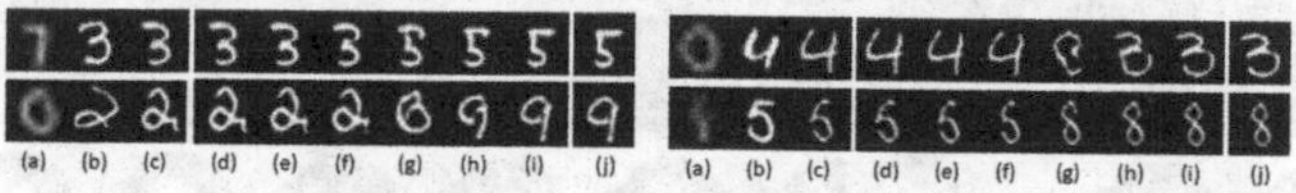

Fig. 5. Interpolation results of digits. Given the low-res inputs in (a), we randomly sample two digits (b) and (j). (c) is the generated results from (a) conditioned on the attribute of (b). Corresponding results of interpolating between attributes of (b) and (j) are shown in (d) to (i). We interpolate between the binary vectors of the digits.

the right. In the next row the outputs adopt the thickness of the input, that is, the relatively thick stroke presented by the low-res '1'. This is a good indicator of the ability of our trained generator: freedom in changing labels based on the high-res images presented as identity attribute, while preserving the essential appearance feature presented by the low-res inputs.

Apart from generating high-res digit images from the low-res inputs, we also perform linear interpolation between two high-res images (as identity features) to show our model is able to learn the digit representation. Specifically, we interpolate between the respective binary vectors of the two digits. Sample results are shown in Fig. 5.

4.2 Attribute-Guided Face Generation

Figure 6 shows sample results for attribute guided face generation. Recall the condition is encoded as a 18-D vector. The 10 results shown in the figure are generated with one attribute label flipped in their corresponding condition vector in conditional CycleGAN. Our generated results conditioned on attributes such as BANGS, BLOND_HAIR, BUSHY_EYEBROWS, GENDER, PALE_SKIN are quite convincing.

Comparison with Conditional GAN. We first compare with conditional GAN framework [13] under the attribute-guided face generation framework. Visualizations are shown in Fig. 7. Generally, our method can generate much better images compared to the competitor, e.g., our methods successfully removes the eyeglasses, as well as generates the right color of hairs. Note that [13] generates different persons while ours are faithful to the inputs.

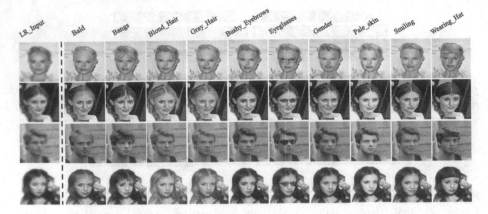

Fig. 6. Attribute-guided face generation. We flip one attribute label for each generated high-res face images, given the low-res face inputs. The 10 labels are: Bald, Bangs, Blond_Hair, Gray_Hair, Bushy_Eyebrows, Eyeglasses, Male, Pale_Skin, Smiling, Wearing_Hat.

Fig. 7. Comparison with [13] by swapping facial attributes. Four paired examples are shown. Generally, our method can generate much better images compared to [13].

Comparison with Unsupervised GAN. We further compare with [9], which is also a unpaired image-to-image translation method. Comparison results are shown in Fig. 8. Note we only provide part of the attribute results according to their paper for fair comparison.

Quantitative Comparison. To quantitatively evaluate the generated results, we use structural similarity (SSIM) [18], which is a widely used image quality metric that correlates well with human visual perception. SSIM ranges from 0 to 1, higher is better. The SSIM of our method, as well as conditional GAN [13] and unsupervised GAN [9], is shown in Table 1 for the generated images.

Our method outperforms [13] and [9] in two aspects: (i) In the unsupervised GAN setting, compared with [9], our method shows significant performance gain with the proposed attributed guided framework. (ii) Compared with conditional GAN [13], the performance gain is even larger with the help of the cyclic network architecture of our conditional CycleGAN.

Blond Hair   No smile -> smiling   Smiling -> no smile

Fig. 8. Comparison results with [9]. Four source images are shown in top row. Images with blue and red bounding boxes indicates transferred results by [9] and results by our method, respectively. (Color figure online)

Table 1. SSIM on CelebA test sets.

Method	Conditional GAN [13]	Unsupervised GAN [9]	Conditional CycleGAN
SSIM	0.74	0.87	**0.92**

4.3 Identity-Guided Face Generation

Figures 9 and 10 show sample face generation results where the identity face features are respectively from the same and *different* persons. There are two interesting points to note: First, the generated high-res results (c) bear high resemblance to the target identity images (b) from which the identity features are computed using Light-CNN. The unique identity features transfer well from (b) to (c), e.g., challenging gender change in the second row of Fig. 10. In the last row, the facial attributes, e.g. beard (example in the blue box), eyeglasses (example in the yellow box) are considered as parts of the identity and faithfully preserved by our model in the high-res outputs, even though the low-res inputs do not have such attributes. The occluded forehead in low-res input (example in the green box) is recovered. Second, the low-res inputs provide overall shape constraint. The head pose and facial expression of the generated high-res images (c) adopt those in the *low*-res inputs (a). Specifically, refer to the example inside the blue box in the last row of Fig. 10, where (b) shows target identity, i.e. man smiling while low-res input (a) shows another man with closed mouth. The generated high-res image in (c) preserves the identity in (b) while the pose of the head follows the input and the mouth is closed as well.

4.4 Face Swapping Within the High-Res Domain

We demonstrate an interesting application *face swapping* where *both* the input and identity images are high-res images. Here, we want to swap the identity while preserving *all* facial details including subtle crease lines and expression, thus both the identity image and the input image must be high-res images. We adopt our identity-guided conditional CycleGAN and utilize Light-CNN as both the source of the identity features and face verification loss. Our face swapping results are shown in Fig. 11. As illustrated, our method swaps the identity by

Fig. 9. Identity-guided face generation results on low-res input and high-res identity of the same person, i.e., identity-preserving face superresolution. (a) Low-res inputs; (b) input identity of the same person; (c) our high-res face outputs (red boxes) from (a); (d) the high-res ground truth of (a). (Color figure online)

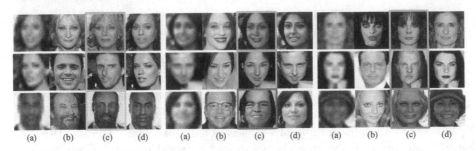

Fig. 10. Identity-guided face generation results on different persons. The last row shows some challenging examples, e.g., , the occluded forehead in low-res input is recovered (example in the green box). (a) Low-res inputs provide overall shape constraint; (b) identity to be transferred; (c) our high-res face outputs (red boxes) from (a) where the man/woman's identity in (b) is transferred; (d) the high-res ground truth of (a). (Color figure online)

transferring the appearance of eyes, eyebrows, hairs, etc., while keeping other factors intact, e.g., head pose, shape of face and facial expression. Without multiple steps (e.g., facial landmark detection followed by warping and blending) in traditional techniques, our identity-guided conditional CycleGAN can still achieve high levels of photorealism of the face-swapped images.

Figure 12 compares face swapping results of our models trained with and without the face verification loss in the auxiliary discriminator. The difference is easy to recognize, and adding face verification loss has a perceptual effect of improving the photorealism of swapped-face image. In this example, the eyebrows and eyes are successfully transformed to the target identity with the face verification loss.

4.5   Frontal Face Generation

Another application of our model consists of generating images of frontal faces from face images in other orientations. By simply providing a low-res frontal face image and adopting our identity-guided conditional CycleGAN model, we can generate the corresponding high-res frontal face images given side-face images

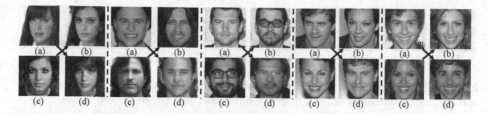

Fig. 11. Face swapping results within the high-res domain. (a)(c) are inputs of two different persons; (b)(d) their face swapping results. The black arrows indicate the guidance of identity, i.e. (d) is transformed from (c) under the identity constraint of (a). Similarly, (b) is transformed from (a) under the identity of (c). Note how our method transforms the identity by altering the appearance of eyes, eyebrows, hairs etc., while keeping other factors intact, e.g., head pose, shape of face and facial expression.

Fig. 12. Results without (c) and with (d) face verification loss. (a) is target identity image to be transferred and (b) is input image. The loss encourages subtle yet important improvement in photorealism, e.g. the eyebrows and eyes in (c) resemble the target identity in (a) by adding the face verification loss.

as high-res face attributes. Figure 13 shows sample results on our frontal face image generation. Note that our frontal face generation is end-to-end and free of human intervention, thus setting it apart from related works of frontalizing the face by landmark detection, warping and blending etc. given a frontal pose.

4.6   Interpolating Conditional Vector

We further explore the conditional attribute vector by linearly interpolating between two different attribute vectors. Figure 14 shows that all the interpolated faces are visually plausible with smooth transition among them, which is a convincing demonstration that the model generalizes well the face representation instead of just directly memorizes the training samples.

Similar to interpolating the attribute vectors, we experiment with interpolating the 256-D identity feature vectors under our identity-guided conditional model. We randomly sample two high-res face images and interpolate between the two identity features. Figure 15 indicates that our model generalizes properly the face representation given the conditional feature vectors.

Fig. 13. Frontal face generation. Given a low-res template (a), our method can generate corresponding frontal faces from different side faces, e.g., (b) to (c), (d) to (e).

(woman, w/o smile, w/o glasses)   (man, smiling, with glasses)

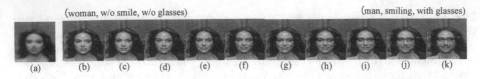

Fig. 14. Interpolation results of the attribute vectors. (a) Low-res face input; (b) generated high-res face images; (c) to (k) interpolated results. Attributes of source and destination are shown in text.

Fig. 15. Interpolating results of the identity feature vectors. Given the low-res input in (a), we randomly sample two target identity face images (b) and (k). (c) is the generated face from (a) conditioned on the identity in (b) and (d) to (j) are interpolations.

5   Conclusion

We have presented the Conditional CycleGAN for attribute-guided and identity-guided face image generation. Our technical contribution consists of the conditional CycleGAN to guide the face image generation process via easy user input of complex attributes for generating high quality results. In the attribute-guided conditional CycleGAN, the adversarial loss is modified to include a conditional feature vector as parts of the inputs to the generator and discriminator networks. We utilize the feature vector from light-CNN in identity-guided conditional CycleGAN. We have presented the first but significant results on identity-guided and attribute-guided face image generation. In the future, we will explore how to further improve the results and extend the work to face video generation.

Acknowledgement. This work was supported in part by Tencent Youtu.

References

1. Choi, Y., Choi, M., Kim, M., Ha, J.W., Kim, S., Choo, J.: StarGAN: unified generative adversarial networks for multi-domain image-to-image translation. In: The IEEE Conference on Computer Vision and Pattern Recognition (CVPR), June 2018

2. Dong, C., Loy, C.C., He, K., Tang, X.: Learning a deep convolutional network for image super-resolution. In: Fleet, D., Pajdla, T., Schiele, B., Tuytelaars, T. (eds.) ECCV 2014. LNCS, vol. 8692, pp. 184–199. Springer, Cham (2014). https://doi.org/10.1007/978-3-319-10593-2_13

3. Dong, C., Loy, C.C., Tang, X.: Accelerating the super-resolution convolutional neural network. CoRR abs/1608.00367 (2016). http://arxiv.org/abs/1608.00367

4. Goodfellow, I., et al.: Generative adversarial nets. In: NIPS, pp. 2672–2680 (2014). http://papers.nips.cc/paper/5423-generative-adversarial-nets.pdf

5. Huang, R., Zhang, S., Li, T., He, R.: Beyond face rotation: global and local perception GAN for photorealistic and identity preserving frontal view synthesis. ArXiv e-prints, April 2017

6. Isola, P., Zhu, J., Zhou, T., Efros, A.A.: Image-to-image translation with conditional adversarial networks. CoRR abs/1611.07004 (2016). http://arxiv.org/abs/1611.07004

7. Johnson, J., Alahi, A., Li, F.: Perceptual losses for real-time style transfer and super-resolution. CoRR abs/1603.08155 (2016). http://arxiv.org/abs/1603.08155

8. Kim, J., Lee, J.K., Lee, K.M.: Deeply-recursive convolutional network for image super-resolution. In: CVPR, pp. 1637–1645 (2016)

9. Kim, T., Cha, M., Kim, H., Lee, J., Kim, J.: Learning to discover cross-domain relations with generative adversarial networks. In: ICML (2017)

10. Ledig, C., et al.: Photo-realistic single image super-resolution using a generative adversarial network. CoRR abs/1609.04802 (2016). http://arxiv.org/abs/1609.04802

11. Liao, J., Yao, Y., Yuan, L., Hua, G., Kang, S.B.: Visual attribute transfer through deep image analogy. In: SIGGRAPH (2017)

12. Liu, Z., Luo, P., Wang, X., Tang, X.: Deep learning face attributes in the wild. CoRR abs/1411.7766 (2014)

13. Perarnau, G., van de Weijer, J., Raducanu, B., Álvarez, J.M.: Invertible conditional GANs for image editing. In: NIPS Workshop on Adversarial Training (2016)

14. Radford, A., Metz, L., Chintala, S.: Unsupervised representation learning with deep convolutional generative adversarial networks. CoRR abs/1511.06434 (2015). http://arxiv.org/abs/1511.06434

15. Schroff, F., Kalenichenko, D., Philbin, J.: FaceNet: a unified embedding for face recognition and clustering. In: CVPR, June 2015

16. Shi, W., et al.: Real-time single image and video super-resolution using an efficient sub-pixel convolutional neural network. In: CVPR, pp. 1874–1883 (2016)

17. Wang, Y., Wang, L., Wang, H., Li, P.: End-to-end image super-resolution via deep and shallow convolutional networks. CoRR abs/1607.07680 (2016). http://arxiv.org/abs/1607.07680

18. Wang, Z., Bovik, A.C., Sheikh, H.R., Simoncelli, E.P.: Image quality assessment: from error visibility to structural similarity. IEEE Trans. Image Process. **13**(4), 600–612 (2004)

19. Wu, X., He, R., Sun, Z.: A lightened CNN for deep face representation. CoRR abs/1511.02683 (2015). http://arxiv.org/abs/1511.02683

20. Yi, Z., Zhang, H., Gong, P.T., et al.: DualGAN: unsupervised dual learning for image-to-image translation. arXiv preprint arXiv:1704.02510 (2017)
21. Zhang, H., et al.: StackGAN: text to photo-realistic image synthesis with stacked generative adversarial networks. In: IEEE International Conference on Computer Vision (ICCV), pp. 5907–5915 (2017)
22. Zhao, B., Wu, X., Cheng, Z.Q., Liu, H., Feng, J.: Multi-view image generation from a single-view. ArXiv e-prints, April 2017
23. Zhu, J.Y., Park, T., Isola, P., Efros, A.A.: Unpaired image-to-image translation using cycle-consistent adversarial networks. In: 2017 IEEE International Conference on Computer Vision (ICCV) (2017)

Deep Structure Inference Network for Facial Action Unit Recognition

Ciprian Corneanu[1,2]([✉]), Meysam Madadi[2], and Sergio Escalera[1,2]

[1] University of Barcelona, Barcelona, Spain
cipriancorneanu@gmail.com, sergio.escalera.guerrero@gmail.com
[2] Computer Vision Center, Barcelona, Spain
meysam.madadi@gmail.com

Abstract. Facial expressions are combinations of basic components called Action Units (AU). Recognizing AUs is key for general facial expression analysis. Recently, efforts in automatic AU recognition have been dedicated to learning combinations of local features and to exploiting correlations between AUs. We propose a deep neural architecture that tackles both problems by combining learned local and global features in its initial stages and replicating a message passing algorithm between classes similar to a graphical model inference approach in later stages. We show that by training the model end-to-end with increased supervision we improve state-of-the-art by 5.3% and 8.2% performance on BP4D and DISFA datasets, respectively.

Keywords: Computer vision · Machine learning · Deep learning
Facial expression analysis · Facial action units · Structure inference

1 Introduction

Facial expressions (FE) are important cues for recognizing non-verbal behaviour. The ability to automatically mine human intentions, attitudes or experiences has many applications like building socially aware systems [4,18], improving e-learning [9], adapting game status according to player's emotions [1], and detecting deception during police interrogations [11].

The Facial Action Unit System (FACS) [5] is a descriptive coding scheme of FEs that focuses on what the face can do without assuming any cognitive or emotional value. Its basic components are called Action Units (AU) and they combine to form a complete representation of FEs.

AUs are patterns of muscular activation and the way they modify facial morphology is localized (Fig. 1a). While initial AU recognition methods (like JPML [25] and APL [28]) were using shallow predefined representations, recent methods (like DRML [26], ROI [12] and GL [7]) applied deep learning to learn richer local features that capture facial morphology. Therefore one could predict specific AUs from informative face regions selected depending on the facial geometry. For instance, contrary to non-adaptive methods like DRML [26] and

© Springer Nature Switzerland AG 2018
V. Ferrari et al. (Eds.): ECCV 2018, LNCS 11216, pp. 309–324, 2018.
https://doi.org/10.1007/978-3-030-01258-8_19

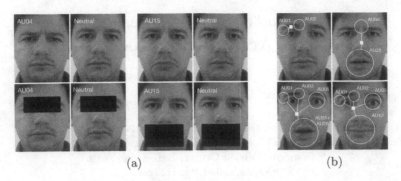

(a)   (b)

Fig. 1. Patch and structure learning are key problems in AU recognition. (a) By masking a region an expressive face becomes indistinguishable from neutral. (b) Multiple, correlated AUs can be active at the same time.

APL [28], ROI [12] and JPML [25] extract features around facial landmarks which are more robust with respect to non-rigid shape changes. Patch learning is challenging as the human face is highly articulated and different patches can contribute to either specific or groups of AUs. Learning the best patch combination together with learning specific features from each patch could be beneficial for AU recognition.

AU recognition is also multi-label. Several AUs can be active at the same time and certain AU combinations are more probable than others (Fig. 1b). AU prediction performance could be improved by considering probabilistic dependencies. In deep learning approaches, correlations can be addressed implicitly in the fully connected layers (e.g. DRML [26], GL [7] and ROI [12]). However, structure is not learned explicitly and inference and sparsity are implicit by design. JPML [25] treats the problem by including pre-learned priors about AU correlations into their learning. Learning structured outputs has also been studied by using Graphical Models [6,19,25]. However, these models are not end-to-end trainable.

In this work, we claim that patch and the structure learning are key problems in dealing with AU recognition. We propose a deep neural network that tackles those problems in an integrated way through an incremental and end-to-end trainable approach. First, the model learns local and holistic representations exhaustively from facial patches. Then it captures structure between patches by predicting specific AUs. Finally, AU correlations are captured by a structure inference network that replicates message passing inference algorithms in a connectionist fashion. Table 1 compares some of the most important features of the proposed method to the state-of-the-art (specifically JPML [25], APL [28], DRML [26], GL [7] and ROI [12]). We show that by separately treating problems in different parts of the network and being able to optimize them jointly, we improve state-of-the-art by 5.3% and 8.2% performance on BP4D and DISFA datasets, respectively. Summarizing, our 2 main contributions are: (1) we propose a model that learns representation, patch and output structure end-to-end, and (2) we introduce a structure inference topology that replicates inference algorithm in probabilistic graphical models by using a recurrent neural network.

Table 1. Features of our model and related work. LRL: local representation learning, AP: adaptive patch, PL: patch learning, SL: structured learning, EE: end-to-end.

Method	LRL	AP	PL	SL	EE	Method	LRL	AP	PL	SL	EE
APL [28]	×	×	✓	×	×	GL [7]	×	×	✓	×	✓
JPML [25]	×	✓	✓	×	×	ROI [12]	✓	✓	✓	×	✓
DRML [26]	✓	✓	×	×	✓	DSIN (ours)	✓	✓	✓	✓	✓

The paper is organized as follows. Section 2 presents related work. Section 3 details the proposed model and Sect. 4 the results. Section 5 concludes the paper.

2 Related Work

Related work is discussed in relation to patch learning or structure learning.

Patch Learning. Inspired by locally connected convolutional layers [17], Zhao et al. [26] proposed a regional connected convolutional layer that learns specific convolutional filters from sub-areas of the input. In [12], different CNNs are trained on different parts of the face merging features in an early fusion fashion with fully connected layers. Zhao et al. [25] performed patch selection and structure learning with shallow representations where patches for each AU were selected by group sparsity learning. Jaiswal et al. [8] used domain knowledge and facial geometry to pre-select a relevant image region for a particular AU, passing it to a convolutional and bi-directional Long Short-Term Memory (LSTM) neural network. Zhong et al. [28] proposed a multi-task sparse learning framework for learning common and specific discriminative patches for different expressions. Patch location was predefined and did not take into account facial geometry.

Structure Learning. Zhang et al. [23] proposed a multi-task approach to learn a common kernel representation that describes AU correlations. Elefteriadis et al. [6] adopted a latent variable Conditional Random Field (CRF) to jointly detect multiple AUs from predesigned features. While existing methods capture local pairwise AU dependencies, Wang et al. [20] proposed a restricted Boltzmann machine that captures higher-order AU interactions. Together with patch-learning, Zhao et al. [25] used positive and negative competitions among AUs to model a discriminative multi-label classifier. Walecki et al. [19] placed a CRF on top of deep representations learned by a CNN. Both components are trained iteratively to estimate AU intensity. Wu et al. [21] used a Restricted Boltzman Machine that captures joint probabilities between facial landmark locations and AUs. More recently, Benitez et al. [7] proposed a loss combining the recognition of isolated and groups of AUs.

3   Method

Let $\mathcal{D} = \{\mathbf{X}, \mathbf{Y}\}$ be a set of pairs of input images $\mathbf{X} = \{\mathbf{x}_1, \ldots, \mathbf{x}_M\}$ and output AU labels $\mathbf{Y} = \{\mathbf{y}_1, \ldots, \mathbf{y}_M\}$ with M number of instances. Each image $\mathbf{x}_i$ is composed of P patches $\{I_1, \ldots, I_P\}$ and output label $\mathbf{y}_i$ is a set of N AUs $\{y_1, \ldots, y_N\}$ taking a binary value $\{0, 1\}$. Several AU classes can be active for an observation as a multi-label problem. Predicting such output is challenging as a softmax function can not be applied on the set of outputs contrary to the standard mono-label/multi-class problems. In addition, using independent AU activation functions in losses like cross-entropy, ignores AU correlations. Including the ability to learn structure in the model design is thus relevant.

Two main ways of solving multi-label learning in AU recognition are either capturing correlations through fully-connected layers [7,12,26] or inferring structure through probabilistic graphical models (PGM) [6,19,25]. While the former can capture correlations between classes, this is not done explicitly. On the other hand, PGMs offer an explicit solution and their optimization is well studied. Unfortunately, placing classical PGMs on top of neural network predictions considerably lowers the capacity of the model to learn high order relationships since it is not end-to-end trainable. One solution is to replicate graphical model inference in a conectionist fashion which would make possible joint optimization. Jointly training CNNs and CRFs has been previously studied in different problems [2,3,27]. Following this trend, in this work we formulate AU recognition by a graphical model and implement it by neural networks, more specifically CNNs and recurrent neural network (RNN). This way, AU predictions from local regions along AU correlations are learned end-to-end.

Let $\mathcal{G} = (\mathcal{V}, \mathcal{E})$ denote a graph with vertices $\mathcal{V} = \mathbf{y}$ specifying AUs and edges $\mathcal{E} \subseteq \mathcal{V} \times \mathcal{V}$ indicating the relationships between AUs. Given the Gibbs distribution we compute conditional probability $P(\mathbf{y}|\mathbf{x}, \Theta)$ as:

$$P(\mathbf{y}|\mathbf{x}, \Theta) = \frac{1}{Z(\mathbf{y}, \mathbf{x}, \Theta)} e^{-E(\mathbf{y}|\mathbf{x}, \Theta)}, \qquad (1)$$

where Θ are model parameters, Z is a normalization function and E is an energy function. The model can be updated by introducing latent variables $\mathbf{p}$ as:

$$P(\mathbf{y}|\mathbf{x}, \Theta) = \sum_{\mathbf{p}} P(\mathbf{y}, \mathbf{p}|\mathbf{x}, \Theta), \qquad (2)$$

where $\mathbf{p}$ is given as the output of CNN. The vertices and edges in the graph $\mathcal{G}$ can be updated as $\mathcal{V} = \mathbf{y} \cup \mathbf{p}$ and $\mathcal{E} = \mathcal{E}_y \cup \mathcal{E}_{py} \cup \mathcal{E}_p$. Although edges $\mathcal{E}_y$ can be defined by a prior knowledge taken from a given dataset, we use a fully connected graph independent to the dataset and assign a mutual gating strategy to control information passing through edges (more details in Sect. 3.3). We define $\mathcal{E}_{py}$ as edges between $\mathbf{p}$ and $\mathbf{y}$, and use a selective strategy to define edges in this set. Finally, edges $\mathcal{E}_p$ is an empty set, since in our model an independent CNN is trained on each image patch I_j and we do not assign any edge among $\mathbf{p}$. Given this assumption, probability distribution $P(\mathbf{y}, \mathbf{p}|\mathbf{x}, \Theta)$ is given by:

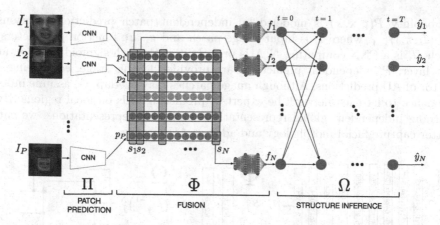

Fig. 2. Deep Structure Inference Network (DSIN) learns independent AU predictions from global and local learned features. It refines each AU prediction by taking into account correlation to the other AUs. Each input image is cropped into a set of patches $\{I_i\}_{i=1}^{P}$ which is used for training an independent CNN for producing a probability vector p_i for N AUs (φ_p in Eq. 4). From s_j (the patch predictions for a specific AU) we learn a combination for producing a single AU prediction f_j (simplified ψ_{py} in Eq. 4). Final predictions y_j are computed by inferring structure among AUs through iterative message passing similar to inference in a probabilistic graph model (ψ_y in Eq. 4).

$$P(\mathbf{y}, \mathbf{p} | \mathbf{x}, \Theta) = P(\mathbf{y} | \mathbf{p}, \mathbf{x}, \Theta) \prod_k P(p_k | \mathbf{x}, \Theta). \tag{3}$$

As in CRF, energy function $E(.)$ is computed by unary and pairwise terms as:

$$E(\mathbf{y}, \mathbf{p}, \mathbf{x}, \Theta) = \sum_k \varphi_p(p_k, \mathbf{x}, \pi) + \sum_{(i,k) \in \mathcal{E}_{py}} \psi_{py}(y_i, p_k, \phi) + \sum_{(i,j) \in \mathcal{E}_y} \psi_y(y_i, y_j, \omega), \tag{4}$$

where $\varphi(.)$ is a unary term, $\psi_*(.)$ are pairwise terms and $\Theta = \pi \cup \phi \cup \omega$. Figure 2 presents our Deep Structure Inference Network (DSIN). It consists of three components each designed to solve a term in Eq. 4. We refer to the initial part as *Patch Prediction* (PP), whose purpose is to exhaustively learn deep local representations from facial patches and produce local predictions. Then, the *Fusion* (F) module performs patch learning per AU. The final stage, *Structure Inference* (SI), refines AU prediction by capturing relationships between AUs. The DSIN is end-to-end trainable and CNN features can be trained based on gradients back-propagated from structure inference in a multi-task learning fashion.

3.1 Patch Prediction

Given image patches $\mathbf{x}$, unary terms $\varphi_p(\mathbf{p}, \mathbf{x}, \pi)$ provide AUs confidences for each patch which are defined as the log probability:

$$\varphi_p(\mathbf{p}, \mathbf{x}, \pi) = \log P(\mathbf{p} | \mathbf{x}, \pi). \tag{5}$$

Probability $P(\mathbf{p}|\mathbf{x}, \pi)$ is modeled by independent patch prediction functions $\{\Pi_i(I_i; \pi_i)\}_{i=1}^{P}$, where I_i is input image patch and π_i are function parameters. Each Π_i is a CNN computing N AUs probabilities through sigmoid function at last layer. P independent predictions are provided at this stage, each being a vector of AU predictions. Although image patches may overlap, we assume independence to let each network be expert at predicting AUs on local regions. By learning independent global representations and local representations, we can better capture facial morphology and address AU locality.

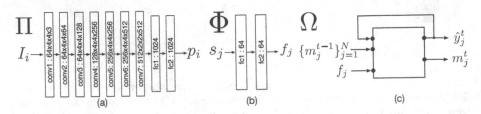

Fig. 3. (a) Topology of patch prediction CNNs. Each convolutional block has stride 2 and batch normalization. Number of filters followed by the size of the kernel are marked. The last layers are fully-connected (FC) layers marked with the number of neurons. All neurons use ReLU activations. (b) Each fusion unit is a stack of 2 FC layers. (c) A structure inference unit. For better visualization, we just show the interface of the unit without the inner topology. See details in Sect. 3.3.

In Fig. 3(a) we detail the topology of the CNNs used for learning the patch prediction functions. Many complex topologies have been proposed in recent years and searching for the best is out of the scope of this work. The chosen topology, a shallow network, follows the intuition behind well known models like VGG [16].

3.2   Fusion

Computational complexity to marginalize pairwise relationships in $\mathcal{E}_{py}$ is high. In our formulation, we simplify edges such that $\mathcal{E}_{py}$ becomes directed from nodes in $\mathbf{p}$ to nodes in $\mathbf{y}$. It means we omit mutual relationships among $\mathbf{p}$ and $\mathbf{y}$. Therefore, nodes in $\mathbf{y}$ are conditioned on the nodes in $\mathbf{p}$. However, we want each AU node in $\mathbf{y}$ to be conditioned on the same AU nodes in $\mathbf{p}$ from different patches. It means different patches can provide complementary information to predict target AU independent to other AUs. Finally, $\psi_{py}(\mathbf{y}, \mathbf{p}, \phi)$ is defined as the log probability of $P(\mathbf{y}|\mathbf{p}, \phi)$ which is modeled by a set of independent functions, so called fusion functions $\{\Phi_j(s_j; \phi_j)\}_{j=1}^{N}$, where $s_j \subset \mathbf{p}$ corresponds to the set of j-th AU predictions from all patches and ϕ_j is function parameters. We simply model each function Φ_j with 2 fully connected layers with 64 hidden units, each followed by a sigmoid layer, as shown in Fig. 3(b). We found 64 hidden units works well in practice while higher dimensionality does not bring any additional performance and quickly starts over-fitting. The output of each Φ_j is the predicted probability f_j for j-th AU.

3.3 Structure Inference

Up to now, we computed individual AU probabilities in a feed-forward neural network without taking AU relationships explicitly into account. The goal is to model pairwise terms ψ_y such that the whole process is end-to-end trainable in a compact way. Belief propagation and message passing between nodes is one of the well known algorithms for PGM inference. Inspired by [3], which proposes a connectionist implementation for action recognition, we build a *Structure Inference* (SI) module in the final part of DSIN.

The SI updates each AU prediction in an iterative manner by taking into account information from other AUs. The intuition behind this is that by passing information between predictions in an explicit way, we can capture AU correlations and improve predictions. The structure inference module is a collection of interconnected recurrent structure interference units (SIU) (see Fig. 3(c)). For each AU there is a dedicated SIU. We denote the computations done by SIU by a function Ω. Let $\{\Omega_j\}_{j=1}^N$ be the set of SIU functions $\Omega_j : \mathbb{R}^{N+2} \to \mathbb{R}^2$ where:

$$\hat{y}_j^t, m_j^t = \Omega_j(f_j, m_1^{t-1}, m_2^{t-1}, ..., m_N^{t-1}, \hat{y}_j^{t-1}; \omega_j). \tag{6}$$

At each iteration t, Ω_j takes as input the initial prediction f_j for its class, a set of incoming messages $\{m_j^{t-1}\}_{j=1}^N$ from the SIUs corresponding to the other classes and its own previous prediction $\hat{y}_j^{t-1}$. Each function Ω_j has two inline units: producing j-th AU prediction $\hat{y}_j^t$ and message m_j^t for next time step. In this way, predictions are improved iteratively by receiving information from other nodes. Computationally, we replicate this iterative message passing mechanism in the collection of SIUs with a recurrent neural network that shares function parameters Ω_j across all time steps. We show a SIU unit in Fig. 3(c).

A message unit basically corresponds to the distribution of the AU node. A message unit from a SIU is a parametrized function of the previous messages, the initial fused prediction and the previous prediction of the same SIU:

$$m_j^t = \sigma\left(\omega_j^m\left[\mu(m_1^{t-1}, ..., m_N^{t-1}), f_j, \hat{y}_j^{t-1}\right] + \beta_j^m\right), \tag{7}$$

where $\sigma(.)$ is the sigmoid function, $\mu(.)$ is the mean function, $\omega_j^m \in \mathbb{R}^3$ and $\beta_j^m \in \mathbb{R}$ are message function parameters. Messages between two nodes at each time step have a mutual relationship which can be controlled by a gating strategy. Therefore, a set of correction factors are computed as:

$$\chi_j^t = \sigma\left(\omega_j^g\left[\mu(m_1^t, ..., m_N^t), f_j, \hat{y}_j^{t-1}\right] + \beta_j^g\right), \tag{8}$$

where $\omega_j^g \in \mathbb{R}^3$ and $\beta_j^g \in \mathbb{R}$ are gating function parameters. Then, a message $m_{i \to j}^t$ that is passed from AU node i to j will be updated by the mutual factors of the gate between nodes i and j as:

$$\overline{m}_j^t = \mu(\chi_i^t, \chi_j^t) m_{i \to j}^t. \tag{9}$$

Finally, updated messages coming to the j-th node along with initial estimation f_j are used to produce output prediction $\hat{y}_j^t$ as:

$$\hat{y}_j^t = \sigma\left(\omega_j^y\left[\mu(\overline{m}_1^t, ..., \overline{m}_N^t), f_j\right] + \beta_j^y\right), \tag{10}$$

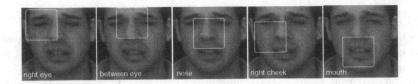

Fig. 4. Each input image is aligned and cropped into 5 patches.

where $\omega_j^y \in \mathbb{R}^2$ and $\beta_j^y \in \mathbb{R}$ are prediction function parameters. By doing this, we are able to combine representation learning in function Π, patch learning in function Φ and structure inference in the Ω in a single end-to-end trainable model. We introduce our training strategy in Sect. 4.1.

4   Experimental Analysis

In the following, we describe experimental settings and results.

4.1   Experimental Setting

Data. We used BP4D [24] and DISFA [13] datasets. BP4D contains 2D and 3D videos of 41 young adults. It has 328 videos (8 videos for 41 participants) with 12 coded AUs, resulting in about 140k valid face images [24]. DISFA contains 27 adults (12 women and 15 men) with ages between 18 to 50 years and relative ethnic diversity. The data corpus consists of approximately 130k frames in total. AU intensity is coded for each video frame on a 0 (not present) to 5 (maximum intensity) ordinal scale. For our purpose we consider all labels with intensity greater than 3 as active and the rest as non-active. Both datasets are widely used in most recent AU recognition works.

Preprocessing. For each image, facial geometry is estimated using [10]. From all neutral faces we compute 3 reference anchors as the mean of the eyes and the mouth landmarks. Faces are resized to $224 \times 224 \times 3$ and a rigid transformation is applied for registering to the anchors, reducing variance to scale and rotation. We crop 5 patches of size $56 \times 56 \times 3$ around points defined by the detected landmarks (see Fig. 4). For reducing redundancy we ignore corresponding, symmetrical patches like the left eye and cheek.

Training. We incrementally train each part of DSIN before end-to-end model training. During training we use supervision on the patch prediction p, the fusion f and the structure inference outputs $\hat{y}$. On p we use a weighted L_2 loss denoted by $L_\Pi(p, y)$. The weights are inversely proportional to the ratio of positives in the total number of observations for each AU class in training. The weighting gives more importance to the minority classes in each training batch which ensures a more equal gradient update across classes and overall better performance. On the fusion and structure inference outputs we apply a binary cross-entropy loss (denoted by $L_\Phi(f, y)$ and $L_\Omega(\hat{y}, y)$). For the structure inference we include a

---

Algorithm 1. Training procedure of DSIN.

Training data: $\{\{I\}_{i=1}^{P}, y\}$
Model parameters: patch prediction: $\{\pi_i\}_{i=1}^{P}$, fusion $\{\phi_i\}_{i=1}^{N}$, structure inference $\{\omega_i\}_{i=1}^{N}$
Step 0: random initialization around 0: $\pi, \phi, \omega \leftarrow \mathcal{N}(0, \sigma^2)$
Step 1: train patch prediction: $\pi_i \leftarrow \min_{\pi}(L_{\Pi}(\Pi_i(I_i; \pi_i)), y), \forall i \in \{1, ..., P\}$
Step 2: freeze patch prediction; train fusion: $\phi \leftarrow \min_{\phi} L_{\Phi}(\Phi(\Pi; \phi), y)$
Step 3: train patch prediction and fusion jointly:
$\quad \pi, \phi \leftarrow \min_{\pi, \phi}(L_{\Pi}(\Pi(I; \pi)), y) + L_{\Phi}(\Phi(\Pi; \phi), y))$
Step 4: freeze patch prediction and fusion; train structure inference:
$\quad \omega \leftarrow \min_{\omega} L_{\Omega}(\Omega(\Phi; \omega), y)$
Step 5. train all:
$\pi, \phi, \omega \leftarrow \min_{\pi, \phi, \omega}(w_1 L_{\Pi}(\Pi(I; \pi)), y) + w_2 L_{\Phi}(\Phi(\Pi; \phi), y) + w_3 L_{\Omega}(\Omega(\Phi; \omega), y))$
Output: optimized parameter: $\pi^{opt}, \phi^{opt}, \omega^{opt}$

---

regularization on the correction factors (denoted by χ in Eqs. 8 and 9) to force sparsity in the message passing. Details of the training procedure are shown in Algorithm 1. We use an Adam optimizer with learning rate of 0.001 and mini-batch size 64 with early stopping. Experimentally, we found the individual loss contributions $w_1 = 0.25$, $w_2 = 0.25$ and $w_3 = 0.5$ to work well in training. For both datasets we perform a subject exclusive 3-fold cross-validation. Similarly to [12], on DISFA we take the best CNNs trained for patch prediction on the BP4D and retrained fully connected layers for the new set of outputs. We fix the convolutional filters throughout the rest of the training.

Methods and Metrics. We compare against CPM [22], APL [28], JPML [25], DRML [26], and ROI [12] state-of-the-art alternatives. We evaluate $F1$ frame score as $F1 = 2\frac{PR}{P+R}$, where $P = \frac{tp}{tp+fp}$, $R = \frac{tp}{tp+fn}$, tp being true positives, fn false negatives and fp false positives. All metrics are computed per AU and then averaged. Targeted AUs shown in Fig. 6.

4.2   Results

In the following, we explore the effect design decisions included in the DSIN followed by comparison against state-of-the-art alternatives in Sect. 4.2 and qualitative examples in Sect. 4.2.

Ablation Study. We analyze DSIN design decisions in the following.

Class Balancing. In both datasets, classes are strongly imbalanced. This can be harmful during training. To alleviate this, we use a weighted loss on patch prediction CNNs. Table 2 shows results with and without class balancing. This overall improves performance, especially on poorly represented classes. On BP4D the classes with ratios of positives in the total of samples lower than 30% are AU01, AU02, AU04, AU17, AU24. These are the classes that are improved the most. AUs like AU07 or AU12 have positives to total rations higher than 50%. Balancing can reduce performance on these classes.

Table 2. Recognition results on BP4D. PP([patch]) stands for patch prediction on the indicated patch. F stands for the fusion and DSIN is the final model. We indicate the results when training on individual AUs with $[method]^{ind}$, fine tuning on the validation dataset of the decision threshold by $DSIN^{tt}$, number of iterations of the structure inference by $DSIN_T$ and training without correction factors as $DSIN^{ncf}$. $VGG(face)^{ft}$ is a pre-trained VGG-16 [14] fine-tuned on BP4D. $PP(face)^{ncb}$ is a patch prediction without class balancing. All results are obtained by 3-fold cross-validation on BP4D.

	Method	AU01	AU02	AU04	AU06	AU07	AU10	AU12	AU14	AU15	AU17	AU23	AU24	Avg
	$VGG(face)^{ft}$	**35.2**	31.2	25.4	73.1	**72.1**	80.1	59.2	35.1	32.1	52.3	26.1	**36.2**	46.5
	$PP(face)^{ncb}$	35.1	**38.1**	**53.9**	77.2	70.7	**83.1**	**86.2**	**56.1**	**39.8**	**54.5**	**37.2**	31.4	**55.3**
PP	$PP(right\ eye)^{ind}$	**46.8**	**40.4**	45.3	68.3	69.2	-	-	-	-	-	-	-	-
	$PP(mouth)^{ind}$	-	-	-	-	-	78.6	82.0	54.2	38.6	54.7	[39.3]	**43.3**	-
	PP(right eye)	38.0	[37.7]	48.3	69.5	71.0	72.4	77.4	50.7	15.0	38.9	13.8	15.3	45.7
	PP(between eye)	41.7	34.8	45.9	64.9	65.5	72.1	73.9	54.9	19.7	33.9	13.9	7.0	44.0
	PP(mouth)	12.4	7.3	22.4	75.5	70.5	78.9	81.3	**66.2**	35.8	59.6	37.6	[42.8]	49.3
	PP(right cheek)	30.5	18.4	41.8	75.2	73.2	79.1	81.9	[61.9]	35.7	55.1	35.5	35.7	52.0
	PP(nose)	41.6	28.4	46.4	71.1	70.5	78.8	78.0	57.1	21.3	43.7	34.0	20.3	49.3
	PP(face)	43.8	37.5	[54.9]	**77.4**	[71.2]	[79.2]	**84.0**	56.6	[39.7]	[59.7]	39.2	39.5	[56.9]
	PP + F	[44.8]	35.8	**57.1**	[76.7]	**74.3**	79.6	[83.7]	56.6	41.1	61.8	**42.2**	40.1	**57.8**
DSIN	$DSIN_2^{ncf}$	46.7	34.1	**62.0**	76.5	**74.1**	[83.1]	84.9	60.9	36.0	57.1	**43.3**	36.1	57.9
	$DSIN_2$	47.7	36.5	55.6	76.3	[73.7]	80.1	85.0	64.0	[39.2]	60.6	[43.1]	39.9	58.2
	$DSIN_5$	[49.7]	36.3	57.3	**76.8**	73.4	81.6	84.5	[64.7]	38.5	[63.0]	39.0	37.3	58.5
	$DSIN_{10}$	**51.7**	[40.4]	56.0	76.1	73.5	79.9	[85.4]	62.7	37.3	62.9	38.6	[41.6]	[58.9]
	$DSIN_{10}^{tt}$	**51.7**	**41.6**	[58.1]	[76.6]	74.1	**85.5**	**87.4**	**72.6**	**40.4**	**66.5**	38.6	**46.9**	**61.7**

Choice of Prediction Topology. In Table 2 we compare the proposed CNN for patch prediction (PP(face)) against VGG-16. The VGG-16 model used was trained for face recognition [14] and fine-tuned on our data for AU recognition. Our model shows superior performance.

Targeting Subsets of AUs. We explore the effect of the considered target set on the overall prediction performance. In Table 2 we show prediction results from the right eye and from the mouth patches when training either on the full set of targets ($[method]$) or on individual targets ($[method]^{ind}$). When training on individual AUs the decision for the classifier is simpler. On the other hand any correlation information between classes that could be captured by the FC layers is ignored. In certain cases the individual prediction is superior to the exhaustive prediction. In the case of the right eye patch this is particularly true for AU01. But this is rather the exception. On average and across patches training on groups of AUs or on all AUs is beneficial as correlation information between classes is employed by the network in the fully connected layers. Additionally, predicting AU individually with independent nets would quickly increase the number of parameters with considerable effects on the training speed and final model performance.

Tables 2 and 3 show AU recognition results on both datasets trained on patches. That proves the locality assumption. When training on the mouth the performance on the upper face AUs is greatly affected. Similarly, training on the eye affects the performance on the lower face AUs. This is expected as the patch prediction can only infer the other AUs from the ones visible in the patch.

Learning Local Representations. On average, face prediction compared to patch prediction performs better on the entire output set. However, when individual AUs are considered, this is no longer the case. For BP4D, the performance on AU15 and AU24 are considerably higher when predicting from the mouth patch than from the face (see Table 2). On DISFA the prediction from the whole face is the best on just 3 AUs (see Table 3). The nose patch is better for predicting AU06 and AU09, the mouth patch is better for AU12, AU25 and AU26, and the between eye patch for AU01.

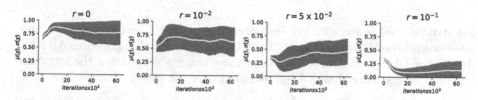

Fig. 5. Different levels of regularization on the mean $\mu(\chi)$ (white line) and standard deviation $\sigma(\chi)$ (envelope) of the correction factors during training. Small regularization values force the correction factors to diverge faster. Increasing regularization collapses the correction factors hurting the message passing.

Patch Learning. Tables 2 and 3 show results of AU-wise fusion for BP4D and DISFA (PP + F). On both, patch learning through fusion is beneficial, but on DISFA benefits are higher. This might be due to the fact that prediction results on DISFA are considerably more balanced across patches. Overall on BP4D the fusion improves results on almost all AUs compared to face prediction. This shows that even though the other patches perform worse on certain classes, there is structure to learn from their prediction that helps to improve performance. However, the fusion is not capable to replicate the result of the mouth prediction on AU14. On DISFA, in almost every case fusion gets close or higher to the best patch prediction. In both cases, fusion has greater problems in improving individual patches in cases where input predictions are already very noisy.

Structure Learning. Tables 2 and 3 show results of the final DSIN model. For BP4D, we also perform a study of the number of iterations T considered for structure inference. Since parameters ω_j are shared across iterations, more iterations are beneficial to capture AU relationships in a fully connected graph with a large number of nodes (12 in our case). We also trained DSIN without correction factors (Eq. 9 is not applied in this case). Results are inferior compared with the same model with correction factors. In the case of DISFA, we only applied

Table 3. Results of DSIN on DISFA. PP([patch]) stands for patch prediction on the indicated patch. F stands for the fusion. DSIN is the final model. For DISFA we only show the DSIN with $T = 10$, the best performing on BP4D.

Method	AU01	AU02	AU04	AU06	AU09	AU12	AU25	AU26	Avg
PP(right eye)	27.2	15.4	58.8	8.0	18.2	53.6	73.3	9.1	33.0
PP(between eye)	34.6	13.2	59.7	15.4	21.1	50.9	72.9	8.5	34.5
PP(mouth)	7.5	6.4	44.6	28.5	23.9	**72.1**	87.5	[27.3]	37.2
PP(right cheek)	24.6	12.2	46.1	31.2	45.2	71.5	84.5	22.4	33.8
PP(nose)	21.9	19.1	52.0	**32.0**	**50.9**	66.5	76.6	8.9	41.0
PP(face)	29.8	[31.4]	64.6	26.8	21.3	70.1	87.0	20.3	43.9
PP+F	[40.1]	18.6	**70.8**	25.4	42.1	[71.8]	[88.8]	26.4	[48.0]
DSIN	**42.4**	**39.0**	[68.4]	[28.6]	[46.8]	70.8	**90.4**	**42.2**	**53.6**

the structure inference with the best previously found $T = 10$ steps. Structure inference is beneficial in both cases. On BP4D, it considerably improves AU2 and AU14. For DISFA, the results are even more conclusive. Adding the structure inference brings more than 5% improvement over the fusion.

Correction Factor Regularization. Figure 5 shows the effect of increasing regularization applied on the correction factors χ. Overall, regularizing χ does not bring significant benefits. When comparing $r = 10^{-2}$ with no regularization the differences are minimal. The network has the ability to learn sparse message passing by itself without regularization. Still, small values of r lead to faster divergence of χ and faster convergence of the network. The difference in performance is not significant. On the other hand values of $r > 5 \times 10^{-2}$ negatively affect performance as most of χ get closer to 0 and no messages are passed anymore. For these reasons, we keep $r = 5 \times 10^{-3}$.

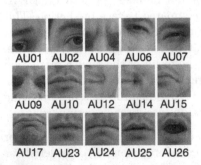

Fig. 6. Facial action units targeted in this work.

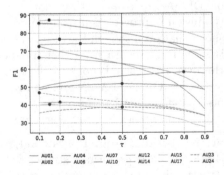

Fig. 7. τ vs AU performance on BP4D validation set. Black circles denote best score.

Threshold Tuning. Prediction value per AU takes values between 0 and 1. In all results, we compute the performance by binarizing the output with respect to threshold $\tau = 0.5$. Although class balancing as a weighted loss is beneficiary, it does not totally solve data imbalance. Figure 7 shows performance in terms of τ for validation set of BP4D. As shown, a threshold $\tau = 0.5$ is not an ideal value. For most classes $\tau \in [0.1, 0.3]$ is preferable. Exception is AU04. Tables 2 and 3 show the performance of the proposed model after tuning τ per class (DSIN^{tt}). This way 2.8% and 3.1% of performance is gained on BP4D and DISFA, respectively.

Comparison with State-of-the-Art. Tables 4 and 5 show how our model compares against the state-of-the-art related methods on BP4D and DISFA, respectively. DSIN and ROI are the best performing in both datasets. Both methods learn deep local representations and patch combinations end-to-end. The worst performing methods, JPML on BP4D and APL on DISFA, use predefined features and are not end-to-end trained. Comparing DSIN and ROI with DRML one can observe the advantage in learning independent local representation. Both ROI and our model learn independent local representations, while DRML disentangles the representation learning in just one layer of their network. Interestingly though, there is also an exception. On BP4D, CPM performs slightly better than DRML even though it is not a deep learning method. When comparing our proposed model with ROI on BP4D our CNN trained just on face without class balancing has inferior results. When we include class balancing and patch learning our topology improves performance, further enhanced by structure inference and end-to-end final training. In the case of DISFA, single CNN trained on the whole face with class balancing has a performance of 43.9, being 4.6% lower than ROI. When we add patch prediction fusion (PP + F) we get just 0.5% lower than ROI while the addition of the structure inference and threshold tuning improves ROI performance. Finally, DSIN shows the best results on both datasets. For BP4D, from the 12 AUs target it performs best on 5 and second best on additional 5. In the case of DISFA the improvement over ROI is greater, DSIN performing best in all but one AU. Overall, we obtain 5.3% absolute and

Table 4. AU recognition results on BP4D. Best results are shown in bold. Second best results are shown in brackets. For the proposed model we show an additional set of results (DSIN$_{tt}$) obtained when the decision threshold is tuned per AU.

Method	AU01	AU02	AU04	AU06	AU07	AU10	AU12	AU14	AU15	AU17	AU23	AU24	AVG
JPML [25]	32.6	25.6	37.4	42.3	50.5	72.2	74.1	[65.7]	38.1	40.0	30.4	[42.3]	45.9
DRML [26]	36.4	**41.8**	43.0	55.0	67.0	66.3	65.8	54.1	33.2	48.0	31.7	30.0	48.3
CPM [22]	[43.4]	40.7	43.3	59.2	61.3	62.1	68.5	52.5	36.7	54.3	**39.5**	37.8	50.0
ROI [12]	36.2	31.6	43.4	**77.1**	[73.7]	[85.0]	[87.0]	62.6	**45.7**	58.0	38.3	37.4	56.4
DSIN	**51.7**	40.4	[56.0]	76.1	73.5	79.9	85.4	62.7	37.3	[62.9]	[38.8]	41.6	[58.9]
DSIN^{tt}	**51.7**	[41.6]	**58.1**	[76.6]	**74.1**	**85.5**	**87.4**	**72.6**	[40.4]	**66.5**	38.6	**46.9**	**61.7**

322   C. Corneanu et al.

Table 5. AU recognition results on DISFA. Best results are shown in bold. Second best results are shown in brackets.

Method	AU01	AU02	AU04	AU06	AU09	AU12	AU25	AU26	Avg
APL [28]	11.4	12.0	30.1	12.4	10.1	65.9	21.4	26.0	23.8
DRML [26]	17.3	17.7	37.4	29.0	10.7	37.7	38.5	20.1	26.7
ROI [12]	41.5	26.4	66.4	**50.7**	8.5	**89.3**	88.9	15.6	48.5
DSIN	[42.4]	[39.0]	[68.4]	28.6	[46.8]	70.8	[90.4]	[42.2]	[53.6]
DSIN^{tt}	**46.9**	**42.5**	**68.8**	[32.0]	**51.8**	[73.1]	**91.9**	**46.6**	**56.7**

9.4% relative performance improvement on BP4D and 8.2% absolute and 16.9% relative performance improvement on DISFA, respectively.

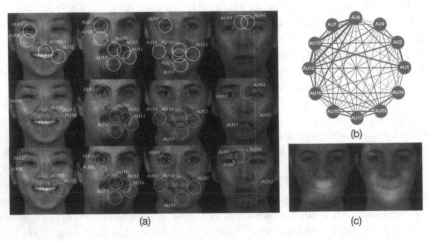

(a)   (b)

                                            (c)

Fig. 8. (a) Examples of AU predictions: ground-truth (top), fusion module (middle) and structure inference (bottom) prediction (∘: true positive, •: false positive). (b) AUs correlation in BP4D (∘: positive, •: negative). Line thickness is proportional with correlation magnitude. (c) Class activation map for AU24 that shows the discriminative regions of simple patch prediction (left) and DSIN (right). Best seen in color.

Qualitative Results. Figure 8(a) shows examples of how structure inference tends to correct predictions following AU correlations. We show the magnitude of AU correlations on BP4D in Fig. 8(b). In the first 3 column examples, AU06 and AU07 are not correctly classified by the fusion model (middle row). Both these AUs are highly correlated with already detected AUs like AU10, AU12 and AU14. Such correlation could be captured by SI (bottom row). The rightmost example shows how AU17, a false positive, is corrected. As shown in Fig. 8(b), AU17 is negatively correlated with AU4, which was already detected. In Fig. 8(c) we show a class activation map [15] for AU24 of the patch prediction (left) vs. the DSIN (right). Contrary to very localized patch prediction, the attention on right expands to a larger area of the face where possible correlated AUs might exist.

5 Conclusion

We proposed the Deep Structured Inference Network, designed to deal with both patch and structure learning for AU recognition. DSIN first learns independent local and global representations and corresponding predictions. Then, it learns relationships between predictions per AU through stacked fully connected layers. Finally, inspired by inference algorithms in graphical models, DSIN replicates a message passing mechanism in a connectionist fashion. This adds the ability to capture correlations in the output space. The model is end-to-end trainable and improves state-of-the-art results by 5.3% and 8.2% performance on BP4D and DISFA datasets, respectively. Future work includes learning patch structure at feature level and a structure inference module with increased capacity.

Acknowledgements. This work has been partially supported by the Spanish project TIN2016-74946-P (MINECO/FEDER, UE) and CERCA Programme/Generalitat de Catalunya. We gratefully acknowledge the support of NVIDIA Corporation with the donation of the GPU used for this research.

References

1. Bakkes, S., Tan, C.T., Pisan, Y.: Personalised gaming. JCT **3**, 4 (2012)
2. Chu, X., Ouyang, W., Wang, X., et al.: CRF-CNN: modeling structured information in human pose estimation. In: Advances in Neural Information Processing Systems, pp. 316–324 (2016)
3. Deng, Z., Vahdat, A., Hu, H., Mori, G.: Structure inference machines: recurrent neural networks for analyzing relations in group activity recognition. In: IEEE CVPR, pp. 4772–4781 (2016)
4. DeVault, D., et al.: A virtual human interviewer for healthcare decision support. In: AAMAS (2014)
5. Ekman, P., Friesen, W., Hager, J.: FACS manual. A human face (2002)
6. Eleftheriadis, S., Rudovic, O., Pantic, M.: Multi-conditional latent variable model for joint facial action unit detection. In: IEEE ICCV, pp. 3792–3800 (2015)
7. Fabian Benitez-Quiroz, C., Wang, Y., Martinez, A.M.: Recognition of action units in the wild with deep nets and a new global-local loss. In: IEEE ICCV, October 2017
8. Jaiswal, S., Valstar, M.: Deep learning the dynamic appearance and shape of facial action units. In: 2016 IEEE Winter Conference on Applications of Computer Vision (WACV), pp. 1–8. IEEE (2016)
9. Kapoor, A., Burleson, W., Picard, R.W.: Automatic prediction of frustration. IJHCS **65**(8), 724–736 (2007)
10. Kazemi, V., Sullivan, J.: One millisecond face alignment with an ensemble of regression trees. In: IEEE CVPR, pp. 1867–1874 (2014)

11. Kulkarni, K., et al.: Automatic recognition of deceptive facial expressions of emotion. arXiv preprint arXiv:1707.04061 (2017)
12. Li, W., Abtahi, F., Zhu, Z.: Action unit detection with region adaptation, multi-labeling learning and optimal temporal fusing. In: IEEE CVPR, pp. 6766–6775 (2017)
13. Mavadati, S.M., Mahoor, M.H., Bartlett, K., Trinh, P., Cohn, J.F.: DISFA: a spontaneous facial action intensity database. IEEE Trans. Affect. Comput. 4(2), 151–160 (2013)
14. Parkhi, O.M., Vedaldi, A., Zisserman, A.: Deep face recognition. In: British Machine Vision Conference (2015)
15. Selvaraju, R.R., Cogswell, M., Das, A., Vedantam, R., Parikh, D., Batra, D.: Grad-CAM: visual explanations from deep networks via gradient-based localization, v3, vol. 7, no. 8 (2016). https://arxiv.org/abs/1610.02391
16. Simonyan, K., Zisserman, A.: Very deep convolutional networks for large-scale image recognition. arXiv preprint arXiv:1409.1556 (2014)
17. Taigman, Y., Yang, M., Ranzato, M., Wolf, L.: DeepFace: closing the gap to human-level performance in face verification. In: IEEE CVPR, pp. 1701–1708 (2014)
18. Vinciarelli, A., Pantic, M., Bourlard, H.: Social signal processing: survey of an emerging domain. IVC 27(12), 1743–1759 (2009)
19. Walecki, R., Rudovic, O., Pavlovic, V., Schuller, B., Pantic, M.: Deep structured learning for facial action unit intensity estimation. In: IEEE CVPR, pp. 5709–5718 (2017)
20. Wang, Z., Li, Y., Wang, S., Ji, Q.: Capturing global semantic relationships for facial action unit recognition. In: IEEE ICCV, pp. 3304–3311 (2013)
21. Wu, Y., Ji, Q.: Constrained joint cascade regression framework for simultaneous facial action unit recognition and facial landmark detection. In: IEEE CVPR, pp. 3400–3408 (2016)
22. Zeng, J., Chu, W.S., De la Torre, F., Cohn, J.F., Xiong, Z.: Confidence preserving machine for facial action unit detection. In: IEEE ICCV, pp. 3622–3630 (2015)
23. Zhang, X., Mahoor, M.H.: Task-dependent multi-task multiple kernel learning for facial action unit detection. Pattern Recognit. 51, 187–196 (2016)
24. Zhang, X., et al.: BP4D-spontaneous: a high-resolution spontaneous 3D dynamic facial expression database. Image Vis. Comput. 32(10), 692–706 (2014)
25. Zhao, K., Chu, W.S., De la Torre, F., Cohn, J.F., Zhang, H.: Joint patch and multi-label learning for facial action unit detection. In: IEEE CVPR, pp. 2207–2216 (2015)
26. Zhao, K., Chu, W.S., Zhang, H.: Deep region and multi-label learning for facial action unit detection. In: IEEE CVPR, pp. 3391–3399 (2016)
27. Zheng, S., et al.: Conditional random fields as recurrent neural networks. In: IEEE CVPR, pp. 1529–1537 (2015)
28. Zhong, L., Liu, Q., Yang, P., Huang, J., Metaxas, D.N.: Learning multiscale active facial patches for expression analysis. IEEE Trans. Cybern. 45(8), 1499–1510 (2015)

Learning Priors for Semantic 3D Reconstruction

Ian Cherabier[1], Johannes L. Schönberger[1]([✉]), Martin R. Oswald[1],
Marc Pollefeys[1,2], and Andreas Geiger[1,3]

[1] ETH Zürich, Zürich, Switzerland
jsch@inf.ethz.ch
[2] Microsoft, Redmond, USA
[3] MPI-IS and University of Tübingen, Tübingen, Germany

Abstract. We present a novel semantic 3D reconstruction framework which embeds variational regularization into a neural network. Our network performs a fixed number of unrolled multi-scale optimization iterations with shared interaction weights. In contrast to existing variational methods for semantic 3D reconstruction, our model is end-to-end trainable and captures more complex dependencies between the semantic labels and the 3D geometry. Compared to previous learning-based approaches to 3D reconstruction, we integrate powerful long-range dependencies using variational coarse-to-fine optimization. As a result, our network architecture requires only a moderate number of parameters while keeping a high level of expressiveness which enables learning from very little data. Experiments on real and synthetic datasets demonstrate that our network achieves higher accuracy compared to a purely variational approach while at the same time requiring two orders of magnitude less iterations to converge. Moreover, our approach handles ten times more semantic class labels using the same computational resources.

1 Introduction

Estimating 3D geometry from images is one of the long-standing goals in computer vision. Despite its long history, however, many problems remain unsolved. In particular, ambiguities arising from textureless or reflective regions, viewpoint changes, and image noise render the problem difficult. Powerful priors are therefore needed to robustly solve the task. One source of prior knowledge which can be exploited are semantics and their interaction with 3D geometry. Consider an urban scene, for example. While the ground is often flat and horizontal, building walls are mostly vertical and located on top of the ground. The availability of reliable semantic image classification methods has therefore recently driven the development of methods that jointly optimize geometry and semantics in 3D.

I. Cherabier and J. L. Schönberger—These authors share first authorship.

Electronic supplementary material The online version of this chapter (https://doi.org/10.1007/978-3-030-01258-8_20) contains supplementary material, which is available to authorized users.

© Springer Nature Switzerland AG 2018
V. Ferrari et al. (Eds.): ECCV 2018, LNCS 11216, pp. 325–341, 2018.
https://doi.org/10.1007/978-3-030-01258-8_20

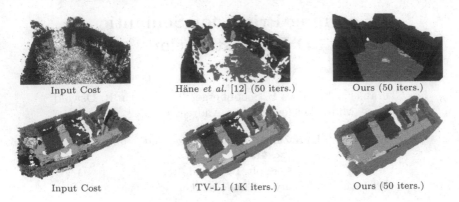

Fig. 1. Semantic 3D reconstruction results. We learn semantic and geometric neighborhood statistics to handle large amounts of noise, outliers, and missing data. Compared to traditional TV-L1 and the state of the art [12], our approach requires significantly less iterations and memory. Besides, it handles much larger label sets.

In their pioneering work, Häne *et al.* [10,12,13] proposed a method for joint volumetric 3D reconstruction and semantic segmentation using depth maps and semantic segmentations as input. They formulate the task as a variational multi-label problem, where each voxel is labeled by either one of the semantic classes or free space. Wulff shapes [28] serve as convex anisotropic regularizers, modeling the relationship between any two neighboring voxel labels. While impressive semantic reconstruction results have been demonstrated, the priors used are hand-tuned and very simplistic, thus not able to fully capture the complex semantic and geometric dependencies of our 3D world. Furthermore, inference in those models requires thousands of iterations for convergence, limiting the applicability of these methods.

This work revisits the problem of jointly estimating geometry and semantics in a multi-view 3D reconstruction setting as shown in Fig. 1. Our approach combines the advantages of classical variational approaches [10,12,13] with recent advances in deep learning [32,39], resulting in a method that is simple, generic, and substantially more scalable than previous solutions. In addition, our approach allows for automatically learning 3D representations from much fewer training data than existing learning-based solutions. As a result, our approach runs orders of magnitude faster than variational methods while producing better reconstructions. Moreover, memory requirements are significantly reduced allowing for larger label spaces. In summary, we make the following **contributions:**

- We present a novel framework for multi-view semantic 3D reconstruction which unifies the advantages of variational methods with those of deep neural networks, resulting in a simple, generic, and powerful model.
- We propose a multi-scale optimization strategy which accelerates inference, increases the receptive field, and allows long-distance information propagation.

Table 1. Qualitative comparison of semantic reconstruction methods. Quantities are approximate and categorized into positive, neutral, negative.

Method	Training scenes	Model complexity	Model parameters	Runtime	Manual tuning	#labels	Semantic interactions
Learned [6,8,9,36,38,40]	> 5K	high	millions	minutes	•	> 40	multi-scale
Variational (TV) [19,31,41]	> 0	low	none	seconds	•	> 40	none
Variational (Wulff-shape) [5,10,12]	> 1	moderate	hundreds	hours	•	< 10	single-scale
Learned-variational [ours]	> 5	low	thousands	seconds	•	> 40	multi-scale

- Compared to existing variational reconstruction methods [13], our approach learns semantic and geometric relationships end-to-end from data. Compared to fully convolutional architectures, our model is lightweight and can be trained from as little as five scenes without overfitting. Besides, formerly required manual and scene-dependent parameter tuning is no longer necessary and all meta-parameters, such as step sizes, are learned implicitly.
- Our experiments demonstrate that our method is able to achieve high quality results with only 50 unrolled optimization iterations compared to several thousands of iterations using traditional variational optimization.

2   Related Work

Our work builds on a variety of computer vision and machine learning works. This section and Table 1 provide an overview of the most relevant prior works.

Semantic 3D Reconstruction. Ladicky et al. [22] presented a model for joint semantic segmentation and stereo matching. They considered simple height-above-ground properties as constraints between semantics and 3D geometry. Kim et al. [17] proposed a conditional random field (CRF) model for labeling the 3D voxel space based on a single RGB-D image and solved the CRF using graph cuts. Joint volumetric 3D reconstruction and semantic segmentation in a multi-view setting has been tackled by Häne et al. [12,13] using variational optimization. Extensions to this seminal work consider object-class specific shape priors [10,23], scalable data-adaptive data structures [1], or larger semantic label spaces [5]. Kundu et al. [21] define a conditional random field to jointly infer semantics and occupancy from monocular video sequences.

A common drawback of these methods is that employed priors are either hand-crafted or not rich enough to capture the complex relationships of our 3D world. We propose to combine the advantages of variational semantic multi-view reconstruction with deep learning in an end-to-end trainable model. This leads to more accurate results and faster runtime as hyperparameters, such as the step size, are learned during training. Furthermore, we propose a novel multi-scale optimization scheme which allows to quickly propagate information across large distances and effectively increases the receptive field of the regularizer.

Variational Regularization. Variational energy minimization methods led to great advances when dealing with noise and missing information. A variety of regularizers have been studied in the literature [2–4,27,28,42] in the context of different vision problems. Although these regularizers haven proven effective for low-level vision problems [3,35] and 3D surface reconstruction [12,19,31,41], they are limited in their expressiveness and do not fully capture the statistics of the underlying problem. In this paper, we propose a more expressive variational regularizer which jointly reasons at multiple scales and can be learned from data.

Learned Regularization. Several works combine the benefits of variational inference and deep learning. Early approaches combine proceed in a sequential manner by either learning the data costs for subsequent energy minimization [43] or by further regularizing the network output [14]. In contrast, several very recent works integrate variational regularization directly into neural networks and apply them to 2D image processing tasks, including depth super-resolution [32], denoising [18,25,39], deblurring [18], stereo matching [39] and image segmentation [30]. Typically, the individual optimization steps are unrolled and embedded as layers into a neural network. Our work builds upon these ideas and tailors them to the multi-view semantic 3D reconstruction problem using a novel multi-scale neural network architecture for joint geometric and semantic reasoning.

Learned Shape Priors. Recently, deep learning based approaches have been proposed for depth map fusion [15], 3D object recognition [16,24], or 3D shape completion [6,8,9,36,38,40] using dense voxel grids as input. As all these approaches rely on generic 3D convolutional neural network architectures, they require a very large number of parameters and enormous amounts of training data. In contrast, our approach is more light-weight as it explicitly incorporates structural constraints via unrolled variational inference, therefore limiting the number of parameters needed. Although there are recent efforts to change the spatial scalability of these approaches using data-adaptive structures [11,33,34,37], current results are mostly limited to single objects or simple scenes and consider relatively small resolutions. However, none of these works have considered the semantic multi-view 3D reconstruction task which is the focus of this paper. Furthermore, our approach is fully convolutional and thus also scales to very large scenes.

3   Method

Using a generic 3D convolutional neural networks for semantic 3D reconstruction requires enormous amounts of memory and training data. In this paper, we therefore propose a more light-weight alternative which embeds a multi-label optimization task into the layers of a semantic 3D reconstruction network. We first introduce our multi-scale network architecture in Sect. 3.1, followed by a detailed description of the embedded variational problem in Sect. 3.2, and a description of the loss function we use for training the model in Sect. 3.3.

3.1   Network Architecture

The proposed network architecture for semantic 3D reconstruction is illustrated in Fig. 2. The input to our network is a set of semantically labeled depth maps aggregated into a 3D volume of truncated signed distance functions (TSDFs). More specifically, we follow [12] and accumulate per label evidence, *e.g.*, using depth maps from stereo and corresponding semantic image segmentations. As in traditional TSDF fusion, we trace rays from every pixel in each depth map to determine which voxels are occupied or empty. However, instead of using a fixed additive cost, we scale it using the semantic scores at the corresponding pixel. The output of our network is a volumetric semantic 3D reconstruction, where every voxel has one of the semantic class labels or the free space label.

Our network comprises three components (see Fig. 2): an encoder (yellow), the unrolled primal dual optimization layers (blue), and a decoder (orange). Our method reasons at multiple scales which allows for (i) modeling semantic interactions at different scales and (ii) propagating information quickly over larger distances during inference, *e.g.*, to complete missing data. We found that (i) results in higher accuracy while (ii) leads to much faster convergence compared to standard solvers [12,42]. We now describe the three network components on a high level before providing a detailed derivation in Sect. 3.2.

Data Cost Encoder. At every voxel, the data cost is encoded by TSDFs computed via fused depth maps (*e.g.*, from stereo or Kinect) and semantic scene segmentations (*e.g.*, obtained from a semantic segmentation algorithm). In the first stage of our network, we pre-process this input using a shallow multi-scale neural network with 3 layers. The encoder serves several purposes: first, it normalizes the influence of the different semantic classes with respect to each other and the data term as a whole. Second, it helps in reducing low-level noise in the input. Finally, our multi-scale optimization requires down-sampling of the data cost which we learn automatically using separate encoders per scale. More concretely, starting at the highest resolution, we process the input with a residual unit that has two pairs of convolution-ReLU operations followed by a final convolution without activation. The encoded input is then down-sampled to the next scale using average pooling, followed by the next encoding stage.

Unrolled Multi-grid Primal Dual. Instead of processing the input with a high-capacity 3D convolutional neural network, we propose to exploit variational optimization for semantic 3D reconstruction as a light-weight regularizer in our model. The advantage of such a regularizer is that it requires relatively few parameters due to temporal weight sharing while being able to propagate information over large distances by unrolling the algorithm for a fixed number of iterations and propagating information across multiple scales. More specifically, we unroll the iterations of the primal-dual (PD) algorithm of Pock and Chambolle [29], tailored to the multi-label semantic 3D reconstruction task, and parameterize it by replacing the gradient operator with matrices which model the interaction of semantics and geometry at multiple scales for efficient label propagation. Each PD update equation defines a layer in the network, as illus-

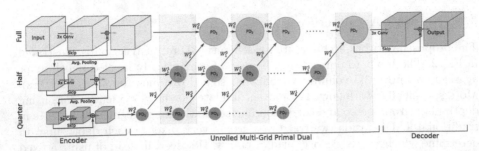

Fig. 2. Proposed network architecture. While the boxes represent data entities, the blue circles represent concurrent primal-dual (PD) processing steps with the iteration number as subscript. The weights W_i^j indicate the information flow (adjoint, primal and dual variables are omitted for brevity). The graph shows an example of our multi-scale optimization for three scales, however, their number is flexible. (Color figure online)

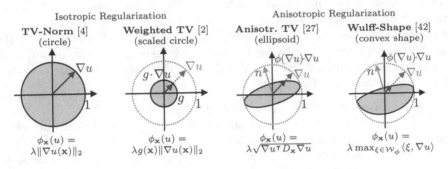

Fig. 3. Overview of hand-crafted regularizers that have been used in volumetric 3D reconstruction, e.g. weighted TV-Norm: [19,41], Anisotropic TV: [20,31], Wulff-shapes: [1,12]. The polar plots show the smoothness cost $\phi_{\mathbf{x}}(\cdot)$ for different gradient directions ∇u. The right two cost functions are aligned to a given normal $\mathbf{n}$. We learn these regularization functions from the training data.

trated with the blue circles in Fig. 2. To learn the parameters of the semantic label interactions and the hyper-parameters of the optimization algorithm, we back-propagate their gradients through the unrolled PD algorithm. A detailed derivation of our algorithm is presented in Sect. 3.2.

Probability Decoder. Similar to the proposed encoding stage, we also decode the obtained solution after the final PD iteration. The main goal here is to smooth and increase contrast, enabling stronger decisions on the final labeling and thereby improving accuracy. Our decoder takes the primal variable after the final iteration of the variational optimizer and feeds it into a residual unit with two pairs of convolution-ReLU operations followed by a final convolution with softmax activation for normalization.

3.2 Learning Variational Energy Minimization

This section describes the multi-grid primal-dual optimization algorithm which we leverage as light-weight, learned regularizer in our network. The traditional variational approach to volumetric 3D reconstruction [1,10,12,13,19,20,31] minimizes the energy

$$\underset{u}{\text{minimize}} \int_{\Omega} (\underbrace{\phi_{\mathbf{x}}(u)}_{\text{regularization}} + \underbrace{fu}_{\text{data fidelity}}) \, d\mathbf{x} \quad \text{subject to} \quad \forall \mathbf{x} \in \Omega : \sum_{\ell} u_{\ell}(\mathbf{x}) = 1$$

(1)

in order to find the best labeling $u : \Omega \to [0,1]^{|\mathcal{L}|}$ that assigns each point in space a probability for each label $\ell \in \mathcal{L}$. The constraint in (1) ensures normalized probabilities across all labels $\ell \in \mathcal{L}$ at every point $\mathbf{x} \in \Omega$. The data cost term $f : \Omega \to \mathbb{R}^{|\mathcal{L}|}$ aggregates the noisy depth measurements of likely surface locations and is usually modeled as a truncated signed distance function (TSDF). To deal with noise, outliers, and missing data, a regularization term is typically added to the energy functional to obtain a smoother and more complete solution. The simplest choice for regularization is the total variation (TV) norm [2,4] $\phi_{\mathbf{x}}(u) = \lambda g(\mathbf{x}) \|\nabla u(\mathbf{x})\|_2$ which corresponds to minimizing the surface area of a 3D shape [19]. In most cases the weight function $g : \Omega \to \mathbb{R}_{\geq 0}$ encodes photoconsistency measures to align the surface with the input data. In many works this model has been extended to better deal with fine geometric details [20,27,31] or multiple semantic labels and directional statistical priors [12,42]. Figure 3 provides an overview of various regularizers which have been proposed for 3D reconstruction. Notably, all these regularizers are convex and a global minimizer of Eq. (1) can be computed efficiently [3]. These hand-crafted regularizers are usually designed for tractability during optimization, but are not powerful enough to represent the true statistics of the underlying problem [18].

Proposed Energy. To overcome the limitations of hand-crafted regularizers, we follow Vogel and Pock [39] and generalize the gradient operator in the regularizer to the general matrix W, i.e. $\phi_{\mathbf{x}}(u) = \|Wu\|_2$. Since we are interested in modeling the complete space of directional and semantic interactions in the 3D multi-label setting, we choose to use a 6-dimensional matrix $W \in \mathbb{R}^{2 \times 2 \times 2 \times |\mathcal{L}| \times |\mathcal{L}| \times 3}$ for our task. This matrix computes gradients using forward-backward differences (modeled by $2 \times 2 \times 2$) and can represent higher-order interactions between any combination of semantic labels (modeled by $|\mathcal{L}| \times |\mathcal{L}|$) in any spatial direction (modeled by last dimension 3). For $W = \nabla$, we obtain a standard TV regularizer. Note that in contrast to the Wulff shapes used by [12], representing W directly leads to a large reduction in the number of parameters and consequently in memory as evidenced by our experimental evaluation. In this work, we aim to learn the weights of this matrix jointly with the other network parameters considering the following energy minimization problem:

$$\underset{u}{\text{minimize}} \int_{\Omega} (\|Wu\|_2 + fu) \, d\mathbf{x} \quad \text{subject to} \quad \forall \mathbf{x} \in \Omega : \sum_{\ell} u_{\ell}(\mathbf{x}) = 1 \quad (2)$$

Optimization. To minimize the convex energy in Eq. (2), we use a first-order primal-dual (PD) algorithm [3] for which the problem is first transformed into a saddle point problem. We introduce the dual variable ξ to replace the TV-norm with its conjugate. We also relax the constraints in Eq. (1) by introducing the Lagrangian variable ν. Then, the corresponding discretized saddle point energy

$$\underset{u}{\text{minimize}} \max_{\|\xi\|_\infty \le 1} \langle Wu, \xi \rangle + \langle f, u \rangle + \nu \left(\sum_\ell u_\ell - 1 \right) \tag{3}$$

can be minimized using the update equations

$$
\begin{aligned}
&1.\ \nu^{t+1} = \nu^t + \sigma \left(\sum_\ell \bar{u}_\ell^t - 1 \right) \quad &3.\ u^{t+1} = \Pi_{[0,1]}\big[u^t - \tau(W^*\xi^{t+1} + f + \nu^{t+1})\big] \\
&2.\ \xi^{t+1} = \Pi_{\|\cdot\| \le 1}\big[\xi^t + \sigma W\bar{u}^t\big] \quad &4.\ \bar{u}^{t+1} = 2u^{t+1} - u^t
\end{aligned}
\tag{4}
$$

at time t with a total of T iterations, W^* the adjoint of W, step sizes τ and σ and projections $\Pi_{[0,1]}$ and $\Pi_{\|\cdot\| \le 1}$, see [3]. Note that the operations $W\bar{u}$ and $W^*\xi$ convolve the kernel W with the variables ξ and $\bar{u}$. This enables efficient integration of these operations into a CNN with shared weights across the primal and dual updates and across the different iterations of the algorithm. We embed this algorithm into our network architecture by unrolling it for a fixed number of iterations. The input to the unrolled PD network is the pre-processed data cost term f provided by the encoder and the output is the optimized primal variable u which is passed to the decoder for post-processing.

Optimization Unrolling. One pass on the updates in Eq. (4) corresponds to one PD iteration. Similar to [32], we unroll the PD algorithm for a fixed number of iterations. Each PD update equation defines a layer in the network, as illustrated with the blue circles in Fig. 2. This unrolled PD algorithm constitutes the core of the network that we use to learn the label interactions represented by W. Note that the step sizes σ and τ that appear in Eq. (4) influence the speed of convergence of the PD algorithm. These parameters are typically selected manually or by preconditioning [29]. In this work, we learn the step sizes automatically by factoring them into W and thereby eliminating them from the update equations, contributing to fast convergence of the proposed algorithm.

Multi-scale Optimization. In the algorithm discussed above, information only propagates between neighboring voxels, generally resulting in slow convergence of the optimization. Therefore, label interactions are relatively low-level and cannot capture more complex statistics arising at larger scales. While it is easy to enlarge the spatial extent of the matrix W, a drawback of naïvely increasing W is the cubic increase in the number of parameters which slows down training and makes the model prone to overfitting. Hence, we consider an alternative in this paper: instead of increasing the size of W, we simultaneously consider the scene at multiple scales.

More specifically, at each PD iteration, information is passed from the lower to the higher scales, as shown in Fig. 2. This enables long-range propagation of information and recovery of fine details while at the same time allowing faster back-propagation of gradients during training. Besides, inference runs in parallel at different scales, which, in practice, results in another speedup of the optimization as compared to traditional coarse-to-fine approaches, where the optimization must wait for coarser scales to converge. Note that even with different regularizer matrices W for each scale, the increase in the number of parameters is at most linear in the number of scale levels. Thus, the increase is sub-linear in the receptive field size compared to the cubic increase of the single-scale approach.

In our network, information is propagated via the matrix W. Thus, we lift our model to multiple scales by modifying update steps 2 and 3 in Eq. (4) to

$$\xi_s^{t+1} = \Pi_{\|\cdot\|\leq 1}\left[\xi_s^t + \sigma\left(W_s^s \bar{u}_s^t + U_{s+1}^s W_{s+1}^s \bar{u}_{s+1}^t\right)\right] \tag{5}$$

$$u_s^{t+1} = \Pi_{[0,1]}\left[u_s^t + \tau\left(W_s^{s*}\xi_s^{t+1} + U_{s+1}^{s*} W_{s+1}^{s*}\xi_{s+1}^{t+1}\right) + \tau\left(v_s^{t+1} - f\right)\right] \tag{6}$$

where s is one of S scale levels (lower level = higher resolution) and U_{s+1}^s upsamples from $s+1$ to s. W_s^s corresponds to the regularizer at level s, while W_{s+1}^s handles the transfer of information from level $s+1$ to the next finer level s.

3.3   Loss Function

We train the network architecture in Fig. 2 using supervised learning. Towards this goal, we define the training objective as the semantic reconstruction loss between our computed solution u and a given ground truth labeling $\hat{u}$. Typically, this loss is defined as the categorical cross entropy. However, several important modifications to the standard definition of this loss are necessary in practice as the ground truth is often not completely observed or labeled. We follow common practice and introduce a separate label $\tilde{\ell}$ for unlabeled regions. Unobserved regions are modeled by a uniform distribution $\mathcal{U}_{\mathcal{L}}$ in label space. To make the loss function agnostic to unobserved areas in the ground truth and to not penalize our solution in unlabeled regions, we use the following weighted loss function

$$H(u, \hat{u}) = -\int_\Omega w(\mathbf{x})\, u(\mathbf{x}) \log \hat{u}(\mathbf{x})\, d\mathbf{x} \tag{7}$$

$$w(\mathbf{x}) = \Delta_{KL}(\hat{u}(\mathbf{x}), \mathcal{U}_{\mathcal{L}})\Delta_{KL}(\hat{u}(\mathbf{x}), \delta_{\tilde{\ell}}) \tag{8}$$

which returns zero if the ground truth at $\mathbf{x}$ is not unobserved or unkown. Here, Δ_{KL} denotes the KL-divergence. The first term measures the similarity between the ground truth and a uniform distribution and the second term the similarity to a Dirac distribution with center $\tilde{\ell}$. In case the ground truth matches exactly the uniform distribution or it is unlabeled with maximum certainty, this is equivalent to masking the loss as a hard constraint. However, as shown in the experiments, we generate ground truth using conventional regularization methods. As a result, it is beneficial to penalize using a soft constrained loss on the imperfectly labeled ground truth. Without the proposed weighting, the training would receive contradicting supervisory signals. Specifically, if the ground truth is incomplete for a specific class, the loss would encourage reconstruction in the observed areas whereas a potentially correct labeling in the unobserved parts would be inadvertently penalized.

4 Results

This section presents our results. We first analyze the memory and runtime complexity of our method wrt. to the state-of-the-art approach of Häne *et al.* [12]. Next, we empirically validate our approach in a controlled setting on a synthetic 2D toy dataset Finally, we present results on challenging indoor and outdoor semantic reconstruction tasks.

4.1 Memory and Runtime Complexity

One of the main advantages of our method over Häne *et al.* [12] is the significantly reduced memory complexity. While the approach of Häne *et al.* has a memory complexity of $(3 + d)|\mathcal{L}| \cdot |\Omega| + (1 + d)|\mathcal{L}|^2|\Omega|$, ours has a complexity of $(3 + d)|\mathcal{L}| \cdot |\Omega| + 3 \cdot 2^d|\mathcal{L}|^2$. Here, d is the dimension of Ω, and $|\mathcal{L}|$ and $|\Omega|$ the number of labels and voxels. Note that using additional scales in our approach only marginally increases the amount of memory, since each successive higher scale has 2^d fewer voxels. While their approach maintain dual variables for all label combinations at each location in the voxel grid, our approach shares this state for all locations. In practice, for a moderate scene size of $|\Omega| = 300^3$ (500^3) voxels with $|\mathcal{L}| = 40$ labels and single-precision floating point data, theirs has an intractable memory usage of around 668 GB (3 TB) versus a tractable 24 GB (111 GB) for ours. In addition to an improved memory complexity, our approach is much faster to compute. Compared to the costly calculation of Wulff shape projections, the convolution operations in our case are much cheaper to compute and, in practice, are implemented efficiently on GPUs. In summary, our proposed approach makes it tractable to perform joint semantic 3D reconstruction for both larger scenes and significantly more labels, as shown in the experiments.

4.2 Experiments on Synthetic 2D Data

Dataset. For validating our model, we created a simple 2D toy dataset with 5 labels, each defined by a color (white for *free space*, gray for *ground*, red for *building*, blue for *roof* and green for *vegetation*). The scenes were generated with shapes like boxes, triangles, and circles, which were randomly positioned subject to interval bounds and ordering constraints, *e.g.*, roof on top of building and building on top of ground. We perturb the images with Gaussian noise and simulate missing data by removing large regions using random shapes (circle, square, triangle). Figure 4 shows examples along with their degraded versions. We created 3000 images of size 160×96 for training and 1200 for testing, respectively. The data cost for label $\ell \in \mathcal{L}$ is defined as $f_\ell = \| I - c_\ell \|_2^2$ where I is the input image and c_ℓ is the color corresponding to label ℓ. For regions with missing pixels, which can only be filled by regularization, we use a uniform data cost.

Quantitative Evaluation. Using this dataset, we evaluate the benefit of the multi-scale approach as well as the feature encoding (E) and the probability

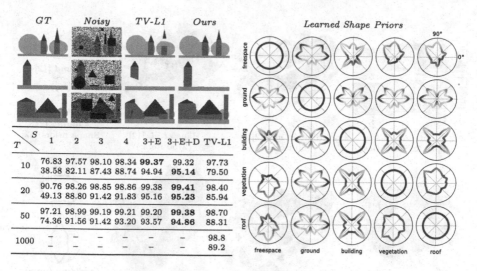

S T	1	2	3	4	3+E	3+E+D	TV-L1
10	76.83	97.57	98.10	98.34	**99.37**	99.32	97.73
	38.58	82.11	87.43	88.74	94.94	**95.14**	79.50
20	90.76	98.26	98.85	98.86	99.38	**99.41**	98.40
	49.13	88.80	91.42	91.83	95.16	**95.23**	85.94
50	97.21	98.99	99.19	99.21	99.20	**99.38**	98.70
	74.36	91.56	91.42	93.20	93.57	**94.86**	88.31
1000	–	–	–	–	–	–	98.8
	–	–	–	–	–	–	89.2

Fig. 4. 2D semantic segmentation on synthetic images. Top Left: 3/1200 test scenes with ground truth (GT), noisy input, results of TV-L1 and ours in comparison. Bottom Left: Reconstruction accuracy for TV-L1 and our method using different numbers of iterations T (TV-L1 converges with 1000) and scales S. First row shows accuracy over *all pixels*, second shows accuracy only over *regions with missing data cost*. Right: Label transition costs between two labels depending on the surface normal. Ours learns more complex cost functions compared to the hand-crafted ones in Fig. 3. The plots have been rescaled for readability, with the magnitude encoded as color. (Color figure online)

decoding (D) networks. All networks are trained from random initialization with a batch size of 32. Figure 4 (left) shows results on the test set with TV-L1 as a baseline. We show the accuracy computed on the whole image and only on the missing regions. The latter emphasizes the performance of the regularizer since in these regions, the data cost has no influence. Our approach consistently outperforms TV-L1, especially in the missing regions. This shows that our method learns more powerful regularizers, encoding statistics about geometry and semantics. Furthermore, increasing the number of scales and including encoding and decoding networks is beneficial.

Qualitative Evaluation. Figure 4 (left) compares the segmentations from our full network ($T = 20$, $S = 3$) to those of TV-L1. While TV-L1 finds the (wrong) minimal surface solution, our network correctly fills in these regions and respects ordering constraints (*e.g.* building above ground).

Learned Priors. Our network learns costs at label transitions in a small 2^d neighborhood at every scale. This cost is influenced by the orientation of the transitions: vertical transitions between building and ground should be penalized more than horizontal transitions. Figure 4 (right) plots the label transition costs against the surface normal for all label combinations. We see that the regularizer has the desired behavior in most cases, *e.g.* for building to ground transitions, we see that vertical transitions are penalized the most.

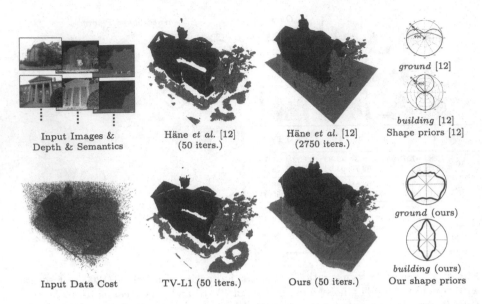

Input Images &   Häne *et al.* [12]   Häne *et al.* [12]   *ground* [12]
Depth & Semantics   (50 iters.)   (2750 iters.)

                                                                        building [12]
                                                                        Shape priors [12]

Input Data Cost   TV-L1 (50 iters.)   Ours (50 iters.)   *ground* (ours)

                                                                        building (ours)
                                                                        Our shape priors

Fig. 5. Semantic 3D reconstruction results. Left: Input. Middle: Reconstruction results. Our method learns semantic and geometric neighborhood statistics to handle large amounts of noise, outliers and missing data. Compared to TV-L1 and the state-of-the-art [12], it needs significantly less iterations and memory. Right: Hand-crafted shape priors from Häne *et al.* [12] (top) vs. our learned shape priors (bottom).

4.3   Experiments on Real 3D Data

We now use the best-performing architecture as determined in our 2D experiments and apply it to the 3D multi-label domain using two challenging datasets. We show that we can replicate hand-crafted Wulff shapes by learning from solutions produced by Häne *et al.* [12]. Using the learned weights, our approach produces equivalent results but two orders of magnitude faster, using only a fraction of the memory. Moreover, we apply our method to datasets with ten times more labels than can be handled by existing Wulff shape approaches.

Datasets. For all datasets, we assume gravity aligned inputs and use a standard multi-label TSDF for data cost aggregation [12]. For comparing against Häne *et al.* [13], we use their 3 outdoor scenes (*Castle, South Building, Providence*) with 5 labels (*freespace, ground, building, vegetation, unkown*). The largest scene has a size of around 300^3 voxels. In addition, we evaluate on the recently released ScanNet dataset [7], comprising 1513 scenes with fine-grain semantic labeling. We adopt the NYU [26] labeling with 40 classes. Using a voxel resolution of 5 cm, the largest scenes have a size of around 400^3 voxels.

Training. Our network can optimize arbitrarily sized scenes both during inference and training, as our architecture is fully convolutional. However, due to the increased memory requirements during back-propagation and the computational benefits of batch processing in stochastic gradient descent, we train on fixed-size,

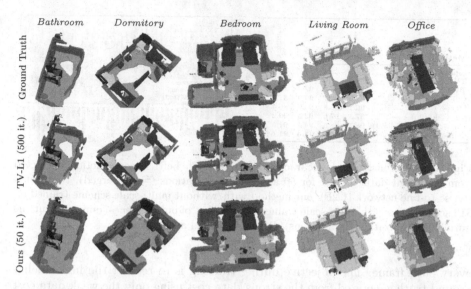

Fig. 6. 3D reconstruction results for ScanNet [7] for different scenes and methods.

random crops of dimension 32^3 with a batch size of 4 and a learning rate of 10^{-4}. We perform data augmentation by randomly rotating and flipping around the gravity axis. For all experiments, we unroll the PD algorithm for $T = 50$ iterations using $S = 3$ scales. As our network uses a few parameters as compared to pure learning approaches, overfitting is not a problem for our approach and training typically converges quickly after a few thousand mini batches.

Wulff Shape Comparison. First, we are interested in replacing the more complex and computationally costly Wulff shape approach [12] by learning from data produced by their method. Figure 5 (right) shows the original Wulff shapes by Häne *et al.* next to our learned shapes at scale $s = 0$. The cost shape visualization is equivalent to the synthetic 2D experiments with the difference that here we compute the average shape around the gravity axis. Our method meaningfully learns the hand-crafted shapes, demonstrating that we can replicate the more complex Wulff shape formulation. This is confirmed by a 98% per-class accuracy when evaluating our learned weights on the full scenes wrt. [12]. Figures 1 and 5 show qualitative results for *Castle* and *South Building*. Moreover, our results are achieved after 50 iterations and 10 s while their approach requires 2750 iterations and around 4000 s to converge. Next, we demonstrate our method in a setting with an order of magnitude more class labels, which would be computationally intractable for their method [12].

Evaluation on ScanNet [7]. For ScanNet we re-integrate the provided depth maps and semantic segmentations using TSDF fusion based on the provided camera poses to establish voxelized ground truth. The resulting data costs provide very strong evidence and we thus use multi-label TV-L1 optimization with $W = \nabla$. For our evaluation, we also generate weak data costs by only integrating

Methods	Overall	Freespace	Occupied	Semantic
Input data	59.8	39.1	99.7	68.4
TV-L1 (50 it.)	92.8	71.0	91.4	87.8
TV-L1 (500 it.)	95.8	86.4	92.3	88.5
C2F (50 it.)	21.0	26.7	99.9	31.4
Ours-5 (50 it.)	96.7	95.8	93.9	86.4
Ours-300 (0 it.)	97.3	97.6	92.3	90.2
Ours-300 (50 it. 1 level)	98.7	98.6	94.4	91.5
Ours-300 (50 it. 3 levels)	**98.7**	**98.6**	**94.4**	**91.5**

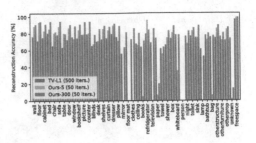

Fig. 7. 3D Reconstruction accuracy for ScanNet [7]. Left: Reconstruction extracted from the input data, TV-L1 for 50 and for 500 iterations ($\hat{=}$ converged), traditional coarse-to-fine network (C2F), our method with/without multi-scale scheme trained on 312 scenes, ours with multi-scale trained on a subset of only 5 scenes, ours without the unrolled optimization (0 iterations). Right: Per-label accuracies.

every 50th frame. The objective during training is to recover the high fidelity ground truth generated from the strong data cost using only the weak data cost as input. We train our network using 312 training scenes and evaluate their performance on 156 test scenes. Figure 7 summarizes quantitative results for a reconstruction extracted from the input data cost, a multi-label TV-L1, a coarse-to-fine version of our network, a version of our network without variational regularization (0 iterations), and our proposed multi-scale architecture. Note that ours without regularization is a simple variant of approaches like SSCNet [36] or ScanComplete [6]. We draw the following conclusions: First, running TV-L1 for the same number of iterations as our method results in significantly worse results. Second, running TV-L1 for an order of magnitude more iterations until convergence still performs worse than our method. Third, a naïve coarse-to-fine approach does not converge during training and produces bad reconstructions. Moreover, integrating multi-scale variational regularization into the network significantly improves the completeness of the results. Lastly, a version trained on only 5 scenes attains almost the same overall accuracy as a version trained on the full training dataset, indicating that our model can be trained with very little data. Furthermore, due to the few learned parameters in our network, we achieve the same accuracy for the training and test scenes which demonstrates the generalization power of our model. Figures 1 and 6 show qualitative results for selected scenes. Surprisingly, our method sometimes produces results which are visually more pleasing than the ground truth used for training. We attribute this to the fact that our method can learn correct label interactions from all training data jointly and can then apply this knowledge to a single instance.

5   Conclusion

We presented a novel method for dense semantic 3D reconstruction. By incorporating variational regularization into a neural network, we can learn powerful semantic priors using a limited number of parameters. In stark contrast to purely learning based approaches, our method requires little training data and generalizes to new scenes without overfitting. The proposed multi-scale optimization jointly reasons about semantics and geometry at different scales and enables inference that is an order of magnitude more efficient than the state of the art. Experiments on synthetic and real data demonstrate the benefits wrt. accuracy, runtime, memory consumption, and algorithmic complexity.

Acknowledgements. This work received funding from the Horizon 2020 research and innovation programme under grant No. 637221 (Built2Spec), No. 688007 (Trim-Bot2020). This research was also supported by the Intelligence Advanced Research Projects Activity (IARPA) via Department of Interior/Interior Business Center (DOI/IBC) contract number D17PC00280. The U.S. Government is authorized to reproduce and distribute reprints for Governmental purposes notwithstanding any copyright annotation thereon.

Disclaimer: The views and conclusions contained herein are those of the authors and should not be interpreted as necessarily representing the official policies or endorsements, either expressed or implied, of IARPA, DOI/IBC, or the U.S. Government.

References

1. Bláha, M., Vogel, C., Richard, A., Wegner, J.D., Pock, T., Schindler, K.: Large-scale semantic 3D reconstruction: an adaptive multi-resolution model for multi-class volumetric labeling. In: Proceedings of Conference on Computer Vision and Pattern Recognition (CVPR) (2016)
2. Bresson, X., Esedoḡlu, S., Vandergheynst, P., Thiran, J.P., Osher, S.: Fast global minimization of the active contour/snake model. J. Math. Imaging Vis. **28**, 151–167 (2007)
3. Chambolle, A., Pock, T.: A first-order primal-dual algorithm for convex problems with applications to imaging. J. Math. Imaging Vis. **40**, 120–145 (2011)
4. Chan, T., Esedoḡlu, S., Nikolova, M.: Algorithms for finding global minimizers of image segmentation and denoising models. SIAM J. Appl. Math. **66**, 1632–1648 (2006)
5. Cherabier, I., Häne, C., Oswald, M.R., Pollefeys, M.: Multi-label semantic 3D reconstruction using voxel blocks. In: International Conference on 3D Vision (3DV) (2016)
6. Dai, A., Ritchie, D., Bokeloh, M., Reed, S., Sturm, J., Nießner, M.: ScanComplete: large-scale scene completion and semantic segmentation for 3D scans. In: Proceedings of Conference on Computer Vision and Pattern Recognition (CVPR) (2017)
7. Dai, A., Chang, A.X., Savva, M., Halber, M., Funkhouser, T., Nießner, M.: ScanNet: richly-annotated 3D reconstructions of indoor scenes. In: Proceedings Conference on Computer Vision and Pattern Recognition (CVPR) (2017)
8. Dai, A., Qi, C.R., Nießner, M.: Shape completion using 3D-encoder-predictor CNNs and shape synthesis. In: Proceedings of Conference on Computer Vision and Pattern Recognition (CVPR) (2017)
9. Han, X., Li, Z., Huang, H., Kalogerakis, E., Yu, Y.: High-resolution shape completion using deep neural networks for global structure and local geometry inference. In: Proceedings of International Conference on Computer Vision (ICCV) (2017)

10. Häne, C., Savinov, N., Pollefeys, M.: Class specific 3D object shape priors using surface normals. In: Proceedings of Conference on Computer Vision and Pattern Recognition (CVPR) (2014)
11. Häne, C., Tulsiani, S., Malik, J.: Hierarchical surface prediction for 3D object reconstruction (2017)
12. Häne, C., Zach, C., Cohen, A., Angst, R., Pollefeys, M.: Joint 3D scene reconstruction and class segmentation. In: Proceedings of Conference on Computer Vision and Pattern Recognition (CVPR) (2013)
13. Häne, C., Zach, C., Cohen, A., Pollefeys, M.: Dense semantic 3D reconstruction. Trans. Pattern Anal. Mach. Intell. (TPAMI) **39**, 1730–1743 (2017)
14. Heber, S., Pock, T.: Convolutional networks for shape from light field. In: Proceedings of Conference on Computer Vision and Pattern Recognition (CVPR) (2016)
15. Ji, M., Gall, J., Zheng, H., Liu, Y., Fang, L.: SurfaceNet: an end-to-end 3D neural network for multiview stereopsis. In: Proceedings of International Conference on Computer Vision (ICCV) (2017)
16. Kar, A., Tulsiani, S., Carreira, J., Malik, J.: Category-specific object reconstruction from a single image. In: Proceedings of Conference on Computer Vision and Pattern Recognition (CVPR) (2015)
17. Kim, B.S., Kohli, P., Savarese, S.: 3D scene understanding by voxel-CRF. In: Proceedings of International Conference on Computer Vision (ICCV) (2013)
18. Kobler, E., Klatzer, T., Hammernik, K., Pock, T.: Variational networks: connecting variational methods and deep learning. In: Roth, V., Vetter, T. (eds.) GCPR 2017. LNCS, vol. 10496, pp. 281–293. Springer, Cham (2017). https://doi.org/10.1007/978-3-319-66709-6_23
19. Kolev, K., Klodt, M., Brox, T., Cremers, D.: Continuous global optimization in multiview 3D reconstruction. Int. J. Comput. Vis. (IJCV) **84**, 80–96 (2009)
20. Kolev, K., Pock, T., Cremers, D.: Anisotropic minimal surfaces integrating photo-consistency and normal information for multiview stereo. In: Daniilidis, K., Maragos, P., Paragios, N. (eds.) ECCV 2010. LNCS, vol. 6313, pp. 538–551. Springer, Heidelberg (2010). https://doi.org/10.1007/978-3-642-15558-1_39
21. Kundu, A., Li, Y., Dellaert, F., Li, F., Rehg, J.M.: Joint semantic segmentation and 3D reconstruction from monocular video. In: Fleet, D., Pajdla, T., Schiele, B., Tuytelaars, T. (eds.) ECCV 2014. LNCS, vol. 8694, pp. 703–718. Springer, Cham (2014). https://doi.org/10.1007/978-3-319-10599-4_45
22. Ladický, L., et al.: Joint optimization for object class segmentation and dense stereo reconstruction. Int. J. Comput. Vis. (IJCV) **100**, 122–133 (2012)
23. Mahabadi, R.K., Hane, C., Pollefeys, M.: Segment based 3D object shape priors. In: Proceedings of Conference on Computer Vision and Pattern Recognition (CVPR) (2015)
24. Maturana, D., Scherer, S.: VoxNet: a 3D convolutional neural network for real-time object recognition. In: International Conference on Intelligent Robots and Systems (IROS) (2015)
25. Meinhardt, T., Möller, M., Hazirbas, C., Cremers, D.: Learning proximal operators: using denoising networks for regularizing inverse imaging problems. In: Proceedings of International Conference on Computer Vision (ICCV) (2017)
26. Silberman, N., Hoiem, D., Kohli, P., Fergus, R.: Indoor segmentation and support inference from RGBD images. In: Fitzgibbon, A., Lazebnik, S., Perona, P., Sato, Y., Schmid, C. (eds.) ECCV 2012. LNCS, vol. 7576, pp. 746–760. Springer, Heidelberg (2012). https://doi.org/10.1007/978-3-642-33715-4_54

27. Olsson, C., Byröd, M., Overgaard, N.C., Kahl, F.: Extending continuous cuts: Anisotropic metrics and expansion moves. In: Proceedings of International Conference on Computer Vision (ICCV) (2009). https://doi.org/10.1109/ICCV.2009.5459206

28. Osher, S.J., Esedoḡlu, S.: Decomposition of images by the anisotropic Rudin-Osher-Fatemi model. Commun. Pure Appl. Math. **57**, 1609–1626 (2004)

29. Pock, T., Chambolle, A.: Diagonal preconditioning for first order primal-dual algorithms in convex optimization. In: Proceedings of International Conference on Computer Vision (ICCV) (2011)

30. Ranftl, R., Pock, T.: A deep variational model for image segmentation. In: Jiang, X., Hornegger, J., Koch, R. (eds.) GCPR 2014. LNCS, vol. 8753, pp. 107–118. Springer, Cham (2014). https://doi.org/10.1007/978-3-319-11752-2_9

31. Reinbacher, C., Pock, T., Bauer, C., Bischof, H.: Variational segmentation of elongated volumetric structures. In: Proceedings of Conference on Computer Vision and Pattern Recognition (CVPR) (2010)

32. Riegler, G., Rüther, M., Bischof, H.: ATGV-Net: accurate depth super-resolution. In: Leibe, B., Matas, J., Sebe, N., Welling, M. (eds.) ECCV 2016. LNCS, vol. 9907, pp. 268–284. Springer, Cham (2016). https://doi.org/10.1007/978-3-319-46487-9_17

33. Riegler, G., Ulusoy, A.O., Bischof, H., Geiger, A.: OctNetFusion: learning depth fusion from data. In: International Conference on 3D Vision (3DV) (2017)

34. Riegler, G., Ulusoy, A.O., Geiger, A.: OctNet: learning deep 3D representations at high resolutions. In: Proceedings of Conference on Computer Vision and Pattern Recognition (CVPR) (2017)

35. Rudin, L.I., Osher, S., Fatemi, E.: Nonlinear total variation based noise removal algorithms. Phys. D Nonlinear Phenom. **60**, 259–268 (1992)

36. Song, S., Yu, F., Zeng, A., Chang, A.X., Savva, M., Funkhouser, T.A.: Semantic scene completion from a single depth image. In: Proceedings of Conference on Computer Vision and Pattern Recognition (CVPR) (2017)

37. Tatarchenko, M., Dosovitskiy, A., Brox, T.: Octree generating networks: efficient convolutional architectures for high-resolution 3D outputs. In: Proceedings of International Conference on Computer Vision (ICCV) (2017)

38. Tulsiani, S., Zhou, T., Efros, A.A., Malik, J.: Multi-view supervision for single-view reconstruction via differentiable ray consistency. In: Proceedings of Conference on Computer Vision and Pattern Recognition (CVPR) (2017)

39. Vogel, C., Pock, T.: A primal dual network for low-level vision problems. In: Roth, V., Vetter, T. (eds.) GCPR 2017. LNCS, vol. 10496, pp. 189–202. Springer, Cham (2017). https://doi.org/10.1007/978-3-319-66709-6_16

40. Wu, Z., et al.: 3D shapeNets: a deep representation for volumetric shapes. In: Proceedings of Conference on Computer Vision and Pattern Recognition (CVPR) (2015)

41. Zach, C., Pock, T., Bischof, H.: A globally optimal algorithm for robust TV-L 1 range image integration. In: Proceedings of International Conference on Computer Vision (ICCV) (2007)

42. Zach, C., Shan, L., Niethammer, M.: Globally optimal finsler active contours. In: Denzler, J., Notni, G., Süße, H. (eds.) DAGM 2009. LNCS, vol. 5748, pp. 552–561. Springer, Heidelberg (2009). https://doi.org/10.1007/978-3-642-03798-6_56

43. Zbontar, J., LeCun, Y.: Computing the stereo matching cost with a convolutional neural network. In: Proceedings of Conference on Computer Vision and Pattern Recognition (CVPR) (2015)

Object Detection in Video with Spatiotemporal Sampling Networks

Gedas Bertasius[1(✉)], Lorenzo Torresani[2], and Jianbo Shi[1]

[1] University of Pennsylvania, Philadelphia, USA
gberta@seas.upenn.edu
[2] Dartmouth College, Hanover, USA

Abstract. We propose a Spatiotemporal Sampling Network (STSN) that uses deformable convolutions across time for object detection in videos. Our STSN performs object detection in a video frame by learning to spatially sample features from the adjacent frames. This naturally renders the approach robust to occlusion or motion blur in individual frames. Our framework does not require additional supervision, as it optimizes sampling locations directly with respect to object detection performance. Our STSN outperforms the state-of-the-art on the ImageNet VID dataset and compared to prior video object detection methods it uses a simpler design, and does not require optical flow data for training.

1 Introduction

In recent years, deep convolutional networks have achieved remarkable results in many computer vision tasks [1–8], including object detection in images [9–19]. However, directly applying these image-level models to object detection in video is difficult due to motion blur, video defocus, unusual poses, or object occlusions (see Fig. 1). Despite these challenges, it is natural to assume that video object detectors should be more powerful than still image detectors because video contains richer information about the same object instance (e.g., its appearance in different poses, and from different viewpoints). The key challenge then is designing a model that effectively exploits temporal information in videos.

Prior work [20–23] has proposed to exploit such temporal information in videos by means of various post-processing steps aimed at making object detections coherent across time. However, since temporal coherence is enforced in a second stage, typically these methods cannot be trained end-to-end. To overcome this limitation, recent work [24] has introduced a flow-based aggregation network that is trainable end-to-end. It exploits optical flow to find correspondences across time and it then aggregates features across temporal correspondences to smooth object detections over adjacent frames. However, one of the downsides

---

Electronic supplementary material The online version of this chapter (https://doi.org/10.1007/978-3-030-01258-8_21) contains supplementary material, which is available to authorized users.

© Springer Nature Switzerland AG 2018
V. Ferrari et al. (Eds.): ECCV 2018, LNCS 11216, pp. 342–357, 2018.
https://doi.org/10.1007/978-3-030-01258-8_21

Fig. 1. An illustration of the common challenges associated with object detection in video. These include video defocus, motion blur, occlusions and unusual poses. The bounding boxes denote the objects that we want to detect in these examples.

of this new model is that in addition to performing object detection, it also needs to predict motion. This is disadvantageous due to the following reasons: (1) designing an effective flow network architecture is not trivial, (2) training such a model requires large amounts of flow data, which may be difficult and costly to obtain, (3) integrating a flow network and a detection network into a single model may be challenging due to factors such as different loss functions, differing training procedures for each network, etc.

To address these shortcomings, in this work, we introduce a simple, yet effective Spatiotemporal Sampling Network (STSN) that uses deformable convolutions [25] across space and time to leverage temporal information for object detection in video. Our STSN learns to spatially sample useful feature points from nearby video frames such that object detection accuracy in a given video frame is maximized. To achieve this, we train our STSN end-to-end on a large set of video frames labeled with bounding boxes. We show that this leads to a better accuracy compared to the state-of-the-art on the ImageNet VID dataset [26], without requiring complex flow network design, or the need to train the network on large amounts of flow data.

2   Related Work

2.1   Object Detection in Images

Modern object detectors [9–19] are predominantly built on some form of deep CNNs [1,3,5]. One of the earliest deep CNN object detection systems was R-CNN [14], which involved a two-stage pipeline where object proposals were extracted in the first stage, and then each proposal was classified using a CNN. To reduce the computational burden, the methods in [9], and [13] leveraged ROI pooling, which led to more efficient learning. Furthermore, to unify the entire object detection pipeline, Faster R-CNN [12] replaced various region proposal methods by another network to make the entire system trainable end-to-end. Following this work, several methods [18,19] extended Faster R-CNN into a system that runs in real time with small reduction in performance. Additionally, recent work [17] introduced position sensitive ROI pooling, which significantly improved the detection efficiency compared to prior object detection systems. Finally, two recent methods, Mask R-CNN [10], and Deformable CNNs [25], improved object detection results even further and they represent the current state-of-the-art in object detection. Whereas Mask-RCNNs use an additional branch that predicts a mask for each region of interest, Deformable CNNs employ deformable convolutions, which allow the network to condition discriminatively its receptive field on the input, and to also model deformations of objects more robustly.

While the aforementioned methods work well on images, they are not designed to exploit temporal relationships in video. Instead, our Spatiotemporal Sampling Network (STSN), is specifically designed for a video object detection task. Unlike standard Deformable CNNs [25], which use deformable convolution in the spatial domain, our STSN learns to sample features temporally across different video frames, which leads to improved video object detection accuracy.

2.2   Object Detection in Videos

Up until the introduction of the ImageNet VID challenge [26], there were no large-scale benchmarks for video object detection. Thus, there are only few methods that we can compare our work to. T-CNNs [20,21] use a video object detection pipeline that involves predicting optical flow first, then propagating image-level predictions according to the flow, and finally using a tracking algorithm to select temporally consistent high confidence detections. Seq-NMS [22] constructs a temporal graph from overlapping bounding box detections across the adjacent frames, and then uses dynamic programming to select bounding box sequences with the highest overall detection score. The work of Lee et al. [23] treats a video object detection task as a multi-object tracking problem. Finally, the method of Feichtenhofer et al. [27] proposes a ConvNet architecture that solves detection and tracking problems jointly, and then applies a Viterbi algorithm to link the detections across time.

The approach most similar to our work is the method of Zhu et al. [24], who proposed an end-to-end trainable network that jointly estimates optical flow and also detects objects in video. This is accomplished by using the predicted optical flow to align the features from the adjacent frames. The aggregated features are then fed as input to the detection network.

Our method is beneficial over the methods that use optical flow CNNs such as the method of Zhu et al. [24]. First, we note that pretrained optical flow CNNs do not always generalize to new datasets, which may hinder video object detection performance. In contrast, our method has a learnable spatiotemporal sampling module that is discriminatively trained from object detection labels, and thus, it does not suffer from this issue. Furthermore, our STSN can be trained for video object detection in a single stage end-to-end. In comparison, methods that rely on optical flow require an additional stage to train an optical flow CNN, which renders the training procedure more cumbersome and lengthy. For example, we note that it would take about four days to train an optical flow CNN of FGFA [24] from scratch and then four additional days to train FGFA [24] for video object detection, making it eight days of total training time. In contrast, our STSN is trained in a single stage in only 4 days. Finally, we point out that our STSN also yields a gain—albeit moderate—in video object detection accuracy.

3 Background: Deformable Convolution

Before describing our method, we first review some background information on deformable convolution [25], which is one of the key components of our STSN. Let us first note that a standard 2D convolution is comprised of two steps: (1) sampling locations on a uniformly-spaced grid $\mathcal{R}$, and (2) performing a weighted summation of sampled values using weights w. For example, if we consider a standard 2D convolution with a 3×3 kernel, and a dilation factor of 1, the grid $\mathcal{R}$ is defined as $\mathcal{R} = \{(-1, -1), (-1, 0), \ldots, (0, 1), (1, 1)\}$. Under a standard 2D convolution, to compute a new value at pixel location p_0 in the output feature map y, we would perform the following operation on the input feature map x:

$$y(p_0) = \sum_{p_n \in \mathcal{R}} w(p_n) \cdot x(p_0 + p_n), \tag{1}$$

Instead, in a deformable 2D convolution, the grid $\mathcal{R}$ is augmented with data-conditioned offsets $\{\Delta p_n | n = 1, \ldots, N\}$, where $N = |\mathcal{R}|$. We can then compute a deformable convolution as:

$$y(p_0) = \sum_{p_n \in \mathcal{R}} w(p_n) \cdot x(p_0 + p_n + \Delta p_n) \tag{2}$$

Since the offset Δp_n is typically fractional, the operation above is implemented using bilinear interpolation. Note that the offsets are obtained by applying a separate convolutional layer to the activation tensor containing the feature map x. This yields an offset map that has the same spatial resolution as the input feature map. Also, note that the offsets are shared across all feature channels of a given activation tensor. During training, the weights for the deformable convolution kernel, and the offsets kernel are learned jointly by propagating gradients through the bilinear interpolation operator. We refer the reader to the original work that introduced deformable convolutions [25] for further details.

4 Spatiotemporal Sampling Network

Our goal is to design a network architecture that incorporates temporal information for object detection in video.

Let us denote with I_t the frame at time t in the video. Let us consider one of the scenarios depicted in Fig. 1, e.g., a setting where I_t is blurry, contains an object in an unusual pose, or perhaps an occlusion. But let us assume that a nearby frame I_{t+k} includes the same object clearly visible and in a relatively standard pose. If we only had access to I_t, accurate object detection would be

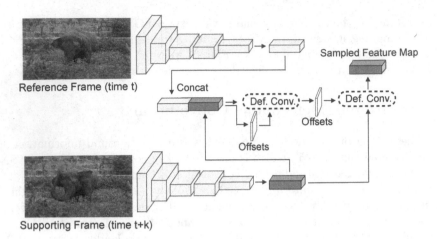

Fig. 2. Our spatiotemporal sampling mechanism, which we use for video object detection. Given the task of detecting objects in a particular video frame (i.e., a reference frame), our goal is to incorporate information from a nearby frame of the same video (i.e., a supporting frame). First, we extract features from both frames via a backbone convolutional network (CNN). Next, we concatenate the features from the reference and supporting frames, and feed them through multiple deformable convolutional layers. The last of such layers produces offsets that are used to sample informative features from the supporting frame. Our spatiotemporal sampling scheme allows us to produce accurate detections even if objects in the reference frame appear blurry or occluded.

very challenging. However, leveraging information from I_{t+k} may enable more robust detection in the frame I_t. Thus, the main challenge in this setting is incorporating object-level information from the *supporting* frame I_{t+k} for an improved object detection accuracy in the *reference* frame I_t. Note that in our system each frame in the video is treated in turn as a reference frame in order to produce object detection in every frame of the video. Furthermore, in practice we use $2K$ supporting frames for detection in the reference frame, by taking the K preceding frames and the K subsequent frames as supporting frames, i.e. $\{I_{t-K}, I_{t-(K-1)}, \ldots, I_{t-1}, I_{t+1}, \ldots, I_{t+(K-1)}, I_{t+K}\}$. However, for ease of explanation we introduce our STSN by considering a single supporting frame I_{t+k}.

To effectively integrate temporal information we need two things: (1) powerful object-level features from an image-level network, and (2) an ability to sample useful object-level features from the supporting frames for the reference frame. We achieve the former by employing a state-of-the-art backbone network. For the latter, we design a spatiotemporal sampling scheme, which we describe below.

Our STSN can be summarized in four steps. First, a backbone convolutional network computes object-level features for each video frame individually. Then, spatiotemporal sampling blocks are applied to the object-level feature maps in order to sample relevant features from nearby frames conditioned on the input *reference* frame. Next, the sampled features from each video frame are temporally aggregated into a single feature tensor for the reference frame using a per-pixel weighted summation. Finally, the feature tensor is provided as input to the detection network to produce final object detection results for the given reference frame. We note that our framework integrates these conceptually-distinct four steps into a single architecture, which we train end-to-end.

Backbone Architecture. Our backbone network is applied to each frame of the video. As backbone network, we use a Deformable CNN [25] based on the ResNet-101 [5] architecture, which is one of the top-performing object detection systems at the moment. Similarly to [25], our backbone network employs 6 deformable convolutional layers. We also note that even though we use a Deformable CNN architecture, our system can easily integrate other architectures and thus it can benefit from future improvements in still-image object detection.

Spatiotemporal Feature Sampling. Our main contribution is the design of a spatiotemporal sampling mechanism, which seamlessly integrates temporal information in a given video. As a first step, we feed the reference frame I_t and the supporting frame I_{t+k} through our image-level backbone network, which produces feature tensors f_t and f_{t+k}, respectively. Note that $f_t, f_{t+k} \in \mathbb{R}^{c \times h \times w}$ where c, h, and w are the number of channels, the height, and the width of the activation tensor. The feature tensors f_t, and f_{t+k} are then concatenated into a new feature tensor $f_{t,t+k} \in \mathbb{R}^{2c \times h \times w}$. Note that this tensor $f_{t,t+k}$ now has twice as many channels as our initial tensors, and that it now contains object-level information from both the reference and the supporting frame.

Next, we use the tensor $f_{t,t+k}$ to predict (x, y) location offsets, which are then used to sample the supporting tensor f_{t+k}. The sampling mechanism is implemented using a deformable convolutional layer, which takes (1) the predicted offsets, and (2) the supporting tensor f_{t+k} as its inputs, and then outputs a newly sampled feature tensor $g_{t,t+k}$, which can be used for object detection in the reference frame. We use subscript $t, t + k$ to denote the resampled tensor because, although g is obtained by resampling the *supporting* tensor, the offset computation uses both the reference as well as the supporting frame. A detailed illustration of our spatiotemporal sampling scheme is presented in Fig. 2.

In practice, our spatiotemporal sampling block has 4 deformable convolution layers (only 2 are shown in Fig. 2). This means that the initially predicted offsets $o_{t,t+k}^{(1)}$ and the concatenated temporal features $f_{t,t+k}$ are first used as inputs to a deformable convolution layer that outputs a new feature map $g_{t,t+k}^{(1)}$. Next, we use $g_{t,t+k}^{(1)}$ to predict offsets $o_{t,t+k}^{(2)}$, and a new feature map $g_{t,t+k}^{(2)}$. This continues for 2 more layers until we obtain offsets $o_{t,t+k}^{(4)}$, which are then used to sample the points out of the supporting feature map f_{t+k}. The final sampled feature map $g_{t,t+k}^{(4)}$ is obtained via another deformable convolutional layer that takes as inputs offsets $o_{t,t+k}^{(4)}$ and the original supporting feature map f_{t+k}.

Our proposed spatiotemporal sampling mechanism learns, which object-level features in the supporting frame are useful for object detection in the reference frame. Conceptually, it replaces the optical flow used in [24] to establish temporal correspondences with a learnable module that is discriminatively trained from object detection labels. In our experimental section, we show that such a sampling scheme allows us to improve video object detection performance over the still-image baseline and the flow-based method of Zhu et al. [24] without training our model on optical flow data.

Feature Aggregation. The spatiotemporal sampling procedure is applied for all the supporting frames in the selected range. Note, that this includes a special case, when the reference frame is treated as a supporting frame to itself to produce $g_{t,t}^{(4)}$, which is a feature tensor computed from only the reference frame.

The resulting feature tensors have the following form: $g_{t,t+k}^{(4)} \in \mathbb{R}^{c^{(4)} \times h \times w}$. These feature tensors are aggregated into an output feature tensor $g_t^{agg} \in \mathbb{R}^{c^{(4)} \times h \times w}$ for the reference frame. This tensor captures information from the reference frame, its K preceding frames and its K subsequent frames. The output tensor value $g_t^{agg}(p)$ for frame t at pixel p is computed as a weighted summation:

$$g_t^{agg}(p) = \sum_{k=-K}^{K} w_{t,t+k}(p) \; g_{t,t+k}^{(4)}(p) \tag{3}$$

Inspired by strong results presented in [24], we use their proposed feature aggregation method where the weights w indicate the importance of each supporting frame to the reference frame. To compute the weights w, we attach a 3-layer subnetwork $S(x)$ to the features $g_{t,t+k}^{(4)}$ and then compute their intermediate feature representations $S(g_{t,t+k}^{(4)})$. We then obtain the weights w by applying an exponential function on the cosine similarity between each corresponding feature point in a reference frame and a supporting frame:

$$w_{t,t+k}(p) = \exp\left(\frac{S(g_{t,t}^{(4)})(p) \cdot S(g_{t,t+k}^{(4)})(p)}{|S(g_{t,t}^{(4)})(p)||S(g_{t,t+k}^{(4)})(p)|} \right) \tag{4}$$

Finally, all weights w are fed into the softmax layer, to ensure that the weights sum up to 1 at each pixel location p (i.e., $\sum_{k=-K}^{K} w_{t,t+k}(p) = 1 \; \forall p$).

Object Detection. Finally, the aggregated feature tensor g_t^{agg} is used as input to the detection network, which outputs the final bounding box predictions and their object class probabilities. We describe more details related to the detection network in the next section along with other implementation details.

4.1   Implementation Details

For our experiments we use the MXNet [28] library. Below we provide details related to our STSN architecture, and our training and inference procedures.

Architecture. For our backbone network we adopt a state-of-the-art Deformable CNN [25] based on the ResNet-101 [5] architecture. Our spatiotemporal sampling block consists of four 3×3 deformable convolutional layers each with 1024 output channels. In addition, it also has four 3×3 convolutional layers predicting (x, y) offsets. To implement a subnetwork $S(x)$ that predicts feature aggregation weights, we use a sequence of 1×1, 3×3 and 1×1 convolutional layers with $512, 512$ and 2048 output channels respectively. Our detection network is implemented based on the deformable R-FCN design [17,25,29]. When feeding the aggregated feature g_t^{agg} to the detection network, we split its 1024 channels into two parts, and feed the first and the last 512 channels to the RPN and R-FCN sub-networks respectively. For the RPN, we use 9 anchors and 300 proposals for each image. Furthermore, for the R-FCN, we use deformable position-sensitive ROI pooling with 7×7 groups.

Training. Our entire STSN model is fully differentiable, and thus, trainable end-to-end. During training, we resize all input images to a shorter side of 600 pixels, and use $T = 3$ frames to train our model (i.e., $K = 1$). More specifically, we randomly sample one supporting frame before and one supporting frame after the reference frame. We observed that using more supporting frames in training does not lead to a higher accuracy.

For the rest of our training procedure, we follow the protocol outlined in [24]. Specifically, we train our model in two stages. First, we pre-train our full model on the Imagenet DET dataset using the annotations of the 30 object classes that overlap with the Imagenet VID dataset. Note that Imagenet DET dataset contains only images, and thus, we cannot sample meaningful supporting frames in this case. Therefore, in the case of images, we use the reference frames as our supporting frames. Afterwards, the entire model is trained for $120K$ iterations on 4 Tesla K40 GPUs with each GPU holding a single mini-batch. The learning rate is set to 0.001 and 0.0001 for the first $80K$ and the last $40K$ iterations respectively. Afterwards, we finetune the entire model on the Imagenet VID dataset for $60K$ iterations with a learning rate of 0.001 and 0.0001 for the first $40K$ and the last $20K$ iterations respectively. Note that in the second stage of training we sample the supporting frames randomly within a certain neighborhood of a reference frame (as described above).

Inference. During inference, we use $T = 27$, meaning that we consider $K = 13$ supporting frames before and after the reference frame. To avoid GPU memory issues, we first extract features from the backbone network for each image individually, and then cache these features in the memory. Afterwards, we feed all these features into our spatiotemporal sampling block. At the end, standard NMS with a threshold of 0.3 is applied to refine the detections. To handle the first and the last $K = 13$ frames in the video—two boundary cases that require sampling the neighboring frames beyond the video start and end, we pad the start of a video with K copies of the first frame, and the end of a video with K copies of the last frame.

5   Experimental Results

In this section, we evaluate our approach for video object detection on the ImageNet VID [26] dataset, which has 3,862 and 555 training and testing video clips respectively. Each video is annotated with bounding boxes. The frames from each video are extracted at 25–30 fps. The dataset contains 30 object categories that are a subset of the 200 categories in the ImageNet DET dataset.

Table 1. We use the ImageNet VID [26] dataset to compare our STSN to the state-of-the-art FGFA [24] and D&T [27] methods. Note that SSN refers to our static baseline, which is obtained by using only the reference frame for output generation (no temporal info). Also note, that D&T+ and STSN+ refer to D&T and STSN baselines with temporal post-processing applied on top of the CNN outputs. Based on these results, we first point out that unlike FGFA, our STSN does not rely on the external optical flow data, and still yields higher mAP (**78.9** vs **78.8**). Furthermore, when no temporal post-processing is used, our STSN produces superior performance in comparison to the D&T baseline (**78.9** vs **75.8**). Finally, we demonstrate that if we use a simple Seq-NMS [22] temporal post-processing scheme on top of our STSN predictions, we can further improve our results and outperform all the other baselines.

	Methods					
	D&T [27]	Our SSN	FGFA [24]	Our STSN	D&T+ [27]	Our STSN+
No FlowNet?	✓	-	✗	✓	✓	✓
Not using flow data?	✓	-	✗	✓	✓	✓
No temporal post-processing?	✓	-	✓	✓	✗	✗
mAP@0.5	75.8	76.0	78.8	78.9	79.8	**80.4**

5.1   Quantitative Results

To assess the effectiveness of our method we compare it to several relevant baselines, mainly two state-of-the-art methods FGFA [24] and D&T [27]. First, to verify that using temporal information from video is beneficial, we include a static image-level variant of our model (SSN) that uses only the reference frame to make its predictions. Furthermore, we also want to show that our spatiotemporal sampling scheme works as effectively as the optical flow network in [24], but without requiring optical flow supervision. To do so, we replace the optical flow network from [24], with our spatiotemporal sampling mechanism. The rest of the architecture and the training details are kept the same for both baselines. Such an experimental design allows us to directly compare the effectiveness of our spatiotemporal sampling scheme and the optical flow network of FGFA [24].

Finally, we demonstrate that our method performs better than the D&T [27] method in two scenarios: (1) when we only use CNN-level outputs for video object detection, and also (2) when we allow temporal post-processing techniques such as Seq-NMS to be applied on top of the CNN outputs. We note that in Table 1, D&T [27] and STSN refer to the CNN-level baselines whereas D&T+ [27] and STSN+ denote these same methods but with temporal post-processing (i.e. Seq-NMS [22], object-tube based linking [27], etc.) applied on top of the CNN outputs.

We present our results in Table 1, where we assess each method according to several criteria. In the first row of Table 1, we list whether a given method requires integrating a separate flow network into its training/prediction pipeline. Ideally, we would want to eliminate this step because optical flow prediction requires designing a highly complex flow network architecture. We also list whether a given method requires pre-training on the external optical flow data, which we would want to avoid since it makes the whole training pipeline more costly. Additionally, we list, whether a given method uses any external temporal post-processing steps, which we would want to eliminate because they typically make the training/prediction pipeline disjoint and more complex. Finally, we assess each method according to the standard mean average precision (mAP) metric at intersection over union (IoU) threshold of 0.5.

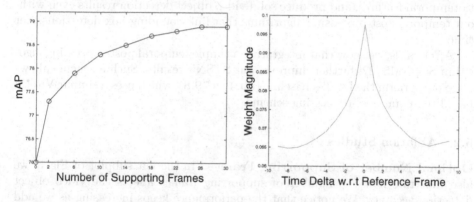

Fig. 3. A figure illustrating some of our ablation experiments. Left: we plot mAP as a function of the number of supporting frames used by our STSN. From this plot, we notice that the video object detection accuracy improves as we use more supporting frames. Right: To understand the contribution of each of the supporting frames, we plot the average weight magnitudes $w_{t,t+k}(p)$ for different values of k. Here, p represents a point at the center of an object. From this plot, we observe that the largest weights are associated with the supporting frames that are near the reference frame. However, note that even supporting frames that are further away from the reference frame (e.g. $k = 9$) contribute quite substantially to the final object detection predictions.

Based on our results in Table 1, we make the following conclusions. First, we note that our STSN produces better quantitative results than the state-of-the-art FGFA method (**78.9** vs **78.8**). We acknowledge that our accuracy improvement over FGFA is moderate. However, we point out that our STSN operates in a much more challenging setting than FGFA. Unlike FGFA, our STSN does not use any optical flow supervision. Instead, it is trained directly for video object detection. The fact that STSN learns temporal correspondences without direct optical flow supervision, and still outperforms FGFA is quite impressive. Such results also show the benefit of discriminative end-to-end training with respect to the final video object detection task objective.

We next compare our STSN to the D&T baseline [27]. We note that unlike for the FGFA [24] baseline, it is much harder to make a direct comparison between STSN and D&T. Whereas our STSN aims to produce powerful spatiotemporal features, the method of D&T [27] is targeted more for smoothing the final bounding box predictions across time. Thus, we believe that these two methods are complementary, and it would be possible to integrate them together for the model that produces both: temporally smooth features, as well as temporally smooth bounding box predictions. We also note that our STSN and D&T [27] use slightly different architectures (both based on ResNet-101 though).

First, we compare STSN and D&T in a setting when no temporal post-processing (i.e. Seq-NMS [22], object-tube linking [27], etc.) is used, and show that our STSN outperforms the D&T baseline by a substantial margin (**78.9** vs **75.8**). These results indicate, that our STSN is able to learn powerful spatiotemporal features, and produce solid video object detection results even without temporal post-processing algorithms that link bounding box detections over time.

Afterwards, we show that integrating a simple temporal post-processing algorithm Seq-NMS [22] further improves our STSN's results. Such a scheme allows us to outperform the D&T+ baseline (**80.4** vs **79.8**), which uses a similar Viterbi based temporal post-processing scheme.

5.2 Ablation Studies

Optimal Number of Supporting Frames. In the left subplot of Fig. 3, we also illustrate how the number of supporting frames affects the video object detection accuracy. We notice that the performance keeps increasing as we add more supporting frames, and then plateaus at $T = 27$.

Increasing the Temporal Stride. We also investigate how the temporal stride k, at which we sample the supporting frames, affects STSN's performance. We report that temporal strides of $k = 2$ and $k = 4$, yield mAP scores of 79.0 and 77.9, respectively. Thus, $k = 2$ yields a slight improvement over our original 78.9 mAP score. However, increasing k to larger values reduces the accuracy.

Feature Aggregation Weight Analysis. To analyze how much each of the supporting frame contributes to the final object detections, we visualize the average weight magnitudes $w_{t,t+k}(p)$ for different values of k. This visualization is presented in the right subplot of Fig. 3. We note that in this case, the weight magnitudes correspond to the point p, which is located at the center of an object.

From this plot, we can conclude that the largest contribution comes from the supporting frames that are near the reference frame ($k = -1, 0, 1$). However, note that even supporting frames that are further away from the reference frame (e.g. $k = -9, 9$) have non-zero weights, and contribute quite substantially to the final object detection predictions.

Reference Frame (t)   Supporting Frame (t+9)   Reference Frame (t)   Supporting Frame (t+9)

Fig. 4. An illustration of our spatiotemporal sampling scheme (zoom-in for a better view). The green square indicates a point in the reference frame, for which we want to compute a new convolutional output. The red square indicates the corresponding point predicted by our STSN in a supporting frame. The yellow arrow illustrates the estimated object motion. Although our model is trained discriminatively for object detection and *not* for tracking or motion estimation, our STSN learns to sample from the supporting frame at locations that coincide almost perfectly with the same object. This allows our method to perform accurate object detection even if objects in the reference frame are blurry or occluded. (Color figure online)

5.3   Qualitative Results

To understand how our STSN exploits temporal information from a given video, we visualize in Fig. 4, the average offsets predicted by the STSN sampling block. These offsets are used by the STSN to decide, which object-level information from the supporting frame should be used to detect an object in the reference frame. The green square in the reference frame depicts a pixel, for which we want to compute a convolution output. The red square in the supporting frame represents an average offset, which is used to determine which feature points from the supporting frame should be sampled. The yellow arrow indicates object's motion between the reference frame and the supporting frame. Note that despite a relatively large motion between the reference and the supporting frames, our STSN samples features from the supporting frame right around the center of the object, which is exactly what we want. Such spatiotemporal sampling allows us to detect objects even if they appear blurry or occluded in the reference frame.

In addition, based on the results in Fig. 4, we observe that even without an explicit optical flow supervision, our STSN learns to accurately capture the motion of the objects, which is another appealing property of our model. In fact, in Fig. 5, we illustrate several examples of using our STSN to track objects in

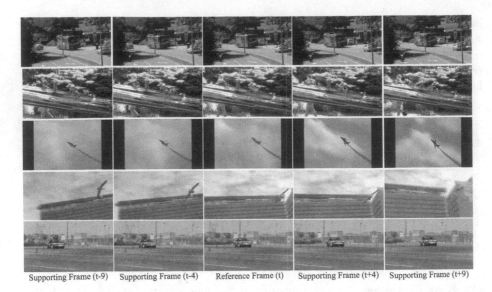

Supporting Frame (t-9)   Supporting Frame (t-4)   Reference Frame (t)   Supporting Frame (t+4)   Supporting Frame (t+9)

Fig. 5. An illustration of using our spatiotemporal sampling scheme in action. The green square indicates a fixed object location in the reference frame. The red square depicts a location in a supporting frame, from which relevant features are sampled. Even without optical flow supervision, our STSN learns to track these objects in video. In our supplementary material, we include more of such examples in the video format. (Color figure online)

a given video. From Fig. 5, we observe that despite a relatively large motion in each sequence, our STSN accurately samples features around objects in every supporting frame. Such results indicate that we may be able to use our sampling mechanism for discriminative object tracking. In fact, we note that the commonly used dense optical flow methods are often redundant because most applications do not require flow prediction for every single pixel. In comparison, we point out that our STSN captures a more discriminative form of motion, which is learned to exclusively benefit a video object detection task. In our supplementary material, we include more of such results in the video form.

In Fig. 6, we also illustrate object detections of the static SSN baseline, and those of our full STSN model (zoom-in to see the probabilities and class predictions). In all of these cases, we observe that incorporating temporal information helps STSN to correct the mistakes made by the static baseline. For instance, in the third row of Fig. 6, a static SSN baseline incorrectly labels an object in the reference frame as a bird, which happens due to the occluded head of the lizard. However, STSN fixes this mistake by looking at the supporting frames, and by sampling around the lizard body and its head (See Row 3, Column 1 in Fig. 6). Furthermore, in the last row, a static SSN baseline fails to detect one of the bicycles because it is occluded in the reference frame. STSN fixes this error, by sampling around the missed bicycle in the supporting frame where the bicycle

| Sampled Points in the Supporting Frame | SSN (Static) | STSN (Ours) |

Fig. 6. A figure illustrating object detection examples where our spatiotemporal sampling mechanism helps STSN to correct the mistakes made by a static SSN baseline (please zoom-in to see the class predictions and their probabilities). These mistakes typically occur due to occlusions, blurriness, etc. STSN fixes these errors by using relevant object level information from supporting frames. In Column 1 we illustrate the points in the supporting frame that STSN considers relevant when computing the output for a point denoted by the green square in Column 2. (Color figure online)

is more clearly visible. Similar behavior also occurs in other cases where STSN successfully resolves occlusion and blurriness issues.

6 Conclusion

In this work, we introduced the Spatiotemporal Sampling Network (STSN) which is a new architecture for object detection in video. Compared to the state-of-the-art FGFA [24] method, our model involves a simpler design, it does not require optical flow computation and it produces higher video object detection accuracy. Our model is fully differentiable, and unlike prior video object detection methods, it does not necessitate optical flow training data. This renders our model easy to train end-to-end. Our future work will include experimenting with more complex design of spatiotemporal sampling blocks.

Acknowledgements. This work was funded in part by NSF award CNS-120552. We gratefully acknowledge NVIDIA and Facebook for the donation of GPUs used for portions of this work.

References

1. Krizhevsky, A., Sutskever, I., Hinton, G.E.: ImageNet classification with deep convolutional neural networks. In: NIPS (2012)
2. Szegedy, C., et al.: Going deeper with convolutions. In: Computer Vision and Pattern Recognition (CVPR) (2015)
3. Simonyan, K., Zisserman, A.: Very deep convolutional networks for large-scale image recognition. In: ICLR (2015)
4. Bertasius, G., Shi, J., Torresani, L.: DeepEdge: a multi-scale bifurcated deep network for top-down contour detection. In: The IEEE Conference on Computer Vision and Pattern Recognition (CVPR), June 2015
5. He, K., Zhang, X., Ren, S., Sun, J.: Deep residual learning for image recognition. In: 2016 IEEE Conference on Computer Vision and Pattern Recognition (CVPR), pp. 770–778 (2016)
6. Xie, S., Girshick, R., Dollár, P., Tu, Z., He, K.: Aggregated residual transformations for deep neural networks. In: CVPR (2017)
7. Toshev, A., Szegedy, C.: DeepPose: human pose estimation via deep neural networks. In: CVPR (2014)
8. Bertasius, G., Torresani, L., Yu, S.X., Shi, J.: Convolutional random walk networks for semantic image segmentation. In: The IEEE Conference on Computer Vision and Pattern Recognition (CVPR), July 2017
9. He, K., Zhang, X., Ren, S., Sun, J.: Spatial pyramid pooling in deep convolutional networks for visual recognition. In: Fleet, D., Pajdla, T., Schiele, B., Tuytelaars, T. (eds.) ECCV 2014. LNCS, vol. 8691, pp. 346–361. Springer, Cham (2014). https://doi.org/10.1007/978-3-319-10578-9_23
10. He, K., Gkioxari, G., Dollár, P., Girshick, R.: Mask R-CNN. In: Proceedings of the International Conference on Computer Vision (ICCV) (2017)
11. Lin, T.Y., Goyal, P., Girshick, R., He, K., Dollár, P.: Focal loss for dense object detection. In: Proceedings of the International Conference on Computer Vision (ICCV) (2017)

12. Ren, S., He, K., Girshick, R., Sun, J.: Faster R-CNN: towards real-time object detection with region proposal networks. In: Neural Information Processing Systems (NIPS) (2015)

13. Girshick, R.: Fast R-CNN. In: Proceedings of the International Conference on Computer Vision (ICCV) (2015)

14. Girshick, R., Donahue, J., Darrell, T., Malik, J.: Rich feature hierarchies for accurate object detection and semantic segmentation. In: Proceedings of the IEEE Conference on Computer Vision and Pattern Recognition (CVPR) (2014)

15. Gupta, S., Girshick, R., Arbeláez, P., Malik, J.: Learning rich features from RGB-D images for object detection and segmentation. In: Fleet, D., Pajdla, T., Schiele, B., Tuytelaars, T. (eds.) ECCV 2014. LNCS, vol. 8695, pp. 345–360. Springer, Cham (2014). https://doi.org/10.1007/978-3-319-10584-0_23

16. Liu, W., et al.: SSD: single shot multibox detector. In: Leibe, B., Matas, J., Sebe, N., Welling, M. (eds.) ECCV 2016. LNCS, vol. 9905, pp. 21–37. Springer, Cham (2016). https://doi.org/10.1007/978-3-319-46448-0_2

17. Dai, J., Li, Y., He, K., Sun, J.: R-FCN: object detection via region-based fully convolutional networks. In: Advances in Neural Information Processing Systems vol. 29, pp. 379–387. Curran Associates Inc. (2016)

18. Redmon, J., Divvala, S.K., Girshick, R.B., Farhadi, A.: You only look once: unified, real-time object detection. In: 2016 IEEE Conference on Computer Vision and Pattern Recognition, CVPR 2016, Las Vegas, NV, USA, 27–30 June 2016, pp. 779–788 (2016)

19. Redmon, J., Farhadi, A.: YOLO9000: better, faster, stronger. In: 2017 IEEE Conference on Computer Vision and Pattern Recognition, CVPR 2017, Honolulu, HI, USA, 21–26 July 2017, pp. 6517–6525 (2017)

20. Kang, K., et al.: T-CNN: tubelets with convolutional neural networks for object detection from videos. IEEE TCSVT 2017 (2017)

21. Kang, K., Ouyang, W., Li, H., Wang, X.: Object detection from video tubelets with convolutional neural networks. CoRR abs/1604.04053 (2016)

22. Han, W., et al.: Soq NMS for video object detection. CoRR abs/1602.08465 (2016)

23. Lee, B., Erdenee, E., Jin, S., Rhee, P.: Multi-class multi-object tracking using changing point detection. CoRR abs/1608.08434 (2016)

24. Zhu, X., Wang, Y., Dai, J., Yuan, L., Wei, Y.: Flow-guided feature aggregation for video object detection. In: International Conference on Computer Vision (ICCV) (2017)

25. Dai, J., et al.: Deformable convolutional networks. In: 2017 IEEE International Conference on Computer Vision (ICCV), pp. 764–773, October 2017

26. Russakovsky, O., et al.: ImageNet large scale visual recognition challenge. Int. J. Comput. Vis. (IJCV) 115(3), 211–252 (2015)

27. Feichtenhofer, C., Pinz, A., Zisserman, A.: Detect to track and track to detect. In: International Conference on Computer Vision (ICCV) (2017)

28. Chen, T., et al.: MXNet: a flexible and efficient machine learning library for heterogeneous distributed systems. CoRR abs/1512.01274 (2015)

29. Zhu, X., Xiong, Y., Dai, J., Yuan, L., Wei, Y.: Deep feature flow for video recognition. In: CVPR (2017)

Video Summarization Using Fully Convolutional Sequence Networks

Mrigank Rochan$^{(\boxtimes)}$ (ID), Linwei Ye (ID), and Yang Wang (ID)

University of Manitoba, Winnipeg R3T 2N2, Canada
{mrochan,ye13,ywang}@cs.umanitoba.ca

Abstract. This paper addresses the problem of video summarization. Given an input video, the goal is to select a subset of the frames to create a summary video that optimally captures the important information of the input video. With the large amount of videos available online, video summarization provides a useful tool that assists video search, retrieval, browsing, etc. In this paper, we formulate video summarization as a sequence labeling problem. Unlike existing approaches that use recurrent models, we propose fully convolutional sequence models to solve video summarization. We firstly establish a novel connection between semantic segmentation and video summarization, and then adapt popular semantic segmentation networks for video summarization. Extensive experiments and analysis on two benchmark datasets demonstrate the effectiveness of our models.

Keywords: Video summarization
Fully convolutional neural networks · Sequence labeling

1 Introduction

With the ever-increasing popularity and decreasing cost of video capture devices, the amount of video data has increased drastically in the past few years. Video has become one of the most important form of visual data. Due to the sheer amount of video data, it is unrealistic for humans to watch these videos and identify useful information. According to Cisco Visual Networking Index 2017 [1], it is estimated that it will take around 5 million years for an individual to watch all the videos that are uploaded on the Internet each month in 2021! It is therefore becoming increasingly important to develop computer vision techniques that can enable efficient browsing of the enormous video data. In particular, video summarization has emerged as a promising tool to help cope with the overwhelming amount of video data.

Given an input video, the goal of video summarization is to create a shorter video that captures the important information of the input video. Video summarization can be useful in many real-world applications. For example, in video surveillance, it is tedious and time-consuming for humans to browse through many hours of videos captured by surveillance cameras. If we can provide a short

V. Ferrari et al. (Eds.): ECCV 2018, LNCS 11216, pp. 358–374, 2018.
https://doi.org/10.1007/978-3-030-01258-8_22

summary video that captures the important information from a long video, it will greatly reduce human efforts required in video surveillance. Video summarization can also provide better user experience in video search, retrieval, and understanding. Since short videos are easier to store and transfer, they can be useful for mobile applications. The summary videos can also help in many downstream video analysis tasks. For example, it is faster to run any other analysis algorithms (e.g. action recognition) on short videos.

In this paper, we consider video summarization as a keyframe selection problem. Given an input video, our goal is to select a subset of the frames to form the summary video. Equivalently, video summarization can also be formulated as a sequence labeling problem, where each frame is assigned a binary label to indicate whether it is selected in the summary video.

Current state-of-the-art methods [24,40] consider video summarization as a sequence labeling problem and solve the problem using a variant of recurrent neural networks known as the long short-term memory (LSTM) [11]. Each time step in the LSTM model corresponds to a frame in the input video. At each time step, the LSTM model outputs a binary value indicating whether this frame is selected in the summary video. The advantage of LSTM is that it can capture long-term structural dependencies among frames. But these LSTM-based models have inherent limitations. The computation in LSTM is usually left-to-right. This means we have to process one frame at a time and each frame must wait until the previous frame is processed. Although bi-directional LSTM (Bi-LSTM) [31] exists, the computation in either direction of Bi-LSTM still suffers the same problem. Due to this sequential nature, the computation in LSTM cannot be easily parallelized to take full advantage of the GPU hardware. In our work, we propose fully convolutional models that can process all the frames simultaneously, and therefore take the full advantage of GPU parallelization. Our model is partly inspired by some recent work [3,7,17] in action detection, audio synthesis, and machine translation showing that convolutional models can outperform recurrent models and can take full advantage of GPU parallelization.

In this paper, we propose to use fully convolutional networks for video summarization. Fully convolutional networks (FCN) [22] have been extensively used in semantic segmentation. Compared with video summarization, semantic segmentation is a more widely studied topic in computer vision. Traditionally, video summarization and semantic segmentation are considered as two completely different problems in computer vision. Our insight is that these two problems in fact share a lot of similarities. In semantic segmentation, the input is a 2D image with 3 color channels (RGB). The output of semantic segmentation is a 2D matrix with the same spatial dimension as the input image, where each cell of the 2D matrix indicates the semantic label of the corresponding pixel in the image. In video summarization, let us assume that each frame is represented as a K-dimensional vector. This can be a vector of raw pixel values or a precomputed feature vector. Then the input to video summarization is a 1D image (over temporal dimension) with K channels. The output is a 1D matrix with the same length as the input video, where each element indicates whether the corresponding frame is selected for the summary. In other words, although semantic segmentation and video summarization are two different problems, they only differ in terms of the dimensions of the input (2D vs. 1D) and the number of channels (3 vs. K). Figure 1 illustrates the relationship between these two tasks. By establishing the connection between these two tasks, we can directly exploit models in semantic segmentation and adapt them for video summarization. In this paper, we develop our video summarization method based on popular semantic segmentation models such as FCN [22]. We call our approach the *Fully Convolutional Sequence Network (FCSN)*.

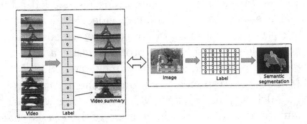

Fig. 1. An illustration of the relationship between video summarization and semantic segmentation. (*Left*) In video summarization, our goal is to select frames from an input video to generate the summary video. This is equivalent to assigning a binary label (0 or 1) to each frame in the video to indicate whether the frame is selected for summary. This problem has a close connection with semantic segmentation (*Right*) where the goal is to label each pixel in an image with its class label.

FCSN is suitable for video summarization due to two important reasons. First, FCSN consist of stack of convolutions whose effective context size grows (though smaller in the beginning) as we go deeper in the network. This allows the network to model the long range complex dependency among input frames that is necessary for video summarization. Second, FCSN is fully convolutional. Compared to LSTM, FCSN allows easier parallelization over input frames.

The contributions of this paper are manifold. (1) To the best of our knowledge, we are the first to propose fully convolutional models for video summarization. (2) We establish a novel connection between two seemingly unrelated problems, namely video summarization and semantic segmentation. We then present a way to adapt popular semantic segmentation networks for video summarization. (3) We propose both supervised and unsupervised fully convolutional models. (4) Through extensive experiments on two benchmark datasets, we show that our model achieves state-of-the-art performance.

2   Related Work

Given an input video, video summarization aims to produce a shortened version that captures the important information in the video. There are various representations proposed for this problem including video synopsis [30], time-lapses [12,16,28], montages [13,35] and storyboards [8–10,18,21,24,38–40]. Our work is most related to storyboards which select a few representative video frames to summarize key events present in the entire video. Storyboard-based summarization has two types of outputs: keyframes [8,18,21] in which certain isolated frames are chosen to form the summary video, and keyshots [9,10,24,39,40] in which a set of correlated consecutive frames within a temporal slot are considered for summary generation.

Early work in video summarization mainly relies on hand-crafted heuristics. Most of these approaches are unsupervised. They define various heuristics to represent the importance or representativeness [14,15,18,23,26,27,34] of the frames and use the importance scores to select representative frames to form the summary video. Recent work has explored supervised learning approaches for video summarization [8–10,39,40]. These approaches use training data consisting of videos and their ground-truth summaries generated by humans. These supervised learning approaches tend to outperform early work on unsupervised methods, since they can implicitly learn high-level semantic knowledge that is used by humans to generate summaries.

Recently deep learning methods [24,32,40] are gaining popularity for video summarization. The most relevant works to ours are the methods that use recurrent models such as LSTMs [11]. The intuition of using LSTM is to effectively capture long-range dependencies among video frames which are crucial for meaningful summary generation. Zhang et al. [40] consider the video summarization task as a structured prediction problem on sequential data and model the variable-range dependency using two LSTMs. One LSTM is used for video sequences in the forward direction and the other for the backward direction. They further improve the diversity in the subset selection by incorporating a determinantal point process model [8,39]. Mahasseni et al. [24] propose an unsupervised generative adversarial framework consisting of the summarizer and discriminator. The summarizer is a variational autoencoder LSTM which first selects video frames and then decodes the output for reconstruction. The discriminator is another LSTM network that learns to distinguish between the input video and its reconstruction. They also extend their method to supervised learning by introducing a keyframe regularization. Different from these LSTM-based approaches, we propose fully convolutional sequence models for video summarization. Our work is the first to use fully convolutional models for this problem.

3   Our Approach

In this section, we first describe the problem formulation (Sect. 3.1). We then introduce our fully convolutional sequence model and the learning algorithm (Sect. 3.2). Finally, we present an extension of the basic model for unsupervised learning of video summarization (Sect. 3.3).

3.1 Problem Formulation

Previous work has considered two different forms of output in video summarization: (1) binary labels; (2) frame-level importance scores. Binary label outputs are usually referred to as either keyframes [5,8,25,40] or keyshots [9,10,29,34,40]. Keyframes consist of a set of non-continuous frames that are selected for the summarization, while keyshots correspond to a set of time-intervals in video where each interval consists of a continuous set of frames. Frame-level importance scores [9,34] indicate how likely a frame should be selected for the summarization. Existing datasets have ground-truth annotations available in at least one of these two forms. Although frame-level scores provide richer information, it is practically much easier to collect annotations in terms of binary labels. It may even be possible to collect binary label annotations automatically from edited video content online. For example, if we have access to professionally edited summary videos and their corresponding raw videos, we can automatically create annotations in the form of binary labels on frames. In this paper, we focus on learning video summarization from only binary label-based (in particular, keyframe-based) annotations.

Let us consider a video with T frames. We assume each frame has been preprocessed (e.g. by a pretrained CNN) and is represented as a feature vector. We denote the frames in a video as $\{F_1, F_2, F_3, ..., F_T\}$ where F_i is the feature descriptor of the t-th ($t \in \{1, 2, .., T\}$) frame in the video. Our goal is to assign a binary label (0 or 1) to each of the T frames. The summary video is obtained by combining the frames that are labeled as 1 (see Fig. 1). We assume access to a training dataset of videos, where each frame has a ground-truth binary label indicating whether this frame should be selected in the summary video.

3.2 Fully Convolutional Sequence Networks

Our models are inspired by fully convolutional models used in semantic segmentation. Our models have the following properties. (1) Semantic segmentation models use 2D convolution over 2D spatial locations in an image. In contrast, our models apply 1D convolution across the temporal sequence domain. (2) Unlike LSTM models [40] for video summarization that process frames in a sequential order, our models process all frames simultaneously using the convolution operation. (3) Semantic segmentation models usually use an encoder-decoder architecture, where an image is first processed by the encoder to extract features, then the decoder is used to produce the segmentation mask using the encoded features. Similarly, our models can also be interpreted as an encoder-decoder architecture. The encoder is used to process the frames to extract both high-level semantic features and long-term structural relationship information among frames, while the decoder is used to produce a sequence of 0/1 labels. We call our model the *fully convolutional sequence network (FCSN)*.

Our models mainly consist of temporal modules such as temporal convolution, temporal pooling, and temporal deconvolution. This is analogous to the modules commonly used in semantic segmentation models, such as 2D convolution, 2D pooling, 2D deconvolution. Due to the underlying relationship between video summarization and semantic segmentation, we can easily borrow the network architecture from existing semantic segmentation models when designing FCSN for video summarization. In this section, we describe a FCSN based on a popular semantic segmentation network, namely FCN [22]. We refer to this FCSN as SUM-FCN. It is important to note that FCSN is certainly not limited to this particular network architecture. We can convert almost any existing semantic segmentation models into FCSN for video summarization.

SUM-FCN: FCN [22] is a widely used model for semantic segmentation. In this section, we adapt FCN (in particular, FCN-16) for the task of video summarization. We call the model SUM-FCN. In FCN, the input is an RGB image of shape $m \times n \times 3$ where m and n are height and width of the image respectively. The output/prediction is of shape $m \times n \times C$ where the channel dimension C corresponds to the number of classes. In SUM-FCN, the input is of dimension $1 \times T \times D$ where T is the number of frames in a video and D is the dimension of the feature vector of a frame. The output of SUM-FCN is of dimension $1 \times T \times C$. Note that the dimension of the output channel is $C = 2$ since we need scores corresponding to 2 classes (keyframe or non-keyframe) for each frame.

Figure 2 shows the architecture of our SUM-FCN model. We convert all the spatial convolutions in FCN to temporal convolutions. Similarly, spatial maxpooling and deconvolution layers are converted to corresponding temporal counterparts. We organize our network similar to FCN. The first five convolutional layers (*conv*1 to

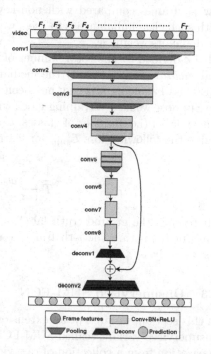

Fig. 2. The architecture of SUM-FCN. It is based on the popular semantic segmentation architecture FCN [22]. Unlike FCN, SUM-FCN performs convolution, pooling and deconvolution operation across time.

*conv*5) consist of multiple temporal convolution layers where each temporal convolution is followed by a batch normalization and a ReLU activation. We add a temporal maxpooling next to each convolution layer. Each of *conv*6 and *conv*7 consists of a temporal convolution, followed by ReLU and dropout. We also have *conv*8 consisting of a 1×1 convolution (to produce the desired output channel), batch normalization, and deconvolution operation along the time axis. We then take the output of *pool*4, apply a 1×1 convolution and batch normalization and then merge (element-wise addition) it with *deconv*1 feature map. This merging corresponds to the skip connection in [22]. Skip connection is widely used in semantic segmentation to combine feature maps at coarse layers with fine layers to produce richer visual features. Our intuition is that this skip connection is also useful in video summarization, since it will help in recovering temporal information required for summarization. Lastly, we apply a temporal deconvolution again and obtain the final prediction of length T.

Learning: In keyframe-based supervised setting, the classes (keyframe vs. non-keyframe) are extremely imbalanced since only a small number of frames in an input video are selected in the summary video. This means that there are very few keyframes compared with non-keyframes. A common strategy for dealing with such class imbalance is to use a weighted loss for learning. For the c-th class, we define its weight $w_c = \frac{median\_freq}{freq_c}$, where $freq_c$ is the number of frames with label c divided by the total number of frames in videos where label c is present, and $median\_freq$ is simply the median of the computed frequencies. Note that this class balancing strategy has been used for pixel labeling tasks as well [6].

Suppose we have a training video with T frames. We also have a ground-truth binary label (i.e. number of classes, $C = 2$) on each frame of this video. We can define the following loss $\mathcal{L}_{sum}$ for learning:

$$\mathcal{L}_{sum} = -\frac{1}{T} \sum_{t=1}^{T} w_{c_t} \log \left(\frac{\exp(\phi_{t,c_t})}{\sum_{c=1}^{C} \exp(\phi_{t,c})} \right) \tag{1}$$

where c_t is the ground-truth label of the t-th frame. $\phi_{t,c}$ and w_c indicate the score of predicting the t-th frame as the c-th class and the weight of class c, respectively.

3.3   Unsupervised SUM-FCN

In this section, we present an extension of the SUM-FCN model. We develop an unsupervised variant (called SUM-FCN$_{unsup}$) of SUM-FCN to learn video summarization from a collection of raw videos without their ground-truth summary videos.

Intuitively, the frames in the summary video should be visually diverse [24, 40]. We use this property of video summarization to design SUM-FCN$_{unsup}$. We develop SUM-FCN$_{unsup}$ by explicitly encouraging the model to generate summary videos where the selected frames are visually diverse. In order to enforce this diversity, we make the following changes to the decoder of SUM-FCN. We first select Y frames (i.e. keyframes) based on the prediction scores from the decoder. Next, we apply a 1×1 convolution to the decoded feature vectors of these keyframes to reconstruct their original feature representations. We then merge the input frame-level feature vectors of these selected Y keyframes using a skip connection. Finally, we use a 1×1 convolution to obtain the final reconstructed features of the Y keyframes such that each keyframe feature vector is of the same dimension as its corresponding input frame-level feature vector.

We use a repelling regularizer [42] $\mathcal{L}_{div}$ to enforce diversity among selected keyframes. We define $\mathcal{L}_{div}$ as the mean of the pairwise similarity between the selected Y keyframes:

$$\mathcal{L}_{div} = \frac{1}{|Y|(|Y|-1)} \sum_{t \in Y} \sum_{t' \in Y, t' \neq t} d(f_t, f_{t'}), \text{ where } (f_t, f_{t'}) = \frac{f_t^T f_{t'}}{\|f_t\|_2 \|f_{t'}\|_2} \qquad (2)$$

where f_t is the reconstructed feature vector of the frame t. Ideally, a diverse subset of frames will lead to a lower value of $\mathcal{L}_{div}$.

We also introduce a reconstruction loss $\mathcal{L}_{recon}$ that computes the mean squared error between the reconstructed features and the input feature vectors of the keyframes. The final learning objective of SUM-FCN$_{unsup}$ becomes $\mathcal{L}_{div}+\mathcal{L}_{recon}$. Since this objective does not require ground-truth summary videos, SUM-FCN$_{unsup}$ is an unsupervised approach.

It is worth noting that SUM-FCN will implicitly achieve diversity to some extent because it is supervised. SUM-FCN learns to mimic the ground-truth human annotations. Presumably, the ground-truth summary videos (annotated by humans) have diversity among the selected frames, since humans are unlikely to annotate two very similar frames as keyframes.

4   Experiments

In this section, we first introduce the datasets in Sect. 4.1. We then discuss the implementation details and setup in Sect. 4.2. Lastly, we present the main results in Sect. 4.3 and additional ablation analysis in Sect. 4.4.

4.1   Datasets

We evaluate our method on two benchmark datasets: SumMe [9] and TVSum [34]. The SumMe dataset is a collection of 25 videos that cover a variety of events (e.g. sports, holidays, etc.). The videos in SumMe are 1.5 to 6.5 min in length. The TVSum dataset contains 50 YouTube videos of 10 different categories (e.g. making sandwich, dog show, changing vehicle tire, etc.) from the TRECVid Multimedia Event Detection (MED) task [33]. The videos in this dataset are typically 1 to 5 min in length.

Since training a deep neural network with small annotated datasets is difficult, previous work [40] has proposed to use additional videos to augment the datasets. Following [40], we use 39 videos from the YouTube dataset [5] and 50 videos from the Open Video Project (OVP) dataset [2,5] to augment the training data. In the YouTube dataset, there are videos consisting of news, sports and cartoon. In the OVP dataset, there are videos of different genres such as documentary. These datasets are diverse in nature and come with different types of annotations. We discuss in Sect. 4.2 on how we handle different formats of ground-truth annotations.

4.2 Implementation Details and Setup

Features: Following [40], we uniformly downsample the videos to 2 fps. Next, we take the output of the *pool*5 layer in the pretrained GoogleNet [36] as the feature descriptor for each video frame. The dimension of this feature descriptor is 1024. Note that our model can be used with any feature representation. We can even use our model with video-based features (e.g. C3D [37]). We use GoogleNet features mainly because they are used in previous work [24,40] and will allow fair comparison in the experiments.

Ground-Truth: Since different datasets provide the ground-truth annotations in various format, we follow [8,40] to generate the single set of ground-truth keyframes (small subset of isolated frames) for each video in the datasets. These keyframe-based summaries are used for training.

To perform fair comparison with state-of-the-art methods (see Evaluation Metrics below), we need summaries in the form of keyshots (interval-based subset of frames [9,10,40]) in both the final generated predictions and the ground-truth annotations for test videos. For the SumMe dataset, ground-truth annotations are available in the form of keyshots, so we use these ground-truth summaries directly for evaluation. However, keyshot annotations are missing from the TVSum dataset. TVSum provides frame-level importance scores annotated by multiple users. To convert importance scores to keyshot-based summaries, we follow the procedure in [40] which includes the following steps: (1) temporally segment a video using KTS [29] to generate disjoint intervals; (2) compute average interval score and assign it to each frame in the interval; (3) rank the frames in the video based on their scores; (4) apply the knapsack algorithm [34] to select frames so that the total length is under certain threshold, which results in the keyshot-based ground-truth summaries of that video. We use this keyshot-based annotation to get the keyframes for training by selecting the frames with the highest importance scores [40]. Note that both the keyframe-based and keyshot-based summaries are represented as 0/1 vector of length equal to the number of frames in the video. Here, a label 0/1 represents whether a frame is selected in the summary video. Table 1 illustrates the ground-truth (training and testing) annotations and their conversion for different datasets.

Training and Optimization: We use keyframe-based ground-truth annotations during training. We first concatenate the visual features of each frame. For a video with T frames, we will have an input of dimension $1 \times T \times 1024$ to the neural network. We also uniformly sample frames from each video such that we end up with $T = 320$. This sampling is similar to the fixed size cropping in semantic segmentation, where training images are usually resized to have the same spatial size. Note that our proposed model, SUM-FCN, can also effectively handle longer and variable length videos (see Sect. 4.4).

During training, we set the learning rate to 10^{-3}, momentum to 0.9, and batch size to 5. Other than using the pretrained GoogleNet to extract frame features, the rest of the network is trained end-to-end using stochastic gradient descent (SGD) optimizer.

Table 1. Ground-truth (GT) annotations used during training and testing for different datasets. ‡We convert frame-level importance scores from multiple users to single keyframes as in [34,40]. †We follow [40] to convert multiple frame-level scores to keyshots. §Following [8,40], we generate one set of keyframes for each video. Note that the YouTube and OVP datasets are only used to supplement the training data (as in [24,40]), so we do not test our methods on them

Dataset	# annotations	Training GT	Testing GT
SumMe	15–18	Frame-level scores‡	Keyshots
TVSum	20	Frame-level scores‡	Frame-level scores †
YouTube	5	Keyframes§	-
OVP	5	Keyframes§	-

Testing: At test time, a uniformly sampled test video with $T = 320$ frames is forwarded to the trained model to obtain an output of length 320. Then this output is scaled to the original length of the video using nearest-neighbor. For simplicity, we use this strategy to handle test videos. But since our model is fully convolutional, it is not limited to this particular choice of video length. In Sect. 4.4, we experiment with sampling the videos to a longer length. We also experiment with directly operating on original non-sampled (variable length) videos in Sect. 4.4.

We follow [24,40] to convert predicted keyframes to keyshots so that we can perform fair comparison with other methods. We first apply KTS [29] to temporally segment a test video into disjoint intervals. Next, if an interval contains a keyframe, we mark all the frames in that interval as 1 and we mark 0 to all the frames in intervals that have no keyframes. This results in keyshot-based summary for the video. To minimize the number of generated keyshots, we rank the intervals based on the number of keyframes in intervals divided by their lengths, and finally apply knapsack algorithm [34] to ensure that the produced keyshot-based summary is of maximum 15% in length of the original test video.

Evaluation Metrics: Following [24,40], we use a keyshot-based evaluation metric. For a given video V, suppose S_O is the generated summary and S_G is the ground-truth summary. We calculate the precision (P) and recall (R) using their temporal overlap:

$$P = \frac{|S_O \cap S_G|}{|S_O|}, R = \frac{|S_O \cap S_G|}{|S_G|} \quad (3)$$

Finally, we use the F-score $F = (2P \times R)/(P + R) \times 100\%$ as the evaluation metric. We follow the standard approach described in [10,34,40] to calculate the metric for videos that have multiple ground-truth summaries.

Experiment Settings: Similar to previous work [39,40], we evaluate and compare our method under the following three different settings.

1. *Standard Supervised Setting:* This is the conventional supervised learning setting where training, validation and test data are drawn (such that they do

not overlap) from the same dataset. We randomly select 20% for testing and leave the rest 80% for training and validation. Since the data is randomly splitted, we repeat the experiment over multiple random splits and report the average F-score performance.

2. *Augmented Setting:* For a given dataset, we randomly select 20% data for testing and leave the rest 80% for training and validation. In addition, we use the other three datasets to augment the training data. For example, suppose we are evaluating on the SumMe dataset, we will then have 80% of SumMe videos combined with all the videos in the TVSum, OVP, and YouTube dataset for training. Likewise, if we are evaluating on TVSum, we will have 80% of TVSum videos combined with all the videos in SumMe, OVP, and YouTube for training. Similar to the standard supervised setting, we run the experiment over multiple random splits and use the average F-score for comparison.

The idea of increasing the size of training data by augmenting with other datasets is well-known in computer vision. This is usually referred as data augmentation. Recent methods [24,40] show that data augmentation improves the performance. Our experimental results show similar conclusion.

3. *Transfer Setting:* This is a challenging supervised setting introduced by Zhang et al. [39,40]. In this setting, the model is not trained using the videos from the given dataset. Instead, the model is trained on other available datasets and tested on the given dataset. For instance, if we are evaluating on the SumMe dataset, we will train the model using videos in the TVSum, OVP, and YouTube datasets. We then use the videos in the SumMe dataset only for evaluation. Similarly, when evaluating on TVSum, we will train on videos from SumMe, OVP, YouTube, and then test on the videos in TVSum. This setting is particularly relevant for practical applications. If we can achieve good performance under this setting, it means that we can perform video summarization in the wild. In other words, we will be able to generate good summaries for videos from domains in which we do not have any related annotated videos during training.

4.3   Main Results and Comparisons

We compare the performance of our approach (SUM-FCN) with prior methods on the SumMe dataset in Table 2. Our method outperforms other state-of-the-art approaches by a large margin.

Table 3 compares the performance of our method with previous approaches on the TVSum dataset. Again, our method achieves state-of-the-art performance. In the *standard supervised* setting, we outperform other approaches. In the *augmented* and *transfer* settings, our performance is comparable to other state-of-the-art. Note that Zhang et al. [40] (vsLSTM) use frame-level importance scores and Zhang et al. [40] (dppLSTM) use both keyframe-based annotation

Table 2. Comparison of summarization performance (F-score) between SUM-FCN and other approaches on the SumMe dataset under different settings

Dataset	Method	Standard supervised	Augmented	Transfer
SumMe	Gygli et al. [9]	39.4	–	–
	Gygli et al. [10]	39.7	–	–
	Zhang et al. [39]	40.9	41.3	38.5
	Zhang et al. [40] (vsLSTM)	37.6	41.6	40.7
	Zhang et al. [40] (dppLSTM)	38.6	42.9	41.8
	Mahasseni et al. [24] (supervised)	41.7	43.6	–
	Li et al. [19]	43.1	–	–
	SUM-FCN (ours)	**47.5**	**51.1**	**44.1**

and frame-level importance scores. But we only use keyframe-based annotation in our method. Previous method [40] has also shown that frame-level importance scores provide richer information than binary labels. Therefore, the performance of our method on TVSum is very competitive, since it does not use frame-level importance scores during training.

Table 3. Performance (F-score) of SUM-FCN and other approaches on the TVSum dataset. †Zhang et al. [40] (vsLSTM) use frame-level importance scores. ‡Zhang et al. [40] (dppLSTM) use both frame-level importance scores and keyframes in their method. Different from these two methods, our method only uses keyframe-based annotations

Dataset	Method	Standard supervised	Augmented	Transfer
TVSum	Zhang et al. [40] (vsLSTM)	54.2	57.9	56.9†
	Zhang et al. [40] (dppLSTM)	54.7	59.6	**58.7‡**
	Mahasseni et al. [24] (supervised)	56.3	**61.2**	–
	Li et al. [19]	52.7	–	–
	SUM-FCN (ours)	**56.8**	59.2	58.2

4.4 Analysis

In this section, we present additional ablation analysis on various aspects of our model.

Unsupervised SUM-FCN$_{unsup}$: Table 4 compares the performance of SUM-FCN$_{unsup}$ with the other unsupervised methods in the literature. SUM-FCN$_{unsup}$ achieves the state-of-the-art performance on both the datasets. These results suggest that our fully convolutional sequence model can effectively learn how to summarize videos in an unsupervised way. This is very appealing since collecting labeled training data for video summarization is difficult.

SUM-DeepLab: To demonstrate the generality of FCSN, we also adapt DeepLab [4] (in particular, DeepLabv2 (VGG16) model), another popular

Table 4. Performance (F-score) comparison of SUM-FCN$_{unsup}$ with state-of-the-art unsupervised methods

Dataset	[5]	[20]	[14]	[34]	[41]	[24]	SUM-FCN$_{unsup}$
SumMe	33.7	26.6	–	26.6	–	39.1	**41.5**
TVSum	–	–	36.0	50.0	46.0	51.7	**52.7**

semantic segmentation model, for video summarization. We call this network SUM-DeepLab. The DeepLab model has two important features: (1) dilated convolution; (2) spatial pyramid pooling. In SUM-DeepLab, we similarly perform temporal dilated convolution and temporal pyramid pooling.

Table 5 compares SUM-DeepLab with SUM-FCN on the SumMe and TVSum datasets under different settings. SUM-DeepLab achieves better performance on SumMe in all settings. On TVSum, the performance of SUM-DeepLab is better than SUM-FCN in the *standard supervised* setting and is comparable in the other two settings.

We noticed that SUM-DeepLab performs slightly worse than SUM-FCN in some settings (e.g. *transfer* setting of TVSum). One possible explanation is that the bilinear upsampling layer in DeepLab may not be the best choice. Unlike semantic segmentation, a smooth labeling (due to bilinear upsampling) is not necessarily desirable in video summarization. In other words, the bilinear upsampling may result in a sub-optimal subset of keyframes. In order to verify this, we replace the bilinear upsampling layers of SUM-DeepLab with learnable deconvolution layers (also used in SUM-FCN) and examine the performance of this modified SUM-DeepLab in the *transfer* setting. The performance of SUM-DeepLab improves as a result of this simple modification. In fact, SUM-DeepLab now achieves the state-of-the-art performance on the *transfer* setting on TVSum as well (see the last column in Table 5).

Table 5. Performance (F-score) of SUM-DeepLab in different settings. We include the performance of SUM-FCN (taken from Tables 2 and 3) in brackets. We also replace the bilinear upsampling with learnable deconvolutional layer and report the result in the transfer setting (last column)

Dataset	Standard supervised	Augmented	Transfer	Transfer (deconv)
SumMe	**48.8** (47.5)	50.2 (51.1)	**45.0** (44.1)	**45.1**
TVSum	**58.4** (56.8)	59.1 (59.2)	57.4 (58.2)	**58.8**

Length of Video: We also perform experiments to analyze the performance of our models on longer-length videos. Again, we select the challenging *transfer* setting to evaluate the models when the videos are uniformly sampled to $T = 640$ frames. Table 6 (first two columns) shows the results of our models for this case.

Compared with $T = 320$ (shown in brackets in Table 6), the performance with $T = 640$ is similar. This shows that the video length is not an issue for our proposed fully convolutional models.

Table 6. Performance (F-score) of our models on longer-length videos (i.e. $T = 640$) and original (i.e. variable length) videos in the *transfer* data setting. In brackets, we show the performance of our model for $T = 320$ (obtained from Tables 2, 3 and 5)

Dataset	SUM-FCN	SUM-DeepLab	SUM-FCN
	$T = 640$ ($T = 320$)	$T = 640$ ($T = 320$)	Variable length
SumMe	45.6 (44.1)	44.5 (45.0)	46.0
TVSum	57.4 (58.2)	57.2 (57.4)	56.7

As mentioned earlier, the main idea behind uniformly sampling videos is to mimic the prevalent cropping strategy in semantic segmentation. Nevertheless, since our model is fully convolutional, it can directly handle variable length videos. The last column of Table 6 shows the results of applying SUM-FCN (in the *transfer* setting) without sampling videos. The performance is comparable (even higher on SumMe) to the results of sampling videos to a fixed length.

Qualitative Results: In Fig. 3, we show example video summaries (good and poor) produced by SUM-FCN on two videos in the SumMe [9] dataset.

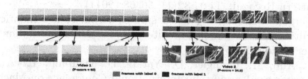

Fig. 3. Example summaries for two videos in the SumMe [9] dataset. The black bars on the green background show the frames selected to form the summary video. For each video, we show the ground-truth (*top bar*) and the predicted labels (*bottom bar*). (Color figure online)

5   Conclusion

We have introduced fully convolutional sequence networks (FCSN) for video summarization. Our proposed models are inspired by fully convolutional networks in semantic segmentation. In computer vision, video summarization and semantic segmentation are often studied as two separate problems. We have shown that these two seemingly unrelated problems have an underlying connection. We have adapted popular semantic segmentation networks for video summarization. Our models achieve very competitive performance in comparison with other supervised and unsupervised state-of-the-art approaches that mainly use LSTMs. We believe that fully convolutional models provide a promising alternative to LSTM-based approaches for video summarization. Finally, our proposed method is not limited to FCSN variants that we introduced. Using similar strategies, we can convert almost any semantic segmentation networks for video summarization. As future work, we plan to explore more recent semantic segmentation models and develop their counterpart models in video summarization.

Acknowledgments. This work was supported by NSERC, a University of Manitoba Graduate Fellowship, and the University of Manitoba GETS program. We thank NVIDIA for donating some of the GPUs used in this work.

References

1. Cisco visual networking index: Forecast and methodology, 2016–2021. https://www.cisco.com/
2. Open video project. https://open-video.org/
3. Bai, S., Kolter, J.Z., Koltun, V.: An empirical evaluation of generic convolutional and recurrent networks for sequence modeling. arXiv:1803.01271 (2018)
4. Chen, L.C., Papandreou, G., Kokkinos, I., Murphy, K., Yuille, A.L.: DeepLab: semantic image segmentation with deep convolutional nets, atrous convolution, and fully connected CRFs. IEEE Trans. Pattern Anal. Mach. Intell. **40**, 834–848 (2017)
5. De Avila, S.E.F., Lopes, A.P.B., da Luz, A., de Albuquerque Araújo, A.: VSUMM: a mechanism designed to produce static video summaries and a novel evaluation method. Pattern Recognit. Lett. **32**(1), 56–68 (2011)
6. Eigen, D., Fergus, R.: Predicting depth, surface normals and semantic labels with a common multi-scale convolutional architecture. In: IEEE International Conference on Computer Vision (2015)
7. Gehring, J., Auli, M., Grangier, D., Yarats, D., Dauphin, Y.N.: Convolutional sequence to sequence learning. In: International Conference on Machine Learning (2017)
8. Gong, B., Chao, W.L., Grauman, K., Sha, F.: Diverse sequential subset selection for supervised video summarization. In: Advances in Neural Information Processing Systems (2014)
9. Gygli, M., Grabner, H., Riemenschneider, H., Van Gool, L.: Creating summaries from user videos. In: Fleet, D., Pajdla, T., Schiele, B., Tuytelaars, T. (eds.) ECCV 2014. LNCS, vol. 8695, pp. 505–520. Springer, Cham (2014). https://doi.org/10.1007/978-3-319-10584-0_33
10. Gygli, M., Grabner, H., Van Gool, L.: Video summarization by learning submodular mixtures of objectives. In: IEEE Conference on Computer Vision and Pattern Recognition (2015)
11. Hochreiter, S., Schmidhuber, J.: Long short-term memory. Neural Comput. **9**(8), 1735–1780 (1997)
12. Joshi, N., Kienzle, W., Toelle, M., Uyttendaele, M., Cohen, M.F.: Real-time hyperlapse creation via optimal frame selection. ACM Trans. Graph. **34**(4), 63 (2015)
13. Kang, H.W., Chen, X.Q.: Space-time video montage. In: IEEE Conference on Computer Vision and Pattern Recognition (2006)

14. Khosla, A., Hamid, R., Lin, C.J., Sundaresan, N.: Large-scale video summarization using web-image priors. In: CVPR (2013)
15. Kim, G., Xing, E.P.: Reconstructing storyline graphs for image recommendation from web community photos. In: IEEE Conference on Computer Vision and Pattern Recognition (2014)
16. Kopf, J., Cohen, M.F., Szeliski, R.: First-person hyper-lapse videos. ACM Trans. Graph. **33**(4), 78 (2014)
17. Lea, C., Flynn, M.D., Vidal, R., Reiter, A., Hager, G.D.: Temporal convolutional networks for action segmentation and detection. In: IEEE Conference on Computer Vision and Pattern Recognition (2017)
18. Lee, Y.J., Ghosh, J., Grauman, K.: Discovering important people and objects for egocentric video summarization. In: IEEE Conference on Computer Vision and Pattern Recognition (2012)
19. Li, X., Zhao, B., Lu, X.: A general framework for edited video and raw video summarization. IEEE Trans. Image Process. **26**(8), 3652–3664 (2017)
20. Li, Y., Merialdo, B.: Multi-video summarization based on video-MMR. In: Workshop on Image Analysis for Multimedia Interactive Services (2010)
21. Liu, D., Hua, G., Chen, T.: A hierarchical visual model for video object summarization. IEEE Trans. Pattern Anal. Mach. Intell. **32**(12), 2178–2190 (2010)
22. Long, J., Shelhamer, E., Darrell, T.: Fully convolutional networks for semantic segmentation. In: IEEE Conference on Computer Vision and Pattern Recognition (2015)
23. Lu, Z., Grauman, K.: Story-driven summarization for egocentric video. In: IEEE Conference on Computer Vision and Pattern Recognition (2013)
24. Mahasseni, B., Lam, M., Todorovic, S.: Unsupervised video summarization with adversarial LSTM networks. In: IEEE Conference on Computer Vision and Pattern Recognition (2017)
25. Mundur, P., Rao, Y., Yesha, Y.: Keyframe-based video summarization using delaunay clustering. Int. J. Digit. Libr. **6**(2), 219–232 (2006)
26. Ngo, C.W., Ma, Y.F., Zhang, H.J.: Automatic video summarization by graph modeling. In: IEEE International Conference on Computer Vision (2003)
27. Panda, R., Roy-Chowdhury, A.K.: Collaborative summarization of topic-related videos. In: IEEE Conference on Computer Vision and Pattern Recognition (2017)
28. Poleg, Y., Halperin, T., Arora, C., Peleg, S.: EgoSampling: fast-forward and stereo for egocentric videos. In: IEEE Conference on Computer Vision and Pattern Recognition (2015)
29. Potapov, D., Douze, M., Harchaoui, Z., Schmid, C.: Category-specific video summarization. In: Fleet, D., Pajdla, T., Schiele, B., Tuytelaars, T. (eds.) ECCV 2014. LNCS, vol. 8694, pp. 540–555. Springer, Cham (2014). https://doi.org/10.1007/978-3-319-10599-4_35
30. Pritch, Y., Rav-Acha, A., Peleg, S.: Nonchronological video synopsis and indexing. IEEE Trans. Pattern Anal. Mach. Intell. **30**(11), 1971–1984 (2008)
31. Schuster, M., Kuldip, P.K.: Bidirectional recurrent neural networks. IEEE Trans. Signal Process. **45**, 2673–2681 (1997)
32. Sharghi, A., Laurel, J.S., Gong, B.: Query-focused video summarization: dataset, evaluation, and a memory network based approach. In: IEEE Conference on Computer Vision and Pattern Recognition (2017)
33. Smeaton, A.F., Over, P., Kraaij, W.: Evaluation campaigns and TRECVid. In: Multimedia Information Retrieval. ACM (2006)

34. Song, Y., Vallmitjana, J., Stent, A., Jaimes, A.: TVSum: summarizing web videos using titles. In: IEEE Conference on Computer Vision and Pattern Recognition (2015)
35. Sun, M., Farhadi, A., Taskar, B., Seitz, S.: Salient montages from unconstrained videos. In: Fleet, D., Pajdla, T., Schiele, B., Tuytelaars, T. (eds.) ECCV 2014. LNCS, vol. 8695, pp. 472–488. Springer, Cham (2014). https://doi.org/10.1007/978-3-319-10584-0_31
36. Szegedy, C., et al.: Going deeper with convolutions. In: IEEE Conference on Computer Vision and Pattern Recognition (2015)
37. Tran, D., Bourdev, L., Fergus, R., Torresani, L., Paluri, M.: Learning spatiotemporal features with 3D convolutional networks. In: IEEE International Conference on Computer Vision (2015)
38. Yang, H., Wang, B., Lin, S., Wipf, D., Guo, M., Guo, B.: Unsupervised extraction of video highlights via robust recurrent auto-encoders. In: IEEE International Conference on Computer Vision (2015)
39. Zhang, K., Chao, W.L., Sha, F., Grauman, K.: Summary transfer: examplar-based subset selection for video summarization. In: IEEE Conference on Computer Vision and Pattern Recognition (2016)
40. Zhang, K., Chao, W.-L., Sha, F., Grauman, K.: Video summarization with long short-term memory. In: Leibe, B., Matas, J., Sebe, N., Welling, M. (eds.) ECCV 2016. LNCS, vol. 9911, pp. 766–782. Springer, Cham (2016). https://doi.org/10.1007/978-3-319-46478-7_47
41. Zhao, B., Xing, E.P.: Quasi real-time summarization for consumer videos. In: IEEE Conference on Computer Vision and Pattern Recognition (2014)
42. Zhao, J., Mathieu, M., LeCun, Y.: Energy-based generative adversarial network. In: International Conference on Learning Representations (2017)

Modeling Visual Context Is Key
to Augmenting Object Detection Datasets

Nikita Dvornik$^{(\boxtimes)}$, Julien Mairal, and Cordelia Schmid

Univ. Grenoble Alpes, Inria, CNRS, Grenoble INP (Institute of Engineering, Univ.
Grenoble Alpes), LJK, 38000 Grenoble, France
{nikita.dvornik,julien.mairal,cordelia.schmid}@inria.fr

Abstract. Performing data augmentation for learning deep neural networks is well known to be important for training visual recognition systems. By artificially increasing the number of training examples, it helps reducing overfitting and improves generalization. For object detection, classical approaches for data augmentation consist of generating images obtained by basic geometrical transformations and color changes of original training images. In this work, we go one step further and leverage segmentation annotations to increase the number of object instances present on training data. For this approach to be successful, we show that modeling appropriately the visual context surrounding objects is crucial to place them in the right environment. Otherwise, we show that the previous strategy actually hurts. With our context model, we achieve significant mean average precision improvements when few labeled examples are available on the VOC'12 benchmark.

Keywords: Object detection · Data augmentation · Visual context

1 Introduction

Object detection is one of the most classical computer vision task and is often considered as a basic proxy for scene understanding. Given an input image, an algorithm is expected to produce a set of tight boxes around objects while automatically classifying them. Obviously, modeling correctly object appearances is important, but it is also well-known that visual context provides important cues for recognition, both for computer vision systems and for humans [1].

Objects from the same class tend indeed to be grouped together in similar environments; sometimes they interact with it and do not even make sense in its absence. Whenever visual information is corrupted, ambiguous, or incomplete (*e.g.*, an image contains noise, bad illumination conditions, or an object is occluded or truncated), visual context becomes a crucial source of information. Frequently, certain object categories may for instance most often appear in specific conditions (*e.g.*, planes in the sky, plates on the table), in co-occurrence with objects of other specific classes (*e.g.*, baseball ball and baseball bat), and more generally, any type of clue for object recognition that is not directly related

© Springer Nature Switzerland AG 2018
V. Ferrari et al. (Eds.): ECCV 2018, LNCS 11216, pp. 375–391, 2018.
https://doi.org/10.1007/978-3-030-01258-8_23

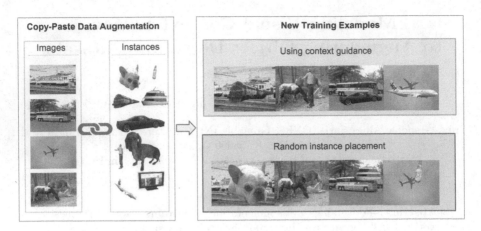

Fig. 1. Examples of data-augmented training examples produced by our approach. Images and objects are taken from the VOC'12 dataset that contains segmentation annotations. We compare the output obtained by pasting the objects with our context model vs. those obtained with random placements. Even though the results are not perfectly photorealistic and display blending artefacts, the visual context surrounding objects is more often correct with the explicit context model.

to the object's appearance is named "context" in the literature. For this reason, a taxonomy of contextual information is proposed in [2] to better understand what type of visual context is useful for object detection.

Before the deep learning/ImageNet revolution, the previous generation of object detectors such as [3–6] modeled the interaction between object locations, categories, and context by manual engineering of local descriptors, feature aggregation methods, and by defining structural relationship between objects. In contrast, recent works based on convolutional neural networks such as [7–10] implicitly model visual context by design since the receptive field of "artificial neurons" grows with the network's depth, eventually covering the full image for the last layers. For this reason, these CNNs-based approaches have shown modest improvements when combined with an explicit context model [11].

Our results are not in contradiction with such previous findings. We show that explicit context modeling is important only for a particular part of object detection pipelines that was not considered in previous work. When training a convolutional neural network, it is indeed important to control overfitting, especially if few labeled training examples are available. Various heuristics are typically used for that purpose such as DropOut [12], penalizing the norm of the network parameters (weight decay), or early stopping. Even though the regularization effect of such approaches is not well understood from a theoretical point of view, these heuristics have been found to be useful in practice.

Besides these heuristics related to the learning procedure, another way to control overfitting consists of artificially increasing the size of training data by using prior knowledge on the task. For instance, all object classes from the VOC'12 dataset [13] are invariant to horizontal flips (*e.g.*, a flipped car is still a car) and to many less-trivial transformations. A more ambitious data augmentation technique consists of leveraging segmentation annotations, either obtained manually, or from an automatic segmentation system, and create new images with objects placed at various positions in existing scenes [14–16]. While not achieving perfect photorealism, this strategy with random placements has proven to be surprisingly effective for *object instance detection* [14], which is a fine-grained detection task consisting of retrieving instances of a particular object from an image collection; in contrast, *object detection* focuses on detecting object instances from a particular category. Unfortunately, the random-placement strategy does not extend to the object detection task, as shown in the experimental section. By placing training objects at unrealistic positions, implicitly modeling context becomes difficult and the detection accuracy drops substantially.

Along the same lines, the authors of [15] have proposed to augment datasets for text recognition by adding text on images in a realistic fashion. There, placing text with the right geometrical context proves to be critical. Significant improvements in accuracy are obtained by first estimating the geometry of the scene, before placing text on an estimated plane. Also related, the work of [16] is using successfully such a data augmentation technique for object detection in indoor scene environments. Modeling context has been found to be critical as well and has been achieved by also estimating plane geometry and objects are typically placed on detected tables or counters, which often occur in indoor scenes.

In this paper, we consider the general object detection problem, which requires more generic context modeling than estimating plane and surfaces as done for instance in [15,16]. To this end, the first contribution of our paper is methodological: we propose a context model based on a convolutional neural network, which will be made available as an open-source software package. The model estimates the likelihood of a particular category of object to be present inside a box given its neighborhood, and then automatically finds suitable locations on images to place new objects and perform data augmentation. A brief illustration of the output produced by this approach is presented in Fig. 1. The second contribution is experimental: We show with extensive tests on the VOC'12 benchmark that context modeling is in fact a key to obtain good results for object detection and that substantial improvements over non-data-augmented baselines may be achieved when few labeled examples are available.

2   Related Work

In this section, we briefly discuss related work for visual context modeling and data augmentation for object detection.

Modeling Visual Context for Object Detection. Relatively early, visual context has been modeled by computing statistical correlation between low-level features of the global scene and descriptors representing an object [17,18]. Later, the authors of [4] introduced a simple context re-scoring approach operating on appearance-based detections. To encode more structure, graphical models were then widely used in order to jointly model appearance, geometry, and contextual relations [19,20]. Then, deep learning approaches such as convolutional neural networks started to be used [7–9]; as mentioned previously, their features already contain implicitly contextual information. Yet, the work of [21] explicitly incorporates higher-level context clues and combines a conditional random field model with detections obtained by Faster-RCNN. With a similar goal, recurrent neural networks are used in [22] to model spatial locations of discovered objects. Another complementary direction in context modeling with convolutional neural networks use a deconvolution pipeline that increases the field of view of neurons and fuse features at different scales [22–24], showing better performance essentially on small objects. The works of [2,25] analyze different types of contextual relationships, identifying the most useful ones for detection, as well as various ways to leverage them. However, despite these efforts, an improvement due to purely contextual information has always been relatively modest [11,26].

Data Augmentation for Object Detection. Data augmentation is a major tool to train deep neural networks. If varies from trivial geometrical transformations such as horizontal flipping, cropping with color perturbations, and adding noise to an image [27], to synthesizing new training images [28,29]. Some recent object detectors [9,10,23] benefit from standard data augmentation techniques more than others [7,8]. The performance of Fast- and Faster-RCNN could be for instance increased by simply corrupting random parts of an image in order to mimic occlusions [30]. Regarding image synthesis, recent works such as [31–33] build and train their models on purely synthetic rendered 2d and 3d scenes. However, a major difficulty for models trained on synthetic images is to guarantee that they will generalize well to real data since the synthesis process introduces significant changes of image statistics [29]. To address this issue, the authors of [15] adopt a different direction by pasting real segmented object into natural images, which reduces the presence of rendering artefacts. For object instance detection, the work [16] estimates scene geometry and spatial layout, before placing objects in the image to create realistic training examples. In [14], the authors propose an even simpler solution to the same problem by pasting images in random positions but modeling well occluded and truncated objects, and making the training step robust to boundary artifacts at pasted locations.

3   Modeling Visual Context for Data Augmentation

Our approach for data augmentation mainly consists of two parts: we first model visual context by using bounding box annotations, where the surrounding of a box is used as an input to a convolutional neural network to predict the presence or absence of an object within the box. Then, the trained context model is used to generate a set of possible new locations for objects. The full pipeline is presented in Fig. 2. In this section, we describe these two steps in details, but before that, we present and discuss a preliminary experiment that has motivated our work.

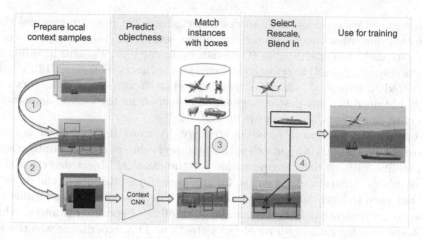

Fig. 2. Illustration of our data augmentation approach. We select an image for augmentation and (1) generate 200 candidate boxes that cover the image. Then, (2) for each box we find a neighborhood that contains the box entirely, crop this neighborhood and mask all pixels falling inside the bounding box; this "neighborhood" with masked pixels is then fed to the context neural network module and (3) object instances are matched to boxes that have high confidence scores for the presence of an object category. (4) We select at most two instances that are rescaled and blended into the selected bounding boxes. The resulting image is then used for training the object detector.

3.1 Preliminary Experiment with Random Positioning

In [14], data augmentation is performed by placing segmented objects at random positions in new scenes. As mentioned previously, the strategy was shown to be effective for object instance detection, as soon as an appropriate procedure is used for preventing the object detector to overfit blending artefacts—that is, the main difficulty is to prevent the detector to "detect artefacts" instead of detecting objects of interest. This is achieved by using various strategies to smooth object boundaries such as Poisson blending [34], and by adding "distractors" objects that do not belong to any of the dataset categories, but which are also synthetically pasted on random backgrounds. With distractors, artefacts occur both in positive and negative examples, preventing the network trained for object detection to overfit them. According to [14], this strategy brings substantial improvements for the object instance detection/retrieval task, where modeling the fine-grain appearance of an object instance seems to be more important than modeling visual context as in the general category object detection task.

Unfortunately, the above context-free strategy does not extend trivially to the object detection task we consider. Our preliminary experiment conducted on the VOC'12 dataset actually shows that it may even hurt the accuracy of the detector, which has motivated us to propose instead an explicit context model. Specifically, we conducted an experiment by following the original strategy of [14] as closely as possible. We use the subset of the VOC'12 train set that has ground-truth segmentation annotations to cut object instances from images and then place them on other images from the training set. As in [14], we experimented with various blending strategies (Gaussian or linear blur, Poisson blending, or using no blending at all) to smooth the boundary artifacts. Following [14], we also considered "distractors", which are then labeled as background. Distractors were simply obtained by copy-pasting segmented objects from the COCO dataset [35] from categories that do not appear in VOC'12.[1]

For any combination of blending strategy, by using distractors or not, the naive data augmentation approach with random placement did not improve upon the baseline without data augmentation for the classical object detection task. A possible explanation may be that for instance object detection, the detector does not need to learn intra-class variability of object/scene representations and seems to concentrate only on appearance modeling of specific instances, which is not the case for category-level object detection. This experiment was the key motivation for proposing a context model, which we now present.

3.2 Modeling Visual Context with Convolutional Neural Networks

Since the context-free data augmentation failed, we propose to learn where to automatically place objects by using a convolutional neural network. Here, we present the data generation, model training, and object placement procedures.

Contextual Data Generation. We consider training data with bounding box and category annotations. For each bounding box B associated to a training image I, we create a set of training contexts, which are defined as subimages of I fully enclosing the bounding box B whose content is masked out, as illustrated in Fig. 3. Several contexts can be created from a single annotated bounding box B by varying the size of the subimage around B and its aspect ratio. In addition, "background" contexts are also created by considering random bounding boxes whose intersection over union with any ground truth doesn't exceed a threshold of 0.3, and whose content is also masked out. The shape of such boxes is defined by aspect ratio a and relative scale s. We draw a pair of parameters from the joint distribution induced by bounding boxes containing positive objects, i.e. a 30×30 bins normalized histogram. Since in general, there is more background samples than the ones actually containing objects, we sample "background" contexts 3 times more often following sampling strategies in [7,9].

Model Training. Given the set of all contexts, gathered from all training data, we train a convolutional neural network to predict the presence of each object in the masked bounding box. The input to the network are the "contextual images" obtained during the data generation step, and which contain a masked bounding box inside. These contextual images are resized to 300×300 pixels, and the output of the network is a label in a set $\{1, 2, ..., K + 1\}$, where K is

---

[1] Note that external data from COCO was used only in this preliminary experiment and not in the experiments reported later in Sect. 4.

Fig. 3. Contextual images - examples of inputs to the context model. A subimage bounded by a magenta box is used as an input to the context model after masking-out the object information inside a red box. The top row lists examples of positive samples encoding real objects surrounded by regular and predictable context. Positive training examples with ambiguous or uninformative context are given in the second row. The bottom row depicts negative examples enclosing background. This figure shows that contextual images could be ambiguous to classify correctly and the task of predicting the category given only the context is challenging. (Color figure online)

the number of object categories and the $(K+1)$-th class represents background. For such a multi-class image classification problem here, we use the classical ResNet50 network [36] pre-trained on ImageNet, and change the last layer to be a softmax with $K+1$ activations (see experimental section for details).

Selection of Object Locations at Test Time. Once the context model is trained by using training data annotated with bounding boxes, we use it to select locations to perform data augmentation on a given image. As input, the trained classifier receives "contextual images" with a bounding box masked out (as in Sect. 3.2). The model is able to provide a set of "probabilities" representing the presence of each object category in a given bounding box, by considering its visual surrounding. Since evaluating all potential bounding boxes from an image is too costly, we randomly draw 200 candidate bounding boxes and retain the ones where an object category has a score greater than 0.8; empirically, the number 200 was found to provide good enough bounding boxes among the top scoring ones, while resulting in a reasonably fast data augmentation procedure.

Fig. 4. Different kinds of blending used in experiments. From left to right: linear smoothing of boundaries, Gaussian smoothing, no processing, motion blur of the whole image, Poisson blending [34].

Blending Objects in Their Environment. Whenever a bounding box is selected by the previous procedure, we need to blend an object at the corresponding location. This step follows closely the findings of [14]. We consider different types of blending techniques (Gaussian or linear blur, simple copy-pasting with no post-processing, or generating blur on the whole image to imitate motion), and randomly choose one of them in order to introduce a larger diversity of blending artefacts. We also do not consider Poisson blending in our approach, which was considerably slowing down the data generation procedure. Unlike [14] and unlike our preliminary experiment described in Sect. 3.1, we do not use distractors, which were found to be less important for our task than in [14]. As a consequence, we do not need to exploit external data to perform data augmentation. Qualitative results are illustrated on Fig. 4.

4   Experiments

In this section, we present experiments demonstrating the importance of context modeling for data augmentation. We evaluate our approach on the subset of the VOC'12 dataset that contains segmentation annotations, and study the impact of data augmentation when changing the amount of training data. In Sect. 4.1, we present data, tools, and evaluation metrics. In Sect. 4.2, we present implementation details that are common to all experiments, in order to make our results reproducible (the source code to conduct our experiments will also be made publicly available in an open-source software package). First, we present experiments for object detectors trained on single categories in Sect. 4.3—that is, detectors are trained individually for each object category, and an experiment for the standard multiple-category setting is presented in Sect. 4.4. Finally, we present an ablation study in Sect. 4.5 to understand the effect of various factors (blending and placement strategies, amount of labeled data).

4.1   Dataset, Tools, and Metrics

Dataset. In all our experiments, we use a subset of the Pascal VOC'12 training dataset [13] that contains segmentation annotations to train all our models (context-model and object detector). We call this training set VOC12train-seg, which contains 1 464 images. Following standard practice, we use the test set of VOC'07 to evaluate the models, which contains 4 952 images with the same 20 object categories as VOC'12. We call this image set VOC07-test.

Object Detector. To test our data-augmentation strategy we chose one of the state-of-the art object detectors with open-source implementation, BlitzNet [23] that achieves 79.1% mAP on VOC07-test when trained on the union of the full training and validation parts of VOC'07 and VOC'12, namely VOC07-train+val and VOC12train+val (see [23]); this network is similar to the DSSD detector of [24] that was also used in the Focal Loss paper [37]. The advantage of such class of detectors is that it is relatively fast (it may work in real time) and supports training with big batches of images without further modification.

Evaluation Metric. In VOC'07, a bounding box is considered to be correct if its Intersection over Union (IoU) with a ground truth box is higher than 0.5. The metric for evaluating the quality of detection for one object class is the average precision (AP), and the mean average precision (mAP) for the dataset.

4.2 Implementation Details

Selecting and Blending Objects. Since we widely use object instances extracted from the training images in all our experiments, we create a database of objects cut out from the VOC12train-seg set to quickly access them during training. For a given candidate box, an instance is considered as matching if after scaling it by a factor in $[0.5, 1.5]$ the re-scaled instance's bounding box fits inside the candidate's one and takes at least 80% of it's area. When blending them into the new background, we follow [14] and use randomly one of the following methods: adding Gaussian or linear blur on the object boundaries, generating blur on the whole image by imitating motion, or just paste an image with no blending. To not introduce scaling artifacts, we keep the scaling factor close to 1.

Training the Context Model. After preparing the "contextual images" as described in 3.2, we re-scale them to the standard size 300×300 and stack them in batches of size 32. We use ResNet50 [36] with ImageNet initialization to train a contextual model in all our experiments. Since we have access only to the training set at any moment we train and apply the model on the same data. To prevent overfitting, we use early stopping. In order to determine when to stop the training procedure, we monitor both training error on our training set and validation error on the VOC'12 validation set VOC12-val. The moment when the loss curves start diverging noticeably is used as a stopping point. To this end, when building context model for one class vs. background, we train a network for 1.5K iterations, then decrease the learning rate by a factor 10 and train for 500 additional iterations. When learning a joint contextual model for all 20 categories, we first run the training procedure for 4K iterations and then for 2K more iterations after decreasing the learning rate. We sample 3 times more background contextual images, as noted in Sect. 3.2. Visual examples of images produced by the context model are presented in Fig. 5. Overall, training the context model is about 5 times faster than training the detector.

Training the Object Detector. In this work, the detector takes images of size 300×300 as an input and produces a set of candidate object boxes with classification scores; like our context model, it uses ResNet50 [36] pre-trained on ImageNet as a backbone. The detector is trained by following [23], with the ADAM optimizer [38] starting from learning rate 10^{-4} and decreasing it later during training by a factor 10 (see Sects. 4.3 and 4.4 for the number of epochs used in each experiment). In addition to our data augmentation approach obtained by copy-pasting objects, all experiments also include classical data augmentation steps obtained by random-cropping, flips, and color transformations, following [23].

4.3   Single-Category Object Detection

In this section, we conduct an experiment to better understand the effect of the proposed data augmentation approach, dubbed "Context-DA" in the different tables, when compared to a baseline with random object placement "Random-DA", and when compared to standard data augmentation techniques called"Base-DA". The study is conducted in a single-category setting, where detectors are trained independently for each object category, resulting in a relatively small number of positive training examples per class. This allows us to evaluate the importance of context when few labeled samples are available and see if conclusions drawn for a category easily generalize to other ones.

The baseline with random object placements on random backgrounds is conducted in a similar fashion as our context-driven approach, by following the strategy described in the previous section. For each category, we treat all images with no object from this category as background images, and consider a collection of cut instances as discussed in Sect. 4.1. During training, we augment a negative (background) image with probability 0.5 by pasting up to two instances on it, either at randomly selected locations (Random-DA), or using our context model in the selected bounding boxes with top scores (Context-DA). The instances are re-scaled by a random factor in $[0.5, 2]$ and blended into an image using a randomly selected blending method mentioned in Sect. 4.1. For all models, we train the object detection network for 6K iterations and decrease the learning rate after 2K and 4K iterations by a factor 10 each time. The results for this experiment are presented in Table 1.

The conclusions are the following: random placement indeed hurts the performance on average. Only the category bird seems to benefit significantly from it, perhaps because birds tend to appear in various contexts in this dataset and some categories significantly suffer from random placement such as boat, table, and sheep. Importantly, the visual context model always improve upon the random placement one, on average by 5%, and upon the baseline that uses only classical data augmentation, on average by 4%. Interestingly, we identify categories for which visual context is crucial (aeroplane, bird, boat, bus, cat, cow, horse), for which context-driven data augmentation brings more than 5% improvement and some categories that display no significant gain or losses (chair, table, persons, train), where the difference with the baseline is less than 1%.

Table 1. Comparison of detection accuracy on VOC07-test for the single-category experiment. The models are trained independently for each category, by using the 1 464 images from VOC12train-seg. The first row represents the baseline experiment that uses standard data augmentation techniques. The second row uses in addition copy-pasting of objects with random placements. The third row presents the results achieved by our context-driven approach and the last row presents the improvement it brings over the baseline. The numbers represent average precision per class in %. Large improvements over the baseline (greater than 5%) are in bold.

method	aero	bike	bird	boat	bott.	bus	car	cat	chair	cow	table	dog	horse	mbike	pers.	plant	sheep	sofa	train	tv	avg.
Base-DA	58.8	64.3	48.8	47.8	33.9	66.5	69.7	68.0	40.4	59.0	61.0	56.2	72.1	64.2	66.7	36.6	54.5	53.0	73.4	63.6	58.0
Random-DA	60.2	66.5	55.1	41.9	29.7	66.5	70.0	70.1	37.4	57.4	45.3	56.7	68.3	66.1	67.0	37.0	49.9	55.8	72.1	62.6	56.9
Context-DA	67.0	68.6	60.0	53.3	38.8	73.3	72.4	74.3	39.7	64.3	61.4	60.3	77.6	69.0	67.3	38.6	56.2	56.9	74.4	66.8	62.0
Impr. Cont.	**8.2**	4.3	**11.2**	**5.5**	4.9	**6.8**	2.7	**6.3**	-0.7	**5.3**	0.4	4.1	**5.5**	4.8	0.6	2.0	1.7	3.9	1.0	3.2	4.0

Table 2. Comparison of detection accuracy on VOC07-test for the multiple-category experiment. The model is trained on all categories at the same time, by using the 1 464 images from VOC12train-seg. The first row represents the baseline experiment that uses standard data augmentation techniques. The second row uses also our context-driven data augmentation. The numbers represent average precision per class in %.

method	aero	bike	bird	boat	bott.	bus	car	cat	chair	cow	table	dog	horse	mbike	pers.	plant	sheep	sofa	train	tv	avg
Base-DA	63.6	73.3	63.2	57.0	31.5	76.0	71.5	79.9	40.0	71.6	61.4	74.6	80.9	70.4	67.9	36.5	64.9	63.0	79.3	64.7	64.6
Context-DA	66.8	75.3	65.9	57.2	33.1	75.0	72.4	79.6	40.6	73.9	63.7	77.1	81.4	71.8	68.1	37.9	67.6	64.7	81.2	65.5	65.9

4.4 Multiple-Categories Object Detection

In this section, we conduct the same experiment as in Sect. 4.3, but we train a single multiple-category object detector instead of independent ones per category. Network parameters are trained with more labeled data (on average 20 times more than for models learned in Sect. 4.3). The results are presented in Table 2 and show a modest improvement of 1.3% on average over the baseline, which is relatively consistent across categories, with 18 categories out of 20 that benefit from the context-driven data augmentation. This confirms that data augmentation is crucial when few labeled examples are available.

4.5 Ablation Study

Finally, we conduct an ablation study to better understand (i) the importance of visual context for object detection, (ii) the impact of blending artefacts, and (iii) the importance of data augmentation when using very few labeled examples. For simplicity, we choose the first 5 categories of VOC'12, namely *aeroplane, bike, bird, boat, bottle,* and train independent detectors per category as in Sect. 4.3, which corresponds to a setting where few samples are available for training.

Baseline When No Object is in Context. Our experiments show that augmenting naively datasets with randomly placed objects slightly hurts the performance. To confirm this finding, we consider a similar experiment, by learning on the same number of instances as in Sect. 4.3, but we consider as positive examples only objects that have been synthetically placed in a random context. This is achieved by removing from the training data all the images that have an object from the category we want to model, and replacing it by an instance of this object placed on a background image. The main motivation for such study is to consider the extreme case where (i) no object is placed in the right context; (ii) all objects may suffer from rendering artefacts. As shown in Table 3, the average precision degrades significantly by about 14% compared to the baseline. As a conclusion, either visual context is indeed crucial for learning, or blending artefacts is also a critical issue. The purpose of the next experiment is to clarify this ambiguity.

Impact of Blending When the Context is Right. In the previous experiment, we have shown that the lack of visual context and the presence of blending artefacts may explain the performance drop observed on the fourth row of Table 3. Here, we propose a simple experiment showing that blending artefacts are not critical when objects are placed in the right context: the experiment consists of extracting each object instance from the dataset, up-scale it by a random factor slightly greater than one (in the interval $[1.2, 1.5]$), and blend it back at the same location, such that it covers the original instance. As a result, the new dataset benefits slightly from data augmentation (thanks to object enlargement), but it also suffers from blending artefacts for *all object instances.* As shown on the fifth row of Table 3, this approach improves over the baseline, though not as much as the full context-driven data augmentation, which suggests that the lack of visual context was the key explaining the result observed before. The experiment also confirms that the presence of blending artefacts is not critical for the object detection task. Visual examples of such artefacts are presented in Fig. 6.

Performance with Very Few Labeled Data. Finally, the last four rows of Table 3 present our results when reducing the amount of labeled data, in a setting where this amount is already small when using all training data. The improvement provided by our approach is significant and consistent (about 6% when using only 50% and 25% of the training data). Even though one may naturally expect larger improvements when a very small number of training examples are available, it

Table 3. Ablation study on the first five categories of VOC'12. All models are learned independently as in Table 1. We compare classical data augmentation techniques (Base-DA), approaches obtained by copy-pasting objects, either randomly (Random-DA) or according to a context model (Context-DA). The line "Removing context" corresponds to the first experiment described in Sect. 4.5; Enlarge-Reblend corresponds to the second experiment, and the last four rows compare the performance of Base-DA and Context-DA when varying the amount of training data from 50% to 25%.

Data portion	Aero	Bike	Bird	Boat	Bottle	Average
Base-DA	58.8	64.3	48.8	47.8	33.9	48.7
Random-DA	60.2	66.5	55.1	41.9	29.7	48.3
Context-DA	67.0	68.6	60.0	53.3	38.8	57.5
Removing context	44.0	46.8	42.0	20.9	15.5	33.9
Enlarge + Reblend-DA	60.1	63.4	51.6	48.0	34.8	51.6
Base-DA 50 %	55.6	60.1	47.6	40.1	21.0	42.2
Context-DA 50 %	62.2	65.9	55.2	46.9	27.2	48.8
Base-DA 25 %	51.3	54.0	33.8	28.2	14.0	32.5
Context-DA 25 %	57.8	59.5	40.6	34.3	19.0	38.3

Fig. 5. Examples of instance placement with context model guidance. The figure presents samples obtained by placing a matched examples into the box predicted by the context model. The top row shows generated images that are visually almost indistinguishable from the real ones. The middle row presents samples of good quality although with some visual artifacts. For the two leftmost examples, the context module proposed an appropriate object class, but the pasted instances do not look visually appealing. Sometimes, the scene does not look natural because of the segmentation artifacts as in the two middle images. The two rightmost examples show examples where the category seems to be in the right environment, but not perfectly placed. The bottom row presents some failure cases.

Fig. 6. Illustration of artifacts arising from enlargement augmentation. In the enlargement data augmentation, an instance is cut out of the image, up-scaled by a small factor and placed back at the same location. This approach leads to blending artefacts. Modified images are given in the top row. Zoomed parts of the images centered on blending artifacts are presented in the bottom line.

should be noted that in such very small regimes, the quality of the context model may degrade as well (e.g., the dataset contains only 87 images of birds, meaning that with 25%, we use only 22 images with positive instances).

5   Discussions and Future Work

In this paper, we introduce a data augmentation technique dedicated to object detection, which exploits segmentation annotations. From a methodological point of view, we show that this approach is effective and goes beyond traditional augmentation approaches. One of the keys to obtain significant improvements in terms of accuracy was to introduce an appropriate context model which allows us to automatically find realistic locations for objects, which can then be pasted and blended at in the new scenes. While the role of explicit context modeling has been unclear so far for object detection, we show that it is in fact crucial when performing data augmentation and learn with few labeled data, which is one of the major issue that deep learning models are facing today.

We believe that these promising results pave the way to numerous extensions. In future work, we will for instance study the application of our approach to other scene understanding tasks, e.g., semantic or instance segmentation, and investigate how to adapt it to larger datasets. Since our approach relies on pre-segmented objects, which are subsequently used for data augmentation, we are also planning to exploit automatic segmentation tools such as [39] in order to use our method when only bounding box annotations are available.

Acknowledgments. This work was supported by a grant from ANR (MACARON project ANR-14-CE23-0003-01), by the ERC grant 714381 (SOLARIS project), the ERC advanced grant ALLEGRO and gifts from Amazon and Intel.

References

1. Oliva, A., Torralba, A.: The role of context in object recognition. Trends Cogn. Sci. **11**(12), 520–527 (2007)
2. Divvala, S.K., Hoiem, D., Hays, J.H., Efros, A.A., Hebert, M.: An empirical study of context in object detection. In: Proceedings of the IEEE Conference on Computer Vision and Pattern Recognition (CVPR) (2009)
3. Murphy, K., Torralba, A., Eaton, D., Freeman, W.: Object detection and localization using local and global features. In: Ponce, J., Hebert, M., Schmid, C., Zisserman, A. (eds.) Toward Category-Level Object Recognition. LNCS, vol. 4170, pp. 382–400. Springer, Heidelberg (2006). https://doi.org/10.1007/11957959_20
4. Felzenszwalb, P.F., Girshick, R.B., McAllester, D., Ramanan, D.: Object detection with discriminatively trained part-based models. IEEE Trans. Pattern Anal. Mach. Intell. (PAMI) **32**(9), 1627–1645 (2010)
5. Park, D., Ramanan, D., Fowlkes, C.: Multiresolution models for object detection. In: Daniilidis, K., Maragos, P., Paragios, N. (eds.) ECCV 2010. LNCS, vol. 6314, pp. 241–254. Springer, Heidelberg (2010). https://doi.org/10.1007/978-3-642-15561-1_18
6. Heitz, G., Koller, D.: Learning spatial context: using stuff to find things. In: Forsyth, D., Torr, P., Zisserman, A. (eds.) ECCV 2008. LNCS, vol. 5302, pp. 30–43. Springer, Heidelberg (2008). https://doi.org/10.1007/978-3-540-88682-2_4
7. Ren, S., He, K., Girshick, R., Sun, J.: Faster R-CNN: towards real-time object detection with region proposal networks. In: Advances in Neural Information Processing Systems (NIPS) (2015)
8. Girshick, R.: Fast R-CNN. In: Proceedings of the International Conference on Computer Vision (ICCV) (2015)
9. Liu, W., et al.: SSD: single shot multibox detector. In: Leibe, B., Matas, J., Sebe, N., Welling, M. (eds.) ECCV 2016. LNCS, vol. 9905, pp. 21–37. Springer, Cham (2016). https://doi.org/10.1007/978-3-319-46448-0_2
10. Redmon, J., Divvala, S., Girshick, R., Farhadi, A.: You only look once: unified, real-time object detection. In: Proceedings of the IEEE Conference on Computer Vision and Pattern Recognition (CVPR) (2016)
11. Yu, R., Chen, X., Morariu, V.I., Davis, L.S.: The role of context selection in object detection. In: British Machine Vision Conference (BMVC) (2016)
12. Srivastava, N., Hinton, G., Krizhevsky, A., Sutskever, I., Salakhutdinov, R.: Dropout: a simple way to prevent neural networks from overfitting. J. Mach. Learn. Res. **15**(1), 1929–1958 (2014)
13. Everingham, M., Van Gool, L., Williams, C.K., Winn, J., Zisserman, A.: The PASCAL visual object classes (VOC) challenge. Int. J. Comput. Vis. (IJCV) **88**(2), 303–338 (2010)
14. Dwibedi, D., Misra, I., Hebert, M.: Cut, paste and learn: surprisingly easy synthesis for instance detection. In: Proceedings of the International Conference on Computer Vision (ICCV) (2017)
15. Gupta, A., Vedaldi, A., Zisserman, A.: Synthetic data for text localisation in natural images. In: Proceedings of the IEEE Conference on Computer Vision and Pattern Recognition (CVPR) (2016)
16. Georgakis, G., Mousavian, A., Berg, A.C., Kosecka, J.: Synthesizing training data for object detection in indoor scenes. arXiv preprint arXiv:1702.07836 (2017)
17. Torralba, A., Sinha, P.: Statistical context priming for object detection. In: Proceedings of the International Conference on Computer Vision (ICCV) (2001)

18. Torralba, A.: Contextual priming for object detection. Int. J. Comput. Vis. (IJCV) **53**(2), 169–191 (2003)
19. Choi, M.J., Lim, J.J., Torralba, A., Willsky, A.S.: Exploiting hierarchical context on a large database of object categories. In: Proceedings of the IEEE Conference on Computer Vision and Pattern Recognition (CVPR) (2010)
20. Gould, S., Fulton, R., Koller, D.: Decomposing a scene into geometric and semantically consistent regions. In: Proceedings of the International Conference on Computer Vision (ICCV) (2009)
21. Chu, W., Cai, D.: Deep feature based contextual model for object detection. Neurocomputing **275**, 1035–1042 (2018)
22. Bell, S., Zitnick, C.L., Bala, K., Girshick, R.: Inside-outside net: detecting objects in context with skip pooling and recurrent neural networks. In: Proceedings of the IEEE Conference on Computer Vision and Pattern Recognition (CVPR) (2016)
23. Dvornik, N., Shmelkov, K., Mairal, J., Schmid, C.: BlitzNet: a real-time deep network for scene understanding. In: Proceedings of the International Conference on Computer Vision (ICCV) (2017)
24. Fu, C.Y., Liu, W., Ranga, A., Tyagi, A., Berg, A.C.: DSSD: deconvolutional single shot detector. arXiv preprint arXiv:1701.06659 (2017)
25. Barnea, E., Ben-Shahar, O.: On the utility of context (or the lack thereof) for object detection. arXiv preprint arXiv:1711.05471 (2017)
26. Yao, B., Fei-Fei, L.: Modeling mutual context of object and human pose in human-object interaction activities. In: Proceedings of the IEEE Conference on Computer Vision and Pattern Recognition (CVPR) (2010)
27. Russakovsky, O., et al.: ImageNet large scale visual recognition challenge. In: Proceedings of the International Conference on Computer Vision (ICCV) (2015)
28. Frid-Adar, M., Klang, E., Amitai, M., Goldberger, J., Greenspan, H.: Synthetic data augmentation using GAN for improved liver lesion classification. arXiv preprint arXiv:1801.02385 (2018)
29. Peng, X., Sun, B., Ali, K., Saenko, K.: Learning deep object detectors from 3D models. In: Proceedings of the International Conference on Computer Vision (ICCV) (2015)
30. Zhong, Z., Zheng, L., Kang, G., Li, S., Yang, Y.: Random erasing data augmentation. arXiv preprint arXiv:1708.04896 (2017)
31. Karsch, K., Hedau, V., Forsyth, D., Hoiem, D.: Rendering synthetic objects into legacy photographs. ACM Trans. Graph. (TOG) **30**(6), 157 (2011)
32. Movshovitz-Attias, Y., Kanade, T., Sheikh, Y.: How useful is photo-realistic rendering for visual learning? In: Hua, G., Jégou, H. (eds.) ECCV 2016. LNCS, vol. 9915, pp. 202–217. Springer, Cham (2016). https://doi.org/10.1007/978-3-319-49409-8_18
33. Su, H., Qi, C.R., Li, Y., Guibas, L.J.: Render for CNN: viewpoint estimation in images using CNNs trained with rendered 3D model views. In: Proceedings of the International Conference on Computer Vision (ICCV) (2015)
34. Prez, P., Gangnet, M., Blake, A.: Poisson image editing. ACM Trans. Graph. (SIGGRAPH 2003) **22**(3), 313–318 (2003)
35. Lin, T.-Y., et al.: Microsoft COCO: common objects in context. In: Fleet, D., Pajdla, T., Schiele, B., Tuytelaars, T. (eds.) ECCV 2014. LNCS, vol. 8693, pp. 740–755. Springer, Cham (2014). https://doi.org/10.1007/978-3-319-10602-1_48
36. He, K., Zhang, X., Ren, S., Sun, J.: Deep residual learning for image recognition. In: Proceedings of the IEEE Conference on Computer Vision and Pattern Recognition (CVPR) (2016)

37. Lin, T.Y., Goyal, P., Girshick, R., He, K., Dollár, P.: Focal loss for dense object detection. In: Proceedings of the International Conference on Computer Vision (ICCV) (2017)
38. Kingma, D., Ba, J.: Adam: a method for stochastic optimization. In: International Conference on Learning Representations (ICLR) (2015)
39. Liao, Z., Farhadi, A., Wang, Y., Endres, I., Forsyth, D.: Building a dictionary of image fragments. In: IEEE Conference on Computer Vision and Pattern Recognition (CVPR) (2012)

Learning Region Features
for Object Detection

Jiayuan Gu[1], Han Hu[2](✉), Liwei Wang[1,3], Yichen Wei[2], and Jifeng Dai[2]

[1] Key Laboratory of Machine Perception, MOE, School of EECS,
Peking University, Beijing, China
{gujiayuan,wanglw}@pku.edu.cn
[2] Microsoft Research Asia, Beijing, China
{hanhu,yichenw,jifdai}@microsoft.com
[3] Center for Data Science, Beijing Institute of Big Data Research,
Peking University, Beijing, China

Abstract. While most steps in the modern object detection methods
are learnable, the region feature extraction step remains largely hand-
crafted, featured by RoI pooling methods. This work proposes a general viewpoint that unifies existing region feature extraction methods
and a novel method that is end-to-end learnable. The proposed method
removes most heuristic choices and outperforms its RoI pooling counterparts. It moves further towards *fully learnable object detection*.

1   Introduction

A noteworthy trait in the deep learning era is that many hand-crafted features,
algorithm components, and design choices, are replaced by their data-driven and
learnable counterparts. The evolution of object detection is a good example. Currently, the leading region-based object detection paradigm [3,4,6–9,14,20] consists of five steps, namely, image feature generation, region proposal generation,
region feature extraction, region recognition, and duplicate removal. Most steps
become learnable in recent years, including image feature generation [6], region
proposal [5,20,21], and duplicate removal [11,12]. Note that region recognition
step is learning based in nature.

The region feature extraction step remains largely hand-crafted. The current
practice, RoI (regions of interest) pooling [6], as well as its variants [8,9], divides a
region into regular grid bins, computes features of the bin from the image features
located nearby to the bin via heuristic rules (avg, max, bilinear interpolation [4,
8], etc.), and concatenates such features from all the bins as the region features.
The process is intuitive and works well, but is more like rules of thumb. There
is no clear evidence that it is optimal in some sensible way.

The recent work of deformable RoI pooling [4] introduces a bin-wise offset
that is adaptively learnt from the image content. The approach is shown better

---

This work is done when Jiayuan Gu is an intern at Microsoft Research Asia.

V. Ferrari et al. (Eds.): ECCV 2018, LNCS 11216, pp. 392–406, 2018.
https://doi.org/10.1007/978-3-030-01258-8_24

than its RoI pooling counterpart. It reveals the potential of making the region feature extraction step *learnable*. However, its form still resembles the regular grid based pooling. The learnable part is limited to bin offsets only.

This work studies *fully learnable* region feature extraction. It aims to improve the performance and enhance the understanding of this step. It makes the following two contributions.

First, a general viewpoint on region feature extraction is proposed. The feature of each bin (or in a general sense, part) of the region is formulated as a weighted summation of image features on different positions over the whole image. Most (if not all) previous region feature extraction methods are shown to be specialization of this formulation by specifying the weights in different ways, mostly hand-crafted.

Based on the viewpoint, the second contribution is a learnable module that represents the weights in terms of the RoI and image features. The weights are affected by two factors: the geometric relation between the RoI and image positions, as well as the image features themselves. The first is modeled using an attention model as motivated by [12,22]. The second is exploited by simply adding one convolution layer over the input image features, as motivated by [4].

The proposed method removes most heuristic choices in the previous RoI pooling methods and moves further towards *fully learnable object detection*. Extensive experiments show that it outperforms its RoI pooling counterparts. While a naive implementation is computationally expensive, an efficient sparse sampling implementation is proposed with little degradation in accuracy. Moreover, qualitative and quantitative analysis on the learnt weights shows that it is feasible and effective to learn the spatial distribution of such weights from data, instead of designing them manually.

2   A General Viewpoint on Region Feature Extraction

Image feature generation step outputs feature maps $\mathbf{x}$ of spatial size $H \times W$ (usually 16× smaller than that of the original image due to down sampling of the network [20]) and C_f channels. Region proposal generation step finds a number of regions of interest (RoI), each a four dimensional bounding box b.

In general, the region feature extraction step generates features $\mathbf{y}(b)$ from $\mathbf{x}$ and an RoI b as

$$\mathbf{y}(b) = \text{RegionFeat}(\mathbf{x}, b). \tag{1}$$

Typically, $\mathbf{y}(b)$ is of dimension $K \times C_f$. The channel number is kept the same as C_f in $\mathbf{x}$ and K represents the number of *spatial parts* of the region. Each part feature $\mathbf{y}_k(b)$ is a partial observation of the region. For example, K is the number of bins (*e.g.*, 7 × 7) in the current RoI pooling practice. Each part is a bin in the regular grid of the RoI. Each $\mathbf{y}_k(b)$ is generated from image features in $\mathbf{x}$ within the bin.

The concepts above can be generalized. A part does not need to have a regular shape. The part feature $\mathbf{y}_k(b)$ does not need to come from certain spatial positions in $\mathbf{x}$. Even, the union of all the parts does not need to be the RoI itself.

A general formulation is to treat the part feature as the weighted summation of image features $\mathbf{x}$ over all positions within a support region Ω_b, as

$$\mathbf{y}_k(b) = \sum_{p \in \Omega_b} w_k(b, p, \mathbf{x}) \odot \mathbf{x}(p). \tag{2}$$

Here, Ω_b is the supporting region. It could simply be the RoI itself or include more context, even the entire image. p enumerates the spatial positions within Ω_b. $w_k(b, p, x)$ is the weight to sum the image feature $\mathbf{x}(p)$ at the position p. $\odot$ denotes element-wise multiplication. Note that the weights are assumed normalized, i.e., $\sum_{p \in \Omega_b} w_k(b, p, x) = 1$.

We show that various RoI pooling methods [4,6,8,9] are specializations of Eq. (2). The supporting region Ω_b and the weight $w_k(\cdot)$ are realized differently in these methods, mostly in hand-crafted ways.

Regular RoI Pooling [6]. The supporting region Ω_b is the RoI itself. It is divided into regular grid bins (*e.g.*, 7×7). Each part feature $\mathbf{y}_k(b)$ is computed as max or average of all image features $\mathbf{x}(p)$ where p is within the kth bin.

Taking averaging pooling as an example, the weight in Eq. (2) is

$$w_k(b, p) = \begin{cases} 1/|R_{bk}| & \text{if } p \in R_{bk} \\ 0 & \text{else} \end{cases} \tag{3}$$

Here, R_{bk} is the set of all positions within the kth bin of the grid.

The regular pooling is flawed in that it cannot distinguish between very close RoIs due to spatial down sampling in the networks, *i.e.*, the spatial resolution of the image feature $\mathbf{x}$ is usually smaller (*e.g.*, $16\times$) than that of the original image. If two RoIs' distance is smaller than 16 pixels, their R_{bk}s are the same, and so are their features.

Spatial Pyramid Pooling [9]. Because it simply applies the regular RoI pooling on different levels of grid divisions, it can be expressed via simple modification of Eqs. (2) and (3). Details are irrelevant and omitted here.

Aligned RoI Pooling [8]. It remedies the quantization issue in the regular RoI pooling above by bilinear interpolation at fractionally sampled positions within each R_{bk}. For simplicity, we assume that each bin only samples one point, *i.e.*, its center (u_{bk}, v_{bk})[1]. Let the position $p = (u_p, v_p)$. The weight in Eq. (2) is

$$w_k(b, p) = g(u_p, u_{bk}) \cdot g(v_p, v_{bk}), \tag{4}$$

where $g(a, b) = \max(0, 1 - |a - b|)$ denotes the 1-D bilinear interpolation weight. Note that the weight in Eq. (4) is only non-zero for the four positions immediately surrounding the sampling point (u_{bk}, v_{bk}).

---

[1] In practical implementation [8], multiple (*e.g.*, 4) points are sampled within each bin and their features are averaged as the bin feature. This is beneficial as more image position features get back-propagated gradients.

Because the weight in Eq. (4) depends on the bin center (u_{bk}, v_{bk}), the region features are sensitive to even subtle changes in the position of the RoI. Thus, aligned pooling outperforms its regular pooling counterpart [8].

Note that everything till now is hand-crafted. Also, image feature $\mathbf{x}$ is not used in $w_k(\cdot)$ in Eqs. (3) and (4).

Deformable RoI Pooling [4]. It generalizes aligned RoI pooling by learning an offset $(\delta u_{bk}, \delta v_{bk})$ for each bin and adding it to the bin center. The weight in Eq. (4) is extended to

$$w_k(b, p, \mathbf{x}) = g(u_p, u_{bk} + \delta u_{bk}) \cdot g(v_p, v_{bk} + \delta v_{bk}). \tag{5}$$

The image feature $\mathbf{x}$ appears here because the offsets are produced by a learnable submodule applied on the image feature $\mathbf{x}$. Specifically, the submodule starts with a regular RoI pooling to extract an initial region feature from image feature, which is then used to regress offsets through an additional learnable fully connected (fc) layer.

As the weight and the offsets depend on the image features now and they are learnt end-to-end, object shape deformation is better modeled, adaptively according to the image content. It is shown that deformable RoI pooling outperforms its aligned version [4]. Note that when the offset learning rate is zero, deformable RoI pooling strictly degenerates to aligned RoI pooling.

Also note that the supporting region Ω_b is no longer the RoI as in regular and aligned pooling, but potentially spans the whole image, because the learnt offsets could be arbitrarily large, in principle.

2.1   More Related Works

Besides the RoI pooling methods reviewed above, there are more region feature extraction methods that can be thought of specializations of Eq. (2) or its more general extension.

Region Feature Extraction in One-Stage Object Detection [15,17,19]. As opposed to the two-stage or region based object detection paradigm, another paradigm is one-stage or dense sliding window based. Because the number of windows (regions) is huge, each region feature is simply set as the image feature on the region's center point, which can be specialized from Eq. (2) as $K = 1$, $\Omega_b = \{\text{center}(b)\}$. This is much faster but less accurate than RoI pooling methods.

Pooling Using Non-grid Bins [1,23]. These methods are similar to regular pooling but change the definition of R_{bk} in Eq. (3) to be non-grid. For example, MaskLab [1] uses triangle-shaped bins other than rectangle ones. It shows better balance in encoding center-close and center-distant subregions. In Interpretable R-CNN [23], the non-grid bins are generated from the grammar defined by an AND-OR graph model.

MNC [2]. It is similar as regular RoI pooling. The difference is that only the bins inside the mask use Eq. (3) to compute weights. The weights of the bins outside are zeros. This equals to relax the normalization assumption on w_k.

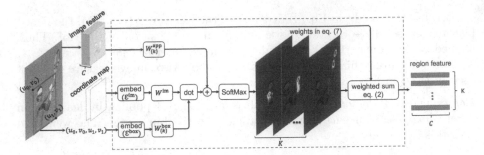

Fig. 1. Illustration of the proposed region feature extraction module in Eqs. (2) and (7).

Deformable Part-Based RoI Pooling [18]. It is similar as deformable RoI pooling [4] that each bin is associated with an offset. Hence, the weight definition also has a term of offset as Eq. (5) but it uses regular pooling instead of bilinear interpolation. Another main difference is that the offsets are determined by minimizing an energy function, while in deformable RoI pooling the offsets are determined by input features through a regular RoI pooling layer and the following fully connected layer.

Position Sensitive RoI Pooling [3,13]. It is similar as regular RoI pooling. The difference is that each bin only corresponds to a subset of channels in the image feature $\mathbf{x}$, instead of all channels. This can be expressed by extending Eq. (2) as

$$\mathbf{y}_k(b) = \sum_{p \in \Omega_b} w_k(b, p, \mathbf{x}_k) \odot \mathbf{x}_k(p), \tag{6}$$

where $\mathbf{x}_k$ only contains a subset of channels in $\mathbf{x}$, according to the kth bin.

3   Learning Region Features

Regular and aligned RoI pooling are fully hand-crafted. Deformable RoI pooling introduces a learnable component, but its form is still largely limited by the regular grid. In this work, we seek to learn the weight $w_k(b, p, \mathbf{x})$ in Eq. (2) with minimum hand crafting.

Intuitively, we consider two factors that should affect the weight. First, the geometric relation between the position p and RoI box b is certainly critical. For example, positions within b should contribute more than those far away from it. Second, the image feature $\mathbf{x}$ should be adaptively used. This is motivated by the effectiveness of deformable RoI pooling [4].

Therefore, the weight is modeled as the exponential of the sum of two terms

$$w_k(b, p, \mathbf{x}) \propto \exp(G_k(b, p) + A_k(\mathbf{x}, p)). \tag{7}$$

The first term $G_k(b, p)$ in Eq. (7) captures *geometric relation* as

$$G_k(b, p) = \langle W_k^{\text{box}} \cdot \mathcal{E}^{\text{box}}(b), W^{\text{im}} \cdot \mathcal{E}^{\text{im}}(p) \rangle. \tag{8}$$

There are three steps. First, the box and image positions are embedded into high dimensional spaces similarly as in [12,22]. The embedding is performed by applying sine and cosine functions of varying wavelengths to a scalar z, as

$$\mathcal{E}_{2i}(z) = \sin(\frac{z}{1000^{2i/C_{\mathcal{E}}}}), \quad \mathcal{E}_{2i+1}(z) = \cos(\frac{z}{1000^{2i/C_{\mathcal{E}}}}).$$

The embedding vector $\mathcal{E}(z)$ is of dimension $C_{\mathcal{E}}$. The subscript i above ranges from 0 to $C_{\mathcal{E}}/2 - 1$. The image position p is embedded into a vector $\mathcal{E}^{\mathrm{im}}(p)$ of dimension $2 \cdot C_{\mathcal{E}}$, as p has two coordinates. Similarly, each RoI box b is embedded into a vector $\mathcal{E}^{\mathrm{box}}(b)$ of dimension $4 \cdot C_{\mathcal{E}}$.

Second, the embedding vectors $\mathcal{E}^{\mathrm{im}}(p)$ and $\mathcal{E}^{\mathrm{box}}(b)$ are linearly transformed by weight matrices W^{im} and W_k^{box}, respectively, which are learnable. The transformed vectors are of the same dimension C_g. Note that the term $W_k^{\mathrm{box}} \cdot \mathcal{E}^{\mathrm{box}}(b)$ has high complexity because the $\mathcal{E}^{\mathrm{box}}(b)$'s dimension $4 \cdot C_{\mathcal{E}}$ is large. In our implementation, we decompose W_k^{box} as $W_k^{\mathrm{box}} = \hat{W}_k^{\mathrm{box}} V^{\mathrm{box}}$. Note that V^{box} is shared for all the parts. It does not have subscript k. Its output dimension is set to $C_{\mathcal{E}}$. In this way, both computation and the amount of parameters are reduced for the term $W_k^{\mathrm{box}} \cdot \mathcal{E}^{\mathrm{box}}(b)$.

Last, the inner product of the two transformed vectors is treated as the geometric relation weight.

Equation (8) is basically an attention model [12,22], which is a good tool to capture dependency between distant or heterogeneous elements, e.g., words from different languages [22], RoIs with variable locations/sizes/aspect ratios [12], and etc, and hence naturally bridges the target of building connections between 4D bounding box coordinates and 2D image positions in our problem. Extensive experiments show that the geometric relations between RoIs and image positions are well captured by the attention model.

The second term $A_k(\mathbf{x}, p)$ in Eq. (7) uses the *image features* adaptively. It applies an 1×1 convolution on the image feature,

$$A_k(\mathbf{x}, p) = W_k^{\mathrm{app}} \cdot \mathbf{x}(p), \tag{9}$$

where W_k^{app} denotes the convolution kernel weights, which are learnable.

The proposed region feature extraction module is illustrated in Fig. 1. During training, the image features $\mathbf{x}$ and the parameters in the module (W_k^{box}, W^{im}, and W_k^{app}) are updated simultaneously.

3.1   Complexity Analysis and an Efficient Implementation

The computational complexity of the proposed region feature extraction module is summarized in Table 1. Note that $A_k(x,p)$ and $W^{\mathrm{im}} \cdot \mathcal{E}^{\mathrm{im}}(p)$ are computed over all the positions in the image feature $\mathbf{x}$ and shared for all RoIs.

A *naive* implementation needs to enumerate all the positions in Ω_b. When Ω_b spans the whole image feature $\mathbf{x}$ densely, its size is $H \times W$ and typically a few thousands. This incurs heavy computational overhead for step 3 and 5 in Table 1. An *efficient* implementation is to sparsely sample the positions in Ω_b,

Table 1. Top: description and typical values of main variables. Bottom: computational complexity of the proposed method. †Using default maximum sample numbers as in Eqs. (10) and (11), the average actual sample number is about 200. See also Table 3. *Note that we decompose W_k^{box} as $W_k^{box} = \hat{W}_k^{box} V^{box}$, and the total computational cost is the sum of two matrix multiplications $V^{box} \cdot \mathcal{E}^{box}$ (the multiplication result is denoted as $\hat{\mathcal{E}}^{box}$) and $\hat{W}_k^{box} \cdot \hat{\mathcal{E}}^{box}$. See also Sect. 3 for details.

notation	description	typical values	notation	description	typical values
$\lvert\Omega_b\rvert$	size of support region	hundreds	N	#RoIs	300
H	height of image feature x	dozens	K	#parts/bins	49
W	width of image feature x	dozens	$C_{\mathcal{E}}$	embed dim. in Eq. (8)	512
C_f	#channels of image feature x	256	C_g	transform dim. in Eq. (8)	256

module	computational complexity	*naive* ($\lvert\Omega_b\rvert$=HW)	*efficient* ($\lvert\Omega_b\rvert$=200†)
(P1) transform position embedding in Eq. (8)	$2HWC_{\mathcal{E}}C_g$	0.59G	0.59G
(P2) transform RoI box embedding in Eq. (8)	$NC_{\mathcal{E}}(KC_g + 4C_{\mathcal{E}})$*	2.1G	2.1G
(P3) inner product in Eq. (8)	$NK\lvert\Omega_b\rvert C_g$	7.2G	**0.72G**
(P4) appearance usage in Eq. (9)	$HWKC_f$	0.03G	0.03G
(P5) weighted aggregation in Eq. (2)	$NK\lvert\Omega_b\rvert C_f$	7.2G	**0.72G**
sum		17.1G	4.16G

during the looping of p in Eq. (2). Intuitively, the sampling points within the RoI should be denser and those outside could be sparser. Thus, Ω_b is split into two sets as $\Omega_b = \Omega_b^{In} \cup \Omega_b^{Out}$, which contain the positions within and outside of the RoI, respectively. Note that Ω_b^{Out} represents the context of the RoI. It could be either empty when Ω_b is the RoI or span the entire image when Ω_b does, too.

Complexity is controlled by specifying a maximum number of sampling positions for Ω_b^{In} and Ω_b^{Out}, respectively (by default, 196 for both). Given an RoI b, the positions in Ω_b^{In} are sampled at stride values $stride_x^b$ and $stride_y^b$, in x and y directions, respectively. The stride values are determined as

$$stride_x^b = \lceil W_b/\sqrt{196}\rceil \text{ AND } stride_y^b = \lceil H_b/\sqrt{196}\rceil, \qquad (10)$$

where W_b and H_b are the width and height of the RoI. The sampling of Ω_b^{Out} is similar. Let $stride^{out}$ be the stride value, it is derived by,

$$stride^{out} = \lceil\sqrt{HW/196}\rceil. \qquad (11)$$

The sparse sampling of Ω_b effectively reduces the computational overhead. Especially, notice that many RoIs have smaller area than the maximum sampling number specified above. So the actual number of sampled positions of Ω_b^{In} in those RoIs is equal to their area, thus even smaller.

Experiments show that the accuracy of sparse sampling is very close to the naive dense sampling (see Table 3).

4   Experiments

All experiments are performed on COCO detection datasets [16]. We follow the COCO 2017 dataset split: 115k images in the *train* split for training; 5k images in the *minival* split for validation; and 20k images in the *test-dev* split for testing. In most experiments, we report the accuracy on the *minival* split.

State-of-the-art Faster R-CNN [20] and FPN [14] object detectors are used. ResNet-50 and ResNet-101 [10] are used as the backbone image feature extractor. By default, Faster R-CNN with ResNet-50 is utilized in ablation study.

For Faster R-CNN, following the practice in [3,4], the *conv4* and *conv5* image features are utilized for region proposal generation and object detection, respectively. The RPN branch is the same as in [3,4,20]. For object detection, the effective feature stride of *conv5* is reduced from 32 pixels to 16 pixels. Specifically, at the beginning of the *conv5* block, stride is changed from 2 to 1. The dilation of the convolutional filters in the *conv5* block is changed from 1 to 2. On top of the *conv5* feature maps, a randomly initialized 1×1 convolutional layer is added to reduce the dimension to 256-D. The proposed module is applied on top to extract regional features, where 49 bins are utilized by default. Two fully-connected (fc) layers of 1024-D, followed by the classification and the bounding box regression branches, are utilized as the detection head. The images are resized to 600 pixels at the shorter side if the longer side after resizing is less than or equal to 1000; otherwise resized to 1000 pixels at the longer side, in both training and inference [6].

For FPN, a feature pyramid is built upon an input image of single resolution, by exploiting multi-scale feature maps generated by top-down and lateral connections. The RPN and Fast R-CNN heads are attached to the multi-scale feature maps, for proposing and detecting objects of varying sizes. Here we follow the network design in [14], and just replace RoI pooling by the proposed learnable region feature extraction module. The images are resized to 800 pixels at the shorter side if the longer side after resizing is less than or equal to 1333; otherwise resized to 1333 pixels at the longer side, in both training and inference.

SGD training is performed on 4 GPUs with 1 image per GPU. Weight decay is 1×10^{-4} and momentum is 0.9. The added parameters in the learnable region feature extraction module, W_k^{box}, W^{im}, and W_k^{app}, are initialized by random Gaussian weights ($\sigma = 0.01$), and their learning rates are kept the same as the existing layers. In both Faster R-CNN and FPN, to facilitate experiments, separate networks are trained for region proposal generation and object detection, without sharing their features. In Faster R-CNN, 6 and 16 epochs are utilized to train the RPN and the object detection networks, respectively. The learning rates are set as 2×10^{-3} for the first $\frac{2}{3}$ iterations and 2×10^{-4} for the last $\frac{1}{3}$ iterations, for both region proposal and object detection networks. In FPN, 12 epochs are utilized to train both the RPN and the object detection networks, respectively. For both networks training, the learning rates start with 5×10^{-3} and decay twice at 8 and 10.667 epochs, respectively. Standard NMS with IoU threshold of 0.5 is utilized for duplication removal.

Table 2. Comparison of three region feature extraction methods using different support regions. Accuracies are reported on COCO detection *minival* set. *It is not clear how to exploit the whole image for regular and aligned RoI pooling methods. Hence the corresponding accuracy numbers are omitted.

Method	mAP	mAP$_{50}$	mAP$_{75}$	mAP$_S$	mAP$_M$	mAP$_L$
1× RoI						
Regular RoI pooling	29.8	52.2	29.9	10.4	32.6	47.8
Aligned RoI pooling	32.9	54.0	34.9	13.9	36.9	48.8
Ours	**33.4**	54.5	35.2	13.9	37.3	50.4
2× RoI						
Regular RoI pooling	30.1	53.2	30.6	10.6	33.3	47.4
Aligned RoI pooling	32.8	54.6	35.1	14.2	37.0	48.5
Ours	**33.8**	55.1	35.8	14.2	37.8	51.1
Whole image						
Regular RoI pooling*	–	–	–	–	–	–
Aligned RoI pooling*	–	–	–	–	–	–
Ours	**34.3**	56.0	36.4	15.4	38.1	51.9

4.1 Ablation Study

Effect of Supporting Region Ω. It is investigated in Table 2. Three sizes of the supporting region Ω are compared: the RoI itself, the RoI expanded with twice the area (with the same center), and the whole image range. Regular and aligned RoI pooling are also compared[2].

There are two observations. First, our method outperforms the other two pooling methods. Second, our method steadily improves from using larger support regions, indicating that exploiting contextual information is helpful. Yet, using larger support regions, e.g., 2× RoI region, has minor and no improvements for regular and aligned RoI pooling, respectively, when compared to using 1× RoI region. Moreover, it is unclear how to exploit the whole image for regular and aligned pooling in a reasonable way.

Effect of Sparse Sampling. Table 3 presents the results of using different numbers of sampling positions for efficient implementation. By utilizing proper number of sampling positions, the accuracy can be very close to that of naive dense enumeration. And the computational overhead can be significantly reduced thanks to the sparse sampling implementation. By default, 196 maximum sampling positions are specified for both Ω_b^{In} and Ω_b^{Out}. The mAP score is 0.2 lower than that of dense enumeration. In runtime, large RoIs will have fewer sampling positions for Ω_b^{Out} and small RoIs will have fewer sampling positions than the maximum threshold for Ω_b^{In}. The average counted sampling positions in runtime

---

[2] Deformable RoI pooling [4] is omitted as it does not have a fixed support region.

are are around 114 and 86 for Ω_b^{In} and Ω_b^{Out}, respectively, as shown in Table 3. The corresponding computational cost is 4.16G FLOPS, which coarsely equals that of the 2-fc head (about 3.9G FLOPs).

For all the following experiments, our method will utilize the sparse sampling implementation with 196 maximum sampling positions for both Ω_b^{In} and Ω_b^{Out}.

Table 3. Detection accuracy and computational times of *efficient* method using different number of sample points. The average samples $|\Omega_b^{Out}|_{avg}$ and $|\Omega_b^{In}|_{avg}$ are counted on COCO *minival* set using 300 ResNet-50 RPN proposals. The bold row ($|\Omega_b^{Out}|_{max} = 196$, $|\Omega_b^{In}|_{max} = 14^2$) are used as our default maximum sample point number. *full* indicates that all image positions are used without any sampling.

$|\Omega_b^{Out}|_{max}$	$|\Omega_b^{In}|_{max}$	mAP	mAP$_{50}$	mAP$_{75}$	mAP$_S$	mAP$_M$	mAP$_L$	$|\Omega_b^{Out}|_{avg}$	$|\Omega_b^{In}|_{avg}$	FLOPS
*full**	7^2	33.4	55.6	35.3	14.1	37.2	50.7	1737	32	15.3G
full	14^2	34.2	56.2	36.3	15.0	38.5	51.3	1737	86	15.7G
full	21^2	34.1	56.0	35.9	14.5	38.3	51.1	1737	158	16.2G
full	*full*	34.3	56.0	36.4	15.4	38.1	51.9	1737	282	17.1G
100	14^2	33.8	55.5	35.9	14.3	38.0	50.8	71	86	3.84G
196	**14^2**	**34.1**	**55.6**	**36.3**	**14.5**	**38.3**	**51.1**	**114**	**86**	**4.16G**
400	14^2	34.0	55.7	36.0	14.4	38.4	51.0	194	86	4.72G
625	14^2	34.1	55.7	36.1	14.5	38.0	51.3	432	86	6.42G
full	14^2	34.2	56.2	36.3	15.0	38.5	51.3	1737	86	15.7G

Table 4. Effect of geometric and appearance terms in Eq. (7) for the proposed region feature extraction module. Detection accuracies are reported on COCO *minival* set.

Method	mAP	mAP$_{50}$	mAP$_{75}$	mAP$_S$	mAP$_M$	mAP$_L$
Regular RoI pooling	29.8	52.2	29.9	10.4	32.6	47.8
Aligned RoI pooling	32.9	54.0	34.9	13.9	36.9	48.8
Deformable pooling	34.0	55.3	36.0	14.7	38.3	50.4
Our (geometry)	**33.2**	55.2	35.4	14.2	37.0	50.0
Our (geometry+appearance)	**34.1**	55.6	36.3	14.5	38.3	51.1

Effect of Geometric Relation and Appearance Feature Terms. Table 4 studies the effect of geometric relation and appearance feature terms in Eq. (7) of the proposed module. Using geometric relation alone, the proposed module is slightly better than aligned RoI pooling, and is noticeably better than regular RoI pooling. By further incorporating the appearance feature term, the mAP score rises by 0.9 to 34.1. The accuracy is on par with deformable RoI pooling, which also exploits appearance features to guide the region feature extraction process.

Comparison on Stronger Detection Backbones. We further compare the proposed module with regular, aligned and deformable versions of RoI pooling on stronger detection backbones, where FPN and ResNet-101 are also utilized.

Table 5 presents the results on COCO *test-dev* set. Using the stronger detection backbones, the proposed module also achieves on par accuracy with deformable RoI pooling, which is noticeably better than aligned and regular versions of RoI pooling. We achieve a final mAP score of 39.9 using FPN+ResNet-101 by the proposed fully learnable region feature extraction module.

It is worth note that although our formulation is more general, it is only slightly better than or comparable with deformable ROI pooling, at some extra computation cost. It reveals the important question: what is the best way of region feature extraction? Previous regular ROI binning methods are clearly limited as they are too hand-crafted and do not exploit the image context well. But, is deformable ROI pooling the best? Practically, probably yes. Theoretically, not necessarily. The proposed method is a first step toward answering this question and we believe future work along this direction will provide better answers. Region-based object detection should not stop at hand-crafted binning based feature extraction, including deformable ROI pooling.

5   What Is Learnt?

Qualitative Analysis. The learnt weights $w_k(*)$ in Eq. (7) are visualized in Fig. 2(a). The supporting region Ω is the whole image.

Table 5. Comparison of different algorithms using different backbones. Accuracies on COCO *test-dev* are reported.

Backbone	Method	mAP	mAP$_{50}$	mAP$_{75}$	mAP$_S$	mAP$_M$	mAP$_L$
Faster R-CNN + ResNet-50	Regular RoI pooling	29.9	52.6	30.1	9.7	31.9	46.3
	Aligned RoI pooling	33.1	54.5	35.1	13.9	36.0	47.4
	Deformable RoI pooling	34.2	55.7	36.7	14.5	37.4	48.8
	Our	**34.5**	56.4	36.4	14.6	37.4	50.3
Faster R-CNN + ResNet-101	Regular RoI pooling	32.7	53.6	23.7	11.4	35.2	50.0
	Aligned RoI pooling	35.6	57.1	38.0	15.3	39.3	51.0
	Deformable RoI pooling	**36.4**	58.1	39.3	15.7	40.2	52.1
	Our	**36.4**	58.6	38.6	15.3	40.2	52.2
FPN + ResNet-50	Regular RoI pooling	35.9	59.0	38.4	19.6	38.8	45.4
	Aligned RoI pooling	36.7	59.1	39.4	20.9	39.5	46.3
	Deformable RoI pooling	37.7	60.6	40.9	21.3	40.7	47.4
	Our	**37.8**	60.9	40.7	21.3	40.4	48.0
FPN + ResNet-101	Regular RoI pooling	38.5	61.5	41.8	21.4	42.0	49.2
	Aligned RoI pooling	39.1	61.4	42.3	21.5	42.5	50.2
	Deformable RoI pooling	**40.0**	62.7	43.5	22.4	43.4	51.3
	Our	39.9	63.1	43.1	22.2	43.4	51.6

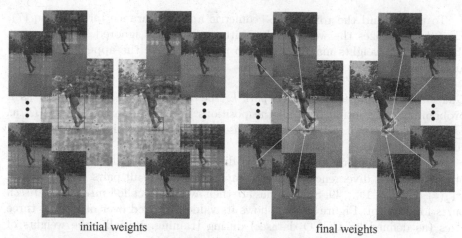

initial weights   final weights

(a) The initial (**left**) and final (**right**) weights $w_k(*)$ in Eq. (7) of two given RoIs (the red boxes). The center images show the maximum value of all $K = 49$ weight maps. The smaller images around show 4 individual weight maps.

(b) Example results of geometric weights (**top**), appearance weights (**median**) and final weights (**bottom**).

Fig. 2. Qualitative analysis of learnt weights. For visualization, all weights are normalized by the maximum value over all image positions and half-half matted with the original image. (Color figure online)

Initially, the weights $w_k(*)$ are largely random on the whole image. After training, weights in different parts are learnt to focus on different areas on the RoI, and they mostly focus on the instance foreground.

To understand the role of the geometric and appearance terms in Eq. (7), Fig. 2(b) visualizes the weights when either of them is ignored. It seems that the geometric weights mainly attend to the RoI, while the appearance weight focuses on all instance foreground.

Quantitative Analysis. For each part k, the weights $w_k(*)$ are treated as a probability distribution over all the positions in the supporting region Ω, as $\sum_{p \in \Omega} w_k(b, p, \mathbf{x}) = 1$. KL divergence is used to measure the discrepancy between such distributions.

We firstly compare the weights in different parts. For each ground truth object RoI, KL divergence value is computed between all pairs of $w_{k_1}(*)$ and $w_{k_2}(*)$, $k_1, k_2 = 1, ..., 49$. Such values are then averaged, called *mean KL between parts* for the RoI. Figure 3 (left) shows its value averaged over objects of three sizes (as defined by COCO dataset) during training. Initially, the weights of different parts are largely indistinguishable. Their KL divergence measure is small. The measure grows dramatically after the first test. This indicates that *the different parts are learnt to focus on different spatial positions*. Note that the divergence is larger for *large* objects, which is reasonable.

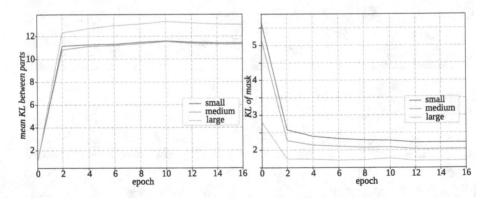

Fig. 3. Quantitative analysis of learnt weights. The two plots are *mean KL between parts* (left) and *KL of mask* (right) during training, respectively. Note that we test KL divergence every two epochs since our training framework saves model weights using such frequency.

We then investigate how the weights resemble the instance foreground, by comparing them to the ground-truth instance foreground mask in COCO. Towards this, for each ground truth object RoI, the weights from all the parts are aggregated together by taking the maximum value at each position, resulting in a "max pooled weight map". The map is then normalized as a distribution (sum is 1). The ground truth object mask is filled with 1 and 0. It is also normalized as a distribution. KL divergence between these two distributions is called *KL of mask*. Figure 3 (right) shows this measure averaged over objects of three sizes during training. It quickly becomes small, indicating that *the aggregation of all part weights is learnt to be similar as the object mask.*

The second observation is especially interesting, as it suggests that learning the weights as in Eq. (7) is related to instance segmentation, in some implicit manner. This is worth more investigation in the future work.

Acknowledgement. Liwei Wang was partially supported by National Basic Research Program of China (973 Program) (grant no. 2015CB352502), NSFC (61573026), BJNSF (L172037), and a grant from Microsoft Research Asia.

References

1. Chen, L.C., Hermans, A., Papandreou, G., Schroff, F., Wang, P., Adam, H.: MaskLab: instance segmentation by refining object detection with semantic and direction features. In: CVPR (2018)
2. Dai, J., He, K., Sun, J.: Instance-aware semantic segmentation via multi-task network cascades. In: CVPR (2016)
3. Dai, J., Li, Y., He, K., Sun, J.: R-FCN: object detection via region-based fully convolutional networks. In: NIPS (2016)
4. Dai, J., et al.: Deformable convolutional networks. In: ICCV (2017)
5. Erhan, D., Szegedy, C., Toshev, A., Anguelov, D.: Scalable object detection using deep neural networks. In: CVPR, pp. 2147–2154 (2014)
6. Girshick, R.: Fast R-CNN. In: ICCV (2015)
7. Girshick, R., Donahue, J., Darrell, T., Malik, J.: Rich feature hierarchies for accurate object detection and semantic segmentation. In: CVPR (2014)
8. He, K., Gkioxari, G., Dollár, P., Girshick, R.: Mask R-CNN. In: ICCV (2017)
9. He, K., Zhang, X., Ren, S., Sun, J.: Spatial pyramid pooling in deep convolutional networks for visual recognition. In: Fleet, D., Pajdla, T., Schiele, B., Tuytelaars, T. (eds.) ECCV 2014. LNCS, vol. 8691, pp. 346–361. Springer, Cham (2014). https://doi.org/10.1007/978-3-319-10578-9_23
10. He, K., Zhang, X., Ren, S., Sun, J.: Deep residual learning for image recognition. In: CVPR (2016)
11. Hosang, J., Benenson, R., Schiele, B.: Learning non-maximum suppression. In: ICCV (2017)
12. Hu, H., Gu, J., Zhang, Z., Dai, J., Wei, Y.: Relation networks for object detection. In: CVPR (2018)
13. Li, Z., Peng, C., Yu, G., Zhang, X., Deng, Y., Sun, J.: Light-head R-CNN: in defense of two-stage object detector. In: CVPR (2018)
14. Lin, T.Y., Dollár, P., Girshick, R., He, K., Hariharan, B., Belongie, S.: Feature pyramid networks for object detection. In: CVPR (2017)
15. Lin, T.Y., Goyal, P., Girshick, R., He, K., Dollár, P.: Focal loss for dense object detection. ICCV (2017)
16. Lin, T.-Y., et al.: Microsoft COCO: common objects in context. In: Fleet, D., Pajdla, T., Schiele, B., Tuytelaars, T. (eds.) ECCV 2014. LNCS, vol. 8693, pp. 740–755. Springer, Cham (2014). https://doi.org/10.1007/978-3-319-10602-1_48
17. Liu, W., et al.: SSD: single shot multibox detector. In: Leibe, B., Matas, J., Sebe, N., Welling, M. (eds.) ECCV 2016. LNCS, vol. 9905, pp. 21–37. Springer, Cham (2016). https://doi.org/10.1007/978-3-319-46448-0_2

18. Mordan, T., Thome, N., Cord, M., Henaff, G.: Deformable part-based fully convolutional network for object detection. arXiv preprint arXiv:1707.06175 (2017)
19. Redmon, J., Divvala, S., Girshick, R., Farhadi, A.: You only look once: unified, real-time object detection. In: CVPR (2016)
20. Ren, S., He, K., Girshick, R., Sun, J.: Faster R-CNN: towards real-time object detection with region proposal networks. In: NIPS (2015)
21. Szegedy, C., Reed, S., Erhan, D., Anguelov, D.: Scalable, high-quality object detection. arXiv preprint arXiv:1412.1441v2 (2014)
22. Vaswani, A., et al.: Attention is all you need. In: NIPS (2017)
23. Wu, T., Li, X., Song, X., Sun, W., Dong, L., Li, B.: Interpretable R-CNN. arXiv preprint arXiv:1711.05226 (2017)

End-to-End Deep Structured Models
for Drawing Crosswalks

Justin Liang[1,2]([✉]) and Raquel Urtasun[1,2]

[1] Uber Advanced Technologies Group, Toronto, Canada
{justin.liang,urtasun}@uber.com
[2] University of Toronto, Toronto, Canada

Abstract. In this paper we address the problem of detecting crosswalks from LiDAR and camera imagery. Towards this goal, given multiple LiDAR sweeps and the corresponding imagery, we project both inputs onto the ground surface to produce a top down view of the scene. We then leverage convolutional neural networks to extract semantic cues about the location of the crosswalks. These are then used in combination with road centerlines from freely available maps (e.g., OpenStreetMaps) to solve a structured optimization problem which draws the final crosswalk boundaries. Our experiments over crosswalks in a large city area show that 96.6% automation can be achieved.

Keywords: Deep structured models · Convolutional neural networks · Drawing crosswalks · Mapping · Autonomous vehicles

1 Introduction

Autonomous vehicles have many potential benefits. Every year, more than 1.2 million people die in traffic accidents. Furthermore, accidents are caused by human factors (e.g., driver distraction) in 96% of the cases. Urban congestion is also changing the landscapes of our cities, where more than 20% of the land is typically dedicated to parking. In recent years, tremendous progress has been made in the field of autonomous vehicles. This is the result of major break-throughs in artificial intelligence, hardware (e.g., sensors, specialized compute) as well as heroic engineering efforts.

Most autonomous driving teams in both industry and academia utilize detailed annotated maps of the environment to drive safely. These maps capture the static information about the scene. As a consequence, very strong prior knowledge can be used to aid perception, prediction and motion planning when the autonomous vehicle is accurately localized. Building such maps is, however, an extremely difficult task. High definition (HD) maps typically contain both geometric and semantic information about the scene. SLAM-based approaches are typically employed to create dense point cloud representations of the world, while human labellers are used to draw the semantic components of the scene such as lanes, roads, intersections, crosswalks, traffic lights, traffic signs, etc.

© Springer Nature Switzerland AG 2018
V. Ferrari et al. (Eds.): ECCV 2018, LNCS 11216, pp. 407–423, 2018.
https://doi.org/10.1007/978-3-030-01258-8_25

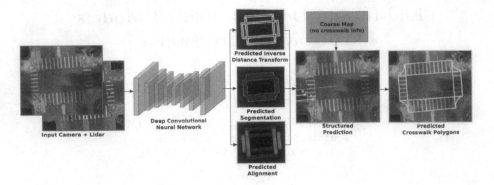

Fig. 1. Overview of our model. LiDAR points and camera images are projected onto the ground to produce input images from bird's eye view. These are then fed into a convolutional neural network (CNN) to produce three feature maps. Next, we perform inference using the three feature maps along with a coarse map which provides the road centrelines and intersection polygons. This is fed into the structured prediction module that finds the best two boundaries x_1 and x_2 along with the best angle β by maximizing a structured energy function.

Most map automation efforts focus on automatically estimating the lanes [7,12,20,22,27,32]. Approaches based on cameras [12,22], LiDAR [20,27] as well as aerial images [19,32] have been proposed. On the other hand, very little to no attention has been paid to other semantic elements.

In this paper, we tackle the problem of accurately drawing crosswalks. Knowledge about where they are is vital for navigation, as it allows the autonomous vehicle to plan ahead and be cautious of potential pedestrians crossing the street. Existing approaches focus on predicting the existence of a crosswalk, but do not provide an accurate localization. Instead, crosswalks are typically crowd-sourced and manually drawn.

Drawing crosswalks is not an easy task. As shown in our experiments, crosswalks come in a variety of shapes and styles even within the same city. Furthermore, paint quality of the crosswalk markings can often be washed out, making the task hard even for humans. Framing the task as semantic segmentation or object detection does not provide the level of reliability that is necessary for autonomous driving. Instead a more structured representation is required.

In this paper, we propose to take advantage of road centerlines and intersection polygons that are typically available in publicly available maps such as the OpenStreetMap (OSM) project. This allows us to parameterize the problem in a structured way, where our crosswalks have the right topology and shape. Towards this goal, we derive a deep structured model that is able to produce accurate estimates and exploit multiple sensors such as LiDAR and cameras. In particular, we use a convolutional net to predict semantic segmentation, semantic edge information, as well as crosswalk directions. These outputs are then used to form a structured prediction problem, whose inference results are our final crosswalk drawings. By leveraging distance transforms and integral accumulators, efficient exact inference is possible.

We demonstrate the effectiveness of our approach in a variety of scenarios, where LiDAR and/or cameras are exploited to build bird's eye view representations of the road on which our model operates. Our approach shows that 96.6% automation is possible when building maps offline and 91.5% when building the map online (as we drive). For comparison, human disagreement is around 0.6%.

2   Related Work

Crosswalk Detection: In [1, 2, 10, 28, 39], methods were developed to detect crosswalks at the street level. Moreover, [24] proposes a model for crosswalk detection in aerial images. However, these methods employ manually created feature extraction techniques, and can only handle zebra-style crosswalks. More recent methods have used deep convolutional neural networks (CNNs) to detect crosswalks. For example, the authors of [25] use deep CNNs to detect the crosswalks in aerial imagery. However, they do no draw the crosswalks. Instead, they only produce the locations of the crosswalks. Similarly, the authors of [8] use deep CNNs to detect crosswalks in satellite imagery, but only predicts whether or not a crosswalk exists in the image. Crosswalk detection is performed for driver assistance systems in [14]. In this paper, they draw the crosswalk in front of a vehicle. However, the method is limited in the sense that there is a maximum distance in which a crosswalk can be detected. Furthermore, the method only works on camera imagery taken at the vehicle level.

Automatic Mapping: There are many methods used to automatically generate different elements of a map. For example, the automatic extraction and segmentation of roads has been tackled in [30–32,41] using techniques such as Markov random fields and deep CNNs. In [18,37], they use LiDAR data in combination with aerial images and/or building address points to perform building shape reconstruction. Reconstruction of both the 2D footprints and the 3D shape of the buildings is tackled in these papers. Recently, the TorontoCity dataset [40] was released, and provides a multitude of map related benchmarks such as building footprints reconstruction, road centerline and curb extraction, road segmentation and urban zoning classification. In [35], a bird's eye view semantic map is produced from multi-view street-level imagery. Here, they perform semantic segmentation on street-level imagery and project this onto the ground plane in overhead view. In [16], they develop a generative algorithm to automatically label regions, roads and blocks with street addresses by extracting relevant features in satellite imagery using deep learning. Many mapping methods have utilized LiDAR data to perform automatic mapping. Examples of this can be seen in [3,4,11,13,29]. In these papers, they utilize LiDAR data to create 3D models of cities, automatically extract pavement markings, and perform semantic segmentation on urban maps to classify features.

Semantic Segmentation: In semantic segmentation, the goal is to label every pixel in an image with a class. Methods involving recurrent neural networks (RNNs) have been proposed [38, 43], however, the RNNs themselves can be computationally expensive to run. In [36], the authors introduced fully convolutional networks (FCNs) which uses skip connections to combine semantic information from feature volumes of various spatial dimensions within the CNN. It utilizes bilinear upsampling to perform semantic segmentation. After this, many variants of FCNs were released. For example, in [34], a deep deconvolutional network followed by a conditional random field (CRF) were used to fine-tune the output segmentation. Similarly, [15] builds upon this idea and uses a deeper network with residual layers and shortcut connections to learn an identity mapping. [5, 6, 9, 21, 26] further expands on these concepts, and use an encoder-decoder network with skip connections. This encoder-decoder architecture is inherently represented as a pyramid which produces a multi-scale feature representation. Since the representation is inherent to the shape of a CNN, inference is less memory and computationally expensive. In [42], they introduce dilated convolutions to aggregate multi-scale contextual information. They show with·their method they can expand the receptive field with no loss in resolution and coverage.

3   Deep Structured Models for Mapping Crosswalks

High definition (HD) maps typically contain both geometric and semantic information about the scene. SLAM-based approaches are typically utilized to create dense point cloud representations of the world, while human labellers are typically employed to draw the semantic components of the scene, e.g., lanes, crosswalks, rules at intersections. In this paper, we focus on automatically drawing crosswalks. Towards this goal, we derived a deep structured model that is able to produce accurate estimates and exploit multiple sensors such as LiDAR and cameras. In particular, we exploit a CNN to predict semantic segmentation, semantic edge information as well as crosswalk directions. These outputs are then used to form a structured prediction problem, whose inference results are our final crosswalk drawings. By leveraging distance transforms and integral accumulators, efficient exact inference is possible. In the remainder of the section, we first define our convolutional potentials, follow by our structured prediction framework.

3.1   Computing Deep Semantic Features

We leverage both images and LiDAR to automatically draw crosswalks. Towards this goal, for each sensor modality we create an overhead view of each intersection. We refer the reader to Fig. 1 for an example of the overhead representation of both LiDAR as well as images. Note that determining where an intersection happens is trivial given the topological graphs of existing freely available coarse maps, such as OpenStreetMaps.

Both LiDAR and Camera overhead images are then concatenated to create our input representation of the scene. This forms a 4-channel input, with

3 dimensions for RGB and one for LiDAR intensity. This 4-channel image is then fed to a multi-task CNN that is trained to produce semantic segmentation, semantic contour detection as well as angles defining the crosswalk direction. In particular, the first output feature map is a pixel-wise foreground/background segmentation of the crosswalks. The second output map is an inverse distance transform from the boundaries of the crosswalks thresholded at a value of 30 pixels (i.e., 1.2 m). By predicting an inverse distance transform, the network learns about the relative distance to the boundaries which makes learning more effective as it contains more supervision than simply predicting the location of the edge. The third output feature map encodes the angles of each crosswalk boundary dilated to a diameter of 30 pixels. We encode this with two outputs per pixel, which correspond to the x and y components of the directional unit vector of the angle. Thus, simply taking the arc tangent of this would produce the predicted angle.

Network Architecture: We use an encoder-decoder architecture with skip connections and residual layers based on the feature pyramids networks in [9, 15, 26] to output the three feature maps. We refer the reader to Fig. 2 for a detail visualization of our network architecture. Note that before each convolutional layer we use batch normalization [17] followed by a ReLU non-linearity [33]. In the encoder network, each residual block consists of three convolutional layers. Because the images can be quite large, we need to ensure the network has a large receptive field, thus, we leverage dilated convolutions [42] in the residual blocks. In the decoder network, we perform nearest neighbor upsampling to upsample back to the original image size. We then split the output into three branches, one for each feature map. To predict the inverse distance transform, we apply a ReLU non-linearity at the end to restrict the output to a positive value. To predict the segmentation, we apply a softmax over the output to get a probability map. To predict the alignment we apply a ReLU non-linearity to restrict the output to a positive value.

Learning: We treat the distance transform and angle predictions as regression and the segmentation as pixel-wise classification tasks. To train our network, we minimize the sum of losses over the three prediction tasks:

$$l(\mathcal{I}) = l_{seg}(\mathcal{I}) + l_{dt}(\mathcal{I}) + \lambda_\ell l_a(\mathcal{I}) \tag{1}$$

where λ_ℓ is a weighting for the alignment loss. In practice we use $\lambda_\ell = 100$ which we found through cross-validation. We define the segmentation loss l_{seg} to be binary cross entropy:

$$l_{seg}(\mathcal{I}) = \frac{1}{N} \sum_p (\hat{y}_p log(y_p) + (1 - \hat{y}_p) log(1 - y_p)) \tag{2}$$

where N is the number of pixels in the bird's eye view image, $\hat{y}_p$ represents the ground truth pixel p's value and y_p represents the predicted probability of the p being a crosswalk.

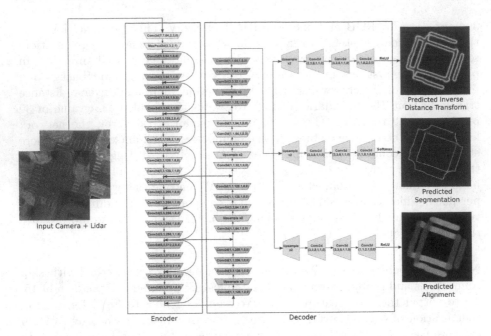

Fig. 2. Overview of our prediction network. Here we use MaxPool2D (kernel width, kernel height, stride, padding) and Conv2D (kernel width, kernel height, out channels, stride, padding, dilation).

We define the boundary loss I_{dt} to be the mean squared loss:

$$l_{dt}(\mathcal{I}) = \frac{1}{N} \sum_p ||d_p - \hat{d}_p||^2 \tag{3}$$

where d_p is pixel p's value in the inverse distance transform feature map ϕ_{dt}.

Finally, we define the alignment loss I_a as the mean squared loss:

$$l_a(\mathcal{I}) = \frac{1}{N} \sum_p ||\text{atan}\left(\frac{v_{p,y}}{v_{p,x}}\right) - \hat{\alpha}_p||^2 \tag{4}$$

where $v_{p,y}$ and $v_{p,x}$ are the y and x components of the unit vector corresponding to the predicted angle, and $\alpha_{p,gt}$ is the ground truth angle. Since a single crosswalk boundary can be represented with multiple angles, we restrict our output to be between $(0, \pi)$.

3.2 Structured Prediction

During inference, we seek to draw the polygon that define each crosswalk. Our approach takes as input the road centerlines, the intersection polygon, as well as the three feature maps predicted by our multi-task convolutional network.

Table 1. This table shows the performance of our model using various inputs. We use the columns N, C and L to denote the Number of passes, camera input and LiDAR input. Here, (Mult) denotes multiple car passes over for offline mapping and (1) denotes a single car pass for online mapping. The first baseline (NN) is a nearest neighbor algorithm on top of VGG features. The second baseline (Seg) is the segmentation output from the model trained on multiple passes of the ground camera and LiDAR. Furthermore, we annotate 100 intersections ourselves and compare these results with the ground truth human annotation.

	N	C	L	Precision at (cm)				Recall at (cm)				IOU
				20	40	60	80	20	40	60	80	
NN	Mult	✓	✓	21.4%	24.8%	25.2%	25.4%	19.4%	22.3%	22.7%	43.1%	35.9%
Seg	Mult	✓	✓	80.1%	93.1%	94.5%	95.0%	77.1%	91.9%	95.2%	97.1%	88.7%
Ours	1	✓	-	78.8%	91.2%	93.8%	94.9%	78.6%	90.5%	92.9%	93.8%	86.9%
Ours	1	-	✓	77.2%	90.6%	93.1%	94.1%	76.8%	89.7%	91.9%	92.8%	85.7%
Ours	1	✓	✓	79.8%	91.5%	93.6%	94.6%	79.9%	91.3%	93.2%	93.9%	87.1%
Ours	Mult	✓	-	83.4%	94.9%	96.6%	97.3%	83.3%	94.6%	96.2%	96.8%	90.2%
Ours	Mult	-	✓	84.5%	95.8%	97.6%	98.4%	85.0%	96.1%	97.8%	98.3%	91.8%
Ours	Mult	✓	✓	**85.6%**	**96.6%**	**98.1%**	**98.8%**	**86.1%**	**96.8%**	**98.2%**	**98.7%**	**92.4%**
Human	-	-	-	88.3%	99.4%	99.7%	99.8%	87.3%	98.3%	98.8%	98.8%	95.3%

Inspired by how humans draw crosswalks, we frame the problem as a 2D search along each centerline to find the two points that describe the boundaries of the crosswalk. This structured representation of the crosswalk drawing problem allows us to produce output estimates that are as good as human annotations.

We use the angle prediction to define a set of candidate hypothesis including the road centerline angle, the mode of the prediction as well as $\pm 2°$ and $\pm 5°$ angles around that prediction. We then formulate the problem as an energy maximization problem, where potentials encode the agreement with the segmentation and boundary semantic features. Here, the inverse distance transform values are maximum right on the boundary, thus, our formulation will favor predicted boundaries that are right on it. The segmentation potential is used to ensure the two boundaries maximize the number of crosswalk pixels inside and maximize the number of background pixels outside. Our energy maximization formulation is below:

$$\max_{x_1, x_2, \beta} \lambda_I (\phi_{seg,\ell,\beta}(x_2) - \phi_{seg,\ell,\beta}(x_1)) + (1 - \lambda_I)(\phi_{dt,\ell,\beta}(x_2) + \phi_{dt,\ell,\beta}(x_1)) \quad (5)$$

where ϕ_{seg} and ϕ_{dt} are the output feature maps of the segmentation and semantic edge tasks. x_1 and x_2 are the two points on the centreline that define the crosswalk. β is the boundary angle. λ_I is the weighting used to balance between the segmentation and semantic edge feature maps. ℓ is the road centreline. Exhaustive search can be computed very efficiently by using non-axis align integral accumulators. In particular we can convert the ϕ_{seg} to a 1D integral image along the road centreline which allows us to easily calculate the number of enclosed crosswalk pixels inside the boundaries defined by x_1 and x_2.

4   Experimental Evaluation

Dataset: We collected a large dataset in a North American city and use all crosswalks in this city with an area of $100\,\mathrm{km}^2$. In total, $9502\,\mathrm{km}$ were driven to create this dataset. Our dataset consists of 1571 training images, 411 validation images and 607 test images. In total, there are 2559 intersections with 8526 crosswalks. This results in 5203 training, 1412 validation and 1911 test crosswalks. Each image represents an intersection with at least one crosswalk, and has a resolution of 4 cm per pixel.

Metrics: We use precision and recall as our base metrics. For precision, the true positive equals the set of predicted crosswalks with a minimal distance smaller than τ and $TP + FP = |P|$. For recall, the true positive equals the set of ground truth crosswalks with minimal distance smaller than τ and $TP + FN = |G|$. We evaluate precision and recall at a τ of 20 cm, 40 cm, 60 cm and 80 cm. We also calculate the Intersection over Union (IoU) of the drawn crosswalks and the ground truth.

Experimental Setup: We trained our models using a batch size of 1 and ADAM [23] with a learning rate of 1e−4 and a weight decay of 5e−4. We decrease the learning rate by a factor of 10 every 100000 training iterations. We then perform data augmentation when training by randomly flipping and rotating the images. The models are trained for 110 epochs over the entire training set.

Importance of Sensor Modality: We trained different models to use camera only, LiDAR only or a combination of both sensors. As shown in Table 1 using both sensors results in better performance. Note that the sensor type is encoded under C (camera) and L (LiDAR) in the table. Furthermore, a histogram of the IoUs using both LiDAR and camera images as input can be seen in Fig. 5 (left). We find that 94.1% of the images have an IoU greater than 85.0%.

Online vs Offline Maps: Table 1 depicts results obtained when using a single pass (online mapping) vs using several passes of driving to create the input feature map (offline mapping). As expected, using multiple passes for offline mapping results in better performance with 96.6% (row 7, prec @ 40 cm), but 91.5% (row 4, prec @ 40 cm) automation can be reached in the online setting. We visualize some of the results from the model trained on both camera and LiDAR in an offline map setting in Fig. 3, while Fig. 4 shows results of the online map setting. Our approach does a very good job at drawing crosswalks with very complex topology in both settings.

Importance of Structured Representation: The first entry in Table 1 shows the results of using a nearest neighbor algorithm on top of VGG features extracted from both the camera and LiDAR. However, this only achieves 24.8%

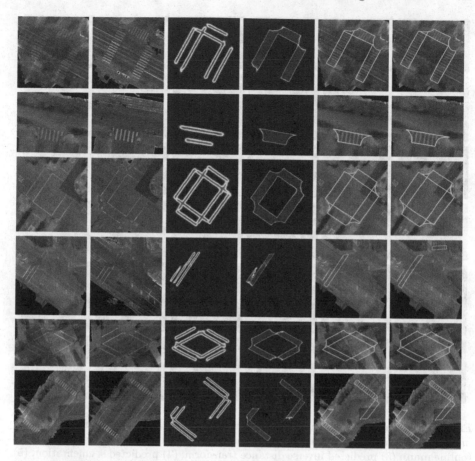

Fig. 3. Offline map model results using the model trained on both camera and LiDAR imagery. Comparisons between col (1) ground camera, (2) ground LiDAR, (3) predicted inverse distance transform, (4) predicted segmentation, (5) predicted crosswalk polygons after inference and (6) GT crosswalk polygons.

automation (precision @ 40 cm). The second entry in Table 1 shows the results of using only the output of the CNN model's semantic segmentation branch for the final prediction. As shown, the network is doing a great job but only 93.1% automation (precision @ 40 cm) can be achieved in the offline setting.

Speed: The CNN forward pass runs at 50 ms per image. The unoptimized structured prediction step runs at 0.75 s on a single core CPU. Optimizing the code would significantly improve the speed.

Qualitative Results: We refer the reader to Figs. 3 and 4 for an illustration of results for both offline and online settings. Despite the complex topology, our approach is still able to accurately draw the crosswalks.

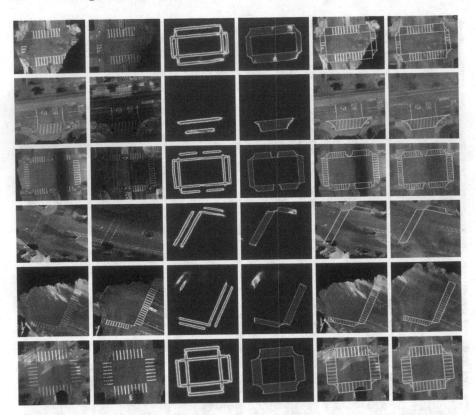

Fig. 4. Online map model results using the model trained on both camera and LiDAR imagery. Comparisons between col (1) ground camera (online map), (2) ground LiDAR (online map), (3) predicted inverse distance transform, (4) predicted segmentation, (5) predicted crosswalk polygons after inference and (6) GT crosswalk polygons overlayed on the ground camera (offline map).

Human Disagreement: We compare the noise in human annotation of the ground truth by annotating 100 intersections with several annotators. Here we calculate the precision, recall and IoU. As shown in the last row in Table 1, there is about a 4.7% error in IOU, and a 11.7% and 12.7% error in the precision and recall at 20 cm between different individuals.

Crosswalk Angle Analysis: Having the correct crosswalk angle is crucial to achieving a high performance on our results. Thus, we perform analysis on the combination of the predicted alignment and centreline angle and compare it to the ground truth. That is, we find the difference between the angle used in inference with the ground truth angle. We plot a histogram and cumulative graph of the differences in Fig. 6. The model we analyze is the model trained on both the camera and LiDAR imagery from the offline maps. We find that 89% of the

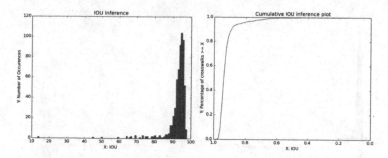

Fig. 5. A histogram of the IOUs (left) and cumulative IOU graph (right) using the LiDAR and camera as input.

crosswalk angles used are within ±5° from the ground truth. After the structured prediction step (which searches over additional angles) this becomes 98%.

Intersection Complexity: We analyze the effect of the number of neighboring roads on our results. A neighboring road is defined as one of the connecting roads to the intersection that provides a road centerline for our structured prediction algorithm. If a street has a divider in the middle, then we split the street into 2 roads. Hence, it is possible for a 4 way intersection to have 8 roads, that is, 2 roads for each approach to the intersection. As shown in Fig. 7, as the number of roads increases, the performance decreases. This is expected, as those intersections are more complex.

Ablation Studies: We perform ablation studies to analyze the contributions of different components in our model in the context of offline mapping with cameras and LiDAR. The results are shown on Table 2. We first explore the effect of removing certain components of the model. We remove the angle search of ±2° and ±5° in row (2) and remove the usage of the centerline angle in row (3). Both result in a slight decrease in performance. In row (4) we do not use the predicted angle when drawing the crosswalks; we see a significant drop of more than 10% for all the performance metrics. This suggests that having the alignment prediction is very important for good inference results.

Oracle Performance: We analyze the upper bound performance of our system by introducing oracle information. Comparing rows (5), (6) and (7) in Table 2 we see that having ground truth segmentation significantly increases the performance of the model. On the other hand, having ground truth distance transform only slightly increases the performance. Interestingly, using ground truth angle performance slightly worse than our result in row (1). This is likely due to the fact that our predicted angles are very accurate. Our angle analysis shows that without ground truth angles we can already achieve 98% angle accuracy. On row (8), we use the ground truth distance transform, segmentation and angle and

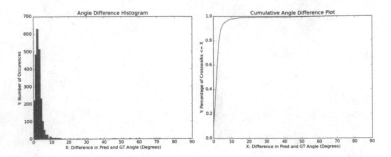

Fig. 6. A histogram of the angle differences (left) and cumulative angle difference graph (right) using the offline model trained on both camera and LiDAR.

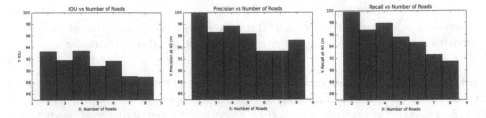

Fig. 7. We visualize the effect of the number of neighbouring roads on the results of the model trained on offline maps using both camera and LiDAR. Histograms of the IoUs vs. number of neighbouring roads (left), Precision at 40 cm vs. number of neighbouring roads (middle) and Recall at 40 cm vs. number of neighbouring roads (right) are plotted here. We use the offline model trained on both camera and LiDAR for this analysis.

see that this performs around the same as using just ground truth segmentation. This suggests that improvements to the semantic segmentation in future models will yield the greatest impact.

Table 2. We report the ablation studies and performance using oracle information in this table. For the ablation studies we analyze the effect of the angle search, road centreline angles and predicted angles in rows (2–4). For the oracle information we inject GT distance transform, segmentation and angles and analyze the results in rows (5–8).

	Precision at (cm)				Recall at (cm)				IOU
	20	40	60	80	20	40	60	80	
Ours	85.6%	96.6%	98.1%	98.8%	86.1%	96.8%	98.2%	98.7%	92.4%
No Ang Search	82.2%	94.4%	97.1%	98.1%	82.7%	94.7%	97.2%	98.2%	91.3%
No Cent Ang	84.5%	96.3%	98.1%	98.8%	84.9%	96.4%	98.0%	98.6%	92.1%
No Pred Ang	74.0%	85.3%	88.9%	91.4%	73.8%	84.8%	88.3%	90.5%	83.7%
GT DT	88.5%	96.6%	97.8%	98.3%	89.5%	97.3%	98.4%	98.8%	92.9%
GT Seg	**94.1%**	**97.8%**	**98.7%**	**99.2%**	94.7%	98.1%	98.8%	99.1%	94.9%
GT Ang	85.5%	96.5%	98.1%	98.7%	85.7%	96.4%	97.9%	98.4%	92.2%
GT DT+S+A	93.9%	97.5%	98.5%	99.0%	**94.9%**	**98.1%**	**98.9%**	**99.2%**	94.9%

Failure Modes: Since we use the weight λ_I to weigh between maximizing segmentation or distance transform energies in our energy formulation, we may at times choose the wrong weighting for a particular input. As seen in Fig. 8 (top), since almost half of the crosswalk boundary in the right crosswalk is missing, our model predicts the wrong segmentation. In this case, our model shows that predicting a boundary that focuses on the segmentation energy gives a larger value and thus produces the wrong inference. The second failure mode can be seen in the bottom image. Here, the paint quality in the ground imagery (although not shown, this is also true for the LiDAR imagery) is of poor quality. Thus, our model mistakes the crosswalk for a stop line at an intersection, and does not predict its presence for the segmentation output. For the online mapping scenario, the major failure mode are holes in the map, as shown in Fig. 9.

Fig. 8. The main failure modes are caused by the trade off between segmentation and distance transform weights (top) and poor image/paint quality (bottom). Here we show comparisons between col (1) ground camera, (2) ground LiDAR, (3) predicted inverse distance transform, (4) predicted segmentation, (5) predicted crosswalk polygons after inference and (6) GT crosswalk polygons.

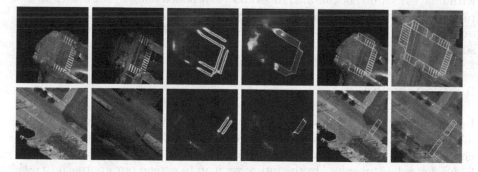

Fig. 9. The main failure mode for the online models is caused by poor data collection when mapping the roads. This poor data collection causes holes and/or poor image quality as seen in this figure. Here we show comparisons between col (1) ground camera (online map), (2) ground LiDAR (online map), (3) predicted inverse distance transform, (4) predicted segmentation, (5) predicted crosswalk polygons after inference and (6) GT crosswalk polygons overlayed on the ground camera (offline map).

Fig. 10. Examples with no crosswalks. (1) Ground camera, (2) ground LiDAR, (3) predicted inverse distance transform, (4) predicted segmentation, (5) predicted crosswalk polygons, (6) GT polygons.

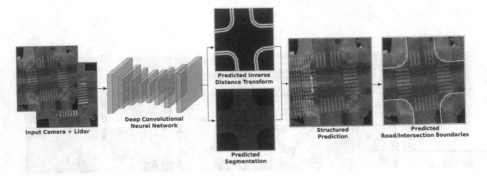

Fig. 11. Generalization of our method to road/intersection boundary prediction.

False Positives: Our dataset was composed of images that contain crosswalks. Without retraining, our approach produces 5.7% false positives. When retrained with images that do not contain crosswalks (45% added images) the false positive rate is 0.04%. The performance of the retrained model is around the same as our result from Table 1 row (8). Examples of the retrained model results can be seen in Fig. 10.

5   Conclusion

In this paper we have proposed a deep structured model that can leverage LiDAR and camera imagery to draw structured crosswalks. Our experiments in a large city has shown that 96.6% automation can be achieved for offline mapping while 91.5% for online mapping. In the future we plan to extend our approach to estimate crosswalks from satellite images. We also plan to extend our approach to predict other semantic elements present in modern HD maps. For example, we can draw stop lines if we predict one boundary instead of two. We can also use this general approach to tackle road/intersection boundaries as seen in Fig. 11. Here the CNN outputs both an inverse distance transform and predicted segmentation. We can use the vehicle's driving path and at every interval we perform a search perpendicular to the vehicle path for the left and right points of the boundary. This can be further extended to draw the lane boundaries.

References

1. Ahmetovic, D., Bernareggi, C., Mascetti, S.: Zebralocalizer: identification and localization of pedestrian crossings. In: Proceedings of the 13th International Conference on Human Computer Interaction with Mobile Devices and Services, MobileHCI 2011, pp. 275–284. ACM, New York (2011). https://doi.org/10.1145/2037373.2037415
2. Ahmetovic, D., Manduchi, R., Coughlan, J.M., Mascetti, S.: Zebra crossing spotter: automatic population of spatial databases for increased safety of blind travelers. In: ASSETS, pp. 251–258. ACM (2015)
3. Babahajiani, P., Fan, L., Kämäräinen, J.K., Gabbouj, M.: Urban 3D segmentation and modelling from street view images and LiDAR point clouds. Mach. Vis. Appl. **28**, 679–694 (2017). https://doi.org/10.1007/s00138-017-0845-3. sJR: h-ind. 45; class. Q1; field rank. 16th (Computer Vision and Pattern Recognition); JuFo-2
4. Babahajiani, P., Fan, L., Kmrinen, J.K., Gabbouj, M.: Comprehensive automated 3D urban environment modelling using terrestrial laser scanning point cloud. IEEE (2016). https://doi.org/10.1109/CVPRW.2016.87. eXT = "Babahajiani, Pouria"
5. Badrinarayanan, V., Handa, A., Cipolla, R.: SegNet: a deep convolutional encoder-decoder architecture for robust semantic pixel-wise labelling. arXiv preprint arXiv:1505.07293 (2015)
6. Badrinarayanan, V., Kendall, A., Cipolla, R.: SegNet: a deep convolutional encoder-decoder architecture for image segmentation. IEEE Trans. Pattern Anal. Mach. Intell. **39**(12), 2481–2495 (2017)
7. Bar Hillel, A., Lerner, R., Levi, D., Raz, G.: Recent progress in road and lane detection: a survey. Mach. Vis. Appl. **25**(3), 727–745 (2014). https://doi.org/10.1007/s00138-011-0404-2
8. Berriel, R.F., Lopes, A.T., de Souza, A.F., Oliveira-Santos, T.: Deep learning-based large-scale automatic satellite crosswalk classification. IEEE Geosc. Remote Sens. Lett. (2017, in press). https://doi.org/10.1109/LGRS.2017.2719863
9. Chaurasia, A., Culurciello, E.: LinkNet: exploiting encoder representations for efficient semantic segmentation. CoRR abs/1707.03718 (2017)
10. Coughlan, J.M., Shen, H.: A fast algorithm for finding crosswalks using figure-ground segmentation. In: Proceedings of the 2nd Workshop on Applications of Computer Vision, in Conjunction with ECCV, p. 2 (2006)
11. Gao, Y., Zhong, R., Tang, T., Wang, L., Liu, X.: Automatic extraction of pavement markings on streets from point cloud data of mobile LiDAR. Meas. Sci. Technol. **28**(8), 085203 (2017)
12. Gurghian, A., Koduri, T., Bailur, S.V., Carey, K.J., Murali, V.N.: Deeplanes: end-to-end lane position estimation using deep neural networks. In: CVPR Workshops, pp. 38–45. IEEE Computer Society (2016)
13. Hackel, T., Savinov, N., Ladicky, L., Wegner, J.D., Schindler, K., Pollefeys, M.: Semantic3D.net: a new large-scale point cloud classification benchmark (2017)
14. Haselhoff, A., Kummert, A.: On visual crosswalk detection for driver assistance systems, pp. 883–888, July 2010
15. He, K., Zhang, X., Ren, S., Sun, J.: Deep residual learning for image recognition. In: CVPR, pp. 770–778. IEEE Computer Society (2016)

16. Demir, I., et al.: Robocodes: towards generative street addresses from satellite imagery. In: IEEE International Conference on Computer Vision and Pattern Recognition, EARTHVISION Workshop (2017)
17. Ioffe, S., Szegedy, C.: Batch normalization: accelerating deep network training by reducing internal covariate shift. In: Proceedings of the 32nd International Conference on International Conference on Machine Learning, ICML 2015, vol. 37, pp. 448–456 (2015). JMLR.org
18. Jarzabek-Rychard, M.: Reconstruction of building outlines in dense urban areas based on lidar data and address point. ISPRS - International Archives of the Photogrammetry, Remote Sensing and Spatial Information Sciences, pp. 121–126 (2012)
19. Jin, H., Feng, Y., Li, M.: Towards an automatic system for road lane marking extraction in large-scale aerial images acquired over rural areas by hierarchical image analysis and Gabor filter. Int. J. Remote Sens. **33**(9), 2747–2769 (2012). https://doi.org/10.1080/01431161.2011.620031
20. Kammel, S., Pitzer, B.: Lidar-based lane marker detection and mapping. In: 2008 IEEE Intelligent Vehicles Symposium, pp. 1137–1142, June 2008. https://doi.org/10.1109/IVS.2008.4621318
21. Kendall, A., Badrinarayanan, V., Cipolla, R.: Bayesian segnet: model uncertainty in deep convolutional encoder-decoder architectures for scene understanding. arXiv preprint arXiv:1511.02680 (2015)
22. Kim, J., Park, C.: End-to-end ego lane estimation based on sequential transfer learning for self-driving cars. In: The IEEE Conference on Computer Vision and Pattern Recognition (CVPR) Workshops, July 2017
23. Kingma, D.P., Ba, J.: Adam: a method for stochastic optimizationadam: a method for stochastic optimization. In: ICLR (2015)
24. Koester, D., Lunt, B., Stiefelhagen, R.: Zebra crossing detection from aerial imagery across countries. In: Miesenberger, K., Bühler, C., Penaz, P. (eds.) ICCHP 2016. LNCS, vol. 9759, pp. 27–34. Springer, Cham (2016). https://doi.org/10.1007/978-3-319-41267-2_5
25. Kurath, S., Gupta, R.D., Keller, S.: OSMDeepOD - object detection on orthophotos with and for VGI, pp. 173–188 (2017)
26. Lin, T.Y., Dollár, P., Girshick, R., He, K., Hariharan, B., Belongie, S.: Feature pyramid networks for object detection. In: CVPR (2017)
27. Lindner, P., Richter, E., Wanielik, G., Takagi, K., Isogai, A.: Multi-channel lidar processing for lane detection and estimation. In: 2009 12th International IEEE Conference on Intelligent Transportation Systems, pp. 1–6, October 2009. https://doi.org/10.1109/ITSC.2009.5309704
28. Mascetti, S., Ahmetovic, D., Gerino, A., Bernareggi, C.: ZebraRecognizer: pedestrian crossing recognition for people with visual impairment or blindness. Pattern Recognit. **60**, 405–419 (2016)
29. Mastin, A., Kepner, J., Fisher, J.: Automatic registration of lidar and optical images of urban scenes. In: IEEE International Conference on Computer Vision and Pattern Recognition (2009)
30. Mattyus, G., Luo, W., Urtasun, R.: DeepRoadMapper: extracting road topology from aerial images. In: The IEEE International Conference on Computer Vision (ICCV), October 2017
31. Máttyus, G., Wang, S., Fidler, S., Urtasun, R.: Enhancing road maps by parsing aerial images around the world. In: ICCV, pp. 1689–1697. IEEE Computer Society (2015)

32. Máttyus, G., Wang, S., Fidler, S., Urtasun, R.: HD maps: fine-grained road segmentation by parsing ground and aerial images. In: CVPR, pp. 3611–3619. IEEE Computer Society (2016)
33. Nair, V., Hinton, G.E.: Rectified linear units improve restricted Boltzmann machines. In: Proceedings of the 27th International Conference on International Conference on Machine Learning, ICML 2010, Omnipress, USA, pp. 807–814 (2010)
34. Noh, H., Hong, S., Han, B.: Learning deconvolution network for semantic segmentation. In: Proceedings of the 2015 IEEE International Conference on Computer Vision (ICCV), ICCV 2015, pp. 1520–1528. IEEE Computer Society, Washington, DC (2015). https://doi.org/10.1109/ICCV.2015.178
35. Sengupta, S., Sturgess, P., Ladicky, L., Torr, P.H.S.: Automatic dense visual semantic mapping from street-level imagery. In: 2012 IEEE/RSJ International Conference on Intelligent Robots and Systems, IROS 2012, Vilamoura, Algarve, Portugal, October 7–12, 2012, pp. 857–862. IEEE (2012). https://doi.org/10.1109/IROS.2012.6385958
36. Shelhamer, E., Long, J., Darrell, T.: Fully convolutional networks for semantic segmentation. IEEE Trans. Pattern Anal. Mach. Intell. **39**(4), 640–651 (2017). https://doi.org/10.1109/TPAMI.2016.2572683
37. Teo, T.A., Rau, J.Y., Chen, L.C., Liu, J.K., Hsu, W.C.: Reconstruction of complex buildings using LIDAR and 2D maps. In: Abdul-Rahman, A., Zlatanova, S., Coors, V. (eds.) Innovations in 3D Geo Information Systems. LNGC, pp. 345–354. Springer, Heidelberg (2006). https://doi.org/10.1007/978-3-540-36998-1_27
38. Visin, F., et al.: ReSeg: a recurrent neural network-based model for semantic segmentation. In: The IEEE Conference on Computer Vision and Pattern Recognition (CVPR) Workshops, June 2016
39. Volodymyr, I., Coughlan, J., Shen, H.: Detecting and locating crosswalks using a camera phone. In: CVPRW (2008)
40. Wang, S., et al.: TorontoCity: seeing the world with a million eyes. In: ICCV, pp. 3028 3036. IEEE (2017)
41. Wegner, J.D., Montoya-Zegarra, J.A., Schindler, K.: A higher-order CRF model for road network extraction. In: CVPR, pp. 1698–1705. IEEE Computer Society (2013)
42. Yu, F., Koltun, V.: Multi-scale context aggregation by dilated convolutions. In: ICLR (2016)
43. Zheng, S., et al.: Conditional random fields as recurrent neural networks. In: Proceedings of the 2015 IEEE International Conference on Computer Vision (ICCV), ICCV 2015, pp. 1529–1537. IEEE Computer Society, Washington, DC (2015). https://doi.org/10.1109/ICCV.2015.179

Sidekick Policy Learning
for Active Visual Exploration

Santhosh K. Ramakrishnan[1(✉)] and Kristen Grauman[2]

[1] The University of Texas at Austin, Austin, TX 78712, USA
srama@cs.utexas.edu
[2] Facebook AI Research, 300 W. Sixth Street, Austin, TX 78701, USA
grauman@fb.com

Abstract. We consider an *active visual exploration* scenario, where an agent must intelligently select its camera motions to efficiently reconstruct the full environment from only a limited set of narrow field-of-view glimpses. While the agent has full observability of the environment during training, it has only partial observability once deployed, being constrained by what portions it has seen and what camera motions are permissible. We introduce *sidekick policy learning* to capitalize on this imbalance of observability. The main idea is a preparatory learning phase that attempts simplified versions of the eventual exploration task, then guides the agent via reward shaping or initial policy supervision. To support interpretation of the resulting policies, we also develop a novel policy visualization technique. Results on active visual exploration tasks with 360° scenes and 3D objects show that sidekicks consistently improve performance and convergence rates over existing methods. Code, data and demos are available (Project website: http://vision.cs.utexas.edu/projects/sidekicks/).

Keywords: Visual exploration · Reinforcement learning

1 Introduction

Visual recognition has witnessed dramatic successes in recent years. Fueled by benchmarks composed of Web photos, the focus has been inferring semantic labels from *human-captured images*—whether classifying scenes, detecting objects, or recognizing activities [41,51,57]. By relying on human-taken images, the common assumption is that an intelligent agent will have already decided where and how to capture the input views. While sufficient for handling static

---

K. Grauman—On leave from University of Texas at Austin (grauman @cs.utexas.edu).

Electronic supplementary material The online version of this chapter (https://doi.org/10.1007/978-3-030-01258-8_26) contains supplementary material, which is available to authorized users.

V. Ferrari et al. (Eds.): ECCV 2018, LNCS 11216, pp. 424–442, 2018.
https://doi.org/10.1007/978-3-030-01258-8_26

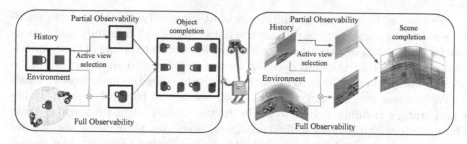

Fig. 1. Embodied agents that actively explore novel objects (left) or 360° environments (right) intelligently select camera motions to gain as much information as possible with very few glimpses. While they naturally face limited observability of the environment, during *learning* fuller observability may be available. We propose sidekicks to guide policy learning for active visual exploration.

repositories of photos (e.g., auto-tagging Web photos and videos), assuming informative observations glosses over a very real hurdle for embodied vision systems.

A resurgence of interest in perception tied to action takes aim at that hurdle. In particular, recent work explores agents that optimize their physical movements to achieve a specific perception goal, e.g., for active recognition [2,28,29,31,43], visual exploration [30], object manipulation [40,46,49], or navigation [2,21,70]. In any such setting, deep reinforcement learning (RL) is a promising approach. The goal is to learn a policy that dictates the best action for the given state, thereby integrating sequential control decisions with visual perception.

However, costly exploration stages and partial state observability are well-known impediments to RL. In particular, an active visual agent [21,30,70,71] has to take a long series of actions purely based on the limited information available from its first person view. Due to poor action selection based on limited information, the most effective viewpoint trajectories are buried among many mediocre ones, impeding the agent's exploration in complex state-action spaces.

We observe that agents lacking full observability when deployed may nonetheless possess full observability *during training*, in some cases. Overall, the imbalance occurs naturally when an agent is trained with a broader array of sensors than available at test-time, or trained free of the hard time pressures that limit test-time exploration. In particular, as we will examine in this work, once deployed, an active exploration agent can only move the camera to "look-around" nearby [30], yet if trained with omnidirectional panoramas, could access any possible viewpoint while learning. Similarly, an active object recognition system [2,28,29,31,65] can only see its previously selected views of the object; yet if trained with CAD models, it could observe all possible views while learning. Additionally, agents can have access to multiple sensors during training in simulation environments [10,13,48], yet operate on first-person observations during test-time. However, existing methods restrict the agent to the same partial observability during training [28–31,65,70].

We propose to leverage the imbalance of observability. To this end, we introduce *sidekick policy learning*. We use the name "sidekick" to signify how a sidekick to a hero (e.g., in a comic or movie) provides alternate points of view, knowledge, and skills that the hero does not have. In contrast to an *expert* [19,61], a sidekick *complements* the hero (agent), yet cannot solve the main task at hand.

We propose two sidekick variants. Both use access to the full state during a preparatory training period to facilitate the agent's ultimate learning task. The first sidekick previews individual states, estimates their value, and shapes rewards to the agent for visiting valuable states during training. The second sidekick provides initial supervision via trajectory selections to accelerate the agent's training, while gradually permitting the agent to act on its own. In both cases, the sidekicks learn to solve *simplified* versions of the main task with full observability, and use insights from those solutions to aid the training of the agent. At test time, the agent has to act without the sidekick.

We validate sidekick policy learning for active visual exploration [30]. The agent enters a novel environment and must select a sequence of camera motions to rapidly understand its entire surroundings. For example, an agent that has explored various grocery stores should enter a *new* one and, with a couple glimpses, (1) conjure a belief state for where different objects are located, then (2) direct its camera to flesh out the harder-to-predict objects and contexts. The task is like active recognition [2,29,31,65], except that the training signal is *pixelwise* reconstruction error for the full environment rather than labeling error. Our sidekicks can look at any part of the environment in any sequence during training, whereas the actual agent is limited to physically feasible camera motions and sees only those views it has selected. On two standard datasets [65,66], we show how sidekicks accelerate training and promote better look around policies.

As a secondary contribution, we present a novel policy visualization technique. Our approach takes the learned policy as input, and displays a sequence of heatmaps showing regions of the environment most responsible for the agent's selected actions. The resulting visualizations help illustrate how sidekick policy learning differs from traditional training.

2 Related Work

Active Vision and Attention: Linking intelligent control strategies to perception has early foundations in the field [1,5,6,63]. Recent work explores new strategies for active object recognition [2,28,29,31,65], object localization [9,20,71], and visual SLAM [32,58], in order to minimize the number of sampled views required to perform accurate recognition or reconstruction. Our work is complementary to any of the above: sidekick policy learning is a means to accelerate and improve active perception when observability is greater during training.

Models of saliency and attention allow a system to prioritize portions of its observation to reduce clutter or save computation [4,42,45,67,68]. However, unlike both our work and the active methods above, they assume full observability at test time, selecting among already-observed regions. Work in active sensor placement aims to place sensors in an environment to maximize *coverage* [11,36,62]. We introduce a model for coverage in our policy learning solution (Sect. 3.3). However, rather than place and fix N static sensors, the visual exploration tasks entail selecting new observations dynamically and in sequence.

Supervised Learning with Observability Imbalance: Prior work in supervised learning investigates ways to leverage greater observability during training, despite more limited observability during test time. Methods for depth estimation [16,22,60] and/or semantic segmentation [25,26,56] use RGBD depth data, multiple views, and/or auxiliary annotations during training, then proceed with single image observations at test time. Similarly, self-supervised losses [27,44] based on auxiliary prediction tasks at training time have been used to aid representation learning for control tasks. Knowledge distillation [24] lets a "teacher" network guide a "student" with the motivation of network compression. In learning with privileged information, an "expert" provides the student with training data having extra information (unavailable during testing) [37,53,61]. At a high level, all the above methods relate to ours in that a simpler learning task facilitates a harder one. However, in strong contrast, they tackle supervised classification/regression/representation learning, whereas our goal is to learn a *policy* for selecting actions. Accordingly, we develop a very different strategy—introducing rewards and trajectory suggestions—rather than auxiliary labels/modalities.

Guiding Policy Learning: There is a wide body of work aimed at addressing sparse rewards and partial observability. Several works explore *reward shaping* motivated by different factors. The intrinsic motivation literature develops parallel reward mechanisms, e.g., based on surprise [7,47], to direct exploration. The TAMER framework [33–35] utilizes expert human rewards about the end-task. Potential-based reward shaping [23] incorporates expert knowledge grounded in potential functions to ensure policy invariance. Others convert control tasks into supervised measurement prediction task by defining goals and rewards as functions of measurements [12]. In contrast to all these approaches, our sidekicks exploit the observability difference between training and testing to transfer knowledge from a simpler version of the task. This external knowledge directly impacts the final policy learned by augmenting task related knowledge via reward shaping.

Behavior cloning provides expert-generated trajectories as supervised (state, action) pairs [8,14,17,50]. *Offline planning*, e.g., with tree search, is another way to prepare good training episodes by investing substantial computation offline [3, 19,54], but observability is assumed to be the same between training and testing. *Guided policy search* uses importance sampling to optimize trajectories within high-reward regions [39] and can utilize full observability [38], yet transfers from an expert in a purely supervised fashion. Our second sidekick also demonstrates good action sequences, but we specifically account for the observability imbalance by annealing supervision over time.

More closely related to our goal is the *asymmetric actor critic*, which leverages synthetic images to train a robot to pick/push an object [48]. Full state information from the graphics engine is exploited to better train the critic. While this approach modifies the advantage expected for a state like our first sidekick, this is only done at the task level. Our sidekick injects a different perspective by solving simpler versions of the task, leading to better performance (Sect. 4.2).

Policy Visualization: Methods for post-hoc explanation of deep networks are gaining attention due to their complexity and limited interpretability. In supervised learning, heatmaps indicating regions of an image most responsible for a decision are generated via backprop of the gradient for a class label [15,52,55]. In reinforcement learning, policies for visual tasks (like Atari) are visualized using t-SNE maps [69] or heatmaps highlighting the parts of a *current* observation that are important for selecting an action [18]. We introduce a policy visualization method that reflects the influence of an agent's *cumulative* observations on its action choices, and use it to illuminate the role of sidekicks.

3 Approach

Our goal is to learn a policy for controlling an agent's camera motions such that it can explore novel environments and objects efficiently. Our key insight is to facilitate policy learning via sidekicks that exploit (1) full observability and (2) unlimited time steps to solve a simpler problem in a preparatory training phase.

We first formalize the problem setup in Sect. 3.1. After overviewing observation completion as a means of active exploration in Sect. 3.2, we introduce our sidekick learning framework in Sect. 3.3. We tie together the observation completion and sidekick components with the overall learning objective in Sect. 3.4. Finally, we present our policy visualization technique in Sect. 3.5.

3.1 Problem Setup: Active Visual Exploration

The problem setting builds on the "learning to look around" challenge introduced in [30]. Formally, the task is as follows. The agent starts by looking at a novel environment (or object) X from some unknown viewpoint[1]. It has a budget T of time to explore the environment. The learning objective is to minimize the error in the agent's pixelwise reconstruction of the full—mostly unobserved—environment using only the sequence of views selected within that budget.

Following [30], we discretize the environment into a set of candidate viewpoints. In particular, the space of viewpoints is a viewgrid indexed by N elevations and M azimuths, denoted by $V(X) = \{x(X, \theta^{(i)}) | 1 \leq i \leq MN\}$, where $x(X, \theta^{(i)})$ is the 2D view of X from viewpoint $\theta^{(i)}$, which is comprised of two angles. More generally, $\theta^{(i)}$ could capture both camera angle and position; however, to best exploit existing datasets, we limit camera motions to rotations.

The agent expends the budget in discrete increments, called "glimpses", by selecting $T - 1$ camera motions in sequence. At each time step, the agent gets

---

[1] For simplicity of presentation, we represent an *environment* as X where the agent explores a novel scene, looking outward in new viewing directions. However, experiments will also use X as an *object* where the agent moves around an object, looking inward at it from new viewing angles.

observation x_t from the current viewpoint. The agent makes an exploratory rotation (δ_t) based on its policy π. When the agent executes action $\delta_t \in \mathcal{A}$, the viewpoint changes according to $\theta_{t+1} = \theta_t + \delta_t$. For each camera motion δ_t executed by the agent, a reward r_t is provided by the environment (Sects. 3.3 and 3.4). Using the view x_t, the agent updates its internal representation of the environment, denoted $\hat{V}(X)$. Because camera motions are restricted to have proximity to the current camera angle (Sect. 4.1) and candidate viewpoints partially overlap, the discretization promotes efficiency without neglecting the physical realities of the problem (following [29–31, 43]).

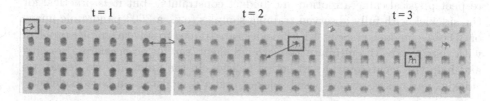

Fig. 2. Active observation completion. The agent receives one view (shown in red), updates its belief and reconstructs the viewgrid at each time step. It executes an action (red arrows) according to its policy to obtain the next view. The active agent must rapidly refine its belief with well-chosen views. (Color figure online)

3.2 Recurrent Observation Completion Network

We start with the deep RL neural network architecture proposed in [30] to represent the agent's recurrent observation completion. The process is deemed "completion" because the agent strives to hallucinate portions of the environment it has not yet seen. It consists of five modules: SENSE, FUSE, AGGREGATE, DECODE, and ACT with parameters W_s, W_f, W_r, W_d and W_a respectively.

- SENSE: Independently encodes the view (x_t) and proprioception (p_t) consisting of elevation at time t and relative motion from time $t-1$ to t, and returns the encoded tuple $s_t = \text{SENSE}(x_t, p_t)$.
- FUSE: Consists of fully connected layers that jointly encode the tuple s_t and output a fused representation $f_t = \text{FUSE}(s_t)$.
- AGGREGATE: An LSTM that aggregates fused inputs over time to build the agent's internal representation $a_t = \text{AGGREGATE}(f_1, f_2, \ldots, f_t)$ of X.
- DECODE: A convolutional decoder which reconstructs the viewgrid $\hat{V}_t = \text{DECODE}(a_t)$ as a set of MN feature maps ($3MN$ for 3 channeled images) corresponding to each view of the viewgrid.
- ACT: Given the aggregated state a_t and proprioception p_t, the ACT module outputs a probability distribution $\pi(\delta|a_t)$ over the candidate camera motions $\delta \in \mathcal{A}$. An action sampled from this distribution $\delta_t = \text{ACT}(a_t, p_t)$ is executed.

At each time step, the agent receives and encodes a new view x_t, then updates its internal representation a_t by sensing, fusing, and aggregating. It decodes the viewgrid $\hat{V}_t$ and executes δ_t to change the viewpoint. It repeats the above steps until the time budget T is reached (see Fig. 2). See Supp. for implementation details and architecture diagram.

3.3   Sidekick Definitions

Sidekicks provide a preparatory learning phase that informs policy learning. Sidekicks have full observability during training: in particular, they can observe the results of arbitrary camera motions in arbitrary sequence. This is impossible for the actual look-around agent—who must enter novel environments and respect physical camera motion and budget constraints—but it *is* practical for the sidekick with fully observed training samples (e.g., a 360° panoramic image or 3D object model, cf. Sect. 4.1). Sidekicks are trained to solve a simpler problem with relevance to the ultimate look-around agent, serving to accelerate training and help the agent converge to better policies. In the following, we define two sidekick variants: a reward-based sidekick and a demonstration-based sidekick.

Reward-Based Sidekick. The reward-based sidekick aims to identify a set of K views $\{x(X, \theta_1), \ldots, x(X, \theta_K)\}$ which can provide maximal information about the environment X. The sidekick is allowed to access X and select views without any restrictions. Hence, it addresses a simplified completion problem.

A candidate view is scored based on how informative it is, i.e., how well the entire environment can be reconstructed given only that view. We train a completion model (cf. Sect. 3.2) that can reconstruct $\hat{V}(X)$ from any single view (i.e., we set $T = 1$). Let $\hat{V}(X|y)$ denote the decoded reconstruction for X given only view y as input. The sidekick scores the information in observation $x(X, \theta)$ as:

$$\text{Info}\left(x(X, \theta), X\right) \quad \propto^{-1} \quad d\left(\hat{V}(X|x(X, \theta)), V(X)\right), \tag{1}$$

where d denotes the reconstruction error and $V(X)$ is the fully observed environment. We use a simple ℓ_2 loss on pixels for d to quantify information. Higher-level losses, e.g., for detected objects, could be employed when available. The scores are normalized to lie in $[0, 1]$ across the different views of X. The sidekick scores each candidate view. Then, in order to sharpen the effects of the scoring function and avoid favoring redundant observations, the sidekick selects the top K most informative views with greedy non-maximal suppression. It iteratively selects the view with the highest score and suppresses all views in the neighborhood of that view until K views are selected (see Supp. for details). This yields a map of favored views for each training environment. See Fig. 3, top row.

The sidekick conveys the results to the agent during policy learning in the form of an augmented reward (to be defined in Sect. 3.4). Thus, the reward-based sidekick previews observations and encourages the selection of those *individually* valuable for reconstruction. Note that while the sidekick indexes views in absolute angles, the agent will not; all its observations are relative to its initial (random) glimpse direction. This works because the sidekick becomes a part of

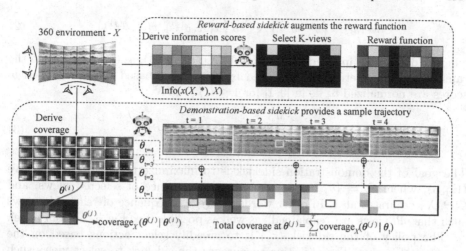

Fig. 3. Top left shows the 360° environment's viewgrid, indexed by viewing elevation and azimuth. **Top: Reward sidekick** scores individual views based on how well they alone permit inference of the viewgrid X (Eq. 1). The grid of scores (center) is post-processed with non-max suppression to prioritize K non-redundant views (right), then is used to shape the agent's rewards. **Bottom: Demonstration sidekick.** Left "grid-of-grids" displays example coverage score maps (Eq. 2) for all $\theta^{(i)}, \theta^{(j)}$ view pairs. The outer $N \times M$ grid considers each $\theta^{(i)}$, and each inner $N \times M$ grid considers each $\theta^{(j)}$ for the given $\theta^{(i)}$ (bottom left). A pixel in that grid is bright if coverage is high for $\theta^{(j)}$ given $\theta^{(i)}$, and dark otherwise. Each $\theta^{(i)}$ denotes an (elevation, azimuth) pair. While observed views and their neighbors are naturally recoverable (brighter), the sidekick uses broader environment context to also anticipate distant and/or different-looking parts of the environment, as seen by the non-uniform spread of scores in the left grid. Given the coverage function and a starting position, this sidekick selects actions to greedily optimize the coverage objective (Eq. 3). The bottom right strip shows the cumulative coverage maps as each of the $T = 4$ glimpses is selected.

the environment, i.e., it attaches rewards to the true views of the environment. In short, the reward-based sidekick shapes rewards based on its exploration with full observability.

Demonstration-Based Sidekick. Our second sidekick generates *trajectories* of informative views. Given a starting view in X, the demonstration sidekick selects a trajectory of T views that are deemed to be most informative about X. Unlike the reward-based sidekick above, this sidekick offers guidance with respect to a starting state, and it is subject to the same camera motion restrictions placed on the main agent. Such restrictions model how an agent cannot teleport its camera using one unit of effort.

To identify informative trajectories, we first define a scoring function that captures *coverage*. Coverage reflects how much information $x(X, \theta)$ contains about each view in X. The coverage score for view $\theta^{(j)}$ upon selecting view $\theta^{(i)}$ is:

$$\text{Coverage}_X\left(\theta^{(j)}|\theta^{(i)}\right) \propto^{-1} d\left(\hat{x}(X,\theta^{(j)}), x(X,\theta^{(j)})\right), \tag{2}$$

where $\hat{x}$ denotes an inferred view within $\hat{V}(X|x(X,\theta^{(i)}))$, as estimated using the same $T = 1$ completion network used by the reward-based sidekick. Coverage scores are normalized to lie in $[0,1]$ for $1 \le i,j \le MN$.

$$\mathcal{C}(\Theta,X) = \sum_{j=1}^{MN}\sum_{\theta\in\Theta} \text{Coverage}_X(\theta^{(j)}|\theta), \tag{3}$$

The goal of the demonstration sidekick is to maximize the coverage objective (Eq. 3), where $\Theta = \{\theta_1,\ldots,\theta_t\}$ denotes the sequence of selected views, and $\mathcal{C}(\Theta,X)$ saturates at 1. In other words, it seeks a sequence of reachable views such that *all* views are "explained" as well as possible. See Fig. 3, bottom panel.

The policy of the sidekick (π_s) is to greedily select actions based on the coverage objective. The objective encourages the sidekick to select views such that the overall information obtained about each view in X is maximized.

$$\pi_s(\Theta) = \arg\max_\delta \mathcal{C}\left(\Theta \cup \{\theta_t + \delta\}, X\right). \tag{4}$$

We use these sidekick-generated trajectories as supervision to the agent for a short preparatory period. The goal is to initialize the agent with useful insights learned by the sidekick to accelerate training of better policies. We achieve this through a hybrid training procedure that combines imitation and reinforcement. In particular, for the first t_{sup} time steps, we let the sidekick drive the action selection and train the policy based on a supervised objective. For steps t_{sup} to T, we let the agent's policy drive the action selection and use REINFORCE [64] or Actor-Critic [59] to update the agent's policy (see Sect. 4). We start with $t_{sup} = T$ and gradually reduce it to 0 in the preparatory sidekick phase (see Supp.). This step relates to behavior cloning [8,14,17], which formulates policy learning as supervised action classification given states. However, unlike typical behavior cloning, the sidekick is not an expert. It solves a simpler version of the task, then backs away as the agent takes over to train with partial observability.

3.4   Policy Learning with Sidekicks

Having defined the two sidekick variants, we now explain how they influence policy learning. The goal is to learn the policy $\pi(\delta|a_t)$ which returns a distribution over actions for the aggregated internal representation a_t at time t. Let $\mathcal{A} = \{\delta_i\}$ denote the set of camera motions available to the agent.

Our agent seeks the policy that minimizes reconstruction error for the environment given a budget of T camera motions (views). If we denote the set of weights of the network $[W_s, W_f, W_r, W_d, W_a]$ by W and W excluding W_a by $W_{/a}$ and W excluding W_d by $W_{/d}$, then the overall weight update is:

$$\Delta W = \frac{1}{n}\sum_{j=1}^{n} \lambda_r \Delta W_{/a}^{rec} + \lambda_p \Delta W_{/d}^{pol} \tag{5}$$

where n is the number of training samples, j indexes over the training samples, λ_r and λ_p are constants and $\Delta W_{/a}^{rec}$ and $\Delta W_{/d}^{pol}$ update all parameters except W_a and W_d, respectively. The pixel-wise MSE reconstruction loss ($\mathcal{L}_t^{rec}$) and corresponding weight update at time t are given in Eq. 6, where $\hat{x}_t(X, \theta^{(i)})$ denotes the reconstructed view at viewpoint $\theta^{(i)}$ and time t, and Δ_0 denotes the offset to account for the unknown starting azimuth (see [30]).

$$\mathcal{L}_{rec}^t(X) = \sum_{i=1}^{MN} d\left(\hat{x}_t(X, \theta^{(i)} + \Delta_0), x(X, \theta^{(i)})\right),$$

$$\Delta W_{/a}^{rec} = -\sum_{t=1}^{T} \nabla_{W_{/a}} \mathcal{L}_{rec}^t(X), \tag{6}$$

The agent's reward at time t (see Eq. 7) consists of the intrinsic reward from the sidekick $r_t^s = \mathrm{Info}(x(X, \theta_t), X)$ (see Sect. 3.3) and the negated final reconstruction loss ($-\mathcal{L}_{rec}^T(X)$).

$$r_t = \begin{cases} r_t^s & 1 \le t \le T-2 \\ -\mathcal{L}_{rec}^T(X) + r_t^s & t = T-1 \end{cases} \tag{7}$$

The update from the policy (see Eq. 8) consists of the REINFORCE update, with a baseline b to reduce variance, and supervision from the demonstration sidekick (see Eq. 9). We consider both REINFORCE [64] and Actor-Critic [59] methods to update the ACT module. For the latter, the policy term additionally includes a loss to update a learned Value Network (see Supp.). For both, we include a standard entropy term to promote diversity in action selection and avoid converging too quickly to a suboptimal policy.

$$\Delta W_{/d}^{pol} = \sum_{t=1}^{T-1} \nabla_{W_{/d}} \log \pi(\delta_t|a_t) \left(\sum_{t'=t}^{T-1} r_{t'} - b(a_t)\right) + \Delta W_{/d}^{demo}, \tag{8}$$

The demonstration sidekick influences policy learning via a cross entropy loss between the sidekick's policy π_s (cf. Sect. 3.3) and the agent's policy π:

$$\Delta W_{/d}^{demo} = \sum_{t=1}^{T-1} \sum_{\delta \in \mathcal{A}} \nabla_{/d}(\pi_s(\delta|a_t) \log \pi(\delta|a_t)). \tag{9}$$

We pretrain the SENSE, FUSE, and DECODE modules with $T = 1$. The full network is then trained end-to-end (with SENSE and FUSE frozen). For training with sidekicks, the agent is augmented either with additional rewards from the reward sidekick (Eq. 7) or an additional supervised loss from the demonstration sidekick (Eq. 9). As we will show empirically, training with sidekicks helps overcome uncertainty due to partial observability and learn better policies.

3.5   Visualizing the Learned Motion Policies

Finally, we propose a visualization technique to qualitatively understand the policy that has been learned. The aggregated state a_t is used by the policy network to determine the action probabilities. To analyze which part of the agent's belief (a_t) is important for the current selected action δ_t, we solve for the change in the aggregated state (Δa_t) which maximizes the change in the predicted action distribution $(\pi(\cdot|a_t))$:

$$\Delta a^* = \arg\max_{\Delta a_t} \sum_{\delta \in \mathcal{A}} \left(\pi(\delta|a_t) - \pi(\delta|a_t + \Delta a_t) \right)^2 \tag{10}$$

$$s.t. \ ||\Delta a_t|| \leq C||a_t||$$

where C is a constant that limits the deviation in norm from the true belief. Equation 10 is maximized using gradient ascent (see Supp.). This change in belief is visualized in the viewgrid space by forward propagating through the DECODE module. The visualized heatmap intensities (H_t) are defined as follows:

$$H_t \propto ||\text{DECODE}(a_t + \Delta a^*) - \text{DECODE}(a_t)||_2^2. \tag{11}$$

The heatmap indicates which parts of the agent's belief *would have to change* to affect its action selection. The views with high intensity are those that affect the agent's action selection the most.

4   Experiments

In Sects. 4.1 and 4.2, we describe our experimental setup and analyze the learning efficiency and test-time performance of different methods. In Sect. 4.3, we visualize learned policies and demonstrate the superiority of our policies over a baseline.

4.1   Experimental Setup

Datasets: We use two popular datasets to benchmark our models.

- **SUN360:** SUN360 [66] consists of high resolution spherical panoramas from multiple scene categories. We restrict our experiments to the 26 category subset used in [30,66]. The viewgrid consists of 32×32 views captured across 4 elevations ($-45°$ to $45°$) and 8 azimuths ($0°$ to $180°$). At each step, the agent sees a $60°$ field-of-view. This dataset represents an agent looking out at a scene in a series of narrow field-of-view glimpses.
- **ModelNet Hard:** ModelNet [65] provides a collection of 3D CAD models for different categories of objects. ModelNet-40 and ModelNet-10 are provided subsets consisting of 40 and 10 object categories respectively, the latter being a subset of the former. We train on objects from the 30 categories not present in ModelNet-10 and test on objects from the unseen 10 categories. We increase

completion difficulty in "ModelNet Hard" by rendering with more challenging lighting conditions, textures and viewing angles than [30]; see Supp. It consists of 32×32 views sampled from 5 elevations and 9 azimuths. This dataset represents an agent looking in at a 3D object and moving it to a series of selected poses.

For both datasets, the candidate motions $\mathcal{A}$ are restricted to a 3 elevations $\times$ 5 azimuths neighborhood, representing the set of unit-cost actions. Neighborhood actions mimic real-world scenarios where the agent's physical motions are constrained (i.e., no teleporting) and is consistent with recent active vision work [2, 28–30, 43]. The budget for number of steps is fixed to $T = 4$.

Baselines: We benchmark our methods against several baselines:

- `one-view`: the agent trained to reconstruct from one view ($T = 1$).
- `rnd-actions`: samples actions uniformly at random.
- `ltla` [30]: our implementation of the "learning to look around" approach [30]. We verified our code reproduces results from [30].
- `rnd-rewards`: naive sidekick where rewards are assigned uniformly at random on the viewgrid.
- `asymm-ac` [48]: approach from [48] adapted for discrete actions. Critic sees the entire panorama/object and true camera poses (no experience replay).
- `demo-actions`: actions selected by demo-sidekick while training/testing.
- `expert-clone`: imitation from an expert policy that uses full observability (similar to critic in Fig. 2 of Supp.)

Evaluation: We evaluate reconstruction error averaged over uniformly sampled elevations, azimuths and all test samples (`avg`). To provide a worst case analysis, we also report an adversarial metric (`adv`), which evaluates each agent on its hardest starting positions in each test sample and averages over the test data.

4.2 Active Exploration Results

Table 1 shows the results on both datasets. For each metric, we report the mean error along with the percentage improvement over the `one-view` baseline. Our methods are abbreviated `ours(rew)` and `ours(demo)` referring to the use of our reward- and demonstration-based sidekicks, respectively. We denote the use of Actor-Critic instead of REINFORCE with `+ac`.

We observe that `ours(rew)` and `ours(demo)` with REINFORCE generally perform better than `ltla` with REINFORCE [30]. In particular, `ours(rew)` performs significantly better than `ltla` on both datasets on all metrics. `ours(demo)` performs better on SUN360, but is only slightly better on ModelNet Hard. Figure 4 shows the validation loss plots; using the sidekicks leads to significant improvement in the convergence rate over `ltla`.

Figure 5 compares example decoded reconstructions. We stress that the vast majority of pixels are unobserved when decoding the belief state, i.e., only 4 views out of the entire viewing sphere are observed. Accordingly, they are blurry.

Table 1. Avg/Adv MSE errors ×1000 (↓ lower is better) and corresponding improvements (%) over the `one-view` model (↑ higher is better), for the two datasets. The best and second best performing models are highlighted in green and blue respectively. Standard errors range from 0.2 to 0.3 on SUN360 and 0.1 to 0.2 on ModelNet Hard.

Method	SUN360				ModelNet Hard			
	Avg (×1000)		Adv (×1000)		Avg (×1000)		Adv (×1000)	
	Mean ↓	% ↑	Mean ↓	% ↑	Mean ↓	% ↑	Mean ↓	% ↑
`one-view`	38.31	-	55.12	-	9.63	-	17.10	-
`rnd-actions`	30.99	19.09	44.85	18.63	7.32	23.93	12.38	27.56
`rnd-rewards`	25.55	33.30	30.20	45.21	7.04	26.89	9.66	43.50
`ltla` [30]	24.94	34.89	31.86	42.19	6.30	34.57	8.78	48.65
`asymm-ac` [48]	23.74	38.01	29.92	45.72	6.24	35.20	8.55	50.00
`expert-clone`	23.98	37.38	28.50	**48.28**	6.41	33.44	8.52	50.13
`ours(rew)`	23.44	**38.82**	28.54	48.22	5.80	**39.79**	7.17	**58.04**
`ours(demo)`	24.24	36.73	29.01	47.36	6.32	34.37	8.64	49.47
`ours(rew)+ac`	23.36	**39.01**	28.26	**48.72**	5.75	**40.26**	7.10	**58.44**
`ours(demo)+ac`	24.05	37.22	28.52	48.26	6.13	36.31	8.26	51.64
`demo-actions`*	26.12	31.82	31.53	42.76	5.82	39.50	7.46	56.40

(* - requires full observability at test time)

Regardless, their differences indicate the differences in belief states between the two methods. A better policy more quickly fleshes out the general shape of the scene or object.

Next, we compare our model to `asymm-ac`, which is an alternate paradigm for exploiting full observability during training. First, we note that `asymm-ac` performs better than `ltla` across all datasets and metrics, making it a strong baseline. Comparing `asymm-ac` with `ours(rew)+ac` and `ours(demo)+ac`, we see our methods still perform considerably better on all metrics and datasets. As we show in the Supp, our methods also lead to faster convergence.

In order to contrast learning from sidekicks with learning from experts, we additionally compare our models to behavior cloning an expert that exploits full observability at training time. As shown in Table 1, `ours(rew)` outperforms `expert-clone` on both the datasets, validating the strength of our approach. It is particularly interesting because training an expert takes a lot longer (17×) than training sidekicks (see Supp.). When compared with `demo-actions`, an ablated version of `ours(demo)` that requires full observability at *test time*, our performance is still significantly better on SUN360 and slightly better on ModelNet Hard. `ours(rew)` and `ours(demo)` also beat the remaining baselines by a significant margin. These results verify our hypothesis that sidekick policy learning can improve over strong baselines by exploiting full observability during training.

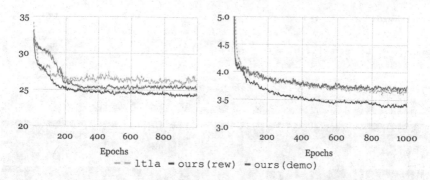

--- ltla   — ours(rew)   — ours(demo)

Fig. 4. Validation errors (×1000) vs. epochs on SUN360 (left) and ModelNet Hard (right). All models shown here use REINFORCE (see Supp. for more curves). Our approach accelerates convergence.

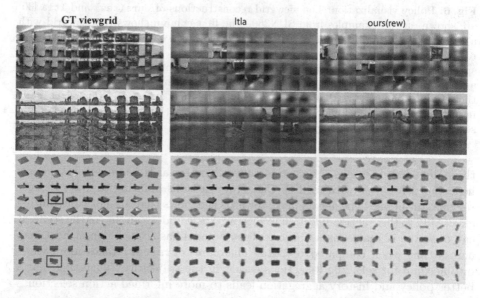

Fig. 5. Qualitative comparison of ours(rew) vs. ltla [30] on SUN360 (first 2 rows) and ModelNet Hard (last 2 rows). The first column shows the groundtruth viewgrid and a randomly selected starting point (marked in red). The 2nd and 3rd columns contain the decoded viewgrids from ltla and ours(rew) after $T = 4$ time steps. The reconstructions from ours(rew) are visibly better. For example, in the 3rd row, our model reconstructs the protrusion more clearly; in the 2nd row, our model reconstructs the sky and central hills more effectively. Best viewed on pdf with zoom. (Color figure online)

4.3   Policy Visualization

We present our policy visualizations for ltla and ours(rew) on SUN360 in Fig. 6; see Supp. for examples with ours(demo). The heatmap from Eq. 10 is shown in pink and overlayed on the reconstructed viewgrids. For both models,

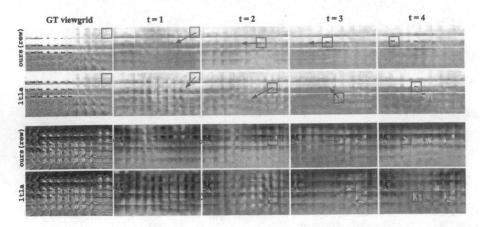

Fig. 6. Policy visualization: The viewgrid reconstructions of `ours(rew)` and `ltla` [30] are shown on two examples from SUN360. The first column shows the viewgrid with a randomly selected view (in red). Subsequent columns show the view received (in red), viewgrid reconstructed, action selected (red arrow), and the parts of the belief space our method deems responsible for the action selection (pink heatmap). Both the agents tend to move towards sparser regions of the heatmap, attempting to improve their beliefs about views that do not contribute to their action selection. `ours(rew)` improves its beliefs much more rapidly and as a result, performs more informed action selection. (Color figure online)

the policies tend to take actions that move them towards views which have low heatmap density, as witnessed by the arrows/actions pointing to lower density regions. Intuitively, the agents move towards the views that are not contributing effectively to their action selection to increase their understanding of the scene. It can observed in many cases that `ours(rew)` model has a much denser heat map across time when compared to `ltla`. Therefore, `ours(rew)` takes more views into account for selecting its actions earlier in the trajectory, suggesting that a better policy and history aggregation leads to more informed action selection.

5   Conclusion

We propose *sidekick policy learning*, a framework to leverage extra observability or fewer restrictions on an agent's motion during training to learn better policies. We demonstrate the superiority of policies learned with sidekicks on two challenging datasets, improving over existing methods and accelerating training. Further, we utilize a novel policy visualization technique to illuminate the different reasoning behind policies trained with and without sidekicks. In future work, we plan to investigate the effectiveness of our framework on other active vision tasks such as recognition and navigation.

Acknowledgements. The authors thank Dinesh Jayaraman, Thomas Crosley, Yu-Chuan Su, and Ishan Durugkar for helpful discussions. This research is supported in part by DARPA Lifelong Learning Machines, a Sony Research Award, and an IBM Open Collaborative Research Award.

References

1. Aloimonos, J., Weiss, I., Bandyopadhyay, A.: Active vision. Int. J. Comput. Vis. **1**, 333–356 (1988)
2. Ammirato, P., Poirson, P., Park, E., Košecká, J., Berg, A.C.: A dataset for developing and benchmarking active vision. In: 2017 IEEE International Conference on Robotics and Automation (2017)
3. Anthony, T., Tian, Z., Barber, D.: Thinking fast and slow with deep learning and tree search. In: Advances in Neural Information Processing Systems (2017)
4. Ba, J., Mnih, V., Kavukcuoglu, K.: Multiple object recognition with visual attention. arXiv preprint arXiv:1412.7755 (2014)
5. Bajcsy, R.: Active perception. In: IEEE Proceedings, vol. 76, no. 8, pp. 996–1006 (1988)
6. Ballard, D.H.: Animate vision. Artif. Intell. **48**(1), 57–86 (1991)
7. Bellemare, M., Srinivasan, S., Ostrovski, G., Schaul, T., Saxton, D., Munos, R.: Unifying count-based exploration and intrinsic motivation. In: Advances in Neural Information Processing Systems (2016)
8. Bojarski, M., et al.: End to end learning for self-driving cars. arXiv preprint arXiv:1604.07316 (2016)
9. Caicedo, J.C., Lazebnik, S.: Active object localization with deep reinforcement learning. In: 2015 IEEE International Conference on Computer Vision (2015)
10. Das, A., Datta, S., Gkioxari, G., Lee, S., Parikh, D., Batra, D.: Embodied Question Answering. In: 2018 IEEE Conference on Computer Vision and Pattern Recognition (2018)
11. Dhillon, S.S., Chakrabarty, K.: Sensor placement for effective coverage and surveillance in distributed sensor networks. In: 2003 Wireless Communications and Networking. WCNC 2003. IEEE (2003)
12. Dosovitskiy, A., Koltun, V.: Learning to act by predicting the future. In: International Conference on Learning Representations (2017)
13. Dosovitskiy, A., Ros, G., Codevilla, F., Lopez, A., Koltun, V.: CARLA: an open urban driving simulator. In: Conference on Robot Learning (2017)
14. Duan, Y., et al.: One-shot imitation learning. In: Advances in Neural Information Processing Systems (2017)
15. Fong, R.C., Vedaldi, A.: Interpretable explanations of black boxes by meaningful perturbation. In: 2017 IEEE International Conference on Computer Vision (2017)
16. Garg, R., Vijay Kumar, B.G., Carneiro, G., Reid, I.: Unsupervised CNN for single view depth estimation: geometry to the rescue. In: Leibe, B., Matas, J., Sebe, N., Welling, M. (eds.) ECCV 2016. LNCS, vol. 9912, pp. 740–756. Springer, Cham (2016). https://doi.org/10.1007/978-3-319-46484-8_45
17. Giusti, A., et al.: A machine learning approach to visual perception of forest trails for mobile robots. IEEE Robot. Autom. Lett. **1**, 661–667 (2016)
18. Greydanus, S., Koul, A., Dodge, J., Fern, A.: Visualizing and understanding atari agents. CoRR (2017)

19. Guo, X., Singh, S., Lee, H., Lewis, R.L., Wang, X.: Deep learning for real-time Atari game play using offline Monte-Carlo tree search planning. In: Advances in Neural Information Processing Systems (2014)

20. Gupta, S., Davidson, J., Levine, S., Sukthankar, R., Malik, J.: Cognitive mapping and planning for visual navigation. In: 2017 IEEE Conference on Computer Vision and Pattern Recognition (2017)

21. Gupta, S., Fouhey, D., Levine, S., Malik, J.: Unifying map and landmark based representations for visual navigation. arXiv preprint arXiv:1712.08125 (2017)

22. Gupta, S., Hoffman, J., Malik, J.: Cross modal distillation for supervision transfer. In: 2016 IEEE Conference on Computer Vision and Pattern Recognition (2016)

23. Harutyunyan, A., Devlin, S., Vrancx, P., Nowe, A.: Expressing arbitrary reward functions as potential-based advice. In: Twenty-Ninth AAAI Conference on Artificial Intelligence (2015)

24. Hinton, G., Vinyals, O., Dean, J.: Distilling the knowledge in a neural network. arXiv preprint arXiv:1503.02531 (2015)

25. Hong, S., Noh, H., Han, B.: Decoupled deep neural network for semi-supervised semantic segmentation. In: Advances in Neural Information Processing Systems (2015)

26. Hong, S., Oh, J., Lee, H., Han, B.: Learning transferrable knowledge for semantic segmentation with deep convolutional neural network. In: 2016 IEEE Conference on Computer Vision and Pattern Recognition (2016)

27. Jaderberg, M., et al.: Reinforcement learning with unsupervised auxiliary tasks. arXiv preprint arXiv:1611.05397 (2016)

28. Jayaraman, D., Grauman, K.: End-to-end policy learning for active visual categorization. IEEE Trans. Pattern Anal. Mach. Intell. (2018). https://doi.org/10.1109/TPAMI.2018.2840991

29. Jayaraman, D., Grauman, K.: Look-ahead before you leap: end-to-end active recognition by forecasting the effect of motion. In: Leibe, B., Matas, J., Sebe, N., Welling, M. (eds.) ECCV 2016. LNCS, vol. 9909, pp. 489–505. Springer, Cham (2016). https://doi.org/10.1007/978-3-319-46454-1_30

30. Jayaraman, D., Grauman, K.: Learning to look around: intelligently exploring unseen environments for unknown tasks. In: 2018 IEEE Conference on Computer Vision and Pattern Recognition (2018)

31. Johns, E., Leutenegger, S., Davison, A.J.: Pairwise decomposition of image sequences for active multi-view recognition. In: 2016 IEEE Conference on Computer Vision and Pattern Recognition (2016)

32. Kim, A., Eustice, R.M.: Perception-driven navigation: active visual slam for robotic area coverage. In: 2013 IEEE International Conference on Robotics and Automation (2013)

33. Knox, W.B., Stone, P.: Interactively shaping agents via human reinforcement: the tamer framework. In: Proceedings of the Fifth International Conference on Knowledge Capture (2009)

34. Knox, W.B., Stone, P.: Combining manual feedback with subsequent MDP reward signals for reinforcement learning. In: Proceedings of the 9th International Conference on Autonomous Agents and Multiagent Systems (2010)

35. Knox, W.B., Stone, P.: Reinforcement learning from simultaneous human and MDP reward. In: Proceedings of the 11th International Conference on Autonomous Agents and Multiagent Systems (2012)

36. Krause, A., Guestrin, C.: Near-optimal observation selection using submodular functions. In: AAAI (2007)

37. Lapin, M., Hein, M., Schiele, B.: Learning using privileged information: SVM+ and weighted SVM. Neural Netw. **53**, 95–108 (2014)
38. Levine, S., Finn, C., Darrell, T., Abbeel, P.: End-to-end training of deep visuomotor policies. J. Mach. Learn. Res. **17**, 1334–1373 (2016)
39. Levine, S., Koltun, V.: Guided policy search. In: International Conference on Machine Learning (2013)
40. Levine, S., Pastor, P., Krizhevsky, A., Quillen, D.: Learning hand-eye coordination for robotic grasping with large-scale data collection. In: Kulić, D., Nakamura, Y., Khatib, O., Venture, G. (eds.) 2016 International Symposium on Experimental Robotics (2017)
41. Lin, T.-Y., et al.: Microsoft COCO: common objects in context. In: Fleet, D., Pajdla, T., Schiele, B., Tuytelaars, T. (eds.) ECCV 2014. LNCS, vol. 8693, pp. 740–755. Springer, Cham (2014). https://doi.org/10.1007/978-3-319-10602-1_48
42. Liu, T., et al.: Learning to detect a salient object. IEEE Trans. Pattern Anal. Mach. Intell. **33**, 353–367 (2011)
43. Malmir, M., Sikka, K., Forster, D., Movellan, J.R., Cottrell, G.: Deep Q-learning for active recognition of germs: baseline performance on a standardized dataset for active learning. In: British Machine Vision Conference (2015)
44. Mirowski, P., et al.: Learning to navigate in complex environments. arXiv preprint arXiv:1611.03673 (2016)
45. Mnih, V., Heess, N., Graves, A., et al.: Recurrent models of visual attention. In: Advances in Neural Information Processing Systems (2014)
46. Nair, A., et al.: Combining self-supervised learning and imitation for vision-based rope manipulation. In: 2017 IEEE International Conference on Robotics and Automation (2017)
47. Pathak, D., Agrawal, P., Efros, A.A., Darrell, T.: Curiosity-driven exploration by self-supervised prediction. In: International Conference on Machine Learning (2017)
48. Pinto, L., Andrychowicz, M., Welinder, P., Zaremba, W., Abbeel, P.: Asymmetric actor critic for image-based robot learning. Robot. Sci. Syst. (2018)
49. Pinto, L., Gupta, A.: Supersizing self-supervision: learning to grasp from 50k tries and 700 robot hours. In: 2016 IEEE International Conference on Robotics and Automation (2016)
50. Ross, S., Gordon, G., Bagnell, D.: A reduction of imitation learning and structured prediction to no-regret online learning. In: Proceedings of the Fourteenth International Conference on Artificial Intelligence and Statistics (2011)
51. Russakovsky, O., et al.: ImageNet large scale visual recognition challenge. Int. J. Comput. Vis. **115**, 211–252 (2015)
52. Selvaraju, R.R., Cogswell, M., Das, A., Vedantam, R., Parikh, D., Batra, D.: Grad-CAM: visual explanations from deep networks via gradient-based localization. In: 2017 IEEE International Conference on Computer Vision (2017)
53. Sharmanska, V., Quadrianto, N., Lampert, C.H.: Learning to rank using privileged information. In: 2013 IEEE International Conference on Computer Vision. IEEE (2013)
54. Silver, D., et al.: Mastering the game of go without human knowledge. Nature **550**, 354 (2017)
55. Simonyan, K., Vedaldi, A., Zisserman, A.: Deep inside convolutional networks: visualising image classification models and saliency maps. arXiv preprint arXiv:1312.6034 (2013)

56. Song, S., Zeng, A., Chang, A.X., Savva, M., Savarese, S., Funkhouser, T.: Im2Pano3D: extrapolating 360 structure and semantics beyond the field of view. In: 2018 IEEE Conference on Computer Vision and Pattern Recognition (2018)

57. Soomro, K., Zamir, A.R., Shah, M.: UCF101: a dataset of 101 human actions classes from videos in the wild. arXiv preprint arXiv:1212.0402 (2012)

58. Spica, R., Giordano, P.R., Chaumette, F.: Active structure from motion: application to point, sphere, and cylinder. IEEE Trans. Robot. **30**, 1499–1513 (2014)

59. Sutton, R.S., Barto, A.G.: Reinforcement Learning: An Introduction. https://mitpress.mit.edu/books/reinforcement-learning

60. Tulsiani, S., Zhou, T., Efros, A.A., Malik, J.: Multi-view supervision for single-view reconstruction via differentiable ray consistency. In: 2017 IEEE Conference on Computer Vision and Pattern Recognition (2017)

61. Vapnik, V., Izmailov, R.: Learning with intelligent teacher. In: Gammerman, A., Luo, Z., Vega, J., Vovk, V. (eds.) COPA 2016. LNCS (LNAI), vol. 9653, pp. 3–19. Springer, Cham (2016). https://doi.org/10.1007/978-3-319-33395-3_1

62. Wang, B.: Coverage problems in sensor networks: a survey. ACM Comput. Surv. **43**, 32 (2011)

63. Wilkes, D., Tsotsos, J.K.: Active object recognition. In: 1992 IEEE Computer Society Conference on Computer Vision and Pattern Recognition (1992)

64. Williams, R.J.: Simple statistical gradient-following algorithms for connectionist reinforcement learning. In: Sutton, R.S. (ed.) Reinforcement Learning, vol. 173, pp. 5–32. Springer, Boston (1992). https://doi.org/10.1007/978-1-4615-3618-5_2

65. Wu, Z., et al.: 3D shapeNets: a deep representation for volumetric shapes. In: 2015 IEEE Conference on Computer Vision and Pattern Recognition (2015)

66. Xiao, J., Ehinger, K.A., Oliva, A., Torralba, A.: Recognizing scene viewpoint using panoramic place representation. In: 2012 IEEE Conference on Computer Vision and Pattern Recognition (2012)

67. Xu, K., et al.: Show, attend and tell: neural image caption generation with visual attention. In: International Conference on Machine Learning (2015)

68. Yang, C., Zhang, L., Lu, H., Ruan, X., Yang, M.H.: Saliency detection via graph-based manifold ranking. In: 2013 IEEE Conference on Computer Vision and Pattern Recognition (2013)

69. Zahavy, T., Ben-Zrihem, N., Mannor, S.: Graying the black box: understanding DQNs. In: International Conference on Machine Learning (2016)

70. Zhu, Y., et al.: Visual semantic planning using deep successor representations. In: 2017 IEEE International Conference on Computer Vision (2017)

71. Zhu, Y., et al.: Target-driven visual navigation in indoor scenes using deep reinforcement learning. In: 2017 IEEE International Conference on Robotics and Automation (2017)

Coloring with Words: Guiding Image Colorization Through Text-Based Palette Generation

Hyojin Bahng[1], Seungjoo Yoo[1], Wonwoong Cho[1],
David Keetae Park[1,3], Ziming Wu[2], Xiaojuan Ma[2],
and Jaegul Choo[1,3(✉)]

[1] Korea University, Seoul, South Korea
{hjj552,seungjooyoo,tyflehd21,heykeetae,jchoo}@korea.ac.kr
[2] Hong Kong University of Science and Technology, Hong Kong, Hong Kong
zwual@connect.ust.hk, mxj@cse.ust.hk
[3] Clova AI Research, NAVER Corporation, Bundang-gu, South Korea

Abstract. This paper proposes a novel approach to generate multiple color palettes that reflect the semantics of input text and then colorize a given grayscale image according to the generated color palette. In contrast to existing approaches, our model can understand rich text, whether it is a single word, a phrase, or a sentence, and generate multiple possible palettes from it. For this task, we introduce our manually curated dataset called Palette-and-Text (PAT). Our proposed model called Text2Colors consists of two conditional generative adversarial networks: the text-to-palette generation networks and the palette-based colorization networks. The former captures the semantics of the text input and produce relevant color palettes. The latter colorizes a grayscale image using the generated color palette. Our evaluation results show that people preferred our generated palettes over ground truth palettes and that our model can effectively reflect the given palette when colorizing an image.

1 Introduction

Humans can associate certain words with certain colors. The real question is, can machines effectively learn the relationship between color and text? Using text to express colors can allow ample room for creativity, and it would be useful to visualize the colors of a certain semantic concept. For instance, since colors can leave a strong impression on people [19], corporations often decide upon the season's color theme from marketing concepts such as 'passion.' Through text input, even people without artistic backgrounds can easily create color palettes that convey high-level concepts. Since our model uses text to visualize aesthetic

---

H. Bahng, S. Yoo and W. Cho Contributed equally.

Electronic supplementary material The online version of this chapter (https://doi.org/10.1007/978-3-030-01258-8_27) contains supplementary material, which is available to authorized users.

© Springer Nature Switzerland AG 2018
V. Ferrari et al. (Eds.): ECCV 2018, LNCS 11216, pp. 443–459, 2018.
https://doi.org/10.1007/978-3-030-01258-8_27

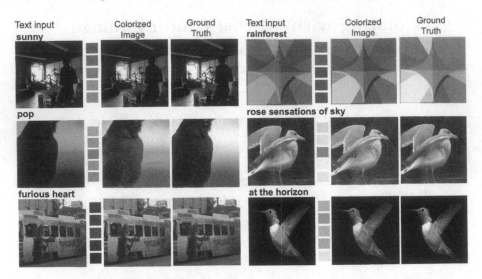

Fig. 1. Colorization results of Text2Colors given text inputs. The text input is shown above the input grayscale image, and the generated palettes are on the right of the grayscale image. The color palette is well-reflected in the colorized image when compared to the ground truth image. Our model is applicable to a wide variety of images ranging from photos to patterns (top right).

concepts, its range of future applications can encompass text to even speech (Fig. 1).

Previous methods have a limited range of applications as they only take a single word as input and can recommend only a single color or a color palette in pre-existing datasets [8,12,15,25]. Other studies have further attempted to link a single word with a multi-color palette [21,36] since multi-color palettes are highly expressive in conveying semantics [18]. Compared to these previous studies, our model can generate multiple plausible color palettes when given rich text input, including both single- and multi-word descriptions, greatly increasing the boundary of creative expression through words.

In this paper, we propose a novel method to generate multiple color palettes that convey the semantics of rich text and then colorize a given grayscale image according to the generated color palette. Perception of color is inherently multimodal [4], meaning that a particular text input can be mapped to multiple possible color palettes. To incorporate such multimodality into our model, our palette generation networks are designed to generate multiple palettes from a single text input. We further apply our generated color palette to the colorization task. Motivated from previous user-guided colorizations that utilize color hints given by users [42,44], we design our colorization networks to utilize color palettes during the colorization process. Our evaluation demonstrates that the colorized outputs do not only reflect the colors in the palette but also convey the semantics of the text input (Fig. 2).

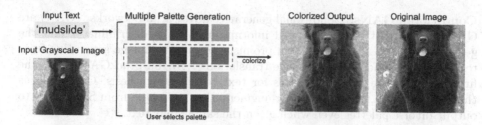

Fig. 2. How Text2Colors works. Our model can produce a diverse selection of palettes when given a text input. Users can optionally choose which palette to be applied to the final colorization output.

The contribution of this paper includes:

(1) We propose a novel deep neural network architecture that can generate multiple color palettes based on natural-language text input.
(2) Our model is able to use the generated palette to produce plausible colorizations of a grayscale image.
(3) We introduce our manually curated dataset called Palette-and-Text (PAT), which includes 10,183 pairs of a multi-word text and a multi-color palette.[1]

2 Related Work

Color Semantics. Meanings associated with a color are both innate and learned [9]. For instance, red can make us instinctively feel alert [9]. Since color has a strong association with high-level semantic concepts [10], producing palettes from text input is useful in aiding artists and designers [18] and allows automatic colorization from palettes [5,42]. A downside to using text to choose a filter is that filter names do not usually convey the filter's colors [21], thus making it difficult for users to find the filter that matches their taste just by looking at filter names. To bridge this discrepancy between color palettes and their names, palette recommendation based on user text input has long been studied. Query-based methods [21,36] use text inputs to query an image from an image dictionary where colors are extracted from the queried image to make an associated palette. This method is problematic in that the text input is mapped to the image content of the queried image rather than the color that the text implies. Instead of looking for a target directly, learning-based approaches [14,23,27] match color palettes to their linguistic descriptions by learning their semantic association from large-scale data. However, our model is the only generative model that supports phrase-level input.

---

[1] Dataset and codes are publicly available at https://github.com/awesome-davian/Text2Colors/.

Conditional GANs. Conditional generative adversarial networks (cGAN) are GAN models that use conditional information for the discriminator and the generator [24]. cGANs have drawn promising results for image generation from text [31,32,43] and image-to-image translation [7,13,16]. StackGAN [43] is the first model to use conditional loss for text to image synthesis. Our model is the first to utilize the conditioning augmentation technique from StackGAN to output diverse palettes even when given the same input text.

Interactive Colorization. Colorization is a multimodal task and desired colorization results for the same object may vary from person to person [4]. A number of studies introduce interactive methods that allow users to control the final colorization output [20,44]. In these models, users directly interact with the model by pinpointing where to color. Even though these methods achieve satisfactory results, a limitation is that users need to have a certain level of artistic skill. Thus instead of making the user directly color an image, other studies take a more indirect approach by utilizing color palettes to recolor an image [3,5]. Palette-based filters of our model are an effective way for non-experts to recolor an image [3].

Sequence-to-Sequence with Attention. Recurrent Neural Networks (RNNs) are a popular tool due to their superior ability to learn from sequential data. RNNs are used in various tasks including sentence classification [39], text generation [37], and sequence-to-sequence prediction [38]. Incorporating attention into a sequence-to-sequence model is known to improve the model performance [22] as networks learn to selectively focus on parts of a source sentence. This allows a model to learn relations between different modalities as is done by our model (e.g., text - colors, text - action [1], and English - French [40]).

3   Palette-and-Text (PAT) Dataset

This section introduces our manually curated dataset named Palette-and-Text (PAT). PAT contains 10,183 text and five-color palette pairs, where the set of five colors in a palette is associated with its corresponding text description as shown in Figs. 3(b)–(d). Words vary with respect to their relationships with colors; some words are direct color words (e.g., pink, blue, etc.) while others evoke a particular set of colors (e.g., autumn or vibrant). To the best of our knowledge, there has been no dataset that matches a multi-word text and its corresponding 5-color palette. This dataset allows us to train our models for predicting semantically consistent color palettes with textual inputs.

Other Color Datasets. Munroe's color survey [26] is a widely used large-scale color corpus. Based on crowd-sourced user judgment, it matches a text to a single color. Another dataset, Kobayashi's Color Image Scale [18], is a well-established multi-color dataset. Kobayashi only uses 180 adjectives to express

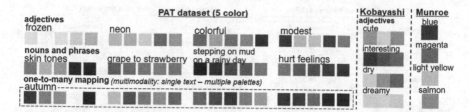

Fig. 3. Our Palette-and-Text (PAT) dataset. On the left are diverse text-palette pairs included in PAT. PAT has a very wide range of expression, especially when compared to existing datasets. Our dataset is designed to address rich text and multimodality, where the same word can be mapped to a wide range of possible colors. (Color figure online)

1170 three-color palettes, which greatly limits its range of expression. In contrast, our dataset is made up of 4,312 unique words. This includes much more text that was not traditionally used to express colors. Our task requires a more sophisticated dataset like PAT, that matches a text to multiple colors and is large enough for a deep learning model to learn from.

Data Collection. We generated our PAT dataset by refining user-named palette data crawled from a community website called color-hex.com. Thousands of users upload custom-made color palettes on color-hex, and thus our dataset was able to incorporate a wide pool of opinions. We crawled 47,665 palette-text pairs and removed non-alphanumerical and non-English words. Among them, we found that users sometimes assign palette names in an arbitrary manner, missing their semantic consistency with their corresponding color palettes. Some names are a collection of random words (e.g., 'mehmeh' and 'i spilled tea all over my laptop rip'), or are riddled with typos (e.g., 'cause iiiiii see right through you boyyyyy' and 'greene gardn'). Thus, using unrefined raw palette names would hinder model performances significantly.

To refine the noisy raw data, four annotators voted whether the text paired with the color palette properly matches its semantic meanings. We then used only the text-palette pairs in which at least three annotators out of four agreed that semantic matching exists between the text and color palette. Including text-palette pairs in the dataset only when all four annotators agree was found to be unnecessarily strict, leaving not much room for personal subjectivity. Annotator's perception is inherently subjective, meaning that a text-palette pair perfectly plausible to one person may not be agreeable to another. We wanted to incorporate such subjectivity by allowing a diverse selection of text-palette pairs. Mis-spelling and punctuation errors were manually corrected after the annotators finished sorting out the data.

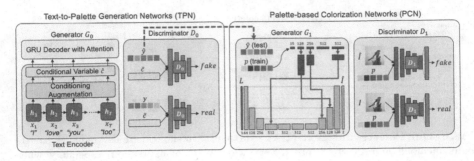

Fig. 4. Overview of our Text2Colors architecture. During training, generator G_0 learns to produce a color palette $\hat{y}$ given a set of conditional variables $\hat{c}$ processed from input text $x = \{x_1, \cdots, x_T\}$. Generator G_1 learns to predict a colorized output of a grayscale image L given a palette p extracted from the ground truth image. At test time, the trained generators G_0 and G_1 are used to produce a color palette from given text and then colorize a grayscale image reflecting the generated palette.

4 Text2Colors: Text-Driven Colorization

Text2Colors consists of two networks: Text-to-Palette Generation Networks (TPN) and Palette-based Colorization Networks (PCN). We train the first networks to generate color palettes given a multi-word text and then train the second networks to predict reasonable colorizations given a grayscale image and the generated palettes. We utilize conditional GANs (cGAN) for both networks.

4.1 Text-to-Palette Generation Networks (TPN)

Objective Function. In this section, we illustrate the Text-to-Palette Generation Networks shown in Figs. 4 and 5. TPN produces reasonable color palettes associated with the text input. Let $x_i \in \mathbb{R}^{300}$ be word vectors initialized by 300-dimensional pre-trained vectors from GloVe [29]. Words not included in the pre-trained set are initialized randomly. Using the CIE *Lab* space for our task, $y \in \mathbb{R}^{15}$ represents a 15-dimensional color palette consisting of five colors with *Lab* values. After a GRU encoder encodes x into hidden states $h = \{h_1, \cdots, h_T\}$, we add random noise to the encoded representation of text by sampling latent variables $\hat{c}$ from a Gaussian distribution $\mathcal{N}(\mu(h), \Sigma(h))$. The sequence of conditioning vectors $\hat{c} = \{\hat{c}_1, \cdots, \hat{c}_T\}$ is given as *condition* for the generator to output a palette $\hat{y}$, while its mean vector $\bar{c} = \frac{1}{T}\sum_{i=1}^{T} \hat{c}$ is given as the condition for the discriminator. Our objective function of the first cGAN can be expressed as

$$L_{D_0} = \mathbb{E}_{y \sim P_{data}}[\log D_0(\bar{c}, y)] + \mathbb{E}_{x \sim P_{data}}[\log(1 - D_0(\bar{c}, \hat{y}))], \tag{1}$$

$$L_{G_0} = \mathbb{E}_{x \sim P_{data}}[\log(1 - D_0(\bar{c}, \hat{y}))], \tag{2}$$

where discriminator D_0 tries to maximize L_{D_0} against generator G_0 that tries to minimize L_{G_0}. The pre-trained word vectors x and the real color palette y is sampled from true data distribution P_{data}.

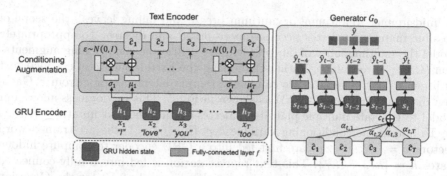

Fig. 5. Model architecture of a generator G_0 that produces the t-th color in the palette given a sequence of conditioning variables $\hat{c} = \{\hat{c}_1, \cdots, \hat{c}_T\}$ processed from an input text $x = \{x_1, \cdots, x_T\}$. Note that randomness is added to the encoded representation of text before it is passed to the generator.

Previous approaches have benefited from mixing the GAN objective with L_2 distance [28] or L_1 distance [13]. We have explored previous loss options and found the Huber (or smooth L_1) loss to be the most effective in increasing diversity among colors in generated palettes. The Huber loss is given by

$$L_H(\hat{y}, y) = \begin{cases} \frac{1}{2}(\hat{y} - y)^2 & \text{for } |\hat{y} - y| \leq \delta \\ \delta |\hat{y} - y| - \frac{1}{2}\delta^2 & \text{otherwise.} \end{cases} \tag{3}$$

This loss term is added to the generator's objective function to force the generated palette to be close to the ground truth palette. We also adopted the Kullback-Leibler (KL) divergence regularization term [43], i.e.,

$$D_{KL}(\mathcal{N}(\mu(h), \Sigma(h)) \parallel \mathcal{N}(0, I)), \tag{4}$$

which is added to the generator's objective function to further enforce the smoothness over the conditioning manifold. Our final objective function is

$$L_{D_0} = \mathbb{E}_{y \sim P_{data}}[\log D_0(\bar{c}, y)] + \mathbb{E}_{x \sim P_{data}}[\log(1 - D_0(\bar{c}, \hat{y}))], \tag{5}$$

$$\begin{aligned} L_{G_0} = \mathbb{E}_{x \sim P_{data}}[\log(1 - D_0(\bar{c}, \hat{y}))] + \lambda_H L_H(\hat{y}, y) \\ + \lambda_{KL} D_{KL}(\mathcal{N}(\mu(h), \Sigma(h)) \parallel \mathcal{N}(0, I)), \end{aligned} \tag{6}$$

λ_H and λ_{KL} are the hyperparameters to balance the three terms in Eq. 6. We set $\delta = 1, \lambda_H = 100, \lambda_{KL} = 0.5$ in our model.

Networks Architecture

Encoding Text Through Conditioning Augmentation. Learning a mapping from text to color is inherently multimodal. For instance, a text 'autumn' can be mapped to a variety of plausible color palettes. As text becomes longer, such as 'midsummer to autumn' or 'autumn breeze and falling leaves', the scope of possible matching palettes becomes more broad and diverse. To appropriately model the multimodality of our problem, we utilize the conditioning augmentation (CA) [43] technique. Rather than using the fixed sequence of encoded text as input to our generator, we randomly sample latent vector $\hat{c}$ from a Gaussian distribution $\mathcal{N}(\mu(h), \Sigma(h))$ as shown in Fig. 5. This randomness allows our model to generate multiple plausible palettes given same text input.

To obtain the conditioning variable $\hat{c} = \{\hat{c}_1, \cdots, \hat{c}_T\}$, the pre-trained word vectors $x = \{x_1, \cdots, x_T\}$ are first fed into a GRU encoder to compute hidden states $h = \{h_1, \cdots, h_T\}$. This text representation is fed into a fully-connected layer to generate μ and σ (the values in the diagonal of Σ) for the Gaussian distribution $\mathcal{N}(\mu(h), \Sigma(h))$. Conditioning variable $\hat{c}$ is computed by $\hat{c} = \mu + \sigma \odot \epsilon$, where $\odot$ is the element-wise multiplication and $\epsilon \sim \mathcal{N}(0, I)$. The resulting set of vectors $\hat{c} = \{\hat{c}_1, \cdots, \hat{c}_T\}$ will be used as *condition* for our generator.

Generator. We design our generator G_0 as a variant of a GRU decoder with attention mechanism [2,6,22]. The i-th color of the palette $\hat{y}_i$ is computed as

$$\hat{y}_i = f(s_i) \text{ where } s_i = g(\hat{y}_{i-1}, c_i, s_{i-1}). \tag{7}$$

s_i is a GRU hidden state vector for time i, having the previously generated color $\hat{y}_{i-1}$, the context vector c_i, and the previous hidden state s_{i-1} as input. The GRU hidden state s_i is given as input to a fully-connected layer f to output the i-th color of the palette $\hat{y}_i \in \mathbb{R}^3$. The resulting five colors are combined to produce a single palette output $\hat{y}$.

The context vector c_i depends on a sequence of conditioning vectors $\hat{c} = \{\hat{c}_1, \cdots, \hat{c}_T\}$ and the previous hidden state s_{i-1}. The context vector c_i is computed as the weighted sum of these conditions $\hat{c}_i$'s, i.e.,

$$c_i = \sum_{j=1}^{T} \alpha_{ij} \hat{c}_j. \tag{8}$$

The weight α_{ij} of each conditional variable $\hat{c}_j$ is computed by

$$\alpha_{ij} = \frac{\exp(e_{ij})}{\sum_{k=1}^{T} \exp(e_{ik})} \text{ where } e_{ij} = a(s_{i-1}, \hat{c}_j). \tag{9}$$

$$a(s_{i-1}, \hat{c}_j) = w^T \sigma(W_s s_{i-1} + W_{\hat{c}} \hat{c}_j), \tag{10}$$

where $\sigma(\cdot)$ is a sigmoid activation function and w is a weight vector. The additive attention [2] $a(s_{i-1}, \hat{c}_j)$ computes how well the j-th word of the text input matches the i-th color of the palette output. The score α_{ij} is computed based on the GRU hidden state s_{i-1} and the j-th condition $\hat{c}_j$. The attention mechanism enables the model to effectively map complex text input to the palette output.

Discriminator. For the discriminator D_0, the conditioning variable $\bar{c}$ and the color palette are concatenated and fed into a series of fully-connected layers. By jointly learning features across the encoded text and palette, the discriminator classifies whether the palettes are real or fake.

4.2   Palette-Based Colorization Networks (PCN)

Objective Function. The goal of the second networks is to automatically produce colorizations of a grayscale image guided by the color palette as a conditioning variable. The inputs are a grayscale image $L \in \mathbb{R}^{H \times W \times 1}$ representing the lightness in CIE *Lab* space and a color palette $p \in \mathbb{R}^{15}$ consisting of five colors in *Lab* values. The output $\hat{I} \in \mathbb{R}^{H \times W \times 2}$ corresponds to the predicted *ab* color channels of the image. The objective function of the second model can be expressed as

$$L_{D_1} = \mathbb{E}_{I \sim P_{data}}[\log D_1(p, I)] + \mathbb{E}_{\hat{I} \sim P_{G_1}}[\log(1 - D_1(p, \hat{I}))], \tag{11}$$

$$L_{G_1} = \mathbb{E}_{\hat{I} \sim P_{G_1}}[\log(1 - D_1(p, \hat{I}))] + \lambda_H L_H(\hat{I}, I). \tag{12}$$

D_1 and G_1 included in the equation are shown in Fig. 4. We have also added the Huber loss to the generator's objective function. In other words, the generator learns to be close to the ground truth image with *plausible* colorizations, while incorporating palette colors to the output image to fool the discriminator. We set $\lambda_H = 10$ in our model.

Networks Architecture

Generator. The generator consists of two sub-networks: the main colorization networks and the conditioning networks. Our main colorization networks adopts the U-Net architecture [33], which has shown promising results in colorization tasks [13,44]. The skip connections help recover spatial information [33], as the input and the output images share the location of prominent edges [13].

The role of the conditioning networks is to apply the palette colors to the generated image. During training, the networks are given a palette $p \in \mathbb{R}^{15}$ extracted from the ground truth image I. We utilize the Color Thief[2] function to extract a palette consisting of five dominant colors of the ground truth image. Similar to the previous work [44], the conditioning palette p is fed into a series of 1×1 *conv-relu* layers as shown in Fig. 4. The feature maps in layers 1, 2, and 4 are duplicated spatially to match the spatial dimension of the *conv9*, *conv8*, and *conv4* features in the main colorization networks and added in an element-wise manner. The palette p is fed into upsampling layers with skip connections as well as the middle of the main networks. This allows the generator to detect prominent edges and apply palette colors to suitable locations of the image. During test time, we use the generated palette $\hat{y}$ from the first networks (TPN) as the conditioning variable, colorizing the grayscale image with the predicted palette colors.

Discriminator. As our discriminator D_1, we use a variant of the DCGAN architecture [30]. The image and conditioning variable p are concatenated and fed into a series of *conv-leaky relu* layers to jointly learn features across the image and the palette. Afterwards, it is fed into a fully-connected layer to classify whether the image is real or fake.

---

[2] http://lokeshdhakar.com/projects/color-thief/.

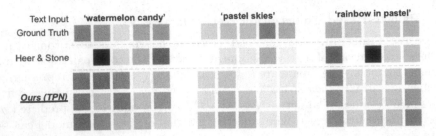

Fig. 6. Comparison to baselines and qualitative analysis on multimodality: Our TPN generates appealing color palettes that reflect all details of the text input. Also our model can generate multiple palettes with the same text input (three rows from bottom). In comparison, Heer and Stone [12]'s model frequently generates unrelated colors and has deterministic outputs.

4.3   Implementation Details

We first train D_0 and G_0 of TPN for 500 epochs using the PAT dataset. We then train D_1 and G_1 of the PCN for 100 epochs, using the extracted palette from a ground truth image. Finally, we use the trained generators G_0 and G_1 during test time to colorize a grayscale image with generated palette $\hat{y}$ from a text input x. All networks are trained using Adam optimizer [17] with a learning rate of 0.0002. Weights were initialized from a Gaussian distribution with zero mean and standard deviation of 0.05. We set other hyper parameters as $\delta = 1, \lambda_H = 100$, and $\lambda_{KL} = 0.5$.

5   Experimental Results

This section presents both quantitative and qualitative analyses of our proposed model. We evaluate the TPN (Sect. 4.1) based on our PAT dataset. For the training of the PCN (Sect. 4.2), we use two different datasets, CUB-200-2011 (CUB) [41] and ImageNet ILSVRC Object Detection (ImageNet dataset) [34].

5.1   Analysis on Multimodality and Diversity of Generated Palettes

This section discusses the evaluation on multimodality and diversity of our generated palettes. Multimodality refers to how many different color palettes a single text input can be mapped to. In other words, if a single text can be expressed with more color palettes, the more multimodal it is. As shown in Fig. 6, our model is multimodal, while previous approaches are deterministic, meaning that it generates only a particular color palette when given a text input. Diversity within a palette refers to how diverse the colors included in a single palette are. Following the current standard for perceptual color distance measurement, we use the CIEDE2000 [35] on CIE *Lab* space to compute a model's multimodality and diversity. To measure multimodality, we compute the average minimum distances between colors from different palettes. To measure diversity of a color

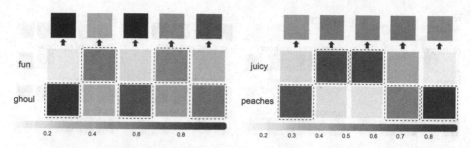

Fig. 7. Attention analysis. Attention scores measured by the TPN for two text input samples. Each box color (in green) denotes the attention score computed in producing the corresponding color shown on top. The dashed-line boxes indicate the word that each color output attended to. (Color figure online)

palette, we measure the average pairwise distance between the five colors within a palette. All measurements are computed based on the test dataset.

Results. Table 1 shows the multimodality and diversity measurement among the variants of our model. The CA module (Sect. 4.1) enables our networks to suggest multiple color palettes when given the same text input. The model variant without CA (the first row in Table 1) results in zero multimodality, indicating that the networks generate identical palettes for the same text input. Another palette generation model by Heer and Stone [12] also has zero multimodality. This shows that TPN is the only existing model that can adequately express multimodality, which is crucial in the domain of colors. Although Heer and Stone's model has higher diversity than TPN, Fig. 6 shows that their palettes contain irrelevant colors that may increase diversity but decrease palette quality. On the other hand, TPN creates those palettes containing colors that well match each other. Results on the fooling rate will be further illustrated in Sect. 5.3.

5.2   Analysis on Attention Outputs

The attention module (Sect. 4.1) plays a role of attending to particular words in text input to predict the most suitable colors for the text input. Figure 7 illustrates how the predicted colors are influenced by attention scores. The green-colored boxes show attention scores computed for each word token when predicting each corresponding color in the palette. Higher scores are indicated by dashed-line boxes. We observe that three colors generated by attending to *ghoul* are all dark and gloomy, while the other two colors attending to *fun* are bright. This attention mechanism enables our model to thoroughly reflect the semantics included in text inputs of varying lengths (Fig. 8).

5.3   User Study

We conduct a user study to reflect universal user opinions on the outputs of our model. Our user study is composed of two parts. The first part measures how

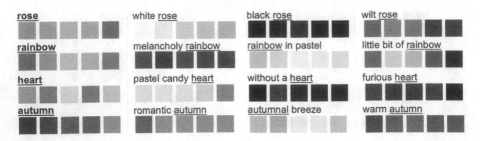

Fig. 8. Qualitative analysis on semantic context. Our model reflects subtle nuance differences in the semantic context of a given text input in the color palette outputs. Except for the first column, all the text combinations shown here are unseen data.

Table 1. Quantitative analysis results

		Palette evaluation				User study: part I			
Model variations		Diversity		Multimodality		Fooling rate (%)			
Objective function	CA	Mean	Std	Mean	Std	Mean	Std	Max	Min
Ours (TPN)	X	19.36	8.74	0.0	0.0	-	-	-	-
Ours (TPN)	O	20.82	7.43	5.43	8.11	**56.2**	12.7	**76.7**	37.1
Heer and stone	-	35.92	12.66	0.0	0.0	39.6	10.8	58.2	25.8
Ground truth palette	-	32.60	21.84	-	-	-	-	-	-

Q1: The palette is reflected in the colorization output.
Q2: The palette colors are evenly used in the colorization process.
Q3: Objects and backgrounds in the colorized image are distinguishable in colors.
Q4: I am satisfied with the quality of the colorized result.
Q5: If I am the painter, I would colorize similarly based on the palette.

Zhang et al. 2017 ■   Ours (PCN) ■

Q1: 2.56 / 3.72
Q2: 2.47 / 3.23
Q3: 3.05 / 3.28
Q4: 2.73 / 3.08
Q5: 2.41 / 2.96

Fig. 9. Colorization performance comparisons. Mean and standard deviation values for each question are reported for the baseline [44] and our PCN. Our PCN scores higher on all of the questions, showing that users are more satisfied with PCN.

the generated palettes match the text inputs. The second part is a survey that compares the performance of our palette-based colorization model to another state-of-the-art colorization model. 53 participants took part in our study.

Part I: Matching Between Text and Generated Palettes. Our goal is to generate a palette with a strong semantic connection with the given text input. A natural way to evaluate it is to quantify the degree of connection between the text input and the generated palette, in comparison to the same text input and its ground truth palette. Given a text input, its generated palette, and the ground truth palette, we ask human observers to select the palette that best suits the text input. A fooling rate (FR) in this study indicates the relative number of generated palettes chosen over ground truth palettes. More people choosing the generated palette results in a higher FR. This measure has often been used to assess the quality of colorization results [11,44]. We will use this metric to measure how much a text input matches its generated palette.

Study Procedure. Users participate in the user study over TPN and Heer and Stone's model [12]. Each consists of 30 evaluations. We randomly choose a single data item out of 992 test data and show the text input along with the generated palette and the ground truth palette.

Results. In Table 1, we measure the FR score for each person and compute the mean and the standard deviation (std) of all of the scores from participants. Max and min scores represent the highest and the lowest FR scores, respectively, recorded by a single person. While Heer and Stone's model [12] shows low FR of 39.6%, our TPN has the FR of 56.2% while maintaining a high level of diversity and multimodality. The FR of 56.2% indicates that the generated palettes are indistinguishable to human eyes and sometimes even match the input text better than the ground truth palettes. Note that the standard deviation of 12.7% implies diverse responses to the same data pairs.

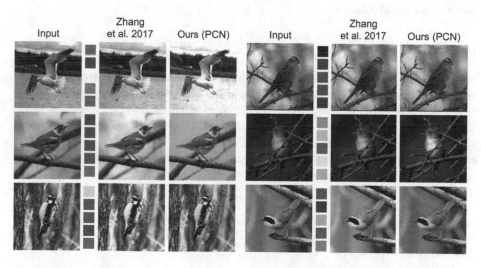

Fig. 10. We compare colorization results with previous work [44]. The five-color palette used for colorization is shown next to the input grayscale image. Note that our PCN performs better at applying various colors included in the palette.

Part II: Colorization Comparisons. In this part of the user study, we conduct a survey on the performance of the PCN given palette inputs. Users are asked to answer five questions based on the given grayscale image, the color palette, and the colored image. For quantitative comparison, we set a state-of-the-art colorization model [44] as our baseline. This model originally contains local and global hint networks. In our implementation of the baseline model, we utilize the global hint networks to infuse our generated palette to the main colorization networks. Note that we modified the baseline model to fit our task. Our novelty is the ability to produce high-quality colorization with only five colors of a palette while our baseline [44] needs 313 bins of ab gamut. Our model is able to colorize with limited information due to novel components such as the conditional adversarial loss and feeding the palette into skip-connection layers.

Study Procedure. We show colorization results of our PCN and the baseline model one-by-one in a random order. Then, we ask each participant to answer five different questions (shown in Fig. 9) based on a five-point Likert scale. The focus of our questions is to evaluate how well the palette was used in colorizing the given grayscale image. The total number of data samples per test is 15.

Results. The resulting statistics are reported in Fig. 9. Our PCN achieves higher scores than the baseline model across all the questions. We can infer that the palettes generated by our model are preferred over palettes created by a human hand. Since our model learns consistent patterns from a large number of human-generated palette-text pairs, our model may have generated color palettes that more users could relate to.

6   Conclusions

We proposed a generative model that can produce multiple palettes from rich text input and colorize grayscale images using the generated palettes. Evaluation results confirm that our TPN can generate plausible color palettes from text input and can incorporate the multimodal nature of colors. Qualitative results on our PCN also show that the diverse colors in a palette are effectively reflected in the colorization results. Future work includes extending our model to a broader range of tasks requiring color recommendation and conducting the detailed analysis of our dataset.

Acknowledgement. This work was partially supported by the National Research Foundation of Korea (NRF) grant funded by the Korean government (MSIP) (No. NRF2016R1C1B2015924).

References

1. Ahn, H., Ha, T., Choi, Y., Yoo, H., Oh, S.: Text2Action: generative adversarial synthesis from language to action. In: Proceedings of the IEEE International Conference on Robotics and Automation (ICRA) (2018)

2. Bahdanau, D., Cho, K., Bengio, Y.: Neural machine translation by jointly learning to align and translate. In: Proceedings of the International Conference on Learning Representations (ICLR) (2014)

3. Chang, H., Fried, O., Liu, Y., DiVerdi, S., Finkelstein, A.: Palette-based photo recoloring. ACM Trans. Graph. (TOG) **34**(4), 139 (2015)

4. Charpiat, G., Hofmann, M., Schölkopf, B.: Automatic image colorization via multimodal predictions. In: Forsyth, D., Torr, P., Zisserman, A. (eds.) ECCV 2008. LNCS, vol. 5304, pp. 126–139. Springer, Heidelberg (2008). https://doi.org/10.1007/978-3-540-88690-7_10

5. Cho, J., Yun, S., Lee, K., Choi, J.Y.: PaletteNet: image recolorization with given color palette. In: Proceedings of the IEEE Conference on Computer Vision and Pattern Recognition Workshops (2017)

6. Cho, K., et al.: Learning phrase representations using RNN encoder-decoder for statistical machine translation. In: Conference on Empirical Methods in Natural Language Processing (EMNLP) (2014)

7. Choi, Y., Choi, M., Kim, M., Ha, J.W., Kim, S., Choo, J.: StarGAN: unified generative adversarial networks for multi-domain image-to-image translation. In: Proceedings of the IEEE Conference on Computer Vision and Pattern Recognition (CVPR) (2017)

8. Chuang, J., Stone, M., Hanrahan, P.: A probabilistic model of the categorical association between colors. In: Proceedings of the IS&T Color and Imaging Conference (CIC), vol. 2008 (2008)

9. Crozier, W.: The psychology of colour preferences. Color. Technol. **26**(1), 63–72 (1996)

10. De Bortoli, M., Maroto, J.: Colours across cultures: translating colours in interactive marketing communications. In: Proceedings of the European Languages and the Implementation of Communication and Information Technologies (ELICIT) (2001)

11. Guadarrama, S., Dahl, R., Bieber, D., Norouzi, M., Shlens, J., Murphy, K.: Pix-Color: pixel recursive colorization. In: Proceedings of the British Machine Vision Conference (BMVC) (2017)

12. Heer, J., Stone, M.: Color naming models for color selection, image editing and palette design. In: Proceedings of the SIGCHI Conference on Human Factors in Computing Systems (SIGCHI) (2012)

13. Isola, P., Zhu, J.Y., Zhou, T., Efros, A.A.: Image-to-image translation with conditional adversarial networks. In: Proc. the IEEE Conference on Computer Vision and Pattern Recognition (CVPR) (2017)

14. Jahanian, A., Keshvari, S., Vishwanathan, S., Allebach, J.P.: Colors-messengers of concepts: visual design mining for learning color semantics. ACM Trans. Comput.-Hum. Interact. (TOCHI) **24**(1), 1 (2017)

15. Kawakami, K., Dyer, C., Routledge, B.R., Smith, N.A.: Character sequence models for colorful words. In: Proceedings of the Conference on Empirical Methods in Natural Language Processing (EMNLP) (2016)

16. Kim, T., Cha, M., Kim, H., Lee, J., Kim, J.: Learning to discover cross-domain relations with generative adversarial networks. In: Proceedings of the International Conference on Machine Learning (ICML) (2017)

17. Kingma, D.P., Ba, J.: Adam: a method for stochastic optimization. In: Proceedings of the International Conference on Learning Representations (ICLR) (2014)

18. Kobayashi, S.: Color image scale (2009). http://www.ncd-ri.co.jp/english/main_0104.html

19. Labrecque, L.I., Milne, G.R.: Exciting red and competent blue: the importance of color in marketing. J. Acad. Mark. Sci. **40**(5), 711–727 (2012)
20. Li, X., Zhao, H., Nie, G., Huang, H.: Image recoloring using geodesic distance based color harmonization. Comput. Vis. Media **1**(2), 143–155 (2015)
21. Liu, Y., Cohen, M., Uyttendaele, M., Rusinkiewicz, S.: AutoStyle: automatic style transfer from image collections to users' images. In: Computer Graphics Forum (CGF), vol. 33, no. 4 (2014)
22. Luong, M.T., Pham, H., Manning, C.D.: Effective approaches to attention-based neural machine translation. In: Proceedings of the Conference on Empirical Methods in Natural Language Processing (EMNLP) (2015)
23. McMahan, B., Stone, M.: A Bayesian model of grounded color semantics. Trans. Assoc. Comput. Linguist. (TACL) **3**(1), 103–115 (2015)
24. Mirza, M., Osindero, S.: Conditional generative adversarial nets. arXiv preprint arXiv:1411.1784 (2014)
25. Monroe, W., Hawkins, R.X., Goodman, N.D., Potts, C.: Colors in context: a pragmatic neural model for grounded language understanding. Trans. Assoc. Comput. Linguist. (ACL) (2017)
26. Munroe, R.: Color survey results (2010). http://blog.xkcd.com/2010/05/03/color-surveyresults
27. Murray, N., Skaff, S., Marchesotti, L., Perronnin, F.: Toward automatic and flexible concept transfer. Comput. Graph. **36**(6) (2012)
28. Pathak, D., Krahenbuhl, P., Donahue, J., Darrell, T., Efros, A.A.: Context encoders: feature learning by inpainting. In: Proceedings of the IEEE Conference on Computer Vision and Pattern Recognition (CVPR) (2016)
29. Pennington, J., Socher, R., Manning, C.: Glove: global vectors for word representation. In: Proceedings of the Conference on Empirical Methods in Natural Language Processing (EMNLP) (2014)
30. Radford, A., Metz, L., Chintala, S.: Unsupervised representation learning with deep convolutional generative adversarial networks. In: Proceedings of the International Conference on Learning Representations (ICLR) (2015)
31. Reed, S., Akata, Z., Lee, H., Schiele, B.: Learning deep representations of fine-grained visual descriptions. In: Proceedings of the IEEE Conference on Computer Vision and Pattern Recognition (CVPR) (2016)
32. Reed, S., Akata, Z., Yan, X., Logeswaran, L., Schiele, B., Lee, H.: Generative adversarial text to image synthesis. In: Proceedings of the International Conference on Machine Learning (ICML) (2016)
33. Ronneberger, O., Fischer, P., Brox, T.: U-Net: convolutional networks for biomedical image segmentation. In: Navab, N., Hornegger, J., Wells, W.M., Frangi, A.F. (eds.) MICCAI 2015. LNCS, vol. 9351, pp. 234–241. Springer, Cham (2015). https://doi.org/10.1007/978-3-319-24574-4_28
34. Russakovsky, O.: ImageNet large scale visual recognition challenge. Int. J. Comput. Vis. (IJCV) **115**(3), 211–252 (2015)
35. Sharma, G., Wu, W., Dalal, E.N.: The CIEDE2000 color-difference formula: implementation notes, supplementary test data, and mathematical observations. Color Res. Appl. **30**(1), 21–30 (2005)
36. Solli, M., Lenz, R.: Color semantics for image indexing. In: Proceedings of the Conference on Colour in Graphics Imaging and Vision (CGIV) (2010)
37. Sutskever, I., Martens, J., Hinton, G.E.: Generating text with recurrent neural networks. In: Proceedings of the International Conference on Machine Learning (ICML) (2011)

38. Sutskever, I., Vinyals, O., Le, Q.V.: Sequence to sequence learning with neural networks. In: Advances in Neural Information Processing Systems (NIPS) (2014)
39. Tang, D., Qin, B., Liu, T.: Document modeling with gated recurrent neural network for sentiment classification. In: Proceedings of the Conference on Empirical Methods in Natural Language Processing (EMNLP) (2015)
40. Vaswani, A., et al.: Attention is all you need. In: Advances in Neural Information Processing Systems (NIPS) (2017)
41. Wah, C., Branson, S., Welinder, P., Perona, P., Belongie, S.: The Caltech-UCSD Birds-200-2011 dataset. Technical report CNS-TR-2011-001, California Institute of Technology (2011)
42. Xiao, Y., Zhou, P., Zheng, Y.: Interactive deep colorization with simultaneous global and local inputs. arXiv preprint arXiv:1801.09083 (2018)
43. Zhang, H., et al.: StackGAN: text to photo-realistic image synthesis with stacked generative adversarial networks. In: Proceedings of the IEEE International Conference on Computer Vision (ICCV) (2017)
44. Zhang, R., et al.: Real-time user-guided image colorization with learned deep priors. ACM Trans. Graph. (TOG) (2017)

Efficient Global Point Cloud Registration by Matching Rotation Invariant Features Through Translation Search

Yinlong Liu[1,2] [iD], Chen Wang[1,2] [iD], Zhijian Song[1,2(✉)] [iD],
and Manning Wang[1,2(✉)] [iD]

[1] Digital Medical Research Center, School of Basic Medical Science,
Fudan University, Shanghai 200032, China
{yinlongliu15,wangchen17,zjsong,mnwang}@fudan.edu.cn
[2] Shanghai Key Laboratory of Medical Imaging Computing and Computer Assisted
Intervention, Shanghai 200032, China

Abstract. Three-dimensional rigid point cloud registration has many applications in computer vision and robotics. Local methods tend to fail, causing global methods to be needed, when the relative transformation is large or the overlap ratio is small. Most existing global methods utilize BnB optimization over the 6D parameter space of $SE(3)$. Such methods are usually very slow because the time complexity of BnB optimization is exponential in the dimensionality of the parameter space. In this paper, we decouple the optimization of translation and rotation, and we propose a fast BnB algorithm to globally optimize the 3D translation parameter first. The optimal rotation is then calculated by utilizing the global optimal translation found by the BnB algorithm. The separate optimization of translation and rotation is realized by using a newly proposed rotation invariant feature. Experiments on challenging data sets demonstrate that the proposed method outperforms state-of-the-art global methods in terms of both speed and accuracy.

Keywords: Point cloud registration · Global optimization
Rotation invariant feature

1 Introduction

Three-dimensional rigid point cloud registration is a common problem in fields such as computer vision, robotics, and computer-assisted intervention [1–4]. Traditional local methods suffice only when the relative transformation is small and there is a large proportion of true overlap [1–3]. In contrast, a global method is

---

Y. Liu and C. Wang—Contributed equally to this work.

Electronic supplementary material The online version of this chapter (https://doi.org/10.1007/978-3-030-01258-8_28) contains supplementary material, which is available to authorized users.

V. Ferrari et al. (Eds.): ECCV 2018, LNCS 11216, pp. 460–474, 2018.
https://doi.org/10.1007/978-3-030-01258-8_28

needed when there is a large relative transformation or when the overlap proportion is small. Example applications include loop closing in simultaneous localization and mapping (SLAM) [1] and spatial registration in computer-assisted intervention [5]. In recent years, there has been a surge in the use of branch-and-bound (BnB) optimization to globally register 3D point clouds. However, the time complexity of BnB optimization is exponential in the dimensionality of the problem. Most existing global methods optimize an objective function in the parameter space of $SE(3)$, which has a dimensionality of six; thus, they are usually very slow.

Motivated by [6], in which $SE(3)$ is decoupled into $SO(3)$ and R^3 and the rotation and translation are optimized separately in $SO(3)$ and R^3, respectively, we also optimize the rotation and translation separately in lower-dimensional spaces to achieve high efficiency via a newly proposed rotation invariant feature. In the method presented in [6], BnB optimization is first used to globally optimize the rotation to align translation invariant features, namely, the surface normal distributions, constructed from the original point clouds. Once the globally optimal rotation in $SO(3)$ has been obtained, BnB optimization in R^3 is performed to calculate the translation. In contrast to [6], we propose a new rotation invariant feature (RIF) that allows us to first globally optimize the translation in R^3 to align the features computed for the original point clouds. The RIF we propose is a triple constructed from a pair of points. The first two elements of the RIF are the distances from the two points to the origin, and the third element is the distance between the two points. Conceptually, the elements of this RIF are the edge lengths of the triangle formed by the two points and the origin, which are obviously invariant with respect to the rotation of the two points around the origin. We maximize an objective function defined in terms of the consensus set between the two RIF sets constructed from the two point clouds to be registered and derive an upper bound on this objective function over the parameter space of translation in R^3. An efficient BnB optimization algorithm is developed based on this upper bound to calculate the translation with guaranteed global optimality. Experiments using real data demonstrate the efficiency and accuracy of the proposed 6D rigid point cloud registration method under challenging real-world conditions, such as large relative transformation and partial overlap.

2   Related Work

Given two 3D point clouds $\mathcal{X}$ and $\mathcal{Y}$, performing 3D rigid registration between them is the process of finding an optimal transformation $\mathbf{T} \in SE(3)$ to align them, as follows:

$$\mathbf{T}^* = \underset{\mathbf{T} \in SE(3)}{\arg\max} \quad O(\mathcal{Y}, \mathbf{T}(\mathcal{X})) \tag{1}$$

where $\mathcal{X}$ is the moving point cloud, $\mathcal{Y}$ is the reference point cloud, and O is a function that measures the alignment. If some correspondences between these two point clouds are known, then the transformation can be robustly calculated analytically. However, this registration becomes a difficult optimization problem if no correspondence is known because the objective function O is highly non-convex.

2.1 Local Methods

As a non-convex optimization problem, point cloud registration is first locally solved with iterative approaches, the most popular of which is the iterative closest point (ICP) method [7]. The ICP method starts from an initial transformation and iterates between finding correspondences with the current transformation and updating the transformation with the newly established correspondences. The optimization scheme of the ICP algorithm is of the expectation maximization (EM) type and can converge only to a local optimum. In addition, the original ICP algorithm finds point-to-point correspondences in accordance with the L2 distance by minimizing the average distance between the corresponding point pairs found during iteration. The objective function and optimization scheme of the ICP algorithm make it very sensitive to outliers, and its convergence basin is very small.

A great number of variants have been proposed to improve the convergence and robustness of the ICP algorithm [8]. Another line of research for improving the convergence is to replace the objective function of the ICP algorithm with a new objective function defined in terms of the probability density [9]. In these methods, the probability densities are constructed from the original point clouds by means of kernels, such as the Gaussian kernel, and the difference between the two probability densities constructed from the two point clouds to be registered is minimized. This kind of objective function can be made much smoother than the ICP objective function can, thereby enlarging the basin of convergence. However, all these methods can still converge only to a local optimum.

2.2 Global Methods

The first attempts at global point cloud registration used heuristic methods, such as simulated annealing [10] or particle swarm optimization [11]. Methods of this kind have an increased probability of reaching the global optimum regardless of the initialization conditions. However, global optimality cannot be guaranteed.

The current trend is to solve the global point cloud registration problem using guaranteed global optimization methods. Most of these methods use BnB optimization, and almost every newly developed method involves deriving a new bound on the objective function. [12] is a pioneer work on global point cloud registration in which the point cloud registration problem is parameterized in terms of both transformation and correspondence and a simplified problem under rotation alone is solved by combining BnB optimization with Lipschitz optimization. Go-ICP [13] is the first practical global point cloud registration method. Based on a lemma presented in [14], which states that when a vector is rotated through two rotations, the angular difference between the two new vectors is no greater than the angular difference between the two rotations, Go-ICP establishes a geometric bound on a point rotated through an arbitrary rotation in a cubic branch of $SO(3)$. Go-ICP optimizes the same objective function as that of the traditional ICP algorithm via BnB optimization, and a trimming technique is used to address outliers. [15] proposes a tighter bound and optimizes a more robust objective function based on a consensus set, and this bound is further tightened in [16]. Another way to address outliers is to define the objective function in terms of the probability density, as is done in GOGMA [17], which minimizes the L2 distance between the two probability densities constructed from the original point clouds with Gaussian kernels.

The above global point cloud registration methods optimize an objective function in the six-dimensional space of $SE(3)$. Asymmetric point matching (APM) optimizes an objective function defined in terms of both transformation and point correspondence matrix [18]. Although the dimensionality of the original parameter space is very high, a bound is developed in a lower-dimensional space, which has the same dimensionality as that of the spatial transformation, by assuming a point-to-point correspondence. This assumption makes it difficult for APM to register partially overlapping point clouds or point clouds with gross outliers. The advantage of this method is that it can perform affine registration.

The time complexity of BnB optimization is exponential in the dimensionality of the problem. Therefore, existing global point cloud registration methods are usually very slow, primarily because the parameter space of $SE(3)$ has six dimensions. One way to improve the time efficiency is to decouple $SE(3)$ into $SO(3)$ and R^3 and then optimize the 3D rotation and the 3D translation separately. [6] utilizes translation invariant features to first optimize the 3D rotation and then optimizes the 3D translation using the calculated globally optimal rotation; however, the process of constructing the translation invariant features is very time consuming.

2.3   Contribution

This paper also optimizes rotation and translation separately to achieve high efficiency. Our first contribution is that we propose a simple RIF that allows us to first globally search for the translation between two point clouds to align the features constructed from the original point clouds. We define a robust objective function based on a consensus set and derive a tight bound to achieve fast BnB optimization for the translation search. Second, we develop a 6D point cloud registration algorithm on the basis of the global translation search. Experiments on challenging real data demonstrate the superiority of the proposed method over state-of-the-art global methods in terms of both run time and accuracy.

3   Method

3.1   Rotation Invariant Feature

Let $\mathcal{Y} = \{\mathbf{y}_j\}_{j=1}^{Y}$ and $\mathcal{X} = \{\mathbf{x}_i\}_{i=1}^{X}$ be two 3D point clouds, which are related by a 3D rigid transformation from $\mathcal{X}$ to $\mathcal{Y}$. For a pair of corresponding points $\mathbf{y}_j$ and $\mathbf{x}_i$, we have

$$\mathbf{y}_j = \mathbf{R}^*(\mathbf{x}_i + \mathbf{t}^*) \tag{2}$$

where $\mathbf{t}^* \in R^3$ and $\mathbf{R}^* \in SO(3)$ are the translation and rotation, respectively, from $\mathcal{X}$ to $\mathcal{Y}$.

For a pair of points $\{\mathbf{x}_{i1}, \mathbf{x}_{i2}\}$ from the moving point cloud, we propose the construction of a triple $\{\|\mathbf{x}_{i1}\|, \|\mathbf{x}_{i2}\|, \|\mathbf{x}_{i1} - \mathbf{x}_{i2}\|\}$, where $\| \cdot \|$ denotes the Euclidean norm in R^3. As shown in Fig. 1, the three elements of this triple are the edge lengths of the triangle formed by the two points $\mathbf{x}_{i1}$ and $\mathbf{x}_{i2}$ and the origin. Obviously, this triple is invariant with respect to rotation around the origin, and thus, we call it a RIF. This means that for any $\mathbf{R} \in SO(3)$, we have

$$\left\{ \begin{array}{c} \|\mathbf{R}\mathbf{x}_{i1}\| \\ \|\mathbf{R}\mathbf{x}_{i2}\| \\ \|\mathbf{R}(\mathbf{x}_{i1} - \mathbf{x}_{i2})\| \end{array} \right\} = \left\{ \begin{array}{c} \|\mathbf{x}_{i1}\| \\ \|\mathbf{x}_{i2}\| \\ \|\mathbf{x}_{i1} - \mathbf{x}_{i2}\| \end{array} \right\} \tag{3}$$

Figure 1(b–d) show the changes in RIFs with the translation of points.

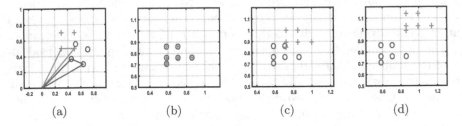

(a)   (b)   (c)   (d)

Fig. 1. Illustration of RIFs and how they change with translation. Only the first two dimensions of the RIFs are illustrated because the third dimension does not change with the translation of the points. (a) Four reference points (blue circles) and four moving points (red crosses). There is a relative rotation but no relative translation between the two point clouds. The two triangles represent two RIFs constructed from corresponding point pairs from the reference and moving point clouds. (b) RIFs constructed from the reference and moving clouds in (a). The two sets of RIFs match each other because there is no relative translation between the reference point cloud and the moving point cloud. (c) and (d) The RIFs when there are relative translations of (0.1, 0.1) and (0.2, 0.2), respectively, between the two point clouds. (Color figure online)

3.2   Objective Function for the Translation Search

We use $\mathbf{p}_{i1,i2} = \{\|\mathbf{x}_{i1}\|, \|\mathbf{x}_{i2}\|, \|\mathbf{x}_{i1} - \mathbf{x}_{i2}\|\}$ to denote the RIF constructed from a pair of moving points $\{\mathbf{x}_{i1}, \mathbf{x}_{i2}\}$ and use $\mathbf{q}_{j1,j2} = \{\|\mathbf{y}_{j1}\|, \|\mathbf{y}_{j2}\|, \|\mathbf{y}_{j1} - \mathbf{y}_{j2}\|\}$ to denote the RIF constructed from a pair of reference points $\{\mathbf{y}_{j1}, \mathbf{y}_{j2}\}$. Following equation (3), if the two point pairs are related by a translation $\mathbf{t}$ and a rotation $\mathbf{R}$, we have

$$\mathbf{q}_{j1,j2} = \left\{ \begin{array}{c} \|\mathbf{y}_{j1}\| \\ \|\mathbf{y}_{j2}\| \\ \|\mathbf{y}_{j1} - \mathbf{y}_{j2}\| \end{array} \right\} = \left\{ \begin{array}{c} \|\mathbf{R}(\mathbf{x}_{i1} + \mathbf{t})\| \\ \|\mathbf{R}(\mathbf{x}_{i2} + \mathbf{t})\| \\ \|\mathbf{R}(\mathbf{x}_{i1} - \mathbf{x}_{i2})\| \end{array} \right\} = \left\{ \begin{array}{c} \|\mathbf{x}_{i1} + \mathbf{t}\| \\ \|\mathbf{x}_{i2} + \mathbf{t}\| \\ \|\mathbf{x}_{i1} - \mathbf{x}_{i2}\| \end{array} \right\} := F(\mathbf{p}_{i1,i2}, \mathbf{t}) \tag{4}$$

We find that the two RIFs are related by the translation $\mathbf{t}$, and we define the function $F(\mathbf{t})$ to express this relationship. The parameter space of the function $F(\mathbf{t})$ is R^3. This means that if two point clouds are related by a translation $\mathbf{t}$ and a rotation $\mathbf{R}$, then the RIFs constructed from corresponding point pairs are related only by the translation $\mathbf{t}$ through the function $F(\mathbf{t})$.

Let $\mathcal{Q} = \{\mathbf{q}_n\}_{n=1}^Q$ be the set of RIFs constructed from point pairs $\{\mathbf{y}_{j1}, \mathbf{y}_{j2}\}$, where $\mathbf{y}_{j1}, \mathbf{y}_{j2} \in \mathcal{Y}$ and $j1 \neq j2$. Let $\mathcal{P} = \{\mathbf{p}_m\}_{m=1}^P$ be the set of RIFs constructed from point pairs $\{\mathbf{x}_{i1}, \mathbf{x}_{i2}\}$, where $\mathbf{x}_{i1}, \mathbf{x}_{i2} \in \mathcal{X}$ and $i1 \neq i2$. The problem of finding the optimal translation from $\mathcal{X}$ to $\mathcal{Y}$ becomes the following optimization problem:

$$\mathbf{t}^* = \arg\max_{\mathbf{t} \in R^3} \quad E(\mathcal{Q}, F(\mathcal{P}, \mathbf{t})) \tag{5}$$

where $E(\mathbf{t})$ is a function that measures the alignment between two RIF sets. By solving the optimization problem in (5) over R^3, we can find the optimal $\mathbf{t}^*$, which forms part of the solution to the optimization problem in (1) over $SE(3)$.

To make the objective function robust to outliers, we define $E(\mathbf{t})$ on the basis of a consensus set as follows:

$$E(\mathcal{Q}, F(\mathcal{P}, \mathbf{t})) = \sum_m \max_n \lfloor \|F(\mathbf{p}_m, \mathbf{t}) - \mathbf{q}_n\|_\infty \leq \varepsilon \rfloor \tag{6}$$

where $\lfloor \cdot \rfloor$ is an indicator function that returns 1 if the condition $\cdot$ is true and 0 otherwise. $\|\cdot\|_\infty$ is the L-infinity norm in R^3 and ε is the inlier threshold. The size of both $\mathcal{Q}$ and $\mathcal{P}$ is very large. From the definition of a RIF, we can see that the third element of a RIF, which is the distance between the two points in the pair, is invariant with respect to translation. This means that the third elements of the corresponding RIFs in $\mathcal{Q}$ and $\mathcal{P}$ are equal to each other. In practice, we do not need to match the entirety of $\mathcal{Q}$ and $\mathcal{P}$. Instead, we match a subset of the RIFs in $\mathcal{Q}$ and $\mathcal{P}$, the third elements of which fall within a specific range. We denote these two subsets by $\mathcal{Q}' = \{\mathbf{q}_n\}_{n=1}^{Q'}$ and $\mathbf{P}' = \{\mathbf{p}_m\}_{m=1}^{P'}$, and the actual objective function used in this paper is

$$E(\mathcal{Q}', F(\mathcal{P}', \mathbf{t})) = \sum_m \max_n \lfloor \|F(\mathbf{p}_m, \mathbf{t}) - \mathbf{q}_n\|_\infty \leq \varepsilon \rfloor \tag{7}$$

3.3   Bounds and Branch-and-Bound-Based Algorithm

To maximize (7) via BnB optimization, we need an upper bound on this objective function in a branch of the parameter space. In our BnB algorithm, we search for the optimal translation in a cube in R^3 and iteratively divide the parameter space into sub-cubes. As shown in Fig. 2, for a translation cube $\mathbb{T}$ with a diagonal length of $2r$ and centred at $\mathbf{t}_c$, we have

$$\|\mathbf{x} + \mathbf{t}_c\| - r \leq \|\mathbf{x} + \mathbf{t}\| \leq \|\mathbf{x} + \mathbf{t}_c\| + r \tag{8}$$

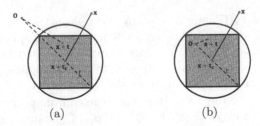

Fig. 2. Bounds on the distance from the origin to a point translated by a translation cube. Two-dimensional coordinates are used for clearer illustration. The translation cube is $\mathbb{T}$, and the possible positions of point $\mathbf{x}$ after being translated by an arbitrary $\mathbf{t} \in \mathbb{T}$ are represented by the grey square. The diagonal length of $\mathbb{T}$ is $2r$, and its centre is at $\mathbf{t}_c$. Therefore, the distance from the origin to an arbitrary point in the grey square is between $\|\mathbf{x} + \mathbf{t}_c\| - r$ and $\|\mathbf{x} + \mathbf{t}_c\| + r$. (a) and (b) illustrate the two cases in which the origin is located outside and inside, respectively, of the circle centred at $\mathbf{t}_c$ with a radius of r.

Let $\mathbf{p}_m$ be the RIF constructed from a point pair $\{\mathbf{x}_{m1}, \mathbf{x}_{m2}\}$ from the moving point cloud and let $\mathbf{q}_n$ be the RIF constructed from a point pair $\{\mathbf{y}_{n1}, \mathbf{y}_{n2}\}$ from the reference point cloud. Then, for any $\mathbf{t} \in \mathbb{T}$, using formula (8), we have

$$\|F(\mathbf{p}_m, \mathbf{t}) - \mathbf{q}_n\|_\infty = \left\| \left\{ \begin{array}{c} \|\mathbf{x}_{m1} + \mathbf{t}\| - \|\mathbf{y}_{n1}\| \\ \|\mathbf{x}_{m2} + \mathbf{t}\| - \|\mathbf{y}_{n2}\| \\ \|\mathbf{x}_{m1} - \mathbf{x}_{m2}\| - \|\mathbf{y}_{n1} - \mathbf{y}_{n2}\| \end{array} \right\} \right\|_\infty := C(\mathbf{t}) \quad (9)$$

where $\|\mathbf{x}_{m1} - \mathbf{x}_{m2}\| - \|\mathbf{y}_{n1} - \mathbf{y}_{n2}\|$ is constant with respect to $\mathbf{t}$. Because we can compute the bounds on $\|\mathbf{x}_{m1} + \mathbf{t}\|$ and $\|\mathbf{x}_{m2} + \mathbf{t}\|$ from equation (8), we can easily compute the bounds on the absolute values of $\|\mathbf{x}_{m1} + \mathbf{t}\| - \|\mathbf{y}_{n1}\|$ and $\|\mathbf{x}_{m2} + \mathbf{t}\| - \|\mathbf{y}_{n2}\|$. Then we can compute the upper and lower bounds on $\|F(\mathbf{p}_m, \mathbf{t}) - \mathbf{q}_n\|_\infty$, and we denote this lower bound by $\underline{C}(\mathbf{t})$. Thus, we have

$$\|F(\mathbf{p}_m, \mathbf{t}) - \mathbf{q}_n\|_\infty \geq \underline{C}(\mathbf{t}) \quad (10)$$

It follows that

$$\lfloor \|F(\mathbf{p}_m, \mathbf{t}) - \mathbf{q}_n\|_\infty \leq \varepsilon \rfloor \leq \lfloor \underline{C}(\mathbf{t}) \leq \varepsilon \rfloor \quad (11)$$

Then, we can define the upper-bound function as

$$\overline{E}(\mathbb{T}) = \sum_m \max_n \lfloor \underline{C}(\mathbf{t}) \leq \varepsilon \rfloor \quad (12)$$

For any $\mathbf{t} \in \mathbb{T}$, we have

$$E(\mathcal{Q}', F(\mathcal{P}', \mathbf{t})) \leq \overline{E}(\mathbb{T}) \quad (13)$$

Utilizing the upper bound given by formula (12), we can search the translation space to find the globally optimal translation that maximizes the objective function (7). The algorithm is outlined in **Algorithm 1**.

3.4   Six-Dimensional Registration

Once the globally optimal translation $\mathbf{t}^*$ between $\mathcal{X}$ and $\mathcal{Y}$ has been found, it is easy to calculate the optimal rotation $\mathbf{R}^*$ between the two point clouds. For

---

Algorithm 1. Globally Optimal Translation Search Based on RIFs

---

Input: Point sets $\mathcal{X}$ and $\mathcal{Y}$
Output: Optimal translation $\mathbf{t}^*$ between $\mathcal{X}$ and $\mathcal{Y}$.
1 Construct two sets of RIF triples, $\mathcal{P}'$ and $\mathcal{Q}'$.
2 Initialize translation branch $\mathbb{T}_0$; $E^* \leftarrow 0, \mathbf{t}^* \leftarrow \mathbf{0}$. Insert $\mathbb{T}_0$ into queue q with
   priority $\overline{E}(\mathbb{T}_0)$.
3 **while** q *is not empty* **do**
4 $\quad$ Obtain the highest-priority cube $\mathbb{T}$ from q.
5 $\quad$ **if** $\overline{E}(\mathbb{T}) = E^*$ **then**
6 $\quad$ $\quad$| Terminate.
7 $\quad$ **end**
8 $\quad$ $\mathbf{t}_c \leftarrow$ centre of cube $\mathbb{T}$
9 $\quad$ **if** $E(\mathbf{t}_c) > E^*$ **then**
10 $\quad$ $\quad$| Update $E^* \longleftarrow E(\mathbf{t}_c), \mathbf{t}^* \leftarrow \mathbf{t}_c$
11 $\quad$ **end**
12 $\quad$ Subdivide $\mathbb{T}$ into eight cubes $\{\mathbb{T}_d\}_{d=1}^8$.
13 $\quad$ **for** *each* $\mathbb{T}_d$ **do**
14 $\quad$ $\quad$ **if** $\overline{E}(\mathbb{T}_d) > E^*$ **then**
15 $\quad$ $\quad$ $\quad$| Insert $\mathbb{T}_d$ into q with priority $\overline{E}(\mathbb{T}_d)$.
16 $\quad$ $\quad$ **end**
17 $\quad$ **end**
18 **end**
19 Obtain the optimal translation $\mathbf{t}^*$.

---

example, we could use the global rotation search methods presented in [15] or [16]; however, the optimal rotation can actually be obtained in a much easier way. When we obtain the optimal $\mathbf{t}^*$ via **Algorithm 1**, we also obtain a set of consensus RIFs between $\mathcal{P}'$ and $\mathcal{Q}'$, which provide us with potential correspondences between points in the original point clouds $\mathcal{X}$ and $\mathcal{Y}$. Of course, there will be some outliers among these correspondences, and the problem of estimating $\mathbf{R}^*$ becomes a robust estimation problem, which can be solved quickly and reliably. In this paper, we estimate $\mathbf{R}^*$ by means of the RANdom SAmple Consensus (RANSAC) algorithm [19]. We refer to our 6D rigid registration method as GoTS. Many global optimization methods sacrifice accuracy for speed and global optimality, and a subsequent local refinement is performed to improve accuracy. Similarly, a local refinement procedure can be added to GoTS; we refer to the algorithm with local refinement as GoTS$^+$.

4 Experiments and Results

In this section, we report the results of evaluating the performance of GoTS and GoTS$^+$ using many different point clouds and compare the proposed algorithms against the following three global methods: Go-ICP [13], Glob-GM [15] and APM [18]. We did not perform comparisons with the methods of [6] and [17], which use GPUs. GoTS and GoTS$^+$ were implemented in MATLAB. The code for the other methods was obtained from the authors. In GoTS, a range is set for the third elements of the RIFs that are used to construct $\mathcal{P}'$ and $\mathcal{Q}'$ for the translation search. We set the lower bound of this range to 65% of the shortest extension of the original point cloud in the X, Y and Z directions, and set the range width to 0.01 times inlier threshold. In the supplementary material, we studied the registration time with respect to the range width used in choosing the RIFs for translation search. The original point clouds used in these experiments are very dense, and we down-sampled them using the *pcdownsample* function of MATLAB with a specified *gridsize*. In the experiments with synthetic data in Sects. 4.1 and 4.2, we scaled the points to make them fall within a cube of $[-1, 1]^3$ and set 0.01 as the inlier threshold for GoTS; in the experiment with real data in Sects. 4.3 and 4.4, we set *gridsize* as the inlier threshold for GoTS. In Glob-GM, the matchlist and local-refinement options were turned on. In Go-ICP, a distance transformation was used to speed up the nearest-neighbour distance calculation. All experiments were performed on a computer with a 2.80 GHz Intel(R) Core(TM) i7-7700HQ CPU and 16 GB of RAM. The run time for each method includes the method-specific pre-processing time.

4.1   Run-Time Comparison with Other Global Methods

We first compared the run times of GoTS for registering point clouds with different numbers of points to the run times of the other three methods. In this experiment, we used the *bunny* point cloud from the Stanford 3D Scanning Repository and down-sampled the original data to point clouds with different numbers of points. The down-sampled point cloud was scaled to fall within a cube of $[-1, 1]^3$ and was regarded as the moving point cloud, and it was transformed to a new position via a random transformation to form the reference point cloud. Therefore, we knew the ground-truth transformation from the moving point cloud to the reference point cloud and the point correspondence between the two point clouds. The moving point cloud was then registered to the reference point cloud with each of the four methods. For each number of points, we performed 20 registrations with different random ground-truth transformations, and the average run times with respect to the number of points are shown in Figs. 3(a) and (b). The run time of Glob-GM and APM exceeded 1000 s when registering 400 points. To better illustrate the difference between GoTS and Go-ICP, we show the run times of only these two methods in Fig. 3(b). We can see that GoTS and Go-ICP are much faster than the other two methods and that GoTS is approximately four times as fast as Go-ICP. In this experiment, all methods could successfully register the moving and reference point clouds.

Figure 3(c) shows the evolution of the upper and lower bounds of **Algorithm 1** during one registration between 1000 moving points and 1000 reference points, in which it took only 5.2 s for GoTS to converge.

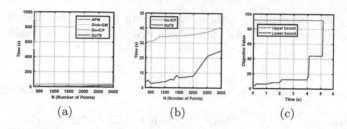

(a)   (b)   (c)

Fig. 3. (a) Run times of GoTS, Go-ICP, APM and Glob-GM with respect to the number of points. (b) Run times of only GoTS and Go-ICP with respect to the number of points, to better illustrate the run time difference between these two methods. (c) Evolution of the upper and lower bounds in the global optimal translation search method (**Algorithm 1**) as a function of time when registering 1000 points.

4.2 Robustness to Outliers

In this experiment, we evaluated the robustness of GoTS to outliers and compared it to the robustness of the other three methods. Outliers are commonly encountered in point cloud registration; in this section, we study only the influence of gross outliers, which do not belong to the true object represented by the point cloud. Gross outliers may originate from imperfections of the device used to obtain the point cloud. In the registration of partially overlapping surfaces, the points in the region that is not overlapped by the other point cloud can also be regarded as outliers; experiments focusing on this scenario are reported in the next section.

We down-sampled the *bunny* data from the Stanford 3D Scanning Repository (http://graphics.stanford.edu/data/3Dscanrep/) with a *gridsize* of 0.0121 to obtain 500 points and then scaled these points to fall within a cube of $[-1, 1]^3$. The scaled data points were used as the clean moving point cloud. Uniformly distributed random outlier points were added to this clean point cloud, and the resulting point cloud was then transformed via a random transformation to form a reference point cloud. Different numbers of outliers were added to generate reference point clouds with five different outlier percentages: 10%, 20%, 30%, 40% and 50%. Figure 4(c) and (d) show examples of reference point clouds with 10% and 50% outliers, respectively. We ran each algorithm 20 times for each outlier ratio.

Table 1 reports the root mean square errors on the inlier points for each method. Both GoTS and Go-ICP achieved high accuracy, indicating that they are both very robust to outliers. Although the errors of Go-ICP were smaller than those of GoTS, the accuracy of GoTS is sufficiently high in practice. The errors of GoTS$^+$ show that two point clouds can be perfectly aligned by means of a subsequent local refinement, which requires less than one second of additional time. The registration error of Glob-GM is much higher than that of GoTS, and it increases as the outlier ratio increases. Considering that all the points lie in a cube with an edge length of 2, the registration errors of Glob-GM indicate that it fails in aligning the two point clouds in many cases. The errors of APM are even higher; the reason for these large errors may be that the assumption of a one-to-one correspondence that is adopted in APM is not valid in these experiments with outliers.

Table 1. Root mean square error between corresponding inlier points after registration.

Method	GoTS	GoTS⁺	Go-ICP	Glob-GM	APM
10%	1.03E−02	1.38E−15	8.95E−06	1.10E−01	2.17E−01
20%	1.20E−02	9.72E−16	7.51E−06	1.21E−01	-
30%	1.14E−02	9.50E−15	4.65E−06	1.14E−01	-
40%	1.09E−02	1.38E−15	4.12E−06	1.12E−01	-
50%	1.17E−02	1.19E−15	6.22E−06	1.41E−01	-

The average run times of the four algorithms with respect to the outlier ratio are shown in Fig. 4(a). The run time of APM increased rapidly as we added more outliers to the 500 inlier points and exceeded 1000 s when the outlier ratio was 20%. The run time of Glob-GM decreased when the outlier ratio was above 20%; this occurred because the algorithm terminated earlier at an incorrect solution in which the two point clouds were not aligned. Again, we plot the average run times of GoTS and Go-ICP separately in Fig. 4(b) to better illustrate the difference between them.

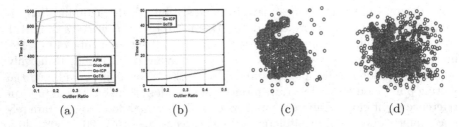

(a)   (b)   (c)   (d)

Fig. 4. (a) Run times of the four methods with respect to the outlier ratio. (b) Run times of only GoTS and Go-ICP with respect to the outlier ratio, to better illustrate the difference between them. (c) and (d) Reference point clouds with 10% outliers and 50% outliers, respectively.

4.3 Partially Overlapping Registration of Real 3D Scans

In this section, we report the results of testing the performance of the proposed method on partially overlapping point clouds using real data. We compared GoTS and GoTS⁺ to Go-ICP and Glob-GM in this experiment. APM was not used here, but we can expect that its registration error would be large in this experiment because of its difficulty in dealing with outliers.

We used bun000, bun045, bun090, ArmadilloStand60, ArmadilloStand30 and ArmadilloStand0 from the Stanford 3D Scanning Repository in this experiment. The first three point clouds are scans of *bunny* from three different directions, and the last three are scans of *Armadillo* from three different directions. The original point clouds were down-sampled to clouds consisting of 1000 to 2000 points, all of which lay in a cube with an edge length of 0.3. The ground-truth transformations between each pair of scans of the same object are provided in the data set. Using the four methods, we performed registrations between four pairs of point clouds: ArmadilloStand60/ArmadilloStand30, ArmadilloStand30/ArmadilloStand0, bun045/bun000 and bun090/bun000. The point cloud pairs before and after registration are shown in the supplementary material.

Table 2. Results of registering *Armadillo* scans using four different methods.

	ArmadilloStand60/30				ArmadilloStand30/0			
Method	GoTS	GoTS$^+$	Go-ICP	Glob-GM	GoTS	GoTS$^+$	Go-ICP	Glob-GM
Tran [m]	0.0037	0.0039	**0.0023**	0.28	0.0065	0.0063	**0.0005**	0.014
Rot [°]	0.94	**0.84**	4.13	172	1.82	**1.70**	1.73	38.10
Time [s]	**27.11**	27.33	30.67	447	**17.00**	17.22	32.08	3136

Table 3. Results of registering *bunny* scans using four different methods.

	bun045/000				bun090/000			
Method	GoTS	GoTS$^+$	Go-ICP	Glob-GM	GoTS	GoTS$^+$	Go-ICP	Glob-GM
Tran [m]	0.0058	0.0057	**0.0024**	0.025	**0.0069**	0.0074	0.10	0.14
Rot [°]	3.95	**3.94**	4.10	19.41	3.82	**3.55**	90.24	137.02
Time [s]	**14.02**	14.25	30.44	2361	**56.39**	56.62	603.63	868

The translation and rotation errors together with the run time of each method are listed in Tables 2 and 3. In these experiments, the inlier threshold of Glob-GM was set to 0.05 for the *Armadillo* data and to 0.029 for the *bunny* data because Glob-GM could not terminate within 1000 s when we used an inlier threshold equal to the *gridsize* of the down-sampling function. We can see that GoTS achieved high accuracy in these challenging registrations. In particular, the translation errors achieved by the global optimal translation search method in **Algorithm 1** are all very small. Go-ICP failed on bun090/000, which is a difficult case because the relative transformation between the two point clouds is very large and the overlap ratio is small. The run time of Go-ICP was extremely long in this case, while in the other three cases, the run time of Go-ICP was slightly longer than or twice as long as that of GoTS. Carefully tuning the trimming ratio may improve the accuracy of Go-ICP, but in practice, the best trimming ratio cannot be known before registration. Glob-GM failed in all four cases, and its run times were very long. The number of RIFs generated for the global translation search was between 150 and 160 in these experiments.

4.4 Registration of Scans of *LivingRoom*

We tested the performance of the proposed method on large-scale field data using "livingRoom.mat" from the MATLAB example "3-D Point Cloud Registration and Stitching", which consists of a series of 3D point sets obtained by continuously scanning a living room. We used GoTS, Go-ICP and Glob-GM to register the point clouds of the first and sixth frames of these data. The original point clouds consist of more than 300,000 points, and all these points lie in a cube with an edge length of 4 m. They were down-sampled with a *gridsize* of 0.1 m.

(a) Init   (b) GoTS   (c) Go-ICP   (d) Glob-GM

Fig. 5. *LivingRoom* point clouds before and after registration.

The results are listed in Table 4. GoTS successfully registered the two point clouds in 25.90 s. In contrast, Go-ICP failed to register the point clouds when the mean square error threshold was set to 0.05. When we used a mean square error threshold of 0.01, the algorithm could not terminate within half an hour. For Glob-GM, when we set the inlier threshold to 0.1, the algorithm could not terminate within half an hour. Then, we set the inlier threshold to 0.8; the algorithm terminated after 633.8 s, but the result was incorrect. The numbers of RIFs generated from the reference and moving point clouds were 1434 and 1866, respectively. More results can be found in the supplementary material.

Table 4. Results of registering *livingRoom* point clouds.

Method	GoTS	Go-ICP	Glob-GM
Tran [m]	**0.1047**	1.158	0.4555
Rot [°]	**4.382**	158.3	97.59
Time [s]	**25.90**	489.6	633.8

5   Conclusion

We introduce a fast global 3D rigid point cloud registration method based on the decoupling of translation and rotation optimization via a newly proposed rotation invariant feature. We first globally optimize the translation by using a BnB algorithm to match sets of rotation invariant features constructed from the two point clouds, and we then calculate the optimal rotation using the optimized translation. Decoupling the optimization of the translation and rotation makes the proposed algorithm more efficient than existing methods. Experiments on real data demonstrate the superiority of the proposed algorithm in cases of partial overlap, large angular differences and high outlier ratios. All code will be available on the web (http://www.fudanmiccai.org).

Acknowledgements. This research was supported by the National Natural Science Foundation of China (grants 81471758, 81701795 and 60972102). This research was also partially supported by the National Key Research and Development Program of China (2017YFC0110700) and the Program of Shanghai Academic/Technology Research Leaders (16XD1424900).

References

1. Whelan, T., Kaess, M., Johannsson, H., Fallon, M., Leonard, J.J., McDonald, J.: Real-time large-scale dense RGB-D SLAM with volumetric fusion. Int. J. Robot. Res. **34**, 598–626 (2015)
2. Henry, P., Krainin, M., Herbst, E., Ren, X., Fox, D.: RGB-D mapping: using Kinect-style depth cameras for dense 3D modeling of indoor environments. Int. J. Robot. Res. **31**, 647–663 (2012)
3. Newcombe, R.A., et al.: KinectFusion: real-time dense surface mapping and tracking. In: International Symposium on Mixed and Augmented Reality, pp. 127–136 (2011)
4. Salvi, J., Matabosch, C., Fofi, D., Forest, J.: A review of recent range image registration methods with accuracy evaluation. Image Vis. Comput. **25**, 578–596 (2007)
5. Fan, Y., Xu, X., Wang, M.: A surface-based spatial registration method based on sense three-dimensional scanner. J. Craniofac. Surg. **28**, 157–160 (2017)
6. Straub, J., Campbell, T., How, J.P., Fisher, J.W.I.: Efficient global point cloud alignment using Bayesian nonparametric mixtures. In: IEEE Conference on Computer Vision and Pattern Recognition, pp. 2403–2412 (2017)
7. Besl, P.J., McKay, N.D.: A method for registration of 3-D shapes. IEEE Trans. Pattern Anal. Mach. Intell. **14**, 239–256 (1992)
8. Chetverikov, D., Stepanov, D., Krsek, P.: Robust euclidean alignment of 3D point sets: the trimmed iterative closest point algorithm. Image Vis. Comput. **23**, 299–309 (2005)
9. Jian, B., Vemuri, B.C.: Robust point set registration using Gaussian mixture models. IEEE Trans. Pattern Anal. Mach. Intell. **33**, 1633–1645 (2011)
10. Kirkpatrick, S., Gelatt, C.D., Vecchi, M.P.: Optimization by simulated annealing. Science **220**, 671–680 (1983)
11. Wachowiak, M.P., Smolikova, R., Zheng, Y.F., Zurada, J.M., Elmaghraby, A.S.: An approach to multimodal biomedical image registration utilizing particle swarm optimization. IEEE Trans. Evol. Comput. **8**, 289–301 (2004)

12. Li, H., Hartley, R.: The 3D–3D registration problem revisited. In: IEEE International Conference on Computer Vision, pp. 1947–1954 (2007)
13. Yang, J., Li, H., Campbell, D., Jia, Y.: Go-ICP: a globally optimal solution to 3D ICP point-set registration. IEEE Trans. Pattern Anal. Mach. Intell. **38**, 2241–2254 (2016)
14. Hartley, R.I., Kahl, F.: Global optimization through rotation space search. Int. J. Comput. Vis. **82**, 64–79 (2009)
15. Bustos, A.P., Chin, T., Eriksson, A., Li, H., Suter, D.: Fast rotation search with stereographic projections for 3D registration. IEEE Trans. Pattern Anal. Mach. Intell. **38**, 2227–2240 (2016)
16. Campbell, D., Petersson, L., Kneip, L., Li, H.: Globally-optimal inlier set maximisation for simultaneous camera pose and feature correspondence. In: IEEE International Conference on Computer Vision, pp. 1–10 (2017)
17. Campbell, D., Petersson, L.: GOGMA: globally-optimal Gaussian mixture alignment. In: IEEE Conference on Computer Vision and Pattern Recognition, pp. 5685–5694 (2016)
18. Lian, W., Zhang, L., Yang, M.: An efficient globally optimal algorithm for asymmetric point matching. IEEE Trans. Pattern Anal. Mach. Intell. **39**, 1281–1293 (2016)
19. Fischler, M.A., Bolles, R.C.: Random sample consensus - a paradigm for model-fitting with applications to image-analysis and automated cartography. Commun. ACM **24**, 381–395 (1981)

Facial Dynamics Interpreter Network: What Are the Important Relations Between Local Dynamics for Facial Trait Estimation?

Seong Tae Kim and Yong Man Ro[✉]

School of Electrical Engineering, KAIST, Daejeon, Republic of Korea
{stkim4978,ymro}@kaist.ac.kr

Abstract. Human face analysis is an important task in computer vision. According to cognitive-psychological studies, facial dynamics could provide crucial cues for face analysis. The motion of a facial local region in facial expression is related to the motion of other facial local regions. In this paper, a novel deep learning approach, named facial dynamics interpreter network, has been proposed to interpret the important relations between local dynamics for estimating facial traits from expression sequence. The facial dynamics interpreter network is designed to be able to encode a relational importance, which is used for interpreting the relation between facial local dynamics and estimating facial traits. By comparative experiments, the effectiveness of the proposed method has been verified. The important relations between facial local dynamics are investigated by the proposed facial dynamics interpreter network in gender classification and age estimation. Moreover, experimental results show that the proposed method outperforms the state-of-the-art methods in gender classification and age estimation.

Keywords: Facial dynamics · Interpretable deep learning
Relation between local dynamics · Facial trait estimation

1 Introduction

Analysis of human face has been an important task in computer vision because it plays a major role in soft biometrics, and human-computer interaction [7,33]. Facial behavior is known to benefit perception of the identity [32,34]. In particular, facial dynamics play crucial roles for improving the accuracy of facial trait estimation such as age estimation or gender classification [6,9].

In recent progress of deep learning, convolutional neural networks (CNN) have shown outstanding performance on many fields of computer vision. Several research efforts have been devoted to developing spatio-temporal feature representation in various applications such as action recognition [13,21,23,40] and activity parsing [26,42]. In [23], a long short-term memory (LSTM) network has

© Springer Nature Switzerland AG 2018
V. Ferrari et al. (Eds.): ECCV 2018, LNCS 11216, pp. 475–491, 2018.
https://doi.org/10.1007/978-3-030-01258-8_29

been designed on top of CNN features to encode dynamics in video. The LSTM network is a variant of recurrent neural network (RNN), which is designed to capture long-term temporal information in sequential data [19]. By using the LSTM, the temporal correlation of CNN features was effectively encoded.

Recently, a few research efforts have been made regarding facial dynamic feature encoding for a facial analysis [6,9,24,25].It is generally known that the dynamic features of local regions are valuable for facial trait estimation [6,9]. Usually, the motion of facial local region in facial expression is related to the motion of other facial regions [39,43]. However, to the best of our knowledge, there are no studies that utilize relations between facial motions and interpret the important relations between local dynamics for facial trait estimation.

In this paper, a novel deep network has been proposed for interpreting relations between local dynamics in facial trait estimation. To interpret the relations between facial local dynamics, the proposed deep network consists of a facial local dynamic feature encoding network and a facial dynamics interpreter network. By the facial dynamics interpreter network, the importance of relations for estimating facial traits is encoded. The main contributions of this study are summarized in following three aspects:

1. We propose a novel deep network which estimates facial traits by using relations between facial local dynamics of smile expression.
2. The proposed deep network has been designed to be able to interpret the relations between local dynamics in facial trait estimation. For that purpose, the relational importance is devised. The relational importance is encoded from the relational features of facial local dynamics. The relational importance is used for interpretation of important relations in facial trait estimation.
3. To validate the effectiveness of the proposed method, comparative experiments have been conducted on two facial trait estimation problems (*i.e.* age estimation and gender classification). In the proposed method, the facial trait estimation is conducted by combining the relational features based on the relational importance. By exploiting the relational features and considering the importance of relations, the proposed method could more accurately estimate facial traits compared with the state-of-the-art methods.

2   Related Work

Age Estimation and Gender Classification. A lot of research efforts have been devoted to development of automatic age estimation and gender classification techniques from face image [2,4,4,16,22,28,29,29,38,38,41]. Recently, deep learning methods show notable potential in various face analysis tasks. One of the main focus of these methods is to design suitable deep network structure for some specific tasks. Parkhi et al. [31] reported VGG-style CNN learned from large-scale static face images. Deep learning based age estimation method and gender classification method have been reported but they were mostly designed on static face image [22,27,28,41].

Facial Dynamic Analysis. The temporal dynamics of face have been ignored in both age estimation and gender classification. Recent studies have reported that facial dynamics could be an important cue for facial trait estimation [6, 8–10, 17]. With aging, the face loses muscle tone and underlying fat tissue, which creates wrinkles, sunken eyes and increases crow's feet around the eyes [9]. Aging also affects facial dynamics along with appearance. As a human being gets older, the elastic fibers of the face show fraying. Therefore facial dynamic features of local facial regions are important cues for age estimation. In cognitive-psychological studies [1, 5, 18, 36], evidence for gender-dimorphism in the human expression has been reported. Females express emotions more frequently compared with males. Males have a tendency to show restricted emotions and to be unwilling to self-disclose intimate feelings [6]. In [6], Dantcheva et al. used dynamic descriptors extracted from facial landmarks for gender classification. However, there are no studies for learning relations of dynamic features in facial trait estimation.

Relational Network. In this paper, we propose a novel deep learning architecture for analyzing relations of facial dynamic features in facial trait estimation. A relational network has been reported in visual question and answering (VQA) [35]. In [35], the authors defined an object as a neuron on feature map obtained from CNN and designed a neural network for relational reasoning. However, it was designed for image-based VQA. In this paper, the proposed method automatically encodes the importance of relations by considering the locational information on face. By utilizing the importance of relations, the proposed method could interpret the relations between facial dynamics in facial trait estimation.

3   Proposed Facial Dynamics Interpreter Network

Overall structure of the proposed facial dynamics interpreter network is shown in Fig. 1. The aim of the proposed method is to interpret the important relations between local dynamics in facial trait estimation from expression sequence. The proposed method largely consists of the facial local dynamic feature encoding network, the facial dynamics interpreter network, and interpretation on important relation between facial local dynamics. The details are described in the following subsections.

3.1   Facial Local Dynamic Feature Encoding Network

Given a face sequence, appearance features are computed by CNN on each frame. For the purpose of appearance feature extraction, we employ the VGG-face network [31] which is trained with large-scale face images. The pre-trained VGG face model is used to get off-the-shelf CNN features in this study. With given CNN features, the proposed facial dynamics interpreter network has been investigated. The output of convolutional layer in the VGG-face network is used as feature map of facial appearance representation.

Based on the feature map, the face is divided into N_0 local regions. The location of local regions was determined to interpret the relation of local dynamics

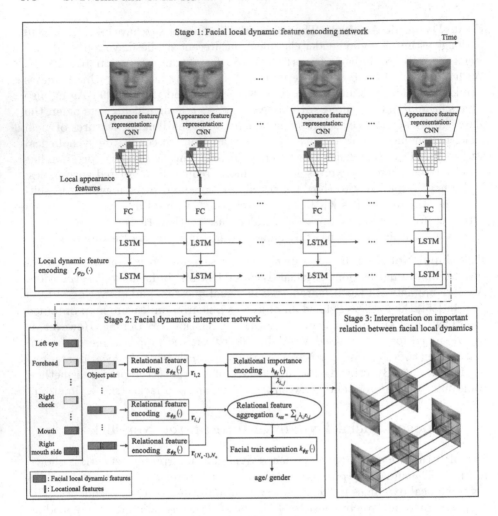

Fig. 1. Overall structure of the proposed facial dynamics interpreter network.

base on semantically meaningful facial local region (*i.e.* left eye, forehead, right eye, left cheek, nose, right cheek, left mouth side, mouth, and right mouth side in this study). Note that each face sequence is automatically aligned based on the landmark detection [3]. Let $\mathbf{x}_i^t$ denote the local appearance features of i-th facial local part at t-th time step. To encode local dynamic features, an LSTM network has been devised with fully-connected layer on top of the local appearance features $\mathbf{X}_i = \left\{ \mathbf{x}_i^1, \ldots, \mathbf{x}_i^t, \ldots, \mathbf{x}_i^T \right\}$ as followings:

$$\mathbf{d}_i = f_{\phi_D}(\mathbf{X}_i), \tag{1}$$

where $\mathbf{d}_i$ denotes the facial local dynamic feature of i-th local part and f_{ϕ_D} is a function with learnable parameters ϕ_D. f_{ϕ_D} consists of the fully-connected layer and the LSTM layers as shown in Fig. 1. T denotes the length of face sequence.

The LSTM network could deal with the different length of sequences. The various dynamic related features including variation of appearance, amplitude, speed, and acceleration could be encoded from the sequence of local appearance features. The detailed configuration of the network used in the experiments will be presented in Sect. 4.1.

3.2   Facial Dynamics Interpreter Network

We extract object features (i.e. facial local dynamic features and locational features) for pairs of objects. The locational features are defined as the central position of the object (i.e. facial local region). For the purpose of telling the location information of objects to the facial dynamics interpreter network, the local dynamic features and the locational features are embedded and defined as object features $\mathbf{o}_i$. The object feature can be written as

$$\mathbf{o}_i = [\mathbf{d}_i, p_i, q_i], \tag{2}$$

where $[p_i, q_i]$ denotes the normalized central position of i-th object.

The design philosophy of the proposed facial dynamics interpreter network is to make the functional form of a neural network which captures the core relations for facial trait estimation. The importance of the relation could be different for each pair of object features. The proposed facial dynamics interpreter network is designed to encode relational importance in facial trait estimation. The relational importance could be used for interpreting the relation between local dynamics in facial trait estimation.

Let $\lambda_{i,j}$ denote a relational importance between i-th and j-th object feature. The relational feature, which represents latent relation between two objects for facial trait estimation, can be written as

$$\mathbf{r}_{i,j} = g_{\phi_R}(\mathbf{s}_{i,j}), \tag{3}$$

where g_{ϕ_R} is a function with learnable parameters ϕ_R. $\mathbf{s}_{i,j} = (\mathbf{o}_i, \mathbf{o}_j)$ is relation pair from i-th and j-th facial local parts. $\mathbf{S} = \{\mathbf{s}_{1,2}, \cdots, \mathbf{s}_{i,j}, \cdots, \mathbf{s}_{(N_0-1),N_0}\}$ is a set of relation pairs where N_0 denotes the number of objects in face. $\mathbf{o}_i$ and $\mathbf{o}_j$ denote the i-th and j-th object features, respectively. The relational importance $\lambda_{i,j}$ for relation between two object features $(\mathbf{o}_i, \mathbf{o}_j)$ is encoded as:

$$\lambda_{i,j} = h_{\phi_I}(\mathbf{r}_{i,j}), \tag{4}$$

where h_{ϕ_I} is a function with learnable parameters ϕ_I. In this paper, h_{ϕ_I} is defined with $\phi_I = \{(\mathbf{W}_{1,2}, \mathbf{b}_{1,2}), \cdots, (\mathbf{W}_{(N_0-1),N_0}, \mathbf{b}_{(N_0-1),N_0})\}$ as followings:

$$h_{\phi_I}(\mathbf{r}_{i,j}) = \frac{\exp(\mathbf{W}_{i,j}\mathbf{r}_{i,j} + \mathbf{b}_{i,j})}{\sum_{i,j} \exp(\mathbf{W}_{i,j}\mathbf{r}_{i,j} + \mathbf{b}_{i,j})}. \tag{5}$$

The aggregated relational features $\mathbf{f}_{agg}$ are represented by

$$\mathbf{f}_{agg} = \sum_{i,j} \lambda_{i,j}\mathbf{r}_{i,j}. \tag{6}$$

Algorithm 1. Calculating relational importance of N_I objects

---
Input
λ: the set of relational importance of two facial local parts
$\left\{\lambda_{1,2}, \cdots, \lambda_{i,j}, \cdots, \lambda_{(N_0-1),N_0}\right\}$
N_I: the number of objects for interpretation
Output: χ: Relational importance of N_I objects
Let N_R denote total number of relations with N_I objects $N_R =_{N_o}C_{N_I}$
for P *from 1 to* N_R **do**
    Let $\chi_P^{N_I}$ denote P-th relational importance of N_I object features (
    $\mathbf{o}_{p1}, \mathbf{o}_{p2}, \cdots, \mathbf{o}_{p(N_I-1)}, \mathbf{o}_{pN_I}$)
    Compute $\chi_P^{N_I}$
     $\chi_P^{N_I} = \lambda_{p_1,p_2} + \cdots + \lambda_{p_1,p_{N_I}} + \cdots + \lambda_{p(N_I-1),p_{N_I}}$
end
$\chi = \left\{\chi_1^{N_I}, \cdots, \chi_P^{N_I}, \cdots, \chi_{N_R}^{N_I}\right\}$

Finally, the facial trait estimation can be performed with

$$\mathbf{y} = k_{\phi_E}(\mathbf{f}_{agg}),\qquad(7)$$

where $\mathbf{y}$ denotes estimated result and k_{ϕ_E} is a function with parameters ϕ_E. k_{ϕ_E} and g_{ϕ_R} are implemented by fully-connected layers.

3.3 Interpretation on Important Relations Between Facial Local Dynamics

The proposed method is useful for interpreting the relations in facial trait estimation. The relational importance calculated in Eq. (4) is utilized to interpret the relations of facial local dynamics. Note that the high relational importance values mean that the relational features of corresponding facial local parts are important for estimating facial traits. The pseudocodes for calculating relational importance of N_I objects are given in Algorithm 1. By analyzing the relational importance, important relations for estimating facial traits could be explained. In Sects. 4.2 and 4.3, we discuss the important relations for age estimation and gender classification, respectively.

4   Experiments

4.1   Experimental Settings

Database. To evaluate the effectiveness of the proposed facial dynamics interpreter network, comparative experiments were conducted. For generalization purpose, we verified the proposed method on both age estimation and gender classification tasks. Age and gender were known as representative facial traits [28]. The public UvA-NEMO Smile database was used for both tasks [10,11].

The UvA-NEMO smile database has been known as the largest smile database [12]. The database consists of 1,240 smile videos collected from 400 subjects. Among 400 subjects, 185 subjects are female and remaining 215 subjects are male. The ages of subjects range from 8 to 76 years. For evaluating the performance of age estimation, we used the experimental protocol defined in [9–11]. The 10-fold cross-validation scheme was used to calculate the performance of the proposed method. Each fold was divided in a way where there was no subject overlap [9–11]. Each time an independent test fold was separated and it was only used for calculating the performance. The remaining 9-folds were used to train the deep network and optimize hyper-parameters. To evaluate the performance of gender classification, we followed the experimental protocol used in [6].

Evaluation Metric. For age estimation, the mean absolute error (MAE) [41] was utilized for evaluation. The MAE could measure the error between the predicted age and the ground-truth. The MAE was computed as follows:

$$\epsilon = \frac{\sum_{n=1}^{N_{test}} \|\hat{\mathbf{y}}_n - \mathbf{y}_n^*\|_1}{N_{test}}, \tag{8}$$

where $\hat{\mathbf{y}}_n$ and $\mathbf{y}_n^*$ denote predicted age and ground-truth age of n-th test sample, respectively. N_{test} denotes the number of the test samples. For the case of gender classification, classification accuracy was used for evaluation. We reported the MAE and classification accuracy averaged over all test folds.

Implementation Details. The face images used in the experiments were automatically aligned based on the two eye locations detected by the facial landmark detection [3]. The face images were cropped and resized to 96×96 pixels. For the appearance representation, the frontal 10 convolutional layers and 4 max-pooling layers of VGG-face network was used. As a result, $6 \times 6 \times 512$ size of feature map was obtained from each face image. Each facial local region was defined on the feature map with size of $2 \times 2 \times 512$. In other words, there were 9 objects in face sequence ($N_0 = 9$). The fully-connected layer with 1024 units and the stacked LSTM layers were used for f_{ϕ_D}. We stacked two LSTMs and each LSTM had 1024 memory cells. Two-layer full-connected layers consisting of 4096 units (with dropout [37]) per layer was used for g_{ϕ_R} with RELU [30]. h_{ϕ_I} was implemented by a fully-connected layer and softmax function. Two-layer fully-connected layers consisting of 2048, 1024 units (with dropout, RELU, and batch normalization [20]) and one fully-connected layer (1 neuron for age estimation and 2 neurons for gender classification) were used for k_{ϕ_E}. The mean squared error was used for training the deep network in age estimation. The cross-entropy loss was used for training the deep network in gender classification.

4.2 Age Estimation

Interpreting Relations Between Facial Local Dynamics in Age Estimation. To understand the mechanism of the proposed facial dynamics interpreter network in age estimation, the relational importance calculated from

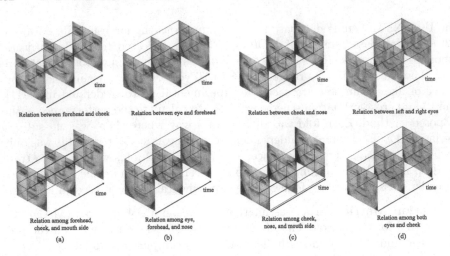

Fig. 2. Example of facial dynamic interpretation in age estimation. Most important relations are visualized with yellow box for the relation between 2 objects in upper side and the relation among 3 objects in bottom side. (a) age group of [13–19], (b) age group of [20–36], (c) age group of [37–66], (d) age group of 66+.

each sequence was analyzed. Figure 2 shows the important relations where the corresponding pair has high relational importance values. We showed the difference of important regions over different ages by presenting the important relations over age groups. Ages were divided into five age groups (8–12, 13–19, 20–36, 37–65, and 66+) according to [15]. To interpret the important relations between each age group, the relational importance values encoded from test set were averaged in each age group, respectively. Four groups were visualized with example face images (there was no subject to be permitted for reporting in age group of [8–12]). As shown in the figure, when estimating age group of [66+], the relation between two eye regions was important. The relation between two eye regions could represent discriminative dynamic features according to crow's feet and sunken eyes, which could be important factors for estimating ages of the older people. In addition, when considering three objects, the relation among left eye, right eye, and left cheek had highest relational importance in age group of [66+]. There was a tendency to symmetry about the relational importance. For example, the relation among left eye, right eye, and right cheek was included in top-5 high relational importance among 84 relations in age group of [66+]. Although the relation of action unit (AU) for determining specific facial expressions has been reported [14], the relation of the motions for estimating age or classifying gender was not investigated. In this study, the facial dynamics interpreter network was designed to interpret the relation of motions in facial trait estimation. It was found that the relation of dynamic features related with AU 2 and AU 6 was highly used by the deep network for estimating ages in range [66+].

In addition, to verify the effect of important relations, we made perturbation on the dynamic features as shown in Fig. 3. For the sequence of 17 years

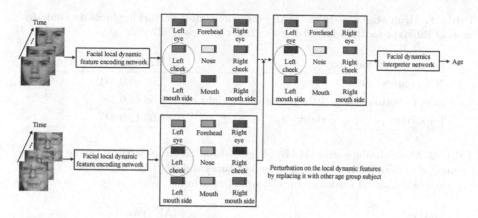

Fig. 3. Perturbing the local dynamic features by replacing it with the local dynamic features of another age group subject (*e.g.*, older subject).

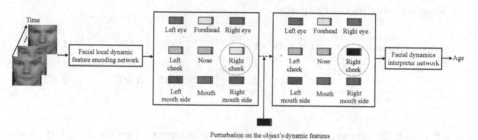

Fig. 4. Perturbing local dynamic features by replacing it with zero vector.

old subject, we changed the local dynamic features of left cheek region with that of 73 years old subject in the experiment. Note that the cheek constructed important pairs for estimating age group of [13–19] as shown in Fig. 2(a). By the perturbation, the absolute error was changed from 0.41 to 2.38. In the same way, we changed the dynamic features of other two regions (left eye and right eye) one by one. The other two regions constructed relatively less important relations and achieved the absolute error of 1.40 and 1.81 (left eye and right eye, respectively). The increase of absolute errors was less than the case which made perturbation on the left cheek. It showed that the relations with the left cheek were important for estimating age compared with the relations with eye in age group of [13–19].

For the same sequence, the facial dynamics interpreter network without the use of relational importance was also analyzed. For the facial dynamics interpreter network without the use of relational importance, the absolute error of the estimated age was increased by perturbation on the local dynamic feature of the left cheek from 1.20 to 7.45. When conducting perturbation on the left eye and the right eye, the absolute errors were 1.87 and 4.21, respectively. The increase of absolute error became much larger when conducting perturbation on

484   S. T. Kim and Y. M. Ro

Table 1. Mean absolute errors (MAE) measured after perturbing local dynamic features of different location for subjects with age groups of [37–66].

Perturbation location	MAE (standard error)
Not contaminated	5.05 (±0.28)
Less important parts (left eye, forehead, right eye)	7.56 (±0.35)
Important part (right cheek)	9.00 (±0.41)

Table 2. Mean absolute error (MAE) of age estimation on UvA-NEMO smile database for analyzing the effectiveness of locational features and relational importance. L.F. and R.I. denote locational features and relational importance, respectively.

Method			MAE (years)		
			Posed	Spontaneous	All
Aggregation of local dynamic features using regional importance			4.27	4.25	4.26
	L.F.	R.I.			
Facial dynamics interpreter network			4.05	4.07	4.06
	✔		3.95	4.05	4.00
	✔	✔	3.83	3.90	3.87

the left cheek. Moreover, the increase of error was larger when the facial dynamics interpreter network did not use relational importance. In other words, the facial dynamics interpreter network with the relational importance was more robust to feature contamination because it adaptively encoded the relational importance from the relational features as in Eq. (4).

In order to statistically analyze the effect of contaminated features in the proposed facial dynamics interpreter network, we also evaluated the MAE when conducting perturbation on each dynamic features of facial local parts with zero vector as shown in Fig. 4. For 402 videos which were collected from the subjects in age group of [37–66] in the UvA-NEMO database, the MAE was calculated as shown in Table 1. As shown in the table, the perturbation on most important facial region (*i.e.* right cheek in age group of [37–66]) had more influenced the accuracy of age estimation compared with the case which made perturbation on less important parts (*i.e.* left eye, forehead, and right eye in age group of [37–66]). The difference of MAE between the cases which made perturbation on important part and less important parts was statically significant ($p < 0.05$).

Assessment of Facial Dynamics Interpreter Network for Age Estimation. We evaluated the effectiveness of the facial dynamics interpreter network. First, the effects of relational importance and locational features were validated for age estimation. Table 2 shows the MAE of the facial dynamics interpreter network with locational feature and relational importance. To verify the

Table 3. Mean absolute error (MAE) on the UvA-NEMO smile database compared with other methods.

Method	MAE (years)
VLBP [17]	15.70
Displacement [10]	11.54
BIF [16]	5.78
BIF + Dynamics [9]	5.03
IEF [2]	4.86
IEF + Dynamics [9]	4.33
Holistic dynamic approach	4.02
Proposed method	**3.87**

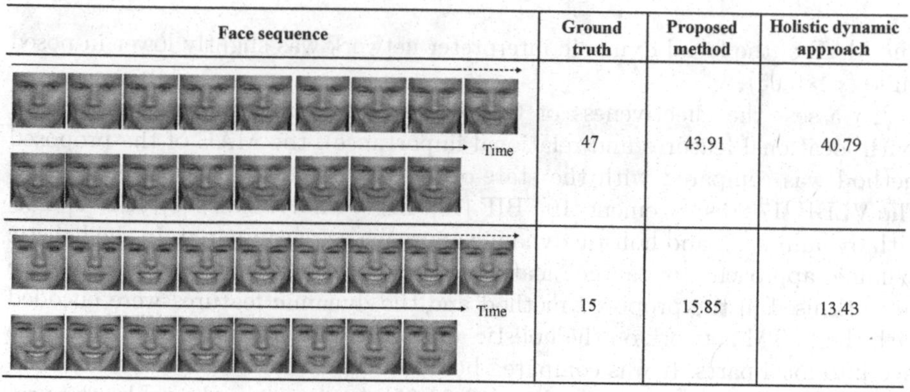

Face sequence	Ground truth	Proposed method	Holistic dynamic approach
Time	47	43.91	40.79
Time	15	15.85	13.43

Fig. 5. Examples of the proposed method on age estimation. For visualization purpose, face sequences are displayed in 5 frames per sec.

effectiveness of the relational features, the aggregation of local dynamic features using regional importance were compared. In the aggregation of local dynamic features using regional importance approach, facial local dynamic features were aggregated with regional importance in unsupervised way. As shown in the table, using the relational features improved the accuracy of age estimation. Moreover, the locational features could improve the performance of the age estimation by making the network know the location information of the object pairs. The locational features of the objects were meaningful as the objects of the face sequence were automatically aligned by the facial landmark detection. By utilizing both the relational importance and the locational features, the proposed facial dynamics interpreter network achieved the lowest MAE of 3.87 over all test set. It was mainly due to the reason that the importance of relations for age estimation was different. By considering the importance of the relational features, the accuracy of age estimation was improved. Moreover, we further analyzed the MAE of the age estimation according to the spontaneity of the smile expression.

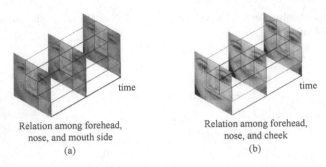

Relation among forehead,
nose, and mouth side
(a)

Relation among forehead,
nose, and cheek
(b)

Fig. 6. Example of interpreting important relations between facial dynamics in gender classification. Most important relations are visualized with yellow box for the relation between 3 objects for recognizing male (a) and for recognizing female (b).

The MAE of the facial dynamic interpreter network was slightly lower in posed smile ($p > 0.05$).

To assess the effectiveness of the proposed dynamics interpreter network (with locational features and relational importance), the MAE of the proposed method was compared with the state-of-the-art methods (please see Table 3). The VLBP [17], displacement [10], BIF [16], BIF with dynamics [9], IEF [2], IEF with dynamics [9], and holistic dynamic approach were compared. In the holistic dynamic approach, appearance features were extracted by the same VGG-face network used in the proposed method and the dynamic features were encoded with the LSTM network on the holistic appearance feature without dividing the face into local parts. It was compared because it has been widely used architecture for a spatio-temporal encoding [13,24,25] As shown in the table, the proposed method achieved lowest MAE. The MAE of the proposed facial dynamics interpreter network was lower than the MAE of the IEF + Dynamics and the difference was statistically significant ($p < 0.05$). It was mainly attributed to the fact that the proposed method encoded the latent relational features from object features (facial local dynamic features and locational features) and effectively combined the relational features based on the relational importance. Examples of age estimation from the proposed method and the holistic dynamic approach are shown in Fig. 5.

4.3   Gender Classification

Interpreting Relations Between Facial Local Dynamics in Gender Classification. In order to interpret important relations in gender classification, the relational importance values encoded from each sequence were analyzed. Figure 6 shows the important relations where the relational importance had high values at classifying gender from face sequence. As shown in the figure, the relation among forehead, nose, and mouth side was important in making decisions on males. Note that there was a tendency to symmetry about the relational importance. For determining male, the relation among forehead, nose, and right

Table 4. Accuracy of gender classification on the UvA-NEMO smile database to analyze the effectiveness of the locational feature and relational importance. L.F. and R.I. denote locational features and relational importance, respectively.

Method			Classification accuracy (%)
Aggregation of local dynamic features using regional importance			88.87
	L.F.	R.I.	
Facial dynamics interpreter network			88.79
	✔		89.35
	✔	✔	**90.08**

Table 5. Accuracy of gender classification on the UvA-NEMO smile database compared with other methods.

Method	Classification accuracy				(%)
	Spontaneous		Posed		All
	Age ≤ 19	Age > 19	Age ≤ 19	Age > 19	
how-old.net + dynamics (tree) [6]	60.80	93.46	N/A	N/A	N/A
how-old.net + dynamics (SVM) [6]	N/A	N/A	60.80	92.89	N/A
COTS + dynamics (tree) [6]	76.92	93.00	N/A	N/A	N/A
COTS + dynamics (bagged trees) [6]	N/A	N/A	76.92	92.89	N/A
Image-based CNN [27]	80.72	89.85	80.58	92.36	86.94
Holistic dynamic approach	74.38	93.52	77.51	93.91	87.10
Proposed method	80.17	94.65	85.14	95.18	**90.08**

mouth side and the relation among forehead, nose, and left mouth side were top-2 important relations among 84 relations of three objects. For the case of female, the relation among forehead, nose, and cheek was important. It could be related to the observation that the females express emotions more frequently compared with males and the males have a tendency to show restricted emotions compared with the females. In other words, the females have a tendency to make smiles bigger than males by using muscles of cheek regions. Therefore, the relations among cheek and other face parts were important for recognizing females.

Assessment of Facial Dynamics Interpreter Network for Gender Classification. We also evaluated the effectiveness of the proposed facial dynamics interpreter network for gender classification. First, the classification accuracy of the facial dynamics interpreter network with relational importance and locational features are summarized in Table 4. For comparison, the aggregation of local dynamic features using regional importance was compared. The proposed facial dynamics interpreter network achieved the highest accuracy by using both locational features and relational importance. The locational features

488   S. T. Kim and Y. M. Ro

and the relational importance in the facial dynamics interpreter network were also important for gender classification.

Table 5 shows the classification accuracy of the proposed facial dynamics interpreter network compared with other methods on UvA-NEMO database. Two types of appearance based approach named "how-old.net" and "commercial off-the-shelf (COTS)" were combined with a hand-crafted dynamic approach for gender classification [6]. How-old.net was a website (http://how-old.net/) launched by Microsoft for online age and gender recognition. COTS was a commercial face detection and recognition software, which included a gender classification. The dynamic approach calculated the facial local region's dynamic descriptors such as amplitude, speed, and acceleration as described in [6]. In holistic dynamic approach, appearance features were extracted by the same VGG-face network used in the proposed method and the dynamic features were encoded on the holistic appearance features. An image based method [27] was also compared to validate the effectiveness of utilizing facial dynamics in gender classification. The accuracy of how-old.net + dynamics and COTS + dynamics were directly from [6] and the accuracy of the image-based CNN and the holistic dynamic approach were calculated in this study. By exploiting the relations between local dynamic features, the proposed method achieved the highest accuracy compared with other methods. The performance difference between the holistic approach and the proposed method was statistically significant ($p < 0.05$).

5   Conclusions

According to cognitive-psychological studies, facial dynamics could provide crucial cues for face analysis. The motion of facial local regions from facial expression is known that it is related to the motion of other facial regions. In this paper, the novel deep learning approach which could interpret the relations between facial local dynamics was proposed to interpret relations of local dynamics in facial trait estimation from the smile expression. Facial traits were estimated by combining relational features of facial local dynamics based on the relational importance. By comparative experiments, the effectiveness of the proposed method was verified for facial trait estimation. The important relations between facial dynamics were interpreted by the proposed method in gender classification and age estimation. The proposed method could accurately estimate facial traits (age and gender) compared with the state-of-the-art methods. We will attempt to extend the proposed method to other facial dynamic analysis such as spontaneity analysis [11] and video facial expression recognition [24].

Acknowledgement. This work was partly supported by Institute for Information & Communications Technology Promotion (IITP) grant funded by the Korea government (MSIT) (No. 2017-0-01778, Development of Explainable Human-level Deep Machine Learning Inference Framework) and (No. 2017-0-00111, Practical Technology Development of High Performing Emotion Recognition and Facial Expression based Authentication using Deep Network).

References

1. Adams Jr., R.B., Hess, U., Kleck, R.E.: The intersection of gender-related facial appearance and facial displays of emotion. Emot. Rev. **7**(1), 5–13 (2015)
2. Alnajar, F., Shan, C., Gevers, T., Geusebroek, J.M.: Learning-based encoding with soft assignment for age estimation under unconstrained imaging conditions. Image Vis. Comput. **30**(12), 946–953 (2012)
3. Asthana, A., Zafeiriou, S., Cheng, S., Pantic, M.: Incremental face alignment in the wild. In: Proceedings of the IEEE Conference on Computer Vision and Pattern Recognition, pp. 1859–1866 (2014)
4. Bekios-Calfa, J., Buenaposada, J.M., Baumela, L.: Robust gender recognition by exploiting facial attributes dependencies. Pattern Recogn. Lett. **36**, 228–234 (2014)
5. Cashdan, E.: Smiles, speech, and body posture: how women and men display socio-metric status and power. J. Nonverbal Behav. **22**(4), 209–228 (1998)
6. Dantcheva, A., Brémond, F.: Gender estimation based on smile-dynamics. IEEE Trans. Inf. Forensics Secur. **12**(3), 719–729 (2017)
7. Dantcheva, A., Elia, P., Ross, A.: What else does your biometric data reveal? a survey on soft biometrics. IEEE Trans. Inf. Forensics Secur. **11**(3), 441–467 (2016)
8. Demirkus, M., Toews, M., Clark, J.J., Arbel, T.: Gender classification from uncon-strained video sequences. In: 2010 IEEE Computer Society Conference on Computer Vision and Pattern Recognition Workshops (CVPRW), pp. 55–62. IEEE (2010)
9. Dibeklioğlu, H., Alnajar, F., Salah, A.A., Gevers, T.: Combining facial dynamics with appearance for age estimation. IEEE Trans. Image Process. **24**(6), 1928–1943 (2015)
10. Dibeklioğlu, H., Gevers, T., Salah, A.A., Valenti, R.: A smile can reveal your age: enabling facial dynamics in age estimation. In: Proceedings of the 20th ACM International Conference on Multimedia, pp. 209–218. ACM (2012)
11. Dibeklioğlu, H., Salah, A.A., Gevers, T.: Are you really smiling at me? Sponta-neous versus posed enjoyment smiles. In: Fitzgibbon, A., Lazebnik, S., Perona, P., Sato, Y., Schmid, C. (eds.) ECCV 2012. LNCS, vol. 7574, pp. 525–538. Springer, Heidelberg (2012). https://doi.org/10.1007/978-3-642-33712-3_38
12. Dibeklioğlu, H., Salah, A.A., Gevers, T.: Recognition of genuine smiles. IEEE Trans. Multimed. **17**(3), 279–294 (2015)
13. Donahue, J., et al.: Long-term recurrent convolutional networks for visual recogni-tion and description. In: Proceedings of the IEEE Conference on Computer Vision and Pattern Recognition, pp. 2625–2634 (2015)
14. Ekman, P.: Facial action coding system (FACS). In: A Human Face (2002)
15. Gallagher, A.C., Chen, T.: Understanding images of groups of people. In: 2009 IEEE Conference on Computer Vision and Pattern Recognition. CVPR 2009, pp. 256–263. IEEE (2009)
16. Guo, G., Mu, G., Fu, Y., Huang, T.S.: Human age estimation using bio-inspired features. In: 2009 IEEE Conference on Computer Vision and Pattern Recognition. CVPR 2009, pp. 112–119. IEEE (2009)
17. Hadid, A.: Analyzing facial behavioral features from videos. In: Salah, A.A., Lepri, B. (eds.) HBU 2011. LNCS, vol. 7065, pp. 52–61. Springer, Heidelberg (2011). https://doi.org/10.1007/978-3-642-25446-8_6
18. Hess, U., Adams Jr., R.B., Kleck, R.E.: Facial appearance, gender, and emotion expression. Emotion **4**(4), 378 (2004)

19. Hochreiter, S., Schmidhuber, J.: Long short-term memory. Neural Comput. **9**(8), 1735–1780 (1997)
20. Ioffe, S., Szegedy, C.: Batch normalization: accelerating deep network training by reducing internal covariate shift. In: International Conference on Machine Learning, pp. 448–456 (2015)
21. Ji, S., Xu, W., Yang, M., Yu, K.: 3D convolutional neural networks for human action recognition. IEEE Trans. Pattern Anal. Mach. Intell. **35**(1), 221–231 (2013)
22. Juefei-Xu, F., Verma, E., Goel, P., Cherodian, A., Savvides, M.: DeepGender: occlusion and low resolution robust facial gender classification via progressively trained convolutional neural networks with attention. In: Proceedings of the IEEE Conference on Computer Vision and Pattern Recognition Workshops, pp. 68–77 (2016)
23. Karpathy, A., Toderici, G., Shetty, S., Leung, T., Sukthankar, R., Fei-Fei, L.: Large-scale video classification with convolutional neural networks. In: Proceedings of the IEEE Conference on Computer Vision and Pattern Recognition, pp. 1725–1732 (2014)
24. Kim, D.H., Baddar, W., Jang, J., Ro, Y.M.: Multi-objective based spatio-temporal feature representation learning robust to expression intensity variations for facial expression recognition. IEEE Trans. Affect. Comput. (2017). https://doi.org/10.1109/TAFFC.2017.2695999
25. Kim, S.T., Kim, D.H., Ro, Y.M.: Facial dynamic modelling using long short-term memory network: analysis and application to face authentication. In: 2016 IEEE 8th International Conference on Biometrics Theory, Applications and Systems (BTAS), pp. 1–6. IEEE (2016)
26. Lea, C., Reiter, A., Vidal, R., Hager, G.D.: Segmental spatiotemporal CNNs for fine-grained action segmentation. In: Leibe, B., Matas, J., Sebe, N., Welling, M. (eds.) ECCV 2016. LNCS, vol. 9907, pp. 36–52. Springer, Cham (2016). https://doi.org/10.1007/978-3-319-46487-9_3
27. Levi, G., Hassner, T.: Age and gender classification using convolutional neural networks. In: Proceedings of the IEEE Conference on Computer Vision and Pattern Recognition Workshops, pp. 34–42 (2015)
28. Li, S., Xing, J., Niu, Z., Shan, S., Yan, S.: Shape driven kernel adaptation in convolutional neural network for robust facial traits recognition. In: Proceedings of the IEEE Conference on Computer Vision and Pattern Recognition, pp. 222–230 (2015)
29. Makinen, E., Raisamo, R.: Evaluation of gender classification methods with automatically detected and aligned faces. IEEE Trans. Pattern Anal. Mach. Intell. **30**(3), 541–547 (2008)
30. Nair, V., Hinton, G.E.: Rectified linear units improve restricted Boltzmann machines. In: Proceedings of the 27th International Conference on Machine Learning (ICML-10), pp. 807–814 (2010)
31. Parkhi, O.M., Vedaldi, A., Zisserman, A., et al.: Deep face recognition. In: BMVC, 1, p. 6 (2015)
32. Pilz, K.S., Thornton, I.M., Bülthoff, H.H.: A search advantage for faces learned in motion. Exp. Brain Res. **171**(4), 436–447 (2006)
33. Reid, D., Samangooei, S., Chen, C., Nixon, M., Ross, A.: Soft biometrics for surveillance: an overview. In: Machine Learning: Theory and Applications, pp. 327–352. Elsevier (2013)
34. Roark, D.A., Barrett, S.E., Spence, M.J., Abdi, H., O'Toole, A.J.: Psychological and neural perspectives on the role of motion in face recognition. Behav. Cogn. Neurosci. Rev. **2**(1), 15–46 (2003)

35. Santoro, A., et al.: A simple neural network module for relational reasoning. In: Advances in Neural Information Processing Systems, pp. 4974–4983 (2017)
36. Simon, R.W., Nath, L.E.: Gender and emotion in the united states: do men and women differ in self-reports of feelings and expressive behavior? Am. J. Sociol. **109**(5), 1137–1176 (2004)
37. Srivastava, N., Hinton, G.E., Krizhevsky, A., Sutskever, I., Salakhutdinov, R.: Dropout: a simple way to prevent neural networks from overfitting. J. Mach. Learn. Res. **15**(1), 1929–1958 (2014)
38. Toews, M., Arbel, T.: Detection, localization, and sex classification of faces from arbitrary viewpoints and under occlusion. IEEE Trans. Pattern Anal. Mach. Intell. **31**(9), 1567–1581 (2009)
39. Tong, Y., Liao, W., Ji, Q.: Facial action unit recognition by exploiting their dynamic and semantic relationships. IEEE Trans. Pattern Anal. Mach. Intell. **29**(10), 1683–1699 (2007)
40. Tran, D., Bourdev, L., Fergus, R., Torresani, L., Paluri, M.: Learning spatiotemporal features with 3D convolutional networks. In: Proceedings of the IEEE International Conference on Computer Vision, pp. 4489–4497 (2015)
41. Uřičař, M., Timofte, R., Rothe, R., Matas, J., et al.: Structured output SVM prediction of apparent age, gender and smile from deep features. In: Proceedings of the 29th IEEE Conference on Computer Vision and Pattern Recognision Workshop (CVPRW 2016), pp. 730–738. IEEE (2016)
42. Yue-Hei Ng, J., Hauswirth, M., Vijayanarasimhan, S., Vinyals, O., Monga, R., Toderici, G.: Beyond short snippets: deep networks for video classification. In: Proceedings of the IEEE Conference on Computer Vision and Pattern Recognition, pp. 4694–4702 (2015)
43. Zhao, K., Chu, W.S., De la Torre, F., Cohn, J.F., Zhang, H.: Joint patch and multi-label learning for facial action unit and holistic expression recognition. IEEE Trans. Image Process. **25**(8), 3931–3946 (2016)

Visual Question Generation for Class Acquisition of Unknown Objects

Kohei Uehara[1]([⊠])(iD), Antonio Tejero-De-Pablos[1], Yoshitaka Ushiku[1],
and Tatsuya Harada[1,2]

[1] The University of Tokyo, Tokyo, Japan
{uehara,antonio-t,ushiku,harada}@mi.t.u-tokyo.ac.jp
[2] RIKEN, Tokyo, Japan

Abstract. Traditional image recognition methods only consider objects belonging to already learned classes. However, since training a recognition model with every object class in the world is unfeasible, a way of getting information on unknown objects (i.e., objects whose class has not been learned) is necessary. A way for an image recognition system to learn new classes could be asking a human about objects that are unknown. In this paper, we propose a method for generating questions about unknown objects in an image, as means to get information about classes that have not been learned. Our method consists of a module for proposing objects, a module for identifying unknown objects, and a module for generating questions about unknown objects. The experimental results via human evaluation show that our method can successfully get information about unknown objects in an image dataset. Our code and dataset are available at https://github.com/mil-tokyo/vqg-unknown.

Keywords: Visual question generation · Unknown object recognition
Unknown object class acquisition · Real world recognition

1 Introduction

In recent years, in large-scale image classification tasks, image classifiers with deep convolutional neural networks (CNN) have achieved accuracies equivalent to humans [7,22]. The recognition capabilities of these methods are limited by the object classes included in the training data. However, for an image recognition system running in the real world, for example a robot, considering all existing object classes in the world during training is unfeasible. If such a robot was able to ask for information about *objects it cannot recognize*, the robot would not have to learn all classes in advance. In this paper, we define an *unknown object* as an object belonging to a class not included in the training data. In order to acquire knowledge about the unknown object class, the most reliable way is to obtain information directly from humans. For example, the robot can present an image to a human and ask them to annotate the class of an object, as in active learning [12]. When the class is unknown, selecting the appropriate object and

© Springer Nature Switzerland AG 2018
V. Ferrari et al. (Eds.): ECCV 2018, LNCS 11216, pp. 492–507, 2018.
https://doi.org/10.1007/978-3-030-01258-8_30

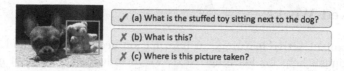

Fig. 1. Examples of suitable/unsuitable questions for unknown objects. A suitable question should specify the target object (*stuffed toy*), so the answer is the class of the unknown object (*teddy bear*). Therefore, questions such as (a) are suitable. On the other hand, simple questions such as (b) and questions about location such as (c) are unsuitable.

generating a suitable question about it is a challenging problem, and has not been tackled yet. The goal of this research is to generate questions that request information about a specific unknown object in an image. As shown in Fig. 1, compared to a simple question such as *"What is this?"*, a specific question such as *"What is the stuffed toy sitting next to the dog?"* targets better the class of the unknown object. There exist several approaches [9,16] for general visual question generation (VQG) by using recurrent neural networks (RNN). Also, VQG with a specific target for a question has also been studied [13] by providing a *target word* (i.e., a word indicating what object the question is targeting) to an RNN as a condition. However, in these works, only the known classes are given as the target word. To the best of our knowledge, VQG targeting unknown objects has not been studied yet. Also, in order to realize a VQG method for unknown objects, first we need to detect and classify the unknown object. However, we cannot rely on object classification methods [7] nor object region proposal methods [21] if they only consider known/labeled classes (i.e., supervised learning).

In this paper, to find unknown objects in an image, we propose object regions by selective search [28], which is not based on supervised learning, and then classify whether the proposed objects are unknown or not. Since our method has to classify all the objects, in order to reduce the execution time we propose an efficient unknown object classification based on uncertainty prediction. In addition, we approach VQG for unknown objects by generating a question containing the *hypernym* of the unknown object. The hypernym of a given word is another word that is higher in the semantic hierarchy, such as *"animal"* for *"dog."*

Contributions: (1) We propose the novel task of automatically generating questions to get information about unknown objects in images. (2) We propose a method to generate questions using the semantic hierarchy of the target word. (3) We construct the whole pipeline by combining modules of object region proposal, unknown object classification, and visual question generation, and show that it can successfully acquire information about unknown objects from humans.

The paper is organized as follows. First, we explain previous studies related to this research in Sect. 2. Next, we introduce our proposed system in Sect. 3. Then, we show experiments on our module for unknown object classification in Sect. 4, and our visual question generation module in Sect. 5. In Sect. 6, we evaluate our entire pipeline to get the class of unknown objects. Finally, in Sect. 7, we discuss the conclusions and future work.

2 Related Works

First, we explain active learning, an information acquisition method that also considers human help for learning. Next, we introduce the research related to each of our modules, namely, object detection, unknown object classification, and visual question generation.

Active Learning. The aim of active learning is achieving efficient learning by automatically selecting data that seems to contribute the most to improve the performance of the classifier and requesting a human annotator to label them. Uncertainty Sampling [12] has been proposed to select the instances whose class is the least certain. There are three methods for Uncertainty Sampling: (1) *Least Confident* [12]: Select the instance whose classification probability is the smallest and whose class has the greatest overall classification probability. (2) *Margin Sampling* [24]: Select the instance whose difference between the most and the second most classification probabilities is the smallest. (3) *Entropy Sampling* [8, 26]: Select the instance whose distribution of classification probabilities has the largest entropy. The main difference between active learning and this research is that active learning targets only instances whose class is included in the training set, whereas we target instances whose class is not in the training set. Also, active learning only presents data to the annotator; it does not generate questions.

Object Region Proposal. Object region proposal methods detect the region surrounding objects in an image. Recent methods perform object detection that performs both object region proposal and object classification at the same time via supervised learning using CNN [20,21]. These methods achieve accurate object detection with a huge amount of labeled data for training. However, they do not consider unknown objects. In contrast, there is some research on *object-ness* that simply estimates the existence objects in a specific region of the image, without classifying the object. Alexe et al. [1] perform objectness estimation by using saliency, contrast, edge, and superpixel information. Cheng et al. [4] learn objectness from image gradients. Also, a method called selective search [23,28] allows object region proposal by using image segmentation, and integrating similar regions with each other. Since it does not require object labels, it can propose regions without learning the object class.

Unknown Object Classification. Unknown object classification performs binary classification of objects in an image as *known* or *unknown*. Traditionally, object classification methods estimate the actual class of an object in an input image. Recent research in object classification are CNN-based methods [7,27]. These methods assume a *closed set*, that is, they only consider the classes included in training and not unknown classes. On the other hand, there is research on the task called *open set recognition* [25] for object classification that includes unknown objects. Open set recognition is a task aimed at classifying to the correct class if the input belongs to the trained class, and if the input is unknown, classifying it as unknown. For open set recognition, methods using SVM [25] and methods extending the nearest neighbor method [2] have been

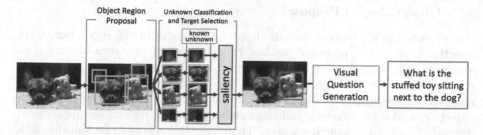

Fig. 2. Overview of the proposed method. First, regions from objects in the image (including unknown objects) are detected. Then, unknown objects are classified and the target region is selected. Finally, the target region along with the whole image is coded into a feature vector, and a question for the unknown object is generated

proposed. Also, Bendale et al. [3] proposed open set recognition using CNN. They classify an object as unknown if its feature distribution extracted from the CNN hidden layers is distant from known classes.

Visual Question Generation. Visual Question Generation (VQG) was recently proposed as an extension of image captioning. Whereas image captioning methods [29] generate descriptive sentences about the content of an image, VQG methods generate questions (e.g., *What color is the car?*). The common approach in VQG is encoding image features via CNN and generating a sentence by decoding those features using an RNN. Methods that use a gated recurrent unit (GRU) [16] and a long short-term memory (LSTM) [9] have been proposed. Traditional VQG methods generate questions from the whole image, without focusing in any particular image region. Only recently, methods that generate questions targeting a particular image region have been proposed. Zhang et al. [30] detect different regions to generate a variety of questions from the same image. In contrast, Li et al. [13] generate questions focusing on a specific region with the goal of distinguishing between two images. For this, they input a target word (e.g., blue) related to the region as a condition to the LSTM. In [13], target words are known classes learned in advance. To the best of our knowledge, VQG targeting an unknown object has not been approached yet.

3 Proposed System

Figure 2 shows the overview of the proposed method. First, objects in the input image are detected by the object region proposal module. Next, the unknown object classification and target selection module identifies whether each object is unknown or not, and selects an object region to be the target of the question. We refer to this region as the *target region*. Finally, the visual question generation module generates a question using features extracted from the whole image and the target region.

3.1   Object Region Proposal

Our object region proposal module detects all objects in the input image via selective search. The proposed method needs to detect unknown objects (i.e., objects never learned before), so supervised learning is not an option since it requires labels for all objects. As mentioned in Sect. 2, selective search provides candidate regions for objects without supervised learning. Thus, unknown objects can also be detected, and the number of object regions can be reduced compared with an exhaustive search. Therefore, this seems to be suitable as a method for object region proposal.

3.2   Unknown Object Classification and Target Selection

This module selects the *target object*, that is, the object to acquire information about. For that, we classify objects into *known* or *unknown*, and then select the most salient unknown object. This prevents generating questions about unimportant regions that may have been proposed by mistake by the object region proposal module. We define unknown object classification as follows: for an input object image, if its class is included in the training set, classify it to the correct class, and if not, classify it as unknown. Specifically, we perform unknown object classification on the classification results of a CNN as follows. The output of the softmax function of the CNN can be regarded as the confidence with which the input is classified into a certain class. We consider that images of unknown objects result in a low confidence value for all classes. That is, the more uniform the confidence distribution, the lower the confidence for all classes and the more possibilities the object is unknown. Therefore, we perform unknown object classification by estimating the dispersion of the probability distribution using an entropy measure, with reference to the method of Uncertainty Sampling in active learning [8, 26]. The entropy measure E is defined as:

$$E = -\sum_{j=1}^{K} p_j \log_2 p_j \tag{1}$$

where p_j is the output of the softmax function when a given input x is classified into class C_j $(j = 1, 2, \ldots, K)$. E takes the maximum value $\log_2 K$ when all p_j are all equal, that is, when $p_j = 1/K$. On the other hand, the larger the dispersion of the probability distribution is, the smaller the entropy becomes.

Also, it is necessary to select which object to generate a question about among the objects classified as unknown. For example, in some cases, the region proposed by selective search contains only the background. Background regions are likely to be classified as unknown, but they do not contain an object to ask about. In order to solve this problem, we calculate the saliency of each proposed region in the image as a criterion for selecting the target region. That is, we ask questions about objects that are unknown and particularly salient in the image. Thus, to select salient objects in the image, we propose using a saliency map. The saliency map is a plot obtained by estimating the saliency for each pixel in

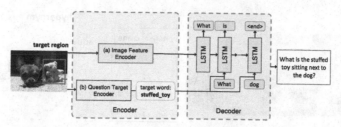

Fig. 3. Overview of the VQG module. First, we obtain the common hypernym of the prediction class of the classifier as the target word. The target word and the image features are input as conditions to the LSTM, and the question is generated

the image. We calculate the saliency map using the method of Zhu et al. [31]. This method estimates low saliency for background pixels and high saliency for foreground pixels. Therefore, it is considered to be suitable for this research. First, we preprocessed the image by applying mask based on saliency map and applied non-maximum suppression to reduce the large number of object regions. Then, the saliency of each proposed object region is expressed by:

$$I_{region} = \sum_{I(p) \geq \theta} I(p) \times \frac{S_{salient}}{S_{region}} \tag{2}$$

where, $I(p)$ is the saliency value of each pixel, θ is the threshold value, $S_{salient}$ is the area in the region where saliency exceeds θ, and S_{region} is the total area of the region. The threshold θ was determined using Otsu method [18]. The region with the highest saliency is selected as the target region.

3.3   Visual Question Generation

Figure 3 depicts the visual question generation module. We generate a question following the encoder-decoder methodology of Mostafazadeh et al. [16] and Li et al. [13]. The encoder extracts visual features of both the entire image and the object region (submodule (a)), and (submodule (b)) the target word into a word embedding vector representation. The decoder takes the encoded features and generates a question via LSTM.

Encoding of Image Features. This submodule uses a pretrained CNN model to extract the features f_I of the entire image and the features f_R of the target region. In our method, we use the output (a 1,000-dimensional vector) of the fc layer of ResNet152 [7]. Then, in order to express the spatial information of the target region, we follow the method by Li et al. [13] to define a five-dimensional vector l_R as:

$$l_R = \left[\frac{x_{tl}}{W}, \frac{y_{tl}}{H}, \frac{x_{br}}{W}, \frac{y_{br}}{H}, \frac{S_R}{S_I} \right] \tag{3}$$

where (x_{tl}, y_{tl}), (x_{br}, y_{br}) is the upper left and the lower right coordinate of the target region, S_R and S_I represent the area of the target region and the entire

498   K. Uehara et al.

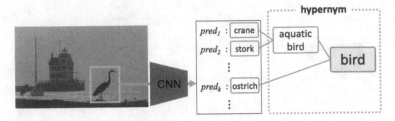

Fig. 4. Overview of the question target module for target word selection using Word-Net [6]. WordNet is used to obtain a hypernym common to the predicted class labels with the highest confidence. The hypernym is then input to the visual question generation module

image respectively, and W and H denote the width and the height of the image respectively. We concatenate f_I, f_R, l_R, and let the 2,005 dimensional vector $f = [f_R, f_I, l_R]$ be the image feature encoding.

Question Target. This submodule selects a target word to represent the object in the target region and embeds it into a vector representation. Since the target object is unknown, that is, is not in the trained classes, it is not possible to use the class label as the target word as in Li et al. [13]. Therefore, we need to devise how to specify the target word. For example, if we do not know the class dog, asking a question referring to an *animal* is natural (e.g., *"What is this animal?"*). In this case, the word *animal* for *dog* is considered to be a hypernym. Such hypernym can be used as the target word. We use WordNet [6] to get the hierarchical relationship of words. Each word in WordNet is hierarchically arranged based on semantic relationships, and thus, it is possible to get the hypernym of a word by going up in the hierarchy.

As shown in Fig. 4, we use the k predicted classes $(pred_1, pred_2, \ldots pred_k)$ with the highest confidence of the classification result, and we select the word with the lowest level among the common hypernyms of the k class labels. If the value of k is too large, the common hypernym becomes a very abstract word such as *whole* or *entity*, and it is not possible to designate the target appropriately. Therefore, the value of k should be chosen carefully.

Then, we use the Poincaré Embeddings [17] to embed words into feature vectors using a neural network similar to Word2Vec [14,15]. However, unlike Word2Vec, Poincaré Embeddings are suitable for expressing a structure in which words are hierarchically represented, such as WordNet, as a vector. Let the target word embedded by Poincaré Embeddings be the vector $\sigma(v)$. Then the input to the decoder LSTM is the visual feature vector f, and the conditional input is the word embedded vector $\sigma(v)$. The decoder LSTM is trained by minimizing the negative log likelihood:

$$L = \sum - \log p(Q \mid f, \ \sigma(v) \ ; \ \theta) \tag{4}$$

where θ is the parameters of the LSTM, and Q denotes the generated question.

4   Evaluation of the Unknown Object Classification

Before evaluating the entire pipeline we performed experiments on independent modules to study their performance. First, we evaluated how accurately the unknown object classification module can classify whether the input image is an unknown object image or not.

4.1   Experimental Settings

We used CaffeNet [11], VGGNet [27], and ResNet152 [7], which are well-known CNN models, to study the variation in unknown classification accuracy when employing different classifiers. We pretrained our classifier with the 1,000 class dataset used in the object classification task of ILSVRC2012. We used 50,000 images of the same dataset for validation. Then, we used the dataset in the object classification task of ILSVRC2010 to create the unknown dataset. We excluded all images whose class is *known* (i.e., included in the ILSVRC2012 dataset), as well as the images whose class is a hypernym of any *known* classes. The reason for removing hypernyms is to avoid including general classes (e.g., "dog") in the unknown dataset when the specific class is already known (e.g., "chihuahua"). Thus, we selected 50,850 images of 339 classes from ILSVRC2010 dataset, which are not included in ILSVRC2012 and its hypernyms.

4.2   Methods

We compare unknown object classification using entropy E, which is the proposed method, with the following two methods.

Least Confident [12]. We used the method of Uncertainty Sampling described in Sect. 2. We set a threshold for the softmax probability of the class label with the highest probability, that is, the most probable label. Then, if the probability is lower than the threshold, the label is considered as unknown.

Bendale et al [3]. We used the method of Bendale et al. mentioned in Sect. 2. We performed this experiment based on the code published by the authors, and change the classification models for CaffeNet, VGGNet, and ResNet.

4.3   Evaluation Metrics

We calculated the F measure as:

$$F = \frac{2TP}{2TP + FP + FN} \tag{5}$$

where TP is defined as the number of known data classified into the correct class, FN as the number of unknown data misclassified into known data, and FP as the number of misclassified known data [3]. We performed the evaluation using a five-fold cross-validation.

Table 1. Comparison of the proposed unknown object classification method in terms of F measure results ± standard error. We performed experiments on CaffeNet, VGGNet, and ResNet. In all three cases, the proposed method outperformed the other methods

	F measure		
	CaffeNet	VGGNet	ResNet
Ours	$\mathbf{0.526 \pm 1.1 \cdot 10^{-3}}$	$\mathbf{0.602 \pm 0.2 \cdot 10^{-3}}$	$\mathbf{0.654 \pm 0.9 \cdot 10^{-3}}$
Least confident	$0.522 \pm 1.1 \cdot 10^{-3}$	$0.590 \pm 1.5 \cdot 10^{-3}$	$0.635 \pm 1.2 \cdot 10^{-3}$
Bendale et al. [3]	$0.524 \pm 0.9 \cdot 10^{-3}$	$0.553 \pm 0.6 \cdot 10^{-3}$	$0.624 \pm 1.7 \cdot 10^{-3}$

Table 2. Comparison of the proposed unknown object classification method in terms of execution time, with CaffeNet as a classifier. We performed classification for 100 images and showed the average time per image ± standard error

	Time (sec/image)
Ours	0.0400 ± 0.0017
Least confident	$\mathbf{0.0365 \pm 0.0019}$
Bendale et al. [3]	15.6 ± 0.7

Also, we measured the execution time of each method. First, we measured the time required by the classifier to calculate the softmax probability distribution of one image. Next, we experimented the calculation time per image for each method, taking the distribution of softmax probability for 100 images as input. We repeated this operation five times and calculated the average execution time.

4.4   Experimental Results

Table 1 shows the resulting F measure per classifier and method. For all three methods, the F measure increased as the classifier was changed from CaffeNet to VGGNet, and to ResNet. The higher the accuracy of the classifier, when inputting known classes, the distribution of the classification probabilities varies more largely, and thus the entropy becomes smaller. In the case of inputting unknown classes, the more accurate the classifier is, the distribution of the classification probabilities is more uniform and thus the entropy becomes larger.

Table 2 shows a comparison of the execution time for each method when CaffeNet is used as a classifier. Our method and the Least Confident method take much less time than the method of Bendale et al. This is because the method of Bendale et al. has to calculate the distance to the average distribution of 1,000 known classes for each image, so the calculation cost is large, but in the method using entropy and the method using threshold of confidence, calculation is performed only with distribution of the input image, so calculation time is shortened.

5   Evaluation of the Visual Question Generation

We studied the performance of the proposed visual question generation module given a target region and compared to other methods.

5.1   Datasets

In this experiment, we used a dataset called Visual Genome [10] with about 100,000 images, and captions and questions. There is a subset of questions that is associated with a specific region in the image. We preprocessed the data as follows. First, we removed questions not beginning with *"What."* Furthermore, since questions about colors are not the goal of our method, we also removed questions beginning with *"What color."* Next, for questions associated with a specific region in the image, if the word representing the object in the region was included in the answer of the question, that word was taken as the target word. For questions not associated with an image region, we searched the object included in the answer among all objects in the image. Then, if there is only one instance of the object in the image, the word and the region where the object exists are set as the target word and the target region corresponding to the question. Furthermore, in order to eliminate the imbalance in the type of questions in the data, we limited to 50 the maximum number of times the same question can be included. Through this preprocessing, we gathered 202,208 questions corresponding to specific target regions in the image (one question per region) and 528 target words.

5.2   Methods

We split the 202,208 questions into 179,997 questions for training, 10,002 questions for validation, and 12,209 questions for testing. At training time, questions were generated by inputting images, regions, and target words. For embedding target words, we used Poincaré Embeddings trained on the tree structure of WordNet. We used the following methods as a baseline to compare our proposed method.

CNN + LSTM. As in Mostafazadeh et al. [16], we generated questions by inputting only the features of the entire image encoded by a CNN.

Retrieval. Following Mostafazadeh et al. [16], we also used retrieval method as baseline. First, we extracted features of the target regions in the training images using the fc layer of ResNet152. Then we retrieved the m regions with the higher cosine similarity between their features and the input target region. Then, for each question associated to the retrieved region, we calculated the similarity with the other $m - 1$ questions using the BLEU score [19], which measures textual similarity. Finally, the question with the highest BLEU score, that is, the most representative question, was taken as the final output.

5.3   Evaluation Metrics

In our experiments, we use BLEU [19] and METEOR [5] for measuring the similarity between the automatically generated questions and the ground truth. The larger the value, the more accurate the result.

Besides the automatic evaluation, we also performed human evaluation via Amazon Mechanical Turk (AMT)[1]. We presented an image with the target region and the target word to the human workers. We asked workers to blindly evaluate each method and the ground truth using a score between 5 (best) and 1 (worst). We used two criteria for evaluation: (1) whether each question is expressed naturally, and (2) whether each question is related to the target region and the target word. For the human evaluation, we used questions generated for 100 images extracted randomly from the test data.

Table 3. Comparison between our method and the baseline in terms of automatic evaluation metrics. The proposed method outperformed baseline methods

	BLEU-1	BLEU-2	BLEU-3	BLEU-4	METEOR
Ours	**0.518**	**0.359**	**0.244**	**0.175**	**0.197**
CNN + LSTM	0.456	0.296	0.175	0.110	0.163
Retrieval	0.438	0.275	0.157	0.094	0.151

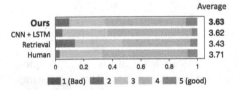

Fig. 5. (1) Human evaluation results on the naturalness of questions

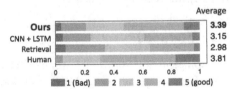

Fig. 6. (2) Human evaluation results on the relevance of questions to their region

5.4   Experimental Results

As shown in Table 3, the proposed method outperformed the baselines for all metrics. This result suggests that inputting the target object (visual features and target word condition) to the decoder LSTM allows generating more accurate questions. Figures 5 and 6 show the results of the human evaluation of our method compared to baselines. From the viewpoint of the naturalness of the question, the difference between the proposed method and CNN + LSTM was small. We believe the reason is that both methods use LSTM as the decoder.

---

[1] https://www.mturk.com/.

When evaluating the relevance of the question to the target region, the proposed method outperformed baselines. This is because, CNN + LSTM does not specify a target object to the decoder, so it may generate questions that are related to the image but not the target region. Also, Retrieval can generate only questions existing in the training data, so the variety of questions is limited, and thus, it may not generate questions related to the target region.

6 Evaluation of VQG for Unknown Objects

Lastly, we performed experiments using the whole pipeline, in which we generate questions to acquire knowledge about the class of unknown objects in the image.

6.1 Datasets

In order to test our VQG method for unknown objects, we used images that include unknown objects extracted from the following two datasets. First, from the test set of Visual Genome, we extracted 50 images with unknown objects, that is, not included in the 1,000 classes of ILSVRC2012. Also, from the dataset of the ILSVRC2010, 50 images of 339 unknown classes as described in Sect. 4 were extracted. In the images from the Visual Genome dataset, target regions contain an average of 8.7 objects, including small objects like "eye" and "button". According to our method, 68.4% of those objects were unknown. Note that we cannot indicate objectively the number of objects in the images from the ILSVRC2010 dataset since its ground truth does not include object regions.

6.2 Methods

The classifier used for unknown object classification was ResNet152, which is the method with the highest accuracy in Sect. 4. We pretrained ResNet152 with the 1,000 class data used in the object classification task of ILSVRC2012. The visual question generation module was pretrained with the dataset created in Sect. 5.1. Furthermore, as described in Sect. 3.3, when choosing a hypernym common to the top k classification results, if the value of k is too large, the target word becomes too abstract. Therefore, we performed experiments with two settings, $k = 2$ and $k = 3$. As baseline methods, we used the CNN + LSTM method and the Nearest Neighbors Retrieval method described in Sect. 5.

6.3 Evaluation Metrics

Since there is no ground truth in this experiment, it is not possible to perform automatic evaluation by comparison with the ground truth. Therefore, we performed only human evaluation via AMT, which consists of the following two tasks.

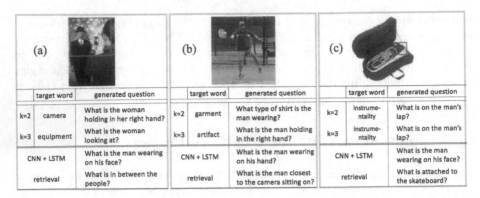

Fig. 7. Examples of input images (upper), the target words and generated questions by our proposed VQG method for unknown objects (middle), and the generated questions by the *CNN + LSTM* and *retrieval* baselines (lower).

(1) We presented to three workers images and the questions generated automatically by our method and the baselines, and asked them to answer the generated questions. When they cannot understand the meaning of the question, we instructed them to answer *"Do not understand."* Note that this task did not present a target region.

(2) Also, we evaluated the question and the answer obtained in task (1). Specifically, we presented to three workers with the question, the answer of each worker in task (1), and the image with the target region, and asked them whether the question and the answer are related to the target region in a 5-point scale. We evaluated only answers different from *"Do not understand."*

As the evaluation value for task (2), we used the median of the evaluation values of the three workers.

Lastly, we evaluated to what extent the generated questions are able to successfully acquire information on unknown objects. We counted only the questions whose answers (task (1)) are not included in the known classes of the classifier, and the relevance of the question and target region in the image (task (2)) is four or more.

6.4 Experimental Results

Figure 7 shows our qualitative results. In Fig. 7(a) and (b), when $k = 2$, the target word is a concrete word (i.e., *"camera"* and *"garment"*), and the generated question refers to an object in the target region. In the case of $k = 3$, the target word is an abstract word such as *"equipment"* and *"artifact"*, and the generated question is not related to the region. Figure 7(c) shows an example where the object region proposal is not performed properly, and thus, it is not possible to generate the question accurately. The lower part of the image shows examples of questions generated by the baselines.

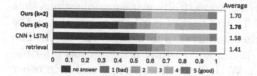

Fig. 8. Comparison of our method with the baseline in terms of the human evaluation in task (2). Task (2) evaluates whether or not the generated question, the image region, and the obtained answer are related. The greater the score, the higher the relevance.

Table 4. The number of generated questions that successfully allowed acquiring information on unknown objects (out of 300). We counted only the questions whose answers (task (1)) are not included in the known classes of the classifier, and the relevance of the question and target region in the image (task (2)) is four or more.

Ours ($k = 2$)	**61**
Ours ($k = 3$)	49
CNN + LSTM	46
Retrieval	45

Figure 8 shows the results of the human evaluation. The answer *"Do not understand"* in task (1) is shown as *"no answer."* The average of evaluation values is calculated by assigning *"no answer"* a score of 0. The proposed method outperformed the baseline in terms of relevance to the region and relevance to the answer. The reason is that the proposed method specifies a target object to the LSTM to generate the question, whereas the baselines do not consider any target. Regarding the number k of class labels used to select the target word, the average score is higher when $k = 3$, but the ratio of the highest score 5 is higher when $k = 2$. Also, the proportion of *"no answer"* is higher when $k = 2$. This means that, when $k = 3$, the target word becomes more generic and the relevance with the target region is less clear than when using $k = 2$. On the other hand, a value of $k = 2$ is more likely to specify a wrong target word for the visual question generation.

Table 4 shows the number of generated questions that successfully allowed acquiring information on unknown objects. We consider successful questions whose answers were not included in the known class of the unknown classifier neither in their hypernym, and whose relevance score in task (2) was 4 or more. We obtained the highest number of successful questions using our method with $k = 2$, since the selected target word is more concrete. On the other hand, our method with $k = 3$ generates questions for a more generic target word, and thus, it does not necessarily get the expected answer, but is still partly related to the target region.

We can conclude that the proposed method can successfully generate questions that allow acquiring information about unknown objects in an image.

7   Conclusions

In this paper, we presented a novel visual question generation (VQG) task to acquire class information of unknown (i.e., not learned previously) objects in the image, and proposed a method that automatically generates questions that target unknown objects in the image. To the best of our knowledge, this is the first research that approaches acquiring unknown information via VQG. The evaluation of our method shows that it can successfully acquire class information of unknown objects from humans. We believe this research will help other researchers in tackling this novel task.

Our future work includes feeding back the acquired information about the unknown object to the system, and learning it as new knowledge. For example, our method could be combined with recent works in few-shot learning and incremental learning to re-train the classifier with the new class. In addition, it is considered that the answers from humans will be noisy, so a system that can use noisy answers for re-training is necessary. If the answer obtained from humans is not the expected, it can be useful to generate multiple questions as necessary.

Acknowledgement. This work was supported by JST CREST Grant Number JPMJCR1403, Japan.

References

1. Alexe, B., Deselaers, T., Ferrari, V.: Measuring the objectness of image windows. IEEE PAMI **34**, 2189–2202 (2012)
2. Bendale, A., Boult, T.E.: Towards open world recognition. In: CVPR (2015)
3. Bendale, A., Boult, T.E.: Towards open set deep networks. In: CVPR (2016)
4. Cheng, M.M., Zhang, Z., Lin, W.Y., Torr, P.: BING: binarized normed gradients for objectness estimation at 300fps. In: CVPR (2014)
5. Denkowski, M., Lavie, A.: Meteor universal: language specific translation evaluation for any target language. In: EACL Workshop on Statistical Machine Translation (2014)
6. Fellbaum, C.: WordNet : An Electronic Lexical Database. MIT Press, Cambridge (1998)
7. He, K., Zhang, X., Ren, S., Sun, J.: Deep residual learning for image recognition. In: CVPR (2016)
8. Hwa, R.: Sample selection for statistical parsing. Comput. Linguist. **30**, 253–276 (2004)
9. Jain, U., Zhang, Z., Schwing, A.G.: Creativity: Generating diverse questions using variational autoencoders. In: CVPR (2017)
10. Krishna, R., et al.: Visual genome: connecting language and vision using crowd-sourced dense image annotations. IJCV **123**, 32–73 (2017)
11. Krizhevsky, A., Sutskever, I., Hinton, G.E.: ImageNet classification with deep convolutional neural networks. In: NIPS (2012)
12. Lewis, D.D., Gale, W.A.: A sequential algorithm for training text classifiers. In: ACM SIGIR (1994)
13. Li, Y., Huang, C., Tang, X., Loy, C.C.: Learning to disambiguate by asking discriminative questions. In: ICCV (2017)
14. Mikolov, T., Chen, K., Corrado, G., Dean, J.: Efficient estimation of word representations in vector space. In: ICLR (2013)

15. Mikolov, T., Sutskever, I., Chen, K., Corrado, G.S., Dean, J.: Distributed representations of words and phrases and their compositionality. In: NIPS (2013)
16. Mostafazadeh, N., Misra, I., Devlin, J., Mitchell, M., He, X., Vanderwende, L.: Generating natural questions about an image. In: ACL (2016)
17. Nickel, M., Kiela, D.: Poincaré embeddings for learning hierarchical representations. In: NIPS (2017)
18. Otsu, N.: A threshold selection method from gray-level histograms. IEEE SMC **9**, 62–66 (1979)
19. Papineni, K., Roukos, S., Ward, T., Zhu, W.J.: BLEU: a method for automatic evaluation of machine translation. In: ACL (2001)
20. Redmon, J., Divvala, S., Girshick, R., Farhadi, A.: You only look once: unified, real-time object detection. In: CVPR (2016)
21. Ren, S., He, K., Girshick, R., Sun, J.: Faster R-CNN: towards real-time object detection with region proposal networks. In: NIPS (2015)
22. Russakovsky, O., et al.: ImageNet large scale visual recognition challenge. IJCV **115**, 211–252 (2015)
23. van de Sande, K.E.A., Uijlings, J.R.R., Gevers, T., Smeulders, A.W.M.: Segmentation as selective search for object recognition. In: ICCV (2011)
24. Scheffer, T., Decomain, C., Wrobel, S.: Active hidden Markov models for information extraction. In: Hoffmann, F., Hand, D.J., Adams, N., Fisher, D., Guimaraes, G. (eds.) IDA 2001. LNCS, vol. 2189, pp. 309–318. Springer, Heidelberg (2001). https://doi.org/10.1007/3-540-44816-0_31
25. Scheirer, W.J., de Rezende Rocha, A., Sapkota, A., Boult, T.E.: Toward open set recognition. IEEE PAMI **35**, 1757–1772 (2013)
26. Settles, B., Craven, M.: An analysis of active learning strategies for sequence labeling tasks. In: EMNLP (2008)
27. Simonyan, K., Zisserman, A.: Very deep convolutional networks for large-scale image recognition. In: ICLR (2015)
28. Uijlings, J.R.R., van de Sande, K.E.A., Gevers, T., Smeulders, A.W.M.: Selective search for object recognition. IJCV **104**, 154–171 (2013)
29. Vinyals, O., Toshev, A., Bengio, S., Erhan, D.: Show and tell: a neural image caption generator. In: CVPR (2015)
30. Zhang, S., Qu, L., You, S., Yang, Z., Zhang, J.: Automatic generation of grounded visual questions. In: IJCAI (2017)
31. Zhu, W., Liang, S., Wei, Y., Sun, J.: Saliency Optimization from Robust Background Detection. In: CVPR (2014)

Efficient Dense Point Cloud Object Reconstruction Using Deformation Vector Fields

Kejie Li[1,2](✉) [iD], Trung Pham[3] [iD], Huangying Zhan[1,2] [iD], and Ian Reid[1,2] [iD]

[1] The University of Adelaide, Adelaide, Australia
{kejie.li,huangying.zhan,ian.reid}@adelaide.edu.au
[2] Australian Center for Robotic Vision, Brisbane, Australia
[3] NVIDIA, Santa Clara, USA
trungp@nvidia.com

Abstract. Some existing CNN-based methods for single-view 3D object reconstruction represent a 3D object as either a 3D voxel occupancy grid or multiple depth-mask image pairs. However, these representations are inefficient since empty voxels or background pixels are wasteful. We propose a novel approach that addresses this limitation by replacing masks with "deformation-fields". Given a single image at an arbitrary viewpoint, a CNN predicts multiple surfaces, each in a canonical location relative to the object. Each surface comprises a depth-map and corresponding deformation-field that ensures every pixel-depth pair in the depth-map lies on the object surface. These surfaces are then fused to form the full 3D shape. During training we use a combination of per-view loss and multi-view losses. The novel multi-view loss encourages the 3D points back-projected from a particular view to be consistent across views. Extensive experiments demonstrate the efficiency and efficacy of our method on single-view 3D object reconstruction.

Keywords: 3D object reconstruction · Dense point clouds
Deep learning

1 Introduction

Although humans can effortlessly infer the 3D structure of an object from a single image, it is, however, an ill-posed problem in computer vision. To make it well-posed, researchers have been using hand-crafted 3D cues such as "Shape from X" (e.g., shading, texture) [1,4,26] , and planarity [23,28]. More recently, there has been considerable interest in using deep networks to regress from an image to its

---

T. Pham—This work was done prior to joining NVIDIA.

Electronic supplementary material The online version of this chapter (https://doi.org/10.1007/978-3-030-01258-8_31) contains supplementary material, which is available to authorized users.

V. Ferrari et al. (Eds.): ECCV 2018, LNCS 11216, pp. 508–524, 2018.
https://doi.org/10.1007/978-3-030-01258-8_31

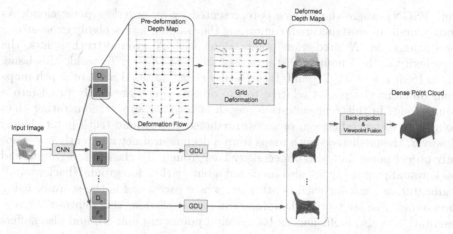

Fig. 1. The overall pipeline of our approach. Given a single RGB image of an object from an arbitrary viewpoint, the CNN outputs a set of 2D pre-deformation depth maps and corresponding deformation fields at pre-defined canonical viewpoints. These are each passed to a Grid Deformation Unit (GDU) that transforms the regular grid of the depth map to a "deformed depth map". Finally, we transform the deformed depth maps into a common coordinate frame to fuse all 3D points into a single dense point cloud. The colors of points indicate different depth values, and the arrow directions represent the image grid deformation (for visualization effect, the magnitude of arrow is not actual scale, the image size is also scaled down) (Color figure online)

depth [8,10,22,38] for scene geometry reconstruction, and in particular from an image of an object to its 3D shape for object geometry reconstruction. There is no settled or best way to represent 3D objects, with methods including meshes [17,29], point clouds [7,21,33], or voxel occupancy grids [5,9,32] , each having both advantages and disadvantages in terms of the efficiency and convenience of the representation, and – importantly for our purposes – for learning.

For volumetric representation methods, most existing CNN-based methods simply extend 2D deconvolutions to 3D deconvolutions on 3D regular grids, as done in [5,9]. For each voxel, the network predicts the score of being occupied by the object. Thresholding the volumetric score map results in a 3D occupancy object representation. Nevertheless, 3D volumetric representations are very expensive in both computation and memory when working with deep networks — the required memory increases cubically with the grid resolution. Importantly, only a small portion of the voxels (less than 10%) are occupied by the object, leaving the rest wasteful. Consequentially, most existing methods are only able to reconstruct objects with low resolutions (i.e., $32 \times 32 \times 32$), thus losing the surface granularity. Furthermore, it is generally non-trivial to find a suitable threshold to generate precise object surfaces for different object classes or even different objects in the same class.

Intuitively, it is more efficient to predict the surface of an object directly, rather than the whole 3D space. Fan *et al.* [7] proposed Point Set Generation

Net (PSGN), where the surface is represented by an orderless point cloud. As point clouds are unstructured, computing the training loss is highly expensive—for instance, for N prediction points along with N ground-truth points, the complexity of the Chamfer Distance used in [7] is $O(N^2)$. To tackle this issue, works from Lin et al. [21] and Tatarchenko et al. [33] used a set of depth maps from different viewpoints relative to the object, which are easily fused into a point cloud. In this representation, depth is used for supervision, rather than point-wise distance between orderless predicted and ground-truth point clouds. However, the predicted depth maps from a deep neural net inherently cover not only object points but also unnecessary background. To classify foreground and background points, [21,33] also predicted a binary (i.e., foreground/background) segmentation mask for each depth map, where each pixel is the score of being foreground. Similar to the 3D volumetric representation, this depth-mask representation is also inefficient as background points are unused, and also suffers from the non-trivial foreground/background thresholding.

Moreover, learning to regress depth from images often generates noisy points around the surface [33]. The fusion of multiple partial-view point clouds escalates the noise. In [21], they propose to improve the quality of fused point clouds by a multi-view consistency supervision based on binary masks and depth maps. The idea is to project the predicted 3D point cloud to novel viewpoints to generate new depth maps and masks at these viewpoints, which are then supervised by the corresponding ground-truth depth maps and binary masks. However, this supervision, being similar to the shape from silhouette technique [24] and voxel based multi-view consistency supervision in deep learning based methods [34,37], encourages masking out the points projected to the background. This further reduces the density of the predicted point clouds and harms the surface coverage.

In this paper, we present a novel and highly efficient framework (shown in Fig. 1) to generate dense point clouds for representing the 3D shape of objects. Given a single image of an object of interest, taken from an arbitrary viewpoint, our network generates multiple partial surfaces of the object, each at a pre-defined canonical viewpoint. Although it looks similar to the depth-mask representation as a multi-view representation, each surface is defined by a depth map and corresponding deformation field (instead of a binary mask). In the Grid Deformation Unit (GDU), a point on the surface is obtained by first shifting a pixel on the depth map image grid by the amount given by the deformation field and then back-projecting (to the corresponding depth). The resulting set of points can then be considered a (dense) point cloud, though it is not an orderless one. The final 3D object representation is obtained by fusing the point-cloud surfaces into a single point cloud.

Both the depth maps and the deformation fields are regressed from the original image using a deep network trained to predict the set of canonical views. At training time we use a combination of per-view and multi-view losses. Our unique representation ensures that the per-view loss can be evaluated in $O(n)$ time (where n is the number of points) because there is no need to establish correspondence between predicted and ground-truth depths. This in contrast to, for instance, Chamfer Distance usually required for unordered point-sets, leading to $O(n^2)$ complexity.

The novel multi-view loss encourages the 3D points back-projected from a particular view to be consistent across novel views. More specifically when a predicted 3D point is re-projected into a novel viewpoint but falls outside of the object silhouette, our network incurs a loss based on the distance of the point to the boundary, rather than penalizing a binary cross entropy loss as done in [21,34,37]. Our extensive experiments demonstrate that using these combined per-view and multi-view losses yields more accurate and dense point cloud representations than any previous method.

Our contributions in this paper are summarized as follows:

- We propose a novel deformed depth map representation for 3D object reconstruction based on multiple canonical views that is efficient and bypasses foreground/background thresholding that lead to structural errors;
- We show how this representation can be effectively regressed using a deep network from a single view;
- We introduce a novel loss for our network that combines a per-view loss – that can be efficiently calculated thanks to our unique representation – with a novel multi-view loss based a distance field.
- We evaluate our method extensively showing more accurate and denser point clouds than current state-of-the-art methods. We include ablation experiments that demonstrate the value of the contributions above separately.

2   Related Work

3D reconstruction from single images has been a long-standing question in computer vision community. While a single image can provide abundant information about scene or object appearance, it barely provides any information about 3D geometry. Therefore, one has to resort to other source of information as additional input for 3D reconstruction.

The use of additional images is a typical example. This branch of works try to find the geometry correspondence between views to recover geometry, such as SfM [12] and SLAM [25]. However, these methods require dense viewpoints because the local appearance has to be preserved for feature matching. To relax the constraint of dense viewpoints, silhouette carving [19,24] and space carving [20] have been proposed. These methods feature the downsides of failure on concave structures and multiple views needed.

Another type of additional information is prior knowledge. Using prior knowledge improves resilience to incorrect feature matching and concavity (e.g., chairs should be concave between two arms). Some prior works used simple geometry entities as shape prior [2,27]. Recently, Kar et al. [16] leveraged the strong regularity of objects. For a specific object category, they learn deformable templates from a large collection of images with object of interest presented and the corresponding segmentation masks. Dame et al. [6] proposed a framework that combines a SLAM with deformable object templates. Rather than learning a single or a few deformable templates, methods like Huang *et al.* [13] and Kurenkov *et al.* [18] used image features to retrieve similar 3D shapes, from which they deform to the target shapes.

Even though our method also uses deformation, the differences between our deformation and that of their approaches are in twofold: firstly, we perform 2D deformation on an image grid, such that the deformed image grid matches the object silhouette, while they deform the 3D shape directly. More importantly, they perform deformation on 3D basis models with small variants while ours deforms a regular grid into any 2D shape.

Since large repositories of CAD models become available (e.g., ShapeNet [39]), it is easy to render vast amount of 2D images from CAD models [30]. The large number of 2D-3D ground-truth pairs make it seamless to use a powerful yet data hungry framework — deep neural net. Different deep learning based methods to generate 3D object shapes from single images are presented.

The pioneering works are from Choy *et al.* [5] and Girdhar *et al.* [9] who use 3D CNNs to perform voxel reconstruction that is limited to low resolution voxel grids. Octree data structure [11,32] and Discrete Cosine Transform technique [15] have been used to scale up the voxel grid. More recently, Fan *et al.* [7] proposed an alternative approach that predicts an orderless point cloud to shape the surface of objects directly. Nevertheless, this method is limited to a sparse point cloud because (1) the number of learnable parameters increases linearly as the number of predicted points and (2) the direct 3D distance metrics (e.g., Chamfer Distance) are also intractable for dense point clouds. Thus, this method is not scalable in terms of memory and training time.

The most relevant works to us are [21,33]. We all advocate that in order to generate dense point clouds, one should resort to partial surfaces each represented by a structured point cloud. However, the fundamental difference between our approach and that of [21,33] is how to shape these surfaces. In their methods, they shape an object surface by predicting a binary mask along with the depth map to filter out points that are not back-projected to the surface in 3D space. Although Lin *et al.* [21] relaxed their network to predict x and y coordinates along with a depth map for more flexibility, they still rely on a binary mask to shape a 3D surface. The side effects of these depth-mask based approaches are firstly, it is a huge computation waste as a large number of points are discarded, especially for objects with thin structure such as lamp, airplane and chairs; secondly, foreground/background thresholding inherits the thresholding issue from 3D voxel grid representation. Instead, we predict the surface directly by deforming the regular depth map to circumvent issues above.

Moreover, although Lin *et al.* [21] have realized that the fusion of multiple partial surfaces generates noisy points and thus developed a multi-view consistency supervision based on binary masks and depths to address this issue. However, the binary cross entropy penalty leads more points to be discarded and thus the surface coverage is sacrificed. In contrast, we develop a novel multi-view supervision framework based on a continuous distance field that does not suffer from the surface coverage trade-off, and the comparison these two supervision

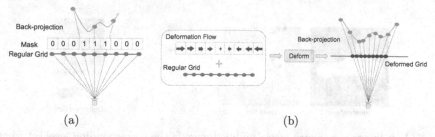

(a)   (b)

Fig. 2. An 1D example of depth-mask back-projection and deformed depth back-projection. Blue points are pixel-depth pairs on 1D regular grid. Dark red arrows are deformation flow. Dark red points are pixel-depth pairs shifted by the deformation flow. Orange lines are the target 2D surface. Green points are 2D points back-projected to reconstruct the 2D surface. (a) In the depth-mask representation, because pixels are filtered out by the mask, there are less points to reconstruct the surface. (b) In our deformed depth representation, the deformed grid is align with the surface, so that all pixels are used to reconstruct the surface. (Color figure online)

frameworks shows that using our multi-view supervision framework outperforms their framework significantly.

3   Method

Our goal is to learn a CNN that is able to reconstruct a dense 3D point cloud to represent 3D object shape from a single RGB image. We first introduce how we represent a partial surface of an object using a deformed depth map and the per-view supervision for the deformed depth map, followed by a multi-view consistency supervision based on distance fields. Lastly, we briefly introduce the network architecture and present the network training algorithm combining the per-view losses and multi-view loss.

3.1   Deformed Depth Map

One way to represent a view-dependent object surface is to use a depth map $\mathbf{D}$. For each pixel p at location (x_p, y_p) with a depth value z_p, we can back-project p to a 3D point $\mathbf{p}$ through an inverse perspective transformation, i.e.,

$$\mathbf{p} = \mathbf{R}^{-1}(\mathbf{K}^{-1}\left[x_p\ y_p\ z_p\right]^T - \mathbf{t}), \tag{1}$$

where $\mathbf{K}$, $\mathbf{R}$ and $\mathbf{t}$ are the camera intrinsic matrix, rotation matrix, and translation vector respectively. Learning a network to reconstruct the 3D object shape becomes learning to predict a set of depth maps, as done in [21,33]. Note that the size of the depth images need not be equal to the size of the input RGB image. The main issue of this representation is that not all pixels are back-projected to the object's surface, therefore the network must additionally predict a binary

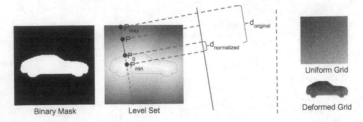

Fig. 3. Left image is a binary mask; middle image is the corresponding level set where the silhouette boundary is shown in red line. To define the deformed position for point p, the closest point on the boundary p_0 is located, followed by finding the point at the maximum level p_{max} and point at the minimum level p_{min} along the line of p and p_0. Then, p should be normalized to the range between p_0 and p_{min}. Right images show a pair of uniform grid and its corresponding deformed grid. The color indicates point correspondence before and after deformation. (Color figure online)

segmentation mask for each depth map to suppress background points. The abandoned points become wasteful.

Notice that in Eq. (1), the pixel locations (x_p, y_p) are fixed in a regular image grid, which is not flexible to model the object's surface. Our insight is that regardless of depth values, the projection ray of every pixel should hit the object's surface. This can be achieved by predicting a deformation flow (vector) $[\mathbf{U}, \mathbf{V}]$ for each pixel p (an 1D illustration is presented in Fig. 2). Specifically, for each pixel p at pixel location (x_p, y_p), our network predicts a deformation vector $[u_p, v_p]$ (besides its depth value z_p). The position of this pixel is shifted by the deformation flow. Then the new position of this pixel after deformation is $x_p' = x_p + u_p$, $y_p' = y_p + v_p$. The same inverse perspective transformation can be applied on the deformed depth map to back-project to 3D space,

$$\mathbf{p} = \mathbf{R}^{-1}(\mathbf{K}^{-1} \left[x_p' \ y_p' \ z_p \right]^T - \mathbf{t}). \qquad (2)$$

Training Losses for Deformed Depth Map. During training, the deformation flow is supervised by a pseudo ground-truth (see the section below). The pixel-wise L_1 deformation flow losses for x and y directions are given below,

$$L_U = \|\mathbf{U} - \mathbf{U_{gt}}\|_1 \quad L_V = \|\mathbf{V} - \mathbf{V_{gt}}\|_1. \qquad (3)$$

where the $\mathbf{U_{gt}}$ and $\mathbf{V_{gt}}$ are the ground-truth deformation fields on x-direction and y-direction respectively.

However, the direct pixel-wise loss cannot be used between a regular ground-truth depth map and a deformed depth map as pixel-wise correspondences have been changed due to deformation. To supervise the deformed depth map, we use the pseudo ground-truth deformation flow to deform the ground-truth depth map to obtain the deformed ground-truth depth map, such that the pixel-wise loss can be used, which is given below,

$$L_d = \|\mathbf{D}' - \mathbf{D'_{gt}}\|, \qquad (4)$$

where the $\mathbf{D}'_{gt}$ and $\mathbf{D}'$ are the deformed ground-truth and predicted depth respectively.

Pseudo Ground-Truth Deformation Flow. We define a function that takes an object binary mask (silhouette as foreground and the rest as background) on a regular grid as input, and outputs a vector field for deformation. This vector field is treated as the pseudo ground-truth for the deformation flow. The criteria of this function are (1) every pixel should be shifted into the silhouette (i.e., the regular grid should be deformed to fit the silhouette), (2) the *deformed* grid should be uniformly dense.

More specifically, we first convert the binary mask into a level set, where inside silhouette is negative levels, background is positive levels and the silhouette boundary is at the zero level set (shown by red line in Fig. 3). For each pixel p at coordinate (x_p, y_p) on the regular grid, it finds its closest pixel at the zero level set (silhouette boundary) called p_0. The deformation direction for a pixel outside of the silhouette is $\overrightarrow{pp_0}$, and that of a point inside of the silhouette is $\overrightarrow{p_0p}$.

After the direction is determined, we then calculate the magnitude for deformation. As illustrated in Fig. 3, along the line of p and p_0, we find the local maximum point p_{max} and the local minimum point p_{min} in the level set. The deformation flow for pixel p is defined below,

$$x'_p = x_p \frac{\|x_{min} - x_0\|}{\|x_{max} - x_{min}\|}, \quad y'_p = y_p \frac{\|y_{min} - y_0\|}{\|y_{max} - y_{min}\|} \qquad (5)$$

$$\mathbf{U}[x_p, y_p] = x'_p - x_p, \quad \mathbf{V}[x_p, y_p] = y'_p - y_p. \qquad (6)$$

The Eq. (5) ensures that a point along the line between p_{max} and p_{min} moves to a point on the line between p_0 and p_{min}, such that the pixel is in the silhouette (the first criteria satisfied). Moreover, no pixels are collided (the second criteria satisfied).

3.2   Distance Field Multi-view Consistency

As mentioned earlier, the 3D points back-projected from a predicted depth map are often noisy viewed from other viewpoints. Figure 4(a) visualizes this problem, where the point cloud back-projected from the front view of a chair contains many noisy points between the front and back legs of the chair. To alleviate this problem, we introduce a novel multi-view consistency supervision, which encourages the 3D points to project into the object silhouette (i.e., foreground) but not the background at novel viewpoints.

To that end, we transform ground-truth binary masks (at novel viewpoints) into a distance field [3], where the values of the foreground pixels are zero in the distance field (meaning no penalty), whereas the values of the background pixels are the distance to the closest boundary. Figure 4(b) demonstrates an example of distance field. Such distance fields are used as the supervision signal to pull

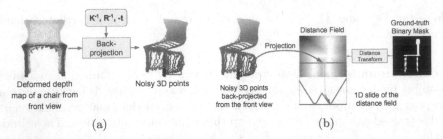

Fig. 4. (a) An example of the noisy reconstruction using only the depth as supervision. (b) Our distance field multi-view consistency. Given a ground-truth binary mask at a novel viewpoint, it is transformed to a distance field using distance transform [3]. 3D points are projected onto the distance field. The projection points are supervised by the multi-view consistency loss L_{df} to move toward the object silhouette. Note that in the example above, the project point move on the 1D surface only for the purpose of visualization. In reality, it moves on the 2D distance field surface.

outliers (i.e., points projected to the outside of the silhouettes) back to the object silhouettes (in 2D).

Technically, a 3D point $\mathbf{p}$ (X_p, Y_p, Z_p) is projected to the distance field using the transformation and camera matrices at the novel viewpoint n, i.e.,

$$[x_p, y_p, 1]^T = \mathbf{K}_n(\mathbf{R}_n \mathbf{p} + \mathbf{t}_n), \tag{7}$$

where $[x_p, y_p]$ is the projection point coordinate in the distance field.

The multi-view consistency training loss L_{df} becomes:

$$L_{df} = \sum_n^N \sum_p^P L_{df}^{(n,p)}, \tag{8}$$

where N is the number of viewpoints and P is the number of 3D points. $L_{df}^{(n,p)}$ is defined as:

$$L_{df}^{(n,p)} = \sum_h^H \sum_w^W \mathbf{F}^n[h, w] \max(0, 1 - |x_p - h|) \max(0, 1 - |y_p - w|), \tag{9}$$

where H and W are the height and width of the distance field respectively, $\mathbf{F}^n$ is the distance field at viewpoint n, and $\mathbf{F}^n[h, w]$ is the distance value at pixel location $[h, w]$.

Given a point at $[x_p, y_p]$, the values (distances) of the 4 neighboring pixels are interpolated to approximate the corresponding distance field $\mathbf{F}[x_p, y_p]$. By minimizing Eq. 9, this point is supervised to move toward the object silhouettes. This technique, called differentiable bilinear interpolation, was used in [14] for differential image warping.

3.3 Network Architecture and Training

We use an autoencoder-like network where the encoder extracts image features and project them into a latent space. The decoder is assembled by several 2D deconvolution layers to generate pairs of a pre-deformation depth map and a deformation flow map from 6 fixed viewpoints which are the faces of a cube centered at the object of interest. More details about the network architecture and training configuration can be found in the supplementary material.

We train the network with the deformed depth map loss, deformation flow loss, and the distance field loss jointly. The final loss function is

$$L = \sum_m^M (L_d^m + L_U^m + L_V^m) + \lambda \sum_n^N L_{df}^n, \tag{10}$$

where M is the 6 fixed viewpoints and N is the number of distance field from novel viewpoints.

4 Experiments

We evaluate our proposed method beginning with ablation study of key components of our framework: deformed depth map and the distance field based multi-view consistency loss, followed by comparison to the state-of-the-art methods on single view 3D object reconstruction. In addition, we test our method on a recently published real dataset to determine whether it can generalize to real images and comparison with other methods reported.

4.1 Data Preparation

Following previous methods, we use a subset of ShapeNet, which contains objects in 13 categories, to train and evaluate our network. We render 6 depth maps along with the binary masks from fixed viewpoints of 6 faces of a cube where a 3D object is centered. The binary mask is used to construct the pseudo ground-truth deformation field. Additionally, we also render 24 RGB images along with its binary mask from arbitrarily sampling azimuth and elevation in $[0,360),[-20,30]$ respectively. The RGB images are input images to the network and the binary masks are preprocessed to a distance field for multi-view consistency loss.

4.2 Quantitative Measurement

To evaluate results quantitatively, we use the average point-wise 3D Euclidean distance called Chamfer Distance between predicted and ground-truth point clouds.

$$D(S_1, S_2) = \sum_{p_i \in S_1} \min_{p_j \in S_2} \|p_i - p_j\|^2 + \sum_{p_j \in S_2} \min_{p_i \in S_1} \|p_i - p_j\|^2 \tag{11}$$

$$D_{S_1 \to S_2} = \sum_{p_i \in S_1} \min_{p_j \in S_2} \|p_i - p_j\|^2 \tag{12}$$

$$D_{S_2 \to S_1} = \sum_{p_j \in S_2} \min_{p_i \in S_1} \|p_i - p_j\|^2 \tag{13}$$

where S_1 is the predicted point cloud and S_2 is the ground-truth point cloud.

As demonstrated by [21], while the Chamfer Distance can evaluate the overall performance, it is also essential to report the prediction to ground-truth distance Eq. (12) and ground-truth to prediction distance Eq. (13) individually as they evaluate different aspects of the prediction point cloud. The former shows how far each prediction point to the closest ground-truth point (i.e., how accurate the prediction is), and the latter reports the distance from each ground-truth point to the closest prediction point indicating the surface coverage. Note that all numbers reported in the experiment section are scaled up by 100 for readability.

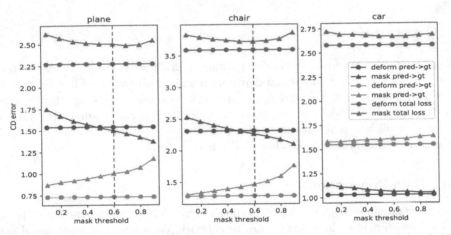

Fig. 5. Chamfer Distance comparison with different foreground/background thresholds for the depth-mask representation. The lower gt → pred loss of our method demonstrates that our method provides better coverage than the baseline. Even though the baseline can achieve lower pred → gt loss when setting the threshold higher (e.g., threshold ≥ 0.6) by only preserve points with high confidence, the penalty of coverage offset the accuracy gain and leading a higher overall loss. (Color figure online)

4.3   Ablation Study

In this section, we evaluate two key components of our framework: the deformed depth map and the distance field based multi-view consistency loss invidiously.

Deformed Depth Map. We train two networks with our proposed deformed depth representation and the depth-mask representation (as a baseline) respectively in an identical training setting.

The networks are trained and evaluated on three categories (plane, car and chair). The per category results are reported in Fig. 5. It shows that the deformed depth representation consistently achieve lower loss under different threshold setting for the depth-mask baseline (shown in two red lines). There is a difficult trade-off between the prediction point accuracy and surface coverage in the baseline. When the $D_{pred \to gt}$ gradually decreases as the threshold rises (i.e., only good prediction points are preserved), the surface coverage loss increases significantly. More importantly, another disadvantage of the depth-mask representation revealed from the experiment is that it is not trivial to select an optimal threshold for different instances. To better visualize this issue, a few qualitative examples from Lin *et al.* [21] that use the depth-mask representation are given in Fig. 6.

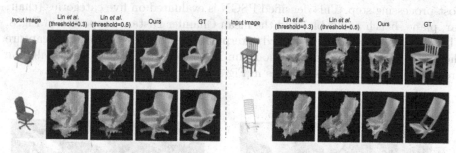

Fig. 6. Visual comparison to Lin *et al.* [21]

Distance Field Multi-view Consistency. To evaluate our distance field based multi-view consistency loss, we compare to a baseline in which the loss is disabled, and a prior art [21] that use a binary mask multi-view consistency loss. The results reported in Table 1 show that after applying our distance field multi-view consistency, the network performs better than the baseline. Since our consistency does not simply mask out more points to reduce outliers, our method also outperforms the binary masked multi-view consistency [21].

Table 1. Comparison on different multi-view consistency losses. The numbers reported in overall CD and the number of prediction points are: without multi-view consistency/with multi-view consistency

Methods	Overall CD	Prediction points
Binary mask multi-view loss [21]	3.240/3.531	31972/25401
Distance field multi-view loss (**Ours**)	**3.102/2.987**	**98304/98304**

4.4 Comparison with Prior Art

We compare our method against previous (state-of-the-art) methods using point cloud or voxel grid representation in a synthetic dataset and a real dataset in this section.

Comparing to PSGN. Because the pre-trained model of PSGN provided by the authors generates a point cloud aligned with the input image while ours is in a canonical pose. To have fair comparison, we use their published code to retrain their network to output point clouds in the canonical pose. Both PSGN and our network train on our rendered input images using the same training-test split.

Our method outperforms PSGN in the overall performance in most of the categories (11 out of 13) as reported in Table 2. To resolve the measurement bias to the density of predicted points, we also report the results of a densified PSGN, where we densify the point cloud size from 1024 to 98304 (the same size of our prediction) using linear interpolation between neighboring points as a post-processing step. This densified PSGN is evaluated on five categories (chair, car, plane, bench and table) and the mean Chamfer Distance reported in Fig. 8. This graph shows that a densified/interpolated reconstruction cannot capture the finer 3D details that our method can. To contrast both methods visually, we present some qualitative examples in Fig. 7.

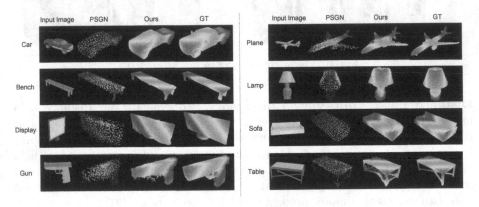

Fig. 7. Visual comparison with PSGN

Comparing to Hierarchical Surface Prediction (HSP) [11]. As PSGN has shown superior performance of point cloud representation over low resolution voxel grid representation (e.g., 3D-R2N2), we provide a quantitative comparison between our method and HSP in Table 3. HSP up-scales the voxel grid to 512^3 by using Octree data structure. Five categories of the ShapeNet are evaluated using input images and a pre-trained model provided by the author of HSP. To calculate Chamfer Distance for HSP outcomes, we generate a mesh from the

Table 2. Comparison with PSGN on 13 classes using Chamfer Distance.

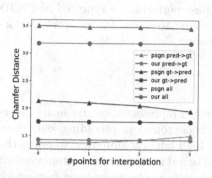

Fig. 8. Densified PSGN comparison

Category	PSGN	Ours
Plane	**2.582**	2.66
Car	3.253	**2.897**
Chair	4.110	**3.731**
Table	3.916	**3.271**
Bench	3.660	**3.357**
Cabinet	4.835	**4.037**
Display	5.010	**4.343**
Lamp	5.105	**4.933**
Speaker	5.707	**5.532**
Gun	**2.949**	3.259
Sofa	4.644	**4.267**
Telephone	3.999	**3.588**
Watercraft	3.921	**3.894**

voxels using the marching cube algorithm and sample uniformly the same number of points as ours from the mesh. Although the Octree method increases the resolution efficiently, it still suffers from the non-trivial occupancy thresholding and the "structurally unaware" cross entropy loss (i.e., missing thin structures), leading to poorer performance than ours.

Table 3. Chamfer Distance between ours and HSP

Methods	Chair	Plane	Car	Table	Bench
HSP	4.716	3.878	3.487	4.072	4.467
Ours	**3.731**	**2.660**	**2.897**	**3.271**	**3.357**

Table 4. Real images evaluated using Earth Mover's Distance and Chamfer Distance

Methods	3D-R2N2 [5]	PSGN [36]	3D-VAE-GAN [36]	DRC [34]	MarrNet [35]	AtlasNet [?]	Pix3D [31]	Ours	Pix3D (w/pose)
EMD	0.211	0.216	0.176	0.144	0.136	0.128	**0.124**	**0.124**	0.118
CD	0.239	0.200	0.182	0.160	0.144	0.125	**0.124**	0.125	0.119

4.5   Generalization to Real Images

Pix3D [31] (a large-scale real dataset with high quality image-shape pairs) has become available and we compare our results to that benchmark in Table 4. We train our method on synthetic images with backgrounds randomly selected from the SUN dataset, then evaluate on Pix3D images directly. Table 4 shows our method generalizes well to real images and achieves comparable performance to the state-of-the-art method. Note that the best performance reported in Pix3D uses joint training of object pose and 3D shape to boost the network performance, and thus excluded from the comparison.

5   Conclusions

In this work, we present a novel deformed depth representation. By using deformation, we bypass the need of foreground/background thresholding leading to denser point clouds and reconstruction with high fidelity. Moreover, to refine the fused point cloud, we propose a distance field based multi-view consistency which outperforms the existing multi-view consistency loss. Our completed framework outperforms the prior art methods in single-view object reconstruction. However, the expedient approach that we adopted in the current paper can be replaced by an energy optimization that might lead to a more uniformly distributed deformed grid.

Acknowledgement. This work was supported by the UoA Scholarship to KL and HZ, the ARC Laureate Fellowship FL130100102 to IR and the Australian Centre of Excellence for Robotic Vision CE140100016.

References

1. Aloimonos, J.: Shape from texture. Biol. Cybern. **58**(5), 345–360 (1988)
2. Biederman, I.: Recognition-by-components: a theory of human image understanding. Psychol. Rev. **94**(2), 115 (1987)
3. Borgefors, G.: Distance transformations in digital images. Comput. Vis. Graph. Image Process. **34**(3), 344–371 (1986)
4. Braunstein, M.L., Liter, J.C., Tittle, J.S.: Recovering three-dimensional shape from perspective translations and orthographic rotations. J. Exp. Psychol.: Hum. Percept. Perform. **19**(3), 598 (1993)
5. Choy, C.B., Xu, D., Gwak, J.Y., Chen, K., Savarese, S.: 3D-R2N2: a unified approach for single and multi-view 3D object reconstruction. In: Leibe, B., Matas, J., Sebe, N., Welling, M. (eds.) ECCV 2016. LNCS, vol. 9912, pp. 628–644. Springer, Cham (2016). https://doi.org/10.1007/978-3-319-46484-8_38
6. Dame, A., Prisacariu, V.A., Ren, C.Y., Reid, I.: Dense reconstruction using 3D object shape priors. In: Proceedings of the IEEE Conference on Computer Vision and Pattern Recognition, pp. 1288–1295. IEEE (2013)
7. Fan, H., Su, H., Guibas, L.: A point set generation network for 3D object reconstruction from a single image. In: Proceedings of the IEEE Conference on Computer Vision and Pattern Recognition, vol. 2, p. 6 (2017)
8. Garg, R., B.G., V.K., Carneiro, G., Reid, I.: Unsupervised CNN for single view depth estimation: geometry to the rescue. In: Leibe, B., Matas, J., Sebe, N., Welling, M. (eds.) ECCV 2016. LNCS, vol. 9912, pp. 740–756. Springer, Cham (2016). https://doi.org/10.1007/978-3-319-46484-8_45

9. Girdhar, R., Fouhey, D.F., Rodriguez, M., Gupta, A.: Learning a predictable and generative vector representation for objects. In: Leibe, B., Matas, J., Sebe, N., Welling, M. (eds.) ECCV 2016. LNCS, vol. 9910, pp. 484–499. Springer, Cham (2016). https://doi.org/10.1007/978-3-319-46466-4_29
10. Godard, C., Mac Aodha, O., Brostow, G.J.: Unsupervised monocular depth estimation with left-right consistency. In: Proceedings of the IEEE Conference on Computer Vision and Pattern Recognition, vol. 2, p. 7 (2017)
11. Häne, C., Tulsiani, S., Malik, J.: Hierarchical surface prediction for 3D object reconstruction. In: 2017 International Conference on 3D Vision (3DV), pp. 412–420. IEEE (2017)
12. Häming, K., Peters, G.: The structure-from-motion reconstruction pipeline - a survey with focus on short image sequences. Kybernetika **46**(5), 926–937 (2010). http://eudml.org/doc/197165
13. Huang, Q., Wang, H., Koltun, V.: Single-view reconstruction via joint analysis of image and shape collections. ACM Trans. Graph. (TOG) **34**(4), 87 (2015)
14. Jaderberg, M., Simonyan, K., Zisserman, A., et al.: Spatial transformer networks. In: Advances in Neural Information Processing Systems, pp. 2017–2025 (2015)
15. Johnston, A., Garg, R., Carneiro, G., Reid, I., van den Hengel, A.: Scaling CNNs for high resolution volumetric reconstruction from a single image. In: Proceedings of the IEEE Conference on Computer Vision and Pattern Recognition, pp. 939–948 (2017)
16. Kar, A., Tulsiani, S., Carreira, J., Malik, J.: Category-specific object reconstruction from a single image. In: Proceedings of the IEEE Conference on Computer Vision and Pattern Recognition, pp. 1966–1974 (2015)
17. Kong, C., Lin, C.H., Lucey, S.: Using locally corresponding cad models for dense 3D reconstructions from a single image. In: Proceedings of the IEEE Conference on Computer Vision and Pattern Recognition, vol. 2 (2017)
18. Kurenkov, A., et al.: Deformnet: free-form deformation network for 3D shape reconstruction from a single image. arXiv preprint arXiv:1708.04672 (2017)
19. Kutulakos, K.N.: Shape from the light field boundary. In: 1997 Proceedings of IEEE Computer Society Conference on Computer Vision and Pattern Recognition, pp. 53–59. IEEE (1997)
20. Kutulakos, K.N., Seitz, S.M.: A theory of shape by space carving. Int. J. Comput. Vis. **38**(3), 199–218 (2000)
21. Lin, C.H., Kong, C., Lucey, S.: Learning efficient point cloud generation for dense 3D object reconstruction. In: AAAI Conference on Artificial Intelligence (AAAI) (2018)
22. Liu, F., Shen, C., Lin, G.: Deep convolutional neural fields for depth estimation from a single image. In: Proceedings of the IEEE Conference on Computer Vision and Pattern Recognition, pp. 5162–5170 (2015)
23. Liu, M., Salzmann, M., He, X.: Discrete-continuous depth estimation from a single image. In: Proceedings of the IEEE Conference on Computer Vision and Pattern Recognition, pp. 716–723. IEEE (2014)
24. Martin, W.N., Aggarwal, J.K.: Volumetric descriptions of objects from multiple views. IEEE Trans. Pattern Anal. Mach. Intell. **2**, 150–158 (1983)
25. Newcombe, R.A., Lovegrove, S.J., Davison, A.J.: DTAM: dense tracking and mapping in real-time. In: 2011 IEEE International Conference on Computer Vision (ICCV), pp. 2320–2327. IEEE (2011)
26. Prados, E., Faugeras, O.: Shape from shading. In: Paragios, N., Chen, Y., Faugeras, O. (eds.) Handbook of Mathematical Models in Computer Vision, pp. 375–388. Springer, Boston (2006). https://doi.org/10.1007/0-387-28831-7_23

27. Roberts, L.G.: Machine perception of three-dimensional solids. Ph.D. thesis, Massachusetts Institute of Technology (1963)
28. Saxena, A., Sun, M., Ng, A.Y.: Make3D: depth perception from a single still image. In: AAAI, pp. 1571–1576 (2008)
29. Sinha, A., Unmesh, A., Huang, Q., Ramani, K.: SurfNet: Generating 3D shape surfaces using deep residual networks. In: Proceedings of the IEEE Conference on Computer Vision and Pattern Recognition (2017)
30. Su, H., Qi, C.R., Li, Y., Guibas, L.J.: Render for CNN: viewpoint estimation in images using CNNs trained with rendered 3D model views. In: Proceedings of the IEEE International Conference on Computer Vision, pp. 2686–2694 (2015)
31. Sun, et al.: Pix3D: dataset and methods for single-image 3D shape modeling. In: CVPR (2018)
32. Tatarchenko, M., Dosovitskiy, A., Brox, T.: Octree generating networks: efficient convolutional architectures for high-resolution 3D outputs. In: IEEE International Conference on Computer Vision (ICCV) (2017). http://lmb.informatik.uni-freiburg.de/Publications/2017/TDB17b
33. Tatarchenko, M., Dosovitskiy, A., Brox, T.: Multi-view 3D models from single images with a convolutional network. In: Leibe, B., Matas, J., Sebe, N., Welling, M. (eds.) ECCV 2016. LNCS, vol. 9911, pp. 322–337. Springer, Cham (2016). https://doi.org/10.1007/978-3-319-46478-7_20
34. Tulsiani, S., Zhou, T., Efros, A.A., Malik, J.: Multi-view supervision for single-view reconstruction via differentiable ray consistency. In: Proceedings of the IEEE Conference on Computer Vision and Pattern Recognition, vol. 1, p. 3 (2017)
35. Wu, J., Wang, Y., Xue, T., Sun, X., Freeman, B., Tenenbaum, J.: MarrNet: 3D shape reconstruction via 2.5 D sketches. In: Advances in Neural Information Processing Systems, pp. 540–550 (2017)
36. Wu, J., Zhang, C., Xue, T., Freeman, B., Tenenbaum, J.: Learning a probabilistic latent space of object shapes via 3D generative-adversarial modeling. In: Advances in Neural Information Processing Systems, pp. 82–90 (2016)
37. Yan, X., Yang, J., Yumer, E., Guo, Y., Lee, H.: Perspective transformer nets: Learning single-view 3D object reconstruction without 3D supervision. In: Advances in Neural Information Processing Systems, pp. 1696–1704 (2016)
38. Zhan, H., Garg, R., Weerasekera, C.S., Li, K., Agarwal, H., Reid, I.: Unsupervised learning of monocular depth estimation and visual odometry with deep feature reconstruction. In: Proceedings of the IEEE Conference on Computer Vision and Pattern Recognition, pp. 340–349 (2018)
39. Chang, A.X., et al.: ShapeNet: an information-rich 3D model repository. arXiv:1512.03012 [cs.GR] (2015)

Improving DNN Robustness to Adversarial Attacks Using Jacobian Regularization

Daniel Jakubovitz[(✉)] and Raja Giryes

School of Electrical Engineering, Tel Aviv University, Tel Aviv, Israel
danielshaij@mail.tau.ac.il, raja@tauex.tau.ac.il

Abstract. Deep neural networks have lately shown tremendous performance in various applications including vision and speech processing tasks. However, alongside their ability to perform these tasks with such high accuracy, it has been shown that they are highly susceptible to *adversarial attacks*: a small change in the input would cause the network to err with high confidence. This phenomenon exposes an inherent fault in these networks and their ability to generalize well. For this reason, providing robustness to adversarial attacks is an important challenge in networks training, which has led to extensive research. In this work, we suggest a theoretically inspired novel approach to improve the networks' robustness. Our method applies regularization using the Frobenius norm of the Jacobian of the network, which is applied as post-processing, after regular training has finished. We demonstrate empirically that it leads to enhanced robustness results with a minimal change in the original network's accuracy.

Keywords: Deep learning · Neural networks · Adversarial examples
Data perturbation · Jacobian regularization · Classification robustness

1 Introduction

Deep neural networks (DNNs) are a widespread machine learning technique, which has shown state-of-the-art performance in many domains such as natural language processing, computer vision and speech processing [7]. Alongside their outstanding performance, deep neural networks have recently been shown to be vulnerable to a specific kind of attacks, most commonly referred to as *Adversarial Attacks*. These cause significant failures in the networks' performance by performing just minor changes in the input data that are barely noticeable by a human observer and are not expected to change the prediction [8]. These attacks pose a possible obstacle for mass deployment of systems relying on deep learning

Electronic supplementary material The online version of this chapter (https://doi.org/10.1007/978-3-030-01258-8_32) contains supplementary material, which is available to authorized users.

© Springer Nature Switzerland AG 2018
V. Ferrari et al. (Eds.): ECCV 2018, LNCS 11216, pp. 525–541, 2018.
https://doi.org/10.1007/978-3-030-01258-8_32

in sensitive fields such as security or autonomous driving, and expose an inherent weakness in their reliability.

In adversarial attacks, very small perturbations in the network's input data are performed, which lead to classifying an input erroneously with a high confidence. Even though these small changes in the input cause the model to err with high probability, they are unnoticeable to the human eye in most cases. In addition, it has been shown in [32] that such adversarial attacks tend to generalize well across models. This transferability trait only increases the possible susceptibility to attacks since an attacker might not need to know the structure of the specific attacked network in order to fool it. Thus, black-box attacks are highly successful as well. This inherent vulnerability of DNNs is somewhat counter intuitive since it exposes a fault in the model's ability to generalize well in very particular cases.

Lately, this phenomenon has been the focus of substantial research, which has focused on effective attack methods, defense methods and theoretical explanations to this inherent vulnerability of the model. Attack methods aim to alter the network's input data in order to deliberately cause it to fail in its task. Such methods include DeepFool [19], Fast Gradient Sign Method (FGSM) [8], Jacobian-based Saliency Map Attack (JSMA) [23], Universal Perturbations [20], Adversarial Transformation Networks [2], and more [3].

Several defense methods have been suggested to increase deep neural networks' robustness to adversarial attacks. Some of the strategies aim at detecting whether an input image is adversarial or not (e.g., [6,12,13,16,17,35]). For example, the authors in [35] suggested to detect adversarial examples using feature squeezing, whereas the authors in [6] proposed to detect adversarial examples based on density estimates and Bayesian uncertainty estimates. Other strategies focus on making the network more robust to perturbed inputs. The latter, which is the focus of this work, aims at increasing the network's accuracy in performing its original task even when it is being fed with perturbed data, intended to mislead it. This increased model robustness has been shown to be achieved by several different methods.

These defense methods include, among others, Adversarial Training [8] which adds perturbed inputs along with their correct labels to the training dataset; Defensive Distillation [24], which trains two networks, where the first is a standard classification network and the second is trained to achieve an output similar to the first network in all classes; the Batch Adjusted Network Gradients (BANG) method [26], which balances gradients in the training batch by scaling up those that have lower magnitudes; Parseval Networks [4] which constrain the Lipschitz constant of each hidden layer in a DNN to be smaller than 1; the Ensemble method [31], which takes the label that maximizes the average of the output probabilities of the classifiers in the ensemble as the predicted label; a Robust Optimization Framework [27], which uses an alternating minimization-maximization procedure in which the loss of the network is minimized over perturbed examples that are generated at each parameter update; Virtual Adversarial Training (VAT) [18], which uses a regularization term to promote the smoothness of the model distribution; Input Gradient Regularization [25] which regularizes the gradient of the cross-entropy loss, and Cross-Lipschitz Regularization [9], which regularizes all the combinations of differences of the gradients of a network's output w.r.t its input. In another recent work [29], the authors suggested an adversarial training procedure that achieves robustness with guarantees on its statistical performance.

In addition to these works, several theoretical explanations for adversarial examples have been suggested. In [8], the authors claim that linear behavior in high-dimensional spaces creates this inherent vulnerability to adversarial examples. In [22], a game theoretical framework is used to study the relationship between attack and defense strategies in recognition systems in the context of adversarial attacks. In [33], the authors examine the transferability of adversarial examples between different models and find that adversarial examples span a contiguous subspace of large dimensionality. The authors also provide an insight into the decision boundaries of DNNs. In [14], the authors claim that first order attacks are universal and suggest the Projected Gradient Descent (PGD) attack which relies on this notion. They also claim that networks require a significantly larger capacity in order to be more robust to adversarial attacks. In another recent work [28], the authors show that the gradient of a network's objective function grows with the dimension of its input and conclude that the adversarial vulnerability of a network increases with the dimension of its input.

In [5], the authors showed the relationship between a network's sensitivity to additive adversarial perturbations and the curvature of the classification boundaries. In addition, they propose a method to discriminate between the original input and perturbed inputs. In [21], the link between a network's robustness to adversarial perturbations and the geometry of the decision boundaries of this network is further developed. Specifically, it is shown that when the decision boundary is positively curved, small universal perturbations are more likely to fool the classifier. However, a direct application of this insight to increase the networks' robustness to adversarial examples is, to the best of our knowledge, still unclear.

In a recent work [30], a relationship between the norm of the Jacobian of the network and its generalization error has been drawn. The authors have shown that by regularizing the Frobenius norm of the Jacobian matrix of the network's classification function, a lower generalization error is achieved. In [34] the authors show that using the Jacobian matrix computed at the logits (before the softmax operation) instead of the probabilities (after the softmax operation) yields better generalization results.

Inspired by the work in [30], we take this notion further and show that using Jacobian regularization as post-processing, i.e. applying it for a second phase of additional training after regular training has finished, also increases deep neural networks' robustness to adversarial perturbations. Besides the relationship to the generalization error, we show also that the Forbenius norm of the Jacobian at a given point is related to its distance to the closest adversarial example and to the curvature of the network's decision boundaries. All these connections provide a theoretical justification to the usage of the Jacobian regularization for decreasing the vulnerability of a network to adversarial attacks.

We apply the Jacobian regularization as post-processing to the regular training, after the network is stabilized with a high test accuracy, thereby allowing to use our strategy with existing pre-trained networks and improve their robustness. In addition, using the Jacobian regularization requires only little additional computational resources as it makes a single additional back-propagation step in each training step, as opposed to other methods that are very computationally demanding such as Distillation [24] which requires the training of two networks.

Two close techniques to our strategy are the Input Gradient regularization technique proposed in [25] and the Cross-Lipschitz regularization proposed in [9]. Our approach differs from the former work by the fact that we regularize the Frobenius norm of the Jacobian matrix of the network itself, and not the norm of the gradient of the cross-entropy loss. Our work differs from the latter work by the fact that we regularize the gradients of the network themselves and not all combinations of their differences, which yields better results at a lower computational cost, as will be later shown.

We compare the methods mentioned above and adversarial training [8] to Jacobian regularization on the MNIST, CIFAR-10 and CIFAR-100 datasets, demonstrating the advantage of our strategy in the form of high robustness to the DeepFool [19], FGSM [8], and JSMA [23] attack methods. Our method surpasses the results of the other strategies on FGSM and DeepFool and achieves competitive performance on JSMA. We also show that using Jacobian regularization combined with adversarial training further improves the robustness results.

This paper is organized as follows. Section 2 introduces the Jacobian regularization method and related strategies. Section 3 shows its connection to some theory of adversarial examples. The relationships drawn in this section suggest that regularizing the Jacobian of deep neural networks can improve their robustness to adversarial examples. In Sect. 4 we demonstrate empirically the advantages of this approach. Section 5 concludes our paper. In the supplementary material, which consists of eight appendices, we provide more theoretical insight and additional experimental results.

2   Jacobian Regularization for Adversarial Robustness

Adversarial perturbations are essentially small changes in the input data which cause large changes in the network's output. In order to prevent this vulnerability, during the post-processing training phase we penalize large gradients of the classification function with respect to the input data. Thus, we encourage the network's learned function to be more robust to small changes in the input space. This is achieved by adding a regularization term in the form of the Frobenius norm of the network's Jacobian matrix evaluated on the input data. The relation between the Frobenius norm and the ℓ_2 (spectral) norm of the Jacobian matrix has been shown in [30], and lays the justification for using the Frobenius norm of the network's Jacobian as a regularization term. We emphasize that we apply this regularization as additional post-processing training which is done after the regular training has finished.

To describe the Jacobian regularization more formally, we use the following notation. Let us denote the network's input as a D-dimensional vector, its output as a K-dimensional vector, and let us assume the training dataset X consists of N training examples. We use the index $l = 1, ..., L$ to specify a certain layer in a network with L layers. $z^{(l)}$ is the output of the lth layer of the network and $z_k^{(l)}$ is the output of the kth neuron in this layer. In addition, let us denote by λ the hyper-parameter which controls the weight of our regularization penalty in the loss function. The input to the network is

$$x_i \in \mathbb{R}^D, \quad i = 1 \ldots N, \quad X = \begin{bmatrix} x_1^T \\ \vdots \\ x_N^T \end{bmatrix} \in \mathbb{R}^{N \times D}, \quad (1)$$

and its output is $f(x_i) \in \mathbb{R}^K$, where the predicted class k_i^* for an input x_i is $k_i^* = \text{argmax}_k f_k(x_i)$, $k = 1, ..., K$.

$f(x_i) = \text{softmax}\{z^{(L)}(x_i)\}$ is the network's output after the softmax operation where $z^{(L)}(x_i)$ is the output of the last fully connected layer in the network for the input x_i. The term $\nabla_x z^{(L)}(x_i)$ is the Jacobian matrix of layer L evaluated at the point x_i, i.e. $J^{(L)}(x_i) = \nabla_x z^{(L)}(x_i)$. Correspondingly, $J_k^{(L)}(x_i) = \nabla_x z_k^{(L)}(x_i)$ is the kth row in the matrix $J^{(L)}(x_i)$.

A network's Jacobian matrix is given by

$$J(x_i) \triangleq J^{(L)}(x_i) = \begin{bmatrix} \frac{\partial z_1^{(L)}(x_i)}{\partial x_{(1)}} & \cdots & \frac{\partial z_1^{(L)}(x_i)}{\partial x_{(D)}} \\ \vdots & \ddots & \vdots \\ \frac{\partial z_K^{(L)}(x_i)}{\partial x_{(1)}} & \cdots & \frac{\partial z_K^{(L)}(x_i)}{\partial x_{(D)}} \end{bmatrix} \in \mathbb{R}^{K \times D}, \quad (2)$$

where $x = (x_{(1)} \ldots x_{(D)})^T$. Accordingly, the Jacobian regularization term for an input sample x_i is

$$\|J(x_i)\|_F^2 = \sum_{d=1}^{D} \sum_{k=1}^{K} \left(\frac{\partial}{\partial x_d} z_k^{(L)}(x_i) \right)^2 = \sum_{k=1}^{K} \|\nabla_x z_k^{(L)}(x_i)\|_2^2. \quad (3)$$

Combining the regularization term in (3) with a standard cross-entropy loss function on the training data, we get the following loss function for training:

$$Loss = -\sum_{i=1}^{N} \sum_{k=1}^{K} y_{ik} \log f_k(x_i) + \lambda \sqrt{\sum_{d=1}^{D} \sum_{k=1}^{K} \sum_{i=1}^{N} \left(\frac{\partial}{\partial x_d} z_k^{(L)}(x_i) \right)^2}, \quad (4)$$

where $y_i \in \mathbb{R}^K$ is a one-hot vector representing the correct class of the input x_i.

The Input Gradient regularization method from [25] uses the following regularization term:

$$\sum_{d=1}^{D}\sum_{i=1}^{N}\left(\frac{\partial}{\partial x_d}\sum_{k=1}^{K}-y_{ik}\log f_k(x_i)\right)^2. \tag{5}$$

The Cross-Lipschitz regularization method from [9] uses the following regularization term:

$$\sum_{i=1}^{N}\sum_{j,k=1}^{K}||\nabla_x z_k^{(L)}(x_i) - \nabla_x z_j^{(L)}(x_i)||_2^2. \tag{6}$$

The adversarial training method [8] adds perturbed inputs along with their correct labels to the training dataset, so that the network learns the correct labels of perturbed inputs during training. This helps the network to achieve a higher accuracy when it is being fed with new perturbed inputs, meaning the network becomes more robust to adversarial examples.

On the computational complexity aspect, Jacobian regularization introduces an overhead of one additional back-propagation step in every iteration. This step involves the computation of mixed partial derivatives, as the first derivative is w.r.t the input, and the second is w.r.t. the model parameters. However, one should keep in mind that Jacobian regularization is applied as a post-processing phase, and not throughout the entire training, which is computationally beneficial. Moreover, it is also more efficient than the Cross-Lipschitz regularization technique [9], which requires the computation of the norm of $\frac{1}{2}K(K-1)$ terms as opposed to our method that only requires the calculation of the norm of K different gradients. This makes Jacobian regularization more scalable for datasets with a large K.

3   Theoretical Justification

3.1   The Jacobian Matrix and Adversarial Perturbations

In essence, for a network performing a classification task, an adversarial attack (a fooling method) aims at making a change as small as possible, which changes the network's decision. In other words, finding the smallest perturbation that causes the output function to cross a decision boundary to another class, thus making a classification error. In general, an attack would seek for the closest decision boundary to be reached by an adversarial perturbation in the input space. This makes the attack the least noticeable and the least prone to being discovered [8].

To gain some intuition for our proposed defense method, we start with a simple informal explanation on the relationship between adversarial perturbations and the Jacobian matrix of a network. Let x be a given input data sample; x_{same} a data sample close to x from the same class that was not perturbed by an adversarial attack; and x_{pert} another data sample, which is the result of an adversarial perturbation of x that keeps it close to it but with a different predicted label. Therefore, we have that for the ℓ_2 distance metric in the input and output of the network

$$\frac{||x_{pert} - x||_2}{||x_{same} - x||_2} \approx 1 \quad \text{and} \quad 1 < \frac{||z^{(L)}(x_{pert}) - z^{(L)}(x)||_2}{||z^{(L)}(x_{same}) - z^{(L)}(x)||_2}, \tag{7}$$

with a high probability. Therefore,

$$\frac{||z^{(L)}(x_{same}) - z^{(L)}(x)||_2}{||x_{same} - x||_2} < \frac{||z^{(L)}(x_{pert}) - z^{(L)}(x)||_2}{||x_{pert} - x||_2}. \tag{8}$$

Let $[x, x_{pert}]$ be the D-dimensional line in the input space connecting x and x_{pert}. According to the mean value theorem there exists some $x' \in [x, x_{pert}]$ such that

$$\frac{||z^{(L)}(x_{pert}) - z^{(L)}(x)||_2^2}{||x_{pert} - x||_2^2} \leq \sum_{k=1}^{K} ||\nabla_x z_k^{(L)}(x')||_2^2 = ||J(x')||_F^2. \tag{9}$$

This suggests that a lower Frobenius norm of the network's Jacobian matrix encourages it to be more robust to small changes in the input space. In other words, the network is encouraged to yield similar outputs for similar inputs.

We empirically examined the average values of the Frobenius norm of the Jacobian matrix of networks trained with various defense methods on the MNIST dataset. The network architecture is described in Sect. 4. Table 1 presents these values for both the original inputs and the ones which have been perturbed by DeepFool [19]. For "regular" training with no defense, it can be seen that as predicted, the aforementioned average norm is significantly larger on perturbed inputs. Interestingly enough, using adversarial training, which does not regularize the Jacobian matrix directly, decreases the average Frobenius norm of the Jacobian matrix evaluated on perturbed inputs (second row of Table 1). Yet, when Jacobian regularization is added (with $\lambda = 0.1$), this norm is reduced much more (third and fourth rows of Table 1). Thus, it is expected to improve the robustness of the network even further. Indeed, this behavior is demonstrated in Sect. 4.

3.2 Relation to Classification Decision Boundaries

As shown in [19], we may locally treat the decision boundaries as hyper-surfaces in the K-dimensional output space of the network. Let us denote $g(x) = w^T x + b = 0$ as a hyper-plane tangent to such a decision boundary hyper-surface in the input space. Using this notion, the following lemma approximates the distance between an input and a perturbed input classified to be at the boundary of a hyper-surface separating between the class of x, k_1, and another class k_2.

Table 1. Average Frobenius norm of the Jacobian matrix at the original data and the data perturbed by DeepFool. DNN is trained on MNIST with various defense methods

Defense method	$\frac{1}{N}\sum_{i=1}^{N}||J(x_i)||_F$	$\frac{1}{N}\sum_{i=1}^{N}||J(x_{i_{pert}})||_F$
No defense	0.14	0.1877
Adversarial training	0.141	0.143
Jacobian regularization	0.0315	0.055
Jacobian regularization & adversarial training	0.0301	0.0545

Lemma 1. *The first order approximation for the distance between an input x, with class k_1, and a perturbed input classified to the boundary hyper-surface separating the classes k_1 and k_2 for an ℓ_2 distance metric is given by*

$$d = \frac{|z_{k_1}^{(L)}(x) - z_{k_2}^{(L)}(x)|}{||\nabla_x z_{k_1}^{(L)}(x) - \nabla_x z_{k_2}^{(L)}(x)||_2}. \tag{10}$$

This lemma is given in [19]. For completeness, we present a short sketch of the proof in Appendix A. Based on this lemma, the following corollary provides a proxy for the minimal distance that may lead to fooling the network.

Corollary 2. *Let k^* be the correct class for the input sample x. Then the ℓ_2 norm of the minimal perturbation necessary to fool the classification function is approximated by*

$$d^* = \min_{k \neq k^*} \frac{|z_{k^*}^{(L)}(x) - z_k^{(L)}(x)|}{||\nabla_x z_{k^*}^{(L)}(x) - \nabla_x z_k^{(L)}(x)||_2}. \tag{11}$$

To make a direct connection to the Jacobian of the network, we provide the following proposition:

Proposition 3. *Let k^* be the correct class for the input sample x. Then the first order approximation for the ℓ_2 norm of the minimal perturbation necessary to fool the classification function is lower bounded by*

$$d^* \geq \frac{1}{\sqrt{2}||J^{(L)}(x)||_F} \min_{k \neq k^*} |z_{k^*}^{(L)}(x) - z_k^{(L)}(x)|. \tag{12}$$

The proof of Proposition 3 is given in Appendix B. The term $|z_{k^*}^{(L)}(x) - z_k^{(L)}(x)|$ in (12) is maximized by the minimization of the cross-entropy term of the loss function, since a DNN aspires to learn the correct output with the largest confidence possible, meaning the largest possible margin in the output space between the correct classification and the other possible classes. The term $||J^{(L)}(x)||_F$ in the denominator is the Frobenius norm of the Jacobian of the last fully connected layer of the network. It is minimized due to the Jacobian regularization part in the loss function. This is essentially a min-max problem, since we wish to maximize the minimal distance necessary to fool the network, d^*. For this reason, applying Jacobian regularization during training increases the minimal distance necessary to fool the DNN, thus providing improved robustness to adversarial perturbations. One should keep in mind that it is important not to deteriorate the network's original test accuracy. This is indeed the case as shown in Sect. 4.

An important question is whether the regularization of the Jacobian at earlier layers of the network would yield better robustness to adversarial examples. To this end, we examined imposing the regularization on the $L-1$ and the $L-2$ layers of the network. Both of these cases generally yielded degraded robustness results compared to imposing the regularization on the last layer of the network. Thus, throughout this work we regularize the Jacobian of the whole network. The theoretical details are given in Appendix C and the corresponding experimental results are given in Appendix D.

3.3 Relation to Decision Boundary Curvature

In [21] the authors show the link between a network's robustness to adversarial perturbations and the geometry of its decision boundaries. The authors show that when the decision boundaries are positively curved the network is fooled by small universal perturbations with a higher probability. Here we show that Jacobian regularization promotes the curvature of the decision boundaries to be less positive, thus reducing the probability of the network being fooled by small universal adversarial perturbations.

Let $H_k(x) = \frac{\partial^2 z_k^{(L)}(x)}{\partial x^2}$ be the Hessian matrix of the network's classification function at the input point x for the class k. As shown in [21], the decision boundary between two classes k_1 and k_2 can be locally referred to as the hypersurface $F_{k_1,k_2}(x) = z_{k_1}^{(L)}(x) - z_{k_2}^{(L)}(x) = 0$. Relying on the work in [15] let us use the approximation $H_k(x) \approx J_k(x)^T J_k(x)$ where $J_k(x)$ is the kth row in the matrix $J(x)$. The matrix $J_k(x)^T J_k(x)$ is a rank one positive semi-definite matrix. Thus, the curvature of the decision boundary $F_{k_1,k_2}(x)$ is given by $x^T(H_{k_1} - H_{k_2})x$, which using the aforementioned approximation, can be approximated by

$$x^T \left(J_{k_1}(x)^T J_{k_1}(x) - J_{k_2}(x)^T J_{k_2}(x) \right) x = \left(J_{k_1}(x)x \right)^2 - \left(J_{k_2}(x)x \right)^2. \tag{13}$$

Thus, we arrive at the following upper bound for the curvature:

$$\left(J_{k_1}(x)x \right)^2 - \left(J_{k_2}(x)x \right)^2 \leq \left(J_{k_1}(x)x \right)^2 + \left(J_{k_2}(x)x \right)^2 \tag{14}$$

$$\leq \sum_{k=1}^{K} \left(J_k(x)x \right)^2 \leq \|J(x)\|_F^2 \|x\|_2^2, \tag{15}$$

where the last inequality stems from the matrix norm inequality. For this reason the regularization of $\|J(x)\|_F$ promotes a less positive curvature of the decision boundaries in the environment of the input samples. This offers a geometric intuition to the effect of Jacobian regularization on the network's decision boundaries. Discouraging a positive curvature makes a universal adversarial perturbation less likely to fool the classifier.

4   Experiments

We tested the performance of Jacobian regularization on the MNIST, CIFAR-10 and CIFAR-100 datasets. The results for CIFAR-100, which are generally consistent with the results for MNIST and CIFAR-10, are given in Appendix E. As mentioned before, we use the training with Jacobian regularization as a post-processing phase to the "regular" training. Using a post-processing training phase is highly beneficial: it has a low additional computational cost as we add the regularization part after the network is already stabilized with a high test accuracy and not throughout the entire training. It also allows taking an existing network and applying the post-processing training phase to it in order to increase its robustness to adversarial examples. We obtained optimal results this way, whereas we found that applying the Jacobian regularization from the beginning of the training yields a lower final test accuracy.

The improved test accuracy obtained using post-processing training can be explained by the advantage of keeping the original training phase, which allows the network to train solely for the purpose of a high test accuracy. The subsequent post-processing training phase with Jacobian regularization introduces a small change to the already existing good test accuracy, as opposed to the case where the regularization is applied from the beginning that results in a worse test accuracy. Table 2 presents a comparison between post-processing training and "regular" training on MNIST. Similar results are obtained for CIFAR-10 and CIFAR-100.

We examine the performance of our method using three different adversarial attack methods: DeepFool [19], FGSM [8] and JSMA [23]. We also assess the performance of our defense combined with adversarial training, which is shown to be effective in improving the model's robustness. However, this comes at the cost of generating and training on a substantial amount of additional input samples as is the practice in adversarial training. We found that the amount of perturbed inputs in the training mini-batch has an impact on the overall achieved robustness. An evaluation of this matter appears in Appendix F. The results for adversarial training, shown hereafter, are given for the amount of perturbed inputs that yields the optimal results in each test case. We also compare the results to the Input Gradient regularization technique [25] and the Cross-Lipschitz regularization technique [9].

For MNIST we used the network from the official TensorFlow tutorial [1]. The network consists of two convolutional layers, each followed by a max pooling layer. These layers are then followed by two fully connected layers. All these layers use the ReLU activation function, except for the last layer which is followed by a softmax operation. Dropout regularization with 0.5 keep probability is applied to the fully connected layers. The training is done using an Adam optimizer [11] and a mini-batch size of 500 inputs. With this network we obtained

Table 2. Effect of post-processing training vs. "regular" training on MNIST, using different defense methods

Defense method	Test accuracy	$\hat{\rho}_{adv}$
No defense	99.08%	20.67 x 10^{-2}
Input Gradient regularization, "regular" training	99.25%	23.43 x 10^{-2}
Input Gradient regularization, post-processing training	99.44%	24.03 x 10^{-2}
Cross-Lipschitz regularization, "regular" training	98.64%	29.03 x 10^{-2}
Cross-Lipschitz regularization, post-processing training	98.91%	29.99 x 10^{-2}
Jacobian regularization, "regular" training	98.35%	32.89 x 10^{-2}
Jacobian regularization, post-processing training	98.44%	34.24 x 10^{-2}

a test accuracy of 99.08%. Training with Jacobian regularization was done with a weight of $\lambda = 0.1$, which we found to provide a good balance between the cross-entropy loss and the Jacobian regularization.

For CIFAR-10 we used a convolutional neural network consisting of four concatenated sets, where each set consists of two convolutional layers followed by a max pooling layer followed by dropout with a 0.75 keep probability. After these four sets, two fully connected layers are used. For CIFAR-10, training was done with a RMSProp optimizer [10] and a mini-batch size of 128 inputs. With this network we obtained a test accuracy of 88.79%. Training with Jacobian regularization was done with a weight of $\lambda = 0.5$, which we found to provide a good balance between the cross-entropy loss and the Jacobian regularization.

The results of an ablation study regarding the influence of variation in the values of λ for MNIST and CIFAR-10 are given in Appendix G.

4.1 DeepFool Evaluation

We start by evaluating the performance of our method compared to the others under the DeepFool attack. The DeepFool attack [19] uses a first order approximation of the network's decision boundaries as hyper-planes. Using this approximation, the method seeks for the closest decision boundary to be reached by a change in the input. Since the decision boundaries are not actually linear, this process continues iteratively until the perturbed input changes the network's decision. The robustness metric associated with this attack is $\hat{\rho}_{adv} = \frac{1}{N} \sum_{i=1}^{N} \frac{d_i}{\|x_i\|_2}$, which represents the average proportion between the ℓ_2 norm of the minimal perturbation necessary to fool the network for an input x_i and the ℓ_2 norm of x_i. This attack is optimized for the ℓ_2 metric.

Tables 3 and 4 present the robustness measured by $\hat{\rho}_{adv}$ under a DeepFool attack for MNIST and CIFAR-10 respectively. As the results show, Jacobian regularization provides a much more significant robustness improvement compared to the other methods. Substantially smaller perturbation norms are required to fool networks that use those defense approaches compared to networks that are trained using Jacobian regularization. Moreover, combining it with adversarial training further enhances this difference in the results.

Table 3. Robustness to DeepFool attack for MNIST

Defense method	Test accuracy	$\hat{\rho}_{adv}$
No defense	99.08%	20.67×10^{-2}
Adversarial training	99.03%	22.38×10^{-2}
Input Gradient regularization	99.25%	23.43×10^{-2}
Input Gradient regularization & adversarial training	98.88%	23.49×10^{-2}
Cross-Lipschitz regularization	98.64%	29.03×10^{-2}
Cross-Lipschitz regularization & adversarial training	98.73%	32.38×10^{-2}
Jacobian regularization	98.44%	34.24×10^{-2}
Jacobian regularization & adversarial training	98%	36.29×10^{-2}

Table 4. Robustness to DeepFool attack for CIFAR-10

Defense method	Test accuracy	$\hat{\rho}_{adv}$
No defense	88.79%	1.21×10^{-2}
Adversarial training	88.88%	1.23×10^{-2}
Input Gradient regularization	88.56%	1.43×10^{-2}
Input Gradient regularization & adversarial training	88.49%	2.17×10^{-2}
Cross-Lipschitz regularization	88.91%	2.08×10^{-2}
Cross-Lipschitz regularization & adversarial training	88.49%	4.04×10^{-2}
Jacobian regularization	89.16%	3.42×10^{-2}
Jacobian regularization & adversarial training	88.49%	6.03×10^{-2}

Notice that neither of the examined defense methods change the test accuracy significantly. For MNIST, the Jacobian and Cross-Lipschitz regularizations and adversarial training cause a small accuracy decrease, whereas the Input Gradient regularization technique improves the accuracy. Conversely, for CIFAR-10, the Jacobian and Cross-Lipschitz regularizations and adversarial training yield a better accuracy, whereas the Input Gradient regularization reduces the accuracy.

4.2   FGSM Evaluation

The FGSM (Fast Gradient Sign Method) attack [8] was designed to rapidly create adversarial examples that could fool the network. The method changes the network's input according to:

$$x_{pert} = x - \epsilon \cdot sign\left(\nabla_x Loss(x)\right), \tag{16}$$

where ϵ represents the magnitude of the attack. This attack is optimized for the ℓ_∞ metric.

We examined the discussed defense methods' test accuracy under the FGSM attack (test accuracy on the perturbed dataset) for different values of ϵ. Figure 1 presents the results comparing Jacobian regularization to adversarial training, Input Gradient regularization and Cross-Lipschitz regularization. In all cases, the minimal test accuracy on the original test set using Jacobian regularization is 98% for MNIST and 88.49% for CIFAR-10.

Similarly to the results under the DeepFool attack, the results under the FGSM attack show that the test accuracy with the Jacobian regularization defense is higher than with the Input Gradient and Cross-Lipschitz regularizations or with adversarial training. Moreover, if adversarial training is combined with Jacobian regularization, its advantage over using the other techniques is even more distinct. This leads to the conclusion that the Jacobian regularization method yields a more robust network to the FGSM attack.

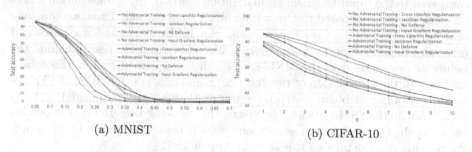

(a) MNIST   (b) CIFAR-10

Fig. 1. Test accuracy for FGSM attack on MNIST (left) and CIFAR-10 (right) for different values of ϵ

4.3 JSMA Evaluation

The JSMA (Jacobian-based Saliency Map Attack) [23] attack relies on the computation of a Saliency Map, which outlines the impact of every input pixel on the classification decision. The method picks at every iteration the most influential pixel to be changed such that the likelihood of the target class is increased. We leave the mathematical details to the original paper. Similarly to FGSM, ϵ represents the magnitude of the attack. The attack is repeated iteratively, and is optimized for the ℓ_0 metric.

We examined the defense methods' test accuracy under the JSMA attack (test accuracy on the perturbed dataset) for different values of ϵ. Figure 2 presents the results for the MNIST and CIFAR-10 datasets. The parameters of the JSMA attack are 80 epochs, 1 pixel attack for the former and 200 epochs, 1 pixel attack, for the latter. In all cases, the minimal test accuracy on the original test set using Jacobian regularization is 98% for MNIST and 88.49% for CIFAR-10.

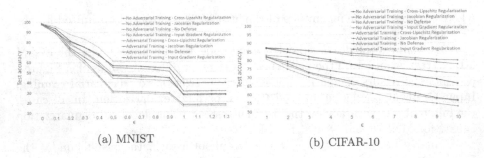

(a) MNIST   (b) CIFAR-10

Fig. 2. Test accuracy for JSMA (1 pixel) attack on MNIST with 80 epochs (left) and CIFAR-10 with 200 epochs (right) for different values of ϵ

Our method achieves superior results compared to the other three methods on CIFAR-10. On the other hand, on MNIST we obtain an inferior performance compared to the Input Gradient regularization method, though we obtain a better performance compared to Cross-Lipschitz regularization. Thus, we conclude that our defense method is effective under the JSMA attack in some cases and presents competitive performance overall. We believe that the reason behind the failure of our method in the MNIST case can be explained by our theoretical analysis. In the formulation of the Jacobian regularization (based on the Frobenius norm of the Jacobian matrix), the metric that is being minimized is the ℓ_2 norm. Yet, in the JSMA attack, the metric that is being targeted by the perturbation is the ℓ_0 pseudo-norm as only one pixel is being changed in every epoch. We provide more details on this issue in Appendix H.

5   Discussion and Conclusions

This paper introduced the Jacobian regularization method for improving DNNs' robustness to adversarial examples. We provided a theoretical foundation for its usage and showed that it yields a high degree of robustness, whilst preserving the network's test accuracy. We demonstrated its improvement in reducing the vulnerability to various adversarial attacks (DeepFool, FGSM and JSMA) on the MNIST, CIFAR-10 and CIFAR-100 datasets. Under all three examined attack methods Jacobian regularization exhibits a large improvement in the network's robustness to adversarial examples, while only slightly changing the network's performance on the original test set. Moreover, in general, Jacobian regularization without adversarial training is better than adversarial training without Jacobian regularization, whereas the combination of the two defense methods provides even better results. Compared to the Input Gradient regularization, our proposed approach achieves superior performance under two out of the three attacks and competitive ones on the third (JSMA). Compared to the Cross-Lipschitz regularization, our proposed approach achieves superior performance under all of the three examined attacks.

We believe that our approach, with its theoretical justification, may open the door to other novel strategies for defense against adversarial attacks.

In the current form of regularization of the Jacobian, its norm is evaluated at the input samples. We empirically deduced that the optimal results are obtained by applying the Jacobian regularization on the original input samples, which is also more efficient computationally, and not on perturbed input samples or on points in the input space for which the Frobenius norm of the Jacobian matrix is maximal. A future work may analyze the reasons for that.

Notice that in the Frobenius norm, all the rows of the Jacobian matrix are penalized equally. Another possible future research direction is providing a different weight for each row. This may be achieved by either using a weighted version of the Frobenius norm or by replacing it with other norms such as the spectral one. Note, though, that the latter option is more computationally demanding compared to our proposed approach.

Acknowledgment. This work is partially supported by the ERC-StG SPADE grant.

References

1. Abadi, M., et al.: Tensorflow: large-scale machine learning on heterogeneous systems, 1 (2015). tensorflow.org
2. Baluja, S., Fischer, I.: Learning to attack: adversarial transformation networks. In: AAAI (2018)
3. Carlini, N., Wagner, D.: Towards evaluating the robustness of neural networks. In: IEEE Symposium on Security and Privacy (2017)
4. Cisse, M., Bojanowski, P., Grave, E., Dauphin, Y., Usunier, N.: Parseval networks: improving robustness to adversarial examples. In: ICML (2017)
5. Fawzi, A., Moosavi-Dezfooli, S., Frossard, P., Soatto, S.: Classification regions of deep neural networks. arXiv abs/1705.09552 (2017)
6. Feinman, R., Curtin, R.R., Shintre, S., Gardner, A.B.: Detecting adversarial samples from artifacts. arXiv abs/1703.00410 (2017). https://arxiv.org/pdf/1703.00410.pdf
7. Goodfellow, I., Bengio, Y., Courville, A.: Deep Learning. MIT Press, Cambridge (2016)
8. Goodfellow, I.J., Shlens, J., Szegedy, C.: Explaining and harnessing adversarial examples. In: ICLR (2015)
9. Hein, M., Andriushchenko, M.: Formal guarantees on the robustness of a classifier against adversarial manipulation. In: Guyon, I., et al. (eds.) Advances in Neural Information Processing Systems 30, pp. 2266–2276. Curran Associates, Inc. (2017). http://papers.nips.cc/paper/6821-formal-guarantees-on-the-robustness-of-a-classifier-against-adversarial-manipulation.pdf
10. Hinton, G.: Networks for machine learning - lecture 6a - overview of mini-batch gradient descent (2012)
11. Kingma, D.P., Ba, J.: Adam: a method for stochastic optimization. In: ICLR (2015). http://arxiv.org/abs/1412.6980
12. Li, X., Li, F.: Adversarial examples detection in deep networks with convolutional filter statistics. In: ICCV (2017)

13. Lu, J., Issaranon, T., Forsyth, D.: SafetyNet: detecting and rejecting adversarial examples robustly. In: ICCV (2017)
14. Madryi, A., Makelov, A., Schmidt, L., Tsipras, D., Vladu, A.: Towards deep learning models resistant to adversarial attacks. arXiv abs/1706.06083 (2017). https://arxiv.org/pdf/1706.06083.pdf
15. Martens, J., Sutskever, I., Swersky, K.: Estimating the hessian by back-propagating curvature. In: Proceedings of the 29th International Conference on Machine Learning, ICML 2012, Edinburgh, Scotland, UK, 26 June 2012–1 July 2012 (2012)
16. Meng, D., Chen, H.: MagNet: a two-pronged defense against adversarial examples. In: ACM SIGSAC Conference on Computer and Communications Security, pp. 135–147 (2017)
17. Metzen, J.H., Genewein, T., Fischer, V., Bischoff, B.: On detecting adversarial perturbations. In: ICLR (2017)
18. Miyato, T., Maeda, S., Koyama, M., Nakae, K., Ishii, S.: Distributional smoothing with virtual adversarial training. In: ICLR (2016). https://arxiv.org/pdf/1507.00677.pdf
19. Moosavi-Dezfooli, S.M., Fawzi, A., Frossard, P.: Deepfool: a simple and accurate method to fool deep neural networks. In: 2016 IEEE Conference on Computer Vision and Pattern Recognition (CVPR), pp. 2574–2582, June 2016
20. Moosavi-Dezfooli, S.M., Fawzi, A., Fawzi, O., Frossard, P.: Universal adversarial perturbations. In: CVPR (2017)
21. Moosavi-Dezfooli, S.M., Fawzi, A., Fawzi, O., Frossard, P., Soatto, S.: Analysis of universal adversarial perturbations. arXiv abs/1705.09554 (2017)
22. Oh, S.J., Fritz, M., Schiele, B.: Adversarial image perturbation for privacy protection a game theory perspective. In: ICCV (2017)
23. Papernot, N., McDaniel, P., Jha, S., Fredrikson, M., Celik, Z.B., Swami, A.: The limitations of deep learning in adversarial settings. In: 1st IEEE European Symposium on Security and Privacy (2016)
24. Papernot, N., McDaniel, P., Wu, X., Jha, S., Swami, A.: Distillation as a defense to adversarial perturbations against deep neural networks. In: 37th IEEE Symposium on Security and Privacy (2016)
25. Ross, A.S., Doshi-Velez, F.: Improving the adversarial robustness and interpretability of deep neural networks by regularizing their input gradients. CoRR abs/1711.09404 (2017). http://arxiv.org/abs/1711.09404
26. Rozsa, A., Gunther, M., E. Boult, T.: Towards robust deep neural networks with BANG. In: WACV (2018)
27. Shaham, U., Yamada, Y., Negahban, S.: Understanding adversarial training: increasing local stability of neural nets through robust optimization. arXiv abs/1511.05432 (2016). https://arxiv.org/pdf/1511.05432.pdf
28. Simon-Gabriel, C.J., Ollivier, Y., Bottou, L., Schlkopf, B., Lopez-Paz, D.: Adversarial vulnerability of neural networks increases with input dimension. arXiv abs/1802.01421 (2018). https://arxiv.org/pdf/1802.01421.pdf
29. Sinha, A., Namkoong, H., Duchi, J.: Certifying some distributional robustness with principled adversarial training. In: ICLR (2018)
30. Sokolic, J., Giryes, R., Sapiro, G., Rodrigues, M.R.D.: Robust large margin deep neural networks. IEEE Trans. Signal Process. 65(16), 4265–4280 (2017)
31. Strauss, T., Hanselmann, M., Junginger, A., Ulmer, H.: Ensemble methods as a defense to adversarial perturbations against deep neural networks. arXiv abs/1709.03423 (2018). https://arxiv.org/pdf/1709.03423.pdf
32. Szegedy, C., et al.: Intriguing properties of neural networks. In: International Conference on Learning Representations (2014). http://arxiv.org/abs/1312.6199

33. Tramer, F., Papernot, N., Goodfellow, I., Boneh1, D., McDaniel, P.: The space of transferable adversarial examples. arXiv abs/1704.03453 (2017). https://arxiv.org/pdf/1704.03453.pdf
34. Varga, D., Csiszarik, A., Zombori, Z.: Gradient regularization improves accuracy of discriminative models. arXiv abs/1712.09936 (2018). https://arxiv.org/pdf/1712.09936.pdf
35. Xu, W., Evans, D., Qi, Y.: Feature squeezing: detecting adversarial examples in deep neural networks. In: Network and Distributed Systems Security Symposium (NDSS) (2018, to appear)

Concept Mask: Large-Scale Segmentation from Semantic Concepts

Yufei Wang[1]([✉])[iD], Zhe Lin[2][iD], Xiaohui Shen[3], Jianming Zhang[2][iD],
and Scott Cohen[2]

[1] Facebook Research, Menlo Park, CA, USA
yufei22@fb.com
[2] Adobe Research, San Jose, CA, USA
{zlin,jianmzha,scohen}@adobe.com
[3] ByteDance AI Lab, Menlo Park, CA, USA
shenxiaohui@bytedance.com

Abstract. Existing works on semantic segmentation typically consider a small number of labels, ranging from tens to a few hundreds. With a large number of labels, training and evaluation of such task become extremely challenging due to correlation between labels and lack of datasets with complete annotations. We formulate semantic segmentation as a problem of image segmentation given a semantic concept, and propose a novel system which can potentially handle an unlimited number of concepts, including objects, parts, stuff, and attributes. We achieve this using a weakly and semi-supervised framework leveraging multiple datasets with different levels of supervision. We first train a deep neural network on a 6M stock image dataset with only image-level labels to learn visual-semantic embedding on 18K concepts. Then, we refine and extend the embedding network to predict an attention map, using a curated dataset with bounding box annotations on 750 concepts. Finally, we train an attention-driven class agnostic segmentation network using an 80-category fully annotated dataset. We perform extensive experiments to validate that the proposed system performs competitively to the state of the art on fully supervised concepts, and is capable of producing accurate segmentations for weakly learned and unseen concepts.

Keywords: Semantic segmentation · Large-scale segmentation
Semi-supervised learning · Weakly-supervised learning
Zero-shot learning

Y. Wang and X. Shen—The work was done when the authors were in Adobe Research.

Electronic supplementary material The online version of this chapter (https://doi.org/10.1007/978-3-030-01258-8_33) contains supplementary material, which is available to authorized users.

V. Ferrari et al. (Eds.): ECCV 2018, LNCS 11216, pp. 542–557, 2018.
https://doi.org/10.1007/978-3-030-01258-8_33

1 Introduction

Image segmentation has attracted a lot of attention in the recent years, and has achieved great progress with the success of Deep Neural Networks (DNN) [1,2,25,31]. Two popular tasks of segmentation problems are semantic segmentation and instance segmentation. Existing semantic segmentation or scene parsing methods mostly consider a small number of classes and their extension to a large number of classes is challenging. The main difficulty comes from arising overlap between labels when the number of labels significantly increases: for the large-scale setting, labels at different levels or different branches in the Word-Net hierarchy could have complex spatial correlations and subsequently confuse the pixel level annotation tasks. For example, for the face of a person, both the fine level annotation of "face" and the higher level annotation of "person" are correct, and for the area of "clothing" on a human body can also be annotated as "person" or "body". This will cause a substantial challenge in training and evaluation of segmentation algorithms. On the other hand, pixel wise annotation for a large number of images and labels takes a lot of manual effort and is costly to obtain, and current publicly available benchmark datasets only have a small number of classes (for example, the MIT Scene Parsing Benchmark, the largest scene parsing dataset, contains annotations for only 150 classes).

As for instance segmentation, the problem only focuses on objects, and the state-of-the-art bounding box proposal-based methods [8,11,22] cannot handle object parts, stuff or other concepts like visual attributes. This is because the region proposal network predicts objectness of a bounding box, and naturally takes object parts or stuff as negative examples.

In this work, we take a step forward and propose a new approach for large-scale semantic segmentation. To overcome the label ambiguity issue, we formulate the task as a problem of image segmentation given an arbitrary semantic concept. For example, the concept can refer to an object, object part, object group, stuff, attribute, etc. By this formulation, we alleviate the issue of label confusion in large-scale semantic segmentation and scene parsing, which makes training and evaluation of segmentation algorithms more well-defined.

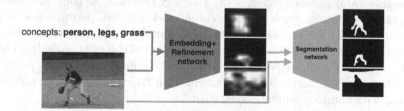

Fig. 1. Overall architecture of the proposed framework. Given a concept (can be object, object parts, stuff, etc.) and an input image, our embedding network and the subsequent attention refinement network predict a low resolution attention map, and a label agnostic segmentation network takes the attention map and the original image as input to predict a segmentation mask for the concept.

However, there is no available dataset for large-scale segmentation. To leverage the existing datasets with different levels of supervision, we use four datasets for training: a 6M Stock dataset (crawled from a stock website) with 18K image level labels; a curated a 750-concept dataset from Open Images [18] and Visual Genome [19], with bounding box annotation; MS-COCO [24] with full segmentation annotation for 80 object classes. In order to evaluate the model's capability on weakly supervised learning, we select a diverse set of 50 test concepts among 18K concepts excluding those 750 concepts with the bounding box annotations.

Given the datasets, we propose a new weakly and semi-supervised learning approach which can leverage all the available training data in an incremental learning framework. The proposed incremental learning framework consists of three steps. First, we train a deep neural network on the stock dataset[1] to learn large-scale visual-semantic embedding between images and 18K concepts [34]. By running the embedding network in a fully convolutional manner, we can compute a coarse attention (heat) map for any given concept. Next, we attach two fully connected layers to the embedding network and fine-tune the refinement network in low resolution using the 750-concept dataset with bounding box annotations to obtain improved attention maps. We use multi-task training to learn from the new 750-concept supervision without affecting the previously learned knowledge on 18K concepts. Finally, we train a label-agnostic segmentation network which takes the attention map and original image as input and predicts a high-resolution segmentation mask without much knowledge of the concept of interest. The segmentation network is trained with only 80 object categories with pixel-level supervision but we show that it generalizes well to any semantic concept, including objects, object parts, and even background stuff, due to the use of attention maps for class-agnostic segmentation.[2] During testing, we can attach the segmentation network to the attention network to form a unified feed-forward network model.

We perform extensive experiments to validate that the proposed approach performs competitively to the state of the art on fully supervised concepts, and is capable of producing accurate segmentations for weakly learned and unseen concepts. The main contributions of this paper are as follows: (1) We address the problem of large-scale semantic segmentation with a new formulation: large-scale segmentation given a concept; (2) To study this task, we construct multiple datasets with different levels of supervision, and establish performance evaluation methods; (3) We propose a new, incremental learning approach that can predict segmentation masks for a very large number of concepts, including object, object parts, and stuff; (4) We propose a novel auxiliary loss called spatial discrimination loss for discriminative segmentation training for a large number of concepts with complex semantic relationships.

---

[1] https://stock.adobe.com.

[2] Note that traditional bounding box proposal-based methods with class-agnostic segmentation could easily fail to detect proposals on object parts or stuff and the bounding box-based class-agnostic segmentation module trained with object categories cannot deal with stuff categories.

2   Related Work

Fully Supervised Semantic Segmentation. Semantic segmentation has made remarkable progress with the recent advancement in deep convolutional neural networks (CNN). Many CNN-based segmentation networks [6,8,11,22, 31,36] perform well on datasets with a small number of labels, such as PASCAL VOC [9] with 20 object classes, ADE20K [38] with 150 stuff/object classes.

For instance aware segmentation which requires segmentation of individual object instances, methods based on region proposals [29] perform well on the COCO dataset with 80 object classes [8,11,22]. However, the region proposal based methods can only handle object classes, and their generation to other concepts such as object parts or stuff is not straightforward.

These methods are all fully supervised, and assume disjoint classes, which enables training segmentation networks with a discriminative soft-max loss.

Weakly/Semi-supervised Semantic Segmentation. In order to reduce annotation efforts needed in fully supervised methods, weakly supervised segmentation methods have been proposed [3,7,14,17,20,28,30]. Image-level annotations require minimum manual effort, but methods with such annotations have a large performance gap compared to fully supervised methods; additional label types such as bounding box annotations are exploited to improve the performance. On the other hand, some works exploit complementary data from the web [14]. Those weakly supervised methods still focus on a small set of disjoint labels.

Different from those works, this paper aims to scale semantic segmentation to a very large number of categories. We make use of all the available annotations in several datasets, thus combining different levels of annotation.

One work related to our model is by Hong et al. [13]. Segmentation is decoupled into two tasks with two separate networks: classification and segmentation. The classification network uses image level annotation, and the segmentation network uses pixel level annotation. However, their work still focuse on a very small number of labels, and their model cannot generalize to unseen concepts.

Another recent work related to ours is by Hu et al. [15]. It aims at instance segmentation on a large number of categories with a small fraction of mask annotations and a large fraction of box annotations. In contrast, our work aims to segment not only objects, but also other concepts such as stuff, parts, and visual attributes (like color); our model is learned to segment concepts trained with only image-level supervisions and can even handle unseen concepts.

Zeroshot Learning. For the problem of zeroshot learning, models are tested on unseen categories by transferring knowledge from the trained categories. Semantic embedding of vectors associated with class labels are obtained from object attribute labels [16,21,27] or word embeddings learned from linguistic tasks [10,26,32]. Zeroshot learning can also be applied to segmentation tasks. With the embedding network that maps an image to a word embedding space, segmentation models have the potential to generate masks given an unseen concept [35].

Large Scale Segmentation/Parsing. Zhao et al. aim to recognize and segment objects with open vocabulary [35], which is in line with our goal of large scale segmentation. Words and images are embedded into a joint space to allow zero-shot learning. Our work is different from theirs in that (1) Zhao *et al.* address only zero-shot segmentation while we aim to solve weakly supervised and zero-shot segmentation in a unified framework, (2) Zhao *et al.* use WordNet for modeling hierarchical label relationships while we consider more complex label relationships including spatial overlap/exclusion which makes trained segmentation models more discriminative, (3) Zhao *et al.* view the open-vocabulary scene parsing as a concept retrieval problem, whereas we assume a target concept is given as an extra input to predict the segmentation mask. Our task is easier to evaluate and with less ambiguity in the ground truth masks.

3   Dataset

Public segmentation datasets typically contain pixel-level annotations on only a small number of labels. On the other hand, datasets with a much larger vocabulary are only weakly annotated, either with bounding box or image-level labels. To make the most of the available datasets, we form a combined dataset, containing different levels of annotations:

- **COCO-80**: MS-COCO dataset [24] pixel level annotation on 80 categories.
- **OIVG-750**: Combined Open Images [18] and Visual Genome [19] dataset with 750 concepts (including COCO concepts) with bounding boxes.[3]
- **Stock-18K**: 6M Stock dataset annotated with 18K tags.

With the combined dataset, we can evaluate the performance of segmentation methods under different levels of supervision by constructing the following test set: (1) strongly supervised concepts: COCO-80 test set, (2) box-level weakly supervised concepts: Weak-Box-670, obtained by excluding 80 COCO categories from OIVG-750, (3) image-level weakly supervised concepts: Weak-Image-50, obtained by choosing 50 new concepts from OIVG excluding OIVG-750.

For testing on weakly-supervised settings, there is no available segmentation ground truth for classes outside COCO-80. Therefore we generate pseudo-ground truth from bounding boxes, using an automatic segmentation model [33]. It is then manually cleaned up, and in the supplementary material we show some examples of the generated pseudo-ground truth masks. Note that we use the pseudo-ground truth masks only for evaluation.

4   Proposed Approach

The overall framework of our large-scale segmentation system is illustrated in Fig. 1. It is composed of an embedding and refinement network that produces an attention map from the input image and a specified concept, and an

---

[3] Visual Genome has more than 10000 classes, and Open Images has 545 trainable classes. We merge the labels of the two datasets, and filtered out classes with very few examples. 750 concepts containing objects, object parts, and stuff are selected.

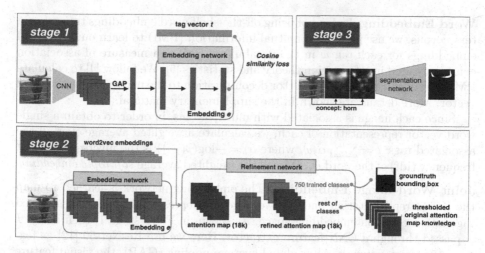

Fig. 2. Three stages of the training framework. Stage 1: embedding network trained on image level annotation. Stage 2: multi-task training of attention network. It finetunes the embedding network while training the refinement network from scratch. It refines the attention map on 750 concepts with bounding box supervision, meanwhile preserves the knowledge learned from embedding network on 18K concepts. Stage 3: label agnostic segmentation network that takes the original image and two refined attention maps (generated from input image with two scales), and predicts the segmentation mask.

attention-driven label-agnostic segmentation network that predicts a final segmentation mask. Utilizing three different levels of supervision, we train the entire framework incrementally in three stages:

1. Train an embedding network on Stock-18K that learns the visual-semantic embedding between images and 18K semantic concepts. Only image-level annotations are used in this stage. After training, we transform the network to fully convolutional, which can generate a low resolution attention map given an input image and any of the 18K concepts.
2. Append a refinement module to the end of the embedding network, and train the refinement network on OIVG-750 with bounding box annotations, aiming at obtaining attention maps of higher quality.
3. Train a label agnostic segmentation network on COCO-80 with 80-class full segmentation supervision. The network takes the initial attention maps together with the image as input, and predicts a higher resolution segmentation mask with more accurate boundaries for the concept.

4.1   Embedding Network

We first utilize the Stock-18K dataset with image-level annotations to learn large-scale visual-semantic embedding. The dataset has 6 million images, each with heavily annotated tags from an 18K vocabulary. The training set is denoted as $\mathcal{D} = \{(I, (w_1, w_2, \ldots, w_n))\}$, where I is an image and w_i is the word vector representation of its associated ground-truth tags.

Word Embedding. Instead of using off-the-shelf word embeddings trained on a text corpus, we use point-wise mutual information (PMI) to learn our own word embeddings for each tag w in the vocabulary. PMI is a measure of association commonly used in information theory and statistics [5]. We follow [4] to calculate PMI matrix and then do eigenvector decomposition to the matrix to get the word vector. More details are shown in the supplementary material.

Since each image is associated with multiple tags, in order to obtain a single word vector representation of each, we calculate a weighted average over all the associated tags: $t = \sum_{i=1}^{n} \alpha_i w_i$ where $\alpha_i = -\log(p(w_i))$ is the inverse document frequency (idf) of the word w_i. We call the weighted average *soft topic embedding*.

Joint Word-Image Embedding. The embedding network is learned to map the image representation and the word vector representation of its associated tags into a common embedding space. As shown in Fig. 2 stage 1, each image I is passed through a CNN feature extractor. Here we use ResNet-50 [12] as feature extraction network. After global average pooling (GAP), the visual feature is then fed into a 3-layer fully connected network, denoted as **Embedding network**, with each fc-layer followed by a batch normalization layer and a ReLU layer. The output is the visual embedding $e = embed\_net(I)$, and is align with the soft topic word vector t by a cosine similarity loss: $L_{embed}(e, t) = 1 - \frac{e^T t}{\|e\|\|t\|}$.

Attention Map. After the embedding network is trained, to predict an attention map for a given concept, we remove the global average pooling layer, and transform the network to a fully-convolutional network by converting the fully connected weights to 1×1 convolution kernels and the batch normalization layers to spatial batch normalization layers. After this transformation, we can obtain a dense embedding map given an image and a word vector, in which the value at each location is the similarity between the word and the image region around that location. Thus the embedding map can also be viewed as an attention map for that word. Note that the way we generate the attention map is similar to [37]. However, we use soft topic embedding instead of discriminative classification so the attention map has better spatial coverage than the one in [37].

Formally, the attention map for a given concept w can be calculated as:

$$\alpha_{(i,j)}^0 = <e_{i,j}, w> \tag{1}$$

where (i, j) is the location index for the attention map. For an unseen concept that is not used in our image-word embedding training, as long as we can obtain its word vector w, we can still obtain its attention map using Eq. 1. Therefore, our embedding network can be generalized to any arbitrary concept.

4.2 Attention Map Refinement

Although the embedding network trained on image level annotation can predict attention maps for any given word vector, the quality of the attention maps is still very coarse due to the lack of annotations with spatial information.

In order to improve the quality of the attention map, we leverage existing finer-level annotations, namely the object bounding box annotations that are available in several large-scale datasets. Specifically, we use the OIVG-750 dataset to train a network for attention map refinement.

Refinement Network Architecture. As shown in Fig. 2 stage 2, the refinement network is appended at the end of the embedding network, and is composed of two convolutional layers with 1×1 kernels followed by a sigmoid layer. By treating word embeddings as convolutional kernels, embedding network can now output 18K coarse attention maps. The two-layer refinement network takes those coarse attention maps as input, and learns a non-linear combination of the concepts to generate refined attention maps for the 750 classes. This encourages the refinement network to consider relationships between concepts during training.

Multi-task Training. For a given concept, training signal for its attention map is a binary mask based on the ground-truth bounding boxes, and a sigmoid cross entropy loss is used. Embedding network is also finetuned for better performance. However, since the bounding box annotations are only available for the 750 concepts, if we only train the network on those classes, the previously learned attention maps for the rest of 18K concepts will be corrupted if we also finetune the embedding network layers. Inspired by [23] on learning without forgetting, in order to preserve the learned knowledge from the rest of 18K concepts, an additional matching loss is added: the original attention maps generated by the embedding network are binarized with a threshold, and sigmoid cross entropy loss is exerted for the refined attention maps to match the original attention maps. The multi-task loss function is therefore as follows:

$$L = L_{xe}(G, \alpha) + c \sum_{k \in \Psi_N} L_{xe}(\text{B}(\alpha_k^0), \alpha_k) \qquad (2)$$

where $L_{xe}(p, q)$ is the cross entropy loss between true distribution p and predicted distribution q. α is the attention map of the given concept, G is the ground truth mask with 1 being inside the bounding box, 0 outside. $\text{B}(\alpha)$ is the binary mask after thresholding the attention map. α_k^0 and α_k are original attention map and refined attention map respectively. Ψ_N is the set of indices of top N attention maps with the highest activation. The matching loss is exerted on attention maps with high activation only to avoid bias toward irrelevant concepts. c is the weight balancing the losses. We choose $N = 800$, and $c = 10^{-6}$.

Spatial Discrimination Loss. The reason we used sigmoid cross entropy loss during training instead of softmax loss as in semantic segmentation is that there are many concepts whose masks are overlapping with each other. It is especially common for objects and their parts. For example, the mask of face is always covered by the mask of person. Using softmax loss therefore would discourage the mask predictions on those concepts one way or another. At the same time, there are still many cases where the masks of two concepts never overlap. To utilize such spatial relationships between label pairs and make training of the attention maps more discriminative, we propose a novel auxiliary loss for discriminating those spatially non-overlapping concepts, referred to as spatial discriminative loss, to discourage high responses for spatially conflicting concepts occuring at the same time.

In particular, we calculate the mask overlap ratio between every co-occurred concept pair in the training data:

$$O(i,j) = \frac{\sum_n |a_n(i) \cap a_n(j)|}{\sum_n |a_n(i)|} \tag{3}$$

where $a_n(i)$ is the mask of the i-th concept in image n, and $|a_n(i) \cap a_n(j)|$ is the overlapping area of between concepts i and j. Here image n has to include both i and j concepts to avoid impact of incomplete annotation. Note that the mask overlap ratio is non-symmetric. In the supplementary material, we show a subset of the overlap ratio matrix $O(i,j)$.

With the overlap ratio matrix $O(i,j)$, a training example of a concept i can serve as a negative training example of its non-overlapping concept j, i.e., for a particular location in the image, the output for concept j should be 0 if the ground-truth for concept i is 1. To soften the constraint, we further weight the auxiliary loss based on the overlap ratio, where the weight γ is calculated as:

$$\gamma_{ij} = \begin{cases} 1 - O(i,j), & \text{if } O(i,j) < 0.5 \\ 0, & \text{otherwise} \end{cases} \tag{4}$$

4.3   Label Agnostic Segmentation Network

Our attention map refinement network now can predict low resolution attention map for an arbitrary concept using its word vector representation. To further obtain the mask of the concept with higher resolution and better boundary quality, we train a label agnostic segmentation network that takes the original image and the attention map as input, and generates a segmentation mask without knowing the concept, as shown in Fig. 2 stage 3. Since the goal of the segmentation network is to generate foreground segmentation mask given the prior knowledge of attention map, the segmentation network can generalize to unseen concepts, even though it is entirely trained on COCO-80 with only 80 object classes.

To segment the masks at different scales, we generate multiple attention maps by feeding the embedding network with different input image sizes (300 and 700 in our experiments). The resultant attention maps are then upsampled to serve as the extra input channel to the segmentation network along with the image.

To make the segmentation network focus on generating accurate masks instead of having the extra burden of predicting the existence of the concept in the image, we normalize the attention maps to $[0, 1]$. We found that such training strategy can learn better segmentation networks. During testing, the attention maps are normalized in the same way, and the verification of the existence of the concept is done separately, with details presented in the supplementary material.

For the architecture of segmentation network, we use an architecture that extracts and combines high level and low level features to predict a concept mask with accurate boundaries. See the supplementary materials for more details.

4.4   Weakly Supervised Segmentation

During testing stage, for the 18K concepts that are only trained with image level supervision, we do not directly use the attention map from the refinement network for that concept as the input to the segmentation network. This is because the segmentation network only sees the examples of the COCO-80 during training, which has the attention map trained with bounding box/pixel-wise segmentation supervision. Thus, the discrepancy between the lower-quality attention maps of the 18K concepts and the higher-quality attention map of the 750 concepts will impact the segmentation performance on 18K concepts.

Therefore, for a concept q from the 18K concepts with image level supervision, we find its nearest neighbor concept p in the embedding space from the 750 concepts, and the attention maps is a linear combination $\alpha = \theta\alpha_q + (1 - \theta)\alpha_p$ of the attention maps from the two concepts, with θ decided on validation set.

5   Experiments

In this section, we provide visual and numerical results on attention map prediction and segmentation mask generation under different levels of supervision. Experimental details are shown in the supplementary material.

5.1   Datasets

For COCO-80, we use the train2014 split, with 80k training images. For OIVG-750, there are 540k training images, and training examples for each concept varies from 8 to 100k. Stock-18K has 6M training images, and 30 tags for each image on average. Test/validation set for OIVG-750, Weak-Box-670, Weak-Image-50 have 5–10 examples per concept, and one example is held for validation.

In Fig. 3, we show the example images and ground truth labels from different datasets. Each row shows an example of a dataset with annotation. In the last column, we also show an example test image from Weak-Image-50, for which the annotation is the pseudo-ground-truth mask.

5.2   Attention Map Evaluation

For attention map generation, we use several ways for evaluation. Following [34], we use Pointing Game for evaluation. For an image, if the maximum point in attention map lies in the ground truth mask, a hit is counted. We can measure the mean accuracy across all the concepts. We can also use IOU for evaluation. The attention map is a probability mask that ranges from 0 to 1, and we calculate IOU as follows:

$$\text{IoU}_n = \frac{\alpha_n * G_n}{\max(\alpha_n, G_n)} \tag{5}$$

where n is image index, α is the attention map, and G is the ground truth. When there is only bounding box ground truth available, we use the pseudo-ground-truth for evaluation.

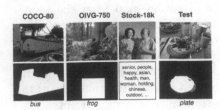

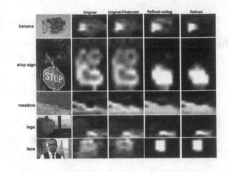

Fig. 3. Examples of our datasets with different levels of annotation. First row is the original image, and second row shows the annotation labels. The Stock-18k image is from **arekmalang - stock.adobe.com**.

Fig. 4. Examples of attention map generated from different models/phases.

Table 1. Performance of different models on attention map generation

	Original	Original-Finetuned	Refined-noNeg	Refined
Pointing Game	0.578	0.631	0.806	**0.810**
IoU	0.262	0.288	0.416	**0.421**

In Table 1, we compare the performance of different models/phases on attention map generation, using OIVG-750 evaluation set. **Original** is the original attention map we obtain from the embedding network, as described in Sect. 4.1. **Original-Finetuned** is the attention map from the embedding network, after finetuning with the refinement network. **Refined-noNeg** is the result from the refinement network as described in Sect. 4.2, without using the negative examples from non-overlapping concept. **Refined** is our full model.

In Fig. 4, we also show the visual result of attention map generated from different models. We can see that the original attention map already generates acceptable attention maps, but it is noisy, and sometimes locating to objects when the concept is object part (see example of *face*). The refined attention map is much cleaner, and is covering the whole object/stuff. The comparison between the result from Refined-noNeg and Refined shows that by using negative samples from non-overlapping concept, the attention map is cleaner visually, and is more discriminative.

5.3 Segmentation Evaluation

In this section, we evaluate our model with different levels of supervision, and compare our results with different baselines. For quantitative evaluation, we simply binarize the soft segmentation outputs using the threshold of 0.5 for all models. Given the binary ground truth mask and prediction mask for one concept, we can calculate precision/recall/IoU. Over different concepts, we calculate mean precision, recall, and mean IoU.

Dataset. Our model uses different levels of supervision, and thus we can evaluate the model performance on concepts with different levels of supervision separately: categories inside **COCO-80** are used to train the attention network and segmentation network, therefore we can evaluate it for full (strong) supervision. We use 5000 miniVal2014 split for evaluation, and all the annotated concepts in the images are evaluated; **Weak-Box-670** is used to evaluate segmentations with bounding box-level supervision; **Weak-Image-50** is used to evaluate our model's performance on concepts with only image-level supervision.

Results. We compare the performance of our model and baselines on different levels of supervision in Tables 2 and 3.

Table 2. Comparison of the performance of our model and baselines, on different levels of supervision. On the left, we show the descriptions of different baselines we use

Model	Description
FCIS	Semantic segmentation trained and tested on COCO[34]. The model generates instance mask for a given concept, and we merge all the instances of one concept to one binary mask.
Mask R-CNN	State-of-the-art semantic segmentation model[11].
Saliency-DSS	The state-of-the-art saliency network for a given image [15].
Mask R-CNN*	Our modified version of Mask-RCNN to better perform on our task. See main paper for details.

Test Dataset	Model	Precision	Recall	IoU
COCO-80	FCIS[34]	**0.864**	0.596	0.442
	Mask R-CNN[11]	0.854	0.668	**0.525**
	Saliency-DSS[15]	0.286	0.492	0.181
	Ours	0.656	**0.722**	0.402
Weak-Box-670	Saliency-DSS[15]	0.592	0.407	0.307
	Mask R-CNN*	0.281	0.111	0.089
	Ours	**0.741**	**0.800**	**0.609**
Weak-Image-50	Saliency-DSS[15]	0.387	0.493	0.283
	Mask R-CNN*	0.268	0.147	0.133
	Ours	**0.580**	**0.539**	**0.412**

Table 3. Ablation study for our model on different levels of supervision. On the left we show the descriptions of the models we compare with

Model	Description
Ours-noNeg	Our model without negative training examples from non-overlapping concepts as described in Section 4.2.
Ours-singleAtt	The segmentation network takes only one attention map from image size 300 × 300 as input.

IoU	Ours	Ours-noNeg	Ours-singleAtt
COCO-80	**0.402**	0.395	0.363
Weak-Box-670	**0.609**	0.594	0.599
Weak-Image-50	**0.412**	0.356	0.390

As shown in Table 2, the performance of our model decreases with less supervision. For the fully supervised concepts, our method performs competitively with semantic segmentation model FCIS, with 4% of gap, and has moderate gap with current state-of-the-art semantic segmentation model Mask R-CNN. The gap is predictable, because our model handles not only 80 categories inside COCO-80, but also orders of magnitude more concepts outside COCO. The closeness between the two models shows that although our model aims at a much bigger concept set, it performs very well on COCO concepts.

For the weakly supervised setting, we first compare our method with the saliency baseline. Since the concepts for evaluation are manually picked and the images used for evaluation are manually filtered for insuring the quality of the groundtruth, one concern is that the test set is not sufficient to test concept segmentation, and a saliency object detection is enough. Here by showing the performance of the saliency detection model is poor, we demonstrate that our test dataset is valid for evaluating our task.

We also train a modified Mask-RCNN (notated as Mask-RCNN*) for weakly supervised results. The original Mask R-CNN [11] predicts a mask independently for each of the 80 COCO classes. For an RoI associated with ground-truth class k, loss is defined as per pixel sigmoid loss only on the kth class. However, this does not apply to our problem, because there is no mask annotation on our large scale OIVG-750 dataset. Therefore, we modify the segmentation head to predict a label-agnostic mask, which is trained only on COCO-80. Mask-RCNN* does not perform well, and the reason can be summarized as follows: First, Mask-RCNN cannot handle stuff classes, such as sky, tree, etc., because the segmentation head only sees 80 object classes with bounding boxes. In contrast, our two-stage model does not rely on bounding boxes, so it can handle stuff very well even though the segmentation head is only trained on 80 object classes. Second, for the large number of classes (750) and highly overlapping concepts, Mask-RCNN has a very low box detection rate, which might be due to conflict of bounding box proposals among object parts, stuff, object classes.

For COCO-80, the IoU for the saliency detection result is very low, whereas for the other test dataset, the saliency performance is higher than that in COCO-80. This is due to the distributions of concepts in OIVG and COCO are essentially different, the former contains more cases with larger objects/stuff. Despite the higher performance on those test sets, we still see a great improvement of our method over saliency.

In Table 3, we show an ablation study of our approach with respect to the final performance. Our full model outperforms Ours-noNeg and Ours-singleAtt on all three cases of supervision setting, indicating the necessity of negative examples and the multi-scale attention map input to the segmentation network.

Figure 5 shows visual examples of our segmentation result. For object, object part, and stuff, we show three examples from each type. All three object categories are from COCO-80. *jean* and *frond* are from Weak-Image-50. The rest four categories are from Weak-Box-670. We also show different baselines' results. We provide more qualitative results and failure cases in the supplementary.

5.4 Zero-Shot Learning

Since we use an embedding network for attention map prediction, with the word embeddings, our model can potentially handle unseen concepts. To test this potential, we curate 10 concepts outside the 18K concepts that our model is trained on, each with 5–10 test examples. The IoU of our method is 0.436, and the IoU of Saliency-DSS is 0.298. Further study with a larger test set is needed to fully justify the zero-shot learning ability of our model.

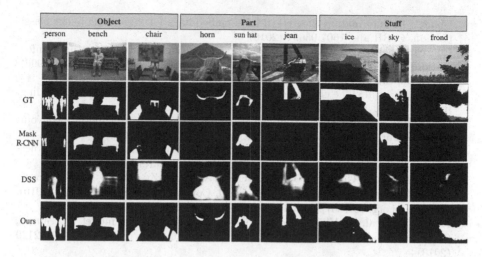

Fig. 5. Example of visual result of our segmentation network.

6 Conclusion

In this paper, we study semantic segmentation at a very large scale. With a large number of labels, training and evaluation of segmentation models are very challenging due to complex correlations between labels. To address the issue, we formulate the problem as conditional image segmentation given a semantic concept. Under this formulation, we propose a powerful weakly and semi-supervised segmentation framework that can handle a large number of concepts including objects, parts, stuff, attributes, and even unseen concepts. The framework consists of three parts: (1) an embedding network that maps the image and a large scale of concepts into the same space; and (2) an attention network which refines the embedding network to predict low resolution attention maps; and (3) a label agnostic segmentation network which generates segmentation masks given the attention map of a concept. Experiments show that our system performs competitively to state-of-the-art semantic segmentation models on concepts with full supervision, and is able to generate segmentation results for a large number of concepts with different levels of weak supervision, and even for unseen concepts.

References

1. Badrinarayanan, V., Kendall, A., Cipolla, R.: SegNet: a deep convolutional encoder-decoder architecture for image segmentation. IEEE Trans. Pattern Anal. Mach. Intell. **39**(12), 2481–2495 (2017)
2. Chen, L., Papandreou, G., Kokkinos, I., Murphy, K., Yuille, A.L.: DeepLab: semantic image segmentation with deep convolutional nets, atrous convolution, and fully connected CRFs. IEEE Trans. Pattern Anal. Mach. Intell. **40**(4), 834–848 (2018)
3. Chen, X., Shrivastava, A., Gupta, A.: Enriching visual knowledge bases via object discovery and segmentation. In: CVPR, pp. 2035–2042. IEEE Computer Society (2014)

4. Chollet, F.: Information-theoretical label embeddings for large-scale image classification. CoRR abs/1607.05691 (2016)
5. Church, K.W., Hanks, P.: Word association norms, mutual information, and lexicography. Comput. Linguist. **16**(1), 22–29 (1990). http://dl.acm.org/citation.cfm?id=89086.89095
6. Cordts, M., et al.: The cityscapes dataset for semantic urban scene understanding. In: CVPR, pp. 3213–3223. IEEE Computer Society (2016)
7. Dai, J., He, K., Sun, J.: BoxSup: exploiting bounding boxes to supervise convolutional networks for semantic segmentation, pp. 1635–1643 (2015)
8. Dai, J., He, K., Sun, J.: Instance-aware semantic segmentation via multi-task network cascades. In: CVPR, pp. 3150–3158. IEEE Computer Society (2016)
9. Everingham, M., Gool, L., Williams, C.K., Winn, J., Zisserman, A.: The pascal visual object classes (VOC) challenge. Int. J. Comput. Vis. **88**(2), 303–338 (2010). https://doi.org/10.1007/s11263-009-0275-4
10. Frome, A., et al.: DeViSE: a deep visual-semantic embedding model. In: Burges, C.J.C., Bottou, L., Ghahramani, Z., Weinberger, K.Q. (eds.) NIPS, pp. 2121–2129 (2013)
11. He, K., Gkioxari, G., Dollár, P., Girshick, R.B.: Mask R-CNN. In: ICCV, pp. 2980–2988. IEEE Computer Society (2017)
12. He, K., Zhang, X., Ren, S., Sun, J.: Deep residual learning for image recognition. In: CVPR, pp. 770–778. IEEE Computer Society (2016)
13. Hong, S., Noh, H., Han, B.: Decoupled deep neural network for semi-supervised semantic segmentation. In: Cortes, C., Lawrence, N.D., Lee, D.D., Sugiyama, M., Garnett, R. (eds.) NIPS, pp. 1495–1503 (2015)
14. Hong, S., Yeo, D., Kwak, S., Lee, H., Han, B.: Weakly supervised semantic segmentation using web-crawled videos, pp. 2224–2232 (2017)
15. Hu, R., Dollár, P., He, K., Darrell, T., Girshick, R.: Learning to segment every thing. In: CVPR (2018)
16. Jayaraman, D., Grauman, K.: Zero-shot recognition with unreliable attributes. In: Ghahramani, Z., Welling, M., Cortes, C., Lawrence, N.D., Weinberger, K.Q. (eds.) NIPS, pp. 3464–3472 (2014)
17. Kolesnikov, A., Lampert, C.H.: Seed, expand and constrain: three principles for weakly-supervised image segmentation. In: Leibe, B., Matas, J., Sebe, N., Welling, M. (eds.) ECCV 2016. LNCS, vol. 9908, pp. 695–711. Springer, Cham (2016). https://doi.org/10.1007/978-3-319-46493-0_42
18. Krasin, I., et al.: OpenImages: a public dataset for large-scale multi-label and multi-class image classification (2017). Dataset available from https://github.com/openimages
19. Krishna, R., et al.: Visual genome: connecting language and vision using crowd-sourced dense image annotations. Int. J. Comput. Vis. **123**(1), 32–73 (2017)
20. Kuettel, D., Guillaumin, M., Ferrari, V.: Segmentation propagation in ImageNet. In: Fitzgibbon, A., Lazebnik, S., Perona, P., Sato, Y., Schmid, C. (eds.) ECCV 2012. LNCS, vol. 7578, pp. 459–473. Springer, Heidelberg (2012). https://doi.org/10.1007/978-3-642-33786-4_34
21. Lampert, C.H., Nickisch, H., Harmeling, S.: Attribute-based classification forzero-shot visual object categorization. IEEE Trans. Pattern Anal. Mach. Intell. **36**(3), 453–465 (2014). https://doi.org/10.1109/TPAMI.2013.140
22. Li, Y., Qi, H., Dai, J., Ji, X., Wei, Y.: Fully convolutional instance-aware semantic segmentation. In: 2017 IEEE Conference on Computer Vision and Pattern Recognition, CVPR 2017, Honolulu, HI, USA, 21–26 July 2017, pp. 4438–4446. IEEE Computer Society (2017). https://doi.org/10.1109/CVPR.2017.472

23. Li, Z., Hoiem, D.: Learning without forgetting. In: Leibe, B., Matas, J., Sebe, N., Welling, M. (eds.) ECCV 2016. LNCS, vol. 9908, pp. 614–629. Springer, Cham (2016). https://doi.org/10.1007/978-3-319-46493-0_37
24. Lin, T.-Y., et al.: Microsoft COCO: common objects in context. In: Fleet, D., Pajdla, T., Schiele, B., Tuytelaars, T. (eds.) ECCV 2014. LNCS, vol. 8693, pp. 740–755. Springer, Cham (2014). https://doi.org/10.1007/978-3-319-10602-1_48
25. Noh, H., Hong, S., Han, B.: Learning deconvolution network for semantic segmentation. In: Proceedings of the 2015 IEEE International Conference on Computer Vision (ICCV), ICCV 2015, pp. 1520–1528. IEEE Computer Society, Washington, DC (2015). https://doi.org/10.1109/ICCV.2015.178
26. Norouzi, M., et al.: Zero-shot learning by convex combination of semantic embeddings. In: International Conference on Learning Representations (ICLR) (2014)
27. Parikh, D., Grauman, K.: Relative attributes. In: Metaxas, D.N., Quan, L., Sanfeliu, A., Gool, L.J.V. (eds.) ICCV, pp. 503–510. IEEE Computer Society (2011)
28. Pathak, D., Krähenbühl, P., Darrell, T.: Constrained convolutional neural networks for weakly supervised segmentation. In: 2015 IEEE International Conference on Computer Vision, ICCV 2015, Santiago, Chile, 7–13 December 2015, pp. 1796–1804. IEEE Computer Society (2015). https://doi.org/10.1109/ICCV.2015.209
29. Ren, S., He, K., Girshick, R.B., Sun, J.: Faster R-CNN: towards real-time object detection with region proposal networks, pp. 91–99 (2015)
30. Rubinstein, M., Joulin, A., Kopf, J., Liu, C.: Unsupervised joint object discovery and segmentation in internet images, pp. 1939–1946 (2013)
31. Shelhamer, E., Long, J., Darrell, T.: Fully convolutional networks for semantic segmentation. IEEE Trans. Pattern Anal. Mach. Intell. 39(4), 640–651 (2017)
32. Socher, R., Ganjoo, M., Manning, C.D., Ng, A.Y.: Zero-shot learning through cross-modal transfer. In: Burges, C.J.C., Bottou, L., Ghahramani, Z., Weinberger, K.Q. (eds.) NIPS, pp. 935–943 (2013)
33. Xu, N., Price, B.L., Cohen, S., Yang, J., Huang, T.S.: Deep GrabCut for object selection. CoRR abs/1707.00243 (2017). http://arxiv.org/abs/1707.00243
34. Zhang, J., Lin, Z., Brandt, J., Shen, X., Sclaroff, S.: Top-down neural attention by excitation backprop. In: Leibe, B., Matas, J., Sebe, N., Welling, M. (eds.) ECCV 2016. LNCS, vol. 9908, pp. 543–559. Springer, Cham (2016). https://doi.org/10.1007/978-3-319-46493-0_33
35. Zhao, H., Puig, X., Zhou, B., Fidler, S., Torralba, A.: Open vocabulary scene parsing. In: ICCV, pp. 2021–2029. IEEE Computer Society (2017)
36. Zhao, H., Shi, J., Qi, X., Wang, X., Jia, J.: Pyramid scene parsing network. In: CVPR, pp. 6230–6239. IEEE Computer Society (2017)
37. Zhou, B., Khosla, A., Lapedriza, A., Oliva, A., Torralba, A.: Learning deep features for discriminative localization. In: CVPR, pp. 2921–2929. IEEE Computer Society (2016)
38. Zhou, B., Zhao, H., Puig, X., Fidler, S., Barriuso, A., Torralba, A.: Scene parsing through ADE20K dataset. In: CVPR, pp. 5122–5130. IEEE Computer Society (2017)

Descending, Lifting or Smoothing:
Secrets of Robust Cost Optimization

Christopher Zach[1]([⊠]) and Guillaume Bourmaud[2]

[1] Toshiba Research Europe, Cambridge, UK
christopher.m.zach@gmail.com
[2] University of Bordeaux, Bordeaux, France

Abstract. Robust cost optimization is the challenging task of fitting a large number of parameters to data points containing a significant and unknown fraction of outliers. In this work we identify three classes of deterministic second-order algorithms that are able to tackle this type of optimization problem: direct approaches that aim to optimize the robust cost directly with a second order method, lifting-based approaches that add so called lifting variables to embed the given robust cost function into a higher dimensional space, and graduated optimization methods that solve a sequence of smoothed cost functions. We study each of these classes of algorithms and propose improvements either to reduce their computational time or to make them find better local minima. Finally, we experimentally demonstrate the superiority of our improved graduated optimization method over the state of the art algorithms both on synthetic and real data for four different problems.

1 Introduction

Robust cost optimization aims to fit parameters to data containing outliers. This generic optimization problem arises in a large number of applications in computer vision such as bundle adjustment [23], optical flow [4], SLAM [8], registration of 3D surfaces [30], etc. In applications where the data contains a small number of outliers, using a convex kernel[1], such as the L_1 kernel or the Huber kernel, sufficiently reduces influence of outliers to obtain a good fit of the parameters to inlier data points. However, when the observations contain a large number of potentially gross outliers, a convex kernel is not "robust" enough and a quasi-convex kernel, such as Tukey's biweight kernel, has to be employed. Optimizing over a sum of quasi-convex kernels produces a highly non-convex cost function with many local minima. In low-dimensional parameter problems poor local minima can be escaped using stochastic/sampling approaches, such

---

[1] In this paper, the word "kernel" refers to a loss function.

Electronic supplementary material The online version of this chapter (https://doi.org/10.1007/978-3-030-01258-8_34) contains supplementary material, which is available to authorized users.

V. Ferrari et al. (Eds.): ECCV 2018, LNCS 11216, pp. 558–574, 2018.
https://doi.org/10.1007/978-3-030-01258-8_34

as RANSAC [10] or simulated annealing [16]. Nevertheless, such methods are impractical for applications that have a large number of parameters and data points (such as bundle adjustment or optical flow). For these large scale problems deterministic second-order approaches are generally considered to be a good compromise between efficiency and accuracy. In return, special care must be taken to escape poor local minima.

Contributions: In this paper, we start with identifying three classes of such algorithms: *direct approaches, lifting-based approaches* and *graduated optimization methods.* Then, we study each of these classes of algorithms and propose improvements either to reduce their computational time or to make them find better local minima. More precisely, we make the following contributions: (i) We show that the *direct approaches* only differ in their quadratic approximation of the quasi-convex kernel. This analysis allows us to outline the limitations and numerical instabilities of some of these algorithms. (ii) We propose to use a convexified Newton approximation to implement *lifting-based approaches* and experimentally demonstrate that this modification leads to better local minima than the classical Gauss-Newton approximation. (iii) We design a novel stopping criterion that allows to significantly speed-up *graduated optimization methods* without harming their ability to avoir poor local minima. (iv) We experimentally demonstrate the superiority of our improved graduated optimization method over the state of the art algorithms both on synthetic and real data for three different problems.

Organization of the Paper: The rest of the paper is organized as follows: Sect. 2 discusses the related work and Sect. 3 introduces our notations as well as some fundamental definitions. Our contributions are gathered in Sects. 4, 5 and 6, where we study three different types of algorithms and make several recommendations to improve their performances. In Sect. 7 numerical evaluations of the methods discussed in the previous three sections are presented. A summary of our recommendations and future work are provided in Sect. 8.

2   Related Work

In this section, we describe the state of the art approaches for robust cost optimization (e.g. redescending m-estimation [15]) and how they are related to the novel method we propose in this paper. We focus on deterministic second-order methods because they are generally considered to be a good compromise between efficiency and accuracy for problems with large numbers of parameters and data points (such as bundle adjustment). In the following literature review we distinguish *direct approaches, graduated optimization methods* and *lifting-based approaches*[2].

---

[2] The "Variable Projection" (VarPro) approach, which can be interpreted as the "opposite" of lifting, was recently shown to be successful for matrix factorization [14].

Direct approaches aim to optimize the original robust objective, usually by utilizing a surrogate model suitable for a second-order method. IRLS [13], the Triggs correction [23] and "square rooting the kernel" [9] are well-known instances of this class of methods. Consequently, these approaches find the local minimum corresponding to the basin of convergence they were initialized in.

Graduated optimization is a meta-algorithm explicitly designed to avoid poor local minima by building a sequence of successively smoother (and therefore easier to optimize) approximations of the original objective. The optimization algorithm consists in successively optimizing the sequence of cost functions (e.g. by using one of the *direct approaches*), with the solution from the previous objective used as starting point for the next one. Homotopy optimization methods (e.g. [7]) and continuation methods (e.g. [20]) are other terms for the same meta-algorithm. Graduated non-convexity [5], multi-scale methods and Gaussian homotopies [19], and deterministic annealing (e.g. [21]) are specific constructions that belong to this family of methods. One drawback of graduated optimization is that they appear to be inefficient as an entire sequence of optimization problems has to be solved.

Instead of explicitly building a sequence of smoothed cost functions, lifting approaches[3] [26,29,31] add so called lifting variables (which can be interpreted as confidence weights) to embed the original robust cost function into a higher dimensional space of unknowns. Initializing the lifting variables to a large value corresponds to smoothing the robust cost function while setting them to their optimal values produces the original robust cost function. The algorithm consists in jointly optimizing over the parameters of interest and the lifting variables. Lifting-based methods can be interpreted as "self-tuned" graduated optimization. One drawback of these methods is, that their performance significantly depends on the initialization of the lifting variables (as demonstrated in our numerical experiments).

3   Background and Notations

Robust cost optimization consists in minimizing functions of the form:

$$\min_{\boldsymbol{\theta}} \; \Psi(\boldsymbol{\theta}) \qquad \text{with} \qquad \Psi(\boldsymbol{\theta}) = \sum_{i=1}^{N} \psi(\|\mathbf{f}_i(\boldsymbol{\theta})\|), \qquad (1)$$

where $\boldsymbol{\theta} \in \mathbb{R}^p$ are the parameters of interest, $\mathbf{f}_i(\boldsymbol{\theta}) : \mathbb{R}^p \to \mathbb{R}^d$ is the i-th vectorial residual function and $\psi(\cdot)$ is a robust kernel function (that will be formally defined hereinafter), that allows to reduce the influence of outlying data points. $\|\cdot\|$ is the usual L_2-norm (leading to isotropic penalization of large residuals). The arguably simplest application of Eq. (1) arises when robustly fitting a "mean" vector $\boldsymbol{\theta}$ to data points $\mathbf{y}_i \in \mathbb{R}^d$ which leads to the following problem:

---

[3] Here, the term "lifting" refers to the "multiplicative" version of lifting [11,29]. We do not consider other types of lifting such as the "additive" version of lifting [12,28].

$\min_\theta \sum_{i=1}^N \psi(\|\mathbf{y}_i - \boldsymbol{\theta}\|)$. From a practical point of view, we would like a robust kernel function to convey the idea that large residuals should always have a smaller influence than smaller residuals when estimating the optimal parameters $\boldsymbol{\theta}^*$. We will now translate this idea into formal properties of a robust kernel function: A robust kernel function $\psi : \mathbb{R} \to \mathbb{R}_0^+$ is a symmetric function sufficiently smooth near 0 with the following properties: (1) $\psi(0) = 0$ and $\psi''(0) = 1$. (2) The mapping $\phi : \mathbb{R}_0^+ \to \mathbb{R}_0^+$ with $\phi(z) := \psi(\sqrt{2z})$ (or $\phi(r^2/2) = \psi(r)$) is concave and monotonically increasing.

In robust cost functions such as Eq. 1 the robust kernel ψ is applied only to non-negative arguments, but it is customary to extend its domain to the entire real line $\mathbb{R}$. The "normalization" property (property 1) allows to compare the robustness of different kernels. Concerning property 2, the fact that ϕ should be monotonically increasing is obvious but the necessity of its concavity requires some justification. To so do, we examine the *weight function* ω associated with a robust kernel ψ that describes how ψ weighs the influence of residuals[4]:

$$\omega(r) := \psi'(r)/r = \phi'(r^2/2). \tag{2}$$

Since we aim for large residuals having a smaller influence than smaller residuals, $\omega(\cdot)$ should be monotonically decreasing in $|r|$, which is guaranteed by the concavity of ϕ. Let us note that this definition of a robust kernel includes both convex and quasi-convex kernels. However, as stated in the introduction, in the experiments we will only consider quasi-convex kernels.

4 Direct Methods: IRLS, Triggs Correction, $\sqrt{\psi}$

In this section, we review the approaches that aim to (iteratively) minimize the objective $\Psi(\boldsymbol{\theta})$ (see Eq. 1) without explicitly modifying the objective, and we outline that each of these approaches can be interpreted as methods trying to locally approximate ψ with a quadratic function. In order to be computationally efficient, these methods try to cast the original problem in a way that allows non-linear least-squares solvers, such as Gauss-Newton or Levenberg-Marquardt, to be employed. As a consequence, at each iteration these approaches perform the following steps:

1. perform a first order approximation of the vectorial residual function around the current value of the parameters $\boldsymbol{\theta} = \bar{\boldsymbol{\theta}}$: $\mathbf{f}_i(\bar{\boldsymbol{\theta}} + \Delta\boldsymbol{\theta}) \approx \bar{\mathbf{f}}_i + \mathbf{J}_i \Delta\boldsymbol{\theta}$ where $\mathbf{J}_i$ is the Jacobian of $\mathbf{f}_i(\bar{\boldsymbol{\theta}} + \Delta\boldsymbol{\theta})$ w.r.t. the increment $\Delta\boldsymbol{\theta}$ evaluated at $\Delta\boldsymbol{\theta} = \mathbf{0}$ and $\bar{\mathbf{f}}_i$ is a short hand notation for $\mathbf{f}_i(\bar{\boldsymbol{\theta}})$,
2. approximate $\psi(\|\bar{\mathbf{f}}_i + \mathbf{J}_i \Delta\boldsymbol{\theta})\|)$ with a quadratic function $\breve{\psi}$ s.t. $\psi(\|\bar{\mathbf{f}}_i\|) = \breve{\psi}(\|\bar{\mathbf{f}}_i\|)$.

While step 1 is the same for all the approaches, step 2 turns out to be very different for each of them.

---

[4] For instance, for the quadratic kernel (which does not try to reduce the influence of large residuals), we have $\omega(r) = 1$.

IRLS [13]: One way to derive the IRLS methods is to interpret it as instance of the majorize-minimize principle (e.g. [17]): given the current solution $\bar{\theta}$, IRLS uses a quadratic majorizer of ψ, i.e $\psi(r) \leq \check{\psi}_{\mathrm{IRLS}}(r)$:

$$\check{\psi}_{\mathrm{IRLS}}(\|\bar{\mathbf{f}}_i + \mathsf{J}_i\Delta\theta)\|) = \omega(\|\bar{\mathbf{f}}_i\|)\left(\|\bar{\mathbf{f}}_i + \mathsf{J}_i\Delta\theta\|^2/2 - \|\bar{\mathbf{f}}_i\|^2/2\right) + \psi(\|\mathbf{f}_i(\bar{\theta})\|). \quad (3)$$

Since robust kernels are by construction sub-quadratic, a non-degenerate quadratic majorizer always exists. The IRLS algorithm iteratively builds and minimizes the quadratic surrogates, which yields a sequence of solutions $\theta^{(k)}$ with monotonically decreasing costs $\Psi(\theta^{(k)})$.

Triggs Correction [23]: Contrary to IRLS, the Triggs correction performs a second order expansion of $F_i(\Delta\theta) := \phi(\|\mathbf{f}_i + \mathsf{J}_i\Delta\theta\|^2/2)$ around $\Delta\theta = \mathbf{0}$. The resulting approximation of ψ is given by

$$\check{\psi}_{\mathrm{Triggs}}(\|\bar{\mathbf{f}}_i + \mathsf{J}_i\Delta\theta)\|) = \psi(\|\bar{\mathbf{f}}_i\|) + \nabla_{\Delta\theta} F_i(\mathbf{0})^\top \Delta\theta + \Delta\theta^\top \mathsf{H}_{F_i}(\mathbf{0})\Delta\theta \quad (4)$$

with the following expressions for the gradient and Hessian at $\Delta\theta = \mathbf{0}$:

$$\nabla_{\Delta\theta} F_i(\mathbf{0}) = \omega(\|\mathbf{f}_i\|)\mathsf{J}_i^\top \mathbf{f}_i \qquad \mathsf{H}_{F_i}(\mathbf{0}) = \mathsf{J}_i^\top \left(\frac{\omega'(\|\mathbf{f}_i\|)}{\|\mathbf{f}_i\|}\mathbf{f}_i\mathbf{f}_i^\top + \omega(\|\mathbf{f}_i\|)\mathsf{I}\right)\mathsf{J}_i.$$

where we used Eq. 2 as well as $\phi''(z) = (\omega(\sqrt{2z}))' = \frac{\omega'(\sqrt{2z})}{\sqrt{2z}}$. Note that $\mathbf{f}_i$ is an eigenvector for $\frac{\omega'}{\|\mathbf{f}_i\|}\mathbf{f}_i\mathbf{f}_i^\top + \omega\mathsf{I}$ (omitting arguments to ω and ω'):

$$\left(\frac{\omega'}{\|\mathbf{f}_i\|}\mathbf{f}_i\mathbf{f}_i^\top + \omega\mathsf{I}\right)\mathbf{f}_i = \omega'\|\mathbf{f}_i\|\mathbf{f}_i + \omega\mathbf{f}_i = (\omega'\|\mathbf{f}_i\| + \omega)\mathbf{f}_i.$$

Hence, if $\omega + \|\mathbf{f}_i\|\omega' < 0$, then $\mathsf{H}_{F_i}(\mathbf{0})$ is negative-definite and the Triggs correction approach cannot be applied. The popular Ceres solver [1], which supports the Triggs correction for robust cost optimization, reverts to IRLS for the current step in this case.

Square-Rooting ψ [9]: A third option consists in square-rooting ψ and performing a first order Taylor expansion of it around $\Delta\theta = \mathbf{0}$. Defining $G_i(\Delta\theta) := g(\bar{\mathbf{f}}_i + \mathsf{J}_i\Delta\theta)$ where $g(\mathbf{v}) = \sqrt{\psi(\|\mathbf{v}\|)} \cdot \mathbf{v}/\|\mathbf{v}\|$, we obtain:

$$\check{\psi}_{\sqrt{}}(\|\bar{\mathbf{f}}_i + \mathsf{J}_i\Delta\theta)\|) = \left(g(\bar{\mathbf{f}}_i) + \mathsf{J}_{G_i}(\mathbf{0})\Delta\theta\right)^2 \quad (5)$$

with

$$\mathsf{J}_{G_i}(\mathbf{0}) = \mathsf{J}_{g_i}(\bar{\mathbf{f}}_i)\mathsf{J}_i \quad \text{and} \quad \mathsf{J}_{g_i}(\mathbf{v}) = \frac{\sqrt{\psi(\|\mathbf{v}\|)}\|\mathbf{v}\|^2 \mathsf{I} - \frac{\gamma(\omega(\mathbf{v}))}{\sqrt{\psi(\|\mathbf{v}\|)}}\mathbf{v}\mathbf{v}^\top}{\|\mathbf{v}\|^3}.$$

where we defined $\gamma(\omega(\mathbf{v})) = \psi(\mathbf{v}) - \omega(\mathbf{v})\frac{\|\mathbf{v}\|^2}{2}$ (more details about that function γ will be provided in Sect. 5). Despite $\|\mathbf{v}\|$ appearing in the denominator, $g(\mathbf{v})$ is smoothly behaving near $\mathbf{0}$. The $\mathbf{v}/\|\mathbf{v}\|$ term cancels out the non-differentiability induced by the square root. Observe that $\sqrt{\psi(\|\mathbf{v}\|)}$ behaves like $\|\mathbf{v}\|/\sqrt{2}$ near $\mathbf{v} = \mathbf{0}$, hence $g(\mathbf{v}) \approx \mathbf{v}/\sqrt{2}$ for $\mathbf{v} \approx \mathbf{0}$. Consequently, $\lim_{\mathbf{v} \to \mathbf{0}} J_{g_i}(\mathbf{v}) = \mathbf{I}/\sqrt{2}$.

In Fig. 1, we plot the different approximations of $\psi(\|\bar{\mathbf{f}}_i + J_i(\bar{\boldsymbol{\theta}})\Delta\boldsymbol{\theta}\|)$ for the 1-D linear function $f_i(\theta) = \theta$ and $\bar{\theta} = 1$. One can see that both "Square-rooting ψ" and the Triggs correction do not preserve the symmetry of ψ, whereas IRLS does. Moreover, the IRLS approximation is the only function that has its minimum at 0 whereas "Square-rooting ψ" has a tendency to overshoot with a minimum at ≈ -0.7 and the Triggs correction produces a negative second-order derivative.

Contribution: Our analysis shows that the underlying quadratic models are very different and that the IRLS model has desirable properties which supports what is pointed out in [29]: the Triggs correction performs poorly and "Square-rooting ψ" is often inferior to IRLS. Nevertheless, the *direct approaches* have a major drawback: their limited ability to escape poor local minima. This leads us to studying fundamentally different approaches in the following sections.

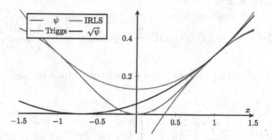

Fig. 1. Quadratic surrogate models used by direct approaches at $\bar{\theta} = 1$ (the x-axis corresponds to $\theta = \bar{\theta} + \Delta\theta$): IRLS (Eq. 3), second order expansion used in the Triggs correction (Eq. 4) (which is concave at $\bar{\theta}$) and "Square-rooting ψ" (Eq. 5). Observe that only the IRLS model preserves the symmetry of ψ and has its minimum at the zero residual.

5   Half-Quadratic Lifting-Based Methods

In this section we review the lifting approach for robust cost minimization proposed in [29], and we unify the formulation with a convexified Newton approximation[5]. In analogy with half-quadratic lifting [11] the robust kernel ψ is reformulated as point-wise minimum over a family of convex parabolas,

$$\psi(x) = \min_{v \in [0,1]} v\frac{x^2}{2} + \gamma(v), \tag{6}$$

where $\gamma : [0,1] \to \mathbb{R}_0^+$ is a convex and monotonically decreasing "bias" function in $[0,1]$. For many interesting choices of ψ the bias function γ can be continuously

---

[5] This is different to a so-called "Lifted Newton method" [3], which addresses "deeply nested functions" and thus is not directly applicable to robust optimization.

extended to the domain $\mathbb{R}_0^+$ (see e.g. [26]). γ is convex but generally increasing in $\mathbb{R}_{\geq 1}$. In order to avoid the constraint $v \in [0,1]$ (or $v \geq 0$, respectively) we reparametrize $v = w(u)$, where $w : \mathbb{R} \to [0,1]$ or $w : \mathbb{R} \to \mathbb{R}_0^+$. Three sensible choices for w are $w(u) = u^2$, $w(u) = e^u$ and $w = \mathrm{sigmoid}(u)$, where sigmoid is the sigmoid function, e.g. $\mathrm{sigmoid}(u) = 1/(1+e^{-u})$. Note that in the objective Eq. 1 one has to introduce an auxiliary unknowns u_i for each term in the sum, but this only induces a moderate increase in run-time in a second order minimization method (e.g. by leveraging the Schur complement [29]).

Using Eq. 6 we can reformulate Eq. 1 as

$$\Psi(\boldsymbol{\theta}) = \min_{u_1,\ldots,u_N} \sum_i \left(w(u_i)\frac{\|\mathbf{f}_i(\boldsymbol{\theta})\|^2}{2} + \gamma(w(u_i)) \right) =: \min_{u_1,\ldots,u_N} \tilde{\Psi}(\boldsymbol{\theta}, (u_i)_i) \quad (7)$$

For notational brevity we will write w_i for $w(u_i)$, w_i' for $w'(u_i)$ etc. in the following.

Gauss-Newton: After linearizing the residual $\mathbf{f}_i(\bar{\boldsymbol{\theta}} + \Delta\boldsymbol{\theta}) \approx \bar{\mathbf{f}}_i + \mathrm{J}_i\Delta\boldsymbol{\theta}$ we can rewrite each term of $\tilde{\Psi}$ as

$$F_i(\Delta\boldsymbol{\theta}, \Delta u_i) := \frac{w_i}{2}\left\|\bar{\mathbf{f}}_i + \mathrm{J}_i\Delta\boldsymbol{\theta}\right\|^2 + \gamma(w_i) = \left\|\begin{matrix}\frac{\sqrt{w_i}}{\sqrt{2}}(\mathrm{J}_i\Delta\boldsymbol{\theta} + \bar{\mathbf{f}}_i) \\ \sqrt{\gamma(w_i)}\end{matrix}\right\|^2. \quad (8)$$

After taking first order derivatives we obtain the Gauss-Newton model for $\tilde{\Psi}$,

$$\tilde{\Psi}^{GN}(\Delta\boldsymbol{\theta}, (\Delta u_i)_i) = \frac{1}{2}\sum_i \begin{pmatrix}\Delta\boldsymbol{\theta} \\ \Delta u_i\end{pmatrix}^\top \begin{pmatrix} w_i\mathrm{J}_i^\top\mathrm{J}_i & \frac{w_i'}{2}\mathrm{J}_i^\top\bar{\mathbf{f}}_i \\ \frac{w_i'}{2}\bar{\mathbf{f}}_i^\top\mathrm{J}_i & \frac{(w_i')^2}{4w_i}\|\bar{\mathbf{f}}_i\|^2 + \frac{(w_i'\gamma_i')^2}{2\gamma_i} \end{pmatrix}\begin{pmatrix}\Delta\boldsymbol{\theta} \\ \Delta u_i\end{pmatrix}$$

$$+ \sum_i \begin{pmatrix} w_i\mathrm{J}_i^\top\bar{\mathbf{f}}_i \\ \frac{w_i'}{2}\|\bar{\mathbf{f}}_i\|^2 + w_i'\gamma_i' \end{pmatrix}^\top \begin{pmatrix}\Delta\boldsymbol{\theta} \\ \Delta u_i\end{pmatrix} + const. \quad (9)$$

By construction the matrices

$$\begin{pmatrix} w_i\mathrm{J}_i^\top\mathrm{J}_i & \frac{w_i'}{2}\mathrm{J}_i^\top\bar{\mathbf{f}}_i \\ \frac{w_i'}{2}\bar{\mathbf{f}}_i^\top\mathrm{J}_i & \frac{(w_i')^2}{4w_i}\|\bar{\mathbf{f}}_i\|^2 + \frac{(w_i'\gamma_i')^2}{2\gamma_i} \end{pmatrix} \quad (10)$$

are positive semi-definite. The bottom right element has two problematic points: when $w_i \to 0$ (then $(w_i')^2/w_i$ is indeterminate) and when $w_i \to 1$ (in this case $(\gamma_i')^2/\gamma_i$ is indeterminate as $\gamma(1) = 0$). It can be shown [27] that the first order Taylor expansions of $(w')^2/w$ and $(\gamma'(v))^2/\gamma(v)$ at the problematic points are given by

$$\frac{(w'(\Delta u))^2}{w(\Delta u)} \approx 2w''(0) + \tfrac{4}{3}w'''(0)\Delta u \qquad \frac{(\gamma'(1+\Delta v))^2}{\gamma(1+\Delta v)} \approx 2\gamma''(1) + \tfrac{4}{3}\gamma'''(1)\Delta v$$

for Δu and Δv small. Consequently, a Gauss-Newton based method can be implemented generically by providing γ and w and the corresponding derivatives.

Newton: The Newton approximation of F_i (Eq. 8) around $\bar{\boldsymbol{\theta}}$ and u_i is given by

$$F_i^N(\Delta\boldsymbol{\theta}, \Delta u_i) \approx \frac{1}{2} \begin{pmatrix} \Delta\boldsymbol{\theta} \\ \Delta u_i \end{pmatrix}^\top \begin{pmatrix} w_i \mathsf{J}_i^\top \mathsf{J}_i & w_i' \mathsf{J}_i^\top \bar{\mathbf{f}}_i \\ w_i' \bar{\mathbf{f}}_i^\top \mathsf{J}_i & \frac{w_i''}{2}\|\bar{\mathbf{f}}_i\|^2 + w_i'' \gamma_i' + (w_i')^2 \gamma_i'' \end{pmatrix} \begin{pmatrix} \Delta\boldsymbol{\theta} \\ \Delta u_i \end{pmatrix}$$

$$+ \begin{pmatrix} w_i \mathsf{J}_i^\top \bar{\mathbf{f}}_i \\ \frac{w_i'}{2}\|\bar{\mathbf{f}}_i\|^2 + w_i' \gamma_i' \end{pmatrix} \begin{pmatrix} \Delta\boldsymbol{\theta} \\ \Delta u_i \end{pmatrix} + const. \tag{11}$$

In this case the Hessian matrices

$$A_i^N := \begin{pmatrix} w_i \mathsf{J}_i^\top \mathsf{J}_i & w_i' \mathsf{J}_i^\top \bar{\mathbf{f}}_i \\ w_i' \bar{\mathbf{f}}_i^\top \mathsf{J}_i & \frac{w_i''}{2}\|\bar{\mathbf{f}}_i\|^2 + w_i'' \gamma_i' + (w_i')^2 \gamma_i'' \end{pmatrix} =: \begin{pmatrix} w_i \mathsf{J}_i^\top \mathsf{J}_i & w_i' \mathsf{J}_i^\top \bar{\mathbf{f}}_i \\ w_i' \bar{\mathbf{f}}_i^\top \mathsf{J}_i & \alpha_i \end{pmatrix} \tag{12}$$

are not guaranteed to be p.s.d. We also denote the bottom right element of A_i^N by $\alpha_i := \frac{w_i''}{2}\|\bar{\mathbf{f}}_i\|^2 + w_i'' \gamma_i' + (w_i')^2 \gamma_i''$. Assuming that $w_i \mathsf{J}_i^\top \mathsf{J}_i$ is strictly positive definite (not just p.s.d. guaranteed by construction)[6], we obtain via the Schur complement that A_i^N is p.s.d. iff $\alpha_i - \frac{(w_i')^2}{w_i}\bar{\mathbf{f}}_i^\top \mathsf{J}_i (\mathsf{J}_i^\top \mathsf{J}_i)^{-1}\mathsf{J}_i^\top \bar{\mathbf{f}}_i \geq 0$. In order to enforce that A_i^N is p.s.d., we add a non-negative value δ_i to α_i

$$\alpha_i + \delta_i - \frac{(w_i')^2}{w_i}\bar{\mathbf{f}}_i^\top \mathsf{J}_i (\mathsf{J}_i^\top \mathsf{J}_i)^{-1}\mathsf{J}_i^\top \bar{\mathbf{f}}_i \geq 0. \tag{13}$$

Since $\mathsf{J}_i(\mathsf{J}_i^\top \mathsf{J}_i)^{-1}\mathsf{J}_i^\top$ is a projection matrix into a respective subspace (the column space of J_i), we deduce that $\bar{\mathbf{f}}_i^\top \mathsf{J}_i (\mathsf{J}_i^\top \mathsf{J}_i)^{-1}\mathsf{J}_i^\top \bar{\mathbf{f}}_i \leq \|\bar{\mathbf{f}}_i\|^2$. Hence, setting $\delta_i = \max\{0, \frac{(w_i')^2}{w_i}\|\bar{\mathbf{f}}_i\|^2 - \alpha_i\}$ is a sufficient condition for Eq. 13 to be satisfied. Note that $\alpha_i + \delta_i = \max\{\alpha_i, \frac{(w_i')^2}{w_i}\|\bar{\mathbf{f}}_i\|^2\}$ and therefore the convexified matrix $\breve{A}_i^N$ is given by

$$\breve{A}_i^N := \begin{pmatrix} w_i \mathsf{J}_i^\top \mathsf{J}_i & w_i' \mathsf{J}_i^\top \bar{\mathbf{f}}_i \\ w_i' \bar{\mathbf{f}}_i^\top \mathsf{J}_i & \max\left\{\alpha_i, \frac{(w_i')^2}{w_i}\|\bar{\mathbf{f}}_i\|^2\right\} \end{pmatrix}. \tag{14}$$

Thus, the (convexified) Newton model for $\tilde{\Psi}$ finally reads as

$$\tilde{\Psi}^N(\Delta\boldsymbol{\theta}, (\Delta u_i)_i) = \frac{1}{2}\sum_i \begin{pmatrix} \Delta\boldsymbol{\theta} \\ \Delta u_i \end{pmatrix}^\top \begin{pmatrix} w_i \mathsf{J}_i^\top \mathsf{J}_i & w_i' \mathsf{J}_i^\top \bar{\mathbf{f}}_i \\ w_i' \bar{\mathbf{f}}_i^\top \mathsf{J}_i & \max\left\{\alpha_i, \frac{(w_i')^2}{w_i}\|\bar{\mathbf{f}}_i\|^2\right\} \end{pmatrix} \begin{pmatrix} \Delta\boldsymbol{\theta} \\ \Delta u_i \end{pmatrix}$$

$$+ \sum_i \begin{pmatrix} w_i \mathsf{J}_i^\top \bar{\mathbf{f}}_i \\ \frac{w_i'}{2}\|\bar{\mathbf{f}}_i\|^2 + w_i' \gamma_i' \end{pmatrix}^\top \begin{pmatrix} \Delta\boldsymbol{\theta} \\ \Delta u_i \end{pmatrix} + const. \tag{15}$$

Contribution: Our novel Newton-based approach (Eq. 15) suggests different updates for $\Delta\boldsymbol{\theta}$ and $(\Delta u_i)_{i=1,...,N}$ than the Gauss-Newton approach (Eq. 9). This is due to the fact that our Newton-based solver leverages second order information. Thus one may expect it to reach better local minima than the Gauss-Newton based solver.

---

[6] Which will be guaranteed in the implementation as we use a damped Newton approach.

6   Graduated Optimization

Graduated optimization aims to avoid poor local minima usually returned by local optimization methods (such as the direct methods presented in Sect. 4) by iteratively optimizing successively better approximations of the original objective. It therefore relies on a sequence of objectives $(\Psi^0, \ldots, \Psi^{k_{\max}})$ such that $\Psi^0 = \Psi$ and Ψ^{k+1} is in some sense easier to optimize than Ψ^k. To our knowledge graduated optimization has not been explored much in the geometric computer vision literature (besides graduated non-convexity, which was specifically developed for a robust and edge-preserving image smoothing method), although it is frequently used in image matching (by leveraging a scale space or image pyramid e.g. [18,24]). Algorithm 1 illustrates the basic graduated optimization method. The construction of Ψ^k and the choices for a stopping criterion are left unspecified and will be described in the following.

Algorithm 1. A generic graduated optimization method.

$\hat{\boldsymbol{\theta}}[k_{\max}] \leftarrow \boldsymbol{\theta}^0$
  for all $k = k_{\max}, \ldots, 0$ **do** $\triangleright$ Traverse towards original cost
    if $k < k_{\max}$ **then** $\hat{\boldsymbol{\theta}}[k] \leftarrow \tilde{\boldsymbol{\theta}}[k+1]$ $\triangleright$ Propagate solution downwards
    repeat
        $\hat{\boldsymbol{\theta}}[k] \leftarrow \text{STEP}(\Psi^k, \hat{\boldsymbol{\theta}}[k])$ $\triangleright$ assuming descent steps
    until a stopping criterion or iteration limit is reached
  end for
  return $\hat{\boldsymbol{\theta}}[0]$

Choice of Ψ^k: For robust costs the natural approach to construct the sequence $(\Psi^0, \ldots, \Psi^{k_{\max}})$ is by appropriate scaling of the kernels. Let $(s_k)_{k=0}^{k_{\max}}$ be a sequence of scaling parameters with $s_0 = 1$ and $s_k < s_{k+1}$. Define

$$\psi^k(r) := s_k^2 \psi(r/s_k) \qquad \text{and} \qquad \Psi^k(\boldsymbol{\theta}) := \sum_i \psi^k(\|\mathbf{f}_i(\boldsymbol{\theta})\|). \qquad (16)$$

In most cases one will choose $s_k = \tau^k$ for a user-specified value τ (a typical choice also used in our experiments is $\tau = 2$). Due to the following lemma this construction of $(\Psi^k)_{k=0}^{k_{\max}}$ is not only natural, but also has a solid justification:

Lemma 1. *Let ψ be a robust kernel and $s \geq 1$. The following statements hold:*

1. *$\psi(r/s) \leq \psi(r) \leq s^2 \psi(r/s)$ for all r.*
2. *Let $0 \leq r' \leq r$. Then we have inequality $\psi(r) - \psi(r') \leq s^2 (\psi(r/s) - \psi(r'/s))$.*

Proof. $\psi(r/s) \leq \psi(r)$ follows from monotonicity of ψ and that $r/s \leq r$ for $s \geq 1$, yielding one part of the first claim. Since ψ is a robust kernel, then the associated mapping $\phi(z) = \psi(\sqrt{2z})$ is concave and monotonically increasing in its domain

$\mathbb{R}_0^+$. Further, ψ is normalized such that $\psi(0) = \phi(0) = 0$. From the concavity of ϕ we deduce that

$$\phi(\alpha z) = \phi(\alpha z + (1 - \alpha) \cdot 0) \geq \alpha \phi(z) + (1 - \alpha)\phi(0) = \alpha \phi(z)$$

for all $\alpha \in [0, 1]$. Now set $\alpha = 1/s^2$ for $s \geq 1$, and we obtain

$$\phi(z/s^2) = \psi(\sqrt{2z}/s) \geq \phi(z)/s^2 = \psi(\sqrt{2z})/s^2.$$

Substituting $z = r^2/2$ (or $r = \sqrt{2z}$) yields $\psi(r/s) \geq \psi(r)/s^2$ or equivalently $s^2\psi(r/s) \geq \psi(r)$. This proves the first claim.

The inequality in the second claim is equivalent to $s^2\psi(r'/s) - \psi(r') \leq s^2\psi(r/s) - \psi(r)$. The function $d(r) := s^2\psi(r/s) - \psi(r) \geq 0$ is monotonically increasing, since $d'(r) = s\psi'(r/s) - \psi'(r) = r(\omega(r/s) - \omega(r)) \geq 0$ (as ω is monotonically decreasing). This verifies the second claim.

The first statement implies that $\Psi^k(\boldsymbol{\theta}) \leq \Psi^{k+1}(\boldsymbol{\theta})$ for all $\boldsymbol{\theta}$, and optimizing Ψ^k means that an upper bound of $\Psi^0 = \Psi$ is minimized.[7] The second statement in the lemma shows that Ψ^k is in a certain sense easier than Ψ^ℓ for $\ell < k$: if $\bar{\boldsymbol{\theta}}$ and $\boldsymbol{\theta}^+$ are solutions such that $\|\mathbf{f}_i(\boldsymbol{\theta}^+)\| \leq \|\mathbf{f}_i(\bar{\boldsymbol{\theta}})\|$ for all i (i.e. going from $\bar{\boldsymbol{\theta}}$ to $\boldsymbol{\theta}^+$ decreases all residuals), then $\Psi^\ell(\bar{\boldsymbol{\theta}}) - \Psi^\ell(\boldsymbol{\theta}^+) \leq \Psi^k(\bar{\boldsymbol{\theta}}) - \Psi^k(\boldsymbol{\theta}^+)$. Thus, Ψ^k is not only an upper bound of Ψ^{k-1}, but also tends to be steeper.

Stopping Criterion: We propose to utilize a relative stopping criterion. Let $\bar{\boldsymbol{\theta}}$ be the current solution and $\boldsymbol{\theta}^+ := \bar{\boldsymbol{\theta}} + \Delta\boldsymbol{\theta}$ be a new solution. Define

$$\mathcal{I}_> := \{i : \mathbf{f}_i(\boldsymbol{\theta}^+) > \mathbf{f}_i(\bar{\boldsymbol{\theta}})\}, \tag{17}$$

i.e. $\mathcal{I}_>$ indexes the strictly increasing residuals after updating the solution. Further, let

$$\Psi_>^k(\boldsymbol{\theta}) := \sum_{i \in \mathcal{I}_>} \psi^k(\mathbf{f}_i(\boldsymbol{\theta})) \qquad \Psi_\leq^k(\boldsymbol{\theta}) := \sum_{i \notin \mathcal{I}_>} \psi^k(\mathbf{f}_i(\boldsymbol{\theta})) \tag{18}$$

(analogously we introduce $\Psi_\leq^{k-1}(\boldsymbol{\theta})$ and $\Psi_>^{k-1}(\boldsymbol{\theta})$). We have $\Psi^k(\boldsymbol{\theta}) = \Psi_\leq^k(\boldsymbol{\theta}) + \Psi_>^k(\boldsymbol{\theta})$ by construction, and $\Psi_\leq^\ell(\bar{\boldsymbol{\theta}}) \leq \Psi_\leq^\ell(\boldsymbol{\theta}^+)$ and $\Psi_\leq^\ell(\boldsymbol{\theta}^+) \leq \Psi_\leq^\ell(\bar{\boldsymbol{\theta}})$ for all $\ell \in \{0, \ldots, k_{max}\}$. We also introduce

$$\Delta_\leq^\ell := \Psi_\leq^\ell(\bar{\boldsymbol{\theta}}) - \Psi_\leq^\ell(\boldsymbol{\theta}^+) \geq 0 \qquad \text{and} \qquad \Delta_>^\ell := \Psi_>^\ell(\boldsymbol{\theta}^+) - \Psi_>^\ell(\bar{\boldsymbol{\theta}}) \geq 0 \tag{19}$$

for all $\ell \in \{0, \ldots, k_{max}\}$ (note the different positions of $\bar{\boldsymbol{\theta}}$ and $\boldsymbol{\theta}^+$ in $\Delta_\leq^\ell$ and $\Delta_>^\ell$). Now if $\bar{\boldsymbol{\theta}}$ is close to a stationary point of Ψ^k, then $\Delta_\leq^k \approx \Delta_>^k$. Since $\boldsymbol{\theta}^+$ is assumed to improve Ψ^k, we read $\Delta_\leq^k \geq \Delta_>^k 0$ and therefore $\Delta_\leq^k - \Delta_>^k \leq \bar{\eta}$ (for a small value $\bar{\eta} > 0$) indicates that $\bar{\boldsymbol{\theta}}$ is close to a stationary point. Since

---

[7] Note that Ψ^k is upper bounding Ψ, but generally it is not a majorizer of Ψ (which would additionally require $\Psi^k(\bar{\boldsymbol{\theta}}) = \Psi(\bar{\boldsymbol{\theta}})$ at the current solution $\bar{\boldsymbol{\theta}}$).

the functions Ψ^k are scaled differently across the hierarchy, we suggest to use a relative stopping criterion,

$$\rho_\Delta^k := \frac{\Delta_\le^k - \Delta_>^k}{\Delta_\le^k + \Delta_>^k} = \frac{\Psi^k(\bar{\theta}) - \Psi^k(\theta^+)}{\Delta_\le^k + \Delta_>^k} \le \eta \qquad (20)$$

for a user-specified value of η. Due to Lemma 1 the denominator monotonically increases with k, hence the criterion becomes looser for larger k.

Contribution: The novel stopping criterion we derived (Eq. 20) allows to speed up particularly the early stages of graduated optimization. Interestingly, there is a connection between the above stopping criterion and the gain ratio

$$\rho_\Psi^k := \frac{\Psi^{k-1}(\bar{\theta}) - \Psi^{k-1}(\theta^+)}{\Psi^k(\bar{\theta}) - \Psi^k(\theta^+)}, \qquad (21)$$

that is commonly used in trust region methods (e.g. [25]) to evaluate the quality of a surrogate model (here Ψ^k) w.r.t. a target cost (Ψ^{k-1}):

Lemma 2. *Let $\eta \in (0,1)$. If $\rho_\Psi^k \ge \frac{\eta+1}{2\eta} > 0$ or $\rho_\Psi^k \le \frac{\eta-1}{2\eta} < 0$ then $\rho_\Delta^k \le \eta$.*

The lemma asserts that if Ψ^{k-1} either increases or decreases sufficiently faster than Ψ^k, then we are near a stationary points of Ψ^k (according to the stopping criterion Eq. 20). It is less relevant in practice, but tells us that Ψ^k and Ψ^{k-1} (or Ψ^ℓ for any $\ell < k$) cannot behave too different when far from a local minimum. The proof uses Lemma 1 and is given in [27].

7   Numerical Results

In this section we compare the performance of the different approaches for robust cost optimization, and we are mostly interested in the quality (i.e. achieved objective value) that is reached after a sensible amount of run-time.

Implementation Remarks: The core of our implementations is a sparse but direct Cholesky solver from the SuiteSparse libraries [6]. We apply Levenberg-type damping $J^\top J + \lambda I$ to (i) ensure the system matrix is sufficiently positive definite for a direct solver and (ii) to obtain a dampled Newton/Gauss-Newton method for non-linear problems. The damping parameter is adjusted using the classical $\times 10 / \div 10$ rule. In the graduated optimization method we used 6 scale levels (i.e. $k_{max} = 5$), where the scale parameter is doubled at each level. The r.h.s. η in the stopping criterion Eq. 20 is set to $\eta = 1/5$. In the figures we abbreviate lifted Gauss-Newton and lifted Newton by l-G-N and l-Newton, respectively. GOM refers to graduated optimization with an uniform allocation of iterations at each level, and GOM+ leverages Eq. 20 as stopping criterion. We use IRLS as direct method inside GOM. We allow 100 iterations (i.e. 100 times solving the underlying system equation for the update $\Delta\theta$) for each method, which results in rather similar wall-clock runtimes for all methods.

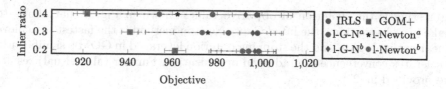

Fig. 2. Final objective values for robust mean instances at varying inlier ratios.

Table 1. Final objective values for the weak membrane energy.

Method	IRLS	l-G-N	l-Newton	GOM+
Objective	231.8133 ± 1.9040	45.0811 ± 0.0861	45.0496 ± 0.0446	$45.0463 \pm 3.66e{-}13$

7.1   Synthetic Data: Robust Mean and Image Smoothing

Estimating the mode (i.e. robust mean) of data points is arguably the simplest robust optimization problem. We follow [26] and create Gaussian distributed inliers and uniformly distributed outliers in a $[-20, 20]^D$ domain. The mean of the Gaussian inlier distribution is also uniformly sampled from the same domain, hence in most cases the outliers will not be symmetrically distributed around the inlier points. Let $(\mathbf{y}_1, \dots, \mathbf{y}_N)$ be the entire set of data points, then the task is to estimate $\boldsymbol{\theta}^* = \arg\min_\theta \Psi^{\mathrm{mean}}(\boldsymbol{\theta}) = \arg\min_\theta \sum_i \psi(\|\boldsymbol{\theta} - \mathbf{y}_i\|)$, where our choice of ψ is the Welsch kernel, $\psi(r) = \frac{1}{2}(1 - e^{-r^2})$. The initial value $\boldsymbol{\theta}^0$ provided to the optimization methods is uniformly sampled as well. We depict in Fig. 2 the average objective values (and corresponding standard deviation using 100 runs) reached by several methods for different choices of inlier ratios and $D = 3$. The included methods are standard IRLS, the accelerated graduated optimization method (GOM+), the lifted Gauss-Newton and Newton methods parametrizing either $w(u) = u^2$ (l-G-N^a, l-Newton^a) or $w(u) = \mathrm{sigmoid}(u)$ (l-G-N^b, l-Newton^b). Graduated optimization (GOM+) is a clear winner, and the lifted Newton method dominates the corresponding lifted Gauss-Newton version. Using the sigmoid parametrization is clearly beneficial, and we will use this parametrization from now on in the lifting-based methods.

Since $\boldsymbol{\theta}$ has very small dimension in the robust mean example, these types of low-parametric robust estimation problems are easily solved by random sampling methods such as RANSAC and variants (e.g. [10,22]). Therefore we now consider a problem with a high dimensional vector of unknowns. We selected the weak membrane energy for image smoothing (e.g. [5]), which is a prototypical instance of a difficult low-level image processing problem. Given an observed image $\mathbf{u}$ the weak membrane energy is given by $\Psi^{\mathrm{Membrane}}(\boldsymbol{\theta}; \mathbf{u}) = \sum_{i \in \mathcal{V}} \psi^{\mathrm{data}}(\theta_i - u_i) + \sum_{(i,j) \in \mathcal{E}} \psi^{\mathrm{smooth}}(\theta_i - \theta_j)$. The node set $\mathcal{V}$ corresponds to pixels, and the edge set $\mathcal{E}$ is induced by the 4-neighborhood. ψ^{data} and ψ^{smooth} are based on the smooth truncated kernel (see [27]). Table 1 lists the reached average objectives (and standard deviation over 25 runs) for the different methods for the 256×256 "Lena" image. The initial guesses $\boldsymbol{\theta}^0$ are uniformly sampled images from $[0, 1]^{|\mathcal{V}|}$. Only IRLS falls clearly behind in terms of reported optimal value. More interesting is the evolution of objective values shown in Fig. 3, that allows to make two observations: the lifted Gauss-Newton method is the fastest to achieve a near optimal value, and the stopping criterion leveraged in GOM+ significantly accelerates convergence of graduated optimization. Further (also visual) results are provided in [27].

7.2   Real Data: Robust Bundle Adjustment

One of the main applications of robust cost minimization in computer vision is bundle adjustment (BA). We took 10 problem instances (the list is provided in [27]) from the "bundle adjustment in the large collection" [2]. The robust bundle objective is given by

$$\Psi^{\mathrm{BA}}(\{\mathbf{R}_i\}, \{\mathbf{t}_i\}, \{\mathbf{X}_j\}) := \sum_{i,j} \psi(\|\pi(\mathbf{R}_i\mathbf{X}_j + \mathbf{t}_i) - \mathbf{q}_{ij}\|), \qquad (22)$$

where $\mathbf{q}_{ij} \in \mathbb{R}^2$ is the observed image observation of the j-th 3D point $\mathbf{X}_j \in \mathbb{R}^3$ point in the i-th image (which has associated parameters $\mathbf{R}_i \in SO(3)$ and $\mathbf{t}_i \in \mathbb{R}^3$). $\pi(X) = X/X_3$ is the projection function of a pinhole camera model. $\mathbf{q}_{ij}$ is measured on the image plane, i.e. the original pixel coordinates are pre-multiplied by the (provided) inverse calibration matrix. ψ is chosen to be the

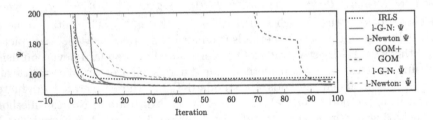

Fig. 3. Evolution of Ψ^{Membrane} w.r.t. the number of iterations. For the lifting based methods we plot the original cost Ψ and lifted one $\tilde{\Psi}$ (Eq. 7).

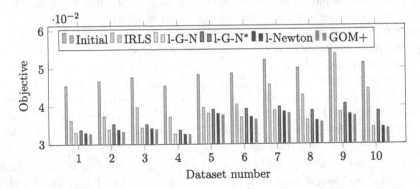

Fig. 4. Objective values (normalized w.r.t. the number of image measurements) reached by the different methods for *linearized* BA.

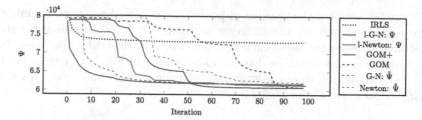

Fig. 5. Evolution of Ψ^{BA} w.r.t. the number of iterations for the Venice-427 instance.

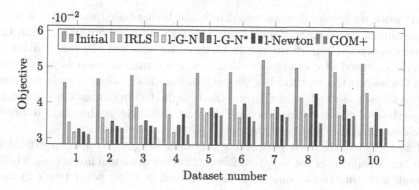

Fig. 6. Objective values (normalized w.r.t. the number of image measurements) reached by the different methods for *metric* BA.

smooth truncated kernel with parameter $\frac{1}{2}$, i.e. $\psi(r) = \frac{1}{16}\left(1 - [1 - 4r^2]_+^2\right)$. This choice makes the problem instances sufficiently difficult, as the initial inlier ratio of image observations ranges between 14% and 50% (depending on the dataset). The inlier ratios obtained after robust cost minimization cluster around 60% for the best obtained local minima.

First, we focus on a *linearized* version of bundle adjustment, where the residuals $\mathbf{f}_{ij} = \pi(R_i\mathbf{X}_j + \mathbf{t}_i) - \mathbf{q}_{ij}$ are replaced by their linearized versions w.r.t. the provided initial values. The non-robust objective is therefore convex, and the performance differences depicted in Fig. 4 indicate how well each method escapes poor local minima. In order to obtain similar objective values regardless of the dataset size, the objective values are normalized w.r.t. the number of image measurements. The unnormalized BA objective values Eq. 22 are approximately between 6000 and 60000 (depending on the dataset and method). Thus, none of the methods is in its respective comfort zone. IRLS is clearly inferior to the other methods, and GOM+ is slightly ahead of the lifted formulations. l-G-N* is the lifted Gauss-Newton method, but the lifted parameters u_i are initialized to their optimal value (given the initial values $\boldsymbol{\theta}^0$). The resulting performance is between IRLS and l-G-N. If we take a closer look on the evolution of objectives (Fig. 5), then the lifted Gauss-Newton method reduces the actual cost Ψ^{BA} very quickly, although graduated optimization eventually reaches a better minimum.

Figure 6 illustrates the reached objectives (normalized w.r.t. the number of image measurements) by the different methods for non-linear metric bundle adjustment. Due to the additional non-linearity introduced by the non-robust objective, the results are more diverse than the ones in Fig. 4. In particular, the lifted Newton method shows an unstable behavior. Details and results for dense disparity estimation are provided in [27].

8 Conclusion and Future Work

In this work we first unified several direct and lifting-based methods for robust cost minimization. We also demonstrated that a graduated optimization method has very competitive performance in terms of the reached objective values and in terms of speed of convergence. Hence, our recommendation is as follows: a lifted Gauss-Newton method is a very strong candidate when very fast decrease of objectives is desired, and the proposed graduated optimization approach is the method of choice when reaching the best objective is the main interest—especially when the quality of the initial solution is unknown.

The fact that the best performing methods "forget" to a large extend the given initial solution is not very satisfactory. Future work will investigate whether methods adapting to the quality of the provided starting point result in faster overall convergence.

References

1. Agarwal, S., Mierle, K., et al.: Ceres solver. https://code.google.com/p/ceres-solver/
2. Agarwal, S., Snavely, N., Seitz, S.M., Szeliski, R.: Bundle adjustment in the large. In: Daniilidis, K., Maragos, P., Paragios, N. (eds.) ECCV 2010. LNCS, vol. 6312, pp. 29–42. Springer, Heidelberg (2010). https://doi.org/10.1007/978-3-642-15552-9_3
3. Albersmeyer, J., Diehl, M.: The lifted newton method and its application in optimization. SIAM J. Optim. **20**(3), 1655–1684 (2010)
4. Black, M.J., Anandan, P.: The robust estimation of multiple motions: parametric and piecewise-smooth flow fields. Comput. Vis. Image Underst. **63**(1), 75–104 (1996)
5. Blake, A., Zisserman, A.: Visual Reconstruction. The MIT Press, Cambridge (1987)
6. Davis, T.A., Hu, Y.: The university of florida sparse matrix collection. ACM Trans. Math. Softw. (TOMS) **38**(1), 1 (2011)
7. Dunlavy, D.M., O'Leary, D.P.: Homotopy optimization methods for global optimization. Technical report, Sandia National Laboratories (2005)
8. Engel, J., Schöps, T., Cremers, D.: LSD-SLAM: large-scale direct monocular SLAM. In: Fleet, D., Pajdla, T., Schiele, B., Tuytelaars, T. (eds.) ECCV 2014. LNCS, vol. 8690, pp. 834–849. Springer, Cham (2014). https://doi.org/10.1007/978-3-319-10605-2_54
9. Engels, C., Stewénius, H., Nistér, D.: Bundle adjustment rules. In: Photogrammetric Computer Vision (PCV) (2006)

10. Fischler, M., Bolles, R.: Random sample consensus: a paradigm for model fitting with applications to image analysis and automated cartography. Commun. ACM **24**(6), 381–395 (1981)
11. Geman, D., Reynolds, G.: Constrained restoration and the recovery of discontinuities. IEEE Trans. Pattern Anal. Mach. Intell. **14**(3), 367–383 (1992)
12. Geman, D., Yang, C.: Nonlinear image recovery with half-quadratic regularization. IEEE Trans. Image Process. **4**(7), 932–946 (1995)
13. Green, P.J.: Iteratively reweighted least squares for maximum likelihood estimation, and some robust and resistant alternatives. J. R. Stat. Soc. Ser. B (Methodol.) **46**, 149–192 (1984)
14. Hong, J.H., Fitzgibbon, A.: Secrets of matrix factorization: approximations, numerics, manifold optimization and random restarts. In: Proceedings of the IEEE International Conference on Computer Vision, pp. 4130–4138 (2015)
15. Huber, P.J.: Robust Statistics. Wiley, New York (1981)
16. Kirkpatrick, S., Gelatt, C.D., Vecchi, M.P.: Optimization by simulated annealing. Science **220**(4598), 671–680 (1983)
17. Lange, K., Hunter, D.R., Yang, I.: Optimization transfer using surrogate objective functions. J. Comput. Graph. Stat. **9**(1), 1–20 (2000)
18. Liwicki, S., Zach, C., Miksik, O., Torr, P.H.S.: Coarse-to-fine planar regularization for dense monocular depth estimation. In: Leibe, B., Matas, J., Sebe, N., Welling, M. (eds.) ECCV 2016. LNCS, vol. 9906, pp. 458–474. Springer, Cham (2016). https://doi.org/10.1007/978-3-319-46475-6_29
19. Mobahi, H., Fisher, J.W.: On the link between Gaussian homotopy continuation and convex envelopes. In: Tai, X.-C., Bae, E., Chan, T.F., Lysaker, M. (eds.) EMMCVPR 2015. LNCS, vol. 8932, pp. 43–56. Springer, Cham (2015). https://doi.org/10.1007/978-3-319-14612-6_4
20. Mobahi, H., Fisher III, J.W.: A theoretical analysis of optimization by Gaussian continuation. In: Twenty-Ninth AAAI Conference on Artificial Intelligence (2015)
21. Rose, K.: Deterministic annealing for clustering, compression, classification, regression, and related optimization problems. Proc. IEEE **86**(11), 2210–2239 (1998)
22. Torr, P.H., Zisserman, A.: MLESAC: a new robust estimator with application to estimating image geometry. Comput. Vis. Image Underst. **78**(1), 138–156 (2000)
23. Triggs, B., McLauchlan, P.F., Hartley, R.I., Fitzgibbon, A.W.: Bundle adjustment — a modern synthesis. In: Triggs, B., Zisserman, A., Szeliski, R. (eds.) IWVA 1999. LNCS, vol. 1883, pp. 298–372. Springer, Heidelberg (2000). https://doi.org/10.1007/3-540-44480-7_21
24. Ye, M., Haralick, R.M., Shapiro, L.G.: Estimating piecewise-smooth optical flow with global matching and graduated optimization. IEEE Trans. Pattern Anal. Mach. Intell. **25**(12), 1625–1630 (2003)
25. Yuan, Y.: A review of trust region algorithms for optimization. In: ICM99: Proceedings of the Fourth International Congress on Industrial and Applied Mathematics (1999)
26. Zach, C., Bourmaud, G.: Iterated lifting for robust cost optimization. In: Proceedings of the BMVC (2017)
27. Zach, C., Bourmaud, G.: Descending, lifting or smoothing: secrets of robust cost optimization. In: Ferrari, V. (ed.) ECCV 2018, Part XII. LNCS, vol. 11216, pp. 558–574. Springer, Cham (2018)
28. Zach, C., Bourmaud, G.: Multiplicative vs. additive half-quadratic minimization for robust cost optimization. In: Proceedings of the BMVC (2018)

29. Zach, C.: Robust bundle adjustment revisited. In: Fleet, D., Pajdla, T., Schiele, B., Tuytelaars, T. (eds.) ECCV 2014. LNCS, vol. 8693, pp. 772–787. Springer, Cham (2014). https://doi.org/10.1007/978-3-319-10602-1_50
30. Zhou, Q.-Y., Park, J., Koltun, V.: Fast global registration. In: Leibe, B., Matas, J., Sebe, N., Welling, M. (eds.) ECCV 2016. LNCS, vol. 9906, pp. 766–782. Springer, Cham (2016). https://doi.org/10.1007/978-3-319-46475-6_47
31. Zollhöfer, M., et al.: Real-time non-rigid reconstruction using an RGB-D camera. In: SIGGRAPH (2014)

Geolocation Estimation of Photos Using a Hierarchical Model and Scene Classification

Eric Müller-Budack[1,2]([✉]) [iD], Kader Pustu-Iren[1] [iD], and Ralph Ewerth[1,2] [iD]

[1] Leibniz Information Centre for Science and Technology (TIB), Hannover, Germany
{eric.mueller,kader.pustu,ralph.ewerth}@tib.eu
[2] L3S Research Center, Leibniz Universität Hannover, Hannover, Germany

Abstract. While the successful estimation of a photo's geolocation enables a number of interesting applications, it is also a very challenging task. Due to the complexity of the problem, most existing approaches are restricted to specific areas, imagery, or worldwide landmarks. Only a few proposals predict GPS coordinates without any limitations. In this paper, we introduce several deep learning methods, which pursue the latter approach and treat geolocalization as a classification problem where the earth is subdivided into geographical cells. We propose to exploit hierarchical knowledge of multiple partitionings and additionally extract and take the photo's scene content into account, i.e., indoor, natural, or urban setting etc. As a result, contextual information at different spatial resolutions as well as more specific features for various environmental settings are incorporated in the learning process of the convolutional neural network. Experimental results on two benchmarks demonstrate the effectiveness of our approach outperforming the state of the art while using a significant lower number of training images and without relying on retrieval methods that require an appropriate reference dataset.

Keywords: Geolocation estimation · Scene classification
Deep learning · Context-based classification

1   Introduction

Predicting the geographical location of photos without any prior knowledge is a very challenging task, since images taken from all over the earth depict a huge amount of variations, e.g., different daytimes, objects, or camera settings. In addition, the images are often ambiguous and therefore provide only very few visual clues about their respective recording location. For these reasons, the majority of approaches simplifies photo geolocalization by restricting the problem to urban photos of, for example, well-known landmarks and

Electronic supplementary material The online version of this chapter (https://doi.org/10.1007/978-3-030-01258-8_35) contains supplementary material, which is available to authorized users.

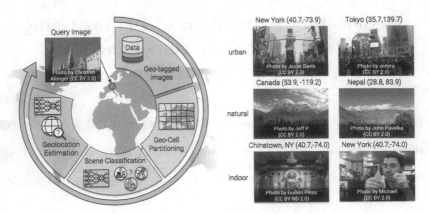

Fig. 1. Left: Workflow of the proposed geolocation estimation approach. Right: Sample images of different locations for specific scene concepts.

cities [3,25,34,43,45,48] or natural areas like deserts or mountains [5,33,38]. Only a few frameworks treat the task at global-scale without relying on specific imagery [13,14,39,42] or any other prior assumptions. These approaches particularly benefit from the advancements in deep learning [15,16,21] and the increasing number of publicly available large-scale image collections from platforms such as *Flickr*. Due to the complexity of the problem and the unbalanced distribution of photos taken from all over the earth, methods based on convolutional neural networks (CNNs) [39,42] treat photo geolocalization as a classification task subdividing the earth into geographical cells with a similar number of images. However, according to Vo et al. [39], even current CNNs are not able to memorize the visual appearance of the entire earth and to simultaneously learn a model for scene understanding. Moreover, geographical partitioning approaches [39,42] entail a trade-off problem. While a finer partitioning leads to a higher accuracy at city-scale (location error less than 1 km), a coarser subdivision increases the performance at country-scale (750 km). In our opinion, one main reason for these problems is the huge diversity caused by various environmental settings, which requires specific features to distinguish different locations. Referring to Fig. 1, we argue that urban images mainly differ in, e.g., architecture, people, and specific objects like cars or street signs. On the contrary, natural scenes like forests or indoor scenarios are most likely defined by features encoding the flora and fauna or the style of the interior furnishings, respectively. Therefore, we claim that photo geolocalization can greatly benefit from contextual knowledge about the environmental scene, since the diversity in the data space could be drastically reduced.

In this paper, we address the aforementioned problems by (1) incorporating hierarchical knowledge at different spatial resolutions in a multi-partitioning approach, as well as (2) extracting and taking information about the respective type of environmental settings (e.g., *indoor*, *natural*, and *urban*) into account. We consider photo geolocalization as a classification task by subdividing the earth into geographical cells with a balanced number of images (similar to *PlaNet* [42]). There are several contributions. We combine the outputs from all scales to exploit the hierarchical information of a CNN that is trained simultaneously with labels from multiple partitionings to encode local and global information. Furthermore, we suggest two strategies to include information about the respective scene type: (a) deep networks that are trained separately with images of distinctive scene categories, and (b) a multi-task network trained with both geographical and scene labels. This should enable the CNN to learn specific features for estimating the GPS (Global Positioning System) coordinate of images in different environmental surroundings. The workflow is illustrated in Fig. 1.

To the best of our knowledge, this is the first approach that considers scene classification and exploits hierarchical (geo)information to improve unrestricted photo geolocalization. Furthermore, we have used a state of the art CNN architecture and our comprehensive experiments include an evaluation of the impact of different scene concepts. Experimental results on two different benchmarks demonstrate that our approach outperforms the state of the art without relying on image retrieval techniques (*Im2GPS* [13,14,39]), while using a significant lower number of training images compared to *PlaNet* [42] – making our approach more feasible.

The remainder of the paper is organized as follows. In Sect. 2, we review related work on photo geolocation estimation. The proposed framework to extract and utilize visual concepts of specific scenes and multiple earth partitionings to estimate the GPS coordinates of images is introduced in Sect. 3. Experimental results on two different benchmarks are presented and discussed in Sect. 4. Section 5 concludes the paper and outlines areas of future work.

2   Related Work

Related work on visual geolocalization can be roughly divided into two categories: (1) proposals which are restricted to specific environments or imagery, and (2) approaches at planet-scale without any restrictions. In this section, we focus on the second category since it is more closely related to our work. For a more comprehensive review, we refer to Brejcha and Čadík's survey [8].

Many proposals of the first category are introduced at city-scale resolution restricting the problem to specific cities or landmarks. These mainly apply retrieval techniques to match a query image against a reference dataset [3, 12,18,20,29,34,46]. Approaches that focus on landmark recognition use either a pre-defined set of landmarks or cluster a given photo collection in an unsupervised manner to retrieve the most interesting areas for geolocalization [4,23,28,48]. Other proposals match query images against 3D models of cities [10,19,24,27,30]. However, the underlying data collections of these methods are restricted to popular scenes and urban environments and therefore lack accuracy when predicting photos that do not have (many) instance matches. For this reason, some approaches additionally make use of satellite aerial imagery to enhance the geolocalization in sparsely covered regions [35,40,44,45]. In this context, solutions are presented that match an aerial query image against a reference dataset containing satellite images in a wide baseline approach [2,6,43]. Some of these proposals [25,26] even address geolocation at planet-scale. But since these frameworks require a reference dataset that contains satellite images, we still consider them as restricted frameworks. Only a minority of proposals has been designed for natural geolocalization of images depicting beaches [9,41], deserts [38], or mountains [5,33].

All of the aforementioned proposals are restricted to well-covered regions, specific imagery, or environmental scenes. As a first attempt for planet-scale geolocation estimation, Hays and Efros [13] have introduced *Im2GPS*. They use a retrieval approach to match a given query image based on a combination of six global image descriptors to a reference dataset consisting of more than six million GPS-tagged images. The authors extend *Im2GPS* [14] by incorporating information on specific geometrical classes like sky and ground as well as an improved retrieval technique. Weyand et al. [42] have introduced *PlaNet*, where the task of geolocalization is treated as a classification problem. The earth is adaptively subdivided into geographical cells with a similar number of images that are used to train a convolutional neural network. This approach noticeably outperformed *Im2GPS*, which encouraged Vo et al. [39] to learn a feature representation with a CNN to improve the *Im2GPS* framework. Using the extracted features of a query photo, the (k)-nearest neighbors in the reference dataset based on kernel density estimation are retrieved. In this way, a multi-partitioning approach is introduced to simultaneously learn photo-geolocation at different spatial resolutions. However, in contrast to our work this approach does not make use of the hierarchical knowledge given by the predictions at each scale.

3   Hierarchical Geolocalization Using Scene Classification

In this section, we present the proposed deep learning framework for geolocation estimation. According to *PlaNet* [42], we treat the task as a classification problem by subdividing the earth into geographical cells C that contain a similar number of images (Sect. 3.1). In contrast to previous work, we exploit contextual information of the environmental scenario solely using the visual content of a given photo to improve the localization accuracy. Therefore, we assign scene labels to all the images based on the 365 categories of the *Places2* dataset [49] (Sect. 3.2). Several approaches that are aimed at integrating the extracted information about the given type of scene and multiple geographical cell partitionings are introduced in Sect. 3.3. Finally, we explain how the proposed approaches are applied to estimate the GPS coordinates of images based on the predicted geo-cell probabilities $\hat{C}$ (Sect. 3.4). In this context, we introduce our hierarchical approach to combine the results of multiple spatial resolutions. An overview of the proposed framework is presented in Fig. 2.

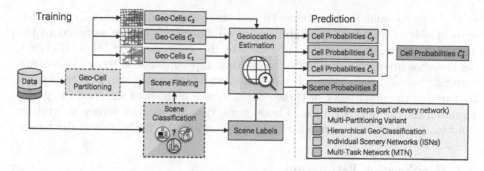

Fig. 2. Pipeline of the proposed geolocation estimation frameworks. Gray: Baseline steps that are part of every network. Additional steps are visualized in different colors. Dashed elements are applied to all images before the training process takes place. (Color figure online)

3.1 Adaptive Geo-Cell Partitioning

The *S2 geometry library*[1] is utilized to generate a set of non-overlapping geographical cells C. In more detail, the earth's surface is projected on an enclosing cube with six sides representing the initial cells. An adaptive hierarchical subdivision based on the GPS coordinates of the images is applied [42], where each cell is the node of a quad-tree. Starting at the root nodes, the respective quad-tree is subdivided recursively until all cells contain a maximum of τ_{max} images. Afterwards, all resulting cells with less than τ_{min} photos are discarded, because they most likely cover areas like poles or oceans which are hard to distinguish.

This approach has several advantages compared to a subdivision of the earth into cells with roughly equally areas. On the one hand side, an adaptive subdivision prevents dataset biases and allows to create classes with a similar number of images. On the other hand, fine cells in photographically well covered areas are generated. This enables a more accurate prediction of image locations which most likely depict interesting regions such as landmarks or cities.

3.2 Visual Scene Classification

To classify scenes and extract scene labels, the ResNet model [16] with 152 layers[2] of the *Places2* dataset [49] is applied. The model has been trained on more than 16 million training images from 365 different place categories. This fits nicely with our approach, since the resulting classifier already distinguishes images that depict specific environments. We predict the scene labels based on the scene set S_{365} of all training images using the maximum probability of the output vector. Based on the provided scene hierarchy[3], we additionally extract labels

---

[1] https://code.google.com/archive/p/s2-geometry-library/.
[2] *Places2* ResNet152 model: https://github.com/CSAILVision/places365.
[3] *Places2* scene hierarchy: http://places2.csail.mit.edu/download.html.

of the sets S_{16} and S_3 containing 16 and three superordinate scene categories, respectively. We add the probabilities of all classes which are assigned to the same superordinate category and generate the corresponding label. However, some scenes like *barn* are allocated to multiple superordinate categories (*outdoor, natural*; *outdoor, man-made*), because they visually overlap. For this reason, we first divide the probability of these classes by the number of assigned categories to maintain the normalization. Please note, that we use the terms *natural* for "*outdoor, natural*" and *urban* for "*outdoor, man-made*" in the rest of the paper.

3.3 Geolocation Estimation

In this section, several approaches based on convolutional neural networks for an unrestricted planet-scale geolocalization are introduced. First, we present a baseline approach which is trained without using scene information and multiple geographical partitionings. In the following, we describe how the information for different spatial resolutions as well as environmental concepts are integrated in the training process. In this context, two different approaches to utilize visual scene labels are proposed. An overview is provided in Fig. 2.

Baseline: To evaluate the impact of the suggested approaches for geolocalization, we first present a baseline system that does not rely on information about the environmental setting and different spatial resolutions. Therefore, we generate a single geo-cell partitioning C as described in Sect. 3.1. For classification, we add a fully-connected layer on top of the global pooling layer of the ResNet architecture [16], where the number of output neurons corresponds to the number of geo-cells $|C|$. During training the cross-entropy geolocalization loss L_{geo}^{single} based on the probability distribution $\hat{C}$ and the ground-truth cell label encoded in a one-hot vector $\hat{C}_{GT}$ is minimized.

Multi-partitioning Variant: We propose to simultaneously learn geolocation estimation at multiple spatial resolutions (according to Vo et al. [39]). In contrast to the baseline approach, we add a fully-connected layer for the geographical cells of all partitionings $P = \{C_1, \ldots, C_n\}$. The multi-partitioning classification loss L_{geo}^{multi} is calculated using the mean of the loss values L_{geo}^{single} for every partitioning. As a consequence, the CNN is able to learn geographical features at different scales resulting in a more discriminative classifier. However, in contrast to Vo et al. [39] we further exploit the hierarchical knowledge for the final prediction. The details are presented in Sect. 3.4.

Individual Scene Networks (ISNs): In a first attempt to incorporate context information about the environmental setting for photo geolocalization, individual networks for images depicting a specific scene are trained. For each photograph, we extract the scene probabilities using the scene classification presented in Sect. 3.2. During the training, every image with a scene probability greater than a threshold of τ_S is used as input for the respective *Individual Scene Network (ISN)*. Following this approach offers the advantage, that the network is solely trained on images depicting specific environmental scenarios. It greatly reduces the diversity in the underlying data space and enables the network to learn more specific features. On the contrary, it is necessary to train individual models for each scene concept, which is hard to manage if the number of different concepts $|S|$ becomes larger. For this reason, we suggest to fine-tune a model, which was initially trained without scene restriction, with images of the respective environmental category.

Multi-Task Network (MTN): Since the aforementioned method for geolocation estimation may become infeasible for a large amount of different environmental concepts, we aim for a more practicable approach using a network which treats photo geolocalization and scene recognition as a multi-task problem. In order to encourage the network to distinguish between images of different environmental scenes, we simultaneously train two classifiers for these complementary tasks. Adding another (complementary) task has proven to be efficient to improve the results of the main task [7,17,32,47]. More specifically, an additional fully-connected layer on top of the global pooling layer of the ResNet CNN architecture [16] is utilized. The number of output neurons of this layer corresponds to the amount of scene categories $|S|$. The weights of all other layers in the network are completely shared. In addition, the scene loss L_{scene} based on the ground-truth one-hot vector $\hat{S}_{GT}$ and the scene probabilities $\hat{S}$ is minimized using the cross-entropy loss. The total loss L_{total} of the *Multi-Task Network (MTN)* is defined by the sum of the geographical and scene loss.

3.4 Predicting Geolocations Using Hierarchical Spatial Information

In order to estimate the GPS coordinate from the classification output, we apply the trained models from Sect. 3.3 on three evenly sampled crops of a given query image according to its orientation. Afterwards, the mean of the resulting class probabilities of each crop is calculated. Please note that an additional step for testing is necessary for the *Individual Scene Networks*. In this case, the scene label is first predicted using the maximum probability as described in Sect. 3.2 in order to feed the image into the respective *ISN* for geolocalization.

Standard Geo-Classification: Without relying on hierarchical information, we solely utilize the probabilities $\hat{C}$ of one given geo-cell partitioning C. In this respect, we assign the class label with the maximum probability to predict the geographical cell. Applying the multi-partitioning approach in Sect. 3.3 we are therefore able to obtain $|P|$ class probabilities at different spatial resolutions. In our opinion, the probabilities at all scales should be exploited to enhance the geolocalization and to combine the capabilities of all partitionings.

Hierarchical Geo-Classification: To ensure that every geographical cell in the finest representation can be uniquely connected to a larger parent area in an upper-level, a fixed threshold parameter τ_{min} for the adaptive subdivision (Sect. 3.1) is applied. Thus, we are able to generate a geographical hierarchy from the different spatial resolutions. Inspired by the hierarchical object classification approach from *YOLO9000* [31], we multiply the respective probabilities at each level of the hierarchy. Consequently, the prediction for the finest subdivision can be refined by incorporating the knowledge of coarser representations.

Class2GPS: Depending on the predicted class we extract the GPS coordinates of the given query image. In contrast to Weyand et al. [42], we use the mean location of all training images in the predicted cell instead of the geographical center. This is more precise for regions containing an interesting area where the majority of photos is taken. Imagine a geographical cell centered around an ocean and a city which is located at the cell boundary. In this example, the error using the geographical center would be very high, even if it is clear that the photo was most likely taken in the city.

4   Experimental Setup and Results

Training Data: We use a subset of the Yahoo Flickr Creative Commons 100 Million dataset (*YFCC100M*) [37] as input data for our approach. This subset was introduced for the MediaEval Placing Task 2016 (*MP-16*) [22] and includes around five million geo-tagged images[4] from Flickr without any restrictions. The dataset contains ambiguous photos of, e.g., indoor environments, food, and humans for which the location is difficult to predict. Like Vo et al. [39] we exclude images from the same authors as in the test datasets, which we use for evaluation. A ResNet model [15] is used which has been pre-trained on ImageNet [11] to avoid duplicate images by comparing the resulting feature vectors from the last pooling layer. Overall, our training dataset consists of $|I| = 4{,}723{,}695$ images.

Partitioning Parameters: As explained in Sect. 3.4, we choose a constant value of $\tau_{min} = 50$ (according to PlaNet [42]) as the minimum threshold for the adaptive subdivision, to enable the hierarchical classification approach. Our goal is to train the geolocation at multiple spatial resolutions. Therefore, the following maximum thresholds $\tau_{max} \in \{1{,}000; 2{,}000; 5{,}000\}$ are used. We select these thresholds because the *MP-16* dataset has approximately 16 times less images than PlaNet [42] and we therefore aim to produce around $\sqrt{16}$ less classes (PlaNet has 26,263 cells) at the middle representation. Since we want to show how fine and coarse representations can be efficiently combined, the other thresholds are specified to produce circa two times more and less classes than the middle representation. The resulting number of classes $|C|$ for different partitionings to train our deep learning approaches are shown in Table 1.

---

4 Available at: http://multimedia-commons.s3-website-us-west-2.amazonaws.com.

Table 1. Number of classes $|C|$ for each partitioning C with different thresholds τ_{min} and τ_{max}.

C	τ_{min}	τ_{max}	$|C|$
Coarse	50	5,000	3,298
Middle	50	2,000	7,202
Fine	50	1,000	12,893

Table 2. Top-1 and Top-5 accuracy on the validation set of the *Places2* benchmark [49] for different scene hierarchies.

Hierarchy	Top-1	Top-5
S_3	91.5%	—
S_{16}	72.1%	97.1%
S_{365}	45.7%	77.3%

Scene Classification Parameters: The performance of the concept classification (Sect. 3.2) is evaluated on the *Places2* validation dataset [49] containing 36,500 images (100 for each scene). In Table 2 results for the different scene hierarchy levels are reported. The quality of the scene classification is very crucial for the *ISNs* presented in Sect. 3.3, because it defines the underlying data space. Since the top-1 accuracy of 91.5% already provides a good basis, we focus on a set of three scene concepts $S_3 = \{indoor, natural, urban\}$. Furthermore, this limits the amount of *ISNs* to a feasible number of three concepts. We suggest to apply a small threshold of $\tau_S = 0.3$. Admittedly, this selection is somewhat arbitrary, but we intend to use images with similar scene probabilities as input for each *ISN*. This could be especially useful for images depicting rural areas, because they share visual information like architecture as well as flora and fauna that are beneficial for both environmental categories *urban* and *natural*. The scene filtering yields a total of around 1.80M, 1.42M, and 2.34M training images for the concepts *indoor, natural, urban*, respectively.

Network Training: The proposed approaches are trained using a ResNet architecture [16] with 101 convolutional layers. The weights are initialized by a pretrained ImageNet model [11]. To avoid overfitting, the data is augmented by randomly selecting an area which covers at least 70% of the image with an aspect ratio R between $3/4 \le R \le 4/3$. Furthermore, the input images are randomly flipped and subsequently cropped to 224×224 pixels. We use the Stochastic Gradient Descend (SGD) optimizer with an initial learning rate of 0.01, a momentum of 0.9, and a weight decay of 0.0001. The learning rate is exponentially lowered by a factor of 0.5 after every five training epochs. We initially train the networks for 15 epochs and a batch size of 128. We validate the CNNs on 25,600 images of the *YFCC100M* dataset [37].

As described in Sect. 3.3, it could be beneficial to fine-tune the *ISNs* based on a model which was initially trained without scene restriction. For a fair comparison, all models are therefore fine-tuned for five epochs or until the loss on the validation set converges. In this respect, the initial learning rate is decreased to 0.001. Finally, the best model on the validation set is used for conducting the experiments. The implementation is realized using the TensorFlow library [1] in Python. The trained models and all necessary data to reproduce our results are available at: https://github.com/TIBHannover/GeoEstimation

Test Setup: We evaluate our approaches on two public benchmarks datasets for geolocation estimation. The *Im2GPS* test dataset [13] contains 237 photos, where 5% are depicting specific tourist sites and the remaining are only recognizable in a generic sense. Because this benchmark is very small, Vo et al. [39] introduced a new datasets called *Im2GPS3k* that contains 3,000 images from *Im2GPS* (2,997 images are provided with a GPS tag). The great circle distance (GCD) between the predicted and ground-truth image location is calculated for evaluation. As suggested by Hays and Efros [13], we report the geolocalization accuracy as the percentage of test images that are predicted within a certain distance to the ground-truth location. The notations of the proposed approaches are presented in Table 3. The most significant results using the suggested multi-partitioning and scene concepts for geolocalization as well a comparison to the state of the art methods are given in the related Sections. A complete list of results is provided in the supplemental material.

Table 3. Notation of the geolocalization approaches. T denotes whether the network was trained with a single/lone (L) or multiple (M) partition(s). $C \in \{c, m, f\}$ indicates which cell partition (coarse (c), middle (m), fine (f)) is used for classification. If C is denoted with a star (*) the hierarchical classification is utilized.

Notation	Description
base (T, C)	*Baseline* trained without scene information
ISNs (T, C, S_3)	*Individual Scene Networks* using the scene set S_3
MTN (T, C, S)	*Multi-Task Network* using a scene set $S \in \{S_3, S_{16}, S_{365}\}$

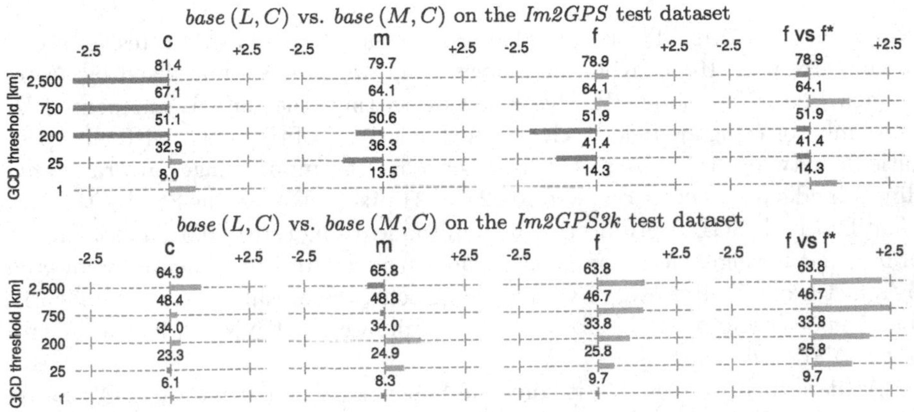

Fig. 3. Comparison of the geolocation approaches trained with and without multiple subdivisions for different geo-cell partitionings C. First mentioned approach *base* (L, C) is used as reference and its accuracy is denoted in the middle of the x-axis.

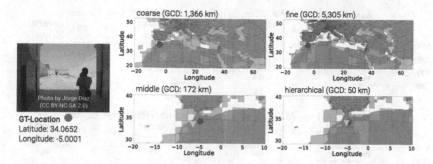

Fig. 4. Quantitative result using the prediction of the different partitioning output layers as well as the hierarchical result.

Table 4. Number of images on the evaluation datasets for different scene concepts in S_3.

Scenes	Im2GPS	Im2GPS3k
All	237	2,997
Indoor	19	545
Natural	80	845
Urban	138	1,607

Table 5. Top-1 and Top-5 scene classification accuracies on the validation set of the *Places2* benchmark [49] for different *Multi-Task Networks*.

Network	Top-1	Top-5
$MTN\ (L, f, S_3)$	92.0%	—
$MTN\ (L, f, S_{16})$	71.7%	97.5%
$MTN\ (L, f, S_{365})$	46.0%	76.5%

4.1 Evaluating the Multi-partitioning Approach

The results for the baseline and the multi-partitioning approach are displayed in Fig. 3. Surprisingly, no significant improvement using multiple partitionings can be observed for the *Im2GPS* test dataset. But it is clearly visible that the results especially for the *fine* partitioning have improved for the *Im2GPS3k* dataset, which is more representative due to its larger size. This demonstrates that the network is able to incorporate features at different spatial resolutions and utilizes this knowledge to learn a more discriminative classifier. A similar observation was made in the latest *Im2GPS* approach [39]. However, by exploiting the hierarchical knowledge at different spatial resolutions the localization accuracy can be indeed further increased. Figure 4 shows that the geo-location of the photo is predicted with a higher accuracy using the coarse and middle partitioning compared to the finest representation. But, the capabilities of the network in terms of spatial resolution are not fully exploited using coarser partitionings. The hierarchical information, however, leads to a more accurate prediction at the finest scale and consequently to a better estimation of the photo's GPS position. Referring to the supplemental material and the next section, it is worth mentioning that the *ISNs* greatly benefit from the knowledge at multiple spatial resolutions. The results on both datasets improve drastically while using the multi-partitioning approach.

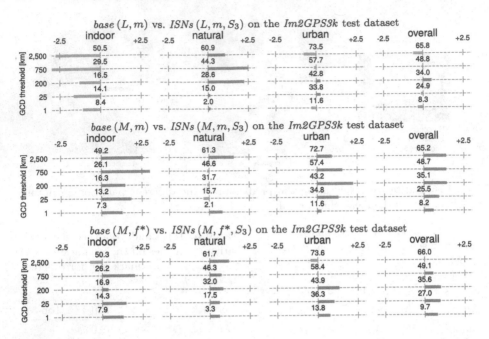

Fig. 5. Comparison of the *Individual Scene Networks* to the baseline approaches for different scene concepts. First mentioned approach is used as reference and its accuracy is denoted in the middle of the x-axis.

4.2   Evaluating the Individual Scene Networks

We apply the scene classifier introduced in Sect. 3.2 to extract the scene labels for all test images to evaluate the results for specific environmental settings. The resulting number of images for every scene is presented in Table 4. Due to the low number of images in the *Im2GPS* test dataset, we analyze the performance of the *ISNs* on the *Im2GPS3k* dataset. However, referring to Table 6 and the supplemental material, similar observations can be made for *Im2GPS*. The geolocation results do not improve when restricting a single-partitioning network to specific concepts (Fig. 5). On the other hand, using a multi-partitioning approach with scene restrictions noticeably improves the geolocation estimation, in particular for urban and indoor photos. One possible explanation is that the intra-class variation for coarser subdivision with more images in larger areas is reduced. Therefore, the network is able to learn specific features for the respective scene concept. The best results are achieved for urban images, which is intuitive since they often contain relevant cues for geolocation. It is also not surprising that the performance of indoor photos is the lowest among all scene concepts, since the images can be ambiguous. Weyand et al. (PlaNet) [42]) even consider indoor images as noise. Despite only 1.42M natural images are available to cover the huge diversity of very different scenes like beaches, mountains, and glaciers, we were able to improve the performance for this concept. We believe that the respective *ISN* mainly benefits from the hierarchical information, because it enables the encoding of more global features such as different climatic zones. Overall, the results show that geolocation estimation benefits from training with specific scene concepts and improves at nearly all GCD thresholds for every scene category.

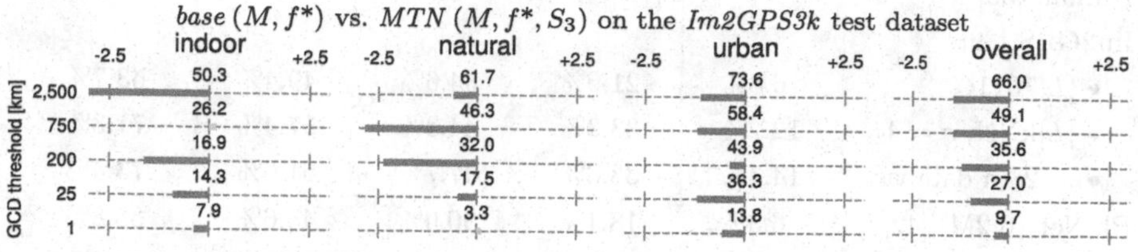

Fig. 6. Comparison of the *Multi-Task Network* to the baseline approach for different scene concepts S. First mentioned approach is used as reference and its accuracy is denoted in the middle of the x-axis.

4.3 Evaluating the Multi-Task Network

We investigate the performance of the *Multi-Task Network* regarding the geolocation estimation (Fig. 6) and scene classification (Table 5). Despite the results demonstrate that the CNNs are able to learn both tasks simultaneously, geolocalization unfortunately does not benefit from learning an additional task no matter which model we analyze. This underlines that the more important fact for predicting the GPS coordinates of photos is to reduce the diversity in the underlying data space. Regarding scene classification, similar results compared to the provided model of the Places2 dataset (Table 2) are achieved.

4.4 Comparison to the State of the Art

We can directly compare the results of our system *base* (L, m) to [L] 7011C network from Im2GPS [39] and PlaNet (6.2M) [42], since they have a similar number of training images and geographical classes. In addition, PlaNet (91M) [42] can be considered as equivalent at larger scale. The multi-partitioning approach *base* (M, m) is comparable to [M] 7011C of Im2GPS [39]. The corresponding results on the *Im2GPS* and *Im2GPS3k* test datasets are presented in Table 6. It is obvious that our proposed approaches significantly outperform the current state of the art methods. Interestingly, already our baseline approach *base* (L, m) noticeably outperforms its equivalents. For this reason, we investigate the influence of the utilized ResNet architecture [16]. Therefore, we train the system *base* (L, m) with VGG16 network [36] used in the *Im2GPS* approach [39]. The result is denoted with *base-vgg* (L, m) and shows that the main improvement is explained by the more powerful ResNet architecture. The system *base-vgg$_c$* (L, m) uses the geographical center of the predicted cell as location (like

Table 6. Results on the *Im2GPS* (top) and *Im2GPS3k* (bottom) test sets. Percentage is the fraction of images localized within the given radius using the GCD distance.

Method	Street	City	Region	Country	Continent
	1 km	25 km	200 km	750 km	2,500 km
Human [39]			3.8%	13.9%	39.3%
Im2GPS [39]					
• $[L]7011C$	6.8%	21.9%	34.6%	49.4%	63.7%
• $[L]$kNN, $\sigma = 4$	12.2%	33.3%	44.3%	57.4%	71.3%
• ... 28m database	14.4%	33.3%	47.7%	61.6%	73.4%
PlaNet (6.2M) [42]	6.3%	18.1%	30.0%	45.6%	65.8%
PlaNet (91M) [42]	8.4%	24.5%	37.6%	53.6%	71.3%
base-vgg$_c$ (L, m)	7.6%	22.8%	35.0%	50.6%	66.7%
base-vgg (L, m)	8.9%	26.6%	36.7%	50.6%	65.8%
base (L, m)	13.5%	36.3%	50.6%	64.1%	79.7%
base (M, m)	13.5%	35.0%	49.8%	64.1%	79.7%
base (M, f^*)	15.2%	40.9%	51.5%	65.4%	78.5%
ISNs (M, f^*, S_3)	**16.9%**	**43.0%**	**51.9%**	**66.7%**	**80.2%**
Method	Street	City	Region	Country	Continent
	1 km	25 km	200 km	750 km	2,500 km
Im2GPS [39]					
• $[L]7011C$	4.0%	14.8%	21.4%	32.6%	52.4%
• $[M]7011C$	3.7%	14.2%	21.3%	33.5%	52.7%
• kNN, $\sigma = 4$	7.2%	19.4%	26.9%	38.9%	55.9%
base-vgg$_c$ (L, m)	4.2%	14.6%	22.2%	34.4%	54.2%
base-vgg (L, m)	4.8%	16.5%	22.6%	34.5%	54.4%
base (L, m)	8.3%	24.9%	34.0%	48.8%	65.8%
base (M, m)	8.2%	25.5%	35.1%	48.7%	65.2%
base (M, f^*)	9.7%	27.0%	35.6%	49.2%	**66.0%**
ISNs (M, f^*, S_3)	**10.5%**	**28.0%**	**36.6%**	**49.7%**	**66.0%**

in *PlaNet* and *Im2GPS*) instead of the mean GPS coordinate of all images that we suggested in Sect. 3.4. This already noticeably improves the performance on street and city level. Compared to Weyand et al. [42] we have used a less noisy training dataset. As described in the previous sections, the geolocalization can be further increased by training the CNN with multiple partitionings and exploiting the hierarchical knowledge at all spatial resolutions. However, the best results are achieved when the *ISNs* are combined with the hierarchical approach that is trained with images of a specific visual scene concept.

5 Conclusions

In this paper, we have presented several deep learning approaches for planet-scale photo geolocation estimation. For this purpose, scene information was exploited to incorporate context about the environmental setting in the convolutional neural network model. We have integrated the extracted knowledge in a classification approach by subdividing the earth into geographical cells. Furthermore, a multi-partitioning approach was leveraged that combines the hierarchical information at different scales. Experimental results on two benchmarks have demonstrated that our framework improves the state of the art in estimating the GPS coordinates of photos. We have shown that the convolutional neural network is enabled to learn specific features for the different environmental settings and spatial resolutions, yielding a more discriminative classifier for geolocalization. Best results were achieved when the hierarchical approach was combined with scene classification. In contrast to previous work, the proposed framework does neither rely on an exemplary dataset for image retrieval nor on a training dataset that consists of several tens of millions images. In the future, we intend to investigate how other contextual information like specific objects, image styles, daytimes and seasons can be exploited to improve geolocalization.

Acknowledgement. This work is financially supported by the German Research Foundation (DFG: Deutsche Forschungsgemeinschaft, project number: EW 134/4-1).

References

1. Abadi, M., et al.: Tensorflow: large-scale machine learning on heterogeneous distributed systems. arXiv preprint arXiv:1603.04467 (2016)
2. Altwaljry, H., Trulls, E., Hays, J., Fua, P., Belongie, S.: Learning to match aerial images with deep attentive architectures. In: IEEE Conference on Computer Vision and Pattern Recognition, pp. 3539–3547. IEEE (2016)
3. Arandjelovic, R., Gronat, P., Torii, A., Pajdla, T., Sivic, J.: NetVLAD: CNN architecture for weakly supervised place recognition. In: IEEE Conference on Computer Vision and Pattern Recognition, pp. 5297–5307. IEEE (2016)
4. Avrithis, Y., Kalantidis, Y., Tolias, G., Spyrou, E.: Retrieving landmark and non-landmark images from community photo collections. In: International Conference on Multimedia, pp. 153–162. ACM (2010)
5. Baatz, G., Saurer, O., Köser, K., Pollefeys, M.: Large scale visual geo-localization of images in mountainous terrain. In: Fitzgibbon, A., Lazebnik, S., Perona, P., Sato, Y., Schmid, C. (eds.) ECCV 2012. LNCS, pp. 517–530. Springer, Heidelberg (2012). https://doi.org/10.1007/978-3-642-33709-3_37
6. Bansal, M., Daniilidis, K., Sawhney, H.: Ultrawide baseline facade matching for geo-localization. In: Zamir, A.R.R., Hakeem, A., Van Van Gool, L., Shah, M., Szeliski, R. (eds.) Large-Scale Visual Geo-Localization. ACVPR, pp. 77–98. Springer, Cham (2016). https://doi.org/10.1007/978-3-319-25781-5_5
7. Bingel, J., Søgaard, A.: Identifying beneficial task relations for multi-task learning in deep neural networks. arXiv preprint arXiv:1702.08303 (2017)
8. Brejcha, J., Čadík, M.: State-of-the-art in visual geo-localization. Pattern Anal. Appl. **20**(3), 613–637 (2017)

9. Cao, L., Smith, J.R., Wen, Z., Yin, Z., Jin, X., Han, J.: Bluefinder: estimate where a beach photo was taken. In: International Conference on World Wide Web, pp. 469–470. ACM (2012)
10. Chen, D.M., et al.: City-scale landmark identification on mobile devices. In: IEEE Conference on Computer Vision and Pattern Recognition, pp. 737–744. IEEE (2011)
11. Deng, J., Dong, W., Socher, R., Li, L.J., Li, K., Fei-Fei, L.: Imagenet: a large-scale hierarchical image database. In: IEEE Conference on Computer Vision and Pattern Recognition, pp. 248–255. IEEE (2009)
12. Gordo, A., Almazán, J., Revaud, J., Larlus, D.: Deep image retrieval: learning global representations for image search. In: Leibe, B., Matas, J., Sebe, N., Welling, M. (eds.) ECCV 2016. LNCS, vol. 9910, pp. 241–257. Springer, Cham (2016). https://doi.org/10.1007/978-3-319-46466-4_15
13. Hays, J., Efros, A.A.: IM2GPS: estimating geographic information from a single image. In: IEEE Conference on Computer Vision and Pattern Recognition, pp. 1–8. IEEE (2008)
14. Hays, J., Efros, A.A.: Large-scale image geolocalization. In: Choi, J., Friedland, G. (eds.) Multimodal Location Estimation of Videos and Images, pp. 41–62. Springer, Cham (2015). https://doi.org/10.1007/978-3-319-09861-6_3
15. He, K., Zhang, X., Ren, S., Sun, J.: Deep residual learning for image recognition. In: IEEE Conference on Computer Vision and Pattern Recognition, pp. 770–778. IEEE (2016)
16. He, K., Zhang, X., Ren, S., Sun, J.: Identity mappings in deep residual networks. In: Leibe, B., Matas, J., Sebe, N., Welling, M. (eds.) ECCV 2016. LNCS, vol. 9908, pp. 630–645. Springer, Cham (2016). https://doi.org/10.1007/978-3-319-46493-0_38
17. Jaderberg, M., et al.: Reinforcement learning with unsupervised auxiliary tasks. arXiv preprint arXiv:1611.05397 (2016)
18. Jin Kim, H., Dunn, E., Frahm, J.M.: Predicting good features for image geo-localization using per-bundle VLAD. In: IEEE International Conference on Computer Vision, pp. 1170–1178. IEEE (2015)
19. Kendall, A., Grimes, M., Cipolla, R.: Posenet: a convolutional network for real-time 6-DOF camera relocalization. In: IEEE International Conference on Computer Vision, pp. 2938–2946. IEEE (2015)
20. Kim, H.J., Dunn, E., Frahm, J.M.: Learned contextual feature reweighting for image geo-localization. In: IEEE International Conference on Computer Vision, pp. 2136–2145. IEEE (2017)
21. Krizhevsky, A., Sutskever, I., Hinton, G.E.: Imagenet classification with deep convolutional neural networks. In: Advances in Neural Information Processing Systems, NIPS, pp. 1097–1105 (2012)
22. Larson, M., Soleymani, M., Gravier, G., Ionescu, B., Jones, G.J.: The benchmarking initiative for multimedia evaluation: MediaEval 2016. IEEE MultiMedia 24(1), 93–96 (2017)
23. Li, Y., Crandall, D.J., Huttenlocher, D.P.: Landmark classification in large-scale image collections. In: International Conference on Computer Vision, pp. 1957–1964. IEEE (2009)
24. Li, Y., Snavely, N., Huttenlocher, D.P., Fua, P.: Worldwide pose estimation using 3D point clouds. In: Zamir, A.R.R., Hakeem, A., Van Van Gool, L., Shah, M., Szeliski, R. (eds.) Large-Scale Visual Geo-Localization. ACVPR, pp. 147–163. Springer, Cham (2016). https://doi.org/10.1007/978-3-319-25781-5_8
25. Lin, T.Y., Belongie, S., Hays, J.: Cross-view image geolocalization. In: IEEE Conference on Computer Vision and Pattern Recognition, pp. 891–898. IEEE (2013)

26. Lin, T.Y., Cui, Y., Belongie, S., Hays, J.: Learning deep representations for ground-to-aerial geolocalization. In: IEEE Conference on Computer Vision and Pattern Recognition, pp. 5007–5015. IEEE (2015)
27. Liu, L., Li, H., Dai, Y.: Efficient global 2D-3D matching for camera localization in a large-scale 3D map. In: 2017 IEEE International Conference on Computer Vision (ICCV), pp. 2391–2400. IEEE (2017)
28. Quack, T., Leibe, B., Van Gool, L.: World-scale mining of objects and events from community photo collections. In: International Conference on Content-based Image and Video Retrieval, pp. 47–56. ACM (2008)
29. Radenović, F., Tolias, G., Chum, O.: CNN image retrieval learns from bow: unsupervised fine-tuning with hard examples. In: Leibe, B., Matas, J., Sebe, N., Welling, M. (eds.) ECCV 2016. LNCS, vol. 9905, pp. 3–20. Springer, Cham (2016). https://doi.org/10.1007/978-3-319-46448-0_1
30. Ramalingam, S., Bouaziz, S., Sturm, P., Brand, M.: SKYLINE2GPS: localization in urban canyons using omni-skylines. In: International Conference on Intelligent Robots and Systems, pp. 3816–3823. IEEE (2010)
31. Redmon, J., Farhadi, A.: Yolo9000: better, faster, stronger. In: IEEE Conference on Computer Vision and Pattern Recognition, pp. 6517–6525. IEEE (2017)
32. Ruder, S.: An overview of multi-task learning in deep neural networks. arXiv preprint arXiv:1706.05098 (2017)
33. Saurer, O., Baatz, G., Köser, K., Pollefeys, M., et al.: Image based geo-localization in the alps. Int. J. Comput. Vis. 116(3), 213–225 (2016)
34. Schindler, G., Brown, M., Szeliski, R.: City-scale location recognition. In: IEEE Conference on Computer Vision and Pattern Recognition, pp. 1–7. IEEE (2007)
35. Shan, Q., Wu, C., Curless, B., Furukawa, Y., Hernandez, C., Seitz, S.M.: Accurate geo-registration by ground-to-aerial image matching. In: International Conference on 3D Vision, vol. 1, pp. 525–532. IEEE (2014)
36. Simonyan, K., Zisserman, A.: Very deep convolutional networks for large-scale image recognition. arXiv preprint arXiv:1409.1556 (2014)
37. Thomee, B., Shamma, D.A., Friedland, G., Elizalde, B., Ni, K., Poland, D., Borth, D., Li, L.J.: YFCC100M: the new data in multimedia research. Commun. ACM 59(2), 64–73 (2016)
38. Tzeng, E., Zhai, A., Clements, M., Townshend, R., Zakhor, A.: User-driven geolocation of untagged desert imagery using digital elevation models. In: IEEE Conference on Computer Vision and Pattern Recognition Workshops, pp. 237–244. IEEE (2013)
39. Vo, N., Jacobs, N., Hays, J.: Revisiting IM2GPS in the deep learning era. arXiv preprint arXiv:1705.04838 (2017)
40. Vo, N.N., Hays, J.: Localizing and orienting street views using overhead imagery. In: Leibe, B., Matas, J., Sebe, N., Welling, M. (eds.) ECCV 2016. LNCS, vol. 9905, pp. 494–509. Springer, Cham (2016). https://doi.org/10.1007/978-3-319-46448-0_30
41. Wang, Y., Cao, L.: Discovering latent clusters from geotagged beach images. In: Li, S., et al. (eds.) MMM 2013. LNCS, vol. 7733, pp. 133–142. Springer, Heidelberg (2013). https://doi.org/10.1007/978-3-642-35728-2_13
42. Weyand, T., Kostrikov, I., Philbin, J.: PlaNet - photo geolocation with convolutional neural networks. In: Leibe, B., Matas, J., Sebe, N., Welling, M. (eds.) ECCV 2016. LNCS, vol. 9912, pp. 37–55. Springer, Cham (2016). https://doi.org/10.1007/978-3-319-46484-8_3
43. Workman, S., Souvenir, R., Jacobs, N.: Wide-area image geolocalization with aerial reference imagery. In: IEEE International Conference on Computer Vision, pp. 3961–3969. IEEE (2015)

44. Zamir, A.R., Shah, M.: Accurate image localization based on Google Maps street view. In: Daniilidis, K., Maragos, P., Paragios, N. (eds.) ECCV 2010. LNCS, vol. 6314, pp. 255–268. Springer, Heidelberg (2010). https://doi.org/10.1007/978-3-642-15561-1_19
45. Zamir, A.R., Shah, M.: Image geo-localization based on multiple nearest neighbor feature matching using generalized graphs. IEEE Trans. Pattern Anal. Mach. Intell. **36**(8), 1546–1558 (2014)
46. Zemene, E., Tariku, Y., Idrees, H., Prati, A., Pelillo, M., Shah, M.: Large-scale image geo-localization using dominant sets. arXiv preprint arXiv:1702.01238 (2017)
47. Zhang, Z., Luo, P., Loy, C.C., Tang, X.: Learning deep representation for face alignment with auxiliary attributes. IEEE Trans. Pattern Anal. Mach. Intell. **38**(5), 918–930 (2016)
48. Zheng, Y.T., et al.: Tour the world: building a web-scale landmark recognition engine. In: IEEE Conference on Computer Vision and Pattern Recognition, pp. 1085–1092. IEEE (2009)
49. Zhou, B., Lapedriza, A., Khosla, A., Oliva, A., Torralba, A.: Places: a 10 million image database for scene recognition. IEEE Trans. Pattern Anal. Mach. Intell. **40**, 1452–1464 (2017)

License Plate Detection and Recognition in Unconstrained Scenarios

Sérgio Montazzolli Silva(✉) ⓘ and Cláudio Rosito Jung ⓘ

Institute of Informatics, Federal University of Rio Grande do Sul,
Porto Alegre, Brazil
{smsilva,crjung}@inf.ufrgs.br

Abstract. Despite the large number of both commercial and academic methods for Automatic License Plate Recognition (ALPR), most existing approaches are focused on a specific license plate (LP) region (e.g. European, US, Brazilian, Taiwanese, etc.), and frequently explore datasets containing approximately frontal images. This work proposes a complete ALPR system focusing on unconstrained capture scenarios, where the LP might be considerably distorted due to oblique views. Our main contribution is the introduction of a novel Convolutional Neural Network (CNN) capable of detecting and rectifying multiple distorted license plates in a single image, which are fed to an Optical Character Recognition (OCR) method to obtain the final result. As an additional contribution, we also present manual annotations for a challenging set of LP images from different regions and acquisition conditions. Our experimental results indicate that the proposed method, without any parameter adaptation or fine tuning for a specific scenario, performs similarly to state-of-the-art commercial systems in traditional scenarios, and outperforms both academic and commercial approaches in challenging ones.

Keywords: License plate · Deep learning
Convolutional neural networks

1 Introduction

Several traffic-related applications, such as detection of stolen vehicles, toll control and parking lot access validation involve vehicle identification, which is performed by Automatic License Plate Recognition (ALPR) systems. The recent advances in Parallel Processing and Deep Learning (DL) have contributed to improve many computer vision tasks, such as Object Detection/Recognition and Optical Character Recognition (OCR), which clearly benefit ALPR systems. In fact, deep Convolutional Neural Networks (CNNs) have been the leading machine learning technique applied for vehicle and license plate (LP) detection [2,3,9,17–19,28,31]. Along with academic papers, several commercial ALPR systems have been also exploring DL methods. They are usually allocated in huge data-centers and work through web-services, being able to process thousands to millions of

© Springer Nature Switzerland AG 2018
V. Ferrari et al. (Eds.): ECCV 2018, LNCS 11216, pp. 593–609, 2018.
https://doi.org/10.1007/978-3-030-01258-8_36

images per day and be constantly improved. As examples of these systems, we can mention Sighthound (https://www.sighthound.com/), the commercial version of OpenALPR (http://www.openalpr.com/) and Amazon Rekognition (https://aws.amazon.com/rekognition/).

Fig. 1. Examples of challenging oblique license plates present in the proposed evaluation dataset.

Despite the advances in the state-of-the-art, most ALPR systems assume a mostly frontal view of the vehicle and LP, which is common in applications such as toll monitoring and parking lot validation, for instance. However, more relaxed image acquisition scenarios (e.g. a law enforcement agent walking with a mobile camera or smartphone) might lead to oblique views in which the LP might be highly distorted yet still readable, as illustrated in Fig. 1, and for which even state-of-the-art commercial systems struggle.

In this work we propose a complete ALPR system that performs well over a variety of scenarios and camera setups. Our main contribution is the introduction of a novel network capable of detecting the LP in many different camera poses and estimate its distortion, allowing a rectification process before OCR. An additional contribution is the massive use of synthetically warped versions of real images for augmenting the training dataset, allowing the network to be trained from scratch using less than 200 manually labeled images. The proposed network and data augmentation scheme also led to a flexible ALPR system that was able to successfully detect and recognize LPs in independent test datasets using the same system parametrization.

We also generalized an existing OCR approach developed for Brazilian LPs [28]. Basically, we re-trained their OCR network using a new training set composed by a mixture of real and artificially generated data using font-types similar to the target regions. As a result, the re-trained network became much more robust for detection and classification of real characters in the original Brazilian scenario, but also for European and Taiwanese LPs, achieving very high precision and recall rates. All the annotated data used for this work is publicly available[1], and the reference images can be obtained by downloading the Cars Dataset [16], the SSIG Database [6], and the AOLP dataset [10].

---

[1] Available at http://www.inf.ufrgs.br/~crjung/alpr-datasets.

The remainder of this work is organized as follows. In Sect. 2 we briefly review related approaches toward ALPR. Details of the proposed method are given in Sect. 3, where we describe the LP detection and unwarping network, as well as the data augmentation process used to train our models. The overall evaluation and final results are presented in Sect. 4. Finally, Sect. 5 summarizes our conclusions and gives perspectives for some future work.

2   Related Work

ALPR is the task of finding and recognizing license plates in images. It is commonly broken into four subtasks that form a sequential pipeline: vehicle detection, license plate detection, character segmentation and character recognition. For simplicity, we refer to the combination of the last two subtasks as OCR.

Many different ALPR systems or related subtasks have been proposed in the past, typically using image binarization or gray-scale analysis to find candidate proposals (e.g. LPs and characters), followed by handcrafted feature extraction methods and classical machine learning classifiers [1,4]. With the rise of DL, the state-of-the-art started moving to another direction, and nowadays many works employ CNNs due to its high accuracy for generic object detection and recognition [8,11,21,23–25].

Related to ALPR are Scene Text Spotting (STS) and number reading in the wild (e.g. from Google Street View images [22]) problems, which goals are to find and read text/numbers in natural scenes. Although ALPR could be seen as a particular case of STS, the two problems present particular characteristics: in ALPR, we need to learn characters and numbers (without much font variability) with no semantic information, while STS is focused on textual information containing high font variability, and possibly exploring lexical and semantic information, as in [30]. Number reading does not present semantic information, but dealing only with digits is simpler than the ALPR context, since it avoids common digit/letter confusions such as B-8, D-0, 1-I, 5-S, for instance.

As the main contribution of this work is a novel LP detection network, we start this section by reviewing DL-based approaches for this specific subtask, as well as a few STS methods that can handle distorted text and could be used for LP detection. Next, we move to complete ALPR DL-based systems.

2.1   License Plate Detection

The success of YOLO networks [23,24] inspired many recent works, targeting real-time performance for LP detection [9,17,28,31]. A slightly modified version of the YOLO [23] and YOLOv2 [24] networks were used by Hsu et al. [9], where the authors enlarged the networks output granularity to improve the number of detections, and set the probabilities for two classes (LP and background). Their network achieved a good compromise between precision and recall, but the paper lacks a detailed evaluation over the bounding boxes extracted. Moreover, it is known that YOLO networks struggle to detect small sized objects, thus further evaluations over scenarios where the car is far from the camera is needed.

In [31], a setup of two YOLO-based networks was trained with the goal of detecting rotated LPs. The first network is used to find a region containing the LP, called "attention model", and the second network captures a rotated rectangular bounding-box of the LP. Nonetheless, they considered only on-plane rotations, and not more complex deformations caused by oblique camera views, such as the ones illustrated in Fig. 1. Also, as they do not present a complete ALPR system, it is difficult to evaluate how well an OCR method would perform on the detected regions.

License plate detectors using sliding window approaches or candidate filtering coupled with CNNs can also be found in the literature [2,3,27]. However, they tend to be computationally inefficient as a result of not sharing calculations like in modern meta-architectures for object detection such as YOLO, SSD [21] and Faster R-CNN [25].

Although Scene Text Spotting (STS) methods focus mostly on large font variations and lexical/semantic information, but it is worth mentioning a few approaches that deal with rotated/distorted text and could be explored for LP detection in oblique views. Jaderberg and colleagues [13] presented a CNN-based approach for text recognition in natural scenes using an entirely synthetic dataset to train the model. Despite the good results, they strongly rely on N-grams, which are not applicable to ALPR. Gupta et al. [7] also explored synthetic dataset by realistically pasting text into real images, focusing mostly on text localization. The output is a rotated bounding box with around the text, which finds limitations for off-plane rotations common in ALPR scenarios.

More recently, Wang et al. [29] presented an approach to detect text in a variety of geometric positions, called Instance Transformation Network (ITN). It is basically a composition of three CNNs: a backbone network to compute features, a transformation network to infer affine parameters where supposedly exists text in the feature map, and a final classification network whose input is built by sampling features according to the affine parameters. Although this approach can (in theory) handle off-plane rotations, it is not able to correctly infer the transformation that actually maps the text region to a rectangle, since there is no physical (or clear psychological) bounding region around the text that should map to a rectangle in an undistorted view. In ALPR, the LP is rectangular and planar by construction, and we explore this information to regress the transformation parameters, as detailed in Sect. 3.2.

2.2   Complete ALPR Methods

The works of Silva and Jung [28] and Laroca et al. [17] presented complete ALPR systems based on a series of modified YOLO networks. Two distinct networks were used in [28], one to jointly detect cars and LPs, and another to perform OCR. A total of five networks were used in [17], basically one for each ALPR subtask, being two for character recognition. Both reported real-time systems, but they are focused only on Brazilian license plates and were not trained to capture distortion, only frontal and nearly rectangular LPs.

Selmi et al. [27] used a series of pre-processing approaches based on morphological operators, Gaussian filtering, edge detection and geometry analysis to find LP candidates and characters. Then, two distinct CNNs were used to (i) classify a set of LP candidates per image into one single positive sample; and (ii) to recognize the segmented characters. The method handles a single LP per image, and according to the authors, distorted LPs and poor illumination conditions can compromise the performance.

Li et al. [19] presented a network based on Faster R-CNN [25]. Shortly, a Region Proposal Network is assigned to find candidate LP regions, whose corresponding feature maps are cropped by a RoI Pooling layer. Then, these candidates are fed into the final part of the network, which computes the probability of being/not being an LP, and performs OCR through a Recurrent Neural Network. Despite promising, the evaluation presented by the authors shows a lack of performance in most challenging scenarios containing oblique LPs.

Commercial systems are good reference points to the state-of-the-art. Although they usually provide only partial (or none) information about their architecture, we still can use them as black boxes to evaluate the final output. As mentioned in Sect. 1, examples are Sighthound, OpenALPR (which is an official NVIDIA partner in the Metropolis platform[2]) and Amazon Rekognition (a general-purpose AI engine including a text detection and recognition module that can be used for LP recognition, as informed by the company).

3 The Proposed Method

The proposed approach is composed by three main steps: vehicle detection, LP detection and OCR, as illustrated in Fig. 2. Given an input image, the first module detects vehicles in the scene. Within each detection region, the proposed Warped Planar Object Detection Network (WPOD-NET) searches for LPs and regresses one affine transformation per detection, allowing a rectification of the LP area to a rectangle resembling a frontal view. These positive and rectified detections are fed to an OCR Network for final character recognition.

3.1 Vehicle Detection

Since vehicles are one of the underlying objects present in many classical detection and recognition datasets, such as PASCAL-VOC [5], ImageNet [26], and COCO [20], we decided to not train a detector from scratch, and instead chose a known model to perform vehicle detection considering a few criteria. On one hand, a high recall rate is desired, since any miss detected vehicle having a visible LP leads directly to an overall LP miss detection. On the other hand, high precision is also desirable to keep running times low, as each falsely detected vehicle

---

[2] NVIDIA platform for video analysis in smart cities (https://www.nvidia.com/en-us/autonomous-machines/intelligent-video-analytics-platform/).

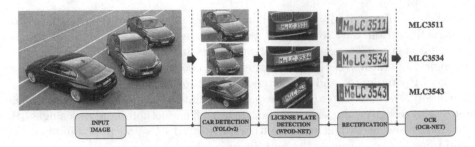

Fig. 2. Illustration of the proposed pipeline.

must be verified by WPOD-NET. Based on these considerations, we decided to use the YOLOv2 network due to its fast execution (around 70 FPS) and good precision and recall compromise (76.8% mAP over the PASCAL-VOC dataset). We did not perform any change or refinement to YOLOv2, just used the network as a black box, merging the outputs related to vehicles (i.e. cars and buses), and ignoring the other classes.

The positive detections are then resized before being fed to WPOD-NET. As a rule of thumb, larger input images allow the detection of smaller objects but increase the computational cost [12]. In roughly frontal/rear views, the ratio between the LP size and the vehicle bounding box (BB) is high. However, this ratio tends to be much smaller for oblique/lateral views, since the vehicle BB tends to be larger and more elongated. Hence, oblique views should be resized to a larger dimension than frontal ones to keep the LP region still recognizable.

Although 3D pose estimation methods such as [32] might be used to determine the resize scale, this work presents a simple and fast procedure based on the aspect ratio of the vehicle BB. When it is close to one, a smaller dimension can be used, and it must be increased as the aspect ratio gets larger. More precisely, the resizing factor f_{sc} is given by

$$f_{sc} = \frac{1}{\min\{W_v, H_v\}} \min\left\{ D_{min} \frac{\max(W_v, H_v)}{\min(W_v, H_v)}, D_{max} \right\}, \quad (1)$$

where W_v and H_v are the width and height of the vehicle BB, respectively. Note that $D_{min} \leq f_{sc}\min(W_v, H_v) \leq D_{max}$, so that D_{min} and D_{max} delimit the range for the smallest dimension of the resized BB. Based on experiments and trying to keep a good compromise between accuracy and running times, we selected $D_{min} = 288$ and $D_{max} = 608$.

3.2 License Plate Detection and Unwarping

License plates are intrinsically rectangular and planar objects, which are attached to vehicles for identification purposes. To take advantage of its shape, we proposed a novel CNN called Warped Planar Object Detection Network. This network learns to detect LPs in a variety of different distortions, and regresses coefficients of an affine transformation that "unwarps" the distorted LP into a rectangular shape resembling a frontal view. Although a planar perspective projection could be learned instead of the affine transform, the division involved in the perspective transformation might generate small values in the denominator, and hence leading to numerical instabilities.

The WPOD-NET was developed using insights from YOLO, SSD and Spatial Transformer Networks (STN) [14]. YOLO and SSD perform fast multiple object detection and recognition at once, but they do not take spatial transformations into account, generating only rectangular bounding boxes for every detection. On the opposite, STN can be used for detecting non-rectangular regions, however it cannot handle multiple transformations at the same time, performing only a single spatial transformation over the entire input.

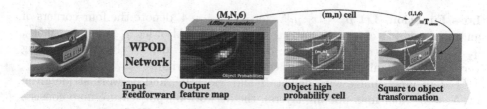

Fig. 3. Fully convolutional detection of planar objects (cropped for better visualization).

The detection process using WPOD-NET is illustrated in Fig. 3. Initially, the network is fed by the resized output of the vehicle detection module. The feed-forwarding results in an 8-channel feature map that encodes object/non-object probabilities and affine transformation parameters. To extract the warped LP, let us first consider an imaginary square of fixed size around the center of a cell (m, n). If the object probability for this cell is above a given detection threshold, part of the regressed parameters is used to build an affine matrix that transforms the fictional square into an LP region. Thus, we can easily unwarp the LP into a horizontally and vertically aligned object.

Network Architecture. The proposed architecture has a total of 21 convolutional layers, where 14 are inside residual blocks [8]. The size of all convolutional filters is fixed in 3×3. ReLU activations are used throughout the entire network, except in the detection block. There are 4 max pooling layers of size 2×2 and stride 2 that reduces the input dimensionality by a factor of 16. Finally, the detection block has two parallel convolutional layers: (i) one for inferring the probability, activated by a softmax function, and (ii) another for regressing the affine parameters, without activation (or, equivalently, using the identity $F(x) = x$ as the activation function). A scheme of the network is shown in Fig. 4.

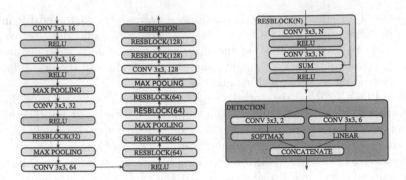

Fig. 4. Detailed WPOD-NET architecture.

Loss Function. Let $p_i = [x_i, y_i]^T$, for $i = 1, \cdots, 4$, denote the four corners of an annotated LP, clockwise starting from top-left. Also, let $q_1 = [-0.5, -0.5]^T$, $q_2 = [0.5, -0.5]^T$, $q_3 = [0.5, 0.5]^T$, $q_4 = [-0.5, 0.5]^T$ denote the corresponding vertices of a canonical unit square centered at the origin.

For an input image with height H and width W, and network stride given by $N_s = 2^4$ (four max pooling layers), the network output feature map consists of an $M \times N \times 8$ volume, where $M = H/N_s$ and $N = W/N_s$. For each point cell (m, n) in the feature map, there are eight values to be estimated: the first two values (v_1 and v_2) are the object/non-object probabilities, and the last six values (v_3 to v_8) are used to build the local affine transformation T_{mn} given by:

$$T_{mn}(q) = \begin{bmatrix} \max(v_3, 0) & v_4 \\ v_5 & \max(v_6, 0) \end{bmatrix} q + \begin{bmatrix} v_7 \\ v_8 \end{bmatrix}, \qquad (2)$$

where the max function used for v_3 and v_6 was adopted to ensure that the diagonal is positive (avoiding undesired mirroring or excessive rotations).

To match the network output resolution, the points p_i are re-scaled by the inverse of the network stride, and re-centered according to each point (m, n) in the feature map. This is accomplished by applying a normalization function

$$A_{mn}(p) = \frac{1}{\alpha} \left(\frac{1}{N_s} p - \begin{bmatrix} n \\ m \end{bmatrix} \right), \qquad (3)$$

where α is a scaling constant that represents the side of the fictional square. We set $\alpha = 7.75$, which is the mean point between the maximum and minimum LP dimensions in the augmented training data divided by the network stride.

Assuming that there is an object (LP) at cell (m, n), the first part of the loss function considers the error between a warped version of the canonical square and the normalized annotated points of the LP, given by

$$f_{affine}(m, n) = \sum_{i=1}^{4} \| T_{mn}(q_i) - A_{mn}(p_i) \|_1. \qquad (4)$$

The second part of the loss function handles the probability of having/not having an object at (m, n). It is similar to the SSD confidence loss [21], and basically is the sum of two log-loss functions

$$f_{probs}(m, n) = \text{logloss}(\mathbb{I}_{obj}, v_1) + \text{logloss}(1 - \mathbb{I}_{obj}, v_2),\tag{5}$$

where $\mathbb{I}_{obj}$ is the object indicator function that returns 1 if there is an object at point (m, n) or 0 otherwise, and $\text{logloss}(y, p) = -y \log(p)$. An object is considered inside a point (m, n) if its rectangular bounding box presents an IoU larger than a threshold γ_{obj} (set empirically to 0.3) w.r.t. another bounding box of the same size and centered at (m, n).

The final loss function is given by a combination of the terms defined in Eqs. (4) and (5):

$$loss = \sum_{m=1}^{M} \sum_{n=1}^{N} [\mathbb{I}_{obj} f_{affine}(m, n) + f_{probs}(m, n)].\tag{6}$$

Training Details. For training the proposed WPOD-NET, we created a dataset with 196 images, being 105 from the Cars Dataset, 40 from the SSIG Dataset (training subset), and 51 from the AOLP dataset (LE subset). For each image, we manually annotated the 4 corners of the LP in the picture (sometimes more than one). The selected images from the Cars Dataset include mostly European LPs, but there are many from the USA as well as other LP types. Images from SSIG and AOLP contain Brazilian and Taiwanese LPs, respectively. A few annotated samples are shown in Fig. 5.

Fig. 5. Examples of the annotated LPs in the training dataset.

Given the reduced number of annotated images in the training dataset, the use of data augmentation is crucial. The following augmentation transforms are used:

- Rectification: the entire image is rectified based on the LP annotation, assuming that the LP lies on a plane;
- Aspect-ratio: the LP aspect-ratio is randomly set in the interval [2, 4] to accommodate sizes from different regions;

- Centering: the LP center becomes the image center;
- Scaling: the LP is scaled so its width matches a value between $40px$ and $208px$ (set experimentally based on the readability of the LPs). This range is used to define the value of α used in Eq. (3);
- Rotation: a 3D rotation with randomly chosen angles is performed, to account for a wide range of camera setups;
- Mirroring: 50% chance;
- Translation: random translation to move the LP from the center of the image, limited to a square of 208×208 pixels around the center;
- Cropping: considering the LP center before the translation, we crop a 208×208 region around it;
- Colorspace: slight modifications in the HSV colorspace;
- Annotation: the locations of the four LP corners are adjusted by applying the same spatial transformations used to augment the input image.

From the chosen set of transformations mentioned above, a great variety of augmented test images with very distinct visual characteristics can be obtained from a single manually labeled sample. For example, Fig. 6 shows 20 different augmentation samples obtained from the same image.

Fig. 6. Different augmentations for the same sample. The red quadrilateral represents the transformed LP annotation. (Color figure online)

We trained the network with $100k$ iterations of mini-batches of size 32 using the ADAM optimizer [15]. The learning rate was set to 0.001 with parameters $\beta_1 = 0.9$ and $\beta_2 = 0.999$. The mini-batches were generated by randomly choosing and augmenting samples from the training set, resulting in new input tensors of size $32 \times 208 \times 208 \times 3$ at every iteration.

3.3   OCR

The character segmentation and recognition over the rectified LP is performed using a modified YOLO network, with the same architecture presented in [28]. However, the training dataset was considerably enlarged in this work by using synthetic and augmented data to cope with LP characteristics of different regions around the world (Europe, United States and Brazil)[3].

---

[3] We also used Taiwanese LPs, but could not find information in English about the font type used by this country in order to include in the artificial data generation.

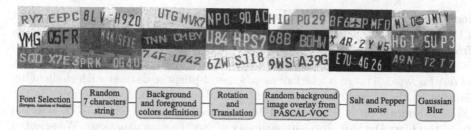

Fig. 7. Artificial LP samples with the proposed generation pipeline (bottom).

The artificially created data consist of pasting a string of seven characters onto a textured background and then performing random transformations, such as rotation, translation, noise, and blur. Some generated samples and a short overview of the pipeline for synthetic data generation are shown in Fig. 7. As shown in Sect. 4, the use of synthetic data helped to greatly improve the network generalization, so that the exact same network performs well for LPs of different regions around the world.

3.4 Evaluation Datasets

One of our goals is to develop a technique that performs well in a variety of unconstrained scenarios, but that should also work well in controlled ones (such as mostly frontal views). Therefore, we chose four datasets available online, namely OpenALPR (BR and EU)[4], SSIG and AOLP (RP), which cover many different situations, as summarized in the first part of Table 1. We consider three distinct variables: LP angle (frontal and oblique), distance from vehicles to the camera (close, intermediate and far), and the region where the pictures were taken.

Table 1. Evaluation datasets.

Database (subset)	LP angle	Vehicle Dist.	#images	Region
OpenALPR (EU)	Mostly frontal	Close	104	Europe
OpenALPR (BR)	Mostly frontal	Close	108	Brazil
SSIG (test-set)	Mostly frontal	Medium,far	804	Brazil
AOLP (Road Patrol)	Frontal + oblique	Close	611	Taiwan
Proposed (CD-HARD)	Mostly oblique	Close, medium, far	102	Various

The more challenging dataset currently used in terms of LP distortion is the AOLP Road Patrol (RP) subset, which tries to simulate the case where a camera is installed in a patrolling vehicle or hand-held by a person. In terms of distance from the camera to the vehicles, the SSIG dataset appears to be the

---

[4] Available at https://github.com/openalpr/benchmarks.

most challenging one. It is composed of high-resolution images, allowing that LPs from distant vehicles might still be readable. None of them present LPs from multiple (simultaneous) vehicles at once.

Although all these databases together cover numerous situations, to the best of our knowledge there is a lack of more general-purpose dataset with challenging images in the literature. Thus, an additional contribution of this work is the manual annotation of a new set of 102 images (named as CD-HARD) selected from the Cars Dataset, covering a variety of challenging situations. We selected mostly images with strong LP distortion but still readable for humans. Some of these images (crops around the LP region) are shown in Fig. 1, which was used to motivate the problem tackled in this work.

4   Experimental Results

This section covers the experimental analysis of our full ALPR system, as well as comparisons with other state-of-the-art methods and commercial systems. Unfortunately, most academic ALPR papers focus on specific scenarios (e.g. single country or region, environment conditions, camera position, etc.). As a result, there are many scattered datasets available in the literature, each one evaluated by a subset of methods. Moreover, many papers are focused only on LP detection or character segmentation, which limits even more the comparison possibilities for the full ALPR pipeline. In this work, we used four independent datasets to evaluate the accuracy of the proposed method in different scenarios and region layouts. We also show comparisons with commercial products and papers that present full ALPR systems.

The proposed approach presents three networks in the pipeline, for which we empirically set the following acceptance thresholds: 0.5 for vehicle (YOLOv2) and LP (WPOD-NET) detection, and 0.4 for character detection and recognition (OCR-NET). Also, it is worth noticing that characters "I" and "1" are identical for Brazilian LPs. Hence, they were considered as a single class in the evaluation of the OpenALPR BR and SSIG datasets. No other heuristic or post-processing was applied to the results produced by the OCR module.

We evaluate the system in terms of the percentage of correctly recognized LPs, where an LP is considered correct if all characters were correctly recognized, and no additional characters were detected. It is important to note that the exact same networks were applied to all datasets: no specific training procedure was used to tune the networks for a given type of LP (e.g. European or Taiwanese). The only slight modification performed in the pipeline was for the AOLP Road Patrol dataset. In this dataset, the vehicles are very close to the camera (causing the vehicle detector to fail in several cases), so that we directly applied the LP detector (WPOD-NET) to the input images.

To show the benefits of including fully synthetic data in the OCR-NET training procedure, we evaluated our system using two sets training data: (i) real augmented data plus artificially generated ones; and (ii) only real augmented data.

Table 2. Full ALPR results for all 5 datasets.

	OpenALPR		SSIG	AOLP	Proposed	Average
	EU	BR	Test	RP	CD-HARD	
Ours	93.52%	91.23%	**88.56%**	**98.36%**	**75.00%**	**89.33%**
Ours (no artf.)	92.59%	88.60%	84.58%	93.29%	73.08%	86.43%
Ours (unrect.)	94.44%	90.35%	87.81%	84.61%	57.69%	82.98%
Commercial systems						
OpenALPR	**96.30%**	85.96%	87.44%	69.72%*	67.31%	81.35%
Sighthound	83.33%	**94.73%**	81.46%	83.47%	45.19%	77.64%
Amazon Rekog.	69.44%	83.33%	31.21%	68.25%	30.77%	56.60%
Literature						
Laroca et al. [17]	-	-	85.45%	-	-	-
Li et al. [18]	-	-	-	88.38%	-	-
Li et al. [19]	-	-	-	83.63%	-	-
Hsu et al. [10]	-	-	-	85.70%**	-	-

*OpenALPR struggled to understand the "Q" letter in Taiwanese LPs.
**In [10] the authors provided an estimative, and not the real evaluation.

These two versions are denoted by "Ours" and "Ours (no artf.)", respectively, in Table 2. As can be observed, the addition of fully synthetic data improved the accuracy in all tested datasets (with a gain ≈5% for the AOLP RP dataset). Moreover, to highlight the improvements of rectifying the detection bounding box, we also present the results of using a regular non-rectified bounding box, identified as "Ours (unrect.)" in Table 2. As expected, the results do not vary much in the mostly frontal datasets (being even slightly better for ALPR-EU), but there was a considerable accuracy drop in datasets with challenging oblique LPs (AOLP-RP and the proposed CD-HARD).

Table 2 also shows the results of competitive (commercial and academic) systems, indicating that our system achieved recognition rates comparable to commercial ones in databases representing more controlled scenarios, where the LPs are mostly frontal (OpenALPR EU and BR, and SSIG). More precisely, it was the second best method in both OpenALPR datasets, and top one in SSIG. In the challenging scenarios (AOLP RP and the proposed CD-HARD dataset), however, our system outperformed all compared approaches by a significant margin (over 7% accuracy gain when compared to the second best result).

It is worth mentioning that the works of Li et al. [18,19], Hsu et al. [10] and Laroca et al. [17] are focused on a single region or dataset. By outperforming them, we demonstrate a strong generalization capacity. It is also important to note that the full LP recognition rate for the most challenging datasets (AOLP-RP and CD-HARD) was higher than directly applying the OCR module to the annotated rectangular LP bounding boxes (79.21% for AOLP-RP and 53.85% for CD-HARD). This gain is due to the unwarping allowed by WPOD-NET, which greatly helps the OCR task when the LP is strongly distorted. To illustrate this behavior, we show in Fig. 8 the detected and unwarped LPs for the images in Fig. 1, as well as the final recognition result produced by OCR-NET. The detection score of the top right LP was below the acceptance threshold, illustrating a false negative example.

Fig. 8. Detected/unwarped LPs from images in Fig. 1 and final ALPR results.

The proposed WPOD-NET was implemented using TensorFlow framework, while the initial YOLOv2 vehicle detection and OCR-NET were created and executed using the DarkNet framework. A Python wrapper was used to integrate the two frameworks. The hardware used for our experiments was an Intel Xeon processor, with 12Gb of RAM and an NVIDIA Titan X GPU. With that configuration, we were able to run the full ALPR system with an average of 5 FPS (considering all datasets). This time is highly dependent of the number of vehicles detected in the input image. Hence, incrementing the vehicle detection threshold will result in higher FPS, but lower recall rates.

5   Conclusions and Future Work

In this work, we presented a complete deep learning ALPR system for unconstrained scenarios. Our results indicate that the proposed approach outperforms existing methods by far in challenging datasets, containing LPs captured at strongly oblique views while keeping good results in more controlled datasets.

The main contribution of this work is the introduction of a novel network that allows the detection and unwarping of distorted LPs by generating an affine transformation matrix per detection cell. This step alleviates the burden of the OCR network, as it needed to handle less distortion.

As an additional contribution, we presented a new challenging dataset for evaluating ALPR systems in captures with mostly oblique LPs. The annotations for the dataset will be made publicly available so that the dataset might be used as a new challenging LP benchmark.

For future work, we want to extend our solution to detect motorcycle LPs. This poses new challenges due to differences in aspect ratio and layout. Moreover, we intend to explore the obtained affine transformations for automatic camera calibration problem in traffic surveillance scenarios.

Acknowledgements. The authors would like to thank the funding agencies CAPES and CNPq, as well as NVIDIA Corporation for donating a Titan X Pascal GPU.

References

1. Anagnostopoulos, C.N., Anagnostopoulos, I., Psoroulas, I., Loumos, V., Kayafas, E.: License plate recognition from still images and video sequences: a survey. IEEE Trans. Intell. Transp. Syst. **9**(3), 377–391 (2008). https://doi.org/10.1109/TITS. 2008.922938. http://ieeexplore.ieee.org/document/4518951/
2. Bulan, O., Kozitsky, V., Ramesh, P., Shreve, M.: Segmentation- and annotation-free license plate recognition with deep localization and failure identification. IEEE Trans. Intell. Transp. Syst. **18**(9), 2351–2363 (2017). https://doi.org/10.1109/ TITS.2016.2639020
3. Delmar Kurpiel, F., Minetto, R., Nassu, B.T.: Convolutional neural networks for license plate detection in images. In: 2017 IEEE International Conference on Image Processing (ICIP), pp. 3395–3399. IEEE (2017) https://doi.org/10.1109/ ICIP.2017.8296912. http://ieeexplore.ieee.org/document/8296912/
4. Du, S., Ibrahim, M., Shehata, M., Badawy, W.: Automatic license plate recognition (ALPR): a state-of-the-art review. IEEE Trans. Circuits Syst. Video Technol. **23**(2), 311–325 (2013). https://doi.org/10.1109/TCSVT.2012.2203741. http://ieeexplore.ieee.org/document/6213519/
5. Everingham, M., Van Gool, L., Williams, C.K.I., Winn, J., Zisserman, A.: The pascal visual object classes (VOC) challenge. Int. J. Comput. Vis. **88**(2), 303–338 (2010)
6. Gonçalves, G.R., da Silva, S.P.G., Menotti, D., Schwartz, W.R.: Benchmark for license plate character segmentation. J. Electron. Imaging **25**(5), 1–5 (2016). http://www.ssig.dcc.ufmg.br/wp-content/uploads/2016/11/JEI-2016-Benchmark. pdf
7. Gupta, A., Vedaldi, A., Zisserman, A.: Synthetic data for text localisation in natural images. In: IEEE Conference on Computer Vision and Pattern Recognition, pp. 2315–2324 (2016)
8. He, K., Zhang, X., Ren, S., Sun, J.: Deep residual learning for image recognition. In: 2016 IEEE Conference on Computer Vision and Pattern Recognition (CVPR), vol. 4, pp. 770–778. IEEE, June 2016. https://doi.org/10.1109/CVPR.2016.90
9. Hsu, G.S., Ambikapathi, A., Chung, S.L., Su, C.P.: Robust license plate detection in the wild. In: 2017 14th IEEE International Conference on Advanced Video and Signal Based Surveillance (AVSS), pp. 1–6. IEEE, August 2017. https://doi.org/ 10.1109/AVSS.2017.8078493. http://ieeexplore.ieee.org/document/8078493/
10. Hsu, G.S., Chen, J.C., Chung, Y.Z.: Application-oriented license plate recognition. IEEE Trans. Veh. Technol. **62**(2), 552–561 (2013). https://doi.org/10.1109/TVT. 2012.2226218
11. Huang, G., Liu, Z., van der Maaten, L., Weinberger, K.Q.: Densely connected convolutional networks. In: 2017 IEEE Conference on Computer Vision and Pattern Recognition (CVPR), pp. 2261–2269. IEEE, July 2017. https://doi.org/ 10.1109/CVPR.2017.243. http://arxiv.org/abs/1608.06993. http://ieeexplore.ieee. org/document/8099726/
12. Huang, J., et al.: Speed/accuracy trade-offs for modern convolutional object detectors. In: 2017 IEEE Conference on Computer Vision and Pattern Recognition (CVPR), pp. 3296–3297. IEEE, July 2017. https://doi.org/10.1109/CVPR.2017. 351. http://ieeexplore.ieee.org/document/8099834/
13. Jaderberg, M., Simonyan, K., Vedaldi, A., Zisserman, A.: Synthetic data and artificial neural networks for natural scene text recognition. In: NIPS, Conference on Neural Information Processing Systems, pp. 1–10 (2014)

14. Jaderberg, M., Simonyan, K., Zisserman, A., kavukcuoglu, k.: Spatial transformer networks. In: Cortes, C., Lawrence, N.D., Lee, D.D., Sugiyama, M., Garnett, R. (eds.) Advances in Neural Information Processing Systems 28, pp. 2017–2025. Curran Associates, Inc. (2015)

15. Kingma, D.P., Ba, J.: Adam: a method for stochastic optimization. CoRR abs/1412.6980 (2014)

16. Krause, J., Stark, M., Deng, J., Fei-Fei, L.: 3D object representations for fine-grained categorization. In: 4th International IEEE Workshop on 3D Representation and Recognition (3dRR-2013), Sydney, Australia (2013)

17. Laroca, R., et al.: A robust real-time automatic license plate recognition based on the YOLO detector. CoRR abs/1802.09567 (2018). http://arxiv.org/abs/1802.09567

18. Li, H., Shen, C.: Reading Car License Plates Using Deep Convolutional Neural Networks and LSTMs. arXiv preprint arXiv:1601.05610, January 2016. http://arxiv.org/abs/1601.05610

19. Li, H., Wang, P., Shen, C.: Towards end-to-end car license plates detection and recognition with deep neural networks. CoRR abs/1709.08828 (2017). http://arxiv.org/abs/1709.08828

20. Lin, T.-Y., et al.: Microsoft COCO: common objects in context. In: Fleet, D., Pajdla, T., Schiele, B., Tuytelaars, T. (eds.) ECCV 2014. LNCS, vol. 8693, pp. 740–755. Springer, Cham (2014). https://doi.org/10.1007/978-3-319-10602-1_48

21. Liu, W., et al.: SSD: single shot multibox detector. In: Leibe, B., Matas, J., Sebe, N., Welling, M. (eds.) ECCV 2016. LNCS, vol. 9905, pp. 21–37. Springer, Cham (2016). https://doi.org/10.1007/978-3-319-46448-0_2

22. Netzer, Y., Wang, T., Coates, A., Bissacco, A., Wu, B., Ng, A.Y.: Reading digits in natural images with unsupervised feature learning. In: NIPS Workshop on Deep Learning and Unsupervised Feature Learning, vol. 2011, p. 5 (2011)

23. Redmon, J., Divvala, S., Girshick, R., Farhadi, A.: You only look once: unified, real-time object detection. In: 2016 IEEE Conference on Computer Vision and Pattern Recognition (CVPR), pp. 779–788. IEEE, June 2016. https://doi.org/10.1109/CVPR.2016.91. http://ieeexplore.ieee.org/document/7780460/

24. Redmon, J., Farhadi, A.: YOLO9000: better, faster, stronger. In: 2017 IEEE Conference on Computer Vision and Pattern Recognition (CVPR), pp. 6517–6525. IEEE, July 2017. https://doi.org/10.1109/CVPR.2017.690. http://arxiv.org/abs/1612.08242. http://ieeexplore.ieee.org/document/8100173/

25. Ren, S., He, K., Girshick, R., Sun, J.: Faster R-CNN: towards real-time object detection with region proposal networks. IEEE Trans. Pattern Anal. Mach. Intell. 39(6), 1137–1149 (2017). https://doi.org/10.1109/TPAMI.2016.2577031

26. Russakovsky, O., et al.: ImageNet large scale visual recognition challenge. Int. J. Comput. Vis. (IJCV) 115(3), 211–252 (2015). https://doi.org/10.1007/s11263-015-0816-y

27. Selmi, Z., Ben Halima, M., Alimi, A.M.: Deep learning system for automatic license plate detection and recognition. In: 2017 14th IAPR International Conference on Document Analysis and Recognition (ICDAR), pp. 1132–1138. IEEE, November 2017. https://doi.org/10.1109/ICDAR.2017.187. http://ieeexplore.ieee.org/document/8270118/

28. Silva, S.M., Jung, C.R.: Real-time Brazilian license plate detection and recognition using deep convolutional neural networks. In: 2017 30th SIBGRAPI Conference on Graphics, Patterns and Images (SIBGRAPI), pp. 55–62, October 2017. https://doi.org/10.1109/SIBGRAPI.2017.14

29. Wang, F., Zhao, L., Li, X., Wang, X., Tao, D.: Geometry-aware scene text detection with instance transformation network. In: IEEE Conference on Computer Vision and Pattern Recognition (CVPR), Salt Lake City, pp. 1381–1389 (2018)
30. Weinman, J.J., Learned-Miller, E., Hanson, A.R.: Scene text recognition using similarity and a lexicon with sparse belief propagation. IEEE Trans. Pattern Anal. Mach. Intell. **31**(10), 1733–1746 (2009)
31. Xie, L., Ahmad, T., Jin, L., Liu, Y., Zhang, S.: A new CNN-based method for multi-directional car license plate detection. IEEE Trans. Intell. Transp. Syst. **19**(2), 507–517 (2018). https://doi.org/10.1109/TITS.2017.2784093
32. Zhou, X., Zhu, M., Leonardos, S., Daniilidis, K.: Sparse representation for 3D shape estimation: a convex relaxation approach. IEEE Trans. Pattern Anal. Mach. Intell. **39**(8), 1648–1661 (2017)

Self-produced Guidance for
Weakly-Supervised Object Localization

Xiaolin Zhang[1], Yunchao Wei[2], Guoliang Kang[1], Yi Yang[1(✉)],
and Thomas Huang[2]

[1] CAI, University of Technology Sydney, Ultimo, NSW, Australia
{Xiaolin.Zhang-3,Guoliang.Kang}@student.uts.edu.au, Yi.Yang@uts.edu.au
[2] University of Illinois Urbana-Champaign, Champaign, IL, USA
{yunchao,t-huang1}@illinois.edu

Abstract. Weakly supervised methods usually generate localization results based on attention maps produced by classification networks. However, the attention maps exhibit the most discriminative parts of the object which are small and sparse. We propose to generate Self-produced Guidance (SPG) masks which separate the foreground *i.e.*, the object of interest, from the background to provide the classification networks with spatial correlation information of pixels. A stagewise approach is proposed to incorporate high confident object regions to learn the SPG masks. The high confident regions within attention maps are utilized to progressively learn the SPG masks. The masks are then used as an auxiliary pixel-level supervision to facilitate the training of classification networks. Extensive experiments on ILSVRC demonstrate that SPG is effective in producing high-quality object localizations maps. Particularly, the proposed SPG achieves the Top-1 localization error rate of 43.83% on the ILSVRC validation set, which is a new state-of-the-art error rate.

Keywords: Object localization · Weakly Supervised Learning

1 Introduction

Weakly Supervised Learning (WSL) has been successfully applied on many tasks, such as object localization [5,6,11,13,26,35,44], relation detection [40] and semantic segmentation [32–34,36,37]. WSL attracts extensive attention from researchers and practitioners because it is less dependent on massive pixel-level annotations. In this paper, we focus on Weakly Supervised Object Localization (WSOL) problem.

Existing WSOL methods locate target object regions using convolutional classification networks. Classification networks recognize various kinds of objects by identifying discriminative regions of an objects. Fully convolutional networks [17] without using fully connected layers can preserve the relative positions of pixels. Therefore, the discovered discriminative regions can indicate the exact

V. Ferrari et al. (Eds.): ECCV 2018, LNCS 11216, pp. 610–625, 2018.
https://doi.org/10.1007/978-3-030-01258-8_37

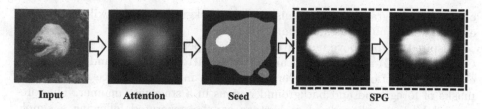

Fig. 1. Learning process of Self-produced guidance. Given an input image, we first generate corresponding attention map with a classification network. Then the attention map is roughly split, following the rule that the region with high confidence should be the object, whereas that with low confidence should be background. The regions with medium confidence remain undefined. All these three regions constitute the seed. Self-produced guidance is defined as the multi-stage pixel-level object mask supervised by the seed.

location of the target objects. Zhou *et al.* revisited classification networks (*e.g.* AlexNet [12], VGG [25] and GoogleNet [27,28]) and proposed a Class Activation Maps (CAM) approach to find the regions of interest using only image-level supervision. Following [14], CAM replaced the top fully connected layers by convolutional layers to keep the object positions and can discover the spatial distribution of discriminative regions for different classes. The key weakness of the localization maps generated by CAM is that only the most discriminative regions are highlighted, as a result we can only locate a small part of target objects. To cope with the weakness, Wei *et al.* [32] proposed to apply additional networks for enriching object-related regions, given images of which the most discriminative regions are erased according to the attention maps from a pre-trained network. Moreover, Zhang *et al.* [43] proved the CAM method can be simplified to enable end-to-end training. Armed with this proof, an Adversarial Complementary Learning approach was proposed in [43] by incorporating one additional classifier for mining complementary object regions, which can finally produce accurate object localization maps. However, all these methods ignore to explore the correlations among pixels.

We observe that images can be roughly divided into foreground and background regions. The foreground pixels usually constitute the object(s) of interests. We found that attention maps inferred from classification networks [32,43,45] can effectively provide the probabilities of each pixel to be foreground or background. Although pixels of high foreground/background probabilities may not cover the entire target object/background, they still provide the important cues for getting some common patterns of target objects. Based on this, we can simply leverage those reliable foreground/background seeds as supervision to encourage the network to sense the distributions of foreground objects and background regions. Since pixels with correlations (*e.g.* within a same object or background) often share similar appearance, more reliable foreground/background pixels can be easily discovered by learning from the discovered seeds. With more reliable guided pixels for supervision, the entire foreground objects can be gradually distinguished from background, which will finally benefit the weakly object localization.

Inspired by the above motivation, in this paper, we propose a Self-produced Guidance (SPG) approach for learning better attention maps and getting precise positions of objects. We leverage attention maps to produce the guidance masks of foreground and background regions in a stagewise manner. The foreground/background seeds of each stage can be generated following a simple rule: (1) the regions with highly confident scores are considered as foreground; (2) the regions with very low scores are background seeds; (3) the regions with medium confidence remain undefined. The undefined regions are meant to be figured out using intermediate features. We adopt a top-down mechanism of using upper layer's output as the supervision of the lower layers to learn better object localizations. The upper layers maintain more abstract semantic information, whereas the lower layers have more specific pixel-related information. We leave the ambiguous area undefined before more regions can be defined as foreground/background using upper layer features. The more regions be defined, the stronger ability to define harder regions. After getting the guidance masks of foreground and background, we use them as auxiliary supervisions. These supervisions are expected to enable the classification network to learn pixel correlations. Consequently, attention maps can clearly indicate class-specific object regions. Figure 1 illustrates the learning process of self-produced guidance. Given an input image, we firstly generate corresponding attention maps through a classification network according to the convenient method in [43]. Then the attention map is roughly split into foreground/background seeds and ignored regions. The self-produced guidance are learned from these seeds with the input of intermediate features in a stagewise manner. Finally, the SPG masks of multiple layers are fused for a more precise and integrate indication of target objects.

To sum up, our main contributions are:

- We propose a stagewise approach to learn high-quality Self-produced Guidance masks which exhibit the foreground and background of a given image.
- We present a weakly object localization method by incorporating self-produced supervision, which can inspire the classification network discover pixel correlations to improve the localization performance.
- The proposed method achieves the new state-of-the-art with the error rate of Top-1 43.83% on ILSVRC dataset with only image-level supervision.

We discuss the proposed SPG approach in detail in Sect. 3. In Sect. 4, we empirically evaluate the proposed method on the ILSVRC2016 dataset, showing that the superiority of SPG in object localization task with only image-level supervision. We also discuss the further insights of the proposed SPG algorithms through additional experiments.

2   Related Work

Convolutional neural network has been widely used in object detection and localization tasks [3,8,10,18,25,42]. One of the earliest deep networks to detect objects in a one-stage manner is OverFeat [23], which employs a multiscale and sliding window approach to predict object boundaries. These boundaries are then applied for accumulating bounding boxes. SSD [16] and YOLO [20] used a similar one-stage method, and these detectors are specifically designed for speeding up the detection process. Faster-RCNN designed by Ren *et al.* [21] has achieved great success in the object detection task. It generates region proposals and predicts highly reliable object locations in an unified network in real time. Lin *et al.* [15] presented that the performance of Faster-RCNN can be significantly improved by constructing feature pyramids with marginal extra cost.

Although these approaches are considerably successful in detecting object of interest in images, the vast number of annotations are unaffordable for training such networks with limited budget. Weakly supervised methods alleviate this problem by using much cheaper annotations like image-level labels. Jie *et al.* [11] proposed a self-taught learning framework by firstly selecting some high-response proposals, and then finetuning the network on the selected regions to progressively improve its detection capacity. This method highly rely on region proposals pre-processed by algorithms like Selective Search [30]. The general-purpose proposal algorithms may not robust to produce accurate bounding boxes. Dong *et al.* [5] adopted two separate networks to jointly refine the region proposals and select positive regions. High-quality attention maps are also critical for object detection and segmentation [19]. Diba *et al.* [4] proposed the attention maps can be leveraged to produce region proposals. With the assistance of these proposals, more detailed information can be easily detected.

However, these methods introduces extra computational as a result of using pre-processed region proposals and multiple networks. Zhou *et al.* [44] discovered that the localization maps for each class can be produced by aggregating top-level feature maps using a class-specific fully connected layer. Zhang *et al.* [41] introduced a different backpropagation scheme to produce contrastive response maps by passing along top-down signals downwards. However, this method supervised by solely using image labels tends to only discover a small part of the target objects. Wei *et al.* [32] applied a similar but more efficient approach to hide discriminative regions under the guidance of a pre-trained network, and then the processed images are trained for discovering more regions of interest. These methods increases the amount of images, thus they need much more precious computational and time resources to train the networks. Zhang *et al.* [43] provided theoretical proof of producing class-specific attention maps during the forward pass by just selecting from the last layer feature maps, which enables the end-to-end attention learning. Also, they proposed the ACoL approach [43] to efficiently mine the integral target object in an enhanced classification network.

3 Self-produced Guidance

3.1 Network Overview

We denote the image set as $I = \{(I_i, y_i)\}_{i=0}^{N-1}$, where $y_i = \{0, 1, ..., C-1\}$ is the label of the image I_i, N is the number of images and C is the number of image

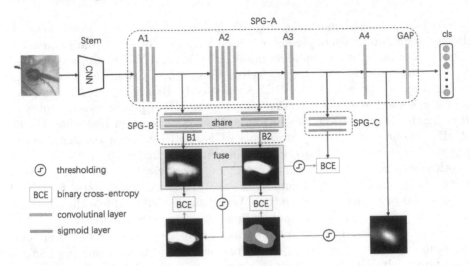

Fig. 2. Overview of the proposed SPG approach. The input images are processed by Stem to extract mid-level feature maps, which are then fed into SPG-A for classification. Attention map is then inferred from the classification network. Self-produced guidance maps are gradually learned with the guide of the attention map. SPG-C utilizes the self-produced guidance map as an auxiliary supervision to reinforce the quality of the attention map. GAP refers to global average pooling

classes. Figure 2 illustrates the architecture of the SPG approach, which mainly has four different components, including Stem, SPG-A, SPG-B and SPG-C. Different components have different structures and functionalities. We use lowercase f to denote functions and capital F to denote output feature maps. Stem is a fully convolutional network denoted as $f^{Stem}(I_i, \theta^{Stem})$, where θ^{Stem} is the parameters. The output feature maps of f^{Stem} is denoted as F^{Stem}. f^{Stem} acts as a feature extractor, which takes the RGB images as input and produces high-level position-aware feature maps of multiple channels. The extracted feature maps F^{Stem} are then fed into the following component SPG-A. We denote the SPG-A component as $f^A(F^{Stem}, \theta^A)$, which is a network for image-level classification. $f^A(F^{Stem}, \theta^A)$ is consisted of four convolutional blocks (i.e. A1, A2, A3 and A4), a global average pooling (GAP) layer [14] and a softmax layer. A4 has one convolutional layer with kernel size 1×1 of C filters. These filters are corresponding to the attention maps of each class, so as to generate attention maps during the forward pass [43]. SPG-B is leveraged to learn Self-produced guidance masks by using the seeds of foreground and background generated from attention maps. The high confident regions within attention maps are extracted to perform as supervision to learn better object regions. SPG-B leverages the intermediate feature maps from the classification network SPG-A to predict Self-produced Guidance masks. Particularly, the output features maps F^{A1} and F^{A2} of A1 and A2 are fed into the two blocks in SPG-B, respectively. Each block of SPG-B contains three convolutional layers followed by a sigmoid layer, where the first layer is to adapt the different number of channels in feature maps F^{A1} and F^{A2}. The output of SPG-B are denoted as F^{B1} and F^{B2} for the two branches, respectively. The component SPG-C uses the auxiliary SPG supervision to encourage the SPG-A to learn pixel-level correlations. SPG-C contains two convolutional layers with 3×3 and 1×1 kernels, followed by a sigmoid layer.

3.2   Self-produced Guidance Learning

Attention maps generated from classification networks can only exhibit the most discriminative parts of target objects. We propose to generate Self-produced Guidance (SPG) masks which separate the foreground, i.e. the object of interest, from the background to provide the classification networks with spatial correlation information of pixels. The generated SPG masks are then leveraged as auxiliary supervision to encourage the networks to learn correlations between pixels. Thus, pixels within the same object will have the same responses in feature maps. As the detailed information (i.e. object edge and boundary) is usually very abstract in the top-level feature maps, we employ the intermediate features to produce precise SPG masks. Indeed, some previous works use low-level feature maps to learn object regions [9,38]. These approaches require pixel-level ground-truth labels as supervision. Differently, we propose to use self-produced guidance by incorporating high confident object regions within attention maps. In detail, for any image I_i, we firstly extract its attention map O by simply from a classification network. We observe that the attention maps usually highlight the most discriminative regions of object. The initial object and background seeds can be easily obtained according to the scores in the attention maps. In particular, the regions with very low scores are considered as background, while the regions with very high scores are foreground. The rest regions are ignored during the learning process. We initialize the SPG learning process by these seeds. B2 is supervised by the seed map and it can learn the patterns of foreground and background. In this way, the pixels within the ignored regions are gradually recognized. Then, we use the same strategy to find the foreground and background seeds in the output map of B2, which are used to train the B1 branch. In such a stagewise way, the intermediate information of the neural network are employed to learn the Self-produced Guidance.

We formally define this process as follows. Given a input image of size $W \times H$, we denote the binarized SPG mask $M \in \{0, 1, 255\}^{W \times H}$, where $M_{x,y} = 0$ if the pixel at x_{th} row and y_{th} column belongs to background regions, $M_{x,y} = 1$ if it belongs to object regions, and $M_{x,y} = 255$ if it is ignored. We denote the attention map as O. The produced guidance masks can be calculated by

$$M_{x,y} = \begin{cases} 0 & if \quad O_{x,y} < \delta_l, 0 < \delta_l < 1 \\ 1 & if \quad O_{x,y} > \delta_h, 0 < \delta_h < 1 \\ 255 & if \quad \delta_l \leq O_{x,y} \leq \delta_h, 0 < \delta_l < \delta_h < 1 \end{cases} \tag{1}$$

where δ_l and δ_h are thresholds to identify regions in localization maps as background and foreground, respectively.

We adopt an stagewise approach to gradually learn the high-quality self-produced supervision maps. B2 is applied to learn better self-produced maps supervised by the seed map M^A. In training, only the positions labeled as 0 and 1 in the self-produced maps are served as pixel-level supervision. The pixels with values of 255 are temporarily ignored. The ignored pixels do not contribute to the loss and their gradients do not back-propagated. The network will learn the patterns from the already labeled pixels and then more regions will be recognized, because the pixels belonging to background or objects usually share much correlation. For example, the regions belong to the same object usually have the same appearance. The output of B2 is then further applied as attention maps, and better self-produced supervision masks can be calculated using the same policy in Eq. (1). After obtaining output maps of B1 and B2, these two maps are fused to generated our final self-produced supervision map. Particularly, we calculate the average of the two maps, then generate the self-produced guidance M^{fuse} according to Eq. (1).

The generated self-produced guidance is leveraged as pixel-level supervision for the classification network SPG-A. Thereby, the classification network will learn the correlation among pixels, and we will obtain better localization maps. The entire network is trained in an end-to-end manner. We adopt the cross-entropy loss function for the classification learning and self-produced guidance learning. Algorithm 1 illustrates the training procedure of the proposed SPG approach.

Algorithm 1. Training algorithm for SPG

Input: Training data $I = \{(I_i, y_i)\}_{i=1}^N$, threshold δ_l and δ_h
1: **while** training is not convergent **do**
2:     Update feature maps $F^{A4} \leftarrow f^A(f^{Stem}(I_i, \theta^{Stem}), \theta^A)$
3:     Extract localization map O from F^{A4} according to image label y_i
4:     Calculate the seeds of foreground/background M^A according to Eq. (1)
5:     Generate the SPG map $F^{B2} \leftarrow f^{B2}(F^{A2}, \theta^{B2})$
6:     Calculate the next stage SPG maps F^{B1}
7:     Calculate the fused maps F^{fuse} by averaging F^{B1} and F^{B2}
8:     Calculate the fused SPG masks $M^{fuse} \leftarrow F^{fuse}$ according to Eq. (1)
9:     Update the entire network $\theta_{Stem}, \theta^A, \theta^B$ and θ_C supervised by M and y_i
10: **end while**
Output: Output the localization map O

During testing, we extract the attention maps according to the class with the highest predicted scores, and then resize the maps to the same size with the original images by bilinear interpolation. For a fair comparison, we apply the same strategy utilized in [44] to produce object bounding boxes based on the generated object localization maps. In particular, we firstly segment the foreground and background by a fixed threshold. Then, we seek the tight bounding boxes covering the largest connected area in the foreground pixels. The thresholds for generating bounding boxes are adjusted to the optimal values using grid search method. For more details please refer to [44].

3.3 Implementation Details

We evaluate the proposed SPG approach by modifying the Inception-v3 network [29]. In particular, we remove the layers after the second Inception block, *i.e.*, the third Inception block, pooling and linear layer. For a fair comparison, we build a plain version network, named SPG-plain. We add two convolutional layers of kernel size 3×3, stride 1, pad 1 with 1024 filters and a convolutional layer of size 1×1, stride 1 with 1000 units (200 for CUB-200-2011). Finally, a GAP layer and a softmax layer are added on the top. We update the plain network by adding two components (SPG-B and SPG-C). The first layers of B1 and B2 are convolutional layers of kernel size 3×3 with 288 and 768 filters, respectively. The second layers are convolutional layers of 512 filters followed by a 1×1 convolutional output layer. The second and third layers share parameters between B1 and B2. The strides are 1 for all convolutional layers. To keep the resolution of feature maps, we set the pad to 1 to the filters whose kernel size is 3×3. SPG-C is consist of two convolutional layers of kernel size 3×3 with 512 filters and a output convolutional layer with kernel size of 1×1. All branches in SPG-B and SPG-C connects to a output sigmoid layer. We use the pre-trained weights on ILSVRC [22]. Following the baseline methods [26,44], input images are randomly cropped to 224×224 pixels after being reshaped to the size of 256×256. During testing, we directly resize the input images to 224×224. For classification results, we average the class scores from the softmax layer with 10 crops (4 corners plus center, same with horizontal flip).

We implement the networks using PyTorch. We finetune the networks with the initial learning rate of 0.001 (0.01 for the added layers) on ILSVRC, and it is decreased by a factor of 10 after every epoch. The batch size is 30 and the weight decay is 0.0005. The momentum of the SGD optimizer is set to 0.9. We randomly sample some images and visualize their localization maps. We adjust δ_h to mine object seeds. The object seeds should include as much object pixels as possible while exclude background pixels. Similarly, δ_l can be adjusted so that the background seeds should be as large as possible while exclude object regions. We choose the parameters for B1 are $\delta_h = 0.5$ and $\delta_l = 0.05$, and the parameters for B2 are $\delta_h = 0.7$ and $\delta_l = 0.1$. We train the networks on NVIDIA GeForce TITAN 1080Ti GPU with 11 GB memory. Code is available at https://github. com/xiaomengyc/SPG.

4 Experiments

4.1 Experiment Setup

Dataset and Evaluation. We evaluate the Top-1 and Top-5 localization accuracy of the proposed approach. We mainly compare our approach with other

Table 1. Localization error on ILSVRC validation set (* indicates methods which improve the Top-5 performance only using predictions with high scores).

Methods	Top-1 err.	Top-5 err.
Backprop on VGGnet [24]	61.12	51.46
Backprop on GoogLeNet [24]	61.31	50.55
AlexNet-GAP [44]	67.19	52.16
VGGnet-GAP [44]	57.20	45.14
GoogLeNet-GAP [44]	56.40	43.00
GoogLeNet-HaS-32 [26]	54.53	-
VGGnet-ACoL [43]	54.17	40.57
GoogLeNet-ACoL [43]	53.28	42.58
SPG-plain	53.71	41.81
SPG	51.40	40.00
SPG*	51.40	35.05

baseline methods on the ILSVRC 2016 dataset, as it has more than 1.2 million images of 1,000 classes for training. We report the accuracy on the *validation* set of 50,000 images. We also tested our algorithm on the bird dataset, CUB-200-2011 [31]. CUB-200-2011 contains 11,788 images of 200 categories with 5,994 images for training and 5,794 for testing. We leverage the localization metric suggested by [22]. An image has the right predicted bounding box if (1) it has the right prediction of image label; (2) and its predicted bounding box has more than 50% overlap with the ground-truth boxes.

Table 2. Localization error on CUB-200-2011 test set (* indicates methods which improve the Top-5 performance only using predictions with high scores).

Methods	Top-1 err.	Top-5 err.
GoogLeNet-GAP [44]	59.00	-
ACoL [43]	54.08	43.49
SPG-plain	56.33	46.47
SPG	53.36	42.28
SPG*	53.36	40.62

4.2   Comparison with the State-of-the-Arts

We compare the proposed SPG approach with the state-of-the-art methods on ILSVRC validation set and CUB-200-2011 test set.

Localization: Table 1 illustrates the localization error of various baseline algorithms on the ILSVRC *val* set. We observe that our baseline SPG-plain model achieves 53.71 and 41.81 of Top-1 and Top-5 localization error. Based on the

Table 3. Localization/Classification error on ILSVRC validation set with the state-of-the-art classification results.

Methods	Top-1 err.	Top-5 err.
GoogLeNet-SPG-ResNet-50	48.79/26.22	38.93/8.47
GoogLeNet-SPG-ResNet-101	48.15/24.90	38.55/7.80
GoogLeNet-SPG-ResNet-152	47.92/24.39	38.53/7.59
GoogLeNet-SPG-DPN-92	45.06/17.70	37.32/3.83
GoogLeNet-SPG-DPN-98	44.92/17.42	37.34/3.67
GoogLeNet-SPG-DPN-131	44.81/17.08	37.24/3.42
GoogLeNet-SPG-DPN-ensemble	43.83/15.47	36.78/2.70
GoogLeNet-SPG-DPN-ensemble*	43.83/15.47	29.36/2.70

SPG-plain network, the SPG strategy further reduces the localization error to Top-1 51.40 and Top-5 40.00. We illustrate the results on CUB-200-2011 in Table 2, the SPG approach achieves the localization error of Top-1 53.36%. Both results on ILSVRC and CUB outperform the state-of-the-art approach, ACoL [43] which applied two classifier branches to discover complementary object regions. Following the baseline methods [43,44], we boost the Top-5 localization error by repeatedly using the predicted bounding boxes with high classification scores. We select two bounding boxes from the top 1st and 2nd predicted classes, and one from the 3rd class. By this way, the Top-5 localization error (indicated by *) on ILSVRC is improved to 35.05%, and that on CUB-200-2011 is improved to 40.62%. To summarize, the improvement of the plain networks mainly attribute to the structure of the Inception-v3 network, which can capture larger object regions. The improvement of the SPG networks attribute to the use of the auxiliary supervision. SPG can encourage the classification network learn more pixel-level correlations, and as a result of this, the localization performance increases.

Localization performance is restricted by the classification accuracy, because the calculation of localization overlap only conducts on images which have the correct prediction of image-level labels. In order to break this limitation, we further improve the localization performance by combining our localization results with the state-of-the-art classification results, *i.e.*, ResNet [7] and DPN [2], As shown in Table 3, the localization performance constantly improves with the classification results getting better. When we use the classification results from the ensemble DPN method (ensemble of DPN-92, DPN-98 and DPN-131), which has very low classification error of Top-1 15.47% and Top-5 2.70%, the localization error decreases to Top-1 43.83% and Top-5 29.36%.

Figure 3 shows the attention maps as well as the predicted bounding boxes with the proposed SPG on ILSVRC and CUB-200-2011. Our proposed approach can highlight nearly the entire object regions and produce precise bounding boxes. Figure 4 visualizes the output of the multiple branches in generating the self-produced guidances. The attention maps generated from the classification network are leveraged to produce the seeds of foreground and background. We

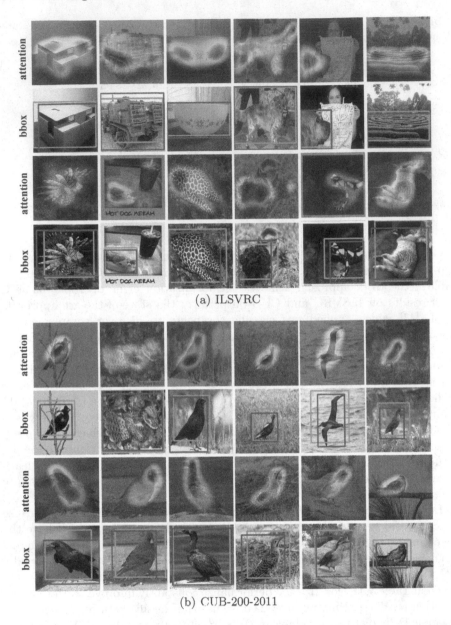

(a) ILSVRC

(b) CUB-200-2011

Fig. 3. Illustration of the attention maps and the predicted bounding boxes of SPG on ILSVRC and CUB-200-2011. The predicted bounding boxes are in green and the ground-truth boxes are in red. Best viewed in color.

can observe the seeds usually cover small region of the object and background pixels. The produced seed masks (Mask-A) are then utilized as supervision for the B2 branch. With such supervision information, B2 can learn more confident patterns of foreground and background pixels, and precisely predict the

Localization map   Mask-A   SPG-B2   SPG-B1   SPG-C

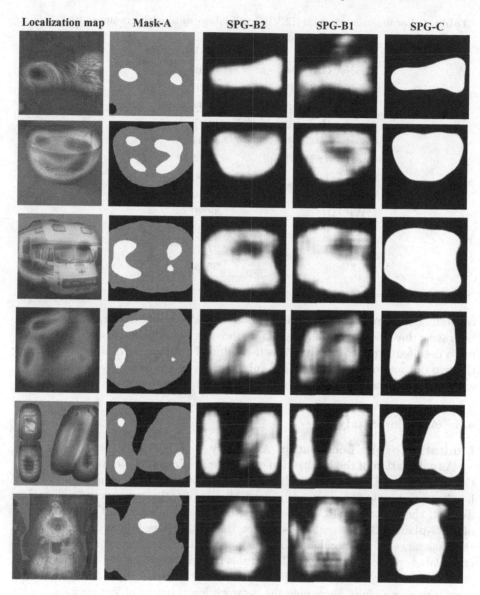

Fig. 4. Output maps of the proposed SPG approach. The localization maps usually only highlight small region of the object. We extract the seeds of the self-produced guidance by segmenting the confident regions of the localization maps as foreground (white) and background (black), and ignore the left regions (grey). These seeds are applied as supervision to learn better self-produced guidance maps. Finally, the learned maps are leveraged to encourage the network to improve the quality of the localization maps.

Table 4. Localization error on ILSVRC validation data with ground-truth labels.

Methods	GT-known loc. err.
AlexNet-GAP [44]	45.01
AlexNet-HaS [26]	41.26
AlexNet-GAP-ensemble [44]	42.98
AlexNet-HaS-emsemble [26]	39.67
GoogLeNet-GAP [44]	41.34
GoogLeNet-HaS [26]	39.43
Deconv [39]	41.60
Feedback [1]	38.80
MWP [41]	38.70
ACoL [43]	37.04
SPG-plain	37.32
SPG	**35.31**

remaining foreground/background regions where leave undefined in Mask-A. B1 leverages the lower level feature maps and the supervision from B2 to learn more detailed regions. Finally, the self-produced guidance is obtained by fusing the two outputs of B1 and B2. This guidance is used as auxiliary supervision to encourage the classification network learn better attention maps.

4.3   Ablation Study

Limitation of the Localization Accuracy

As calculation of the localization error rate is affected by network's classification performance. We compare the localization performance using ground-truth labels to eliminate the influence caused by classification accuracy As shown in Table 4, the proposed SPG outperforms the other approaches. The Top-1 error of SPG-plain is 37.32%, which is better than other baseline approaches. With the assistance of the auxiliary supervision, the localization error with ground-truth labels reduces to 35.31%. This reveals the superiority of the attention maps generated by our method, and shows that the proposed self-produced guidance maps can successfully encourage the network learn better object regions.

Effect of the Cascade Learning Strategy

In the proposed method, we learn the self-produced guidance maps in a two-stage way. The branch B2 is supervised by the guidance maps generated by the localization maps from SPG-A, while the branch B1 is supervised by self-produced guidance from the output of B2. In order to verify the effectiveness of this two-stage method, we break this structure and use the initial seed masks as supervision for the both branches. As a result, we obtain a higher Top-1 error rate of 35.58% when providing the ground-truth classification labels. So, we can conclude that the two-stage structure utilized in SPG-B is useful to generate better self-produced guidance maps, and it is more effective for generating better attention maps. Also, we find it is helpful to share the second and third layers of B1 and B2. By removing the shared setting, the localization *error rate* will increase from 35.31% to 36.31%.

Effect of the Auxiliary Supervision

We propose to use the self-produced guidance maps as a pixel-level auxiliary supervision to encourage the classification network to learn better localization maps using SPG-C. Thus, we remove SPG-C to test whether SPG-C influence the classification network. After removing SPG-C, the performance becomes worse with the Top-1 error rate of 36.06% on ILSVRC validation set when providing ground-truth labels. This reveals that the proposed self-produced guidance maps is effective to improve the quality of the localization maps by adding auxiliary supervision with SPG-C. It is notable that, the localization performance with only using SPG-B is still better than the plain version. So, the branches in SPG-B can also contribute to the improvement of localization accuracy.

5   Conclusions

In this paper, we proposed the Self-produced Guidance approach for locating target object regions given only image-level labels. The proposed approach can generate high-quality self-produced guidance maps for encouraging the classification network to learn pixel-level correlations. Thereby, the networks can detect much more object regions for localization. Extensive experiments show the proposed method can detect more object regions and outperform the state-of-the-art localization methods.

Acknowledgement. Xiaolin Zhang (No. 201606180026) is partially supported by the Chinese Scholarship Council. This work is partially supported by IBM-ILLINOIS Center for Cognitive Computing Systems Research (C3SR) - a research collaboration as part of the IBM AI Horizons Network. We acknowledge the Data to Decisions CRC (D2D CRC) and the Cooperative Research Centres Programme for funding this research.

References

1. Cao, C., et al.: Look and think twice: capturing top-down visual attention with feedback convolutional neural networks. In: Proceedings of the IEEE International Conference on Computer Vision, pp. 2956–2964 (2015)
2. Chen, Y., Li, J., Xiao, H., Jin, X., Yan, S., Feng, J.: Dual path networks. arXiv preprint arXiv:1707.01629 (2017)
3. Cheng, B., Wei, Y., Shi, H., Feris, R., Xiong, J., Huang, T.: Revisiting RCNN: on awakening the classification power of faster RCNN. In: ECCV (2018)
4. Diba, A., Sharma, V., Pazandeh, A., Pirsiavash, H., Van Gool, L.: Weakly supervised cascaded convolutional networks. arXiv preprint (2017)
5. Dong, X., Meng, D., Ma, F., Yang, Y.: A dual-network progressive approach to weakly supervised object detection. In: ACM Multimedia (2017)

6. Dong, X., Zheng, L., Ma, F., Yang, Y., Meng, D.: Few-example object detection with model communication. arXiv preprint arXiv:1706.08249 (2017)
7. He, K., Zhang, X., Ren, S., Sun, J.: Deep residual learning for image recognition. In: Proceedings of the IEEE Conference on Computer Vision and Pattern Recognition, pp. 770–778 (2016)
8. He, S., Jiao, J., Zhang, X., Han, G., Lau, R.W.: Delving into salient object subitizing and detection. In: 2017 IEEE International Conference on Computer Vision (ICCV), pp. 1059–1067. IEEE (2017)
9. Hou, Q., Cheng, M.M., Hu, X., Borji, A., Tu, Z., Torr, P.: Deeply supervised salient object detection with short connections. In: 2017 IEEE Conference on Computer Vision and Pattern Recognition (CVPR), pp. 5300–5309. IEEE (2017)
10. Jiang, H., Wang, J., Yuan, Z., Wu, Y., Zheng, N., Li, S.: Salient object detection: a discriminative regional feature integration approach. In: IEEE CVPR, pp. 2083–2090 (2013)
11. Jie, Z., Wei, Y., Jin, X., Feng, J., Liu, W.: Deep self-taught learning for weakly supervised object localization. In: IEEE CVPR (2018)
12. Krizhevsky, A., Sutskever, I., Hinton, G.E.: Imagenet classification with deep convolutional neural networks. In: NIPS, pp. 1097–1105 (2012)
13. Liang, X., Liu, S., Wei, Y., Liu, L., Lin, L., Yan, S.: Towards computational baby learning: a weakly-supervised approach for object detection. In: IEEE ICCV, pp. 999–1007 (2015)
14. Lin, M., Chen, Q., Yan, S.: Network in network. In: ICLR (2013)
15. Lin, T.Y., Dollár, P., Girshick, R., He, K., Hariharan, B., Belongie, S.: Feature pyramid networks for object detection. In: CVPR, vol. 1, p. 4 (2017)
16. Liu, W., et al.: SSD: single shot MultiBox detector. In: Leibe, B., Matas, J., Sebe, N., Welling, M. (eds.) ECCV 2016. LNCS, vol. 9905, pp. 21–37. Springer, Cham (2016). https://doi.org/10.1007/978-3-319-46448-0_2
17. Long, J., Shelhamer, E., Darrell, T.: Fully convolutional networks for semantic segmentation. In: IEEE CVPR (2015)
18. Luo, Y., Guan, T., Pan, H., Wang, Y., Yu, J.: Accurate localization for mobile device using a multi-planar city model. In: 2016 23rd International Conference on Pattern Recognition (ICPR), pp. 3733–3738. IEEE (2016)
19. Luo, Y., Zheng, Z., Zheng, L., Tao, G., Junqing, Y., Yang, Y.: Macro-micro adversarial network for human parsing. In: ECCV (2018)
20. Redmon, J., Divvala, S., Girshick, R., Farhadi, A.: You only look once: unified, real-time object detection. In: Proceedings of the IEEE Conference on Computer Vision and Pattern Recognition, pp. 779–788 (2016)
21. Ren, S., He, K., Girshick, R., Sun, J.: Faster R-CNN: towards real-time object detection with region proposal networks. In: Advances in Neural Information Processing Systems, pp. 91–99 (2015)
22. Russakovsky, O., et al.: ImageNetLarge scale visual recognition challenge. Int. J. Comput. Vis. (IJCV) 115(3), 211–252 (2015). https://doi.org/10.1007/s11263-015-0816-y
23. Sermanet, P., Eigen, D., Zhang, X., Mathieu, M., Fergus, R., LeCun, Y.: OverFeat: integrated recognition, localization and detection using convolutional networks. In: International Conference on Learning Representations (2014)
24. Simonyan, K., Vedaldi, A., Zisserman, A.: Deep inside convolutional networks: visualising image classification models and saliency maps. arXiv preprint arXiv:1312.6034 (2013)

25. Simonyan, K., Zisserman, A.: Very deep convolutional networks for large-scale image recognition. In: International Conference on Learning Representations (2015)
26. Singh, K.K., Lee, Y.J.: Hide-and-seek: forcing a network to be meticulous for weakly-supervised object and action localization. arXiv preprint arXiv:1704.04232 (2017)
27. Szegedy, C., et al.: Going deeper with convolutions. arXiv preprint arXiv:1409.4842 (2014)
28. Szegedy, C., et al.: Going deeper with convolutions. In: IEEE CVPR, pp. 1–9 (2015)
29. Szegedy, C., Vanhoucke, V., Ioffe, S., Shlens, J., Wojna, Z.: Rethinking the inception architecture for computer vision. In: Proceedings of the IEEE Conference on Computer Vision and Pattern Recognition, pp. 2818–2826 (2016)
30. Uijlings, J.R., van de Sande, K.E., Gevers, T., Smeulders, A.W.: Selective search for object recognition. IJCV **104**(2), 154–171 (2013)
31. Wah, C., Branson, S., Welinder, P., Perona, P., Belongie, S.: The Caltech-UCSD Birds-200-2011 Dataset. Technical report, CNS-TR-2011-001, California Institute of Technology (2011)
32. Wei, Y., Feng, J., Liang, X., Cheng, M.M., Zhao, Y., Yan, S.: Object region mining with adversarial erasing: a simple classification to semantic segmentation approach. In: IEEE CVPR (2018)
33. Wei, Y., et al.: Learning to segment with image-level annotations. Pattern Recognit. **59**, 234–244 (2016)
34. Wei, Y., et al.: STC: a simple to complex framework for weakly-supervised semantic segmentation. IEEE TPAMI **39**(11), 2314–2320 (2016)
35. Wei, Y., et al.: TS2C: tight box mining with surrounding segmentation context for weakly supervised object detection. In: ECCV (2018)
36. Wei, Y., Xiao, H., Shi, H., Jie, Z., Feng, J., Huang, T.S.: Revisiting dilated convolution: a simple approach for weakly-and semi-supervised semantic segmentation. In: IEEE CVPR, pp. 7268–7277 (2018)
37. Xiao, H., Wei, Y., Liu, Y., Zhang, M., Feng, J.: Transferable semi-supervised semantic segmentation. In: AAAI (2018)
38. Xie, S., Tu, Z.: Holistically-nested edge detection. In: Proceedings of the IEEE International Conference on Computer Vision, pp. 1395–1403 (2015)
39. Zeiler, M.D., Fergus, R.: Visualizing and understanding convolutional networks. In: Fleet, D., Pajdla, T., Schiele, B., Tuytelaars, T. (eds.) ECCV 2014. LNCS, vol. 8689, pp. 818–833. Springer, Cham (2014). https://doi.org/10.1007/978-3-319-10590-1_53
40. Zhang, H., Kyaw, Z., Yu, J., Chang, S.F.: PPR-FCN: weakly supervised visual relation detection via parallel pairwise R-FCN. In: IEEE ICCV (2017)
41. Zhang, J., Lin, Z., Brandt, J., Shen, X., Sclaroff, S.: Top-down neural attention by excitation backprop. In: Leibe, B., Matas, J., Sebe, N., Welling, M. (eds.) ECCV 2016. LNCS, vol. 9908, pp. 543–559. Springer, Cham (2016). https://doi.org/10.1007/978-3-319-46493-0_33
42. Zhang, Q., Jiao, J., Cao, Y., Lau, R.W.: Task-driven webpage saliency. In: ECCV (2018)
43. Zhang, X., Wei, Y., Feng, J., Yang, Y., Huang, T.: Adversarial complementary learning for weakly supervised object localization. In: IEEE CVPR (2018)
44. Zhou, B., Khosla, A., Lapedriza, A., Oliva, A., Torralba, A.: Learning deep features for discriminative localization. In: IEEE CVPR (2016)
45. Zhu, J., Mao, J., Yuille, A.L.: Learning from weakly supervised data by the expectation loss SVM (e-SVM) algorithm. In: NIPS, pp. 1125–1133 (2014)

Occlusions, Motion and Depth Boundaries with a Generic Network for Disparity, Optical Flow or Scene Flow Estimation

Eddy Ilg, Tonmoy Saikia[✉], Margret Keuper, and Thomas Brox

University of Freiburg, Freiburg im Breisgau, Germany
{ilg,saikia,keuper,brox}@cs.uni-freiburg.de

Abstract. Occlusions play an important role in disparity and optical flow estimation, since matching costs are not available in occluded areas and occlusions indicate depth or motion boundaries. Moreover, occlusions are relevant for motion segmentation and scene flow estimation. In this paper, we present an efficient learning-based approach to estimate occlusion areas jointly with disparities or optical flow. The estimated occlusions and motion boundaries clearly improve over the state-of-the-art. Moreover, we present networks with state-of-the-art performance on the popular KITTI benchmark and good generic performance. Making use of the estimated occlusions, we also show improved results on motion segmentation and scene flow estimation.

1 Introduction

When applying dense correspondences to higher level tasks, there is often the desire for additional information apart from the raw correspondences. The areas in one image that are occluded in the other image are important to get an indication of potentially unreliable estimates due to missing measurements. A typical approach to estimate occluded areas is by computing correspondences in both directions and verifying their consistency post-hoc. However, since occlusions and correspondences are mutually dependent [17,32] and the presence of occlusions already negatively influences the correspondence estimation itself, postprocessing is suboptimal and leads to unreliable occlusion estimates.

Another valuable extra information in disparity maps and flow fields are explicit depth and motion boundaries, respectively. Referring to the classic work of Black and Fleet [4], "motion boundaries may be useful for navigation, structure from motion, video compression, perceptual organization and object recognition".

E. Ilg and T. Saikia—Equal contribution.

Electronic supplementary material The online version of this chapter (https://doi.org/10.1007/978-3-030-01258-8_38) contains supplementary material, which is available to authorized users.

© Springer Nature Switzerland AG 2018
V. Ferrari et al. (Eds.): ECCV 2018, LNCS 11216, pp. 626–643, 2018.
https://doi.org/10.1007/978-3-030-01258-8_38

In this paper, we integrate occlusion estimation as well as depth or motion boundary estimation elegantly with a deep network for disparity or optical flow estimation based on FlowNet 2.0 [18] and provide these quantities explicitly as output. In contrast to many prior works, this leads to much improved occlusion and boundary estimates and much faster overall runtimes. We quantify this improvement directly by measuring the accuracy of the occlusions and motion boundaries. We also quantify the effect of this improved accuracy on motion segmentation.

Furthermore we improved on some details in the implementation of the disparity and optical flow estimation networks from [11,18,29], which gives us state-of-the-art results on the KITTI benchmarks. Moreover, the networks show good generic performance on various datasets if we do not fine-tune them to a particular scenario. While these are smaller technical contributions, they are very relevant for applications of optical flow and disparity. Finally, with state-of-the-art optical flow, disparity and occlusion estimates in place, we put everything together to achieve good scene flow performance at a high frame-rate, using only 2D motion information. Using our predicted occlusions as input, we present a network that learns to interpolate the occluded areas to avoid the erroneous or missing information when computing the motion compensated difference between two disparity maps for scene flow.

2   Related Work

Optical Flow Estimation with CNNs. Optical flow estimation based on deep learning was pioneered by Dosovitsky et al. [11], who presented an end-to-end trainable encoder-decoder network. The work has been improved by Ilg et al. [18], who introduced a stack of refinement networks. Ranjan and Black [34] focused on efficiency and proposed a much smaller network based on the coarse-to-fine principle. Sun et al. [42] extended this idea by introducing correlations at the different pyramid levels. Their network termed PWC-Net currently achieves state-of-the-art results. The coarse-to-fine approach, however, comes with the well-known limitation that the flow for small, fast-moving objects cannot be estimated. While this does not much affect the average errors of benchmarks, small objects can be very important for decisions in application scenarios.

Disparity Estimation with CNNs. For disparity estimation, Zbontar et al. [52] were the first to present a Siamese CNN for matching patches. Post-processing with the traditional SGM method [14] yielded disparity maps. Other approaches to augment SGM with CNNs were presented by [28,38]. The first end-to-end learning framework was presented by Mayer et al. [29]. The network named DispNetC was derived from the FlowNetC of Dosovitskiy et al. [11] restricted to rectified stereo images. It includes a correlation layer that yields a cost volume, which is further processed by the network. Kendall et al. [21] presented GC-Net, which uses 3D convolutions to process the cost volume also along the disparity dimension and by using a differentiable softargmin operation. Pang et al. [31] extended DispNetC by stacking a refinement network on top, similar to FlowNet 2.0 [18], with the difference that the second network is posed in a residual setting. In this work we also make use of network stacks with up to three networks and use their residual refinement.

Occlusion Estimation. Occlusion and optical flow estimation mutually depend on each other and are thus a typical chicken-and-egg problem [17,32]. Humayun et al. [16] determine occlusions post-hoc by training a classifier on a broad spectrum of visual features and precomputed optical flow. Pérez-Rúa et al. [32] do not require a dense optical flow field, but motion candidates, which are used to determine if a "plausible reconstruction" exists. Many other methods try to estimate optical flow and occlusions jointly. Leordeanu et al. [27] train a classifier based on various features, including the current motion estimate and use it repeatedly during energy minimization of the flow. Sun et al. [41] make use of superpixels and local layering for an energy formulation that is optimized jointly for layers, optical flow and occlusions. The most recent work from Hur et al. [17] uses consistency between forward and backward flows of two images, by integrating a corresponding constraint into an energy formulation. Since occlusions are directly related to changes in depth [12], it was quite common to consider them explicitly in disparity estimation methods [9,12,19,44].

In this paper, we show that training a network for occlusion estimation is clearly beneficial, especially if the trained network is combined with a network formulation of disparity or optical flow estimation. We do not try to disentangle the chicken-and-egg problem, but instead solve this problem using the joint training procedure.

Depth and Motion Boundary Estimation. In many energy minimization approaches, depth or motion boundary estimation is implicitly included in the form of robustness to outliers in the smoothness constraint. Typically, these boundaries are not made explicit. An exception is Black and Fleet [4], who estimate translational motion together with motion boundaries. Motion boundaries are also explicit in layered motion segmentation approaches. Most of these assume a precomputed optical flow, and only few estimate the segmentation and the flow jointly [8,40]. Leordeanu et al. [26] introduced a method for combined optimization of a boundary detector that also covers motion boundaries, while most other approaches make use of an external image boundary detector [1,10]. Sundberg et al. [43] use gPb [1] and LDOF [6] to compute motion differences between regions adjacent to image boundaries. Weinzaepfel et al. [49] use a structured random forest trained on appearance and motion cues. Lei et al. [25] present a fully convolutional Siamese network that is trained on annotated video segmentation. Using only the video segmentation ground-truth for training, they are able to infer the motion of boundary points during inference. For disparity and depth boundaries, the problem is very similar and most of the above mentioned methods could be applied to disparities, too. Jia et al. [20] infer depth boundaries from color and depth images with a Conditional Random Field. In this paper, we obtain depth and motion boundaries also by a joint training procedure and by joint refinement together with occlusions and disparity or flow.

Scene Flow Estimation. Scene flow estimation was popularized for the first time by the work of Vedula et al. [45] and was later dominated by variational methods [15,33,47]. Vogel et al. [46] combined the task of scene flow estimation with superpixel segmentation using a piecewise rigid model for regularization. Schuster et al. [37] proposed a variational approach to interpolate sparse scene flow estimates from sparse matches. Behl et al. [3] proposed a 3D scene flow method, which exploits instance recognition and 3D geometry information to obtain improved performance in texture-less, reflective and fast moving regions.

In this paper, we investigate scene flow estimation based on estimating correspondences only, without the use of 3D geometry information. The only learning based approach in a similar setting was proposed by Mayer et al. [29], but did not perform similarly well.

3   Network Architectures

We investigate estimating occlusions and depth or motion boundaries with CNNs together with disparity and optical flow. To this end, we build upon the convolutional encoder-decoder architectures from FlowNet [11] and the stacks from FlowNet 2.0 [18]. Our modifications are shown in Fig. 1(a). For simplicity, in the following we mention the flow case. The disparity case is analogous.

In our version of [18], we leave away the small displacement network. In fact, the experiments from our re-implemented version show that the stack can perform well on small displacements without it. We still keep the former fusion network as it also performs smoothing and sharpening (see Fig. 1(a)). We denote this network by the letter "R" in network names (e.g. FlowNet-CSSR). This network is only for refinement and does not see the second image. We further modify the stack by integrating the suggestion of Pang et al. [31] and add residual connections to the refinement networks. As in [18], we also input the warped images, but omit the brightness error inputs, as these can easily be computed by the network.

Finally, we add the occlusions and depth or motion boundaries. While occlusions are important for refinement from the beginning, boundaries are only required in later refinement stages. Therefore we add the boundaries in the third network. Experimentally, we also found that when adding depth or motion boundary prediction in earlier networks, these networks predicted details better, but failed more rigorously in case of errors. Predicting exact boundaries early would be contrary to the concept of a refinement pipeline.

Generally, in an occluded area, the forward flow from the first to the second image does not match the backward flow from the second to the first image. If the forward flow is correctly interpolated into the occluded regions, it resembles the flow of the background object. Since this object is not visible in the second image, the backward flow of the target location is from another object and forward and backward flows are inconsistent. Many classical methods use this fact to determine occlusions.

We bring this into the network architecture from Fig. 1(b). In this version, we let the network estimate forward and backward flows and occlusions jointly.

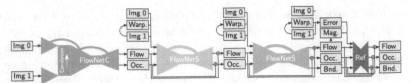

(a) Extension of FlowNet2 with occlusions and residual connections.

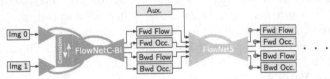

(b) Architecture for joint estimation of forward/backward flows and occlusions. See figure caption for symbol explanation.

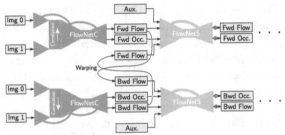

(c) Dual forward and backward estimation architecture with mutual warping. See figure caption for symbol explanation.

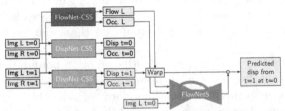

(d) Extending FlowNet-CSS and DispNet-CSS to a full scene flow network.

Fig. 1. Overview of possible refinement stacks for flow, occlusions and motion boundaries. The residual connections are only shown in the first figure and indicated by + elsewhere. Aux. refers to the images plus a warped image for each input flow, respectively. Architectures for the disparity case are analogous.

Therefore we modify FlowNetC to include a second correlation that takes a feature vector from the second image and computes the correlations to a neighborhood in the first image. We concatenate the outputs and also add a second skip connection for the second image. This setup is shown as FlowNetC-Bi in

Fig. 1(b). Throughout the stack, we then estimate flow and occlusions in forward and backward directions.

In the third variant from Fig. 1(c), we model forward and backward flow estimation as separate streams and perform mutual warping to the other direction after each network. E.g., we warp the estimated backward flow after the first network to the coordinates of the first image using the forward flow. Subsequently we flip the sign of the warped flow, effectively turning it into a forward flow. The network then has the forward and the corresponding backward flow at the same pixel position as input.

Finally, we use our networks for flow and disparity to build a scene flow extension. For the scene flow task, the disparity at $t = 0$ is required and the flow is extended by disparity change [29] (resembling the change in the third coordinate). To compute this disparity change, one can estimate disparities at $t = 1$, warp them to $t = 0$ and compute the difference. However, the warping will be incorrect or undefined everywhere, where an occlusion is present. We therefore add the network shown in Fig. 1(d) to learn a meaningful interpolation for these areas given the warped disparity, the occlusions and the image.

4 Experiments

4.1 Training Data

For training our flow networks, we use the FlyingChairs [11], FlyingThings3D [29] and ChairsSDHom [18] datasets. For training the disparity networks, we only use the FlyingThings3D [29] dataset. These datasets do not provide the ground-truth required for our setting per-se. For FlyingChairs, using the code provided by the authors of [11], we recreate the whole dataset including also backward flows, motion boundaries and occlusions. For FlyingThings3D, depth and motion boundaries are directly provided. We use flow and object IDs to determine occlusions. For ChairsSDHom, we compute motion boundaries by finding discontinuities among object IDs and in the flow, by using a flow magnitude difference threshold of 0.75. To determine the ground-truth occlusions, we also use the flow and the object IDs.

4.2 Training Schedules and Settings

For training our networks, we also follow the data and learning rate schedules of FlowNet 2.0 [18]. We train the stack network by network, always fixing the already trained networks. Contrary to [18], for each step we only use half the number of iterations. The initial network is then a bit worse, but it turns out that the refinement can compensate for it well. We also find that the residual networks converge much faster. Therefore, we train each new network on the stack for $600k$ iterations on FlyingChairs and for $250k$ iterations on FlyingThings3D. Optionally, we follow the same fine-tuning procedure for small-displacements on ChairsSDHom as in [18] (we add "-ft-sd" to the network names in this case).

Table 1. Training a FlowNetS to estimate occluded regions from different inputs. Since Sintel [7] does not provide the ground-truth backward flow, we additionally report numbers on FlyingThings3D [29]. The results show that contrary to literature [16, 27,32], occlusion estimation is even possible from just the two images. Providing the optical flow, too, clearly improves the results

Input	F-measure	
	FlyingThings3D [29]	Sintel clean [7]
Images 0+1	0.790	0.545
Images 0+1, GT fwd Flow	0.932	**0.653**
Images 0+1, GT fwd Flow, GT bwd flow	0.930	-
Images 0+1, GT fwd Flow, GT bwd flow warped+flipped	**0.943**	-
Images 0+1, GT fwd Flow, GT fwd/bwd consistency	**0.943**	-

We use the caffe framework and the same settings as in [18], with one minor modification: we found that numerically scaling the ground truth flow vectors (by a factor of $\frac{1}{20}$) yields noise for small displacements during optimization. We propose to change this factor to 1. Since these are all minor modifications, we present details in the supplemental material.

To train for flow and disparity, we use the normal EPE loss. For small displacement training we also apply the suggested non-linearity of [18]. To train for occlusions and depth or motion boundaries, we use a normal cross entropy loss with classes 0 and 1 applied to each pixel. To combine multiple losses of different kind, we balance their coefficients during the beginning of the training, such that their magnitudes are approximately equal.

4.3 Estimating Occlusions with CNNs

We first ran some basic experiments on estimating occlusions with a FlowNetS architecture and the described ground truth data. In the past, occlusion estimation was closely coupled with optical flow estimation and in the literature is stated as "notoriously difficult" [27] and a chicken-and-egg problem [17,32]. However, before we come to joint estimation of occlusions and disparity or optical flow, we start with a network that estimates occlusions independently of the optical flow or with optical flow being provided as input.

In the most basic case, we only provide the two input images to the network and no optical flow, i.e., the network must figure out by itself on how to use the relationship between the two images to detect occluded areas. As a next step, we additionally provide the ground-truth forward optical flow to the network, to see if a network is able to use flow information to find occluded areas. Since a classical way to detect occlusions is by checking the consistency between the

Table 2. Joint estimation of flow and occlusions with a FlowNetC from Sintel train clean. Estimating occlusions neither improves nor degrades flow performance

Configuration	EPE	F-measure
FlowNetC estimating flow	3.21	-
FlowNetC estimating occlusions	-	**0.546**
FlowNetC estimating flow + occlusions	**3.20**	0.539
FlowNetC-Bi estimating fwd/bwd flow and fwd occlusions	3.26	0.542

forward and the backward flow as mentioned in Sect. 3, we provide different versions of the backward flow: (1) backward flow directly; (2) using the forward flow to warp the backward flow to the first image and flipping its sign (effectively turning the backward flow into a forward flow up to the occluded areas); (3) providing the magnitude of the sum of forward and backward flows, i.e., the classical approach to detect occlusions. From the results of these experiments in Table 1, we conclude:

Occlusion Estimation without Optical Flow is Possible. In contrast to existing literature, where classifiers are always trained with flow input [16,26, 27,32] or occlusions are estimated jointly with optical flow [17,41], we show that a deep network can learn to estimate the occlusions directly from two images.

Using the Flow as Input Helps. The flow provides the solution for correspondences and the network uses these correspondences. Clearly, this helps, particularly since we provided the correct optical flow.

Adding the Backward Flow Marginally Improves Results. Providing the backward flow directly does not help. This can be expected, because the information for a pixel of the backward flow is stored at the target location of the forward flow and a look-up is difficult for a network to perform. Warping the backward flow or providing the forward/backward consistency helps a little.

4.4   Joint Estimation of Occlusions and Optical Flow

Within a Single Network. In this section we investigate estimating occlusions jointly with optical flow, as many classical methods try to do [17,41]. Here, we provide only the image pair and therefore can use a FlowNetC instead of a FlowNetS. The first row of Table 2 shows that just occlusion estimation with a FlowNetC performs similar to the FlowNetS of the last section. Surprisingly, from rows one to three of Table 2 we find that joint flow estimation neither improves nor deproves the flow or the occlusion quality. In row four of the table we additionally estimate the backward flow to enable the network to reason about forward/backward consistency. However, we find that this also does not affect performance much.

When finding correspondences, occlusions need to be regarded by deciding that no correspondence exists for an occluded pixel and by filling the occlusion

Table 3. Results of refinement stacks on Sintel train clean. Simply adding occlusions in a straightforward manner performs better or similar to more complicated approaches. In general, adding occlusions does not perform better than estimating only flow

Configuration	EPE	F-measure
Only flow as in FlowNet2-CS [18]	2.28	-
+ occlusions (Fig. 1(a))	**2.25**	**0.590**
+ bwd direction (Fig. 1(b))	2.77	0.572
+ mutual warping (Fig. 1(c))	2.25	0.589

Table 4. Comparison of estimated disparity occlusions from our DispNet-CSS to other methods on examples from the Middlebury 2001 and 2003 datasets (results of Kolmogorov et al. [24] and Tan et al. [44] taken from [44]) and the Sintel train dataset. Only in the scene Teddy of Middlebury our occlusions are outperformed by Kolmogorov et al. [24]

Method	F-Measure					
	Cones	Teddy	Tsukuba	Venus	Sintel clean	Sintel final
Kolmogorov et al. [24]	0.45	**0.63**	0.60	0.41	-	-
Tan et al. [44]	0.44	0.40	0.50	0.33	-	-
Ours	**0.91**	0.57	**0.68**	**0.44**	**0.76**	**0.72**

area with some value inferred from the surroundings. Therefore, knowledge about occlusions is mandatory for correspondence and correct flow estimation. Since making the occlusion estimation in our network explicit does not change the result, we conclude that an end-to-end trained network for only flow already implicitly performs all necessary occlusion reasoning. By making it explicit, we obtain the occlusions as an additional output at no cost, but the flow itself remains unaffected.

4.5   With a Refinement Network

In the last section we investigated the joint estimation of flow and occlusions, which in the literature is referred to as a "chicken-and-egg" problem. With our first network already estimating flow and occlusions, we investigate if the estimated occlusions can help refine the flow ("if a chicken can come from an egg").

To this end, we investigate the three proposed architectures from Sect. 2. We show the results of the three variants in Table 3. While the architectures from Fig. 1(a) and (c) are indifferent about the additional occlusion input, the architecture with joint forward and backward estimation performs worse.

Overall, we find that providing explicit occlusion estimates to the refinement does not help compared to estimating just the optical flow. This means, either the occluded areas are already filled correctly by the base network, or

Table 5. Comparison of the occlusions from FlowNet-CSSR-ft-sd to other occlusion estimation methods on the Sintel train dataset. For the first entry, occlusions were computed using forward/backward consistency post-hoc. The proposed approach yields much better occlusions

Method	Type	F-Measure	
		Clean	Final
FlowNet2 [18]	Consistency	0.377	0.348
MirrorFlow [17]	Estimated	0.390	0.348
S2DFlow [27]	Estimated	0.470	0.403
Ours	Estimated	**0.703**	**0.654**

in a stack without explicit occlusion estimation, the second network can easily recover occlusions from the flow and does not require the explicit input.

We finally conclude that occlusions can be obtained at no extra cost, but do not actually influence the flow estimation, and that it is best to leave the inner workings to the optimization by using only the baseline variant (Fig. 1(a)). This is contrary to the findings from classical methods.

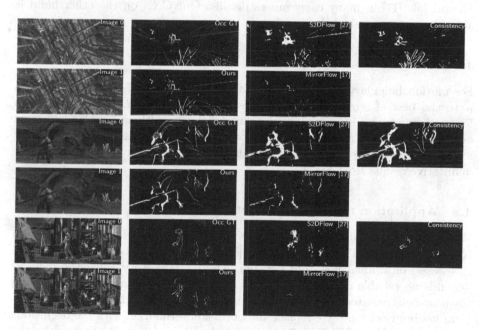

Fig. 2. Qualitative results for occlusions. In comparison to other methods and the forward-backward consistency check, our method is able to capture very fine details.

Table 6. Comparison of our motion boundary estimation to Weinzaepfel et al. [49] on the Sintel train dataset. The table shows the mean average precision computed with their evaluation code. Although Weinzaepfel et al. [49] trained on Sintel train clean, our method outperforms theirs by a large margin

Method	Sintel clean	Sintel final
Weinzaepfel et al. [49]	76.3	68.5
Ours	**86.3**	**79.5**

4.6   Comparing Occlusion Estimation to Other Methods

In Tables 4 and 5 we compare our occlusion estimations to other methods. For disparity our method outperforms Kolmogorov et al. [24] for all except one scene. For the more difficult case of optical flow, we outperform all existing methods by far. This shows that the chicken-and-egg problem of occlusion estimation is much easier to handle with a CNN than with classical approaches [17,24,27,44] and that CNNs can perform very well at occlusion reasoning. This is confirmed by the qualitative results of Fig. 2. While consistency checking is able to capture mainly large occlusion areas, S2DFlow [27] also manages to find some details. MirrorFlow [17] in many cases misses details. Our CNN on the other hand is able to estimate most of the fine details.

4.7   Motion Boundary Estimation

For motion boundary estimation we compare to Weinzaepfel et al. [49], which is to the best of our knowledge the best available method. It uses a random forest classifier and is trained on the Sintel dataset. Although we do not train on Sintel, from the results of Table 6, our CNN outperforms their method by a large margin. The improvement in quality is also very well visible from the qualitative results from Fig. 3.

4.8   Application to Motion Segmentation

We apply the estimated occlusions to the motion segmentation framework from Keuper et al. [22]. This approach, like [5], computes long-term point trajectories based on optical flow. For deciding when a trajectory ends, the method depends on reliable occlusion estimates. These are commonly computed using the post-hoc consistency of forward and backward flow, which was shown to perform badly in Sect. 4.6. We replace the occlusion estimation with the occlusions from our FlowNet-CSS. Table 7 shows the clear improvements obtained by the more reliable occlusion estimates on the common FBMS-59 motion segmentation benchmark. In row four, we show how adding our occlusions to flow estimations of FlowNet2 can improve results. This shows that by only adding occlusions, we recover 30 objects instead of 26. The last result from our flow and occlusions

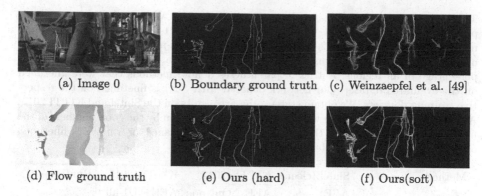

(a) Image 0   (b) Boundary ground truth   (c) Weinzaepfel et al. [49]

(d) Flow ground truth   (e) Ours (hard)   (f) Ours(soft)

Fig. 3. Motion boundaries on Sintel train clean. Our approach succeeds to detect the object in the background and has less noise around motion edges than existing approaches (see green arrows). Weinzaepfel et al. detect some correct motion details in the background. However, these details are not captured in the ground-truth. (Color figure online)

Table 7. Results of motion segmentation from Keuper et al. [22] on the FBMS-59 test set [5,30] (with sampling density 8px). The fourth row uses flows from FlowNet2 [18] combined with our occlusions. The improved results show that occlusions help the motion segmentation in general. The last row shows the segmentation using our flow and occlusions, which performs best and also improves over the recent state-of-the-art on sparse motion segmentation using higher order motion models [23]

Method	FBMS test set (30 sequences)			
	Precision	Recall	F-Measure	#Objects
Third order multicut [23]	87.77%	71.96%	79.08%	29/69
DeepFlow [48]	88.20%	69.39%	77.67%	26/69
FlowNet2	86.73%	68.77%	76.71%	26/69
FlowNet2 + our occ	85.67%	70.15%	77.14%	30/69
Ours	**88.71%**	**73.60%**	**80.45%**	**31/69**

together further improve the results. Besides the direct quantitative and qualitative evaluation from the last sections, this shows the usefulness of our occlusion estimates in a relevant application. Our final results can produce results that are even better than the ones generated by the recently proposed third order motion segmentation with multicuts [23].

4.9 Benchmark Results for Disparity, Optical Flow, and Scene Flow

Finally, we show that besides the estimated occlusions and depth and motion boundaries, our disparities and optical flow achieve state-of-the-art performance. In Table 8 we show results for the common disparity benchmarks. We also present smaller versions of our networks by scaling the number of channels in each layer

Table 8. Benchmark results for **disparity estimation**. We report the average end-point error (AAE) for Sintel. On KITTI, Out-noc and D1-all are used for the bench-mark ranking on KITTI 2012 and 2015, respectively. Out-noc shows the percentage of outliers with errors more than 3px in non-occluded regions, whereas D1-all shows the percentage in all regions. Entries in parentheses denote methods that were finetuned on the evaluated dataset. Our network denoted with "-ft" is finetuned on the respec-tive training datasets. We obtain state-of-the-art results on the Sintel and KITTI 2015. Also, our networks generalize well across domains, as shown by the good numbers of the non-finetuned networks and the reduced drop in performance for a network finetuned on KITTI and tested on Sintel

Method	Sintel (clean)	KITTI (2012)		KITTI (2015)		Runtime *(s)*
	AEE	AEE	Out-noc	AEE	D1-all	
	train	*train*	*test*	*train*	*test*	
Standard						
SGM [14]	19.62	10.06	-	7.21	10.86%	1.1
CNN based						
DispNetC [29]	5.66	1.75	-	1.59	-	0.06
DispNetC-ft [29]	21.88	1.48	4.11%	(0.68)	4.34%	0.06
CRL [31]	16.13	1.11	-	(0.52)	2.67%	0.47
GC-Net [21]	-	-	**1.77%**	-	2.87%	0.90
MC-CNN-acrt [52]	-	-	2.43%	-	3.89%	67
DRR [13]	-	-	-	-	3.16%	0.4
L-ResMatch [39]	-	-	2.27%	-	3.42%	42
With joint occ. est.						
SPS stereo [51]	-	-	3.39%	-	5.31%	2
Our DispNet-CSS	**2.33**	1.40	-	1.37	-	0.07
Our DispNet-CSS-ft	5.53	(0.72)	1.82%	(0.71)	**2.19%**	0.07
Our DispNet-css	2.95	1.53	-	1.49	-	0.03

down to 37.5% as suggested in [18] (denoted by css). While this small ver-sion yields a good speed/accuracy trade-off, the larger networks rank second on KITTI 2015 and are the top ranked methods on KITTI 2012 and Sintel.

In Table 9 we show the benchmark results for optical flow. We perform on-par on Sintel, while we set the new state-of-the-art on both KITTI datasets.

In Table 10 we report numbers on the KITTI 2015 scene flow benchmark. The basic scene flow approach warps the next frame disparity maps into the current frame (see [36]) using forward flow. Out of frame occluded pixels cannot be estimated this way. To mitigate this problem we train a CNN to reason about disparities in occluded regions (see the architecture from Fig. 1(d)). This yields clearly improved results that get close to the state-of-the-art while the approach is orders of magnitude faster.

Table 9. Benchmark results for **optical flow estimation**. We report the average end-point error (AAE) for all benchmarks, except KITTI, where Out-noc and F1-all are used for the benchmark ranking on KITTI 2012 and 2015, respectively. Out-noc shows the percentage of outliers with errors more than 3px in non-occluded regions, whereas F1-all shows the percentage in all regions. Entries in parentheses denote methods that were finetuned on the evaluated dataset. On the Sintel dataset, the performance of our networks is on par with FlowNet2. When comparing to other methods with joint occlusion estimation we are faster by multiple orders of magnitude. On KITTI 2012 and 2015 we obtain state-of-the-art results among all optical flow methods (two frame, non-stereo)

Method	Sintel (clean)		Sintel (final)		KITTI (2012)		KITTI (2015)		Runtime (s)
	AEE		AEE		AEE	OUT-noc	AEE	$F1$-all	
	train	test	train	test	train	test	train	test	
Standard									
EpicFlow [35]	2.27	4.12	3.56	6.29	**3.09**	7.88%	9.27	26.29%	42
FlowfieldsCNN [2]	-	3.78	-	5.36	-	4.89%	-	18.68%	23
DCFlow [50]	-	**3.54**	-	5.12	-	-	-	14.86%	9
CNN based									
FlowNet2 [18]	**2.02**	3.96	**3.14**	6.02	4.09	-	10.06	-	0.123
FlowNet2-ft [18]	(1.45)	4.16	(2.01)	5.74	(1.28)	-	(2.30)	11.48%	0.123
SpyNet [34]	4.12	6.69	5.57	8.43	9.12	-	-	-	**0.016**
SpyNet-ft [34]	(3.17)	6.64	(4.32)	8.36	(4.13)	12.31%	-	35.07%	**0.016**
PWC-Net [42]	2.55	-	3.93	-	4.14	-	10.35	33.67%	0.030
PWC-Net-ft [42]	(2.02)	4.39	(2.08)	**5.04**	-	4.22%	(2.16)	9.80%	0.030
With joint occ est.									
MirrorFlow [17]	-	3.32	-	6.07	-	4.38%	-	10.29%	660
S2D flow [27]	-	18.48	-	6.82	-	-	-	-	2280
Our FlowNet-CSS	2.08	3.94	3.61	6.03	3.69	-	**9.33**	-	0.068
Our FlowNet-CSS-ft	(1.47)	4.35	(2.12)	5.67	(1.19)	**3.45%**	(1.79)	**8.60%**	0.068
Our FlowNet-css	2.65	-	4.05	-	5.05	-	11.74		0.033

Table 10. Benchmark results for **scene flow estimation**. "Interp." means the disparity values were automatically interpolated by the KITTI benchmark suite in the sparse regions. Compared to [37] we obtain much improved results and close the performance gap to much slower state-of-the-art methods, such as [3], which use 2D information by a large margin

Method	D1-all	D2-all	Fl-all	SF-all	Runtime (s)
ISF [3]	4.46	5.95	6.22	8.08	600
SGM+FlowFields (interp.) [36]	13.37	27.80	22.82	33.57	29
SceneFFields (dense) [37]	6.57	10.69	12.88	15.78	65
Ours (interp.)	2.16	13.71	8.60	17.73	0.22
Ours (dense)	2.16	6.45	8.60	11.34	0.25

5 Conclusion

We have shown that, in contrast to traditional methods, CNNs can very easily estimate occlusions and depth or motion boundaries, and that their performance surpasses traditional approaches by a large margin. While classical methods often use the backward flow to determine occlusions, we have shown that a simple extension from the forward FlowNet 2.0 stack performs best in the case of CNNs. We have also shown that this generic network architecture performs well on the tasks of disparity and flow estimation itself and yields state-of-the-art results on benchmarks. Finally, we have shown that the estimated occlusions can significantly improve motion segmentation.

Acknowledgements. We acknowledge funding by the EU Horizon2020 project Trim-Bot2020 and by Gala Sports, and donation of a GPU server by Facebook. Margret Keuper acknowledges funding by DFG grant KE 2264/1-1.

References

1. Arbelaez, P., Maire, M., Fowlkes, C., Malik, J.: Contour detection and hierarchical image segmentation. PAMI **33**(5), 898–916 (2011)
2. Bailer, C., Varanasi, K., Stricker, D.: CNN-based patch matching for optical flow with thresholded hinge embedding loss. In: CVPR (2017)
3. Behl, A., Jafari, O.H., Mustikovela, S.K., Alhaija, H.A., Rother, C., Geiger, A.: Bounding boxes, segmentations and object coordinates: how important is recognition for 3D scene flow estimation in autonomous driving scenarios? In: International Conference on Computer Vision (ICCV) (2017)
4. Black, M.J., Fleet, D.J.: Probabilistic detection and tracking of motion boundaries. Int. J. Comput. Vis. **38**(3), 231–245 (2000)
5. Brox, T., Malik, J.: Object segmentation by long term analysis of point trajectories. In: Daniilidis, K., Maragos, P., Paragios, N. (eds.) ECCV 2010. LNCS, vol. 6315, pp. 282–295. Springer, Heidelberg (2010). https://doi.org/10.1007/978-3-642-15555-0_21
6. Brox, T., Malik, J.: Large displacement optical flow: descriptor matching in variational motion estimation. PAMI **33**(3), 500–513 (2011)
7. Butler, D.J., Wulff, J., Stanley, G.B., Black, M.J.: A naturalistic open source movie for optical flow evaluation. In: Fitzgibbon, A., Lazebnik, S., Perona, P., Sato, Y., Schmid, C. (eds.) ECCV 2012. LNCS, vol. 7577, pp. 611–625. Springer, Heidelberg (2012). https://doi.org/10.1007/978-3-642-33783-3_44
8. Cheng, J., Tsai, Y.H., Wang, S., Yang, M.H.: SegFlow: joint learning for video object segmentation and optical flow (2017)
9. Deng, Y., Yang, Q., Lin, X., Tang, X.: Stereo correspondence with occlusion handling in a symmetric patch-based graph-cuts model (2007)
10. Dollár, P., Zitnick, C.L.: Structured forests for fast edge detection (2013)
11. Dosovitskiy, A., et al.: FlowNet: learning optical flow with convolutional networks. In: IEEE International Conference on Computer Vision (ICCV) (2015)
12. Geiger, D., Ladendorf, B., Yuille, A.: Occlusions and binocular stereo. IJCV **14**(3), 211–226 (1995)

13. Gidaris, S., Komodakis, N.: Detect, replace, refine: deep structured prediction for pixel wise labeling. In: IEEE Conference on Computer Vision and Pattern Recognition (CVPR) (2017)
14. Hirschmüller, H.: Stereo processing by semiglobal matching and mutual information. PAMI **30**(2), 328–341 (2008)
15. Huguet, F., Devernay, F.: A variational method for scene flow estimation from stereo sequences. In: 2007 IEEE 11th International Conference on Computer Vision, pp. 1–7, October 2007. https://doi.org/10.1109/ICCV.2007.4409000
16. Humayun, A., Aodha, O.M., Brostow, G.J.: Learning to find occlusion regions. In: IEEE Conference on Computer Vision and Pattern Recognition (CVPR) (2011)
17. Hur, J., Roth, S.: MirrorFlow: exploiting symmetries in joint optical flow and occlusion estimation (2017)
18. Ilg, E., Mayer, N., Saikia, T., Keuper, M., Dosovitskiy, A., Brox, T.: FlowNet 2.0: evolution of optical flow estimation with deep networks. In: IEEE Conference on Computer Vision and Pattern Recognition (CVPR) (2017)
19. Ishikawa, H., Geiger, D.: Global optimization using embedded graphs (2000)
20. Jia, Z., Gallagher, A., Chen, T.: Learning boundaries with color and depth (2013)
21. Kendall, A., et al.: End-to-end learning of geometry and context for deep stereo regression (2017)
22. Keuper, M., Andres, B., Brox, T.: Motion trajectory segmentation via minimum cost multicuts. In: ICCV (2015)
23. Keuper, M.: Higher-order minimum cost lifted multicuts for motion segmentation. In: The IEEE International Conference on Computer Vision (ICCV), October 2017
24. Kolmogorov, V., Monasse, P., Tan, P.: Kolmogorov and Zabih's graph cuts stereo matching algorithm. Image Process. Line **4**, 220–251 (2014). https://doi.org/10.5201/ipol.2014.97. https://hal-enpc.archivesouvertes.fr/hal-01074878
25. Lei, P., Li, F., Todorovic, S.: Joint spatio-temporal boundary detection and boundary flow prediction with a fully convolutional siamese network. In: CVPR (2018)
26. Leordeanu, M., Sukthankar, R., Sminchisescu, C.: Efficient closed-form solution to generalized boundary detection. In: Fitzgibbon, A., Lazebnik, S., Perona, P., Sato, Y., Schmid, C. (eds.) ECCV 2012. LNCS, vol. 7575, pp. 516–529. Springer, Heidelberg (2012). https://doi.org/10.1007/978-3-642-33765-9_37
27. Leordeanu, M., Zanfir, A., Sminchisescu, C.: Locally affine sparse-to-dense matching for motion and occlusion estimation. In: IEEE International Conference on Computer Vision (ICCV) (2013)
28. Luo, W., Schwing, A.G., Urtasun, R.: Efficient deep learning for stereo matching (2016)
29. Mayer, N., et al.: A large dataset to train convolutional networks for disparity, optical flow, and scene flow estimation. In: IEEE Conference on Computer Vision and Pattern Recognition (CVPR) (2016)
30. Ochs, P., Malik, J., Brox, T.: Segmentation of moving objects by long term video analysis. IEEE TPAMI **36**(6), 1187–1200 (2014)
31. Pang, J., Sun, W., Ren, J.S.J., Yang, C., Yan, Q.: Cascade residual learning: a two-stage convolutional neural network for stereo matching. In: IEEE International Conference on Computer Vision (ICCV) Workshop (2017)
32. Perez-Rua, J.M., Crivelli, T., Bouthemy, P., Perez, P.: Determining occlusions from space and time image reconstructions. In: IEEE Conference on Computer Vision and Pattern Recognition (CVPR) (2016)

33. Quiroga, J., Brox, T., Devernay, F., Crowley, J.: Dense semi-rigid scene flow estimation from RGBD images. In: Fleet, D., Pajdla, T., Schiele, B., Tuytelaars, T. (eds.) ECCV 2014. LNCS, vol. 8695, pp. 567–582. Springer, Cham (2014). https://doi.org/10.1007/978-3-319-10584-0_37. https://hal.inria.fr/hal-01021925

34. Ranjan, A., Black, M.: Optical flow estimation using a spatial pyramid network. In: IEEE Conference on Computer Vision and Pattern Recognition (CVPR) (2017)

35. Revaud, J., Weinzaepfel, P., Harchaoui, Z., Schmid, C.: EpicFlow: edge-preserving interpolation of correspondences for optical flow. In: IEEE Conference on Computer Vision and Pattern Recognition (CVPR) (2015)

36. Schuster, R., Bailer, C., Wasenmüller, O., Stricker, D.: Combining stereo disparity and optical flow for basic scene flow. In: Berns, K. (ed.) Commercial Vehicle Technology 2018, pp. 90–101. Springer, Wiesbaden (2018). https://doi.org/10.1007/978-3-658-21300-8_8

37. Schuster, R., Wasenmüller, O., Kuschk, G., Bailer, C., Stricker, D.: SceneFlowFields: dense interpolation of sparse scene flow correspondences. In: IEEE Winter Conference on Applications of Computer Vision (WACV) (2018)

38. Seki, A., Pollefeys, M.: SGM-Nets: semi-global matching with neural networks (2017)

39. Shaked, A., Wolf, L.: Improved stereo matching with constant highway networks and reflective confidence learning. In: IEEE Conference on Computer Vision and Pattern Recognition (CVPR) (2017)

40. Sun, D., Liu, C., Pfister, H.: Local layering for joint motion estimation and occlusion detection (2014)

41. Sun, D., Liu, C., Pfister, H.: Local layering for joint motion estimation and occlusion detection. In: IEEE Conference on Computer Vision and Pattern Recognition (CVPR) (2014)

42. Sun, D., Yang, X., Liu, M.Y., Kautz, J.: PWC-Net: CNNs for optical flow using pyramid, warping, and cost volume. In: CVPR (2018)

43. Sundberg, P., Brox, T., Maire, M., Arbeláez, P., Malik, J.: Occlusion boundary detection and figure/ground assignment from optical flow. In: IEEE Conference on Computer Vision and Pattern Recognition (CVPR) (2011)

44. Tan, P., Chambolle, A., Monasse, P.: Occlusion detection in dense stereo estimation with convex optimization. In: 2017 IEEE International Conference on Image Processing (ICIP), pp. 2543–2547, September 2017. https://doi.org/10.1109/ICIP.2017.8296741

45. Vedula, S., Baker, S., Rander, P., Collins, R., Kanade, T.: Three-dimensional scene flow. IEEE Trans. Pattern Anal. Mach. Intell. **27**(3), 475–480 (2005). https://doi.org/10.1109/TPAMI.2005.63

46. Vogel, C., Schindler, K., Roth, S.: Piecewise rigid scene flow. In: 2013 IEEE International Conference on Computer Vision, pp. 1377–1384, December 2013. https://doi.org/10.1109/ICCV.2013.174

47. Wedel, A., Brox, T., Vaudrey, T., Rabe, C., Franke, U., Cremers, D.: Stereoscopic scene flow computation for 3D motion understanding. Int. J. Comput. Vis. **95**(1), 29–51 (2011). https://doi.org/10.1007/s11263-010-0404-0

48. Weinzaepfel, P., Revaud, J., Harchaoui, Z., Schmid, C.: DeepFlow: large displacement optical flow with deep matching. In: ICCV - IEEE International Conference on Computer Vision, Sydney, Australia, pp. 1385–1392. IEEE, December 2013. https://doi.org/10.1109/ICCV.2013.175, https://hal.inria.fr/hal-00873592

49. Weinzaepfel, P., Revaud, J., Harchaoui, Z., Schmid, C.: Learning to detect motion boundaries. In: CVPR 2015 - IEEE Conference on Computer Vision & Pattern Recognition. Boston, United States, June 2015. https://hal.inria.fr/hal-01142653

50. Xu, J., Ranftl, R., Koltun, V.: Accurate optical flow via direct cost volume processing. In: IEEE Conference on Computer Vision and Pattern Recognition (CVPR) (2017)
51. Yamaguchi, K., McAllester, D., Urtasun, R.: Efficient joint segmentation, occlusion labeling, stereo and flow estimation. In: Fleet, D., Pajdla, T., Schiele, B., Tuytelaars, T. (eds.) ECCV 2014. LNCS, vol. 8693, pp. 756–771. Springer, Cham (2014). https://doi.org/10.1007/978-3-319-10602-1_49
52. Zbontar, J., LeCun, Y.: Stereo matching by training a convolutional neural network to compare image patches. J. Mach. Learn. Res. **17**(1–32), 2 (2016)

Is Robustness the Cost of Accuracy? – A Comprehensive Study on the Robustness of 18 Deep Image Classification Models

Dong Su[1]([✉]), Huan Zhang[2], Hongge Chen[3], Jinfeng Yi[4], Pin-Yu Chen[1], and Yupeng Gao[1]

[1] IBM Research, New York, USA
sudong.tom@gmail.com, {pin-yu.chen,yupeng.gao}@ibm.com
[2] University of California, Davis, Davis, USA
ecezhang@ucdavis.edu
[3] Massachusetts Institute of Technology, Cambridge, USA
chenhg@mit.edu
[4] JD AI Research, Beijing, China
yijinfeng@jd.com

Abstract. The prediction accuracy has been the long-lasting and sole standard for comparing the performance of different image classification models, including the ImageNet competition. However, recent studies have highlighted the lack of robustness in well-trained deep neural networks to adversarial examples. Visually imperceptible perturbations to natural images can easily be crafted and mislead the image classifiers towards misclassification. To demystify the trade-offs between robustness and accuracy, in this paper we thoroughly benchmark 18 ImageNet models using multiple robustness metrics, including the distortion, success rate and transferability of adversarial examples between 306 pairs of models. Our extensive experimental results reveal several new insights: (1) linear scaling law - the empirical ℓ_2 and ℓ_∞ distortion metrics scale linearly with the logarithm of classification error; (2) model architecture is a more critical factor to robustness than model size, and the disclosed accuracy-robustness Pareto frontier can be used as an evaluation criterion for ImageNet model designers; (3) for a similar network architecture, increasing network depth slightly improves robustness in ℓ_∞ distortion; (4) there exist models (in VGG family) that exhibit high adversarial transferability, while most adversarial examples crafted from one model can only be transferred within the same family. Experiment code is publicly available at https://github.com/huanzhang12/Adversarial_Survey.

Keywords: Deep neural networks · Adversarial attacks · Robustness

---

D. Su and H. Zhang—Contribute equally to this work.

Electronic supplementary material The online version of this chapter (https://doi.org/10.1007/978-3-030-01258-8_39) contains supplementary material, which is available to authorized users.

© Springer Nature Switzerland AG 2018
V. Ferrari et al. (Eds.): ECCV 2018, LNCS 11216, pp. 644–661, 2018.
https://doi.org/10.1007/978-3-030-01258-8_39

1 Introduction

Image classification is a fundamental problem in computer vision and serves as the foundation of multiple tasks such as object detection, image segmentation, object tracking, action recognition, and autonomous driving. Since the breakthrough achieved by AlexNet [1] in ImageNet Challenge (ILSVRC) 2012 [2], deep neural networks (DNNs) have become the dominant force in this domain. From then on, DNN models with increasing depth and more complex building blocks have been proposed. While these models continue to achieve steadily increasing accuracies, their robustness has not been thoroughly studied, thus little is known if the high accuracies come at the price of reduced robustness.

A common approach to evaluate the robustness of DNNs is via adversarial attacks [3–11], where imperceptible adversarial examples are crafted to mislead DNNs. Generally speaking, the easier an adversarial example can be generated, the less robust the DNN is. Adversarial examples may lead to significant property damage or loss of life. For example, [12] has shown that a subtly-modified physical Stop sign can be misidentified by a real-time object recognition system as a Speed Limit sign. In addition to adversarial attacks, neural network robustness can also be estimated in an attack-agnostic manner. For example, [13] and [14] theoretically analyzed the robustness of some simple neural networks by estimating their global and local Lipschitz constants, respectively. [15] proposes to use extreme value theory to estimate a lower bound of the minimum adversarial distortion, and can be efficiently applied to any neural network classifier. [16] proposes a robustness lower bound based on linear approximations of ReLU activations. In this work, we evaluate DNN robustness by using specific attacks as well as attack-agnostic approaches. We also note that the adversarial robustness studied in this paper is different from [17], where "robustness" is studied in the context of label semantics and accuracy.

Since the last ImageNet challenge has ended in 2017, we are now at the beginning of post-ImageNet era. In this work, we revisit 18 DNN models submitted to the ImageNet Challenge or achieved state-of-the-art performance. These models have different sizes, classification performance, and belong to multiple architecture families such as AlexNet [1], VGG Nets [18], Inception Nets [19], ResNets [20], DenseNets [21], MobileNets [22], and NASNets [23]. Therefore, they are suitable to analyze how different factors influence the model robustness. Specifically, we aim to examine the following questions in this study:

1. *Has robustness been sacrificed for the increased classification performance?*
2. *Which factors influence the robustness of DNNs?*

In the course of evaluation, we have gained a number of insights and we summarize our contributions as follows:

- Tested on a large number of well-trained deep image classifiers, we find that robustness is scarified when solely pursuing a higher classification performance. Indeed, Fig. 2(a) and (b) clearly show that the ℓ_2 and ℓ_∞ adversarial distortions scale almost linearly with the logarithm of model classification errors. Therefore, the classifiers with very low test errors are highly

vulnerable to adversarial attacks. We advocate that ImageNet network designers should evaluate model robustness via our disclosed accuracy-robustness
Pareto frontier.
- The networks of a same family, e.g., VGG, Inception Nets, ResNets, and
  DenseNets, share similar robustness properties. This suggests that network
  architecture has a larger impact on robustness than model size. Besides, we
  also observe that the ℓ_∞ robustness slightly improves when ResNets, Inception Nets, and DenseNets become deeper.
- The adversarial examples generated by the VGG family can transfer very well
  to all the other 17 models, while most adversarial examples of other models
  can only transfer within the same model family. Interestingly, this finding
  provides us an opportunity to reverse-engineer the architecture of black-box
  models.
- We present the first comprehensive study that compares the robustness of 18
  popular and state-of-the-art ImageNet models, offering a complete picture of
  the accuracy v.s. robustness trade-off. In terms of transferability of adversarial
  examples, we conduct thorough experiments on each pair of the 18 ImageNet
  networks (306 pairs in total), which is the largest scale to date.

2   Background and Experimental Setup

In this section, we introduce the background knowledge and how we set up
experiments. We study both untargeted attack and targeted attack in this paper.
Let x_0 denote the original image and x denote the adversarial image of x_0. The
DNN model $F(\cdot)$ outputs a class label (or a probability distribution of class
labels) as the prediction. Without loss of generality, we assume that $F(x_0) = y_0$,
which is the ground truth label of x_0, to avoid trivial solution. For untargeted
attack, the adversarial image x is crafted in a way that x is close to x_0 but
$F(x) \neq y_0$. For targeted attack, a target class t $(t \neq y_0)$ is provided and the
adversarial image x should satisfy that (i) x is close to x_0, and (ii) $F(x) = t$.

2.1   Deep Neural Network Architectures

In this work, we study the robustness of 18 deep image classification models
belonging to 7 architecture families, as summarized below. Their basic properties
of these models are given in Table 1.

- **AlexNet.** AlexNet [1] is one of the pioneering and most well-known deep convolutional neural networks. Compared to many recent architectures, AlexNet
  has a relatively simple layout that is composed of 5 convolutional layers followed by two fully connected layers and a softmax output layer.
- **VGG Nets.** The overall architecture of VGG nets [18] are similar to AlexNet,
  but they are much deeper with more convolutional layers. Another main difference between VGG nets and AlexNet is that all the convolutional layers

of VGG nets use a small (3×3) kernel while the first two layers of AlexNet use 11×11 and 5×5 kernels, respectively. In our paper, we study VGG networks with 16 and 19 layers, with 138 million and 144 million parameters, respectively.

- **Inception Nets.** The family of Inception nets utilizes the inception modules [24] that act as multi-level feature extractors. Specifically, each inception module consists of multiple branches of 1×1, 3×3, and 5×5 filters, whose outputs will stack along the channel dimension and be fed into the next layer in the network. In this paper, we study the performance of all popular networks in this family, including Inception-v1 (GoogLeNet) [19], Inception-v2 [25], Inception-v3 [26], Inception-v4, and Inception-ResNet [27]. All these models are much deeper than AlexNet/VGG but have significantly fewer parameters.
- **ResNets.** To solve the vanishing gradient problem for training very deep neural networks, the authors of [20] proposes ResNets, where each layer learns the residual functions with reference to the input by adding skip-layer paths, or "identity shortcut connections". This architecture enables practitioners to train very deep neural networks to outperform shallow models. In our study, we evaluate 3 ResNets with different depths.
- **DenseNets.** To further exploit the "identity shortcut connections" techniques from ResNets, [21] proposes DenseNets that connect all layers with each other within a dense block. Besides tackling gradient vanishing problem, the authors also claimed other advantages such as encouraging feature reuse and reducing the number of parameters in the model. We study 3 DenseNets with different depths and widths.
- **MobileNets.** MobileNets [22] are a family of light weight and efficient neural networks designed for mobile and embedded systems with restricted computational resources. The core components of MobileNets are depthwise separable filters with factorized convolutions. Separable filters can factorize a standard convolution into two parts, a depthwise convolution and a 1×1 pointwise convolution, which can reduce computation and model size dramatically. In this study, we include 3 MobileNets with different depths and width multipliers.
- **NASNets.** NASNets [23] are a family of networks automatically generated by reinforcement learning using a policy gradient algorithm to optimize architectures [28]. Building blocks of the model are first searched on a smaller dataset and then transfered to a larger dataset.

2.2 Robustness Evaluation Approaches

We use both adversarial attacks and attack-agnostic approaches to evaluate network robustness. We first generate adversarial examples of each network using multiple state-of-the-art attack algorithms, and then analyze the attack success rates and the distortions of adversarial images. In this experiment, we assume to have full access to the targeted DNNs, known as the white-box attack. To further study the transferability of the adversarial images generated by each network, we consider all the 306 network pairs and for each pair, we conduct

Table 1. 18 ImageNet models under robustness examination

Models	Year	# layers	# parameters	Top-1/5 ImageNet accuracies
AlexNet [1]	2012	8	60 million	56.9%/80.1%[a]
VGG 16 [18]	2014	16	138 million	71.5%/89.8% [29]
VGG 19 [18]	2014	19	144 million	71.1%/89.8% [29]
Inception-v1 [19]	2014	22	6.7 million	69.8%/89.6% [29]
Inception-v2 [25]	2015	48	11.3 million	73.9%/91.8% [29]
Inception-v3 [26]	2015	48	23.9 million	78.0%/93.9% [29]
Inception-v4 [27]	2016	76	42.9 million	80.2%/95.2% [29]
Inception-ResNet-v2 [27]	2016	96	56.1 million	80.4%/95.3% [29]
ResNet-v2-50 [30]	2016	50	25.7 million	75.6%/92.8% [29]
ResNet-v2-101 [30]	2016	101	44.8 million	77.0%/93.7% [29]
ResNet-v2-152 [30]	2016	152	60.6 million	77.8%/94.1% [29]
DenseNet-121-k32 [21]	2017	121	8.2 million	74.9%/92.2[b]
DenseNet-169-k32 [21]	2017	169	14.4 million	76.1%/93.1 %[b]
DenseNet-161-k48 [21]	2017	161	29.0 million	77.6%/93.8 %[b]
MobileNet-0.25-128 [22]	2017	128	0.5 million	41.5%/66.3% [29]
MobileNet-0.50-160 [22]	2017	160	1.4 million	59.1%/81.9% [29]
MobileNet-1.0-224 [22]	2017	224	4.3 million	70.9%/89.9% [29]
NASNet [23]	2017	-	88.9 million	82.7%/96.2% [29]

[a]https://github.com/BVLC/caffe/wiki/Models-accuracy-on-ImageNet-2012-val
[b]https://github.com/pudae/tensorflow-densenet

transfer attack that uses one model's adversarial examples to attack the other model. Since transfer attack is widely used in the black-box setting [31–36], where an adversary has no access to the explicit knowledge of the target models, this experiment can provide some evidence on networks' black-box robustness. Finally, we compute CLEVER [15] score, a state-of-the-art attack-agnostic network robustness metric, to estimate each network's intrinsic robustness. Below, we briefly introduce all the evaluation approaches used in our study.

We evaluate the robustness of DNNs using the following adversarial attacks:

- **Fast Gradient Sign Method (FGSM).** FGSM [3] is one of the pioneering and most efficient attacking algorithms. It only needs to compute the gradient once to generate an adversarial example $\mathbf{x}$:

$$\mathbf{x} \leftarrow \text{clip}[\mathbf{x}_0 - \epsilon \, \mathbf{sgn}(\nabla J(\mathbf{x}_0, t))],$$

where $\mathbf{sgn}(\nabla J(\mathbf{x}_0, t))$ is the sign of the gradient of the training loss with respect to $\mathbf{x}_0$, and $\text{clip}(\mathbf{x})$ ensures that $\mathbf{x}$ stays within the range of pixel values. It is efficient for generating adversarial examples as it is just an one-step attack.
- **Iterative FGSM (I-FGSM).** Albeit efficient, FGSM suffers from a relatively low attack success rate. To this end, [37] proposes iterative FGSM

to enhance its performance. It applies FGSM multiple times with a finer distortion, and is able to fool the network in more than 99% cases. When we run I-FGSM for T iterations, we set the per-iteration perturbation to $\frac{\epsilon}{T} \, \mathbf{sgn}(\nabla J(\mathbf{x}_0, t))$. I-FGSM can be viewed as a projected gradient descent (PGD) method inside an ℓ_∞ ball [38], and it usually finds adversarial examples with small ℓ_∞ distortions.

– **C&W attack.** [39] formulates the problem of generating adversarial examples $\mathbf{x}$ as the following optimization problem

$$\min_{\mathbf{x}} \; \lambda f(\mathbf{x}, t) + \|\mathbf{x} - \mathbf{x}_0\|_2^2$$
$$\text{s.t.} \;\; \mathbf{x} \in [0, 1]^p,$$

where $f(\mathbf{x}, t)$ is a loss function to measure the distance between the prediction of $\mathbf{x}$ and the target label t. In this work, we choose

$$f(\mathbf{x}, t) = \max\{\max_{i \neq t}[(\mathbf{Logit}(\mathbf{x}))_i - (\mathbf{Logit}(\mathbf{x}))_t], -\kappa\}$$

as it was shown to be effective by [39]. $\mathbf{Logit}(\mathbf{x})$ denotes the vector representation of $\mathbf{x}$ at the logit layer, κ is a confidence level and a larger κ generally improves transferability of adversarial examples.

C&W attack is by far one of the strongest attacks that finds adversarial examples with small ℓ_2 perturbations. It can achieve almost 100% attack success rate and has bypassed 10 different adversary detection methods [40].

– **EAD-L1 attack.** EAD-L1 attack [41] refers to the **E**lastic-**N**et **A**ttacks to **D**NNs, which is a more general formulation than C&W attack. It proposes to use elastic-net regularization, a linear combination of ℓ_1 and ℓ_2 norms, to penalize large distortion between the original and adversarial examples. Specifically, it learns the adversarial example $\mathbf{x}$ via

$$\min_{\mathbf{x}} \; \lambda f(\mathbf{x}, t) + \|\mathbf{x} - \mathbf{x}_0\|_2^2 + \beta \|\mathbf{x} - \mathbf{x}_0\|_1$$
$$\text{s.t.} \;\; \mathbf{x} \in [0, 1]^p,$$

where $f(\mathbf{x}, t)$ is the same as used in the C&W attack. [41–44] show that EAD-L1 attack is highly transferable and can bypass many defenses and analysis.

We also evaluate network robustness using an attack-agnostic approach:

– **CLEVER.** CLEVER [15] (Cross-Lipschitz Extreme Value for nEtwork Robustness) uses extreme value theory to estimate a lower bound of the minimum adversarial distortion. Given an image $\mathbf{x}_0$, CLEVER provides an estimated lower bound on the ℓ_p norm of the minimum distortion δ required to misclassify the distorted image $\mathbf{x}_0 + \delta$. A higher CLEVER score suggests that the network is likely to be more robust to adversarial examples. CLEVER is attack-agnostic and reflects the intrinsic robustness of a network, rather than the robustness under a certain attack.

2.3 Dataset

In this work, we use the ImageNet [45] as the benchmark dataset, due to the following reasons: (i) ImageNet dataset can take full advantage of the studied DNN models since all of them were designed for ImageNet challenges; (ii) comparing to the widely-used small-scale datasets such as MNIST, CIFAR-10 [46], and GTSRB [47], ImageNet has significantly more images and classes and is more challenging; and (iii) it has been shown by [39,48] that ImageNet images are easier to attack but harder to defend than the images from MNIST and CIFAR datasets. Given all these observations, ImageNet is an ideal candidate to study the robustness of state-of-the-art deep image classification models.

A set of randomly selected 1,000 images from the ImageNet validation set is used to generate adversarial examples from each model. For each image, we conduct targeted attacks with a random target and a least likely target as well as an untargeted attack. Misclassified images are excluded. We follow the setting in [15] to compute CLEVER scores for 100 out of the all 1,000 images, as CLEVER is relatively more computational expensive. Additionally, we conducted another experiment by taking the subset of images (327 images in total) that are correctly classified by *all* of 18 examined ImageNet models. The results are consistent with our main results and are given in supplementary material.

2.4 Evaluation Metrics

In our study, the robustness of the DNN models is evaluated using the following four metrics:

- **Attack success rate.** For non-targeted attack, success rate indicates the percentage of the adversarial examples whose predicted labels are different from their ground truth labels. For targeted attack, success rate indicates the percentage of the adversarial examples that are classified as the target class. For both attacks, a higher success rate suggests that the model is easier to attack and hence less robust. When generating adversarial examples, we only consider original images that are correctly classified to avoid trial attacks.
- **Distortion.** We measure the distortion between adversarial images and the original ones using ℓ_2 and ℓ_∞ norms. ℓ_2 norm measures the Euclidean distance between two images, and ℓ_∞ norm is a measure of the maximum absolute change to any pixel (worst case). Both of them are widely used to measure adversarial perturbations [39–41]. A higher distortion usually suggests a more robust model. To find adversarial examples with minimum distortion for each model, we use a binary search strategy to select the optimal attack parameters ϵ in I-FGSM and λ in C&W attack. Because each model may have different input sizes, we divide ℓ_2 distortions by the number of total pixels for a fair comparison.
- **CLEVER score.** For each image, we compute its ℓ_2 CLEVER score for target attacks with a random target class and a least-likely class, respectively. The reported number is the averaged score of all the tested images. The higher the CLEVER score, the more robust the model is.

– **Transferability.** We follow [31] to define targeted and non-targeted transferability. For non-targeted attack, transferability is defined as the percentage of the adversarial examples generated for one model (*source model*) that are also misclassified by another model (*target model*). We refer to this percentage as *error rate*, and a higher error rate means better non-targeted transferability. For targeted attack, transferability is defined as *matching rate*, i.e., the percentage of the adversarial examples generated for source model that are misclassified as the target label (or within top-k labels) by the target model. A higher matching rate indicates better targeted transferability.

3   Experiments

After examining all the 18 DNN models, we have learned insights about the relationships between model architectures and robustness, as discussed below.

3.1   Evaluation of Adversarial Attacks

We have carefully conducted a controlled experiment by pulling images from a *common* set of 1000 test images when evaluating the robustness of different models. For assessing the robustness of each model, the originally misclassified images are excluded. We compare the success rates of targeted attack with a *random* target of FGSM, I-FGSM, C&W and EAD-L1 with different parameters for all 18 models. The success rate of FGSM targeted attack is low so we also show its untargeted attack success rate in Fig. 1(b).

For targeted attack, the success rate of FGSM is very low (below 3% for all settings), and unlike in the untargeted setting, increasing ϵ in fact *decreases* attack success rate. This observation further confirms that FGSM is a weak attack, and targeted attack is more difficult and needs iterative attacking methods. Figure 1(c) shows that, with *only 10* iterations, I-FGSM can achieve a very good targeted attack success rate on all models. C&W and EAD-L1 can also achieve almost 100% success rate on almost all of the models when $\kappa = 0$.

For C&W and EAD-L1 attacks, increasing the confidence κ can significantly make the attack harder to find a feasible adversarial example. A larger κ usually makes the adversarial distortion more universal and improves transferability (as we will show shortly), but at the expense of decreasing the success rate and increasing the distortion. However, we find that the attack success rate with large κ *cannot be used as a robustness measure*, as it is not aligned with the ℓ_p norm of adversarial distortions. For example, for MobileNet-0.50-160, when $\kappa = 40$, the success rate is close to 0, but in Fig. 2 we show that it is one of the most vulnerable networks. The reason is that the range of the logits output can be different for each network, so the difficulty of finding a fixed logit gap κ is different on each network, and is not related to its intrinsic robustness.

We defer the results for targeted attack with the *least likely* target label to the Supplementary section because the conclusions made are similar.

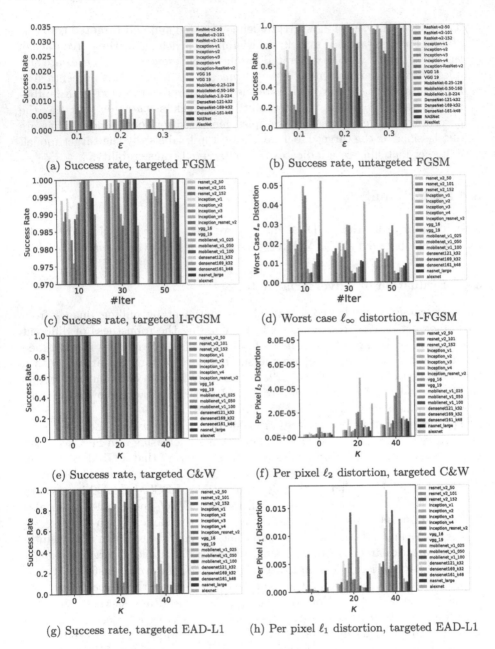

(a) Success rate, targeted FGSM

(b) Success rate, untargeted FGSM

(c) Success rate, targeted I-FGSM

(d) Worst case ℓ_∞ distortion, I-FGSM

(e) Success rate, targeted C&W

(f) Per pixel ℓ_2 distortion, targeted C&W

(g) Success rate, targeted EAD-L1

(h) Per pixel ℓ_1 distortion, targeted EAD-L1

Fig. 1. Comparison of FGSM, I-FGSM, CW and EAD-L1 attacks by varying attack parameters.

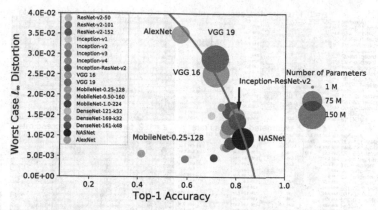

(a) Fitted Pareto frontier of ℓ_∞ distortion (I-FGSM attack) vs. top-1 accuracy:
ℓ_∞ dist $= [2.9 \cdot \ln(1 - \mathrm{acc}) + 6.2] \times 10^{-2}$

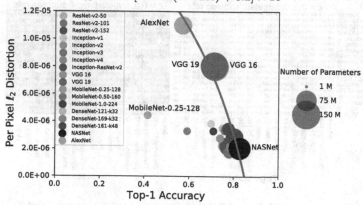

(b) Fitted Pareto frontier of ℓ_2 distortion (C&W attack) vs. top-1 accuracy:
ℓ_2 dist $= [1.1 \cdot \ln(1 - \mathrm{acc}) + 2.1] \times 10^{-5}$

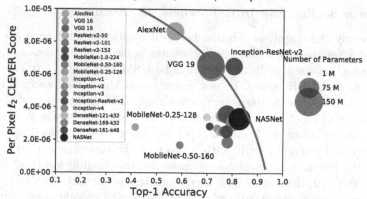

(c) Fitted Pareto frontier of ℓ_2 CLEVER score vs. top-1 accuracy:
ℓ_2 score $= [4.6 \cdot \ln(1 - \mathrm{acc}) + 12.5] \times 10^{-6}$

Fig. 2. Robustness vs. classification accuracy plots of I-FGSM attack [37], C&W attack [39] and CLEVER [15] score on random targets over 18 ImageNet models.

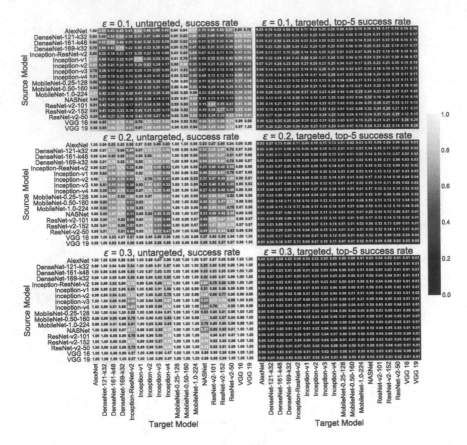

Fig. 3. Transferability of FGSM attack over 18 ImageNet models.

3.2   Linear Scaling Law in Robustness v.s. Accuracy

Here we study the empirical relation between robustness and accuracy of different ImageNet models, where the robustness is evaluated in terms of the ℓ_∞ and ℓ_2 distortion metrics from successful I-FGSM and C&W attacks respectively, or ℓ_2 CLEVER scores. In our experiments the attack success rates of these attacks are nearly 100% for each model. The scatter plots of distortions/scores v.s. top-1 prediction accuracy are displayed in Fig. 2. We define the classification error as 1 minus top-1 accuracy (denoted as $1 - \mathrm{acc}$). By regressing the distortion metric with respect to the classification error of networks on the Pareto frontier of robustness-accuracy distribution (i.e., AlexNet, VGG 16, VGG 19, ResNet_v2_152, Inception_ResNet_v2 and NASNet), we find that the distortion scales linearly with the logarithm of classification error. That is, the distortion and classification error has the following relation: $\mathrm{distortion} = a + b \cdot \log(\mathrm{classification\text{-}error})$. The fitted parameters of a and b are given in the captions of Fig. 2. Take I-FGSM attack as an example, the linear scaling law suggests that to reduce the classification error by a half, the ℓ_∞ distortion of

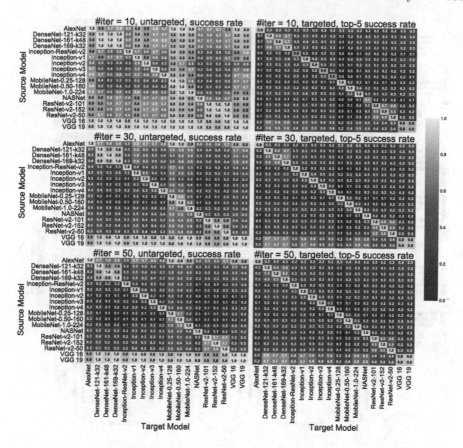

Fig. 4. Transferability of I-FGSM attack over 18 ImageNet models, $\epsilon = 0.3$.

the resulting network will be expected to reduce by approximately 0.02, which is roughly 60% of the AlexNet distortion. Following this trend, if we naively pursue a model with low test error, the model robustness may suffer. Thus, when designing new networks for ImageNet, we suggest to evaluate the model's accuracy-robustness tradeoff by comparing it to the disclosed Pareto frontier.

3.3 Robustness of Different Model Sizes and Architectures

We find that model architecture is a more important factor to model robustness than the model size. Each family of networks exhibits a similar level of robustness, despite different depths and model sizes. For example, AlexNet has about 60 million parameters but its robustness is the best; on the other hand, Mobilenet-0.50-160 has only 1.5 million parameters but is more vulnerable to adversarial attacks in all metrics.

We also observe that, within the same family, for DenseNet, ResNet and Inception, models with *deeper architecture yields a slight improvement* of the

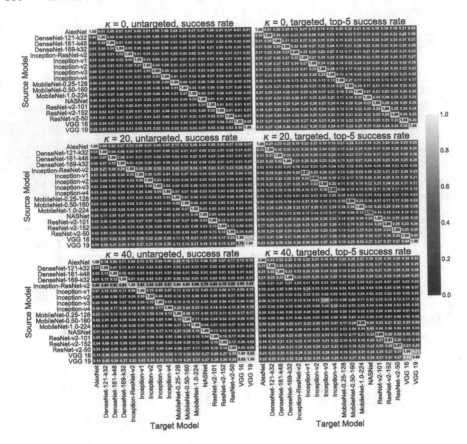

Fig. 5. The transferability of EAD-L1 attack over 18 ImageNet models.

robustness in terms of the ℓ_∞ distortion metric. This might provide new insights for designing robust networks and further improve the Pareto frontier. This result also echoes with [49], where the authors use a larger model to increase the ℓ_∞ robustness of a CNN based MNIST model.

3.4   Transferability of Adversarial Examples

Figures 3, 4 and 5 show the transferability heatmaps of FGSM, I-FGSM and EAD-L1 over all 18 models (306 pairs in total). The value in the i-th row and j-th column of each heatmap matrix is the proportion of the adversarial examples successfully transferred to target model j out of all adversarial examples generated by source model i (including both successful and failed attacks on the source model). Specifically, the values on the diagonal of the heatmap are the attack success rate of the corresponding model. For each model, we generate adversarial images using the aforementioned attacks and pass them to the target model to perform black-box untargeted and targeted transfer attacks. To evaluate each model, we use the success rate for evaluating the untargeted transfer attacks and the top-5 matching rate for evaluating targeted transfer attacks.

Note that not all models have the same input image dimension. We also find that simply resizing the adversarial examples can significantly decrease the transfer attack success rate [50]. To alleviate the disruptive effect of image resizing on adversarial perturbations, when transferring an adversarial image from a network with larger input dimension to a smaller dimension, we crop the image from the center; conversely, we add a white boarder to the image when the source network's input dimension is smaller.

Generally, the transferability of untargeted attacks is significantly higher than that of targeted attacks, as indicated in Figs. 3, 4 and 5. We highlighted some interesting findings in our experimental results:

1. In the *untargeted* transfer attack setting, FGSM and I-FGSM have much higher transfer success rates than those in EAD-L1 (despiting using a large κ). Similar to the results in [41], we find that the transferability of C&W is even worse than that of EAD-L1 and we defer the results to the supplement. The ranking of attacks on transferability in untargeted setting is given by

$$FGSM \succeq I\text{-}FGSM \succeq EAD\text{-}L1 \succeq C\&W.$$

2. Again in the untargeted transfer attack setting, for FGSM, a larger ϵ yields better transferability, while for I-FGSM, *less iterations* yield better transferability. For untargeted EAD-L1 transfer attacks, a higher κ value (confidence parameter) leads to better transferability, but it is still far behind I-FGSM.
3. Transferability of adversarial examples is sometimes *asymmetric*; for example, in Fig. 4, adversarial examples of VGG 16 are highly transferable to Inception-v2, but adversarial examples of Inception v2 do not transfer very well to VGG.
4. We find that VGG 16 and VGG 19 models achieve *significantly better transferability* than other models, in both targeted and untargeted setting, for all attacking methods, leading to the "stripe patterns". This means that adversarial examples generated from VGG models are empirically more transferable to other models. This observation might be explained by the simple convolutional nature of VGG networks, which is the stem of all other networks. VGG models are thus a good starting point for mounting black-box transfer attacks. We also observe that the most transferable model family may vary with different attacks.
5. Most recent networks have some unique features that might restrict adversarial examples' transferability to only within the same family. For example, as shown in Fig. 4, when using I-FGSM in the untargeted transfer attack setting, for DenseNets, ResNets and VGG, transferability between different depths of the same architecture is *close to 100%*, but their transfer rates to other architectures can be much worse. This provides us an opportunity to reserve-engineer the internal architecture of a black-box model, by feeding it with adversarial examples crafted for a certain architecture and measure the attack success rates.

4   Conclusions

In this paper, we present the largest scale to date study on adversarial examples in ImageNet models. We show comprehensive experimental results on 18 state-of-the-art ImageNet models using adversarial attack methods focusing on ℓ_1, ℓ_2 and ℓ_∞ norms and also an attack-agnostic robustness score, CLEVER. Our results show that there is a clear trade-off between accuracy and robustness, and a better performance in testing accuracy in general reduces robustness. Tested on the ImageNet dataset, we discover an empirical linear scaling law between distortion metrics and the logarithm of classification errors in representative models. We conjecture that following this trend, naively pursuing high-accuracy models may come with the great risks of lacking robustness. We also provide a thorough adversarial attack transferability analysis between 306 pairs of these networks and discuss the robustness implications on network architecture.

In this work, we focus on image classification. To the best of our knowledge, the scale and profound analysis on 18 ImageNet models have not been studied thoroughly in the previous literature. We believe our findings could also provide insights to robustness and adversarial examples in other computer vision tasks such as object detection [51] and image captioning [5], since these tasks often use the same pre-trained image classifiers studied in this paper for feature extraction.

References

1. Krizhevsky, A., Sutskever, I., Hinton, G.E.: Imagenet classification with deep convolutional neural networks. In: Advances in Neural Information Processing Systems (NIPS), pp. 1097–1105 (2012)
2. Russakovsky, O., et al.: Imagenet large scale visual recognition challenge. Int. J. Comput. Vis. **115**(3), 211–252 (2015)
3. Goodfellow, I., Shlens, J., Szegedy, C.: Explaining and harnessing adversarial examples. In: International Conference on Learning Representations (ICLR) (2015)
4. Xu, X., Chen, X., Liu, C., Rohrbach, A., Darell, T., Song, D.: Fooling vision and language models despite localization and attention mechanism. In: Proceedings of the Thirtieth IEEE/CVF Conference on Computer Vision and Pattern Recognition (CVPR) (2018)
5. Chen, H., Zhang, H., Chen, P.Y., Yi, J., Hsieh, C.J.: Attacking visual language grounding with adversarial examples: a case study on neural image captioning. In: Proceedings of the 56th Annual Meeting of the Association for Computational Linguistics, vol. 1: Long Papers, pp. 2587–2597 (2018)
6. Metzen, J.H., Kumar, M.C., Brox, T., Fischer, V.: Universal adversarial perturbations against semantic image segmentation. Statistics **1050**, 19 (2017)
7. Cheng, M., Yi, J., Zhang, H., Chen, P.Y., Hsieh, C.J.: Seq2Sick: evaluating the robustness of sequence-to-sequence models with adversarial examples. arXiv preprint arXiv:1803.01128 (2018)
8. Carlini, N., Wagner, D.: Audio adversarial examples: targeted attacks on speech-to-text. In: Deep Learning and Security Workshop (2018)

9. Sun, M., Tang, F., Yi, J., Wang, F., Zhou, J.: Identify susceptible locations in medical records via adversarial attacks on deep predictive models. In: Proceedings of the 24th ACM SIGKDD International Conference on Knowledge Discovery and Data Mining (KDD), pp. 793–801 (2018)

10. Xiao, C., Li, B., Zhu, J.Y., He, W., Liu, M., Song, D.: Generating adversarial examples with adversarial networks. In: Proceedings of the Twenty-Seventh International Joint Conference on Artificial Intelligence, IJCAI 2018, International Joint Conferences on Artificial Intelligence Organization, pp. 3905–3911, July 2018

11. Xiao, C., Zhu, J.Y., Li, B., He, W., Liu, M., Song, D.: Spatially transformed adversarial examples. In: International Conference on Learning Representations (ICLR) (2018)

12. Eykholt, K., et al.: Robust physical-world attacks on deep learning visual classification. In: Proceedings of the IEEE Conference on Computer Vision and Pattern Recognition, pp. 1625–1634 (2018)

13. Szegedy, C., et al.: Intriguing properties of neural networks. In: International Conference on Learning Representations (ICLR) (2014)

14. Hein, M., Andriushchenko, M.: Formal guarantees on the robustness of a classifier against adversarial manipulation. In: Advances in Neural Information Processing Systems 30: Annual Conference on Neural Information Processing Systems (NIPS), pp. 2263–2273 (2017)

15. Weng, T.W., et al.: Evaluating the robustness of neural networks: an extreme value theory approach. In: International Conference on Learning Representations (ICLR) (2018)

16. Weng, T.W., et al.: Towards fast computation of certified robustness for ReLU networks. In: Proceedings of the 35th International Conference on Machine Learning (ICML) (2018)

17. Stock, P., Cisse, M.: Convnets and imagenet beyond accuracy: explanations, bias detection, adversarial examples and model criticism. arXiv preprint arXiv:1711.11443 (2017)

18. Simonyan, K., Zisserman, A.: Very deep convolutional networks for large-scale image recognition. In: International Conference on Learning Representations (ICLR) (2015)

19. Szegedy, C., et al.: Going deeper with convolutions. In: IEEE Conference on Computer Vision and Pattern Recognition, CVPR 2015, Boston, MA, USA, 7–12 June 2015, pp. 1–9 (2015)

20. He, K., Zhang, X., Ren, S., Sun, J.: Deep residual learning for image recognition. In: 2016 IEEE Conference on Computer Vision and Pattern Recognition, CVPR 2016, Las Vegas, NV, USA, 27–30 June 2016, pp. 770–778 (2016)

21. Huang, G., Liu, Z., van der Maaten, L., Weinberger, K.Q.: Densely connected convolutional networks. In: 2017 IEEE Conference on Computer Vision and Pattern Recognition (CVPR) (2017)

22. Howard, A.G., et al.: MobileNets: efficient convolutional neural networks for mobile vision applications. CoRR abs/1704.04861 (2017)

23. Zoph, B., Vasudevan, V., Shlens, J., Le, Q.V.: Learning transferable architectures for scalable image recognition. In: 2018 IEEE Conference on Computer Vision and Pattern Recognition (CVPR) (2018)

24. Lin, M., Chen, Q., Yan, S.: Network in network. In: International Conference on Learning Representations, ICLR (ICLR) (2014)

25. Ioffe, S., Szegedy, C.: Batch normalization: accelerating deep network training by reducing internal covariate shift. In: Proceedings of the 32nd International Conference on Machine Learning, ICML 2015, Lille, France, 6–11 July 2015, pp. 448–456 (2015)

26. Szegedy, C., Vanhoucke, V., Ioffe, S., Shlens, J., Wojna, Z.: Rethinking the inception architecture for computer vision. In: 2016 IEEE Conference on Computer Vision and Pattern Recognition, CVPR 2016, Las Vegas, NV, USA, 27–30 June 2016, pp. 2818–2826 (2016)

27. Szegedy, C., Ioffe, S., Vanhoucke, V., Alemi, A.A.: Inception-v4, inception-resnet and the impact of residual connections on learning. In: Proceedings of the Thirty-First AAAI Conference on Artificial Intelligence, San Francisco, California, USA, 4–9 February 2017, pp. 4278–4284 (2017)

28. Zoph, B., Le, Q.V.: Neural architecture search with reinforcement learning. In: International Conference on Learning Representations (ICLR) (2017)

29. Wu, N., Sivakumar, S., Guadarrama, S., Andersen, D.: TensorFlow-Slim Image Classification Model Library (2017). Github https://github.com/tensorflow/models/tree/master/research/slim

30. He, K., Zhang, X., Ren, S., Sun, J.: Identity mappings in deep residual networks. In: Leibe, B., Matas, J., Sebe, N., Welling, M. (eds.) ECCV 2016. LNCS, vol. 9908, pp. 630–645. Springer, Cham (2016). https://doi.org/10.1007/978-3-319-46493-0_38

31. Liu, Y., Chen, X., Liu, C., Song, D.: Delving into transferable adversarial examples and black-box attacks. In: International Conference on Learning Representations (ICLR) (2017)

32. Papernot, N., McDaniel, P., Goodfellow, I.: Transferability in machine learning: from phenomena to black-box attacks using adversarial samples. arXiv preprint arXiv:1605.07277 (2016)

33. Chen, P.Y., Zhang, H., Sharma, Y., Yi, J., Hsieh, C.J.: ZOO: zeroth order optimization based black-box attacks to deep neural networks without training substitute models. In: Proceedings of the 10th ACM Workshop on Artificial Intelligence and Security, pp. 15–26. ACM (2017)

34. Tu, C., et al.: AutoZOOM: autoencoder-based zeroth order optimization method for attacking black-box neural networks. CoRR abs/1805.11770 (2018)

35. Cheng, M., Le, T., Chen, P.Y., Yi, J., Zhang, H., Hsieh, C.J.: Query-efficient hard-label black-box attack: an optimization-based approach. arXiv preprint arXiv:1807.04457 (2018)

36. Tu, C.C., et al.: AutoZOOM: autoencoder-based zeroth order optimization method for attacking black-box neural networks. arXiv preprint arXiv:1805.11770 (2018)

37. Kurakin, A., Goodfellow, I.J., Bengio, S.: Adversarial machine learning at scale. In: International Conference on Learning Representations (ICLR) (2017)

38. Cisse, M., Bojanowski, P., Grave, E., Dauphin, Y., Usunier, N.: Parseval networks: improving robustness to adversarial examples. In: International Conference on Machine Learning (ICML), pp. 854–863 (2017)

39. Carlini, N., Wagner, D.A.: Towards evaluating the robustness of neural networks. In: 2017 IEEE Symposium on Security and Privacy (Oakland) 2017, San Jose, CA, USA, 22–26 May 2017, pp. 39–57 (2017)

40. Carlini, N., Wagner, D.: Adversarial examples are not easily detected: bypassing ten detection methods. In: Proceedings of the 10th ACM Workshop on Artificial Intelligence and Security, AISec 2017, pp. 3–14. ACM, New York (2017)

41. Chen, P.Y., Sharma, Y., Zhang, H., Yi, J., Hsieh, C.J.: EAD: elastic-net attacks to deep neural networks via adversarial examples. In: AAAI (2018)

42. Sharma, Y., Chen, P.Y.: Attacking the Madry defense model with L_1-based adversarial examples. arXiv preprint arXiv:1710.10733 (2017)
43. Lu, P.H., Chen, P.Y., Chen, K.C., Yu, C.M.: On the limitation of magnet defense against L_1-based adversarial examples. In: IEEE/IFIP DSN Workshop (2018)
44. Lu, P.H., Chen, P.Y., Yu, C.M.: On the limitation of local intrinsic dimensionality for characterizing the subspaces of adversarial examples. In: ICLR Workshop (2018)
45. Deng, J., Dong, W., Socher, R., Li, L.J., Li, K., Fei-Fei, L.: ImageNet: a large-scale hierarchical image database. In: IEEE Conference on Computer Vision and Pattern Recognition, CVPR 2009, pp. 248–255. IEEE (2009)
46. Krizhevsky, A.: Learning multiple layers of features from tiny images (2009)
47. Stallkamp, J., Schlipsing, M., Salmen, J., Igel, C.: Man vs. computer: benchmarking machine learning algorithms for traffic sign recognition. Neural Netw. **32**, 323–332 (2012)
48. Moosavi-Dezfooli, S., Fawzi, A., Frossard, P.: DeepFool: a simple and accurate method to fool deep neural networks. In: 2016 IEEE Conference on Computer Vision and Pattern Recognition, CVPR 2016, Las Vegas, NV, USA, 27–30 June 2016, pp. 2574–2582 (2016)
49. Madry, A., Makelov, A., Schmidt, L., Tsipras, D., Vladu, A.: Towards deep learning models resistant to adversarial attacks. In: International Conference on Learning Representations (ICLR) (2018)
50. Athalye, A., Engstrom, L., Ilyas, A., Kwok, K.: Synthesizing robust adversarial examples. In: 35th International Conference on Machine Learning (ICML) (2018)
51. Xie, C., Wang, J., Zhang, Z., Zhou, Y., Xie, L., Yuille, A.: Adversarial examples for semantic segmentation and object detection. In: International Conference on Computer Vision (ICCV). IEEE (2017)

Improving Shape Deformation in Unsupervised Image-to-Image Translation

Aaron Gokaslan[1]([✉])[iD], Vivek Ramanujan[1][iD], Daniel Ritchie[1][iD],
Kwang In Kim[2], and James Tompkin[1][iD]

[1] Brown University, Providence, USA
agokasla@cs.brown.edu
[2] University of Bath, Bath, UK

Abstract. Unsupervised image-to-image translation techniques are able to map local texture between two domains, but they are typically unsuccessful when the domains require larger shape change. Inspired by semantic segmentation, we introduce a discriminator with dilated convolutions that is able to use information from across the entire image to train a more context-aware generator. This is coupled with a multi-scale perceptual loss that is better able to represent error in the underlying shape of objects. We demonstrate that this design is more capable of representing shape deformation in a challenging toy dataset, plus in complex mappings with significant dataset variation between humans, dolls, and anime faces, and between cats and dogs.

Keywords: Generative adversarial networks · Image translation

1 Introduction

Unsupervised image-to-image translation is the process of learning an arbitrary mapping between image domains without labels or pairings. This can be accomplished via deep learning with generative adversarial networks (GANs), through the use of a discriminator network to provide instance-specific generator training, and the use of a cyclic loss to overcome the lack of supervised pairing. Prior works such as DiscoGAN [19] and CycleGAN [43] are able to transfer sophisticated local texture appearance between image domains, such as translating between paintings and photographs. However, these methods often have difficulty with objects that have both related appearance and shape changes; for instance, when translating between cats and dogs.

Coping with shape deformation in image translation tasks requires the ability to use spatial information from across the image. For instance, we cannot expect to transform a cat into a dog by simply changing the animals' local

---

Electronic supplementary material The online version of this chapter (https://doi.org/10.1007/978-3-030-01258-8_40) contains supplementary material, which is available to authorized users.

V. Ferrari et al. (Eds.): ECCV 2018, LNCS 11216, pp. 662–678, 2018.
https://doi.org/10.1007/978-3-030-01258-8_40

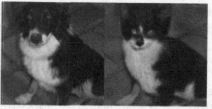

Fig. 1. Our approach translates texture appearance and complex head and body shape changes between the cat and dog domains (left: input; right: translation).

texture. From our experiments, networks with fully connected discriminators, such as DiscoGAN, are able to represent larger shape changes given sufficient network capacity, but train much slower [17] and have trouble resolving smaller details. Patch-based discriminators, as used in CycleGAN, work well at resolving high frequency information and train relatively quickly [17], but have a limited 'receptive field' for each patch that only allows the network to consider spatially local content. These networks reduce the amount of information received by the generator. Further, the functions used to maintain the cyclic loss prior in both networks retains high frequency information in the cyclic reconstruction, which is often detrimental to shape change tasks.

We propose an image-to-image translation system, designated *GANimorph*, to address shortcomings present in current techniques. To allow for patch-based discriminators to use more image context, we use dilated convolutions in our discriminator architecture [39]. This allows us to treat discrimination as a semantic segmentation problem: the discriminator outputs per-pixel real-vs.-fake decisions, each informed by global context. This per-pixel discriminator output facilitates more fine-grained information flow from the discriminator to the generator. We also use a multi-scale structure similarity perceptual reconstruction loss to help represent error over image areas rather than just over pixels. We demonstrate that our approach is more successful on a challenging shape deformation toy dataset than previous approaches. We also demonstrate example translations involving both appearance and shape variation by mapping human faces to dolls and anime characters, and mapping cats to dogs (Fig. 1).

The source code to our GANimorph system and all datasets are online: https://github.com/brownvc/ganimorph/.

2   Related Work

Image-to-Image Translation. Image analogies provides one of the earliest examples of image-to-image translation [14]. The approach relies on non-parametric texture synthesis and can handle transformations such as seasonal scene shifts [20], color and texture transformation, and painterly style transfer. Despite the ability of the model to learn texture transfer, the model cannot affect the shape of objects. Recent research has extended the model to perform visual

attribute transfer using neural networks [13, 23]. However, despite these improvements, deep image analogies are unable to achieve shape deformation.

Neural Style Transfer. These techniques show transfer of more complex artistic styles than image analogies [10]. They combine the style of one image with
the content of another by matching the Gram matrix statistics of early-layer
feature maps from neural networks trained on general supervised image recognition tasks. Further, Duomiln et al. [8] extended Gatys et al.'s technique to
allow for interpolation between pre-trained styles, and Huang et al. [15] allowed
real-time transfer. Despite this promise, these techniques have difficulty adapting to shape deformation, and empirical results have shown that these networks
only capture low-level texture information [2]. Reference images can affect brush
strokes, color palette, and local geometry, but larger changes such as anime-style
combined appearance and shape transformations do not propagate.

Generative Adversarial Networks. Generative adversarial networks (GANs) have
produced promising results in image editing [22], image translation [17], and
image synthesis [11]. These networks learn an adversarial loss function to distinguish between real and generated samples. Isola et al. [17] demonstrated with
Pix2Pix that GANs are capable of learning texture mappings between complex
domains. However, this technique requires a large number of explicitly-paired
samples. Some such datasets are naturally available, e.g., registered map and
satellite photos, or image colorization tasks. We show in our supplemental material that our approach is also able to solve these limited-shape-change problems.

Unsupervised Image Translation GANs. Pix2Pix-like architectures have been
extended to work with unsupervised pairs [19, 43]. Given image domains X and
Y, these approaches work by learning a cyclic mapping from X $\rightarrow$ Y $\rightarrow$ X and
Y $\rightarrow$ X $\rightarrow$ Y. This creates a bijective mapping that prevents mode collapse in
the unsupervised case. We build upon the DiscoGAN [19] and CycleGAN [43]
architectures, which themselves extend Coupled GANs for style transfer [25]. We
seek to overcome their shape change limitations through more efficient learning
and expanded discriminator context via dilated convolutions, and by using a
cyclic loss function that considers multi-scale frequency information (Table 1).

Other works tackle complementary problems. Yi et al. [38] focus on improving high frequency features over CycleGAN in image translation tasks, such as
texture transfer and segmentation. Ma et al. [27] examine adapting CycleGAN to
wider variety in the domains—so-called instance-level translation. Liu et al. [24]
use two autoencoders to create a cyclic loss through a shared latent space with
additional constraints. Several layers are shared between the two generators and
an identity loss ensures that both domains resolve to the same latent vector.
This produces some shape transformation in faces; however, the network does
not improve the discriminator architecture to provide greater context awareness.

One qualitatively different approach is to introduce object-level segmentation
maps into the training set. Liang et al.'s ContrastGAN [22] has demonstrated
shape change by learning segmentation maps and combining multiple conditional

Table 1. Translating a human to a doll, and a cat to a dog. Dilated convolutions in the discriminator outperform both patch-based and dense convolution methods for image translations that require larger shape changes and small detail preservation.

Input	Patch based	Dense	Dilated

cyclic generative adversarial networks. However, this additional input is often unavailable and time consuming to declare.

3   Our Approach

Crucial to the success of translation under shape deformation is the ability to maintain consistency over global shapes as well as local texture. Our algorithm adopts the cyclic image translation framework [19,43] and achieves the required consistency by incorporating a new dilated discriminator, a generator with residual blocks and skip connections, and a multi-scale perceptual cyclic loss.

3.1   Dilated Discriminator

Initial approaches used a global discriminator with a fully connected layer [19]. Such a discriminator collapses an image to a single scalar value for determining image veracity. Later approaches [22,43] used a patch-based DCGAN [32] discriminator, initially developed for style transfer and texture synthesis [21]. In this type of discriminator, each image patch is evaluated to determine a fake or real score. The patch-based approach allows for fast generator convergence by operating on each local patch independently. This approach has proven effective for texture transfer, segmentation, and similar tasks. However, this patch-based view limits the networks' awareness of global spatial information, which limits the generator's ability to perform coherent global shape change.

Reframing Discrimination as Semantic Segmentation. To solve this issue, we reframe the discrimination problem from determining real/fake images or subimages into the more general problem of finding real or fake regions of the image, i.e., a *semantic segmentation* task. Since the discriminator outputs a higher-resolution segmentation map, the information flow between the generator and

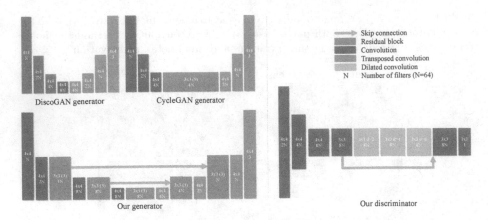

Fig. 2. (Left) Generators from different unsupervised image translation models. The skip connections and residual blocks are combined via concatenation as opposed to addition. (Right) Our discriminator network architecture is a fully-convolutional segmentation network. Each colored block represents a convolution layer; block labels indicate filter size. In addition to global context from the dilations, the skip connection bypassing the dilated convolution blocks preserves the network's view of local context. (Color figure online)

discriminator increases. This allows for faster convergence than using a fully connected discriminator, such as in DiscoGAN.

Current state-of-the-art networks for segmentation use dilated convolutions, and have been shown to require far fewer parameters than conventional convolutional networks to achieve similar levels of accuracy [39]. Dilated convolutions provide advantages over both global and patch-based discriminator architectures. For the same parameter budget, they allow the prediction to incorporate data from a larger surrounding region. This increases the information flow between the generator and discriminator: by knowing which regions of the image contribute to making the image unrealistic, the generator can focus on that region of the image. An alternative way to think about dilated convolutions is that they allow the discriminator to implicitly learn context. While multi-scale discriminators have been shown to improve results and stability for high resolution image synthesis tasks [35], we will show that incorporating information from farther away in the image is useful in translation tasks as the discriminator can determine where a region should fit into an image based on surrounding data. For example, this increased spatial context helps localize the face of a dog relative to its body, which is difficult to learn from small patches or patches learned in isolation from their neighbors. Figure 2 (right) illustrates our discriminator architecture.

3.2 Generator

Our generator architecture builds on those of DiscoGAN and CycleGAN. DiscoGAN uses a standard encoder-decoder architecture (Fig. 2, top left). However, its narrow bottleneck layer can lead to output images that do not preserve all the important visual details from the input image. Furthermore, due to the low capacity of the network, the approach remains limited to low resolution images of size 64×64. The CycleGAN architecture seeks to increase capacity over DiscoGAN by using a residual block to learn the image translation function [12]. Residual blocks have been shown to work in extremely deep networks, and they are able to represent low frequency information [2,40].

However, using residual blocks at a single scale limits the information that can pass through the bottleneck and thus the functions that the network can learn. Our generator includes residual blocks at multiple layers of both the decoder and encoder, allowing the network to learn multi-scale transformations that work on both higher and lower spatial resolution features (Fig. 2, bottom left).

3.3 Objective Function

Perceptual Cyclic Loss. As per prior unsupervised image-to-image translation work [19,22,24,38,43], we use a cyclic loss to learn a bijective mapping between two image domains. However, not all image translation functions can be perfectly bijective, e.g., when one domain has smaller appearance variation, like human face photos vs. anime drawings. When all information in the input image cannot be preserved in the translation, the cyclic loss term should aim to preserve the most important information. Since the network should focus on image attributes of importance to human viewers, we should choose a perceptual loss that emphasizes shape and appearance similarity between the generated and target images.

Defining an explicit shape loss is difficult, as any explicit term requires known image correspondences between domains. These do not exist for our examples and our unsupervised setting. Further, including a more-complex perceptual neural network into the loss calculation imparts a significant computational and memory overhead. While using pretrained image classification networks as a perceptual loss can speed up style transfer [18], these do not work on shape changes as the pretrained networks tend only to capture low-level texture information [2].

Instead, we use multi-scale structure similarity loss (MS-SSIM) [36]. This loss better preserves features visible to humans instead of noisy high frequency information. MS-SSIM can also better cope with shape change since it can recognize geometric differences through area statistics. However, MS-SSIM alone can ignore smaller details, and does not capture color similarity well. Recent work has shown that mixing MS-SSIM with L1 or L2 losses is effective for super resolution and segmentation tasks [41]. Thus, we also add a lightly-weighted L1 loss term, which helps increase the clarity of generated images.

Feature Matching Loss. To increase the stability of the model, our objective function uses a feature matching loss [33]:

$$\mathcal{L}_{\text{FM}}(G, D) = \frac{1}{n-1} \sum_{i=1}^{n-1} \|\mathbb{E}_{x \sim p_{\text{data}}} f_i(x) - \mathbb{E}_{z \sim p_z} f_i(G(z))\|_2^2. \tag{1}$$

Where $f_i \in D(x)$ represents the raw activation potentials of the ith layer of the discriminator D, and n is the number of discriminator layers. This term encourages fake and real samples to produce similar activations in the discriminator, and so encourages the generator to create images that look more similar to the target domain. We have found this loss term to prevent generator mode collapse, to which GANs are often susceptible [19,33,35].

Scheduled Loss Normalization (SLN). In a multi-part loss function, linear weights are often used to normalize the terms with respect to one another, with previous works often optimizing a single set of weights. However, finding appropriately-balanced weights can prove difficult without ground truth. Further, often a single set of weights is inappropriate because the magnitude of the loss terms changes over the course of training. Instead, we create a procedure to periodically renormalize each loss term and so control their relative values. This lets the user intuitively provide weights that sum to 1 to balance the loss terms in the model, without having knowledge of how their magnitudes will change over training.

Let $\mathcal{L}$ be a loss function, and let $\mathcal{X}_n = \{x_t\}_{t=1}^{bn}$ be a sequence of n batches of training inputs, each b images large, such that $\mathcal{L}(x_t)$ is the training loss at iteration t. We compute an exponentially-weighted moving average of the loss:

$$\mathcal{L}_{\text{moavg}}(\mathcal{L}, \mathcal{X}_n) = (1 - \beta) \sum_{x_t \in \mathcal{X}_n} \beta^{bn-t} \mathcal{L}(x_t)^2 \qquad (2)$$

where β is the decay rate. We can renormalize the loss function by dividing it by this moving average. If we do this on every training iteration, however, the loss stays at its normalized average and no training progress is made. Instead, we schedule the loss normalization:

$$\text{SLN}(\mathcal{L}, \mathcal{X}_n, s) = \begin{cases} \mathcal{L}(\mathcal{X}_n)/(\mathcal{L}_{\text{moavg}}(\mathcal{L}, \mathcal{X}_n) + \epsilon) & \text{if } n \ (\text{mod } s) = 1 \\ \mathcal{L}(\mathcal{X}_n) & \text{otherwise} \end{cases}$$

Here, s is the scheduling parameter such that we apply normalization every s training iterations. For all experiments, we use $\beta = 0.99$, $\epsilon = 10^{-10}$, and $s = 200$.

One other normalization difference between CycleGAN/DiscoGAN and our approach is the use of instance normalization [15] and batch normalization [16], respectively. We found that batch normalization caused excessive over-fitting to the training data, and so we used instance normalization.

Final Objective. Our final objective comprises three loss normalized terms: a standard GAN loss, a feature matching loss, and two cyclic reconstruction losses. Given image domains X and Y, let $G : X \to Y$ map from X to Y and $F : Y \to X$ map from Y to X. D_X and D_Y denote discriminators for G and F, respectively.

For GAN loss, we combine normal GAN loss terms from Goodfellow et al. [11]:

$$\mathcal{L}_{\text{GAN}} = \mathcal{L}_{\text{GAN}_X}(F, D_X, Y, X) + \mathcal{L}_{\text{GAN}_Y}(G, D_Y, X, Y) \qquad (3)$$

For feature matching loss, we use Eq. 1 for each domain:

$$\mathcal{L}_{FM} = \mathcal{L}_{FM_X}(G, D_X) + \mathcal{L}_{FM_Y}(F, D_Y) \tag{4}$$

For the two cyclic reconstruction losses, we consider structural similarity [36] and an $\mathbb{L}_1$ loss. Let $X' = F(G(X))$ and $Y' = G(F(Y))$ be the cyclically-reconstructed input images. Then:

$$\mathcal{L}_{SS} = (1 - \text{MS-SSIM}(X', X)) + (1 - \text{MS-SSIM}(Y', Y)) \tag{5}$$
$$\mathcal{L}_{L1} = \|X' - X\|_1 + \|Y' - Y\|_1 \tag{6}$$

where we compute MS-SSIM without discorrelation.

Our total objective function with scheduled loss normalization (SLN) is:

$$\mathcal{L}_{total} = \lambda_{GAN}\text{SLN}(\mathcal{L}_{GAN}) + \lambda_{FM}\text{SLN}(\mathcal{L}_{FM}) + $$
$$\lambda_{CYC}\text{SLN}(\lambda_{SS}\mathcal{L}_{SS} + \lambda_{L1}\mathcal{L}_{L1}) \tag{7}$$

with $\lambda_{GAN} + \lambda_{FM} + \lambda_{CYC} = 1$, $\lambda_{SS} + \lambda_{L1} = 1$, and all coefficients ≥ 0. We set $\lambda_{GAN} = 0.49$, $\lambda_{FM} = 0.21$, and $\lambda_{CYC} = 0.3$, and $\lambda_{SS} = 0.7$ and $\lambda_{L1} = 0.3$. Empirically, these helped to reduce mode collapse and worked across all datasets. For all training details, we refer the reader to our supplemental material.

4 Experiments

4.1 Toy Problem: Learning 2D Dot and Polygon Deformations

We created a challenging toy problem to evaluate the ability of our network design to learn shape- and texture-consistent deformation. We define two domains: the regular polygon domain X and its deformed equivalent Y (Fig. 3). Each example $X_{s,h,d} \in X$ contains a centered regular polygon with $s \in \{3 \dots 7\}$ sides, plus a deformed matrix of dots overlaid. The dot matrix is computed by taking a unit dot grid and transforming it via h, a Gaussian random normal 2×2 matrix, and a displacement vector d, a Gaussian normal vector in $\mathbb{R}^2$.

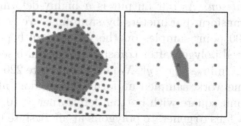

Fig. 3. Toy dataset (128×128). *Left:* $\mathcal{X}$ instance; a regular polygon with deformed dot matrix overlay. *Right:* $\mathcal{Y}$ instance; a deformed polygon and dot lattice. The dot lattice provides information from across the image to the true deformation.

Table 2. Toy dataset. When estimating complex deformation, DiscoGAN collapses to the mean dataset value (near white). CycleGAN approximates the deformation of the polygon but not the dot lattice (right-hand side). Our approach learns both.

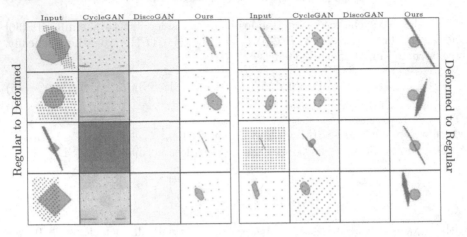

The corresponding domain equivalent in Y is $Y_{s,h,d}$, with instead the polygon transformed by h and the dot matrix remaining regular. This construction forms a bijection from X to Y, and so the translation problem is well-posed.

Learning a mapping from X to Y requires the network to use the large-scale cues present in the dot matrix to successfully deform the polygon, as local patches with a fixed image location cannot overcome the added displacement d. Table 2 shows that DiscoGAN is unable to learn to map between either domain, and produces an output that is close to the mean of the dataset (off-white). CycleGAN is able to learn only local deformation, which produces hue shifts towards the blue of the polygon when mapping from regular to deformed spaces, and which in most cases produces an undeformed dot matrix when mapping from deformed to regular spaces. In contrast, our approach is significantly more successful at learning the deformation as the dilated discriminator is able to incorporate information from across the image.

Quantitative Comparison. As our output is a highly-deformed image, we estimate the learned transform parameters by sampling. We compute a Hausdorff distance between 500 point samples on the ground truth polygon and on the image of the generated polygon after translation: for finite sets of points X and Y, $d(X,Y) = \max_{y \in Y} \min_{x \in X} \|x - y\|$. We hand annotate 220 generated polygon boundaries for our network, sampled uniformly at random along the boundary. Samples exist in a unit square with bottom left corner at $(0, 0)$.

First, DiscoGAN fails to generate polygons at all, despite being able to reconstruct the original image. Second, for 'regular to deformed', CycleGAN fails to produce a polygon, whereas our approach produces average Hausdorff distance of 0.20 ± 0.01. Third, for 'deformed to regular', CycleGAN produces a polygon with distance of 0.21 ± 0.04, whereas our approach has distance of 0.10 ± 0.03.

In the true dataset, note that regular polygons are centered, but CycleGAN only constructs polygons at the position of the original distorted polygon. Our network constructs a regular polygon at the center of the image as desired.

4.2 Real-World Datasets

We evaluate GANimorph on several image datasets. For human faces, we use the aligned version of the CelebFaces Attribute dataset [26], with 202,599 images.

Table 3. GANimorph is able to translate shape and style changes while retaining input attributes such as hair color, pose, glasses, headgear, and background.

Anime Faces. Previous works have noted that anime images are challenging for style transfer methods, since translating between photoreal and anime faces involves both shape and appearance changes. We create a large 966,777 image anime dataset crowdsourced from Danbooru [1]. The Danbooru dataset has a wide variety of styles from super-deformed chibi-style faces, to realistically-proportioned faces, to rough sketches. Since traditional face detectors yield poor results on drawn datasets, we ran the Animeface filter [29] on both datasets.

When translating humans to anime, we see an improvement in our approach for head pose and accessories such as glasses (Table 3, 3rd row, right), plus a larger degree of shape deformation such as reduced face vertical height. The final line of each group represents a particularly challenging example.

Doll Faces. Translating human faces to dolls provides an informative test case: both domains have similar photorealistic appearance, so the translation task focuses on shape more than texture. Similar to Morishita et al. [28], we extracted 13,336 images from the Flickr100m dataset [30] using specific doll manufacturers as keywords. Then, we extract local binary patterns [31] using OpenCV [4], and use the Animeface filter for facial alignment [29].

Table 3, bottom, shows that our architecture handles local deformation and global shape change better than CycleGAN and DiscoGAN, while preserving local texture similarity. Either the shape is malformed (DiscoGAN), or the shape shows artifacts from the original image or unnatural skin texture (CycleGAN). Our method matches skintones from the CelebA dataset, while capturing the overall facial structure and hair color of the doll. For a more difficult doll to human example in the bottom right-hand corner, while our transformation is not realistic, our method still creates more shape change than existing networks.

Pets in the Wild. To demonstrate our network on unaligned data, we evaluate on the Kaggle cat and dog dataset [9]. This contains 12,500 images of each species, across many animal breeds at varying scales, lighting conditions, poses, backgrounds, and occlusion factors.

When translating between cats and dogs (Table 4), the network is able to change both the local features such as the addition and removal of fur and whiskers, plus the larger shape deformation required to fool the discriminator, such as growing a snout. Most errors in this domain come from the generator failing to identify an animal from the background, such as forgetting the rear or tail of the animal. Sometimes the generator may fail to identify the animal at all.

We also translate between humans and cats. Table 5 demonstrates how our architecture handles large scale translation with these two variable data distributions. Our failure cases are approximately the same as that of the cats to dogs translation, with some promising results. Overall, we translate a surprising degree of shape deformation even when we might not expect this to be possible.

4.3   Quantitative Study

To quantify GANimorph's translation ability, we consider classification-based metrics to detect class change, e.g., whether a cat was successfully translated into a dog. Since there is no per pixel ground truth in this task for any real-world

Table 4. Pets in the Wild: Between dogs and cats, our approach is able to generate shape transforms across pose and appearance variation.

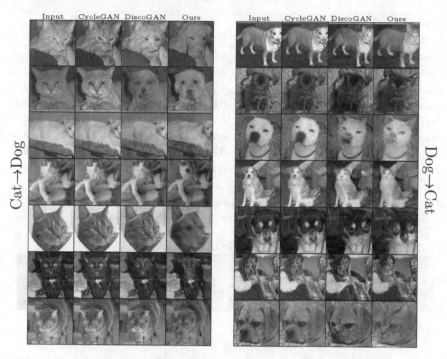

Table 5. Human and Pet Faces (dataset details in supplemental): As a challenge, we map humans to cats and cats to humans. Pose is reliably translated; semantic appearance like hair color is sometimes translated; some inputs still fail (bottom left).

Table 6. Percentage of pixels classified in translated images via CycleGAN, DiscoGAN, and our algorithm (with design choices). Target classes are in blue.

Class (%)	Cat → Dog				Dog → Cat			
Networks	Cat	**Dog**	Person	Other	**Cat**	Dog	Person	Other
Initial Domain	100.00	0.00	0.00	0.00	0.00	98.49	1.51	0.00
CycleGAN	99.99	0.01	0.00	0.00	2.67	97.27	0.06	0.00
DiscoGAN	24.37	75.38	0.25	0.00	96.95	0.00	2.71	0.34
Ours w/ L1	100.00	0.00	0.00	0.00	0.00	0.00	0.00	100.00
Ours w/o feature match loss	5.03	93.64	0.81	0.53	85.62	14.15	0.00	0.23
Ours w/ fully conn. discrim	6.11	93.60	0.29	0.00	91.41	8.45	0.03	0.10
Ours w/ patch discrim	46.02	42.90	0.05	11.03	91.77	8.22	0.00	0.01
Ours (dilated discrim.)	1.00	**98.57**	0.41	0.02	**100.00**	0.00	0.00	0.00

Table 7. Example segmentation masks from DeepLabV3 for Table 6 for Cat → Dog. Red denotes the cat class, and blue denotes the intended dog class.

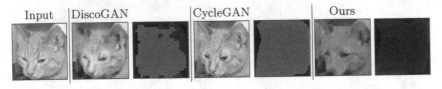

datasets, we cannot use Fully Convolution Score. Using Inception Score [33] is uninformative since simply outputting the original image would score highly.

Further, similar to adversarial examples, CycleGAN is able to convince many classification networks that the image is translated even though to a human the image appears untranslated: all CycleGAN results from supplemental Table 3 convince both ResNet50 [12] and the traditional segmentation network of Zheng et al. [42], even though the image is unsuccessfully translated.

However, semantic segmentation networks that use dilated convolutions can distinguish CycleGAN's 'adversarial examples' from true translations, such as DeepLabV3 [5]. As such, we run each test image through the DeepLabV3 network to generate a segmentation mask. Then, we compute the percent of non-background-labeled pixels per class, and average across the test set (Table 6). Our approach is able to more fully translate the image in the eyes of the classification network, with images also appearing translated to a human (Table 7).

4.4   Ablation Study

We use these quantiative settings for an ablation study (Table 6). First, we removed MS-SSIM to leave only L1 ($\mathcal{L}_{SS}$, Eq. 7), which causes our network to mode collapse. Next, we removed feature match loss, but this decreases both our segmentation consistency and the stability of the network. Then, we replaced our

Table 8. In qualitative comparisons, GANimorph outperforms all of its ablated versions. For instance, our approach better resolves fine details (e.g., second row, cat eyes) while also better translating the overall shape (e.g., last row, cat nose and ears).

Input	No FM Loss	L1 Loss	Patch Discr.	FC Discr.	Ours

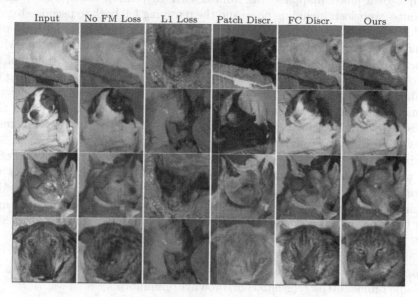

dilated discriminator with a patch discriminator. However, the patch discriminator cannot use global context, and so the network confuses facial layouts. Finally, we replace our dilated discriminator with a fully connected discriminator. We see that our generator architecture and loss function allow our network to outperform DiscoGAN even with the same type of discriminator (fully connected).

Qualitative ablation study results are shown in Table 8. The patch based discriminator translates texture well, but fails to create globally-coherent images. Decreasing the information flow by using a fully-connected discriminator or removing feature match leads to better results. Maximizing the information flow ultimately leads to the best results (last column). Using L1 instead of a perceptual cyclic loss term leads to mode collapse.

5   Discussion

There exists a trade off in the relative weighting of the cyclic loss. A higher cyclic loss term weight λ_{cyc} will prevent significant shape change and weaken the generator's ability to adapt to the discriminator. Setting it too low will cause the collapse of the network and prevent any meaningful mapping from existing between domains. For instance, the network can easily hallucinate objects in the other domain if the reconstruction loss is too low. Likewise, setting it too high will prevent the network from deforming the shape properly. As such, an architecture that allowed modifying the weighting of this term at test time would prove valuable for allowing the user control over how much deformation to allow.

One counter-intuitive result we discovered is that in domains with little variety, the mappings can lose semantic meaning (see supplemental material). One example of a failed mapping was from celebA to bitmoji faces [34, 37]. Many attributes were lost, including pose, and the mapping fell back to pseudo-steganographic encoding of the faces [7]. For example, background information would be encoded in color gradients of hair styles, and minor variations in the width of the eyes were used similarly. As such, the cyclic loss limits the ability of the network to abstract relevant details. Approaches such as relying on mapping the variance within each dataset, similar to Benaim et al. [3], may prove an effective means of ensuring the variance in either domain is maintained. We found that this term over-constrained the amount of shape change in the target domain; however, this may be worth further investigation.

Finally, trying to learn each domain simultaneously may also prove an effective way to increase the accuracy of image translation. Doing so allows the discriminator(s) and generator to learn how to better determine and transform regions of interest for either network. Better results might be obtained by mapping between multiple domains using parameter-efficient networks (e.g., StarGAN [6]).

Repository: The source code to our GANimorph system and all datasets are available online: https://github.com/brownvc/ganimorph/.

Acknowledgement. Kwang In Kim thanks RCUK EP/M023281/1.

References

1. Anonymous, Branwen, G., Gokaslan, A.: Danbooru 2017: a large-scale crowd-sourced and tagged anime illustration dataset, April 2017. https://www.gwern.net/Danbooru2017
2. Bau, D., Zhou, B., Khosla, A., Oliva, A., Torralba, A.: Network dissection: quantifying interpretability of deep visual representations. In: Computer Vision and Pattern Recognition (2017)
3. Benaim, S., Wolf, L.: One-sided unsupervised domain mapping. In: Advances in Neural Information Processing Systems (2017)
4. Bradski, G.: The OpenCV library. Dr. Dobb's J. Softw. Tools **120**, 122–125 (2000)
5. Chen, L.C., Papandreou, G., Schroff, F., Adam, H.: Rethinking atrous convolution for semantic image segmentation. arXiv preprint arXiv:1706.05587 (2017)
6. Choi, Y., Choi, M., Kim, M., Ha, J.W., Kim, S., Choo, J.: StarGAN: unified generative adversarial networks for multi-domain image-to-image translation. In: Computer Vision and Pattern Recognition (2018)
7. Chu, C., Zhmoginov, A., Sandler, M.: CycleGAN: a master of steganography. arXiv preprint arXiv:1712.02950 (2017)
8. Dumoulin, V., Shlens, J., Kudlur, M.: A learned representation for artistic style. In: International Conference on Learning Representations (2017)
9. Elson, J., Douceur, J., Howell, J., Saul, J.: Asirra: a CAPTCHA that exploits interest-aligned manual image categorization. In: Proceedings of the 14th ACM Conference on Computer and Communications Security, CCS 2007 (2007)

10. Gatys, L.A., Ecker, A.S., Bethge, M.: Image style transfer using convolutional neural networks. In: Computer Vision and Pattern Recognition (2016)
11. Goodfellow, I., et al.: Generative adversarial nets. In: Advances in Neural Information Processing Systems (2014)
12. He, K., Zhang, X., Ren, S., Sun, J.: Deep residual learning for image recognition. In: Computer Vision and Pattern Recognition (2016)
13. He, M., Liao, J., Yuan, L., Sander, P.V.: Neural color transfer between images. arXiv preprint arXiv:1710.00756 (2017)
14. Hertzmann, A., Jacobs, C.E., Oliver, N., Curless, B., Salesin, D.H.: Image analogies. In: Proceedings of the 28th Annual Conference on Computer Graphics and Interactive Techniques. ACM (2001)
15. Huang, X., Belongie, S.J.: Arbitrary style transfer in real-time with adaptive instance normalization. In: International Conference on Computer Vision (2017)
16. Ioffe, S., Szegedy, C.: Batch normalization: accelerating deep network training by reducing internal covariate shift. In: International Conference on Machine Learning (2015)
17. Isola, P., Zhu, J.Y., Zhou, T., Efros, A.A.: Image-to-image translation with conditional adversarial networks. In: Computer Vision and Pattern Recognition (2017)
18. Johnson, J., Alahi, A., Fei-Fei, L.: Perceptual losses for real-time style transfer and super-resolution. In: Leibe, B., Matas, J., Sebe, N., Welling, M. (eds.) ECCV 2016. LNCS, vol. 9906, pp. 694–711. Springer, Cham (2016). https://doi.org/10.1007/978-3-319-46475-6_43
19. Kim, T., Cha, M., Kim, H., Lee, J.K., Kim, J.: Learning to discover cross-domain relations with generative adversarial networks. In: International Conference on Machine Learning (2017)
20. Laffont, P.Y., Ren, Z., Tao, X., Qian, C., Hays, J.: Transient attributes for high-level understanding and editing of outdoor scenes. ACM Trans. Graph. (TOG) **33**(4), 149 (2014)
21. Li, C., Wand, M.: Precomputed real-time texture synthesis with markovian generative adversarial networks. In: Leibe, B., Matas, J., Sebe, N., Welling, M. (eds.) ECCV 2016. LNCS, vol. 9907, pp. 702–716. Springer, Cham (2016). https://doi.org/10.1007/978-3-319-46487-9_43
22. Liang, X., Zhang, H., Xing, E.P.: Generative semantic manipulation with contrasting GAN. arXiv preprint arXiv:1708.00315 (2017)
23. Liao, J., Yao, Y., Yuan, L., Hua, G., Kang, S.B.: Visual attribute transfer through deep image analogy. ACM Trans. Graph. (2017)
24. Liu, M.Y., Breuel, T., Kautz, J.: Unsupervised image-to-image translation networks. In: Advances in Neural Information Processing Systems (2017)
25. Liu, M.Y., Tuzel, O.: Coupled generative adversarial networks. In: Advances in Neural Information Processing Systems (2016)
26. Liu, Z., Luo, P., Wang, X., Tang, X.: Deep learning face attributes in the wild. In: International Conference on Computer Vision (2015)
27. Ma, S., Fu, J., Chen, C.W., Mei, T.: DA-GAN: instance-level image translation by deep attention generative adversarial networks. In: Conference on Computer Vision and Pattern Recognition (2018)
28. Morishita, M., Ueno, M., Isahara, H.: Classification of doll image dataset based on human experts and computational methods: a comparative analysis. In: International Conference On Advanced Informatics: Concepts, Theory And Application (ICAICTA) (2016)
29. Nagadomi: lbpcascade_animeface (2017). https://github.com/nagadomi/lbpcascade_animeface

30. Ni, K., et al.: Large-scale deep learning on the YFCC100M dataset. arXiv preprint arXiv:1502.03409 (2015)
31. Ojala, T., Pietikainen, M., Harwood, D.: Performance evaluation of texture measures with classification based on kullback discrimination of distributions. In: International Conference on Pattern Recognition (1994)
32. Radford, A., Metz, L., Chintala, S.: Unsupervised representation learning with deep convolutional generative adversarial networks. arXiv e-prints, November 2015
33. Salimans, T., Goodfellow, I., Zaremba, W., Cheung, V., Radford, A., Chen, X.: Improved techniques for training GANs. In: Advances in Neural Information Processing Systems (2016)
34. Taigman, Y., Polyak, A., Wolf, L.: Unsupervised cross-domain image generation. arXiv preprint arXiv:1611.02200 (2016)
35. Wang, T.C., Liu, M.Y., Zhu, J.Y., Tao, A., Kautz, J., Catanzaro, B.: High-resolution image synthesis and semantic manipulation with conditional GANs. In: Computer Vision and Pattern Recognition (2018)
36. Wang, Z., Bovik, A.C., Sheikh, H.R., Simoncelli, E.P.: Image quality assessment: from error visibility to structural similarity. Trans. Image Process. **13**(4), 600–612 (2004)
37. Wolf, L., Taigman, Y., Polyak, A.: Unsupervised creation of parameterized avatars. In: International Conference on Computer Vision (2017)
38. Yi, Z., Zhang, H.R., Tan, P., Gong, M.: DualGAN: unsupervised dual learning for image-to-image translation. In: International Conference on Computer Vision (2017)
39. Yu, F., Koltun, V.: Multi-scale context aggregation by dilated convolutions. In: International Conference on Learning Representations (2015)
40. Zeiler, M.D., Fergus, R.: Visualizing and understanding convolutional networks. In: Fleet, D., Pajdla, T., Schiele, B., Tuytelaars, T. (eds.) ECCV 2014. LNCS, vol. 8689, pp. 818–833. Springer, Cham (2014). https://doi.org/10.1007/978-3-319-10590-1_53
41. Zhao, H., Gallo, O., Frosio, I., Kautz, J.: Loss functions for image restoration with neural networks. IEEE Trans. Comput. Imaging **3**(1), 47–57 (2017)
42. Zheng, S., et al.: Conditional random fields as recurrent neural networks. In: International Conference on Computer Vision (2015)
43. Zhu, J.Y., Park, T., Isola, P., Efros, A.A.: Unpaired image-to-image translation using cycle-consistent adversarial networkss. In: International Conference on Computer Vision (2017)

SwapNet: Image Based Garment Transfer

Amit Raj[1]([⊠]), Patsorn Sangkloy[1], Huiwen Chang[2], James Hays[1,3], Duygu Ceylan[4], and Jingwan Lu[4]

[1] Georgia Institute of Technology, Atlanta, USA
amit.raj@gatech.edu
[2] Princeton University, Princeton, USA
[3] Argo AI, San Francisco, USA
[4] Adobe Research, San Jose, USA

Abstract. We present *Swapnet*, a framework to transfer garments across images of people with arbitrary body pose, shape, and clothing. Garment transfer is a challenging task that requires (i) disentangling the features of the clothing from the body pose and shape and (ii) realistic synthesis of the garment texture on the new body. We present a neural network architecture that tackles these sub-problems with two task-specific sub-networks. Since acquiring pairs of images showing the same clothing on different bodies is difficult, we propose a novel weakly-supervised approach that generates training pairs from a single image via data augmentation. We present the first fully automatic method for garment transfer in unconstrained images without solving the difficult 3D reconstruction problem. We demonstrate a variety of transfer results and highlight our advantages over traditional image-to-image and analogy pipelines.

1 Introduction

Imagine being able to try on different types of clothes from celebrities' red carpet appearance within the comfort of your own home, within minutes, and without hours of shopping. In this work, we aim to fulfill this goal with an algorithm to transfer garment information between two single view images depicting people in arbitrary pose, shape, and clothing (Fig. 1). Beyond virtual fitting room applications, such a system could be useful as an image editing tool. For example, after a photo-shoot a photographer might decide that the subject would look better in a different outfit for the photographic setting and lighting condition. Garment transfer is also useful for design ideation to answer questions like "how does this style of clothing look on different body shapes and proportions?"

These applications require solving the challenging problem of jointly inferring the body pose, shape, and clothing of a person. Most virtual try-on applications address this challenge by making simplifying assumptions. They either use predefined virtual avatars in a small set of allowed poses or require an accurate 3D scan of the individual to demonstrate a limited selection of clothes using physical cloth simulation [1]. The recent approach for garment recovery and transfer [2]

© Springer Nature Switzerland AG 2018
V. Ferrari et al. (Eds.): ECCV 2018, LNCS 11216, pp. 679–695, 2018.
https://doi.org/10.1007/978-3-030-01258-8_41

Fig. 1. SwapNet can interchange garment appearance between two single view images (A and B) of people with arbitrary shape and pose.

involves 3D reconstruction of the human body and estimation of the parameters of pre-defined cloth templates. The proposed model fitting approach is computationally expensive and the quality is limited by the representational power of the pre-defined templates. None of these approaches address the problem of transferring arbitrary clothes to an arbitrary person and pose in the image space.

Transferring garment information between images inherently requires solving three sub-problems. First, the garment pieces need to be identified from the input images. Second, the shape, e.g., the outline of each garment piece, needs to be transferred across two bodies with potentially different pose and shape. Finally, the texture of the garment needs to be synthesized realistically in this new shape. Our approach focuses on solving the last two stages, *warping* (Fig. 2) and *texturing* (Fig. 6), using a learning approach.

Assume we have an image A, depicting the desired clothing, and B, showing the target body and pose. Learning to directly transfer detailed clothing from A to B is challenging due to large differences in body shape, cloth outlines, and pose between the two images. Instead, we propose to first transfer the clothing segmentation A_{cs} of A, based on the body segmentation B_{bs} of B to generate the appropriate warped clothing segmentation B'_{cs} which is different from B's original clothing segmentation B_{cs}. This segmentation warping operation is easier to learn since it does not require the transfer of high frequency texture details. Once the desired clothing segmentation B'_{cs} is generated, we next transfer the clothing details from A to B conditioned on B'_{cs} for final result.

In the ideal scenario, given pairs of photos (A, B) of people in different poses with different proportions wearing the exact same clothing, we could train a 2-stage pipeline in a supervised manner. However, such a dataset is hard to obtain and therefore we propose a novel weakly supervised approach where we use a single image and its augmentations as exemplars of A and B to train *warping* and *texturizing* networks. We introduce mechanisms to prevent the networks from learning the identity mapping such that *warping* and *texturizing* can be applied when A and B depict different individuals at test time. At both training and

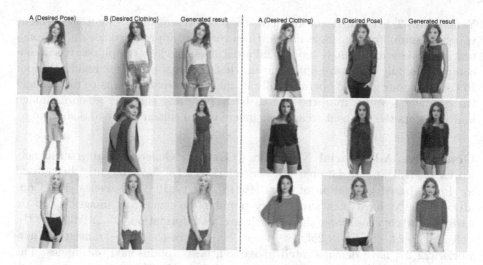

Fig. 2. Demonstration of clothing transfer.

test time, we assume that we have access to the body and clothing segmentation of the image from state-of-the-art human parsing pipelines.

No previous works address the problem we have at hand – transferring garment from the picture of one person to the picture of another with no constraints on identity, poses, body shapes and clothing categories in the source and target images. We argue that garment transfer in our unconstrained setting is a more challenging task. It requires disentangling the target clothing from the corresponding body and retargetting it to a different body where ideal training data for supervised learning are hard to obtain.

To summarize, we make the following contributions: (1) We present the first method that operates in image-space to transfer garment information across images with arbitrary clothing, body poses, and shapes. Our approach eschews the need for 3D reconstruction or parameter estimation of cloth templates. (2) With the absence of ideal training data for supervision, we introduce a weakly supervised learning approach to accomplish this task.

2   Related Work

Human Parsing and Understanding. There is significant work in the computer vision community for human understanding from monocular images. We can group the related work under two main methodologies, where, one line of work explicitly focuses on parsing clothing items from images [3], while the other approaches focus on modeling the human body in terms of 2D pose [4], body part segmentation [5], 3D pose [6], or 3D body shape [7]. A few approaches tackle the problem of jointly modeling the 3D body shape and garments but require additional information in the form of depth scans [8,9]. The recent work of

682   A. Raj et al.

Yang et al. [2] is the first automatic method to present high-resolution garment transfer results from a single image. However, this approach relies on the existence of a deformable body model and a database of cloth templates. It solves a computationally expensive optimization that requires priors for regularization. In contrast, our method operates fully in the image space, learns to disentangle the garment features from the human body pose and shape in a source image and transfers the garment to another image with arbitrary pose and shape.

Generative Adversarial Networks (GANs). Generative adversarial networks [10–13] and variational auto-encoders [14,15] have recently been used for image-based generation of faces [16–18], birds [19], and scenes [12]. Conditional GANs have been particularly popular for generating images based on various kinds of conditional signals such as class information [20], attributes [21], sketch [22–24], text [19,25], or pose [26]. Image-to-image translation networks [22,27] have demonstrated image synthesis conditioned on images. The texturing stage of our framework is inspired from the U-Net architecture [28]. However, we have *two* conditioning images where one provides the desired garment and the other shows the desired body pose and shape.

Image-Based Garment Synthesis. Several recent works attempt to solve problems similar to ours. The work by Lassner et al. [29] presents an approach to generate images of people in arbitrary clothing conditioned on pose. More recent methods [26,30] propose a framework to modify the viewpoint or the pose of a person from an image while keeping the clothing the same. Some recent works [31,32] attempt to transfer a stand-alone piece of clothing to an image of a person, whilst another work [33] solves the opposite task of generating a stand-alone piece of clothing given a person image. Finally, the work of Zhu et al. [34] generates different clothing from a given image based on textual descriptions, whilst retaining the pose of the original image. Yang et al. [2] propose a pipeline different from generative models, which involves estimation of the 3D body model followed by cloth simulation. Ma et al. [35] propose an approach to disentangle pose, foreground, and background from an image in an unsupervised manner such that different disentangled representations can be used to generate new images. They did not solve our exact problem of transferring the garment from source to target while maintaining the target picture's identity. In fact, the identity is often lost in their transfer process. Another difference is that they represent the desired pose to transfer garments to as silhouette derived from sparse pose key points while we operate on individual cloth segments. Clothing segmentation provides more informative signals than pose key points, which allows us to transfer the garment from source to target more precisely.

Visual Analogies. There has been recent interest in visual analogy pipelines which synthesize an image by inferring the transformation between a pair of images and then applying that transformation to a new image. The work by

Reed et al. [36] generates the analogous image for a particular input instance given the relationship between a similar pair of images. They show good generation results on simple 2D shapes, 3D car models and video game sprites. The more recent work by Liao et al. [37] presents a framework that, given two images, A and B', generates two additional images A' and B, such that each input and output image form an analogical pair (A, A') and (B, B'). Our work is similar in spirit to this work in that, given two full-body images of people in clothing, we can transfer the clothing between the pair of images. However, our formulation is more challenging, as the system has to reason about the concept of clothing explicitly.

3   SwapNet

We present a garment transfer system that can swap clothing between a pair of images while preserving the pose and body shape. We achieve this by disentangling the concept of *clothing* from that of *body shape and pose*, so that we can change either the person or the clothing and recombine them as we desire.

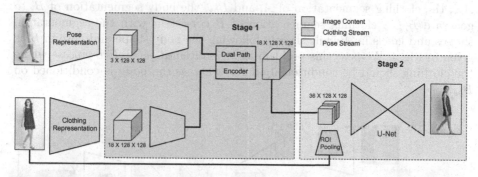

Fig. 3. Our pipeline consists of two stages: (1) the *warping* stage, which generates a clothing segmentation consistent with the desired pose and (2) the *texturing* stage, which uses clothing information from desired clothing image to synthesize detailed clothing texture consistent with the clothing segmentation from the previous stage.

Given an image A containing a person wearing desired clothing and an image B portraying another person in the target body shape and pose, we generate an image B' composed of the same person as in B wearing the desired clothing in A. Note that A and B can depict different persons of diverse body shape and pose wearing arbitrary clothing.

Increasingly popular conditional generative models use encoder-decoder types of network architectures to transform an input image to produce output pixels directly. Recent work such as pix2pix and Scribbler [22,27] have shown high quality results on image translation tasks where the structure and shape in the output does not deviate much from the input. However, our garment

transfer task presents unique challenges. A successful transfer involves significant structural changes to the input images. As shown in previous work [34],
directly transferring both the shape and the texture details of the desired clothing to a target body gives the network too much burden resulting in poor transfer
quality.

We propose a two-stage pipeline (Fig. 3) to tackle the shape and texture
synthesis separately. Specifically, we argue that clothing and body segmentations
provide a concise and necessary representation of the desired clothing and the
target body. Thus, we first operate on these segmentations to perform the desired
shape change, i.e., generate a clothing segmentation in the target body shape
and pose of B but with the clothing in A. We assume the clothing segmentation
of image A and the body segmentation of image B are given or are computed by
previous work [3,7]. In a second stage, we propose a texturization network that
takes as input the synthesized clothing segmentation and image of the desired
clothing to generate the final transfer result.

3.1 Warping Module

The first stage of our pipeline, which we call the *warping module*, operates on
A_{cs}, the clothing segmentation of A, and B_{bs}, the body segmentation of B, to
generate B'_{cs}, a clothing segmentation of B consistent with the segmentation
shapes and labels in A while strictly following the body shape and pose in B as
given in Fig. 4. We pose this problem as a *conditioned generative process* where
the clothing should be conditioned on A_{cs} whereas the body is conditioned on
B_{bs}.

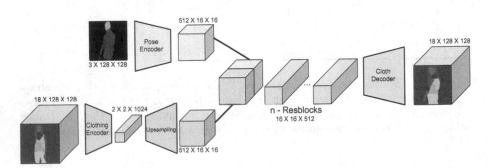

Fig. 4. Architecture of stage 1 module. The warp module consists of a dual-path U-net
strongly conditioned on the body segmentation and weakly conditioned on the clothing
segmentation.

We use a dual path [28] network to address the dual conditioning problem.
The dual path network consists of two streams of encoders, one for the body
and one for the clothing, and one decoder that combines the two encoded hidden
representations to generate the final output. We represent the clothing with a 18-
channel segmentation mask where we exclude small accessories such as belts or

glasses. Given this 18-channel segmentation map where each channel contains the probability map of one clothing category, the cloth encoder produces a feature map of size $512 \times 16 \times 16$ (16×16 features of size 512). Given a color-coded 3-channel body segmentation, the body encoder similarly produces a feature map of size $512 \times 16 \times 16$ to represent the target body. These encoded feature maps are concatenated and passed through 4 residual blocks. The resulting feature map is then up-sampled to generate the desired 18-channel clothing segmentation.

The generated image is strongly conditioned on the body segmentation and weakly conditioned on the clothing segmentation. This is achieved by encoding the clothing segmentation into a narrow representation of $2 \times 2 \times 1024$, before upsampling it to a feature map of the required size. This compact representation encourages the network to distill high-level information such as the types of clothing items (top, bottom, shoes, skin, etc.) and the general shape of each item from the clothing stream, whilst restricting the generated segmentation to closely follow the target pose and body shape embedded in the body segmentation.

To supervise the training, ideally we need ground-truth triplets ($B_{bs} + A_{cs} \Rightarrow B'_{cs}$) as in [26]. However, such a dataset is hard to obtain and is often not scalable for larger variation in clothing. Instead, we use a self-supervised approach to generate the required triplets. Specifically, given a single image B, we consider the triplet ($B_{bs} + B_{cs} \Rightarrow B'_{cs}$) for which we can directly supervise. With this setting, however, there is a danger for the network to learn the identity mapping since $B_{cs} = B'_{cs}$. To avoid this, we use augmentations of B_{cs} instead. We perform random affine transformations (including random crops and flips). This encourages the network to discard locational cues from B_{cs} and pick up only high-level cues regarding the types and structures of the clothing segments.

We choose to represent the clothing segmentation as a 18-channel probability map instead of a 3-channel color-coded segmentation image to allow the model more flexibility to warp each individual segment separately. During training, each channel of the segmentation image undergoes a different affine transform, and hence the network should learn higher level relational reasoning between each channel and the corresponding body segment. For the body segmentation, in contrast, we use the 3-channel color-coded image, similar to Lassner et al. [29] as we observe a more fine-grained encoding of the body segmentation does not offer much more information. The color-coded body segmentation image also provides guidance as to where each clothing segment should be aligned, which overall provides a stronger cue about body shape and pose. Additionally, since clothing segments span over multiple body segments, keeping the structure of the entire body image is more beneficial than splitting the body segment into individual channels.

The warping module is trained with the combination of cross entropy loss and GAN loss. Specifically, our warping module $z_{cs} = f1(A_{cs}, B_{bs})$ has the the following learning objectives:

$$\mathcal{L}_{CE} = -\sum_{c=1}^{18} \mathbb{1}(A_{cs}(i,j) = c)(\log(z_{cs}(i,j))) \tag{1}$$

$$\mathcal{L}_{adv} = \mathbb{E}_{x\sim p(A_{cs})}[D(x)] + \mathbb{E}_{z\sim p(f1_{enc}(A_{cs},B_{bs}))}[1 - D(f1_{dec}(z))] \tag{2}$$

$$\mathcal{L}_{warp} = \mathcal{L}_{CE} + \lambda_{adv}\mathcal{L}_{adv} \tag{3}$$

where $\lambda_{adv}\mathcal{L}_{adv}$ refers to the adversarial component of the loss and $f1_{enc}$ and $f1_{dec}$ are the encoder and decoder components of the warp module. The weights of each component are tuned such that the gradient contribution from each loss is around the same order of magnitude. In our experiments, we observe that adding a small adversarial weight helps produce better convergence and shape retention of the generated segmentation.

Finally, to train and test this network, we use the DeepFashion dataset [38], where we use the LIP_SSL pretrained network [3] to generate clothing segmentations and use "Unite the People" [39] to obtain the body segmentation as in Fig. 5.

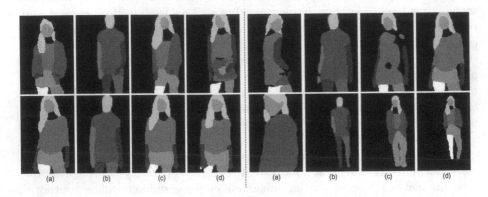

Fig. 5. Stage 1 segmentation visualization. (a) Clothing segmentation of A; (b) Body segmentation of B; (c) Generated clothing segmentation for B by warping module; (d) Original clothing segmentation of B.

3.2   Texturing Module

Our second stage network, the *texturing module*, is a U-Net architecture trained to generate texture details given the clothing segmentation at the desired body shape and pose, B'_{cs}, and an embedding of the desired clothing shown in image A. We obtain this embedding by ROI pooling on each of the 6 body parts (main body, left arm, right arm, left leg, right leg and face) of A and generating feature maps of size $3 \times 16 \times 16$, which are then upsampled to the original image size. We stack these feature maps with B'_{cs} before feeding them into the U-Net. The idea is to use the clothing segmentation to control the high-level structure and shape and use the clothing embedding to guide the hallucination of low-level color and details.

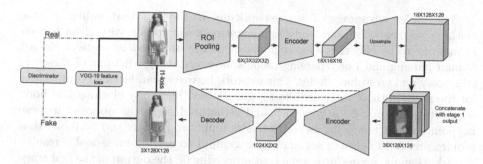

Fig. 6. Architecture of the stage 2 module. The texturing module is trained in a self supervised manner. The shape information input to the encoder is obtained from clothing segmentation and the texture information is obtained using ROI pooling.

Similar to the first stage, we train the texturing module in a weakly supervised way. Specifically, given an input image B, we consider the inputs to be $(B_{cs} +$ embedding of the clothing in $B \Rightarrow B)$. To avoid learning the identity mapping, we compute an embedding of the desired clothing from augmentations of B by performing random flips and crops. We use the L1 reconstruction loss, feature loss (VGG-19) and the GAN loss with DRAGAN gradient penalty [40] which has been shown to improve the sharpness of the results and stabilize the training of GANs. The learning objective of the second stage texturing module $f2$ is given as follows:

$$\mathcal{L}_{L1} = ||f2(z'_{cs}, A) - A||_1 \tag{4}$$

$$\mathcal{L}_{feat} = \sum_l \lambda_l ||\phi_l(f2(z'_{cs}, A)) - \phi_l(A)||_2 \tag{5}$$

$$\mathcal{L}_{adv} = \mathbb{E}_{x \sim p(A)}[D(x)] + \mathbb{E}_{z \sim p(f2_{enc})}[1 - D(f2_{dec}(z))] \tag{6}$$

where, ϕ_l accounts for loss w.r.t activations of some layer of a pretrained VGG-19 network. The discriminator for this stage has the following objective:

$$\mathcal{L}_{adv_d} = \mathbb{E}_{x \sim p(A)}[D(x)] + \mathbb{E}_{z \sim p(f2_{enc})}[1 - D(f2_{dec}(z))] + \lambda_{gp} \mathbb{E}_{z \sim P(z)}[|||\nabla_z D(z)||_2] \tag{7}$$

During testing, we use the clothing segmentation generated by the previous stage. Note that we flatten the 18 channel segmentation map by performing an argmax operation across the channels. This is done mainly to prevent artifacts due to output of stage 1 having non-zero values in more than 1 channel at a particular pixel location. This step is non-differentiable, and therefore disallows end-to-end training. However, we can perform an end-to-end fine-tuning of these pretrained networks by skipping the argmax step and employing a softmax instead. We would like to point out that our framework is robust to the noise in the input clothing and body segmentation. The second stage operates on noisy clothing segmentation generated from the first stage and learns to ignore the noise while filling in textures and colors.

The major advantage of our network lies in the fact that unlike [29] the clothing segmentation and body segmentation need not be very clean for our framework to be effective. Our segmentations are obtained by state of the art human parsing and body parsing models, however the predictions of these are still noisy and often have holes. Our network however, can learn to compensate for the noise in these intermediate representation. The noisy clothing and body segmentations provide a very rich and structured signal as opposed to pose keypoints whilst not being as restrictive as inputs to pix2pix and Scribbler that require precise sketches or segmentation as input to generate reasonable results.

Additionally, we perform some post processing on the output of the first stage to preserve the identity of the target individual before feeding it into the second stage. In particular, in the generated clothing segmentation B'_{cs}, we replace the "face" and "hair" segments with corresponding segments in the original clothing segmentation B_{cs}. Similarly, at the end of the second stage, we copy the face and hair pixels from B into the result. Without these steps, the whole framework becomes akin to reposing the same individual instead of re-targeting the clothing to a different individual.

4 Experiments

In this section, we show results of each stage and provide detailed quantitative and qualitative comparisons with baselines. We first explain the baseline methods and then discuss our findings.

4.1 Qualitative Evaluation

Need for Augmentation: To analyze the effects of different types of augmentation, we present an ablation study (Fig. 7), where stage 1 is trained (a) with no augmentation, (b) with only affine transforms, (c) with random flips and small affine transforms and (d) with flips and large affine transforms. While flips help to handle cases when source and target are on different regions of the frame, affine transformations are necessary in part to handle scale changes between source and target. We also show that crops and flips reduce leaking artifacts for the second stage (e).

Comparison with PG2: We compare SwapNet with the work of Ma et al. [26] on their provided test split (Fig. 8). We notice visible high frequency artifacts as a result of the second stage network in PG2. In contrast, as demonstrated by many previous work, adding feature loss makes the generated quality better because we match higher level feature statistics in addition to the color of the clothing component. Furthermore, we see that a "learned" representation of pose, such as body segmentation, provides richer guidance to the original target pose, as opposed to extracting a hand engineered mask from pose keypoints as in [26]. Additionally, body segmentations allow for just as much control as

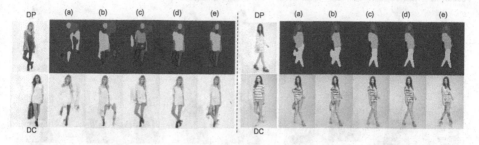

Fig. 7. Ablation study showing the need for various augmentations. Results from models trained with (a) no augmentations, (b) no flips + affine transforms, (c) flips + small affine transforms, (d) flips + large affine transforms (e) no flip on stage 2

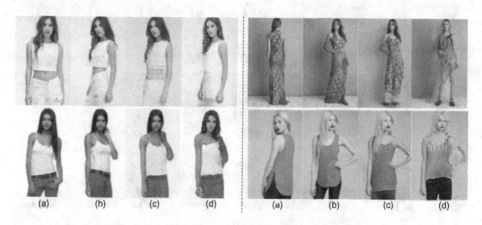

Fig. 8. Comparision with PG2. (a) Source pose, (b) Target Pose, (c) Ours (d) PG2.

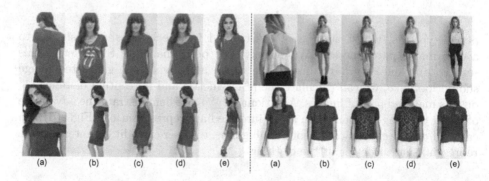

Fig. 9. Comparision with PG2. (a) Source pose, (b) Target Pose, (c) Ours, (d) Ours after user corrects intermediate clothing segmentation (e) PG2.

Fig. 10. Results of SwapNet, VITON and Visual Analogy on the Zolando dataset. Additional results on SwapNet-Feat (trained without Feature loss) and SwapNet-Gan (trained without GAN loss)

pose keypoints, whilst still being constrained by the body shape (similar to a deformable parts model). We evaluate the performance of SwapNet in this setting, and since we have direct supervision as to what the generated image should look like, we can calculate the SSIM metric and perceptual distance (1) on this matched pair of images. Additionally, We also demonstrate the advantage of using clothing segmentation as an intermediate representation (Fig. 9(d)). In cases where the clothing segment is ambiguous, the user can edit the intermediate representation to better fit the clothing.

Comparison with VITON and Visual Analogy: We present additional comparisons with VITON [32] and Deep Visual Analogy [37]. VITON transfers a product image of a clothing item onto an image of an individual using a two-stage approach, where the first stage involves generating a coarse transferred image using an Encoder-decoder network, and the second stage involves refining the generated image by warping the product image. Deep Visual Analogies produce images to complete analogies of the form A:A'::B:B'. Particularly, it generates images A' and B, given style and content image A and B'. We highlight that VITON and Deep Visual Analogy are not strict baselines since our target task of swapping clothing between portrait images in the wild is different from the task of VITON (virtual try-on based on product image) and Deep Visual Analogy (Style transfer). We cannot find other previous work addressing the same problem as ours, so we modify our problem setting slightly to compare with these related but different works. We use the test split used by VITON for fair comparison. VITON demonstrates clothing transfer on the Zolando dataset [32]. We observe that our model trained on the DeepFashion dataset is able to generalize to the Zolando dataset without additional finetuning.

4.2   Quantitative Results

We present the performance of different models on some of the common metrics for evaluating generative models. The inception score is a measure of how realistic images from a set look and how diverse they are. We also present the SSIM on a subset of data for which we have paired information.

Additionally, we use the VGG perceptual metric (PD) as suggested by [41]. We present PD(TP) – the perceptual distance to the target pose and PD(TC) – the perceptual distance to the target clothing image.

Table 1. Quantitative metrics for different models. Higher score is better for IS and SSIM and smaller is better for PD

Model	IS	SSIM	PD(TP)	PD(TC)
CGAN	2.11	0.22	-	-
PG2	**3.06**	0.09	-	-
Ours (w/o GAN w/o feat)	2.63 ± 0.061	**0.84**	0.075	0.114
Ours (w/o feat)	2.72 ± 0.032	0.82	0.057	0.100
Ours (w/o GAN)	2.75 ± 0.13	0.81	0.061	0.101
Ours	**3.04 ± 0.052**	0.83	**0.056**	**0.099**
Dataset	3.28	-		

For the most part we see that scores of all methods are clustered around similar values. The IS and SSIM metrics provide a good proxy to measure the performance but are not a true measurement of how well the model is performing the required task. The perceptual losses provide some more insights about the transfer performance. Particularly, we see that the SSIM scores favourably for a model trained without the GAN loss and feature loss. Since the network is trained with only L1 loss, the SSIM predicts that the generations are very close to ground truth. However, with the perceptual metric it can be clearly seen that the model w/o GAN and w/o feature loss performs worse perceptually. We see that our SwapNet model performs the best both in terms of inception score and the perceptual distance on the task of reposing a given clothing image (Table 1).

4.3 Limitations

Our framework has difficulty handling large pose changes between source and target images (top row of Fig. 11). If one of the images contain a truncated body and the other contains a full body, our model is not able to hallucinate appropriate details for the missing lower limbs. Furthermore, our framework is sensitive to occlusions by classes like hats and sunglasses, and might generate blending artifacts (the bottom row Fig. 11). The third row in Fig. 10 also shows that the network is sometimes unable to handle partial self occlusion.

Fig. 11. Limitations of SwapNet for clothing transfer. First row demonstrates extreme pose changes (DP: Desired pose; DC: Desired clothing; Gen: Generated image). Second row demonstrates occlusion by rare classes (hat, purse).

5   Conclusion

We present SwapNet, a framework for single view garment transfer. We motivate the need for a two-stage approach as opposed to a traditional "end-to-end" training pipeline and highlight the use of split channel segmentation as an intermediary stage for garment transfer. Additionally, we employ a novel weakly supervised training procedure to train the warping and texturization modules in the absence of supervised data for same clothing in different poses. In the future we aim to leverage a supervised subset that could potentially enable the model to handle larger pose and scale variations. We could also leverage approaches like warping as in [32], to further improve the details in the generated clothing.

Acknowledgements. This work was partially funded by Adobe Research and NSF award 1561968.

References

1. Zhou, Z., Shu, B., Zhuo, S., Deng, X., Tan, P., Lin, S.: Image-based clothes animation for virtual fitting. In: SIGGRAPH Asia 2012 Technical Briefs, p. 33. ACM (2012)
2. Yang, S., et al.: Detailed garment recovery from a single-view image. arXiv e-prints, August 2016
3. Gong, K., Liang, X., Zhang, D., Shen, X., Lin, L.: Look into person: self-supervised structure-sensitive learning and a new benchmark for human parsing. In: The IEEE Conference on Computer Vision and Pattern Recognition (CVPR), July 2017
4. Cao, Z., Simon, T., Wei, S.E., Sheikh, Y.: Realtime multi-person 2D pose estimation using part affinity fields. In: CVPR (2017)
5. Varol, G., et al.: Learning from synthetic humans. In: CVPR (2017)
6. Rogez, G., Weinzaepfel, P., Schmid, C.: LCR-Net: localization-classification-regression for human pose. In: CVPR (2017)
7. Bogo, F., Kanazawa, A., Lassner, C., Gehler, P., Romero, J., Black, M.J.: Keep it SMPL: automatic estimation of 3D human pose and shape from a single image. In: Leibe, B., Matas, J., Sebe, N., Welling, M. (eds.) ECCV 2016. LNCS, vol. 9909, pp. 561–578. Springer, Cham (2016). https://doi.org/10.1007/978-3-319-46454-1_34
8. Chen, X., Zhou, B., Lu, F., Wang, L., Bi, L., Tan, P.: Garment modeling with a depth camera. ACM Trans. Graph. **34**(6), 203:1–203:12 (2015)
9. Pons-Moll, G., Pujades, S., Hu, S., Black, M.: ClothCap: seamless 4D clothing capture and retargeting. ACM Trans. Graph. (Proc. SIGGRAPH) **36**(4), 73 (2017)
10. Goodfellow, I., et al.: Generative adversarial nets. In: Advances in Neural Information Processing Systems, pp. 2672–2680 (2014)
11. Radford, A., Metz, L., Chintala, S.: Unsupervised representation learning with deep convolutional generative adversarial networks. arXiv preprint arXiv:1511.06434 (2015)
12. Denton, E.L., Chintala, S., Fergus, R., et al.: Deep generative image models using a Laplacian pyramid of adversarial networks. In: Advances in Neural Information Processing Systems, pp. 1486–1494 (2015)
13. Zhao, J., Mathieu, M., LeCun, Y.: Energy-based generative adversarial network. In: International Conference on Learning Representations (ICLR) (2017)
14. Kingma, D.P., Welling, M.: Auto-encoding variational bayes. In: International Conference on Learning Representations (ICLR) (2014)
15. Pu, Y., et al.: Variational autoencoder for deep learning of images, labels and captions. In: Advances in Neural Information Processing Systems, pp. 2352–2360 (2016)
16. Yin, X., Yu, X., Sohn, K., Liu, X., Chandraker, M.: Towards large-pose face frontalization in the wild. In: International Conference on Computer Vision (ICCV) (2017)
17. Berthelot, D., Schumm, T., Metz, L.: Began: Boundary equilibrium generative adversarial networks. arXiv preprint arXiv:1703.10717 (2017)

18. Karras, T., Aila, T., Laine, S., Lehtinen, J.: Progressive growing of GANs for improved quality, stability, and variation. In: International Conference on Learning Representations (ICLR) (2018)
19. Reed, S., Akata, Z., Yan, X., Logeswaran, L., Schiele, B., Lee, H.: Generative adversarial text-to-image synthesis. In: Proceedings of The 33rd International Conference on Machine Learning (2016)
20. Mirza, M., Osindero, S.: Conditional generative adversarial nets. arXiv preprint arXiv:1411.1784 (2014)
21. Karacan, L., Akata, Z., Erdem, A., Erdem, E.: Learning to generate images of outdoor scenes from attributes and semantic layouts. arXiv preprint arXiv:1612.00215 (2016)
22. Sangkloy, P., Lu, J., Fang, C., Yu, F., Hays, J.: Scribbler: controlling deep image synthesis with sketch and color. In: IEEE Conference on Computer Vision and Pattern Recognition, CVPR (2017)
23. Liu, Y., Qin, Z., Luo, Z., Wang, H.: Auto-painter: cartoon image generation from sketch by using conditional generative adversarial networks. arXiv preprint arXiv:1705.01908 (2017)
24. Xian, W., Sangkloy, P., Lu, J., Fang, C., Yu, F., Hays, J.: Texturegan: controlling deep image synthesis with texture patches. In: IEEE Conference on Computer Vision and Pattern Recognition (CVPR) (2018)
25. Zhang, H., et al.: Stackgan: text to photo-realistic image synthesis with stacked generative adversarial networks. In: International Conference on Computer Vision (ICCV) (2017)
26. Ma, L., Jia, X., Sun, Q., Schiele, B., Tuytelaars, T., Van Gool, L.: Pose guided person image generation. In: Advances in Neural Information Processing Systems (2017)
27. Isola, P., Zhu, J.Y., Zhou, T., Efros, A.A.: Image-to-image translation with conditional adversarial networks. In: IEEE Conference on Computer Vision and Pattern Recognition (CVPR) (2017)
28. Ronneberger, O., Fischer, P., Brox, T.: U-Net: convolutional networks for biomedical image segmentation. In: Navab, N., Hornegger, J., Wells, W.M., Frangi, A.F. (eds.) MICCAI 2015. LNCS, vol. 9351, pp. 234–241. Springer, Cham (2015). https://doi.org/10.1007/978-3-319-24574-4_28
29. Lassner, C., Pons-Moll, G., Gehler, P.V.: A generative model of people in clothing. CoRR abs/1705.04098 (2017)
30. Zhao, B., Wu, X., Cheng, Z.Q., Liu, H., Feng, J.: Multi-view image generation from a single-view. CoRR abs/1704.04886 (2017)
31. Jetchev, N., Bergmann, U.: The conditional analogy GAN: swapping fashion articles on people images (2017)
32. Han, X., Wu, Z., Wu, Z., Yu, R., Davis, L.S.: Viton: an image-based virtual try-on network. In: CVPR (2018)
33. Yoo, D., Kim, N., Park, S., Paek, A.S., Kweon, I.: Pixel-level domain transfer. CoRR abs/1603.07442 (2016)
34. Zhu, S., Fidler, S., Urtasun, R., Lin, D., Loy, C.C.: Be your own prada: fashion synthesis with structural coherence. In: International Conference on Computer Vision (ICCV) (2017)
35. Ma, L., Sun, Q., Georgoulis, S., Van Gool, L., Schiele, B., Fritz, M.: Pose guided person image generation. In: Neural Information Processing Systems (NIPS) (2017)
36. Reed, S.E., Zhang, Y., Zhang, Y., Lee, H.: Deep visual analogy-making. In: Advances in Neural Information Processing Systems (NIPS), pp. 1252–1260 (2015)

37. Liao, J., Yao, Y., Yuan, L., Hua, G., Kang, S.B.: Visual attribute transfer through deep image analogy. In: SIGGRAPH (2017)
38. Liu, Z., Luo, P., Qiu, S., Wang, X., Tang, X.: Deepfashion: powering robust clothes recognition and retrieval with rich annotations. In: Proceedings of IEEE Conference on Computer Vision and Pattern Recognition (CVPR) (2016)
39. Lassner, C., Romero, J., Kiefel, M., Bogo, F., Black, M.J., Gehler, P.V.: Unite the people: closing the loop between 3D and 2D human representations. In: IEEE Conference on Computer Vision and Pattern Recognition (CVPR), July 2017
40. Kodali, N., Abernethy, J.D., Hays, J., Kira, Z.: On convergence and stability of GANs (2017)
41. Zhang, R., Isola, P., Efros, A.A., Shechtman, E., Wang, O.: The unreasonable effectiveness of deep networks as a perceptual metric. In: CVPR (2018)

Optimization

Deterministic Consensus Maximization
with Biconvex Programming

Zhipeng Cai[1]([✉]), Tat-Jun Chin[1], Huu Le[2], and David Suter[3]

[1] School of Computer Science, The University of Adelaide, Adelaide, Australia
{zhipeng.cai,tat-jun.chin}@adelaide.edu.au
[2] School of Electrical Engineering and Computer Science,
Queensland University of Technology, Brisbane, Australia
huu.le@qut.edu.au
[3] School of Computing and Security, Edith Cowan University, Joondalup, Australia
d.suter@ecu.edu.au

Abstract. Consensus maximization is one of the most widely used robust fitting paradigms in computer vision, and the development of algorithms for consensus maximization is an active research topic. In this paper, we propose an efficient *deterministic optimization* algorithm for consensus maximization. Given an initial solution, our method conducts a *deterministic search* that forcibly increases the consensus of the initial solution. We show how each iteration of the update can be formulated as an instance of biconvex programming, which we solve efficiently using a novel biconvex optimization algorithm. In contrast to our algorithm, previous consensus improvement techniques rely on random sampling or relaxations of the objective function, which reduce their ability to significantly improve the initial consensus. In fact, on challenging instances, the previous techniques may even return a worse off solution. Comprehensive experiments show that our algorithm can consistently and greatly improve the quality of the initial solution, without substantial cost. (Matlab demo program is available in the supplementary material)

Keywords: Robust fitting · Consensus maximization · Biconvex programming

1 Introduction

Due to the existence of noise and outliers in real-life data, robust model fitting is necessary to enable many computer vision applications. Arguably the most prevalent robust technique is random sample consensus (RANSAC) [11], which aims to find the model that has the largest consensus set. The RANSAC algorithm approximately solves this optimization problem, by repetitively sampling

Electronic supplementary material The online version of this chapter (https://doi.org/10.1007/978-3-030-01258-8_42) contains supplementary material, which is available to authorized users.

© Springer Nature Switzerland AG 2018
V. Ferrari et al. (Eds.): ECCV 2018, LNCS 11216, pp. 699–714, 2018.
https://doi.org/10.1007/978-3-030-01258-8_42

minimal subsets of the data, in the hope of "hitting" an all-inlier minimal subset that gives rise to a model hypothesis with high consensus.

Many variants of RANSAC have been proposed [7]. Most variants attempt to conduct guided sampling using various heuristics, so as to speed up the retrieval of all-inlier minimal subsets. Fundamentally, however, taking minimal subsets reduces the span of the data and produces biased model estimates [20,27]. Thus, the best hypothesis found by RANSAC often has much lower consensus than the maximum achievable, especially on higher-dimensional problems. In reality, the RANSAC solution should only be taken as a rough initial estimate [9].

To "polish" a rough RANSAC solution, one can perform least squares (LS) on the consensus set of the RANSAC estimate (i.e. the Gold Standard Algorithm [12, Chap. 4]). Though justifiable from a maximum likelihood point of view, the efficacy of LS depends on having a sufficiently large consensus set to begin with.

A more useful approach is Locally Optimized RANSAC (LO-RANSAC) [9,18], which attempts to enlarge the consensus set of an initial RANSAC estimate, by generating hypotheses from *larger-than-minimal subsets* of the consensus set.[1] The rationale is that hypotheses fitted on a larger number of inliers typically lead to better estimates with even higher support. Ultimately, however, LO-RANSAC is also a randomized algorithm. Although it conducts a more focused sampling, the algorithm cannot guarantee improvements to the initial estimate. As we will demonstrate in Sect. 5.2, often on more challenging datasets, LO-RANSAC is unable to significantly improve upon the RANSAC result.

Due to its combinatorial nature, consensus set maximization is NP-hard [4]. While this has not deterred the development of globally optimal algorithms [3, 5,6,10,19,21,25,30], the fundamental intractability of the problem means that global algorithms are essentially variants of exhaustive search-and-prune procedures, whose runtime scales exponentially in the general case. While global algorithms have their place in computer vision, currently they are mostly confined to problems with low-dimensions and/or small number of measurements.

1.1 Deterministic Algorithms—A New Class of Methods

Recently, efficient deterministic algorithms for consensus maximization are gaining attention [17,22]. Different from random sampling, such algorithms begin with an initial solution (obtained using least squares or a random sampling method) and iteratively performs *deterministic updates* on the solution to improve its quality. While they do not strive for the global optimum, such algorithms are able to find excellent solutions due to the directed search.

To perform deterministic updating, the previous methods relax the objective function (Le et al. [17] use ℓ_1 penalization, and Purkait et al. [22] use a smooth surrogate function). Invariably this necessitates the setting of a smoothing parameter that controls the degree of relaxation, and the progressive tightening of the relaxation to ensure convergence to a good solution. As we will

---

[1] This is typically invoked from within a main RANSAC routine.

demonstrate in Sect. 5.4, incorrect settings of the smoothing parameter and/or its annealing rate may actually lead to a worse solution than the starting point.

1.2 Our Contributions

We propose a novel deterministic optimization algorithm for consensus maximization. The overall structure of our method is a bisection search to increase the consensus of the current solution. The key to the effectiveness of our method is to formulate the feasibility test in each iteration as a *biconvex program*, which we solve efficiently via a biconvex optimization algorithm. Unlike [17,22], our method neither relaxes the objective function, nor requires tuning of smoothing parameters. On both synthetic and real datasets, we demonstrate the superior performance of our method over previous consensus improvement techniques.

2 Problem Definition

Given a set of N outlier contaminated measurements, consensus maximization aims to find the model $\mathbf{x} \in D$ that is consistent with the largest data subset

$$\underset{\mathbf{x} \in D}{\text{maximize}}\ \mathcal{I}(\mathbf{x}), \tag{1}$$

where D is the domain of model parameters (more details later), and

$$\mathcal{I}(\mathbf{x}) = \sum_{i=1}^{N} \mathbb{I}\left(r_i(\mathbf{x}) \leq \epsilon\right) \tag{2}$$

counts the number of inliers (consensus) of $\mathbf{x}$. Function $r_i(\mathbf{x})$ gives the *residual* of the i-th measurement w.r.t. $\mathbf{x}$, ϵ is the inlier threshold and $\mathbb{I}$ is the indicator function which returns 1 if the input statement is true and 0 otherwise.

Figure 1 illustrates the objective function $\mathcal{I}(\mathbf{x})$. As can be appreciated from the inlier counting operations, $\mathcal{I}(\mathbf{x})$ is a step function with uninformative gradients.

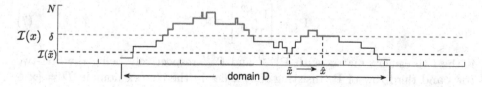

Fig. 1. Illustrating the update problem. Given the current solution $\tilde{\mathbf{x}}$ and a target consensus δ, where $\delta > \mathcal{I}(\tilde{\mathbf{x}})$, the update problem (3) aims to find another solution $\hat{\mathbf{x}}$ with $\mathcal{I}(\hat{\mathbf{x}}) \geq \delta$. Later in Sect. 4, problem (3) will be embedded in a broader algorithm that searches over δ to realize deterministic consensus maximization.

2.1 The Update Problem

Let $\tilde{\mathbf{x}}$ be an initial solution to (1); we wish to improve $\tilde{\mathbf{x}}$ to yield a better solution. We define this task formally as

$$\text{find} \quad \mathbf{x} \in D, \quad \text{such that} \quad \mathcal{I}(\mathbf{x}) \geq \delta, \tag{3}$$

where $\delta > \mathcal{I}(\tilde{\mathbf{x}})$ is a target consensus value. See Fig. 1 for an illustration. For now, assume that δ is given; later in Sect. 4 we will embed (3) in a broader algorithm to search over δ.

Also, although (3) does not demand that the revised solution be "close" to $\tilde{\mathbf{x}}$, it is strategic to employ $\tilde{\mathbf{x}}$ as a starting point to perform the update. In Sect. 3, we will propose such an algorithm that is able to efficiently solve (3).

2.2 Residual Functions and Solvable Models

Before embarking on a solution for (3), it is vital to first elaborate on the form of $r_i(\mathbf{x})$ and the type of models that can be fitted by the proposed algorithm. Following previous works [5,14,15], we focus on residual functions of the form

$$r_i(\mathbf{x}) = \frac{q_i(\mathbf{x})}{p_i(\mathbf{x})}, \tag{4}$$

where $q_i(\mathbf{x})$ is convex quadratic and $p_i(\mathbf{x})$ is linear. We also insist that $p_i(\mathbf{x})$ positive. We call $r_i(\mathbf{x})$ the *quasiconvex geometric residual* since it is quasiconvex [2, Sect. 3.4.1] in the domain

$$D = \{\mathbf{x} \in \mathbb{R}^d \mid p_i(\mathbf{x}) > 0, i = 1, \ldots, N\}, \tag{5}$$

Note that D in the above form specifies a convex domain in $\mathbb{R}^d$.

Many model fitting problems in computer vision have residuals of the type (4). For example, in multiple view triangulation where we aim to estimate the 3D point $\mathbf{x} \in \mathbb{R}^3$ from multiple (possibly incorrect) 2D observations $\{\mathbf{u}_i\}_{i=1}^N$,

$$r_i(\mathbf{x}) = \frac{\|(\mathbf{P}_i^{(1:2)} - \mathbf{u}_i \mathbf{P}_i^{(3)})\bar{\mathbf{x}}\|_2}{\mathbf{P}_i^{(3)}\mathbf{x}} \tag{6}$$

is the reprojection error in the i-th camera, where $\bar{\mathbf{x}} = [\mathbf{x}^T \ 1]^T$,

$$\mathbf{P}_i = \begin{bmatrix} \mathbf{P}_i^{(1:2)} \\ \mathbf{P}_i^{(3)} \end{bmatrix} \in \mathbb{R}^{3 \times 4} \tag{7}$$

is the i-th camera matrix with $\mathbf{P}_i^{(1:2)}$ and $\mathbf{P}_i^{(3)}$ respectively being the first-two rows and third row of $\mathbf{P}$. Insisting that $\mathbf{x}$ lies in the convex domain $D = \{\mathbf{x} \in \mathbb{R}^3 \mid \mathbf{P}_i^{(3)}\bar{\mathbf{x}} > 0, \forall i\}$ ensures that the estimated $\mathbf{x}$ lies in front of all the cameras.

Other model fitting problems with quasiconvex geometric residuals include homography fitting, camera resectioning, and the known rotation problem; see [14] for details and other examples. However, note that fundamental matrix estimation is not a quasiconvex problem [14]; in Sect. 5, we will show how the proposed technique can be adapted to robustly estimate the fundamental matrix.

3   Solving the Update Problem

As the decision version of (1), the update problem (3) is NP-complete [4] and thus can only be approximately solved. In this section, we propose an algorithm that works well in practice, i.e., able to significantly improve $\tilde{\mathbf{x}}$.

3.1   Reformulation as Continuous Optimization

With quasicovex geometric residuals (4), the inequality $r_i(\mathbf{x}) \leq \epsilon$ becomes

$$q_i(\mathbf{x}) - \epsilon p_i(\mathbf{x}) \leq 0. \tag{8}$$

Since $q_i(\mathbf{x})$ is convex and $p_i(\mathbf{x})$ is linear, the constraint (8) specifies a convex region in D. Defining

$$r_i'(\mathbf{x}) := q_i(\mathbf{x}) - \epsilon p_i(\mathbf{x}) \tag{9}$$

and introducing for each $r_i'(\mathbf{x})$ an indicator variable $y_i \in [0, 1]$ and a slack variable $s_i \geq 0$, we can write (3) using complementarity constraints [13] as

$$\text{find} \qquad\qquad \mathbf{x} \in D \tag{10a}$$

$$\text{subject to} \qquad\qquad \sum_i y_i \geq \delta, \tag{10b}$$

$$y_i \in [0, 1], \ \forall i, \tag{10c}$$

$$y_i s_i = 0, \ \forall i, \tag{10d}$$

$$s_i - r_i'(\mathbf{x}) \geq 0, \ \forall i, \tag{10e}$$

$$s_i \geq 0, \ \forall i. \tag{10f}$$

Intuitively, y_i reflects whether the i-th datum is an inlier w.r.t. $\mathbf{x}$. In the following, we establish the integrality of y_i and the equivalence between (10) and (3).

Lemma 1. *Problems (10) and (3) are equivalent.*

Proof. Observe that for any $\mathbf{x}$,

a1: If $r_i'(\mathbf{x}) > 0$, the i-th datum is outlying to $\mathbf{x}$, and (10d) and (10e) will force $s_i \geq r_i'(\mathbf{x}) > 0$ and $y_i = 0$.

a2: If $r_i'(\mathbf{x}) \leq 0$, the i-th datum is inlying to $\mathbf{x}$, and (10f) and (10d) allow s_i and y_i to have only one of the following settings: **a2.1:** $s_i > 0$ and $y_i = 0$; or **a2.2:** $s_i = 0$ and y_i being indeterminate.

If $\mathbf{x}$ is infeasible for (3), i.e., $\mathcal{I}(\mathbf{x}) < \delta$, condition **a1** ensures that (10b) is violated, hence $\mathbf{x}$ is also infeasible for (10). Conversely, if $\mathbf{x}$ is infeasible for (10), i.e., $\sum_i y_i < \delta$, then $\mathcal{I}(\mathbf{x}) < \delta$, hence $\mathbf{x}$ is also infeasible for (3).

If $\mathbf{x}$ is feasible for (3), we can always set $y_i = 1$ and $s_i = 0$ for all inliers to satisfy (10b), ensuring the feasibility of $\mathbf{x}$ to (10). Conversely, if $\mathbf{x}$ is feasible for (10), by **a1** there are at least δ inliers, thus $\mathbf{x}$ is also feasible to (3). $\square$

From the computational standpoint, (10) is no easier to solve than (3). How-ever, by constructing a cost function from the bilinear constraints (10d), we arrive at the following continuous optimization problem

$$
\underset{\mathbf{x} \in D,\ \mathbf{s} \in \mathbb{R}^N,\ \mathbf{y} \in \mathbb{R}^N}{\text{minimize}} \qquad \sum_i y_i s_i \tag{11a}
$$

$$
\text{subject to} \qquad \sum_i y_i \geq \delta, \tag{11b}
$$

$$
y_i \in [0, 1], \quad \forall i, \tag{11c}
$$

$$
s_i - r_i'(\mathbf{x}) \geq 0, \quad \forall i, \tag{11d}
$$

$$
s_i \geq 0, \quad \forall i, \tag{11e}
$$

where $\mathbf{s} = [s_1, \ldots, s_N]^T$ and $\mathbf{y} = [y_1, \ldots, y_N]^T$. The following lemma establishes the equivalence between (11) and (3).

Lemma 2. *If the globally optimal value of (11) is zero, then there exists $\mathbf{x}$ that satisfies the update problem (3).*

Proof. Due to (11c) and (11e), the objective value of (11) is lower bounded by zero. Let $(\mathbf{x}^*, \mathbf{s}^*, \mathbf{y}^*)$ be a global minimizer of (11). If $\sum_i y_i^* s_i^* = 0$, then $\mathbf{x}^*$ satisfies all the constraints in (10) thus $\mathbf{x}^*$ is feasible to (3). ◻

3.2   Biconvex Optimization Algorithm

Although all the constraints in (11) are convex (including $\mathbf{x} \in D$), the objective function is not convex. Nonetheless, the primary value of formulation (11) is to enable the usage of convex solvers to approximately solve the update problem. Note also that (11) does not require any smoothing parameters.

To this end, observe that (11) is in fact an instance of *biconvex programming* [1]. If we fix $\mathbf{x}$ and $\mathbf{s}$, (11) reduces to the linear program (LP)

$$
\underset{\mathbf{y} \in \mathbb{R}^N}{\text{minimize}} \qquad \sum_i y_i s_i \tag{12a}
$$

$$
\text{subject to} \qquad \sum_i y_i \geq \delta, \tag{12b}
$$

$$
y_i \in [0, 1], \quad \forall i, \tag{12c}
$$

which can be solved in close form.[2] On the other hand, if we fix $\mathbf{y}$, (11) reduces to the second order cone program (SOCP)

$$
\underset{\mathbf{x} \in D, \mathbf{s} \in \mathbb{R}^N}{\text{minimize}} \qquad \sum_i y_i s_i \tag{13a}
$$

$$
\text{subject to} \qquad s_i - r_i'(\mathbf{x}) \geq 0, \quad \forall i, \tag{13b}
$$

$$
s_i \geq 0, \quad \forall i. \tag{13c}
$$

---

[2] Set $y_i = 1$ if s_i is one of the δ-smallest slacks, and $y_i = 0$ otherwise.

Algorithm 1. Biconvex optimization (BCO) for the continuous problem (11).

Require: Initial solution $\tilde{\mathbf{x}}$, target consensus δ.
1: Initialize $\hat{\mathbf{x}} \leftarrow \tilde{\mathbf{x}}$, set $\hat{\mathbf{s}}$ using (14).
2: **while** not converged **do**
3:    $\hat{\mathbf{y}} \leftarrow$ solve LP (12).
4:    $(\hat{\mathbf{x}}, \hat{\mathbf{s}}) \leftarrow$ solve SOCP (13).
5: **end while**
6: **return** $\hat{\mathbf{x}}$, $\hat{\mathbf{s}}$ and $\hat{\mathbf{y}}$.

Note that s_i does not have influence if the corresponding $y_i = 0$; these slack variables can be removed from the problem to speed up optimization.[3]

The proposed algorithm (called *Biconvex Optimization* or *BCO*) is simple: we initialize $\mathbf{x}$ as the starting $\tilde{\mathbf{x}}$ from (3), and set the slacks as

$$s_i = \max\left\{0, r_i'(\tilde{\mathbf{x}})\right\}, \quad \forall i. \tag{14}$$

Then, we alternate between solving the LP and SOCP until convergence. Since (11) is lower-bounded by zero, and each invocation of the LP and SOCP are guaranteed to reduce the cost, BCO will always converge to a *local optimum* $(\hat{\mathbf{x}}, \hat{\mathbf{s}}, \hat{\mathbf{y}})$.

In respect to solving the update problem (3), if the local optimum $(\hat{\mathbf{x}}, \hat{\mathbf{s}}, \hat{\mathbf{y}})$ turns out to be the global optimum (i.e., $\sum_i \hat{y}_i \hat{s}_i = 0$), then $\hat{\mathbf{x}}$ is a solution to (3), i.e., $\mathcal{I}(\hat{\mathbf{x}}) \geq \delta$. Else, $\hat{\mathbf{x}}$ might still represent an improved solution over $\tilde{\mathbf{x}}$. Compared to randomized search, our method is by design more capable of improving $\tilde{\mathbf{x}}$. This is because optimizing (11) naturally reduces the residual of outliers that "should be" an inlier, i.e., with $y_i = 1$, which may still lead to a local refinement, i.e., $\mathcal{I}(\hat{\mathbf{x}}) > \delta_l = \mathcal{I}(\tilde{\mathbf{x}})$, regardless of whether problem (3) is feasible or not. In the next section, we will construct an effective deterministic consensus maximization technique based on Algorithm 1.

4 Main Algorithm—Deterministic Consensus Maximization

Given an initial solution $\mathbf{x}^{(0)}$ to (1), e.g., obtained using least squares or a random sampling heuristic, we wish to update $\mathbf{x}^{(0)}$ to a better solution. The main structure of our proposed algorithm is simple: we conduct bisection over the consensus value to search for a better solution; see Algorithm 2.

A lower and upper bound δ_l and δ_h for the consensus, which are initialized respectively to $\mathcal{I}(\mathbf{x}^{(0)})$ and N, are maintained and progressively tightened. Let $\tilde{\mathbf{x}}$ be the current best solution (initialized to $\mathbf{x}^{(0)}$); then, the midpoint

---

[3] Given the optimal $\hat{\mathbf{x}}$ for (13), the values of the slack variables that did not participate in the problem can be obtained as $s_i = \max\{0, r_i'(\hat{\mathbf{x}})\}$.

Algorithm 2. Bisection (non-global) for deterministic consensus maximization.

Require: Initial solution $\mathbf{x}^{(0)}$ for (1) obtained using least squares or random sampling.
1: $\tilde{\mathbf{x}} \leftarrow \mathbf{x}^{(0)}$, $\delta_h \leftarrow N$, $\delta_l \leftarrow \mathcal{I}(\mathbf{x}^{(0)})$.
2: **while** $\delta_h > \delta_l + 1$ **do**
3:     $\delta \leftarrow \lfloor 0.5(\delta_l + \delta_h) \rfloor$.
4:     $(\hat{\mathbf{x}}, \hat{\mathbf{s}}, \hat{\mathbf{y}}) \leftarrow \text{BCO}(\tilde{\mathbf{x}}, \delta)$ (see Algorithm 1).
5:     **if** $\mathcal{I}(\hat{\mathbf{x}}) > \mathcal{I}(\tilde{\mathbf{x}})$ **then**
6:         $\tilde{\mathbf{x}} \leftarrow \hat{\mathbf{x}}$, $\delta_l \leftarrow \mathcal{I}(\hat{\mathbf{x}})$.
7:     **end if**
8:     **if** $\mathcal{I}(\hat{\mathbf{x}}) < \delta$ **then**
9:         $\delta_h \leftarrow \delta$.
10:    **end if**
11: **end while**
12: **return** $\tilde{\mathbf{x}}$, δ_l.

$\delta = \lfloor 0.5(\delta_l + \delta_h) \rfloor$ is obtained and the update problem via the continuous bicon-vex formulation (11) is solved using Algorithm 1. If the solution $\hat{\mathbf{x}}$ for (11) has a higher quality than the incumbent, $\tilde{\mathbf{x}}$ is revised to become $\hat{\mathbf{x}}$ and δ_l is increased to $\mathcal{I}(\hat{\mathbf{x}})$. And if $\mathcal{I}(\hat{\mathbf{x}}) < \delta$, δ_h is decreased to δ. Algorithm 2 ends when $\delta_h = \delta_l + 1$.

Since the "feasibility test" in Algorithm 2 (Step 4) is solved via a non-convex subroutine, the bisection technique does not guarantee finding the global solution, i.e., the quality of the final solution may underestimate the maximum achievable quality. However, our technique is fundamentally advantageous compared to previous methods [9,17,22] since it is not subject to the vagaries of randomization or require tuning of hyperparameters. Empirical results in the next section will demonstrate the effectiveness of the proposed algorithm.

5   Results

We call the proposed algorithm *IBCO* (for *iterative biconvex optimization*). We compared IBCO against the following random sampling methods:

- RANSAC (RS) [11] (baseline): the confidence ρ was set to 0.99 for computing the termination threshold.
- PROSAC (PS) [8] and Guided MLESAC (GMS) [26] (RS variants with guided sampling): only tested for fundamental matrix and homography estimation since inlier priors like matching scores for correspondences were needed.
- LO-RANSAC (LRS) [9]: subset size in inner sampling was set to half of the current consensus size, and the max number of inner iterations was set to 10.
- Fixing LO-RANSAC (FLRS) [18]: subset size in inner sampling was set to 7× minimal subset size, and the max number of inner iterations was set to 50.
- USAC [23]: a modern technique that combines ideas from PS and LRS.[4] USAC was evaluated only on fundamental matrix and homography estimation since the available code only implements these models.

---

[4] Code from http://www.cs.unc.edu/~rraguram/usac/USAC-1.0.zip.

Table 1. Convex solvers used in deterministic methods.

Convex subproblem	LP	SOCP
Solvers used	Gurobi	Sedumi
Methods using the solver	EP, SS	IBCO

Except USAC which was implemented in C++, the other sampling methods were based on MATLAB [16]. Also, least squares was executed on the final consensus set to refine the results of all the random sampling methods.

In addition to the random sampling methods, we also compared IBCO against the following deterministic consensus maximization algorithms:

- Exact Penalty (EP) method [17]: The method[5] was retuned for best performance on our data: we set the penalty parameter α to 1.5 for fundamental matrix estimation and 0.5 for all other problems. The annealing rate κ for the penalty parameter was set to 5 for linear regression and 2D homography estimation and 1.5 for triangulation and fundamental matrix estimation.
- Smooth Surrogate (SS) method [22]: Using our own implementation. The smoothing parameter γ was set to 0.01 as suggested in [22].

For the deterministic methods, Table 1 lists the convex solvers used for their respective subproblems. Further, results for these methods with both FLRS and random initialization ($\mathbf{x}^{(0)}$ was generated randomly) were provided, in order to show separately the performance with good (FLRS) and bad (random) initialization. We also tested least squares initialization, but under high outlier rates, its effectiveness was no better than random initialization. All experiments were executed on a laptop with Intel Core 2.60 GHz i7 CPU and 16GB RAM.

5.1 Robust Linear Regression on Synthetic Data

Data of size $N = 1000$ for 8-dimensional linear regression (i.e., $\mathbf{x} \in \mathbb{R}^8$) were synthetically generated. In linear regression, the residual takes the form

$$r_i(\mathbf{x}) = \|\mathbf{a}_i^T \mathbf{x} - b_i\|_2, \tag{15}$$

which is a special case of (4) (set $p_i(\mathbf{x}) = 1$), and each datum is represented by $\{\mathbf{a}_i \in \mathbb{R}^8, b_i \in \mathbb{R}\}$. First, the independent measurements $\{\mathbf{a}_i\}_{i=1}^N$ and parameter vector $\mathbf{x}$ were randomly sampled. The dependent measurements were computed as $b_i = \mathbf{a}_i^T \mathbf{x}$ and added with noise uniformly distributed between $[-0.3, 0.3]$. A subset of $\eta\%$ of the dependent measurements were then randomly selected and added with Gaussian noise of $\sigma = 1.5$ to create outliers. To guarantee the outlier rate, each outlier is regenerated until the noise is not within $[-0.3, 0.3]$. The inlier threshold ϵ for (1) was set to 0.3.

Figure 2 shows the optimized consensus, runtime and model accuracy of the methods for $\eta \in \{0, 5, ..., 70, 75\}$, averaged over 10 runs for each data instance.

---

[5] Code from https://cs.adelaide.edu.au/~huu/.

Note that the actual outlier rate was sometimes slightly lower than expected since the largest consensus set included some outliers with low noise value. For $\eta = 75$ the actual outlier rate was around 72% (see Fig. 2(a)). To prevent inaccurate analysis caused by this phenomenon, results for $\eta > 75$ were not provided.

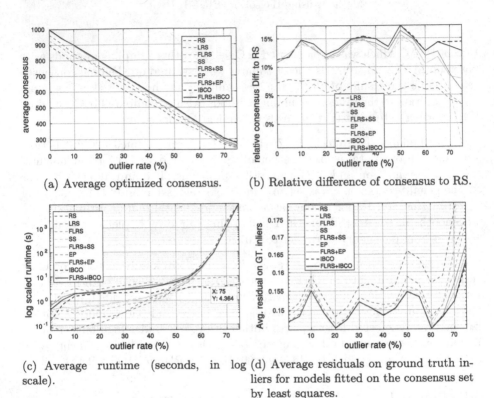

(a) Average optimized consensus.   (b) Relative difference of consensus to RS.

(c) Average runtime (seconds, in log scale).

(d) Average residuals on ground truth inliers for models fitted on the consensus set by least squares.

Fig. 2. Robust linear regression results with varied η (approx. outlier rate).

Figure 2(b) demonstrates for each method the relative consensus difference to RS. It is evident that both IBCO variants outperformed other methods in general. Unlike other methods, whose improvement to RS was low at high outlier rates, both IBCO variants were consistently better than RS by more than 11%. Though IBCO was only marginally better than EP for outlier rates lower than 65%, Fig. 2(a) shows that for most of the data instances, both IBCO variants found consensus very close or exactly equal to the maximum achievable. The cost of IBCO was fairly practical (less than 5 seconds for all data instances, see the data tip in Fig. 2(c)). Also the runtime of the random sampling methods (RS, LRS, FLRS) increased exponentially with η. Hence, at high η, the major cost of FLRS+EP, FLRS+SS and FLRS+IBCO came from FLRS.

To demonstrate the significance of having higher consensus, we further performed least squares fitting on the consensus set of each method. Given a least

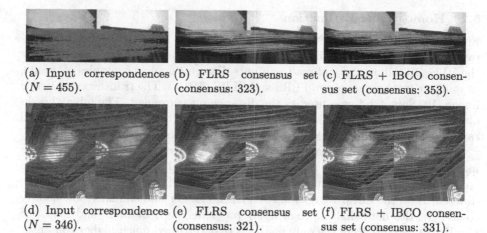

(a) Input correspondences (b) FLRS consensus set (c) FLRS + IBCO consen-
($N = 455$). (consensus: 323). sus set (consensus: 353).

(d) Input correspondences (e) FLRS consensus set (f) FLRS + IBCO consen-
($N = 346$). (consensus: 321). sus set (consensus: 331).

Fig. 3. Data and results of robust homography estimation for *Building1* (top) and
Ceiling1 (bottom). Consensus sets were downsampled for visual clearance.

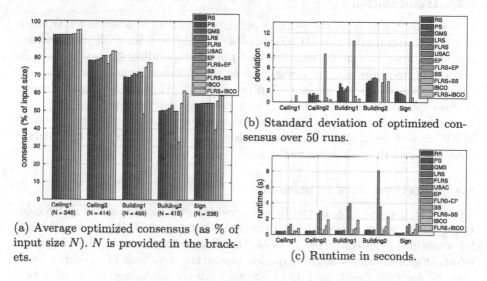

(b) Standard deviation of optimized consensus over 50 runs.

(a) Average optimized consensus (as % of
input size N). N is provided in the brackets.

(c) Runtime in seconds.

Fig. 4. Robust homography estimation results.

squares fitted model $\mathbf{x}_{LS}$, define the average residual on ground truth inliers (the
data assigned with less than 0.3 noise level) as:

$$e(\mathbf{x}_{LS}) = \frac{\sum_{i^* \in \mathcal{I}^*} r_{i^*}(\mathbf{x}_{LS})}{|\mathcal{I}^*|}, \tag{16}$$

where $\mathcal{I}^*$ was the set of all ground truth inliers. Figure 2(d) shows $e(\mathbf{x}_{LS})$ for all
methods on all data instances. Generally, higher consensus led to a lower average
residual, suggesting a more accurate model.

5.2 Homography Estimation

Five image pairs from the NYC Library dataset [29] were used for 2D homography estimation. On each image pair, SIFT correspondences were produced by the VLFeat toolbox [28] and used as inputs. Figure 3 depicts examples of inputs, as well as consensus sets from FLRS and FLRS+IBCO. The transfer error in one image [12, Sect. 4.2.2] was used as the distance measurement. The inlier threshold ϵ was set to 4 pixels. The 4-Point algorithm [12, Sect. 4.7.1] was used in all random sampling approaches for model fitting on minimal samples.

Figure 4, shows the quantitative results, averaged over 50 runs. Though marginally costlier than SS and random approaches, both IBCO variants found considerably larger consensus sets than other methods for all data. Meanwhile, different from the linear regression case, EP no longer had similar result quality to IBCO. Also note that for challenging problems, e.g., *Ceiling1* and *Sign*, the two IBCO variants were the only methods that returned much higher consensus than RS.

5.3 Triangulation

Five feature tracks from the NotreDame dataset [24] were selected for triangulation, i.e., estimating the 3D coordinates. The input from each feature track contained a set of camera matrices and the corresponding 2D feature coordinates. The re-projection error was used as the distance measurement [15] and the inlier threshold ϵ was set to 1 pixel. The size of minimal samples was 2 (views) for all RANSAC variants. The results are demonstrated in Fig. 5. For triangulation, the quality of the initial solution largely affected the performance of EP, SS and IBCO. Initialized with FLRS, IBCO managed to find much larger consensus sets than all other methods.

5.4 Effectiveness of Refinement

Though all deterministic methods were provided with reliable initial FLRS solutions, IBCO was the only one that effectively refined all FLRS results. EP and SS sometimes even converged to worse than initial solutions. To illustrate these effects, Fig. 6 shows the solution quality during the iterations of the three deterministic methods (initialized by FLRS) on *Ceiling1* for homography estimation and *Point 16* for triangulation. In contrast to EP and SS which progressively made the initial solution worse, IBCO steadily improved the initial solution.

It may be possible to rectify the behaviour of EP and SS by choosing more appropriate smoothing parameters and/or their annealing rates. However, the need for data-dependent tuning makes EP and SS less attractive than IBCO.

5.5 Fundamental Matrix Estimation

Image pairs from the two-view geometry corpus of CMP[6] were used for fundamental matrix estimation. As in homography estimation, SIFT correspondences

---

[6] http://cmp.felk.cvut.cz/data/geometry2view/.

were used as the input data. Since the Sampson error [12, Sect. 11.4.3] and the reprojection error [12, Sect. 11.4.1] for fundamental matrix estimation are not linear or quasiconvex, the deterministic algorithms (EP, SS, IBCO) cannot be directly applied. Thus, we linearize the epipolar constraint and use the algebraic error [12, Sect. 11.3] as the residual. The inlier threshold ϵ was set to 0.006 for all data.

Further, a valid fundamental matrix satisfies the rank-2 constraint [12, Sect. 11.1.1], which is non-convex. For EP, SS, IBCO, we impose the rank-2 constraint using SVD after each parameter vector updates (for IBCO, after each BCO run).

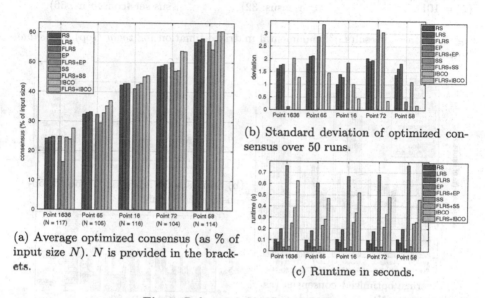

(a) Average optimized consensus (as % of input size N). N is provided in the brackets.

(b) Standard deviation of optimized consensus over 50 runs.

(c) Runtime in seconds.

Fig. 5. Robust triangulation results.

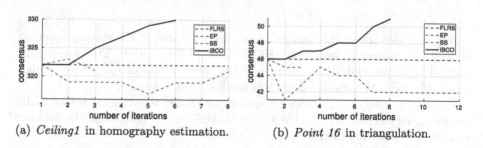

(a) *Ceiling1* in homography estimation.

(b) *Point 16* in triangulation.

Fig. 6. Consensus size in each iteration, given FLRS results as the initialization. Observe that EP and SS converged to worse off solutions.

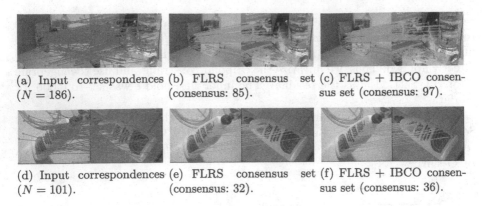

(a) Input correspondences (N = 186).

(b) FLRS consensus set (consensus: 85).

(c) FLRS + IBCO consensus set (consensus: 97).

(d) Input correspondences (N = 101).

(e) FLRS consensus set (consensus: 32).

(f) FLRS + IBCO consensus set (consensus: 36).

Fig. 7. Data and results of fundamental matrix estimation for *zoom* (top) and *shout* (bottom).

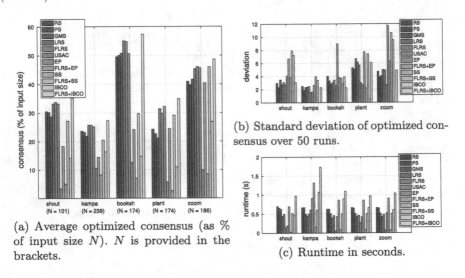

(a) Average optimized consensus (as % of input size N). N is provided in the brackets.

(b) Standard deviation of optimized consensus over 50 runs.

(c) Runtime in seconds.

Fig. 8. Robust fundamental matrix estimation results.

Figure 7 depicts sample image pairs and generated SIFT correspondences, as well as consensus sets from FLRS and FLRS+IBCO. The seven-point method [12, Sect. 11.1.2] was used in USAC and the normalized 8-point algorithm [12, Sect. 11.2] was used in all other RANSAC variants.

As shown in Fig. 8(a), unlike EP and SS who failed to refine the initial FLRS results for all the tested data, IBCO was still effective even though the problem contains non-convex constraints.

6   Conclusions

We proposed a novel deterministic algorithm for consensus maximization with non-linear residuals. The basis of our method lies in reformulating the decision version of consensus maximization into an instance of biconvex programming, which enables the use of bisection for efficient guided search. Compared to other deterministic methods, our method does not relax the objective of consensus maximization problem and is free from the tuning of smoothing parameters, which makes it much more effective at refining the initial solution. Experiments show that our method is able to greatly improve upon initial results from widely used random sampling heuristics.

Acknowledgements. This work was supported by the ARC grant DP160103490.

References

1. Biconvex optimization. https://en.wikipedia.org/wiki/Biconvex_optimization
2. Boyd, S., Vandenberghe, L.: Convex Optimization. Cambridge University Press, Cambridge (2004)
3. Campbell, D., Petersson, L., Kneip, L., Li, H.: Globally-optimal inlier set maximisation for simultaneous camera pose and feature correspondence. arXiv preprint arXiv:1709.09384 (2017)
4. Chin, T.J., Cai, Z., Neumann, F.: Robust fitting in computer vision: easy or hard? arXiv preprint arXiv:1802.06464 (2018)
5. Chin, T.J., Heng Kee, Y., Eriksson, A., Neumann, F.: Guaranteed outlier removal with mixed integer linear programs. In: Proceedings of the IEEE Conference on Computer Vision and Pattern Recognition, pp. 5858–5866 (2016)
6. Chin, T.J., Purkait, P., Eriksson, A., Suter, D.: Efficient globally optimal consensus maximisation with tree search. In: Proceedings of the IEEE Conference on Computer Vision and Pattern Recognition, pp. 2413–2421 (2015)
7. Choi, S., Kim, T., Yu, W.: Performance evaluation of RANSAC family. In: British Machine Vision Conference (BMVC) (2009)
8. Chum, O., Matas, J.: Matching with PROSAC-progressive sample consensus. In: 2005 IEEE Computer Society Conference on Computer Vision and Pattern Recognition (CVPR 2005), vol. 1, pp. 220–226. IEEE (2005)
9. Chum, O., Matas, J., Kittler, J.: Locally optimized RANSAC. In: Michaelis, B., Krell, G. (eds.) DAGM 2003. LNCS, vol. 2781, pp. 236–243. Springer, Heidelberg (2003). https://doi.org/10.1007/978-3-540-45243-0_31
10. Enqvist, O., Ask, E., Kahl, F., Åström, K.: Tractable algorithms for robust model estimation. Int. J. Comput. Vis. **112**(1), 115–129 (2015)
11. Fischler, M.A., Bolles, R.C.: Random sample consensus: a paradigm for model fitting with applications to image analysis and automated cartography. Commun. ACM **24**(6), 381–395 (1981)
12. Hartley, R., Zisserman, A.: Multiple View Geometry in Computer Vision. Cambridge University Press, Cambridge (2003)
13. Hu, J., Mitchell, J.E., Pang, J.S., Yu, B.: On linear programs with linear complementarity constraints. J. Glob. Optim. **53**(1), 29–51 (2012)

14. Kahl, F., Hartley, R.: Multiple-view geometry under the l_∞-norm. IEEE Trans. Pattern Anal. Mach. Intell. **30**(9), 1603–1617 (2008)
15. Ke, Q., Kanade, T.: Quasiconvex optimization for robust geometric reconstruction. IEEE Trans. Pattern Anal. Mach. Intell. **29**(10), 1834–1847 (2007)
16. Kovesi, P.D.: MATLAB and octave functions for computer vision and image processing. http://www.peterkovesi.com/matlabfns/
17. Le, H., Chin, T.J., Suter, D.: An exact penalty method for locally convergent maximum consensus. In: 2017 IEEE Conference on Computer Vision and Pattern Recognition (CVPR). IEEE (2017)
18. Lebeda, K., Matas, J., Chum, O.: Fixing the locally optimized RANSAC-full experimental evaluation. In: British Machine Vision Conference, pp. 1–11. Citeseer (2012)
19. Li, H.: Consensus set maximization with guaranteed global optimality for robust geometry estimation. In: 2009 IEEE 12th International Conference on Computer Vision, pp. 1074–1080. IEEE (2009)
20. Meer, P.: Robust techniques for computer vision. In: Emerging Topics in Computer Vision pp. 107–190 (2004)
21. Olsson, C., Enqvist, O., Kahl, F.: A polynomial-time bound for matching and registration with outliers. In: 2008 IEEE Conference on Computer Vision and Pattern Recognition, CVPR 2008, pp. 1–8. IEEE (2008)
22. Purkait, P., Zach, C., Eriksson, A.: Maximum consensus parameter estimation by reweighted ℓ_1 methods. In: Pelillo, M., Hancock, E. (eds.) EMMCVPR 2017. LNCS, vol. 10746, pp. 312–327. Springer, Cham (2018). https://doi.org/10.1007/978-3-319-78199-0_21
23. Raguram, R., Chum, O., Pollefeys, M., Matas, J., Frahm, J.M.: USAC: a universal framework for random sample consensus. IEEE Trans. Pattern Anal. Mach. Intell **35**(8), 2022–2038 (2013)
24. Snavely, N., Seitz, S.M., Szeliski, R.: Photo tourism: exploring photo collections in 3D. ACM Trans. Graph. (TOG) **25**, 835–846 (2006)
25. Speciale, P., Paudel, D.P., Oswald, M.R., Kroeger, T., Gool, L.V., Pollefeys, M.: Consensus maximization with linear matrix inequality constraints. In: 2017 IEEE Conference on Computer Vision and Pattern Recognition (CVPR), pp. 5048–5056. IEEE (2017)
26. Tordoff, B.J., Murray, D.W.: Guided-MLESAC: faster image transform estimation by using matching priors. IEEE Trans. Pattern Anal. Mach. Intell. **27**(10), 1523–1535 (2005)
27. Tran, Q.H., Chin, T.J., Chojnacki, W., Suter, D.: Sampling minimal subsets with large spans for robust estimation. Int. J. Comput. Vis. **106**(1), 93–112 (2014)
28. Vedaldi, A., Fulkerson, B.: VLFeat: an open and portable library of computer vision algorithms (2008). http://www.vlfeat.org/
29. Wilson, K., Snavely, N.: Robust global translations with 1DSfM. In: Fleet, D., Pajdla, T., Schiele, B., Tuytelaars, T. (eds.) ECCV 2014. LNCS, vol. 8691, pp. 61–75. Springer, Cham (2014). https://doi.org/10.1007/978-3-319-10578-9_5
30. Zheng, Y., Sugimoto, S., Okutomi, M.: Deterministically maximizing feasible subsystem for robust model fitting with unit norm constraint. In: 2011 IEEE Conference on Computer Vision and Pattern Recognition (CVPR), pp. 1825–1832. IEEE (2011)

Robust Fitting in Computer Vision: Easy or Hard?

Tat-Jun Chin$^{(\boxtimes)}$, Zhipeng Cai, and Frank Neumann

School of Computer Science, The University of Adelaide, Adelaide, Australia
tat-jun.chin@adelaide.edu.au

Abstract. Robust model fitting plays a vital role in computer vision, and research into algorithms for robust fitting continues to be active. Arguably the most popular paradigm for robust fitting in computer vision is *consensus maximisation*, which strives to find the model parameters that maximise the number of inliers. Despite the significant developments in algorithms for consensus maximisation, there has been a lack of fundamental analysis of the problem in the computer vision literature. In particular, whether consensus maximisation is "tractable" remains a question that has not been rigorously dealt with, thus making it difficult to assess and compare the performance of proposed algorithms, relative to what is theoretically achievable. To shed light on these issues, we present several computational hardness results for consensus maximisation. Our results underline the fundamental intractability of the problem, and resolve several ambiguities existing in the literature.

Keywords: Robust fitting · Consensus maximisation
Inlier set maximisation · Computational hardness

1 Introduction

Robustly fitting a geometric model onto noisy and outlier-contaminated data is a necessary capability in computer vision [1], due to the imperfectness of data acquisition systems and preprocessing algorithms (e.g., edge detection, keypoint detection and matching). Without robustness against outliers, the estimated geometric model will be biased, leading to failure in the overall pipeline.

In computer vision, robust fitting is typically performed under the framework of *inlier set maximisation*, a.k.a. *consensus maximisation* [2], where one seeks the model with the most number of inliers. For concreteness, say we wish to estimate the parameter vector $\mathbf{x} \in \mathbb{R}^d$ that defines the linear relationship $\mathbf{a}^T\mathbf{x} = b$ from a set of outlier-contaminated measurements $\mathcal{D} = \{(\mathbf{a}_i, b_i)\}_{i=1}^N$. The consensus maximisation formulation for this problem is as follows.

Problem 1 (MAXCON). Given input data $\mathcal{D} = \{(\mathbf{a}_i, b_i)\}_{i=1}^N$, where $\mathbf{a}_i \in \mathbb{R}^d$ and $b_i \in \mathbb{R}$, and an inlier threshold $\epsilon \in \mathbb{R}_+$, find the $\mathbf{x} \in \mathbb{R}^d$ that maximises

$$\Psi_\epsilon(\mathbf{x} \mid \mathcal{D}) = \sum_{i=1}^N \mathbb{I}\left(|\mathbf{a}_i^T\mathbf{x} - b_i| \le \epsilon\right), \tag{1}$$

© Springer Nature Switzerland AG 2018
V. Ferrari et al. (Eds.): ECCV 2018, LNCS 11216, pp. 715–730, 2018.
https://doi.org/10.1007/978-3-030-01258-8_43

where $\mathbb{I}$ returns 1 if its input predicate is true, and 0 otherwise.

The quantity $|\mathbf{a}_i^T \mathbf{x} - b_i|$ is the *residual* of the i-th measurement with respect to $\mathbf{x}$, and the value given by $\Psi_\epsilon(\mathbf{x} \mid \mathcal{D})$ is the *consensus* of $\mathbf{x}$ with respect to $\mathcal{D}$. Intuitively, the consensus of $\mathbf{x}$ is the number of inliers of $\mathbf{x}$. For the robust estimate to fit the inlier structure well, the inlier threshold ϵ must be set to an appropriate value; the large number of applications that employ the consensus maximisation framework indicate that this is usually not an obstacle.

Developing algorithms for robust fitting, specifically for consensus maximisation, is an active research area in computer vision. Currently, the most popular algorithms belong to the class of randomised sampling techniques, i.e., RANSAC [2] and its variants [3,4]. Unfortunately, such techniques do not provide certainty of finding satisfactory solutions, let alone optimal ones [5].

Increasingly, attention is given to constructing *globally optimal* algorithms for robust fitting, e.g., [6–14]. Such algorithms are able to deterministically calculate the best possible solution, i.e., the model with the highest achievable consensus. This mathematical guarantee is regarded as desirable, especially in comparison to the "rough" solutions provided by random sampling heuristics.

Recent progress in globally optimal algorithms for consensus maximisation seems to suggest that global solutions can be obtained efficiently or tractably [6–14]. Moreover, decent empirical performances have been reported. This raises hopes that good alternatives to the random sampling methods are now available. However, to what extent is the problem solved? Can we expect the global algorithms to perform well in general? Are there fundamental obstacles toward efficient robust fitting algorithms? What do we even mean by "efficient"?

1.1 Our Contributions and Their Implications

Our contributions are *theoretical*. We resolve the above ambiguities in the literature, by proving the following computational hardness results. The implications of each result are also listed below.

> MAXCON is NP-hard (Section 2).

$\implies$ There are no algorithms that can solve MAXCON in time polynomial to the input size, which is proportional to N and d.

> MAXCON is W[1]-hard in the dimension d (Section 3.2).

$\implies$ There are no algorithms that can solve MAXCON in time $f(d)\mathrm{poly}(N)$, where $f(d)$ is an arbitrary function of d, and $\mathrm{poly}(N)$ is a polynomial of N.

> MAXCON is APX-hard (Section 4).

$\implies$ There are no polynomial time algorithms that can approximate MAXCON up to $(1-\delta)\psi^*$ for any known factor δ, where ψ^* is the maximum consensus.

As usual, the implications of the hardness results are subject to the standard complexity assumptions P$\neq$NP [15] and FPT$\neq$W[1]-hard [16].

Our analysis indicates the "extreme" difficulty of consensus maximisation. MAXCON is not only *intractable* (by standard notions of intractability [15, 16]), the W[1]-hardness result also suggests that any global algorithm will scale exponentially in a function of d, i.e., $N^{f(d)}$. In fact, if a conjecture of Erickson et al. [17] holds, MAXCON cannot be solved faster than N^d. Thus, the decent performances in [6–14] are unlikely to extend to the general cases in practical settings, where $N \geq 1000$ and $d \geq 6$ are common. More pessimistically, APX-hardness shows that MAXCON is impossible to approximate, in that there are no polynomial time approximation schemes (PTAS) [18] for MAXCON[1].

A slightly positive result is as follows.

MAXCON is FPT (fixed parameter tractable) in the number of outliers o and dimension d (Section 3.3).

This is achieved by applying a special case of the algorithm of Chin et al. [13] on MAXCON to yield a runtime of $\mathcal{O}(d^o)\mathrm{poly}(N, d)$. However, this still scales exponentially in o, which can be large in practice (e.g., $o \geq 100$).

1.2   How Are Our Theoretical Results Useful?

First, our results clarify the ambiguities on the efficiency and solvability of consensus maximisation alluded to above. Second, our analysis shows how the effort scales with the different input size parameters, thus suggesting more cogent ways for researchers to test/compare algorithms. Third, since developing algorithms for consensus maximisation is an active topic, our hardness results encourage researchers to consider alternative paradigms of optimisation, e.g., deterministically convergent heuristic algorithms [19–21] or preprocessing techniques [22–24].

1.3   What About Non-linear Models?

Our results are based specifically on MAXCON, which is concerned with fitting linear models. In practice, computer vision applications require the fitting of non-linear geometric models (e.g., fundamental matrix, homography, rotation). While a case-by-case treatment is ideal, it is unlikely that non-linear consensus maximisation will be easier than linear consensus maximisation [25–27].

1.4   Why Not Employ Other Robust Statistical Procedures?

Our purpose here is not to benchmark or advocate certain robust criteria. Rather, our primary aim is to establish the fundamental difficulty of consensus maximisation, which is widely used in computer vision. Second, it is unlikely that other robust criteria are easier to solve [28]. Although some that use differentiable robust loss functions (e.g., M-estimators) can be solved up to local optimality, it is unknown how far the local optima deviate from the global solution.

The rest of the paper is devoted to developing the above hardness results.

---

[1] Since RANSAC does not provide any approximation guarantees, it is not an "approximation scheme" by standard definition [18].

2 NP-hardness

The decision version of MAXCON is as follows.

Problem 2 (MAXCON-D). Given data $\mathcal{D} = \{(\mathbf{a}_i, b_i)\}_{i=1}^N$, an inlier threshold $\epsilon \in \mathbb{R}_+$, and a number $\psi \in \mathbb{N}_+$, does there exist $\mathbf{x} \in \mathbb{R}^d$ such that $\Psi_\epsilon(\mathbf{x} \mid \mathcal{D}) \geq \psi$?

Another well-known robust fitting paradigm is least median squares (LMS), where we seek the vector $\mathbf{x}$ that minimises the median of the residuals

$$\min_{\mathbf{x}\in\mathbb{R}^d} \ \mathrm{med}\left(|\mathbf{a}_1^T\mathbf{x} - b_1|, \ldots, |\mathbf{a}_N^T\mathbf{x} - b_N|\right). \tag{2}$$

LMS can be generalised by minimising the k-th largest residual instead

$$\min_{\mathbf{x}\in\mathbb{R}^d} \ \mathrm{kos}\left(|\mathbf{a}_1^T\mathbf{x} - b_1|, \ldots, |\mathbf{a}_N^T\mathbf{x} - b_N|\right), \tag{3}$$

where function kos returns its k-th largest input value.

Geometrically, LMS seeks the *slab* of the *smallest width* that contains *half* of the data points $\mathcal{D}$ in $\mathbb{R}^{d+1}$. A slab in $\mathbb{R}^{d+1}$ is defined by a normal vector $\mathbf{x}$ and width w as

$$h_w(\mathbf{x}) = \left\{(\mathbf{a}, b) \in \mathbb{R}^{d+1} \ \middle| \ |\mathbf{a}^T\mathbf{x} - b| \leq \frac{1}{2}w\right\}. \tag{4}$$

Problem (3) thus seeks the thinnest slab that contains k of the points. The decision version of (3) is as follows.

Problem 3 (k-SLAB). Given data $\mathcal{D} = \{(\mathbf{a}_i, b_i)\}_{i=1}^N$, an integer k where $1 \leq k \leq N$, and a number $w' \in \mathbb{R}_+$, does there exist $\mathbf{x} \in \mathbb{R}^d$ such that k of the members of $\mathcal{D}$ are contained in a slab $h_w(\mathbf{x})$ of width at most w'?

k-SLAB has been proven to be NP-complete in [17].

Theorem 1. *MAXCON-D is NP-complete.*

Proof. Let $\mathcal{D}$, k and w' define an instance of k-SLAB. This can be reduced to an instance of MAXCON-D by simply reusing the same $\mathcal{D}$, and setting $\epsilon = \frac{1}{2}w'$ and $\psi = k$. If the answer to k-SLAB is positive, then there is an $\mathbf{x}$ such that k points from $\mathcal{D}$ lie within vertical distance of $\frac{1}{2}w'$ from the hyperplane defined by $\mathbf{x}$, hence $\Psi_\epsilon(\mathbf{x} \mid \mathcal{D})$ must be at least ψ and the answer to MAXCON-D is also positive. Conversely, if the answer to MAXCON-D is positive, then there is an $\mathbf{x}$ such that ψ points have vertical distance of less than ϵ to $\mathbf{x}$, hence a slab that is centred at $\mathbf{x}$ of width at most w' can enclose k of the points, and the answer to k-SLAB is also positive. □

The NP-completeness of MAXCON-D implies the NP-hardness of the optimisation version MAXCON. See Sect. 1.1 for the implications of NP-hardness.

3 Parametrised Complexity

Parametrised complexity is a branch of algorithmics that investigates the inherent difficulty of problems with respect to structural parameters in the input [16]. In this section, we report several parametrised complexity results of MAXCON.

First, the *consensus set* $\mathcal{C}_\epsilon(\mathbf{x} \mid \mathcal{D})$ of $\mathbf{x}$ is defined as

$$\mathcal{C}_\epsilon(\mathbf{x} \mid \mathcal{D}) := \{i \in \{1, \ldots, N\} \mid |\mathbf{a}_i^T \mathbf{x} - b_i| \leq \epsilon\}. \tag{5}$$

An equivalent definition of consensus (1) is thus

$$\Psi_\epsilon(\mathbf{x} \mid \mathcal{D}) = |\mathcal{C}_\epsilon(\mathbf{x} \mid \mathcal{D})|. \tag{6}$$

Henceforth, we do not distinguish between the integer subset $\mathcal{C} \subseteq \{1, \ldots, N\}$ that indexes a subset of $\mathcal{D}$, and the actual data that are indexed by $\mathcal{C}$.

3.1 XP in the Dimension

The following is the *Chebyshev approximation* problem [29, Chapter 2] defined on the input data indexed by $\mathcal{C}$:

$$\min_{\mathbf{x} \in \mathbb{R}^d} \max_{i \in \mathcal{C}} |\mathbf{a}_i^T \mathbf{x} - b_i| \tag{7}$$

Problem (7) has the linear programming (LP) formulation

$$\min_{\mathbf{x} \in \mathbb{R}^d, \gamma \in \mathbb{R}} \gamma$$
$$\text{s.t.} \quad |\mathbf{a}_i^T \mathbf{x} - b_i| \leq \gamma, \ i \in \mathcal{C}, \tag{LP[$\mathcal{C}$]}$$

which can be solved in polynomial time. Chebyshev approximation also has the following property.

Lemma 1. *There is a subset $\mathcal{B}$ of $\mathcal{C}$, where $|\mathcal{B}| \leq d + 1$, such that*

$$\min_{\mathbf{x} \in \mathbb{R}^d} \max_{i \in \mathcal{B}} r_i(\mathbf{x}) = \min_{\mathbf{x} \in \mathbb{R}^d} \max_{i \in \mathcal{C}} r_i(\mathbf{x}) \tag{8}$$

Proof. See [29, Sect. 2.3]. $\qquad\square$

We call $\mathcal{B}$ a *basis* of $\mathcal{C}$. Mathematically, $\mathcal{B}$ is the set of active constraints to LP[$\mathcal{C}$], hence bases can be computed easily. In fact, LP[$\mathcal{B}$] and LP[$\mathcal{C}$] have the same minimisers. Further, for any subset $\mathcal{B}$ of size $d + 1$, a method by de la Vallée-Poussin can solve LP[$\mathcal{B}$] analytically in time polynomial to d; see [29, Chapter 2] for details.

Let $\mathbf{x}$ be an arbitrary candidate solution to MAXCON, and $(\hat{\mathbf{x}}, \hat{\gamma})$ be the minimisers to LP[$\mathcal{C}_\epsilon(\mathbf{x} \mid \mathcal{D})$], i.e., the Chebyshev approximation problem on the consensus set of $\mathbf{x}$. The following property can be established.

Lemma 2. $\Psi_\epsilon(\hat{\mathbf{x}} \mid \mathcal{D}) \geq \Psi_\epsilon(\mathbf{x} \mid \mathcal{D})$.

Proof. By construction, $\hat{\gamma} \leq \epsilon$. Hence, if $(\mathbf{a}_i, b_i)$ is an inlier to $\mathbf{x}$, i.e., $|\mathbf{a}_i^T \mathbf{x} - b_i| \leq \epsilon$, then $|\mathbf{a}_i^T \hat{\mathbf{x}} - b_i| \leq \hat{\gamma} \leq \epsilon$, i.e., $(\mathbf{a}_i, b_i)$ is also an inlier to $\hat{\mathbf{x}}$. Thus, the consensus of $\hat{\mathbf{x}}$ is no smaller than the consensus of $\mathbf{x}$. $\qquad\square$

Lemmas 1 and 2 suggest a rudimentary algorithm for consensus maximisation that attempts to find the basis of the maximum consensus set, as encapsulated in the proof of the following theorem.

Theorem 2. *MAXCON is XP (slice-wise polynomial) in the dimension d.*

Proof. Let $\mathbf{x}^*$ be a witness to an instance of MAXCON-D with positive answer, i.e., $\Psi_\epsilon(\mathbf{x}^* \mid \mathcal{D}) \geq \psi$. Let $(\hat{\mathbf{x}}^*, \hat{\gamma}^*)$ be the minimisers to $\text{LP}[\mathcal{C}_\epsilon(\mathbf{x}^* \mid \mathcal{D})]$. By Lemma 2, $\hat{\mathbf{x}}^*$ is also a positive witness to the instance. By Lemma 1, $\hat{\mathbf{x}}^*$ can be found by enumerating all $(d+1)$-subsets of $\mathcal{D}$, and solving Chebyshev approximation (7) on each $(d+1)$-subset. There are a total of $\binom{N}{d+1}$ subsets to check; including the time to evaluate $\Psi_\epsilon(\mathbf{x} \mid \mathcal{D})$ for each candidate, the runtime of this simple algorithm is $\mathcal{O}(N^{d+2}\text{poly}(d))$, which is polynomial in N for a fixed d. $\qquad\square$

Theorem 2 shows that for a fixed dimension d, MAXCON can be solved in time polynomial in the number of measurements N (this is consistent with the results in [8,12]). However, this does not imply that MAXCON is tractable (following the standard meaning of tractability in complexity theory [15,16]). Moreover, in practical applications, d could be large (e.g., $d \geq 5$), thus the rudimentary algorithm above will not be efficient for large N.

3.2   W[1]-Hard in the Dimension

Can we remove d from the exponent of the runtime of a globally optimal algorithm? By establishing W[1]-hardness in the dimension, this section shows that it is not possible. Our proofs are inspired by, but extends quite significantly from, that of [30, Sect. 5]. First, the source problem is as follows.

Problem 4 (k-CLIQUE). Given undirected graph $G = (V, E)$ with vertex set V and edge set E and a parameter $k \in \mathbb{N}_+$, does there exist a clique in G with k vertices?

k-CLIQUE is W[1]-hard w.r.t. parameter k [31]. Here, we demonstrate an FPT reduction from k-CLIQUE to MAXCON-D with fixed dimension d.

Generating the Input Data. Given input graph $G = (V, E)$, where $V = \{1, \ldots, M\}$, and size k, we construct a $(k+1)$-dimensional point set $\mathcal{D}_G = \{(\mathbf{a}_i, b_i)\}_{i=1}^N = \mathcal{D}_V \cup \mathcal{D}_E$ as follows:

– The set $\mathcal{D}_V$ is defined as

$$\mathcal{D}_V = \{(\mathbf{a}_\alpha^v, b_\alpha^v)\}_{\alpha=1,\ldots,k}^{v=1,\ldots,M}, \tag{9}$$

where

$$\mathbf{a}_\alpha^v = [0, \dots, 0, 1, 0, \dots, 0]^T \tag{10}$$

is a k-dimensional vector of 0's except at the α-th element where the value is 1, and

$$b_\alpha^v = v. \tag{11}$$

- The set $\mathcal{D}_E$ is defined as

$$\begin{aligned}
\mathcal{D}_E = \{ (\mathbf{a}_{\alpha,\beta}^{u,v}, b_{\alpha,\beta}^{u,v}) \mid \ & u, v = 1, \dots, M, \\
& \langle u, v \rangle \in E, \langle v, u \rangle \in E, \\
& \alpha, \beta = 1, \dots, k, \\
& \alpha < \beta \},
\end{aligned} \tag{12}$$

where

$$\mathbf{a}_{\alpha,\beta}^{u,v} = [0, \dots, 0, 1, 0, \dots, 0, M, 0, \dots, 0]^T \tag{13}$$

is a k-dimensional vector of 0's, except at the α-th element where the value is 1 and the β-th element where the value is M, and

$$b_{\alpha,\beta}^{u,v} = u + Mv. \tag{14}$$

The size N of $\mathcal{D}_G$ is thus $|\mathcal{D}_V| + |\mathcal{D}_E| = kM + 2|E|\binom{k}{2}$.

Setting the Inlier Threshold. Under our reduction, $\mathbf{x} \in \mathbb{R}^d$ is responsible for "selecting" a subset of the vertices V and edges E of G. First, we say that $\mathbf{x}$ selects vertex v if a point $(\mathbf{a}_\alpha^v, b_\alpha^v) \in \mathcal{D}_V$, for some α, is an inlier to $\mathbf{x}$, i.e., if

$$|(\mathbf{a}_\alpha^v)^T \mathbf{x} - b_\alpha^v| \le \epsilon \equiv x_\alpha \in [v - \epsilon, v + \epsilon], \tag{15}$$

where x_α is the α-th element of $\mathbf{x}$. The key question is how to set the value of the inlier threshold ϵ, such that $\mathbf{x}$ selects no more than k vertices, or equivalently, such that $\Psi_\epsilon(\mathbf{x} \mid \mathcal{D}_V) \le k$ for all $\mathbf{x}$.

Lemma 3. *If $\epsilon < \frac{1}{2}$, then $\Psi_\epsilon(\mathbf{x} \mid \mathcal{D}_V) \le k$, with equality achieved if and only if $\mathbf{x}$ selects k vertices of G.*

Proof. For any u and v, the ranges $[u - \epsilon, u + \epsilon]$ and $[v - \epsilon, v + \epsilon]$ cannot overlap if $\epsilon < \frac{1}{2}$. Hence, x_α lies in at most one of the ranges, i.e., each element of $\mathbf{x}$ selects at most one of the vertices; see Fig. 1. This implies that $\Psi_\epsilon(\mathbf{x} \mid \mathcal{D}_V) \le k$. □

Second, a point $(\mathbf{a}_{\alpha,\beta}^{u,v}, b_{\alpha,\beta}^{u,v})$ from $\mathcal{D}_E$ is an inlier to $\mathbf{x}$ if

$$|(\mathbf{a}_{\alpha,\beta}^{u,v})^T \mathbf{x} - b_{\alpha,\beta}^{u,v}| \le \epsilon \equiv |(x_\alpha - u) + M(x_\beta - v)| \le \epsilon. \tag{16}$$

As suggested by (16), the pairs of elements of $\mathbf{x}$ are responsible for selecting the edges of G. To prevent each element pair x_α, x_β from selecting more than one edge, or equivalently, to maintain $\Psi_\epsilon(\mathbf{x} \mid \mathcal{D}_E) \le \binom{k}{2}$, the setting of ϵ is crucial.

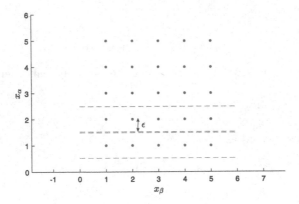

Fig. 1. The blue dots indicate the integer values in the dimensions x_α and x_β. If $\epsilon < \frac{1}{2}$, then the ranges defined by (15) for all $v = 1, \ldots, M$ do not overlap. Hence, x_α can select at most one vertex of the graph. (Color figure online)

Lemma 4. *If $\epsilon < \frac{1}{2}$, then $\Psi_\epsilon(\mathbf{x} \mid \mathcal{D}_E) \leq \binom{k}{2}$, with equality achieved if and only if $\mathbf{x}$ selects $\binom{k}{2}$ edges of G.*

Proof. For each α, β pair, the constraint (16) is equivalent to the two linear inequalities

$$
\begin{aligned}
x_\alpha + M x_\beta - u - Mv &\leq \epsilon, \\
x_\alpha + M x_\beta - u - Mv &\geq -\epsilon,
\end{aligned}
\tag{17}
$$

which specify two opposing half-planes (i.e., a slab) in the space (x_α, x_β). Note that the slopes of the half-plane boundaries do not depend on u and v. For any two unique pairs (u_1, v_1) and (u_2, v_2), we have the four linear inequalities

$$
\begin{aligned}
x_\alpha + M x_\beta - u_1 - Mv_1 &\leq \epsilon, \\
x_\alpha + M x_\beta - u_1 - Mv_1 &\geq -\epsilon, \\
x_\alpha + M x_\beta - u_2 - Mv_2 &\leq \epsilon, \\
x_\alpha + M x_\beta - u_2 - Mv_2 &\geq -\epsilon.
\end{aligned}
\tag{18}
$$

The system (18) can be simplified to

$$
\begin{aligned}
\frac{1}{2} \left[u_2 - u_1 + M(v_2 - v_1) \right] &\leq \epsilon, \\
\frac{1}{2} \left[u_1 - u_2 + M(v_1 - v_2) \right] &\leq \epsilon.
\end{aligned}
\tag{19}
$$

Setting $\epsilon < \frac{1}{2}$ ensures that the two inequalities (19) cannot be consistent for all unique pairs (u_1, v_1) and (u_2, v_2). Geometrically, with $\epsilon < \frac{1}{2}$, the two slabs defined by (17) for different (u_1, v_1) and (u_2, v_2) pairs do not intersect; see Fig. 2 for an illustration.

Hence, if $\epsilon < \frac{1}{2}$, each element pair x_α, x_β of $\mathbf{x}$ can select at most one of the edges. Cumulatively, $\mathbf{x}$ can select at most $\binom{k}{2}$ edges, thus $\Psi_\epsilon(\mathbf{x} \mid \mathcal{D}_E) \leq \binom{k}{2}$. $\square$

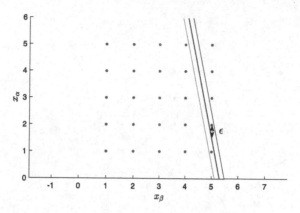

Fig. 2. The blue dots indicate the integer values in the dimensions x_α and x_β. If $\epsilon < \frac{1}{2}$, then any two slabs defined by (17) for different (u_1, v_1) and (u_2, v_2) pairs do not intersect. The figure shows two slabs corresponding to $u_1 = 1$, $v_1 = 5$, $u_2 = 2$, $v_2 = 5$. (Color figure online)

Up to this stage, we have shown that if $\epsilon < \frac{1}{2}$, then $\Psi_\epsilon(\mathbf{x} \mid \mathcal{D}_G) \leq k + \binom{k}{2}$, with equality achievable if there is a clique of size k in G. To establish the FPT reduction, we need to establish the reverse direction, i.e., if $\Psi_\epsilon(\mathbf{x} \mid \mathcal{D}_G) = k + \binom{k}{2}$, then there is a k-clique in G. The following lemma shows that this can be assured by setting $\epsilon < \frac{1}{M+2}$.

Lemma 5. *If* $\epsilon < \frac{1}{M+2}$, *then* $\Psi_\epsilon(\mathbf{x} \mid \mathcal{D}_G) \leq k + \binom{k}{2}$, *with equality achievable if and only if there is a clique of size k in G.*

Proof. The 'only if' direction has already been proven. To prove the 'if' direction, we show that if $\epsilon < \frac{1}{M+2}$ and $\Psi_\epsilon(\mathbf{x} \mid \mathcal{D}_G) = k + \binom{k}{2}$, the subgraph $S(\mathbf{x}) = \{\lfloor x_1 \rceil, \ldots, \lfloor x_k \rceil\}$ is a k-clique, where each $\lfloor x_\alpha \rceil$ represents a vertex index in G. Since $\epsilon < \frac{1}{2}$, $\lfloor x_\alpha \rceil = u$ if and only if $(\mathbf{a}_\alpha^u, b_\alpha^u)$ is an inlier. Therefore, $S(\mathbf{x})$ consists of all vertices selected by $\mathbf{x}$. From Lemmas 3 and 4, when $\Psi_\epsilon(\mathbf{x} \mid \mathcal{D}_G) = k + \binom{k}{2}$, $\mathbf{x}$ is consistent with k points in $\mathcal{D}_V$ and $\binom{k}{2}$ points in $\mathcal{D}_E$. The inliers in $\mathcal{D}_V$ specifies the k vertices in $S(\mathbf{x})$. The 'if' direction is true if all selected $\binom{k}{2}$ edges are only edges in $S(\mathbf{x})$, i.e., for each inlier point $(\mathbf{a}_{\alpha,\beta}^{u,v}, b_{\alpha,\beta}^{u,v}) \in \mathcal{D}_E$, $(\mathbf{a}_\alpha^u, b_\alpha^u)$ and $(\mathbf{a}_\beta^v, b_\beta^v)$ are also inliers w.r.t. $\mathbf{x}$. The prove is done by contradiction:

If $\epsilon < \frac{1}{M+2}$, given an inlier $(\mathbf{a}_{\alpha,\beta}^{u,v}, b_{\alpha,\beta}^{u,v})$, from (16) we have:

$$|(x_\alpha - u) + M(x_\beta - v)| =$$

$$|[(\lfloor x_\alpha \rceil - u) + M(\lfloor x_\beta \rceil - v)] + [(x_\alpha - \lfloor x_\alpha \rceil) + M(x_\beta - \lfloor x_\beta \rceil)]| < \frac{1}{M+2} \cdot \quad (20)$$

Assume at least one of $(\mathbf{a}_\alpha^u, b_\alpha^u)$ and $(\mathbf{a}_\beta^v, b_\beta^v)$ is not an inlier, from (15) and $\epsilon < \frac{1}{M+2}$, we have $\lfloor x_\alpha \rceil \neq u$ or $\lfloor x_\beta \rceil \neq v$, which means that at least one of $(\lfloor x_\alpha \rceil - u)$ and $(\lfloor x_\beta \rceil - v)$ is not zero. Since all elements of $\mathbf{x}$ satisfy (15), both $(\lfloor x_\alpha \rceil - u)$

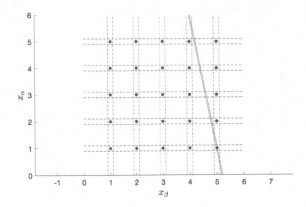

Fig. 3. If $\epsilon < \frac{1}{M+2}$, then the slab (17) that contains a point $(\mathbf{a}_{\alpha,\beta}^{u,v}, b_{\alpha,\beta}^{u,v}) \in \mathcal{D}_E$, where (u,v) is an edge in $\mathcal{G}$, does not intersect with any grid region besides the one formed by $(\mathbf{a}_\alpha^u, b_\alpha^u)$ and $(\mathbf{a}_\beta^v, b_\beta^v)$. In this figure, $u = 1$ and $v = 5$.

and $(\lfloor x_\beta \rceil - v)$ are integers between $[-(M-1),(M-1)]$. If only one of $(\lfloor x_\alpha \rceil - u)$ and $(\lfloor x_\beta \rceil - v)$ is not zero, then $|(\lfloor x_\alpha \rceil - u) + M(\lfloor x_\beta \rceil - v)| \geq |1 + M \cdot 0| = 1$. If both are not zero, then $|(\lfloor x_\alpha \rceil - u) + M(\lfloor x_\beta \rceil - v)| \geq |(M-1) + M \cdot 1| = 1$ Therefore, we have

$$|(\lfloor x_\alpha \rceil - u) + M(\lfloor x_\beta \rceil - v)| \geq 1. \tag{21}$$

Also due to (15), we have

$$|(x_\alpha - \lfloor x_\alpha \rceil) + M(x_\beta - \lfloor x_\beta \rceil)| \leq (M+1) \cdot \epsilon = \frac{M+1}{M+2}. \tag{22}$$

Combining (21) and (22), we have

$$\begin{aligned} &|[(\lfloor x_\alpha \rceil - u) + M(\lfloor x_\beta \rceil - v)] + [(x_\alpha - \lfloor x_\alpha \rceil) + M(x_\beta - \lfloor x_\beta \rceil)]| \geq \\ &|[(\lfloor x_\alpha \rceil - u) + M(\lfloor x_\beta \rceil - v)]| - |[(x_\alpha - \lfloor x_\alpha \rceil) + M(x_\beta - \lfloor x_\beta \rceil)]| \geq \\ &1 - \frac{M+1}{M+2} = \frac{1}{M+2}, \end{aligned} \tag{23}$$

which contradicts (20). It is obvious that $S(\mathbf{x})$ can be computed within linear time. Hence, the 'if' direction is true when $\epsilon < \frac{1}{M+2}$. $\qquad\square$

To illustrate Lemma 5, Fig. 3 depicts the value of $\Psi_\epsilon(\mathbf{x} \mid \mathcal{D}_G)$ in the subspace (x_α, x_β) for $\epsilon < \frac{1}{M+2}$. Observe that $\Psi_\epsilon(\mathbf{x} \mid \mathcal{D}_G)$ attains the highest value of 3 in this subspace if and only if x_α and x_β select a pair of vertices that are connected by an edge in G.

Completing the Reduction. We have demonstrated a reduction from k-CLIQUE to MAXCON-D, where the main work is to generate data $\mathcal{D}_G$ which has number of measurements $N = k|V| + 2|E|\binom{k}{2}$ that is linear in $|G|$ and polynomial in k, and dimension $d = k$. In other words, the reduction is FPT in k. Setting $\epsilon < \frac{1}{M+2}$ and $\psi = k + \binom{k}{2}$ completes the reduction.

Theorem 3. *MAXCON is W[1]-hard w.r.t. the dimension d.*

Proof. Since k-CLIQUE is W[1]-hard w.r.t. k, by the above FPT reduction, MAXCON is W[1]-hard w.r.t. d. □

The implications of Theorem 3 have been discussed in Sect. 1.1.

3.3 FPT in the Number of Outliers and Dimension

Let $f(\mathcal{C})$ and $\hat{\mathbf{x}}_\mathcal{C}$ respectively indicate the minimised objective value and minimiser of LP[$\mathcal{C}$]. Consider two subsets $\mathcal{P}$ and $\mathcal{Q}$ of $\mathcal{D}$, where $\mathcal{P} \subseteq \mathcal{Q}$. The statement

$$f(\mathcal{P}) \leq f(\mathcal{Q}) \tag{24}$$

follows from the fact that LP[$\mathcal{P}$] contains only a subset of the constraints of LP[$\mathcal{Q}$]; we call this property *monotonicity*.

Let $\mathbf{x}^*$ be a global solution of an instance of MAXCON, and let $\mathcal{I}^* := \mathcal{C}_\epsilon(\mathbf{x}^* \mid \mathcal{D}) \subset \mathcal{D}$ be the maximum consensus set. Let $\mathcal{C}$ index a subset of $\mathcal{D}$, and let $\mathcal{B}$ be the basis of $\mathcal{C}$. If $f(\mathcal{C}) > \epsilon$, then by Lemma 1

$$f(\mathcal{D}) \geq f(\mathcal{C}) = f(\mathcal{B}) > \epsilon. \tag{25}$$

The monotonicity property affords us further insight.

Lemma 6. *At least one point in $\mathcal{B}$ do not exist in $\mathcal{I}^*$.*

Proof. By monotonicity,

$$\epsilon < f(\mathcal{B}) \leq f(\mathcal{I}^* \cup \mathcal{B}). \tag{26}$$

Hence, $\mathcal{I}^* \cup \mathcal{B}$ cannot be equal to $\mathcal{I}^*$, for if they were equal, then $f(\mathcal{I}^* \cup \mathcal{B}) = f(\mathcal{I}^*) \leq \epsilon$ which violates (26). □

The above observations suggest an algorithm for MAXCON that recursively removes basis points to find a consensus set, as summarised in Algorithm 1. This algorithm is a special case of the technique of Chin et al. [13]. Note that in the worst case, Algorithm 1 finds a solution with consensus d (i.e., the minimal case to fit $\mathbf{x}$), if there are no solutions with higher consensus to be found.

Theorem 4. *MAXCON is FPT in the number of outliers and dimension.*

Proof. Algorithm 1 conducts a depth-first tree search to find a recursive sequence of *basis* points to remove from $\mathcal{D}$ to yield a consensus set. By Lemma 6, the longest sequence of basis points that needs to be removed is $o = N - |\mathcal{I}^*|$, which is also the maximum tree depth searched by the algorithm (each descend of the

---

Algorithm 1. FPT algorithm for MAXCON.

Require: $\mathcal{D} = \{\mathbf{a}_i, b_i\}_{i=1}^N$, threshold ϵ.
1: $\mathcal{C} \leftarrow \{1, \ldots, N\}$, $\hat{\mathbf{x}} \leftarrow$ NULL, $\hat{\psi} \leftarrow 0$.
2: $[\hat{\mathbf{x}}, \hat{\psi}] \leftarrow$ fitRem$(\mathcal{C}, \epsilon, \hat{\mathbf{x}}, \hat{\psi})$.
3: **return** $\hat{\mathbf{x}}$.

$[\hat{\mathbf{x}}, \hat{\psi}] =$ fitRem$(\mathcal{C}, \epsilon, \hat{\mathbf{x}}, \hat{\psi})$
1: Solve LP$[\mathcal{C}]$ to obtain $f(\mathcal{C})$, $\hat{\mathbf{x}}_\mathcal{C}$, and the basis $\mathcal{B}$ of $\mathcal{C}$.
2: **if** $f(\mathcal{C}) \leq \epsilon$ **then**
3:    **if** $|\mathcal{C}| > \hat{\psi}$ **then**
4:        $\hat{\mathbf{x}} \leftarrow \hat{\mathbf{x}}_\mathcal{C}$, $\hat{\psi} \leftarrow |\mathcal{C}|$. //Found a better consensus set.
5:    **end if**
6: **else**
7:    **for** each $i \in \mathcal{B}$ **do**
8:        $[\hat{\mathbf{x}}, \hat{\psi}] \leftarrow$ fitRem$(\mathcal{C} \setminus i, \epsilon, \hat{\mathbf{x}}, \hat{\psi})$. //Remove points from basis and refit.
9:    **end for**
10: **end if**
11: **return** $\hat{\mathbf{x}}$ and $\hat{\psi}$.

---

tree removes one point). The number of nodes visited is of order $(d + 1)^o$, since the branching factor of the tree is $|\mathcal{B}|$, and by Lemma 1, $|\mathcal{B}| \leq d + 1$.

At each node, LP$[\mathcal{C}]$ is solved, with the largest of these LPs having $d + 1$ variables and N constraints. Algorithm 1 thus runs in $\mathcal{O}(d^o \mathrm{poly}(N, d))$ time, which is exponential only in the number of outliers o and dimension d.   □

Using [32, Theorem 2.3] and the repeated basis detection and avoidance procedure in [13, Sec. 3.1], the complexity of Algorithm 1 can be improved to $\mathcal{O}((o + 1)^d \mathrm{poly}(N, d))$. See [33, Sec. 3.5] for details.

4   Approximability

Given the inherent intractability of MAXCON, it is natural to seek recourse in approximate solutions. However, this section shows that it is not possible to construct PTAS [18] for MAXCON.

Our development here is inspired by [34, Sec. 3.2]. First, we define our source problem: given a set of k Boolean variables $\{v_j\}_{j=1}^k$, a *literal* is either one of the variables, e.g., v_j, or its negation, e.g., $\neg v_j$. A *clause* is a disjunction over a set of literals, i.e., $v_1 \vee \neg v_2 \vee v_3$. A *truth assignment* is a setting of the values of the k variables. A clause is *satisfied* if it evaluates to true.

Problem 5 (MAX-2SAT). Given M clauses $\mathcal{K} = \{\mathcal{K}_i\}_{i=1}^M$ over k Boolean variables $\{v_j\}_{j=1}^k$, where each clause has exactly two literals, what is the maximum number of clauses that can be satisfied by a truth assignment?

MAX-2SAT is APX-hard [35], meaning that there are no algorithms that run in polynomial time that can approximately solve MAX-2SAT up to a desired error ratio. Here, we show an L-reduction [36] from MAX-2SAT to MAXCON, which unfortunately shows that MAXCON is also APX-hard.

Generating the Input Data. Given an instance of MAX-2SAT with clauses $\mathcal{K} = \{\mathcal{K}_i\}_{i=1}^{M}$ over variables $\{v_j\}_{j=1}^{k}$, let each clause $\mathcal{K}_i$ be represented as $(\pm v_{\alpha_i}) \vee (\pm v_{\beta_i})$, where $\alpha_i, \beta_i \in \{1, \ldots, k\}$ index the variables that exist in $\mathcal{K}_i$, and $\pm$ here indicates either a "blank" (no negation) or $\neg$ (negation). Define

$$\text{sgn}(\alpha_i) = \begin{cases} +1 & \text{if } v_{\alpha_i} \text{ occurs without negation in } \mathcal{K}_i, \\ -1 & \text{if } v_{\alpha_i} \text{ occurs with negation in } \mathcal{K}_i; \end{cases} \quad (27)$$

similarly for $\text{sgn}(\beta_i)$. Construct the input data for MAXCON as

$$\mathcal{D}_{\mathcal{K}} = \{(\mathbf{a}_i^p, b_i^p)\}_{i=1,\ldots,M}^{p=1,\ldots,6}, \quad (28)$$

where there are six measurements for each clause. Namely, for each clause $\mathcal{K}_i$,

- $\mathbf{a}_i^1$ is a k-dimensional vector of zeros, except at the α_i-th and β_i-th elements where the values are respectively $\text{sgn}(\alpha_i)$ and $\text{sgn}(\beta_i)$, and $b_i^1 = 2$.
- $\mathbf{a}_i^2 = \mathbf{a}_i^1$ and $b_i^2 = 0$.
- $\mathbf{a}_i^3$ is a k-dimensional vector of zeros, except at the α_i-th element where the value is $\text{sgn}(\alpha_i)$, and $b_i^3 = -1$.
- $\mathbf{a}_i^4 = \mathbf{a}_i^3$ and $b_i^4 = 1$.
- $\mathbf{a}_i^5$ is a k-dimensional vector of zeros, except at the β_i-th element where the value is $\text{sgn}(\beta_i)$, and $b_i^5 = -1$.
- $\mathbf{a}_i^6 = \mathbf{a}_i^5$ and $b_i^6 = 1$.

The number of measurements N in $\mathcal{D}_{\mathcal{K}}$ is $6M$.

Setting the Inlier Threshold. Given a solution $\mathbf{x} \in \mathbb{R}^k$ for MAXCON, the six input measurements associated with $\mathcal{K}_i$ are inliers under these conditions:

$$\begin{aligned} (\mathbf{a}_i^1, b_i^1) \text{ is an inlier} &\iff |\text{sgn}(\alpha_i)x_{\alpha_i} + \text{sgn}(\beta_i)x_{\beta_i} - 2| \le \epsilon, \\ (\mathbf{a}_i^2, b_i^2) \text{ is an inlier} &\iff |\text{sgn}(\alpha_i)x_{\alpha_i} + \text{sgn}(\beta_i)x_{\beta_i}| \le \epsilon, \end{aligned} \quad (29)$$

$$\begin{aligned} (\mathbf{a}_i^3, b_i^3) \text{ is an inlier} &\iff |\text{sgn}(\alpha_i)x_{\alpha_i} + 1| \le \epsilon, \\ (\mathbf{a}_i^4, b_i^4) \text{ is an inlier} &\iff |\text{sgn}(\alpha_i)x_{\alpha_i} - 1| \le \epsilon, \end{aligned} \quad (30)$$

$$\begin{aligned} (\mathbf{a}_i^5, b_i^5) \text{ is an inlier} &\iff |\text{sgn}(\beta_i)x_{\beta_i} + 1| \le \epsilon, \\ (\mathbf{a}_i^6, b_i^6) \text{ is an inlier} &\iff |\text{sgn}(\beta_i)x_{\beta_i} - 1| \le \epsilon, \end{aligned} \quad (31)$$

where x_α is the α-th element $\{x\}$. Observe that if $\epsilon < 1$, then at most one of (29), one of (30), and one of (31) can be satisfied. The following result establishes an important condition for L-reduction.

Lemma 7. *If $\epsilon < 1$, then*

$$\text{OPT}(MAXCON) \le 6 \cdot \text{OPT}(MAX\text{-}2SAT), \quad (32)$$

OPT(MAX-2SAT) is the maximum number of clauses that can be satisfied for a given MAX-2SAT instance, and OPT(MAXCON) is the maximum achievable consensus for the MAXCON instance generated under our reduction.

Proof. If $\epsilon < 1$, for all $\mathbf{x}$, at most one of (29), one of (30), and one of (31), can be satisfied, hence OPT(MAXCON) cannot be greater than $3M$. For any MAX-2SAT instance with M clauses, there is an algorithm [37] that can satisfy at least $\lceil \frac{M}{2} \rceil$ of the clauses, thus OPT(MAX-2SAT) $\geq \lceil \frac{M}{2} \rceil$. This leads to (32). □

Note that, if $\epsilon < 1$, rounding $\mathbf{x}$ to its nearest bipolar vector (i.e.,, a vector that contains only -1 or 1) cannot decrease the consensus w.r.t. $\mathcal{D}_\mathcal{K}$. It is thus sufficient to consider $\mathbf{x}$ that are bipolar in the rest of this section.

Intuitively, $\mathbf{x}$ is used as a proxy for truth assignment: setting $x_j = 1$ implies setting $v_j = true$, and vice versa. Further, if one of the conditions in (29) holds for a given $\mathbf{x}$, then the clause $\mathcal{K}_i$ is satisfied by the truth assignment. Hence, for $\mathbf{x}$ that is bipolar and $\epsilon < 1$,

$$\Psi_\epsilon(\mathbf{x} \mid \mathcal{D}_\mathcal{K}) = 2M + \sigma, \tag{33}$$

where σ is the number of clauses satisfied by $\mathbf{x}$. This leads to the final necessary condition for L-reduction.

Lemma 8. *If $\epsilon < 1$, then*

$$|\mathrm{OPT}(\textit{MAX-2SAT}) - \mathrm{SAT}(\mathbf{t}(\mathbf{x}))| = |\mathrm{OPT}(\textit{MAXCON}) - \Psi_\epsilon(\mathbf{x} \mid \mathcal{D}_\mathcal{K})|, \tag{34}$$

where $\mathbf{t}(\mathbf{x})$ returns the truth assignment corresponding to $\mathbf{x}$, and $\mathrm{SAT}(\mathbf{t}(\mathbf{x}))$ returns the number of clauses satisfied by $\mathbf{t}(\mathbf{x})$.

Proof. For any bipolar $\mathbf{x}$ with consensus $2M + \sigma$, the truth assignment $\mathbf{t}(\mathbf{x})$ satisfies exactly σ clauses. Since the value of OPT(MAXCON) must take the form $2M + \sigma^*$, then OPT(MAX-2SAT) $= \sigma^*$. The condition (34) is immediately seen to hold by substituting the values into the equation.   □

We have demonstrated an L-reduction from MAX-2SAT to MAXCON, where the main work is to generate $\mathcal{D}_\mathcal{K}$ in linear time. The function $\mathbf{t}$ also takes linear time to compute. Setting $\epsilon < 1$ completes the reduction.

Theorem 5. *MAXCON is APX-hard.*

Proof. Since MAX-2SAT is APX-hard, by the above L-reduction, MAXCON is also APX-hard.   □

See Sect. 1.1 for the implications of Theorem 5.

5   Conclusions and Future Work

Given the fundamental difficulty of consensus maximisation as implied by our results (see Sect. 1.1), it would be prudent to consider alternative paradigms for optimisation, e.g., deterministically convergent heuristic algorithms [19–21] or preprocessing techniques [22–24].

Acknowledgements. This work was supported by ARC Grant DP160103490.

References

1. Meer, P.: Robust techniques for computer vision. In: Medioni, G., Kang, S.B. (eds.) Emerging Topics in Computer Vision. Prentice Hall, Upper Saddle River (2004)
2. Fischler, M.A., Bolles, R.C.: Random sample consensus: a paradigm for model fitting with applications to image analysis and automated cartography. Commun. ACM 24(6), 381–395 (1981)
3. Choi, S., Kim, T., Yu, W.: Performance evaluation of RANSAC family. In: British Machine Vision Conference (BMVC) (2009)
4. Raguram, R., Chum, O., Pollefeys, M., Matas, J., Frahm, J.M.: USAC: a universal framework for random sample consensus. IEEE Trans. Pattern Anal. Mach. Intell. 35(8), 2022–2038 (2013)
5. Tran, Q.H., Chin, T.J., Chojnacki, W., Suter, D.: Sampling minimal subsets with large spans for robust estimation. Int. J. Comput. Vis. (IJCV) 106(1), 93–112 (2014)
6. Li, H.: Consensus set maximization with guaranteed global optimality for robust geometry estimation. In: IEEE International Conference on Computer Vision (ICCV) (2009)
7. Zheng, Y., Sugimoto, S., Okutomi, M.: Deterministically maximizing feasible subsystems for robust model fitting with unit norm constraints. In: IEEE Computer Society Conference on Computer Vision and Pattern Recognition (CVPR) (2011)
8. Enqvist, O., Ask, E., Kahl, F., Åström, K.: Robust fitting for multiple view geometry. In: Fitzgibbon, A., Lazebnik, S., Perona, P., Sato, Y., Schmid, C. (eds.) ECCV 2012. LNCS, vol. 7572, pp. 738–751. Springer, Heidelberg (2012). https://doi.org/10.1007/978-3-642-33718-5_53
9. Bazin, J.C., Li, H., Kweon, I.S., Demonceaux, C., Vasseur, P., Ikeuchi, K.: A branch-and-bound approach to correspondence and grouping problems. IEEE Trans. Pattern Anal. Mach. Intell. 35(7), 1565–1576 (2013)
10. Yang, J., Li, H., Jia, Y.: Optimal essential matrix estimation via inlier-set maximization. In: Fleet, D., Pajdla, T., Schiele, B., Tuytelaars, T. (eds.) ECCV 2014. LNCS, vol. 8689, pp. 111–126. Springer, Cham (2014). https://doi.org/10.1007/978-3-319-10590-1_8
11. Parra Bustos, A., Chin, T.J., Suter, D.: Fast rotation search with stereographic projections for 3D registration. In: IEEE Computer Society Conference on Computer Vision and Pattern Recognition (CVPR) (2014)
12. Enqvist, O., Ask, E., Kahl, F., Åström, K.: Tractable algorithms for robust model estimation. Int. J. Comput. Vis. 112(1), 115–129 (2015)
13. Chin, T.J., Purkait, P., Eriksson, A., Suter, D.: Efficient globally optimal consensus maximisation with tree search. In: IEEE Computer Society Conference on Computer Vision and Pattern Recognition (CVPR) (2015)
14. Campbell, D., Petersson, L., Kneip, L., Li, H.: Globally-optimal inlier set maximisation for simultaneous camera pose and feature correspondence. In: IEEE International Conference on Computer Vision (ICCV) (2017)
15. Garey, M.R., Johnson, D.S.: Computers and Intractability: A Guide to the Theory of NP-Completeness. W H Freeman & Co, New York (1990)
16. Downey, R.G., Fellows, M.R.: Parametrized Complexity. Springer, New York (1999). https://doi.org/10.1007/978-1-4612-0515-9
17. Erickson, J., Har-Peled, S., Mount, D.M.: On the least median square problem. Discret. Comput. Geom. 36(4), 593–607 (2006)

18. Vazirani, V.: Approximation Algorithms. Springer, Berlin (2001). https://doi.org/10.1007/978-3-662-04565-7
19. Le, H., Chin, T.J., Suter, D.: An exact penalty method for locally convergent maximum consensus. In: IEEE Computer Society Conference on Computer Vision and Pattern Recognition (CVPR) (2017)
20. Purkait, P., Zach, C., Eriksson, A.: Maximum consensus parameter estimation by reweighted ℓ_1 methods. In: Pelillo, M., Hancock, E. (eds.) EMMCVPR 2017. LNCS, vol. 10746, pp. 312–327. Springer, Cham (2018). https://doi.org/10.1007/978-3-319-78199-0_21
21. Cai, Z., Chin, T.J., Le, H., Suter, D.: Deterministic consensus maximization with biconvex programming. In: Ferrari, V. (ed.) ECCV 2018, Part XII. LNCS, vol. 11216, pp. 699–714. Springer, Cham (2018)
22. Svärm, L., Enqvist, O., Oskarsson, M., Kahl, F.: Accurate localization and pose estimation for large 3D models. In: IEEE Computer Society Conference on Computer Vision and Pattern Recognition (CVPR) (2014)
23. Parra Bustos, A., Chin, T.J.: Guaranteed outlier removal for rotation search. In: IEEE International Conference on Computer Vision (ICCV) (2015)
24. Chin, T.J., Kee, Y.H., Eriksson, A., Neumann, F.: Guaranteed outlier removal with mixed integer linear programs. In: IEEE Computer Society Conference on Computer Vision and Pattern Recognition (CVPR) (2016)
25. Johnson, D.S., Preparata, F.P.: The densest hemisphere problem. Theor. Comput. Sci. **6**, 93–107 (1978)
26. Ben-David, S., Eiron, N., Simon, H.: The computational complexity of densest region detection. J. Comput. Syst. Sci. **64**(1), 22–47 (2002)
27. Aronov, B., Har-Peled, S.: On approximating the depth and related problems. SIAM J. Comput. **38**(3), 899–921 (2008)
28. Bernholt, T.: Robust estimators are hard to compute. Technical report 52, Technische Universität Dortmund (2005)
29. Cheney, E.W.: Introduction to Approximation Theory. McGraw-Hill, New York (1966)
30. Giannopoulos, P., Knauer, C., Rote, G.: The parameterized complexity of some geometric problems in unbounded dimension. In: Chen, J., Fomin, F.V. (eds.) IWPEC 2009. LNCS, vol. 5917, pp. 198–209. Springer, Heidelberg (2009). https://doi.org/10.1007/978-3-642-11269-0_16
31. https://en.wikipedia.org/wiki/Parameterized_complexity
32. Matoušek, J.: On geometric optimization with few violated constraints. Discret. Comput. Geom. **14**(4), 365–384 (1995)
33. Chin, T.J., Purkait, P., Eriksson, A., Suter, D.: Efficient globally optimal consensus maximisation with tree search. IEEE Trans. Pattern Anal. Mach. Intell. (TPAMI) **39**(4), 758–772 (2017)
34. Amaldi, E., Kann, V.: The complexity and approximability of finding maximum feasible subsystems of linear relations. Theor. Comput. Sci. **147**, 181–210 (1995)
35. https://en.wikipedia.org/wiki/2-satisfiability
36. https://en.wikipedia.org/wiki/L-reduction
37. Johnson, D.S.: Approximation algorithms for combinatorial problems. J. Comput. Syst. Sci. **9**, 256–278 (1974)

Highly-Economized Multi-view Binary Compression for Scalable Image Clustering

Zheng Zhang[1,2,3], Li Liu[3], Jie Qin[4], Fan Zhu[3], Fumin Shen[5], Yong Xu[1(✉)],
Ling Shao[3], and Heng Tao Shen[5]

[1] Harbin Institute of Technology (Shenzhen), Shenzhen, China
yongxu@ymail.com
[2] The University of Queensland, Brisbane, Australia
[3] Inception Institute of Artificial Intelligence, Abu Dhabi, UAE
[4] Computer Vision Laboratory, ETH Zurich, Zürich, Switzerland
[5] University of Electronic Science and Technology of China, Chengdu, China

Abstract. How to economically cluster large-scale multi-view images
is a long-standing problem in computer vision. To tackle this challenge, we introduce a novel approach named **Highly-economized Scalable Image Clustering (HSIC)** that radically surpasses conventional
image clustering methods via binary compression. We intuitively unify
the binary representation learning and efficient binary cluster structure learning into a joint framework. In particular, common binary
representations are learned by exploiting both sharable and individual
information across multiple views to capture their underlying correlations. Meanwhile, cluster assignment with robust binary centroids is
also performed via effective discrete optimization under ℓ_{21}-norm constraint. By this means, heavy continuous-valued Euclidean distance computations can be successfully reduced by efficient binary XOR operations during the clustering procedure. To our best knowledge, HSIC is
the first binary clustering work specifically designed for scalable multi-
view image clustering. Extensive experimental results on four large-scale
image datasets show that HSIC consistently outperforms the state-of-
the-art approaches, whilst significantly reducing *computational time* and
memory footprint.

Keywords: Large-scale image clustering · Binary code learning
Binary clustering · Multi-view features

1 Introduction

Image clustering is a commonly used unsupervised analytical technique for practical computer vision applications [17]. The aim of image clustering is to discover the natural and interpretable structure of image representations, so as

---

Z. Zhang, L. Liu and J. Qin—Equal contributions.

© Springer Nature Switzerland AG 2018
V. Ferrari et al. (Eds.): ECCV 2018, LNCS 11216, pp. 731–748, 2018.
https://doi.org/10.1007/978-3-030-01258-8_44

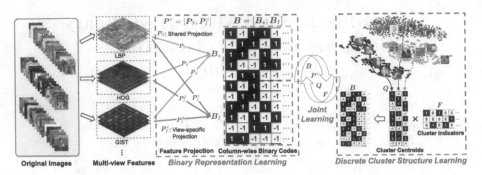

Fig. 1. The pipeline of HSIC. Common binary representation learning and discrete cluster structure learning are jointly and efficiently solved by alternating optimization.

to group images that are similar to each other into the same cluster. Based on the number of sources where images are collected or number of features how images are described, existing clustering methods can be divided into single-view image clustering (SVIC) [1,16,32,36] and multi-view[1] image clustering (MVIC) [3,4,22,47,48]. Recently, MVIC [3,48,51] has been evoking more and more attention due to the flexibility of extracting multiple heterogeneous features from a single image. Compared to SVIC, MVIC has access to more characteristics and structural information of the data, and the features from diverse views can potentially complement each other and produce more effective clustering performance.

Existing MVIC methods can be roughly divided into three groups: multi-view spectral clustering [19,30,31], multi-view matrix factorization [4,22,37], and multi-view subspace clustering [13,45,49]. Multi-view spectral clustering [47] constructs multiple similarity graphs to achieve a common or similar eigenvector matrix on all views, and then generates consensus data partitions, which hinge crucially on the single-view spectral clustering [29]. Due to the straightforward interpretability of matrix factorization [20], multi-view matrix factorization methods [4,22] integrate information from multiple views towards a compatible common consensus, or decompose the heterogeneous features into specified centroid and cluster indicator matrices. Different from the above strategies, multi-view subspace clustering [13] employs the complementary properties across multiple views to uncover the common latent subspace and quantify the genuine similarities. Some other kernel-based MVIC methods [10,42] exploit a linear or a non-linear kernel on each view. Note that SVIC (*e.g.*, k-means [16] and spectral clustering [29]) can also be leveraged to deal with multi-view clustering problem. A common practice for them is to perform clustering on either any single-view feature or simply concatenated multiple features [47,48].

Although SVIC and MVIC methods have achieved much progress on small- and middle-scale data, both of them will become intractable (because of unaf-

---

[1] Despite 'multi-view' can refer to multiple features, domains or modalities, in this paper, we solely focus on the clustering problem for images with multiple features (*e.g.*, LBP, HOG and GIST).

fordable computation and memory overhead) when dealing with large-scale data with high dimensionality, which is a typical case in the era of 'big data'. As pointed out in [15,41], we argue that real-valued features are the essential bottleneck restricting the scalability of existing clustering methods. To address this issue, inspired by the recent advances on compact binary coding (*a.k.a.* hashing) [5,23,24,27,34,39,40,43], we aim to develop a feasible binary clustering technique for large-scale MVIC. Specifically, we transform the original real-valued Euclidean space to the low-dimensional binary Hamming space, based on which an efficient clustering solution can then be devised. In this way, time-consuming Euclidean distance measures (typically of $\mathcal{O}(Nd)$ complexity, where N and d respectively indicate the data size and dimension) for real-valued data can be substantially eliminated by the extremely fast XOR operations (of $\mathcal{O}(1)$ complexity) for compact binary codes. Note that the proposed method is also potentially promising in practical use cases where computation and memory resources are limited (*e.g.*, on wearable or mobile devices).

As shown in Fig. 1, we particularly develop a *Highly-economized Scalable Image Clustering* (HSIC) framework for efficient large-scale MVIC. HSIC jointly learns the effective common binary representations and robust discrete cluster structures. The former can maximally preserve both sharable and view-specific/individual information across multiple views; the latter can significantly promote the computational efficiency and robustness of clustering. The joint learning strategy is superior to separately learning each objective by facilitating the collaboration between both objectives. An efficient alternating optimization algorithm is developed to address the joint discrete optimization problem. The main contributions of this work include:

(1) To the best of our knowledge, HSIC is the pioneering work with large-scale MVIC capability, where common binary representations and robust binary cluster structures can be obtained in a unified learning framework.
(2) HSIC captures both sharable and view-specific information from multiple views to fully exploit the complementation and individuality of heterogeneous image features. The sparsity-induced ℓ_{21}-norm is imposed on the clustering model to further alleviate its sensitivity against outliers and noise.
(3) Extensive experimental results on four image datasets clearly show that HSIC can reduce the *memory footprint* and *computational time* up to **951** and **69.35** times respectively over the classical k-means algorithm, whilst consistently outperform the state-of-the-art approaches.

Notably, two works [15,41] in the literature are most relevant to ours. [15] introduced a two-step binary k-means approach, in which clustering is performed on the binary codes obtained by Iterative Quantization (ITQ) [14], and [41] integrated binary structural SVM and k-means. Our HSIC fundamentally differs from them in the following aspects: (1) [15] and [41] are SVIC methods, while HSIC is specially designed for MVIC; (2) [15] divides the clustering task into two unconnected procedures, which completely eliminate the important tie between the binary coding and cluster structure learning. Meanwhile, the binary codes learned by [41] are too weak to achieve satisfactory results because of lacking adequate representative capability. More importantly, both methods cannot make full use of the complementary properties of multiple views for scalable MVIC, which is also shown in [50].

In the next section, we will introduce the detailed framework of our HSIC and then elaborate on the alternating optimization algorithm. The analysis in terms of computational complexity and memory load will also be presented.

2   Highly-Economized Scalable Image Clustering

Suppose we have a set of multi-view image features $\mathcal{X} = \{\boldsymbol{X}^1, \cdots, \boldsymbol{X}^m\}$ from m views, where $\boldsymbol{X}^v = [\boldsymbol{x}_1^v, \cdots, \boldsymbol{x}_N^v] \in \Re^{d_v \times N}$ is the accumulated feature matrix from the v-th view. d_v and N denote the dimensionality and the number of data points in $\boldsymbol{X}^v$, respectively. $\boldsymbol{x}_i^v \in \Re^{d_v \times 1}$ is the i-th feature vector from the v-th view. The main objective of unsupervised MVIC is to partition $\mathcal{X}$ into c groups, where c is the number of clusters. In this work, to address the large-scale MVIC problem, our HSIC aims to perform binary clustering in the much lower-dimensional Hamming space. Particularly, we perform multi-view compression (*i.e.*, project multi-view features onto the common Hamming space) by learning the compatible **common binary representation** via the complimentary characteristics of multiple views. Meanwhile, **robust binary cluster structures** are formulated in the learned Hamming space for efficient clustering.

As a preprocessing step, we first normalize the features from each view as zero-centered vectors. Inspired by [26,40], in this work, each feature vector is encoded by the simple nonlinear RBF kernel mapping, *i.e.*, $\psi(\boldsymbol{x}_i^v) = [exp(-\|\boldsymbol{x}_i^v - \boldsymbol{a}_1^v\|^2/\gamma), \cdots, exp(-\|\boldsymbol{x}_i^v - \boldsymbol{a}_l^v\|^2/\gamma)]^\top$, where γ is the pre-defined kernel width, and $\psi(\boldsymbol{x}_i^v) \in \Re^{l \times 1}$ denotes an l-dimensional nonlinear embedding for the i-th feature from the v-th view. Similar to [25,26,40], $\{\boldsymbol{a}_i^v\}_{i=1}^l$ are randomly selected l anchor points from $\boldsymbol{X}^v$ ($l = 1000$ is used for each view in this work). Subsequently, we will introduce how to learn the common binary representation and robust binary cluster structure respectively, and finally end up with a joint learning objective.

(1) Common Binary Representation Learning. We consider a family of K hashing functions to be learned in HSIC, which quantize each $\psi(\boldsymbol{x}_i^v)$ into a binary representation $\boldsymbol{b}_i^v = [b_{i1}^v, \cdots, b_{iK}^v]^T \in \{-1, 1\}^{K \times 1}$. To eliminate the semantic gaps between different views, HSIC generates the common binary representation by combining multi-view features. Specifically, HSIC simultaneously projects features from multiple views onto a common Hamming space, *i.e.*, $\boldsymbol{b}_i = sgn((\boldsymbol{P}^v)^\top \psi(\boldsymbol{x}_i^v))$, where $\boldsymbol{b}_i$ is the common binary code of the i-th features from different views (*i.e.*, $\boldsymbol{x}_i^v$, $\forall v = 1, ..., m$), $sgn(\cdot)$ is an element-wise sign function, $\boldsymbol{P}^v = [\boldsymbol{p}_1^v, \cdots, \boldsymbol{p}_K^v] \in \Re^{l \times K}$ is the mapping matrix for the v-th view and $\boldsymbol{p}_i^v$ is the projection vector for the i-th hashing function. As such, we construct the learning function by minimizing the following quantization loss:

$$\min_{\boldsymbol{P}^v, \boldsymbol{b}_i} \sum_{v=1}^m \sum_{i=1}^N \|\boldsymbol{b}_i - (\boldsymbol{P}^v)^\top \psi(\boldsymbol{x}_i^v)\|_F^2. \tag{1}$$

Since different views describe the same subject from different perspectives, the projection $\{P^v\}_{v=1}^m$ should capture the shared information that maximizes the similarities of multiple views, as well as the view-specific/individual information that distinguishes individual characteristics between different views. To this end, we decompose each projection into the combination of sharable and individual projections, i.e., $P^v = [P_S, P_I^v]$. Specifically, $P_S \in \Re^{l \times K_S}$ is the shared projection across multiple views, while $P_I^v \in \Re^{l \times K_I}$ is the individual projection for the v-th view, where $K = K_S + K_I$. Therefore, HSIC collectively learns the common binary representation from multiple views using

$$\min_{P^v, B, \alpha^v} \sum_{v=1}^m (\alpha^v)^r \left(\|B - (P^v)^\top \psi(X^v)\|_F^2 + \lambda_1 \|P^v\|_F^2 \right),$$

$$s.t. \sum_v \alpha^v = 1, \alpha^v > 0, B = [B_s; B_I] \in \{-1,1\}^{K \times N}, P^v = [P_s, P_I^v], \qquad (2)$$

where $B = [b_1, \cdots, b_N]$, $\alpha = [\alpha^1, \cdots, \alpha^m] \in \Re^m$ weighs the importance of different views, $r > 1$ is a constant managing the weight distributions, and λ_1 is a regularization parameter. The second term is a regularizer to control the parameter scales.

Moreover, from the information-theoretic point of view, the information provided by each bit of the binary codes needs to be maximized [2]. Based on this point and motivated by [14,44], we adopt an additional regularizer for the binary codes B using maximum entropy principle, i.e., $\max var[B] = var[sgn((P^v)^\top \psi(x_i^v))]$. This additional regularization on B can ensure the *balanced partition* and *reduce the redundancy* of the binary codes. Here we replace the sign function by its signed magnitude, and formulate the relaxed regularization as follows

$$\max \sum_k \mathbb{E}[\|(p_i^v)^\top \psi(x_i^v)\|^2] = \frac{1}{N} tr\left((P^v)^\top \psi(X^v)\psi(X^v)^\top P^v\right) = g(P^v). \qquad (3)$$

Finally, we combine problems (2) and (3) together and reformulate the overall common binary representation learning problem as the following

$$\min_{P^v, B} \sum_{v=1}^m (\alpha^v)^r \left(\|B - (P^v)^\top \psi(X^v)\|_F^2 + \lambda_1 \|P^v\|_F^2 - \lambda_2 g(P^v) \right)$$

$$s.t. \sum_v \alpha^v = 1, \alpha^v > 0, B = [B_s; B_I] \in \{-1,1\}^{K \times N}, P^v = [P_s, P_I^v], \qquad (4)$$

where λ_2 is a weighting parameter.

(2) Robust Binary Cluster Structure Learning. For binary clustering, HSIC directly factorizes the learned binary representation B into the binary clustering centroids Q and discrete clustering indicators F using

$$\min_{Q,F} \|B - QF\|_{21}, \ s.t. \ Q1 = 0, Q \in \{-1,1\}^{K \times c}, F \in \{0,1\}^{c \times N}, \sum_j f_{ji} = 1,$$

$$(5)$$

Algorithm 1. Highly-economized Scalable Image Clustering (HSIC)

Input   : Multi-view features $\{\boldsymbol{X}^v\}_{v=1}^m \in \Re^{d_v \times N}$, $m \geq 3$; code length K;
              number of centroids c; maximum iterations κ and t; λ_1, λ_2 and λ_3.
Output: Binary representation $\boldsymbol{B}$, cluster centroid $\boldsymbol{Q}$ and cluster indicator $\boldsymbol{F}$.
Initial. : Randomly select l anchor points from each view to calculate the
              kernelized feature embedding $\psi(\boldsymbol{X}^v) \in \Re^{l \times N}$, and normalize them to
              have zero-centered mean.
repeat
    P_S-**Step**: Update $\boldsymbol{P}_S$ by Eqn.(8);
    P_I^v-**Step**: Update $\boldsymbol{P}_I^v$ by Eqn. (9), $\forall v = 1, \cdots, m$;
    B-**Step**: Update $\boldsymbol{B}$ by Eqn. (12);
    repeat
        Q-**Step**: Iteratively update $\boldsymbol{Q}$ by Eqn. (14);
        F-**Step**: Update $\boldsymbol{F}$ by Eqn. (16);
    until *convergence or reach κ iterations*;
    α-**Step**: Update α by Eqn. (18);
until *convergence or reach t iterations*;

---

where $\|\boldsymbol{A}\|_{21} = \sum_i \|\boldsymbol{a}^i\|_2$, and $\boldsymbol{a}^i$ is the i-th row of matrix $\boldsymbol{A}$. The first constraint of (5) ensures the balanced property on the clustering centroids as with the binary codes. Note that the ℓ_{21}-norm imposed on the loss function can also be replaced by the F-norm, *i.e.*, $\|\boldsymbol{B} - \boldsymbol{QF}\|_F^2$. However, the F-norm based loss function can amplify the errors induced from noise and outliers. Therefore, to achieve more stable and robust clustering performance, we employ the sparsity-induced ℓ_{21}-norm. It is also observed in [12] that the ℓ_{21}-norm not only preserves the rotation invariance within each feature, but also controls the reconstruction error, which significantly mitigates the negative influence of the representation outliers.

(3) Joint Objective Function. To preserve the semantic interconnection between the learned binary codes and the robust cluster structures, we incorporate the common binary representation learning and the discrete cluster structure constructing into a joint learning framework. In this way, the unified framework can interactively enhance the qualities of the learned binary representation and cluster structures. Hence, we have the following joint objective function:

$$\min_{\boldsymbol{P}^v, \boldsymbol{B}, \boldsymbol{Q}, \boldsymbol{F}, \alpha^v} \sum_{v=1}^m (\alpha^v)^r \left(\|\boldsymbol{B} - (\boldsymbol{P}^v)^\top \psi(\boldsymbol{X}^v)\|_F^2 + \lambda_1 \|\boldsymbol{P}^v\|_F^2 - \lambda_2 g(\boldsymbol{P}^v) \right) + \lambda_3 \|\boldsymbol{B} - \boldsymbol{QF}\|_{21},$$

$$s.t. \sum_v \alpha^v = 1, \alpha^v > 0, \boldsymbol{B} = [\boldsymbol{B}_s; \boldsymbol{B}_I] \in \{-1, 1\}^{K \times N}, \boldsymbol{P}^v = [\boldsymbol{P}_s, \boldsymbol{P}_I^v],$$

$$\boldsymbol{Q}\mathbf{1} = \mathbf{0}, \boldsymbol{Q} \in \{-1, 1\}^{K \times c}, \boldsymbol{F} \in \{0, 1\}^{c \times N}, \sum_j f_{ji} = 1, \tag{6}$$

where λ_1, λ_2 and λ_3 are trade-off parameters to balance the effects of different terms. To optimize the difficult discrete programming problem, a newly-derived alternating optimization algorithm is developed as shown in the next section.

2.1   Optimization

The solution to problem (6) is non-trivial as it involves a mixed binary integer program with three discrete constraints, which lead to an NP-hard problem. In the following, we introduce an alternating optimization algorithm to iteratively update each variable while fixing others, $i.e.$, update $\boldsymbol{P}_s \rightarrow \boldsymbol{P}_I^v \rightarrow \boldsymbol{B} \rightarrow \boldsymbol{Q} \rightarrow \boldsymbol{F} \rightarrow \boldsymbol{\alpha}$ in each iteration.

Due to the intractable ℓ_{21}-norm loss function, we first rewrite the last term in (6) as $\lambda_3 tr(\boldsymbol{U}^\top \boldsymbol{D} \boldsymbol{U})$, where $\boldsymbol{U} = \boldsymbol{B} - \boldsymbol{Q}\boldsymbol{F}$, and $\boldsymbol{D} \in \Re^{K \times K}$ is a diagonal matrix, the i-th diagonal element of which is defined as $\boldsymbol{d}_{ii} = 1/2\|\boldsymbol{u}^i\|$, where $\boldsymbol{u}^i$ is the i-th row of $\boldsymbol{U}$.

(1) $\boldsymbol{P}_s$-Step: When fixing other variables, we update the sharable projection by

$$\min_{\boldsymbol{P}_s} \sum_{v=1}^{m} (\alpha^v)^r \left(\|\boldsymbol{B}_s - \boldsymbol{P}_s^\top \psi(\boldsymbol{X}^v)\|_F^2 + \lambda_1 \|\boldsymbol{P}_s\|_F^2 - \frac{\lambda_2}{N} tr\left(\boldsymbol{P}_s^\top \psi(\boldsymbol{X}^v)\psi^\top(\boldsymbol{X}^v)\boldsymbol{P}_s\right)\right).$$

(7)

For notational convenience, we rewrite $\psi(\boldsymbol{X}^v)\psi^\top(\boldsymbol{X}^v)$ as $\tilde{\boldsymbol{X}}$. Taking derivation of $\mathcal{L}$ with respect to $\boldsymbol{P}_s$ and let $\frac{\partial \mathcal{L}}{\partial \boldsymbol{P}_s} = 0$, we can obtain the closed-form solution of $\boldsymbol{P}_s$, $i.e.$,

$$\boldsymbol{P}_s = (\boldsymbol{A} + \lambda_1 \sum_{v=1}^{m} (\alpha^v)^r \boldsymbol{I})^{-1} \boldsymbol{T}\boldsymbol{B}^\top,$$

(8)

where $\boldsymbol{A} = (1 - \frac{\lambda_2}{N}) \sum_{v=1}^{m} (\alpha^v)^r \tilde{\boldsymbol{X}}$ and $\boldsymbol{T} = \sum_{v=1}^{m} (\alpha^v)^r \psi(\boldsymbol{X}^v)$.

(2) $\boldsymbol{P}_I^v$-Step: Similarly, when fixing other parameters, the optimal solution of the v-th individual projection matrix can be determined by solving

$$\min_{\boldsymbol{P}_I^v} \|\boldsymbol{B}_I - (\boldsymbol{P}_I^v)^\top \psi(\boldsymbol{X}^v)\|_F^2 + \lambda_1 \|\boldsymbol{P}_I^v\|_F^2 - \frac{\lambda_2}{N} tr(\boldsymbol{P}_I^v \tilde{\boldsymbol{X}}(\boldsymbol{P}_I^v)^\top),$$

(9)

and its closed-form solution can be obtained by $\boldsymbol{P}_I^v = \boldsymbol{W}\psi(\boldsymbol{X}^v)\boldsymbol{B}^\top$, where $\boldsymbol{W} = \left((1 - \frac{\lambda_2}{N})\tilde{\boldsymbol{X}} + \lambda_1 \boldsymbol{I}\right)^{-1}$ can be calculated beforehand.

(3) $\boldsymbol{B}$-Step: Problem (6) w.r.t. $\boldsymbol{B}$ can be rewritten as:

$$\min_{\boldsymbol{B}} \sum_{v=1}^{m} (\alpha^v)^r \left(\|\boldsymbol{B} - (\boldsymbol{P}^v)^\top \psi(\boldsymbol{X}^v)\|_F^2 \right) + \lambda_3 tr(\boldsymbol{U}^\top \boldsymbol{D} \boldsymbol{U}), \ s.t. \ \boldsymbol{B} \in \{-1,1\}^{K \times N}.$$

(10)

Since $\boldsymbol{B}$ only has '1' and '-1' entries and $\boldsymbol{D}$ is a diagonal matrix, both $tr(\boldsymbol{B}\boldsymbol{B}^\top) = tr(\boldsymbol{B}^\top \boldsymbol{B}) = KN$ and $tr(\boldsymbol{B}^\top \boldsymbol{D} \boldsymbol{B}) = N * tr(\boldsymbol{D})$ are constant terms w.r.t. $\boldsymbol{B}$. Based on this and with some further algebraic computations, (10) can be reformulated as

$$\min_{\boldsymbol{B}} -2tr\left[\boldsymbol{B}^\top\left(\sum_{v=1}^m(\alpha^v)^r((\boldsymbol{P}^v)^\top\psi(\boldsymbol{X}^v))+\lambda_3\boldsymbol{Q}\boldsymbol{F}\right)\right]+const, s.t.\ \boldsymbol{B}\in\{-1,1\}^{K\times N},$$

(11)

where '*const*' denotes the constant terms. This problem has a closed-form solution:

$$\boldsymbol{B}=sgn\left(\sum_{v=1}^m(\alpha^v)^r((\boldsymbol{P}^v)^\top\psi(\boldsymbol{X}^v))+\lambda_3\boldsymbol{Q}\boldsymbol{F}\right).$$

(12)

(4) $\boldsymbol{Q}$-Step: First, we degenerate (6) into the following computationally feasible problem (by removing some irrelevant parameters and discarding the first constraint):

$$\min_{\boldsymbol{Q},\boldsymbol{F}} tr\left(\boldsymbol{U}^\top\boldsymbol{D}\boldsymbol{U}\right)+\nu\|\boldsymbol{Q}^\top\mathbf{1}\|_F^2,\ s.t.\ \boldsymbol{Q}\in\{-1,1\}^{K\times c},\ \boldsymbol{F}\in\{0,1\}^{c\times N},\sum_j f_{ji}=1.$$

(13)

With sufficiently large $\nu>0$, problems (6) and (13) will be equivalent. Then, by fixing the variable $\boldsymbol{F}$, problem (13) becomes

$$\min_{\boldsymbol{Q}}\mathcal{L}(\boldsymbol{Q})=-2tr(\boldsymbol{B}^\top\boldsymbol{D}\boldsymbol{Q}\boldsymbol{F})+\nu\|\boldsymbol{Q}^\top\mathbf{1}\|_F^2+const,\ s.t.\ \boldsymbol{Q}\in\{-1,1\}^{K\times c}.$$ (14)

Inspired by the efficient discrete optimization algorithm in [35, 38], we develop an adaptive discrete proximal linearized optimization algorithm, which iteratively updates $\boldsymbol{Q}$ in the $(p+1)$-th iteration by $\boldsymbol{Q}^{p+1}=sgn(\boldsymbol{Q}^p-\frac{1}{\eta}\nabla\mathcal{L}(\boldsymbol{Q}^p))$, where $\nabla\mathcal{L}(\boldsymbol{Q})$ is the gradient of $\mathcal{L}(\boldsymbol{Q})$, $\frac{1}{\eta}$ is the learning step size and $\eta\in(C,2C)$, where C is the Lipschitz constant. Intuitively, for the very special $sgn(\cdot)$ function, if the step size $1/\eta$ is too small/large, the solution of $\boldsymbol{Q}$ will get stuck in a bad local minimum or diverge. To this end, a proper η is adaptively determined by enlarging or reducing based on the changing values of $\mathcal{L}(\boldsymbol{Q})$ between adjacent iterations, which can accelerate its convergence.

(5) $\boldsymbol{F}$-Step: Similarly, when fixing $\boldsymbol{Q}$, the problem w.r.t. $\boldsymbol{F}$ turns into

$$\min_{\boldsymbol{f}_i}\sum_{i=1}^N d_{ii}\|\boldsymbol{b}_i-\boldsymbol{Q}\boldsymbol{f}_i\|_{21},\ s.t.\ \boldsymbol{f}_i\in\{0,1\}^{c\times 1},\sum_j f_{ji}=1.$$

(15)

We can divide the above problem into N subproblems, and independently optimize the cluster indicator in a column-wise fashion. That is, one column of $\boldsymbol{F}$ (*i.e.*, $\boldsymbol{f}_i$) is computed at each time. Specifically, we solve the subproblems in an exhaustive search manner, similar to the conventional k-means algorithm. Regarding the i-th column $\boldsymbol{f}_i$, the optimal solution of its j-th entry can be efficiently obtained by

$$f_{ji}=\begin{cases}1,& j=\arg\min_k H(d_{ii}*\boldsymbol{b}_i,\boldsymbol{q}_\wp),\\0,&otherwise,\end{cases}$$

(16)

where $q_\wp$ is the $\wp$-th vector of Q, and $H(\cdot,\cdot)$ denotes the Hamming distance metric. Note that computing the Hamming distance is remarkably faster than the Euclidean distance, so the assigned vector f_i will efficiently constitute the matrix F.

(6) α-Step: Let $h^v = \|B-(P^v)^\top \phi(X^v)\|_F^2 + \lambda_1\|P^v\|_F^2 - \lambda_2 g(P^v)$, then problem (6) w.r.t. α can be rewritten as

$$\min_{\alpha^v} \sum_{v=1}^m (\alpha^v)^r h^v, \ s.t. \ \sum_v \alpha^v = 1, \alpha^v > 0. \tag{17}$$

The Lagrange function of (17) is $\min \mathcal{L}(\alpha^v, \zeta) = \sum_{v=1}^m (\alpha^v)^r h^v - \zeta(\sum_{v=1}^m \alpha^v - 1)$, where ζ is the Lagrange multiplier. Taking the partial derivatives w.r.t. α^v and ζ, respectively, we can get

$$\begin{cases} \dfrac{\partial \mathcal{L}}{\partial \alpha^v} = r(\alpha^v)^{r-1} h^v - \zeta, \\ \dfrac{\partial \mathcal{L}}{\partial \zeta} = \displaystyle\sum_{v=1}^m \alpha^v - 1. \end{cases} \tag{18}$$

Following [47], by setting $\nabla_{\alpha^v, \zeta}\mathcal{L} = 0$, the optimal solution of α^v is $\dfrac{(h^v)^{\frac{1}{1-r}}}{\sum_v (h^v)^{\frac{1}{1-r}}}$.

To obtain the locally optimal solution of problem (6), we update the above six variables iteratively until convergence. To deal with the out-of-example problem in image clustering, HSIC needs to generate the binary code for a new query image $\hat{x}$ from the v-th view (*i.e.*, $\hat{x}^v$) by $b^v = sgn\left((P^v)^\top \psi(\hat{x}^v)\right)$, and then assigns it to the j-th cluster decided by $j = \arg\min_k H(b^v, q_k)$ in the fast Hamming space. For multi-view clustering, the common binary code of $\hat{x}$ is $b = sgn\left(\sum_{v=1}^m (\alpha^v)^r (P^v)^\top \psi(\hat{x}^v)\right)$. Then the optimal cluster assignment of $\hat{x}$ is determined by the solution of F. The full learning procedure of HSIC is illustrated in Algorithm 1.

2.2 Complexity and Memory Load Analysis

(1) The major computation burden of HSIC lies in the compressive binary representation learning and robust discrete cluster structures learning. The computational complexities of calculating P_S and P_I^v are $\mathcal{O}(K_S lN)$ and $\mathcal{O}(m(K_I lN))$, respectively. Computing B consumes $\mathcal{O}(KlN)$. Similar to [15], constructing the discrete cluster structures needs $\mathcal{O}(N)$ on bit-wise operators for κ iterations, where the distance computation requires only $\mathcal{O}(1)$ per time. The total computational complexity of HSIC is $\mathcal{O}(t((K_S + mK_I + K)lN + \kappa N))$, where t and κ are empirically set to 10 in all the experiments. In general, the computational complexity of optimizing HSIC is linear to the number of samples, *i.e.*, $\mathcal{O}(N)$. (2) For memory cost in HSIC, it is unavoidable to store the mapping matrices P_s and P_I^v, demanding $\mathcal{O}(lK_S)$ and $\mathcal{O}(lK_I)$ memory costs, respectively. Notably, the learned binary representation and discrete cluster centroids only need the ***bit-wise*** memory load $\mathcal{O}(K(N + c))$, which is much less than that of k-means requiring $\mathcal{O}(d(N + c))$ ***real-valued*** numerical storage footprint.

3   Experimental Evaluation

In this section, we conducted multi-view image clustering experiments on four scalable image datasets to evaluate the effectiveness of HSIC with four frequently-used performance measures. All the experiments are implemented based on Matlab 2013a using a standard Windows PC with an Intel 3.4 GHz CPU.

3.1   Experimental Settings

Datasets and Features: We perform experiments on four image datasets, including **ILSVRC2012 1K** [11], **Cifar-10** [18], **YouTube Faces** (YTBF) [46] and **NUS-WIDE** [9]. Specifically, we randomly select 10 classes from ILSVRC2012 1 K with 1, 300 images per class, denoted as *ImageNet-10*, for *middle-scale* multi-view clustering study. *Cifar-10* contains 60, 000 tiny color images in 10 classes, with 6, 000 images per class. A subset of *YTBF* contains 182, 881 face images from 89 different people ($> 1, 200$ for each one). Similar to [38], we collect the subset of *NUS-WIDE* including the 21 most frequent concepts, resulting in 195, 834 images with at least 3, 091 images per category. Because some images in NUS-WIDE were labeled by multiple concepts, we only select one of the most representative labels as their true categories for simplicity. Multiple features are extracted on all datasets. Specifically, for ImageNet-10, Cifar-10 and YTBF, we use three different types of features, *i.e.*, 1450-d LBP, 1024-d GIST, and 1152-d HOG. For NUS-WIDE, five publicly available features are employed for experiments, *i.e.*, 64-d color Histogram (CH), 225-d color moments (CM), 144-d color correlation (CORR), 73-d edge distribution (EDH) and 128-d wavelet texture (WT).

Metrics and Parameters: We adopt four widely-used evaluation measures [28] for clustering, including clustering accuracy (ACC), normalized mutual information (NMI), purity, and F-score. In addition, both computational time and memory footprint are compared to show the efficiency of HSIC. To fairly compare different methods, we run the provided codes with default or fine-tuned parameter settings according to the original papers. For binary clustering methods, 128-bit code length is used for all datasets. For hyper-parameters λ_1, $\frac{\lambda_2}{N}$, and λ_3 of HSIC, we first employ the grid search strategy on ImageNet-10 to find the best values (*i.e.*, 10^{-3}, 10^{-3}, and 10^{-5}, respectively), which are then directly adopted on other datasets for simplicity. We empirically set r and $\delta = \frac{K_s}{K}$ (*i.e.*, the ratio of shared binary codes) as 5 and 0.2 respectively in all experiments. The multi-view clustering results are denoted as 'MulView'. We report the averaged clustering results with 10 times randomly initialization for each method.

We conduct the following experiments from *three* perspectives. *Firstly*, we verify various characteristics of HSIC on the *middle-scale* dataset, *i.e.*, ImageNet-10. Here we compare HSIC with both SVIC and MVIC methods (including real-valued and binary ones). *Secondly*, three large-scale datasets are exploited to evaluate HSIC on the challenging large-scale MVIC problem. **Remark:** Based on the results on ImageNet-10 (see Table 2), the real-valued MVIC methods only

Table 1. Performance comparisons on ImageNet-10. The bold **black** and **blue** numbers indicate the best single-view and multi-view clustering results, respectively.

Metric / Feature	ACC				NMI				Purity				F-Score			
	LBP	GIST	HOG	MulView	LBP	GIST	HOG	MulView	LBP	GIST	HOG	MulView	LBP	GIST	HOG	MulView
k-means	0.2265	0.3085	0.2492	0.3073	0.1120	**0.1853**	0.1134	0.1803	**0.2361**	0.3098	0.2439	0.3133	0.1628	0.1970	0.1363	0.1996
k-Medoids	0.1925	0.2634	0.2268	0.2605	0.0755	0.1721	0.1298	0.1461	0.1988	0.2852	0.2329	0.2690	0.1110	**0.1973**	0.1836	0.1874
Ak-kmeans	0.2159	0.2988	0.2515	0.3113	0.1000	0.1541	0.1279	0.1966	0.2255	0.2805	0.2761	0.3254	0.1662	0.1827	0.1870	0.2122
Nyström	0.2234	0.2459	0.2544	0.2950	0.0936	0.1222	0.1317	0.1719	0.2181	0.2585	0.2741	0.3320	0.1490	0.1749	0.1639	0.2050
NMF	0.2178	0.2540	0.2509	0.2737	0.1076	0.1353	0.1434	0.1610	0.2178	0.2614	0.2705	0.2887	0.1571	0.1798	0.1609	0.1854
LSC-K	**0.2585**	**0.3192**	0.2529	0.3284	0.1356	0.1806	0.1254	0.2215	0.2260	0.2660	0.2797	0.3447	**0.1748**	0.1748	0.1625	0.2301
AMGL	0.2093	0.2843	0.2516	0.2822	0.1131	0.1301	0.1368	0.2110	0.2149	0.3090	0.2796	0.2902	0.1311	0.1571	**0.2021**	0.2305
MVKM	0.2321	0.2882	0.2535	0.3058	0.1181	0.1612	0.1372	0.1881	0.2115	0.3091	0.2538	0.3082	0.1461	0.1730	0.1861	0.2161
MLAN	0.2109	0.2197	0.2127	0.3182	0.1173	0.1255	0.1152	0.1648	0.2117	0.2258	0.2168	0.3248	0.1403	0.1614	0.1813	0.1813
MultiNMF	0.2113	0.2639	0.2574	0.2632	0.0986	0.1732	**0.1605**	0.1708	0.2202	0.2735	**0.2855**	0.2905	0.1531	0.1789	0.1802	0.1906
OMVC	0.2062	0.2706	0.2544	0.2739	0.1196	0.1613	0.1222	0.1744	0.1925	0.2611	0.2592	0.2637	0.1333	0.1739	0.1761	0.1885
MVSC	0.2248	0.2629	**0.2732**	0.3191	0.1293	0.1593	0.1294	0.2097	0.2132	0.3126	0.2828	0.3393	0.1481	0.1909	0.1911	0.2180
ITQ+*bk*-means [15]	0.1861	0.2923	0.2562	0.3101	0.0604	0.1746	0.1200	0.2304	0.1879	0.2842	0.2644	0.3168	0.1214	0.1954	0.1643	0.2032
CKM [40]	0.1712	0.2382	0.1906	0.2794	0.0394	0.1352	0.0738	0.1823	0.1784	0.2556	0.1962	0.2844	0.1107	0.1687	0.1389	0.1990
HSIC-TS	0.1829	0.3030	0.2523	0.3568	0.1367	0.1672	0.1013	0.2376	0.1935	0.3247	0.2577	0.3665	0.1194	0.1945	0.1525	0.2309
HSIC-F	0.1951	0.2923	0.2516	0.3749	0.1289	0.1592	0.1015	0.2411	0.2062	0.3165	0.2625	0.3795	0.1252	0.1832	0.1566	0.2321
HSIC(ours)	0.2275	0.3128	0.2597	**0.3865**	**0.1396**	0.1692	0.1219	**0.2515**	0.2131	**0.3253**	0.2723	**0.3905**	0.1353	0.1929	0.1739	**0.2530**

For all single-view methods, features from all views are simply concatenated to obtain the 'MulView' results.

Table 2. Time costs (in seconds) of different methods on ImageNet-10.

Alg.	*k*-means Time / Speedup		Ak-kmeans Tim. / Speedup		Nyström Tim. / Speedup		LSC-K Tim. / Speedup		AMGL Tim. / Speedup		MLAN Tim. / Speedup		OMVC Tim. / Speedup		CKM Tim. / Speedup		HSIC-TS Tim. / Speedup		HSIC (ours) Tim. / Speedup	
LBP	69	1×	16	4.31×	15	4.60×	211	0.33×	1693	0.04×	1431	0.05×	696	0.10×	17	4.06×	18	3.83×	4	17.25×
GIST	43	1×	11	3.91×	11	3.91×	226	0.19×	1730	0.03×	1557	0.03×	616	0.07×	11	3.91×	16	2.69×	4	10.75×
HOG	82	1×	11	7.46×	12	6.83×	331	0.25×	1862	0.04×	2226	0.04×	643	0.13×	18	4.56×	16	5.13×	3	27.33×
MulView	201	1×	21	9.57×	19	10.58×	503	0.40×	3820	0.05×	3336	0.06×	1109	0.18×	27	7.44×	20	10.05×	5	40.20×

obtain comparable results to *k*-means, but they are very time-consuming. Moreover, when applying those MVIC methods (*e.g.*, AMGL and MLAN) to larger datasets, we encounter the 'out-of-memory' error. Therefore, the real-valued MVIC methods are not compared on the three large-scale datasets. *Thirdly*, some empirical analyses of our HSIC are also provided.

3.2 Experiments on the Middle-Scale ImageNet-10

We compare HSIC to several state-of-the-art clustering methods including SVIC methods (*i.e.*, *k*-means [16], *k*-Medoids [33], Approximate kernel *k*-means [8], Nyström [6], NMF [20], LSC-K [7]), MVIC methods, (*i.e.*, AMGL [31], MVKM [4], MLAN [30], MultiNMF [22], OMVC [37], MVSC [21]) and two existing binary clustering methods (*i.e.*, ITQ+*bk*-means [15] and CKM [41]). Additionally, two variants of HSIC are also compared to show its efficacy, *i.e.*, HSIC with *F*-norm regularized binary clustering (HSIC-F), and HSIC with two separate steps of binary code learning and discrete clustering (HSIC-TS). Similar to [21,22], for all the SVIC methods, we simply concatenate the feature vectors of all views for the 'MulView' clustering.

Table 1 demonstrates the performance of all clustering methods. From Table 1, we can observe in most cases that our HSIC can achieve comparable SVIC results but superior MVIC results in comparison with all the real-valued and binary clustering methods. This indicates the effectiveness of HSIC on the common representation learning and robust cluster structures learning, especially for the MVIC cases. Furthermore, it is clear that HSIC is superior to HSIC-F and HSIC-ST, which demonstrates the robustness and effectiveness of the joint learning framework.

The computational costs are illustrated in Table 2. From its last three columns, we can see that the binary clustering methods can reduce the computational time compared with the real-valued ones such as k-means and LSC-K, due to the highly efficient distance calculation in the Hamming space. Particularly, our HSIC is much faster than the compared real-valued and binary clustering methods, which also proves the superiority of the developed efficient optimization algorithm. Specifically, the speed-up of our HSIC for MVIC is very clear by a margin of 40.20 times compared to k-means. For memory footprint, k-means and our HSIC respectively require 361 MB and 2.73 MB, *i.e.*, ≈ 132 times memory can be reduced using HSIC.

Why does HSIC Outperform the Real-Valued Methods? Table 1 clearly shows that HSIC achieves competitive or superior clustering performance compared to the real-valued clustering methods. The favorable performance mainly comes from: (1) HSIC greatly benefits from the proposed effective discrete optimization algorithm such that the learned binary representations can eliminate some redundant and noisy information in the original real-valued features. As can be seen in Fig. 2, the similarity structures of the same clusters are enhanced in the coding space, meanwhile, some disturbances from the original features are excluded to refine the learned representation. (2) For image clustering, binary features are more robust to local changes since small variations caused by varying environments can be eliminated by quantized binary codes. (3) HSIC is a unified interactive learning framework of the optimal binary codes and clustering structures, which is shown to be better than those disjoint learning approaches (*e.g.*, LSC-K, NMF, MVSC, AMGL and MLAN).

3.3   Experiments on Large-Scale Datasets

To show the strong scalability of HSIC on the large-scale MVIC problem, we compare HSIC with several state-of-the-art scalable clustering methods on three

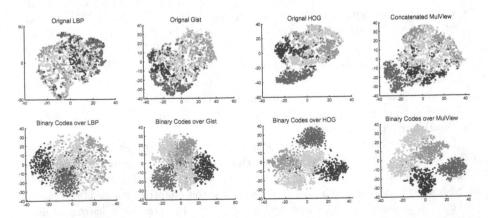

Fig. 2. t-SNE visualization of randomly selected 5 classes from ImageNet-10. The two rows show the real-valued features and 128-bit HSIC-based binary codes, respectively.

Table 3. Performance comparisons on the three large-scale datasets. The bold **black** and **blue** numbers indicate the best single-view and multi-view results, respectively.

	Metric	Alg.	k-means	k-mean++	k-Medoids	Ak-kmeans	LSC-K	Nyström	ITQ+ bk-means	CKM	HSIC-TS	HSIC-F	HSIC
Cifar-10	ACC	LBP	0.2185	0.2182	0.2171	0.2066	0.2550	0.2339	0.2322	0.2225	0.2440	0.2536	**0.2681**
		GIST	0.2842	0.2845	0.2419	0.2847	0.3010	0.2592	0.2777	0.2521	0.3209	0.3456	**0.3595**
		HOG	0.2661	0.2703	0.2456	0.2608	0.2838	0.2408	0.2481	0.2294	0.3178	0.3394	**0.3389**
		MulView	0.2877	0.2882	0.2630	0.2879	0.3488	0.2747	0.2787	0.2703	0.3742	0.3809	**0.3951**
	NMI	LBP	0.1044	0.1044	0.0862	0.1021	0.1303	0.0922	0.0963	0.1092	0.1105	0.1094	**0.1220**
		GIST	0.1692	0.1691	0.1238	0.1692	0.1869	0.1226	0.1502	0.1184	0.2063	0.2134	**0.2299**
		HOG	0.1634	0.1645	0.1328	0.1607	0.1668	0.1415	0.1570	0.1034	0.2053	**0.2199**	0.2170
		MulView	0.1803	0.1805	0.1565	0.1808	0.2382	0.1511	0.1613	0.1499	0.2547	0.2596	**0.2629**
	Purity	LBP	0.2401	0.2400	0.2339	0.2275	0.2768	0.2445	0.2490	0.2476	0.2526	0.2697	**0.2837**
		GIST	0.3056	0.3052	0.2483	0.3054	0.3306	0.2626	0.2882	0.2649	0.3650	0.3651	**0.3828**
		HOG	0.2943	0.2953	0.2561	0.2847	0.3039	0.2655	0.2756	0.2319	0.3199	**0.3589**	0.3481
		MulView	0.3136	0.3138	0.2921	0.3148	0.3787	0.2975	0.2953	0.2846	0.3956	0.4045	**0.4204**
	F-score	LBP	0.1677	0.1676	0.1703	0.1643	0.1692	0.1517	0.1685	0.1509	0.1717	0.1670	**0.1721**
		GIST	0.1866	0.1866	0.1744	0.1867	0.2044	0.1654	0.1808	0.1606	0.2318	0.2318	**0.2397**
		HOG	0.1887	0.1895	0.1808	0.1882	0.1878	0.1680	0.1769	0.1479	0.2221	0.2337	**0.2383**
		MulView	0.1998	0.2001	0.2035	0.2001	0.2477	0.1793	0.1863	0.1807	0.2422	0.2564	**0.2595**
YouTube-Faces (YTBF)	ACC	LBP	0.5870	0.5994	0.5262	0.5584	0.6017	0.5647	0.5765	0.5319	0.5930	0.6208	**0.6471**
		GIST	0.4081	0.4068	0.3584	0.2937	0.4638	0.4497	0.3547	0.3760	0.5432	0.6059	**0.6121**
		HOG	0.5751	0.5821	0.4810	0.5542	0.5830	0.5642	0.5574	0.5584	0.5436	**0.6133**	0.6099
		MulView	0.5927	0.6067	0.5290	0.5562	0.6099	0.6190	0.5852	0.5574	0.5974	0.6315	**0.6547**
	NMI	LBP	0.7473	0.7460	0.6835	0.7251	**0.7725**	0.7515	0.6870	0.6222	0.7256	0.7478	0.7690
		GIST	0.5528	0.5472	0.5062	0.4165	0.6237	0.6630	0.5146	0.5094	0.6889	0.7272	**0.7436**
		HOG	0.7442	0.7375	0.6640	0.7206	**0.7536**	0.7193	0.6827	0.6805	0.6965	0.7342	0.7483
		MulView	0.7492	0.7488	0.6774	0.7215	0.7515	0.7307	0.6921	0.6827	0.7579	0.7785	**0.7899**
	Purity	LBP	0.6744	0.6760	0.6033	0.6155	0.6782	0.6697	0.6529	0.5695	0.6597	0.6600	**0.6915**
		GIST	0.4641	0.4622	0.4315	0.3157	0.5366	0.5729	0.4405	0.4398	0.6099	0.6530	**0.6766**
		HOG	0.6499	0.6481	0.5733	0.6218	0.6602	0.6602	0.6257	0.6369	0.6105	0.6606	**0.6682**
		MulView	0.6712	0.6692	0.5969	0.6376	0.6687	0.6778	0.6642	0.6257	0.6615	0.6955	**0.7023**
	F-score	LBP	0.4240	0.4378	0.4034	0.4412	0.5058	0.4375	0.4421	0.4105	0.4286	0.4982	**0.5123**
		GIST	0.2567	0.2551	0.2310	0.1666	0.3390	0.3455	0.2308	0.2578	0.3367	0.4871	**0.4914**
		HOG	0.4813	0.4572	0.3715	0.4464	0.4627	0.3990	0.4303	0.4663	0.3379	0.4960	**0.5016**
		MulView	0.4886	0.4853	0.4236	0.4209	0.4650	0.4211	0.4650	0.4303	0.4517	0.5113	**0.5425**
NUS-WIDE	ACC	CH	0.1321	0.1370	**0.1433**	0.1351	0.1253	0.1391	0.1193	0.1244	0.1243	0.1314	0.1282
		CM	0.1334	**0.1379**	0.1305	0.1300	0.1297	0.1130	0.1123	0.1202	0.1346	0.1376	0.1360
		CORR	0.1352	**0.1358**	0.1222	0.1301	0.1344	0.1277	0.1143	0.1161	0.1349	0.1253	0.1279
		EDH	0.1402	**0.1425**	0.1382	0.1399	0.1266	0.1129	0.1180	0.1223	0.1343	0.1343	0.1396
		WT	0.1145	0.1182	0.1176	0.1169	0.1110	0.1226	0.1240	0.1172	0.1242	0.1147	**0.1293**
		MulView	0.1434	0.1458	0.1545	0.1499	0.1567	0.1452	0.1295	0.1296	0.1607	0.1639	**0.1661**
	NMI	CH	0.0687	0.0675	0.0706	0.0682	0.0638	0.0684	0.0629	0.0613	0.0668	0.0662	**0.0938**
		CM	0.0755	0.0687	0.0615	0.0747	0.0746	0.0656	0.0625	0.0580	0.0775	0.0870	**0.0944**
		CORR	0.0701	0.0699	0.0639	0.0714	0.0691	0.0661	0.0655	0.0589	0.0784	0.0652	**0.0882**
		EDH	0.0844	0.0877	0.0830	0.0900	0.0866	0.0707	0.0758	0.0731	**0.0961**	0.0872	0.0925
		WT	0.0571	0.0593	0.0559	0.0558	0.0661	0.0711	0.0632	0.0645	0.0878	0.0652	**0.0748**
		MulView	0.0944	0.0967	0.0823	0.0947	0.0980	0.0880	0.0773	0.0696	0.0937	0.0989	**0.1032**
	Purity	CH	0.2459	0.2418	0.2498	0.2439	0.2432	0.2443	0.2422	0.2390	0.2437	0.2397	**0.2589**
		CM	0.2453	0.2459	0.2284	0.2507	0.2516	0.2495	0.2433	0.2414	**0.2601**	0.2371	0.2515
		CORR	0.2370	0.2341	0.2402	0.2413	0.2408	0.2387	0.2404	0.2344	0.2564	0.2337	**0.2589**
		EDH	0.2388	0.2448	0.2365	0.2467	0.2393	0.2193	0.2354	0.2308	0.2451	0.2296	**0.2587**
		WT	0.2256	0.2274	0.2235	0.2237	0.2297	0.2328	0.2273	0.2256	0.2339	0.2306	**0.2393**
		MulView	0.2625	0.2634	0.2446	0.2711	0.2657	0.2546	0.2487	0.2413	0.2647	0.2653	**0.2753**
	F-score	CH	0.1128	0.1134	**0.1147**	0.1095	0.0946	0.1031	0.0867	0.0882	0.0863	0.0901	0.1009
		CM	0.1011	**0.1128**	0.0981	0.0956	0.0896	0.0867	0.0836	0.0879	0.0941	0.1095	0.1010
		CORR	0.1005	**0.1027**	0.0954	0.0947	0.0945	0.0969	0.0854	0.0841	0.0985	0.0888	0.0965
		EDH	**0.1163**	0.1150	0.1079	0.1149	0.0972	0.0865	0.0892	0.0899	0.0966	0.1130	0.1033
		WT	0.0933	0.0949	0.0940	0.0975	0.0893	0.0914	0.0889	0.0892	0.0903	0.0912	**0.1019**
		MulView	0.1106	0.1125	0.1105	0.1061	0.1071	0.1006	0.0905	0.0903	0.1076	0.1055	**0.1216**

For all single-view methods, features from all views are simply concatenated to obtain the 'MulView' results.

large-scale multi-view datasets. The clustering performance is summarized in Table 3. Given these results, we have the following observations: (1) Generally, MVIC performs better than SVIC, which implies the necessity of incorporating complementary traits of multiple features for image clustering. Particularly, our

Table 4. Time costs (in seconds) on the three large-scale multi-view datasets.

Alg.	k-means Time	Speedup	k-means++ Time	Speedup	Ak-kmeans Time	Speedup	LSC-K Time	Speedup	Nyström Time	Speedup	ITQ+bk-means Time	Speedup	CKM Time	Speedup	HSIC-TS Time	Speedup	HSIC (ours) Time	Speedup
Cifar-10 LBP	409	1×	294	1.39×	61	6.71×	112	3.65×	26	15.73×	24	17.04×	29	14.10×	29	14.10×	10	40.90×
GIST	305	1×	334	0.91×	56	5.44×	834	0.37×	28	10.89×	23	13.26×	28	10.89×	30	10.17×	10	30.50×
HOG	412	1×	266	1.55×	58	7.10×	913	0.45×	32	12.87×	27	15.26×	30	13.73×	25	16.48×	10	41.20×
MulView	977	1×	791	1.23×	77	12.69×	1877	0.52×	58	16.85×	48	20.35×	46	21.24×	34	28.74×	17	57.47×
YTBF LBP	2344	1×	1974	1.18×	533	4.40×	3546	0.66×	766	3.06×	90	26.04×	141	16.62×	97	24.17×	40	58.60×
GIST	2299	1×	1705	1.34×	515	4.46×	3796	0.61×	828	2.78×	107	21.49×	153	15.03×	98	23.46×	36	63.86×
HOG	3329	1×	1508	2.21×	523	6.37×	4042	0.83×	870	3.83×	104	32.01×	197	16.90×	105	31.71×	48	69.35×
MulView	5879	1×	4250	1.38×	539	10.91×	12546	0.47×	998	5.89×	110	53.45×	309	19.03×	162	36.29×	139	42.30×
NUS-WIDE CH	1027	1×	852	1.21×	464	2.21×	1693	0.61×	327	3.14×	91	11.29×	83	12.37×	85	12.08×	34	30.21×
CM	1206	1×	937	1.29×	464	2.60×	1987	0.61×	352	3.43×	82	14.71×	93	12.97×	89	13.55×	35	34.46×
CORR	1101	1×	876	1.26×	467	2.36×	1854	0.59×	382	2.88×	83	13.27×	83	13.26×	89	12.37×	35	31.46×
EDH	1000	1×	829	1.21×	454	2.21×	1825	0.55×	371	2.70×	99	10.10×	91	10.99×	98	10.20×	34	29.41×
WT	1206	1×	784	1.54×	491	2.46×	1984	0.61×	427	2.82×	82	14.71×	99	12.18×	81	14.89×	34	35.47×
MulView	1711	1×	1147	1.49×	479	3.57×	8978	0.19×	485	3.53×	105	16.30×	142	12.05×	112	15.28×	81	21.12×

Table 5. Memory footprint of 'MulView' k-means and HSIC on the three large-scale datasets. 'Reduction' denotes the times of memory reduction against k-means.

Datasets	Memory w.r.t. k-means Data (Real-valued features)	Centroids	Reduction	Memory w.r.t. HSIC (ours) Data (128-bit binary codes)	Centroids	Projection	Reduction
Cifar-10 (60,000 images)	1.62GB	0.28MB	1×	0.92MB	0.15×10^{-3}MB	2.53MB	481×
YTBF (182,881 images)	4.94GB	2.46MB	1×	2.79MB	1.36×10^{-3}MB	2.53MB	951×
NUS-WIDE (195,834 images)	961MB	0.10MB	1×	2.99MB	0.32×10^{-3}MB	2.53MB	174×

HSIC achieves competitive or better SVIC results but consistent best MVIC performance. This mainly owes to the adaptive weights learning strategy and the exploiting of sharable and individual information from heterogeneous features. (2) From the last three columns of Table 3, we can observe that HSIC and its variants tend to be better than the real-valued ones. This shows that the binary codes learned by HISC are competitive to the real-valued ones. (3) When comparing to HSIC-TS and HSIC-F, HSIC in most cases achieves superior performance. This further reflects the advantages of the unified learning strategy and robust binary cluster structure construction.

The comparisons of running time and memory footprint are illustrated in Tables 4 and 5, respectively. From Table 4, we can observe that our HSIC is the fastest method in most cases. Table 5 shows that HSIC significantly reduces the memory load for large-scale MVIC compared to k-means. The memory cost of HSIC is similar to other binary clustering methods but clearly less than the real-valued methods. Moreover, as shown in Tables 4 and 5, for MVIC on NUS-WIDE with 5 views, HSIC can cluster near one million ($195,834 \times 5$) features in 81 seconds using only 5.52 MB memory, while k-means needs about 29 minutes with 961 MB memory. Thus, HSIC can effectively address large-scale MVIC with much less computational time and memory footprint.

3.4   Empirical Analysis

Component Analysis: We evaluate the effectiveness of different components of HSIC in Fig. 3. Specifically, in addition to 'HSIC-TS' and 'HSIC-F', we have 'HSIC-U' by removing the balanced and independence constraints on binary

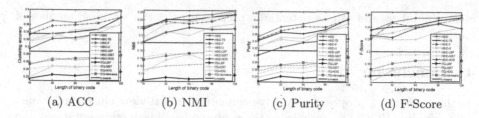

(a) ACC   (b) NMI   (c) Purity   (d) F-Score

Fig. 3. Performance of different clustering methods vs. code lengths on Cifar-10.

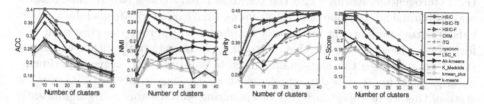

Fig. 4. Performance of different clustering methods vs. numbers of clusters on Cifar-10.

codes and clustering centroids. HSIC-'view' and ITQ-'view' respectively refer to the SVIC results obtained using HSIC and ITQ+bk-means on the 'view'-specific features. From Fig. 3, we can observe that each component contributes essentially to the enhanced performance, and lacking any component will deteriorate the performance.

Effect of Code Length: We show our performance changes with the increasing code lengths in Fig. 3. In general, longer codes may provide more information for higher clustering performance. Specifically, both ITQ and HSIC based methods tend to achieve improved performance with increasing numbers of bits. Moreover, HSIC-based methods are superior to the baseline k-means when the code length is larger than 32. The best clustering results are established by HSIC w.r.t. different code lengths, because HSIC can effectively coordinate the importance of different views and mine the semantic correlations between them.

Effect of Number of Clusters: All the above experiments are evaluated based on the ground-truth cluster numbers. However, if the number of clusters is unknown, how will the performance change with different cluster numbers? To this end, we perform experiments on Cifar-10 to evaluate the stabilities of different methods w.r.t. number of clusters. Figure 4 illustrates the performance changes by varying the cluster numbers from 5 to 40 with an interval of 5. Interestingly, the performance (*i.e.*, ACC, NMI and F-score) of HSIC-based methods increases when the cluster number increases from 5 to 10, but then sharply drops using more than 10 clusters. This suggests that 10 is the optimal number of clusters. Notably, 'purity' can not trade off the precise clustering evaluation against the number of clusters [28]. Importantly, the clustering performance of HSIC in most cases is better than all the compared methods, and HSIC-based methods hold the first three best results. This shows that HSIC is adaptive to different cluster numbers and can be potentially used to predict the 'optimal' number of clusters.

4 Conclusion

In this paper, we proposed a highly-economized multi-view clustering framework, dubbed HSIC, to jointly learn the compressive binary representations and robust discrete cluster structures. Specifically, HSIC collaboratively integrated the heterogeneous features into the common binary codes, where the sharable and individual information of multiple views were exploited. Meanwhile, a robust cluster structure learning model was developed to improve the clustering performance. Moreover, an effective alternating optimization algorithm was introduced to guarantee the high-quality discrete solutions. Extensive experiments on large-scale multi-view datasets demonstrate the superiority of HSIC over the state-of-the-art methods in terms of clustering performance with significantly reduced computational time and memory footprint.

References

1. Avrithis, Y., Kalantidis, Y., Anagnostopoulos, E., Emiris, I.Z.: Web-scale image clustering revisited. In: ICCV (2015)
2. Baluja, S., Covell, M.: Learning to hash: forgiving hash functions and applications. Data Mining Knowl. Discov. **17**(3), 402–430 (2008)
3. Bickel, S., Scheffer, T.: Multi-view clustering. In: ICDM (2004)
4. Cai, X., Nie, F., Huang, H.: Multi-view k-means clustering on big data. In: IJCAI (2013)
5. Chen, J., Wang, Y., Qin, J., Liu, L., Shao, L.: Fast person re-identification via cross-camera semantic binary transformation. In: CVPR (2017)
6. Chen, W.Y., Song, Y., Bai, H., Lin, C.J., Chang, E.Y.: Parallel spectral clustering in distributed systems. IEEE TPAMI **33**(3), 568–586 (2011)
7. Chen, X., Cai, D.: Large scale spectral clustering with landmark-based representation. In: AAAI (2011)
8. Chitta, R., Jin, R., Havens, T.C., Jain, A.K.: Approximate kernel k-means: solution to large scale kernel clustering. In: SIGKDD (2011)
9. Chua, T.S., Tang, J., Hong, R., Li, H., Luo, Z., Zheng, Y.: NUS-WIDE: a real-world web image database from national university of Singapore. In: ACM International Conference on Image and Video Retrieval (2009)
10. De Sa, V.R., Gallagher, P.W., Lewis, J.M., Malave, V.L.: Multi-view kernel construction. Mach. Learn. **79**(1–2), 47–71 (2010)
11. Deng, J., Dong, W., Socher, R., Li, L.J., Li, K., Li, F.F.: ImageNet: a large-scale hierarchical image database. In: CVPR (2009)
12. Ding, C., Zhou, D., He, X., Zha, H.: R1-PCA: rotational invariant ℓ1-norm principal component analysis for robust subspace factorization. In: ICML (2006)
13. Gao, H., Nie, F., Li, X., Huang, H.: Multi-view subspace clustering. In: ICCV (2015)
14. Gong, Y., Lazebnik, S., Gordo, A., Perronnin, F.: Iterative quantization: a procrustean approach to learning binary codes for large-scale image retrieval. IEEE TPAMI **35**(12), 2916–2929 (2013)

15. Gong, Y., Pawlowski, M., Yang, F., Brandy, L., Bourdev, L., Fergus, R.: Web scale photo hash clustering on a single machine. In: CVPR (2015)
16. Hartigan, J.A., Wong, M.A.: Algorithm as 136: a k-means clustering algorithm. J. R. Stat. Soc. Ser. C **28**(1), 100–108 (1979)
17. Jain, A.K.: Data clustering: 50 years beyond k-means. PRL **31**(8), 651–666 (2010)
18. Krizhevsky, A., Hinton, G.: Learning multiple layers of features from tiny images. Technical report (2009)
19. Kumar, A., Rai, P., Daume, H.: Co-regularized multi-view spectral clustering. In: NIPS (2011)
20. Lee, D.D., Seung, H.S.: Algorithms for non-negative matrix factorization. In: NIPS (2001)
21. Li, Y., Nie, F., Huang, H., Huang, J.: Large-scale multi-view spectral clustering via bipartite graph. In: AAAI (2015)
22. Liu, J., Wang, C., Gao, J., Han, J.: Multi-view clustering via joint nonnegative matrix factorization. In: ICDM (2013)
23. Liu, L., Shao, L.: Sequential compact code learning for unsupervised image hashing. IEEE TNNLS **27**(12), 2526–2536 (2016)
24. Liu, L., Yu, M., Shao, L.: Latent structure preserving hashing. IJCV **122**(3), 439–457 (2017)
25. Liu, W., Mu, C., Kumar, S., Chang, S.F.: Discrete graph hashing. In: NIPS (2014)
26. Liu, W., Wang, J., Kumar, S., Chang, S.F.: Hashing with graphs. In: ICML (2011)
27. Lu, J., Liong, V.E., Zhou, J.: Simultaneous local binary feature learning and encoding for homogeneous and heterogeneous face recognition. IEEE TPAMI **40**(8), 1979–1993 (2017)
28. Manning, C.D., Raghavan, P., Schütze, H., et al.: Introduction to Information Retrieval, vol. 1. Cambridge University Press, Cambridge (2008)
29. Ng, A.Y., Jordan, M.I., Weiss, Y.: On spectral clustering: analysis and an algorithm. In: NIPS (2002)
30. Nie, F., Cai, G., Li, X.: Multi-view clustering and semi-supervised classification with adaptive neighbours. In: AAAI (2017)
31. Nie, F., Li, J., Li, X., et al.: Parameter-free auto-weighted multiple graph learning: A framework for multiview clustering and semi-supervised classification. In: IJCAI (2016)
32. Otto, C., Wang, D., Jain, A.K.: Clustering millions of faces by identity. IEEE TPAMI **40**(2), 289–303 (2018)
33. Park, H.S., Jun, C.H.: A simple and fast algorithm for k-medoids clustering. Expert Syst. Appl. **36**(2), 3336–3341 (2009)
34. Qin, J., et al.: Binary coding for partial action analysis with limited observation ratios. In: CVPR (2017)
35. Qin, J., et al.: Zero-shot action recognition with error-correcting output codes. In: CVPR (2017)
36. Sculley, D.: Web-scale k-means clustering. In: WWW (2010)
37. Shao, W., He, L., Lu, C.T., Philip, S.Y.: Online multi-view clustering with incomplete views. In: ICBD (2016)
38. Shen, F., Zhou, X., Yang, Y., Song, J., Shen, H.T., Tao, D.: A fast optimization method for general binary code learning. IEEE TIP **25**(12), 5610–5621 (2016)
39. Shen, F., et al.: Classification by retrieval: binarizing data and classifier. In: ACM SIGIR (2017)
40. Shen, F., Shen, C., Liu, W., Tao Shen, H.: Supervised discrete hashing. In: CVPR (2015)

41. Shen, X.B., Liu, W., Tsang, I.W., Shen, F., Sun, Q.S.: Compressed k-means for large-scale clustering. In: AAAI (2017)
42. Tzortzis, G., Likas, A.: Kernel-based weighted multi-view clustering. In: ICDM (2012)
43. Wang, J., Zhang, T., Sebe, N., Shen, H.T., et al.: A survey on learning to hash. IEEE TPAMI **40**(4), 769–790 (2017)
44. Wang, J., Kumar, S., Chang, S.F.: Semi-supervised hashing for scalable image retrieval. In: CVPR (2010)
45. Wang, X., Guo, X., Lei, Z., Zhang, C., Li, S.Z.: Exclusivity-consistency regularized multi-view subspace clustering. In: CVPR (2017)
46. Wolf, L., Hassner, T., Maoz, I.: Face recognition in unconstrained videos with matched background similarity. In: CVPR (2011)
47. Xia, T., Tao, D., Mei, T., Zhang, Y.: Multiview spectral embedding. IEEE TCYB **40**(6), 1438–1446 (2010)
48. Xu, C., Tao, D., Xu, C.: A survey on multi-view learning. arXiv preprint (2013)
49. Zhang, C., Hu, Q., Fu, H., Zhu, P., Cao, X.: Latent multi-view subspace clustering. In: CVPR (2017)
50. Zhang, Z., Liu, L., Shen, F., Shen, H.T., Shao, L.: Binary multi-view clustering. IEEE TPAMI (2018). https://doi.org/10.1109/TPAMI.2018.2847335
51. Zhang, Z., Shao, L., Xu, Y., Liu, L., Yang, J.: Marginal representation learning with graph structure self-adaptation. IEEE TNNLS **29**(10), 4645–4659 (2018)

Efficient Semantic Scene Completion Network with Spatial Group Convolution

Jiahui Zhang[1], Hao Zhao[2], Anbang Yao[3(✉)], Yurong Chen[3], Li Zhang[2], and Hongen Liao[1(✉)]

[1] Department of Biomedical Engineering, Tsinghua University, Beijing, China
jiahui-z15@mails.tsinghua.edu.cn, liao@tsinghua.edu.cn
[2] Department of Electronic Engineering, Tsinghua University, Beijing, China
zhao-h13@mails.tsinghua.edu.cn, chinazhangli@mail.tsinghua.edu.cn
[3] Intel Labs China, Beijing, China
{anbang.yao,yurong.chen}@intel.com

Abstract. We introduce Spatial Group Convolution (SGC) for accelerating the computation of 3D dense prediction tasks. SGC is orthogonal to group convolution, which works on spatial dimensions rather than feature channel dimension. It divides input voxels into different groups, then conducts 3D sparse convolution on these separated groups. As only valid voxels are considered when performing convolution, computation can be significantly reduced with a slight loss of accuracy. The proposed operations are validated on semantic scene completion task, which aims to predict a complete 3D volume with semantic labels from a single depth image. With SGC, we further present an efficient 3D sparse convolutional network, which harnesses a multiscale architecture and a coarse-to-fine prediction strategy. Evaluations are conducted on the SUNCG dataset, achieving state-of-the-art performance and fast speed.

Keywords: Spatial group convolution
Sparse convolutional network · Efficient neural network
Semantic scene completion

1 Introduction

3D shape processing has attracted increased attention recently, because large scale 3D datasets and deep learning based methods open new opportunities for understanding and synthesizing 3D data, such as segmentation and shape completion. These 3D dense prediction tasks are quite useful for many applications. For example, robots need semantic information to understand the world, while knowing complete scene geometry can help them to grasp objects [43] and avoid obstacles. However, it is not a trivial task to adopt 3D Convolutional Neural Network (CNN) by just adding one dimension to 2D CNN. Dense 3D CNN

J. Zhang and H. Zhao—Indicates interns at Intel Labs China.

V. Ferrari et al. (Eds.): ECCV 2018, LNCS 11216, pp. 749–765, 2018.
https://doi.org/10.1007/978-3-030-01258-8_45

methods [30,45] face the problem of cubic growth of computational and memory requirements with the increase of voxel resolution.

But meanwhile, we observe that 3D data has some attractive characteristics, which inspire us to build efficient 3D CNN blocks. Firstly, intrinsic sparsity in 3D data. Most of the voxels in a dense 3D grid are empty. Non-trivial voxels usually exist near the boundaries of objects. This property has been explored in several recent works [9,11,37,44]. Secondly, redundancy in 3D voxels. Dense 3D voxels are usually redundant, discarding a large portion of voxels (e.g. 70%) randomly does not prevent humans from reasoning the overall semantic information, as shown in Fig. 1. Thirdly, different subsets of original dense voxels contain complementary information. It is hard to recognize objects with small size and complex geometry when giving only partial voxels. These properties motivate us to design computation-efficient 3D CNNs for dense prediction tasks. We adopt Sparse Convolutional Network (SCN) [11][1] to exploit the intrinsic sparsity of 3D data, which encodes sparse 3D data with Hash Table and presents sparse convolution design. These designs can avoid unnecessary memory or computation cost on empty voxels. However, the computation is still intensive when the resolution is high or input is not so sparse. For example, the complexity of the baseline SCN used in this paper is about 80 GFLOPs while only outputting 1/64 sized predictions. Our work takes advantage of SCN and steps further by encouraging higher sparsity in feature maps. We propose SGC to exploit the redundancy of 3D voxels, which partitions features into different groups and makes voxels sparser. Then we conduct sparse convolution on each group. Because only valid voxels are considered in sparse convolution rather than all voxels in a regular grid, and only partial voxels exist in each group after partition, the computation of networks with SGC can be significantly reduced compared to previous SCN. Besides, in order to utilize the complementary information of different groups, results of different groups after certain SGC operations are gathered for further processing.

Network acceleration methods in 2D CNN such as weight pruning, quantization, and Group Convolution (GC) design [20,50] can also be used, but these methods have not been well explored in 3D CNNs for now. Different from these methods, **SGC speeds up 3D CNNs from another perspective by encouraging sparsity in feature maps**. Though recently there are works [6,13] exploiting sparsity in feature maps, they are not suitable for dense prediction tasks because some voxels need to be predicted are deactivated in the network. **Our method is orthogonal to Group Convolution**, which is an operation widely used in recent CNN architectures [3,24,46]. SGC is defined on spatial dimensions while GC is defined on channel dimension. Besides, because voxels in different groups are similar, weights are shared between different groups in SGC, which is not the case in GC.

We validate our method on semantic scene completion as test case to show its effectiveness on 3D dense prediction tasks. This task not only aims to predict semantic labels, but also needs to output complete structure which is different

---

[1] Or called Submaniflod Sparse Convolutional Network in [11].

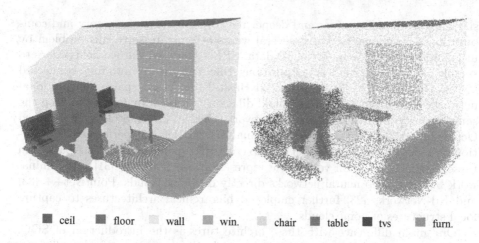

| ■ ceil | ■ floor | wall | ■ win. | chair | ■ table | ■ tvs | ■ furn. |

Fig. 1. A 3D scene image from the SUNCG dataset. Left is the ground truth image. Right is a sampled image with only 30% voxels reserved. Giving only partial voxels does not prevent humans in reasoning the overall semantic information, but it imposes a challenge to recognize small objects such as chair's leg. (**Best viewed in color**)

from the input. We introduce a novel SCN architecture that is applicable to scenarios where output has a different structure with input. Dense deconvolution layer and Abstract Module are designed to generate voxels which are absent in input and remove trivial voxels respectively. Multiscale encoder-decoder architecture and coarse-to-fine prediction strategy are used for final predictions. We evaluate our network on the SUNCG dataset [40] and achieve state-of-the-art results. Our SGC operation can reduce about 3/4 of the computation while losing only 0.7% and 1.2% in terms of Intersection over Union (IoU) for scene completion and semantic scene completion compared to networks without SGC.

Our main contributions are as follows:

- We propose SGC by exploiting sparsity in features for 3D dense prediction tasks, which can significantly reduce computation with slight loss of accuracy.
- We present a novel end-to-end sparse convolutional network design to generate unknown structures for 3D semantic scene completion.
- We achieve state-of-the-art results on the SUNCG dataset, reaching an IoU of 84.5% for scene completion and 70.5% for semantic segmentation.

2   Related Works

2.1   3D Deep Learning

The success of deep learning in 2D computer vision areas has inspired researchers to employ CNN in 3D tasks, such as object recognition [30,32,45], shape completion [4,40,45], and segmentation [1,40]. However, the cubic growth in data size impedes building wider and deeper networks because of memory and computation restrictions. Recently, several works attempt to solve this problem by utilizing the intrinsic sparsity of 3D data. FPNN [28] used learned field probes to sample 3D data at a small set of positions, then fed features into fully connected layers. Graham et al. [9,11] proposed Hash Table based sparse convolutional networks and solved the "submanifold dilation" problem by forcing to keep the same sparsity level throughout the network. OctNet [37] and O-CNN [44] used Octree-based 3D CNN for 3D shape analysis. SBNet [35] performed convolution on blockwise decomposition of the structured sparsity patterns. Apart from these methods based on volumetric representation, PointNet [31] is a seminal work building deep neural networks directly on point clouds. PointNet++ [33] and Kd-Networks [23] further employed hierarchical architectures to capture local structures of point clouds.

Our main difference with these architectures is the introduction of SGC, which encourages higher sparsity in features and makes networks more efficient.

2.2   Computation-Efficient Networks

Most previous computation-efficient networks focus on reducing model size to accelerate inference, such as pruning weight connections [14,25] and quantizing weights [8]. Another line of works uses GC to reduce the computation, such as MobileNet [20] and ShuffleNets [50]. GC separates features to different groups along channel dimension and performs convolution on each group parallelly. Besides, Graham [9] used smaller filters on different lattices to decrease the computation.

However, there are seldom works designing computation-efficient networks by exploiting higher sparsity in feature maps for 3D dense prediction tasks. Vote3deep [6] encouraged sparsity in feature maps using L_1 regularization. ILA-SCNN [13] used adaptive rectified linear unit to control the sparsity of features. But these methods are not suitable for dense prediction tasks, because some desired voxels are deactivated in the network and cannot be recovered. Besides, Li et al. [26] also exploited sparsity and reduced the computation of 2D segmentation task with cascaded networks, and only hard pixels are handled by deeper sub-models.

Different with these methods, we create groups along the spatial dimensions and make voxels in each group sparser. Computation of convolution can be largely reduced because only partial valid voxels are used in each computation.

2.3   3D Semantic Segmentation and Shape Completion

3D semantic segmentation [2,29,34,48] and Shape Completion [4,7,15,45] are both active areas in computer vision. 3D segmentation gives semantic labels to observed voxels, while shape completion completes missing voxels. SSCNet [40] combined these two tasks together and showed that segmentation and completion can benefit from each other. In order to generate high resolution 3D structure, various methods had been explored, such as long short-term memorized [15], coarse-to-fine strategy [5], 3D generative adversarial network [47], and inverse discrete cosine transform [22]. Recently, segmentation and completion are both benefited from these advanced 3D deep learning methods described in Sect. 2.1. Different methods have been presented in the 3D segmentation challenge [49], such as SCN, Pd-Network, densely connected PointNet, and Point CNN [27]. For 3D completion tasks, advanced Octree-based CNN methods [17, 36, 41] were also used for generating high resolution 3D outputs. Our network architecture shares some similarities with [36, 41], while the main difference is that we focus on efficient model design in this paper.

3   Method

In this section, we firstly give a brief introduction to previous SCN architecture [11], and then introduce SGC for computation-efficient 3D dense prediction tasks. Thirdly, a novel sparse convolutional network architecture which can predict unknown structures will be presented for semantic scene completion. Finally, details about training and networks will be given.

3.1   Sparse Convolutional Network

Previous dense 3D convolution is neither computational nor memory efficient because of the usage of dense 3D grid for representation. Another problem is that traditional "dense" convolution has the "dilation" problem [11] which will destroy the sparsity of 3D feature maps. For example, after a $3 \times 3 \times 3$ convolution, surrounding 26 voxels will be filled in. SCN addressed these problems by only storing non-empty voxels in 3D feature maps using Hash Table. **Only non-empty voxels are considered in sparse convolutional network.** Besides, **it forces to keep sparsity at the same level throughout the network** when performing convolution, which means the activation pattern of next layer is the same as the previous layer. These designs can largely decrease computation and memory requirements, enabling the usage of deeper 3D CNNs.

However, there is still intensive computation in 3D sparse CNN as mentioned above. Thus reducing the computation of 3D sparse CNN is necessary for real-time applications. Another problem of previous SCN is that it cannot be directly used for scene completion task. Because completion needs to output a complete structure which is different from the input, while previous SCN can only output predictions with the same structure as input. We introduce a novel sparse convolutional network to predict unknown structures.

3.2   Spatial Group Convolution

This section introduce SGC which can significantly reduce the computation of 3D dense prediction tasks. Our design makes use of those three properties of 3D data described in Sect. 1 (see Fig. 2). We partition voxels uniformly into different

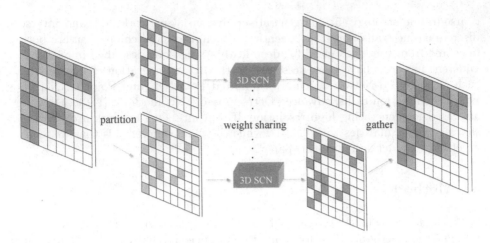

Fig. 2. Illustration of SGC. Feature maps are partitioned uniformly into different groups along the spatial dimensions (only two groups are shown here). 3D CNNs are conducted on different groups and give the final dense prediction for all voxels. Weights are shared between different groups.

groups, then conduct 3D sparse convolution on each group. Weights are shared among different groups because these groups are similar. Features of different groups are gathered later in order to utilize the complementary information of different groups.

In the implementation of SGC, we partition features along the spatial dimensions and then stack different groups along the batch dimension. For one sparse feature map whose size is $B \times D \times H \times W \times C$ ($batchsize \times depth \times height \times width \times channel$), after the partition operation, it becomes $(G \times B) \times D \times H \times W \times C$, where G is the group number. Note that because we use Hash Table based representation, only non-empty voxels are stored. So this operation does not require extra memory. In each convolution computation, only part of original non-empty voxels in its receptive filed participate in the calculation, and the number of valid voxels in each group is about $1/G$ of the original non-empty voxels after partition. The final computation cost is thus about $1/G = \frac{N \times \frac{1}{G} \times k^3}{N \times k^3}$ of original convolution when ignoring the bias computation, where N is the total number of valid voxels, and k is the filter size. SGC can readily replace plain 3D sparse convolution in existing CNNs.

Obviously, partition strategy plays an important role in SGC. Here we present two different partition strategies:

- Random partition method. Voxels of feature maps are partitioned into different groups randomly and uniformly.
- Partition with a fixed pattern. Random partition expects convolutional filters to be invariant to all possible patterns of activation, which may be hard for CNN to learn. We propose to partition input voxels with a fixed regular

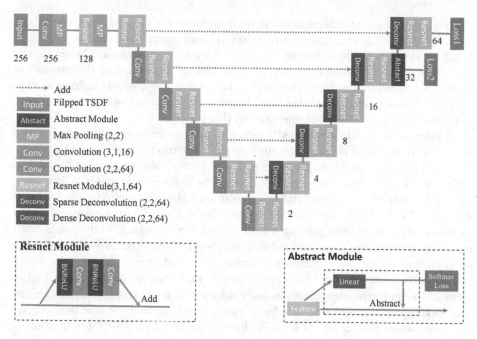

Fig. 3. Network architecture for semantic scene completion. Taking flipped TSDF as input, the network predicts occupancy and object labels in 1/4 size. **The resolution of each layer is marked nearby.** Parameters of each layer are shown in the order of (filter size, stride, output channel). Dense deconvolution layers can generate new voxels. The abstract module can abstract non-trivial voxels to high resolution according to the prediction in low resolution. (**Best viewed in color**)

pattern for all input voxels throughout training and testing. For example, we can partition voxels by the following formulation:

$$i = mod(ax + by + cz, G) \tag{1}$$

where i is the group index, (x, y, z) is the position of the voxel, G is the total group number, mod is the modulus operation, (a, b, c) controls the distribution of different groups. This strategy can also partition voxels uniformly but in a fixed pattern manner. Different (a, b, c) and G give different patterns.

3.3 Sparse Convolutional Networks for Semantic Scene Completion

This section will present a novel SCN architecture for semantic scene completion. Previous SCN [10] keeps the sparsity unchanged to avoid "submanifold dilation" problem. The output of previous SCN has the same known structure as input. This design restricts its application in shape completion, RGB-D fusion and etc., which aim to predict unknown structures. In order to generate unknown voxels for semantic scene completion task, we have to break this restriction.

Here we use multiscale encoder-decoder architecture [38]. As shown in Fig. 3, encoder modules are constituted of sparse convolutions described in Sect. 3.1. While in decoder modules, we implement a "dense" deconvolution layer to generate new voxels. More specifically, after a "dense" up-sampling deconvolution layer, each voxel in low resolution will generate $2 \times 2 \times 2$ voxels in high resolution. The sparsity changes rather than keeping the same as the layers in encoder modules. New voxels can be generated in this process.

Applying this module repeatedly in each scale can generate all missing structures but it will soon destroy the sparsity of 3D feature maps just as the "submanifold dilation" problem. So we introduce Abstract Module similar to [36,41], which abstracts a coarse structure and removes unnecessary voxels in low resolution. Details will be refined in high resolution. The Abstract Module contains a $1 \times 1 \times 1$ convolution layer and a softmax layer, these layers give a prediction in this scale and provide guiding information for abstracting. Only voxels with non-empty labels and their surrounding voxels are abstracted. Abstracting these surrounding empty voxels within a distance of k could provide fine details. $k = 1$ works well in our practice. We apply the abstract module in resolution higher than 32 because removing voxels in early stages may hurt the performance. Since our setting exploits resolution 64 for output, one Abstract module is enough.

Voxel-wise softmax loss is used in the two scales which give a prediction:

$$L_i = \frac{1}{\sum w_j} \sum_j w_j L_{sm}(p_j, y_j), \tag{2}$$

where $i \in \{0, 1\}$ means resolution scale as shown in Fig. 3, L_{sm} is softmax loss, y_j is ground truth label of voxel j, p_j is the predicted possibility, and $w_j \in \{0, 1\}$ is the weight of this voxel. The final loss is a summation of all losses as follows:

$$L = \sum_i \alpha_i L_i, \tag{3}$$

where α_i is the weight for each scale. We found $\alpha_i = 1$ works well.

3.4   Implementation Details

Dataset. We train and evaluate our network on the SUNCG dataset, which is a manually created large-scale synthetic scene dataset [40]. It contains 139368 valid pairs of depth map and complete labels for training, and 470 pairs for testing. Depth maps are converted to volumes with a size of $240 \times 144 \times 240$. The ground truth labels are 12-class volumes with 1/4 size of input volume.

Network Details. The detailed network architecture is illustrated in Fig. 3. For volumetric data encoding, we use flipped Truncated Signed Distance Function (fTSDF), which can enhance performance because it eliminates strong gradients in empty space [40]. The input size of our network is 256^3, and we put the original fTSDF volume in the middle of input volume. The input volume is down-sampled twice using Max-pooling layer. Then a U-Net architecture follows, which contains six resolution scales, from 64^3 to 2^3. Features from encoding stages and decoding stages are summed, and zeros are filled at missing locations. The network uses pre-activation Resnet block in encoding and decoding modules [18,19], and each block has two $3 \times 3 \times 3$ convolutions. Down-sampling and up-sampling are implemented by convolution layers with stride 2 and kernel size 2. SGC is used in resolution scales not less than 32^3, which account for most of the computation. Partition operation is performed again once the resolution scale changes, which can help information flow across each other group.

The weight of each voxel is computed by randomly sampling empty and non-empty voxels at a ratio of 1:2 [40]. All non-empty voxels are positive examples. For negative examples, we mainly consider empty voxels around the surface as hard examples, which can be determined by the TSDF value of GT labels ($|TSDF| < 1$). The ratio of hard negative and easy negative examples is 9:1.

Training Policy. Networks are trained using stochastic gradient descent with a momentum of 0.9. The initial learning rate is 0.1, and L2 weight decay is 1e-4. We train our network for 10 epochs with a batch size of 4, and decay learning rate by a factor of $exp(-0.5)$ in each epoch. In order to reduce training time, we randomly select 40000 samples in each epoch, and the total training time is about 5 days with a GTX TitanX GPU and two Intel E5-2650 CPUs.

4   Evaluation

In this section, we evaluate our network on the standard SUNCG test dataset. Both semantic scene completion results and scene completion results are given. Voxel-level IoU evaluation metric is used. Semantic scene completion results are evaluated on both observed and unobserved voxels, and completion results are evaluated on unobserved voxels. Tables 1 and 2 show the quantitative results of our network without or with SGC. Fig. 4 shows the qualitative comparison with previous work. We also give results on real-word noisy NYU dataset [39].

4.1   Comparision to SSCNet

Table 1 shows the result of our baseline network without SGC (group number is 1). We outperform the previous SSCNet by a significant margin, having an improvement of 24.1% in semantic scene completion and 11.0% in scene completion, and achieving state-of-the-art results. Our network exceeds SSCNet in almost all classes, especially in small and hard categories such as chair, tvs and objects. We attribute this improvement to the novel SCN architecture that enables the usage of several advanced deep learning techniques such as deeper networks (15-layer vs 57-layer), multiscale network architecture (3 resolution scales vs 8 resolution scales), batch normalization layer [21] and stacked Resnet style blocks. Figure 4 shows the visualization results of semantic scene completion from a single depth image. Obviously our baseline network produces visually better results compared to SSCNet, especially around the object boundaries.

4.2   Spatial Group Convolution Evaluation

This section describes the results of networks with SGC (see Table 2). We conduct experiments on 2, 3, 4, 6 groups with different partition strategies.

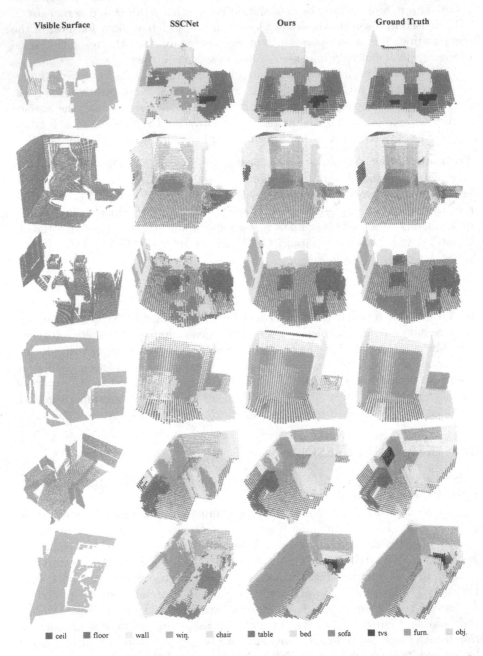

Visible Surface   SSCNet   Ours   Ground Truth

█ ceil   █ floor   ░ wall   ▓ win.   ▒ chair   █ table   ░ bed   █ sofa   █ tvs   ▓ furn.   ░ obj.

Fig. 4. Qualitative results of our network and SSCNet. We achieve obviously much better results, such as predictions around object boundaries.

Table 1. Quantitative results of our network and SSCNet on the SUNCG dataset. Scene completion IoU is measured on unobserved voxels, and all non-empty classes are treated as one category. Semantic scene completion IoU is measured on both observed and unobserved voxels. Overall, our method outperforms SSCNet by a large margin. Better results of each category are bold.

Method	Scene completion			Semantic scene completion											
	prec.	recall	IoU	ceil.	floor	wall	win.	chair	bed	sofa	table	tvs	furn.	objs.	avg.
SSCNet [40]	76.3	**95.2**	73.5	96.3	**84.9**	56.8	28.2	21.3	56.0	52.7	33.7	10.9	44.3	25.4	46.4
Our	**92.6**	90.4	**84.5**	**96.6**	83.7	**74.9**	**59.0**	**55.1**	**83.3**	**78.0**	**61.5**	**47.4**	**73.5**	**62.9**	**70.5**

Table 2. Quantitative IoU (%) results of networks using SGC with random partition strategy or fixed pattern partition strategy. Both accuracy and FLOPs are given. For fixed pattern partition method, flexible parameters (a, b, c) are also given and we select the best results in our experiments. Best trade-off is bolded.

Group no.	Method	Scene completion	Semantic scene completion	FLOPs/G
1(Baseline)		84.5	70.5	79
2	Random	83.9	69.9	42
	Pattern(1,1,1)	84.0	69.6	39
3	Random	82.6	67.6	29
	Pattern(1,1,1)	84.0	69.6	27
4	Random	83.1	67.6	23
	Pattern(1,2,3)	**83.8**	**69.3**	**22**
6	Random	82.3	66.6	17
	Pattern(1,2,1)	82.6	66.9	16

The efficiency is evaluated with FLOPs, i.e., the number of floating-point multiplication-adds of the whole network. As shown in Table 2, SGC can reduce about $(G-1)/G$ of the whole computation. Experiments show that 3D sparse CNNs can be sparsity-invariant to some extent, because accuracy only drops about 0.5% when dividing voxels into two groups even randomly, while only about 50% voxels preserved in this case. Increasing group number will reduce more computation at the cost of a little drop of performance. Compared to random partition method, fixed pattern partition strategy can give better performance yet requires less computation. For example, 1.7% IoU enhancement for semantic completion can be achieved using fixed pattern partition method when dividing voxels into four groups. Overall, SGC can significantly reduce the computation while maintaining accuracy, achieving a drop of only 0.7% and 1.2% in terms of IoU for scene completion and semantic completion task while using only 27.8% computation.

Table 3 shows the detailed semantic scene completion results of different categories using SGC. The accuracies of best and worst three categories compared to baseline network are marked in the table. It can be found that the IoUs of

Table 3. Influence of SGC on each category. The numbers in third to sixth row mean IoU (%) drop when using SGC. The best or worst three are underlined or bolded.

Group no.	Method	ceil.	floor	wall	win.	chair	bed	sofa	table	tvs	furn.	objs.	avg.
Baseline		96.6	83.7	74.9	58.9	55.1	83.3	78.0	61.5	47.4	73.5	62.9	70.5
4	Random	0.4	−0.6	−2.0	−2.9	−4.4	−3.0	−3.2	−4.1	−3.5	−4.4	−4.7	−2.9
	Pattern	0.2	−0.3	−0.8	0.7	−3.7	−1.7	−1.5	−3.1	1.1	−1.9	−2.1	−1.2
6	Random	0.1	−0.7	−3.7	−2.8	−5.7	−2.9	−3.5	−5.6	−5.4	−6.8	−6.0	−3.9
	Pattern	0.2	−0.4	−2.3	−3.8	−5.5	−1.8	−3.7	−6.9	−4.0	−5.5	−5.8	−3.6

Table 4. Scene completion (IoU %) and semantic scene completion results (IoU %) on NYU dataset.

	Scene completion			Semantic scene completion											
Method	prec.	recall	IoU	ceil.	floor	wall	win.	chair	bed	sofa	table	tvs	furn.	objs.	avg.
SSCNet	57.0	94.5	55.1	15.1	94.7	24.4	0	12.6	32.1	35	13	7.8	27.1	10.1	24.7
Ours	71.9	71.9	56.2	17.5	75.4	25.8	6.7	15.3	53.8	42.4	11.2	0	33.4	11.8	26.7

categories with small physical sizes such as chair, furniture, and objects drop more than categories with large size such as ceiling and floor. This may be caused by the fact that those small objects have fewer voxels. Dividing these voxels into different groups may lose important geometric information and makes it harder to distinguish these objects (see chair's leg in Fig. 1). While large objects have surplus voxels, sparser voxels can still keep a rough structure. So, a possible future work to increase the accuracy of semantic scene completion is to adaptively handle large easy objects and small hard objects, sampling small objects with high density while sampling large objects with relatively low density.

We also tried sparsity invariant convolution [42] in random partition method, which normalizes convolution by a factor of valid voxels number, but it does not work in our task.

4.3   Evaluation on NYU Dataset

NYU [39] contains 1449 depth maps captured by Kinect. Following SSCNet [40], we use Guo et al.'s algorithm [12] to generate ground truth annotations for semantic scene completion task. The object categories are mapped based on Handa et al. [16]. We trained the network described above from scrath on NYU dataset. The base of exponential learning rate decay is 0.12 and we trained it for 40 epochs using the whole dataset. Other hyperparameters are same as experiments on SUNCG. Table 4 shows that our network achieves an improvement of 2.0% in semantic scene completion and 1.1% in scene completion compared to SSCNet. Table 5 gives detail results on NYU dataset. It shows that SGC operation is still effective on real data. The fixed pattern partition method gives comparable or even better results than baseline network, and it is consistently better than the random partition method. Note that there exists a gap between the improvements on SUNCG and NYU. We attribute this gap to the fact that

Table 5. Results (IoU%) of networks with SGC using different partition strategies on NYU dataset. (SSC stands for semantic scene completion)

Group no.	1	2		3		4	
Method	Baseline	Random	Pattern	Random	Pattern	Random	Pattern
SSC	26.4	24.1	26.5	23	**26.7**	22.6	25.9
Completion	55.7	53	54.8	52.2	**56.2**	52.6	55.1

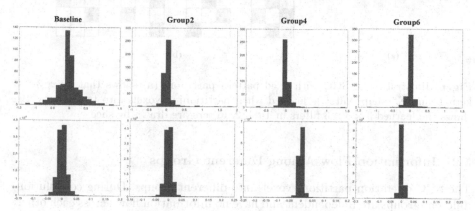

Fig. 5. Histograms of learned weight values of SCN and SGC with different groups. The first row shows the statistics of the first convolution layer, and the second row shows that of the last convolution layer. Filters of SGC have "sharper" histograms.

misalignment and incomplete annotations are common in the generated labels [12]. This may both mislead the training and evaluation procedures, and it may be unfavorable for our network considering the sparisty geometry representation.

5 Discussion

5.1 What Does Spatial Group Convolution Learn?

In Fig. 5, we visualize the histograms of learned weight values of networks without or with SGC using random partition method. It can be observed that filters of SGC have "sharper" histograms while normal SCN filters have relative "flat" histograms, which means the values of SGC filters are pretty close. The histograms become "sharper" with the increase of group number. This may be caused by that filters of SGC need to be invariant to different sparsity patterns, so the values of filters at different locations had better be close to adapt to different sparsity patterns.

As for SGC with fixed pattern partition, we find it learned an irregular convolutional kernel. In Fig. 6a, we show a simple case in a 2D convolution which divides voxels into two groups. The valid convolutional kernel shape is always "X" because the sparsity pattern keeps the same when sliding the convolutional kernel. Figure 6b shows the valid convolutional filter shapes used in Table 2.

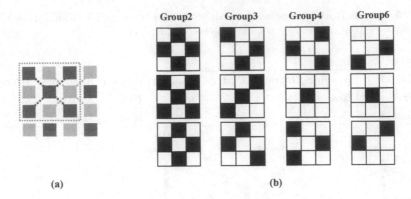

Fig. 6. Illustration of SGC with fixed pattern partition. (a) shows that for a 3 × 3 kernel, an "X" shape filter is learned when partitioning voxels into two groups. (b) shows the learned 3 × 3 × 3 filters in Table 2. Filters are drawn by slice.

5.2 Information Flow Among Different Groups

The SGC operation partitions voxels into different groups. During convolution, different groups are independent and have no information flow across each other. However, after SGC, the voxels are gathered and fed into down-sampling convolution or up-sampling deconvolution layers, in which information of different groups can communicate. Besides, we also explored more complicated methods to help information exchange among different groups. For example, Shuffled SGC, which is inspired by ShuffleNet [50]. ShuffleNet uses channel shuffle to help information flow across feature channels, while we shuffle the features across spatial dimensions which is implemented by using different partition patterns in the two convolution layers of Resnet block. But no obvious improvement is observed in our case.

6 Conclusions

The paper presents an efficient semantic scene completion network with Spatial Group Convolution. SGC partitions feature maps into different groups along the spatial dimensions and can significantly reduce the computation with slight loss of accuracy. Besides, we propose a novel end-to-end sparse convolutional network architecture for 3D semantic scene completion and set a new accuracy record on the SUNCG dataset.

Acknowledgment. This work was supported in part by National Key Research and Development Program of China (2017YFC0108000), National Natural Science Foundation of China (81427803, 81771940, 61132007, 61172125, 61601021, and U1533132), Beijing Municipal Natural Science Foundation (7172122, L172003), and Soochow-Tsinghua Innovation Project (2016SZ0206).

References

1. Ben-Shabat, Y., Lindenbaum, M., Fischer, A.: 3D point cloud classification and segmentation using 3D modified fisher vector representation for convolutional neural networks. arXiv preprint arXiv:1711.08241 (2017)
2. Chang, A., et al.: Matterport3D: learning from RGB-D data in indoor environments. In: 3DV, pp. 667–676. IEEE (2017)
3. Chollet, F.: Xception: deep learning with depthwise separable convolutions. In: CVPR, pp. 1251–1258 (2017)
4. Dai, A., Qi, C.R., Nießner, M.: Shape completion using 3D-encoder-predictor CNNs and shape synthesis. In: CVPR, vol. 3 (2017)
5. Dai, A., Ritchie, D., Bokeloh, M., Reed, S., Sturm, J., Nießner, M.: Scancomplete: large-scale scene completion and semantic segmentation for 3D scans. In: CVPR, vol. 1, p. 2 (2018)
6. Engelcke, M., Rao, D., Wang, D.Z., Tong, C.H., Posner, I.: Vote3Deep: fast object detection in 3D point clouds using efficient convolutional neural networks. In: ICRA, pp. 1355–1361. IEEE (2017)
7. Firman, M., Mac Aodha, O., Julier, S., Brostow, G.J.: Structured prediction of unobserved voxels from a single depth image. In: CVPR, pp. 5431–5440 (2016)
8. Gong, Y., Liu, L., Yang, M., Bourdev, L.: Compressing deep convolutional networks using vector quantization. arXiv preprint arXiv:1412.6115 (2014)
9. Graham, B.: Sparse 3D convolutional neural networks. arXiv preprint arXiv:1505.02890 (2015)
10. Graham, B., Engelcke, M., van der Maaten, L.: 3D semantic segmentation with submanifold sparse convolutional networks. In: CVPR (2018)
11. Graham, B., van der Maaten, L.: Submanifold sparse convolutional networks. arXiv preprint arXiv:1706.01307 (2017)
12. Guo, R., Zou, C., Hoiem, D.: Predicting complete 3D models of indoor scenes. arXiv preprint arXiv:1504.02437 (2015)
13. Hackel, T., Usvyatsov, M., Galliani, S., Wegner, J.D., Schindler, K.: Inference, learning and attention mechanisms that exploit and preserve sparsity in convolutional networks. arXiv preprint arXiv:1801.10585 (2018)
14. Han, S., Pool, J., Tran, J., Dally, W.: Learning both weights and connections for efficient neural network. In: NIPS, pp. 1135–1143 (2015)
15. Han, X., Li, Z., Huang, H., Kalogerakis, E., Yu, Y.: High-resolution shape completion using deep neural networks for global structure and local geometry inference. In: CVPR, pp. 85–93 (2017)
16. Handa, A., Patraucean, V., Badrinarayanan, V., Stent, S., Cipolla, R.: Understanding real world indoor scenes with synthetic data. In: CVPR, pp. 4077–4085 (2016)
17. Häne, C., Tulsiani, S., Malik, J.: Hierarchical surface prediction for 3D object reconstruction. In: 3DV (2017)
18. He, K., Zhang, X., Ren, S., Sun, J.: Deep residual learning for image recognition. In: CVPR, pp. 770–778 (2016)
19. He, K., Zhang, X., Ren, S., Sun, J.: Identity mappings in deep residual networks. In: Leibe, B., Matas, J., Sebe, N., Welling, M. (eds.) ECCV 2016. LNCS, vol. 9908, pp. 630–645. Springer, Cham (2016). https://doi.org/10.1007/978-3-319-46493-0_38
20. Howard, A.G., et al.: MobileNets: efficient convolutional neural networks for mobile vision applications. arXiv e-prints, April 2017

21. Ioffe, S., Szegedy, C.: Batch normalization: accelerating deep network training by reducing internal covariate shift. In: ICML, pp. 448–456 (2015)
22. Johnston, A., Garg, R., Carneiro, G., Reid, I., vd Hengel, A.: Scaling CNNs for high resolution volumetric reconstruction from a single image. In: ICCV Workshops (2017)
23. Klokov, R., Lempitsky, V.: Escape from cells: deep KD-networks for the recognition of 3D point cloud models. In: ICCV, pp. 863–872. IEEE (2017)
24. Krizhevsky, A., Sutskever, I., Hinton, G.E.: Imagenet classification with deep convolutional neural networks. In: NIPS, pp. 1097–1105 (2012)
25. Le Cun, Y., Denker, J.S., Solla, S.A.: Optimal brain damage. In: NIPS, NIPS 1989, pp. 598–605. MIT Press, Cambridge (1989)
26. Li, X., Liu, Z., Luo, P., Change Loy, C., Tang, X.: Not all pixels are equal: difficulty-aware semantic segmentation via deep layer cascade. In: CVPR, pp. 3193–3202 (2017)
27. Li, Y., Bu, R., Sun, M., Chen, B.: PointCNN. arXiv e-prints, January 2018
28. Li, Y., Pirk, S., Su, H., Qi, C.R., Guibas, L.J.: FPNN: field probing neural networks for 3D data. In: NIPS, pp. 307–315 (2016)
29. Liu, F., et al.: 3DCNN-DQN-RNN: a deep reinforcement learning framework for semantic parsing of large-scale 3D point clouds. In: CVPR, pp. 5678–5687 (2017)
30. Maturana, D., Scherer, S.: VoxNet: a 3D convolutional neural network for real-time object recognition. In: IROS, pp. 922–928. IEEE (2015)
31. Qi, C.R., Su, H., Mo, K., Guibas, L.J.: PointNet: deep learning on point sets for 3D classification and segmentation. In: CVPR, pp. 652–660 (2017)
32. Qi, C.R., Su, H., Nießner, M., Dai, A., Yan, M., Guibas, L.J.: Volumetric and multi-view CNNs for object classification on 3D data. In: CVPR, pp. 5648–5656 (2016)
33. Qi, C.R., Yi, L., Su, H., Guibas, L.J.: Pointnet++: deep hierarchical feature learning on point sets in a metric space. In: NIPS, pp. 5105–5114 (2017)
34. Qi, X., Liao, R., Jia, J., Fidler, S., Urtasun, R.: 3D graph neural networks for RGBD semantic segmentation. In: ICCV (2017)
35. Ren, M., Pokrovsky, A., Yang, B., Urtasun, R.: SBNet: sparse blocks network for fast inference. In: CVPR, pp. 8711–8720 (2018)
36. Riegler, G., Ulusoy, A.O., Bischof, H., Geiger, A.: OctNetFusion: learning depth fusion from data. In: 3DV (2017)
37. Riegler, G., Ulusoy, A.O., Geiger, A.: OctNet: learning deep 3D representations at high resolutions. In: CVPR, vol. 3 (2017)
38. Ronneberger, O., Fischer, P., Brox, T.: U-net: convolutional networks for biomedical image segmentation. In: Navab, N., Hornegger, J., Wells, W.M., Frangi, A.F. (eds.) MICCAI 2015. LNCS, vol. 9351, pp. 234–241. Springer, Cham (2015). https://doi.org/10.1007/978-3-319-24574-4_28
39. Silberman, N., Hoiem, D., Kohli, P., Fergus, R.: Indoor segmentation and support inference from RGBD images. In: Fitzgibbon, A., Lazebnik, S., Perona, P., Sato, Y., Schmid, C. (eds.) ECCV 2012. LNCS, vol. 7576, pp. 746–760. Springer, Heidelberg (2012). https://doi.org/10.1007/978-3-642-33715-4_54
40. Song, S., Yu, F., Zeng, A., Chang, A.X., Savva, M., Funkhouser, T.: Semantic scene completion from a single depth image. In: CVPR, pp. 190–198. IEEE (2017)
41. Tatarchenko, M., Dosovitskiy, A., Brox, T.: Octree generating networks: efficient convolutional architectures for high-resolution 3D outputs. In: CVPR, pp. 2088–2096 (2017)
42. Uhrig, J., Schneider, N., Schneidre, L., Franke, U., Brox, T., Geiger, A.: Sparsity invariant CNNs. In: 3DV (2017)

43. Varley, J., DeChant, C., Richardson, A., Ruales, J., Allen, P.: Shape completion enabled robotic grasping. In: IROS, pp. 2442–2447. IEEE (2017)
44. Wang, P.S., Liu, Y., Guo, Y.X., Sun, C.Y., Tong, X.: O-CNN: octree-based convolutional neural networks for 3D shape analysis. TOG **36**(4), 72 (2017)
45. Wu, Z., et al.: 3D ShapeNets: a deep representation for volumetric shapes. In: CVPR, pp. 1912–1920 (2015)
46. Xie, S., Girshick, R., Dollár, P., Tu, Z., He, K.: Aggregated residual transformations for deep neural networks. In: CVPR, pp. 5987–5995. IEEE (2017)
47. Yang, B., Rosa, S., Markham, A., Trigoni, N., Wen, H.: 3D object dense reconstruction from a single depth view. arXiv preprint arXiv:1802.00411 (2018)
48. Yi, L., Guibas, L., Hertzmann, A., Kim, V.G., Su, H., Yumer, E.: Learning hierarchical shape segmentation and labeling from online repositories. TOG **36**(4), 70 (2017)
49. Yi, L., et al.: Large-Scale 3D Shape Reconstruction and Segmentation from ShapeNet Core55 (2017)
50. Zhang, X., Zhou, X., Lin, M., Sun, J.: ShuffleNet: an extremely efficient convolutional neural network for mobile devices. In: CVPR (2018)

Asynchronous, Photometric Feature Tracking Using Events and Frames

Daniel Gehrig$^{(\boxtimes)}$, Henri Rebecq, Guillermo Gallego, and Davide Scaramuzza

Departments of Informatics and Neuroinformatics,
University of Zurich and ETH Zurich, Zürich, Switzerland
`rebecq@ifi.uzh.ch`

Abstract. We present a method that leverages the complementarity of event cameras and standard cameras to track visual features with low-latency. Event cameras are novel sensors that output pixel-level brightness changes, called "events". They offer significant advantages over standard cameras, namely a very high dynamic range, no motion blur, and a latency in the order of microseconds. However, because the same scene pattern can produce different events depending on the motion direction, establishing event correspondences across time is challenging. By contrast, standard cameras provide intensity measurements (frames) that do not depend on motion direction. Our method extracts features on frames and subsequently tracks them asynchronously using events, thereby exploiting the best of both types of data: the frames provide a photometric representation that does not depend on motion direction and the events provide low-latency updates. In contrast to previous works, which are based on heuristics, this is the first principled method that uses raw intensity measurements directly, based on a generative event model within a maximum-likelihood framework. As a result, our method produces feature tracks that are both more accurate (subpixel accuracy) and longer than the state of the art, across a wide variety of scenes.

1   Introduction

Event cameras, such as the Dynamic Vision Sensor (DVS) [1], work very differently from traditional cameras (Fig. 1). They have independent pixels that send information (called "events") only in presence of brightness changes in the scene at the time they occur. Thus, their output is not an intensity image but a *stream of asynchronous events*. Event cameras excel at sensing motion, and they do so with very low-latency (1 μs). However, they do not provide absolute intensity measurements, rather they measure only *changes of intensity*. Conversely, standard cameras provide *direct* intensity measurements for every pixel,

---

Multimedia Material. A supplemental video for this work is available at https://youtu.be/A7UfeUnG6c4.

Electronic supplementary material The online version of this chapter (https://doi.org/10.1007/978-3-030-01258-8_46) contains supplementary material, which is available to authorized users.

© Springer Nature Switzerland AG 2018
V. Ferrari et al. (Eds.): ECCV 2018, LNCS 11216, pp. 766–781, 2018.
https://doi.org/10.1007/978-3-030-01258-8_46

but with comparatively much higher latency (10–20 ms). Event cameras and standard cameras are, thus, complementary, which calls for the development of novel algorithms capable of combining the specific advantages of both cameras to perform computer vision tasks with low-latency. In fact, the Dynamic and Active-pixel Vision Sensor (DAVIS) [2] was recently introduced (2014) in that spirit. It is a sensor comprising an asynchronous event-based sensor and a standard frame-based camera in the same pixel array.

We tackle the problem of feature tracking using both events and frames, such as those provided by the DAVIS. Our goal is to combine both types of intensity measurements to maximize tracking accuracy and age, and for this reason we develop a maximum likelihood approach based on a generative event model.

Feature tracking is an important research topic in computer vision, and has been widely studied in the last decades. It is a core building block of numerous applications, such as object tracking [3] or Simultaneous Localization and Mapping (SLAM) [4–7]. While feature detection and tracking methods for frame-based cameras are well established, they cannot track in the blind time between consecutive frames, and are expensive because they process information from all pixels, even in the absence of motion in the scene. Conversely, event cameras acquire only relevant information for tracking and respond asynchronously, thus, filling the blind time between consecutive frames.

In this work we present a feature tracker which works by extracting corners in frames and subsequently tracking them using only events. This allows us to take advantage of the asynchronous, high dynamic range and low-latency nature of the events to produce feature tracks with high temporal resolution. However, this asynchronous nature means that it becomes a challenge to associate individual events coming from the same object, which is known as the data association problem. In contrast to previous works which used heuristics to solve for data association, we propose a maximum likelihood approach based on a generative event model that uses the photometric information from the frames to solve the problem. In summary, our contributions are the following:

- We introduce the first feature tracker that combines events and frames in a way that (*i*) fully exploits the strength of the brightness gradients causing the events, (*ii*) circumvents the data association problem between events and pixels of the frame, and (*iii*) leverages a generative model to explain how events are related to brightness patterns in the frames.
- We provide a comparison with state-of-the-art methods [8,9], and show that our tracker provides feature tracks that are both more accurate and longer.
- We thoroughly evaluate the proposed tracker using scenes from the publicly available Event Camera Dataset [10], and show its performance both on man-made environments with large contrast and in natural scenes.

2   Related Work

Feature detection and tracking with event cameras is a major research topic [8, 9,12–18], where the goal is to unlock the capabilities of event cameras and use

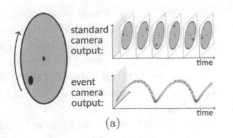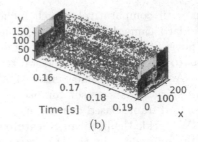

(a)   (b)

Fig. 1. (a): Comparison of the output of a standard frame-based camera and an event camera when facing a black dot on a rotating disk (figure adapted from [11]). The standard camera outputs frames at a fixed rate, thus sending redundant information when there is no motion in the scene. Event cameras respond to pixel-level *brightness changes* with microsecond latency. (b): A combined frame and event-based sensor such as the DAVIS [2] provides both standard frames and the events that occurred in between. Events are colored according to polarity: blue (brightness increase) and red (brightness decrease). (Color figure online)

them to solve these classical problems in computer vision in challenging scenarios inaccessible to standard cameras, such as low-power, high-speed and high dynamic range (HDR) scenarios. Recently, extensions of popular image-based keypoint detectors, such as Harris [19] and FAST [20], have been developed for event cameras [17,18]. Detectors based on the distribution of optical flow [21] for recognition applications have also been proposed for event cameras [16]. Finally, most event-based trackers use binary feature templates, either predefined [13] or built from a set of events [9], to which they align events by means of iterative point-set–based methods, such as iterative closest point (ICP) [22].

Our work is most related to [8], since both combine frames and events for feature tracking. The approach in [8] detects patches of Canny edges around Harris corners in the grayscale frames and then tracks such local edge patterns using ICP on the event stream. Thus, the patch of Canny edges acts as a template to which the events are registered to yield tracking information. Under the simplifying assumption that events are mostly generated by strong edges, the Canny edgemap template is used as a proxy for the underlying grayscale pattern that causes the events. The method in [8] converts the tracking problem into a geometric, point-set alignment problem: the event coordinates are compared against the point template given by the pixel locations of the Canny edges. Hence, pixels where no events are generated are, efficiently, not processed. However, the method has two drawbacks: (*i*) the information about the strength of the edges is lost (since the point template used for tracking is obtained from a binary edgemap) (*ii*) explicit correspondences (i.e., data association) between the events and the template need to be established for ICP-based registration. The method in [9] can be interpreted as an extension of [8] with (*i*) the Canny-edge patches replaced by motion-corrected event point sets and (*ii*) the correspondences computed in a soft manner using Expectation-Maximization (EM)-ICP.

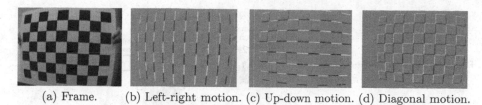

(a) Frame.   (b) Left-right motion. (c) Up-down motion. (d) Diagonal motion.

Fig. 2. Result of moving a checkerboard (a) in front of an event camera in different directions. (b)–(d) Show brightness increment images (Eq. (2)) obtained by accumulating events over a short time interval. Pixels that do not change intensity are represented in gray, whereas pixels that increased or decreased intensity are represented in bright and dark, respectively. Clearly, (b) (only vertical edges), (c) (only horizontal edges), and (d) cannot be related to each other without the prior knowledge of the underlying photometric information provided by (a).

Like [8,9], our method can be used to track generic features, as opposed to constrained edge patterns. However, our method differs from [8,9] in that (i) we take into account the strength of the edge pattern causing the events and (ii) we do not need to establish correspondences between the events and the edgemap template. In contrast to [8,9], which use a point-set template for event alignment, our method uses the spatial gradient of the raw intensity image, directly, as a template. Correspondences are implicitly established as a consequence of the proposed image-based registration approach (Sect. 4), but before that, let us motivate why establishing correspondences is challenging with event cameras.

3   The Challenge of Data Association for Feature Tracking

The main challenge in tracking scene features (i.e., edge patterns) with an event camera is that, because this sensor responds to temporal changes of intensity (caused by moving edges on the image plane), the appearance of the feature varies depending on the motion, and thus, continuously changes in time (see Fig. 2). Feature tracking using events requires the establishment of correspondences between events at different times (i.e., data association), which is difficult due to the above-mentioned varying feature appearance (Fig. 2).

Instead, if additional information is available, such as the absolute intensity of the pattern to be tracked (i.e., a time-invariant representation or "map" of the feature), such as in Fig. 2(a), then event correspondences may be established indirectly, via establishing correspondences between the events and the additional map. This, however, additionally requires to continuously estimate the motion (optic flow) of the pattern. This is in fact an important component of our approach. As we show in Sect. 4, our method is based on a model to generate a prediction of the time-varying event-feature appearance using a given frame and an estimate of the optic flow. This generative model has not been considered in previous feature tracking methods, such as [8,9].

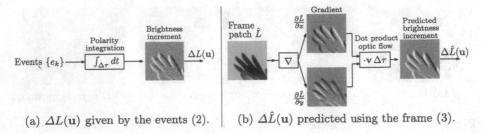

(a) $\Delta L(\mathbf{u})$ given by the events (2). | (b) $\Delta \hat{L}(\mathbf{u})$ predicted using the frame (3).

Fig. 3. Brightness increments given by the events (2) vs. predicted from the frame and the optic flow using the generative model (3). Pixels of $L(\mathbf{u})$ that do not change intensity are represented in gray in ΔL, whereas pixels that increased or decreased intensity are represented in bright and dark, respectively.

4   Methodology

An event camera has independent pixels that respond to changes in the continuous brightness signal[1] $L(\mathbf{u}, t)$. Specifically, an event $e_k = (x_k, y_k, t_k, p_k)$ is triggered at pixel $\mathbf{u}_k = (x_k, y_k)^\top$ and at time t_k as soon as the brightness increment since the last event at the pixel reaches a threshold $\pm C$ (with $C > 0$):

$$\Delta L(\mathbf{u}_k, t_k) \doteq L(\mathbf{u}_k, t_k) - L(\mathbf{u}_k, t_k - \Delta t_k) = p_k C, \tag{1}$$

where Δt_k is the time since the last event at the same pixel, $p_k \in \{-1, +1\}$ is the event polarity (i.e., the sign of the brightness change). Equation (1) is the event generation equation of an ideal sensor [23, 24].

4.1   Brightness-Increment Images from Events and Frames

Pixel-wise accumulation of event polarities over a time interval $\Delta \tau$ produces an image $\Delta L(\mathbf{u})$ with the amount of brightness change that occurred during the interval (Fig. 3a),

$$\Delta L(\mathbf{u}) = \sum_{t_k \in \Delta \tau} p_k C \, \delta(\mathbf{u} - \mathbf{u}_k), \tag{2}$$

where δ is the Kronecker delta due to its discrete argument (pixels on a lattice).

For small $\Delta \tau$, such as in the example of Fig. 3a, the brightness increments (2) are due to moving edges according to the formula[2]:

$$\Delta L(\mathbf{u}) \approx -\nabla L(\mathbf{u}) \cdot \mathbf{v}(\mathbf{u}) \Delta \tau, \tag{3}$$

---

[1] Event cameras such as the DVS [1] respond to logarithmic brightness changes, i.e., $L \doteq \log I$, with brightness signal I, so that (1) represents logarithmic changes.

[2] Equation (3) can be shown [24] by substituting the brightness constancy assumption (i.e., optical flow constraint) $\frac{\partial L}{\partial t}(\mathbf{u}(t), t) + \nabla L(\mathbf{u}(t), t) \cdot \dot{\mathbf{u}}(t) = 0$, with image-point velocity $\mathbf{v} \equiv \dot{\mathbf{u}}$, in Taylor's approximation $\Delta L(\mathbf{u}, t) \doteq L(\mathbf{u}, t) - L(\mathbf{u}, t - \Delta \tau) \approx \frac{\partial L}{\partial t}(\mathbf{u}, t) \Delta \tau$.

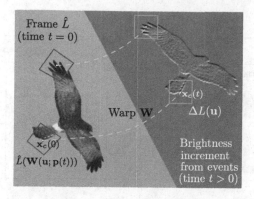

Fig. 4. Illustration of tracking for two independent patches. Events in a space-time window at time $t > 0$ are collected into a patch of brightness increments $\Delta L(\mathbf{u})$ (in orange), which is compared, via a warp (i.e., geometric transformation) $\mathbf{W}$ against a predicted brightness increment image based on $\hat{L}$ (given at $t = 0$) around the initial feature location (in blue). Patches are computed as shown in Fig. 5, and are compared in the objective function (6). (Color figure online)

that is, increments are caused by brightness gradients $\nabla L(\mathbf{u}) = \left(\frac{\partial L}{\partial x}, \frac{\partial L}{\partial y} \right)^{\top}$ moving with velocity $\mathbf{v}(\mathbf{u})$ over a displacement $\Delta \mathbf{u} \doteq \mathbf{v}\Delta\tau$ (see Fig. 3b). As the dot product in (3) conveys, if the motion is parallel to the edge ($\mathbf{v} \perp \nabla L$), the increment vanishes, i.e., no events are generated. From now on (and in Fig. 3b) we denote the modeled increment (3) using a hat, $\Delta\hat{L}$, and the frame by $\hat{L}$.

4.2 Optimization Framework

Following a maximum likelihood approach, we propose to use the difference between the observed brightness changes ΔL from the events (2) and the predicted ones $\Delta\hat{L}$ from the brightness signal $\hat{L}$ of the frames (3) to estimate the motion parameters that best explain the events according to an optimization score.

More specifically, we pose the feature tracking problem using events and frames as that of *image registration* [25, 26], between images (2) and (3). Effectively, frames act as feature templates with respect to which events are registered. As is standard, let us assume that (2) and (3) are compared over small patches ($\mathcal{P}$) containing distinctive patterns, and further assume that the optic flow $\mathbf{v}$ is constant for all pixels in the patch (same regularization as [25]).

Letting $\hat{L}$ be given by an intensity frame at time $t = 0$ and letting ΔL be given by events in a space-time window at a later time t (see Fig. 4), our goal is to find the registration parameters $\mathbf{p}$ and the velocity $\mathbf{v}$ that maximize the similarity between $\Delta L(\mathbf{u})$ and $\Delta\hat{L}(\mathbf{u}; \mathbf{p}, \mathbf{v}) = -\nabla\hat{L}(\mathbf{W}(\mathbf{u}; \mathbf{p})) \cdot \mathbf{v}\Delta\tau$, where $\mathbf{W}$ is the warping map used for the registration. We explicitly model optic flow $\mathbf{v}$ instead of approximating it by finite differences of past registration parameters to avoid introducing approximation errors and to avoid error propagation from past

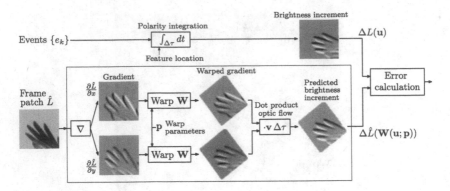

Fig. 5. Block diagram showing how the brightness increments being compared are computed for a patch of Fig. 4. Top of the diagram is the brightness increment from event integration (2). At the bottom is the generative event model from the frame (3).

noisy feature positions. A block diagram showing how both brightness increments are computed, including the effect of the warp $\mathbf{W}$, is given in Fig. 5. Assuming that the difference $\Delta L - \Delta \hat{L}$ follows a zero-mean additive Gaussian distribution with variance σ^2 [1], we define the likelihood function of the set of events $\mathcal{E} \doteq \{e_k\}_{k=1}^{N_e}$ producing ΔL as

$$p(\mathcal{E} \mid \mathbf{p}, \mathbf{v}, \hat{L}) = \frac{1}{\sqrt{2\pi\sigma^2}} \exp\left(-\frac{1}{2\sigma^2} \int_{\mathcal{P}} \left(\Delta L(\mathbf{u}) - \Delta \hat{L}(\mathbf{u}; \mathbf{p}, \mathbf{v})\right)^2 d\mathbf{u}\right). \quad (4)$$

Maximizing this likelihood with respect to the motion parameters $\mathbf{p}$ and $\mathbf{v}$ (since $\hat{L}$ is known) yields the minimization of the L^2 norm of the photometric residual,

$$\min_{\mathbf{p}, \mathbf{v}} \|\Delta L(\mathbf{u}) - \Delta \hat{L}(\mathbf{u}; \mathbf{p}, \mathbf{v})\|_{L^2(\mathcal{P})}^2 \quad (5)$$

where $\|f(\mathbf{u})\|_{L^2(\mathcal{P})}^2 \doteq \int_{\mathcal{P}} f^2(\mathbf{u})d\mathbf{u}$. However, the objective function (5) depends on the contrast sensitivity C (via (2)), which is typically unknown in practice. Inspired by [26], we propose to minimize the difference between unit-norm patches:

$$\min_{\mathbf{p}, \mathbf{v}} \left\| \frac{\Delta L(\mathbf{u})}{\|\Delta L(\mathbf{u})\|_{L^2(\mathcal{P})}} - \frac{\Delta \hat{L}(\mathbf{u}; \mathbf{p}, \mathbf{v})}{\|\Delta \hat{L}(\mathbf{u}; \mathbf{p}, \mathbf{v})\|_{L^2(\mathcal{P})}} \right\|_{L^2(\mathcal{P})}^2, \quad (6)$$

which cancels the terms in C and $\Delta\tau$, and only depends on the direction of the feature velocity $\mathbf{v}$. In this generic formulation, the same type of parametric warps $\mathbf{W}$ as for image registration can be considered (projective, affine, etc.). For simplicity, we consider warps given by rigid-body motions in the image plane,

$$\mathbf{W}(\mathbf{u}; \mathbf{p}) = \mathtt{R}(\mathbf{p})\mathbf{u} + \mathbf{t}(\mathbf{p}), \quad (7)$$

where $(\mathtt{R}, \mathbf{t}) \in SE(2)$. The objective function (6) is optimized using the non-linear least squares framework provided in the Ceres software [27].

Algorithm 1. Photometric feature tracking using events and frames

---
Feature initialization:
- Detect Harris corners [19] on the frame $\hat{L}(\mathbf{u})$, extract intensity patches around corner points and compute $\nabla \hat{L}(\mathbf{u})$.
- Set patches $\Delta L(\mathbf{u}) = 0$, set initial registration parameters $\mathbf{p}$ to those of the identity warp, and set the number of events N_e to integrate on each patch.
Feature tracking:
for each incoming event **do**
  - Update the patches containing the event (i.e., accumulate polarity pixel-wise (2)).
  for each patch $\Delta L(\mathbf{u})$ (once N_e events have been collected (2)) **do**
    - Minimize the objective function (6), to get parameters $\mathbf{p}$ and optic flow $\mathbf{v}$.
    - Update the registration parameters $\mathbf{p}$ of the feature patch (e.g., position).
    - Reset the patch ($\Delta L(\mathbf{u}) = 0$) and recompute N_e.

4.3 Discussion of the Approach

One of the most interesting characteristics of the proposed method (6) is that it is based on a generative model for the events (3). As shown in Fig. 5, the frame $\hat{L}$ is used to produce a registration template $\Delta \hat{L}$ that changes depending on $\mathbf{v}$ (weighted according to the dot product) in order to best fit the motion-dependent event data ΔL, and so does our method not only estimate the warping parameters of the event-feature but also its optic flow. This optic flow dependency was not explicitly modeled in previous works, such as [8,9]. Moreover, for the template, we use the full gradient information of the frame $\nabla \hat{L}$, as opposed to its Canny (i.e., binary-thresholded) version [8], which provides higher accuracy and the ability to track less salient patterns.

Another characteristic of our method is that it does not suffer from the problem of establishing event-to-feature correspondences, as opposed to ICP methods [8,9]. We borrow the implicit pixel-to-pixel data association typical of image registration methods by creating, from events, a convenient image representation. Hence, our method has smaller complexity (establishing data association in ICP [8] has quadratic complexity) and is more robust since it is less prone to be trapped in local minima caused by data association (as will be shown in Sect. 5.3). As optimization iterations progress, all event correspondences evolve jointly as a single entity according to the evolution of the warped pixel grid.

Additionally, monitoring the evolution of the minimum cost values (6) provides a sound criterion to detect feature track loss and, therefore, initialize new feature tracks (e.g., in the next frame or by acquiring a new frame on demand).

4.4 Algorithm

The steps of our asynchronous, low-latency feature tracker are summarized in Algorithm 1, which consists of two phases: (i) initialization of the feature patch and (ii) tracking the pattern in the patch using events according to (6). Multiple patches are tracked independently from one another. To compute a patch $\Delta L(\mathbf{u})$, (2), we integrate over a given number of events N_e [28–31] rather than over a fixed time $\Delta\tau$ [32,33]. Hence, tracking is asynchronous, as soon as N_e events are acquired on the patch (2), which typically happens at rates higher than the frame rate of the standard camera ($\sim$ 10 times higher). The supplementary material provides an analysis of the sensitivity of the method with respect to N_e and a formula to compute a sensible value, to be used in Algorithm 1.

5   Experiments

To illustrate the high accuracy of our method, we first evaluate it on simulated data, where we can control scene depth, camera motion, and other model parameters. Then we test our method on real data, consisting of high-contrast and natural scenes, with challenging effects such as occlusions, parallax and illumination changes. Finally, we show that our tracker can operate using frames reconstructed from a set of events [34,35], which have higher dynamic range than those of standard cameras, thus opening the door to feature tracking in high dynamic range (HDR) scenarios.

For all experiments we use patches $\Delta L(\mathbf{u})$ of 25×25 pixel size[3] and the corresponding events falling within the patches as the features moved on the image plane. On the synthetic datasets, we use the 3D scene model and camera poses to compute the ground truth feature tracks. On the real datasets, we use KLT [25] as ground truth. Since our feature tracks are produced at a higher temporal resolution than the ground truth, interpolating ground truth feature positions may lead to wrong error estimates if the feature trajectory is not linear in between samples. Therefore, we evaluate the error by comparing each ground truth sample with the feature location given by linear interpolation of the two closest feature locations in time and averaging the Euclidean distance between ground truth and the estimated positions.

5.1   Simulated Data. Assessing Tracking Accuracy

By using simulated data we assess the accuracy limits of our feature tracker. To this end, we used the event camera simulator presented in [10] and 3D scenes with different types of texture, objects and occlusions (Fig. 6). The tracker's accuracy can be assessed by how the average feature tracking error evolves over time (Fig. 6(c)); the smaller the error, the better. All features were initialized using the first frame and then tracked until discarded, which happened if they left the field of view or if the registration error (6) exceeded a threshold of 1.6. We define a feature's age as the time elapsed between its initialization and its disposal. The longer the features survive, the more robust the tracker.

The results for simulated datasets are given in Fig. 6 and Table 1. Our method tracks features with a very high accuracy, of about 0.4 pixel error on average, which can be regarded as a lower bound for the tracking error (under noise-free conditions). The remaining error is likely due to the linearization approximation in (3). Note that feature age is just reported for completeness, since simulation time cannot be compared to the physical time of real data (Sect. 5.2).

---

[3] A justification of the choice of patch size can be found in the supplementary material.

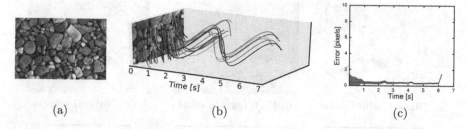

(a)   (b)   (c)

Fig. 6. Feature tracking results on simulated data. (a) Example texture used to generate synthetic events in the simulator [10]. (b) Qualitative feature tracks represented as curves in space-time. (c) Mean tracking error (center line) and fraction of surviving features (width of the band around the center line) as a function of time. Our features are tracked with 0.4 pixel accuracy on average.

Table 1. Average pixel error and average feature age for simulated data.

Datasets	Error [px]	Feature age [s]
sim_april_tags	0.20	1.52
sim_3planes	0.29	0.78
sim_rocks	0.42	1.00
sim_3wall	0.67	0.40

5.2 Real Data

We compare our method against the state-of-the-art [8,9]. The methods were evaluated on several datasets. For [8] the same set of features extracted on frames was tracked, while for [9] features were initialized on motion-corrected event images and tracked with subsequent events. The results are reported in Fig. 7 and in Table 2. The plots in Fig. 7 show the mean tracking error as a function of time (center line). The width of the colored band indicates the proportion of features that survived up to that point in time. The width of the band decreases with time as feature tracks are gradually lost. The wider the band, the more robust the feature tracker. Our method outperforms [8] and [9] in both tracking accuracy and length of the tracks.

In simple, black and white scenes (Fig. 7(a) and (d)), such as those in [8], our method is, on average, twice as accurate and produces tracks that are almost three times longer than [8]. Compared to [9] our method is also more accurate and robust. For highly textured scenes (Fig. 7(b) and (e)), our tracker maintains the accuracy even though many events are generated everywhere in the patch, which leads to significantly high errors in [8,9]. Although our method and [9] achieve similar feature ages, our method is more accurate. Similarly, our method performs better than [8] and is more accurate than [9] on natural scenes (Fig. 7(c) and (f)). For these scenes [9] exhibits the highest average feature age. However, being a purely event-based method, it suffers from drift due to changing event appearance, as is most noticeable in Fig. 7(f). Our method does not drift since

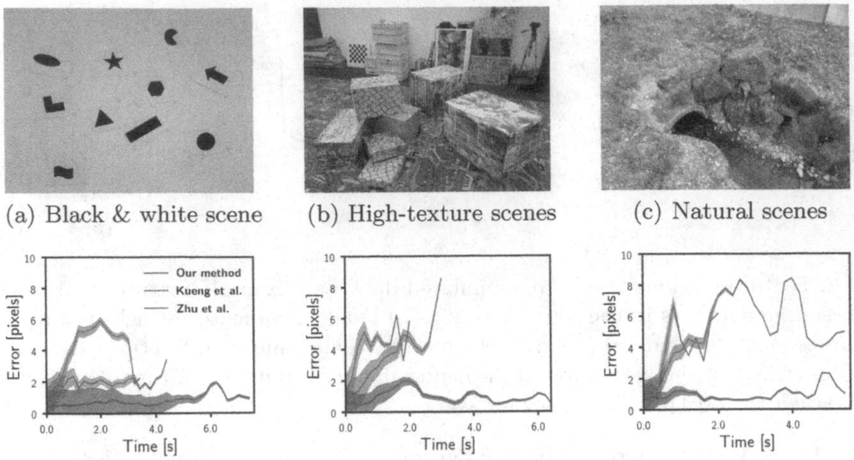

(a) Black & white scene   (b) High-texture scenes   (c) Natural scenes

(d) shapes_6dof   (e) boxes_6dof   (f) rocks

Fig. 7. Feature tracking on simple black and white scenes (a), highly textured scenes (b) and natural scenes (c). Plots (d) to (f) show the mean tracking error (center line) and fraction of surviving features (band around the center line) for our method and [8,9] on three datasets, one for each type of scene in (a)–(c). More plots are provided in the supplementary material.

Table 2. Average pixel error and average feature age for various datasets.

Scene	Datasets	Error [px]			Feature age [s]		
		Our method	Kueng [8]	Zhu [9]	Our method	Kueng [8]	Zhu [9]
Black and white	shapes_6dof	**0.64**	1.75	3.04	**3.94**	1.53	1.30
	checkerboard	**0.78**	1.58	2.36	**8.23**	2.76	7.12
High texture	poster_6dof	**0.67**	2.86	2.99	**2.65**	0.65	2.56
	boxes_6dof	**0.90**	3.10	2.47	**1.56**	0.78	1.56
Natural	bicycles	**0.75**	3.65	3.66	1.15	0.49	**1.26**
	rocks	**0.80**	2.11	3.24	0.78	0.85	**1.13**

it uses a time invariant template and a generative model to register events, as opposed to an event-based template [9]. Additionally, unlike previous works, our method also exploits the full range of the brightness gradients instead of using simplified, point-set–based edge maps, thus yielding higher accuracy. A more detailed comparison with [8] is further explored in Sect. 5.3, where we show that our objective function is better behaved.

The tracking error of our method on real data is larger than that on synthetic data, which is likely due to modeling errors concerning the events, including noise and dynamic effects (such as unequal contrast thresholds for events of different polarity). Nevertheless, our tracker achieves subpixel accuracy and consistently outperforms previous methods, leading to more accurate and longer tracks.

Patch on frame   Events   Cost (6)   Cost (8), [8]   Track (position history)

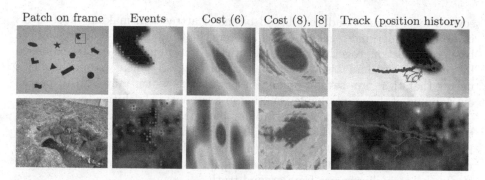

Fig. 8. Our cost function (6) is better behaved (smoother and with fewer local minima) than that in [8], yielding a better tracking (last column). The first two columns show the datasets and feature patches selected, with intensity (grayscale) and events (red and blue). The third and fourth columns compare the cost profiles of (6) and (8) for varying translation parameters in x and y directions (± 5 pixel around the best estimate from the tracker). The point-set–based cost used in [8] shows many local minima for more textured scenes (second row) which is not the case of our method. The last column shows the position history of the features (green is ground truth, red is [8] and blue is our method). (Color figure online)

5.3 Objective Function Comparison Against ICP-Based Method [8]

As mentioned in Sect. 4, one of the advantages of our method is that data association between events and the tracked feature is implicitly established by the pixel-to-pixel correspondence of the compared patches (2) and (3). This means that we do not have to explicitly estimate it, as was done in [8,9], which saves computational resources and prevents false associations that would yield bad tracking behavior. To illustrate this advantage, we compare the cost function profiles of our method and [8], which minimizes the alignment error (Euclidean distance) between two 2D point sets: $\{\mathbf{p}_i\}$ from the events (data) and $\{\mathbf{m}_j\}$ from the Canny edges (model),

$$\{\mathbf{R}, \mathbf{t}\} = \arg\min_{\mathbf{R}, \mathbf{t}} \sum_{(\mathbf{p}_i, \mathbf{m}_i) \in \text{Matches}} b_i \|\mathbf{R}\mathbf{p}_i + \mathbf{t} - \mathbf{m}_i\|^2. \qquad (8)$$

Here, $\mathbf{R}$ and $\mathbf{t}$ are the alignment parameters and b_i are weights. At each step, the association between events and model points is done by assigning each $\mathbf{p}_i$ to the closest point $\mathbf{m}_j$ and rejecting matches which are too far apart (> 3pixel). By varying the parameter $\mathbf{t}$ around the estimated value while fixing $\mathbf{R}$ we obtain a slice of the cost function profile. The resulting cost function profiles for our method (6) and (8) are shown in Fig. 8.

For simple black and white scenes (first row of Fig. 8), all events generated belong to strong edges. In contrast, for more complex, highly-textured scenes (second row), events are generated more uniformly in the patch. Our method clearly shows a convex cost function in both situations. In contrast, [8] exhibits several local minima and very broad basins of attraction, making exact localization of the optimal registration parameters challenging. The broadness of the basin of attraction, together with the multitude of local minima can be explained by the fact that data association changes for each alignment parameter. This means that there are several alignment parameters which may lead to partial overlapping of the point-clouds resulting in a suboptimal solution.

To show how non-smooth cost profiles affect tracking performance, we show the feature tracks in the last column of Fig. 8. The ground truth derived from KLT is marked in green. Our tracker (in blue) is able to follow the ground truth with high accuracy. On the other hand [8] (in red) exhibits jumping behavior leading to early divergence from ground truth.

5.4   Tracking Using Frames Reconstructed from Event Data

Recent research [34–37] has shown that events can be combined to reconstruct intensity frames that inherit the outstanding properties of event cameras (high dynamic range (HDR) and lack of motion blur). In the next experiment, we show that our tracker can be used on such reconstructed images, thus removing the limitations imposed by standard cameras. As an illustration, we focus here on demonstrating feature tracking in HDR scenes (Fig. 9). However, our method could also be used to perform feature tracking during high-speed motions by using motion-blur–free images reconstructed from events.

Standard cameras have a limited dynamic range (60 dB), which often results in under- or over-exposed areas of the sensor in scenes with a high dynamic range (Fig. 9(b)), which in turn can lead to tracking loss. Event cameras, however, have a much larger dynamic range (140 dB) (Fig. 9(b)), thus providing valuable tracking information in those problematic areas. Figure 9(c)–(d) show qualitatively how our method can exploit HDR intensity images reconstructed from a set of events [34,35] to produce feature tracks in such difficult conditions. For example, Fig. 9(d) shows that some feature tracks were initialized in originally over-exposed areas, such as the top right of the image (Fig. 9). Note that our tracker only requires a limited number of reconstructed images since features can be tracked for several seconds. This complements the computationally-demanding task of image reconstruction.

Supplementary Material. We encourage the reader to inspect the video, additional figures, tables and experiments provided in the supplementary material.

6   Discussion

While our method advances event-based feature tracking in natural scenes, there remain directions for future research. For example, the generative model we use to predict events is an approximation that does not account for severe dynamic effects and noise. In addition, our method assumes uniform optical flow in the vicinity of features. This assumption breaks down at occlusions and at objects

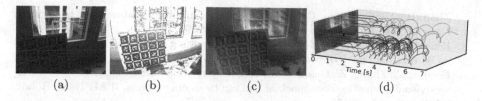

(a)   (b)   (c)   (d)

Fig. 9. Our feature tracker is not limited to intensity frames from a real camera. In this example, we use an intensity image reconstructed from a stream of events [34,35] in a scene with high dynamic range (a). The DAVIS frame, shown in (b) with events overlaid on top, cannot capture the full dynamic range of the scene. By contrast, the reconstructed image in (c) captures the full dynamic range of the scene. Our tracker (d) can successfully use this image to produce accurate feature tracks everywhere, including the badly exposed areas of (b).

undergoing large flow distortions, such as motion along the camera's optical axis. Nevertheless, as shown in the experiments, many features in a variety of scenes and motions do not suffer from such effects, and are therefore tracked well (with sub-pixel accuracy). Finally, we demonstrated the method using a Euclidean warp since it was more stable than more complex warping models (e.g., affine). Future research includes ways to make the method more robust to sensor noise and to use more accurate warping models.

7   Conclusion

We presented a method that leverages the complementarity of event cameras and standard cameras to track visual features with low-latency. Our method extracts features on frames and subsequently tracks them asynchronously using events. To achieve this, we presented the first method that relates events directly to pixel intensities in frames via a generative event model. We thoroughly evaluated the method on a variety of sequences, showing that it produces feature tracks that are both more accurate (subpixel accuracy) and longer than the state of the art. We believe this work will open the door to unlock the advantages of event cameras on various computer vision tasks that rely on accurate feature tracking.

Acknowledgment. This work was supported by the DARPA FLA program, the Swiss National Center of Competence Research Robotics, through the Swiss National Science Foundation, and the SNSF-ERC starting grant.

References

1. Lichtsteiner, P., Posch, C., Delbruck, T.: A 128×128 120 dB 15 μs latency asynchronous temporal contrast vision sensor. IEEE J. Solid-State Circ. **43**(2), 566–576 (2008)
2. Brandli, C., Berner, R., Yang, M., Liu, S.C., Delbruck, T.: A 240×180 130 dB 3 μs latency global shutter spatiotemporal vision sensor. IEEE J. Solid-State Circ. **49**(10), 2333–2341 (2014)

3. Zhou, H., Yuan, Y., Shi, C.: Object tracking using SIFT features and mean shift. Comput. Vis. Image. Und. **113**(3), 345–352 (2009)
4. Klein, G., Murray, D.: Parallel tracking and mapping on a camera phone. In: IEEE ACM International Symposium on Mixed and Augmented Reality (ISMAR) (2009)
5. Forster, C., Zhang, Z., Gassner, M., Werlberger, M., Scaramuzza, D.: SVO: semidirect visual odometry for monocular and multicamera systems. IEEE Trans. Robot. **33**(2), 249–265 (2017)
6. Mur-Artal, R., Montiel, J.M.M., Tardós, J.D.: ORB-SLAM: a versatile and accurate monocular SLAM system. IEEE Trans. Robot. **31**(5), 1147–1163 (2015)
7. Rosinol Vidal, A., Rebecq, H., Horstschaefer, T., Scaramuzza, D.: Ultimate SLAM? Combining events, images, and IMU for robust visual SLAM in HDR and high speed scenarios. IEEE Robot. Autom. Lett. **3**(2), 994–1001 (2018)
8. Kueng, B., Mueggler, E., Gallego, G., Scaramuzza, D.: Low-latency visual odometry using event-based feature tracks. In: IEEE/RSJ International Conference on Intelligent Robots and Systems (IROS), Daejeon, Korea, pp. 16–23, October 2016
9. Zhu, A.Z., Atanasov, N., Daniilidis, K.: Event-based feature tracking with probabilistic data association. In: IEEE International Conference on Robotics and Automation (ICRA), pp. 4465–4470 (2017)
10. Mueggler, E., Rebecq, H., Gallego, G., Delbruck, T., Scaramuzza, D.: The event-camera dataset and simulator: event-based data for pose estimation, visual odometry, and SLAM. Int. J. Robot. Res. **36**, 142–149 (2017)
11. Mueggler, E., Huber, B., Scaramuzza, D.: Event-based, 6-DOF pose tracking for high-speed maneuvers. In: IEEE/RSJ International Conference on Intelligent Robots and Systems (IROS), pp. 2761–2768 (2014). Event camera animation: https://youtu.be/LauQ6LWTkxM?t=25
12. Ni, Z., Bolopion, A., Agnus, J., Benosman, R., Regnier, S.: Asynchronous event-based visual shape tracking for stable haptic feedback in microrobotics. IEEE Trans. Robot. **28**, 1081–1089 (2012)
13. Lagorce, X., Meyer, C., Ieng, S.H., Filliat, D., Benosman, R.: Asynchronous event-based multikernel algorithm for high-speed visual features tracking. IEEE Trans. Neural Netw. Learn. Syst. **26**(8), 1710–1720 (2015)
14. Clady, X., Ieng, S.H., Benosman, R.: Asynchronous event-based corner detection and matching. Neural Netw. **66**, 91–106 (2015)
15. Tedaldi, D., Gallego, G., Mueggler, E., Scaramuzza, D.: Feature detection and tracking with the dynamic and active-pixel vision sensor (DAVIS). In: International Conference on Event-Based Control, Communication, and Signal Processing (EBCCSP), pp. 1–7 (2016)
16. Clady, X., Maro, J.M., Barré, S., Benosman, R.B.: A motion-based feature for event-based pattern recognition. Front. Neurosci. **10**, 594 (2017)
17. Vasco, V., Glover, A., Bartolozzi, C.: Fast event-based Harris corner detection exploiting the advantages of event-driven cameras. In: IEEE/RSJ International Conference on Intelligent Robots and Systems (IROS) (2016)
18. Mueggler, E., Bartolozzi, C., Scaramuzza, D.: Fast event-based corner detection. In: British Machine Vision Conference (BMVC) (2017)
19. Harris, C., Stephens, M.: A combined corner and edge detector. In: Proceedings of Fourth Alvey Vision Conference, Manchester, UK, vol. 15, pp. 147–151 (1988)
20. Rosten, E., Drummond, T.: Machine learning for high-speed corner detection. In: Leonardis, A., Bischof, H., Pinz, A. (eds.) ECCV 2006. LNCS, vol. 3951, pp. 430–443. Springer, Heidelberg (2006). https://doi.org/10.1007/11744023_34

21. Chaudhry, R., Ravichandran, A., Hager, G., Vidal, R.: Histograms of oriented optical flow and Binet-Cauchy kernels on nonlinear dynamical systems for the recognition of human actions. In: IEEE International Conference on Computer Vision and Pattern Recognition (CVPR), pp. 1932–1939, June 2009

22. Besl, P.J., McKay, N.D.: A method for registration of 3-D shapes. IEEE Trans. Pattern Anal. Mach. Intell. **14**(2), 239–256 (1992)

23. Gallego, G., Lund, J.E.A., Mueggler, E., Rebecq, H., Delbruck, T., Scaramuzza, D.: Event-based, 6-DOF camera tracking from photometric depth maps. IEEE Trans. Pattern Anal. Machi. Intell. **40**(10), 2402–2412 (2017)

24. Gallego, G., Forster, C., Mueggler, E., Scaramuzza, D.: Event-based camera pose tracking using a generative event model. arXiv:1510.01972 (2015)

25. Lucas, B.D., Kanade, T.: An iterative image registration technique with an application to stereo vision. In: International Joint Conference on Artificial Intelligence (IJCAI), pp. 674–679 (1981)

26. Evangelidis, G.D., Psarakis, E.Z.: Parametric image alignment using enhanced correlation coefficient maximization. IEEE Trans. Pattern Anal. Mach. Intell. **30**(10), 1858–1865 (2008)

27. Agarwal, A., Mierle, K., et al.: Ceres solver. http://ceres-solver.org

28. Gallego, G., Scaramuzza, D.: Accurate angular velocity estimation with an event camera. IEEE Robot. Autom. Lett. **2**, 632–639 (2017)

29. Gallego, G., Rebecq, H., Scaramuzza, D.: A unifying contrast maximization framework for event cameras, with applications to motion, depth, and optical flow estimation. In: IEEE International Conference on Computer Vision and Pattern Recognition (CVPR), pp. 3867–3876 (2018)

30. Rebecq, H., Gallego, G., Mueggler, E., Scaramuzza, D.: EMVS: event-based multi-view stereo–3D reconstruction with an event camera in real-time. Int. J. Comput. Vis. 1–21 (2017)

31. Rebecq, H., Horstschaefer, T., Scaramuzza, D.: Real-time visual-inertial odometry for event cameras using keyframe-based nonlinear optimization. In: British Machine Vision Conference (BMVC), September 2017

32. Maqueda, A.I., Loquercio, A., Gallego, G., García, N., Scaramuzza, D.: Event-based vision meets deep learning on steering prediction for self-driving cars. In: IEEE International Conference on Computer Vision and Pattern Recognition (CVPR), pp. 5419–5427 (2018)

33. Bardow, P., Davison, A.J., Leutenegger, S.: Simultaneous optical flow and intensity estimation from an event camera. In: IEEE International Conference on Computer Vision and Pattern Recognition (CVPR), pp. 884–892 (2016)

34. Kim, H., Handa, A., Benosman, R., Ieng, S.H., Davison, A.J.: Simultaneous mosaicing and tracking with an event camera. In: British Machine Vision Conference (BMVC) (2014)

35. Rebecq, H., Horstschäfer, T., Gallego, G., Scaramuzza, D.: EVO: a geometric approach to event-based 6-DOF parallel tracking and mapping in real-time. IEEE Robot. Autom. Lett. **2**, 593–600 (2017)

36. Reinbacher, C., Graber, G., Pock, T.: Real-time intensity-image reconstruction for event cameras using manifold regularisation. In: British Machine Vision Conference (BMVC) (2016)

37. Munda, G., Reinbacher, C., Pock, T.: Real-time intensity-image reconstruction for event cameras using manifold regularisation. Int. J. Comput. Vis. 1–13 (2018)

Author Index

Alahari, Karteek   241

Babenko, Artem   209
Bahng, Hyojin   443
Bai, Yalong   21
Baranchuk, Dmitry   209
Belov, Roman   55
Bertasius, Gedas   342
Bethge, Matthias   225
Bhagoji, Arjun Nitin   158
Bourmaud, Guillaume   558
Brox, Thomas   626
Bugaev, Bogdan   55

Cadena, Santiago A.   225
Cai, Jianfei   38
Cai, Zhipeng   699, 715
Camps, Octavia   175
Castro, Francisco M.   241
Ceylan, Duygu   679
Chang, Huiwen   679
Chen, Hongge   644
Chen, Pin-Yu   644
Chen, Yurong   749
Cherabier, Ian   325
Chin, Tat-Jun   699, 715
Cho, Wonwoong   443
Choo, Jaegul   443
Cohen, Scott   542
Corneanu, Ciprian   309

Dai, Jifeng   392
Davidson, James   89
Deng, Ruizhi   192
Deng, Zhiwei   192
Dubey, Abhimanyu   71
Dvornik, Nikita   375

Ecker, Alexander S.   225
Escalera, Sergio   309
Ewerth, Ralph   575

Farrell, Ryan   71
Freeman, William T.   3
Fu, Jianlong   21

Gallego, Guillermo   766
Gan, Chuang   141
Gao, Yupeng   644
Gatys, Leon A.   225
Gehrig, Daniel   766
Geiger, Andreas   325
Giryes, Raja   525
Gokaslan, Aaron   662
Grauman, Kristen   424
Gu, Jiayuan   392
Guil, Nicolás   241
Guo, Pei   71
Gupta, Abhinav   89
Gupta, Otkrist   71

Harada, Tatsuya   492
Hays, James   679
He, Warren   158
Hospedales, Timothy   106
Hu, Guosheng   106
Hu, Han   392
Hua, Yang   106
Huang, Qixing   141
Huang, Thomas   610

Ilg, Eddy   626

Jakubovitz, Daniel   525
Jung, Cláudio Rosito   593

Kang, Guoliang   610
Karpur, Arjun   141
Keuper, Margret   626
Kiapour, M. Hadi   258
Kim, Kwang In   662
Kim, Seong Tae   475

Kordas, Paige 258
Kryshchenko, Anton   55

Lazebnik, Svetlana   258
Le, Huu 699
Li, Bo 158
Li, Kejie 508
Li, Yonglu 124
Liang, Justin 407
Liao, Hongen 749
Lin, Zhe 542
Liu, Li 106, 731
Liu, Wenqian 175
Liu, Yinlong 460
Liu, Zhijian 3
Lu, Cewu 124
Lu, Jingwan 679
Lu, Yongyi 293
Luo, Linjie 141

Ma, Xiaojuan 443
Madadi, Meysam 309
Mairal, Julien 375
Maire, Michael 192
Malkov, Yury 209
Marín-Jiménez, Manuel J.   241
Mei, Tao 21
Mori, Greg 192
Müller-Budack, Eric   575

Naik, Nikhil 71
Neumann, Frank 715

Oswald, Martin R.   325

Park, David Keetae 443
Paudel, Danda Pani 275
Pham, Trung 508
Piramuthu, Robinson 258
Plummer, Bryan A. 258
Pollefeys, Marc 325
Pustu-Iren, Kader 575

Qin, Jie 731

Raj, Amit 679
Ramakrishnan, Santhosh K.   424
Ramanujan, Vivek 662

Raskar, Ramesh 71
Rebecq, Henri 766
Reid, Ian 508
Ritchie, Daniel 662
Ro, Yong Man 475
Robertson, Neil 106
Rochan, Mrigank 358

Saikia, Tonmoy 626
Sangkloy, Patsorn 679
Scaramuzza, Davide 766
Schmid, Cordelia 241, 375
Schönberger, Johannes L.   325
Shao, Ling 106, 731
Sharma, Abhishek 175
Shen, Fumin 106, 731
Shen, Heng Tao 731
Shen, Xiaohui 542
Shi, Jianbo 342
Silva, Sérgio Montazzolli 593
Song, Dawn 158
Song, Zhijian 460
Su, Dong 644
Suter, David 699
Sznaier, Mario 175

Tai, Yu-Wing 293
Tan, Ping 192
Tang, Chi-Keung 293
Tejero-De-Pablos, Antonio 492
Tenenbaum, Joshua B. 3
Tompkin, James 662
Torresani, Lorenzo 342

Uehara, Kohei 492
Urtasun, Raquel 407
Ushiku, Yoshitaka 492

Van Gool, Luc 275

Wang, Chen 460
Wang, Liwei 392
Wang, Manning 460
Wang, Xiaolong 89
Wang, Yang 358
Wang, Yufei 542
Wei, Yichen 392
Wei, Yunchao 610
Weis, Marissa A. 225

Wu, Jiajun   3
Wu, Ziming   443

Xu, Wenqiang   124
Xu, Yong   731

Yang, Xu   38
Yang, Yi   610
Yang, Yongxin   106
Yao, Anbang   749
Ye, Linwei   358
Ye, Tian   89
Yi, Jinfeng   644
Yoo, Seungjoo   443
Yu, Zehao   106
Yuan, Yang   106

Zach, Christopher   558
Zhan, Huangying   508
Zhang, Hanwang   38
Zhang, Huan   644
Zhang, Jiahui   749
Zhang, Jianming   542
Zhang, Li   749
Zhang, Xiaolin   610
Zhang, Zheng   731
Zhang, Zhihong   106
Zhao, Hao   749
Zhao, Tiejun   21
Zheng, Shuai   258
Zhou, Xingyi   141
Zhu, Fan   731
Zhu, Ligeng   192

Printed in the United States
By Bookmasters